Dear Reader

With the aim of giving a maximum amount of information in a limited number of pages Michelin has adopted a system of symbols which is today known the world over.

Failing this system the present publication would run to six volumes.

Judge for yourselves by comparing the descriptive text below with the equivalent extract from the Guide in symbol form.

🏨 ✻✻ **Cheval Blanc** (Durand) Ⓜ, ✆ 28 31 42, ≤ lake, « garden » – wc . AE
closed December and Wednesday – **M** 90/185 **st** – 25 – **32 rm** 175/290
Spec. Ris de veau à la crème, Poularde bressanne, tarte flambée. **Wines.** Viré, Morgon.

A comfortable hotel where you will enjoy a pleasant stay and be tempted to prolong your visit.
The excellence of the cuisine, which is personally supervised by the proprietor Mr Durand, is worth a detour.
The hotel in its quiet secluded setting away from the built-up-area offers every modern amenity.
To reserve phone 28 31 42.

The hotel affords a fine view of the lake ; in good weather it is possible to eat out of doors. The hotel is enhanced by an attractive garden.

Bedrooms with private bathroom with toilet or private shower without toilet. Telephone in room.

Parking facilities, under cover, are available to all guests with this Guide.

The hotel accepts payment by American Express credit cards.

The establishment is closed throughout December and every Wednesday.

Prices : st = service is included in all prices. There should be no supplementary charge for service, taxes or VAT on your bill.

The set meal prices range from 90 F for the lowest to 185 F for the highest.

The cost of continental breakfast served in the bedroom is 25 F.

32 bedroomed hotel. The charges vary from 175 F for a single to 290 F for the best twin bedded room.

Included for the gourmet are some culinary specialities, recommended by the hotelier : Ris de veau à la crème, Poularde bressanne, tarte flambée. In addition to the best quality wines you will find many of the local wines worth sampling : Viré, Morgon.

This demonstration clearly shows that each entry contains a great deal of information. The symbols are easily learnt and to know them will enable you to understand the Guide and to choose those establishments that you require.

CONTENTS

In addition to those situated in the main cities, restaurants renowned for their exceptional cuisine will be found in the towns printed in italics.

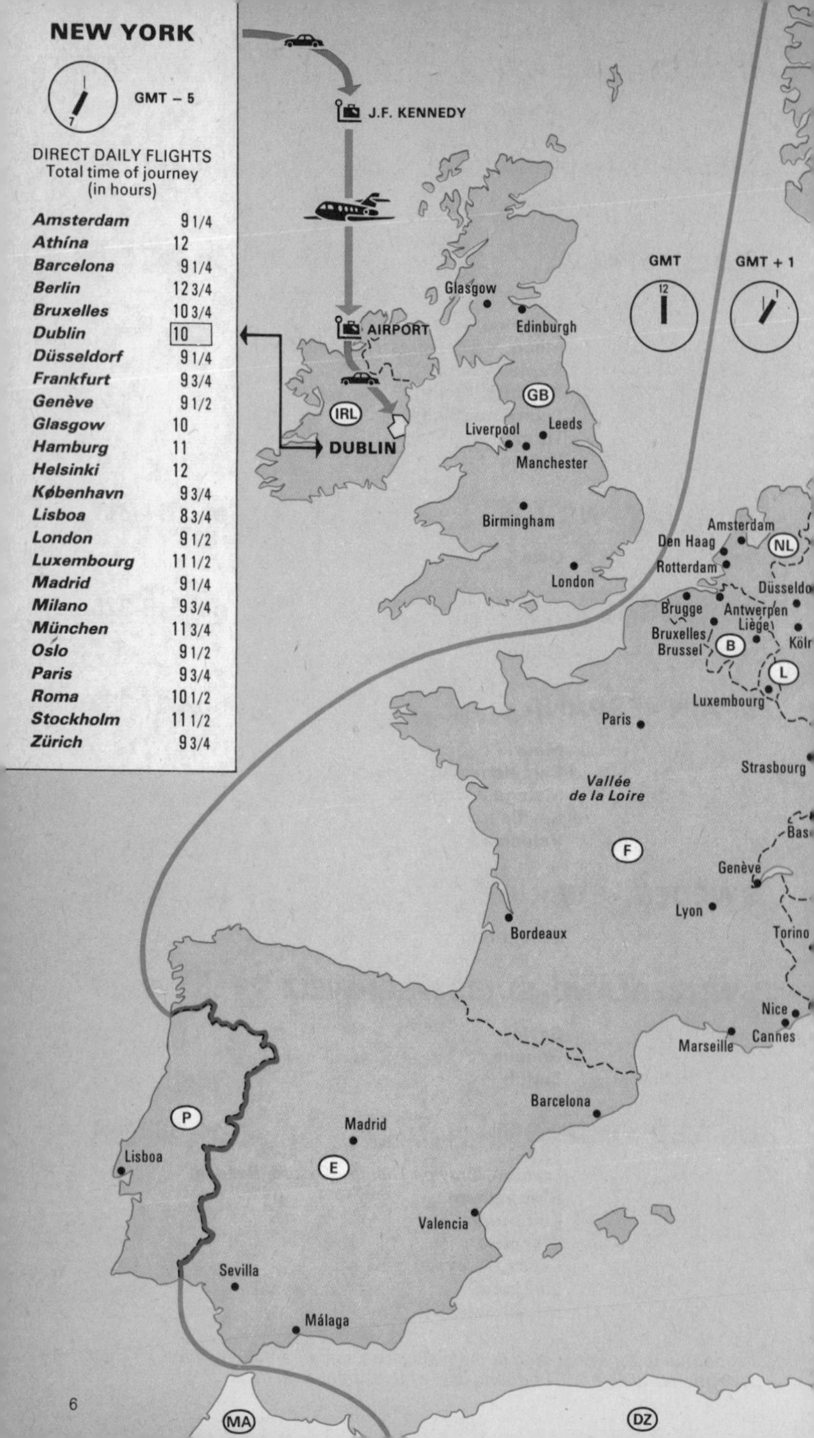
NEW YORK
GMT – 5
DIRECT DAILY FLIGHTS
Total time of journey
(in hours)
Amsterdam 9 1/4
Athína 12
Barcelona 9 1/4
Berlin 12 3/4
Bruxelles 10 3/4
Dublin 10
Düsseldorf 9 1/4
Frankfurt 9 3/4
Genève 9 1/2
Glasgow 10
Hamburg 11
Helsinki 12
København 9 3/4
Lisboa 8 3/4
London 9 1/2
Luxembourg 11 1/2
Madrid 9 1/4
Milano 9 3/4
München 11 3/4
Oslo 9 1/2
Paris 9 3/4
Roma 10 1/2
Stockholm 11 1/2
Zürich 9 3/4
J.F. KENNEDY
AIRPORT
DUBLIN
IRL
GMT
GMT + 1
Glasgow
Edinburgh
GB
Liverpool
Leeds
Manchester
Birmingham
London
Amsterdam
Den Haag
NL
Rotterdam
Düsseldo
Brugge
Antwerpen
Liège
Bruxelles/
Brussel
B
Köln
L
Luxembourg
Paris
Strasbourg
Vallée
de la Loire
F
Bas
Genève
Lyon
Bordeaux
Torino
Nice
Cannes
Marseille
Barcelona
P
Madrid
Lisboa
E
Valencia
Sevilla
Málaga
MA
DZ

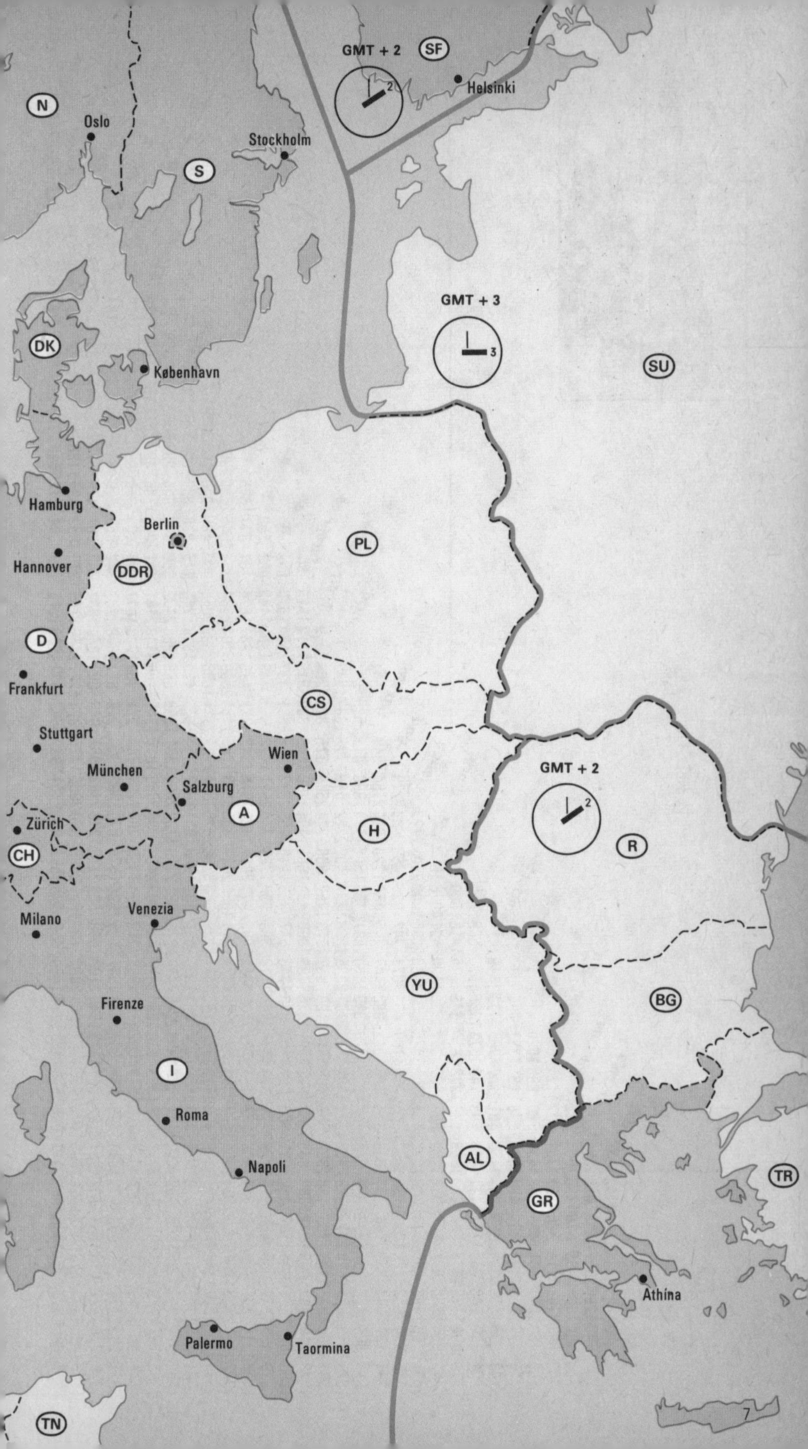
GMT + 2
SF
Helsinki
N
Oslo
Stockholm
S
GMT + 3
DK
København
SU
Hamburg
Berlin
PL
Hannover
DDR
D
Frankfurt
CS
Stuttgart
Wien
München
GMT + 2
Salzburg
A
Zürich
H
R
CH
Venezia
Milano
YU
BG
Firenze
I
Roma
AL
Napoli
TR
GR
Athína
Palermo
Taormina
TN

DISTANCES BY ROAD

(in kilometres)

	Amsterdam	Antwerp	Barcelona	Basle	Berlin	Birmingham	Bordeaux	Brussels	Cologne	Copenhagen	Dublin	Edinburg	Frankfort	Geneva	Glasgow	Hamburg	Lisbon	London	Luxembourg	Lyons	Madrid	Manchester	Marseilles	Milan	Münich	Nice	Oslo	Palermo	Paris	Rome	Stockholm	Strasbourg	Stuttgart	Venice	Vienna
Antwerp	159																																		
Barcelona	1592	1433																																	
Basle	745	599	1007																																
Berlin	671	725	1855	864																															
Birmingham	374	531	1703	1003	1255																														
Bordeaux	1081	922	631	834	1634	1192																													
Brussels	205	48	1396	552	783	522	885																												
Cologne	263	206	1336	489	576	755	1063	212																											
Copenhagen	739	851	2105	1114	385	1381	1781	897	723																										
Dublin	608	769	1941	1241	1493	246	1432	760	993	1620																									
Edinburg	743	936	2109	1409	1661	484	1598	928	1161	1787	416																								
Frankfort	443	395	1320	329	553	943	1158	401	187	788	1164	1349																							
Geneva	904	752	748	259	1123	1127	693	705	748	1373	1365	1533	588																						
Glasgow	779	1004	2176	1476	1728	483	1665	995	1228	1854	343	74	1416	1600																					
Hamburg	442	554	1808	817	297	1084	1484	600	426	305	1323	1490	491	1076	1557																				
Lisbon	2319	2160	1280	2066	2873	2430	1229	2123	2302	3020	2668	2836	2396	2009	2903	2723																			
London	196	324	1502	802	1054	196	992	315	554	1180	433	671	742	926	669	883	2229																		
Luxembourg	391	261	1147	333	764	747	946	219	189	911	980	1147	245	486	1220	614	2184	540																	
Lyons	963	804	629	387	1226	1074	548	767	707	1476	1313	1480	691	156	1547	1179	1890	873	518																
Madrid	1818	1659	627	1620	2372	1929	728	1622	1801	2519	2167	2335	1895	1361	2402	2222	653	1728	1683	1242															
Manchester	501	660	1833	1133	1385	138	1322	652	885	1511	196	357	1073	1257	355	1214	2560	325	871	1204	2059														
Marseilles	1278	1119	499	693	1541	1389	648	1082	1022	1791	1628	1795	1006	434	1862	1494	1760	1188	833	315	1112	1519													
Milan	1093	947	971	348	1162	1440	995	900	837	1462	1678	1846	677	323	1913	1165	2232	1239	681	437	1584	1570	504												
Münich	829	765	1338	396	585	1313	1273	771	573	1076	1551	1719	393	590	1786	779	2511	1112	517	749	1951	1443	1052	559											
Nice	1408	1274	654	736	1339	1544	803	1237	1152	1777	1783	1950	992	477	2017	1480	1915	1343	988	470	1267	1674	187	317	865										
Oslo	1322	1434	2688	1697	968	1964	2364	1480	1306	583	2203	2370	1371	1956	2437	888	3603	1763	1494	2059	3102	2094	2374	2045	1659	2360									
Palermo	2675	2447	2270	1848	2431	2925	2419	2400	2419	2922	3163	3331	2239	1808	3398	2625	3531	2724	2181	1888	2883	3055	1803	1495	1828	1616	3505								
Paris	504	345	1090	551	1057	615	579	308	486	1204	854	1021	586	537	1088	907	1817	414	375	460	1316	745	776	826	832	931	1787	2311							
Rome	1752	1524	1347	925	1508	2002	1496	1477	1496	1999	2240	2408	1316	885	2475	1702	2608	1801	1258	965	1960	2132	880	572	905	693	2582	929	1388						
Stockholm	1369	1481	2735	1744	1015	2011	2411	1527	1353	630	2250	2417	1418	2003	2484	935	3650	1810	1541	2106	3149	2141	2421	2092	1706	2407	522	3552	1834	2629					
Strasbourg	634	487	1110	145	753	947	927	440	378	1003	1186	1353	218	404	1420	706	2298	746	221	480	1723	1077	796	493	359	951	1586	1993	488	1070	1633				
Stuttgart	621	553	1256	265	632	1101	1068	559	365	967	1339	1507	205	524	1574	670	2306	900	312	627	1869	1231	942	530	219	845	1550	2030	627	1107	1597	154			
Venice	1326	1213	1227	610	1082	1702	1257	1162	1070	1573	1940	2108	890	585	2175	1276	2488	1501	943	699	1840	1832	760	267	479	573	2156	1451	1088	528	2203	755	668		
Vienna	1143	1095	1843	826	642	1626	1799	1101	887	1257	1864	2032	707	1021	2099	960	2966	1425	924	1287	2456	1756	1376	883	435	1189	1840	2054	1227	1131	1887	814	674	620	
Zurich	827	683	1026	85	850	1088	913	636	570	1185	1326	1494	410	278	1561	888	2151	887	449	437	1639	1218	713	304	312	619	1768	1804	636	881	1815	229	222	566	742

Lisbon – Strasbourg: 2298

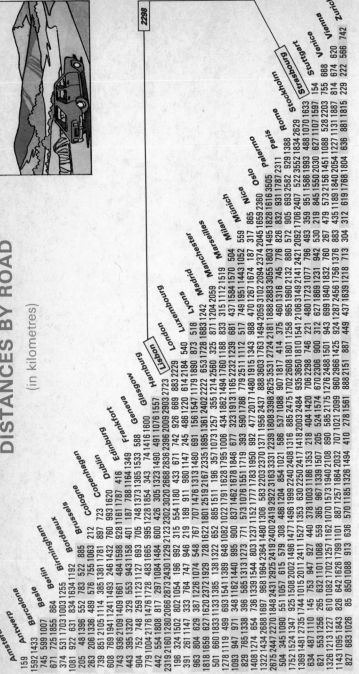

AIR LINKS (in hours)

3 1/2 not daily

	Amsterdam	Antwerp	Barcelona	Basle	Berlin	Birmingham	Bordeaux	Brussels	Cologne	Copenhagen	Dublin	Edinburgh	Frankfort	Geneva	Glasgow	Hamburg	Lisbon	London	Luxembourg	Lyons	Madrid	Manchester	Marseilles	Milan	Munich	Nice	Oslo	Palermo	Paris	Rome	Stockholm	Strasbourg	Stuttgart	Venice	Vienna
Antwerp	2 1/4																																		
Barcelona	3 3/4	6																																	
Basle	3 1/4	4 3/4	4 1/2																																
Berlin	3	6	5 3/4	4 1/2																															
Birmingham	2 3/4	5 1/4	8	5 1/4	5 1/4																														
Bordeaux	2 3/4			4 1/4	8 1/2	5 3/4																													
Brussels	2 1/2		3 3/4	3	4 1/4	3 1/4	5 1/2																												
Cologne			5 1/4	4	2 3/4	4 1/4	7 1/4																												
Copenhagen	3	4 3/4	4 1/2	4 3/4	4	4 1/2	6	3 1/4	4 1/4																										
Dublin	3 1/4	4 3/4	6 1/2	5	5 1/2	2 1/2	5 3/4	3 1/4	5 1/2	4																									
Edinburgh	3 3/4	5 1/2	6 1/4	4 1/4	6	2 3/4	5 1/2	4 3/4	5 1/4	5 1/2	2 3/4																								
Frankfort	2 3/4	4 1/4	3 3/4	2 3/4	2 3/4	3 1/4	6 1/4	2 3/4	2 1/2	3 1/4	3 3/4	5 3/4																							
Geneva	3	4 1/2	3	2 1/4	4 1/2	5	3	3	4 1/2	3 3/4	4	5 1/2	3																						
Glasgow	3 1/4	5 1/4	6 3/4	5 1/2	6 3/4	2 3/4	6	4 3/4	5 1/2	3 1/2	2 1/2	2 1/4	5 1/2	5 1/2																					
Hamburg	2 3/4	4 1/2	5 1/2	4 1/2	2 1/2	5	5 3/4	3	2 3/4	2 1/2	5 1/2	6 1/4	2 3/4	4 3/4	6																				
Lisbon	4 1/2	6 1/4	3 1/4	5 1/2	7 1/2	7		4 1/2	7 1/2	5 1/2	6 3/4	7 1/4	4 3/4	3 1/4	7	6 1/4																			
London	2 3/4	3 1/4	4 1/4	3 1/2	7	3	3 3/4	3 1/4	3 1/2	4	3 1/4	3 1/2	3 1/2	3 1/2	3 1/2	3 3/4	4 3/4																		
Luxembourg	2 1/2		6 3/4	3 3/4	4 3/4	6	6 1/4	2 1/4	4 1/2	4 3/4	5 1/2		2 1/2	4	5 1/2	4 3/4	6 3/4	3 1/4																	
Lyons	3 1/2	5 1/2	3	3	4	4 3/4	3	3 1/4	5	4	6	6	3 1/4		6	5 1/2	4 1/4	4																	
Madrid	3	5 3/4	2 3/4	6	6 1/4	6 1/4	3	4	5 1/2	4 3/4	4	6	4 1/4	3 1/2	6 1/4	6	2 3/4	4 1/4	6	4 3/4															
Manchester	3	4 1/2	6	5 1/2	5 1/2	2 1/2	5 3/4	3	5 1/2	3 3/4	2 3/4	3	3 3/4	4	2	5	4 3/4	3 1/4	5 3/4	6	4 1/4														
Marseilles	4 1/2		2 3/4	4 1/4	7 1/4	4 3/4	2 3/4	3 1/2	6 1/2	5 1/4	6 1/4	6 1/4	4 1/2	2 1/2	6 1/2	6 1/2	4	4	6	2 3/4	3 1/4	5 3/4													
Milan	3	5 1/4	3 1/4	3 1/2	5	4 3/4	5 1/4	3 1/4	4 1/4	3 3/4	5 1/4	6 1/4	3	2 1/2	5 1/2	4 3/4	5 1/4	4	4 3/4	3	3 3/4	4	3												
Munich	3 1/4	5	3 3/4	2 3/4	3	5	6	3	2 3/4	3 1/4	4 1/4	6 1/4	2 3/4	3 1/2	6	3	6 1/2	4	4 1/4	5 1/4	5 1/2	5 1/2	8	2 3/4											
Nice	3 1/4	4 3/4	2 3/4	4 1/4	6 1/4	5 3/4	3	3	5 1/4	4	5 1/2	6 1/2	3 1/4	2 1/2	6	5 1/2	4	4	4	2 3/4	3 1/4	4	2 1/4	2 3/4	3										
Oslo	3	6	6 1/4	6 1/4	4 1/2	4 3/4	7 1/4	4 3/4	6 3/4	3 1/2	6	7 1/2	3 1/2	5 1/4	4 1/4	2 3/4	7 1/4	3	6	5 3/4	6 1/2	5 1/4	7	5 1/4	5	5 3/4									
Palermo	3		7			8 1/2		6 1/2	9 3/4	9 1/2	10		5 1/4	6 3/4	10 3/4			7	6	7 3/4	7 1/2	9 3/4	8	3 1/2	6 1/2	5 1/2	11								
Paris	2	4 1/2	3 1/2	2 3/4	4 3/4	3	3	2 3/4	3	3 3/4	3 3/4	5	3 1/4	3	3 3/4	3 1/2	4 1/2	3 1/2	2 3/4	3	3 3/4	3 1/4	3	3 1/4	3 1/2	3 1/4	4	6 3/4							
Rome	3	6	3 1/2	4 3/4	5 1/4	6 1/4	8 1/4	4	5 3/4	4 1/2	4 1/4	6 3/4	3 3/4	3 1/2	7 1/4	5 3/4	4 3/4	4 3/4	3 3/4	5	4 1/4	5	3 1/2	3	3 1/2	2 3/4	6 1/2	3 1/4	4 1/4						
Stockholm	4	5 3/4	7 3/4	6 1/4	5	5 1/4	6 3/4	5 1/4	6 1/2	3 1/4	7	7 1/4	4	6	7	3 1/2	9 1/4	5	6 3/4	6 1/2	7	6	7 3/4	6	5 3/4	6	2 3/4		4 3/4	7					
Strasbourg	2 1/2		6 3/4	4 1/2		5 1/2	4 1/2	2 1/2		5 3/4	6 1/2	5 3/4		2 3/4	6 1/2		6 1/2	4 1/2		3 1/4	7	4 3/4	3 3/4	2 3/4		2 3/4	6 3/4		3	4 3/4	8 1/2				
Stuttgart	3 3/4	4 1/2	3 3/4	4	3	5	8	3 3/4	2 1/2	3 1/4	5 1/2	6 3/4	2 1/2	3 3/4	6	3	4 3/4	3 3/4	4 1/4	5	4 1/4	5	6 1/4	2 3/4	2 1/2	2 3/4	5		3 1/4	5 1/2	5 1/2				
Venice	5 1/2		5 3/4		5	5 3/4		4 3/4	5 1/4	5 3/4	6 1/4		3	4 3/4	6	5	7	4 1/4	5	5	5 1/4	6 1/2	4 3/4	2 1/2	3	3 1/4	6	4 3/4	3 1/2	3	6 1/2		5		
Vienna	3 1/2	5	4	4	5	4 3/4	6	3 1/2	4 1/2	3 1/4	5 3/4	6 1/4	3	3 1/4	6	4 3/4	6 1/2	4 1/2	4 3/4	5 1/2	4 3/4	5 3/4	6	3	2 3/4	3 1/4	5	6	3 3/4	3 1/2	4 1/4		3	3 1/4	
Zurich	3	5 1/4	3 1/4	2	3 1/4	4 1/4	6	3	2 3/4	3 1/2	5 3/4	5 1/2	2 3/4	2 1/2	5 1/4	3	4 1/2	3 3/4	2 1/2	3 1/4	3 3/4	3 3/4	5	2 1/2	2 1/2	2 3/4	5	5 1/2	3 1/4	3 1/2	4 1/2	2 1/2	2 1/2	3 3/4	3

Hamburg — Oslo: 2 3/4

HAMBURG

FUHLSBÜTTEL

FORNEBU

OSLO

This revised edition from
Michelin Tyre Company's Tourism Department
offers you a selection of
hotels and restaurants in the main European cities.
The latter have been chosen for
their business or tourist interest.

In addition the guide indicates establishments,
located in other towns,
renowned for the excellence of their cuisine.

We hope that the guide will help you
with your choice of a hotel or restaurant
and prove useful for your sightseeing.
Have an enjoyable stay.

Signs and symbols

HOTELS AND RESTAURANTS

CLASS, STANDARD OF COMFORT

Luxury in the traditional style
Top class comfort
Very comfortable
Good average
Quite comfortable
In its class, hotel with modern amenities — M

AMENITY

Pleasant hotels — ...
Pleasant restaurants — ...
Particularly attractive feature — « Park »
Very quiet or quiet secluded hotel
Quiet hotel
Exceptional view – Panoramic view — sea,
Interesting or extensive view

CUISINE

Exceptional cuisine in the country, worth a special journey
Excellent cooking : worth a detour
An especially good restaurant in its class
Other recommended carefully prepared meals

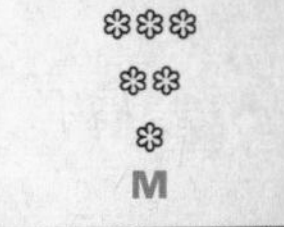

HOTEL FACILITIES

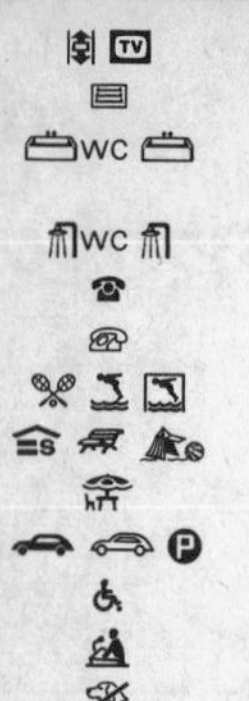

Lift (elevator) – Television in room

Air conditioning

Private bathroom with toilet, private bathroom without toilet

Private shower with toilet, private shower without toilet

Telephone in room : direct dialling for outside calls

Telephone in room : outside calls connected by operator

Hotel tennis court(s) – Outdoor or indoor swimming pool

Sauna – Garden – Beach with bathing facilities

Meals served in garden or on terrace

Free garage – Charge made for garage – Car park

Bedrooms accessible to the physically handicapped

Equipped conference hall

Dogs are not allowed

without rest. The hotel has no restaurant

PRICES

These prices are given in the currency of the country in question. Valid for 1987 the rates shown should only vary if the cost of living changes to any great extent.

Meals

M 75/130 — Set meal prices

M a la carte 110/180 — " a la carte " meals

Hotels

30 rm 185/300 — Lowest price for a comfortable single and highest price for the best double room

Breakfast

Price of breakfast

Bb — Breakfast with choice from buffet

Service and taxes

s. **t.** — Service only included. V.A.T. only included.

In Austria, Benelux, Denmark, Germany, Italy, Norway, Sweden and Switzerland, prices shown are inclusive, that is to say service and V.A.T. included.

SIGHTS

Worth a journey
Worth a detour
Interesting

TOWN PLANS

Main conventional signs

Tourist Information Centre

Hotel, restaurant – Reference letter on the town plan

Place of interest and its main entrance } Reference letter on the town plan
Interesting church or chapel

Shopping street – Public car park

Tram

Underground station

One-way street

Church or chapel – Poste restante, telegraph – Telephone

Public buildings located by letters:

Police (in large towns police headquarters) – Theatre – Museum

Coach station – Airport – Hospital – Covered market

Ruins – Monument, statue – Fountain

Garden, park, wood – Cemetery, Jewish cemetery

Outdoor or indoor swimming pool – Racecourse – Golf course

Cable-car – Funicular

Sports ground, stadium – View – Panorama

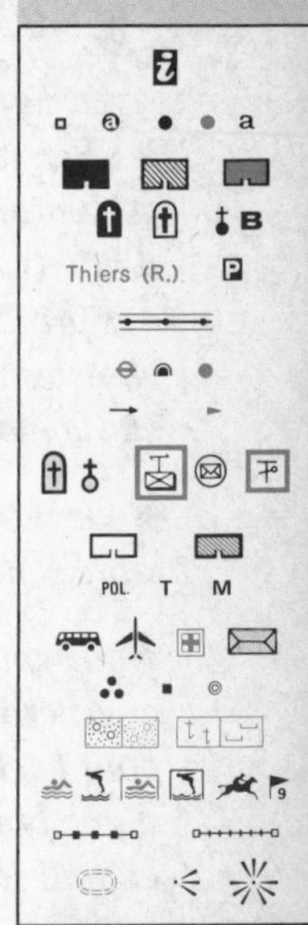

Names shown on the street plans are in the language of the country to conform to local signposting.

Avec cette nouvelle édition,
les Services de Tourisme du Pneu Michelin
vous proposent une sélection
d'hôtels et restaurants
des principales villes d'Europe,
choisies en raison de leur vocation internationale
sur le plan des affaires et du tourisme.

Vous y trouverez également les grandes tables
situées hors de ces grandes villes.

Nous vous souhaitons d'agréables séjours
et espérons que ce guide vous aidera utilement
pour le choix d'un hôtel,
d'une bonne table
et pour la visite des principales curiosités.

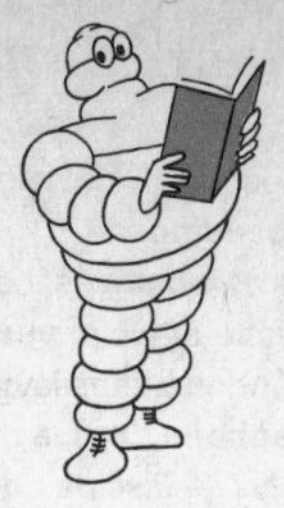

Signes et symboles

HOTELS ET RESTAURANTS

CLASSE ET CONFORT

Grand luxe et tradition		XXXXX
Grand confort		XXXX
Très confortable		XXX
Bon confort		XX
Assez confortable		X
Dans sa catégorie, hôtel d'équipement moderne	M	

L'AGRÉMENT

Hôtels agréables	...
Restaurants agréables	XXXXX ... X
Élément particulièrement agréable	« Park »
Hôtel très tranquille, ou isolé et tranquille	
Hôtel tranquille	
Vue exceptionnelle, panorama	sea,
Vue intéressante ou étendue	

LA TABLE

Une des meilleures tables du pays, vaut le voyage
Table excellente, mérite un détour
Une très bonne table dans sa catégorie
Autre table soignée

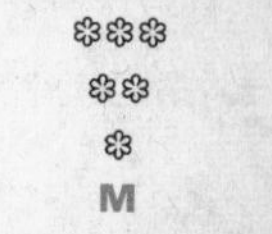

L'INSTALLATION

without rest.

Ascenseur, Télévision dans la chambre
Air conditionné
Bain et wc privés, bain sans wc
Douche et wc privés, douche privée sans wc
Téléphone dans la chambre direct avec l'extérieur
Téléphone dans la chambre relié par standard
Tennis – Piscine : de plein air ou couverte
Sauna – Jardin – Plage aménagée
Repas servis au jardin ou en terrasse
Garage gratuit – Garage payant – Parc à voitures
Chambres accessibles aux handicapés physiques
L'hôtel reçoit les séminaires
Accès interdit aux chiens
L'hôtel n'a pas de restaurant

LES PRIX

Les prix sont indiqués dans la monnaie du pays. Établis pour l'année 1987, ils ne doivent être modifiés que si le coût de la vie subit des variations importantes.

Au restaurant

M 75/130 — Prix des repas à prix fixes

M a la carte 110/180 — Prix des repas à la carte

A l'hôtel

30 rm 185/300 — Prix minimum pour une chambre d'une personne et maximum pour la plus belle chambre occupée par deux personnes

Petit déjeuner

25 20 — Prix du petit déjeuner.

Bb — Petit déjeuner buffet

Service et taxes

s. **t.** — Service compris T.V.A. comprise

En Allemagne, Autriche, Benelux, Danemark, Italie, Norvège, Suède et Suisse, les prix indiqués sont nets.

LES CURIOSITÉS

Vaut le voyage
Mérite un détour
Intéressante

LES PLANS

Principaux signes conventionnels

Information touristique
Hôtel, restaurant – Lettre les repérant sur le plan
Monument intéressant et entrée principale } Lettre les repérant sur le plan
Église ou chapelle intéressante } Lettre les repérant sur le plan
Rue commerçante – Parc de stationnement public
Tramway
Station de métro
Sens unique
Église ou chapelle – Poste restante, télégraphe – Téléphone
Édifices publics repérés par des lettres :
Police (dans les grandes villes commissariat central) – Théâtre – Musée
Gare routière – Aéroport – Hôpital – Marché couvert
Ruines – Monument, statue – Fontaine
Jardin, parc, bois – Cimetière, cimetière israélite
Piscine de plein air, couverte – Hippodrome – Golf
Téléphérique – Funiculaire
Stade – Vue – Panorama

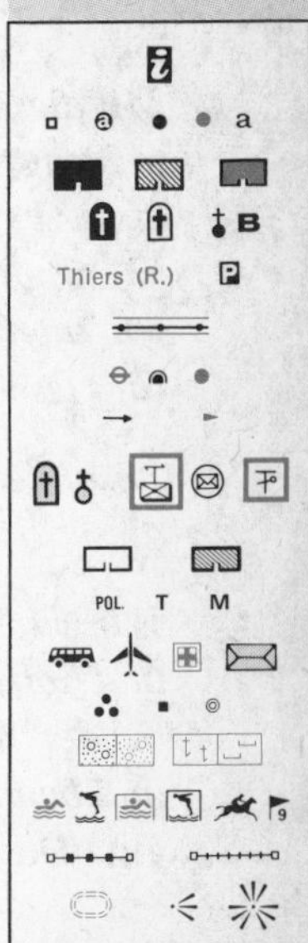

Les indications portées sur les plans sont dans la langue du pays, en conformité avec la dénomination locale.

Mit dieser Neuauflage
präsentieren Ihnen die Michelin-Touristikabteilungen
eine Auswahl von Hotels und Restaurants
in europäischen Hauptstädten
von internationaler Bedeutung
für Geschäftsreisende und Touristen.

Besonders gute Restaurants in der näheren Umgebung
dieser Städte wurden ebenfalls aufgenommen.

Wir wünschen einen angenehmen Aufenthalt
und hoffen, daß Ihnen dieser Führer
bei der Wahl eines Hotels, eines Restaurants
und beim Besuch der Hauptsehenswürdigkeiten
gute Dienste leisten wird.

Zeichen und Symbole

HOTELS UND RESTAURANTS

KLASSENEINTEILUNG UND KOMFORT

Großer Luxus und Tradition		
Großer Komfort		
Sehr komfortabel		
Mit gutem Komfort		
Mit ausreichendem Komfort		
Moderne Einrichtung	M	

ANNEHMLICHKEITEN

Angenehme Hotels	...
Angenehme Restaurants	...
Besondere Annehmlichkeit	« Park »
Sehr ruhiges oder abgelegenes und ruhiges Hotel	
Ruhiges Hotel	
Reizvolle Aussicht, Rundblick	sea,
Interessante oder weite Sicht	

KÜCHE

Eine der besten Küchen des Landes : eine Reise wert
Eine hervorragende Küche : verdient einen Umweg
Eine sehr gute Küche : verdient Ihre besondere Beachtung
Andere sorgfältig zubereitete Mahlzeiten

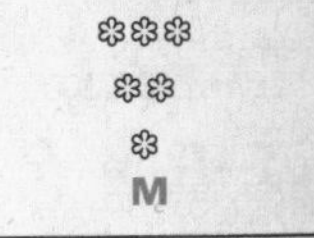

EINRICHTUNG

without rest

Fahrstuhl – Fernsehen im Zimmer
Klimaanlage
Privatbad mit wc, Privatbad ohne wc
Privatdusche mit wc, Privatdusche ohne wc
Zimmertelefon mit direkter Außenverbindung
Zimmertelefon mit Außenverbindung über Telefonzentrale
Tennis – Freibad – Hallenbad
Sauna – Garten – Strandbad
Garten-, Terrassenrestaurant
Garage kostenlos – Garage wird berechnet – Parkplatz
Für Körperbehinderte leicht zugängliche Zimmer
Konferenzraum
Das Mitführen von Hunden ist unerwünscht
Hotel ohne Restaurant

DIE PREISE

Die Preise sind in der jeweiligen Landeswährung angegeben. Sie gelten für das Jahr 1987 und können nur geändert werden, wenn die Lebenshaltungskosten starke Veränderungen erfahren.

Im Restaurant

M 75/130 — Feste Menupreise

M a la carte 110/180 — Mahlzeiten "a la carte"

Im Hotel

30 rm 185/300 — Mindestpreis für ein Einzelzimmer und Höchstpreis für das schönste Doppelzimmer für zwei Personen

Frühstück

25 — Preis des Frühstücks

20 Bb — Frühstücksbuffet

Bedienungsgeld und Gebühren

s. **t.** — Bedienung inbegriffen – MWSt inbegriffen.

In Benelux, Dänemark, Deutschland, Italien, Norwegen, Österreich, Schweden und Schweiz sind die angegebenen Preise Inklusivpreise.

SEHENSWÜRDIGKEITEN

Eine Reise wert
Verdient einen Umweg
Sehenswert

STADTPLÄNE

Erklärung der wichtigsten Zeichen

Informationsstelle ....

Hotel, Restaurant – Referenzbuchstabe auf dem Plan ....

Sehenswertes Gebäude mit Haupteingang } Referenzbuchstabe auf dem Plan ...
Sehenswerte Kirche oder Kapelle .... }

Einkaufsstraße – Öffentlicher Parkplatz, Parkhaus

Straßenbahn ....

U-Bahnstation ....

Einbahnstraße ....

Kirche oder Kapelle – Postlagernde Sendungen, Telegraph – Telefon ....

Öffentliche Gebäude, durch Buchstaben gekennzeichnet :

Polizei (in größeren Städten Polizeipräsidium) – Theater – Museum ....

Autobusbahnhof – Flughafen – Krankenhaus – Markthalle ....

Ruine – Denkmal, Statue – Brunnen ....

Garten, Park, Wald – Friedhof, Jüd. Friedhof ....

Freibad – Hallenbad – Pferderennbahn – Golfplatz und Lochzahl ....

Seilschwebebahn – Standseilbahn ....

Sportplatz – Aussicht – Rundblick ....

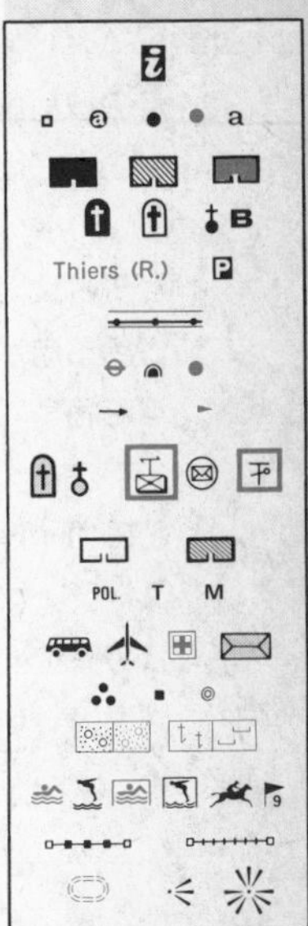

Die Angaben auf den Stadtplänen erfolgen, übereinstimmend mit der örtlichen Beschilderung, in der Landessprache.

この改訂版ガイドブックはミシュラン・タイヤ社観光部がおとどけするものです。

ビジネスに、観光に、国際的な拠点ヨーロッパ主要都市が誇る自慢のホテルとレストランを、そして郊外にたたずむ名うてのレストランをあわせて、御紹介いたします。

このガイドブックが、より快適なホテル、味わい深いレストランやあこがれの地と出逢うきっかけとなり、皆さまの旅をより素晴らしいものにするお手伝いができれば幸いです。

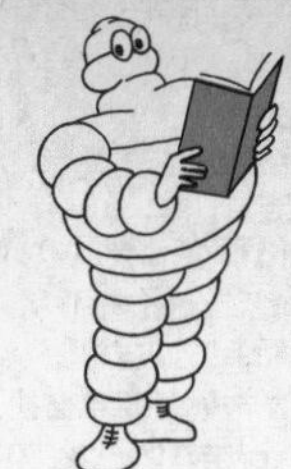

記号とシンボルマーク

ホテルとレストラン

等級と快適さ

豪華で伝統的様式
トップクラス
たいへん快適
快適
かなり快適
等級内での近代的設備のホテル

M

居心地

居心地よいホテル
居心地よいレストラン
特に魅力的な特徴
大変静かなホテル又は人里離れた静かなホテル
静かなホテル
見晴らしがよい展望（例：海）、パノラマ
素晴らしい風景

« Park »
sea,

料理

最上の料理、出かける価値あり
素晴らしい料理、寄り道の価値あり
等級内では大変おいしい料理
その他の心のこもった料理

M

設備

TV	エレベーター、室内テレビ
	空調設備
wc	専用のバスとトイレ。専用のバスのみでトイレなし
wc	専用のシャワーとトイレ。専用のシャワーのみでトイレなし
	室内に電話あり、外線直通
	室内に電話あり、外線は交換台経由
	テニスコート。屋外プール。屋内プール。
s	サウナ。くつろげる庭。整備された海水浴場
	食事が庭またはテラスでできる
P	無料駐車場。有料駐車場。駐車場
	体の不自由な方のための設備あり
	会議又は研修会の出来るホテル
	犬の連れ込みおことわり
without rest.	レストランの無いホテル

料金

料金は1987年のその国の貨幣単位で示してありますが、物価の変動などで変わる場合もあります。

レストラン

M 75/130
M a la carte 110/180

定食、ア・ラ・カルトそれぞれの最低料金と最高料金。

ホテル

30 rm 185/300

一人部屋の最低料金と二人部屋の最高料金。

朝食

25　20
Bb

朝食代
朝食はビュッフェ形式

サービス料と税金

s.　**t.**

サービス料込み。付加価値税込み。

オーストリア、ベネルクス、デンマーク、ドイツ、イタリア、ノルウェー、スウェーデン、スイスに関しては正価料金。

名所

出かける価値あり……………………………………………… ★★★
立ち寄る価値あり……………………………………………… ★★
興味深い………………………………………………………… ★

地図

主な記号

ツーリストインフォメーション……………………………

ホテル・レストラン――地図上での目印番号……………

興味深い歴史的建造物と、その中央入口 } 地図上での目印番号……………
興味深い教会または聖堂

商店街――公共駐車場……………………………………

路面電車………………………………………………………

地下鉄駅………………………………………………………

一方通行路……………………………………………………

教会または聖堂――局留郵便、電報――電話……………

公共建造物、記号は下記の通り……………………………

警察(大都市では、中央警察署)――劇場――美術館、博物館……

長距離バス発着所――空港――病院――屋内市場………

遺跡――歴史的建造物、像――泉…………………………

庭園、公園、森林――墓地――ユダヤ教の墓地…………

屋外プール、屋内プール――競馬場――ゴルフ場………

ロープウェイ――ケーブルカー……………………………

スタジアム――風景――パノラマ…………………………

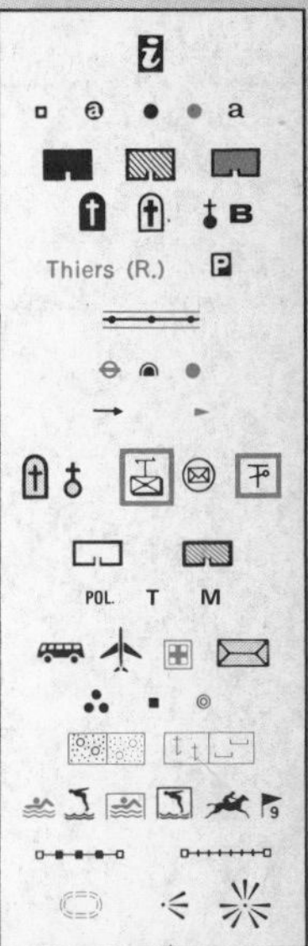

地図上の名称は、地方の標識に合わせてその国の言葉で表記されています。

Austria
Österreich

Vienna
Salzburg

PRACTICAL INFORMATION

LOCAL CURRENCY

Austrian Schilling ; 100 S = 7.33 US $ (Jan. 87)

TOURIST INFORMATION

In Vienna : Österreich-Information, 1040 Wien, Margaretenstr. 1, ☏ (0222) 5 87 57 24
Niederösterreich-Information, 1010 Wien, Heidenschuß 2, ☏ (0222) 63 31 14

In Salzburg : Landesverkehrsamt, Mozartplatz 5, ☏ (0662) 4 15 61

AIRLINES

AUSTRIAN AIRLINES : 1107 Wien, Kärntner Ring 18, ☏ (0222) 68 00

AIR FRANCE : 1010 Wien, Kärntnerstr. 49, ☏ (0222) 52 66 55

BRITISH AIRWAYS : 1010 Wien, Kärntner Ring 10, ☏ (0222) 65 76 91

DEUTSCHE LUFTHANSA : 1015 Wien, Opernring 1, ☏ (0222) 5 88 35

PAN AM : 1010 Wien, Kärntner Ring 5, ☏ (0222) 52 66 46

FOREIGN EXCHANGE

Hotels, restaurants and shops do not always accept foreign currencies and it is wise, therefore, to change money and cheques at the banks and exchange offices which are found in the larger stations, airports and at the frontier.

SHOPPING and BANK HOURS

Shops are open from 9am to 6pm, but often close for a lunch break. They are closed Saturday afternoon, Sunday and Bank Holidays (except the shops in railway stations).

Branch offices of banks are open from Monday to Friday between 8am and 12.30pm (in Salzburg 12am) and from 1.30pm to 3pm (in Salzburg 2pm to 4.30pm), Thursday to 5.30pm (only in Vienna).

In the index of street names those printed in red are where the principal shops are found.

BREAKDOWN SERVICE

ÖAMTC : See addresses in the text of Vienna and Salzburg

ARBÖ : in Vienna : Mariahilfer Str. 180, ☏ (0222) 85 35 35
in Salzburg : Münchner Bundesstr. 9, ☏ (0662) 3 36 01

In Austria the ÖAMTC and the ARBÖ make a special point of assisting foreign motorists. They have motor patrols covering main roads.

TIPPING

Service is generally included in hotel and restaurant bills. But in Austria, it is usual to give more than the expected tip in hotels, restaurants and cafés. Taxi-drivers, porters, barbers and theatre attendants also expect tips.

SPEED LIMITS

The speed limit in built up areas (indicated by place name signs at the beginning and end of such areas) is 50 km/h - 31 mph ; on motorways 130 km/h - 80 mph and on all other roads 100 km/h - 62 mph.

SEAT BELTS

The wearing of seat belts in Austria is compulsory for drivers and front seat passengers.

VIENNA

SIGHTS

HOFBURG★★★ BV

Imperial Palace of the Habsburgs (Kaiserpalast der Habsburger) : Swiss Court – Royal Chapel – Amalienhof – Stallburg – Leopold Wing – Ballhausplatz – Imperial Chancellery – Spanish Riding School – Neue Burg – Josefsplatz – Michaelerplatz – In der Burg – Capuchins Crypt – Church of the Augustinians. Art Collections : Imperial Treasury★★★ – Imperial Apartments★★ – Austrian National Library (Great Hall★) – Collection of Court Porcelain and Silver★★ – Collection of Arms and Armour★★ – Collection of Old Musical Instruments★ – Albertina (Dürer Collection★) – Museum of Ephesian Sculpture (Reliefs of Ephesus★★).

BUILDINGS AND MONUMENTS

St Stephen's Cathedral★★ (Stephansdom) CV – Schönbrunn★★ (Apartments★★★, Park★★, Coach Room★) S – Upper and Lower Belvedere★★ (Oberes und Unteres Belvedere) (Terraced Gardens and Art Collections★) DX and S – Opera★ (Staatsoper)★ CV – Church of St Charles★ (Karlskirche) CX – Church of St Michael (Michaeler Kirche) BCV – Church of the Minor Friars (Minoritenkirche) BV – Church of the Teutonic Order (Deutschordenskirche) (Altarpiece★, Treasure★) CV – Church of the Jesuits (Jesuitenkirche) CV **B** – Church of Our Lady of the River Bank (Maria am Gestade) CU – Church of the Faithful Virgin (Maria Treu) S **F** – Mozart Memorial (Mozart-Gedenkstätte) CV **D** – Dreimäderlhaus BU **K**.

STREETS, PLACES, PARKS

Kärntner Straße CVX – Graben (Plague Column) CV – Am Hof (Column to the Virgin) BV – Herrengasse★ BV – Maria-Theresien-Platz BV – Prater★ (Giant Whell, ⋞★) S – Oberlaapark★ S – Heldenplatz BV – Burggarten BV – Volksgarten BV – Rathausplatz BV.

IMPORTANT MUSEUMS (Hofburg and Belvedere see above)

Museum of Fine Arts★★★ (Kunsthistorisches Museum) BV – Historical Museum of the City of Vienna★★ (Historisches Museum der Stadt Wien) CX **M1** – Austrian Folklore Museum★★ (Österreichisches Museum für Volkskunde) S **M2** – Gallery of Painting and Fine Arts★ (Gemäldegalerie der Akademie der Bildenden Künste) BX **M3** – Natural History Museum★ (Naturhistorisches Museum) BV **M4** – Birthplace of Schubert (Schubert-Museum) R **M5** – Austrian Museum of Applied Arts★ (Österreichisches Museum für angewandte Kunst) DV **M6**.

EXCURSIONS

Danube Tower★★ (Donauturm) R – Leopoldsberg⋞★★ R – Kahlenberg⋞★ R – Klosterneuburg Abbey (Stift Klosterneuburg) (Altarpiece by Nicolas of Verdun★) R – Grinzing R – Baden★ S – Vienna Woods★ (Wienerwald) S.

VIENNA (WIEN) Austria 987 ⑩, 426 ⑫ – pop. 1 530 000 – alt. 156 m. – ☎ 0222.

✈ Wien-Schwechat by ②, ☎ 7 77 00 – 🚗 ☎ 56 50 29 89.

Exhibition Centre, Messeplatz 1, ☎ 9 31 52 40.

ℹ Tourist-Information, Opernpassage (Basement), ☎ 43 16 08 – **ÖAMTC**, Schubertring, ☎ 72 99

Budapest 208 ③ – München 435 ⑥ – Praha 292 ① – Salzburg 292 ⑥ – Zagreb 362 ⑤.

Town Centre, city districts (Stadtbezirke) 1-9 :

Imperial - Restaurant zur Majestät (converted 19 C palace), Kärntner Ring 16, A-1015, 6 51 76 50/5 01 10, Telex 112630 – AE E VISA. rest M *(closed Saturday - Sunday)* a la carte 340/730 (booking essential) – **Café Imperial M** a la carte 210/550 – **162 rm** 1820/4440. CX **a**

Bristol - Restaurant Korso, Kärntner Ring 1, A-1015, 51 51 60, Telex 112474, – rest (with). AE E VISA. rest CX **m**
M *(closed Saturday lunch)* a la carte 360/840 – **Rôtisserie Sirk M** a la carte 300/520 – **152 rm** 1820/3940.

Sacher, Philharmonikerstr. 4, A-1015, 5 14 56, Telex 112520, « Antique furniture, restaurant Sacherstöckl » – . AE E VISA. rest CV **x**
M a la carte 335/620 – **124 rm** 1150/3700.

Marriott, Parkring 12a, A-1010, 51 51 80, Telex 112249, , – . AE E VISA. rest CV **d**
Restaurants : – **Symphonika** *(dinner only)* **M** a la carte 350/560 – **Parkring-Restaurant M** a la carte 225/475 – **304 rm** 2590/3330.

Hilton International-Rôtisserie Prinz Eugen, Landstraßer Hauptstr. 2 (near Stadtpark), A-1030, 7 52 65 20, Telex 136799, – . AE E VISA. rest DV **e**
M *(closed Saturday lunch)* a la carte 340/750 (booking essential) – **Café am Park M** a la carte 200/410 – **620 rm** 1590/3340
Spec. Suprême vom Steinbutt in Basilikumfond, Lammkarrée mit Senfkörnern und Kräutern, Waldbeeren in Blätterkrokant.

Intercontinental, Johannesgasse 28, A-1037, 7 50 50, Telex 131235, – . AE E VISA. rest DX **p**
Restaurants : – **Vier Jahreszeiten M** a la carte 300/600 – **Brasserie M** a la carte 195/500 – **500 rm** 2260/3340.

Hotel im Palais Schwarzenberg, Schwarzenbergplatz 9, A-1030, 78 45 15, Telex 136124, « Converted 1727 baroque palace, park » – . AE E VISA
M a la carte 460/820 (booking essential) – **38 rm** 3200/4500 CX
Spec. Gänselebercarpaccio, Buchweizenschmarrn mit Lachsvariationen, Perlhuhnbrust mit Krebsravioli.

Hotel de France, Schottenring 3, A-1010, 34 35 40, Telex 114360, – rest . AE E VISA BU **b**
M a la carte 300/480 – **190 rm** 1455/3700 Bb.

SAS-Palais-Hotel (modern hotel in a historical building), Parkring/Weihburggasse 32, A-1010, 51 51 70, Telex 136127, – . AE E VISA. CV **z**
M a la carte 390/580 – **165 rm** 1700/3200 Bb.

Biedermeier, Landstraßer Hauptstr. 28 (at Sünnhof), A-1030, 75 55 75, Telex 111039 – . AE E VISA S **w**
M a la carte 235/460 – **200 rm** 1600/1900.

Ambassador, Neuer Markt 5, A-1010, 5 14 66, Telex 111906 – . AE VISA. rest CV **s**
M a la carte 305/615 – **107 rm** 1050/2600 Bb.

Europa, Neuer Markt 3, A-1015, 51 59 40, Telex 112292 – . AE E VISA. rest CV **a**
M a la carte 245/470 – **102 rm** 1200/1860 Bb.

Rathauspark without rest, Rathausstr. 17, A-1010, 4 23 66 10, Telex 112817 – wc wc . AE E VISA S **t**
117 rm 1010/1290.

K u. K Palais Hotel without rest (modern hotel in a former palace), Rudolfsplatz 11, A-1010, 6 31 35 30/53 31 35 30, Telex 134049 – wc wc . AE E VISA. CU **h**
66 rm 1300/1650 Bb.

Stefanie, Taborstr. 12, A-1020, 24 24 12, Telex 134589, – wc wc DU **d**
130 rm Bb.

Capricorno without rest, Schwedenplatz 3, A-1010, 6 33 10 40/53 33 10 40, Telex 115266 – wc wc . AE VISA DV **f**
46 rm 1020/1640.

Amadeus without rest, Wildpretmarkt 5, A-1010, 63 87 38, Telex 111102 – wc wc . AE VISA CV **y**
closed 22 December - 6 January – **30 rm** 890/1680.

Hungaria, Rennweg 51, A-1030, 73 25 21, Telex 131797 – wc wc . AE E VISA. rest S **h**
M a la carte 155/310 – **168 rm** 1100/1600 Bb.

Etap Hotel Belvedere, Am Heumarkt 35, A-1030, 75 25 35, Telex 111822 – wc – **211 rm** Bb. CX **e**

Dorkahof without rest, Breite Gasse 9, A-1070, 9 31 34 50, Telex 136614 – wc wc . AE E VISA S **u**
closed 23 to 26 December – **55 rm** 930/1420 Bb.

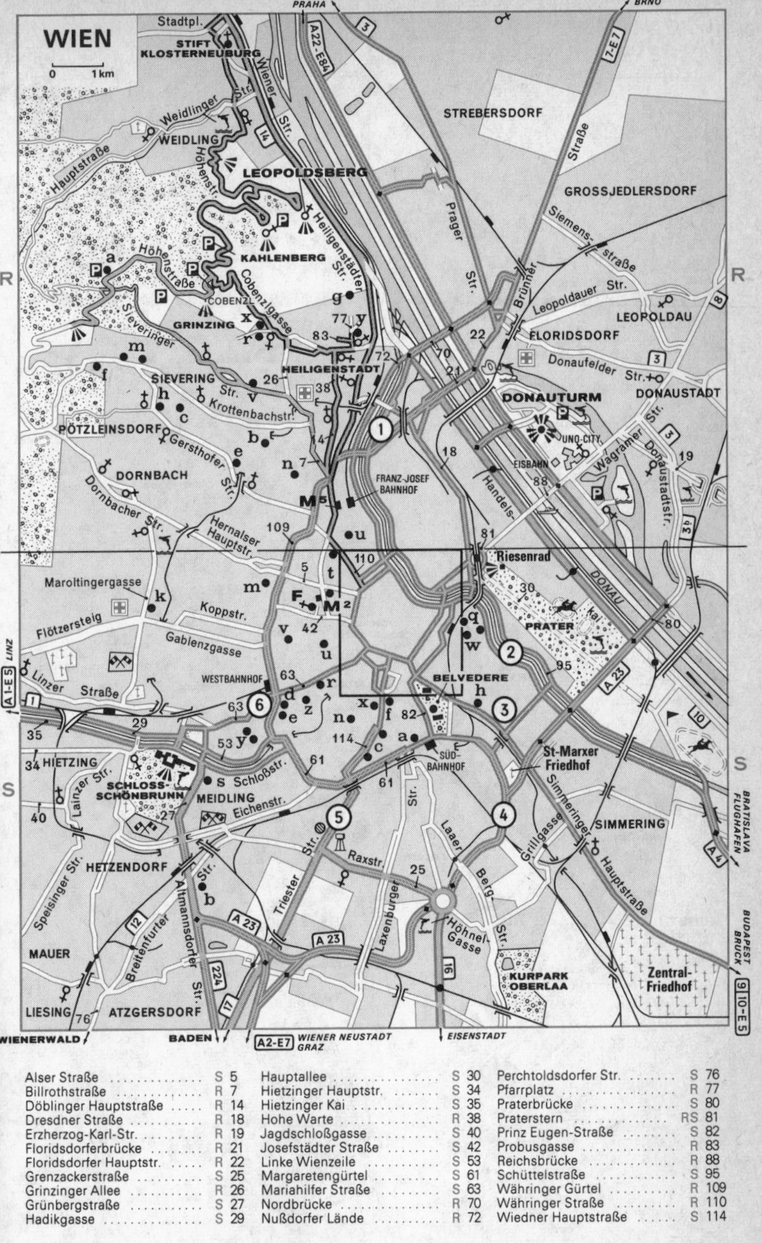

Alser Straße	S 5	Hauptallee	S 30	Perchtoldsdorfer Str.	S 76
Billrothstraße	R 7	Hietzinger Hauptstr.	S 34	Pfarrplatz	R 77
Döblinger Hauptstraße	R 14	Hietzinger Kai	S 35	Praterbrücke	S 80
Dresdner Straße	R 18	Hohe Warte	R 38	Praterstern	RS 81
Erzherzog-Karl-Str.	R 19	Jagdschloßgasse	S 40	Prinz Eugen-Straße	S 82
Floridsdorferbrücke	R 21	Josefstädter Straße	S 42	Probusgasse	R 83
Floridsdorfer Hauptstr.	R 22	Linke Wienzeile	S 53	Reichsbrücke	R 88
Grenzackerstraße	S 25	Margaretengürtel	S 61	Schüttelstraße	S 95
Grinzinger Allee	R 26	Mariahilfer Straße	S 63	Währinger Gürtel	R 109
Grünbergstraße	S 27	Nordbrücke	R 70	Währinger Straße	R 110
Hadikgasse	S 29	Nußdorfer Lände	R 72	Wiedner Hauptstraße	S 114

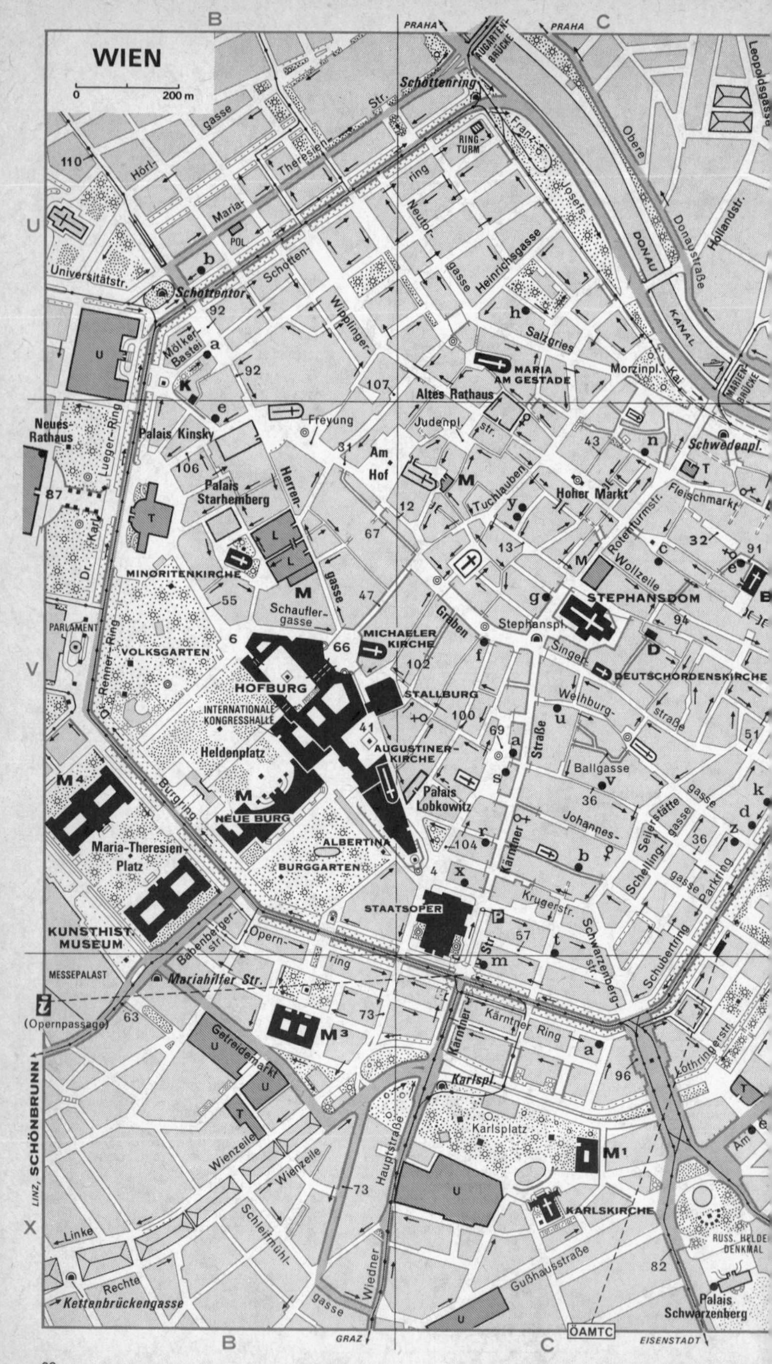
WIEN
0
200 m
B
C
U
V
X
PRAHA
Schottenring
Schottentor
Universitätsstr.
Hörlgasse
Maria-Theresien-Str.
Franz-Josefs-Kai
RINGTURM
Obere Donaustraße
Leopoldsgasse
Hollandstr.
DONAU KANAL
Neutorgasse
Heinrichsgasse
Schottengasse
Wipplingerstr.
Salzgries
MARIA AM GESTADE
Morzinpl.
MARIENBRÜCKE
AUGARTENBRÜCKE
Mölker-Bastei
Altes Rathaus
Freyung
Judenpl.
Am Hof
Neues Rathaus
Palais Kinsky
Palais Starhemberg
Herrengasse
Tuchlauben
Hoher Markt
Schwedenpl.
Fleischmarkt
Rotenturmstr.
Wollzeile
Dr.-Karl-Lueger-Ring
MINORITENKIRCHE
Schauflergasse
Graben
Stephanspl.
STEPHANSDOM
Singerstr.
DEUTSCHORDENSKIRCHE
PARLAMENT
VOLKSGARTEN
MICHAELERKIRCHE
HOFBURG
STALLBURG
INTERNATIONALE KONGRESSHALLE
Heldenplatz
AUGUSTINERKIRCHE
Palais Lobkowitz
Weihburgg.
Ballgasse
Dr.-Renner-Ring
Burgring
NEUE BURG
ALBERTINA
BURGGARTEN
Kärntner Straße
Johannesg.
Seilerstätte
Schellinggasse
Parkring
Maria-Theresien-Platz
KUNSTHIST. MUSEUM
STAATSOPER
Krugerstr.
Schwarzenbergstr.
Schubertring
Babenbergerstr.
Opernring
MESSEPALAST
Mariahilfer Str.
(Opernpassage)
Getreidemarkt
Kärntner Ring
Lothringerstr.
Karlspl.
Karlsplatz
Linke Wienzeile
Rechte Wienzeile
Hauptstraße
Wiedner
Schleifmühlgasse
KARLSKIRCHE
Gußhausstraße
RUSS. HELDENDENKMAL
Palais Schwarzenberg
Kettenbrückengasse
LINZ, SCHÖNBRUNN
GRAZ
ÖAMTC
EISENSTADT
POL

STREET INDEX TO WIEN TOWN PLANS

President, Wallgasse 23, ✉ A-1060, ☎ 5 99 90, Telex 112523 – [lift] [air] [TV] [bath]wc ☎ [car] [conf]. AE ⓓ E VISA S **e**
M a la carte 190/370 – **77 rm** 1080/1580.

Astoria, Führichgasse 1, ✉ A-1015, ☎ 51 57 70, Telex 112856 – [lift] [air] rest [TV] [bath]wc ☎. AE ⓓ E VISA CV **r**
M 255/440 a la carte 235/440 – **108 rm** 1140/2310 Bb.

Strudlhof without rest, Pasteurgasse 1, ✉ A-1090, ☎ 31 25 22, Telex 135256 – [lift] [TV] [bath]wc ☎ [car] R **u**
48 rm Bb.

Kummer, Mariahilfer Str. 71 A, ✉ A-1061, ☎ 5 88 95, Telex 111417 – [lift] [TV] [bath]wc [shower]wc ☎. AE ⓓ E VISA S **r**
M a la carte 215/375 – **108 rm** 870/1950.

Erzherzog Rainer, Wiedner Hauptstr. 27, ✉ A-1041, ☎ 6 54 64 60/50 11 10, Telex 132329 – [lift] [air] rest [TV] [bath]wc [shower]wc ☎ [conf]. AE ⓓ E VISA S **f**
M a la carte 235/445 – **84 rm** 930/1760.

Prinz Eugen, Wiedner Gürtel 14, ✉ A-1040, ☎ 65 17 41, Telex 132483 – [lift] [TV] [bath]wc [shower]wc ☎. AE ⓓ E VISA S **a**
M a la carte 195/400 – **106 rm** 915/1950.

Graben, Dorotheergasse 3, ✉ A-1010, ☎ 5 12 15 31 – [lift] [bath]wc [shower]wc ☎ CV **f**
Restaurants : – **Altenberg** – **Trattoria Santo Stefano** – **46 rm** Bb.

Mailberger Hof without rest, Annagasse 7, ✉ A-1010, ☎ 51 20 64 10, Telex 133828 – [lift] [TV] [bath]wc ☎ CV **b**
40 rm.

Mercure, Fleischmarkt 1a, ✉ A-1010, ☎ 63 47 31, Telex 112048 – [lift] [TV] [bath]wc ☎. AE ⓓ E VISA CV **n**
M a la carte 190/350 – **105 rm** 1120/1160 Bb.

Ibis, Mariahilfer Gürtel 22, ✉ A-1060, ☎ 56 56 26, Telex 133833 – [lift] [bath]wc [shower]wc ☎ [disabled] [P] [conf]. AE ⓓ E VISA S **d**
M a la carte 165/325 – **341 rm** 890/1360 Bb.

Attaché without rest, Wiedner Hauptstr. 71, ✉ A-1040, ☎ 65 18 18, Telex 111146 – [lift] [TV] [bath]wc [shower]wc ☎. AE ⓓ E VISA S **c**
23 rm 790/1580.

Am Parkring, Parkring 12, ✉ A-1015, ☎ 52 65 24/5 12 65 24, Telex 113420, ≤ – [lift] [air] [TV] [bath]wc ☎ [car]. AE ⓓ E VISA. [no dogs] CV **k**
M a la carte 180/435 – **64 rm** 1020/1760 Bb.

Am Stephansplatz, Stephansplatz 9, ✉ A-1010, ☎ 6 35 60 50/53 40 50, Telex 114334 – [lift] [air] rest [TV] [bath]wc [shower]wc ☎. AE ⓓ E VISA CV **g**
M a la carte 190/320 – **62 rm** 1040/1540 Bb.

Alpha without rest, Boltzmanngasse 8, ✉ A-1090, ☎ 31 16 46, Telex 115749 – [lift] [bath]wc [shower]wc ☎ [car]. AE ⓓ E VISA R **u**
70 rm 775/1435.

Alba, Margaretenstr. 53, ✉ A-1050, ☎ 5 88 50, Telex 113264 – [lift] [TV] [bath]wc [shower]wc ☎ [car]. AE ⓓ E VISA. [no dogs] rest S **n**
M a la carte 170/290 – **46 rm** 1090/1540 Bb.

Atlanta without rest, Währinger Str. 33, ✉ A-1090, ☎ 42 12 30, Telex 115002 – [lift] [bath]wc [shower]wc ☎. AE ⓓ E VISA RS **t**
57 rm 690/1300.

XXX ✿ **Steirereck**, Rasumofskygasse 2 / Ecke Weißgerberlände, ✉ A-1030, ☎ 73 31 68 – AE S **q**
closed Saturday, Sunday and Bank Holidays – **M** a la carte 385/565 (booking essential) (remarkable wine list)
Spec. Rote Paprikatorte mit Wachtelbrüstchen, Crépinette vom Milchlamm, Apfel-Weißbrotauflauf mit Zimteis.

XXX ✿ **Gottfried**, Untere Viaduktgasse 45/Maxgasse 3, ✉ A-1010, ☎ 73 82 56/7 13 82 56 – AE ⓓ E VISA S **q**
closed Sunday and Bank Holidays, Saturday lunch only – **M** a la carte 400/745 (booking essential)
Spec. Fische und Krustentiere, Rohe Rinderfiletscheiben mit Rührei und Schalottenrahm.

XXX **Zu den drei Husaren**, Weihburggasse 4, ✉ A-1010, ☎ 5 12 10 92 – AE ⓓ E VISA CV **u**
closed mid July - mid August – **M** (dinner only) a la carte 400/720 (booking essential).

XXX ✿ **Hauswirth**, Otto-Bauer-Gasse 20, ✉ A-1060, ☎ 5 87 12 61 – AE ⓓ E VISA S **z**
closed Sunday and Bank Holidays – **M** a la carte 315/495 (booking essential)
Spec. Roulade von der Bachforelle, Kalbsbriesrose mit Gänseleber in Blätterteig, Rehrückenfilet in der Semmelhülle auf Wacholdersauce.

XXX **Belvedere Stöckl**, Prinz-Eugen-Str. 25, ✉ A-1030, ☎ 78 41 98, « Garden » – AE E VISA
M a la carte 265/455. S

XXX Kervansaray, Mahlerstr. 9, ✉ A-1010, ☎ 51 12 88 43 – [air]. [no dogs] CVX **t**
(booking essential) – **Hummer Bar** *(dinner only, mainly Seafood)*.

XX ❀ **Mattes**, Schönlaterngasse 8, ✉ A-1010, ℘ 52 62 75 – AE ⓓ E VISA. ⌀ CV **e**
closed Sunday, Bank Holidays, August and 22 December - 2 January – **M** (dinner only) a la carte 380/630 (booking essential)
Spec. Kalbsbriessuppe mit Gänseleber, Ravioli von Jakobsmuscheln im Basilikumsud, Täubchenbrüstchen im Salzteig.

XX **Kupferdachl**, Schottengasse 7, ✉ A-1010, ℘ 63 93 81 – AE ⓓ E VISA BU **a**
closed Saturday lunch, Sunday and 26 July - 17 August – **M** a la carte 290/470 – **Leupold M** a la carte 185/355.

XX **Schubertstüberln**, Schreyvogelgasse 4, ✉ A-1010, ℘ 63 71 87 – AE ⓓ E VISA BV **e**
closed Saturday in July - August, Sunday and 24 December - 6 January – **M** a la carte 170/450 ♁.

XX **Steinerne Eule**, Halbgasse 30, ✉ A-1070, ℘ 93 72 68, 孟 – AE ⓓ E VISA S **v**
closed Sunday and Monday – **M** a la carte 240/455.

XX **Steirer Stüberl**, Wiedner Hauptstr. 111, ✉ A-1050, ℘ 55 43 49 – ⓓ E VISA S **c**
closed Sunday – **M** a la carte 210/390 ♁.

XX **Zum Kuckuck**, Himmelpfortgasse 15, ✉ A-1010, ℘ 5 12 84 70 – AE ⓓ E VISA CV **v**
closed Saturday and Sunday – **M** a la carte 280/450(booking essential).

XX **Salut**, Wildpretmarkt 3, ✉ A-1010, ℘ 63 13 22/5 33 13 22 – AE ⓓ E VISA CV **y**
lunch only except Saturday, closed Sunday and Bank Holidays – **M** a la carte 300/480.

XX Wiener Rathauskeller (vaults with murals turn of the century), Rathausplatz 1, ✉ A-1010, ℘ 42 12 19 BV

X **Wein-Comptoir** (old vaulted wine cellar), Bäckerstr. 6, ✉ A-1010, ℘ 5 12 17 60 – AE ⓓ E VISA CV **c**
closed Saturday, Sunday, 3 to 21 August and Bank Holidays – **M** a la carte 205/430 (booking essential) ♁.

X Goldener Hecht, Waaggasse 5, ✉ A-1040, ℘ 5 87 06 95, « Court-terrace » S **x**

X Do und Co (Bistro in a delicatessen store), Akademiestr. 3, ✉ A-1010, ℘ 52 64 74 – ⌀ (booking essential). CV **t**

City districts south (Stadtbezirke) 12-15 :

🏨 **Garten Hotel Altmannsdorf** ⛰, Hoffingergasse 26, ✉ A-1120, ℘ 84 75 27, Telex 135327, 孟, Park, ≘s – |♦| TV ⌂wc ⋒wc ☎ ⇔ P 🏃. AE ⓓ E VISA S **b**
closed 3 to 7 January and 24 to 28 December – **M** a la carte 200/370 – **41 rm** 890/1290 Bb.

🏨 **Reither**, Graumanngasse 16, ✉ A-1150, ℘ 85 61 65, Telex 136430, ≘s, ⊠ – |♦| TV ⌂wc ☎ ⇔. AE ⓓ E VISA. ⌀ rest S **y**
M *(dinner only, closed Saturday, Sunday and Bank Holidays)* a la carte 165/315 – **50 rm** 850/1200 Bb.

🏨 **Arabella - Hotel Jagdschloß** without rest, Jagdschloßgasse 79, ✉ A-1130, ℘ 84 35 08, ⛱, ⛱ – |♦| TV ⌂wc ⋒wc ☎ by Jagdschloßgasse S
closed 5 January - 8 February – **40 rm** 640/980.

🏨 Kaiserpark-Schönbrunn, Grünbergstr. 11, ✉ A-1120, ℘ 83 86 10, Telex 134754 – |♦| TV ⌂wc ⋒wc ☎ – *(dinner only)* – **46 rm** Bb. S **s**

XX **Altwienerhof** with rm (wine list with 400 wines), Herklotzgasse 6, ✉ A-1150, ℘ 83 71 45, « Winter garden, court terrace » – |♦| ⋒wc ☎. AE S **y**
closed 1 to 21 January – **M** *(closed Sunday)* a la carte 305/600 (booking essential) – **22 rm** 490/1600 Bb.

City districts (Stadtbezirke) 16-19 :

🏨 **Modul** M, Peter-Jordan-Str. 78, ✉ A-1190, ℘ 4 71 58 40, Telex 116736 – |♦| ▤ TV ♿ ⇔ P 🏃. AE ⓓ E VISA R **b**
M a la carte 210/410 – **42 rm** 1110/2300 Bb.

🏨 **Cottage** without rest, Hasenauerstr. 12, ✉ A-1190, ℘ 31 25 71, Telex 134146 – |♦| TV ⌂wc ⋒wc ☎ 🏃. AE ⓓ E VISA R **n**
closed 22 to 28 December – **23 rm** 900/1400 Bb.

🏨 **Clima Villenhotel** ⛰, Nussberggasse 2c, ✉ A-1190, ℘ 37 15 16, Telex 115670, « Rest. Bockkeller, vaulted cellar with Tyrolian farmhouse furniture », ≘s, ⛱, ⊠, ⛱ – |♦| TV ⌂wc ☎ ⇔ P 🏃. AE ⓓ E VISA R **g**
M *(dinner only, closed Sunday)* a la carte 185/340 ♁ – **33 rm** 1300/1700 Bb – 8 apartments.

🏨 Maté, Ottakringer Str. 34, ✉ A-1170, ℘ 43 61 33, Telex 115485, ≘s, ⊠ – |♦| ▤ rest TV ⌂wc ⋒wc ☎ P S **m**
125 rm Bb.

🏨 **Gartenhotel Glanzing** ⛰ without rest, Glanzinggasse 23, ✉ A-1190, ℘ 47 42 72 – |♦| TV ⌂wc ⋒wc ☎ ⇔ R **c**
20 rm 820/1260 Bb.

🏨 **Hadrigan**, Maroltinger Gasse 68, ✉ A-1160, ℘ 92 54 26, Telex 135951 – |♦| ⌂wc ⋒wc ☎ S **k**
(closed Saturday, Sunday and Bank Holidays) a la carte 135/270 – **47 rm** 440/760.

🏨 **Schild** without rest, Neustift am Walde 97, ✉ A-1190, ℘ 4 42 19 10, ⛱ – |♦| ⌂wc ⋒wc ☎ ♿ P – **32 rm** 560/930 Bb. R **f**

XX **Fischerhaus**, an der Höhenstraße, ✉ A-1190, ℘ 44 13 20, « Terrace and winter garden with ≤ » – P. AE ⊙ E VISA R a
closed 15 December - 15 January, Sunday dinner and Monday – **M** a la carte 320/600.

XX **Sailer**, Gersthofer Str. 14, ✉ A-1180, ℘ 47 21 21, 🍽, « Kellerstuben » – AE ⊙ E VISA
closed Sunday and Bank Holidays – **M** a la carte 255/430. R e

X **Eckel**, Sieveringer Str. 46, ✉ A-1190, ℘ 32 32 18, 🍽 – AE ⊙ R v
closed Sunday, Monday, 15 to 24 August and 24 December - 11 January – **M** a la carte 170/455 🍷.

X **Römischer Kaiser**, Neustift am Walde 2, ✉ A-1190, ℘ 44 11 04, « Terraced garden with ≤ Vienna » R h
closed Tuesday, Wednesday and 8 January - 8 February – **M** a la carte 155/300.

Heurigen and Buschen-Schänken (wine gardens) – **(mostly self-service, hot and cold dishes from buffet, prices according to weight of chosen meals, Buschen-Schänken sell their own wines only) :**

X **Kirchenstöckl**, Himmelstr. 4, ℘ 32 15 71 – AE ⊙ E VISA R x
closed Sunday and July - August – **M** *(dinner only)* a la carte 205/360 🍷.

X **Oppolzer**, Himmelstr. 22, ✉ A-1190, ℘ 32 24 16, « Garden » R r
closed Sunday and 20 December - 15 January – **M** (dinner only) a la carte 150/250 (buffet) (booking essential).

X **Altes Preßhaus**, Cobenzlgasse 15, ✉ A-1190, ℘ 32 23 93, 🍽, « Old vaulted wine cellar » – AE ⊙ E VISA R x
closed until 4 p.m and 5 January - 28 February – **M** a la carte 195/275 (and buffet) 🍷.

X **Fuhrgassl Huber** (Wine-garden with Viennese Schrammelmusik), Neustift am Walde 68, ✉ A-1190, ℘ 44 14 05, « Court-terrace » R m
closed until 2.30 p.m. – **M** a la carte 130/250 (buffet) 🍷.

X **Grinzinger Hauermandl**, Cobenzlgasse 20, ✉ A-1190, ℘ 32 30 27, 🍽 – AE ⊙ E VISA
closed until 5.30 p.m. and Sunday – **M** a la carte 155/300 🍷. R x

X **Wolff** (Buschenschank), Rathstr. 44, ✉ A-1190, ℘ 44 23 35, « Terraced Garden »
closed Monday to Saturday until 2.30 p.m., Sunday until 11.30 a.m. – **M** a la carte 130/300 (buffet) 🍷. R m

X **Grinzinger Weinbottich**, Cobenzlgasse 28, ✉ A-1190, ℘ 32 42 37, « Shady garden » – AE ⊙ E VISA R x
closed until 5.30 p.m. and Monday – **M** a la carte 155/300 🍷.

X **Mayer** (Buschenschank with Viennese Schrammelmusik), Pfarrplatz 2, ✉ A-1190, ℘ 37 12 87, « Shady garden » – AE E VISA R y
closed until 4 p.m.and 20 December - 10 January – **M** a la carte 120/300 (buffet) 🍷.

at Perchtoldsdorf ⑤ : 10 km :

XXX ❀ **La Tour**, Hochstr. 17, ✉ A-2380, ℘ (0222) 86 47 65 – AE ⊙ E VISA
closed August, Saturday lunch, Sunday dinner and Monday – **M** a la carte 360/660 (booking essential)
Spec. Marinierte Gänsestopfleber, Crépinette von Saibling und Lachs, Lammkoteletts mit Buchweizen-Kruste.

X **Killermann** (Heurigen-Lokal), Sonnbergstr. 22, ✉ A-2380 Perchtoldsdorf, ℘ (0222) 86 81 81, 🍽 – 🚫
closed until 6 p.m., Sunday, Monday, Bank Holidays, April 2 weeks, August and 23 December - 12 January – **M** *(self-service)* a la carte 150/250 (buffet, booking essential) 🍷.

at Vösendorf S : 11 km by A 2 or B 17 S :

🏨 **Novotel Wien-Süd**, Nordring 4 (Shopping City Süd), ✉ A-2334 Vösendorf, ℘ (0222) 69 26 01, Telex 134793, 🍽, 🏊 – 🛗 ▤ rest 📺 ⛀wc ☎ ♿ P 🏋. AE ⊙ E VISA
M a la carte 175/360 – **102 rm** 980/1300 Bb.

at Schwechat ③ : 13 km by B 9 :

🏨 **Jesuitenmühle**, Mühlgasse 30, ✉ A-2320 Schwechat, ℘ (0222) 77 66 14, Telex 135020, ≘s – 🛗 📺 ⛀wc 🚿wc ☎ P 🏋. AE
M *(closed Sunday from December to March)* a la carte 150/270 – **62 rm** 650/860 Bb.

🏨 **Reinisch**, Mannswörther Str. 76 (Mannswörth), ✉ A-2323 Schwechat, ℘ (0222) 77 82 18, 🍽 – 📺 🚿wc ☎ P. VISA
M *(closed Sunday and Bank Holidays)* a la carte 115/275 – **36 rm** 530/740.

at Vienna-Schwechat airport ② : 20 km :

🏨 **Novotel Wien Airport**, ✉ A-1300 Schwechat, ℘ (0222) 77 66 66, Telex 111566, 🍽, 🏊 – 🛗 ▤ rest 📺 ⛀wc ☎ ♿ P 🏋. AE ⊙ E VISA
M a la carte 180/270 – **127 rm** 980/1300 Bb.

at Groß-Enzersdorf E : 16 km, by Erzherzog-Karl-Str. R :

🏨 **Am Sachsengang**, Schloßhofer Str. 60 (B 3), ✉ A-2301 Groß-Enzersdorf, ℘ (02249) 2 90 10, Telex 136236, « Terrace », Massage, ≘s, 🏊, 🌳 – ⛀wc ☎ ♿ P 🏋. AE ⊙ E VISA
closed 22 to 25 December – **M** a la carte 240/350 – **54 rm** 690/970 Bb.

at Baden ⑤ : 28 km by B 17 or A 2 – Spa – 02252 :

Grand-Hotel Sauerhof zu Rauhenstein, Weilburgstr. 11, A-2500 Baden, 4 12 51, Telex 14334, Massage, – rest (with). AE E
M a la carte 220/445 – **87 rm** 900/1500 Bb.

Krainerhütte, Helenental (W : 6 km), A-2500 Baden, 4 45 11, Telex 14303, – wc wc . AE E
M a la carte 225/590 – **67 rm** 750/1480 Bb.

Parkhotel, Kaiser-Franz-Ring 5, A-2500 Baden, 4 43 86, Telex 14461, Massage, – wc . AE E VISA. rest
M a la carte 240/450 – **90 rm** 870/1350 Bb.

Gutenbrunn, Pelzgasse 22, A-2500 Baden, 4 81 71, Telex 14304, direct entrance to the spa-centre – wc . AE E VISA
M a la carte 225/410 – **80 rm** 870/1850 Bb.

by motorway A 1 W : 8 km :

Novotel Wien-West, Wientalstraße (Auhof motorway station), A-1140, (0222) 97 25 42, Telex 135584, – wc . AE E VISA
M a la carte 195/475 – **115 rm** 980/1280 Bb.

by motorway A 1 W : 30 km :

Motor-Hotel Grossram, A-3033 Großram, (02773) 66 51, Telex 15692 – wc . AE E VISA
M a la carte 160/350 – **42 rm** 650/900.

SALZBURG 5020. Austria 987 ㊳, 426 ⑲ ⑳, 413 W 23 – pop. 140 000 – alt. 425 m – 0662.

See : Site (Stadtbild) ≤ ** Y **K** – Hohensalzburg** Z : ≤** (from the Kuenburg Bastion), ** (from the Reck Tower), Museum (Burgmuseum) * Z **M3** – St. Peter's Churchyard (Petersfriedhof)** Z – St. Peter's Church (Stiftskirche St. Peter)** Z – Residenz** Z – Natural History Museum (Haus der Natur)** Y **M2** – Franciscan's Church (Franziskanerkirche)* Z **A** – Getreidegasse* Y – Mirabell Gardens (Mirabellgarten)* V – Hettwer Bastei* : ≤* Y – Mozart's Birthplace (Mozarts Geburtshaus) Y **D**.

Envir. : Road to the Gaisberg (Gaisbergstraße)** (≤*) by ① – Untersberg* by ② : 10 km (with) – Mondsee* ① : 28 km (by motorway A 1).

71 54 14 22.

Exhibition Centre (Messegelände), Linke Glanzeile 65, 3 45 66.

Tourist Information (Stadtverkehrsbüro), Auerspergstr. 7, 7 15 11.

ÖAMTC, Alpenstr. 102, 2 05 01.

Wien 292 ① – Innsbruck 177 ③ – München 140 ③.

Plans on following pages

Salzburg Sheraton Hotel M, Auerspergstr. 4, 79 32 10, Telex 632518, entrance to the spa facilities – . AE E VISA. rest V **s**
Restaurants : – **Mirabell M** a la carte 310/545 – **Bistro M** a la carte 180/380 – **165 rm** 1650/3250 Bb.

Bristol, Makartplatz 4, 7 35 57, Telex 633337, « Tastefully furnished, collection of pictures » – rest . AE E VISA Y **a**
closed 2 January - 15 March – **M** a la carte 370/600 – **80 rm** 1300/3450.

Österreichischer Hof, Schwarzstr. 5, 7 25 41, Telex 633590, « Salzach-side setting, terrace with ≤ old town and castle » – (with). AE E VISA Y **b**
Restaurants : – **Roter Salon M** a la carte 190/490 – **Salzach Grill M** a la carte 115/370 – **120 rm** 980/2530.

Goldener Hirsch, Getreidegasse 37, 84 85 11, Telex 632967, « 15 C Patrician house, tastefully furnished » – rest . AE E VISA Y **e**
M a la carte 280/520 – **57 rm** 1700/4400.

Schloß Mönchstein, Am Mönchsberg 26, 8 41 36 30, Telex 632080, ≤, « Park », – X **e**
17 rm.

Pitter, Rainerstr. 6, 78 57 10, Telex 633532, – . AE E VISA. rest
M a la carte 165/330 – **220 rm** 590/1650. V **n**

Europa, Rainerstr. 31, 73 39 10, Telex 633424, rest. on the 14th floor with ≤ Salzburg and environs – rest wc wc (with). AE E VISA V **b**
M a la carte 180/380 – **104 rm** 820/1570 Bb.

Winkler, Franz-Josef-Str. 7, 7 35 13, Telex 633961 – wc . AE E VISA V **f**
M a la carte 160/460 – **103 rm** 980/1980 Bb.

Kasererhof, Alpenstr. 6, 2 12 65, Telex 633477, – wc wc . AE E VISA by ②
closed February – **M** *(closed Saturday and Sunday)* a la carte 220/440 – **51 rm** 810/2420 Bb.

SALZBURG

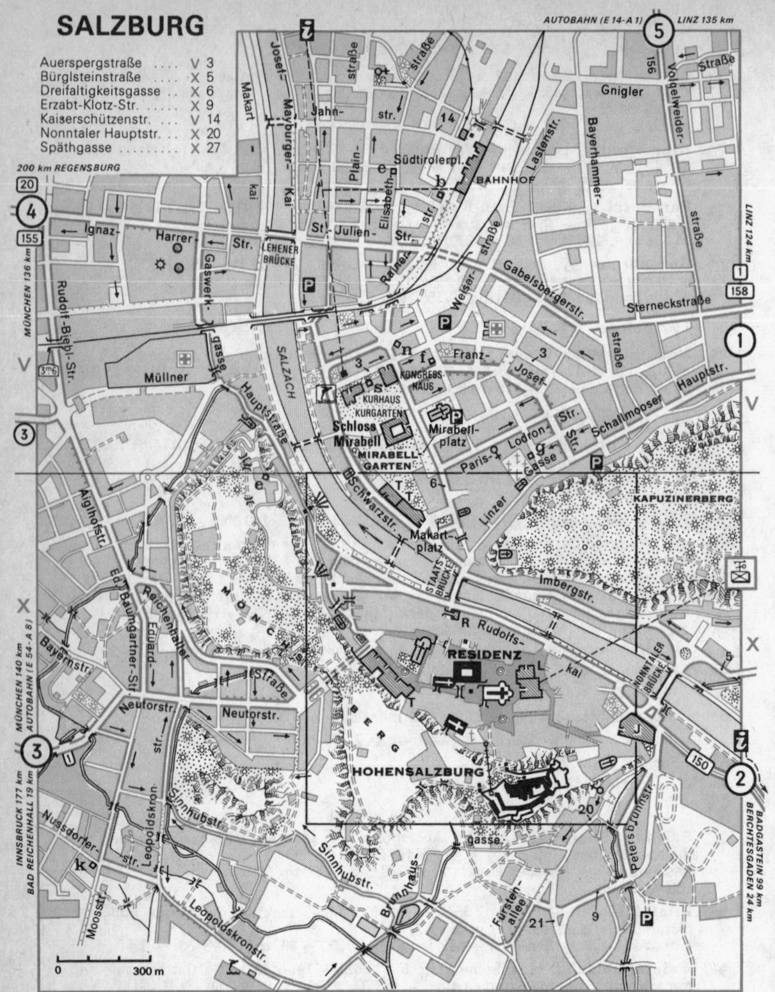

🏨 **Fuggerhof** without rest, Eberhard-Fugger-Str. 9, ☎ 2 04 79, Telex 632533, ≤, sauna, garden – bath wc shower wc ☎ garage P by Bürglsteinstr. X
closed 23 December - 7 January – **20 rm** 650/1600.

🏨 **Hohenstaufen** without rest, Elisabethstr. 19, ☎ 7 21 93 – lift bath wc shower wc ☎ garage. AE DC E VISA – **28 rm** 620/1290. V **e**

🏨 **Schaffenrath**, Alpenstr. 115, ☎ 2 31 53, Telex 633207, Massage, sauna – lift TV bath wc shower wc ☎ P. AE DC E VISA by ②
M a la carte 125/310 – **50 rm** 590/1400 Bb.

🏨 Elefant, Sigmund-Haffner-Gasse 4, ☎ 84 33 97, Telex 632725 – lift bath wc shower wc ☎
36 rm. Y **f**

🏨 **Weiße Taube** without rest, Kaigasse 9, ☎ 84 24 04, Telex 633065 – lift bath wc shower wc ☎. AE DC E VISA. – **30 rm** 380/1250. Z **r**

🏨 **Nußdorfer Hof** without rest, Moosstr. 36, ☎ 84 52 24, Telex 632515, sauna, pool (heated), garden, tennis – lift bath wc shower wc ☎ disabled garage P. AE E VISA X **k**
35 rm 490/1180.

🏨 **Wolf-Dietrich**, Wolf-Dietrich-Str. 7, ☎ 7 12 75, Telex 633877, sauna, indoor pool – lift bath wc shower wc ☎. AE DC E VISA. rest V **g**
closed 8 February - 8 March – **M** *(closed Sunday)* a la carte 150/350 – **32 rm** 590/1320.

XX **Café Winkler**, Mönchsberg 32 (access by lift, 15 A.S.), ☎ 8 41 21 50, ≤ Salzburg, « Modern café-rest. on the Mönchsberg, terraces » – AE ⓓ E VISA Y
closed Monday September - July – **M** a la carte 270/450.

XX **K u. K Restaurant am Waagplatz**, Waagplatz 2, ☎ 84 21 56, « Medieval dinner with period performance in the Freysauff-Keller (by arrangement) » – AE ⓓ E VISA
M a la carte 170/390 (booking essential). Z **h**

XX **Zum Mohren**, Judengasse 9, ☎ 84 23 87 Y **g**
closed Sunday, Bank Holidays and November – **M** a la carte 170/310 (booking essential).

XX Purzelbaum (Rest. in Bistro-style), Zugallistr. 7, ☎ 84 88 43 – Ⓟ. Z **e**
M *(dinner only)*.

at Salzburg-Aigen **5026** by Bürglsteinstr. X :

Doktorwirt, Glaser Str. 9, ☎ 2 29 73, Telex 632938, beer-garden, ≘s, (heated), – wc wc ☎ Ⓟ. AE E VISA
closed 25 October - 10 December – **M** *(closed Monday)* a la carte 115/270 – **39 rm** 400/850.

at Salzburg-Liefering by ④ :

Brandstätter, Münchner Bundesstr. 69, ☎ 3 45 35, beer-garden, ≘s, – wc wc ☎ Ⓟ. AE
closed 23 December - 13 January – **M** a la carte 195/430 – **36 rm** 560/1180.

at Salzburg-Maria Plain **5101** by Plainstr. V :

Maria Plain (17 C inn), Plainbergweg 33, ☎ 5 07 01, Telex 632801, « Garden with ≤ » – wc ☎ Ⓟ – **40 rm**.

at Salzburg-Parsch **5020** by Bürglsteinstr. X :

Fondachhof, Gaisbergstr. 46, ☎ 2 09 06, Telex 632519, ≤, « 18 C Manor house in a park », ≘s, (heated), – Ⓟ. AE ⓓ VISA. rest
April - October – (rest. for residents only) – **30 rm** 800/2700.

Cottage, Joseph-Messner-Str. 12, ☎ 2 45 71, Telex 632011, Massage, ≘s, ⊠ – |≑| TV ⊟wc ☎ ⟹ P ⛰. AE ⓓ E VISA
M a la carte 210/360 ⸗ – **115 rm** 995/3300 Bb.

Haus Ingeborg ⛰, Sonnleitenweg 9, ☎ 2 17 49, Telex 631141, ≤ town and Hohensalzburg, ≘s, ⛱, ⚘ – TV ⊟wc ☎ P
season only – (rest. for residents only) – **11 rm.**

on the Heuberg NE : 3 km by ① – alt. 565 m :

Schöne Aussicht ⛰, ✉ 5023 Salzburg, ☎ (0662) 7 82 26, Telex 631153, « Garden with ≤ Salzburg and Alps », ≘s, ⛱ (heated), ⚘, ✂ – ⊟wc ⋒wc ☎ P ⛰. AE ⓓ
March - October – **M** a la carte 160/450 ⸗ – **30 rm** 550/1000 Bb.

on the Gaisberg by ① :

Kobenzl ⛰, Judenbergalpe (E : 9 km alt. 750 m), ✉ 5020 Salzburg, ☎ (0662) 21 77 60, Telex 633833, ⛱, « Beautiful panoramic-location with ≤ Salzburg and Alps », Massage, ≘s, ⊠, ⚘ – TV ⟹ P ⛰. AE VISA. ⚹ rest
mid April - October – **M** a la carte 255/505 – **35 rm** 1200/3200 Bb.

Berghotel Zistel-Alm ⛰, (E : 12 km alt. 1 001 m), ✉ 5026 Salzburg-Aigen, ☎ (0662) 2 01 04, ≤ Alps, ⛱, ⛱, ⚘, ⚡ – ⊟wc ⋒wc ☎ ⟹ P. AE ⓓ E VISA
closed November - 21 December – **M** a la carte 160/380 ⸗ – **24 rm** 250/880 – 6 apartments 1400.

at Anif **5081** by ② : 7 km :

Romantik-Hotel Schloßwirt (17 C inn with Biedermeier furniture), ☎ (06246) 21 75, Telex 631169, « Garden », ⚘ – |≑| ⊟wc ⋒wc ☎ ⟹ P. AE ⓓ E VISA
closed February – **M** a la carte 220/390 – **32 rm** 490/1170 Bb.

Friesacher, ☎ (06246) 20 75, Telex 632943, « Garden », ⚘, ✂ – |≑| TV ⊟wc ⋒wc ☎ P ⛰. ⓓ
closed 23 December - 15 January – **M** *(closed Wednesday)* a la carte 160/350 ⸗ – **70 rm** 510/990.

at Hof **5322** by ① : 20 km :

Schloß Fuschl ⛰ (former 15C hunting seat with 3 annexes), ☎ (06229) 25 30/2 25 30, Telex 633454, ≤, ⛱, Massage, ≘s, ⊠, ⛵, ⚘, ✂, ⛳ – |≑| TV ⟹ P ⛰. AE ⓓ E VISA. ⚹ rest
closed 1 to 23 February – **M** a la carte 340/600 (booking essential) – **86 rm** 1000/3800 Bb.

Jagdhof am Fuschlsee, ☎ (06229) 37 20/2 37 20, Telex 633454, ≤, « Hunting museum », ≘s, ⊠, ⚘ – TV ⊟wc ⋒wc ☎ P ⛰. AE ⓓ E VISA
M a la carte 180/330 ⸗ – **50 rm** 450/950 Bb.

at Fuschl am See **5330** by ① : 26 km :

Parkhotel Waldhof ⛰, ☎ (06226) 2 64, Telex 632795, ≤, ⛱, Massage, ≘s, ⊠, ⛵, ⚘, ✂ – |≑| P ⛰. AE
closed 10 January - 20 March and November - 20 December – **M** a la carte 210/380 ⸗ – **63 rm** 490/1400.

XX **Brunnwirt**, ☎ (06226) 2 36, ⛱ – P. AE ⓓ E VISA. ⚹
closed Tuesday and 15 January - 15 February – **M** (week-days dinner only) a la carte 320/470 (booking essential).

at Mondsee **5310** ① : 28 km (by motorway A 1) :

❀ **Weißes Kreuz**, Herzog-Odilo-Str. 25, ☎ (06232) 22 54, « Garden » – |≑| ⊟wc ⋒wc ☎ ⟹ P
closed 10 November - 10 December – **M** *(closed Wednesday and Thursday lunch)* a la carte 290/520 (booking essential) – **10 rm** 400/1200.

XXX ❀ **Plomberg-Eschlböck** with rm, NE : 5 km, ☎ (06232) 29 12, ≤, ⛱, ≘s, ⛵, ⚘ – TV ⋒wc ☎ P. AE ⓓ E VISA
M *(closed Monday November - mid April)* a la carte 330/550 (booking essential) – **11 rm** 480/2000.

Benelux

Belgium

Brussels
Antwerp
Bruges
Liège

Luxembourg

Netherlands

Amsterdam
The Hague
Rotterdam

PRACTICAL INFORMATION

LOCAL CURRENCY

Belgian Franc : 100 F = 2.47 US $ (Jan. 87) can also be used in Luxembourg
Dutch Florin : 100 Fl. = 45.65 US $ (Jan. 87)

TOURIST INFORMATION

In Belgium : The B.B.B. Tourist House, rue du Marché-aux-Herbes 61, Brussels, open from 9am to 6pm (Sundays 1 to 5pm) in winter, and 9am to 8pm (weekends 9am to 7pm) in Summer.

In the Netherlands : Offices in Amsterdam open daily from 9am to 11.30pm ; in Den Haag (Scheveningen) weekdays from 9am to 9pm, Sundays 9am to 6pm, and in Rotterdam weekdays 9am to 6pm, Sundays 10am to 6pm.

FOREIGN EXCHANGE

In Belgium, banks close at 3.30pm and weekends ; **in the Netherlands,** banks close at 5.00pm and weekends, Schiphol Airport exchange offices open daily from 6.30am to 11.30pm.

TRANSPORT

Taxis : may be hailed in the street, found day and night at taxi ranks or called by telephone.

Bus, tramway : practical for long and short distances and good for sightseeing.

POSTAL SERVICES

Post offices open Monday to Friday from 9am to 5pm in Benelux.

SHOPPING

Shops and boutiques are generally open from 9am to 7pm in Belgium and Luxembourg, and from 9am to 6pm in the Netherlands. The main shopping areas are :

in Brussels : Rue Neuve, Porte de Namur, Avenue Louise - Second-hand goods and antiques : Brussels antique market on Saturday from 9am to 3pm, and Sunday from 9am to 1pm (around place du Grand-Sablon) - Flower market (Grand-Place) on Sunday morning.

in Antwerp : Bird Market : Sunday from 8.30am to 1pm - Antwerp diamond quarter.

in Bruges : Calashes on the Market Place for shopping and town sightseeing.

in Amsterdam : Kalverstraat, Leidsestraat, Nieuwendijk, P.C. Hoofstraat and Utrechtsestraat. Second-hand goods and antiques. Amsterdam Flea Market (near Waterlooplein).

in Den Haag : Hoogstraat, Korte Poten, Paleispromenade, De Passage and Spuistraat.

in Rotterdam : Binnenweg, Hoogstraat, Karel Doormanstraat, Lijnbaan and Stadhuisplein.

BREAKDOWN SERVICE

RACB : rue d'Arlon 53, Brussels ✆ (02) 230 08 68 and **TCB** : rue de la Loi 44, Brussels ✆ (02) 233 22 11 operate a 24 hour breakdown service. In the Netherlands, **ANWB**-Wegenwacht also offer 24 hour assistance.

TIPPING

In Benelux, prices include service and taxes. You may choose to leave a tip if you wish but there is no obligation to do so.

SPEED LIMITS

In Belgium and Luxembourg, the maximum speed limits are 120 km/h-74 mph on motorways and dual carriageways, 90 km/h-56 mph on all other roads and 60 km/h-37 mph in built-up areas. In the Netherlands, 100 km/h-62 mph on motorways and "autowegen", 80 km/h-50 mph on other roads and 50 km/h-31 mph in built-up areas.

SEAT BELTS

In each country, the wearing of seat belts is compulsory.

BRUSSELS

SIGHTS

See : Market Square*** (Grand-Place) LZ – Manneken Pis** KZ – Rue des Bouchers LZ – St. Michael's Cathedral** FU – Place du Grand Sablon* and the Church of Notre-Dame du Sablon* FV **D** – Anderlecht : Erasmus's House*.

Museums : Old Masters Gallery*** (Musée d'Art ancien : Brueghel) FV – Royal museum of Art and History*** (antiques, Belgian decorative art) – Musical Instruments** FV **M**[18].

Env. Forest of Soignes** – Tervuren : Royal Museum of Central Africa* ⑥ : 13 km – Beersel : Castle* S : 11 km – Gaasbeek : castle and grounds* SW : 12 km by rue de Lennick – Meise : Bouchout Estate*(Domaine de Bouchout) : Plant Palace** by ① : 13 km – Grimbergen : Confessional* in the abbey (Abdijkerk) by ①: 18 km – Vilvoorde : Choir stalls* of Our Lady's Church (O.L. Vrouwkerk).

BRUSSELS (BRUXELLES - BRUSSEL) 1000 Brabant **213** ⑱ and **409** ⑬ – Pop. 980 196 agglomeration – 02.

Château de Ravenstein at Tervuren by ⑥ : 13 km ✆ 7675801.

National NE : 12 km ✆ 7518080 – Air Terminal : Air Terminus, r. du Cardinal-Mercier 35 LZ **✆ 5119060.**

✆ 2186050 ext. 4106.

Town Hall (Hôtel de Ville), Grand'Place ✆ 5138940 – Tourist Association of the Province, r. Marché-aux-Herbes 61 ✆ 5130750.

Paris 308 ⑨ – Amsterdam 205 ① – Düsseldorf 222 ⑤ – Lille 116 ⑫ – Luxembourg 219 ⑦.

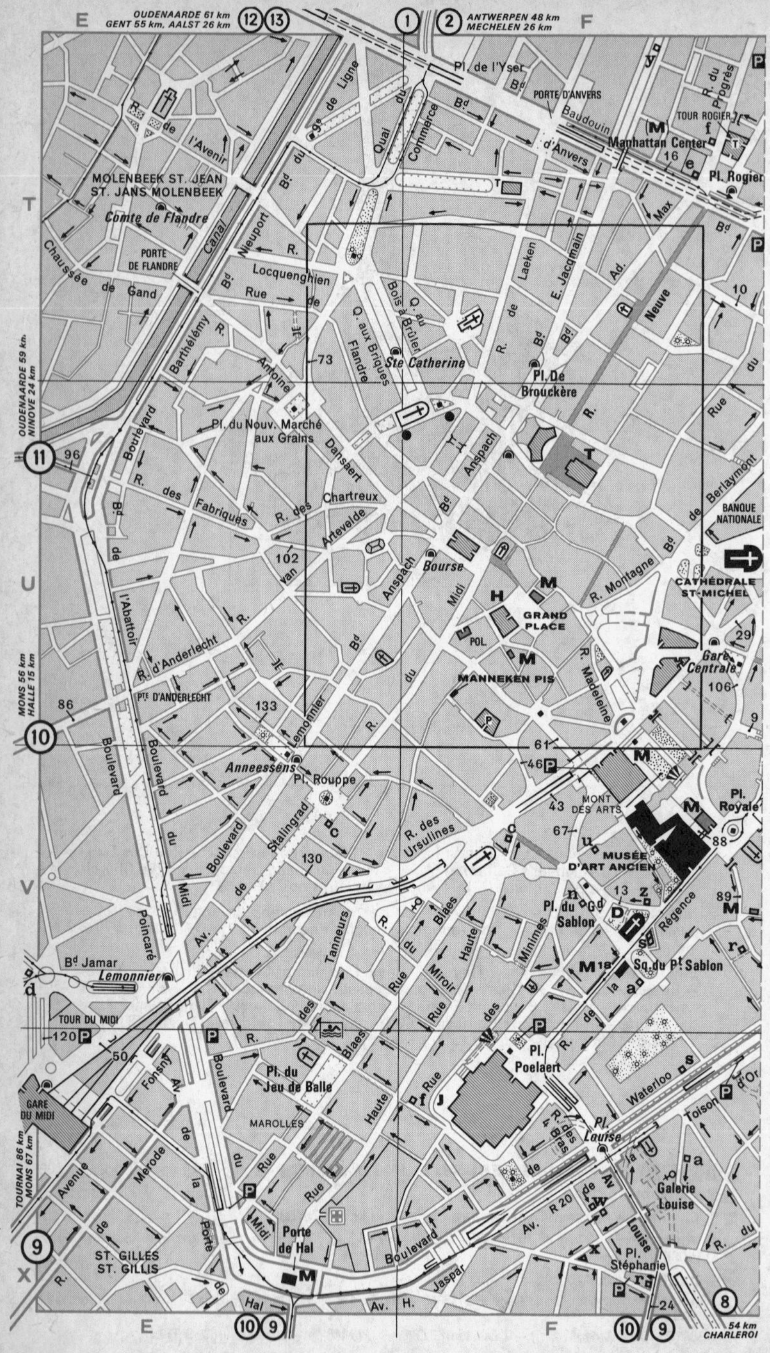
OUDENAARDE 61 km
GENT 55 km, AALST 26 km
ANTWERPEN 48 km
MECHELEN 26 km
Pl. de l'Yser
PORTE D'ANVERS
Bd Baudouin
d'Anvers
TOUR ROGIER
R. du Progrès
Manhattan Center
Pl. Rogier
MOLENBEEK ST. JEAN
ST. JANS MOLENBEEK
Comte de Flandre
PORTE DE FLANDRE
Chaussée de Gand
Canal
R. de l'Avenir
Quai du Commerce
Bd de Nieuport
Pce de Ligne
R. Locquenghien
Rue de Flandre
Q. au Bois à Brûler
Q. aux Briques
Ste Catherine
R. de Laeken
Bd E. Jacqmain
Bd Ad. Max
R. Neuve
Pl. De Brouckère
R. Barthélémy
R. Antoine Dansaert
Pl. du Nouv. Marché aux Grains
OUDENAARDE 59 km
NINOVE 24 km
Boulevard de l'Abattoir
R. des Fabriques
R. des Chartreux
R. van Artevelde
Bd Anspach
Bourse
Bd du Midi
BANQUE NATIONALE
Bd de Berlaymont
Rue du Marais
CATHÉDRALE ST-MICHEL
R. Montagne
GRAND PLACE
POL.
MANNEKEN PIS
R. Madeleine
Gare Centrale
R. d'Anderlecht
Pte D'ANDERLECHT
MONS 56 km
HALLE 15 km
Lemonnier
Anneessens
Pl. Rouppe
R. des Ursulines
Av. de Stalingrad
Boulevard Poincaré
MONT DES ARTS
MUSÉE D'ART ANCIEN
Pl. Royale
Pl. du Gd Sablon
R. de la Régence
R. des Minimes
R. du Miroir
Rue Haute
Rue des Tanneurs
Rue Blaes
Sq. du Pt Sablon
Bd Jamar
Lemonnier
TOUR DU MIDI
GARE DU MIDI
Av. Fonsny
Pl. du Jeu de Balle
MAROLLES
Pl. Poelaert
Bd de Waterloo
R. des 4 Bras
Pl. Louise
Toison d'Or
Galerie Louise
Av. de la Porte de Hal
Rue Haute
Porte de Hal
Boulevard
R. Jaspar
Av. H. Jaspar
Av. Louise
Pl. Stéphanie
TOURNAI 86 km
MONS 67 km
Avenue de Merode
ST. GILLES
ST. GILLIS
Hal
54 km CHARLEROI
E
F
T
U
V
X

BRUXELLES BRUSSEL CENTRE

Baron-Horta (R.) .... FU 9
Blanchisserie (R. de la) . FT 10
Bodenbroek (R.) .... FV 13
Boulevard (Av. du) ..... FT 16
Charleroi (Chaussée de) .... FX 24
Colonies (R. des) ...... FGU 29
Empereur (Bd de l') ..... FV 43
Ernest-Solvay (R.) ...... GX 45
Escalier (R. de l') .... FV 46
Esplanade (R. de l') ..... GV 47
Europe (Bd de l') .... EX 50
Hôpital (R. de l') ...... FUV 61
Joseph-Lebeau (R.) .... FV 67
Léon-Lepage (R.) ...... ET 73
Mons (Chée de) .... EU 86
Musée (R. du) .... FV 88
Namur (R. de) .... FGV 89

Ninove (Chée de) ..... EU 96
Pletinckx (R.) .... EU 102
Ravenstein (R.) .... FU 106
Remorqueur (R. du) ... HV 109
Spaak (Av.) .... EX 120
Vander Weyden (R.) ... EV 130
Verbist (R.) .... HU 132
Verdure (R. de la) ..... EU 133
Willems (R.) .... HU 143

Room prices are subject to the addition of a local tax of 6%

Centre

North (Porte d'Anvers, Place Rogier) FT :

Brussels-Sheraton M, pl. Rogier 3, ✉ 1210, ☎ 2193400, Telex 26887, – ▯ ▭ TV ☎ ♿ – 🅰. AE ⓓ E VISA. ✱ rest FT e
M a la carte 640/1250 – ☐ 495 – **483 rm** and **43** apartments 5000/5800.

President World Trade Center M, bd Emile Jacqmain 180, ✉ 1210, ☎ 2172020, Telex 21066 – ▯ ▭ rest TV ☎ – 🅰. AE ⓓ E VISA FT y
M 600/1900 – **305 rm** ☐ 5500/6600.

New Hotel Siru and Rest. Le Couvert, pl. Rogier 1, ✉ 1210, ☎ 2177580 and 2178308 (rest.), Telex 21722 – ▯ TV ⌂wc ⌂wc ☎. AE ⓓ E VISA. ✱ FT f
M *(closed Saturday lunch and Sunday)* 1100 – **100 rm** ☐ 2525/3320.

North (Botanique, Porte de Schaerbeek) GHT :

Hyatt Regency Brussels M, r. Royale 250, ✉ 1210, ☎ 2194640, Telex 61871 – ▯ ▭ TV ☎ ♿ – 🅰. AE ⓓ VISA. ✱ rest GT r
M 990/1290 – ☐ 420 – **315 rm** 6900/8010.

Ambassade, pl. des Barricades 1a, ✉ 1000, ☎ 2182061, Telex 62358 – ▯ TV ⌂wc ☎. AE ⓓ E VISA GT a
M *(closed lunch Saturday and Sunday)* a la carte 740/1060 – **17 rm** ☐ 1800/2200.

XX **Den Botaniek,** r. Royale 328, ✉ 1210, ☎ 2184838, « Garden-terrace » – Ⓟ. AE ⓓ E VISA GT n
closed Saturday, Sunday and 25 December-3 January – **M** 1375/1850.

XX **De Ultieme Hallucinatie** r. Royale 316, ✉ 1210, ☎ 2170614, « Art Nouveau Interior » – AE ⓓ E VISA. ✱ GT u
closed Saturday lunch, Sunday and 1 to 17 August – **M** 950/1750.

Town Centre (Bourse, Grand'Place, Pl. de Brouckère, Ste-Catherine)

Amigo, r. Amigo 1, ✉ 1000, ☎ 5115910, Telex 21618, « Tasteful decor » – ▯ ▭ rest TV ☎ – 🅰. AE ⓓ E VISA. ✱ rest KZ h
M a la carte 780/1250 – **183 rm** ☐ 4600/5250.

Royal Windsor H. and Rest. les 4 Saisons M, r. Duquesnoy 5, ✉ 1000, ☎ 5114215, Telex 62905 – ▯ ▭ TV ☎ – 🅰. AE ⓓ E VISA. ✱ LZ k
M 1090/2100 – **300 rm** ☐ 6425/7535 – P 8495/9115.

Jolly H. Atlanta without rest., bd A.-Max 7, ✉ 1000, ☎ 2170120, Telex 21475 – ▯ TV ☎ – 🅰. AE ⓓ E VISA LY a
244 rm ☐ 5130/5430.

Président Nord without rest., bd A.-Max 107, ✉ 1000, ☎ 2190060, Telex 61417 – ▯ TV ☎. AE ⓓ E VISA LY b
63 rm ☐ 2700/3150.

Métropole, pl. de Brouckère 31, ✉ 1000, ☎ 2172300, Telex 21234, « Elegant rest. » – ▯ ▭ rest TV ☎ – 🅰. AE ⓓ E VISA. ✱ rest LY r
M *(closed Saturday and Sunday)* 980 – **320 rm** ☐ 2800/4500.

Bedford, r. Midi 135, ✉ 1000, ☎ 5127840, Telex 24059 – ▯ TV ☎ – 🅰. AE ⓓ E VISA. ✱ KZ r
M *(closed 20 December-5 January)* a la carte 870/1300 – **275 rm** ☐ 3600/4250 – P 4310/4850.

Arenberg, r. d'Assaut 15, ✉ 1000, ☎ 5110770, Telex 25660 – ▯ TV ⌂wc ⌂wc ☎. AE ⓓ E VISA LZ p
M *(closed last 2 weeks December)* a la carte 580/970 – **155 rm** ☐ 2600/3600.

Sainte-Catherine M without rest., r. Joseph Plateau 2 (Pl. Ste-Catherine), ✉ 1000, ☎ 5137620, Telex 22476 – ▯ TV ⌂wc ☎ ♿ – 🅰. VISA KY s
☐ 175 – **234 rm** 1715/2265.

XXXX ✿✿ **Maison du Cygne,** Grand'Place 9, ✉ 1000, ☎ 5118244, « Ancient mansion, elegant decor » – AE ⓓ E VISA. ✱ LZ q
closed 10 to 17 August, Christmas-New Year, Saturday lunch and Sunday – **M** a la carte 1450/2500
Spec. Mousseline de brochet homardine, Dos d'agneau façon du Cygne, Faisan 2 assiettes (15 Oct.-10 February).

XXX **Huîtrière,** quai aux Briques 20, ✉ 1000, ☎ 5120866, Seafood – AE ⓓ E VISA KY v
M 925/1350.

XXX **Cheval Marin,** Marché-aux-Porcs 25, ✉ 1000, ☎ 5130287, « Ancient decor » – Ⓟ. AE ⓓ E VISA KY u
closed Sunday dinner – **M** a la carte 940/1600.

XX ✿ **Sirène d'Or** (Van Duuren), pl. Ste-Catherine 1 a, ✉ 1000, ☎ 5135198 – AE ⓓ E VISA
closed Sunday, Monday, 30 June-1 August and 22 to 28 December – **M** a la carte 1240/2400
Spec. Fricassée de sole et ris de veau aux jets de houblon (March), Bouillabaisse, Poêlée de langouste au Sauternes et poivre rose. KY n

XX ✿ **La Belle Maraîchère** (Devreker), pl. Ste-Catherine 11, ✉ 1000, ✆ 5129759 – AE ⓓ E VISA KY **f**
closed Wednesday and Thursday – **M** a la carte 1030/1930
Spec. Soupe de poissons, Fricassée de homard aux petits légumes, Turbot grillé.

XX **Filet de Boeuf,** r. Harengs 8, ✉ 1000, ✆ 5119559, « Ancient mansion » – AE ⓓ E VISA LZ **s**
closed Saturday, Sunday, Bank Holidays and 15 July-1 August – **M** a la carte 1270/1880.

XX **Tête d'Or,** r. Tête d'Or 9, ✉ 1000, ✆ 5110201, « Old Brussels decor » – AE ⓓ E VISA KZ **t**
closed Saturday and Sunday – **M** a la carte 1200/1850.

XX **Éperon d'Or,** r. Éperonniers 8, ✉ 1000, ✆ 5125239, « Ancient Brussels residence » – AE ⓓ E VISA LZ **w**
closed Saturday, Sunday and 21 July-15 August – **M** a la carte 920/1700.

XX **Le Chablis,** r. Flandre 6, ✉ 1000, ✆ 5124631 – AE ⓓ E VISA KY **r**
closed Sunday and 7 to 31 July – **M** 1690.

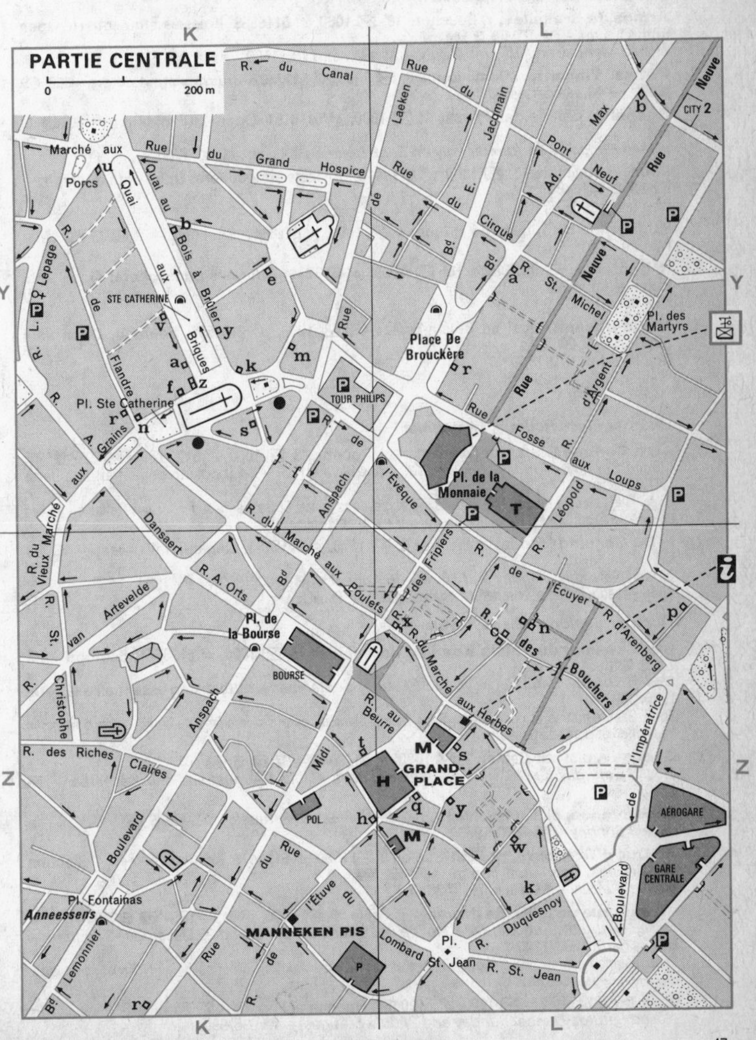

XX **François,** quai aux Briques 2, ✉ 1000, ☎ 5116089, Seafood – AE ⓓ E VISA KY **z**
closed Monday and June – **M** a la carte 900/1620.

XX **Rôtiss. Au Cochon d'Or,** quai au Bois-à-Brûler 15, ✉ 1000, ☎ 2180771 – AE ⓓ E VISA
closed Sunday dinner, Monday and 15 August-15 September – **M** 650/980. KY **y**

XX **Serge et Anne,** r. Peuplier 23, ✉ 1000, ☎ 2181662 – AE ⓓ E VISA KY **e**
closed Wednesday and 15 July-15 August – **M** a la carte 690/1260.

XX **Les Algues,** pl. Ste-Catherine 15, ✉ 1000, ☎ 2179012, Seafood – AE ⓓ E VISA KY **k**
M a la carte 1140/1760.

XX **Crustacés,** quai aux Briques 8, ✉ 1000, ☎ 5131493, Seafood – AE ⓓ E VISA. ✻
M a la carte 950/1850. KY **a**

XX **L'Ami Michel,** pl. du Samedi 17, ✉ 1000, ☎ 2175377, Seafood – AE E KY **m**
closed Saturday lunch, Sunday, Monday and 15 July-15 August – **M** a la carte 1280/1780.

XX **Bon Vieux Temps,** 1st floor, r. Marché-aux-Herbes 12, ✉ 1000, ☎ 2181546, « Ancient Brussels residence » – AE ⓓ E VISA LZ **x**
closed Saturday lunch and Sunday – **M** 650/1105.

XX **Armes de Bruxelles,** r. Bouchers 13, ✉ 1000, ☎ 5115598, Brussels atmosphere, Open until 11 p.m. – ▤. AE ⓓ E VISA LZ **c**
closed Monday and 15 June-2 July – **M** a la carte 700/1400.

X **Rôtiss. Vincent,** r. Dominicains 8, ✉ 1000, ☎ 5112302, Brussels atmosphere – AE ⓓ E VISA – **M** a la carte 600/1160. LZ **n**

X **Ogenblik,** Galerie des Princes 1, ✉ 1000, ☎ 5116151, Open until midnight – AE ⓓ E VISA LZ **n**
closed Sunday – **M** *(dinner only on Bank Holidays)* a la carte 1180/1760.

X **Léon,** r. Bouchers 18, ✉ 1000, ☎ 5111415, Brussels atmosphere, Open until midnight – AE ⓓ E VISA. ✻ LZ **c**
M a la carte 670/1160.

X **Rugbyman Nr 1,** quai aux Briques 4, ✉ 1000, ☎ 5125640, Shellfish – AE ⓓ E VISA
M 650/1350. KY **z**

X **'t Kelderke,** Grand'Place 15, ✉ 1000, ☎ 5137344, Brussels atmosphere, Open until 2 a.m. – AE E VISA LZ **y**
M a la carte 600/990.

X **Marie-Joseph,** quai au Bois-à-Brûler 47, ✉ 1000, ☎ 2180596, Seafood, Open until 11 p.m. – AE ⓓ VISA KY **b**
M a la carte 1070/1650.

Centre South

Quartier Place Rouppe, Lemonnier EV :

XXX ✿✿✿ **Comme Chez Soi** (Wynants), pl. Rouppe 23, ✉ 1000, ☎ 5122921 – ▤. AE ⓓ
closed Sunday, Monday, July and Christmas-New Year – **M** (booking essential) a la carte 1700/2250 EV **c**
Spec. Filets de sole mousseline au Riesling et crevettes grises, Côtes d'agneau farcies aux truffes et graines de sésame (April-Sept.), Tartelette aux pommes, sorbet et sauce aux pêches.

XXX ✿ **Da Gesuino** (Todde), r. Fiennes 3, ✉ 1070, ☎ 5215163, Elegant, Italian rest. – AE ⓓ E EV **d**
closed Saturday, Sunday and 18 July-16 August – **M** 1200/1900
Spec. Assaggi di Pasta, Gamberi citronella, Agneau de Pauillac.

Quartier Sablon et Place Royale FV :

XXX ✿✿ **L'Écailler du Palais Royal,** r. Bodenbroek 18, ✉ 1000, ☎ 5128751, Seafood – AE ⓓ E VISA FV **z**
closed Sunday, Bank Holidays and 30 July-1 September – **M** (booking essential) a la carte 1530/2380
Spec. Banc d'huîtres et coquillages (Sept.-April), Blanc de barbue à la crème de curry, Homard sauté au Sauvignon et potée de poireaux.

XXX **Debussy,** pl. Petit-Sablon 2, ✉ 1000, ☎ 5128041 – AE ⓓ E VISA FV **s**
closed Saturday lunch, Sunday, Bank Holidays, 4 July-4 August and end December – **M** 1450/1950.

XXX **En Provence,** pl. Petit-Sablon 1, ✉ 1000, ☎ 5111208, Rustic – AE ⓓ E VISA FV **s**
closed Sunday – **M** 1300/1950.

XX **Au Duc d'Arenberg,** pl. Petit-Sablon 9, ✉ 1000, ☎ 5111475, Rustic Pub-rest., Collection of paintings, Open until 11 p.m. – AE ⓓ VISA FV **a**
closed Sunday – **M** a la carte 1430/2500.

X ✿ **Trente rue de la Paille** (Martiny), r. Paille 30, ✉ 1000, ☎ 5120715 – ⓓ E VISA FV **u**
closed Saturday, Sunday, Bank Holidays, 28 June-3 August and 20 December-3 January – **M** a la carte 1200/1740
Spec. Saumon mariné, dés d'anguille fumée et foie de canard poêlé, Turbot poché au Noilly et ris de veau, Glace au nougat et au miel.

X **J. et B.,** r. Baudet 5, ✉ 1000, ☎ 5120484, Open until 11 p.m. – AE ⓓ E VISA FV **r**
closed Saturday lunch, Sunday and 21 July-5 August – **M** 695/995.

X **Les Années Folles,** r. Haute 17, ✉ 1000, ✆ 5135858 FV **c**
closed Saturday lunch and Sunday – **M** 1050/1500.

X **Au Vieux Saint-Martin,** Grand Sablon 38, ✉ 1000, ✆ 5126476, Pub-rest., Open until midnight FV **n**
M a la carte 1020/1350.

Quartier Porte Louise, Palais Justice, Place Stéphanie FX :

Hilton International Brussels M, bd Waterloo 38, ✉ 1000, ✆ 5138877, Telex 22744, « Rest. Plein Ciel on 27th floor with ≤ of town » – AE E VISA. FX **s**
M (Maison du Boeuf) 1075/1475 – 590 – **365 rm** 6300/7900.

Ramada-Brussels M, chaussée de Charleroi 38, ✉ 1060, ✆ 5393000, Telex 25539 – AE E VISA
M *(closed Sunday)* a la carte 1250/1800 – 410 – **201 rm** 3600/4450.

Delta M without rest., quick-lunch, chaussée de Charleroi 17, ✉ 1060, ✆ 5390160, Telex 63225 – wc wc – AE E VISA FX **r**
253 rm 2900/3600.

Diplomat M without rest., r. Jean-Stas 32, ✉ 1060, ✆ 5374250, Telex 61012 – wc AE E VISA FX **x**
68 rm 2900/3600.

Argus without rest., r. Capitaine Crespel 6, ✉ 1050, ✆ 5140770, Telex 29393 – wc AE E VISA FX **a**
41 rm 2200/2500.

La Cascade without rest., r. Source 14, ✉ 1060, ✆ 5388830, Telex 26637 – wc – AE E VISA.
42 rm 2235/2775.

Ascot without rest., pl. Loix 1, ✉ 1060, ✆ 5388835, Telex 25010 – wc AE E VISA – **59 rm** 1720/2150.

XX **Al Piccolo Mondo,** r. Jourdan 19, ✉ 1060, ✆ 5388794, Italian rest., Open until 1 a.m. – AE E VISA FX **w**
M a la carte 600/1200.

XX **Meo Patacca,** r. Jourdan 20, ✉ 1060, ✆ 5381546, Italian rest., Open until 1 a.m. – AE E VISA FX **w**
closed Sunday – **M** a la carte 780/1580.

X ✿ **Au Beurre Blanc** (Hella), r. Faucon 2a, ✉ 1000, ✆ 5130111 – AE E VISA FX **f**
closed Saturday lunch, Sunday, Easter, 10 August-2 September and Christmas-New Year – **M** a la carte 830/1600
Spec. Emincé de coquilles St. Jacques au miel (end Sept.-mid May), Assiette du pêcheur au beurre blanc, Cervelas de homard aux truffes et pistaches.

Quartier Porte de Namur, Luxembourg, Palais des Académies GV :

Chambord without rest., r. Namur 82, ✉ 1000, ✆ 5134119, Telex 20373 – wc AE E VISA. GV **v**
69 rm 1975/3925.

XXX **Bernard,** 1st floor, r. Namur 93, ✉ 1000, ✆ 5126805, Seafood – AE E GV **c**
closed Sunday, Monday dinner and July – **M** a la carte 1160/2100.

Quartier Porte de Namur (côté Tour), Quartier St. Boniface GX :

Sun without rest., r. Berger 38, ✉ 1050, ✆ 5112119 – wc. AE E VISA GX **s**
200 – **22 rm** 1295/1695.

XX **Charles-Joseph,** r. E. Solvay 9, ✉ 1050, ✆ 5134390 – AE E VISA GX **r**
closed Saturday lunch and Sunday – **M** 850/1800.

XX Old Mario, r. Alsace Lorraine 44, ✉ 1050, ✆ 5116161, Italian rest. – AE E VISA GX **e**
closed Saturday and Sunday.

Centre East

Quartier St. Josse, Square Marie-Louise, Square Ambiorix, Cité Européenne HU :

Archimède M without rest., r. Archimède 22, ✉ 1040, ✆ 2310909, Telex 20420 – AE E VISA. HU **y**
56 rm 3550/4200.

Euro-Flat without rest., bd Charlemagne 50, ✉ 1040, ✆ 2300010, Telex 21120 – AE E VISA. HU **p**
134 rm 3550/4300.

XX **Gigotin,** r. Stevin 102, ✉ 1040, ✆ 2303091, – AE E. HU **n**
closed Saturday, Sunday, Bank Holidays and 5 August-5 September – **M** a la carte 640/1230.

Rue de la Loi, Quartier Schuman, Quartier Léopold HV :

Brussels Europa, r. de la Loi 107, ✉ 1040, ✆ 2301333, Telex 25121 – – AE E VISA. rest HV **s**
M a la carte 1100/1750 – 390 – **240 rm** 4500/5500.

Quartier Cité Administrative, Madou, Parc de Bruxelles GU :

Astoria and Rest. Palais Royal, r. Royale 103, ✉ 1000, ✆ 2176290, Telex 25040 – |$| 📺 ☎ – 🏛. AE ⓓ E VISA. ✻ rest GTU **b**
M *(closed Saturday lunch, Sunday dinner and Bank Holidays)* 1250/1670 – ☐ 440 – **125 rm** 2970/4980.

City Garden 🄼 without rest., with suites, **r. Joseph II 59,** ✉ **1040,** ✆ **2300945, Telex** 63570 – |$| 📺 ☎ 🚗. AE ⓓ E VISA. ✻ GU **r**
☐ 200 – **94 rm** 2610/3040.

Président Centre without rest., r. Royale 160, ✉ 1000, ✆ 2190065, Telex 26784 – |$| ▤ 📺 ☎. AE ⓓ E VISA GU **a**
73 rm ☐ 2970/3630.

Congrès and Rest. Le Carrousel, r. Congrès 42, ✉ 1000, ✆ 2171890 – |$| ⛀wc ⛆ ☎. AE ⓓ E VISA GU **c**
M *(closed weekends in August)* – **38 rm** ☐ 1075/1330.

Résidence Sabina without rest., r. Nord 78, ✉ 1000, ✆ 2182637 – ⛆wc ☎ GU **e**
22 rm ☐ 720/1230.

XXX **Astrid "Chez Pierrot",** r. de la Presse 21, ✉ 1000, ✆ 2173831, Classic – ▤. VISA
closed Sunday, Easter and 15 July-15 August – **M** 700/1500. GU **d**

Suburbs

North

Quartier Basilique (Koekelberg, Ganshoren, Jette) :

XXX ✿✿ **Dupont,** av. Vital-Riethuisen 46, ✉ 1080, ✆ 4275450, Classic-elegant – AE ⓓ E VISA
closed Monday, Tuesday and mid July-mid August – **M** a la carte 1330/2180
Spec. Panaché de poissons arc-en-ciel, Beurrée d'huîtres au champagne et caviar (15 Sept.-April), Selle de chevreuil au thym frais (Oct.-10 Dec.).

XXX ✿✿ **Bruneau,** av. Broustin 73, ✉ 1080, ✆ 4276978, Classic-elegant – AE ⓓ E VISA
closed holiday Thursdays, Tuesday dinner, Wednesday, mid June-mid July and Christmas-New Year – **M** a la carte 2040/2640
Spec. Salade de homard nordique aux pommes vertes, Filet de bar tartiné au caviar, Galette de pigeon aux légumes et ses cuisses caramélisées au soja.

XXX ✿ **Le Sermon** (Kobs), av. Jacques-Sermon 91, ✉ 1090, ✆ 4268935 – AE E VISA
closed Sunday, Monday and July – **M** a la carte 1100/1740
Spec. Moules au champagne (Sept.-April), Sole Sermon, Waterzooi de homard.

XX **Cambrils** 1st floor, av. Charles-Quint 365, ✉ 1080, ✆ 4669582, ⛱ – AE E VISA
closed Sunday, Monday dinner and 6 July-4 August – **M** 495/1250.

XX **Pannenhuis,** r. Léopold-1er 317, ✉ 1090, ✆ 4258373, « Converted 17C inn » – AE ⓓ E VISA
closed Saturday lunch, Sunday and 1 to 22 August – **M** a la carte 930/1450.

XX **Au Chaudron d'Or,** Drève du Château 71, ✉ 1080, ✆ 4283737, « Rustic farmhouse » – AE ⓓ E VISA
closed Sunday dinner, Monday and August – **M** a la carte 1420/2430.

XX **Le Barolo,** av. de Laeken 57, ✉ 1090, ✆ 4254576, ⛱ – AE ⓓ E VISA
closed Tuesday, Wednesday and 28 July-26 August – **M** a la carte 960/1920.

Quartier Centenaire and Atomium (Laeken, Wemmel, Strombeek-Bever) :

Fimotel Expo, av. Impératrice Charlotte, ✉ 1020, ✆ 4791910, Telex 20907 – |$| 📺 ⛀wc ☎ ♿ Ⓟ – 🏛
80 rm.

XXX ✿✿ **Eddie Van Maele,** chaussée Romaine 964, ✉ 1810, ✆ 4606145, « Flower terrace and garden » – Ⓟ. AE ⓓ. ✻
closed Saturday lunch, Sunday, Monday, July and Christmas-New Year – **M** (booking essential) a la carte 1800/2500
Spec. Marinade d'agneau au thym et légumes farcis, Petites folies du marché, Minestrone de turbot au safran.

XXX **De Kam,** chaussée de Bruxelles 7, ✉ 1810, ✆ 4600374, ⛱, Rustic – Ⓟ. AE ⓓ E VISA
closed dinner Sunday, Tuesday and Wednesday, Monday and August – **M** 1050/1750.

XXX **Centenaire,** av. J.-Sobieski 84, ✉ 1020, ✆ 4786623 – AE ⓓ E
closed Sunday dinner, Monday, July and Christmas-New Year – **M** 1150/1850.

XX **Val Joli,** r. Leestbeek 16, ✉ 1820, ✆ 4606543, ⛱, « Garden-terrace » – Ⓟ. E VISA
closed Monday, Tuesday and 1 to 22 November – **M** 1000/1490.

XX ✿ **Les Baguettes Impériales** (Ma), av. J. Sobieski 70, ✉ 1020, ✆ 4796732, Vietnamese rest. – AE. ✻
closed Sunday dinner, Tuesday, Easter and 2 August-2 September – **M** a la carte 1090/1370
Spec. Délices de vulcain, Canette de Barbarie Baguettes Impériales, Dessert chaud - froid.

XX **Aub. Arbre Ballon,** chaussée de Bruxelles 416, ✉ 1810, ✆ 4606259 – Ⓟ. AE ⓓ E VISA
closed Monday except Bank Holidays and last 3 weeks July – **M** 695/1295.

XX **Castel,** av. Houba-de-Strooper 96, ✉ 1020, ✆ 4784392 – AE ⓓ E VISA
closed Tuesday dinner – **M** 675/895.

XX **Figaro,** r. Émile-Wauters 137, ✉ 1020, ✆ 4786529
closed Sunday dinner, Monday and July – **M** a la carte approx. 1400.

X **Adrienne Atomium,** Parc Expositions, ✉ 1020, ✆ 4783000, ≤, Hors d'œuvre – AE ⓓ E VISA
closed Sunday, Bank Holidays and July – **M** (lunch only) 650.

West

Anderlecht :

XXX **La Réserve,** chaussée de Ninove 675, ✉ 1080, ✆ 5222653 – AE ⓓ E VISA. ✻
closed Saturday lunch, Monday dinner, Tuesday and 14 July-3 August – **M** a la carte 1130/1850.

Molenbeek St-Jean **(Sint-Jans Molenbeek) :**

XXX ✿ **Béarnais** **(Dela Rue), bd Mettewie 318, ✉ 1080, ✆ 5231151, Classic** – ▤. AE ⓓ E VISA
closed Sunday and Monday dinner – **M** 1650/2195
Spec. Côtelette de homard au beurre de corail, Ris de veau aux écrevisses, Crêpe soufflée sur coulis de framboise.

Berchem Ste Agathe **(Sint-Agatha Berchem) :**

XX **Saule,** chaussée de Gand 1110, ✉ 1080, ✆ 4656682 – AE ⓓ E VISA
closed Sunday dinner, Monday and July – **M** a la carte 870/1510.

South

Bois de la Cambre :

🏨 **Lloyd George** without rest., **av. Lloyd George 12, ✉ 1050, ✆ 6483072** – |♦| ⛀wc ⋒ ☎. AE ⓓ E VISA
14 rm ☕ 1060/1985.

XXXX ✿✿ **Villa Lorraine,** **av. Vivier-d'Oie 75, ✉ 1180, ✆ 3743163, Classic-elegant** – Ⓟ. AE ⓓ E VISA
closed Sunday and 29 June-28 July – **M** (booking essential) a la carte 1900/3400
Spec. Huîtres au champagne (Sept.-April), Turbotin Belle Alliance, Soufflé au chocolat amer et jus de noix vertes.

Quartier "Ma Campagne" **(Ixelles, St-Gilles) :**

XXX **Chouan,** av. Brugmann 100, ✉ 1060, ✆ 3440999, Seafood – ▤. AE ⓓ VISA
closed Saturday lunch, Sunday dinner, Monday and 20 June-3 August – **M** a la carte 1230/2140.

XX **Fruit de ma Passion,** r. Jean-Baptiste Meunier 53a, ✉ 1180, ✆ 3473294 – AE ⓓ E VISA
closed Saturday, Sunday and 3 weeks July – **M** a la carte 1060/1450.

XX **Palatino,** r. Aqueduc 7, ✉ 1050, ✆ 5386415, with Italian rest. – AE ⓓ E VISA
closed Saturday lunch and 1 to 21 July – **M** a la carte 1060/1450.

XX **Le Fronton Basque,** chaussée de Waterloo 361, ✉ 1060, ✆ 5372118, Oyster bar and seafood – AE ⓓ E VISA. ✻
M a la carte 1170/1950.

XX **L'Auvergne,** r. Aqueduc 61, ✉ 1050, ✆ 5373125, Rustic interior – AE ⓓ E VISA
closed Sunday, Monday, 21 July-21 August and 22 to 31 December – **M** 740.

Quartier Avenue Louise et Bascule **(Ixelles) :**

🏨 **Mayfair,** av. Louise 381, ✉ 1050, ✆ 6499800, Telex 24821 – |♦| TV ☎ 🚗 – 🏛. AE ⓓ E. ✻ rest
M a la carte 1170/1700 – ☕ 250 – **90 rm** 5080.

🏨 **Arcade Stéphanie** Ⓜ, av. Louise 91, ✉ 1050, ✆ 5390240, Telex 25558, 🏊 – |♦| TV ☎ 🚗. AE ⓓ E VISA. ✻
M 695 – **142 rm** ☕ 3995/4600.

🏨 **L'Agenda** Ⓜ without rest., r. Florence 6, ✉ 1050, ✆ 5390031, Telex 63947 – |♦| TV ☎ 🚗. AE ⓓ E VISA
☕ 190 – **38 rm** 2250/2600.

🏨 **Alfa Louise** without rest., r. Blanche 4, ✉ 1050, ✆ 5379210, Telex 62434 – |♦| TV ☎ 🚗 – 🏛. AE ⓓ E VISA
65 rm ☕ 3350.

🏨 **Brussels** without rest., av. Louise 315, ✉ 1050, ✆ 6402415, Telex 25075 – |♦| TV ☎. AE ⓓ E VISA. ✻
40 rm ☕ 3300/3700.

🏨 **Au Tagawa** without rest., quick-lunch, av. Louise 321, ✉ 1050, ✆ 6408029, Telex 22322 – |♦| TV ☎ 🚗 – 🏛. AE ⓓ E VISA. ✻
77 rm ☕ 4450.

XXX ✿ **Cravache d'Or,** pl. A.-Leemans 10, ✉ 1050, ☎ 5383746 – ▤. AE ⓓ E VISA
closed Saturday lunch – **M** a la carte 2090/2720
Spec. Foie de canard confit sur gelée de homard, Loup fumé à la minute, vinaigrette au jus de truffes, Homard au four.

XX **La Porte des Indes,** av. Louise 455, ✉ 1050, ☎ 6478651, Indian rest., « Exotic decor » – AE ⓓ E VISA
closed Sunday – **M** a la carte 1290/1790.

XX **Comme Ça,** r. Châtelain 61, ✉ 1050, ☎ 6496290, 🍽 – AE ⓓ E VISA
closed Sunday, Monday dinner, Easter and 3 weeks July – **M** 690/950.

XX **Armagnac,** chaussée de Waterloo 591, ✉ 1060, ☎ 3459279 – AE ⓓ E VISA
closed Sunday, Monday dinner and 21 July-15 August – **M** 800.

XX **Tagawa,** av. Louise 279, ✉ 1050, ☎ 6405095, Japanese rest. – ▤ Ⓟ. AE ⓓ E. ✂
closed Sunday – **M** 760/2600.

X **La Thailande,** av. Legrand 29, ✉ 1050, ☎ 6402462, 🍽, Thaï rest.
closed Sunday – **M** a la carte approx. 700.

X **Les Cadets de Gascogne,** r. Florence 26, ✉ 1050, ☎ 5384640, 🍽 – VISA
closed Saturday lunch, Sunday and 21 July-15 August – **M** 695.

X **Arche de Noé,** r. Beau-Site 27, ✉ 1050, ☎ 6475383 – AE ⓓ
closed Sunday – **M** a la carte 780/1760.

Forest (Vorst) :

XX ✿ **De Reu,** chaussée de Bruxelles 226, ✉ 1190, ☎ 3435460 – AE ⓓ E VISA
closed Tuesday, 18 August-15 September and 3 February-3 March – **M** (booking essential) a la carte 1100/1950
Spec. Foie d'oie frais au naturel, Agneau sarladaise, Mousse glacée au marc de Gewürztraminer.

Quartier Boondael (Ixelles) :

XXXX ✿✿ **L'Oasis** (Beyls), Place Marie-José 9, ✉ 1050, ☎ 6484545, « Elegant » – ▤ Ⓟ. AE ⓓ E VISA. ✂
closed Sunday and 1 to 22 August – **M** a la carte 1770/2700
Spec. Epinards farcis aux huîtres et au caviar, Turbot au four en croûte de mie de pain au basilic, Assiette de foie d'oie et de canard.

XX **Aub. de Boendael,** square du Vieux-Tilleul 12, ✉ 1050, ☎ 6727055, Grill, Rustic – Ⓟ. AE ⓓ E VISA
closed Saturday, Sunday and last week July-15 August – **M** a la carte 1230/1950.

XX **Le Chalet Rose,** av. Bois de la Cambre 49, ✉ 1050, ☎ 6727864, 🍽 – Ⓟ. AE ⓓ E VISA
closed Saturday lunch, Sunday and Bank Holidays – **M** a la carte 1520/2200.

Uccle (Ukkel) :

🏨 **County House,** Square des Héros 2, ✉ 1180, ☎ 3754420, Telex 22392 – |♦| TV ⇔wc ☎ 🚗 – 🏛. ⓓ E VISA
M 650/1200 – **96 rm** ☕ 2800/3450.

XXX **L'Orangeraie,** av. Winston Churchill 81, ✉ 1180, ☎ 3457147, « Tasteful decor » – AE ⓓ E VISA
closed Saturday lunch, Sunday and 15 August-1 September – **M** a la carte approx. 1400.

XXX **Prince d'Orange,** av. Prince-d'Orange 1, ✉ 1180, ☎ 3744871, 🍽, Classic – Ⓟ. AE ⓓ E VISA
closed Monday except Bank Holidays – **M** 875/1275.

XXX **Dikenek,** chaussée de Waterloo 830, ✉ 1180, ☎ 3748346, 🍽, Rustic tavern – AE ⓓ E VISA
closed Saturday lunch, Wednesday in winter, Easter and end August – **M** a la carte 1350/1920.

XX ✿ **Villa d'Este,** r. Etoile 142, ✉ 1180, ☎ 3778646, 🍽 – Ⓟ. ⓓ VISA. ✂
closed Sunday dinner, Monday, 29 June-3 August and 22 December-5 January – **M** a la carte 1300/1950
Spec. Sole farcie aux poireaux, Chausson de homard à l'aneth beurre corail, Coquelet à la moutarde de Meaux.

XX **Les Délices de la Mer,** chaussée de Waterloo 1020, ✉ 1180, ☎ 3755467, 🍽, Oyster-bar – Ⓟ. AE ⓓ E VISA
closed Easter – **M** 1250/1750.

XX **L'Ascoli,** chaussée de Waterloo 940, ✉ 1180, ☎ 3755775, 🍽, Italian rest. – Ⓟ. AE ⓓ E VISA
closed Sunday and August – **M** a la carte 1150/1730.

XX **L'Éléphant Bleu,** chaussée de Waterloo 1120, ✉ 1180, ☎ 3744962, Thaï rest. – ▤. AE ⓓ E VISA
closed Wednesday – **M** a la carte 810/1160.

XX **Les Pélerins,** av. de Fré 190, ✉ 1180, ☎ 3742046 – Ⓟ. AE ⓓ E VISA
closed Saturday and Sunday – **M** 750/1050.

XX **Le Calvados,** av. de Fré 182, ✉ 1180, ☎ 3747098, 🍽, 1900 decor – AE ⓓ E VISA
closed Sunday dinner and Monday except Bank Holidays – **M** a la carte 1100/1780.

XX **Pierrot au Surcouf,** r. Doyenné 89, ✉ 1180, ℘ 3457538 – AE ① E VISA
closed Sunday dinner, Monday and August – **M** 975/1695.

XX **Ventre-Saint-Gris,** r. Basse 10, ✉ 1180, ℘ 3752755 – AE ① E VISA – **M** 790.

XX **Pavillon Impérial,** chaussée de Waterloo 1296, ✉ 1180, ℘ 3746751, Chinese rest. – ▤. AE ① VISA. ✈
closed Wednesday and July-August – **M** a la carte 630/1250.

X **De Hoef,** r. Edith-Cavell 218, ✉ 1180, ℘ 3743417, 🏠, Grill, 17C inn – AE ① E VISA
closed 10 to 31 July – **M** 575.

East

Quartier Cinquantenaire (Etterbeek) :

🏨 **Chelton Concorde** without rest., r. Véronèse 48, ✉ 1040, ℘ 7364095, Telex 64253 – ⧉ TV ⛀wc ☎ – 🏋. AE ① E VISA
☕ 220 – **41 rm** 2730/2940.

XX **Fontaine de Jade,** av. Tervuren 5, ✉ 1040, ℘ 7363210, Chinese rest. – ▤. AE ① E VISA – *closed Tuesday* – **M** a la carte 660/1570.

XX **St-Laurent,** bd Louis Schmidt 30, ✉ 1040, ℘ 7360398 – AE ① E VISA
closed Monday and 15 June-1 July – **M** a la carte 860/1300.

XX **Casse-Dalle,** av. Celtes 37, ✉ 1040, ℘ 7336625 – AE
closed Saturday lunch, Sunday and Christmas-New Year – **M** a la carte 1000/1410.

Quartier Place Eugène-Flagey (Ixelles) :

XX **Piano à Bretelles,** r. A.-Dewitte 40, ✉ 1050, ℘ 6476105 – AE
closed Saturday lunch, Sunday and August – **M** a la carte 820/1320.

X **Le Prévot,** r. V. Greyson 95, ✉ 1050, ℘ 6491465 – AE ① E VISA
closed 19 to 27 April, 12 July-1 September, Saturday lunch and Sunday – **M** a la carte 1050/1560.

Quartier Place Meiser (Schaerbeek) :

🏨 **Lambermont** Ⓜ without rest., bd Lambermont 322, ✉ 1030, ℘ 2425595, Telex 62220 – ⧉ TV ⛀wc ☎. AE ① E VISA
42 rm ☕ 2300/2450.

XXX **Le Meiser,** bd Gén.-Wahis 55, ✉ 1030, ℘ 7353769 – AE ① E VISA
closed Saturday and Sunday – **M** a la carte 1120/1860.

XX **Philippe Riesen** 1st floor, bd Aug. Reyers 163, ✉ 1040, ℘ 7364138 – AE ① E VISA
closed Saturday dinner Easter-October, Saturday lunch and Sunday – **M** a la carte 1200/1700.

XX **L'Armor,** av. Milcamps 126, ✉ 1040, ℘ 7331981 – ▤. AE ① E VISA. ✈
closed Saturday lunch, Sunday and 13 July-3 August – **M** a la carte 1060/1470.

X **Au Cadre Noir,** av. Milcamps 158, ✉ 1040, ℘ 7341445 – AE ① E VISA
closed Saturday lunch, Sunday dinner, Monday and 1 to 22 July – **M** a la carte 950/1500.

X **Anak Timoer,** pl. de la Patrie 26, ✉ 1030, ℘ 7338987, Indonesian and Chinese rest. – AE ① E VISA
closed Tuesday – **M** a la carte 630/1100.

Auderghem (Oudergem) :

XX **L'Abbaye de Rouge Cloître,** Rouge Cloître 8, ✉ 1160, ℘ 6724525, ←, 🏠, « Garden setting » – Ⓟ. AE ① E VISA
closed Sunday dinner, Monday and February – **M** 1175.

XX **Le Chèvrefeuille,** bd du Souverain 145, ✉ 1160, ℘ 6720877 – AE ① E
closed Sunday dinner and Monday – **M** 850.

X ✲ **La Grignotière** (Chanson), chaussée de Wavre 2045, ✉ 1160, ℘ 6728185 – AE ① VISA
closed Sunday, Monday and first 2 weeks August – **M** (booking essential) 1200
Spec. Foie gras de canard au Sauternes, Anguilles aux herbes du jardin (April-Oct.).

X **New Asia,** chaussée de Wavre 1240, ✉ 1160, ℘ 6606206, Chinese rest. – AE ① E VISA
closed Saturday lunch, Monday and 15 to 29 July – **M** a la carte 600/1020.

Evere :

🏨 **Belson** Ⓜ without rest., quick-lunch until 1 a.m., chaussée de Louvain 805, ✉ 1140, ℘ 7350000, Telex 64921 – ⧉ TV ☎. AE ① E VISA
☕ 430 – **90 rm** 3310/4795.

Woluwé-St-Lambert (Sint-Lambrechts-Woluwé) :

🏨 **Armorial** without rest., bd Brand-Whitlock 101, ✉ 1200, ℘ 7345636 – TV ⛀wc 🚿 ☎. AE ① E VISA
15 rm ☕ 800/2100.

🏨 **Léopold III** without rest., square Jos.-Charlotte 11, ✉ 1200, ℘ 7628288 – ⛀ 🚿 ☎
15 rm ☕ 1100/1550.

🏨 **Résidence Lambeau** without rest., av. Lambeau 150, ✉ 1200, ℘ 7338414 – TV ⛀ ☎
12 rm ☕ 1500/1750.

XXX ✿✿ **Mon Manège à Toi,** r. Neerveld 1, ✉ 1200, ✆ 7700238, « Villa with flower garden » – Ⓟ. AE ⓓ E VISA
closed 6 to 31 July, 24 December-3 January, Saturday, Sunday and Bank Holidays – **M** a la carte 1780/2630
Spec. Terrine de turbot et cervelle de veau, Foie de canard poêlé aux pommes caramélisées, Poêlée de bar au beurre fin.

XXX **Coq en Pâte,** r. Tomberg 259, ✉ 1200, ✆ 7621971 – AE ⓓ E VISA
closed Monday and 21 July-25 August – **M** a la carte 1070/1470.

XX **Le Grand Veneur,** r. Tomberg 253, ✉ 1200, ✆ 7706122, Rustic – AE ⓓ E VISA
closed Tuesday and July – **M** 1280/1580.

XX **Lindekemale,** av. J.F. Debecker 6, ✉ 1200, ✆ 7709057, 🍽 – Ⓟ. AE ⓓ E VISA
closed Saturday, Sunday, Bank Holidays and March-April – **M** 1300/1600.

XX **Le Relais de la Woluwe,** pl. Verheyleweghen 2, ✉ 1200, ✆ 7626636 – AE ⓓ E VISA
closed Saturday lunch, Sunday and 24 December-1 January – **M** a la carte 1180/1540.

XX **Michel Servais,** r. Th. Decuyper 136, ✉ 1200, ✆ 7626295 – AE ⓓ E VISA
closed Sunday, Monday and 21 July-20 August – **M** 950/1600.

XX **Sugito,** 1st floor, bd Brand-Whitlock 107, ✉ 1200, ✆ 7335045, Indonesian rest. – AE ⓓ E VISA
closed Monday – **M** a la carte 850/1420.

Woluwé-St-Pierre (Sint-Pieters Woluwé) :

XXX **Des 3 Couleurs,** av. Tervuren 453, ✉ 1150, ✆ 7703321
closed Saturday lunch, Sunday dinner, Monday and 1 to 29 September – **M** a la carte 1030/1780.

XX **La Madonette,** r. Eglise 92, ✉ 1150, ✆ 7310298, 🍽 – AE ⓓ E VISA
closed Tuesday lunch, Monday and 1 to 21 June – **M** a la carte 770/1190.

XX **Médicis,** av. de l'Escrime 124, ✉ 1150, ✆ 7820711, 🍽 – AE ⓓ E VISA
M a la carte 1170/1550.

XX **La Salade Folle,** av. Jules Dujardin 9, ✉ 1150, ✆ 7701961, Grill – AE ⓓ E VISA
closed Sunday dinner, Monday, 17 February-5 March and 12 August-2 September – **M** a la carte 960/1400.

Watermael-Boitsfort (Watermael-Bosvoorde) :

🏠 **Aub. du Souverain** without rest., av. Fauconnerie 1, ✉ 1170, ✆ 6721601 – ⋒. AE E VISA
10 rm ☕ 1300/1800.

XXX **Trois Tilleuls** 🐌 with rm, Berensheide 8, ✉ 1170, ✆ 6723014, 🍽 – 📺 ⊟wc ⋒ ☎. AE ⓓ E VISA. ✻ rm
M *(closed 15 July-14 August)* a la carte 1180/1980 – **8 rm** ☕ 1720/3035.

XX **Samambaia,** r. Philippe Dewolfs 7, ✉ 1170, ✆ 6728720, 🍽, Brazilian rest., « Tasteful decor » – AE ⓓ E
closed Sunday, Monday and 21 July-19 August – **M** a la carte 980/1160.

XX **Le Canard Sauvage,** chaussée de la Hulpe 194, ✉ 1170, ✆ 6730975 – AE ⓓ E VISA
closed Saturday and August – **M** a la carte 1050/1630.

Brussels environs

at Diegem : 🄲 Machelen, Brussels-Zaventem motorway Diegem exit – pop. 11 322 – ✉ 1920 Diegem – ⊚ 02 :

🏨 **Sofitel** Ⓜ, Bessenveldstraat 15, ✆ 7206050, Telex 26595, 🏊, 🌳 – ▤ 📺 ☎ Ⓟ – 🏛. AE ⓓ E VISA. ✻ rest
M a la carte 1290/1940 – ☕ 480 – **125 rm** 4000/4300.

🏨 **Holiday Inn** Ⓜ, Holidaystraat 7, ✆ 7205865, Telex 24285, 🏊, 🎾 – ⇅ ▤ 📺 ☎ ♿ Ⓟ – 🏛. AE ⓓ E VISA. ✻ rest
M a la carte 1160/1450 – **288 rm** ☕ 4200/6000.

🏨 **Novotel** Ⓜ, Olmenstraat, ✆ 7205830, Telex 26751, 🏊 heated – ⇅ ▤ 📺 ⊟wc ☎ Ⓟ – 🏛. AE ⓓ E VISA
M a la carte 700/1280 – ☕ 330 – **159 rm** 3430/3760.

🏨 **Fimotel Aéroport,** Berkenlaan, ✆ 7214801, Telex 20906 – ⇅ 📺 ⊟wc ☎ ♿ Ⓟ – 🏛. AE ⓓ E VISA
M 600/890 – **79 rm** ☕ 2400/2800.

XX **Diegemhof,** Calenbergstraat 51, ✆ 7201134, 🍽 – AE ⓓ E VISA. ✻
closed Saturday, Sunday, Bank Holidays and August – **M** a la carte 1020/1520.

at Essene 🄲 Hekelgem, by ⑫ : 18 km, by E 40 outway Ternat – pop. 11 165 – ✉ 1705 Essene – ⊚ 053 :

XXXX ✿ **Host. Bellemolen** 🐌 with rm, Stationstraat 11, SW : 1,5 km, ✆ 666238, ⋖, « Tastefully converted 12C mill », 🌳 – ▤ ⊟wc Ⓟ – 🏛. AE ⓓ E. ✻
closed 6 to 31 July, 23 December-1 January, Sunday dinner and Monday – **M** a la carte 1450/2130 – 6 rm ☕ 1850/2500
Spec. Langoustines poêlées aux jeunes poireaux, Blanc de turbot Bellemolen, Agneau aux primeurs et gratin dauphinois.

at Groenendaal : – ✉ 1990 Hoeilaart – ☎ 02 :

XXXX ✿✿✿ **Romeyer,** chaussée de Groenendaal 109, ✆ 6570581, « Stately home, ≤ garden and private lake » – Ⓟ. AE ⓓ E VISA
closed Sunday dinner, Monday except Bank Holidays and February – **M** a la carte 2100/2680
Spec. Foie d'oie au naturel, Canard colvert chasseur (mid July-January), Ecrevisses farcies nantua.

XXX ✿ **Aloyse Kloos,** chaussée de la Hulpe 2, ✆ 6573737, ⛱, Classic-elegant – Ⓟ. ⓓ E VISA
closed Sunday dinner, Monday, 31 March-26 April and 18 August-13 September – **M** a la carte 1230/1740
Spec. Jambon de nos fumoirs, Asperges au saumon, Agneau aux amandes et vinaigre de Xérès.

at Groot-Bijgaarden (Grand-Bigard) Ⓒ Dilbeek, by ⑫ : 7 km – pop. 35 885 – ✉ 1720 Groot-Bijgaarden – ☎ 02 :

XXXX ✿✿ **De Bijgaarden,** I. Van Beverenstraat 20 (near castle), ✆ 4664485, ≤ – AE ⓓ E VISA
closed 20 to 28 April, 17 August-7 September, Saturday lunch and Sunday – **M** 2250/2850
Spec. Sauté de homard au Sancerre, Selle d'agneau cloutée aux truffes, Turbot rôti au four, sabayon à la graine de moutarde.

XXX ✿ **Michel** (Coppens), Schepen Gossetlaan 31, ✆ 4666591 – Ⓟ. AE ⓓ VISA
closed Sunday, Monday and August – **M** 1350/2200
Spec. Turbotin au beurre de champagne (Oct.-March), Blanc de Bresse et ris de veau au Sauternes et estragon, Oranges marinées et glace à la cannelle.

at Jezus-Eik by ⑦ : 12 km – ✉ 1900 Overijse – ☎ 02 :

XXXX ✿✿ **Barbizon** (Deluc), Welriekendedreef 95, ✆ 6570462 – Ⓟ. AE ⓓ E VISA
closed Tuesday, Wednesday, mid July-early August and February – **M** (booking essential) 1675/2700
Spec. Homard en chemise beurre Barbizon, Chariot de desserts maison.

ANTWERP (ANTWERPEN) 2000 212 ⑮ and 409 ④ – pop. 486 576 – ☎ 03.

See : Old Antwerp★★★ : Cathedral★★★ and Market Square★ (Grote Markt) FY – Rubens' House★★ (Rubenshuis) GZ – Butchers' House★ (Vleeshuis) : museum FY **D** – Rubens' burial chapel★ in the St. James' church (St-Jacobskerk) GY – The port★★★ (Haven) ⛴ FY – Zoo★★ (Dierentuin) EU.

Museums : Royal Art Gallery★★★ (Koninklijk Museum voor Schone Kunsten) CV – Plantin-Moretus★★★ (ancient printing-office) FZ – Mayer Van den Bergh★★ (Brueghel) GZ – Maritime Steen★ (Nationaal Scheepvaartmuseum Steen) FY **M¹**.

18 9 Kapellen by ② : 22 km, Georges Capiaulei 2 ✆ 6668456 – 18 Uilenbaan 15 at Wommelgem by ⑥ ✆ 3530292.

ℹ Gildekamerstraat 7 ✆ 2320103 and 2322284 – Koningin Astridplein ✆ 2330570 – Tourist association of the province, Karel Oomsstraat 11, ✉ 2018, ✆ 2162810.

Brussels 48 ⑩ – Amsterdam 158 ④ – Luxembourg 261 ⑨ – Rotterdam 103 ④.

Plans on following pages

Room prices are subject to the addition of a local tax of 6%

Town Centre

Switel Ⓜ, Copernicuslaan 2, ✉ 2018, ✆ 2316780, Telex 33965, ⛶, ✂ – |♦| ▤ rest TV ☎ 🚗 – 🏋. AE ⓓ E VISA — EV **k**
M a la carte approx. 1400 – ☕ 645 – **350 rm** 2600/4350.

De Keyser Ⓜ, De Keyserlei 66, ✉ 2018, ✆ 2340135, Telex 34219 – |♦| ▤ TV ☎ – 🏋. AE ⓓ E VISA. ✱ — EU **b**
M a la carte 1000/1500 – **117 rm** ☕ 3490/4940.

Plaza without rest., Charlottalei 43, ✉ 2018, ✆ 2189240, Telex 31531 – |♦| TV ☎. AE ⓓ E VISA — EV **v**
☕ 275 – **79 rm** 2600/4200.

Alfa Empire Ⓜ without rest., Appelmansstraat 31, ✉ 2018, ✆ 2314755, Telex 33909 – |♦| TV ☎. AE ⓓ E VISA — DU **s**
70 rm ☕ 2470/3900.

Waldorf, Belgiëlei 36, ✉ 2018, ✆ 2309950, Telex 32948 – |♦| TV ☎ Ⓟ – 🏋. AE ⓓ E VISA. ✱ — EV **n**
M a la carte 900/1200 – **100 rm** ☕ 1735/2545.

Alfa Congress Ⓜ, Plantin en Moretuslei 136, ✉ 2018, ✆ 2353000, Telex 31959 – |♦| TV ⛀wc ☎ 🚗 Ⓟ – 🏋. AE ⓓ E VISA — EV **s**
M *(closed Saturday and Sunday)* a la carte 730/1200 – **61 rm** ☕ 2350/2700.

Antwerp Tower Hotel Ⓜ without rest. with 11 apartments in annex, Van Ertbornstraat 10, ✉ 2018, ✆ 2340120, Telex 34478 – |♦| TV ⛀wc ☎. AE ⓓ E VISA. ✱ — DU **b**
40 rm ☕ 2400/3300.

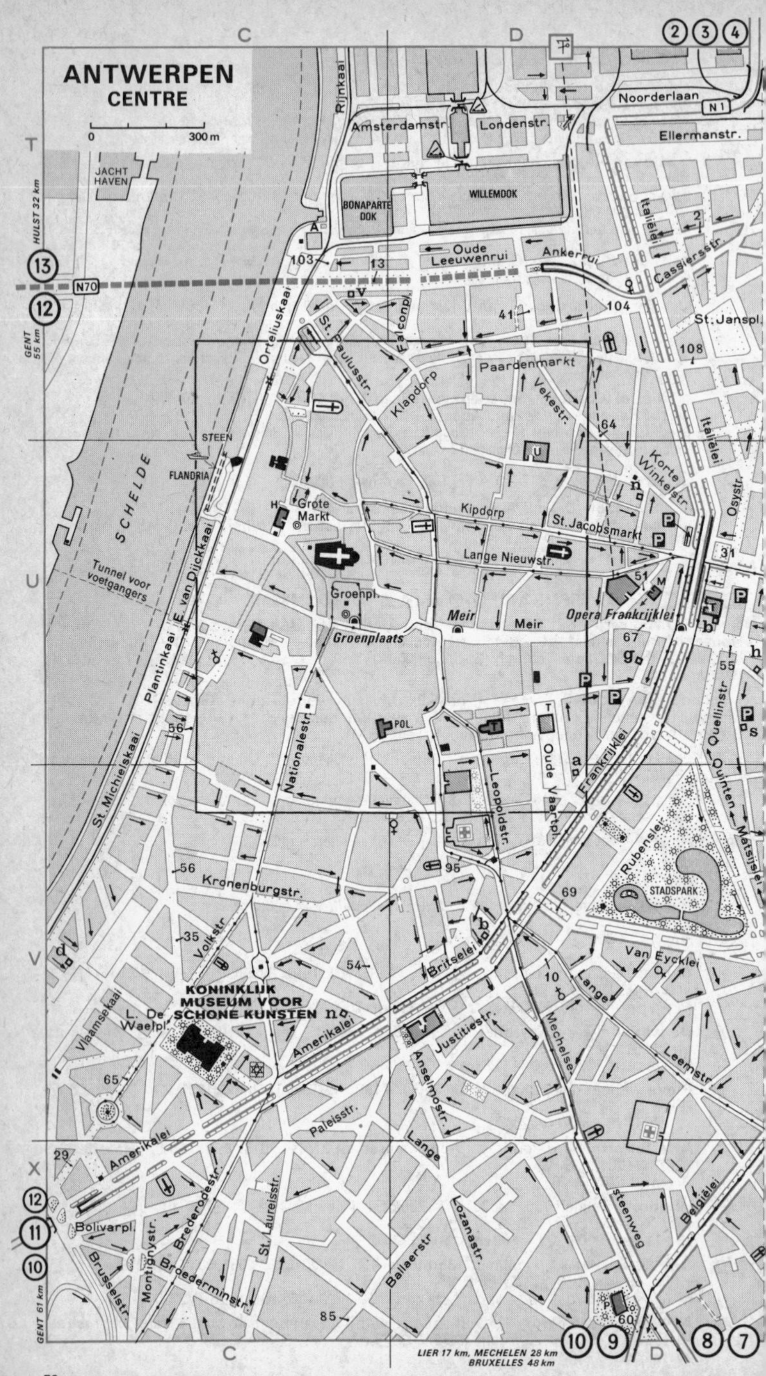
ANTWERPEN
CENTRE
0
300 m
JACHT HAVEN
HULST 32 km
GENT 55 km
N70
SCHELDE
Tunnel voor voetgangers
STEEN
FLANDRIA
BONAPARTE DOK
WILLEMDOK
Rijnkaai
Amsterdamstr.
Londenstr.
Noorderlaan
N1
Ellermanstr.
Oude Leeuwenrui
Ankerrui
Cassiersstr.
St. Jansplein
Italiëlei
Orteliuskaai
St. Paulusstr.
Falconpl.
Klapdorp
Paardenmarkt
Vekestr.
Korte Winkelstr.
Osystr.
Grote Markt
Kipdorp
St. Jacobsmarkt
Lange Nieuwstr.
Groenpl.
Groenplaats
Meir
Opera
Frankrijklei
E. van Dijckkaai
Plantinkaai
St. Michielskaai
Nationalestr.
POL.
Oude Vaartpl.
Leopoldstr.
Quellinstr.
Quinten Matsijslei
Rubenslei
STADSPARK
Kronenburgstr.
Volkstr.
Britselei
Van Eycklei
Lange
Mechelse steenweg
Leemstr.
KONINKLIJK MUSEUM VOOR SCHONE KUNSTEN
L. De Waelpl.
Vlaamsekaai
Amerikalei
Justitiestr.
Anselmostr.
Paleisstr.
Lange Lozanastr.
Belgiëlei
Bolivarpl.
Brusselstr.
Montignystr.
Brederodestr.
Broederminstr.
St. Laureisstr.
Ballaerstr
GENT 61 km
LIER 17 km, MECHELEN 28 km
BRUXELLES 48 km

STREET INDEX TO ANTWERPEN TOWN PLANS

Continued on next page

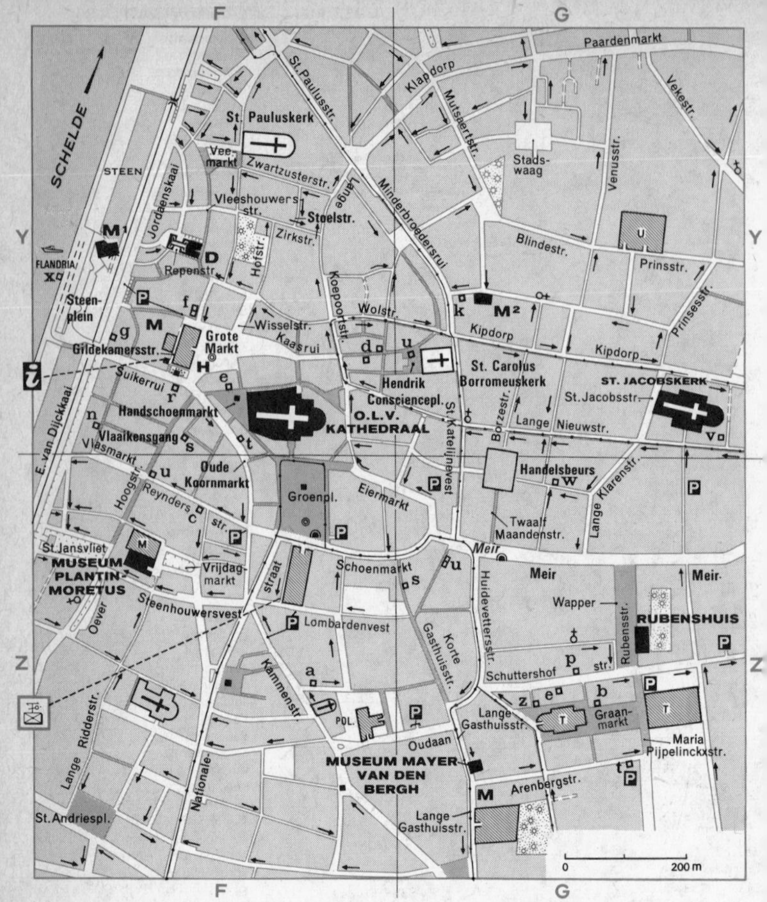

STREET INDEX TO ANTWERPEN TOWN PLANS (Concluded)

XXX ✿ **Vateli,** Kipdorpvest 50, ✆ 2331781, Classic – ▤ Ⓟ. AE ⓓ E VISA DU **g**
closed Sunday, Monday, Bank Holidays, July and Christmas-New Year – **M** a la carte 1600/2300
Spec. Caneton à la rouennaise, Terrine d'anguille et saumon fumés, Rognon de veau à la bière.

XXX **De Lepeleer,** Lange St-Annastr. 8, ✆ 2342225, « Rustic interior » – Ⓟ. AE ⓓ E VISA
closed 9 to 25 August, 20 December-3 January, Saturday lunch, Sunday and Bank Holidays – **M** a la carte 1750/2000. DU **n**

XXX **Relais Estérel,** Tolstraat 70, ✆ 2373261, Open until midnight – ▤. AE ⓓ E VISA CV **n**
closed lunch Saturday and Sunday, Monday, Thursday and July – **M** a la carte 1400/2050.

XX **De Poterne,** Desguinlei 186, ✉ 2018, ✆ 2382824 – AE ⓓ
closed Saturday, Sunday, 21 July-16 August and Christmas-New Year – **M** a la carte 1200/1820.

XX **Sawadee,** 1st floor, Britselei 16, ✆ 2330859, Thaï rest., « Ancient mansion » – AE ⓓ E VISA DV **b**
closed Tuesday – **M** (closed lunch in August) a la carte 950/1100.

XX **Panaché,** Statiestr. 17, ✉ 2018, ✆ 2326905, Open until 1.30 a.m. - quick lunch – ▤. AE ⓓ E VISA EU **q**
closed 29 July-26 August – **M** 465/925.

XX **La Moule Parquée,** Wapenstraat 18, ✆ 2384908, Seafood – ▤. ⓓ E VISA CV **d**
closed Monday, Saturday lunch and 3 weeks in May – **M** a la carte 850/1050.

XX **Liang's Garden,** Markgravelei 141, ✉ 2018, ✆ 2372222, Chinese rest. – AE ⓓ VISA. ⚘
closed Wednesday and 3 to 20 August – **M** a la carte 1200/1620.

X **Solmar,** Breidelstraat 23, ✉ 2018, ✆ 2325053, Portuguese rest. – AE ⓓ E VISA. ⚘
closed Tuesday and August – **M** a la carte 860/1580. EU **r**

X **Rimini,** Vestingstraat 5, ✉ 2018, ✆ 2314290, Italian rest. DU **h**
closed Wednesday and August – **M** a la carte 700/1320.

Old Antwerp.

Alfa Theater Ⓜ, Arenbergstraat 30, ✆ 2311720, Telex 33910 – ⇕ ▤ rest TV ☎ – 🅰. AE ⓓ E VISA GZ **t**
M *(closed Saturday and Sunday)* 600/800 – **83 rm** ☕ 2460/3320 – P 3310/3600.

Arcade Ⓜ without rest., Meistraat 39 (Theaterplein), ✆ 2318830, Telex 31104 – ⇕ TV ⋔wc ☎ ♿ – 🅰. VISA DV **a**
☕ 160 – **150 rm** 1810/1965.

XXXX ✿✿ **La Pérouse,** Steenplein (pontoon), ✆ 2323528, ≤, « Anchored vessel » – ▤ Ⓟ. AE ⓓ E VISA. ⚘ FY **x**
30 September-end May except Sunday, Monday, Bank Holidays, 25 December-5 January and Good Friday – **M** (booking essential) a la carte 1650/2040
Spec. Ravioli de St.Jacques aux girolles et mousserons, Côtelettes de homard et de barbue au lait d'amandes, Bar poêlé et beignets de langoustines.

XXX ✿✿ **Sir Anthony Van Dijck** (Paesbrugghe), Oude Koornmarkt 16 (Vlaeykensgang), ✆ 2316170, « Situated in a 16C lane, tasteful ancient interior » – AE ⓓ E. ⚘ FY **s**
closed 20 to 27 April, 1 to 25 August, 22 to 31 December, Saturday and Sunday – **M** a la carte 1450/2080
Spec. Salade d'huîtres au saumon mariné et witloof (Oct.-March), Selle d'agneau en croûte, Gratin de poires à la vanille.

XXX St. Jacob in Galicië, Braderijstraat 14, ✆ 2318043, « In a 16C house complex » FY **f**

XXX **Den Gulden Greffoen,** Hoogstraat 37, ✆ 2315046, « Elegant interior in a 15C restored house » – ▤. AE ⓓ E VISA. ⚘ FZ **u**
closed Saturday lunch, Sunday, Bank Holidays, last 3 weeks July and Christmas-New Year – **M** a la carte 1800/2420.

XXX **La Rade,** 1st floor, Van Dijckkaai 8, ✆ 2334963, « 19C mansion » – AE ⓓ E VISA FY **g**
closed 2 to 8 March, 6 to 28 July, Saturday lunch and Sunday – **M** 1800.

XXX ✿ **'t Fornuis** (Segers), Reyndersstraat 24, ✆ 2336270, « Rustic » – AE ⓓ E. ⚘ FZ **c**
closed Saturday, Sunday, last 3 weeks August and Christmas-New Year – **M** a la carte 1650/2400
Spec. Nage de sole et d'écrevisses au Chablis, Filets de sole meunière et cervelle de veau à la moelle et champignons des bois, Ris de veau au gratin de nouilles, foie gras et truffes.

XX **Petrus,** Kelderstraat 1, ✆ 2252734 – AE ⓓ E VISA. ⚘ GZ **z**
closed Monday, Saturday lunch and last 3 weeks July – **M** a la carte 1180/1680.

XX Cigogne d'Alsace, Wiegstraat 9, ✆ 2339716 GZ **u**

XX **Criterium,** Schuttershofstraat 39, ✆ 2328346, Elegant interior – AE ⓓ E VISA. ⚘
closed Saturday lunch, Sunday, Bank Holidays, 27 July-16 August and 24 December-1 January – **M** a la carte 1410/2030. GZ **p**

XX **Koperen Ketel,** Wiegstraat 5, ✆ 2331274 – AE ⓓ E VISA GZ **u**
closed Saturday lunch, Sunday and Bank Holidays – **M** a la carte 930/1420.

XX **V.I.P. Diners,** Lange Nieuwstraat 95, ✆ 2331317 – AE ⓓ E VISA GY **v**
closed Saturday lunch, Sunday, Bank Holidays, Easter and 19 July-3 August – **M** 1400.

XX **De Kerselaar,** Grote Pieter Potstraat 22, ✆ 2335969 – AE ⓓ E VISA. ✻ FY **n**
closed lunch Saturday and Monday, Sunday, Easter and 7 to 28 July – **M** a la carte 1200/1540.

XX **De Zeven Schaken,** Braderijstraat 24 (Grote Markt), ✆ 2337003, « Rustic » – AE ⓓ E VISA. ✻ FY **f**
closed Sunday, Bank Holidays and August – **M** 900/1600.

XX **De Manie,** H. Conscienceplein 3, ✆ 2326438 – AE ⓓ E VISA. ✻ GY **u**
closed Sunday, Wednesday and 25 February-11 March – **M** 1950.

XX **Bistro 15,** Schrijnwerkerstraat 15, ✆ 2337826 – AE ⓓ E VISA GZ **s**
closed Sunday and 15 August-3 September – **M** (lunch only except Friday) a la carte approx. 1300.

XX **Neuze-Neuze,** Wijngaardstraat 19, ✆ 2325783 – AE ⓓ E VISA. ✻ FY **d**
closed Saturday lunch, Sunday and 2 to 17 August – **M** a la carte 1350/1680.

XX **Laurent,** Korte Klarenstraat 5, ✆ 2329547 – AE ⓓ E VISA. ✻ GZ **w**
closed 18 to 27 April, 23 August-7 September, Saturday lunch and Sunday – **M** a la carte 1150/2650.

XX **Manoir,** Everdijstraat 13, ✆ 2327697, « Carved and painted panelling » – AE ⓓ E VISA
closed Wednesday and 15 July-15 August – **M** a la carte 840/1580. FZ **a**

XX **Preud'homme,** Suikerrui 28, ✆ 2334200 – AE ⓓ E VISA. ✻ FY **r**
closed Tuesday and 3 February-5 March – **M** a la carte 1300/1980.

XX **Zagreb,** Brouwersvliet 30, ✆ 2260102, Yugoslavian rest. – AE ⓓ E VISA. ✻ CT **v**
closed Saturday, Sunday and 15 July-14 August – **M** a la carte 1000/1530.

XX **De Twee Atheners,** Keizerstraat 2, ✆ 2320851, Greek rest., Open until 2 a.m. – AE ⓓ
closed Wednesday except Bank Holidays and September – **M** a la carte 650/1100. GY **k**

X **Fourchette,** Schuttershofstraat 28, ✆ 2313335 – AE ⓓ E VISA GZ **e**
closed Saturday lunch, Sunday, Monday, Bank Holidays and 12 July-3 August – **M** a la carte 1100/1400.

X **Rooden-Hoed,** Oude Koornmarkt 25, ✆ 2332844, Mussels in season, Antwerp atmosphere – ▤. AE. ✻ FY **t**
closed 28 February-8 March, 17 June-15 July and Wednesday – **M** a la carte 910/1530.

X **Peerdestal,** Wijngaardstraat 8, ✆ 2319503 – AE ⓓ E VISA. ✻ FY **d**
M a la carte 600/1420.

X **In de Schaduw van de Kathedraal,** Handschoenmarkt 17, ✆ 2324014, ☂ – AE ⓓ E VISA FY **e**
closed Monday November-April, Tuesday and 4 to 16 May – **M** a la carte 810/1350.

X **Henri,** Graanmarkt 3, ✆ 2329258 – AE ⓓ E VISA. ✻ GZ **b**
closed Saturday lunch, Sunday and September – **M** a la carte 800/1390.

Left Bank (Linker Oever)

XX **Lido,** Hanegraefstraat 8, ✉ 2050, ✆ 2193590, Chinese rest. – ▤. AE ⓓ E
closed Tuesday, Wednesday and 15 July-early August – **M** a la carte 600/1060.

Suburbs

North – ✉ 2030 :

🏨 **Novotel** Ⓜ, Luithagen-Haven 6, ✆ 5420320, Telex 32488, ⛱, 🎾 – 🛗 ▤ 📺 🛁wc ☎ ♿ 🅟 – 🏛. AE ⓓ E VISA
M a la carte 830/1180 – ☕ 295 – **119 rm** 2300/2850.

XXX **Terminal,** Leopolddok 214, ✆ 5412680, ≤ harbour – 🅟
closed Saturday, Sunday, Bank Holidays and August – **M** (lunch only) a la carte 1160/1800.

South – ✉ 2020 :

🏨 **Crest H.** Ⓜ, G. Legrellelaan 10, ✆ 2372900, Telex 33843 – 🛗 ▤ 📺 ☎ 🅟 – 🏛. AE ⓓ E VISA
M 1050/1450 – ☕ 300 – **253 rm** 3450/3750.

at Berchem – ✉ 2600 Berchem – ☎ 03 :

X Ten Carvery et Den Ossenaert, Rooiplein 6, ✆ 2304733, Grill, « Converted ancient farm » – 🅟.

X **Euterpia,** Generaal Capiaumontstraat 2, ✆ 2368356, ☂
closed Monday, Tuesday and first 2 weeks August – **M** (dinner only) a la carte 1120/1670.

X **Willy,** Generaal Lemanstraat 54, ✆ 2188807 – AE ⓓ E VISA
closed July – **M** 295.

at Borgerhout – ✉ 2200 Borgerhout – ☎ 03 :

🏨 **Quality Inn,** Luitenant Lippenslaan 66, ✆ 2359191, Telex 34479, ⛱ – 🛗 ▤ 📺 ☎ ♿ 🅟 – 🏛. AE ⓓ E VISA
M a la carte 860/1600 – **176 rm** ☕ 2835/3785.

at Deurne – ✉ 2100 Deurne – ☎ 03 :

XXX **Den Uyl,** Bosuil 1, ☎ 3243404, « Converted farm » – Ⓟ. AE ⓓ E VISA. ✻
closed Saturday lunch, Sunday and July – **M** a la carte 1330/1690.

XX **Périgord,** Turnhoutsebaan 273, ☎ 3255200 – AE ⓓ E VISA. ✻
closed Tuesday dinner, Wednesday, Saturday lunch and 1 to 29 July – **M** 1125/1525.

at Mortsel – pop. 26 401 – ✉ 2510 Mortsel – ☎ 03 :

Bristol International without rest., Edegemstraat 1, ☎ 4498049 – lift TV wc ☎. AE ⓓ E VISA
closed 26 December-3 January – **26 rm** ☕ 890/1300.

Environs

at Aartselaar : by ⑩ : 10 km – pop. 12 921 – ✉ 2630 Aartselaar – ☎ 03 :

XXXX **Host. Kasteelhoeve Groeninghe** with rm, Kontichsesteenweg 78, ☎ 4579586, ←, terrace, « Restored Flemish farm, country atmosphere » – TV wc ☎ Ⓟ. ✻
closed 21 to 30 December – **M** *(closed Saturday lunch, Sunday and 20 July-9 August)* a la carte 1830/2600 – ☕ 500 – **7 rm** *(closed 13 July-2 August)* 5250/6750.

XXX **Lindenbos,** Boomsesteenweg 139, ☎ 8880965, « Converted castle with park and lake » – Ⓟ. AE ⓓ E. ✻
closed Monday and August – **M** 1200/1850.

at Brasschaat : by ② and ③ : 11 km – pop. 32 880 – ✉ 2130 Brasschaat – ☎ 03 :

XXX **Halewijn,** Donksesteenweg 212 (Ekeren-Donk), ☎ 6472010, terrace – ▤. AE ⓓ E
closed Monday – **M** 900/1400.

XXX **Het Villasdal,** Kapelsesteenweg 480, ☎ 6645821 – Ⓟ. AE ⓓ E
closed Saturday lunch, Monday and 13 July-10 August – **M** a la carte 1500/2000.

at Ekeren : by ② : 11 km – ✉ 2070 Ekeren – ☎ 03 :

XX **Hof de Bist,** Veltwijcklaan 258, ☎ 6646130 – Ⓟ. AE ⓓ E
closed Sunday and Monday – **M** a la carte approx. 1700.

XX **Het Laer,** Kapelsesteenweg 75, ☎ 6460299 – Ⓟ. AE ⓓ E VISA
closed Sunday, Monday and 28 June-28 July – **M** a la carte 1270/1950.

at Kapellen : by ② : 15,5 km – pop. 22 549 – ✉ 2080 Kapellen – ☎ 03 :

XXX ✻ **De Bellefleur** (Buytaert), Antwerpsesteenweg 253, ☎ 6646719, « Winter garden » – Ⓟ. AE ⓓ E
closed Saturday, Sunday and 4 July-2 August – **M** (booking essential) a la carte 1630/2380
Spec. Assiette du pêcheur zélandais, Chevreuil aux cêpes (Oct.-March), Blanc de coucou de Malines au vieux Madère.

XX **De Graal,** Kapellenboslei 11 (N : 5 km by N 122 direction Kalmthout), ☎ 6665510, « Terrace and garden » – AE ⓓ E
M a la carte 1400/1800.

XX **De Pauw,** Antwerpsesteenweg 48, ☎ 6642282, terrace – AE ⓓ E VISA
closed Tuesday dinner, Wednesday and 16 to 31 August – **M** 900/1500.

X **Cappelleke,** Dorpstraat 70, ☎ 6646728 – AE ⓓ E VISA
closed Tuesday, Wednesday and 17 August-9 September – **M** 950.

at Kontich : by ⑨ : 12 km – pop. 18 081 – ✉ 2550 Kontich – ☎ 03 :

XX **Alexander's,** Mechelsesteenweg 318, ☎ 4572631 – Ⓟ. AE ⓓ E VISA. ✻
closed Sunday dinner, Monday and July – **M** 1395.

at Merksem : 10 km – ✉ 2060 Merksem – ☎ 03 :

XXX **Maritime,** Bredabaan 978, ☎ 6462223, terrace, Seafood, « Elegant interior » – Ⓟ. AE ⓓ VISA
closed Sunday – **M** 1850.

at Schoten : 10 km – pop. 30 738 – ✉ 2120 Schoten – ☎ 03 :

XXX **Kleine Barreel,** Bredabaan 1147, ☎ 6458584, Classic – ▤ Ⓟ. AE ⓓ E VISA
M a la carte 1200/1900.

XX **Uilenspiegel,** Brechtsebaan 277, ☎ 6516145, terrace, « Terrace and garden » – Ⓟ. AE ⓓ E VISA
closed Saturday lunch and Monday – **M** 1275/1775.

XX **Witte Raaf,** Horstebaan 97, ☎ 6588664, ←, terrace – Ⓟ. AE ⓓ E VISA
closed Wednesday dinner and Sunday – **M** a la carte 1220/2000.

XX **Ten Weyngaert,** Winkelstapstraat 151, ☎ 6455516, Grill, « Converted 17C farm » – ▤ Ⓟ. AE ⓓ E VISA. ✻
M 1055.

at Wijnegem : 10 km – pop. 8 176 – ✉ 2110 Wijnegem – ☎ 03 :

XXX **Ter Vennen,** Merksemsebaan 278, ✆ 3538140, « Converted farm, elegant interior » – P. AE ⓓ E VISA
closed Saturday lunch, Monday, Easter and 1 to 15 September – **M** a la carte approx. 1700.

at Wilrijk : by ⑩ : 6 km – ✉ 2610 Wilrijk – ☎ 03 :

XX **Schans XV,** Moerelei 155, ✆ 8284564, 帝, « Early 20C redoubt » – ⓓ E VISA. ✻
closed Thursday dinner, Saturday lunch, Sunday, Bank Holidays, last 2 weeks February and 9 to 31 August – **M** a la carte approx. 1700.

BRUGES (BRUGGE) 8000 West-Vlaanderen 213 ③ and 409 ② – pop. 117 747 agglomeration – ☎ 050.

See : Trips on the canals★★★ (Boottocht) CY – Procession of the Holy Blood★★★ – Belfry and Halles★★★ (Belfort en Hallen) CY – Market square★★ (Markt) CY – Market-town★★ (Burg) CY – Beguinage★★ (Begijnhof) CZ – Basilica of the Holy Blood★ CY **A** – Church of Our Lady★ : tower★★, statue of the Madonna★★, tombstone of Mary of Burgundy★★ CZ **S** – Rosery quay (Rozenhoedkaai) ≤★★ CY – Dijver ≤★★ CZ – St. Boniface bridge (Bonifaciusbrug) : site★★ CZ – Chimney of the "Brugse Vrijë" in the Court of Justice (Gerechtshof) CY **B.**

Museums : Groeninge★★★ CZ – Memling (St. John's Hospital)★★★ CZ – Gruuthuse★ CZ **M**[1] – Arents House★ (Arentshuis) CZ **M**[4].

Envir. : Zedelgem : baptismal font★ in the St.Lawrence's church by ⑥ : 10,5 km.

ℹ Markt 7 ✆ 330711 – Tourist association of the province, Vlamingstraat 55 ✆ 337344.

Brussels 96 ③ – Ghent 45 ③ – Lille 72 ⑪ – Ostend 28 ⑤.

Plans on following pages

Orangerie ⛢ without rest., Karthuizerinnestraat 10, ✆ 341649, Telex 82443, « Ancient mansion with tasteful decor » – 🛗 TV ☎ – 🅰. AE ⓓ E VISA — CY **y**
18 rm ☕ 3375/5750.

Oud Huis Amsterdam ⛢, Spiegelrei 3, ✆ 341810, ≤, « 17C mansion, ancient Dutch Hanse » – 🛗 TV ☎ – 🅰. AE VISA. ✻ — CY **w**
M (see 't Bourgoensche Cruyce) – **17 rm** ☕ 2625/5250.

Karos M without rest., Hoefijzerlaan 37, ✆ 341448, Telex 82377 – 🛗 ▤ TV ☎ ♿ – 🅰. AE ⓓ E VISA. ✻ — BY **r**
closed 5 January-5 February – **20 rm** ☕ 2870/5730.

Portinari M ⛢ without rest., 't Zand 15, ✆ 341034, Telex 82400 – 🛗 TV ☎ ♿ P – 🅰. AE ⓓ E VISA. ✻ — CZ **x**
32 rm ☕ 2500/3400.

Holiday Inn, Boeveriestraat 2, ✆ 340971, Telex 81369, ⛶ – 🛗 ▤ TV ☎ ♿ 🚗 – 🅰. AE ⓓ E VISA — CZ **a**
M 650/1925 – **128 rm** ☕ 3300/4200.

Park H. without rest., Vrijdagmarkt 5, ✆ 333364, Telex 81686 – 🛗 TV ☎ ♿ – 🅰. AE ⓓ E VISA — CZ **g**
62 rm ☕ 2500/3000.

Die Swaene ⛢ without rest., Steenhouwersdijk 1, ✆ 342798, Telex 82446, ≤, « Tasteful decor » – 🛗 TV ⛀wc ☎ – 🅰. AE ⓓ E VISA — CY **g**
27 rm ☕ 2500/4200.

Pand H. ⛢ without rest., Pandreitje 16, ✆ 334434, Telex 81018 – 🛗 TV ⛀wc ⛆wc ☎ – 🅰. AE ⓓ E VISA — CY **u**
18 rm ☕ 2050/3000.

Erasmus M without rest., quick-lunch, Wollestraat 35, ✆ 335781, ≤, « Terrace ≤ inner courtyard (classified historic monument) » – 🛗 TV ⛀wc ☎. AE E VISA. ✻ — CY **a**
10 rm ☕ 2650/4900.

Prinsenhof ⛢ without rest., Ontvangersstraat 9, ✆ 342690, Telex 81315, « Tasteful decor » – 🛗 TV ⛀wc ☎. AE ⓓ E VISA — CY **c**
16 rm ☕ 2175/3250.

Adornes without rest., St-Annarei 26, ✆ 341336, ≤, « Tasteful decor » – 🛗 TV ⛀wc ☎ ♿. AE E VISA. ✻ — DY **r**
closed 4 January-12 February – **20 rm** ☕ 1700/2900.

Europ H. ⛢ without rest., Augustijnenrei 18, ✆ 337975, Telex 82490 – 🛗 TV ⛀wc ⛆wc ☎ – 🅰. AE ⓓ E VISA. ✻ — CY **b**
March-15 November – **30 rm** ☕ 2055/3070.

De Biskajer M ⛢ without rest., Biskajersplein 4, ✆ 341506 – 🛗 TV ⛀wc ⛆wc ☎. AE ⓓ E VISA — CY **j**
17 rm ☕ 2600/3200.

Ter Brughe ⛢ without rest., Oost-Gisthelhof 2, ✆ 340324 – TV ⛀wc ☎. AE ⓓ E VISA
closed January-February – **20 rm** ☕ 2050/2500. — CY **x**

Azalea without rest., Wulfhagestraat 43, ✆ 331478, Telex 81282 – TV ⛀wc ⛆wc ☎ ♿ 🚗 – 🅰. AE ⓓ E VISA — CY **p**
18 rm ☕ 2175/3350.

't Putje with apartments in annex, 't Zand 31, ℘ 332847, Buffet lunch, open until 2 a.m. – TV 🛁wc 🚿wc ☎ – AE ① E VISA CZ **t**
M a la carte 760/1070 – **16 rm** 2300/2950.

Aragon without rest., Naaldenstraat 24, ℘ 333533 – TV 🛁wc 🚿wc ☎. AE E VISA CY **t**
16 rm 2250/3100.

Bourgoensch Hof without rest., Wollestraat 39, ℘ 331645, ⇐ canals and ancient Flemish houses – TV 🛁wc 🚿wc ☎. ✽ CY **a**
15 November-15 March weekends only – **11 rm** 1850/3950.

Bryghia without rest., Oosterlingenplein 4, ℘ 338059 – 🛁wc 🚿wc ☎. AE ① E VISA. ✽ CY **f**
18 rm 2120/2320.

Groeninghe without rest., Korte Vuldersstraat 29, ℘ 340769 – 🛁wc ☎. AE E VISA
closed January – **8 rm** 1800/2300. CZ **c**

Navarra without rest., St-Jacobsstraat 41, ℘ 340561, Telex 81037 – 🛁wc 🚿wc ☎ Ⓟ – AE ① E VISA CY **k**
78 rm 2400/2950.

Egmond without rest., Minnewater 15, ℘ 341445, « Garden setting » – 🚿wc ☎ Ⓟ. AE ① E VISA CZ **v**
15 March-14 November – **9 rm** 1600/2800.

Anselmus without rest., Ridderstraat 15, ℘ 341374 – TV 🛁wc 🚿wc ☎. AE VISA DY **n**
10 rm 1775/2050.

Ter Duinen without rest., Langerei 52, ℘ 330437 – 🛁wc ☎. AE ① E VISA
10 rm 1240/1880. CX **a**

Hans Memling without rest., Kuipersstraat 18, ℘ 332096 – 🚿wc ☎. VISA CY **e**
17 rm 1750/1950.

Jacobs without rest., Baliestraat 1, ℘ 339831, Telex 81693 – 🛁wc 🚿wc ☎. AE VISA CX **n**
closed 31 December-January – **27 rm** 1150/1800.

Fevery without rest., Collaert Mansionstraat 3, ℘ 331269 – 🛁wc 🚿wc ☎. AE ① E VISA CX **d**
11 rm 1315/1680.

Post Hotel without rest., Hoogstraat 18, ℘ 337889, Telex 26937 – 🚿wc – VISA
closed 20 December-1 January – **19 rm** 1600/1900. DY **y**

De Pauw without rest., St-Gilliskerkhof 8, ℘ 337118 – 🚿wc ☎. AE ① E VISA CX **d**
8 rm 950/1650.

XXX ✿ **De Witte Poorte** (Van Boven), Jan Van Eyckplein 6, ℘ 330883, « Former vaulted store, garden » – AE ① VISA CY **v**
closed February, last week August, Sunday and Monday – **M** a la carte 1800/2550
Spec. Terrine de foie d'oie, Queues de langoustines aux petits légumes et beurre blanc, Médaillon de homard aux filets de sole.

XXX **De Zilveren Pauw,** Zilverstraat 41, ℘ 335566, « Belle-époque interior, patio » – AE ① E VISA CY **z**
closed 11 to 26 February, 15 to 31 July, Tuesday dinner and Wednesday – **M** 980/2000.

XXX **Den Braamberg,** Pandreitje 11, ℘ 337370, Classic-elegant – AE ① VISA CY **u**
closed Sunday dinner and Thursday – **M** 1700.

XXX ✿ **De Karmeliet** (Van Hecke), Jeruzalemstraat 1, ℘ 338259 – AE ① E VISA DY **u**
closed Sunday dinner, Monday, 30 August-15 September and 1 week February – **M** a la carte 1630/2040
Spec. Trois petits plats aux oursins (Oct.-March), Salade d'escargots et pommes de terre aux herbes vertes, Ris de veau et volaille fumée au foie gras.

XXX **'t Pandreitje,** Pandreitje 6, ℘ 331190, « Elegant interior » – AE ① E VISA CDY **s**
closed 1 to 24 March, 13 to 31 December, Sunday and Monday – **M** a la carte 1350/2150.

XX **Den Gouden Harynck,** Groeninge 25, ℘ 337637 – AE ① E VISA CZ **e**
closed Sunday and Monday except Bank Holidays – **M** 1750.

XX **Kardinaalshof,** Sint-Salvatorkerkhof 14, ℘ 341691, Seafood – AE E VISA CZ **r**
closed Sunday dinner, Tuesday, 2 weeks January and 2 weeks June – **M** a la carte 1130/1900.

XX **'t Bourgoensche Cruyce** with rm, Wollestraat 41, ℘ 337926, ⇐ canals and old Flemish houses – TV 🛁wc 🚿. AE VISA. ✽ CY **a**
closed February, 2 weeks November, Tuesday May-October, Sunday and Monday lunch October-May – **M** a la carte 1600/2100 – **6 rm** 1430/1865.

XX **Boudewijn I** with rm, 't Zand 21, ℘ 336962, Telex 81163 – TV 🛁wc ☎ – AE ① E VISA CZ **t**
M *(closed Tuesday)* 600/1300 – **11 rm** 1650/3000.

XX **'t Lammetje,** Braambergstraat 3, ℘ 332495 – AE E VISA CY **q**
closed Monday, 25 August-2 September and February – **M** a la carte 1150/1720.

XX **Criterium,** 't Zand 12, ℘ 331984, – AE ① E VISA CZ **x**
closed 1 to 17 July, 2 weeks October, Tuesday dinner except July and Wednesday – **M** 795/1395.

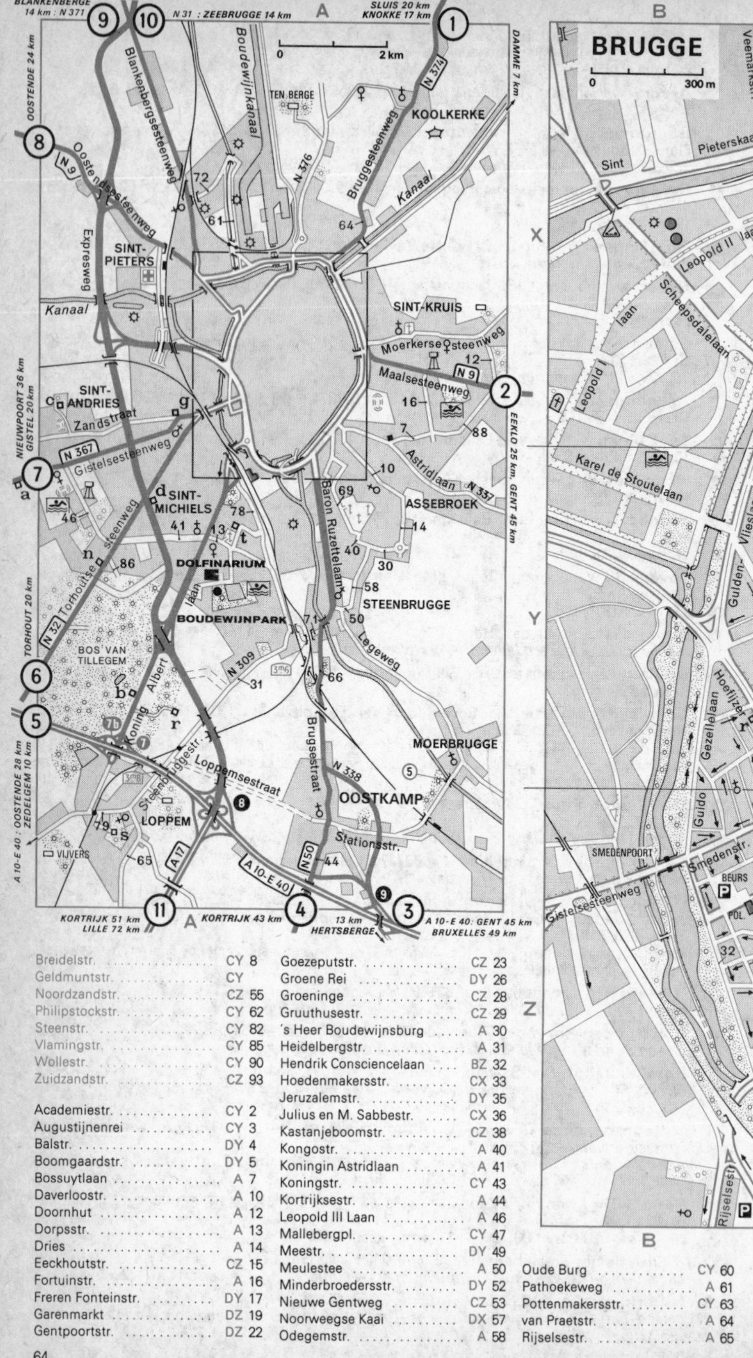

Breidelstr. .... CY 8
Geldmuntstr. .... CY
Noordzandstr. .... CZ 55
Philipstockstr. .... CY 62
Steenstr. .... CY 82
Vlamingstr. .... CY 85
Wollestr. .... CY 90
Zuidzandstr. .... CZ 93

Academiestr. .... CY 2
Augustijnenrei .... CY 3
Balstr. .... DY 4
Boomgaardstr. .... DY 5
Bossuytlaan .... A 7
Daverloostr. .... A 10
Doornhut .... A 12
Dorpsstr. .... A 13
Dries .... A 14
Eeckhoutstr. .... CZ 15
Fortuinstr. .... A 16
Freren Fonteinstr. .... DY 17
Garenmarkt .... DZ 19
Gentpoortstr. .... DZ 22
Goezeputstr. .... CZ 23
Groene Rei .... DY 26
Groeninge .... CZ 28
Gruuthusestr. .... CZ 29
's Heer Boudewijnsburg .... A 30
Heidelbergstr. .... A 31
Hendrik Consciencelaan .... BZ 32
Hoedenmakersstr. .... CX 33
Jeruzalemstr. .... DY 35
Julius en M. Sabbestr. .... CX 36
Kastanjeboomstr. .... CZ 38
Kongostr. .... A 40
Koningin Astridlaan .... A 41
Koningstr. .... CY 43
Kortrijksestr. .... A 44
Leopold III Laan .... A 46
Mallebergpl. .... CY 47
Meestr. .... DY 49
Meulestee .... A 50
Minderbroedersstr. .... DY 52
Nieuwe Gentweg .... CZ 53
Noorweegse Kaai .... DX 57
Odegemstr. .... A 58
Oude Burg .... CY 60
Pathoekeweg .... A 61
Pottenmakersstr. .... CY 63
van Praetstr. .... A 64
Rijselsestr. .... A 65

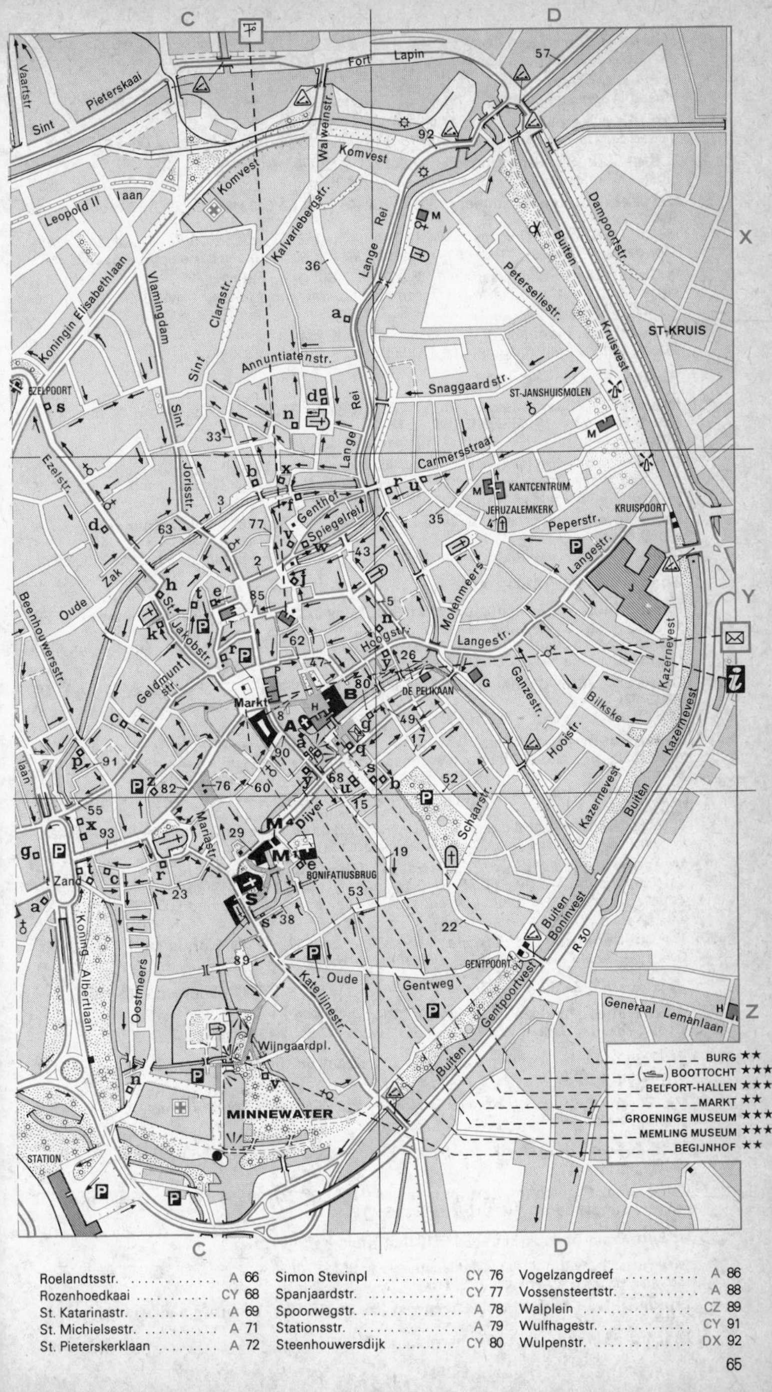

Roelandtsstr. .... A 66	Simon Stevinpl .... CY 76	Vogelzangdreef .... A 86
Rozenhoedkaai .... CY 68	Spanjaardstr. .... CY 77	Vossensteertstr. .... A 88
St. Katarinastr. .... A 69	Spoorwegstr. .... A 78	Walplein .... CZ 89
St. Michielsestr. .... A 71	Stationsstr. .... A 79	Wulfhagestr. .... CY 91
St. Pieterskerklaan .... A 72	Steenhouwersdijk .... CY 80	Wulpenstr. .... DX 92

X **Eglantier,** Ezelstraat 120, ✆ 332946 – AE ⓞ VISA CX **s**
closed Sunday dinner and Monday – **M** a la carte 890/1370.

X **'t Presidentje,** Ezelstraat 21, ✆ 339521 – AE ⓞ E VISA CY **d**
closed Wednesday dinner, Sunday and 22 June-12 July – **M** a la carte 950/1550.

X **Postiljon,** Katelijnestraat 3, ✆ 335616 – AE ⓞ E VISA CZ **s**
closed Sunday dinner, Tuesday and 15 November-10 December – **M** a la carte 810/1260.

X **'t Kluizeke,** Sint Jacobstraat 58, ✆ 341224 – AE ⓞ VISA. ✄ CY **h**
closed Wednesday and 11 to 27 February – **M** 1050.

X **De Watermolen,** Oostmeers 130, ✆ 332448 (will be 343348), ≤, ☂, « Terrace » – E VISA CZ **n**
closed first 2 weeks Oct., last 2 weeks February, Thursday dinner 16 Sept.-May and dinner Monday and Tuesday, Wednesday except July-August – **M** a la carte approx. 1200.

X **'t Cipiertje,** Gevangenisstraat 1, ✆ 332056, Grill, Open until 2 a.m. DY **b**
closed 1 to 24 March, 13 to 31 December, Sunday and Monday – **M** (dinner only) a la carte 800/1100.

X **Malpertuus,** Eiermarkt 9, ✆ 333038 – AE ⓞ E VISA CY **r**
closed Wednesday and July – **M** 420/825.

South – ✉ 8200 – ☎ 050 :

Novotel Ⓜ, Chartreuseweg 20, ✆ 382851, Telex 81507, ☂, ⛱, ⛰ – 🛗 ▤ rest 📺 ⛀wc ☎ ♿ Ⓟ – 🏛. AE ⓞ E VISA A **r**
M a la carte 680/1170 – ☕ 300 – **101 rm** 2375/3000.

XXXX ✿✿ **Weinebrugge** (Galens), Koning Albertlaan 242, ✆ 384440 – Ⓟ. AE A **b**
closed Sunday dinner in December and February, Wednesday, Thursday and January – **M** (weekend booking essential) a la carte 1730/2550.

XXX **Casserole** (Hotel. school), Groene Poortdreef 17, ✆ 383888, « Country atmosphere » – Ⓟ. AE E VISA A **t**
closed 30 June-18 August – **M** (lunch only except Friday and Saturday) a la carte 1160/1930.

South-West – ✉ 8200 – ☎ 050 :

Pannenhuis ⛰, Zandstraat 2, ✆ 311907, Telex 82345, ≤, ☂, « Garden-terrace » – 📺 ☎ ♿ Ⓟ – 🏛. AE ⓞ E VISA. ✄ rest A **g**
closed 15 to 31 January – **M** *(closed 1 to 15 July, Tuesday dinner October-July and Wednesday)* a la carte 1200/1750 – **20 rm** ☕ 1250/3300 – P 2400.

Climat Ⓜ, Jozef Wauterstraat 61, ✆ 380988, Telex 85461 – 📺 ⛀wc ☎ ♿ Ⓟ – 🏛. AE ⓞ E VISA A **d**
M 600/785 – ☕ 330 – **48 rm** 1650.

XXX ✿ **Ter Heyde** (Hanbuckers) ⛰ with rm, Torhoutsesteenweg 620 (by ⑥ : 8 km on N 32), ✆ 383858, ≤, « Stately home in extensive grounds » – ⛀wc ☎ 🚗 Ⓟ. AE ⓞ E VISA. ✄ rm
closed Wednesday dinner, Thursday and 15 December-23 January – **M** 1850 – 5 rm ☕ 2000/3250
Spec. Rognon de veau au fumet rouge et moelle, Magret de canard au parfum de laurier, Langue de veau avec choucroute de poireaux et aiguillettes de canard fumé.

XX **Vossenburg** ⛰ with rm, Zandstraat 272 (Coude Ceuken), ✆ 317026, ≤, « Converted castle in a park » – ⛆wc Ⓟ. AE ⓞ E VISA. ✄ A **c**
closed 12 to 30 November – **M** *(closed Tuesday and Sunday dinner)* 600/895 – 8 rm ☕ 920/1530 – P 1750/1950.

X **De Boekeneute,** Torhoutsesteenweg 380, ✆ 382632, ☂, Converted farm – Ⓟ. AE ⓞ E VISA – *closed Sunday and Monday dinner* – **M** 850/1800. A **n**

at Loppem Ⓒ Zedelgem, South : 5 km – pop. 19 600 – ✉ 8021 Loppem – ☎ 050 :

XX **Bakkershof,** Parklaan 16, ✆ 824987, ☂ – Ⓟ. AE ⓞ A **s**
closed Tuesday dinner, Wednesday and 2 weeks July – **M** 650/1350.

at Oostkamp by ④ bridge E40 then 2nd street on the left – pop. 20 000 – ✉ 8020 Oostkamp – ☎ 050 :

XX **De Kampveldhoeve,** Kampveldstraat 16, ✆ 824258, ≤, « Country atmosphere » – Ⓟ
closed Tuesday – **M** 890/1295.

at Ruddervoorde Ⓒ Oostkamp, by ④ : 12 km – pop. 20 000 – ✉ 8040 Ruddervoorde – ☎ 050 :

XXX Leegendael, ⛰ with rm, Kortrijkstraat 486 (N 50), ✆ 277699, ≤, « Ancient residence in a country atmosphere », ⛰ – 📺 ⛀wc ☎ Ⓟ – 7 rm.

at Sint-Kruis by ② : 6 km – ✉ 8310 Sint-Kruis – ☎ 050 :

Morfeus ⛰ without rest., Maalsesteenweg 351, ✆ 363030 – ⛀wc ♿ Ⓟ. AE ⓞ E VISA
closed February – **7 rm** ☕ 1875/2150.

Lodewijk van Male, Maalsesteenweg 488, ✆ 355763, « Extensive park with lake », ⛰ – ⛀wc ⛆wc Ⓟ. ✄ rm
M *(closed Monday)* 600/895 – **16 rm** ☕ 1170/1785.

XX **Jonkman,** Maalsesteenweg 438, ✆ 360767, ←, 🏡, « Terrace-garden » – Ⓟ. AE ⓓ E VISA
closed Sunday and Monday lunch – **M** a la carte approx. 1900.

at Varsenare by ⑦ : 6,5 km – ✉ 8202 Varsenare – ☎ 050 :

XX **Stuivenberg,** Gistelsteenweg 27, ✆ 381502, 🏡 – Ⓟ. AE ⓓ E VISA A **a**
closed Sunday dinner, Monday and Tuesday lunch – **M** a la carte 1660/1950.

at Waardamme C Oostkamp, by ④ : 11 km – pop. 20 000 – ✉ 8041 Waardamme – ☎ 050 :

XXX **Ter Talinge,** Rooiveldstraat 46, ✆ 279061, 🏡, « Country atmosphere, terrace » – Ⓟ. AE ⓓ VISA
closed 23 February-13 March and 24 August-4 September – **M** a la carte 940/1350.

at Zedelgem by ⑥ : 10,5 km – pop. 19 600 – ✉ 8210 Zedelgem – ☎ 050 :

🏨 **Zuidwege** M without rest., Torhoutsesteenweg 126, ✆ 201339 – ⛀wc ⛆wc ☎ Ⓟ. AE E VISA. ✻
17 rm ☕ 1300/2200.

🏨 **Bonne Auberge,** Torhoutsesteenweg 201, ✆ 209525, Telex 81227 – ⇕ ⛀wc ⛆ ☎ Ⓟ – 🏊. AE ⓓ E VISA
M *(closed December-January)* a la carte 780/1410 – **27 rm** ☕ 1315/2530 – P 2000/2900.

XX **Ter Leepe,** Torhoutsesteenweg 168, ✆ 200197 – Ⓟ. AE ⓓ VISA
closed 21 July-4 August, Sunday and Wednesday dinner – **M** a la carte 1030/1340.

Oostende 8400 West-Vlaanderen 213 ② and 409 ① – pop. 68 850 – ☎ 059 – 27 km.

XXXX ✿✿ **Au Vigneron and Oostendse Compagnie** (Daue) with rm, Koningstraat 79, ✆ 704816, 🏡 – ⇕ TV ⛀wc ☎ 🚗 Ⓟ. AE ⓓ E VISA
closed October – **M** *(closed Sunday dinner and Monday)* (Saturday and Sunday booking essential) a la carte 1680/2650 – ☕ 350 – **13 rm** 2100/3250
Spec. Trois services de homard, Coquelet aux truffes Lucien Tendret, Sole à la ciboulette.

Knokke 8300 West-Vlaanderen 212 ⑪ and 409 ② – pop. 30 095 – ☎ 050 – 17 km.

XXX ✿✿ **Aquilon** (De Spae), 1st floor, Lippenslaan 306 (transfer planned), ✆ 601274 – AE ⓓ E. ✻
closed 15 November-1 February, Sunday dinner, Monday and Tuesday 15 September-Easter, Tuesday dinner Easter-15 September and Wednesday – **M** (Saturday and Sunday booking essential) a la carte 1700/2600
Spec. Mousseline de St. Jacques aux huîtres (Sept.-April), Foie d'oie au naturel, Canette au poivre rose et pistaches.

Oostkerke 8350 West-Vlaanderen 213 ③ and 409 ② – ☎ 050 – 7 km.

XX ✿✿ **Bruegel** (Fonteyne), Damse Vaart Zuid 26, ✆ 500346, ←, « Rustic interior » – Ⓟ. AE ⓓ E VISA
closed Tuesday, Wednesday, January and February – **M** (Saturday and Sunday booking essential) a la carte 1850/2550
Spec. Sole Pieter Bruegel, Homard Maman Jenny, Châteaubriand des gastronomes.

Waregem 8790 West-Vlaanderen 213 ⑮ and 409 ⑪ – pop. 33 626 – ☎ 056 – 47 km.

South : 2 km, near motorway :

XXX ✿✿ **'t Oud Konijntje** (Desmedt), Bosstraat 53, ✆ 601937, 🏡, « Elegant inn - garden setting » – Ⓟ. AE ⓓ E VISA
closed dinner Sunday and Thursday, Friday, 22 July-13 August and 23 December-6 January – **M** a la carte 1370/1900
Spec. Petite soupe de homard, Pavé de turbot moutardé, Crépinette de veau et gâteau de légumes.

LIÈGE 4000 213 ㉒ and 409 ⑮ – pop. 202 314 – ☎ 041.

See : Old town★★ – Baptismal font★★★ of St. Bartholomew's church DX – Citadel ←★★ DX – Treasury★★ of St. Paul's Cathedral FZ – Palace of the Prince-Bishops : court of honour★★ GY J – The Perron★ (market cross) GY A – Aquarium★ DY D – St. James church★ DY – Cointe Park ←★ CZ – Altarpiece★ in the St. Denis church GZ – Church of St John : statues★ in wood of the Calvary FZ.

Museums : Life in Wallonia★★ GY – Curtius★ : evangelistary★★★, glassware museum : collection★ EX M¹ – Ansembourg★ DX M² – Arms★ DX M³.

Envir. : Visé : Reliquary★ of St. Hadelin in the Collegiate church by ① : 17 km – Baptismal font★ in the church of St. Severin-en-Condroz by ⑥ : 23 km.

⛳18 rte du Condroz 541 at Ougrée by ⑥ : 7 km ✆ 362021.

🚗 ✆ 425214.

ℹ En Féronstrée 92 ✆ 222456 and Place des Guillemins (May-Sept.) ✆ 524419 – Tourist association of the province, bd de la Sauvenière 77 ✆ 224210.

Brussels 97 ⑨ – Amsterdam 242 ① – Antwerp 119 ⑫ – Köln 122 ② – Luxembourg 159 ⑤.

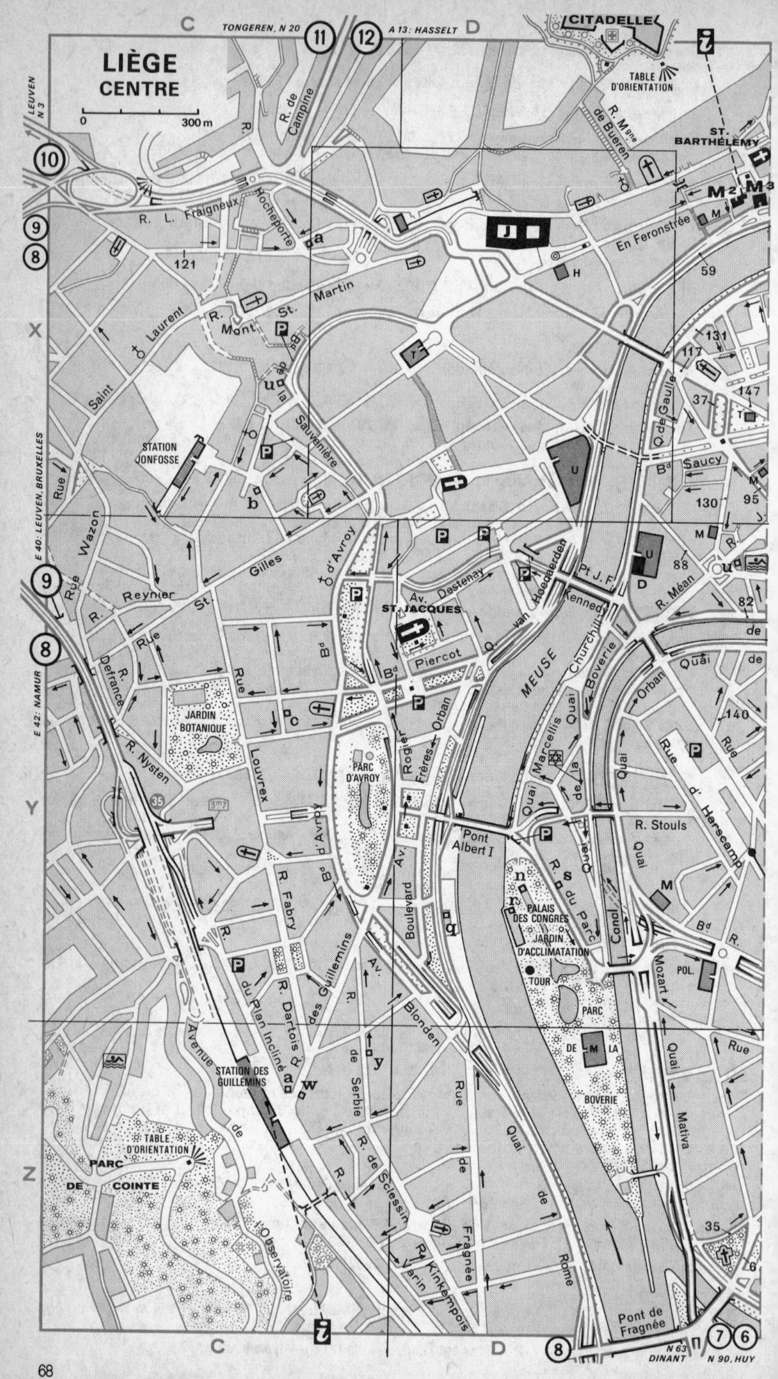

LIÈGE
CENTRE
0
300 m
TONGEREN, N 20
A 13: HASSELT
LEUVEN N 3
E 40: LEUVEN, BRUXELLES
E 42: NAMUR
N 63 DINANT
N 90, HUY
CITADELLE
TABLE D'ORIENTATION
ST. BARTHÉLEMY
R. de Campine
R. L. Fraigneux
Hocheporte
R. Mgne de Bueren
En Feronstrée
R. Mont St. Martin
Saint Laurent
Bd de la Sauvenière
STATION JONFOSSE
Rue Wazon
Rue Reynier
R. St. Gilles
Bd d'Avroy
Av. Destenay
ST. JACQUES
Bd Piercot
Q. van Hoegaerden
Pt J. F. Kennedy
Quai Churchill
MEUSE
Q. de Gaulle
Bd Saucy
R. Méan
Quai de la Boverie
Quai Orban
Rue d'Harscamp
R. Stouls
R. Defrance
JARDIN BOTANIQUE
R. Nysten
Rue Louvrex
PARC D'AVROY
Av. Rogier
Frères Orban
Quai Marcellis
Pont Albert I
R. du Parc
PALAIS DES CONGRES
JARDIN D'ACCLIMATATION
TOUR
PARC DE LA BOVERIE
Canal
Bd R. Mozart
POL.
R. Fabry
Boulevard
R. Dartois
R. du Plan Incliné
R. des Guillemins
Av. R. Blonden
STATION DES GUILLEMINS
Avenue de l'Observatoire
R. de Serbie
R. de Sclessin
Rue de Fragnée
R. Varin
Kinkempois
Quai de Rome
Quai Mativa
Pont de Fragnée
TABLE D'ORIENTATION
PARC DE COINTE
C
D
X
Y
Z

To obtain a general view of Benelux,
use the Michelin Map 987
Germany - Austria - Benelux
(1 in: 16 miles)

Room prices are subject to the addition of a local tax of 6 %

Ramada-Liége [M], bd Sauveniére 100, ✆ 224910, Telex 41896 – AE ① E VISA CX **u**
M a la carte 800/1300 – ☕ 375 – **105 rm** 2800/3300.

Holiday Inn [M] without rest., Esplanade de l'Europe 2, ✉ 4020, ✆ 426020, Telex 41156, ≤, – AE ① VISA DY **n**
224 rm ☕ 3645/3810.

Cygne d'Argent without rest., r. Beeckman 49, ✆ 237001, Telex 42617 – wc. AE ① E VISA CY **c**
☕ 225 – **20 rm** 1560/1760.

H. de l'Univers without rest., r. Guillemins 116, ✆ 522650, Telex 42424 – wc. AE ① E VISA CZ **a**
☕ 245 – **51 rm** 1400/1780.

XXX ✿ **Vieux Liège,** quai Goffe 41, ✆ 237748, « Ancient decor in a 16C house » – AE ① E VISA GY **c**
closed Wednesday dinner, Sunday, Bank Holidays, Easter and August – **M** a la carte 1320/2100
Spec. Bûche de homard enrobée de saumon fumé au Sauternes, Tartare de saumon au caviar.

XXX **Héliport,** bd Frère Orban, ✆ 521321, ≤ – Ⓟ DY **q**
closed Sunday, Monday dinner and last 3 weeks July – **M** a la carte 1200/1800.

XXX **Rôtiss. de l'Empereur,** pl. du 20-Août 15, ✆ 235373, Grill – AE ① E VISA GZ **n**
closed 3 to 31 August and Tuesday except Bank Holidays – **M** a la carte 660/1130.

XX **Dauphin,** r. du Parc 53, ✉ 4020, ✆ 434753 – AE ① E VISA DY **s**
closed Monday and July – **M** a la carte 1070/1630.

XX **As Ouhès,** pl. Marché 21, ✆ 233225, Seafood, Open until 11 p.m. – AE ① E VISA GY **r**
closed Saturday lunch, Sunday and last 3 weeks July – **M** a la carte 790/1520.

XX **Y Sing,** bd Sauvenière 50, ✆ 233578, Chinese rest. – AE ① FY **r**
closed Wednesday, Easter, last 2 weeks August and Christmas-New Year – **M** (dinner only) 600/855.

XX **Ile de Meuse,** Esplanade de l'Europe 2 (Palais des Congrès), ✉ 4020, ✆ 431552, ≤ – Ⓟ. AE ① E VISA DY **r**
M 600/890.

XX **La Bécasse,** r. Casquette 21, ✆ 231520, Open until 11 p.m. – AE ① E VISA FZ **b**
closed Wednesday, Thursday lunch and 18 August-5 September – **M** a la carte approx. 1200.

XX **Le Picotin,** pl. des Béguinages 8, ✆ 231763 – AE ① E VISA. ✻ CX **b**
closed Saturday lunch, Sunday, Bank Holidays and 15 July-15 August – **M** a la carte 890/1220.

XX **Romantique,** r. Pot-d'Or 54, ✆ 235036 – ✻ FZ **f**
closed Tuesday, Wednesday and 18 August-16 September – **M** 525/650.

XX **Beaujolais,** pl. Saint-Séverin 46, ✆ 230006. AE ① E VISA CX **a**
closed 2 to 13 February, 27 July-10 August and Monday – **M** a la carte 800/1130.

XX **La Sardegna,** r. Université 33, ✆ 230913, Italian rest., Open until 11 p.m. – AE ① E VISA. ✻ GZ **v**
closed Tuesday – **M** a la carte 630/1170.

X **Le Bistroquet,** r. Serbie 73, ✆ 531641, Open until 11 p.m. – AE ① E VISA CZ **y**
closed Saturday lunch, Wednesday and July-15 August – **M** a la carte 950/1560.

X **Les Cyclades,** r. Ourthe 4, ✉ 4020, ✆ 422586 – AE ① E VISA. ✻ DY **u**
closed Wednesday and Thursday – **M** 950/1250.

X **Chambord,** r. Pont-d'Avroy 25, ✆ 237011 – AE ① E VISA FZ **t**
closed Monday, Tuesday and August – **M** 425/825.

X **Écu de France,** r. Vinâve-d'Ile 9, ✆ 233917, « Tavern, tea-room » – AE ① E VISA
M (lunch only except Saturday) 600. FZ **d**

X **Le Duc d'Anjou,** r. Guillemins 127, ✆ 522858, Mussels in season, Open until 11 p.m. – AE ① E VISA CZ **w**
closed 2 May-June – **M** 675.

X **Chez Marcel,** r. Moulin 49, ✉ 4020, ✆ 432937 – AE ① VISA EX **b**
closed Sunday, Monday and 10 July-8 August – **M** a la carte 750/1160.

X **Shanghai** 1st floor, Galeries Cathédrale 104, Chinese rest. – AE ① E VISA. ✻ FZ **m**
closed Tuesday and 17 August-9 September – **M** 540/1250.

at Angleur – ✉ 4900 Angleur – ☎ 041 :

XXX **Sart Tilman,** r. Sart Tilman 343, ✆ 654224, « Classic-elegant » – Ⓟ. AE ① E VISA
closed Monday, dinner Sunday and Wednesday and August – **M** a la carte 970/1720.

XXX **Orchidée Blanche,** rte du Condroz 457, ✆ 651118, – Ⓟ. AE ① E VISA
closed Tuesday dinner, Wednesday and July – **M** a la carte 930/1500.

X **Devinière,** r. Tilff 39, ✆ 650032 – ① E VISA
closed Thursday dinner, Sunday and 15 July-5 August – **M** a la carte 920/1260.

at Awans by ⑩ : 8 km by N 3 – pop. 7 363 – ✉ 4341 Awans – ☎ 041 :

XX **En Provence,** rte de Bruxelles 215, ✆ 638218 – Ⓟ. AE ⓓ E VISA
closed Saturday, Sunday and 15 July-15 August – **M** (lunch only except Tuesday) a la carte 1030/1700.

at Boncelles Ⓒ Seraing, by ⑥ : 8 km – pop. 62 592 – ✉ 4208 Boncelles – ☎ 041 :

XXX **Franc Canard,** rte du Condroz 94, ✆ 367465 – Ⓟ. AE ⓓ E VISA
closed Saturday lunch, Sunday and 15 to 31 July – **M** 875/1300.

at Flémalle-Haute Ⓒ Flémalle, by r. Samuel-Donnay – pop. 27 801 – ✉ 4110 Flémalle-Haute – ☎ 041 :

XX **Gourmet Gourmand,** Grand Route 411, ✆ 330756 – AE ⓓ E VISA
closed Wednesday, dinner Tuesday and Thursday and 15 July-15 August – **M** a la carte 1000/1340.

at Hermalle-sous-Argenteau Ⓒ Oupeye, by ① : 14 km – pop. 23 134 – ✉ 4530 Hermalle-sous-Argenteau – ☎ 041 :

XXX **Au Comte de Mercy,** r. Tilleul 5, ✆ 793535, « Rustic interior » – Ⓟ. AE ⓓ E VISA
closed Sunday dinner, Monday and July – **M** 1100/1500.

X **Le Pichet,** r. J.-Verkruijts 7, ✆ 792033 – AE ⓓ E VISA
closed Tuesday dinner, Wednesday and 7 to 31 July – **M** a la carte 800/1400.

at Herstal – pop. 37 446 – ✉ 4400 Herstal – ☎ 041 :

Post House and Rest. La Diligence Ⓜ, r. Hurbise (by motorway E 40 exit Hermée - Haut-Sarts N 34), ✆ 646400, Telex 41103, heated – rest Ⓟ – . AE ⓓ E
M a la carte 940/1580 – 315 – **96 rm** 2690/3350.

at Neuville-en-Condroz Ⓒ Neupré, by ⑥ : 18 km – pop. 8 329 – ✉ 4121 Neuville-en-Condroz – ☎ 041 :

XXXX ❀❀ **Chêne Madame** (Tilkin), av. de la Chevauchée 70, dans le bois de Rognac SE : 2 km, ✆ 714127 – Ⓟ. AE ⓓ.
closed Sunday dinner, Monday, Easter, 2 August-3 September and 23 December-6 January – **M** a la carte 1600/2000
Spec. Huîtres au champagne (Sept.-February), Escalope de turbot au Bouzy et échalotes confites, Canette au citron vert et mangue.

at Plainevaux Ⓒ Neupré, by ⑥ : 18 km – pop. 8 329 – ✉ 4051 Plainevaux – ☎ 041 :

XXX Vieux Moulin, Grand'Route 115, N 683-N 639 at Hout-si-Plout, ✆ 801144 – Ⓟ. AE ⓓ E VISA
closed Tuesday.

at Rotheux-Rimière Ⓒ Neupré, by ⑥ : 16 km – pop. 8 329 – ✉ 4051 Plainevaux – ☎ 041 :

XX **Vieux Chêne,** r. Bonry 146, near N 63, ✆ 714651 – Ⓟ. AE ⓓ E VISA.
closed Wednesday, dinner Monday and Tuesday, mid August-mid September and 22 December-6 January – **M** a la carte 860/1260.

at Tilff-sur-Ourthe Ⓒ Esneux, S : 12 km by N 633 – pop. 11 840 – ✉ 4040 Tilff-sur-Ourthe – ☎ 041 :

XXX **Casino** with rm, pl. Roi-Albert 3, ✆ 881015 – wc . rm
closed 15 December-15 January – **M** *(closed Monday)* a la carte approx. 1400 – 200 – **6 rm** 1200/1500.

XX **Romeo et Michette,** r. Damry 11, ✆ 881869, , « Flower terrace with ≤ garden » – AE ⓓ E VISA
closed Monday, Tuesday and February – **M** a la carte 750/1160.

XX **La Mairie,** r. Blandot 15, ✆ 882424, , « Garden » – AE ⓓ E VISA
closed Sunday dinner, Monday and February – **M** a la carte 940/1310.

Stevoort 3512 Limburg 213 ⑨ and 409 ⑥ – ☎ 011 – 42 km.

XXXX ❀❀ **Scholteshof** (Souvereyns) Ⓜ with rm, Kermtstraat 118, ✆ 250202, Telex 39684, ≤, , « 18C converted farm with tasteful decor, country atmosphere » – wc wc Ⓟ – . AE ⓓ E VISA
closed 2 to 31 January – **M** *(closed Wednesday)* a la carte 1250/2300 – 300 – **18 rm** 1900/4300
Spec. Filet de sole farci à la crème de caviar, Composit de la mer, Ris de veau Brandewijn de Hasselt.

LUXEMBOURG

SIGHTS

See : Site★★ – Old Luxembourg★★ – "Promenade de la Corniche" ≤★★ and the rocks of the city ≤★★ DY – The Bock cliff ≤★★, Bock Casemates★★ DY – Place de la Constitution ≤★★ DY – Grand-Ducal Palace★ DY **K** – Our Lady's Cathedral (Notre Dame)★ DY **L** – Grand-Duchess Charlotte Bridge★ DY – State Museum★★ DY.

LUXEMBOURG 8 ⑧ and 409 ㉖ – pop. 78 912.

18 Höhenhof, near Airport ✆ 34090.

✈ Findel by ③ : 6 km ✆ 47981 and 47983 – **Air terminal** : pl. de la Gare ✆ 481820.

i pl. d'Armes. ✉ 2011. ✆ 22809.

Amsterdam 391 ⑧ – Bonn 190 ③ – Brussels 219 ⑧.

Plan on next page

Luxembourg-Centre :

Le Royal M, bd Royal 12, ✉ 2449, ✆ 41616, Telex 2979, – AE E VISA. rest CY **e**
M *(closed Saturday dinner and 25 July-16 August)* a la carte 1210/1860 – **170 rm** 5400/6450.

Cravat, bd Roosevelt 29, ✉ 2450, ✆ 21975, Telex 2846 – . AE E VISA. rest – **M** 700/1000 – **59 rm** 2900/3900 DY **a**

Rix H. without rest., bd Royal 20, ✉ 2449, ✆ 27545, Telex 1234 – wc wc P – . CY **b**
closed 20 December-4 January – **19 rm** 1450/2950.

XXX ✿✿ **St-Michel** (Guillou), 1st floor, r. Eau 32, ✉ 1449, ✆ 23215, Seafood, « Rustic interior » – AE E VISA DY **e**
closed 1 to 31 August, Christmas-New Year, Saturday and Sunday – **M** (booking essential) a la carte 1580/2700
Spec. Langoustines au gingembre, Bar aux moules de bouchots, Filet de boeuf à la ficelle. **Wines** Wousselt.

XXX **Le Vert Galant,** 1st floor, r. Aldringen 23 (r. Poste), ✉ 1118, ✆ 470822 – . AE E VISA CY **r**
closed Saturday lunch, Sunday and Bank Holidays – **M** a la carte 1370/1770.

XXX **La Cigogne,** r. du Curé 24, ✉ 1368, ✆ 28250 – AE E VISA. DY **r**
closed Saturday, Sunday, Bank Holidays and August – **M** a la carte 1340/1950.

XXX **Astoria,** av. du X-Septembre 14, ✉ 2550, ✆ 446223 – AE E VISA CY **y**
closed 9 to 24 August, 24 December-3 January and Saturday – **M** (lunch only) a la carte 1410/1790.

XXX **Gourmet,** r. Chimay 8, ✉ 1333, ✆ 25561 – AE DY **h**
closed Sunday dinner, Monday and 23 July-15 August – **M** a la carte 990/2010.

Theatre Musculus, r. Beaumont 3, ✉ 1219, ℘ 460534, Luxemburg rustic – AE VISA. DY **n**
closed Sunday dinner, Monday and 15 August-10 September – **M** a la carte 1230/1820.

Caesar, av. Monterey 18, ✉ 2163, ℘ 470925, Tavern restaurant, « Tasteful decor » – AE E VISA CY **u**
closed Sunday – **M** a la carte 800/1640.

Roma, r. Louvigny 5, ✉ 1946, ℘ 23692, Italian rest. – AE E VISA CY **z**
closed Sunday dinner, Monday, 10 August-10 September and 24 December-2 January – **M** a la carte 830/1220.

Gëlle Fra, r. Notre-Dame 10, ✉ 2240, ℘ 471794, Tavern restaurant – AE E VISA DY **s**
closed Wednesday dinner, Thursday and August – **M** 600/770.

Luxembourg-Station :

Kons, pl. Gare 24, ✉ 1616, ℘ 486021, Telex 2306 – AE E VISA. rest DZ **v**
M 600/2200 – **136 rm** 2190/3490.

Arcotel M without rest., av. Gare 43, ✉ 1611, ℘ 494001, Telex 3776 – AE E VISA. – **30 rm** 2600/2900. DZ **u**

Nobilis and Rest. Calao M, av. Gare 47, ✉ 1611, ℘ 494971, Telex 3212 – AE E VISA DZ **m**
M 600/845 – 345 – **43 rm** 2750/2900.

Central-Molitor, av. Liberté 28, ✉ 1930, ℘ 489911, Telex 2613 – AE E VISA. rest DZ **x**
M *(closed Friday and mid December-mid January)* 600/860 – **36 rm** 2100/2800.

President, pl. Gare 32, ✉ 1616, ℘ 486161, Telex 1510 – AE E VISA DZ **v**
M *(closed August)* (dinner only) 600/1200 – **40 rm** 2500/3900.

Ardennes M without rest., av. Liberté 59, ✉ 1931, ℘ 488141 – wc. AE VISA DZ **e**
21 rm 2100/2400.

Bristol without rest., r. Strasbourg 11, ✉ 2561, ℘ 485829, Telex 2328 – wc. AE E VISA. – 180 – **29 rm** 1700/1900. DZ **d**

City without rest., r. Strasbourg 1, ✉ 2561, ℘ 484608 – wc. AE E VISA DZ **t**
closed December-3 January – **30 rm** 950/2400.

Cordial, 1st floor, pl. Paris 1, ✉ 2314, ℘ 488538, « Elegant interior » – VISA. DZ **w**
closed Friday, Saturday lunch, 15 July-15 August and 8 to 15 February – **M** a la carte 1600/2100.

Arlecchino, rte d'Esch 100, ✉ 1470, ℘ 446456, Italian rest. – E VISA CZ **s**
closed Saturday lunch, Sunday and 24 December-4 January – **M** a la carte 1080/1520.

Italia with rm, r. Anvers 15, ✉ 1130, ℘ 486626, Telex 3644, Italian rest. – wc wc. AE E VISA DZ **q**
M a la carte 820/1430 – **20 rm** 1800/2300 – P 1900.

Upland of Kirchberg – ✉ Luxembourg :

Holiday Inn and Rest. Les Trois Glands M, Kirchberg, ✉ 2015, ℘ 437761, Telex 2751 – AE E VISA. rest
M *(closed Saturday lunch)* (Open until midnight) a la carte 950/1480 – **260 rm** 3650/5100.

North, at Limpertsberg – ✉ Luxembourg :

Europe without rest., av. du Bois 1, ✉ 1251, ℘ 470444, Telex 3707 – wc. AE E VISA – **51 rm** 2150/2400. CY **f**

Osteria del Teatro, Allée Scheffer 21, ✉ 2520, ℘ 28811, Italian rest. – AE E VISA CY **a**
closed Sunday – **M** a la carte 810/1220.

at Dommeldange – ✉ Dommeldange :

Inter-Continental M, r. Jean Engling, ✉ 1466, ℘ 43781, Telex 3754 – AE E VISA. rest
M *(closed Saturday lunch)* a la carte 1720/2180 – 500 – **344 rm** 3900/6900.

Novotel M, rte d'Echternach, ✉ 1453, ℘ 435643, Telex 1418 – AE E VISA
M a la carte 710/1620 – **221 rm** 2500/3200.

Host. Grünewald, rte d'Echternach 10, ✉ 1453, ℘ 431882, Telex 605432, « Tasteful decor » – rest wc wc. AE E VISA.
closed 2 to 26 January – **M** *(closed Saturday lunch and Sunday)* a la carte 1350/1820 – **28 rm** 2550/3600.

at Hesperange – pop. 9 090 – ✉ Hespérange :

L'Agath (Steichen) with rm, rte de Thionville 274, ✉ 5884, ℘ 488687, « Classic-elegant » – wc wc. AE E VISA
closed Sunday, mid July-mid August and 1 November – **M** *(closed lunch Monday and Saturday and Sunday)* a la carte 1780/2430 – **7 rm** 1600/3200
Spec. Saumon mariné aux légumes, Œuf poché aux langoustines et ravioli de poireaux au beurre d'huîtres, Loup de mer à la vapeur de fenouil. **Wines** Riesling, Pinot gris.

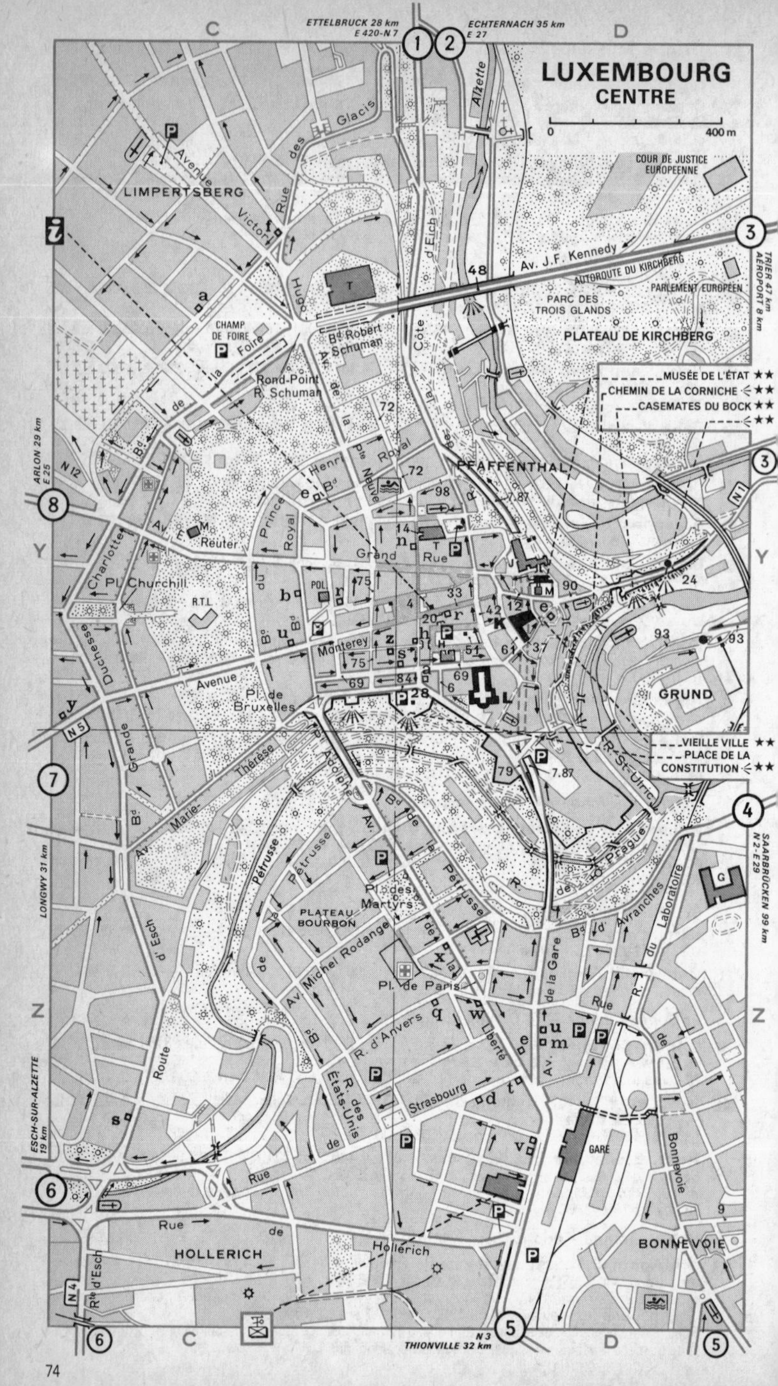
LUXEMBOURG
CENTRE
0
400 m
ETTELBRUCK 28 km
E 420-N 7
ECHTERNACH 35 km
E 27
TRIER 47 km
AÉROPORT 8 km
ARLON 29 km
E 25
LONGWY 31 km
ESCH-SUR-ALZETTE 19 km
SAARBRÜCKEN 99 km
N 2-E 29
N 3
THIONVILLE 32 km
COUR DE JUSTICE EUROPEENNE
Av. J.F. Kennedy
AUTOROUTE DU KIRCHBERG
PARLEMENT EUROPÉEN
PARC DES TROIS GLANDS
PLATEAU DE KIRCHBERG
LIMPERTSBERG
CHAMP DE FOIRE
Rond-Point R. Schuman
Bd Robert Schuman
PFAFFENTHAL
GRUND
MUSÉE DE L'ÉTAT ★★
CHEMIN DE LA CORNICHE ★★
CASEMATES DU BOCK ★★
VIEILLE VILLE ★★
PLACE DE LA CONSTITUTION ★★
Grand Rue
Pl. Churchill
R.T.L.
Pl. de Bruxelles
Av. Marie-Thérèse
PLATEAU BOURBON
Pl. des Martyrs
Av. Michel Rodange
Pl. de Paris
R. d'Anvers
R. des États-Unis
Strasbourg
GARE
BONNEVOIE
HOLLERICH
Rue de Hollerich
Route d'Esch
Av. de la Gare
Bd d'Avranches
R. du Laboratoire
R. St-Ulric
R. de Prague
Av. de la Liberté
Pétrusse
Bd de la Pétrusse
Av. Monterey
Av. E. Reuter
Bd Charlotte
Bd Grande-Duchesse
Bd Prince Henri
Bd Royal
Av. de la Pte Neuve
Côte d'Eich
Alzette
Rue des Glacis
Avenue Victor Hugo
R. St-Ulric
Bonnevoie

STREET INDEX TO LUXEMBOURG TOWN PLAN

at the skating-rink of Kockelscheuer – ✉ **Luxembourg :**

XXX ✿ **Patin d'Or** (Berring), **r. Bettembourg 40, ✉ 1899, ℘ 26499 – ▤ Ⓟ. E VISA**
closed Saturday lunch, Sunday dinner, Monday, 24 August-6 September and 21 December-10 January – **M** a la carte 1470/2180
Spec. Blanc de turbot rôti aux artichauts et truffes, Chartreuse de foie d'oie et volaille, Croustillant aux poires William's. **Wines** Riesling.

Airport **by ③ : 8 km – ✉ Luxembourg :**

🏨 **Aérogolf-Sheraton** Ⓜ 🐎, **rte de Trèves, ✉ 1973, ℘ 34571, Telex 2662,** ← – |$| ▤ TV ☎ Ⓟ – 🏃. AE ⓞ E VISA
M a la carte approx. 1100 – ☕ 450 – **148 rm** 3280/4980 – P 3540/4030.

Diekirch 8 ③ **and** 409 ㉖ – **pop. 5 585 – 35 km :**

XXX ✿✿ **Hiertz** (Pretty) with rm, **r. Clairefontaine 1, ✉ 9220, ℘ 803562, « Tasteful decoration, terrace and flower garden » –** ⇔wc. AE E VISA
closed Monday dinner, Tuesday, 24 August-8 September and 21 December-12 January – **M** (booking essential) a la carte 1450/2030 – **7 rm** ☕ 1700/2100
Spec. Ravioli de homard sauce coraline, Ballottine de pigeonneau périgourdine, Soufflé chaud au citron vert et au miel d'acacia. **Wines** Riesling.

Echternach 8 ④ **and** 409 ㉗ – **pop. 4 159 – 35 km :**

at Geyershof **SW : 7 km by E 42** C **Consthum – pop. 278 – ✉ Echternach :**

XXX ✿✿ **La Bergerie** (Phal), **✉ 6251, ℘ 79464,** ←, 🌳, **« Converted farm, country atmosphere » –** Ⓟ. AE ⓞ E VISA
closed Monday lunch except Bank Holidays, dinner Monday and Sunday and February – **M** a la carte 1350/2130
Spec. Foie gras au naturel, Homard-5 services, Vacherin moka. **Wines** Riesling, Pinot gris.

AMSTERDAM

SIGHTS

See : Old Amsterdam★★★ : the canals★★★ (Grachten) : Singel, Herengracht, Reguliersgracht, Keizersgracht, boattrip★ (Rondvaart) – Beguine Convent★★ (Begijnhof) LY – Dam : New Church★ (Nieuwe Kerk) LXY – Flower market★ (Bloemenmarkt) LY – Rembrandt Square (Rembrandtsplein) MY – Small Bridge (Magere Brug) MZ.

Museums : Rijksmuseum★★★ KZ – Rijksmuseum Vincent van Gogh★★★ – Municipal★★ (Stedelijk Museum) : Modern Art – History of Amsterdam★★ (Amsterdams Historisch Museum) LY – Madame Tussaud★ : wax museum LY **M**[1] – Museum Amstelkring Ons'Lieve Heer op Solder : ancient secret chapel★ MX **M**[4] – Rembrandt's House★ (Rembrandthuis) : (graphic arts of the master) MY **M**[5] – Maritime Museum of the Netherlands★ (Nederlands Scheepvaart Museum) – The Tropics Museum★ (Tropenmuseum) – Allard Pierson★ : archaeological collections.

AMSTERDAM Noord-Holland 211 ③ and 408 ⑩ ㉗ ㉘ – Pop. 675 579 – ☎ 0 20.

18 Zwarte Laantje 4 at Duivendrecht ☎ (0 20) 943650.

9 Sportpark Overamstel, Jan Vroegopsingel ☎ (0 20) 651863.

✈ at Schiphol SW : 9,5 km ☎ (0 20) 5110432 (information) and (0 20) 747747 (reservations) – Air Terminal : Central Station ☎ (0 20) 495575.

🚗 (Departure from 's-Hertogenbosch) ☎ (0 20) 238383 and (0 20) 141959 (Schiphol).

ℹ Stationsplein (Koffiehuis), ✉ 1012 AB ☎ 266444 – Tourist Association of the Province, Rokin 9-15, ✉ 1012 KK, ☎ 221016, Telex 12324.

Bruxelles 205 ③ – Düsseldorf 227 ③ – Den Haag 55 ④ – Luxembourg 391 ③ – Rotterdam 76 ④.

Centre

Amstel and Rest. La Rive, Professor Tulpplein 1, ⊠ 1018 GX, ✆ 226060, Telex 11004, « Shaded terrace ≤ Amstel » – rest – . AE VISA. rest MZ **f**
M (dinner only) 70/115 – 24 – **111 rm** 395/500.

Sonesta and Rest. Rib Room M, Kattengat 1, ⊠ 1012 SZ, ✆ 212223, Telex 17149 – rest – . AE E VISA. rest LX **a**
M *(closed Saturday lunch)* a la carte 69/86 – 31 – **425 rm** 395/500.

Amsterdam Marriott and Rest. Port O'Amsterdam M, Stadhouderskade 21, ⊠ 1054 ES, ✆ 835151, Telex 15087 – – . AE E VISA. JZ **p**
M a la carte 63/107 – 30 – **395 rm** 420/495.

Europe and Rest. Excelsior M, Nieuwe Doelenstraat 2, ⊠ 1012 CP, ✆ 234836, Telex 12081, ≤ – – . AE E VISA LY **r**
M *(closed Saturday lunch)* 65/150 – 28 – **79 rm** 350/650.

Victoria, Damrak 1, ⊠ 1012 LG, ✆ 234255 – rest – . AE E VISA. rest MX **a**
M *(closed Sunday)* 45/115 – **160 rm** 335/365.

Gd H. Krasnapolsky and Rest. Le Reflet d'Or, Dam 9, ⊠ 1012 JS, ✆ 5549111, Telex 12262, with Japanese rest. Edo – rest – . AE E VISA. rest LY **m**
M a la carte 51/70 – **370 rm** 275/390.

Doelen and Rest. Café Savarin, Nieuwe Doelenstraat 24, ⊠ 1012 CP, ✆ 220722, Telex 14399 – – . AE E VISA MY **q**
M 40/70 – 23 – **85 rm** 250/325 – P 322.

Ascot, M, Damrak 95, ⊠ 1012 LP, ✆ 260066, Telex 16620 – – LY **b**
110 rm.

Pulitzer and Rest. Goudsbloem, Prinsengracht 323, ⊠ 1016 GZ, ✆ 228333, Telex 16508 – rest – – 194 rm. KY **r**

American, Leidsekade 97, ⊠ 1017 PN, ✆ 245322, Telex 11379, – – . AE E VISA. rest JKZ **v**
M (Café Américain) 35/55 – 27 – **185 rm** 240/360.

Barbizon Centre, Stadhouderskade 7, ⊠ 1054 ES, ✆ 851351, Telex 12601 – – . AE E VISA. rest JZ **c**
M a la carte 40/90 – 25 – **242 rm** 300/425.

Caransa and Rest. Four Seasons, Rembrandtsplein 19, ⊠ 1017 CT, ✆ 229455, Telex 13342 – – . AE E VISA MY **x**
M a la carte 48/57 – 22 – **66 rm** 250/325.

Carlton without rest., Vijzelstraat 2, ⊠ 1017 HK, ✆ 222266, Telex 11670 – – . AE VISA LY **v**
27 – **156 rm** 195/290.

Capitool without rest., Nieuwe Zijds Voorburgwal 67, ⊠ 1012 RE, ✆ 275900, Telex 14494 – – . AE E VISA LX **r**
148 rm 240/274.

Port van Cleve, Nieuwe Zijds Voorburgwal 178, ⊠ 1012 SJ, ✆ 244860, Telex 13129 – – . AE E VISA LX **d**
M a la carte 50/66 – **110 rm** 178/273 – P 250/288.

Arthur Frommer and Rest. Oranjehof, Noorderstraat 46, ⊠ 1017 TV, ✆ 220328, Telex 14047 – . AE E VISA. LZ **k**
M (dinner only) 33 – **90 rm** 189/216.

Schiller, Rembrandtsplein 26, ⊠ 1017 CV, ✆ 231660, Telex 14058 – – . AE E. MZ **z**
M a la carte 68/100 – 22 – **97 rm** 245/330.

Rembrandt without rest., Herengracht 255, ⊠ 1016 BJ, ✆ 221727, Telex 15424 – . AE E VISA KY **p**
22 – **111 rm** 230/290.

Ambassade without rest., Herengracht 341, ⊠ 1016 AZ, ✆ 262333, Telex 10158 – wc . AE E VISA KY **f**
41 rm 165/190.

Parkhotel, Stadhouderskade 25, ⊠ 1071 ZD, ✆ 717474, Telex 11412 – rest wc – . AE E VISA. rest KZ **f**
M 38/48 – 23 – **186 rm** 325/390.

Owl Hotel without rest., Roemer Visscherstraat 1, ⊠ 1054 EV, ✆ 189484, Telex 13360 – wc wc . AE E VISA JZ **e**
34 rm 122/155.

Choura without rest., Marnixstraat 372, ⊠ 1016 XX, ✆ 237524, Telex 15362 – wc wc . AE E JY **a**
22 rm 89/207.

Estheréa without rest., Singel 305, ⊠ 1012 WJ, ✆ 245146, Telex 14019 – wc . AE E VISA. – **72 rm** 140/195. KY **t**

Nicolaas Witsen without rest., Nicolaas Witsenstraat 6, ⊠ 1017 ZH, ✆ 266546 – wc wc – **32 rm** 65/145. MZ **b**

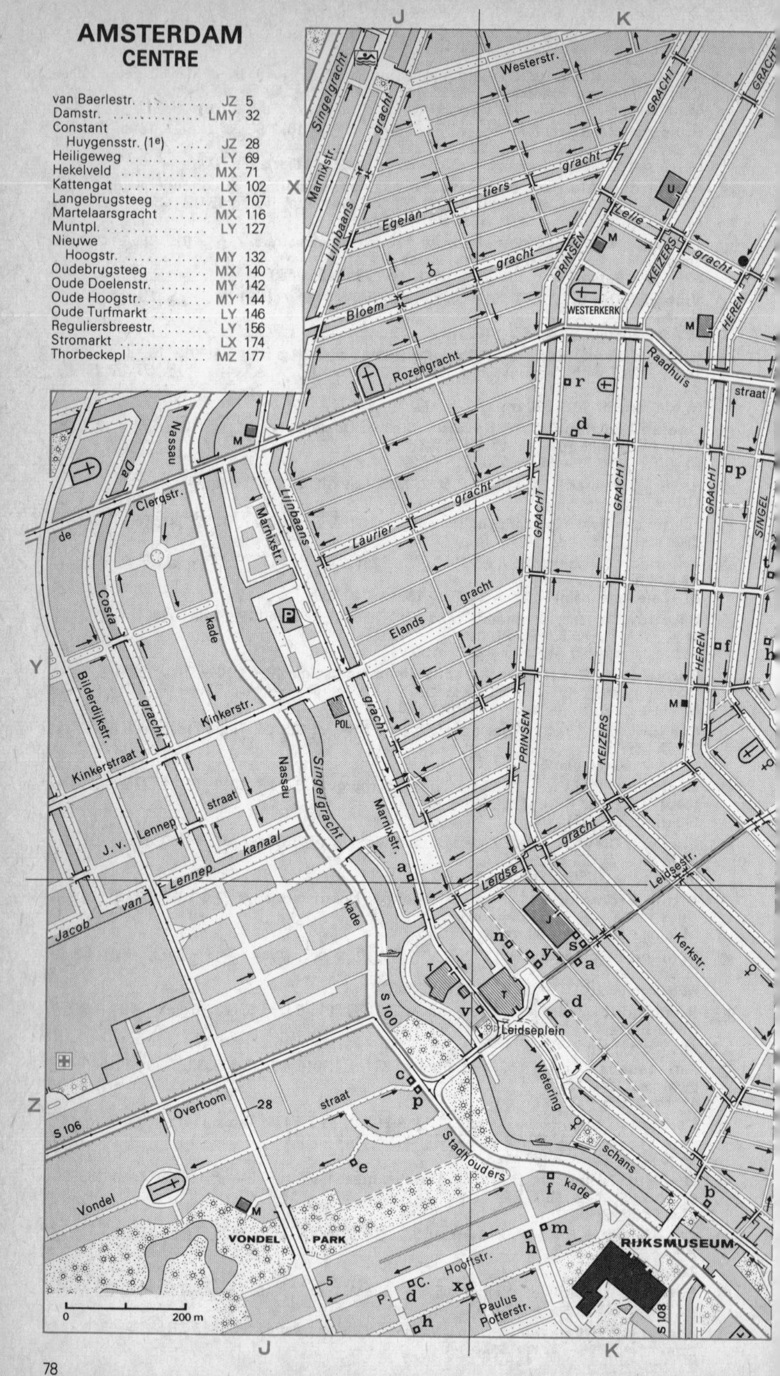

AMSTERDAM
CENTRE
van Baerlestr. JZ 5
Damstr. LMY 32
Constant Huygensstr. (1e) JZ 28
Heiligeweg LY 69
Hekelveld MX 71
Kattengat LX 102
Langebrugsteeg LY 107
Martelaarsgracht MX 116
Muntpl. LY 127
Nieuwe Hoogstr. MY 132
Oudebrugsteeg MX 140
Oude Doelenstr. MY 142
Oude Hoogstr. MY 144
Oude Turfmarkt LY 146
Reguliersbreestr. LY 156
Stromarkt LX 174
Thorbeckepl MZ 177
J
K
X
Y
Z
Westerstr.
Singelgracht
Marnixstr.
Lijnbaans gracht
Egelantiers gracht
Bloem gracht
PRINSEN GRACHT
KEIZERS GRACHT
HEREN GRACHT
Leliegracht
WESTERKERK
Rozengracht
Raadhuisstraat
SINGEL
Nassaukade
Da Costa kade
de Clercqstr.
Laurier gracht
Elands gracht
Bilderdijkstr.
Kinkerstr.
Kinkerstraat
POL.
Jacob van Lennep straat
J. v. Lennep kanaal
Leidse gracht
Leidsestr.
Kerkstr.
Leidseplein
Weteringschans
Stadhouderskade
S 100
S 106
S 108
Overtoom
28
Vondel
VONDEL PARK
Hooftstr.
P. C. Hooftstr.
Paulus Potterstr.
RIJKSMUSEUM
5
0
200 m

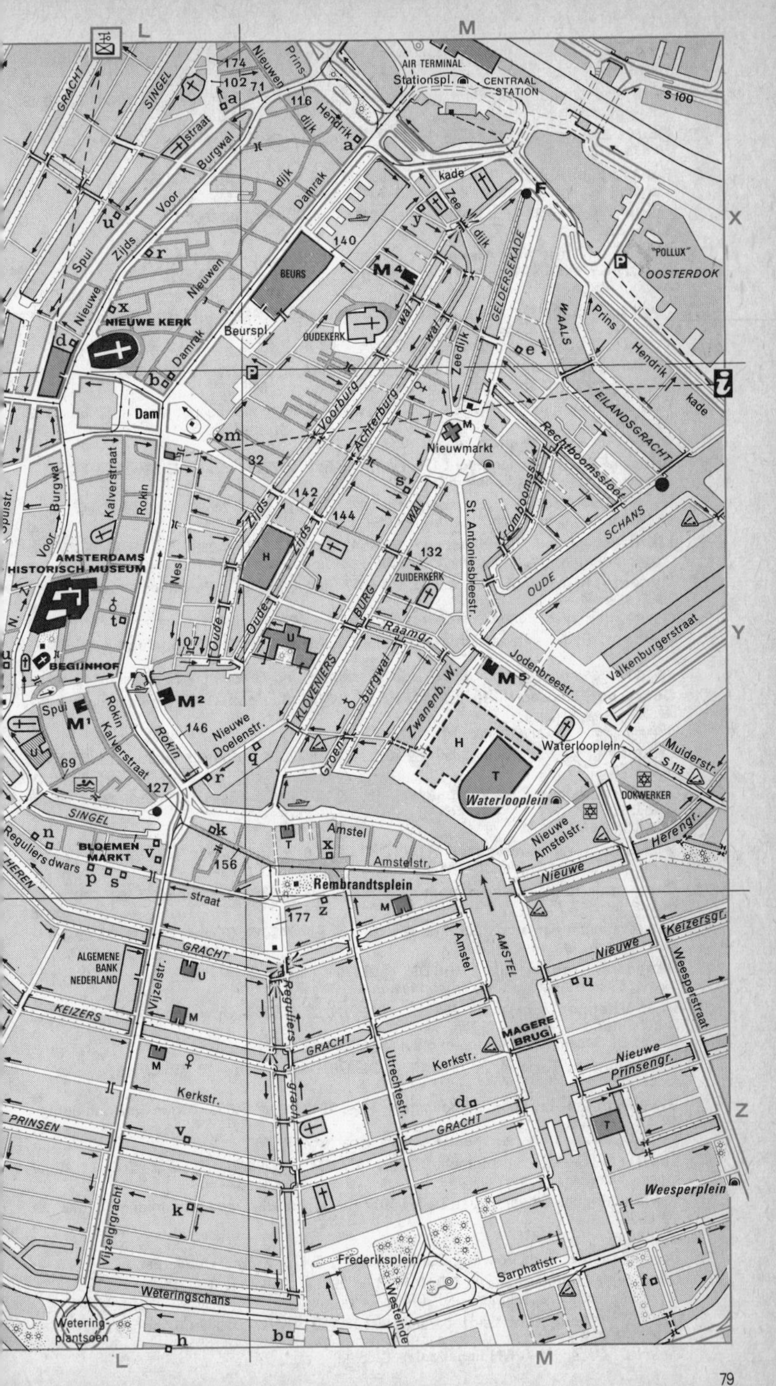

L
M
X
Y
Z
AIR TERMINAL
Stationspl.
CENTRAAL STATION
S 100
"POLLUX"
OOSTERDOK
BEURS
Beurspl.
OUDEKERK
NIEUWE KERK
Dam
Damrak
Nieuwmarkt
ZUIDERKERK
AMSTERDAMS HISTORISCH MUSEUM
BEGIJNHOF
Spui
Waterlooplein
Jodenbreestr.
Valkenburgerstraat
Muiderstr.
S 113
DOKWERKER
Rembrandtsplein
BLOEMEN MARKT
ALGEMENE BANK NEDERLAND
MAGERE BRUG
Weesperplein
Frederiksplein
Sarphatistr.
Weteringschans
Wetering-plantsoen
Westeinde
Utrechtestr.
Vijzelgracht
Vijzelstr.
Kerkstr.
KEIZERS
PRINSEN
GRACHT
HEREN
Reguliersdwars
straat
Reguliers
gracht
AMSTEL
Amstel
Amstelstr.
Nieuwe Amstelstr.
Nieuwe Herengr.
Nieuwe Keizersgr.
Nieuwe Prinsengr.
Weesperstraat
Kalverstraat
Rokin
Nes
SINGEL
Oude Zijds
Voorburg
Achterburg
KLOVENIERS BURG WAL
Groenburgwal
Raamgr.
Zwanenb. W.
Nieuwe Doelenstr.
St. Antoniesbreestr.
Kromboomssl.
Rechtboomssloot
OUDE SCHANS
GELDERSEKADE
WAALS EILANDSGRACHT
Prins Hendrik kade
Zeedijk
Nieuwendijk
Nieuwe Zijds Voorburgwal
Spuistr.
Voor Burgwal

Asterisk without rest., Den Texstraat 16, ✉ 1017 ZA, ☎ 262396 – wc wc. E VISA
19 rm 63/150. LZ **h**

Parklane without rest., Plantage Parklaan 16, ✉ 1018 ST, ☎ 224804 – wc. AE ⓓ E VISA – **10 rm** 80/125.

Roode Leeuw, Damrak 93, ✉ 1012 LP, ☎ 240396 – wc – . AE VISA LXY **b**
M a la carte 33/44 – **82 rm** 77/158.

Fantasia without rest., Nieuwe Keizersgracht 16, ✉ 1018 DR, ☎ 238259 – wc.
closed 9 November-21 December – **19 rm** 55/105. MZ **u**

Linda without rest., Stadhouderskade 131, ✉ 1074 AW, ☎ 625668 – .
17 rm 95/135.

XXXX **Dikker en Thijs and Alexander H.** with rm, Prinsengracht 444, angle Leidsestraat, ✉ 1017 KE, ☎ 267721, Telex 13161 – TV wc wc . AE ⓓ E VISA. KZ **s**
M *(closed Sunday)* (dinner only) 45/105 – 21 – **25 rm** 210/310.

XXX **Swarte Schaep,** 1st floor, Korte Leidsedwarsstraat 24, ✉ 1017 RC, ☎ 223021, « 17C interior » – . AE ⓓ E VISA KZ **d**
closed 5, 25, 26, 31 December and 1 January – **M** 78/90.

XXX **Martinn,** 12th floor, De Ruyterkade 7, ✉ 1013 AA, ☎ 256277, ← – . ⓓ E VISA
closed Saturday, Sunday and 24 December-1 January – **M** 55/88.

XXX **Bali,** 1st floor, Leidsestraat 89, ✉ 1017 NZ, ☎ 227878, Indonesian rest. – . AE ⓓ E VISA KZ **a**
closed Sunday lunch and 5, 24, 31 December – **M** 30/70.

XX **Prinsenkelder,** Prinsengracht 438, ✉ 1017 KE, ☎ 267721 – AE ⓓ E VISA. KZ **s**
closed Monday – **M** (dinner only) 55.

XX **Les Quatre Canetons,** Prinsengracht 1111, ✉ 1017 JJ, ☎ 246307 – AE ⓓ E VISA.
closed Saturday lunch and Sunday – **M** 59/83. MZ **d**

XX **L'Entrée,** 1st floor, Reguliersdwarsstraat 42, ✉ 1017 BM, ☎ 258788 – AE ⓓ E VISA.
closed Saturday lunch, Sunday and 29 June-22 July – **M** a la carte 58/114. LY **s**

XX **Dynasty,** Reguliersdwarsstraat 30, ✉ 1017 BM, ☎ 268400, , Oriental rest. – . AE ⓓ E VISA. LY **p**
closed Tuesday and mid December-mid January – **M** (dinner only) a la carte 51/77.

XX **Pêcheur,** Reguliersdwarsstraat 32, ✉ 1017 BM, ☎ 243121, , Seafood – AE ⓓ E LY **s**
closed lunch Saturday and Sunday, 5, 31 December and 1 January – **M** a la carte 46/108.

XX **Oesterbar,** Leidseplein 10, ✉ 1017 PT, ☎ 263463, Seafood, Open until midnight – . AE. KZ **y**
closed 25 and 26 December – **M** a la carte 53/87.

XX **Indonesia,** 1st floor, Singel 550, ✉ 1017 AZ, ☎ 232035, Indonesian rest. – . AE ⓓ E VISA – **M** 30/40 LY **v**

XX **Treasure,** Nieuwe Zijds Voorburgwal 115, ✉ 1012 RH, ☎ 234061, Chinese rest. – AE ⓓ E VISA. LX **x**
M a la carte 30/55.

XX **Da Canova,** Warmoesstraat 9, ✉ 1012 HT, ☎ 266725, Italian rest. – AE ⓓ E MX **y**
closed Sunday and Monday – **M** (dinner only) a la carte 57/71.

XX **Camargue,** Reguliersdwarsstraat 7, ✉ 1017 BJ, ☎ 239352 – . AE ⓓ E VISA.
M a la carte 47/75. LY **n**

XX **Lotus,** Binnen Bantammerstraat 5, ✉ 1011 CH, ☎ 242614, Chinese rest. – . AE ⓓ E VISA. – **M** *(dinner only)* 39/70. MX **e**

XX **Sancerre,** Reestraat 28, ✉ 1016 DN, ☎ 278794 – AE ⓓ E VISA. KY **d**
closed Easter, Whitsuntide, Christmas and New Year – **M** 50/85.

XX **Vijff Vlieghen,** Spuistraat 294, ✉ 1012 VX, ☎ 248369, Open until midnight, « Old Dutch interior » – AE ⓓ E VISA KY **h**
closed 31 December – **M** (dinner only) 45/85.

XX **Kopenhagen,** Rokin 84, ✉ 1012 KX, ☎ 249376, Danish rest. – . AE ⓓ VISA LY **t**
closed Sunday – **M** 30/55.

XX **Gravenmolen,** 1st floor, Lijnbaansteeg 5, ✉ 1012 TE, ☎ 246531, Open until midnight – . AE ⓓ E VISA LX **u**
closed lunch Saturday and Sunday – **M** a la carte 64/75.

XX **Les Trois Neufs,** Prinsengracht 999, ✉ 1017 KM, ☎ 229044 – AE ⓓ E VISA LZ **v**
closed Monday and mid July-mid August – **M** a la carte 43/70.

XX **Adrian,** Reguliersdwarsstraat 21, ✉ 1017 BJ, ☎ 239582, Open until midnight – . AE ⓓ E VISA LY **n**
M (dinner only) 40/93.

XX Dorrius, Nieuwe Zijds Voorburgwal 336, ✉ 1012 RX, ☎ 235245, Dutch rest. LY **u**

XX **Opatija,** Weteringschans 93, ✉ 1017 RZ, ☎ 225184, Balkan rest. – KZ **b**
closed Monday – **M** (dinner only) 30/43.

XX **Djawa,** 1st floor, Korte Leidsedwarsstraat 18, ✉ 1017 RC, ☎ 246016, Indonesian rest. – . AE ⓓ E VISA. KZ **n**
closed 31 December – **M** (dinner only) 30/55.

X **Valentijn,** Kloveniersburgwal 6, ✉ 1012 CT, ✆ 242028 – ▤. AE ⓓ E VISA. ✻ MY **s**
closed Monday, Tuesday and 8 to 30 June – **M** (dinner only) 55/98.

X **Ardjuna,** 1st floor, Reguliersbreestraat 21, ✉ 1017 CL, ✆ 220204, Indonesian rest. – AE ⓓ E VISA LY **k**
M 30.

South and West Quarters

Amsterdam Hilton M with Japanese rest. **Kei**, Apollolaan 138, ✉ 1077 BG, ✆ 780780, Telex 11025 – |♦| ▤ rest TV ☎ ♿ P – ♣. AE ⓓ E VISA. ✻
M 75 – ⊐ 28 – **274 rm** 340/490.

✻ **Garden Hotel and Rest. De Kersentuin** M, Dijsselhofplantsoen 7, ✉ 1077 BJ, ✆ 642121, Telex 15453 – |♦| ▤ TV ☎ P – ♣. AE ⓓ E VISA
M *(closed Saturday lunch, Sunday, 1 January, 31 March, 8, 19 May and 5, 24, 31 December)* a la carte 80/164 – ⊐ 28 – **97 rm** 325/350
Spec. Foie gras et giroflées à la choucroute, Saumon mi-cuit et fumé au beurre de balsamine, Pintade en demi-deuil.

Okura and Rest. Ciel Bleu M with Japanese rest. **Yamazato**, Ferdinand Bolstraat 333, ✉ 1072 LH, ✆ 787111, Telex 16182, « Rest. on the 23rd floor with ≤ town » – |♦| ▤ TV ☎ 🚗 P – ♣. AE ⓓ E VISA. ✻ rest
M (Ciel Bleu) (dinner only, open until midnight) 65/95 – ⊐ 28 – **403 rm** 370/410.

Apollohotel, Apollolaan 2, ✉ 1077 BA, ✆ 735922, Telex 14084, « Terrace with ≤ canal » – |♦| TV ☎ ♿ P – ♣. AE ⓓ E VISA
M 39/116 – ⊐ 29 – **217 rm** 240/400.

Crest H. Amsterdam M, De Boelelaan 2, ✉ 1083 HJ, ✆ 462300, Telex 13647 – |♦| ▤ TV ☎ P – ♣. AE ⓓ E VISA. ✻
M a la carte 58/89 – ⊐ 25 – **260 rm** 280/390.

Novotel Amsterdam M, Europaboulevard 10, ✉ 1083 AD, ✆ 5411123, Telex 13375 – |♦| ▤ rest TV ☎ P – ♣. AE ⓓ E VISA. ✻
M 35 – **600 rm** ⊐ 205/255.

Jan Luyken without rest., Jan Luykenstraat 58, ✉ 1071 CS, ✆ 764111, Telex 16254 – |♦| TV ☎. AE ⓓ E VISA JZ **x**
63 rm ⊐ 213/245.

Cok First Class H. M without rest., Koninginnelaan 30, ✉ 1075 CZ, ✆ 646111, Telex 11679 – |♦| TV ☎. AE ⓓ E VISA
40 rm ⊐ 170/210.

Memphis Hotel, De Lairessestraat 87, ✉ 1071 NX, ✆ 733141, Telex 12450 – |♦| TV. AE ⓓ E VISA. ✻ rest
M (Saturday and Sunday dinner only) 30/60 – **81 rm** ⊐ 204/257 – P 259/274.

Acca M, Van de Veldestraat 3 a, ✉ 1071 CW, ✆ 625262, Telex 10840 – |♦| TV ⛀ ⛆wc ☎ – ♣. AE ⓓ E VISA JZ **h**
M 30/40 – ⊐ 26 – **25 rm** 220/320 – P 280.

Beethoven M, Beethovenstraat 43, ✉ 1077 HN, ✆ 644816, Telex 14275 – |♦| TV ⛀wc ⛆wc ☎. AE ⓓ E VISA. ✻ rest
M a la carte 37/62 – **55 rm** ⊐ 213/254.

Borgmann M ⛲ without rest., Koningslaan 48, ✉ 1075 AE, ✆ 735252, Telex 10984 – |♦| TV ⛀wc ⛆wc ☎. AE ⓓ E VISA. ✻
15 rm ⊐ 153/190.

Delphi without rest., Apollolaan 105, ✉ 1077 AN, ✆ 795152, Telex 16659 – |♦| TV ⛀wc ⛆wc ☎. AE ⓓ E VISA
46 rm ⊐ 128/205.

Apollofirst, Apollolaan 123, ✉ 1077 AP, ✆ 730333, Telex 13446 – |♦| TV ⛀wc ⛆wc ☎. AE ⓓ E VISA
M *(closed Sunday)* (dinner only) a la carte 45/97 – **35 rm** ⊐ 179/290.

Atlas H., Van Eeghenstraat 64, ✉ 1071 GK, ✆ 766336, Telex 17081 – |♦| TV ⛀wc ☎. AE ⓓ E VISA
M 40/50 – **24 rm** ⊐ 140/190 – P 205/225.

Casa 400, James Wattstraat 75, ✉ 1097 DL, ✆ 651171, Telex 14677 – |♦| ⛆wc ☎ – ♣. AE VISA
June-September – **M** 30 – **387 rm** ⊐ 136/166 – P 149.

Zandbergen without rest., Willemsparkweg 205, ✉ 1071 HB, ✆ 769321, Telex 33756 – TV ⛀wc ⛆wc ☎. AE ⓓ E VISA
17 rm ⊐ 118/155.

Wilhelmina without rest., Koninginneweg 169, ✉ 1075 CN, ✆ 625467 – TV ⛆wc. AE ⓓ E VISA
15 rm ⊐ 100/145.

Toro ⛲ without rest., Koningslaan 64, ✉ 1075 AG, ✆ 737223 – ⛀wc ⛆ ☎. AE ⓓ E VISA
12 rm ⊐ 65/140.

Belfort, Surinameplein 53, ✉ 1058 GN, ✆ 174333 – TV ⛆wc. AE ⓓ E VISA. ✻ rm
M a la carte 31/55 – **20 rm** ⊐ 94/155.

XXX **Parkrest. Rosarium,** Europa boulevard, Amstelpark 1, ✉ 1083 HZ, ✆ 444085, « Flowered park » – . AE ⓓ E VISA
closed Sunday – **M** 53/85.

XX **Petit Culinair,** P.C. Hooftstraat 87, ✉ 1071 BP, ✆ 624747 – . AE ⓓ E VISA JZ **d**
closed Sunday and 6 to 28 July – **M** 58/98.

XX **Henri Smits,** Beethovenstraat 55, ✉ 1077 HN, ✆ 791715 – . AE ⓓ E VISA
closed Sunday lunch, 25 and 26 December – **M** a la carte 35/57.

XX **In den Nederhoven,** Nederhoven 13, ✉ 1083 AM, ✆ 425619, – AE ⓓ E VISA
closed lunch Saturday and Sunday – **M** a la carte 55/83.

XX ✿ **Trechter** (de Wit), Hobbemakade 63, ✉ 1071 XL, ✆ 711263 – AE ⓓ E.
closed 5 July-3 August, 24 December-4 January, Sunday, Monday and Bank Holidays – **M** (dinner only)(booking essential) a la carte approx. 80
Spec. Consommé froid de tomates aux langoustines (June-Sept.), Solette fumée à la vinaigrette de lavande, Côte de porc fumée et rôtie aux poireaux.

XX **Castheele,** Kastelenstraat 172, ✉ 1082 EJ, ✆ 447267 – AE ⓓ E.
closed Sunday, Bank Holidays and last week July-first 2 weeks August – **M** a la carte 50/68.

XX **Bistro Lapin,** 1st floor, Scheldeplein 3, ✉ 1078 GR, ✆ 642211 – . AE ⓓ.
closed Monday – **M** (dinner only) 30/68.

XX **Keijzer,** Van Baerlestraat 96, ✉ 1071 BB, ✆ 711441 – AE ⓓ E.
closed Sunday and 25, 26 December – **M** a la carte 32/58.

XX **Miranda Paviljoen,** Amsteldijk 223, ✉ 1079 LK, ✆ 445768 – Ⓟ. AE ⓓ E VISA
closed New Year – **M** 50.

XX **Hamilcar,** Overtoom 306, ✉ 1054 JC, ✆ 837981, Tunisian rest. – AE ⓓ E VISA.
closed Monday and 4 July-8 August – **M** (dinner only) a la carte 31/56.

X **Rembrandt,** P.C. Hooftstraat 31, ✉ 1071 BM, ✆ 629011 – . AE ⓓ E VISA KZ **h**
closed Monday – **M** 35/70.

X **Beddington's,** Roelof Hartstraat 6, ✉ 1071 VH, ✆ 765201 – AE ⓓ E VISA.
closed Saturday, Sunday and 22 December-5 January – **M** a la carte 58/71.

X **Sama Sebo,** P.C. Hooftstraat 27, ✉ 1071 BL, ✆ 628146, Indonesian rest. – . AE ⓓ E
closed Sunday and 12 July-2 August – **M** 30/38. KZ **m**

Environs

at Schiphol – ✆ 0 20 :

Hilton International Schiphol and Rest. Dutch Oven Ⓜ, Herbergierstraat 1, ✉ 1118 ZK (near airport), ✆ 5115911, Telex 15186, – – . AE ⓓ E VISA. rest
M a la carte 63/106 – 26 – **204 rm** 350/410.

XXX Aviorama, with Indonesian rest. **Ken Dedes, 3rd Floor, Schipholweg 1, airport,** ✉ 1118 AA, ✆ 152150, ← – .

near The Hague motorway A 4 :

Euromotel Amsterdam Ⓜ, Oude Haagseweg 20, ✉ 1066 BW, ✆ 179005, Telex 15524 – Ⓟ – . AE ⓓ E VISA
M 30/70 – **157 rm** 125/175 – P 190.

XX **De Boekanier,** Oude Haagseweg 49, ✉ 1066 BV, ✆ 173525 – Ⓟ. AE ⓓ E VISA
closed Saturday, Sunday, 18 July-9 August and 24 December-3 January – **M** 80/125.

on The Hague motorway A 4 by ④ : 15 km – ✆ 0 2503 :

Schiphol Ⓜ, Kruisweg 495, Hoofddorp, ✉ 2132 NA, ✆ 15851, Telex 74546 – Ⓟ – . AE ⓓ E VISA
M 50/95 – 20 – **168 rm** 285/315.

Amstelveen Noord-Holland **211** ③ and **408** ⑩㉗ – pop. 68 189 – ✆ 0 20 – 11 km.

XXXX ✿ **Molen De Dikkert,** Amsterdamseweg 104a, ✉ 1182 HG, ✆ 411378, « 17C converted mill » – Ⓟ. AE ⓓ E VISA
closed Saturday lunch, Sunday and 25 July-14 August – **M** 73/135
Spec. Brandade glacée de turbot aux truffes, Foie gras de canard braisé enrobé de chou, Râble de lièvre aux pruneaux sauce poivrade (15 Oct.-Dec.).

XXX ✿ **Rôtiss. Ile de France,** Pieter Lastmanweg 9, ✉ 1181 XG, ✆ 453509 – . AE.
closed Saturday lunch, Sunday, Monday and 27 December-11 January – **M** a la carte 60/82
Spec. Crêpe au foie d'oie, sauce calvados, Saumon en papillote, sauce à l'oseille, Côtelettes d'agneau au gratin de pleurotes.

Bosch en Duin Utrecht **211** ⑭ – ✆ 0 30 – 50 km.

XXX ✿✿ **Hoefslag,** Vossenlaan 28, ✉ 3735 KN, ✆ 784395, ← – Ⓟ. AE ⓓ E VISA
closed Sunday and Monday – **M** a la carte 73/105
Spec. Potage de petits pois à l'anguille fumée (May-Sept.), Filet d'agneau gratiné aux fines herbes (Jan.-July), Canard sauvage à la sauge (August-Nov.).

The HAGUE (Den HAAG or 's-GRAVENHAGE) Zuid-Holland 211 ⑪ and 408 ⑨ – pop. 443 456 – ✆ 0 70.

See : Scheveningen★★ – Binnenhof★ : The Knights' Room★ (Ridderzaal) JV **A** – Hofvijver (Court pool) ≤★ JV – Lange Voorhout★ JV – Panorama Mesdag★ HV **B** – Madurodam★.

Museums : Mauritshuis★★★ JV – Municipal★★ (Gemeentemuseum) – Mesdag★ HU **M²**.

Gr. Haesebroekseweg 22 at Wassenaar N : 4 km ✆ (0 1751) 79607.

Amsterdam-Schiphol NE : 37 km ✆ (0 70) 824141, (0 20) 5110432 (informations) and (0 20) 747747 (reservations) – Rotterdam-Zestienhoven SE : 17 km ✆ (0 10) 4157633 (informations) and (0 10) 4372745, 4155430 (reservations).

(departs from 's-Hertogenbosch) ✆ (0 70) 471681.

Kon. Julianaplein 30, ✉ 2595 AA, ✆ 546200.

Amsterdam 55 – Brussels 175 – Rotterdam 24 – Delft 13

Plan on next page

Promenade and Rest. Cigogne M, van Stolkweg 1, ✉ 2585 JL, ✆ 525161, Telex 31162, « Elegant decoration, collection of modern paintings » – rest – AE E VISA
M *(closed Saturday and Sunday)* a la carte 56/94 – 25 – **101 rm** 235/265.

Sofitel M, Koningin Julianaplein 35, ✉ 2595 AA, ✆ 814901, Telex 34001 – – AE E VISA. rest
M a la carte 57/115 – 27 – **144 rm** 235/340.

Des Indes and Le Restaurant, Lange Voorhout 54, ✉ 2514 EG, ✆ 469553, Telex 31196 – rest – AE E VISA JV **s**
M 49/89 – 30 – **77 rm** 341/435 – P 458.

Bel Air, Johan de Wittlaan 30, ✉ 2517 JR, ✆ 502021, Telex 31444, – – AE E VISA
M a la carte 60/93 – 18 – **350 rm** 150/220 – P 160/250.

Parkhotel-De Zalm without rest. (annex), Molenstraat 53, ✉ 2513 BJ, ✆ 624371, Telex 33005 – – AE E VISA HV **a**
130 rm 64/197.

Corona, Buitenhof 42, ✉ 2513 AH, ✆ 637930, Telex 31418, – rest wc wc – AE E VISA HV **v**
M 50/75 – 15 – **26 rm** 200/400.

Paleis M without rest., Molenstraat 26, ✉ 2513 BL, ✆ 624621, Telex 34349 – wc . AE E VISA HV **r**
20 rm 149/237.

XXXX Royal, Lange Voorhout 44, ✉ 2514 EG, ✆ 600772 – AE E VISA. JV **t**
closed Sunday.

XXX ✿ **Saur,** 1st floor, Lange Voorhout 51, ✉ 2514 EC, ✆ 463344, Seafood – . AE E VISA. JV **h**
closed Saturday lunch, Sunday and Bank Holidays – **M** 80/135
Spec. Turbot en papillote, Homard nonante-huit, Sole Lafayette.

XXX **Da Roberto,** Noordeinde 196, ✉ 2514 GS, ✆ 464977, Italian rest. – AE E VISA
closed Saturday lunch, Sunday lunch and Tuesday – **M** a la carte 77/95. HV **k**

XXX **Raden Ajoe,** Lange Poten 31, ✉ 2511 CM, ✆ 644592, Indonesian rest. – . AE E VISA. JV **a**
M a la carte approx. 50.

XX **Pastel** 1st floor, Laan van Roos en Doorn 51a, ✉ 2514 BC, ✆ 643750 – . AE E VISA
closed 25, 31 December and 1 January – **M** (dinner only) 35. JU **z**

XX **Aubergerie,** Nieuwe Schoolstraat 19, ✉ 2514 HT, ✆ 648070 – AE E VISA JV **b**
closed Tuesday – **M** (dinner only) 55/75.

XX **Gemeste Schaap,** Raamstraat 9, ✉ 2512 BX, ✆ 639572, Old Dutch interior – AE E VISA HX **y**
closed Thursday – **M** a la carte 52/83.

XX **Hof van Brederode,** Grote Halstraat 3, ✉ 2513 AX, ✆ 646455, « Converted cellar of a 16C townhall » – AE E VISA HV **s**
closed Saturday and Sunday – **M** (dinner only) 30/60.

XX **Gobelet,** Noordeinde 143, ✉ 2514 GG, ✆ 465838 – . AE E HV **k**
closed Saturday lunch and Sunday – **M** 35/63.

XX **La Grande Bouffe,** Maziestraat 10, ✉ 2514 GT, ✆ 654274 – AE E VISA HV **k**
closed Sunday, lunch Saturday and Monday, 15 July-15 August and 27 December-4 January – **M** 57/85.

XX **Julien,** Vos in Tuinstraat 2a, ✉ 2514 BX, ✆ 658602, Open until midnight – AE E VISA. JV **s**
closed Sunday lunch – **M** a la carte 59/74.

XX **Table du Roi,** Prinsestraat 130, ✉ 2513 CH, ✆ 461908 – . AE HV **g**
closed Monday, Tuesday, first 3 weeks August and 1 week January – **M** a la carte 50/75.

XX **De Verliefde Kreeft,** Bleijenburg 11, ✉ 2511 VC, ✆ 644522, Seafood – AE E VISA
closed Easter and 25, 31 December – **M** 33/70. JV **r**

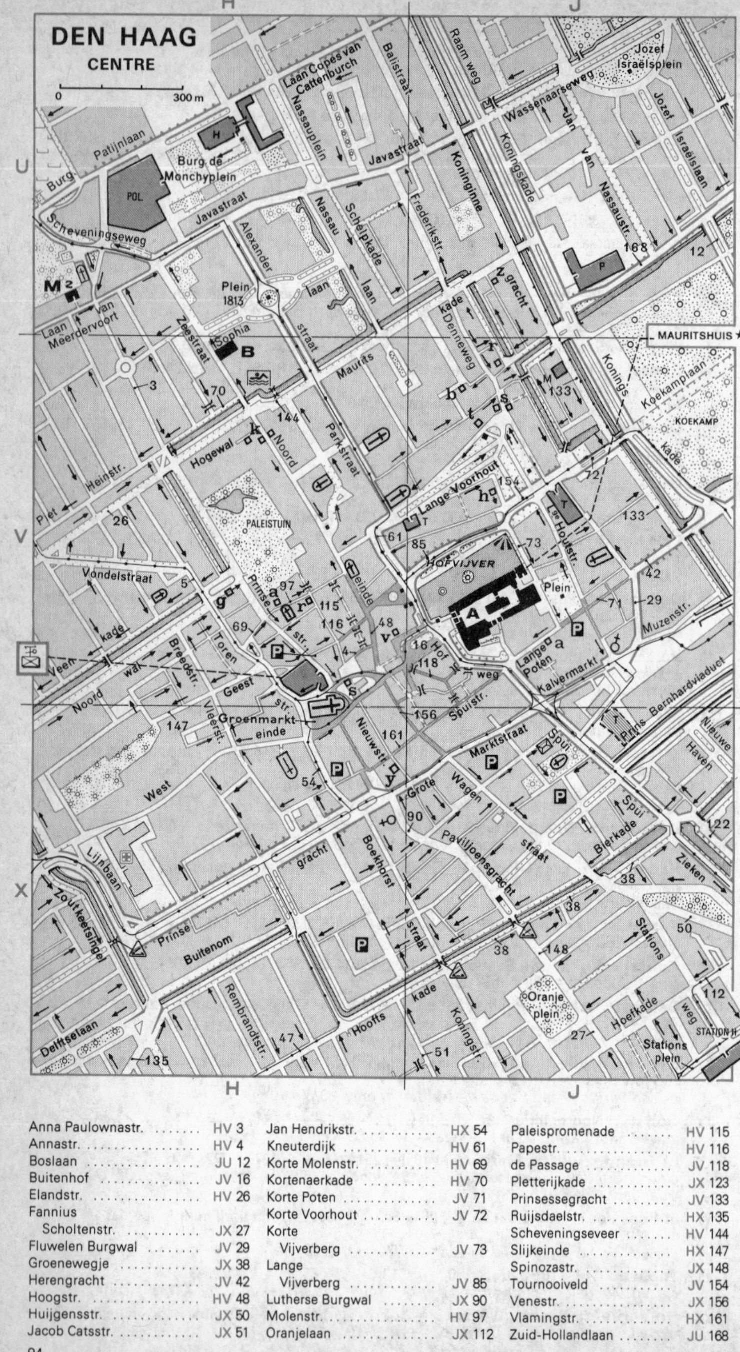

Anna Paulownastr.	HV 3	Jan Hendrikstr.	HX 54	Paleispromenade	HV 115
Annastr.	HV 4	Kneuterdijk	HV 61	Papestr.	HV 116
Boslaan	JU 12	Korte Molenstr.	HV 69	de Passage	JV 118
Buitenhof	JV 16	Kortenaerkade	HV 70	Pletterijkade	JX 123
Elandstr.	HV 26	Korte Poten	JV 71	Prinsessegracht	JV 133
Fannius Scholtenstr.	JX 27	Korte Voorhout	JV 72	Ruijsdaelstr.	HX 135
Fluwelen Burgwal	JV 29	Korte Vijverberg	JV 73	Scheveningseveer	HV 144
Groenewegje	JX 38	Lange Vijverberg	JV 85	Slijkeinde	HX 147
Herengracht	JV 42	Lutherse Burgwal	JX 90	Spinozastr.	JX 148
Hoogstr.	HV 48	Molenstr.	HV 97	Tournooiveld	JV 154
Huijgensstr.	JX 50	Oranjelaan	JX 112	Venestr.	JX 156
Jacob Catsstr.	JX 51			Vlamingstr.	HX 161
				Zuid-Hollandlaan	JU 168

at Scheveningen – 0 70 :

Shipping connections with Great Yarmouth : Norfolk Line, Kranenburgweg 211 527400.

Zwolsestraat 30, 2587 VJ, 546200.

Kurhaus and Rest. Kandinsky, Gevers Deijnootplein 30, 2586 CK, 520052, Telex 33295, ≤, Casino on ground-floor – rest – . AE E VISA. rest
M *(Open until midnight)* 88/115 – **250 rm** 255/375.

Carlton Beach H. and Rest. Le Homard M, Gevers Deijnootweg 201, 2586 HZ, 541414, Telex 33687, ≤, – – . AE E VISA
M 33/68 – **95 rm** 145/195.

Europa Crest H. and Rest. New Orleans Ribhouse, Zwolsestraat 2, 2587 VJ, 512651, Telex 33138, – – . AE E VISA
M 50/75 – 19 – **174 rm** 205/285.

Flora Beach H. and Rest. Le Bouquet, Gevers Deijnootweg 63, 2586 BJ, 543300, Telex 32123 – wc wc – . AE E VISA
M 35/65 – **88 rm** 90/180 – P 140.

Badhotel, Gevers Deijnootweg 15, 2586 BB, 512221, Telex 31592 – wc wc – . AE E VISA
M (dinner only) a la carte 43/75 – **96 rm** 130/187 – P 146.

XXX **Seinpost** (Savelberg), Zeekant 60, 2586 AD, 555250, ≤ – AE E VISA
closed Saturday lunch, Sunday, Monday, 12 July-4 August and 20 December-4 January – **M** 73/98
Spec. Pigeon à la sauge, Huîtres chaudes au safran et caviar (15 Sept.-April), Soufflé au chocolat.

XXX **Lee Towers Palace,** Strandweg 155, 2586 JM, 547373, ≤, Tavern and nightclub – . AE E VISA
closed Monday, Tuesday and 5, 24, 31 December – **M** 65/135.

XXX **Raden Mas,** Gevers Deijnootplein 125, 2586 CX, 545432, Indonesian rest. – . AE E VISA.
M a la carte 49/82.

XX **The Lobsterpot,** Dr Lelykade 23, 2583 CL, 501039, Lobster and seafood – AE E VISA
closed Wednesday – **M** a la carte 61/89.

XX Les Pieds dans l'Eau, Dr. Lelykade 33, 2583 CL, 550040 – **M** (dinner only).

XX **La Galleria,** Gevers Deijnootplein 120, 2586 CP, 521156, Italian rest., Open until midnight – . AE E
M a la carte 41/64.

XX **Bali** with rm, Badhuisweg 1, 2587 CA, 502434, Indonesian rest. – wc . AE E VISA. rm
M 38/55 – **34 rm** 43/105.

on the way to Wassenaar : 3 km :

XXX **Boerderij De Hoogwerf,** Zijdelaan 20, 2594 BV, 475514, , « 17C farm » – AE E VISA.
closed Saturday lunch and Sunday – **M** 75/80.

at Kijkduin : 4 km – 0 70 :

Atlantic, Deltaplein 200, 2554 EJ, 254025, Telex 33399, ≤, – – . AE E VISA
M 38/60 – 18 – **60 rm** and **58** apartments 155/200.

Zeehaghe M without rest., Deltaplein 675, 2554 GK, 256262, Telex 31407, ≤ – – . AE E VISA
18 – **42 rm** and **28** apartments 145/170.

XX **Turpin,** Deltaplein 616, 2554 GJ, 687881 – AE E VISA
M 38/60.

Leidschendam

Leidschendam Zuid-Holland 211 ⑫ and 408 ⑩ – pop. 30 944 – 0 70 – 50 km.

XXX **Chagall,** Weigelia 20, 2262 AB, 276910, « Lake side setting » – . AE E VISA
closed Sunday lunch and Monday – **M** 73/105
Spec. Terrine de foie gras de canard, Escalope de saumon à l'oseille.

XXX **Villa Rozenrust,** Veursestraatweg 104, 2265 CG, 277460, , « Elegant interior » – . AE E VISA
closed Saturday lunch and Sunday – **M** a la carte 65/100
Spec. Filet de boeuf au raifort, Pâtes fraîches, Truffes blanches et noires (Oct.-February).

If you would like a more complete selection of hotels and restaurants, consult the ***Michelin Guides*** *for the following countries:*
Benelux, Deutschland, España Portugal, France,
Great Britain and Ireland, Italia.

ROTTERDAM Zuid-Holland 211 ⑫ and 408 ㉔㉕ – pop. 571 081 – 0 10.

See : The harbour*** KZ – Lijnbaan* (Shopping center) JKY – St. Laurence Church (Grote-of St. Laurenskerk) : interior* KY **D** – Euromast* (tower) (**, <*) JZ.

Museums : Boymans-van Beuningen*** JZ – "De Dubbele Palmboom"*.

Kralingseweg 200 4527646.

Zestienhoven 4157633 (informations) and 4155430, 4372745 (reservations).

(departs from 's-Hertogenbosch) 4117100.

Europoort to Kingston-upon-Hull : Shipping connections North Sea Ferries (Cie Noordzee Veerdiensten) (0 1819) 55500.

Stadhuisplein 19, 3012 AR, 4136000, Telex 21228 and Central Station 4136006.

Amsterdam 76 – The Hague 24 – Antwerp 103 – Brussels 149 – Utrecht 57.

Plan opposite

Hilton International Rotterdam, Weena 10, 3012 CM, 4144044, Telex 22666 – rest – . AE VISA. rest JKY **a**
M a la carte 68/89 – 24 – **261 rm** 260/375.

Parkhotel, Westersingel 70, 3015 LB, 4363611, Telex 22020 – rest – . AE E. JZ **a**
M a la carte 49/89 – **157 rm** 130/260.

Atlanta, Aert van Nesstraat 4, 3012 CA, 4110420, Telex 21595 – – . AE E VISA KY **e**
M a la carte 60/93 – 18 – **169 rm** 170/200 – P 250.

Central and Rest. Alexander, Kruiskade 12, 3012 EH, 4140744, Telex 24040 – rest – . AE E VISA. rest KY **u**
M 30/38 – **64 rm** 119/208 – P 145/228.

Rijnhotel and Rest. Falstaff, Schouwburgplein 1, 3012 CK, 4333800, Telex 21640 – – . AE E VISA. rest JY **e**
M *(closed Sunday)* 38/43 – **140 rm** 140/305 – P 200/310.

Savoy, Hoogstraat 81, 3011 PJ, 4139280, Telex 21525 – wc wc . AE E VISA KY **n**
M *(closed Saturday and Sunday)* (dinner only) 30/70 – 20 – **94 rm** 125/155 – P 200.

Scandia, Willemsplein 1, 3016 DN, 4134790, Telex 21662, < – wc wc – . AE E VISA
M a la carte 49/72 – 18 – **52 rm** 78/175.

Pax without rest., Schiekade 658, 3032 AK, 4663344 – wc wc . AE E VISA JY **m**
44 rm 92/128.

Emma without rest, Nieuwe Binnenweg 6, 3015 BA, 4365533, Telex 25320 – wc . AE E VISA JZ **w**
26 rm 120/150.

Van Walsum, Mathenesserlaan 199, 3014 HC, 4363275 – wc wc . AE E VISA. rest JZ **e**
M *(closed after 8 p.m.)* 30 – **28 rm** 60/120 – P 95.

Holland without rest., Provenierssingel 7, 3033 ED, 4653100 – AE VISA JY **n**
24 rm 68/85.

Baan without rest., Rochussenstraat 345, 3023 DH, 4770555 – wc.
closed 15 December-5 January – **14 rm** 55/90.

Bienvenue without rest., Spoorsingel 24, 3033 GL, 4669394 – wc. AE E VISA JY **d**
10 rm 50/90.

Breitner without rest., Breitnerstraat 23, 3015 XA, 4360262 – wc . AE E VISA JZ **d**
23 rm 40/100.

Heemraad without rest., Heemraadssingel 90, 3021 DE, 4775461 – wc. AE E VISA
8 – **10 rm** 50/80.

Geervliet without rest., 's-Gravendijkwal 14, 3014 EA, 4366109 – wc JZ **b**
closed 2 December-2 January – **15 rm** 45/90.

XXXX **Raden Mas** 1st floor, Kruiskade 72, 3012 EG, 4117244, Indonesian rest. – . AE E VISA. JY **a**
closed lunch Saturday and Sunday – **M** a la carte 55/68.

XXX ✿ **La Vilette,** Westblaak 160, 3012 KM, 4148692 – . AE E VISA JZ **t**
closed Saturday lunch, Sunday and Bank Holidays – **M** 73/98.

XXX ✿ **Coq d'Or,** 1st floor, Van Vollenhovenstraat 25, 3016 BG, 4366405, , Quick bar lunch – . AE E VISA KZ **a**
closed Saturday, Sunday and 24 December-3 January – **M** 58/98
Spec. Caille à la sauce framboise, Magret de canard au miel et suprême de pigeon au foie gras truffé (July-January), Lotte au caviar rouge et coulis de homard.

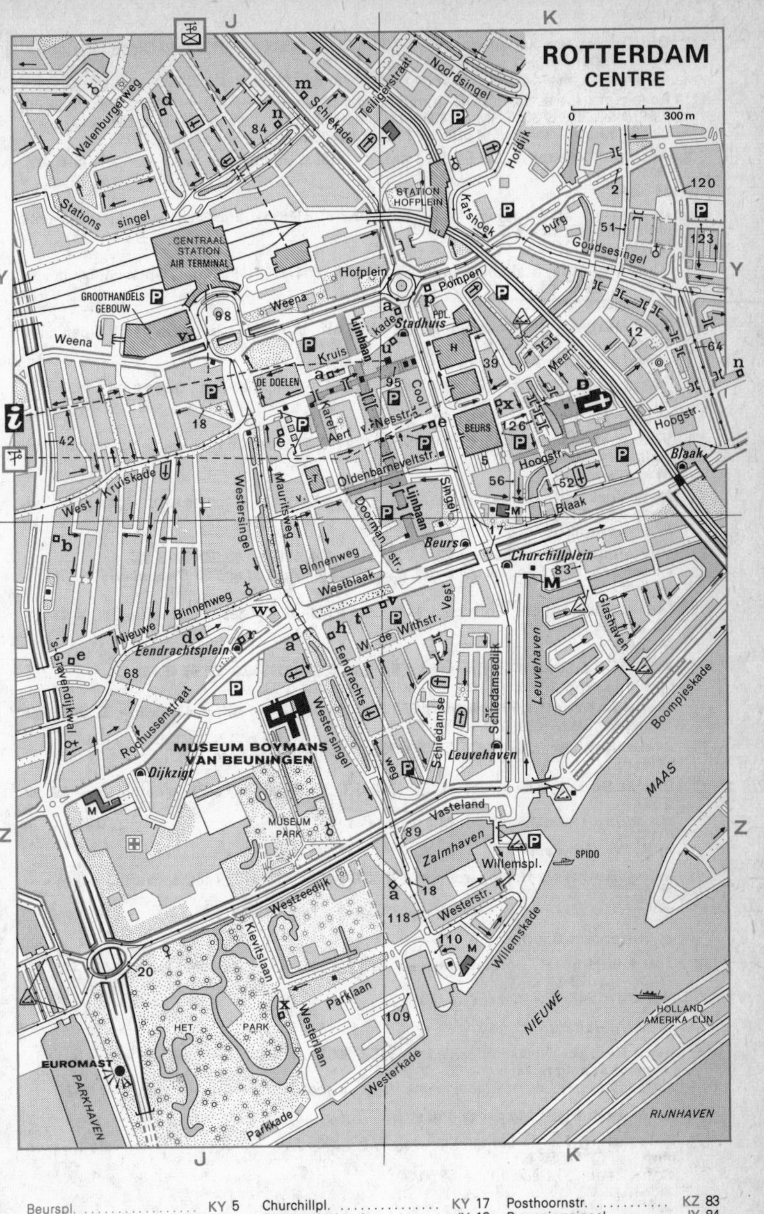

Beurspl. . . . . KY 5
Binnenweg . . . . JZ
Hoogstr. . . . . KY
Karel Doormanstr. . . . . JY
Korte Hoogstr. . . . . KY 56
Lijnbaan . . . . KYZ
Stadhuispl. . . . . KY 95

Admiraal
de Ruyterweg . . . . KY 2
Botersloot . . . . KY 12

Churchillpl. . . . . KY 17
Diergaardesingel . . . . JY 18
Droogleever
Fortuynpl. . . . . JZ 20
Haagsever . . . . KY 39
Henegouwerlaan . . . . JY 42
Jonker
Fransstr. . . . . KY 51
Keizerstr. . . . . KY 52
Mariniersweg . . . . KY 64
Mathenesserlaan . . . . JZ 68

Posthoornstr. . . . . KZ 83
Provenierssingel . . . . JY 84
Scheepstimmermanslaan . . . . KZ 89
Stationspl. . . . . JY 98
Veerhaven . . . . KZ 109
Veerkade . . . . KZ 110
van
Vollenhovenstr. . . . . KZ 118
Vondelweg . . . . KY 120
Warande . . . . KY 123
Westewagenstr. . . . . KY 126

XXX **Old Dutch,** Rochussenstraat 20, ✉ 3015 EK, ✆ 4360344, 佘, « Old Dutch interior » – AE ⓓ E VISA JZ **r**
closed Saturday, Sunday, Easter and Whitsuntide – **M** a la carte 65/125.

XXX **Euromast** (Rest. **La Rôtisserie mid-height of a tower of 180 m - Entrance : 7,50 Fl),** Parkhaven 20, ✉ 3016 GM, ✆ 4364811, ✳ city and port – ▤ Ⓟ. AE ⓓ E VISA. ✻ JZ
closed Saturday lunch and Sunday 15 October-15 March – **M** a la carte 43/86.

XXX **Archipel,** Westblaak 82, ✉ 3012 KM, ✆ 4116533, Indonesian rest. – ▤. AE ⓓ E VISA. ✻ JKZ **v**
M 30/43.

XX **Beefeater,** Stationsplein 45, ✉ 3013 AK, ✆ 4119551, English Pub rest., Open until midnight – ▤. AE ⓓ E VISA JY **v**
M a la carte 42/73.

XX **Chez François,** Stationsplein 45, ✉ 3013 AK, ✆ 4119551, Pub rest., Open until midnight – ▤. AE ⓓ E VISA JY **v**
M a la carte 42/73.

XX **Don Quijote,** Stationsplein 45, ✉ 3013 AK, ✆ 4119551, Spanish rest., Open until midnight – ▤. AE ⓓ E VISA JY **v**
closed Monday – **M** (dinner only) a la carte 42/73.

XX **Tokaj,** Stationsplein 45, ✉ 3013 AK, ✆ 4119551, Hungarian rest., Open until midnight – ▤. AE ⓓ E VISA JY **v**
M a la carte 42/73.

XX **Viking,** Stationsplein 45, ✉ 3013 AK, ✆ 4119551, Scandinavian rest., Open until midnight – ▤. AE ⓓ E VISA JY **v**
M a la carte 42/73.

XX **New Yorker,** Stationsplein 45, ✉ 3013 AK, ✆ 4119551, Counter rest., Open until midnight – ▤. AE ⓓ E VISA JY **v**
M a la carte 42/73.

XX **Castellane,** Eendrachtsweg 22, ✉ 3012 LB, ✆ 4141159 – ▤. AE ⓓ E VISA JZ **h**
closed Saturday, Sunday, Bank Holidays, 20 July-9 August and 23 December-3 January – **M** 75/95.

XX **Indonesia,** 1st floor, Rodezand 34, ✉ 3011 AN, ✆ 4148588, Indonesian rest. – ▤. AE ⓓ VISA. ✻ KY **x**
M 30/40.

XX **Aub. Marie Louise,** Bergweg 64, ✉ 3036 BC, ✆ 4671919 – AE ⓓ E VISA
closed Monday and last 2 weeks July – **M** a la carte 63/93.

XX **Marie Antoinette,** Pompenburg 652 (Hofplein), ✉ 3011 AX, ✆ 4333595 – AE ⓓ E VISA KY **p**
closed Monday – **M** a la carte 55/85.

XX **Statenhof,** Bentinckplein 1, ✉ 3039 KL, ✆ 4661508 – E
M 38/88.

XX **Chalet Suisse,** Kievitslaan 31, ✉ 3016 CG, ✆ 4365062, « Parkside cottage » – AE ⓓ E VISA JZ **x**
closed 25 and 26 December – **M** a la carte 44/63.

at Rotterdam-East :

XXX **In den Rustwat,** Honingerdijk 96, ✉ 3062 NX, ✆ 4134110, « 16C converted house » – ▤ Ⓟ. AE ⓓ E
closed Saturday, Sunday and 27 July-9 August – **M** a la carte 60/78.

at Rotterdam-South :

🏨 **Zuiderparkhotel,** Dordtsestraatweg 285, ✉ 3083 AJ, ✆ 4850055, Telex 28755 – |≑| TV ☎ Ⓟ – 🏃. AE ⓓ E VISA
M a la carte 48/65 – **120 rm** 120/180.

at Hillegersberg – ✆ 0 10 :

XXX **Beau Rivage,** Weissenbruchlaan 149, ✉ 3054 LM, ✆ 4184040, 佘, « Elegant interior, lake side setting terrace » – AE ⓓ E VISA
closed Saturday lunch, Sunday, Bank Holidays and 25 December-4 January – **M** 60/80.

at Ommoord NE : 7 km – ✆ 0 10 :

XXX **Keizershof,** Martin Luther Kingweg 7, ✉ 3069 EW, ✆ 4551333, « Renovated Saxon farm » – Ⓟ. AE ⓓ E
closed 24 and 31 December – **M** 60/90.

Denmark
Danmark

Copenhagen

PRACTICAL INFORMATION

LOCAL CURRENCY

Danish Kroner : 100 D.Kr = 13.62 US $ (Jan. 87)

TOURIST INFORMATION

The telephone number and address of the Tourist Information office is given in the text under 🅸.

FOREIGN EXCHANGE

Banks are open between 9.30am and 4.00pm (6.00pm on Thursdays) on weekdays except Saturdays. The main banks in the centre of Copenhagen, the Central Station and the Airport have exchange facilities outside these hours.

SHOPPING IN COPENHAGEN

Strøget (Department stores, exclusive shops, boutiques).

Kompagnistraede (Antiques).

See also in the index of street names, those printed in red are where the principal shops are found.

CAR HIRE

The international car hire companies have branches in Copenhagen - Your hotel porter will be able to give details and help you with your arrangements.

TIPPING

In Denmark, all hotels and restaurants include a service charge. As for the taxis, there is no extra charge to the amount shown on the meter.

SPEED LIMITS

The maximum permitted speed in cities is 50 km/h - 31mph, outside cities 80 km/h - 50mph and 100 km/h - 62mph on motorways.

SEAT BELTS

The wearing of seat belts is compulsory for drivers and front seat passengers.

COPENHAGEN

SIGHTS

See : Tivoli★★★ : May 1 to September 15 BZ – Harbour and Canal Tour★★★ (Kanaltur) : May to September 15 (Gammel Strand and Nyhavn) – Little Mermaid★★★ (Den Lille Havfrue) DX – Strøget★★ BCYZ – Nyhavn★★ DY – Amalienborg★★ : Changing of the Guard at noon DY – Rosenborg Castle★★ (Rosenborg Slot) CX Christiansborg Palace★★ (Christiansborg Slot) CZ – Old Stock Exchange★★ (Børsen) CZ – Round Tower★★ (Rundetårn) CY **D** Gråbrødretorv★ CY **28** – Gammel Strand★ CZ **26** – Marble Church★ (Marmorkirke) DY **E** – Royal Chapel and Naval Church★ (Holmen's Kirke) CZ **B** – King's Square★ (Kongens Nytorv) DY – Charlottenborg Palace★ (Charlottenborg Slot) DY **F** – Citadel★ (Kastellet) DX – Christianshavn★ DZ – Botanical Garden★ (Botanisk Have) BX – Frederiksberg Garden★ (Frederiksberg Have) AZ – Town Hall (Radhus) : World Clock★ (Jen Olsen's Verdensur) BZ **H**. Breweries – Porcelain Factories – Danish Design Centre (" Den Permanente ") AZ.

Museums : Ny Carlsberg Glyptotek★★★ (Glyptoteket) BZ – National Museum★★ (Nationalmuseet) CZ – Royal Museum of Fine Arts★★ (Statens Museum for Kunst) CX – Thorvaldsen Museum★ CZ **M1** – Royal Arsenal Museum★ (Tøjhusmuseet) CZ **M2** – Royal Theatre Museum★ (Teaterhistoriskmuseum) CZ **M3** – Copenhagen City Museum★ (By Museum) AZ **M4**.

Outskirts : Open Air Museum★★ (Frilandsmuseet) NW : 12 km BX – Ordrupgaard Museum★ (Ordrupgaardsamlingen) N : 10 km CX – Dragør★ SW : 13 km DZ.

COPENHAGEN (KØBENHAVN) Danmark **920** L 3 – pop. 622 000 – ✆ 01.

18 Dansk Golf Union 56 ✆ (01) 13.12.21.

✈ Copenhagen/Kastrup SW : 10 km ✆ (01) 54.17.01 – Air Terminal : main railway station.

Motorail for Southern Europe : ✆ (01) 14.17.01.

Further information from the D S B, main railway station or tourist information centre (see below).

ℹ Danmarks Turistråd, H.C. Andersens Bould. 22 A - 1553 København.V ✆ (01) 11.13.25

Berlin 385 – Hamburg 305 – Oslo 583 – Stockholm 630.

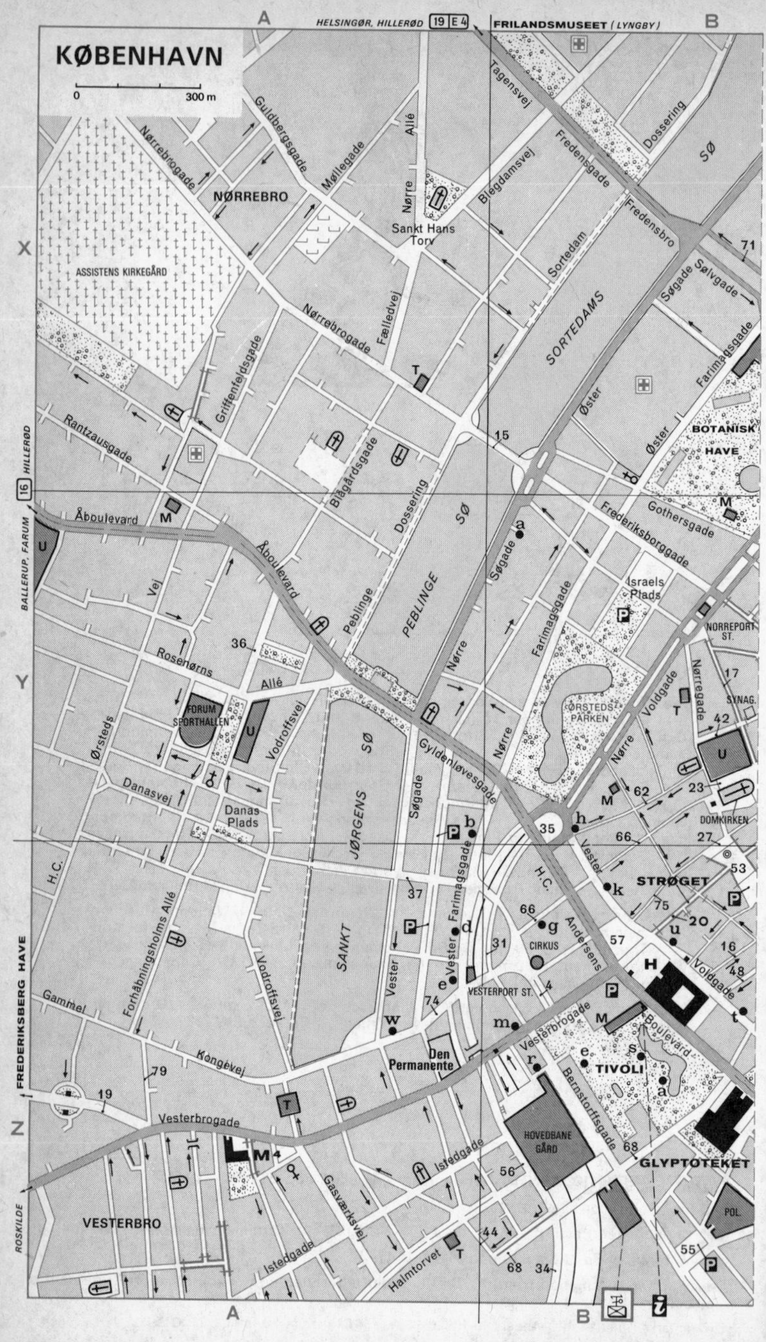
KØBENHAVN
0
300 m
HELSINGØR, HILLERØD
19
E 4
FRILANDSMUSEET (LYNGBY)
NØRREBRO
ASSISTENS KIRKEGÅRD
Sankt Hans Torv
SORTEDAMS
SØ
PEBLINGE
SØ
SANKT JØRGENS SØ
BOTANISK HAVE
Israels Plads
ØRSTEDS-PARKEN
NØRREPORT ST.
SYNAG.
DOMKIRKEN
STRØGET
FORUM SPORTHALLEN
Danas Plads
CIRKUS
VESTERPORT ST.
Den Permanente
TIVOLI
HOVEDBANE GÅRD
GLYPTOTEKET
POL.
VESTERBRO
FREDERIKSBERG HAVE
BALLERUP, FARUM
16
HILLERØD
ROSKILDE
Vesterbrogade
Istedgade
Halmtorvet
Gasværksvej
Kongevej
Åboulevard
Nørrebrogade
Gothersgade
Frederiksborggade
Farimagsgade
Vodroffsvej
Rantzausgade
Griffenfeldsgade
Blågårdsgade
Guldbergsgade
Møllegade
Fælledvej
Tagensvej
Blegdamsvej
Fredensgade
Fredensbro
Sølvgade
Voldgade
Nørregade
Bernstorffsgade
Gyldenløvesgade
Forhåbningsholms Allé
Danasvej
Rosenørns Allé
H.C. Andersens Boulevard
A
B
X
Y
Z

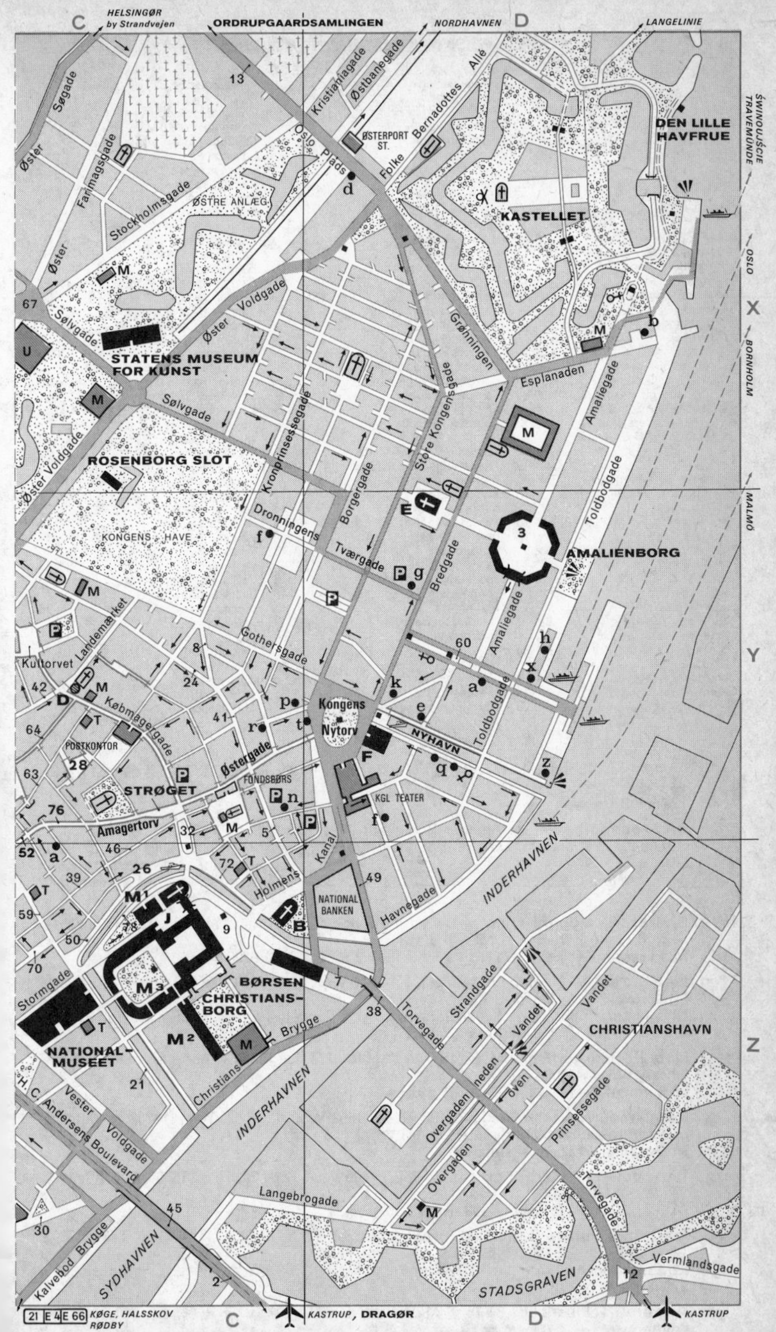
HELSINGØR by Strandvejen
ORDRUPGAARDSAMLINGEN
NORDHAVNEN
LANGELINIE
ŚWINOUJŚCIE TRAVEMÜNDE
OSLO
BORNHOLM
MALMÖ
C
D
X
Y
Z
DEN LILLE HAVFRUE
KASTELLET
ØSTERPORT ST.
Oslo Plads
Folke Bernadottes Allé
Kristianiagade
Østbanegade
Søgade
Øster
Farimagsgade
Stockholmsgade
ØSTRE ANLÆG
Øster Voldgade
Sølvgade
STATENS MUSEUM FOR KUNST
ROSENBORG SLOT
KONGENS HAVE
Kronprinsessegade
Borgergade
Store Kongensgade
Grønningen
Esplanaden
Amaliegade
Toldbodgade
Bredgade
AMALIENBORG
Dronningens Tværgade
Gothersgade
Landemærket
Kultorvet
Købmagergade
POSTKONTOR
STRØGET
Østergade
FONDSBØRS
Amagertorv
Kongens Nytorv
NYHAVN
KGL TEATER
Holmens Kanal
NATIONAL BANKEN
Havnegade
INDERHAVNEN
BØRSEN
CHRISTIANSBORG
Christians Brygge
NATIONALMUSEET
Stormgade
H. C. Andersens Boulevard
Vester Voldgade
Kalvebod Brygge
SYDHAVNEN
Langebrogade
Torvegade
Strandgade
Overgaden neden Vandet
Overgaden oven Vandet
Prinsessegade
CHRISTIANSHAVN
STADSGRAVEN
Vermlandsgade
21 E 4 E 66 KØGE, HALSSKOV RØDBY
KASTRUP, DRAGØR
KASTRUP

STREET INDEX TO KØBENHAVN TOWN PLAN

Amagertorv (Strøget) ..... CY
Bredgade ..... DY
Frederiksberggade (Strøget) ..... BZ 20
Købmagergade ..... CY
Nygade (Strøget) ..... CYZ 52
Nørre Voldgade ..... BY
Store Kongensgade ..... DX
Vesterbrogade ..... ABZ
Vimmelskaftet (Strøget) ..... CY 76
Østergade (Strøget) ..... CY

Amager Boulevard ..... CZ 2
Amaliegade ..... DXY
Amalienborg Plads ..... DY 3
Axeltorv ..... BZ 4
Bernstorffsgade ..... BZ
Blegdamsvej ..... BX
Blågårdsgade ..... AX
Borgergade ..... DXY
Bremerholm ..... CY 5
Børsgade ..... DZ 7
Christan IX's Gade ..... CY 8
Christiansborg Slotsplads ..... CZ 9
Christians Brygge ..... CZ
Christmas Møllers Plads ..... DZ 12
Dag Hammarskjölds Allé ..... CX 13
Danas Plads ..... AY
Danasvej ..... AY
Dronningens Tvaergade ..... CDY
Dronning Louises Bro ..... BX 15
Esplanaden ..... DX
Farvergade ..... BZ 16
Fiolstraede ..... BY 17
Folke Bernadottes Allé ..... DX
Forhåbningsholms Allé ..... AZ
Fredensbro ..... BX
Fredensgade ..... BX
Frederiksberg Allé ..... AZ 19
Frederiksborggade ..... BY
Frederiksholms Kanal ..... CZ 21
Frue Plads ..... BY 23
Faelledvej ..... AX
Gammel Kongevej ..... AZ
Gammel Mønt ..... CY 24
Gammel Strand ..... CZ 26
Gammeltorv ..... BYZ 27
Gasvaerksvej ..... AZ
Gothersgade ..... BCY
Griffenfeldsgade ..... AX
Grønningen ..... DX
Gråbrødretorv ..... CY 28
Guldbergsgade ..... AX
Gyldenløvesgade ..... AY
Halmtorvet ..... AZ
Hambrosgade ..... CZ 30
Hammerichsgade ..... BZ 31
Havnegade ..... DZ
H.C.Andersens Boulevard ..... BCZ
H.C.Ørsteds Vej ..... AY
Holmens Kanal ..... CDZ
Højbro Plads ..... CY 32
Ingerslevsgade ..... BZ 34
Israels Plads ..... BY
Istedgade ..... AZ
Jarmers Plads ..... BY 35
Julius Thomsens Gade ..... AY 36
Kalvebod Brygge ..... CZ
Kampmannsgade ..... AZ 37
Knippelsbro ..... DZ 38
Kompagnistraede ..... CZ 39
Kongens Nytorv ..... DY
Kristen Bernikows Gade ..... CY 41
Kristianiagade ..... DX
Kronprinsessegade ..... CXY
Krystalgade ..... BCY 42
Kultorvet ..... CY
Kvaegtorvsgade ..... ABZ 44
Landemaerket ..... CY
Langebro ..... CZ 45
Langebrogade ..... CDZ
Laederstraede ..... CYZ 46
Løngangstraede ..... BZ 48
Møllegade ..... AX
Niels Juels Gade ..... DZ 49
Nybrogade ..... CZ 50
Nyhavn ..... DY
Nytorv ..... BZ 53
Nørre Allé ..... AX
Nørrebrogade ..... AX
Nørre Farimagsgade ..... BY
Nørregade ..... BY
Nørre Søgade ..... ABY
Oslo Plads ..... DX
Overgaden neden Vandet ..... DZ
Overgaden oven Vandet ..... DZ
Peblinge Dossering ..... AY
Polititorvet ..... BZ 55
Prinsessegade ..... DZ
Rantzausgade ..... AX
Reventlowsgade ..... BZ 56
Rosenørns Allé ..... AY
Rådhuspladsen ..... BZ 57
Rådhusstraede ..... CZ 59
Sankt Annae Plads ..... DY 60
Sankt Hans Torv ..... AX
Sankt Peders Straede ..... BY 62
Skindergade ..... CY 63
Sortedam Dossering ..... BX
Stockholmsgade CX
Store Kannikestraede ..... CY 64
Stormgade ..... CZ
Strandgade ..... DZ
Studiestraede ..... BYZ 66
Sølvgade ..... BCX
Sølvtorvet ..... CX 67
Tagensvej ..... BX
Tietgensgade ..... BZ 68
Toldbodgade ..... DXY
Torvegade ..... DZ
Vandkunsten ..... CZ 70
Webersgade ..... BX 71
Ved Stranden ..... CZ 72
Ved Vesterport ..... AZ 74
Vermlandsgade ..... DZ
Vester Farimagsgade ..... AZ
Vestergade ..... BZ 75
Vester Søgade ..... AYZ
Vester Voldgade ..... BCZ
Vindebrogade ..... CZ 78
Vodroffsvej ..... AYZ
Vaernedamsvej ..... AZ 79
Østbanegade ..... DX
Øster Farimagsgade ..... BCX
Øster Søgade ..... BCX
Øster Voldgade CX
Åboulevard ..... AY

Angleterre, Kongens Nytorv 34, ⊠ 1050 K, ℘ 12 00 95, Telex 15877 – rest. CDY **t**
139 rm, 9 suites.

SAS Scandinavia M, Amager Boulevard 70, ⊠ 2300 S, ℘ 11 23 24, Telex 31330, ≤ city, « Panoramic restaurant on 25th floor », – AE E VISA by Amager Boulevard CZ
M buffet lunch 120 and a la carte 70/288 – 90 – **543 rm** 1250/1450, **48 suites** 1500/8200.

Sheraton - Copenhagen M, 6 Vester Søgade, ⊠ 1601 K, ℘ 14 35 35, Telex 27450, – rest. AE E VISA AZ **w**
M a la carte 200/390 – **471 rm** 1350/1700, **2 suites** 2100/5200.

SAS Royal M, Hammerichsgade 1, ⊠ 1611 V, ℘ 14 14 12, Telex 27155, ≤, – AE E VISA BZ **m**
M a la carte 108/265 – **Royal Garden** *(closed Sunday) (dinner only) a la carte* 315/510
275 rm 1350/1950, **4 suites** 2250/9850.

Plaza M, Bernstorffsgade 4, ⊠ 1577 V, ℘ 14 92 62, Telex 15330, « Antiques and paintings, Library bar » – BZ **r**
M Baron of Beef – – 96 rm, 10 suites.

Kong Frederik, Vester Voldgade 23-27, ⊠ 1552 V, ℘ 12 59 02, Telex 19702, « Victorian pub and restaurant, antiques » – BZ **k**
M Queen's – 127 rm, 4 suites.

Impérial M, Vester Farimagsgade 9, ⊠ 1606 V, ℘ 12 80 00, Telex 15556 – AE E VISA. AZ **e**
M 165/230 and a la carte – **163 rm** 830/1070.

Ladbroke Palace (Ladbroke), Raadhuspladsen 57, ⊠ 1550 V, ℘ 14 40 50, Telex 19693, – AE E VISA BZ **u**
M buffet lunch 110/dinner 125/250 and a la carte – **163 rm** 940/1215, **4 suites** 1890/3700.

Admiral, Toldbodgade 24-28, ⊠ 1253 K, ℘ 11 82 82, Telex 15841, ≤, « Former 18C warehouse » – rest. E VISA DY **h**
M (buffet lunch) 120/dinner a la carte 143/265 – 64 – **366 rm** 485/815.

Sophie Amalie M without rest., Sankt Annae Plads 21, 1250 K, 13 34 00, Telex 15815, <, – AE ⓓ E VISA DY **x**
M (see Admiral Hotel) – 64 – **134 rm** 485/815, **10 suites**.

Richmond, Vester Farimagsgade 33, 1625 V, 12 33 66, Telex 19767 – . AE ⓓ E VISA AY **b**
closed 23 to 31 December – **M** 175/325 (see also **La Cocotte** below) – **132 rm** 825/1120, **5 suites** 1700.

Mercur, Vester Farimagsgade 17, 1625 V, 12 57 11, Telex 19767, – wc . AE ⓓ E VISA. AZ **d**
M *(closed Sunday lunch)* a la carte 88/284 – **110 rm** 825/1275, **3 suites** 1700.

Neptun (Best Western) without rest., Sankt Annae Plads 18, 1250 K, 13 89 00, Telex 19554 – wc wc . AE ⓓ E VISA DY **a**
66 rm 550/900, **10 suites** 1400/2600.

Opera, Tordenskjoldsgade 15, 1055 K, 12 15 19, Telex 15812 – wc wc
66 rm 728/1148, **1 suite**. DY **f**

71 Nyhavn, Nyhavn 71, 1051 K, 11 85 85, Telex 27558, <, « Former warehouse » – wc wc . AE ⓓ E VISA DY **z**
closed 24 to 26 December – **M** (buffet lunch) 142 a la carte 132/298 – **82 rm** 828/1498, **6 suites** 1618/1938.

Kong Arthur without rest., Nørre Søgade 11, 1370 K, 11 12 12, Telex 16512, – wc wc . AE ⓓ E VISA BY **a**
closed 15 December-4 January – **60 rm** 595/835.

Ascot without rest., Studiestraede 57, 1554 V, 12 60 00, Telex 15730 – wc wc . AE ⓓ E VISA BZ **g**
60 rm 520/870, **1 suite** 890/1600.

Park without rest., Jamers Plads 3, 1551 V, 13 30 00, Telex 15692 – wc wc . AE ⓓ E VISA. BY **h**
50 – **66 rm** 595/810.

Danmark without rest., Vester Voldgade 89, 1552 V, 11 48 06 – wc wc BZ **t**
51 rm, **2 suites**.

XXX **Kong Hans,** Vingardsstraede 6, 1070 K, 11 68 68, « Ancient vaulted cellar » – AE ⓓ E VISA CY **n**
closed Sunday, mid July-mid August and Bank Holidays – **M** (dinner only) a la carte 385/565
Spec. Home-Smoked salmon, Assortment of fish daily from the Market, Beef tender-loin, baked in a salted dough.

XXX **Bourgogne,** Dronningens Tvaergade 2, 1302 K, 12 03 17 – AE ⓓ E VISA DY **g**
closed July, August and Bank Holidays – **M** *(Closed Sunday lunch and Saturday)* a la carte 195/359.

XXX **La Cocotte,** (at Richmond H.), Vester Farimagsgade 33, 1606 V, 14 04 07 – AE ⓓ E VISA AY **b**
closed Sunday, Christmas-New Year and Bank Holidays – **M** 180/300 and a la carte 185/307.

XX Les Etoiles, Dronningens Tvaergade 43, 1302 K, 15 05 54 CY **f**

XX **Leonore Christine,** Nyhavn 9, 1051 K, 13 50 40 – AE ⓓ E VISA DY **e**
closed Saturday lunch, Sunday, last 2 weeks July, 23 December-2 January and Bank Holidays – **M** 168/298 and a la carte 178/344.

XX Remis, Badstuestraede 10, 1209 K, 32 80 81 CYZ **a**

XX **Fridtjof,** Fridtjof Nansens Plads 5, 2100 ø, 42 42 44 – AE ⓓ E VISA
closed Sunday, Monday and July – **M** a la carte 80/300. by Kristianagade DX

XX **Saison,** (at østerport H.), Oslo Plads 5, 2100, 11 22 66, Telex 15888 – AE ⓓ E VISA DX **d**
closed Saturday lunch, Sunday, Monday, July, 23 December-2 January and Bank Holidays – **M** 300/450 and a la carte 175/365
Spec. Poissons, crustacés, coquillages, Menu végétarien, Gibier pendant la saison de chasse (November-December).

XX **Den Sorte Ravn,** Nyhavn 14, 1051 K, 13 12 33 – AE ⓓ E VISA DY **q**
M a la carte 90/317.

XX **L'Alsace,** Ny østergade 9, 1101 K, 14 57 43 – . AE ⓓ E VISA CY **r**
closed Sunday – **M** 147/315 and a la carte.

XX **Els,** Store Strandstraede 3, 1255 K, 14 13 41, « 19C murals » – . AE ⓓ E VISA
M 174/378 and a la carte. DY **k**

X **Lumskebugten,** Esplanaden 21, 1263 K, 15 60 29, « Mid 19C café-pavilion » – AE ⓓ E VISA DX **b**
closed Sunday and 21 December-4 January – **M** 250/465 and a la carte 145/347.

X **Egoisten,** Hovedvagtsgade 2, 1103 K, 12 79 71 – AE ⓓ E VISA CY **p**
closed Saturday, Sunday and Bank Holidays – **M** a la carte 250/360.

X **Gilleleje,** Nyhavn 10, 1051 K, 12 58 58, « Old sailors inn » – AE ⓓ E VISA DY **q**
closed Sunday and Bank Holidays – **M** (buffet lunch) 20/118 and a la carte 193/313.

in Tivoli :

XXX **Divan 2,** Tivoli Gardens, Vesterbrogade 3, ✉ 1620 V, ☎ 12 51 51, « Floral decoration and terrace » – AE ⓓ E VISA BZ **a**
May-13 September – **M** 275/395 and a la carte 198/443.

XXX **Belle Terrasse,** Tivoli Gardens, Vesterbrogade 3, ✉ 1620 V, ☎ 12 11 36, « Floral decoration and terrace » – AE ⓓ E VISA BZ **s**
May-13 September – **M** 210/345 and a la carte 98/398.

XXX **La Crevette,** Tivoli Gardens, Vesterbrogade 3, 1620 V, ☎ 14 68 47, Seafood, « Floral decoration and terrace » – AE ⓓ E VISA BZ **e**
May-14 September – **M** 275/425 and a la carte 250/360.

at Søllerød N : 19 km by exit Tagensvej – BX – and A 43 – ✉ 2840 Holte – ⊕ 02 Holte :

XXX **Søllerød Kro,** Søllerødvej 35, ☎ 80 25 05, « 17C thatched inn » – AE ⓓ E VISA
closed 24 December – **M** 310/450 and a la carte 190/325.

Finland
Suomi

Helsinki

PRACTICAL INFORMATION

LOCAL CURRENCY

Finnish Mark : 100 FIM = 20.86 $ (Jan. 87)

TOURIST INFORMATION

The Tourist Office is situated near the Market Square, Pohjoisesplanadi 19 ✆ 169 3757 and 169 2277. Open from 15 May to 15 September, Monday to Friday 8.30am - 6pm, Saturday 8.30am - 1pm, and from 16 September to 14 May, Monday to Friday 8.30am - 4pm.

FOREIGN EXCHANGE

Banks are open between 9.15am and 4.15pm on weekdays only. Exchange office at the Railway Station open daily from 11.30am to 6pm and at Helsinki-Vantaa airport also daily between 7am and 11pm.

SHOPPING IN HELSINKI

Furs, jewelry, china, glass and ceramics, finnish handicraft and wood.
In the index of street names, those printed in red are where the principal shops are found. Your hotel porter will be able to help you and give you information.

THEATRE BOOKINGS

A ticket service - Lippupalvelu, Aleksanterinkatu 23, is selling tickets for cinema, concert and theatre performances - Telephone 643 043, open Mon-Fri 9am to 5pm.

CAR HIRE

The international car hire companies have branches in Helsinki city and at Vantaa airport. Your hotel porter will be able to help you with your arrangements.

TIPPING

Service is normally included in hotel and restaurant bills - Doormen, baggage porters etc. are generally given a gratuity ; taxi drivers are usually not tipped.

SPEED LIMITS

The maximum permitted speed on motorways is 120 km/h - 74 mph, 80 km/h - 50 mph on other roads and 50 km/h - 31 mph in built-up areas.

SEAT BELTS

The wearing of seat belts in Finland is compulsory for drivers and front seat passengers.

HELSINKI

SIGHTS

See : Senate Square★★★ (Senaatintori) DY **53** : Lutheran Cathedral (Tuomiokirkko) DY, University Library (Yliopiston kirjasto) CY **B**, Senate House (Valtioneuvosto) DY **C**, Sederholm House DY **E** – Market Square★★ (Kauppatori) DY **26** : Uspensky Cathedral (Uspenskin katedraali) DY, Presindential Palace (Presidentinlinna) DY **F**, Havis Amanda Fountain DY **K** – Finnish Design Center★ CZ **R** ; Spa Park★ (Kaivopuisto) DZ ; Esplanade★★ (Eteläesplanadi CY **8**, Pohjoisesplanadi CY **43**) ; Aleksanterinkatu★ CDY **2** ; Atheneum Art Museum★★ (Ateneumintaidemuseo) CY **M¹** – Mannerheimintie★★ BCXY : Parliament House (Eduskuntatalo) BX, Rock Church (Temppeliaukion kirkko) BX, National Museum (Kansallismuseo) BX **M²**, Helsinki City Museum (Helsingin kaupunginmuseo) BX **M³**, Finlandia Hall (Finlandiatalo) BX – Sibelius Monument★★ (Sibeliuksen puisto) AX ; Stadium tower (Olympia-stadion) BX : view★★.

Sightseeing by sea : Fortress of Suomenlinna★★ ; Seurasaari Open-Air Museum★ (from Kauppatori) ; Helsinki zoo★ (Korkeasaari).

Entertainment : Helsinki Festival★★ (June 12th to September).

HELSINKI Finland 920 P 2 – Pop. 484 120 – ✆ 90.

18 Tali Manor ✆ 556 271.

✈ Helsinki-Vantaa N : 19 km ✆ 829 21 - Finnair Head Office, Mannerheimintie 102 ✆ 410 411, Telex 124 404 - Air Terminal : Hotel Intercontinental.

⛴ To Sweden, USSR and boat excursions : contact the City Tourist Office (see below) - Car Ferry : Silja Line - Finnjet Line ✆ 659 722.

ℹ City Tourist Office, Pohjoisesplanadi 19 ✆ 169 3757 – Automobile and Touring Club of Finland : Autoliitto ✆ 694 0022, Telex 124 839.

Lahti 103 – Tampere 176 – Turku 165.

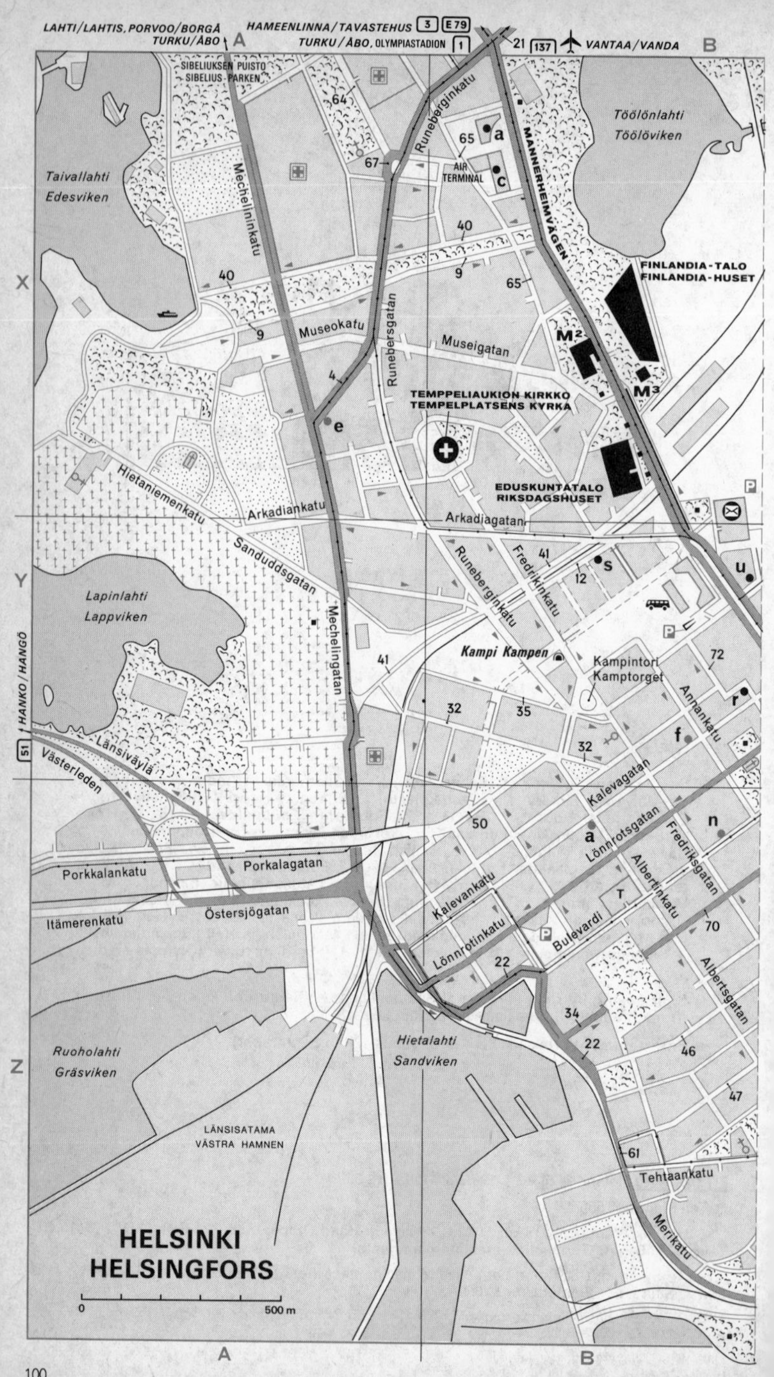
LAHTI/LAHTIS, PORVOO/BORGÅ
TURKU/ÅBO
HAMEENLINNA/TAVASTEHUS 3 E79
TURKU/ÅBO, OLYMPIASTADION 1
21 137 VANTAA/VANDA
SIBELIUKSEN PUISTO
SIBELIUS-PARKEN
Töölönlahti
Töölöviken
Taivallahti
Edesviken
Mechelininkatu
Runeberginkatu
AIR TERMINAL
MANNERHEIMVÄGEN
FINLANDIA-TALO
FINLANDIA-HUSET
Museokatu
Museigatan
Runebersgatan
TEMPPELIAUKION KIRKKO
TEMPELPLATSENS KYRKA
EDUSKUNTATALO
RIKSDAGSHUSET
Hietaniemenkatu
Arkadiankatu
Arkadiagatan
Sanduddsgatan
Fredrikinkatu
Lapinlahti
Lappviken
Mechelingatan
Kampi Kampen
Kampintori
Kamptorget
Annankatu
HANKO/HANGÖ
Länsiväylä
Västerleden
Kalevagatan
Lönnrotsgatan
Fredriksgatan
Albertinkatu
Porkalagatan
Porkkalankatu
Kalevankatu
Östersjögatan
Itämerenkatu
Lönnrotinkatu
Bulevardi
Albertsgatan
Ruoholahti
Gräsviken
Hietalahti
Sandviken
LÄNSISATAMA
VÄSTRA HAMNEN
Tehtaankatu
Merikatu
HELSINKI
HELSINGFORS
0
500 m

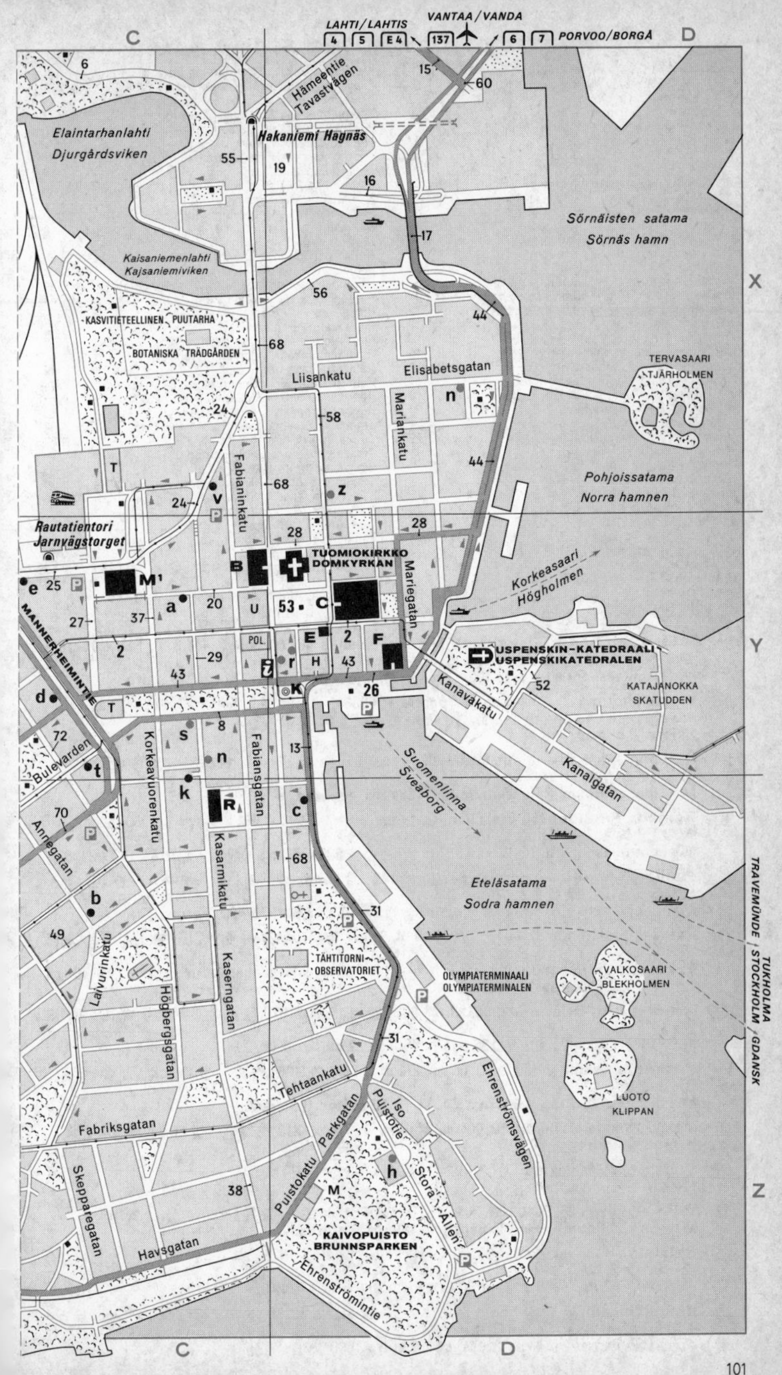

LAHTI/LAHTIS
VANTAA/VANDA
PORVOO/BORGÅ
Hämeentie
Tavastvägen
Hakaniemi Hagnäs
Elaintarhanlahti
Djurgårdsviken
Kaisaniemenlahti
Kajsaniemiviken
Sörnäisten satama
Sörnäs hamn
KASVITIETEELLINEN PUUTARHA
BOTANISKA TRÄDGÅRDEN
Liisankatu
Elisabetsgatan
Mariankatu
TERVASAARI
TJÄRHOLMEN
Fabianinkatu
Pohjoissatama
Norra hamnen
Rautatientori
Jarnvägstorget
TUOMIOKIRKKO
DOMKYRKAN
Mariegatan
Korkeasaari
Högholmen
MANNERHEIMINTIE
USPENSKIN-KATEDRAALI
USPENSKIKATEDRALEN
Kanavakatu
KATAJANOKKA
SKATUDDEN
Bulevarden
Korkeavuorenkatu
Fabiansgatan
Suomenlinna
Sveaborg
Kanalgatan
Annegatan
Kasarmikatu
Eteläsatama
Sodra hamnen
TRAVEMÜNDE
TUKHOLMA
STOCKHOLM
GDANSK
Laivurinkatu
Högbergsgatan
Kaserngatan
TÄHTITORNI
OBSERVATORIET
OLYMPIATERMINAALI
OLYMPIATERMINALEN
VALKOSAARI
BLEKHOLMEN
Tehtaankatu
Ehrenströmsvägen
LUOTO
KLIPPAN
Fabriksgatan
Iso Puistotie
Stora Allén
Puistokatu
Parkgatan
Skepparegatan
KAIVOPUISTO
BRUNNSPARKEN
Havsgatan
Ehrenströmintie

STREET INDEX TO HELSINKI/HELSINGFORS TOWN PLAN

Aleksanterinkatu/Alexandersgatan .... CDY 2
Fabianinkatu/Fabiansgatan .... CXYZ
Keskuskatu/Centralgatan .... CY 27
Kluuvikatu/Glogatan .... CY 29
Mannerheimintie/Mannerheimvägen .... BCXY
Mikonkatu/Mikaelsgatan .... CY 37
Pohjoisesplanadi/Norra esplanaden .... CDY 43

Albertinkatu/Albertsgatan .... BZ
Annankatu/Annegatan .... BCYZ
Arkadiankatu/Arkadiagatan .... ABX
Bulevardi/Bulevarden .... BCXY
Caloniuksenkatu/Caloniusgatan .... AX 4
Ehrenströmintie/Ehrenströmsvägen .... DZ
Eläintarhantie/Djurgårdsvägen .... CX 6
Eteläesplanadi/Södra esplanaden .... CY 8
Eteläinen Hesperiankatu/Södra Hesperiagatan ABX 9
Eteläinen Rautatiekatu/Södra Järnvägsgatan . BY 12
Eteläranta/Södra kajen .... DY 13
Fredrikinkatu/Fredriksgatan .... BYZ
Haapaniemenkatu/Aspnäsgatan .... DX 15
Hakaniemenranta/Hagnäskajen .... DX 16
Hakaniemen silta/Hagnäs bro .... DX 17
Hakaniemen tori/Hagnäs torg .... DX 19
Hallituskatu/Regeringsgatan .... CY 20
Helsinginkatu/Helsingegatan .... BX 21
Hietalahdenranta/Sandvikskajen .... BZ 22
Hietaniemenkatu/Sanduddsgatan .... AXY
Hämeentie/Tavastvägen .... DX
Iso Puistotie/Stora Allen .... DZ
Itämerenkatu/Östersjögatan .... AZ
Kaisaniemenkatu/Kajsaniemigatan .... CX 24
Kaivokatu/Brunnsgatan .... CY 25
Kalevankatu/Kalevagatan .... BYZ
Kampintori/Kamptorget .... BY
Kanavakatu/Kanalgatan .... DXY
Kasarmikatu/Kaserngatan .... CZ
Kauppatori/Salutorget .... DY 26
Kirkkokatu/Kyrkogatan .... DY 28

Korkeavuorenkatu/Högbergsgatan .... CYZ
Laivasillankatu/Skeppsbrogatan .... DZ 31
Laivurinkatu/Skepparegatan .... CZ
Lapinlahdenkatu/Lappviksgatan .... BY 32
Liisankatu/Elisabetsgatan .... DX
Länsiväylä/Västerleden .... AYZ
Lönnrotinkatu/Lönnrotsgatan .... BZ
Mallaskatu/Maltgatan .... BZ 34
Malminkatu/Malmgatan .... BY 35
Mariankatu/Mariegatan .... DXY
Mechelininkatu/Mechelingatan .... AXY
Merikatu/Havsgatan .... BCZ
Museokatu/Museigatan .... ABX
Neitsytpolku/Jungfrustigen .... CZ 38
Pohjoinen Hesperiankatu/Norra Hesperiagatan ABX 40
Pohjoinen Rautatiekatu/Norra Järnvägsgatan . ABY 41
Pohjoisranta/Norra kajen .... DX 44
Porkkalankatu/Porkalagatan .... AZ
Puistokatu/Parkgatan .... DZ
Punavuorenkatu/Rödbergsgatan .... BZ 46
Pursimiehenkatu/Båtsmansgatan .... BZ 47
Ratakatu/Bangatan .... CZ 49
Rautatientori/Järnvägstorget .... CY
Runeberginkatu/Runebersgatan .... ABXY
Ruoholahdenkatu/Gräsviksgatan .... BZ 50
Satamakatu/Hamngatan .... DY 52
Senaatintori/Senatstorget .... DY 53
Siltasaarenkatu/Broholmsgatan .... CX 55
Siltavuorenranta/Brobergskajen .... DX 56
Snellmaninkatu/Snellmansgatan .... DX 58
Sörnäisten rantatie/Sörnäs strandväg .... DX 60
Tehtaankatu/Fabriksgatan .... BCDZ
Telakkakatu/Docksgatan .... BZ 61
Topeliuksenkatu/Topeliusgatan .... AX 64
Töölönkatu/Tölögatan .... BX 65
Töölöntori/Tölötorg .... AX 67
Unioninkatu/Unionsgatan .... DXYZ 68
Uudenmaankatu/Nylandsgatan .... BCZ 70
Yrjönkatu/Georgsgatan .... BCY 72

Inter-Continental (Inter-Con), Mannerheimintie 46, 00260, 441 331, Telex 122159, BX **c**
M – **Ambassador** a la carte 102/220 – **Brasserie** – **555 rm** 710/830, **16 suites** 1600.

Kalastajatorppa, Kalastajatorpantie 1, 00330, 488 011, Telex 121571, « In private park beside the sea », by Mannerheimintie BX
235 rm, **8 suites**.

Hesperia, Mannerheimintie 50, 00 260, 431 01, Telex 122117, BX **a**
M – **French Room** – **Russian Room** – **384 rm**, **4 suites**.

Ramada Presidentti, Eteläinen Ravtatiekatu 4, 00100, 6911, Telex 121953, BY **s**
M - **Four Seasons** (buffet lunch) 95/dinner 145 – **500 rm** 595/740, **5 suites** 1700/2200.

Pasila M, Maistraatinportti 3, 00240, 142 211, Telex 125809, squash – by Mannerheimintie BX
M (buffet lunch) 100/dinner a la carte 97/170 – **253 rm** 370/480, **1 suite** 900.

Palace, Eteläranta 10, 00130, 171 114, Telex 121570, DZ **c**
M **La Vista** 95/180 and a la carte lunch – (see also rest. **Palace Gourmet** below) – **59 rm** 650/1050, **6 suites** 1400/2000.

Klaus Kurki, Bulevardi 2, 00120, 602 322, Telex 121670, CY **t**
M 130/150 and a la carte – **135 rm** 430/560, **2 suites** 600/700.

Vaakuna, Asema-aukio 2, 00100, 171 811, Telex 121381, – rest BY **u**
M a la carte 125/215 – **290 rm** 450/710, **10 suites** 1000/3000.

Marski, Mannerheimintie 10, 00100, 641 717, Telex 121240, CY **d**
163 rm, **6 suites**.

Seurahuone, Kaivokatu 12, 00100, 170 441, CY **e**
114 rm.

Torni, Yrjönkatu 26, 00100, 644 611, Telex 125153, wc wc BY **r**
M – **Balkan Room** – **Parrilla Espanola** **155 rm**, **8 suites**.

Helsinki, Hallituskatu 12, 00100, 171 401, Telex 121022, wc wc CY **a**
closed Christmas – **M** a la carte 80/156 – **130 rm** 410/540.

Rivioli Jardin M without rest., Kasarmikatu 40, 00130, 177 880, Telex 125881, wc CYZ **k**
closed Christmas – **54 rm** 520/660, **1 suite** 1600.

Aurora, Helsinginkatu 50, 00530, ✆ 717 400, Telex 125643, squash – rm wc. AE E VISA by Helsinginkatu BX
closed 24 December-3 January – **M** *(closed Sunday dinner)* 45/60 and a la carte – **74 rm** 280/480, **1 suite** 620.

Olympia, Läntinen Brahenkatu 2, 00510, ✆ 750 801, Telex 122101, – wc. AE E VISA by Helsinginkatu BX
M 150/180 and a la carte – **170 rm** 370/480, **1 suite** 550/600.

Metrocity without rest. Kaisaniemenkatu 7, 00100, ✆ 171 146, Telex 125419 – wc. AE E VISA CX **v**
62 rm 320/440, **2 suites** 540.

Anna without rest., Annankatu 1, 00120, ✆ 648 011, Telex 125514, – wc. AE E VISA. CZ **b**
closed Christmas – **58 rm** 285/490.

XXX ✿ **Palace Gourmet,** (at Palace H.), Eteläranta 10 (10th floor), 00130, ✆ 171 114, Telex 121570, ≤ Harbour and city – . AE E VISA DZ **c**
closed Saturday, Sunday, 1 to 26 July and Bank Holidays – **M** 165/275 and a la carte 250/255
Spec. Slightly salted salmon seasoned with aquavit, Willow grouse in flaky pastry, Pudding of fresh cheese with cloudberry sauce.

XXX **Havis Amanda,** Unioninkatu 23, 00170, ✆ 666 882, Seafood – . AE E VISA DY **r**
closed Sunday and Bank Holidays – **M** a la carte 170/295.

XXX **Kauppakilta,** Snellmaninkatu 13, 00170, ✆ 662 889 – . AE E VISA DX **z**
closed Saturday and Sunday – **M** (lunch) 165 and a la carte 149/209.

XXX **Savoy,** Eteläesplanadi 14, 00130, ✆ 176 571, Telex 121369, ≤, . AE E VISA CY **s**
closed Saturday lunch in July, Saturday dinner, Sunday and 24 December-5 January – **M** 155/1300 and a la carte.

XXX **Kaivohuone,** Kaivopuisto, 00140, ✆ 177 881, Telex 123312, ≤, , « In Kaivopuisto Park » – . AE E VISA DZ **h**
closed Sunday, Monday and 24 to 28 December – **M** *(closed lunch October-March)* 98/225 and a la carte dinner.

XX **George,** Kalevankatu 17, 00100, ✆ 647 662 – AE E VISA BY **f**
closed Sunday, Midsummer Day and Christmas – **M** 116/280 and a la carte 108/221.

XX **Svenska Klubben,** Mavrinkatu 6, 00170, ✆ 628 706, « Scottish style house » – . AE E VISA DX **n**
closed Sunday and 6 June-17 August – **M** 140/195 and a la carte.

XX Suomalainen Ravintola, Sibeliuksenkatu 2, 00260, ✆ 491 568, , Finnish rest. by Mannerheimintie BX

XX **Amadeus,** Sofiankatu 4, 00170, ✆ 626 676 – . AE E VISA DY **r**
closed Sunday – **M** (lunch) 160 dinner a la carte 88/228.

XX **Céline,** Kasarminkatu 23, 00130, ✆ 636 921 – AE E VISA CY **n**
closed Saturday and Sunday – **M** a la carte 80/190.

XX **Rivoli (Kala and Cheri),** Albertinkatu 38, 00180, ✆ 643 455. AE E VISA BZ **a**
closed lunch Saturday and Sunday – **M** (lunch) 89 dinner a la carte 99/187.

X **Troikka,** Caloniuksenkatu 3, 00100, ✆ 445 229, Russian rest. AE E VISA AX **e**
closed Saturday and Sunday on public holidays – **M** 55/245 and a la carte 195/198.

X Kreisi, Bulevardi 7, 00120, ✆ 611 081, « A funny original interior » – BZ **n**

on 137 N : 15 km – ✉ Vanta – 90 Helsinki :

Airport Hotel Rantasipi M, Takamaartie 4, PL 53, 01511, ✆ 826 822, Telex 121812, – wc. AE E VISA by Helsinginkatu BX
closed Christmas – **M** (buffet lunch) 92/a la carte approx. 115 – **300 rm** 470/630, **4 suites** 1000/1500

on Suomenlinna Island by ferry from Market Square – ✉ 90 Helsinki :

XX **Walhalla,** 00190, ✆ 668 552, « Vaulted restaurant in 18C fortress » – . AE E VISA
12 May-4 September – **M** (buffet lunch) 170/dinner a la carte 107/272. by ferry from Market Square DY

France

Paris and Environs
Bordeaux
Cannes
Lyons
Marseilles
Monaco (Principality of)
Nice
Strasbourg
Valley of the Loire

PRACTICAL INFORMATION

LOCAL CURRENCY

French Franc : 100 F = 15.56 US $ (Jan. 87)

TOURIST INFORMATION IN PARIS

Paris "Welcome" Office (Office de Tourisme de Paris - Accueil de France) : 127 Champs-Élysées, 8th, ✆ 47 23 61 72, Telex 611984

American Express 11 Rue Scribe, 9th, ✆ 42 66 09 99

AIRLINES

T.W.A. : 101 Champs Élysées, 8th, ✆ 47 20 62 11
PAN AM : 1 Rue Scribe, 9th, ✆ 42 66 45 45
BRITISH AIRWAYS : 91 Champs Élysées, 8th, ✆ 47 78 14 14
AIR FRANCE : 119 Champs Élysées, 8th, ✆ 45 35 61 61
AIR INTER : 12 Rue de Castiglione, 1st, ✆ 45 39 25 25
U.T.A. : 3 Boulevard Malesherbes, 8th, ✆ 42 66 30 30

FOREIGN EXCHANGE OFFICES

Banks : close at 5pm and at weekends

Orly Airport : daily 6.30am to 11.30pm

Charles de Gaulle Airport : daily 6am to 11.30pm

TRANSPORT IN PARIS

Taxis : may be hailed in the street when showing the illuminated sign-available day and night at taxi ranks or called by telephone

Bus-Métro (subway) : for full details see the Michelin Plan de Paris no 11. The metro is quickest but the bus is good for sightseeing and practical for short distances.

POSTAL SERVICES

Local post offices : open Mondays to Fridays 8am to 7pm ; Saturdays 8am to noon

General Post Office, 52 rue du Louvre, 1st : open 24 hours

SHOPPING IN PARIS

Department stores : Boulevard Haussmann, Rue de Rivoli and Rue de Sèvres

Exclusive shops and boutiques : Faubourg St-Honoré, Rue de la Paix and Rue Royale

Second-hand goods and antiques : Flea Market (Porte Clignancourt) ; Swiss Village (Avenue de la Motte Picquet), Louvre des Antiquaires (Place du Palais Royal), Flea Market - type shops around the "Halles" (the old Paris Central Market)

TIPPING

Service is generally included in hotel and restaurants bills. But you may choose to leave more than the expected tip to the staff. Taxi-drivers, porters, barbers and theatre or cinema attendants also expect a small gratuity.

BREAKDOWN SERVICE

Certain garages in central and outer Paris operate a 24 hour breakdown service. If you breakdown the police are usually able to help by indicating the nearest one.

SPEED LIMITS

The maximum permitted speed in built up areas is 60 km/h - 37 mph ; on motorways the speed limit is 130 km/h - 80 mph and 110 km/h - 68 mph on dual carriageways. On all other roads 90 km/h - 56 mph.

SEAT BELTS

The wearing of seat belts is compulsory for drivers and front seat passengers.

PARIS

and environs

PARIS 75 Maps : **10**, **11**, **12** and **14** G. Paris.

Population : Paris 2 176 243 ; Ile-de-France region : 9 878 500.
Altitude : Observatory : 60 m ; Place Concorde : 34 m
Air Terminals : Esplanade des Invalides, 7th, ✆ 43 23 97 10 – Palais des Congrès, Porte Maillot, 17th, ✆ 42 99 20 18
Airports : see Orly and Charles de Gaulle (Roissy)
Railways, motorail, sleepers : apply to the appropriate railway station (S.N.C.F.)

ARRONDISSEMENTS

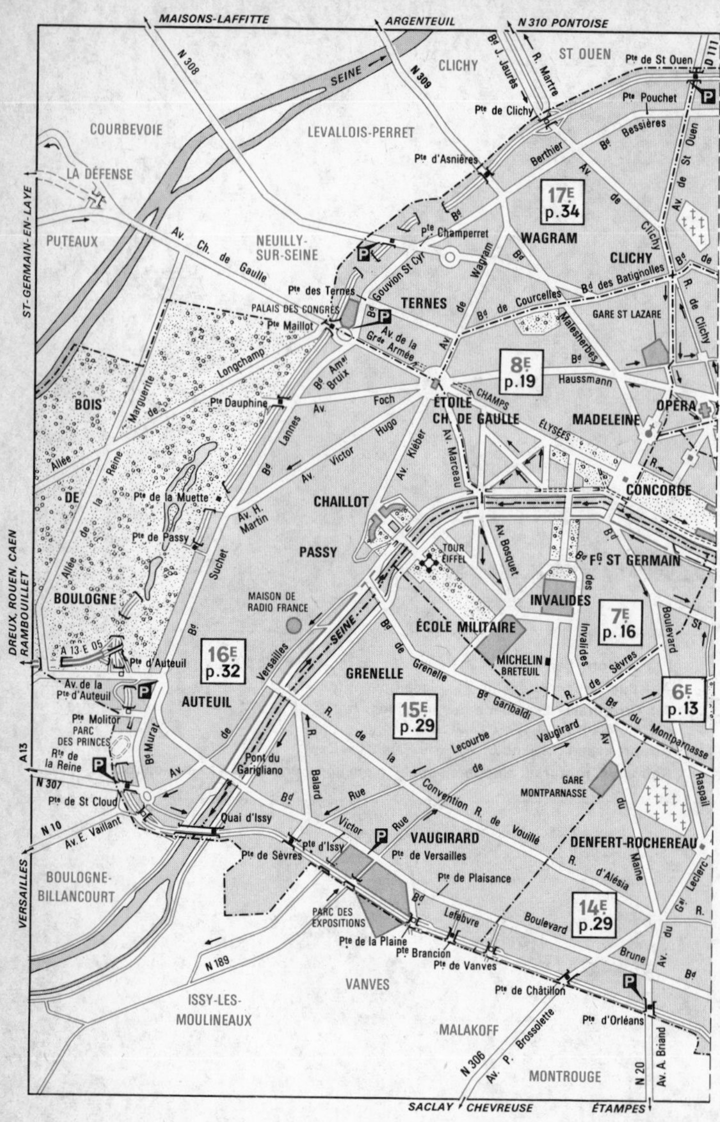

P Car park
-.-.- Arrondissement boundary
One-way street
Ring road (interchange: ▪ complete, ▫ partial)

AND DISTRICTS

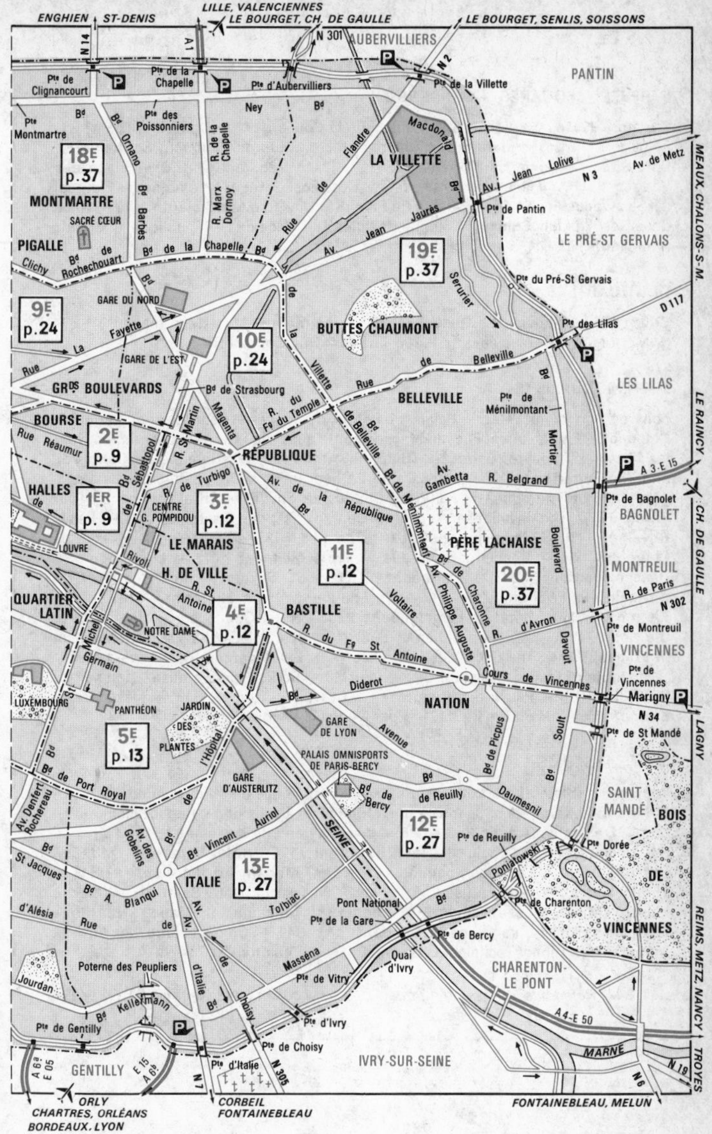

To find your way in the capital, use the **Michelin street plans of Paris**

10 sheet map, **12** sheet map with street index,

11 atlas with street index and practical information,

14 atlas with street index.

SIGHTS

STREETS – SQUARES – GARDENS

Champs-Élysées*** F 8, F 9, G 10 – Place de la Concorde*** (Obelisk of Luxor) G 11 – Tuileries Gardens** (Jardin des Tuileries) H 12 – Rue du Faubourg St-Honoré** G 11, G 12 – Avenue de l'Opéra** G 13 – Place Vendôme** G 12 – Place des Vosges** J 17 – Place du Tertre** D 14 – Botanical Gardens** (Jardin des Plantes) L 16 – Avenue Foch* F 6, F 7 – Rue de Rivoli* G 12 – Rue Mouffetard* M 15 – Place de la Bastille (July Column : Colonne de Juillet) – Place de la République – Grands Boulevards F 13, F 14.

OLD QUARTERS

Cité*** (Ile St-Louis, The Quays) J 14, J 15 – Le Marais*** – Montmartre*** D 14 – Montagne Ste Geneviève** (Latin Quarter : Quartier Latin) K 14.

MAIN MONUMENTS

Louvre*** (Royal Palace : Palais des Rois de France ; Cour Carrée, Perrault's Colonnade, Embankment Façade : façade sur le quai, the "two arms" of the Louvre : les "bras" du Louvre, Carrousel Triumphal Arch : Arc de Triomphe du Carrousel, and The Parterres.) H 13 – Notre Dame Cathedral*** K 15 – Sainte Chapelle*** J 14 – Arc de Triomphe*** F 8 (Place Charles de Gaulle) – Eiffel Tower*** (Tour Eiffel) J 7 – The Invalides*** (Dôme Church : Napoléon's tomb) J 10 – Palais Royal** H 13 – Madeleine** G 11 – Opera** F 12 – St. Germain l'Auxerrois Church** H 14 – Conciergerie** J 14 – Ecole Militaire** K 9 – Luxembourg** (Palace, gardens) KL 13 – Panthéon** L 14 – St. Séverin Church** K 14 – St. Germain des Prés Church** J 13 – St. Etienne du Mont Church** – St. Sulpice Church** K 13 – Hôtel de Lamoignon** J 16 – Hôtel Guénégaud** (Museum of the Chase) H 16 – Hôtel de Rohan** H 16 – Soubise Palace** (Historical Museum of France) H 16 – The Sacré Cœur Basilica** D 14 – Montparnasse Tower** LM 11 – Institute of France* (Institut de France) J 13 – Radio France House* (Maison de Radio France) – Palais des Congrès* – St. Roch Church* G 13 – Alexandre III Bridge* (Pont Alexandre III) H 10 – Pont Neuf J 14 – Pont des Arts J 13.

MAIN MUSEUMS

Louvre*** (Stele of the Vultures, Seated Scribe, Vénus de Milo, Winged Victory of Samothrace, Nymphs of Jean Goujon, Mona Lisa : La Joconde, Regent diamond...) H 13 – Decorative Arts** H 13 – Hôtel de Cluny and its museum** (The Lady and the Unicorn) K 14 – Rodin** (Hôtel de Biron) J 10 – Hôtel Carnavalet** J 17 – Orsay*** H 12 – Georges Pompidou Centre** (Modern Art Museum***) H 15 – The Invalides*** (Army Museum***) J 10 – Picasso** (Hôtel Salé) H 17 – Chaillot Palace (Museum of French Monuments**, Museum of Man**, Maritime Museum**) H 7 – Palais de la Découverte** G 10 – Conservatoire des Arts et Métiers** (National Technical Museum) G 16 – La Villette* BC 20.

K 14, G 10 : *Reference letters and numbers on the Michelin town plans* **10**, **11**, **12** *or* **14**.

ALPHABETICAL LIST OF HOTELS AND RESTAURANTS

HOTELS, RESTAURANTS

Listed by districts and arrondissements

(List of Hotels and Restaurants in alphabetical order, see pp 5 to 8)

G 12: These reference letters and numbers correspond to the squares on the Michelin **Map of Paris** n° **10**, **Paris Atlas** n° **11**, **Map with street index** n° **12** and **Map of Paris** n° **14**.

Consult any of the above publications when looking for a car park nearest to a listed establishment.

Opéra, Palais-Royal,
Halles, Bourse.
1st et 2nd arrondissements.
1st : ✉ 75001
2nd : ✉ 75002

Ritz, 15 pl. Vendôme (1st) ☎ **42 60 38 30, Telex 220262, « Indoor garden »** – |♦| ▤ TV ☎ ♿ P – 30-80. AE ⓓ E VISA. ✻ rest G 12
st. : M see rest. **Ritz-Espadon** below – ☐ 92 – **163 rm** 1 955/2 460, 45 apartments.

Inter-Continental, 3 r. Castiglione (1st) ☎ **42 60 37 80, Telex 220114,** ☂ – |♦| ▤ TV ☎ – 1000. AE ⓓ E VISA. ✻ rest G 12
st. : Rôtiss. Rivoli M 250/350 - **Café Tuileries M** 90/180 – ☐ 90 – **420 rm** 1 270/2 138, 52 apartments.

Meurice, 228 r. Rivoli (1st) ☎ **42 60 38 60, Telex 230673** – |♦| ▤ rest TV ☎ ♿ – 40-80. AE ⓓ E VISA. ✻ rest G 12
st. : M 280 – ☐ 100 – **151 rm** 1 660/2 350, 36 apartments.

Lotti, 7 r. Castiglione (1st) ☎ **42 60 37 34, Telex 240066** – |♦| TV ☎ – 25. AE ⓓ E VISA. ✻ rest G 12
st. : M a la carte 225/350 – ☐ 86 – **126 rm** 1 185/1 690.

Westminster, 13 r. Paix (2nd) ☎ **42 61 57 46, Telex 680035** – |♦| ▤ rm TV ☎ – 80. AE ⓓ E VISA G 12
st. : M see rest. **Le Céladon** below – ☐ 85 – **85 rm** 1 050/1 600, 18 apartments.

Résidence St-James et Albany M, 202 r. Rivoli (1st) ☎ **42 60 31 60, Telex 213031,** ☂ – |♦| TV ☎ – 30 - 120. AE ⓓ E VISA. ✻ H 12
rest. **Le St-James M** a la carte 140/210 – ☐ 50 – **138 rm** 595/800, 69 apartments 655/2 000.

Louvre-Concorde, pl. A.-Malraux (1st) ☎ **42 61 56 01, Telex 220412** – |♦| ▤ rest TV ☎ ♿ – 50 - 100. AE ⓓ E VISA H 13
st. : M a la carte 130/240 – ☐ 55 – **216 rm** 880/1 900.

Édouard VII, 39 av. Opéra (2nd) ☎ **42 61 56 90, Telex 680217** – |♦| TV ☎ – 25. AE ⓓ VISA G 13
M see rest. **Delmonico** below – **96 rm** ☐ 700/880, 4 apartments 2 500.

Mayfair M without rest, **3 r. Rouget-de-Lisle (1st)** ☎ **42 60 38 14, Telex 240037** – |♦| TV ☎ ♿. AE ⓓ E VISA G 12
st. : 52 rm ☐ 676/968.

France et Choiseul without rest, **239 r. St-Honoré (1st)** ☎ **42 61 54 60, Telex 680959** – |♦| TV ☎ – 30-200. AE ⓓ E VISA. ✻ G 12
st. : ☐ 50 – **120 rm** 700/1 100, 23 apartments 1 400/1 600.

Royal St Honoré M without rest, **221 r. St Honoré (1st)** ☎ **42 60 32 79, Telex 680429** – |♦| TV ☎ – 25. AE ⓓ E VISA G 12
st. : ☐ 30 – **80 rm** 610/790.

Novotel Paris Halles M, **8 pl. M. de Navarre (1st)** ☎ **42 21 31 31, Telex 216389,** ☂ – |♦| ▤ TV ☎ P – 40-100. AE ⓓ E VISA H 14
M a la carte 90/160 ♨ – ☐ 47 – **285 rm** 624/680, 5 apartments.

Normandy, 7 r. Échelle (1st) ☎ **42 60 30 21, Telex 670250** – |♦| TV ☎ – 50. AE ⓓ E VISA H 13
st. : M *(closed Saturday and Sunday)* 150 – ☐ 45 – **120 rm** 560/940, 8 apartments 1 100/1 390.

Cusset M without rest, **95 r. Richelieu (2nd)** ☎ **42 97 48 90, Telex 670245** – |♦| TV ☎. E VISA F 13
st. : ☐ 25 – **115 rm** 350/500.

Cambon M without rest, 3 r. Cambon (1st) ✆ 42 60 38 09, Telex 240814 – lift TV ☎. AE ⓓ E VISA G 12
st. : 44 rm ☕ 620/880.

François without rest., 3 bd Montmartre (2nd) ✆ 42 33 51 53, Telex 211097 – lift TV ☎. AE E VISA. ⚹ F 14
st. : ☕ 28 – **64 rm** 550/770, 11 apartments 770.

Favart without rest, 5 r. Marivaux (2nd) ✆ 42 97 59 83, Telex 213126 – lift TV bathwc showerwc ☎ F 13
st. : 37 rm ☕ 380/450.

Montana H. Tuileries M without rest, 12 r. St-Roch (1st) ✆ 42 60 35 10, Telex 214404 – lift TV bathwc showerwc ☎. AE E VISA G 12
st. : ☕ 25 – **25 rm** 375/499.

Duminy-Vendôme without rest, 3 r. Mont-Thabor (1st) ✆ 42 60 32 80, Telex 213492 – lift TV bathwc showerwc ☎ – 🏛 40. AE ⓓ E VISA. ⚹ G 12
st. : 79 rm ☕ 450/800.

Gaillon Opéra M without rest, 9 r. Gaillon (2nd) ✆ 47 42 47 74, Telex 215716 – lift TV bathwc ☎. AE ⓓ E VISA G 13
st. : ☕ 25 – **26 rm** 465/540.

Richepanse without rest, 14 r. Richepanse (1st) ✆ 42 60 36 00, Telex 210811 – lift TV bathwc showerwc ☎. AE. ⚹ G 12
st. : 43 rm ☕ 442/464.

Louvre-Forum M without rest, 25 r. du Bouloi (1st) ✆ 42 36 54 19, Telex 240288 – lift TV bathwc showerwc ☎. AE ⓓ E VISA. ⚹ H 14
st. : ☕ 20 – **28 rm** 280/350.

Du Piémont without rest, 22 r. Richelieu (1st) ✆ 42 96 44 50 – lift TV bathwc showerwc ☎. AE ⓓ E VISA G 13
☕ 26 – **27 rm** 290/486.

Ascot Opéra without rest, 2 r. Monsigny (2nd) ✆ 42 96 87 66, Telex 216679 – lift TV bathwc showerwc ☎. AE ⓓ E VISA G 13
☕ 27 – **36 rm** 153/456.

Gd H. Champagne without rest, 17 r. J.-Lantier (1st) ✆ 42 36 60 00, Telex 215955 – lift TV bathwc showerwc ☎. AE ⓓ VISA J 14
st. : ☕ 30 – **45 rm** 301/402.

Ducs de Bourgogne without rest, 19 r. Pont-Neuf (1st) ✆ 42 33 95 64, Telex 216367 – lift TV bathwc showerwc ☎. E VISA. ⚹ H 14
st. : ☕ 25 – **49 rm** 260/340.

Ducs d'Anjou without rest, 1 r. Ste-Opportune (1st) ✆ 42 36 92 24 – lift bathwc showerwc ☎. E VISA H 14
st. : 38 rm ☕ 253/319.

Family without rest, 35 r. Cambon (1st) ✆ 42 61 54 84 – lift bathwc showerwc ☎ ♿ G 12
st. : ☕ 20 – **25 rm** 200/400.

XXXXX ✿✿ **Ritz-Espadon,** 15 pl. Vendôme (1st) ✆ 42 60 38 30, ⛱ – AE ⓓ E VISA. ⚹ G 12
M a la carte 320/460
Spec. Foie gras d'oie au vin de paille, Omble chevalier (November-December), Noisettes de chevreuil Grand Veneur (season).

XXXX ✿✿ **Grand Vefour,** 17 r. Beaujolais (1st) ✆ 42 96 56 27, « Pre-Revolutionary (late 18C) Café Style » – ▤. AE ⓓ E VISA. ⚹ G 13
closed August, Saturday (except dinners from 15 September-31 May) and Sunday – **M** 250 (lunch) and a la carte 320/450
Spec. Bar farci aux herbes, Canon d'agneau rôti, Soufflé au chocolat.

XXXX ✿✿ **Carré des Feuillants** (Dutournier), 14 r. Castiglione (1st) ✆ 42 86 82 82 – E VISA
closed Saturday and Sunday – **st. : M** a la carte 260/360 G 12
Spec. Ravioles de homard (June-November), Agneau de Pauillac rôti (January-April), Râble de lièvre aux saveurs du nouveau monde (mid October-mid December).

XXXX **Prunier Madeleine,** 9 r. Duphot (1st) ✆ 42 60 36 04, seafood – ▤. AE ⓓ E VISA
M a la carte 260/390.

XXXX ✿✿ **Gérard Besson,** 5 r. Coq Héron (1st) ✆ 42 33 14 74 – VISA H 14
closed 7 to 31 July, 15 to 31 December, Saturday and Sunday – **M** 180 (lunch) and a la carte 195/340
Spec. Gibier (season), Poissons et crustacés.

XXX ✿ **Mercure Galant,** 15 r. Petits-Champs (1st) ✆ 42 97 53 85 – AE ⓓ E VISA G 13
closed Saturday lunch, Sunday and Bank Holidays – **M** a la carte 225/275
Spec. Sauté de langoustines aux lasagnes, Coeur de Charolais à la moëlle, Millefeuille du Mercure.

XXX ✿ **Le Céladon,** 13 r. Paix (2nd) ✆ 47 03 40 42 – AE ⓓ E VISA G 12
closed August, Saturday and Sunday – **st. : M** a la carte 220/370
Spec. Julienne d'anguille, Etuvée de Joue de boeuf à la moëlle, Croûte de noix au chocolat amer.

XXX ✿ **Hubert,** 25 r. Richelieu (1st) ✆ 42 96 08 47 – ▤. AE ⓓ VISA G 13
closed Monday lunch and Sunday – **M** a la carte 210/290
Spec. Salade de pigeon, Turbot rôti au jus de truffes, Feuillantine de poires.

XXX **Delmonico,** 39 av. Opéra (2nd) ✆ 42 61 44 26 – ▤. AE ⓓ VISA G 13
closed Saturday and Sunday – **st. : M** 220 b.i./250 b.i.

XXX **Chez Vong,** 10 r. Grande-Truanderie (1st) ✆ 42 96 29 89, Chinese and Vietnamese cuisine – AE ⓓ E VISA H 15
closed Sunday – **M** a la carte 130/205.

XXX **Pierre "A la Fontaine Gaillon",** pl. Gaillon (2nd) ✆ 42 65 87 04 – AE ⓓ E VISA G 13
closed August, Saturday lunch and Sunday – **M** a la carte 150/260.

XXX ✿ **Goumard,** 17 r. Duphot (1st) ✆ 42 60 36 07 – ▤. AE ⓓ E VISA G 12
closed 15 to 24 August, 21 December-4 January and Sunday – **M** a la carte 210/315
Spec. Escalope de loup à l'huile d'olive, Rouget de roches aux olives, Feuilleté tiède de fruits rouges (May-October).

XX ✿ **Chez Pauline** (Génin), 5 r. Villedo (1st) ✆ 42 96 20 70 – ▤. VISA G 13
closed 4 July-4 August, Saturday lunch from April-September, Saturday dinner and Sunday – **M** (▤ 1st floor) a la carte 140/245
Spec. Fricassée de filets de sole et langoustines, Ris de veau en croûte, Gibier (October-February).

XX ✿ **Pierre Traiteur,** 10 r. Richelieu (1st) ✆ 42 96 09 17 – AE ⓓ E VISA H 13
closed August, Saturday, Sunday and Bank Holidays – **M** a la carte 170/265
Spec. Foie gras chaud, St-Jacques à l'éffilochée d'endives (October-April), Rognon de veau rôti à l'échalote confite.

XX **Capeline,** 18 r. Louvre (1st) ✆ 42 86 95 05 – ▤. AE ⓓ E VISA H 14
closed July, February Holidays, Saturday lunch and Sunday – **M** 144/260.

XX **Velloni,** 22 r. des Halles (1st) ✆ 42 21 12 50, Italian cuisine – AE ⓓ VISA. ✱ H 14
closed 9 to 18 August, Saturday lunch and Sunday – **st. : M** a la carte 140/200.

XX **Pavillon Baltard,** 9 r. Coquillière (1st) ✆ 42 36 22 00 – ▤. AE ⓓ E VISA H 14
M a la carte 115/205.

XX **La Main à la Pâte,** 35 r. St-Honoré (1st) ✆ 45 08 85 73, Italian cuisine – AE ⓓ VISA H 14
closed Sunday – **st. : M** a la carte 155/225 ♁.

XX **Le Petit Coin de la Bourse,** 16 r. Feydeau (2nd) ✆ 45 08 00 08 – AE ⓓ E VISA F 14
closed Saturday and Sunday – **M** a la carte 130/230.

XX **La Corbeille,** 154 r. Montmartre (2nd) ✆ 42 61 30 87 – AE E VISA G 14
closed 9 to 17 August, 27 December-4 January, Saturday (except dinners from September-April) and Sunday – **st. : M** 350 b.i./149.

XX **La Barrière Poquelin,** 17 r. Molière (1st) ✆ 42 96 22 19 – AE ⓓ VISA G 13
closed 1 to 18 August, Saturday lunch and Sunday – **M** 200 b.i./300 b.i.

XX **Les Délices du Foie Gras,** 7 r. Gomboust (1st) ✆ 42 61 02 93 – AE ⓓ E VISA G 13
closed August and Sunday – **st. : M** (booking essential) 130.

XX **Pile ou Face,** 52 bis r. N.-D. des Victoires (2nd) ✆ 42 33 64 33 G 14
closed August, Saturday, Sunday and Bank Holidays – **M** a la carte 165/240.

XX **Le Soufflé,** 36 r. Mt-Thabor (1st) ✆ 42 60 27 19 – ▤. AE ⓓ E VISA G 12
closed Sunday and Bank Holidays – **M** a la carte 120/180.

XX **Saudade,** 34 r. Bourdonnais (1st) ✆ 42 36 30 71, Portuguese cuisine – AE ⓓ VISA H 14
closed 1 August-6 September, 23 to 27 December and Sunday – **st. : M** 130 b.i./200 b.i.

XX **Vaudeville,** 29 r. Vivienne (2nd) ✆ 42 33 39 31 – AE ⓓ VISA FG 14
M a la carte 135/210.

XX **La Ferme Irlandaise,** 30 pl. Marché St.-Honoré (1st) ✆ 42 96 02 99 – AE VISA G 12
closed 23 to 30 December and Sunday dinner – **st. : M** a la carte 150/220.

XX ✿ **Pharamond** (Hyvonnet), 24 r. Grande-Truanderie (1st) ✆ 42 33 06 72 – AE ⓓ VISA H 15
closed July, Monday lunch and Sunday – **M** a la carte 140/180
Spec. Tripes à la mode de Caen, St-Jacques au cidre (season), Canette rôtie.

XX **Pied de Cochon** (24hr service), 6 r. Coquillière (1st) ✆ 42 36 11 75 – AE ⓓ VISA H 14
M a la carte 125/230.

XX **Coup de Coeur,** 19 r. St-Augustin (2nd) ✆ 47 03 45 70 – AE ⓓ E VISA G 13
closed Saturday lunch and Sunday – **st. : M** 112.

XX **Kinugawa** 8 r. Mont-Thabor (1st) ✆ 42 60 65 07, Japanese cuisine – AE ⓓ VISA G 12
closed 10 to 31 August, 24 December-5 January and Sunday – **M** 220 b.i./350 b.i.

XX **Caveau du Palais,** 19 pl. Dauphine (1st) ✆ 43 26 04 28 – AE VISA J 14
closed Saturday and Sunday – **M** a la carte 150/235.

XX **Chez Gabriel,** 123 r. St-Honoré (1st) ✆ 42 33 02 99 – AE ⓓ E VISA H 14
closed 7 to 20 August, Sunday and Bank Holidays – **M** 80/160.

XX **Pasadena,** 7 r. du 29-Juillet (1st) ✆ 42 60 68 96 – AE VISA G 12
closed August, Saturday dinner and Sunday – **M** 68/140 ♁.

XX **Le Saint-Amour,** 8 r. Port-Mahon (2nd) ✆ 47 42 63 82 – AE ⓓ E VISA G 13
closed Saturday (except dinners from September-June), Sunday and Bank Holidays – **M** 130.

✗ ✿ **Aux Petits Pères "Chez Yvonne",** 8 r. N.-D.-des-Victoires (2nd) ✆ 42 60 91 73 – AE E VISA G 14
closed August, Saturday and Sunday – **M** (booking essential) a la carte 120/220
Spec. St-Jacques à la provençale (October-April), Ris de veau toulousaine, Faisan (season) or pintade aux choux.

✗ **Chez Georges,** 1 r. Mail (2nd) ✆ 42 60 07 11 – ▤. AE ⓓ E VISA G 14
closed Sunday and Bank Holidays – **M** a la carte 125/200.

✗ **Cochon Doré,** 16 r. Thorel (2nd) ✆ 42 33 29 70 – ▤. E VISA G 15
closed 1 to 20 August and Monday dinner – **M** 62/127.

✗ **Louis XIV,** 1bis pl. Victoires (1st) ✆ 42 61 39 44 – VISA G 14
closed August, Saturday, Sunday and Bank Holidays – **st. : M** 145.

✗ **Paul,** 15 pl. Dauphine (1st) ✆ 43 54 21 48 – ✻ J 14
closed August, Monday and Tuesday – **M** a la carte 100/145 ⚱.

✗ **Le Pistou Chez Fernande,** 29 r. Tiquetonne (2nd) ✆ 42 61 94 85 – AE VISA G 15
closed Sunday – **st. : M** a la carte 135/175.

Bastille, République,
Hôtel de Ville.
3rd, 4th et 11th arrondissements.
3rd : ✉ 75003
4th : ✉ 75004
11th : ✉ 75011

Pavillon de la Reine Ⓜ ⛰ without rest, 28 pl. Vosges (3rd) ✆ 42 77 96 40, Telex 216160 – |♦| ▤ TV ☎ 🚗. AE ⓓ E VISA J 17
st. : ☕ 60 – **29 rm** 850/900, 20 apartments 1 100/1 850.

Holiday Inn Ⓜ, 10 pl. République (11th) ✆ 43 55 44 34, Telex 210651 – |♦| kitchenette ▤ TV ☎ ♿ Ⓟ – 🏛 200. AE ⓓ E VISA G 17
st. : rest **Belle Époque** (Classic) **M** a la carte 150/250 - **Le Jardin d'hiver** (Coffee-Shop) **M** a la carte 120/160 ⚱ – **316 rm** ☕ 910/1 400, bedrooms for non smokers, 7 apartments.

Atlantide without rest, 114 bd Richard-Lenoir (11th) ✆ 43 38 29 29, Telex 216907 – |♦| TV 🛁wc 🚿wc ☎. AE ⓓ E VISA H 18
closed 24 December to 5 January – **st. :** ☕ 28 – **27 rm** 400/480.

Méridional Ⓜ without rest, 36 bd Richard Lenoir (11th) ✆ 48 05 75 00, Telex 211324 – |♦| TV 🛁wc 🚿wc ☎. AE ⓓ E VISA J 18
st. : ☕ 22 – **36 rm** 380/420.

Deux Iles Ⓜ without rest, 59 r. St.-Louis-en-l'Ile (4th) ✆ 43 26 13 35 – |♦| TV 🛁wc 🚿wc ☎ – **st. :** ☕ 28 – **17 rm** 385/485. K 16

Lutèce Ⓜ without rest, 65 r. St-Louis-en-l'Ile (4th) ✆ 43 26 23 52 – |♦| TV 🛁wc 🚿wc ☎. ✻ – ☕ 30 – **23 rm** 550. K 16

Bretonnerie without rest, 22 r. Ste-Croix-de-la-Bretonnerie (4th) ✆ 48 87 77 63, Telex 305551 – |♦| 🛁wc 🚿wc ☎. E. ✻ J 16
st. : ☕ 25 – **29 rm** 250/450.

Vieux Marais without rest, 8 r. Plâtre (4th) ✆ 42 78 47 22 – |♦| 🛁wc 🚿wc ☎. ✻ H 16
st. : 30 rm ☕ 205/350.

Place des Vosges without rest, 12 r. Birague (4th) ✆ 42 72 60 46 – |♦| 🛁wc 🚿wc ☎. AE ⓓ E VISA J 17
st. : 16 rm ☕ 180/300.

Nord et Est without rest, 49 r. Malte (11th) ✆ 47 00 71 70 – |♦| 🛁wc 🚿wc ☎. E VISA. ✻
closed 25 July-31 August and 24 December-2 January – **st. :** ☕ 20 – **45 rm** 200/260. G 17

Notre-Dame without rest, 51 r. Malte (11th) ✆ 47 00 78 76 – |♦| 🛁wc 🚿wc ☎. ✻ G 17
closed August – **st. :** ☕ 24 – **54 rm** 160/240.

✗✗✗✗ ✿✿ **L'Ambroisie** (Pacaud), 9 pl. des Vosges (4th) ✆ 42 78 51 45 – E VISA J 17
closed August, Monday lunch and Sunday – **M** 190 (lunch) and a la carte 250/360
Spec. Feuilleté de truffes (mid December-mid March), Dariole de foie gras aux morilles (mid March-mid May), Bar à l'huile parfumée.

✗✗✗ **Ambassade d'Auvergne,** 22 r. Grenier St-Lazare (3rd) ✆ 42 72 31 22 – ▤. VISA H 15
closed Sunday – **st. : M** a la carte 140/220.

✗✗ ✿ **Quai des Ormes** (Masraff), 72 quai Hôtel de Ville (4th) ✆ 42 74 72 22, ☂ – ▤. VISA
closed August, Saturday and Sunday – **M** a la carte 200/300 J 15
Spec. Ravioli de champignons des bois (September-March), Bar grillé au basilic, Millefeuille de fruits de saison.

✗✗ **Le Dômarais,** 53 bis r. Francs-Bourgeois (4th) ✆ 42 74 54 17 – AE E VISA J 16
closed August, 24 December-2 January, Sunday and Monday – **st. : M** a la carte 180/275.

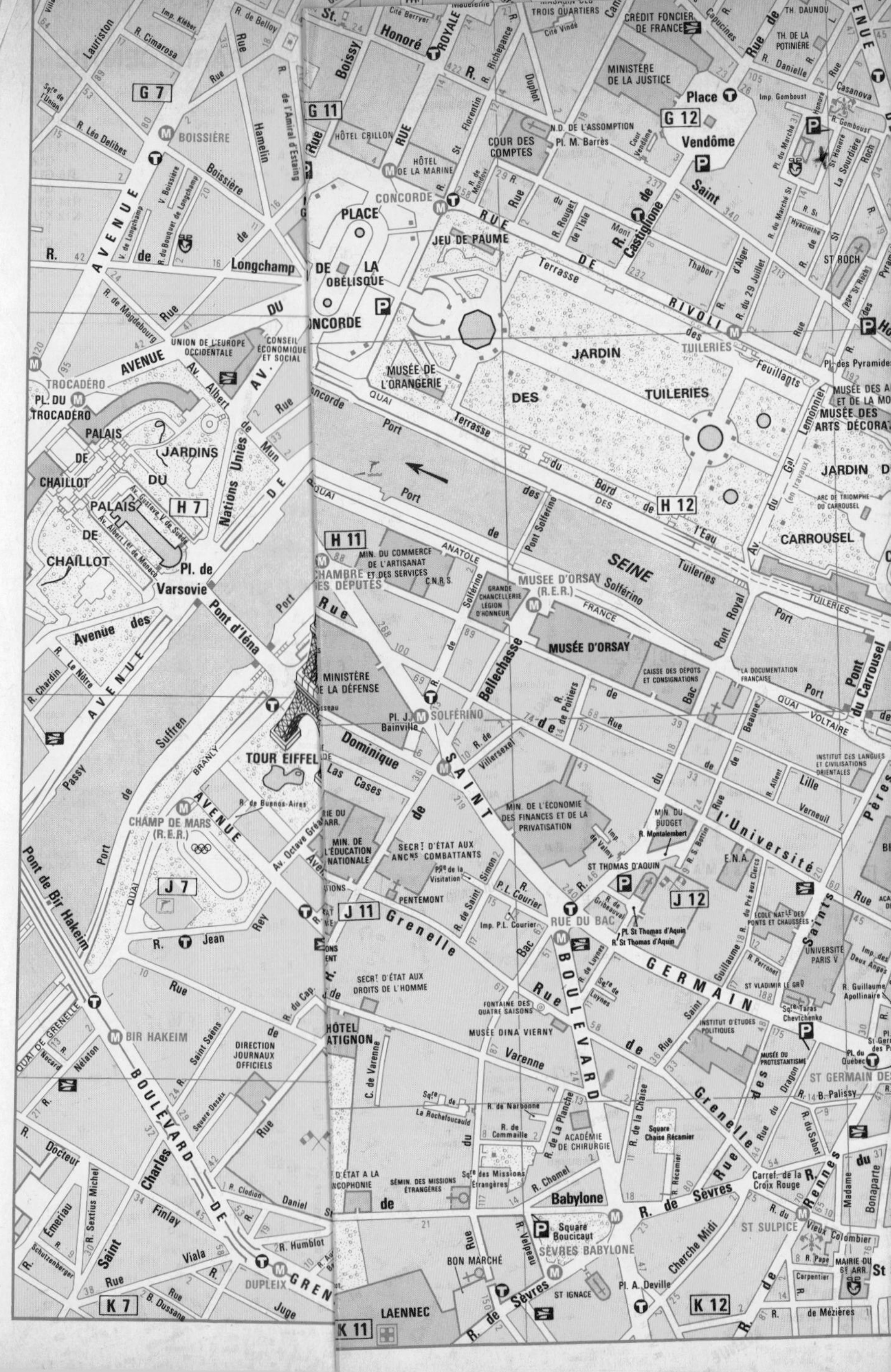

G 7
G 11
G 12
H 7
H 11
H 12
J 7
J 11
J 12
K 7
K 11
K 12
Lauriston
R. Cimarosa
Imp. Kléber
R. de Belloy
R. Léo Delibes
BOISSIÈRE
Boissière
Hamelin
de l'Amiral d'Estaing
AVENUE
de
Longchamp
R. de Magdebourg
UNION DE L'EUROPE OCCIDENTALE
CONSEIL ÉCONOMIQUE ET SOCIAL
TROCADÉRO
PL. DU TROCADÉRO
PALAIS DE CHAILLOT
JARDINS DU PALAIS DE CHAILLOT
Av. Albert de Mun
Nations Unies
Pl. de Varsovie
Pont d'Iéna
Avenue des
R. Chardin
R. Le Nôtre
Passy
Suffren
BRANLY
TOUR EIFFEL
R. de Buenos-Aires
CHAMP DE MARS (R.E.R.)
Pont de Bir Hakeim
R. Jean Rey
BIR HAKEIM
QUAI DE GRENELLE
R. Nélaton
R. Nocard
BOULEVARD DE GRENELLE
Saint Saëns
DIRECTION JOURNAUX OFFICIELS
R. Docteur
R. Sextius Michel
Émeriau
R. Schutzenberger
Saint Charles
Finlay
Viala
R. Humblot
R. Clodion
DUPLEIX
Juge
R. Dussane
St. Honoré
ROYALE
Boissy
Cité Berryer
TROIS QUARTIERS
CRÉDIT FONCIER DE FRANCE
Capucines
Rue de la Paix
R. Richepance
R. St Florentin
Duphot
HÔTEL CRILLON
HÔTEL DE LA MARINE
CONCORDE
PLACE DE LA CONCORDE
OBÉLISQUE
JEU DE PAUME
COUR DES COMPTES
N.D. DE L'ASSOMPTION
Pl. M. Barrès
MINISTÈRE DE LA JUSTICE
Place Vendôme
R. de Castiglione
Mont Thabor
R. d'Alger
R. du 29 Juillet
Saint Honoré
RUE DE RIVOLI
Terrasse
JARDIN DES TUILERIES
TUILERIES
Feuillants
MUSÉE DE L'ORANGERIE
Pl. des Pyramides
ST ROCH
R. Gomboust
Imp. Gomboust
TH. DAUNOU
TH. DE LA POTINIÈRE
R. Danielle Casanova
MUSÉE DES ARTS DÉCORATIFS
JARDIN DU CARROUSEL
ARC DE TRIOMPHE DU CARROUSEL
CARROUSEL
Lemonnier
QUAI
Port
Port Solférino
Port des Tuileries
Pont Solférino
Pont Royal
Pont du Carrousel
QUAI VOLTAIRE
QUAI ANATOLE FRANCE
SEINE
MIN. DU COMMERCE DE L'ARTISANAT ET DES SERVICES
CHAMBRE DES DÉPUTÉS
C.N.R.S.
GRANDE CHANCELLERIE LÉGION D'HONNEUR
MUSÉE D'ORSAY (R.E.R.)
MUSÉE D'ORSAY
CAISSE DES DÉPÔTS ET CONSIGNATIONS
LA DOCUMENTATION FRANÇAISE
MINISTÈRE DE LA DÉFENSE
Pl. J. Bainville
SOLFÉRINO
Bellechasse
R. de Poitiers
Rue de Lille
Rue du Bac
Beaune
Verneuil
R. Allent
INSTITUT DES LANGUES ET CIVILISATIONS ORIENTALES
Saint Dominique
Las Cases
R. de Villersexel
MIN. DE L'ÉCONOMIE DES FINANCES ET DE LA PRIVATISATION
Imp. de Valmy
MIN. DU BUDGET
R. Montalembert
Rue de l'Université
E.N.A.
MIN. DE L'ÉDUCATION NATIONALE
SECRT D'ÉTAT AUX ANCNS COMBATTANTS
Pge de la Visitation
PENTEMONT
R. de Saint Simon
R. P.L. Courier
Imp. P.L. Courier
ST THOMAS D'AQUIN
Pl. St Thomas d'Aquin
R. St Thomas d'Aquin
R. de Gribeauval
RUE DU BAC
BOULEVARD SAINT GERMAIN
R. de Luynes
Sqre de Luynes
R. du Pré aux Clercs
ÉCOLE NATLE DES PONTS ET CHAUSSÉES
UNIVERSITÉ PARIS V
R. Perronet
ST VLADIMIR LE GRD
R. Guillaume Apollinaire
Sqre Taras Chevtchenko
Saints Pères
Rue de Grenelle
SECRT D'ÉTAT AUX DROITS DE L'HOMME
FONTAINE DES QUATRE SAISONS
MUSÉE DINA VIERNY
Varenne
HÔTEL MATIGNON
C. de Varenne
INSTITUT D'ÉTUDES POLITIQUES
MUSÉE DU PROTESTANTISME
R. du Dragon
ST GERMAIN DES PRÉS
Pl. du Québec
R. B. Palissy
R. du Sabot
Sqre de La Rochefoucauld
R. de Narbonne
R. de Commaille
R. de La Planche
ACADÉMIE DE CHIRURGIE
R. de la Chaise
Square Chaise Récamier
R. Récamier
SÉMIN. DES MISSIONS ÉTRANGÈRES
Sqre des Missions Étrangères
R. Chomel
Babylone
R. de Sèvres
Carrel. de la Croix Rouge
Rue de Rennes
Madame
Bonaparte
ST SULPICE
R. du Vieux Colombier
R. Pape Carpentier
MAIRIE DU 6E ARR.
Square Boucicaut
SÈVRES BABYLONE
R. Velpeau
BON MARCHÉ
ST IGNACE
Pl. A. Deville
Cherche Midi
LAENNEC
de Mézières

G 13
G 14
G 15
H 13
H 14
H 15
J 13
J 14
J 15
K 13
K 14
K 15
BOURSE
SENTIER
BIBLIOTHÈQUE NATIONALE
MAIRIE DU 2E ARR.
BASILIQUE N.D. DES VICTOIRES
TH. DES BOUFFES PARISIENS
HÔTEL COLBERT
TH. DU PALAIS ROYAL
PYRAMIDES
JARDIN DU PALAIS ROYAL
BANQUE DE FRANCE
COMÉDIE FRANÇAISE
CONSEIL CONSTITUTIONNEL
PALAIS ROYAL
MIN. DE LA CULTURE ET DE LA COMMUNICATION
CONSEIL D'ÉTAT
Pl. du Palais Royal
Pl. A. Malraux
Pl. Colette
LE LOUVRE DES ANTIQUAIRES
MIN. DE L'ÉCONOMIE, DES FINANCES ET DU BUDGET
MIN. DE LA PRIVATISATION
PALAIS DU LOUVRE
MUSÉE DU LOUVRE
JARDIN DE L'INFANTE
ORATOIRE DU LOUVRE
HÔTEL DES POSTES
CAISSE D'ÉPARGNE DE PARIS
ST EUSTACHE
BOURSE DU COMMERCE
Place R. Cassin
LES HALLES
PAVILLON DES ARTS
MAISON DE LA POÉSIE
FORUM
TOUR DE JEAN SANS PEUR
ÉTIENNE MARCEL
RÉAUMUR SÉBASTOPOL
CHÂTELET LES HALLES (R.E.R.)
CENTRE NATL D'ART ET DE CULTURE G. POMPIDOU
Pl. Georges Pompidou
RAMBUTEAU
IRCAM
Pl. I. Stravinsky
TH. ESSAÏON
LOUVRE
MAIRIE DU 1ER ARR.
ST GERMAIN L'AUXERROIS
SAMARITAINE
PONT NEUF
Pl. de l'École
CHÂTELET
CHAMBRE DES NOTAIRES
TH. MUSICAL DE PARIS-CHÂTELET
TOUR ST JACQUES
TH. DE LA VILLE
Pl. du Châtelet
ASSISTANCE PUBLIQUE
HÔTEL DE VILLE
MAIRIE DE PARIS
BAZAR DE L'HÔTEL DE VILLE
Pl. St Gervais
ST GERVAIS ST PROTAIS
Sq.re du Vert Galant
Pl. Dauphine
CONCIERGERIE
PALAIS DE JUSTICE
STE CHAPELLE
TRIBUNAL DE COMMERCE
Pl. L. Lépine
CITÉ
PRÉFECTURE DE POLICE
HÔTEL DIEU
ÎLE DE LA CITÉ
Place du Parvis Notre Dame
NOTRE DAME
Square Jean XXIII
Square de l'Île de France
Pl. de l'Institut
INSTITUT DE FRANCE
HÔTEL DES MONNAIES
ÉCOLE NATLE SUPRE DES BEAUX ARTS
DIRECTION R.A.T.P.
MUSÉE DELACROIX
ST GERMAIN DES PRÉS
ALCAZAR
Carref. de Buci
MABILLON
Pl. d'Acadie
ST MICHEL (R.E.R.)
Pl. St Michel
LYCÉE FÉNELON
Pl. St André des Arts
ODÉON
Carref. de l'Odéon
UNIVERSITÉ PARIS V R. DESCARTES
UNIVERSITÉ PARIS VI (CORDELIERS)
UNIVERSITÉ PARIS VII
ST SULPICE
ST SÉVERIN
ST JULIEN LE PAUVRE
Square de Cluny
MUSÉE DE CLUNY
ÉCOLE SPÉCIALE DES TRAVAUX PUBLICS DU BÂTIMENT ET DE L'INDUSTRIE
Pl. Maubert
MUSÉE DE L'ASSISTANCE PUBLIQUE
Rue Réaumur
Rue Étienne Marcel
R. Montmartre
R. Montorgueil
Bd de Sébastopol
R. de Turbigo
R. Rambuteau
R. St Denis
R. St Martin
R. Beaubourg
R. du Renard
R. du Temple
Rue de Rivoli
Rue St Honoré
R. Berger
R. du Pont Neuf
Bd du Palais
Av. Victoria
Voie Georges Pompidou
Quai de la Mégisserie
Quai du Louvre
Quai Malaquais
Quai de Conti
Quai des Grands Augustins
Quai St Michel
Quai de Montebello
Quai des Orfèvres
Quai de l'Horloge
Quai de Gesvres
Quai de Corse
Quai aux Fleurs
Quai de l'Hôtel de Ville
Quai d'Orléans
Quai de Bourbon
Pont des Arts
Pont St Michel
Pont au Change
Pont Notre Dame
Pont d'Arcole
Pont Louis Philippe
Pont St Louis
Bd St Germain
Bd St Michel
R. St Jacques
R. de Seine
R. Bonaparte
R. Jacob
R. Mazarine
R. Dauphine
R. de l'Odéon
R. de Condé
R. de Tournon
R. St Sulpice
R. du Four
R. de Richelieu
R. de l'Opéra
R. du Louvre
R. du Mail
R. Vivienne
R. du Croissant
R. St Joseph
R. d'Aboukir
R. de Cléry
R. des Petits Carreaux
Pl. des Victoires
R. Croix des Petits Champs
R. J. J. Rousseau
R. de la Ferronnerie
R. des Lombards
R. de la Verrerie
R. de Lobau
R. de Rohan
R. des Écoles
R. Monge

XX **Bofinger,** 5 r. Bastille (4th) ✆ 42 72 87 82 – AE ⓓ VISA J 17
M a la carte 130/190 ₰.

XX ⚙ **Péché Mignon** (Rousseau), 5 r. Guillaume-Bertrand (11th) ✆ 43 57 02 51 – ▤ Ⓟ. VISA
closed 21 to 28 April, August, Sunday and Monday – **st. : M** a la carte 160/220 H 19
Spec. Mosaïque des trois poissons, Panaché de la mer et du jardin, Filet de boeuf à la ficelle.

XX ⚙ **A Sousceyrac** (Asfaux), 35 r. Faidherbe (11th) ✆ 43 71 65 30 – AE VISA J 19
closed August, Saturday and Sunday – **M** a la carte 160/220
Spec. Foie gras frais, Ris de veau étuvé aux champignons, Lièvre à la royale (season).

XX **Repaire de Cartouche,** 8 bd Filles-du-Calvaire (11th) ✆ 47 00 25 86 – AE VISA H 17
closed 26 July-24 August, Sunday and Monday – **M** 72.

XX **Coconnas,** 2 bis pl. Vosges (4th) ✆ 42 78 58 16 – AE ⓓ E VISA J 17
closed 15 December-15 January, Monday and Tuesday – **M** 160 b.i./280.

XX **Guirlande de Julie,** 25 pl. des Vosges (3rd) ✆ 48 87 94 07 – AE E VISA J 17
closed February, Monday (except from June-September) and Tuesday – **M** 160 b.i.

XX **Franc Pinot,** 1 quai Bourbon (4th) ✆ 43 29 46 98, « Former wine cellar » – ⓓ E VISA
closed Sunday and Monday – **M** 120 (lunch) and a la carte 150/290. K 16

XX **Wally,** 16 r. Le Regrattier (4th) ✆ 43 25 01 39, North African cuisine – ⓓ VISA. ✻ K 15
closed Sunday – **st. : M** (dinner only) 250 b.i.

XX **Pyrénées Cévennes,** 106 r. Folie-Méricourt (11th) ✆ 43 57 33 78 G 17
closed August, Saturday and Sunday – **M** a la carte 140/200.

XX **Taverne des Templiers,** 106 r. Vieille-du-Temple (3rd) ✆ 42 78 74 67 – AE VISA H 17
closed August, Saturday and Sunday – **M** a la carte 155/210.

XX **Au Gourmet de l'Isle,** 42 r. St-Louis-en-l'Ile (4th) ✆ 43 26 79 27 – ▤ K 16
closed 25 July-1 September, February Holidays, Monday and Thursday – **M** 85.

X ⚙ **Benoît,** 20 r. St-Martin (4th) ✆ 42 72 25 76 J 15
closed August, Christmas, 1 January, Saturday and Sunday – **st. : M** a la carte 225/305
Spec. Soupe de moules, Compotiers de boeuf en salade, Cassoulet.

Quartier Latin, Luxembourg,

Jardin des Plantes,

5th et 6th arrondissements.
5th : ✉ 75005
6th : ✉ 75006

🏨 **Lutétia,** 45 bd Raspail (6th) ✆ 45 44 38 10, Telex 270424 – |♦| ▤ TV ☎ – 🏟 25-600. AE ⓓ E VISA K 12
st. : M see rest. **Le Paris** below - **brasserie Lutetia M** a la carte 135/260 ₰ – ☕ 55 – **282 rm** 850/1 500, 18 apartments 2 400.

🏨 **Victoria Palace** ⛱, 6 r. Blaise-Desgoffe (6th) ✆ 45 44 38 16, Telex 270557 – |♦| TV ☎ 🚗. AE E VISA. ✻ L 11
st. : M 130 – **110 rm** ☕ 560/750.

🏨 **Littré** ⛱, 9 r. Littré (6th) ✆ 45 44 38 68, Telex 203852 – |♦| TV ☎ – 🏟 25. AE E VISA. ✻
st. : M 130 – **96 rm** ☕ 560/700, 4 apartments 835. L 11

🏨 **Relais Christine** M ⛱ without rest, 3 r. Christine (6th) ✆ 43 26 71 80, Telex 202606 – |♦| ▤ TV ☎ 🚗 – 🏟 25. AE ⓓ E VISA J 14
st. : ☕ 60 – **50 rm** 1 100.

🏨 **Jardin de Cluny** M without rest, 9 r. Sommerard (5th) ✆ 43 54 22 66, Telex 206975 – |♦| TV ☎. AE ⓓ E VISA K 14
st. : 40 rm ☕ 380/550.

🏨 **Sainte Beuve** M without rest, 9 r. Ste Beuve (6th) ✆ 45 48 20 07, Telex 270182 – |♦| TV. AE E VISA L 12
st. : ☕ 50 – **23 rm** 550/880.

🏨 **Abbaye St-Germain** M ⛱ without rest, 10 r. Cassette (6th) ✆ 45 44 38 11, 🌳 – |♦| ☎. ✻ K 12
st. : 45 rm ☕ 500/630.

🏨 **Angleterre** without rest, 44 r. Jacob (6th) ✆ 42 60 34 72 – |♦| ☎. AE ⓓ VISA. ✻ J 13
st. : ☕ 25 – **29 rm** 350/750.

🏨 **Madison H.** without rest, 143 bd St-Germain (6th) ✆ 43 29 72 50, Telex 201628 – |♦| ☎. AE VISA J 13
st. : 55 rm ☕ 500/900.

🏨 **Odéon H.,** M without rest, 3 r. Odéon (6th) ✆ 43 25 90 67, Telex 202943 – |♦| ☎. AE E VISA. ✻ K 13
st. : ☕ 25 – **34 rm** 550/600.

St-Germain-des-Prés without rest, 36 r. Bonaparte (6th) 43 26 00 19 – TV wc wc ☎. AE. J 13
st. : 40 – **30 rm** 500/900.

Ferrandi without rest, 92 r. Cherche-Midi (6th) 42 22 97 40, Telex 205201 – wc wc ☎. AE E VISA L 11
st. : 35 – **41 rm** 340/480.

Panthéon M without rest, 19 pl. Panthéon (5th) 43 54 32 95, Telex 206435 – TV wc ☎. AE E VISA. L 14
st. : 25 – **34 rm** 425/520.

Grands Hommes M without rest, 17 pl. Panthéon (5th) 46 34 19 60, Telex 200185 – TV wc ☎. AE E VISA. L 14
st. : 25 – **32 rm** 420/530.

des Saints-Pères without rest, 65 r. des Sts-Pères (6th) 45 44 50 00, Telex 205424 – wc ☎. E VISA. J 12
st. : 35 – **34 rm** 400/1 000, 3 apartments.

Aramis St-Germain M without rest, 124 r. Rennes (6th) 45 48 03 75, Telex 205098 – TV wc wc ☎ – 30 - 40. AE E VISA. L 12
st. : 25 – **42 rm** 420/540.

Collège de France M without rest, 7 r. Thénard (5th) 43 26 78 36 – TV wc wc ☎. AE. K 14
st. : 25 – **29 rm** 295/350.

Louis II without rest, 2 r. St.-Sulpice (6th) 46 33 13 80 – wc wc ☎. AE VISA K 13
st. : 25 – **22 rm** 350/450.

Scandinavia without rest, 27 r. Tournon (6th) 43 29 67 20, « Rural setting » – wc ☎. K 13
closed August – **st.** : 25 – **22 rm** 350.

Pas-de-Calais without rest, 59 r. Sts-Pères (6th) 45 48 78 74 – wc ☎ J 12
st. : 41 rm 410/460.

Gd H. des Principautés Unies without rest, 42 r. Vaugirard (6th) 46 34 11 80 – wc wc ☎. K 13
closed August – **st.** : 25 – **25 rm** 170/370.

Marronniers without rest, 21 r. Jacob (6th) 43 25 30 60, – wc wc ☎. J 13
st. : 25 – **37 rm** 250/450.

Aviatic without rest, 105 r. Vaugirard (6th) 45 44 38 21, Telex 200372 – TV wc ☎. AE VISA. L 11
st. : 43 rm 380/550.

De l'Odéon without rest, 13 r. St-Sulpice (6th) 43 25 70 11, Telex 206731 – TV wc ☎. AE E VISA K 13
st. : 30 – **26 rm** 520/560.

Avenir without rest, 65 r. Madame (5th) 45 48 84 54, Telex 200428 – TV wc wc ☎. AE E VISA. L 12
st. : 22 – **35 rm** 300/340.

Delavigne without rest, 1 r. C.-Delavigne (6th) 43 29 31 50, Telex 201579 – wc wc ☎. K 13
st. : 25 – **34 rm** 330/430.

Terminus Montparnasse without rest, 59 bd Montparnasse (6th) 45 48 99 10, Telex 202636 – TV wc wc ☎. E VISA L 11
closed August – **st.** : 29 – **63 rm** 386/467.

Bréa without rest, 14 r. Bréa (6th) 43 25 44 41 – TV wc wc ☎. AE E VISA L 12
st. : 25 – **21 rm** 420/520.

Le Régent without rest, 61 r. Dauphine (6th) 46 34 59 80, Telex 206257 – TV wc wc ☎. AE E VISA J 13
st. : 25 – **25 rm** 490/540.

Seine without rest, 52 r. Seine (6th) 46 34 22 80 – TV wc wc ☎. AE E VISA. J 13
st. : 25 – **30 rm** 195/385.

Rennes Montparnasse without rest, 151 bis r. Rennes (6th) 45 48 97 38, Telex 250048 – TV wc wc ☎. AE E VISA L 12
closed August – **st.** : 30 – **35 rm** 240/420.

La Sorbonne M without rest, 6 r. Victor Cousin (5th) 43 54 58 08, Telex 206373 – TV wc wc ☎. AE E VISA K 14
st. : 21 – **37 rm** 278/338.

Nations without rest, 54 r. Monge (5th) 43 26 45 24, Telex 200397 – wc wc ☎. AE E VISA L 15
st. : 25 – **38 rm** 320/420.

Trois Collèges M without rest, 16 r. Cujas (5th) 43 54 67 30, Telex 206034 – TV wc wc ☎. AE E VISA H 14
25 – **44 rm** 250/400.

Gd H. Suez without rest, 31 bd St-Michel (5th) ✆ 46 34 08 02, Telex 202019 – wc wc ☎. AE ⓓ E VISA. K 14
st. : 49 rm 210/370.

Albe without rest, 1 r. Harpe (5th) ✆ 46 34 09 70 – wc wc ☎. E VISA. K 14
st. : 20 – **41 rm** 250/320.

Muséum without rest, 9 r. Buffon (5th) ✆ 43 31 51 90 – TV wc wc ☎. AE VISA L 16
st. : 22 – **24 rm** 214/300.

Welcome without rest, 66 r. Seine (6th) ✆ 46 34 24 80 – wc wc ☎. J 13
st. : 23 – **30 rm** 210/350.

St-Sulpice without rest, 7 r. C.-Delavigne (6th) ✆ 46 34 23 90 – wc wc ☎. E VISA K 13
st. : 21 – **42 rm** 210/310.

XXXXX ✻✻✻ **Tour d'Argent** (Terrail), 15 quai Tournelle (5th) ✆ 43 54 23 21, **« Little museum showing the development of eating utensils, ≤ Notre-Dame. In the cellar : an illustrated history of wine »** – AE ⓓ VISA K 16
closed Monday – **M** 250 (lunch) and a la carte 470/590
Spec. Canard au sang Tour d'Argent, Tourin au jus de truffes, Croquant de chocolat.

XXXX ✻ **Le Paris,** 45 bd Raspail (6th) ✆ 45 44 38 10 – AE ⓓ VISA K 12
closed August, Sunday and Monday – **st. : M** a la carte 260/345
Spec. Salade de langoustines aux trois brunoises, Tournedos à la croûte au pot, Filets de sole en habit rose.

XXX ✻✻ **Jacques Cagna,** 14 r. Gds-Augustins (6th) ✆ 43 26 49 39, **« Old Parisian house »** – ▤. AE ⓓ E VISA J 14
closed August, 23 December-2 January, Saturday and Sunday – **M** a la carte 330/430
Spec. Pétoncles en coquilles, Filet de barbue farci d'huîtres, Canard de Challans aux zestes d'orange et citron.

XXX ✻✻ **Relais Louis XIII,** 1 r. Pont de Lodi (6th) ✆ 43 26 75 96, **« 16C cellar, fine furniture »** – ▤. AE ⓓ E VISA J 14
closed 20 July-17 August, Monday lunch and Sunday – **M** a la carte 280/365
Spec. Dégustation de poissons de petite pêche, Millefeuille de rognons et ris de veau, Crème à l'ancienne caramélisée.

XXX **Lapérouse,** 51 quai Gds Augustins (6th) ✆ 43 26 68 04, **« Belle Epoque decor »** – ▤. AE VISA
st. : M 200.

XXX ✻ **Villars Palace,** 8 r. Descartes (5th) ✆ 43 26 39 08 – AE ⓓ E VISA L 15
closed Saturday lunch – **M** (rest.) a la carte 180/300 – **La Saumoneraie M** 79
Spec. Aïoli, Bouillabaise, Pochouse (July-September).

XXX ✻✻ **Duquesnoy,** 30 r. Bernardins (5th) ✆ 43 54 21 13 – AE E VISA K 15
closed August, Saturday and Sunday – **M** 175 (lunch) and a la carte 260/360
Spec. Terrine tiède de poireaux, Ravioli de tourteau et homard, Chartreuse de pigeon au foie gras.

XXX **Chat Grippé,** 87 r. d'Assas (6th) ✆ 43 54 70 00 – ▤. E VISA. LM 13
closed August, Saturday lunch and Monday – **M** 155/260 ♁.

XX **Aub. des Deux Signes,** 46 r. Galande (5th) ✆ 43 25 46 56, **« Medieval decor »** – AE ⓓ E VISA K 14
closed Sunday and Bank Holidays – **M** a la carte 230/340.

XX ✻ **Dodin-Bouffant,** 25 r. F.-Sauton (5th) ✆ 43 25 25 14 – ▤. ⓓ E VISA K 15
closed Sunday – **M** 135 (lunch) and a la carte 180/250
Spec. Feuilleté aux huîtres, Timbale du pêcheur, Ragoût de canard et ris de veau.

XX **Clavel,** 65 quai de la Tournelle (5th) ✆ 46 33 18 65 – VISA. K 15
closed August, Monday lunch and Sunday – **st. : M** a la carte 210/290.

XX **Au Pactole,** 44 bd St-Germain (5th) ✆ 46 33 31 31 – AE E VISA K 15
closed Saturday lunch and Sunday – **st. : M** 160 (lunch) and a la carte 240/310.

XX **L'Épicurien,** 11 r. Nesle (6th) ✆ 43 29 55 78 – AE ⓓ E VISA J 13
closed August, Monday lunch and Sunday – **M** 140.

XX **Sud Ouest,** 40 r. Montagne Ste Geneviève (5th) ✆ 46 33 30 46, **« 13C Crypt »** – AE ⓓ E VISA K 15
closed August and Sunday – **M** 127/160.

XX ✻ **Miravile** (Keller), 25 quai de la Tournelle (5th) ✆ 46 34 07 78 – AE ⓓ VISA K 15
closed Sunday – **st. : M** a la carte 220/300
Spec. Salade de caille au chou, Queue de boeuf au Bourgogne, Crêpes soufflées à la liqueur.

XX **La Marlotte,** 55 r. Cherche-Midi (6th) ✆ 45 48 86 79 – AE ⓓ. K 12
closed August, Saturday and Sunday – **M** a la carte 135/195.

XX **Le Clos des Bernardins,** 14 r. Pontoise (5th) ✆ 43 54 70 07 – AE ⓓ E VISA K 15
closed Monday and Tuesday – **st. : M** 130.

XX **Atelier Maître Albert,** 1 r. Maître-Albert (5th) ✆ 46 33 13 78 – ▤ K 15
closed Sunday and Bank Holidays – **M** (dinner only) 150 b.i.

XX **La Truffière,** 4 r. Blainville (5th) ✆ 46 33 29 82 – ▤. AE ⓓ E VISA L 15
closed 20 July-24 August and Monday – **M** 140/220.

XX **L'Arrosée,** 12 r. Guisarde (6 th) ℰ 43 54 66 59 – AE E VISA — K 13
closed Saturday lunch and Sunday – **st. : M** 190 b.i./300 b.i.

XX **L'Apollinaire,** 168 bd St.-Germain (6th) ℰ 43 26 50 30 – ▤. AE ⓓ E VISA — J 12
closed 20 December-5 January – **M** 129/200.

XX **Le Port de St Germain,** 155 bd St Germain (6th) ℰ 45 48 22 66 – ▤. AE ⓓ VISA — J 12
M a la carte 170/250.

XX **Taverne Basque,** 45 r. Cherche-Midi (6th) ℰ 42 22 51 07 – AE E VISA — K 12
closed 9 to 17 August, Sunday dinner and Monday – **M** 150 b.i.

XX **La Foux,** 2 r. Clément (6th) ℰ 43 54 09 53 – ▤. AE ⓓ VISA — K 13
closed Sunday – **st. : M** a la carte 130/230.

XX **Au Régent,** 97 r. Cherche Midi (6th) ℰ 42 22 32 44 – AE ⓓ E VISA — L 11
closed August, Sunday and Monday – **st. : M** 110/220.

XX **Chez Tante Madée,** 11 r. Dupin (6th) ℰ 42 22 64 56 – AE ⓓ — K 12
closed Saturday lunch and Sunday – **st. : M** 140 (lunch) and a la carte 200/300.

XX **Le Sybarite,** 6 r. Sabot (6th) ℰ 42 22 21 56 – ▤. AE ⓓ VISA. ✱ — K 12
closed Saturday lunch – **st. : M** 150 ₰.

XX **Au Grilladin,** 13 r. Mézières (6th) ℰ 45 48 30 38 – E VISA — K 12
closed 18 to 27 April, August, 23 December-4 January, Monday lunch and Sunday – **st. : M** a la carte 130/190.

XX **Joséphine** (Chez Dumonet), 117 r. Cherche-Midi (6th) ℰ 45 48 52 40 – E VISA — L 11
closed July, 22 to 28 December, Saturday and Sunday – **M** a la carte 150/270.

XX **Dominique,** 19 r. Bréa (6th) ℰ 43 27 08 80, Russian cuisine – AE ⓓ E VISA — L 12
closed July and February Holidays – **M** a la carte 110/190.

X **Allard,** 41 r. St-André-des-Arts (6th) ℰ 43 26 48 23 – AE ⓓ E VISA — K 14
closed August, Christmas-1 January, Saturday and Sunday – **st. : M** (booking essential) a la carte 220/310.

X **Balzar,** 49 r. Écoles (5th) ℰ 43 54 13 67 – ✱ — K 14
closed August and Tuesday – **M** a la carte 110/175.

X **Moissonnier,** 28 r. Fossés-St-Bernard (5th) ℰ 43 29 87 65 — K 15
closed August, Sunday dinner and Monday – **M** a la carte 125/170.

X **L'Ange Gourmand,** 31 quai Tournelle (5th) ℰ 43 54 11 31 – AE — K 15
closed Monday – **st. : M** 145/220.

X **Chez Maître Paul,** 12 r. Monsieur-le-Prince (6th) ℰ 43 54 74 59 – AE ⓓ E VISA — K 13
closed August, 24 December-2 January, Sunday and Monday – **M** a la carte 110/160 ₰.

X **Xavier-Grégoire,** 80 r. Cherche-Midi (6th) ℰ 45 44 72 72 – AE VISA — L 11
closed 2 to 24 August, Saturday lunch and Sunday – **st. : M** a la carte 155/215.

X **Moulin à Vent,** 20 r. Fossés-St-Bernard (5th) ℰ 43 54 99 37 – AE VISA — K 15
closed August and Sunday – **M** a la carte 150/225.

X **L'Agronome,** 35 quai Tournelle (5th) ℰ 43 25 44 42 — K 16
closed Saturday lunch and Sunday – **st. : M** a la carte 140/185.

X **Le Mange Tout,** 30 r. Lacépède (5th) ℰ 45 35 53 93 – ⓓ VISA — L 15
closed August, February Holidays, Monday lunch and Sunday – **st. : M** 80 b.i./160 b.i.

X **La Vigneraie,** 16 r. Dragon (6th) ℰ 45 48 57 04 – AE ⓓ E VISA — J 12
closed Sunday – **st. : M** a la carte 130/215.

Faubourg-St-Germain, Invalides, École Militaire.

7th arrondissement.
7th : ✉ 75007

Pont Royal and rest. Les Antiquaires, 7 r. Montalembert ℰ 45 44 38 27, Telex 270113 – |☰| kitchenette ▤ TV ☎ – 🏛 50. AE ⓓ E VISA — J 12
st. : M *(closed August and Sunday)* 190 b.i. – **75 rm** ☕ 920/1 300, 5 apartments.

Sofitel Bourbon Ⓜ, 32 r. St-Dominique ℰ 45 55 91 80, Telex 250019 – |☰| ▤ TV ☎ ♿ 🚗 – 🏛 50. AE ⓓ E VISA — H 10
st. : M see rest. **Le Dauphin** below – ☕ 75 – **112 rm** 1 050/1 300.

Cayré-Copatel Ⓜ without rest, 4 bd Raspail ℰ 45 44 38 88, Telex 270577 – |☰| TV ☎ – 🏛 40. AE ⓓ E VISA – **st. : 130 rm** ☕ 774/796. — J 12

St-Simon without rest, 14 r. St-Simon ℰ 45 48 35 66, « Antique furniture » – |☰| ☎. ✱
st. : ☕ 30 – **29 rm** 550/850, 5 apartments 1 000. — J 11

Université without rest, 22 r. Université ℰ 42 61 09 39 – |☰| ☎. ✱ — J 12
st. : ☕ 35 – **27 rm** 360/570.

Montalembert without rest, 3 r. Montalembert ✆ 45 48 68 11, Telex 200132 – |\$| ☎. E VISA
st. : **61 rm** ☐ 520/720. J 12

La Bourdonnais, 111 av. La Bourdonnais ✆ 47 05 45 42, Telex 201416 – |\$| TV ☎. ⊙ E VISA
st. : **M** see rest. **La Cantine des Gourmets** below – **60 rm** ☐ 300/420. J 9

Les Jardins d'Eiffel M without rest, 8 r. Amélie ✆ 47 05 46 21, Telex 206582 – |\$| TV ⊟wc ☎ 🚗. AE ⊙ E VISA
st. : **44 rm** ☐ 400/590, 4 apartments 1 100. H 9

Suède without rest, 31 r. Vaneau ✆ 47 05 00 08, Telex 200596 – |\$| ⊟wc ⋔wc ☎. AE. ✻ – st. : **40 rm** ☐ 393/593 K 11

De Varenne M ⊗ without rest, 44 r. Bourgogne ✆ 45 51 45 55 – |\$| TV ⊟wc ⋔wc ☎. AE – st. : ☐ 28 – **24 rm** 280/430 J 10

Résidence Elysées Maubourg M without rest, 35 bd Latour-Maubourg ✆ 45 56 10 78, Telex 206227 – |\$| TV ⊟wc ☎. AE ⊙ E VISA
st. : **30 rm** ☐ 430/600. H 10

Lenox without rest, 9 r. Université ✆ 42 96 10 95, Telex 260745 – |\$| TV ⊟wc ⋔wc ☎. AE ⊙ E VISA
st. : ☐ 25 – **32 rm** 302/430. J 12

Académie without rest, 32 r. des Sts-Pères ✆ 45 48 36 22, Telex 205650 – |\$| TV ⊟wc ⋔wc ☎. AE ⊙ E VISA
st. : ☐ 26 – **33 rm** 370/450. J 12

Beaugency M without rest, 21 r. Duvivier ✆ 47 05 01 63, Telex 201494 – |\$| TV ⊟wc ⋔wc ☎. AE ⊙ E VISA. ✻
st. : ☐ 20 – **30 rm** ☐ 350/410. J 9

St-Germain without rest, 88 r. Bac ✆ 45 48 62 92 – |\$| ⊟wc ⋔wc ☎. AE. ✻ J 11
st. : ☐ 24 – **29 rm** 240/480.

Bourgogne et Montana, 3 r. Bourgogne ✆ 45 51 20 22, Telex 270854 – |\$| ⊟wc ☎ ☎. AE E VISA H 11
M *(closed August, Saturday and Sunday)* a la carte 110/170 – **30 rm** ☐ 335/560, 5 apartments 800.

Verneuil-St-Germain without rest, 8 r. Verneuil ✆ 42 60 82 16, Telex 205650 – |\$| TV ⊟wc ⋔wc ☎. AE E VISA
st. : ☐ 26 – **26 rm** 370/440. J 12

Derby H. without rest, 5 av. Duquesne ✆ 47 05 12 05, Telex 206236 – |\$| ⊟wc ⋔wc ☎. AE ⊙ E VISA
st. : ☐ 30 – **44 rm** 440. J 9

Lindbergh without rest, 5 r. Chomel ✆ 45 48 35 53, Telex 201777 – |\$| TV ⊟wc ⋔wc ☎. AE ⊙ E VISA
st. : ☐ 25 – **26 rm** 310/390. K 12

Tourville M without rest, 16 av. Tourville ✆ 47 05 52 15, Telex 250786 – |\$| TV ⊟wc ⋔wc ☎. AE VISA
st. : ☐ 18 – **31 rm** 288. J 9

Londres without rest, 1 r. Augereau ✆ 45 51 63 02, Telex 206398 – |\$| TV ⊟wc ⋔wc ☎. AE ⊙ E VISA
st. : ☐ 25 – **30 rm** 390/490.

Solférino without rest, 91 r. Lille ✆ 47 05 85 54 – |\$| ⊟wc ⋔wc ☎. E VISA. ✻ H 11
closed 22 December-3 January – **st. :** ☐ 24 – **32 rm** 275/350.

Chomel without rest, 15 r. Chomel ✆ 45 48 55 52, Telex 206522 – ⊟wc ⋔wc. AE ⊙ E VISA. ✻
st. : ☐ 26 – **23 rm** 395/505. K 12

Bersoly's without rest, 28 r. Lille ✆ 42 60 73 79 – |\$| TV ⊟wc ⋔wc ☎. AE E VISA. ✻
st. : ☐ 26 – **16 rm** 400/510. J 13

Tour Eiffel M without rest, 17 r. Exposition ✆ 47 05 14 75 – |\$| TV ⊟wc ⋔wc ☎ ♿. AE E VISA – **st. :** ☐ 21 – **23 rm** 315/400. J 9

Mars H. without rest, 117 av. La Bourdonnais ✆ 47 05 42 30 – |\$| ⊟wc ⋔wc ☎. E VISA
st. : ☐ 19 – **24 rm** 110/260. J 9

Kensington without rest, 79 av. La Bourdonnais ✆ 47 05 74 00 – |\$| ⊟wc ⋔wc ☎. AE ⊙ E VISA
st. : ☐ 19 – **26 rm** 210/320. J 9

Turenne without rest, 20 av. Tourville ✆ 47 05 99 92, Telex 203407 – |\$| ⊟wc ⋔wc ☎. AE VISA – **st. :** ☐ 23 – **34 rm** 179/374. J 9

Résidence d'Orsay without rest, 93 r. Lille ✆ 47 05 05 27 – |\$| ⊟wc ⋔wc ☎. VISA. ✻
closed August – **st. :** ☐ 23 – **31 rm** 150/320. H 11

Champ de Mars without rest, 7 r. Champ de Mars ✆ 45 51 52 30 – |\$| ⊟wc ⋔wc ☎. VISA
closed 10 to 30 August – **st. :** ☐ 22 – **25 rm** 260/300. J 9

L'Empereur without rest, 2 r. Chevert ✆ 45 55 88 02 – |\$| TV ⊟wc ⋔wc ☎ J 9
☐ 20 – **34 rm** 280/325.

XXXX ✿ **Jules Verne,** Eiffel Tower : 2nd platform, lift in south leg ℘ 45 55 61 44, Telex 205789, < Paris – ▤ P. AE ⓓ E VISA. ✗ J 7
M 180 (lunch) and a la carte 235/375
Spec. Fricassée de langoustines aux poivres et au gingembre, Grouse d'Ecosse rôtie aux choux verts (October-February), Grand dessert "Jules Verne".

XXXX ✿✿ **Le Divellec,** 107 r. Université ℘ 45 51 91 96 – ▤. AE ⓓ E VISA. ✗ H 10
closed August, Sunday and Monday – **M** a la carte 250/405
Spec. Langoustines marinées et foie gras poêlé, Saumon et bar au basilic, Rouget poêlé en laitue.

XXX ✿ **L'Arpège** (Passard), 84 r. Varenne ℘ 45 51 20 02 – ▤. AE ⓓ VISA J 10
closed 1 to 15 August, Saturday lunch and Sunday – **st.** : **M** a la carte 155/275
Spec. Chou braisé au foie gras, Haricot de pigeonneau, Ravioli cacao.

XXX ✿ **Le Dauphin** (Sofitel Bourbon), 32 r. St-Dominique ℘ 45 55 91 80 – ▤. AE ⓓ E VISA
st. : **M** a la carte 250/365 H 10
Spec. Crème d'asperges aux crustacés, Bar poêlé, Panaché de pied de porc et tête de veau.

XXX ✿ **Chez les Anges,** 54 bd Latour-Maubourg ℘ 47 05 89 86 – ▤. AE ⓓ E VISA J 9
closed Sunday dinner – **M** a la carte 230/365
Spec. Oeufs en meurette, Turbot "Albert Benoist", Foie de veau rosé.

XXX ✿ **La Flamberge** (Albistur), 12 av. Rapp ℘ 47 05 91 37 – ▤. AE ⓓ E VISA H 8
closed 1 to 24 August, Saturday lunch and Sunday – **st.** : **M** a la carte 220/300
Spec. Salade d'artichauts aux rougets tièdes, Gibier (season), Tarte chaude aux fruits.

XXX ✿ **La Cantine des Gourmets,** 113 av. La Bourdonnais ℘ 47 05 47 96 – ▤. AE ⓓ VISA
closed Sunday – **st.** : **M** 200 b.i. (lunch) and a la carte 220/330 J 9
Spec. Biscuit de sardines et olives, Consommé de rougets à la moelle, Arlequin aux deux chocolats.

XXX **La Bourgogne,** 6 av. Bosquet ℘ 47 05 96 78 – AE ⓓ E VISA H 9
closed Saturday lunch and Sunday – **M** a la carte 170/280.

XXX ✿ **La Boule d'Or,** 13 bd Latour-Maubourg ℘ 47 05 50 18 – AE ⓓ VISA H 10
closed August, Saturday lunch and Monday – **M** a la carte 195/260
Spec. Foie gras frais de canard, Millefeuille de sole et langoustines, Soufflé au citron.

XXX **Beato,** 8 r. Malar ℘ 47 05 94 27, Italian cuisine – ▤. AE VISA. ✗ H 9
closed August and Christmas-1 January – **st.** : **M** 200 b.i./300 b.i.

XX **Chez Françoise,** Aérogare des Invalides ℘ 47 05 49 03 – P. AE ⓓ VISA H 10
closed August, Sunday dinner and Monday – **M** 170 b.i./95.

XX ✿ **Récamier** (Cantegrit), 4 r. Récamier ℘ 45 48 86 58, ☂ – ▤. ⓓ E VISA K 12
closed 25 December-1 January and Sunday – **M** a la carte 205/320
Spec. Oeufs en meurette, Mousse de brochet, Boeuf bourguignon.

XX ✿ **Ferme St-Simon** (Vandenhende), 6 r. St-Simon ℘ 45 48 35 74 – VISA J 11
closed 1 to 25 August, Saturday lunch and Sunday – **M** 150 b.i (lunch) and a la carte 175/240
Spec. Feuillantine de lièvre au foie gras (October-December), Marinière de barbue au Sauternes, Desserts.

XX ✿ **Labrousse,** 4 r. Pierre-Leroux ℘ 43 06 99 39 – ▤. AE VISA K 11
closed 25 July-18 August, Saturday lunch and Sunday – **M** 180/310
Spec. Oeufs en meurette, Croustade de rougets au beurre de basilic, Ris de veau braisés aux morilles.

XX **Le Florence,** 22 r. Champ-de-Mars ℘ 45 51 52 69, Italian cuisine – AE VISA. ✗ J 9
closed July – **M** a la carte 170/230.

XX ✿ **Bistrot de Paris,** 33 r. Lille ℘ 42 61 16 83, bistro style – VISA J 12
closed Saturday lunch and Sunday – **M** a la carte 180/235
Spec. Daube de pied de porc aux ravioli (season), St-Jacques au chou croquant (season), Tournedos de canard et de volaille.

XX **Le Galant Verre,** 12 r. Verneuil ℘ 42 60 84 56 – AE ⓓ E VISA J 12
closed Saturday lunch and Sunday – **M** 200 b.i./250 b.i.

XX **Les Glénan,** 54 r. Bourgogne ℘ 45 51 61 09, seafood – AE ⓓ E VISA J/10
closed 3 to 30 August and Sunday – **st.** : **M** a la carte 150/245.

XX **Vert Bocage,** 96 bd Latour-Maubourg ℘ 45 51 48 54 – ▤. AE ⓓ VISA J 9
closed Saturday and Sunday – **M** a la carte 180/270.

XX **Bellecour,** 22 r. Surcouf ℘ 45 51 46 93 – AE ⓓ E VISA H 9
closed 10 August-1 September, Saturday (except dinner from 1 October to 30 June) and Sunday – **M** 200/280.

XX **Aux Délices de Szechuen,** 40 av. Duquesne ℘ 43 06 22 55, Chinese cuisine – ▤. AE E VISA K 10
closed 1 to 21 August and Monday – **st.** : **M** a la carte 115/175 ♨.

XX **Chez Ribe,** 15 av. Suffren ℘ 45 66 53 79 – AE ⓓ E VISA J 7
closed August, Sunday and Monday – **M** 130 b.i.

XX ✿ **Gildo** (Bellini), 153 r. Grenelle ℘ 45 51 54 12, Italian cuisine J 9
closed 14 July-1 September, Christmas Holidays, Sunday and Monday – **M** a la carte 135/190
Spec. Tagliarini aux champignons sauvages (July-January), Filets de rouget, Escalope Gildo.

XX **Le Champ de Mars,** 17 av. Motte-Picquet ℘ 47 05 57 99 – AE ⓓ VISA J 9
closed 14 July-15 August, Tuesday dinner and Monday – **M** a la carte 110/160.

X ✪ **Tan Dinh,** 60 r. Verneuil ☎ 45 44 04 84, Vietnamese cuisine J 12
closed 1 to 15 August and Sunday – **M** a la carte 130/180
Spec. Rouleaux de crevettes Asam, Beignets de langoustines au vinaigre de Shin Kiang, Bouchées de veau à la citronelle.

X **La Calèche,** 8 r. Lille ☎ 42 60 24 76 – AE ⓓ E VISA J 12
closed 8 to 31 August, 25 December-1 January, Saturday and Sunday – **st. : M** 100 b.i./130 b.i.

X **Pantagruel,** 20 r. Exposition ☎ 45 51 79 96 – AE ⓓ E VISA. ✂ J 9
closed August and Sunday – **st. : M** a la carte 150/260.

X **Aub. Champ de Mars,** 18 r. Exposition ☎ 45 51 78 08 – AE ⓓ VISA J 9
closed August, Saturday lunch and Sunday – **st. : M** 101.

X **Nuits de St-Jean,** 29 r. Surcouf ☎ 45 51 61 49 – AE ⓓ E VISA. ✂ H/9
closed Sunday dinner and Saturday – **M** a la carte 120/170.

X **Vin sur Vin,** 20 r. Monttessuy ☎ 47 05 14 20 H 8
closed 9 August-1 September, 23 December-4 January, Saturday lunch and Sunday – **M** a la carte 150/210.

Champs-Élysées, St-Lazare, Madeleine.

8th arrondissement.

8th : ✉ 75008

Plaza-Athénée, 25 av. Montaigne ☎ 47 23 78 33, Telex 650092 – |♦| ▤ TV ☎ – 🏛 30-100. AE ⓓ E VISA G 9
M see rest. **Régence and Relais Plaza** below – ☕ 80 – **218 rm** 1 800/2 100, 44 apartments.

Bristol, 112 fg St-Honoré ☎ 42 66 91 45, Telex 280961, 🏊, 🌳 – |♦| ▤ TV ☎ 🚗 – 🏛 40-150. AE ⓓ E VISA. ✂ F 10
st. : M see rest. **Bristol** below – ☕ 88 – **145 rm** 1 425/2 490, 45 apartments.

Crillon, 10 pl. Concorde ☎ 42 65 24 24, Telex 290204, 🍴 – |♦| ▤ TV ☎ – 🏛 30-60. AE ⓓ E VISA. ✂ rest G 11
st. : M see rest **Les Ambassadeurs** below - **L'Obelisque** *(closed August and Sunday)* **M** a la carte 135/225 – ☕ 85 – **146 rm** 1 460/2 100, 41 apartments.

Résidence Maxim's, 42 av. Gabriel ☎ 45 61 96 33, Telex 642794, 🍴 – |♦| ▤ TV ☎ Ⓟ – 🏛 60. AE ⓓ VISA. ✂ rest G 11
st. : M a la carte 225/375 – ☕ 90 – **4 rm** 2 000, 39 apartments.

George V, 31 av. George-V ☎ 47 23 54 00, Telex 650082, 🍴 – |♦| ▤ TV ☎ – 🏛 500. AE ⓓ E VISA G 8
st. : M see rest. **Les Princes** below – ☕ 85 – **288 rm** 1 575/2 100, 63 apartments.

Prince de Galles, 33 av. George-V ☎ 47 23 55 11, Telex 280627, 🍴 – |♦| ▤ TV ☎ – 🏛 40-200. AE ⓓ E VISA. ✂ rest G 8
st. : M 195/350 – ☕ 90 – **140 rm** 1 500/1 950, 30 apartments.

Royal Monceau, 37 av. Hoche ☎ 45 61 98 00, Telex 650361, 🍴, 🏊 – |♦| ▤ TV ☎ – 🏛 500. AE ⓓ E VISA. ✂ E 8
st. : Le Jardin M a la carte 290/420 - **Le Carpaccio** *(closed August)* **M** a la carte 260/380 – ☕ 100 – **180 rm** 1 542/2 372, 40 apartments.

Balzac and rest Le Sallambier Ⓜ, 6 r. Balzac ☎ 45 61 97 22, Telex 290298 – |♦| ▤ rest TV ☎ Ⓟ. AE ⓓ E VISA. ✂ rest F 8
M *(closed August, Saturday and Sunday)* 195 – ☕ 60 – **56 rm** 1 000/1 400, 14 apartments.

La Trémoille, 14 r. La Trémoille ☎ 47 23 34 20, Telex 640344 – |♦| ▤ rest TV ☎. AE ⓓ E VISA G 9
M a la carte 145/205 – ☕ 55 – **97 rm** 1 070/1 800, 14 apartments 1 800/1 920.

Warwick Ⓜ, 5 r. Berri ☎ 45 63 14 11, Telex 642295 – |♦| ▤ TV ☎ – 🏛 25-150. AE ⓓ E VISA F 9
st. : M see rest. **La Couronne** below – ☕ 85 – **144 rm** 1 390/1 950, 4 apartments.

Pullman Windsor Ⓜ, 14 r. Beaujon ☎ 45 63 04 04, Telex 650902 – |♦| ▤ rest TV ☎ – 🏛 25-120. AE ⓓ E VISA F 8
st. : M see rest. **Le Clovis** below – ☕ 58 – **135 rm** 955/1 300.

San Regis Ⓜ, 12 r. J. Goujon ☎ 43 59 41 90, Telex 643637, « Tasteful decor » – |♦| ▤ rm TV ☎. AE ⓓ VISA. ✂ G 9
st. : M (residents only) a la carte 160/235 – ☕ 65 – **44 rm** 950/1 800, 10 apartments.

Lancaster, 7 r. Berri ☎ 43 59 90 43, Telex 640991, 🍴 – |♦| ▤ rm TV ☎. AE ⓓ E VISA. ✂ rest F 9
M *(closed Saturday and Sunday)* a la carte 165/370 – ☕ 85 – **47 rm** 1 300/1 800, 10 apartments.

Claridge Bellman M, 37 r. François 1er 47 23 54 42, Telex 641150 – rest . AE VISA. G 9
st. : **M** *(closed August, 25 December-2 January, Saturday and Sunday)* a la carte 180/270 – 54 – **42 rm** 695/995.

Château Frontenac, 54 r. P.-Charron 47 23 55 85, Telex 660994 – – 30. AE E VISA. G 9
st. : **Ludmila Pavillon Russe** *(closed 15 July-31 August, Sunday and Bank Holidays)* **M** 160 b.i. (lunch) and a la carte 185/335 – 52 – **99 rm** 660/990, 4 apartments 1 190.

Napoléon, 40 av. Friedland 47 66 02 02, Telex 640609 – kitchenette – 100. AE E VISA F 8
st. : **M** see rest. **Napoléon Baumann** below – 40 – **108 rm** 840/1 150, 32 apartments.

Bedford, 17 r. Arcade 42 66 22 32, Telex 290506 – rest – 80. E VISA. rest F 11
st. : **M** *(closed August, Saturday and Sunday)* (lunch only) a la carte 125/195 – **137 rm** 500/680, 10 apartments 1 000/1 300.

California without rest, 16 r. Berri 43 59 93 00, Telex 660634 – – 35-70. AE E VISA F 9
st. : 42 – **184 rm** 860/1 230, 3 apartments 1 800/2 500.

Concorde-St-Lazare, 108 r. St-Lazare 42 94 22 22, Telex 650442 – rest – 100. AE E VISA E 12
st. : **Café Terminus M** 130/280 – 55 – **324 rm** 730/1 500.

Queen Elizabeth, 41 av. Pierre-1er-de-Serbie 47 20 80 56, Telex 641179 – – 25. AE E VISA G 8
st. : **M** *(closed August, Sunday and dinner Monday to Friday)* 100 b.i./155 b.i. – 70 – **50 rm** 850/1 500, 17 apartments 1 600/2 000.

Etap St-Honoré M without rest, 15 r. Boissy d'Anglas 42 66 93 62, Telex 240366 – . AE E VISA G 11
st. : 45 – **104 rm** 485/650, 8 apartments 865.

Royal Malesherbes M, 24 bd Malesherbes 42 65 53 30, Telex 660190 – – 30. AE E VISA F 11
st. : **M** a la carte 120/210 – **102 rm** 720/800.

Royal-Madeleine M without rest, 29 r. Arcade 42 66 13 81, Telex 641458 – . AE E VISA. F 11
49 – **70 rm** 710/915.

Castiglione, 40 r. Fg-St-Honoré 42 65 07 50, Telex 240362 – . AE E VISA
M 120 b.i. (lunch) and a la carte 165/280 – **96 rm** 1 220/1 285, 16 apartments 1 530/2 033. G 11

L'Horset Astor, 11 r. Astorg 42 66 56 56, Telex 642718 – . AE E VISA F 11
st. : **M** *(closed Saturday and Sunday)* a la carte 170/270 – **128 rm** 750/830.

Résidence Champs-Elysées M without rest, 92 r. La Boëtie 43 59 96 15, Telex 650695 – . AE E VISA F 9
st. : 42 – **84 rm** 676/930.

Elysées-Marignan, 12 r. Marignan 43 59 58 61, Telex 660018 – – 100-130. AE E VISA G 9
st. : **M** *(closed Saturday, Sunday and Bank Holidays)* 130 – 50 – **57 rm** 650/1 180, 22 apartments 1 500/1 700.

Résidence St-Honoré without rest, 214 r. Fg St-Honoré 42 25 26 27, Telex 640524 – . AE E VISA
st. : **91 rm** 586/681.

Printemps and rest Chez Martin, 1 r. Isly 42 94 12 12, Telex 290744 – – 25. E VISA F 12
st. : **M** *(closed Sunday)* 92 b.i./55 – **67 rm** 330/760.

Roblin and rest Le Mazagran, 6 r. Chauveau-Lagarde 42 65 57 00, Telex 640154 – . AE E VISA F 11
M *(closed August, Saturday and Sunday)* a la carte 150/220 - **Grill** *(closed August, Saturday and Sunday)* **M** a la carte approx. 100/170 – **70 rm** 488/620.

Vernet, 25 r. Vernet 47 23 43 10, Telex 290347 – . AE E VISA F 8
st. : **M** *(closed Saturday and Sunday)* 180 – **63 rm** 745/1 110.

Royal H. without rest, 33 av. Friedland 43 59 08 14, Telex 280965 – . AE E VISA F 8
st. : 38 – **57 rm** 672/900.

Concortel without rest, 19 r. Pasquier 42 65 45 44, Telex 660228 – . AE
st. : 30 – **38 rm** 360/440, 8 apartments 540. F 11

Powers without rest, 52 r. François-1er 47 23 91 05, Telex 642051 – . AE VISA. G 9
st. : 30 – **53 rm** 450/610.

Alison M without rest, 21 r. Surène 42 65 54 00, Telex 640435 – wc wc . AE E VISA. F 11
st. : 30 – **35 rm** 280/480.

L'Arcade without rest, 7 r. Arcade ℘ 42 65 43 85 – wc ☎ F 11
st. : **47 rm** 320/430.

Bradford without rest, 10 r. St-Philippe-du-Roule ℘ 43 59 24 20, Telex 648530 – wc wc ☎. F 9
st. : **48 rm** 380/490.

Colisée M without rest, 6 r. Colisée ℘ 43 59 95 25, Telex 643101 – wc ☎. AE E VISA F 9
st. : **44 rm** 430/590.

St Augustin without rest, 9 r. Roy ℘ 42 93 32 17, Telex 641919 – wc wc ☎. AE E VISA F 11
st. : 25 – **62 rm** 524/631.

Plaza Haussmann M without rest, 177 bd Haussmann ℘ 45 63 93 83, Telex 673716 – wc ☎. AE E VISA F 9
st. : **41 rm** 515/620.

Elysées Ponthieu M without rest, 24 r. Ponthieu ℘ 42 25 68 70, Telex 640053 – wc wc ☎. AE E VISA F 9
st. : 25 – **60 rm** 450/610.

Angleterre-Champs-Élysées M without rest, 91 r. La Boétie ℘ 43 59 35 45, Telex 640317 – wc wc ☎. AE VISA F 9
st. : 25 – **40 rm** 295/400.

Royal Alma without rest, 35 r. Jean-Goujon ℘ 42 25 83 30, Telex 641428 – wc wc ☎. AE E VISA. G 9
st. : 35 – **82 rm** 798/920.

Astoria M without rest, 42 r. Moscou ℘ 42 93 63 53, Telex 210408 – wc wc. AE E VISA D 11
st. : 25 – **82 rm** 550.

Résidence St-Philippe without rest, 123 r. Fg-St-Honoré ℘ 43 59 86 99 – wc wc ☎. F 9-10
st. : **38 rm** 350/550.

Franklin Roosevelt without rest, 18 r. Clément-Marot ℘ 47 23 61 66, Telex 614797 – wc wc ☎. AE VISA. G 9
st. : **45 rm** 520/550.

Rond-Point des Champs-Elysées without rest, 10 r. Ponthieu ℘ 43 59 55 58, Telex 642386 – wc wc ☎. AE E VISA. F 10
st. : **45 rm** 335/450.

West End without rest, 7 r. Clément-Marot ℘ 47 20 30 78, Telex 611972 – wc ☎. AE E VISA G 9
st. : 40 – **60 rm** 550/900.

Rochambeau without rest, 4 r. La Boétie ℘ 42 65 27 54, Telex 640030 – wc wc ☎. AE E VISA
st. : **50 rm** 580/620.

Brescia M without rest, 16 r. Edimbourg ℘ 45 22 14 31, Telex 660714 – wc wc ☎ ♿. AE E VISA E 11
st. : 22 – **38 rm** 210/300.

Washington without rest, 43 r. Washington ℘ 45 63 33 36 – wc wc ☎. VISA. F 9
23 – **18 rm** 220/380.

Atlantic without rest, 44 r. Londres ℘ 43 87 45 40, Telex 650477 – wc wc ☎. AE VISA. E 12
st. : 27 – **93 rm** 250/390.

Queen Mary without rest, 9 r. Greffulhe ℘ 42 66 40 50, Telex 640419 – wc wc ☎. VISA. F 12
st. : 33 – **36 rm** 340/495.

Lido without rest, 4 passage Madeleine ℘ 42 66 27 37, Telex 281039 – wc wc ☎. AE E VISA F 11
st. : 25 – **32 rm** 465/580.

Lord Byron without rest, 5 r. Chateaubriand ℘ 43 59 89 98, Telex 649662, – wc wc ☎. F 9
st. : 26 – **30 rm** 355/630.

Opal without rest, 19 r. Tronchet ℘ 42 65 77 97, Telex 217152 – wc ☎. AE VISA. F 12
st. : 30 – **36 rm** 360/500.

Élysées without rest, 100 r. La Boétie ℘ 43 59 23 46 – wc wc ☎. AE E VISA F 9
st. : **30 rm** 366/403.

Ministère without rest, 31 r. Surène ℘ 42 66 21 43 – wc wc ☎ F 11
st. : **32 rm** 185/400.

Lavoisier-Malesherbes without rest, 21 r. Lavoisier ℘ 42 65 10 97 – wc wc ☎. F 11
st. : **32 rm** 280/340.

XXXXX ✿✿✿ **Lucas-Carton** (Senderens), 9 pl. Madeleine ✆ 42 65 22 90, **« Fine 1900's decor »** – VISA. ✻ G 11
closed 1 to 25 August, 23 December-4 January, Saturday and Sunday – **M** a la carte 395/515
Spec. Ravioli de pétoncles aux courgettes, Millefeuille de foie gras de Canard, Emincé de veau et sa chartreuse de poivrons rouges.

XXXXX ✿✿ **Bristol,** 112 r. Fg St-Honoré ✆ 42 66 91 45 – Ⓟ. AE ⓓ E VISA. ✻ F 10
st. : **M** a la carte 360/470
Spec. Salade landaise au Mesclum, Escalope de turbot au Sauternes, Filets de sole aux morilles.

XXXXX ✿✿ **Lasserre,** 17 av. Franklin-D.-Roosevelt ✆ 43 59 53 43, **Roof open in fine weather** – ▤. ✻ G 10
closed 2 to 31 August, Monday lunch and Sunday – **M** a la carte 330/460
Spec. Blanc de sandre à la nage d'étrilles, Emincé de volaille de Bresse en papillote, Parfait aux noisettes grillées.

XXXXX ✿✿✿ **Taillevent,** 15 r. Lamennais ✆ 45 61 12 90 – ▤. ✻ F 9
closed 25 July-24 August, February Holidays, Saturday, Sunday and Bank Holidays – **M** (booking essential) a la carte 300/400
Spec. Millefeuille de homard aux pointes d'asperges, Noisettes d'agneau en chevreuil, Turban glacé à la liqueur de mandarine.

XXXXX ✿✿ **Les Ambassadeurs** (Crillon), 10 pl. Concorde ✆ 42 65 24 24, ⛱, **« 18C decor »** – AE ⓓ E VISA. ✻ G 11
st. : **M** 320 (lunch) and a la carte 320/530
Spec. Pigeonneau en terrine, Poêlée de St-Jacques (October-April), Crêpe aux griottes.

XXXXX ✿ **Ledoyen,** carré Champs-Élysées ✆ 42 66 54 77 – Ⓟ. AE E VISA G 10
closed August and Sunday – **M** a la carte 335/420
Spec. Terrine de homard océane, Blanc de turbot à l'oseille, Mignon de veau poêlé au citron.

XXXXX ✿ **Laurent,** 41 av. Gabriel ✆ 42 25 00 39 – AE ⓓ. ✻ G 11
closed Saturday lunch, Sunday and Bank Holidays – **M** a la carte 340/530
Spec. Langouste tiède en salade, Canard aux deux cuissons, Deux soufflés Laurent.

XXXXX ✿ **Régence,** 25 av. Montaigne ✆ 47 23 78 33, ⛱ – AE ⓓ E VISA. ✻ G 9
M a la carte 325/435
Spec. Langoustines et St-Jacques en salade, St-Pierre et ravioles Régence, Canette de Challans aux deux poivres.

XXXXX ✿✿ **Pavillon Elysée** (Lenôtre), 10 av. Champs-Elysées (1st floor) ✆ 42 65 85 10 – Ⓟ. AE ⓓ VISA G 10
closed August, Saturday lunch, Sunday and Bank Holidays – **M** a la carte 300/430 and see **Les Jardins Lenôtre** (ground floor) below
Spec. Soufflé au corail d'oursins (October-April), Croquet d'agneau, Canard rouennais Madeleine Brument.

XXXX ✿ **Les Princes,** 31 av. Georges-V ✆ 47 23 54 00, ⛱ – ▤. AE ⓓ E VISA. ✻ G 8
closed Saturday, Sunday and Bank Holidays – **M** a la carte 280/390
Spec. Poularde de Bresse en terrine, Blanc de turbot à la mousseline de langoustines, Tarte au sucre roux et rhubarbe.

XXXX ✿ **Lamazère,** 23 r. Ponthieu ✆ 43 59 66 66 – ▤. AE ⓓ E VISA. ✻ F 9
closed August and Sunday – **M** a la carte 245/390
Spec. Truffe Lamazère, Foie gras de canard au sabayon de truffes, Cassoulet aux trois confits.

XXXX ✿ **Chiberta,** 3 r. Arsène-Houssaye ✆ 45 63 77 90 – ▤. AE ⓓ E VISA F 8
closed 1 to 25 August, 25 December-1 January, Saturday, Sunday and Bank Holidays – **M** a la carte 285/400
Spec. Fricassée de champignons des bois (September-December), Langoustines tièdes à la vinaigrette de poivron, Foie gras de canard.

XXXX ✿✿ **La Marée,** 1 r. Daru ✆ 47 63 52 42 – ▤. AE ⓓ. ✻ E 8
closed August, Saturday and Sunday – **M** a la carte 255/390
Spec. Belons au champagne, Loup au gingembre.

XXXX ✿ **Fouquet's Élysées,** 99 av. Champs-Élysées (1st floor) ✆ **47 23 70 60, Telex 648227** – AE ⓓ E VISA F 8
closed 15 July-31 August, Saturday and Sunday – **M** a la carte 220/320
Spec. Aiguillettes de canard au citron vert, Filets de sole et turbot à l'Antiboise, Flan d'aubergines au coulis de tomates.

XXX ✿ **La Couronne,** 5 r. Berri ✆ 45 63 14 11 – AE ⓓ E VISA F 9
closed August, Sunday and Bank Holidays – **st.** : **M** 195/280
Spec. Salade de la Couronne, Rôti de lotte au safran, Pot au feu maigre d'agneau.

XXX ✿ **Les Jardins Lenôtre,** 10 av. Champs Élysées (ground-floor) ✆ 42 65 85 10 – Ⓟ. AE ⓓ VISA G 10
M 200
Spec. St-Jacques en coque lutée, Turbotin aux oignons et lard confit, Joue de boeuf braisée.

XXX **Alain Rayé,** 49 r. Colysée ✆ 42 25 66 76 – ⓓ E VISA F 10
closed Saturday lunch and Sunday – **M** a la carte 265/350.

XXX ✿ **Copenhague,** 142 av. Champs-Élysées (1st floor) ✆ 43 59 20 41, ⛱ – ▤. AE ⓓ E VISA. ✻ F 8
closed 2 to 30 August, 1 to 8 January, Sunday and Bank Holidays – **M** a la carte 210/300
Spec. Saumon mariné à l'aneth, Canard salé à la danoise, Mignon de renne au vinaigre de pin.

XXX ✿ **Le Clovis,** 4 r. B.-Albrecht ✆ 45 61 15 32 – AE ⓓ E VISA F 8
closed August, 24 December-2 January, Saturday and Sunday – **st. : M** a la carte 260/380
Spec. Tartare de daurade rose et saumon mariné, Filets de sole au curry, Filet d'agneau et son ragoût de légumes verts.

XXX **Napoléon Baumann,** 38 av. Friedland ✆ 42 27 99 50 – ▤. AE ⓓ E VISA F 8
st. : M 188/290 ₰.

XXX **Le Marcande,** 52 r. Miromesnil ✆ 42 65 19 14 – AE ⓓ VISA F 10
closed 1 to 25 August, Saturday and Sunday – **M** 250/350.

XXX **Chez Vong,** 27 r. Colisée ✆ 43 59 77 12, Chinese and Vietnamese cuisine – AE ⓓ E VISA F 10
closed Sunday – **M** a la carte 140/200.

XXX **Al Amir,** 66 r. François 1er ✆ 47 23 79 05, Lebanese cuisine – AE ⓓ E VISA. ✂ F 8
st. : M 180 b.i./230 b.i.

XXX **Relais-Plaza,** 21 av. Montaigne ✆ 47 23 46 36 – ▤. AE ⓓ E VISA. ✂ G 9
closed August – **M** a la carte 240/315 ₰.

XXX **Indra,** 10 r. Cdt-Rivière ✆ 43 59 46 40, Indian cuisine – AE ⓓ E VISA F 9
closed Saturday lunch and Sunday – **st. : M** a la carte 150/220.

XXX **Au Vieux Berlin,** 32 av. George-V ✆ 47 20 88 96, German cuisine – ▤. AE ⓓ E VISA
closed Sunday – **M** a la carte 180/270. G 8

XX **Baumann Marbeuf,** 15 r. Marbeuf ✆ 47 20 11 11 – AE ⓓ E VISA G 9
st. : M a la carte 130/215 ₰.

XX **Fermette Marbeuf,** 5 r. Marbeuf ✆ 47 20 63 53, « 1900's decor with genuine ceramics and leaded glass windows » – AE ⓓ VISA G 9
M a la carte 125/210 ₰.

XX **Chez Tante Louise,** 41 r. Boissy d'Anglas ✆ 42 65 06 85 – ▤. AE ⓓ E VISA F 11
closed August, Saturday and Sunday – **st. : M** a la carte 200/290.

XX **Le Boeuf sur le toit,** 34 r. Colisée ✆ 43 53 83 80 – ▤. AE ⓓ VISA
M a la carte 135/210.

XX **Le Petit Montmorency,** 5 r. Rabelais ✆ 42 25 11 19 – ▤. E VISA. ✂ F 10
closed August, Saturday from 1 April-31 July and Sunday – **st. : M** a la carte 220/350.

XX **Ruc,** 2 r. Pépinière ✆ 45 22 66 70 – ▤. AE ⓓ E VISA F 11
M (1st floor) 190 b.i.

XX **Le Drugstorien** (1st floor), 1 av. Matignon ✆ 43 59 38 70 – ▤. AE ⓓ E VISA
M a la carte 160/200.

XX **Marius et Janette,** 4 av. George V ✆ 47 23 41 88 – AE E VISA F 8
closed Saturday and Sunday – **M** a la carte 250/400.

XX **Le Grenadin,** 46 r. Naples ✆ 45 63 28 92 – AE E VISA E 11
closed 10 to 31 August, 24 December-4 January, Saturday and Sunday – **M** a la carte 200/270.

XX **Chez Bosc,** 7 r. Richepanse ✆ 42 60 10 27 – VISA G 12
closed August, Saturday and Sunday – **M** a la carte 160/240.

XX **Chez Modeste,** 8 r. Miromesnil ✆ 42 65 20 39 – ▤. AE VISA F 10
closed Saturday and Sunday – **M** a la carte 180/270.

XX **Artois,** 13 r. Artois ✆ 42 25 01 10 F 9
closed 14 July-5 September, Saturday, Sunday and Bank Holidays – **M** (booking essential) a la carte 130/190.

XX **St Germain,** 74 av. Champs-Elysées ✆ 45 63 55 45 – AE ⓓ E VISA G 9
closed Saturday, Sunday and Bank Holidays – **M** 160 b.i./240 b.i.

XX **Tong Yen,** 1 bis r. Jean-Mermoz ✆ 42 25 04 23, Chinese and Vietnamese cuisine – ▤. AE ⓓ E VISA F 10
closed 1 to 22 August – **M** a la carte 160/230.

XX **Le Bonaventure,** 35 r. J. Goujon ✆ 42 25 02 58, ⛱, 🍽 – AE VISA. ✂ G 9
closed Saturday lunch and Sunday – **M** a la carte 140/210.

XX **Androuët,** 41 r. Amsterdam ✆ 48 74 26 90 – AE ⓓ E VISA E 12
closed Sunday and Bank Holidays – **M** a la carte 128/200.

XX **Le Sarladais,** 2 r. Vienne ✆ 45 22 23 62 – ▤. E VISA E 11
closed August, Saturday lunch, Sunday and Bank Holidays – **M** a la carte 120/195.

XX **Chez Max,** 19 r. Castellane ✆ 42 65 33 81 – VISA F 11
closed 31 July-2 September, 24 December-2 January, Thursday dinner, Saturday, Sunday and Bank Holidays – **M** a la carte 175/275.

XX **l'Addition,** 10 r. La Trémoille ✆ 47 23 53 53 – AE ⓓ E VISA G 9
closed Saturday lunch and Sunday – **M** a la carte 165/215.

XX **Le Manoir Normand,** 77 bd Courcelles ✆ 42 27 38 97 – AE ⓓ VISA E 8
closed Sunday – **M** 100 b.i./250 b.i.

XX **Rose des Sables,** 19 r. Washington ✆ 45 63 36 73, Moroccan cuisine – VISA F 9
closed Saturday lunch and Sunday – **M** a la carte 120/200.

XX **Annapurna,** 32 r. Berri ✆ 45 63 91 56, Indian cuisine – AE ⓓ VISA F 9
closed Saturday lunch and Sunday – **M** a la carte 145/190.

X **Olsson's,** 62 r. P. Charron ✆ 45 61 49 11, Scandinavian cuisine – VISA
M a la carte 145/210.

X **Stresa,** 7 r. Chambiges ✆ 47 23 51 62, Italian cuisine – AE ⓓ G 9
closed 10 to 25 August, 20 December-5 January, Saturday dinner and Sunday – **M** a la carte 165/215.

X **Martin Alma,** 44 r. J. Goujon ✆ 43 59 28 25, North African cuisine – VISA
closed 29 July-30 August, Sunday dinner and Monday – **M** a la carte 115/160.

X **Le Capricorne,** 81 r. Rocher ✆ 45 22 64 99 – VISA E 10-11
closed 18 to 26 April, August, Saturday, Sunday and Bank Holidays – **M** a la carte 100/155 🌡.

X **Al Dente,** 182 bd Haussmann ✆ 45 62 88 68, Italian cuisine – VISA F 8
closed 8 to 16 August and Sunday – **M** a la carte 125/190.

X **La Petite Auberge,** 48 r. Moscou ✆ 43 87 91 84 – E VISA D 11
closed Saturday (except dinner from 1 September-31 November and 1 March-31 July) and Sunday – **M** 84 (lunch) and a la carte 125/200.

Opéra, Gare du Nord,
Gare de l'Est,
Grands Boulevards.

9th et 10th arrondissements.
9th : ✉ 75009
10th : ✉ 75010

Le Gd Hôtel, 2 r. Scribe (9th) ✆ 42 68 12 13, Telex 220875 – lift ▤ rm TV ☎ – 🏢 25-500. AE ⓓ E VISA. ❄ rest F 12
st. : rest. **Le Patio** *(closed August)* **M** (lunch only) 230 b.i. and see rest. **Opéra - Café de la Paix** and **Relais Capucines - Café de la paix** below – ☕ 80 – **300 rm** 1 260/1 740, 20 apartments.

Scribe Ⓜ, 1 r. Scribe (9th) ✆ 47 42 03 40, Telex 214653 – lift ▤ TV ☎ ♿ – 🏢 150. AE ⓓ E VISA. ❄ rest F 12
st. : **Les Muses** *(closed August, Saturday, Sunday and Bank Holidays)* **M** 160 - **Le Jardin des Muses** (snack) **M** 75/160 🌡 – ☕ 80 – **217 rm** 1 150/2 000, 11 apartments.

Ambassador, 16 bd Haussmann (9th) ✆ 42 46 92 63, Telex 650912 – lift TV ☎ ♿ – 🏢 30. AE ⓓ E VISA. ❄ rm F 13
st. : **M** *(closed 7 to 27 December)* a la carte 140/275 – **300 rm** ☕ 1 005/1 610, 6 apartments.

Commodore, 12 bd Haussmann (9th) ✆ 42 46 72 82, Telex 280601 – lift TV ☎ ♿ F 13
st. : **M** 175 (lunch) and a la carte 130/205 🌡 – ☕ 46 – **165 rm** 935/1 045, 11 apartments 1 300/1 900.

Brébant Ⓜ, 32 bd Poissonnière (9th) ✆ 47 70 25 55, Telex 280127 – lift ▤ rest TV ☎ F 14
128 rm.

St-Pétersbourg without rest, 33 r. Caumartin (9th) ✆ 42 66 60 38, Telex 680001 – lift TV ☎. AE ⓓ E VISA F 12
st. : ☕ 25 – **120 rm** 495/520.

Astra Ⓜ without rest, 29 r. Caumartin (9th) ✆ 42 66 15 15, Telex 210408 – lift TV ☎. AE ⓓ E VISA F 15
st. : ☕ 25 – **85 rm** ☕ 580/630.

Blanche Fontaine 🐚 without rest, 34 r. Fontaine (9th) ✆ 45 26 72 32, Telex 660311 – lift TV ☎ 🚗. AE VISA. ❄ D 13
st. : **49 rm** ☕ 315/460.

Terminus Nord without rest, 12 bd Denain (10th) ✆ 42 80 20 00, Telex 660615 – lift TV ☎ ♿ – 🏢 40. AE ⓓ E VISA. ❄ E 15-16
st. : **225 rm** ☕ 295/480.

Paris Est Ⓜ without rest, cour d'Honneur (10th) ✆ 42 41 00 33, Telex 217916 – lift TV ☎ – 🏢 50-450. E VISA E 16
st. : ☕ 25 – **33 rm** 350/450.

Franklin et du Brésil, 19 r. Buffault (9th) ✆ 42 80 27 27, Telex 640988 – lift TV ☎. AE ⓓ E VISA. ❄ rest E 14
rest. **Les Années Folles** *(closed 15 July-15 August, Saturday, Sunday and Bank Holidays)* **M** a la carte 150/220 – **64 rm** ☕ 460/575.

Léman Ⓜ without rest, 20 r. Trévise (9th) ✆ 42 46 50 66, Telex 281086 – lift TV 🛁wc ☎. AE ⓓ E VISA F 14
st. : **24 rm** ☕ 500/800.

Moulin Rouge Ⓜ without rest, 39 r. Fontaine (9th) ✆ 42 82 08 56, Telex 660055 – lift TV 🛁wc 🚿wc ☎. AE ⓓ E VISA D 13
st. : ☕ 30 – **50 rm** 460/800.

🏨 **Gotty** Ⓜ without rest, 11 r. Trévise (9th) ✆ 47 10 12 90, Telex 660330 – |$| TV ⛀wc ☎. AE ⓓ E VISA F 14
st. : **44 rm** ☕ 520/600.

🏨 **Carlton's H.** without rest, 55 bd Rochechouart (9th) ✆ 42 81 91 00, Telex 640649 – |$| TV ⛀wc ☎. AE ⓓ E VISA D 14
st. : ☕ 30 – **103 rm** 400/420.

🏨 **du Pré** without rest, 10 r. Pierre Sémard (9th) ✆ 42 81 37 11, Telex 660549 – |$| TV ⛀wc ⛆wc ☎. AE VISA
st. : ☕ 20 – **41 rm** 340/380.

🏨 **Caumartin** Ⓜ without rest, 27 r. Caumartin (9th) ✆ 47 42 95 95, Telex 680702 – |$| TV ⛀wc ⛆wc ☎. AE ⓓ E VISA F 12
st. : ☕ 25 – **40 rm** 450/610.

🏨 **Athènes** Ⓜ without rest, 21 r. d'Athènes (9th) ✆ 48 74 00 55, Telex 640715 – |$| TV ⛀wc ⛆wc ☎. AE ⓓ E VISA. ⛒ E 12
☕ 30 – **36 rm** 400/450.

🏨 **Alpha** Ⓜ without rest, 11 r. Geoffroy Marie (9th) ✆ 45 23 14 04, Telex 643939 – |$| TV ⛀wc ☎. AE ⓓ E VISA. ⛒ F 14
st. : **28 rm** ☕ 450/550.

🏨 **Chamonix** Ⓜ without rest, 8 r. d'Hauteville (10th) ✆ 47 70 19 49, Telex 641177 – |$| TV ⛀wc ⛆wc ☎. AE ⓓ E VISA. ⛒ F 15
st. : ☕ 29 – **35 rm** 490/670.

🏨 **Printania** Ⓜ without rest, 19 r. Chateau d'Eau (10th) ✆ 42 01 84 20, Telex 215425 – |$| TV ⛀wc ⛆wc ☎. AE ⓓ E VISA. ⛒ F 16
st. : ☕ 25 – **51 rm** 390/480.

🏨 **Florida** without rest, 7 r. Parme (9th) ✆ 48 74 47 09, Telex 640410 – |$| TV ⛀wc ⛆wc ☎. AE ⓓ E VISA D 12
st. : **31 rm** ☕ 323/490.

🏨 **Anjou-Lafayette** without rest, 4 r. Riboutté (9th) ✆ 42 46 83 44, Telex 281001 – |$| ⛀wc ⛆wc ☎. AE ⓓ E VISA E 14
st. : **39 rm** ☕ 400/590.

🏨 **Moris** Ⓜ without rest, 13 r. R.-Boulanger (10th) ✆ 46 07 92 08, Telex 212024 – |$| TV ⛀wc ⛆wc ☎. AE ⓓ E VISA. ⛒ G 16
☕ 25 – **48 rm** 375/430.

🏨 **Modern' Est** without rest, 91 bd Strasbourg (10th) ✆ 46 07 24 72 – |$| ⛀wc ⛆wc ☎. VISA. ⛒ E 16
st. : ☕ 25 – **30 rm** 250/310.

🏨 **Gisendre** without rest, 6 r. Fromentin (9th) ✆ 42 80 36 86, Telex 641797 – |$| TV ⛀wc ⛆wc ☎. AE ⓓ E VISA. ⛒ D 13
st. : **32 rm** ☕ 303/338.

🏨 **Morny** without rest, 4 r. Liège (9th) ✆ 42 85 47 92, Telex 660822 – |$| TV ⛀wc ☎. AE ⓓ E VISA E 12
st. : **43 rm** ☕ 414/614.

🏨 **Capucines** without rest, 6 r. Godot-de-Mauroy (9th) ✆ 47 42 06 37 – |$| ⛀wc ⛆wc ☎ F 12
st. : ☕ 19 – **46 rm** 190/310.

🏨 **London Palace** without rest, 32 bd Italiens (9th) ✆ 48 24 54 64, Telex 642360 – |$| ⛀wc ⛆wc ☎. AE E VISA. ⛒ F 13
st. : ☕ 25 – **48 rm** 280/420.

🏨 **Gare du Nord** without rest, 33 r. St-Quentin (10th) ✆ 48 78 02 92, Telex 642415 – |$| TV ⛀wc ⛆wc ☎. AE E VISA. ⛒ E 16
st. : ☕ 24 – **49 rm** 200/380.

🏨 **Hélios** without rest, 75 r. Victoire (9th) ✆ 48 74 28 64, Telex 641255 – |$| TV ⛀wc ⛆wc ☎. AE ⓓ E VISA F 13
st. : ☕ 26 – **50 rm** 302/357.

🏨 **Baccarat** Ⓜ without rest, 19 r. Messageries (10th) ✆ 47 70 96 92, Telex 648895 – |$| TV ⛀wc ⛆wc ☎. AE ⓓ E VISA. ⛒ E 15
st. : ☕ 25 – **30 rm** 260/360.

🏨 **Résidence Mauroy** without rest, 11 bis r. Godot-de-Mauroy (9th) ✆ 47 42 50 78 – |$| TV ⛀wc ⛆wc ☎. AE ⓓ E VISA F 12
closed August – **st. :** ☕ 30 – **26 rm** 230/420.

🏨 **Florence** without rest, 26 r. Mathurins (9th) ✆ 47 42 63 47 – |$| ⛀wc ⛆wc ☎. AE ⓓ F 12
st. : ☕ 28 – **20 rm** 280/450.

🏨 **Royal Medoc** without rest, 14 r. Geoffroy Marie (9th) ✆ 47 70 37 33, Telex 660053 – |$| TV ⛀wc ☎. AE ⓓ E VISA. ⛒
st. : **41 rm** ☕ 460.

🏨 **Montréal** without rest, 23 r. Godot-de-Mauroy (9th) ✆ 42 65 99 54 – |$| TV ⛀wc ⛆wc ☎. AE ⓓ E VISA F 12
closed August – **st. :** ☕ 27 – **14 rm** 230/380, 5 apartments 550.

🏨 **Gd H. Haussmann** without rest, 6 r. Helder (9th) ✆ 48 24 76 10, Telex 650018 – |$| TV ⛀wc ⛆wc ☎. AE. ⛒ F 13
st. : ☕ 24 – **59 rm** 300/402.

Français without rest, 13 r. 8 Mai 1945 (10th) ☎ 46 07 42 02, Telex 230431 – |‡| 🛁wc 🚿wc ☎. E VISA E 16
st. : ☕ 19 – **71 rm** 250/280.

Pax without rest, 47 r. Trévise (9th) ☎ 47 75 52 81, Telex 650197 – |‡| 🛁wc 🚿wc ☎. E VISA E 14
st. : ☕ 15 – **52 rm** 270/350.

Peyris without rest, 10 r. Conservatoire (9th) ☎ 47 70 50 83 – |‡| 🛁wc 🚿wc ☎. E VISA F 14
st. : ☕ 15 – **50 rm** 270/350.

Gd H. Lafayette Buffault without rest, 6 r. Buffault (9th) ☎ 47 70 70 96, Telex 642180 – |‡| TV 🛁wc 🚿wc ☎ E 14
st. : ☕ 20 – **47 rm** 175/295.

Campaville Montmartre without rest, 21 bd Clichy (9th) ☎ 48 74 01 12, Telex 643572 – |‡| TV 🛁wc 🚿wc ☎. VISA D 13
st. : ☕ 23 – **78 rm** 227/305.

Campaville-Montholon without rest, 11 r. P.-Sémard (9th) ☎ 48 78 28 94, Telex 643861 – |‡| TV 🛁wc 🚿wc ☎. VISA E 15
st. : ☕ 23 – **47 rm** 255/305.

Ribouité Lafayette without rest, 5 r. Ribouité (9th) ☎ 47 70 62 36 – |‡| 🛁wc 🚿wc ☎
st. : ☕ 18 – **24 rm** 232/284.

Victor Massé without rest, 32 bis r. Victor-Massé (9th) ☎ 48 74 37 53 – |‡| 🛁wc 🚿wc ☎. ⊕ VISA. ⊀ E 13
st. : ☕ 19 – **40 rm** 138/240.

Résidence Magenta without rest, 35 r. Y.-Toudic (10th) ☎ 46 07 63 13 – |‡| TV 🚿wc ☎. AE F 17
st. : ☕ 16,50 – **29 rm** 218/234.

Blanche H. without rest, 69 r. Blanche (9th) ☎ 48 74 16 94 – |‡| 🛁wc 🚿 ☎. ⊀ D 12
st. : ☕ 16,50 – **53 rm** 75/220.

Fénelon without rest, 23 r. Buffault (9th) ☎ 48 78 32 18 – |‡| 🛁wc 🚿wc ☎. E VISA. ⊀ E 14
st. : ☕ 18 – **36 rm** 135/270.

Laffon without rest, 25 r. Buffault (9th) ☎ 48 78 49 91 – |‡| 🛁wc 🚿wc ☎. E VISA E 14
closed 27 July-24 August – **st.** : ☕ 18 – **46 rm** 100/262.

XXXX ✿ **Rest. Opéra - Café de la Paix,** pl. Opéra (9th) ☎ 47 42 97 02, « Second Empire décor » – ▤. AE ⊕ E VISA F 12
closed August – **st.** : **M** a la carte 260/370 - see rest. **Relais Capucines - Café de la Paix** below
Spec. Chartreuse de rouget et homard sauce souveraine, Aiguillettes de saumon et turbot rôties, Trois mignons sauce velours.

XXX **Charlot "Roi des Coquillages",** 12 pl. Clichy (9th) ☎ 48 74 49 64 – ▤ P. AE ⊕ E D 12
M 147/280.

XXX ✿ **Nicolas,** 12 r. Fidélité (10th) ☎ 47 70 10 72 – AE ⊕ E VISA F 16
closed Saturday – **M** a la carte 145/215
Spec. Foie gras frais, Canard aux fruits, Tournedos Nicolas.

XX **La Table d'Anvers,** 2 pl. d'Anvers (9th) ☎ 48 78 35 21 – ▤. VISA D 14
M 120/180.

XX **Au Chateaubriant,** 23 r. Chabrol (10th) ☎ 48 24 58 94, Italian cuisine, Collection of paintings – ▤. AE E VISA. ⊀ E 15
closed August, 14 to 21 February, Sunday and Monday – **M** a la carte 130/250.

XX **Relais Capucines - Café de la Paix,** 12 bd Capucines (9 th) ☎ 42 68 12 13 – ▤. AE ⊕ E VISA F 12
M Coffee shop a la carte 145/180 ♁.

XX ✿✿ **Chez Michel** (Tounissoux), 10 r. Belzunce (10th) ☎ 48 78 44 14 – ▤. AE ⊕ VISA E 15
closed 1 to 21 August, Christmas-February Holidays, Friday and Saturday – **M** (booking essential) a la carte 210/350
Spec. Salade d'avocat aux noix, St-Jacques au safran (15 October-15 April), Fondant au chocolat crème menthe.

XX **Le Newport,** 79 r. fg St-Denis (10th) ☎ 48 24 19 38, Seafood – AE VISA E 15
closed August, 23 December-4 January, Saturday lunch and Sunday – **M** a la carte 170/205.

XX **Grand Café Capucines** (24 hr service), 4 bd Capucines ☎ 47 42 75 77, Early 20C decor – AE ⊕ E VISA F 13
M a la carte 145/210 ♁.

XX **Mövenpick,** 12 bd Madeleine (9th) ☎ 47 42 47 93 – ▤. AE ⊕ E VISA G 12
Café des Artistes M a la carte 150/250 - **La Fontaine M** a la carte 100/160 ♁.

XX **Cartouche Edouard VII,** 18 r. Caumartin (9th) ☎ 47 42 08 82 – ▤. AE VISA E 12
closed 26 July-23 August and Sunday – **M** a la carte 130/200.

XX **Le Quercy,** 36 r. Condorcet (9th) ☎ 48 78 30 61 – AE ⊕ E VISA E 14
closed August and Sunday – **st.** : **M** 118.

XX **Rest. du Casino,** 41 r. Clichy (9th) ✆ 42 80 34 62 – AE ⓓ E VISA E 12
closed Saturday, Sunday and Bank Holidays – **M** a la carte 210/270.

XX **Le Saintongeais,** 62 r. Fg Montmartre (9th) ✆ 42 80 39 92 – AE VISA E 14
closed 8 to 24 August, Saturday lunch and Sunday – **st. : M** a la carte 140/185.

XX **Chez Casimir,** 6 r. Belzunce (10th) ✆ 48 78 32 53 – AE ⓓ E VISA E 15
closed Saturday lunch and Sunday – **st. : M** 160 b.i./230.

XX **Ty Coz,** 35 r. St-Georges (9th) ✆ 48 78 34 61, seafood only – AE ⓓ VISA E 13
closed 8 to 17 August, Christmas Holidays, Sunday and Monday – **st. : M** a la carte 140/250.

XX **Julien,** 16 r. Fg St-Denis (10th) ✆ 47 70 12 06, Early 20C decor – AE ⓓ VISA F 15
M a la carte 110/195 ♫.

XX **Brasserie Flo,** 7 cour Petites-Écuries (10th) ✆ 47 70 13 59, 1900 Setting – ▤. AE ⓓ VISA – **M** a la carte 110/195 ♫ F 15

XX **Petit Riche,** 25 r. Le Peletier (9th) ✆ 47 70 68 68, late 19C decor – AE ⓓ VISA F 13
closed Sunday – **M** a la carte 140/190 ♫.

XX **Terminus Nord,** 23 r. Dunkerque (10th) ✆ 42 85 05 15 – AE ⓓ VISA E 16
M a la carte 110/195 ♫.

XX **Bistrot Papillon,** 6 r. Papillon (9th) ✆ 47 70 90 03 – AE ⓓ VISA E 15
closed 18 to 26 April, August, Saturday and Sunday – **M** 86 ♫.

XX **Pagoda,** 50 r. Provence (9th) ✆ 48 74 81 48, Chinese cuisine – VISA F 13
closed Sunday in August – **M** a la carte 85/160.

XX **La P'tite Tonkinoise,** 56 fg Poissonnière (10th) ✆ 42 46 85 98, Vietnamese cuisine – VISA – *closed 1 August-15 September, 22 December-5 January, Sunday and Monday* – **M** a la carte 110/150 F 15

X **Le Mas,** 26 r. Bergère (9th) ✆ 47 70 85 81 – AE VISA
closed 7 to 15 August, Saturday and Sunday – **st. : M** 120.

X **Relais Beaujolais,** 3 r. Milton (9th) ✆ 48 78 77 91 E 14
closed August, Saturday, Sunday and Bank Holidays – **M** a la carte 110/170.

X **La Grille,** 80 fg Poissonnière (10th) ✆ 47 70 89 73 – ⓓ. ✻ E 15
closed August, February Holidays, Saturday, Sunday and Bank Holidays – **st. : M** a la carte 115/170.

Bastille, Gare de Lyon,
Place d'Italie,
Bois de Vincennes.
12th et 13th arrondissements.
12th : ✉ 75012
13th : ✉ 75013

Équinoxe Ⓜ without rest, 40 r. Le Brun (13th) ✆ 43 37 56 56, Telex 201476 – ⧉ TV ☎ ⇔. AE ⓓ E VISA N 15
st. : 49 rm ☐ 370/480.

Paris-Lyon-Palace without rest, 11 r. Lyon (12th) ✆ 43 07 29 49, Telex 213310 – ⧉ TV ☎ – 🏛 150. AE ⓓ E VISA L 18
st. : ☐ 29 – **128 rm** 410/440.

Modern H. Lyon without rest, 3 r. Parrot (12th) ✆ 43 43 41 52, Telex 230369 – ⧉ TV ☎. AE VISA. ✻ – **st. :** ☐ 29 – **53 rm** 265/415. L 18

Relais de Lyon Ⓜ without rest, 64 r. Crozatier (12th) ✆ 43 44 22 50, Telex 216690 – ⧉ TV ☎ – 🏛 25. AE ⓓ E VISA. ✻ K 19
st. : ☐ 25 – **34 rm** 350/400.

Terminus-Lyon without rest, 19 bd Diderot (12th) ✆ 43 43 24 03, Telex 230702 – ⧉ TV ⊟wc ⋒wc ☎. AE E VISA L 18
st. : ☐ 26 – **61 rm** 349/389.

Slavia without rest, 51 bd St-Marcel (13th) ✆ 43 37 81 25, Telex 205542 – ⧉ TV ⊟wc ⋒wc ☎. ✻ M 16
st. : ☐ 20 – **37 rm** 240/280, 6 apartments 330.

Gd H. Gobelins without rest, 57 bd St-Marcel (13th) ✆ 43 31 79 89 – ⧉ TV ⊟wc ⋒wc ☎ – **st. :** ☐ 16 – **45 rm** 195/280 M 16

Terrasses without rest, 74 r. Glacière (13th) ✆ 47 07 73 70, Telex 203488 – ⧉ ⊟wc ⋒wc ☎. VISA. ✻ – **st. :** ☐ 19 – **52 rm** 130/270. N 14

Corail without rest, 23 r. Lyon (12 th) ✆ 43 43 23 54, Telex 212002 – ⧉ TV ⊟wc ⋒wc ☎. AE ⓓ E VISA L 18
st. : ☐ 19 – **50 rm** 250/340.

Claret, 44 bd Bercy (12e) ✆ 46 28 41 31, Telex 217115 – ⧉ TV ⊟wc ⋒wc ☎ – 🏛 40. AE ⓓ E VISA M 19
M *(closed Saturday lunch and Sunday)* a la carte 95/140 ♫ – ☐ 25 – **52 rm** 380/600.

Marceau without rest, 13 r. Jules-César (12th) ✆ 43 43 11 65, Telex 214006 – |$| ⇔wc fl wc ☎. 🐕 K 17
closed August – **st.** : ☕ 20 – **51 rm** 101/300.

Timhôtel without rest, 22 r. Barrault (13th) ✆ 45 80 67 67, Telex 205461 – |$| TV ⇔wc fl wc ☎. AE ⦿ E VISA P 15
st. : ☕ 25 – **73 rm** 281/320.

Viator without rest, 1 r. Parrot (12th) ✆ 43 43 11 00 – |$| TV ⇔wc fl wc ☎. VISA. 🐕 L 18
st. : ☕ 20 – **45 rm** 200/260.

Jules César without rest, 52 av. Ledru-Rollin (12th) ✆ 43 43 15 88, Telex 670945 – |$| fl wc ☎. 🐕 K 18
st. : ☕ 20 – **48 rm** 200/250.

Rubens without rest, 35 r. Banquier (13th) ✆ 43 31 73 30 – |$| ⇔wc fl wc ☎ N 16
st. : ☕ 15 – **50 rm** 120/215.

Arts without rest, 8 r. Coypel (13th) ✆ 47 07 76 32 – |$| fl wc ☎ N 16
st. : ☕ 18 – **38 rm** 110/250.

Terminus et Sports without rest, 96 cours Vincennes (12th) ✆ 43 43 97 93 – |$| TV ⇔wc fl wc ☎. 🐕 L 23
st. : ☕ 20 – **43 rm** 135/260.

Résidence des Gobelins without rest, 9 r. Gobelins (13th) ✆ 47 07 26 90, Telex 206566 – |$| TV ⇔wc fl wc ☎. AE ⦿ E VISA N 15
st. : ☕ 20 – **32 rm** 220/320.

Nouvel H. without rest, 24 av. Bel Air (12th) ✆ 43 43 01 81, Telex 240139, 🌳 – ⇔wc fl wc ☎. AE ⦿ VISA L 21
st. : ☕ 33 – **28 rm** 155/400.

Palym H. without rest, 4 r. E.-Gilbert (12th) ✆ 43 43 24 48 – |$| TV fl wc ☎ L 18
st. : **51 rm** ☕ 150/290.

XXX ✿ **Au Pressoir** (Seguin), 257 av. Daumesnil (12th) ✆ 43 44 38 21 – ▤. E VISA M 22
closed August, February Holidays, Saturday and Sunday – **st.** : **M** a la carte 230/340
Spec. St-Jacques aux betteraves (October-May), Coeur de filet au coulis de truffes, Queues de langoustines.

XXX **Train Bleu,** Gare de Lyon (12th) ✆ 43 43 09 06, « Fine murals recalling the journey from Paris to the Mediterranean » – AE ⦿ E VISA L 18
M (1st floor) a la carte 180/250.

XX ✿ **Au Trou Gascon,** 40 r. Taine (12th) ✆ 43 44 34 26 – ▤. E VISA M 21
closed August, 25 December-1 January, Saturday and Sunday – **st.** : **M** (booking essential) a la carte 240/300
Spec. Foie gras de canard, Saumon rôti au lard et chou, Truffé de chocolat noir.

XX **Sologne,** 164 av. Daumesnil (12th) ✆ 43 07 68 97 – ▤. VISA M 21
closed Monday dinner and Sunday – **st.** : **M** a la carte 120/260.

XX **La Flambée,** 4 r. Taine (12th) ✆ 43 43 21 80 – VISA M 20
closed dinner Sunday, Monday and Tuesday and 7 to 20 August – **st.** : **M** 115 🍷.

XX **La Gourmandise,** 271 av. Daumesnil (12th) ✆ 43 43 94 41 – AE ⦿ VISA N 22
closed 16 to 23 April and 9 to 23 August – **st.** : **M** a la carte 175/260.

XX **La Frégate,** 30 av. Ledru-Rollin (12th) ✆ 43 43 90 32 – VISA. 🐕 L 18
closed August, Saturday and Sunday – **M** a la carte 185/220.

XX **Le Traversière,** 40 r. Traversière (12th) ✆ 43 44 02 10 – AE ⦿ E VISA K 18
closed 14 July-1 September, Sunday dinner and Bank Holidays – **M** a la carte 140/230.

XX **L'Escapade en Touraine,** 24 r. Traversière (12e) ✆ 43 43 14 96 – E VISA L 18
closed August, Saturday, Sunday and Bank Holidays – **M** a la carte 105/145.

XX **Potinière du Lac,** 4 pl. E.-Renard (12th) ✆ 43 43 39 98 – ⦿ VISA N 23
closed 15 to 25 September, 8 December-4 January, Sunday dinner and Monday – **M** 90.

X **Petit Marguery,** 9 bd. Port-Royal (13th) ✆ 43 31 58 59 – AE ⦿ E VISA M 15
closed August, 24 December-2 January, Sunday and Monday – **st.** : **M** a la carte 155/235.

X **Etchegorry,** 41 r. Croulebarbe (13th) ✆ 43 31 63 05 – AE ⦿ E VISA N 15
closed Sunday – **st.** : **M** 113 b.i./170 b.i..

X **Quincy,** 28 av. Ledru-Rollin (12th) ✆ 46 28 46 76 – AE ⦿ L 17
closed 10 August-15 September, Saturday, Sunday and Monday – **M** a la carte 130/200.

X **Les Algues,** 66 av. Gobelins (13th) ✆ 43 31 58 22 – AE VISA N 15
closed 2 to 23 August, 20 December-4 January, Sunday and Monday – **M** a la carte 160/205.

X **Le Rhône,** 40 bd Arago (13th) ✆ 47 07 33 57, 🏡 – E VISA N 14
closed August, Saturday, Sunday and Bank Holidays – **M** (booking essential) 63/80 🍷.

X **Relais du Périgord,** 15 r. Tolbiac (13th) ✆ 45 83 07 48, 🏡 – AE ⦿ VISA P 18
closed 15 August-15 September, Christmas Day-1 January, Saturday, Sunday and Bank Holidays – **M** (booking essential) 120/170 🍷.

X **Chez Michel,** 39 r. Daviel (13th) ✆ 45 80 09 13 – AE VISA P 14
closed August and Sunday – **st.** : **M** a la carte 115/175 🍷.

Vaugirard,
Gare Montparnasse, Grenelle,
Denfert-Rochereau.

14th et 15th arrondissements.
14th : ✉ 75014
15th : ✉ 75015

Hilton M, 18 av. Suffren (15th) ✆ 42 73 92 00, Telex 200955, – ☎ ♿ – 40 - 1200. AE ⓓ E VISA. ✻ rest J 7
st. : Le Toit de Paris ≤ Paris, *(closed August and Sunday)* **M** (dinner only) a la carte 260/390 - **Western M** 185 b.i. - **la Terrasse M** 108 b.i./171 b.i. – ☕ 65 – **445 rm** 1 205/1 865, 31 apartments.

Sofitel Paris M, 8 r. L.-Armand (15th) ✆ 40 60 30 30, Telex 200432, indoor pool overlooking Paris – ☎ ♿ – 30 - 1 200. AE ⓓ E VISA N 5
st. : M see rest. **Le Relais de Sèvres** below - **La Tonnelle** (Brasserie) **M** a la carte 130/180 – ☕ 60 – **618 rm** 980/1 140, 17 apartments.

Nikko M, 61 quai Grenelle (15th) ✆ 45 75 62 62, Telex 260012, ≤, – ☎ – 40 - 800. AE ⓓ E VISA K 6
st. : M see rest. **Les Célébrités** below - **Brasserie Pont Mirabeau M** a la carte 130/180 - **Japanese rest. Benkay M** a la carte 180/300 – ☕ 65 – **777 rm** 895/1 800, 9 apartments.

Méridien Montparnasse M, 19 r. Cdt-Mouchotte (14th) ✆ 43 20 15 51, Telex 200135, ≤, – ☎ ♿ – 25 - 1 400. AE ⓓ E VISA. ✻ rest M 11
st. : Montparnasse 25 *(closed August and Sunday)* **M** a la carte 270/360 - **La Ruche M** 150 – ☕ 71 – **912 rm** 1 100/1 300, 38 apartments.

Pullman St-Jacques M, 17 bd St-Jacques (14th) ✆ 45 89 89 80, Telex 270740 – ☎ – 40 - 1000. AE ⓓ E VISA N 13-14
st. : Café Français (1st floor) **M** 170 b.i./225 b.i. - **Le Patio** (3rd floor) **M** a la carte 100/155 – ☕ 46 – **783 rm** 830/927, 14 apartments 1 150/1 400.

Mercure Paris Porte de Versailles M, r. Moulin at Vanves ✉ 92170 Vanves ✆ 46 42 93 22, Telex 202195 – ☎ ♿ – 350. AE ⓓ E VISA P 7
M (brasserie) a la carte 100/150 – ☕ 40 – **395 rm** 525/560.

L'Aiglon without rest., 232 bd Raspail (14th) ✆ 43 20 82 42 – ☎. AE VISA. ✻ M 12
st. : ☕ 25 – **41 rm** 320/390, 8 apartments 540.

Holiday Inn M, porte Versailles (15th) ✆ 45 33 74 63, Telex 260844 – ☎ ♿ – 130. AE ⓓ E VISA. ✻ rest N 7
st. : M 90/165 – ☕ 45 – **90 rm** 650/1 030.

Montcalm M without rest., 50 av. F.-Faure (15th) ✆ 45 54 97 27, Telex 203174, – ☎ ♿. AE ⓓ E VISA M 6
st. : 41 rm ☕ 430/470.

Lenox M without rest, 15 r. Delambre (14th) ✆ 43 35 34 50, Telex 260745 – ☎. AE ⓓ E VISA M 12
st. : ☕ 25 – **52 rm** 360/520.

Orléans Palace H. without rest, 185 bd Brune (14th) ✆ 45 39 68 50, Telex 260725 – ☎ – 35. AE ⓓ E VISA R 11
st. : ☕ 25 – **92 rm** 270/430.

Wallace M without rest, 89 r. Fondary (15th) ✆ 45 78 83 30, Telex 205277 – wc ☎. AE ⓓ E VISA L 8
st. : ☕ 25 – **35 rm** 390/430.

Waldorf M without rest, 17 r. Départ (14th) ✆ 43 20 64 79, Telex 201677 – wc wc ☎ L 11
30 rm.

Versailles M without rest, 213 r. Croix-Nivert (15th) ✆ 48 28 48 66, Telex 200473 – wc wc ☎ ♿. AE VISA N 7
st. : ☕ 26 – **41 rm** 400/470.

Arès without rest., 7 r. Gén.-de-Larminat (15th) ✆ 47 34 74 04, Telex 206083 – wc wc ☎. E VISA. ✻ K 8
st. : ☕ 21 – **43 rm** 290/345.

Messidor M without rest, 330 r. Vaugirard (15th) ✆ 48 28 03 74, Telex 204606, – wc wc ☎. VISA M 8
☕ 36 – **74 rm** 201/405.

Châtillon H. without rest, 11 square Châtillon (14th) ✆ 45 42 31 17 – wc wc ☎. ✻ P 11
closed August – **st. :** ☕ 18 – **31 rm** 180/230.

Joigny without rest, 8 r. St-Charles (15th) ✆ 45 79 33 35, Telex 204057 – wc wc ☎. AE ⓓ E VISA. ✻ K 7
st. : ☕ 32 – **39 rm** 315/400.

Tourisme without rest, 66 av. La-Motte-Picquet (15th) 47 34 28 01 – wc wc. st. : 17 – **60 rm** 210/270. K 8

France without rest, 46 r. Croix-Nivert (15th) 47 83 67 02, Telex 206453 – wc wc st. : 22 – **30 rm** 230/325. L 8

Fondary without rest, 30 r. Fondary (15th) 45 75 14 75, Telex 206761 – TV wc. AE VISA st. : 22 – **20 rm** 240/290. L 8

Baldi without rest, 42 bd Garibaldi (15th) 47 83 20 10 – TV wc wc 20 – **28 rm** 220/280. L 9

Pasteur without rest, 33 r. Dr.-Roux (15th) 47 83 53 17 – TV wc wc. E VISA *closed 28 July-1 September* – **st.** : 20 – **19 rm** 220/350. M 10

Virgina without rest, 66 r. Père Corentin (14th) 45 40 70 90 – wc wc. AE. st. : 18 – **54 rm** 95/220. R 12

Pacific H. without rest, 11 r. Fondary (15th) 45 75 20 49, Telex 201346 – wc wc. E. st. : **66 rm** 126/254. K 7

Atlantique without rest, 54 r. Falguière (15th) 43 20 70 70 – TV wc wc. E VISA st. : 20 – **26 rm** 210/330.

XXXX ❀ **Les Célébrités,** 61 quai Grenelle (15th) 45 75 62 62, ← – . AE E VISA K 6
st. : **M** 245 b.i. (lunch) and a la carte 390/455
Spec. Salade de langoustines et St-Jacques rôties, Blanc de turbot au basilic, Escalope de foie d'oie poêlée.

XXX ❀ **Morot Gaudry,** 6 r. Cavalerie (15th) (8th floor) 45 67 06 85, ←, open-air terrace, – . VISA K 8
closed Saturday and Sunday – **st.** : **M** a la carte 220/320
Spec. Mousseline d'huîtres homardine, Rognon de veau à l'échalote confite, Grouse rôtie (1 October-28 February).

XXX ❀ **Olympe** (Mme Nahmias), 8 r. Nicolas Charlet (15th) 47 34 86 08 – . AE VISA
closed 1 to 24 August, 23 December-3 January, lunch Saturday and Sunday and Monday – **st.** : **M** a la carte 330/450 L 10
Spec. Ravioli de homard, Lapin rôti au pistou, Ecrevisses sautées à l'ail et persil (season).

XXX **Armes de Bretagne,** 108 av. du Maine (14th) 43 20 29 50 – . AE E VISA N 11
closed August, Sunday dinner and Monday except Bank Holidays – **M** a la carte 180/280.

XXX ❀ **Relais de Sèvres,** 8 r. L.-Armand (15th) 40 60 30 30 – . AE E VISA N 5
closed August, Christmas Day, Saturday and Sunday – **st.** : **M** a la carte 215/305
Spec. St-Jacques en papillotes de céleri (October-April), Pâté chaud de canard en croûte, Millefeuille chocolat et pistache.

XXX **Moniage Guillaume** with rm, 88 r. Tombe Issoire (14th) 43 22 96 15 – TV . AE E VISA P 12
closed Sunday – **M** 190 – 21 – **5 rm** 190/241.

XXX ❀ **Aquitaine** (Mme Massia), 54 r. Dantzig (15th) 48 28 67 38, – . AE E VISA N 8
closed Sunday and Monday – **st.** : **M** a la carte 260/325
Spec. Escalope de foie gras au chasselas (September-November), Panaché de poissons beurre blanc, Confit de Canard.

XX ❀ **Bistro 121,** 121 r. Convention (15th) 45 57 52 90 – . AE E VISA M 7
closed 12 July-17 August, 23 to 31 December, Sunday dinner and Monday – **M** a la carte 200/300
Spec. Pétoncles aux trois sauces, Foie gras de canard au verjus.

XX **Le Pfister,** 1 r. Dr.-Jacquemaire-Clemenceau (15th) 48 28 51 38 – VISA L 8
closed Saturday lunch and Sunday – **st.** : **M** 145/250.

XX **Chez Albert,** 122 av. Maine (14th) 43 20 21 69 – AE VISA N 11
closed August, Saturday lunch and Monday – **st.** : **M** 120/250.

XX ❀ **Gérard et Nicole** (Faucher), 6 av. J.-Moulin (14th) 45 42 39 56 – E VISA P 12
closed mid July-mid August, Saturday and Sunday – **st.** : **M** a la carte 235/340
Spec. Ravioli de langoustines, St-Jacques (October-February), Rouget à l'huile d'olive.

XX **La Chaumière des Gourmets,** 22 pl. Denfert-Rochereau (14th) 43 21 22 59 – E VISA N 12
closed August, 7 to 15 March, Saturday and Sunday – **M** 205.

XX ❀ **Le Dôme,** 108 bd du Montparnasse (14th) 43 35 25 81 – . AE VISA LM 12
closed Monday – **M** a la carte 185/295
Spec. Langoustines grillées au sel de Guérande, Ragoût de sole au foie gras, Coquilles St. Jacques à la Coque (October-May).

XX **Maison Blanche,** 82 bd Lefèbvre (15th) ☎ 48 28 38 83 – AE VISA P 7
closed 1 to 15 September, 24 December-3 January, Saturday lunch, Sunday and Monday – **st. : M** a la carte 190/270.

XX **Napoléon et Chaix,** 46 r. Balard (15th) ☎ 45 54 09 00 – ▤. E VISA M 5
closed August and Sunday – **M** a la carte 170/220.

XX ✿ **Pierre Vedel,** 19 r. Duranton (15th) ☎ 45 58 43 17 – VISA. ✻ M 6
closed 5 July-2 August, 24 December-3 January, Saturday and Sunday – **st. : M** (booking essential) a la carte 170/210
Spec. Safranade de filets de rascasse (March-October), Blanquette d'huîtres (October-March), Bourride de lotte.

XX **Chaumière Paysanne,** 7 r. L.-Robert (14th) ☎ 43 20 76 55 – AE ◑ E VISA M 12
closed 10 to 25 August and Sunday – **st. : M** a la carte 190/270.

XX **Vallon de Vérone,** 53 r. Didot (14th) ☎ 45 43 18 87 – VISA P 11
closed August, Saturday lunch and Sunday – **st. : M** a la carte 150/235.

XX **Le Clos Morillons,** 50 r. Morillons (15th) ☎ 48 28 04 37 – VISA N 8
closed Saturday lunch and Sunday – **st. : M** 95/230.

XX **Chez Maître Albert,** 8 r. Abbé Groult (15th) ☎ 48 28 36 98 – AE ◑ E VISA L 7
closed mid July-mid August and Monday – **st. : M** 160 b.i.

XX **L'Étape,** 89 r. Convention (15th) ☎ 45 54 73 49 – VISA M 6
closed Saturday lunch and Sunday – **M** 95/220.

XX **Petite Bretonnière,** 2 r. Cadix (15th) ☎ 48 28 34 39 – AE VISA N 7
closed August, Saturday lunch and Sunday – **st. : M** a la carte 185/240.

XX **La Giberne,** 42 bis av. Suffren (15th) ☎ 47 34 82 18 – AE ◑ E VISA J 8
closed 7 to 30 August, Saturday lunch and Sunday – **M** a la carte 150/225.

XX **La Gauloise,** 59 av. La Motte-Picquet (15th) ☎ 47 34 11 64 – AE ◑ VISA K 8
closed Saturday and Sunday – **st. : M** a la carte 170/240.

XX **Le Copreaux,** 15 r. Copreaux (15th) ☎ 43 06 83 35 – ▤. AE E VISA M 9
closed August, 24 December-3 January, Saturday and Sunday – **M** a la carte 155/240.

XX **La Chaumière,** 54 av. F.-Faure (15th) ☎ 45 54 13 91 – AE ◑ VISA M 7
closed August, Monday dinner and Tuesday – **M** a la carte 130/180.

XX **Le Caroubier,** 8 av. Maine (15th) ☎ 45 48 14 38, North African cuisine – VISA M 11
closed August and Sunday dinner – **M** 100 b.i./180 b.i.

XX **Mina Mahal,** 25 r. Cambronne (15th) ☎ 47 34 26 17, Indian cuisine – ▤. AE ◑ VISA. ✻
M a la carte 105/150. L 8

XX **Les Brémailles,** 9 r. G.-Saché (14th) ☎ 45 39 05 55 – AE E VISA N 11
closed August, Saturday lunch and Sunday – **st. : M** a la carte 170/225.

XX **Rest. du 15e,** 48 r. Balard (15th) ☎ 45 54 18 32 – AE ◑ E VISA M 5
closed August, Saturday lunch and Sunday – **M** 118/300.

XX **Monsieur Lapin,** 11 r. R.-Losserand (14th) ☎ 43 20 21 39 – VISA. ✻ N 11
closed August, Saturday lunch and Monday – **st. : M** a la carte 145/215.

X ✿ **La Cagouille** (Allemandou), 89 rue Daguerre (14th) ☎ 43 22 09 01 N 11
closed August, Sunday and Monday – **st. : M** (booking essential) a la carte 160/240
Spec. Seafood.

X **La Bonne Table,** 42 r. Friant (14th) ☎ 45 39 74 91 – E VISA R 11
closed 4 July-4 August, 25 December-4 January, Saturday and Sunday – **st. : M** a la carte 140/230.

X **Senteurs de Provence,** 295 r. Lecourbe (15th) ☎ 45 57 11 98 – AE ◑ E VISA M 6
closed 4 to 25 August, Sunday and Monday – **M** a la carte 130/205.

X **Bonne Auberge,** 33 r. Volontaires (15th) ☎ 47 34 65 49 – AE ◑ E VISA M 9
closed August, February Holidays, Saturday, Sunday and Bank Holidays – **st. : M** a la carte 100/165.

X **Le Clos de la Tour,** 22 r. Falguière (15th) ☎ 43 22 34 73 – AE ◑ E VISA L 10
closed Saturday lunch and Sunday – **M** a la carte 130/210.

X **Chaumière du Petit Poucet,** 10 r. Desnouettes (15th) ☎ 48 28 60 91 – E VISA N 7
closed July, Saturday dinner and Sunday – **M** 50/82 ♁.

X **Au Passé Retrouvé,** 13 r. Mademoiselle (15th) ☎ 42 50 35 29 – AE VISA L 7
closed August, Sunday and Monday – **M** a la carte 110/160.

X **La Hérissonnière,** 104 r. Balard (15th) ☎ 45 54 35 41 – AE ◑ VISA. ✻ M 5
closed August, Saturday lunch and Monday – **st. : M** 140/230.

X **Trois Horloges,** 73 r. Brancion (15th) ☎ 48 28 24 08 – AE ◑ VISA N 9
closed July – **st. : M** a la carte 125/170.

X **La Datcha Lydie** 7 r. Dupleix (15th) ☎ 45 66 67 77, Russian cuisine – VISA K 8
closed 15 July-28 August and Wednesday – **M** 92 b.i.

X **Le Troquet,** 21 r. F.-Bonvin (15th) ☎ 47 34 66 16 – E VISA L 9
closed August and Sunday – **M** a la carte 90/120 ♁.

Passy, Auteuil,
Bois de Boulogne,
Chaillot, Porte Maillot.
16th arrondissement.

La Pérouse and rest. l'Astrolabe M, 40 r. La Pérouse ✉ 75116, ✆ 45 00 83 47, Telex 613420 – ▮ ▤ TV ☎. AE ① E VISA. ✂ rest F 7
st. : M *(closed Saturday, Sunday and Bank Holidays)* 160 – ☕ 49 – **11 rm** 900/1 100, 25 apartments 1 390/1 870.

Baltimore M, 88 bis av. Kléber ✉ 75116, ✆ 45 53 83 33, Telex 611591 – ▮ TV ☎ – 🎓 30-100. AE ① E VISA. ✂ rest G 7
L'Estournel *(closed August, Saturday , Sunday and Bank Holidays)* **M** 185 – ☕ 50 – **120 rm** 650/1 180.

Raphaël, 17 av. Kléber ✉ 75116, ✆ 45 02 16 00, Telex 610356 – ▮ TV ☎ – 🎓 25 - 50. AE ① E VISA F 7
st. : M 180 – ☕ 65 – **52 rm** 770/1 180, 36 apartments.

Résidence du Bois without rest, 16 r. Chalgrin ✉ 75116, ✆ 45 00 50 59, « Refined decor, garden » – TV ☎ F 7
st. : 16 rm ☕ 750/1 140, 3 apartments 1 410.

Alexander M without rest, 102 av. Victor-Hugo ✉ 75116, ✆ 45 53 64 65, Telex 610373 – ▮ TV ☎. AE VISA. ✂ G 6
st. : 60 rm ☕ 500/780.

Union H. Étoile without rest, 44 r. Hamelin ✉ 75116, ✆ 45 53 14 95, Telex 611394 – ▮ kitchenette TV ☎. AE G 7
st. : ☕ 32 – **29 rm** 500/580, 13 apartments 700/850.

Victor Hugo without rest, 19 r. Copernic ✉ 75116, ✆ 45 53 76 01, Telex 630939 – ▮ TV ☎ – 🎓 25. AE ① E VISA. ✂ G 7
st. : ☕ 30 – **75 rm** 400/540.

Rond-Point de Longchamp and rest Belles Feuilles M, 86 r. Longchamp ✉ 75116, ✆ 45 05 13 63, Telex 620653 – ▮ ▤ rest TV ☎. AE ① G 6
st. : M *(closed August, 1 to 7 January, Saturday and Sunday)* a la carte 160/280 – ☕ 32 – **59 rm** 485/510.

Régina de Passy without rest, 6 r. Tour ✉ 75116, ✆ 45 24 43 64, Telex 630004 – ▮ kitchenette TV ☎. AE ① E VISA. ✂ H6-J6
st. : ☕ 28 – **60 rm** 430/460.

Majestic without rest, 29 r. Dumont-d'Urville ✉ 75116, ✆ 45 00 83 70 – ▮ TV ☎. AE ① E VISA F 7
st. : ☕ 30 – **27 rm** 700/900, 3 apartments 1 250.

Frémiet without rest, 6 av. Frémiet ✉ 75016, ✆ 45 24 52 06, Telex 630329 – ▮ TV ☎ ♿. AE ① E VISA J 6
st. : ☕ 20 – **34 rm** 395/590.

Massenet without rest, 5 bis r. Massenet ✉ 75116, ✆ 45 24 43 03, Telex 620682 – ▮ TV ☎. AE ① E VISA. ✂ J 6
st. : 41 rm ☕ 395/630.

Elysées Bassano M without rest, 24 r. Bassano ✉ 75116, ✆ 47 20 49 03, Telex 611559 – ▮ TV ☎. AE ① E VISA G 8
st. : ☕ 25 – **40 rm** 450/610.

Floride Etoile M without rest, 14 r. St-Didier ✉ 75116, ✆ 47 27 23 36, Telex 615087 – ▮ TV ☎ – 🎓 40. AE ① E VISA. ✂ G 7
st. : ☕ 30 – **60 rm** 510.

Residence Foch without rest, 10 r. Marbeau ✉ 75116, ✆ 45 00 46 50, Telex 630886 – ▮ TV ☎. AE ① E VISA F 6
st. : ☕ 25 – **21 rm** 425/580, 4 apartments 730.

Kléber without rest, 7 r. Belloy ✉ 75116, ✆ 47 23 80 22, Telex 612830 – ▮ TV ☎. AE ① E G 7
st. : 21 rm ☕ 534/760.

Sévigné without rest 6 r. Belloy ✉ 75116, ✆ 47 20 88 90, Telex 610219 – ▮ TV ☎. AE ① E G 7
st. : 30 rm ☕ 365/510.

Résidence Kléber M without rest, 97 r. Lauriston ✉ 75116, ✆ 45 53 83 30, Telex 613106 – ▮ TV 🛁wc 🚿wc ☎. AE ① E VISA G 7
st. : ☕ 30 – **45 rm** 650.

Sylva Pergolèse without rest, 3 r. Pergolèse ✉ 75116, ✆ 45 00 38 12, Telex 612245 – ▮ TV 🛁wc ☎. AE ① E VISA E 6
st. : ☕ 30 – **37 rm** 410/450.

Ambassade M without rest, 79 r. Lauriston ✉ 75116, ✆ 45 53 41 15, Telex 613643 – ▮ TV 🛁wc 🚿wc ☎. AE ① E VISA G 7
closed Christmas Holidays – **st. :** ☕ 27 – **38 rm** 350/420.

Murat M without rest, 119 bis bd Murat ✉ 75016, ✆ 46 51 12 32, Telex 648963 – TV wc wc ☎. AE VISA. M 3
st. : 28 – **28 rm** 320/450.

Passy Eiffel without rest, 10 r. Passy ✉ 75016, ✆ 45 25 55 66, Telex 612753 – wc wc ☎. AE ⓓ E VISA. J 6
st. : 25 – **50 rm** 380/430.

Longchamp without rest, 68 r. Longchamp ✉ 75116, ✆ 47 27 13 48, Telex 610342 – TV wc wc ☎. AE ⓓ E VISA G 6
st. : 30 – **23 rm** 430/480.

Queen's H. M without rest, 4 r. Bastien Lepage ✉ 75016, ✆ 42 88 89 85 – TV wc wc ☎. VISA. K 4
st. : 20 – **22 rm** 190/420.

Keppler without rest, 12 r. Keppler ✉ 75116 ✆ 47 20 65 05, Telex 620440 – TV wc wc ☎. AE ⓓ E VISA F 8
st. : 20 – **49 rm** 250/290.

Eiffel Kennedy without rest, 12 r. Boulainvilliers ✉ 75016, ✆ 45 24 45 75, Telex 614895 – TV wc wc ☎. AE ⓓ E VISA. J 5
st. : 25 – **30 rm** 383/414.

XXXX ✿✿ **Faugeron,** 52 r. Longchamp ✉ 75116, ✆ 47 04 24 53 – ▤. G 7
closed August, 24 December-2 January, Saturday and Sunday – **M** 200 (lunch) and a la carte 295/400
Spec. Salade de gambas aux choux (October-December), Cervelas de ris de veau, Nougat glacé aux pistaches.

XXXX ✿✿✿ **Jamin (Robuchon),** 32 r. Longchamp ✉ 75116, ✆ 47 27 12 27 – ▤. VISA G 7
closed 29 June-26 July, Saturday and Sunday – **M** (booking essential) a la carte 340/600
Spec. Gelée de caviar à la crème de chou-fleur, Galette de truffes (December-March), Blanc de bar sauce verjutée.

XXXX ✿✿ **Vivarois** (Peyrot), 192 av. V.-Hugo ✉ 75116, ✆ 45 04 04 31 – ▤. AE ⓓ VISA G 5
closed August, Saturday and Sunday – **M** a la carte 260/370
Spec. Feuilleté de truffe, Poissons, Pieds de porc farcis.

XXX ✿ **Toit de Passy** (Jacquot) (6th floor), 94 av. P.-Doumer ✉ 75016, ✆ 45 24 55 37, – ▤ Ⓟ. E VISA HJ 5
closed 8 to 18 August, 19 December-11 January, Saturday (except dinner 18 Aug.-19 Déc.), Sunday and Bank Holidays – **M** 170 (lunch) and a la carte 275/370
Spec. Soupe d'huîtres (1 October-15 April), Pigeon en croûte de sel, Millefeuille aux fruits rouges (15 May-30 September).

XXX **Tsé-Yang,** 25 av. Pierre 1er de Serbie ✉ 75016 ✆ 47 20 68 02, Chinese cuisine – ▤. AE ⓓ E VISA G 8
st. : **M** a la carte 200/300.

XXX **Pavillon des Princes,** 69 av. Porte d'Auteuil ✉ 75016, ✆ 47 43 15 15, – AE ⓓ VISA K 1
st. : **M** 230.

XXX ✿ **Ferrero,** 38 r. Vital ✉ 75016, ✆ 45 04 42 42 – AE ⓓ VISA H 5
closed 1 to 11 May, 14 August-1 September, 23 December-3 January, Saturday and Sunday – **M** a la carte 250/370
Spec. Volaille en vessie aux légumes, Bar en croûte, Les Trois soufflés.

XXX ✿✿ **Le Petit Bedon** (Ignace), 38 r. Pergolèse ✉ 75116, ✆ 45 00 23 66 – ▤. AE ⓓ VISA F 6
closed August, Saturday and Sunday – **M** a la carte 200/330
Spec. Foie gras frais de canard, Feuilleté de St-Jacques au champagne (October-March), Ris de veau aux morilles.

XXX ✿ **Michel Pasquet,** 59 r. La-Fontaine ✉ 75016, ✆ 42 88 50 01 – ▤. AE ⓓ VISA K 4
closed 15 July-16 August, 24 to 27 December, Saturday (except dinner from 16 August-1 May) and Sunday – **st. : M** 160 lunch and a la carte 245/315
Spec. Salade tiède de St-Jacques (October-March), Ravioles de langoustines et fondue de poireaux, Tuiles dentelles à l'orange.

XXX **Le Duret,** 28 r. Duret, ✉ 75116, ✆ 45 00 17 67 – ▤. VISA. F 6
closed 14 July-4 August, 24 December-6 January, Saturday and Sunday – **M** a la carte 150/230.

XXX **Sully d'Auteuil,** 78 r. d'Auteuil ✉ 75016, ✆ 46 51 71 18 – ▤. AE VISA K 3
closed 3 to 31 August, Saturday lunch and Sunday – **M** 200 b.i./350 b.i.

XXX **Shogun,** Port Debilly, bateau Nomadic ✉ 75116, ✆ 47 20 05 04, ≤, Japanese cuisine – Ⓟ. AE ⓓ E VISA. H 7
closed Monday – **st. : M** a la carte 225/315.

XXX **Morens,** 10 av. New-York ✉ 75116, ✆ 47 23 75 11 – AE ⓓ E VISA H 8
closed August, 24 December-1 January, Friday dinner and Saturday – **M** a la carte 1565/275.

XXX **Ramponneau,** 21 av. Marceau ✉ 75116 ✆ 47 20 59 51 – AE ⓓ VISA G 8
closed August – **M** a la carte 155/265.

XX **Al Mounia,** 16 r. Magdebourg ✉ 75116, ✆ 47 27 57 28, Moroccan cuisine – AE. ✻ G 7
closed mid July-31 August and Sunday – **M** a la carte 130/200.

XX **Paul Chêne,** 123 r. Lauriston ✉ 75116, ✆ 47 27 63 17 – ▤. AE ⓓ VISA G 6
closed August, 24 December-3 January, Saturday and Sunday – **M** a la carte 210/280.

XX **Relais d'Auteuil,** 31 bd Murat ✉ 75016, ✆ 46 51 09 54 – AE ⓓ E VISA L 3
closed Saturday lunch and Sunday – **st. : M** a la carte 195/245.

XX ✲ **Conti,** 72 r. Lauriston ✉ 75116, ✆ 47 27 74 67 – ▤. AE VISA. ✻ G 7
closed Saturday and Sunday – **M** 140 (lunch) and a la carte 200/300
Spec. Ravioli de chou aux grillons de ris de veau (November-March), Filets de rouget barigoule (April-September), Gâteau au Mascarpone.

XX **Sous l'Olivier,** 15 r. Goethe ✉ 75116, ✆ 47 20 84 81 – E VISA G 8
closed Saturday, Sunday and Bank Holidays – **st. : M** a la carte 150/240.

XX **Palais du Trocadéro,** 7 av. d'Eylau, ✉ 75116, ✆ 47 27 05 02, Chinese cuisine – ▤. AE E VISA H 6
M a la carte 140/210.

XX **Le Gd Chinois,** 6 av. New-York ✉ 75116, ✆ 47 23 98 21, Chinese and Vietnamese cuisine – AE ⓓ H 8
closed 10 to 25 August and Monday – **M** a la carte 120/170.

X **Au Clocher du Village,** 8 bis r. Verderet ✉ 75016, ✆ 42 88 35 87 – VISA L 4
closed August, Saturday lunch and Sunday – **st. : M** a la carte 125/210.

X **Le Valéry,** 55 r. Lauriston ✉ 75016, ✆ 45 53 55 48 – E VISA F 7
closed August, Saturday and Sunday – **st. : M** a la carte 140/240 ♁.

in the Bois de Boulogne :

XXXX ✲✲ **Pré Catelan,** ✉ 75016, ✆ 45 24 55 58, Telex 614983, 🏛, 🌳 – Ⓟ. AE ⓓ VISA H 2
closed February Holidays, Sunday dinner and Monday – **M** a la carte 320/430
Spec. Soufflé d'oursins (October-April), Rougets de roche au pamplemousse, Caneton au vinaigre de framboises.

XXXX ✲ **Grande Cascade,** ✉ 75016, ✆ 45 27 33 51, ←, 🏛 – Ⓟ. AE E VISA
closed 20 December-20 January – **M** *(lunch only from 1 October-14 April)* 200 (lunch) and a la carte 260/340
Spec. Langoustines rôties (May-September), Huîtres chaudes (October-May), Pigeonneau en cocotte à l'ancienne.

Clichy, Ternes, Wagram.

17th arrondissement.
17th : ✉ 75017

🏨 **Méridien** Ⓜ, 81 bd Gouvion-St-Cyr (pte Maillot) ✆ 47 58 12 30, Telex 290952 – |♦| ▤ TV ☎ 🚗 – 🎤 100-900. AE ⓓ E VISA. ✻ E 6
st. : M see rest. **Le Clos de Longchamp** below - **Café l'Arlequin M** a la carte 110/190 ♁ – **Le Yamato** (Japanese rest) - **M** a la carte 100/160 - **La Maison Beaujolaise M** 140 b.i./300 b.i. – ☕ 68 – **1 027 rm** 990/1 735, 15 apartments.

🏨 **Concorde Lafayette** Ⓜ, 3 pl. Gén.-Koenig ✆ 47 58 12 84, Telex 650892, « Bar with ✳ on 34th floor » – |♦| kitchenette ▤ TV ☎ – 🎤 4 000. AE ⓓ E VISA E 6
st. : M see rest. **L'Étoile d'Or** below - **L'Arc-en-Ciel M** 153/200 ♁ - Coffee Shop **Les Saisons M** a la carte 135/170 ♁ – ☕ 55 – **940 rm** 1 250/1 450, 30 apartments.

🏨 **Splendid Étoile** Ⓜ without rest, 1 bis av. Carnot ✆ 47 66 41 41, Telex 280773 – |♦| TV ☎. AE ⓓ E VISA. ✻ F 7
st. : ☕ 52 – **49 rm** 580/720, 8 apartments 820/920.

🏨 **Regent's Garden** 🔇 without rest, 6 r. P.-Demours ✆ 45 74 07 30, Telex 640127, « Garden » – |♦| TV ☎. AE ⓓ E VISA E 7
st. : ☕ 30 – **39 rm** 550/800.

🏨 **Résidence St-Ferdinand** Ⓜ without rest, 36 r. St-Ferdinand ✆ 45 72 66 66, Telex 649565 – |♦| ▤ TV ☎. AE ⓓ E VISA E 6-7
st. : ☕ 550/732.

🏨 **Mercure** Ⓜ without rest, 27 av. Ternes ✆ 47 66 49 18, Telex 650679 – |♦| ▤ TV ☎ Ⓟ. AE ⓓ E VISA E 8
st. : ☕ 34 – **56 rm** 475/500.

🏨 **Balmoral** without rest, 6 r. Gén.-Lanrezac ✆ 43 80 30 50, Telex 642435 – |♦| TV ☎. AE ⓓ E 7
st. : ☕ 25 – **57 rm** 400/500.

🏨 **Magellan** 🔇 without rest, 17 r. J.B.-Dumas ✆ 45 72 44 51, Telex 660728, 🌳 – |♦| ☎. AE ⓓ E VISA D 7
st. : 75 rm ☕ 370/390.

Pierre [M] without rest, 25 r. Th.-de-Bainville ✆ 47 63 76 69, Telex 643003 – |♦| TV ⇔wc ☎ ♿ – 🏊 50. AE ⦿ E VISA D 8
st. : ☐ 30 – **50 rm** 440/570.

De Neuville [M], 3 pl. Verniquet ✆ 43 80 26 30, Telex 648822 – |♦| TV ⇔wc ☎. AE ⦿ VISA C 8
M *(closed Saturday and Sunday)* a la carte 80/120 🍷 – **28 rm** ☐ 380/480.

Étoile Péreire [M] without rest, 146 bd Péreire ✆ 42 67 60 00 – |♦| TV ⇔wc ⋒wc ☎. AE ⦿ E VISA. ⚘ D 7
st. : ☐ 35 – **26 rm** 350/520, 5 duplex 760.

Courcelles [M] without rest, 184 r. Courcelles ✆ 47 63 65 30, Telex 642252 – |♦| TV ⇔wc ⋒wc ☎. AE ⦿ E VISA D 8
st. : ☐ 25 – **42 rm** 395/450.

Cheverny [M] without rest, 7 villa Berthier ✆ 43 80 46 42, Telex 648848 – |♦| TV ⇔wc ⋒wc ☎. AE ⦿ E VISA D 7
st. : ☐ 25 – **26 rm** 350/550.

Banville without rest, 166 bd Berthier ✆ 42 67 70 16, Telex 643025 – |♦| ⇔wc ⋒wc ☎. E VISA D 8
st. : **40 rm** ☐ 395/420.

Belfast without rest, 10 av. Carnot ✆ 43 80 12 10, Telex 642777 – |♦| TV ⇔wc ⋒wc ☎. AE ⦿ E VISA. ⚘ E 7
st. : ☐ 30 – **54 rm** 430/530.

Mercédès without rest, 128 av. Wagram ✆ 42 27 77 82, Telex 660751 – |♦| TV ⇔wc ⋒wc ☎. AE ⦿ E VISA D 9
st. : ☐ 25 – **37 rm** 350.

Régence-Étoile without rest, 24 av. Carnot ✆ 43 80 75 60, Telex 641914 – |♦| TV ⇔wc ⋒wc ☎. AE VISA. ⚘ E 7
st. : ☐ 32 – **38 rm** 360/480.

Royal Magda without rest, 7 r. Troyon ✆ 47 64 10 19, Telex 641068 – |♦| TV ⇔wc ☎. AE ⦿ E VISA E 8
st. : **28 rm** ☐ 407/506, 10 apartments 540/688.

Stella without rest, 20 av. Carnot ✆ 43 80 84 50, Telex 660845 – |♦| TV ⇔wc ⋒wc ☎. AE ⦿ E VISA. ⚘ E 7
st. : ☐ 25 – **36 rm** 280/450.

Empire H. without rest, 3 r. Montenotte ✆ 43 80 15 55, Telex 643232 – |♦| TV ⇔wc ⋒wc ☎. AE ⦿ E VISA E 8
st. : ☐ 30 – **42 rm** 245/490.

Trois Couronnes [M] without rest, 30 r. Arc de Triomphe ✆ 43 80 46 81, Telex 660182 – |♦| TV ⇔wc ⋒wc ☎. AE ⦿ E VISA E 7
st. : ☐ 20 – **20 rm** 375/385.

Monceau Étoile without rest, 64 r. Levis ✆ 42 27 33 10, Telex 643170 – |♦| TV ⇔wc ⋒wc ☎. E VISA. ⚘ D 10
st. : ☐ 26 – **26 rm** 400/440.

Tivoli Étoile without rest, 7 r. Brey ✆ 43 80 31 22, Telex 643107 – |♦| TV ⇔wc ☎. AE ⦿ E VISA E 8
☐ 20 – **30 rm** 430/460.

Astor without rest, 36 r. P.-Demours ✆ 42 27 44 93, Telex 650078 – |♦| TV ⇔wc ⋒wc ☎. E VISA. ⚘ D 8
st. : ☐ 22 – **48 rm** 260/355.

Palma without rest, 46 r. Brunel ✆ 45 74 74 51, Telex 660183 – |♦| TV ⇔wc ⋒wc ☎. E VISA. ⚘ E 7
st. : ☐ 18 – **37 rm** 240/300.

Prima H., 167 r. Rome ✆ 46 22 21 09, Telex 642186 – |♦| TV ⇔wc ⋒wc ☎. AE VISA C 10
st. : **M** *(closed Sunday)* 120/180 🍷 – ☐ 25 – **30 rm** 220/280.

Astrid without rest, 27 av. Carnot ✆ 43 80 56 20, Telex 642065 – |♦| ⇔wc ⋒wc ☎. VISA. ⚘ E 7
st. : **40 rm** ☐ 230/350.

Néva without rest, 14 r. Brey ✆ 43 80 28 26, Telex 649041 – |♦| TV ⇔wc ⋒wc ☎. AE E VISA. ⚘ E 8
☐ 22 – **35 rm** 300/360.

Bel'Hôtel without rest, 20 r. Pouchet ✆ 46 27 34 77, Telex 642396, 🚗 – |♦| TV ⇔wc ☎ 🚘. VISA B 11
closed August – **st. :** ☐ 22 – **30 rm** 110/290.

XXXX ✿✿ **Michel Rostang,** 20 r. Rennequin ✆ 47 63 40 77, Telex 649629 – ▤. VISA D 8
closed 10 to 15 August, Saturday lunch, Sunday and Bank Holidays – **M** 200 (lunch) and a la carte 270/350
Spec. Oeufs de caille en coque d'oursins (October-March), Canette de Bresse au sang (season).

XXX ✿ **Le Clos de Longchamp,** 81 bd. Gouvion-St-Cyr (Pte Maillot) ✆ 47 58 80 00 – AE ⓓ E VISA. ✂ E 6
closed Saturday and Sunday – **st.** : **M** a la carte 260/370.

XXX ✿✿ **Guy Savoy,** 18 r. Troyon ✆ 43 80 40 61 – VISA. ✂ E 8
closed 14 July-4 August, 26 December-6 January, Saturday and Sunday – **M** a la carte 210/370
Spec. Escargots et ravioles au coulis d'herbes, Tronçons de homard sautés (May-October), Pigeon "poché-grillé".

XXX ✿ **Étoile d'Or,** 3 pl. Gén.-Koenig ✆ 47 58 12 84 – ▤. AE ⓓ E VISA E 6
closed August – **st.** : **M** a la carte 260/330
Spec. Saumon mi-doux en vinaigrette, Rouelle de turbot au chou, Gigot de sept heures aux pâtes fraîches.

XXX ✿ **Michel Comby,** 116 bd Péreire ✆ 43 80 88 68 – AE ⓓ VISA D 8
closed 13 July-2 August, 23 February-9 March, Saturday (except dinner from June to October) and Sunday – **M** 135 (lunch) and a la carte 190/280
Spec. Oeufs pochés en meurette, St-Jacques (October-April), Croustillant aux pommes caramélisées.

XXX ✿ **Timgad** (Laasri), 21 r. Brunel ✆ 45 74 23 70, « Moorish decor » – ▤. AE ⓓ E VISA. ✂ E 7
M 188/284
Spec. Tagine, Couscous, Méchoui.

XXX ✿ **Manoir de Paris,** 6 r. Pierre-Demours ✆ 45 72 25 25 – AE ⓓ E VISA E 7
closed 11 July-2 August, Saturday and Sunday – **M** a la carte 240/340
Spec. Mesclun de chinchards aux aromates, Ravioli de saumon fumé au caviar, Etuvée de merlan.

XXX ✿ **Sormani** (Fayet), 4 r. Gén.-Lanrezac ✆ 43 80 13 91 – VISA. ✂ E 7
closed 18 to 26 April, 1 to 23 August, 24 December-2 January, Saturday, Sunday and Bank Holidays – **M** a la carte 200/270
Spec. Assiette de l'artiste, Ravioli aux cèpes, Friture de scampi et chipirons.

XXX ✿✿ **Apicius** (Vigato), 122 av. Villiers ✆ 43 80 19 66 – ▤. AE VISA D 8
closed August, Saturday and Sunday – **M** a la carte 230/300
Spec. Pieds de porc en crépinette, Rougets tièdes à l'huile d'olive, Grand dessert au chocolat amer.

XXX **Chez Laudrin,** 154 bd Péreire ✆ 43 80 87 40 – AE E VISA D 7
closed Saturday and Sunday – **st.** : **M** a la carte 180/280.

XXX **Lacanthe,** 123 av. Wagram ✆ 42 27 61 50 – ⓓ E VISA D 8
closed Saturday lunch and Sunday – **st.** : **M** a la carte 130/250.

XXX ✿ **Paul et France** (Romano), 27 av. Niel ✆ 47 63 04 24 – AE ⓓ E VISA. ✂ D 8
closed 15 July-15 August, Saturday and Sunday – **M** a la carte 235/320
Spec. Ravioli de tourteaux, Barbue au beurre de poivron rouge, Rognon de veau Paul-France.

XX **Andrée Baumann,** 64 av. Ternes ✆ 45 74 16 66 – ▤. AE ⓓ E VISA E 7
st. : **M** a la carte 140/200 ♁.

XX **L'Écrevisse,** 212 bis bd Péreire ✆ 45 72 17 60 – ▤ Ⓟ. AE ⓓ E VISA E 6
closed August, Saturday lunch and Sunday – **M** a la carte 145/210.

XX ✿ **Le Petit Colombier** (Fournier), 42 r. Acacias ✆ 43 80 28 54 – VISA E 7
closed 1 to 17 August, Sunday lunch and Saturday – **M** 180 (lunch) and a la carte 165/255
Spec. Gâteau de brochet au beurre de caviar, Tourte de lapereau aux cèpes, Civet de lièvre à la française (October-January).

XX **Épicure,** 22 r. Foucroy ✆ 47 63 34 00 – VISA D 8
closed Saturday lunch and Sunday – **st.** : **M** a la carte 210/300.

XX **La Coquille,** 6 r. Débarcadère ✆ 45 74 25 95 – ▤. AE VISA E 7
closed August, 24 December-1 January, Sunday and Monday – **M** a la carte 175/300.

XX ✿ **Chez Guyvonne** (Cros), 14 r. Thann ✆ 42 27 25 43 – VISA D 9-10
closed 10 July-3 August, 24 December-5 January, Saturday, Sunday and Bank Holidays – **M** a la carte 180/260
Spec. Foie gras de canard aux cèpes, Aileron de raie au chou vert, Emincé de rognon de veau au vin.

XX **Lajarrige,** 16 av. Villiers ✆ 47 63 25 61 – AE VISA D 10
closed Saturday lunch and Sunday – **M** a la carte 185/250.

XX ✿ **Chez Augusta,** 98 r. Tocqueville ✆ 47 63 39 97 – E VISA C 9
closed August, Sunday and Bank Holidays – **M** a la carte 185/290
Spec. Salade Augusta, Bouillabaisse, St-Jacques à la purée de brocolis et champignons (October-March).

XX **Ma Cuisine,** 18 r. Bayen ✆ 45 72 02 19 – AE ⓓ E VISA E 8
closed Saturday lunch and Sunday – **M** 205.

XX **Epicure 108,** 108 r. Cardinet ✆ 47 63 50 91 – VISA D 10
closed Sunday and Monday – **st.** : **M** 160.

XX **Santenay,** 75 av. Niel ✆ 42 27 88 44 – AE ⓓ E VISA D 8
closed 1 to 21 August, Sunday dinner and Monday – **M** a la carte 140/210.

XX **La Braisière,** 54 r. Cardinet ✆ 47 63 40 37 – VISA D 9
closed Easter, August, Saturday and Sunday – **st.** : **M** a la carte 180/270.

XX **Chez Georges,** 273 bd Péreire ✆ 45 74 31 00 – VISA E 6
closed August – **M** a la carte 125/200.

XX ✿ **La Petite Auberge** (Harbonnier), 38 r. Laugier ✆ 47 63 85 51 – ◑ E VISA D 7-8
closed 2 to 31 August, Sunday and Monday – **M** (booking essential) a la carte 175/270
Spec. Foie de canard chaud, Turbot Camille Renault, Millefeuille.

XX **La Grosse Tartine,** 91 bd Gouvion St-Cyr ✆ 45 74 02 77 – ▤. AE ◑ E VISA E 6
M 100/140.

XX **Le Beudant,** 97 r. des Dames ✆ 43 87 11 20 – AE ◑ VISA D 11
closed Saturday lunch and Sunday – **M** 197 b.i. (lunch) and a la carte 180/260.

XX **La Gourmandine,** 26 r. d'Armaillé ✆ 45 72 00 82 – AE ◑ E VISA E 7
closed 2 to 30 August, Saturday lunch and Sunday – **st. : M** 145/250.

XX **Cap Dauphin,** 94 bd Batignolles ✆ 43 87 26 84 – ▤. AE VISA D 11
M a la carte 130/250.

XX **Relais d'Anjou,** 15 r. Arc-de-Triomphe ✆ 43 80 43 82 – E VISA E 7
closed 25 July-25 August, Saturday lunch and Sunday – **M** a la carte 145/200.

XX **Le Gouberville,** 1 pl. Ch.-Fillon ✆ 46 27 33 37, 余 – E VISA C 10-11
closed 1 to 21 August, February Holidays, Sunday and Monday – **st. : M** 130.

XX **La Toque,** 16 r. Tocqueville ✆ 42 27 97 75 – VISA D 10
closed 10 July-9 August, 24 December-1 January, Saturday and Sunday – **st. : M** 180 b.i./220 b.i.

X **Chez Léon,** 32 r. Legendre ✆ 42 27 06 82 – ◑ VISA D 10
closed August, February Holidays, Saturday and Sunday – **st. : M** 120.

X **Pommeraie Jouffroy,** 36 r. Jouffroy ✆ 42 27 39 41, 余 – AE ◑ E VISA D 9
closed August and Sunday – **st. : M** 120 b.i.

X **La Soupière,** 154 av. Wagram ✆ 42 27 00 73 – ▤. AE VISA D 9
closed 8 to 16 August, Saturday and Sunday – **st. : M** 130.

X ✿ **Mère Michel** (Gaillard), 5 r. Rennequin ✆ 47 63 59 80 – VISA E 8
closed 18 to 26 April, August, Saturday and Sunday – **st. : M** (booking essential) a la carte 175/225
Spec. Cressonnette de foies de volaille au Xérès, Poissons beurre blanc, Omelette soufflée.

X **Le Messager,** 101 av. Ternes ✆ 45 74 87 07, 余 – ▤. AE VISA
closed Sunday – **M** 80 b.i./120 b.i.

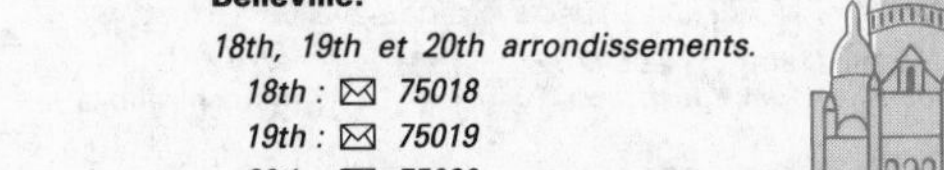

Montmartre, La Villette, Belleville.

18th, 19th et 20th arrondissements.
18th : ✉ 75018
19th : ✉ 75019
20th : ✉ 75020

Terrass'H. Ⓜ, 12 r. J.-de-Maistre (18th) ✆ 46 06 72 85, Telex 280830 – 歯 ▤ rest TV ☎ ♿ – 🔔 30. AE ◑ E VISA C 13
st. : Le Guerlande **M** a la carte 175/235 - **l'Albaron M** a la carte 100/135 ₰ – **95 rm** ☕ 460/760, 13 apartments 800/840 – P 630/840.

Mercure Paris Montmartre Ⓜ without rest, 1 r. Caulaincourt (18th) ✆ 42 94 17 17, Telex 640605 – 歯 ▤ TV ☎ ♿. AE ◑ E VISA D 12
st. : ☕ 42 – **308 rm** 520/550.

Mercure Porte de Pantin Ⓜ, 25 r. Scandicci à Pantin ✉ 93500 Pantin ✆ 48 46 70 66, Telex 230742 – 歯 ▤ TV ☎ 🚗 – 🔔 25-150. AE ◑ E VISA B 21
st. : M *(closed Sunday lunch and Saturday)* a la carte 100/200 – ☕ 40 – **129 rm** 470/495, 9 appartments 750.

Palma Ⓜ without rest, 77 av. Gambetta (20th) ✆ 46 36 13 65, Telex 216056 – 歯 TV 🛁wc 🚿wc ☎. AE VISA. ✂ G 21
st. : ☕ 21 – **32 rm** 270/300.

H. Le Laumière without rest, 4 r. Petit (19th) ✆ 42 06 10 77 – 歯 🛁wc 🚿wc ☎ D 19
st. : ☕ 18 – **54 rm** 92/240.

Super H., 208 r. Pyrénées (20th) ✆ 46 36 97 48, Telex 215588 – 歯 ▤ rest 🛁wc 🚿wc ☎. VISA G 21
hotel : closed August ; rest. : closed 8 to 22 August and Sunday – **st. : M** 75/150 ₰ – **28 rm** ☕ 152/390.

Regyn's Montmartre without rest, 18 pl. Abbesses (18th) ✆ 42 54 45 21 – 歯 TV 🛁wc 🚿wc ☎. AE ◑ VISA D 13
st. : ☕ 17 – **22 rm** 300/350.

Pyrénées Gambetta without rest, 12 av. Père Lachaise (20th) ✆ 47 97 76 57, Telex 213533 – 歯 TV 🛁wc 🚿wc ☎ H 21
st. : 30 rm ☕ 125/300.

Prima-Lepic without rest, 29 r. Lepic (18th) ✆ 46 06 44 64, Telex 281162 – 歯 🛁wc 🚿wc ☎. AE ◑ E VISA. ✂ D 13
st. : ☕ 28 – **38 rm** 160/250.

Roma Sacré Coeur M without rest, 101 r. Caulaincourt (18th) ✆ 42 62 02 02, Telex 643492 – |\$| TV ⇔wc ⋒wc ☎. AE ⓓ E VISA C 14
st. : ☕ 19 – **57 rm** 335/340.

Capucines Montmartre without rest, 5 r. A.-Bruant (18th) ✆ 42 52 89 80, Telex 281648 – |\$| TV ⇔wc ⋒wc ☎. AE ⓓ E VISA D 13
st. : ☕ 17 – **29 rm** 198/300.

Eden H. without rest, 90 r. Ordener (18th) ✆ 42 64 61 63, Telex 290504 – |\$| TV ⇔wc ⋒wc ☎. AE ⓓ E VISA. ✻ B 14
st. : ☕ 20 – **35 rm** 170/260.

Luxia without rest, 8 r. Seveste (18th) ✆ 46 06 84 24 – |\$| ⇔wc ⋒wc ☎. AE ⓓ D 14
st. : ☕ 17 – **48 rm** 135/265.

XXX ✿ **Beauvilliers** (Carlier), 52 r. Lamarck (18th) ✆ 42 54 54 42, ⛱, « 1900's decor, terrace » – E VISA. ✻ C 14
closed 31 August-14 September, Monday lunch and Sunday – **M** a la carte 240/335
Spec. Cassolette de Civelles (January-March), Turbot rôti, Rot-de-bif de filet d'agneau.

XXX ✿ **Cochon d'Or,** 192 av. J.-Jaurès (19th) ✆ 46 07 23 13 – AE ⓓ E VISA C 20
M a la carte 180/295
Spec. Grillades, Darne de turbot grillée Béarnaise, Rognon de veau grillé.

XXX **Pavillon Puebla,** Parc Buttes Chaumont, entrance : Corner av. S. Bolivar and r. Botzaris (19th) ✆ 42 08 92 62, <, ⛱, « Pleasant situation in the park », ⛱ – Ⓟ. VISA E 19
closed Sunday and Monday – **st. : M** a la carte 205/285.

XXX **Charlot 1er "Merveilles des Mers",** 128 bis bd Clichy (18th) ✆ 45 22 47 08, Seafood – AE ⓓ E VISA D 12
closed 22 July-26 August – **M** a la carte 200/280.

XXX **Relais Pyrénées,** 1 r. Jourdain (20th) ✆ 46 36 65 81 – AE ⓓ VISA F 20
closed end of July-31 August and Saturday – **M** a la carte 190/250.

XX **Le Clodenis,** 57 r. Caulaincourt (18th) ✆ 46 06 20 26 – AE ⓓ E VISA. ✻ C 13
closed Sunday and Monday – **M** 170 (lunch) and a la carte 245/340.

XX **Chez le Baron,** 65 r. Manin (19th) ✆ 42 05 72 72 – AE VISA D 19
closed 10 to 20 August, Saturday lunch and Sunday – **M** 130 (lunch) and a la carte 190/255.

XX **Moucharabieh,** 4 r. A.-Lavy (18th) ✆ 42 64 48 70, « Moorish decor » – ⓓ VISA B 14
closed Monday – **st. : M** 210 b.i.

XX **Sanglier Bleu,** 102 bd Clichy (18th) ✆ 46 06 07 61 – ▤. AE ⓓ E VISA D 12
M a la carte 150/220.

XX **Deux Taureaux,** 206 av. J.-Jaurès (19th) ✆ 46 07 39 31 – AE ⓓ VISA C 21
closed Saturday and Sunday – **st. : M** a la carte 155/215.

XX **Boeuf Couronné,** 188 av. J.-Jaurès (19th) ✆ 46 07 89 52 – AE ⓓ E VISA C 20
closed Sunday – **M** a la carte 130/260 🍾.

XX **Au Clair de la Lune,** 9 r. Poulbot (18th) ✆ 42 58 97 03 – AE ⓓ E VISA D 14
closed February Holidays, Monday lunch and Sunday – **st. : M** 155.

XX **Grandgousier,** 17 av. Rachel (18th) ✆ 43 87 66 12 – AE ⓓ E VISA D 12
closed 10 to 23 August, Saturday lunch and Sunday – **M** 100.

XX **La Chaumière,** 46 av. Secrétan (19th) ✆ 46 07 98 62 – AE ⓓ E VISA E 18
closed August and Sunday – **st. : M** 71/135.

XX **Chez Frézet,** 181 r. Ordener (18th) ✆ 46 06 64 20 – AE VISA B 13
closed August, Saturday, Sunday and Bank Holidays – **M** a la carte 135/185.

X **La Marbouille,** 41 r. Trois Frères (18th) ✆ 42 64 49 15 – E VISA D 14
closed Sunday – **st. : M** (dinner only) 90.

X **Poulbot-Gourmet,** 39 r. Lamarck (18th) ✆ 46 06 86 00 – VISA C 14
closed Sunday except lunch out of season – **M** a la carte 120/175.

X **Le Pichet,** 174 r. Ordener (18th) ✆ 46 27 85 28 – AE E VISA B 13
closed 20 to 26 April, August, Thursday dinner and Sunday – **M** a la carte 100/170 🍾.

X **Relais Normand,** 32 bis r. d'Orsel (18th) ✆ 46 06 92 57 – AE ⓓ E VISA D 14
closed 2 to 27 August, February Holidays, Friday dinner and Saturday – **st. : M** 59/104.

X **Marie-Louise,** 52 r. Championnet (18th) ✆ 46 06 86 55 – ⓓ VISA B 15
closed 31 July-2 September, Sunday, Monday and Bank Holidays – **M** a la carte 95/145.

X **Le Sancerre,** 13 av. Corentin-Cariou (19th) ✆ 46 07 80 44 – ✻ B 19
closed Saturday and Sunday – **M** a la carte 115/160.

Environs

Bagnolet 93170 Seine-St-Denis 101 ⑯ – pop. 32 557 – alt. 86.

Paris 7,5 – Bobigny 10 – Lagny 27 – Meaux 40.

Novotel Paris Bagnolet M, av. République, Porte de Bagnolet interchange ☎ 43 60 02 10, Telex 670216, – – 25 - 800. AE E VISA
rest. **Le Clos Gourmand M** a la carte 130/200 - **Grill M** a la carte 90/160 – 37 – **611 rm** 510.

Bougival 78380 Yvelines 101 ⑬ – pop. 8 487 – alt. 40.

Paris 18 – Rueil-Malmaison 3,5 – St-Germain-en-Laye 7 – Versailles 7 – Le Vésinet 4.

Château de la Jonchère M, 10 côte la Jonchère ☎ 39 18 57 03, Telex 699491, , park – – 30-200. AE E VISA
st. : M *(closed Sunday dinner and Monday)* a la carte 180/260 - **Bistrot Les Années Trente M** a la carte 100/180 – 35 – **48 rm** 510/1 000.

XXXX ✿ **Coq Hardy,** 16 quai Rennequin-Sualem (N 13) ☎ 36 69 01 43, , « Terraced flower gardens, elegant setting » – . AE E VISA
closed Wednesday – **M** (Sunday booking essential) 300/400
Spec. Foie gras de canard, Millefeuille de St-Jacques aux épinards (October-March), Poulet de Bresse à l'estragon.

XXX ✿ **Le Camelia** (Delaveyne), 7 quai G.-Clemenceau ☎ 39 69 03 02 – AE VISA.
closed Sunday dinner and Monday – **M** a la carte 280/350
Spec. Champignons (September-January), Sole Lafayette, Pièce d'agneau à la sauge en cocotte.

XX **L'Huître et la Tarte,** 6 quai Clemenceau ☎ 39 18 45 55 – VISA.
closed August, Sunday dinner and Monday – **st. : M** a la carte 110/180.

XX Cheval Noir, 14 quai G.-Clemenceau ☎ 39 69 00 96, .

Boulogne-Billancourt 92100 Hauts-de-Seine 101 ㉔ – pop. 102 595 – alt. 35.

See : Bois de Boulogne★★ : Municipal Floral Garden★ (Fleuriste municipal) – Albert Kahn Gardens★ – Paul Landowski Museum★.

Paris 15 – Nanterre 7 – Versailles 11.

Sélect H. M without rest, 66 av. Gén.-Leclerc ☎ 46 04 70 47, Telex 206029 – wc wc . E VISA
st. : 22 – **64 rm** 270/300.

Olympic H. M without rest, 69 av. V.-Hugo ☎ 46 05 20 69, Telex 201443 – wc wc . AE VISA
closed 1 to 15 August – **st. :** 20 – **36 rm** 230/280.

Excelsior without rest, 12 r. Ferme ☎ 46 21 08 08, Telex 203114 – wc . AE
st. : 20 – **52 rm** 220/300.

XXXX ✿ **Au Comte de Gascogne,** 89 av. J.-B.-Clément ☎ 46 03 47 27, « Winter garden » – . AE VISA
closed August, 24 December-1 January, Saturday and Sunday – **M** a la carte 240/340
Spec. Foie frais de canard, Gigotin de lapereau, Homard rôti entier.

XX **L'Avant Seine,** 1 rond-point Rhin et Danube ☎ 48 25 58 00 – . VISA
closed Sunday and Monday – **M** 90/135.

XX ✿ **La Bretonnière,** 120 av. J.-B.-Clément ☎ 46 05 73 56 – AE E VISA
closed Saturday and Sunday – **M** a la carte 185/280.

XX La Bergerie, 87 av. J.-B.-Clément ☎ 46 05 39 07.

XX **La Petite Auberge Franc Comtoise,** 86 av. J.-B.-Clément ☎ 46 05 67 19 – AE E VISA
closed August, Sunday and Bank Holidays – **M** a la carte 155/220.

XX Laux... à la Bouche, 117 av. J.-B.-Clément ☎ 48 25 43 88.

X **La Galère,** 112 r. Gén.-Gallieni ☎ 46 05 64 51 – E VISA.
closed August, Saturday and Sunday – **M** a la carte 120/170.

Le Bourget 93350 Seine-St-Denis 101 ⑰ – pop. 11 021 – alt. 66.

See : Aviation Museum★★.

Paris 15 – Bobigny 5 – Chantilly 34 – Meaux 38 – St-Denis 6,5 – Senlis 36.

Novotel M, at Blanc-Mesnil ZA pont Yblon ✉ 93150 Le Blanc-Mesnil ☎ 48 67 48 88, Telex 230115, , – – 25-250. AE E VISA
M a la carte 90/160 – 33 – **143 rm** 340.

Châteaufort 78117 Yvelines 101 ㉒ – pop. 780 – alt. 153.

Paris 27 – Arpajon 28 – Rambouillet 25 – Versailles 10.

XXX ✿ **La Belle Epoque** (Peignaud), 10 pl. Mairie ☎ 39 56 21 66, «Country inn overlooking a small valley» – AE ⓓ E VISA
closed 12 August-12 September, 22 December-6 January, Sunday dinner and Monday – **M** a la carte 210/390
Spec. Délices des Samouraïs, Canard de Soullans à la façon de Pékin, Compotée de perdrix aux choux (1 October-late December).

Clichy 92110 Hauts-de-Seine 101 ⑮ – pop. 47 000 – alt. 30.

Paris 7,5 – Argenteuil 7 – Nanterre 10 – Pontoise 27 – St-Germain-en-Laye 17.

XXX ✿ **Barrière de Clichy** (Le Galles), 1 r. de Paris ☎ 47 37 05 18 – ▤. AE ⓓ E VISA
closed 8 to 23 August, Saturday lunch and Sunday – **M** 230 (lunch) and a la carte 210/280
Spec. Encornets farcis, Fricassée de sole et ris de veau, Noisettes d'agneau au chèvre frais.

Courbevoie 92400 Hauts-de-Seine 101 ⑭ – pop. 59 931 – alt. 34.

See : La Défense★★ : perspective★ from the parvis.

Paris 11 – Asnières 3 – Levallois-Perret 3,5 – Nanterre 4 – St-Germain-en-Laye 14.

the Défense quarter :

Novotel Paris La Défense [M], 2 bd Neuilly ☎ **47 78 16 68, Telex 630288,** ≤ – ▤ TV ☎ ♿ – 25 - 150. AE ⓓ E VISA
M Grill a la carte 90/160 ⅄ – ☕ 45 – **276 rm** 555/590.

the Charras quarter :

Penta, 18 r. Baudin ☎ **47 88 50 51, Telex 610470** – ▤ rest TV wc ☎ – 25 - 300. AE ⓓ E VISA. ✂ rest
st. : rest. **l'Atelier M** 145 b.i. – ☕ 41 – **494 rm** 460/495.

Créteil P 94000 Val-de-Marne 101 ㉗ – pop. 71 705 – alt. 49.

See : Town Hall★ : parvis★ – ℹ 1 r. F.-Mauriac ☎ 48 98 58 18.

Paris 13 – Bobigny 19 – Évry 22 – Lagny 26 – Melun 36.

Novotel [M] ⛰, **near the lake** ☎ **42 07 91 02, Telex 670395,** – ▤ TV ☎ Ⓟ – 100. AE ⓓ E VISA
M a la carte 90/160 ⅄ – ☕ 33 – **110 rm** 357.

Enghien-les-Bains 95880 Val d'Oise 101 ⑤ – pop. 9 739 – alt. 50 – Spa – Casino.

See : Lake★ – 18 of Domont ☎ 39 91 07 50, N : 8 km – ℹ 2 bd Cotte ☎ 34 12 41 15.

Paris 16 – Argenteuil 6 – Chantilly 32 – Pontoise 20 – St-Denis 6 – St-Germain-en-Laye 23.

Grand Hôtel, 85 r. Gén.-de-Gaulle ☎ **34 12 80 00, Telex 697842,** «**Attractive flower garden**» – TV ☎ Ⓟ – 35. AE ⓓ VISA. ✂ rest
st. : M 140/200 – ☕ 38 – **48 rm** 345/505, 3 apartments 715.

Villa Marie Louise ⛰ without rest, **49 r. Malleville** ☎ **39 64 82 21** – wc wc ☎
st. : ☕ 16 – **22 rm** 140/214.

XXXX ✿✿ **Duc d'Enghien,** at the Casino ☎ **34 12 90 00,** ≤ lake – ▤. AE ⓓ E VISA
closed January, Sunday dinner and Monday – **M** 280 b.i. (lunch) and a la carte 265/380
Spec. Langoustines rôties au gingembre, Raviole de homard aux truffes (November-March), Pigeon et foie gras en paupiette de chou.

XX **Aub. Landaise,** 32 bd d'Ormesson ☎ **34 12 78 36** – AE E VISA
closed August, Sunday dinner and Wednesday – **st. : M** a la carte 140/190.

XX **A la Carpe d'Or,** 91 r. Gén.-de-Gaulle ☎ **34 12 79 53** – AE ⓓ VISA
M a la carte 140/230 ⅄.

Gennevilliers 92230 Hauts-de-Seine 101 ⑮ – pop. 45 445 – alt. 29.

ℹ 177 av. Gabriel Péri (closed morning) ☎ 47 99 33 92.

Paris 10 – Nanterre 12 – Pontoise 23 – St-Denis 4 – St-Germain-en-Laye 20.

XX ✿ **Julius,** 6 bd Camélinat ☎ **47 98 79 37** – ▤. VISA
closed Saturday lunch and Sunday – **st. : M** a la carte 205/285
Spec. Poissons du marché, Blanquette de lapereau, Mousseline de fromage blanc.

Longjumeau 91160 Essonne 101 ㉟ – pop. 18 395 – alt. 72.

Paris 21 – Chartres 70 – Dreux 82 – Évry 16 – Melun 39 – Orléans 96 – Versailles 21.

Relais des Chartreux [M], **at Saulxier SW : 2 km, on N 20** ✉ **91160 Longjumeau** ☎ **69 09 34 31, Telex 691245,** ≤, – TV ☎ Ⓟ – 150. E VISA
st. : M 110/175 – ☕ 35 – **100 rm** 330/350 – P 345/530.

Relais St-Georges [M] ⛰, **at Saulx-les-Chartreux SW : 3 km** ✉ **91160 Longjumeau** ☎ **64 48 36 40, Telex 603038,** ≤, park – TV ☎ Ⓟ – 80. AE ⓓ E VISA
closed August – **st. : M** 140/250 – **40 rm** ☕ 250/350 – P 400/450.

Maisons-Laffitte 78600 Yvelines 101 ⑬ – pop. 22 892 – alt. 40 – **See : Château★.**

Paris 21 – Argenteuil 8,5 – Mantes-la-Jolie 37 – Poissy 8 – Pontoise 18 – St-Germain 8 – Versailles 24.

XXX ✿✿ **Le Tastevin** (Blanchet), 9 av. Eglé ✆ 39 62 11 67, ☂, ⚘ – Ⓟ. AE ⓓ VISA
closed 17 August-9 September, 1 to 15 February, Monday dinner and Tuesday – **st. : M** a la carte 220/300
Spec. Escalope de foie gras chaud, Assiette du pêcheur au Bouzy, Sanciaux aux pommes (season).

XXX ✿ **Vieille Fontaine** (Clerc), 8 av. Gretry ✆ 39 62 01 78, ☂, « Garden » – AE ⓓ VISA
closed August, Sunday and Monday – **M** a la carte 290/400
Spec. Cuisses de grenouilles à la coque, St Jacques à la fondue d'endives (October-March), Millefeuille aux noisettes.

XX **Le Laffitte,** 5 av. St-Germain ✆ 39 62 01 53 – AE E VISA
closed August, 10 to 17 February, dinner Sunday and Tuesday and Wednesday – **st. : M** 200 b.i./250 b.i.

Marne-la-Vallée 77206 S.-et-M. 101 ⑲

Paris 26 – Meaux 28 – Melun 35.

S.E : 6 km by Lagny traffic interchange A 4 :

Novotel Ⓜ, ✆ 60 05 91 15, Telex 691990, ☂, ⛱ – ⇅ ▤ TV ☎ ♿ Ⓟ – 🏛 130. AE ⓓ E VISA
M a la carte 90/160 ♪ – ☕ 30 – **92 rm** 340/355.

Meudon 92190 Hauts-de-Seine 101 ㉔ – pop. 49 004 – alt. 100.
See : Terrace★ : ✹★ – Meudon Forest★.

Paris 11 – Boulogne-Billancourt 3 – Clamart 3,5 – Nanterre 11 – Versailles 10.

XXX ✿ **Relais des Gardes,** at Bellevue, 42 av. Gallieni ✆ 45 34 11 79, ☂ – AE ⓓ VISA
closed August, Sunday dinner and Saturday – **st. : M** a la carte 190/290
Spec. Aumonière Côte d'Emeraude, Estouffade de turbot, Baba au rhum.

Montrouge 92120 Hauts-de-Seine 101 ㉕ – pop. 38 632 – alt. 74.

Paris 6 – Boulogne-Billancourt 6,5 – Longjumeau 14 – Nanterre 15 – Versailles 16.

Mercure Ⓜ, 13 r. F.-Ory ✆ 46 57 11 26, Telex 202528 – ⇅ ▤ TV ☎ ♿ 🚗 – 🏛 150. AE ⓓ E VISA
st. : M a la carte 135/190 – ☕ 42 – **186 rm** 520/550.

Neuilly-sur-Seine 92200 Hauts-de-Seine 101 ⑮ – pop. 64 450 – alt. 36.
See : Bois de Boulogne★★ : Jardin d'acclimatation★, (Children's Amusement Park, Miniature Railway and Zoo in the Bois de Boulogne), Bagatelle★ (Park and Garden) National Museum of Popular Art and Traditions★★ – Palais des Congrès★ : main conference hall★★, ≤★ from hotel Concorde-Lafayette.

Paris (by Porte Neuilly) 8 – Argenteuil 12 – Nanterre 5,5 – Pontoise 37 – St-Germain 14 – Versailles 18.

H. Club Méditerranée Ⓜ, 58 bd. V.-Hugo ✆ 47 58 11 00, Telex 610971, ☂, Club atmosphere, ⚘ – ⇅ ▤ TV ☎ – 🏛 150. AE ⓓ VISA
st. : M 200 b.i./220 b.i. – ☕ 50 – **335 rm** 825/945, 3 apartments.

Parc Neuilly without rest, 4 bd Parc ✆ 46 24 32 62, Telex 613689 – ⇅ TV 🛁wc 🚿wc ☎. VISA
st. : ☕ 18 – **71 rm** 194/277.

Roule without rest, 37 bis av. du Roule ✆ 46 24 60 09 – ⇅ TV 🛁wc 🚿wc ☎
st. : ☕ 20 – **35 rm** 180/300.

XXX ✿ **Jacqueline Fénix,** 42 av. Ch.-de-Gaulle ✆ 46 24 42 61 – ▤. AE VISA
closed August, 23 December-4 January Saturday, Sunday and Bank Holidays – **st. : M** a la carte 250/340
Spec. Millefeuille de lapereau, Filet d'agneau et rognon de veau au beurre de persil, Meringué aux noix.

XXX **Le Manoir,** r. Église ✆ 46 24 04 61 – ▤. AE ⓓ VISA
closed 14 July-15 August, Saturday lunch and Sunday – **st. : M** a la carte 200/285.

XXX **Truffe Noire** (Jacquet), 2 pl. Parmentier ✆ 46 24 94 14 – VISA. ⚘
closed 10 to 15 August, Saturday lunch and Sunday – **M** a la carte 165/235
Spec. Mousseline de brochet au beurre blanc, Aiguillettes de canette au citron, Coeur de filet à la moelle.

XX **Jarrasse,** 4 av. Madrid ✆ 46 24 07 56 – AE ⓓ E VISA
closed 4 July-1 September, Sunday dinner and Monday – **M** a la carte 185/310.

XX **Tonnelle Saintongeaise,** 32 bd Vital Bouhot ✆ 46 24 43 15, ☂
closed 1 to 21 August, 20 December-3 January, Saturday and Sunday – **M** a la carte 135/190.

XX **Chau'veau,** 59 r. Chauveau ✆ 46 24 46 22 – ⓓ VISA
closed August, Saturday and Sunday – **M** a la carte 105/175.

XX **Bourrier,** 1 pl. Parmentier ✆ 46 24 11 19 – AE VISA
closed 1 to 20 August, 23 December-3 January, Saturday (except dinner in winter) and Sunday – **st. : M** 180/250.

XX **Focly,** 10 r. P.-Chatrousse ✆ 46 24 43 36, Chinese cuisine – AE VISA
closed 13 to 27 July – **M** 70 b.i./150 b.i.

XX **Carpe Diem,** 10 r. Église ✆ 46 24 95 01
closed 1 to 9 May, 7 to 31 August, 26 December-5 January, Saturday lunch and Sunday – **st.** : **M** a la carte 200/260.

X **Chez Livio,** 6 r. longchamp ✆ 46 24 81 32, , Italian cuisine – VISA
closed 24 to 31 December and week-ends in August – **M** 110 b.i.

Nogent-sur-Marne **94130** Val-de-Marne **101** ㉗ – pop. 24 696 – alt. 56.
5 av. Joinville (closed morning) ✆ 48 73 75 90.
Paris 14 – Créteil 6,5 – Montreuil 5 – Vincennes 4.

Nogentel M, 8 r. Port ✆ 48 72 70 00, Telex 210116, ← – – 250. AE E VISA
rest. **Le Panoramic** *(closed August)* **M** a la carte 185/250 - Grill **Le Canotier M** a la carte 95/145 – 35 – **61 rm** 330/360.

Orly (Paris Airport) **94396** Val-de-Marne **101** ㉖ – pop. 23 886 – alt. 89.
Information : ✆ 48 84 32 10.
Paris 16 – Corbeil-Essonnes 17 – Créteil 12 – Longjumeau 9 – Villeneuve-St-Georges 12.

Hilton Orly M, near air terminal ✆ 46 87 33 88, Telex 250621, ← – – 300. AE E VISA
st. : rest. **Le Café du Marché M** a la carte 105/155 - **La Louisiane** *(closed August, Saturday and Sunday* **M** a la carte 165/220 – 36 – **380 rm** 520/970.

Orly Airport South :

XX **Le Grillardin,** ✆ 46 87 24 25, ← – . AE E VISA
st. : **M** (lunch only) 140.

Orly Airport West :

XXX **Maxim's,** ✆ 46 87 16 16, ← – . AE VISA
st. : **M** (lunch only) a la carte 210/290.

XX **Jardin d'Orly,** ✆ 46 87 16 16, ← – . AE VISA
closed August, Saturday and Sunday – **st.** : **M** a la carte 140/175.

X **La Galerie,** ✆ 46 87 16 16, ← – . VISA
st. : **M** a la carte 110/140 .

Le Pré St-Gervais **93310** Seine-St-Denis **101** ⑯ – pop. 13 313 – alt. 71.
Paris 7 – Bobigny 5 – Lagny 27 – Meaux 38 – Senlis 44.

X ✿ **Au Pouilly Reuilly** (Thibault), 68 r. A.-Joineau ✆ 48 45 14 59 – AE VISA.
closed 1 August-5 September, Sunday and Bank Holidays – **M** a la carte 90/180
Spec. Pâté de grenouilles, Foie de veau aux girolles, Rognon de veau dijonnaise.

Puteaux **92800** Hauts-de-Seine **101** ⑭ – pop. 36 143 – alt. 36.
See : La Défense★★ : perspective★★ of the parvis.
Paris 11 – Nanterre 3 – Pontoise 35 – St-Germain-en-Laye 11 – Versailles 14.

XX ✿ **Gasnier,** 7 bd Richard-Wallace ✆ 45 06 33 63 – AE VISA
closed 26 June-3 August, February Holidays, Saturday, Sunday and Bank Holidays – **st.** : **M** (booking essential) a la carte 205/270
Spec. Petit Gris du contrebandier, Cassoulet, Confit de canard aux cèpes.

Roissy-en-France **95700** Val-d'Oise **101** ⑧ – pop. 1 411.
Charles de Gaulle ✆ 48 62 22 80.
Paris 25 – Chantilly 28 – Meaux 36 – Pontoise 44 – Senlis 28.

in the airport area :

Sofitel M, ✆ 48 62 23 23, Telex 230166, , – – 25 - 500. AE E VISA
st. : Panoramic rest. **Les Valois** *(closed lunch Saturday and Sunday)* **M** 175 - **Le Jardin** (brasserie) (ground floor) **M** a la carte 130/195 – 42 – **344 rm** 590/705, 8 apartments 995.

in the airport nr. 1 :

XXXX ✿ **Maxim's,** ✆ 48 62 16 16 – . AE E VISA
st. : **M** (lunch only) a la carte 310/430
Spec. Poêlée de lotte et langoustines au basilic, Chartreuse de ris et rognon de veau, Poulet de Bresse aux ravioles de truffes.

XX **Grill Maxim's,** ✆ 48 62 16 16 – . AE E VISA
st. : **M** a la carte 230/290.

Rueil-Malmaison **92500** Hauts-de-Seine **101** ⑬ – pop. **64 545** – alt. 15.

See : Museum★★ of the Château de Malmaison – Château de Bois-Préau★ – Church (organ-corse★).

Paris 15 – Argenteuil 12 – Nanterre 1,5 – St-Germain-en-Laye 7,5 – Versailles 11.

Cardinal M without rest, 1 pl. Richelieu ✆ 47 08 20 20, Telex 204113 – 30. AE E VISA
st. : 39 – **55 rm** 330/470.

XXX ❀ **El Chiquito,** 126 av. Paul-Doumer ✆ 47 51 00 53, « Garden » – E VISA
closed August, Saturday and Sunday – **M** a la carte 200/300
Spec. Médaillon de lotte au vinaigre et miel, Saumon frais au beurre de homard, Gigot de mer aux pâtes fraiches.

XX **Relais de St-Cucufa,** 114 r. Gén.-Miribel ✆ 47 49 79 05, – VISA
closed 13 to 31 August, dinner Sunday and Monday – **st.** : **M** a la carte 155/250.

at Nanterre P N : 2 km – pop. 90 371 – ✉ **92000** Nanterre :

XXX **Ile de France,** 83 av. Mar. Joffre ✆ 47 24 10 44, – . AE VISA
closed August and Sunday except Bank Holidays – **M** 110/136.

Rungis **94150** Val-de-Marne **101** ㉖ – pop. **2 650** – alt. 80 - Main wholesale produce market for Paris.

Paris 13 – Antony 5,5 – Corbeil-Essonnes 26 – Créteil 11 – Longjumeau 10.

Pullman Orly M Access : from Paris, Highway A6 and take Orly Airport exit, from outside of Paris, A6 and Rungis-Orly exit, 20 av. Ch.-Lindbergh ✉ 94656 ✆ 46 87 36 36, Telex 260738, <, – – 50 - 300. AE E VISA
st. : rest. **La Rungisserie M** a la carte 170/260 – 45 – **205 rm** 495/595.

Holiday Inn M Access : from Paris, Highway A6 and take Orly Airport exit, from outside of Paris, A6 and Rungis-Orly exit ✆ 46 87 26 66, Telex 204679, , – – 50 - 250. AE E VISA
st. : **M** 90/105 – 50 – **168 rm** 517/594.

XXX **Le Charolais,** 13 r. N-Dame at Rungis Ville ✆ 46 86 16 42 – AE VISA
closed 10 to 31 August, 21 December-4 January, Saturday and Sunday – **M** 180 (lunch) and a la carte 180/245 .

Saclay **91400** Essonne **101** ㉓ – pop. **1 865** – alt. 157.

18 St-Aubin ✆ 69 41 25 19, SW : 2,5 km.

Paris 26 – Arpajon 22 – Chartres 68 – Evry 28 – Rambouillet 30 – Versailles 11.

Novotel M, near Christ-de-Saclay circle ✆ 69 41 81 40, Telex 691856, , , – – 450. AE E VISA
M Grill a la carte 90/160 – 33 – **134 rm** 350.

St-Germain-en-Laye SP **78100** Yvelines **101** ⑫ – pop. **40 829** – alt. 78.

See : Château★ BZ **: Museum of National Antiquities★★ – Terrace★★** BY **– English Garden★** BY **– Priory Museum ★** AZ.

9 ; 18 ✆ 34 51 75 90 by ④ : 3 km ; 9 ; 9 ; 9 of Fourqueux ✆ 34 51 41 47 by r. de Mareil AZ - 4 km.

1 bis r. République ✆ 44 51 05 12.

Paris 29 ② – Beauvais 73 ① – Chartres 81 ③ – Dreux 70 ③ – Mantes-la-J. 34 ④ – Versailles 13 ③.

Plan on next page

Pavillon Henri IV M , 21 r. Thiers ✆ 34 51 62 62, Telex 695822, < Paris and the River Seine, , – – 200. AE E VISA BZ **s**
st. : **M** a la carte 275/400 – **42 rm** 600/1 400, 3 apartments 2 000.

Le Cèdre , 7 r. Alsace ✆ 34 51 84 35, – wc – 30. AY **u**
closed 1 February-7 March – **st.** : **M** 83/96 – **31 rm** 175/255 – P 270/355.

XXX **Le 7 Rue des Coches,** 7 r. Coches ✆ 39 73 66 40 – . AE E VISA AZ **e**
closed Sunday dinner and Monday – **st.** : **M** a la carte 215/275.

X **Petite Auberge,** 119 bis r. L.-Desoyer - AZ - ✆ 34 51 03 99 – VISA
closed July, 3 to 10 March, Tuesday dinner and Wednesday – **st.** : **M** (booking essential) a la carte 100/135 .

X **La Résidence,** 149 r. Pdt Roosevelt by r. Joffre - AZ - ✆ 34 51 03 07, – VISA
closed Sunday dinner and Monday – **st.** : **M** a la carte 135/185.

to the NW by ① : 2,5 km on N 284 and route des Mares – ✉ **78100** St-Germain-en-Laye :

La Forestière M , 1 av. Prés.-Kennedy ✆ 39 73 36 60, Telex 696055, – – 40. E VISA
st. : **M** see rest **Cazaudehore** below – 40 – **24 rm** 520/590, 6 apartments 690/760.

XXX ❀ **Cazaudehore,** 1 av. Prés.-Kennedy ✆ 34 51 93 80, , « Rustic decor, flower garden in woods » – . E VISA
closed Monday except Bank Holidays – **M** a la carte 185/250
Spec. Foie gras de canard, Saumon rôti sur sa peau, Aiguillettes de canard à l'orange.

ST-GERMAIN EN-LAYE

Bonnenfant (R. A.) .... AZ 3
Marché-Neuf (Pl. du) .... AZ 17
Pain (R. au) .... AZ 20
Paris (R. de) .... AZ
Poissy (R. de) .... AZ 22
Vieux-Marché (R. du) .... AZ 33

Alain (Pl. Jéhan) .... AY 2
Coches (R. des) .... AZ 4
Denis (R. M.) .... AZ 5
Detaille (Pl.) .... AY 6
Gaulle (Pl. Ch. de) .... BZ 7
Giraud-Teulon (R.) .... BZ 9
Gde-Fontaine (R.) .... AZ 10
Gréban (R. R.) .... AZ 12

Lattre-de-T. (Av. Mar. de) .... BZ 13
Loges (Av. des) .... AY 14
Lyautey (R. Mar.) .... BZ 15
Malraux (Pl. A.) .... BZ 16
Mareil (Pl.) .... AZ 19
Pologne (R. de) .... AY 23
Pontoise (R. de) .... AY 25
St-Louis (R.) .... BZ 26
Victoire (Pl. de la) .... AY 30
Vieil-Abreuvoir (R. du) .... AZ 32

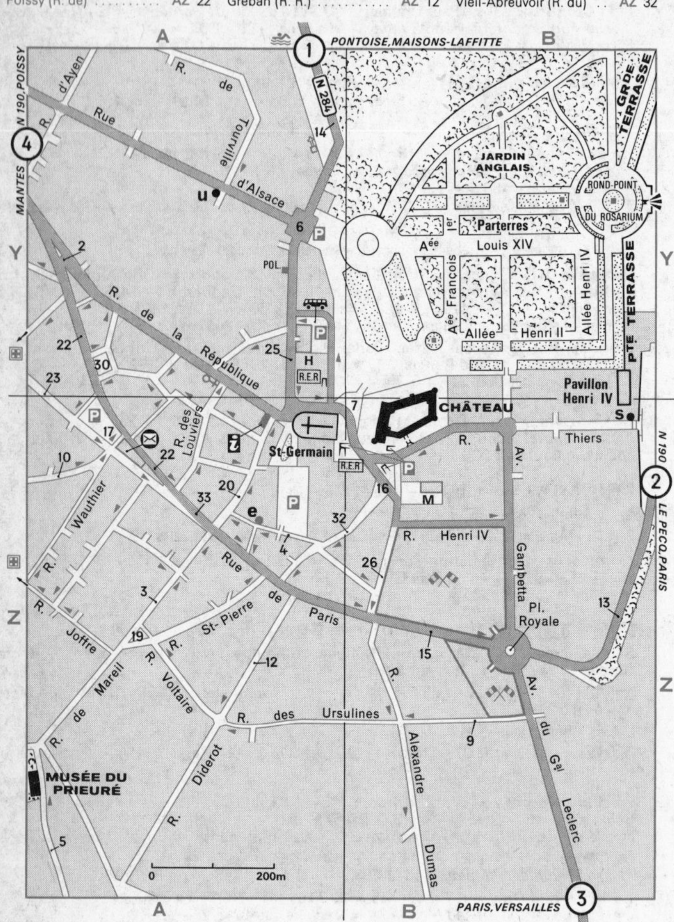

*If you would like a more complete selection of hotels and restaurants, consult the **Michelin Guides** for the following countries:*
Benelux, Deutschland, España Portugal, France, Great Britain and Ireland, Italia.

Vélizy-Villacoublay **78140** Yvelines **101** ㉓ – pop. 23 886 – alt. 174.

Paris 18 – Antony 11 – Chartres 79 – Meudon 7,5 – Versailles 6,5.

Holiday Inn M, av. Europe, near commercial centre Vélizy II ☎ 39 46 96 98, Telex 696537, – – 400. AE ① E VISA
st. : M 80/180 – 50 – **183 rm** 565/650.

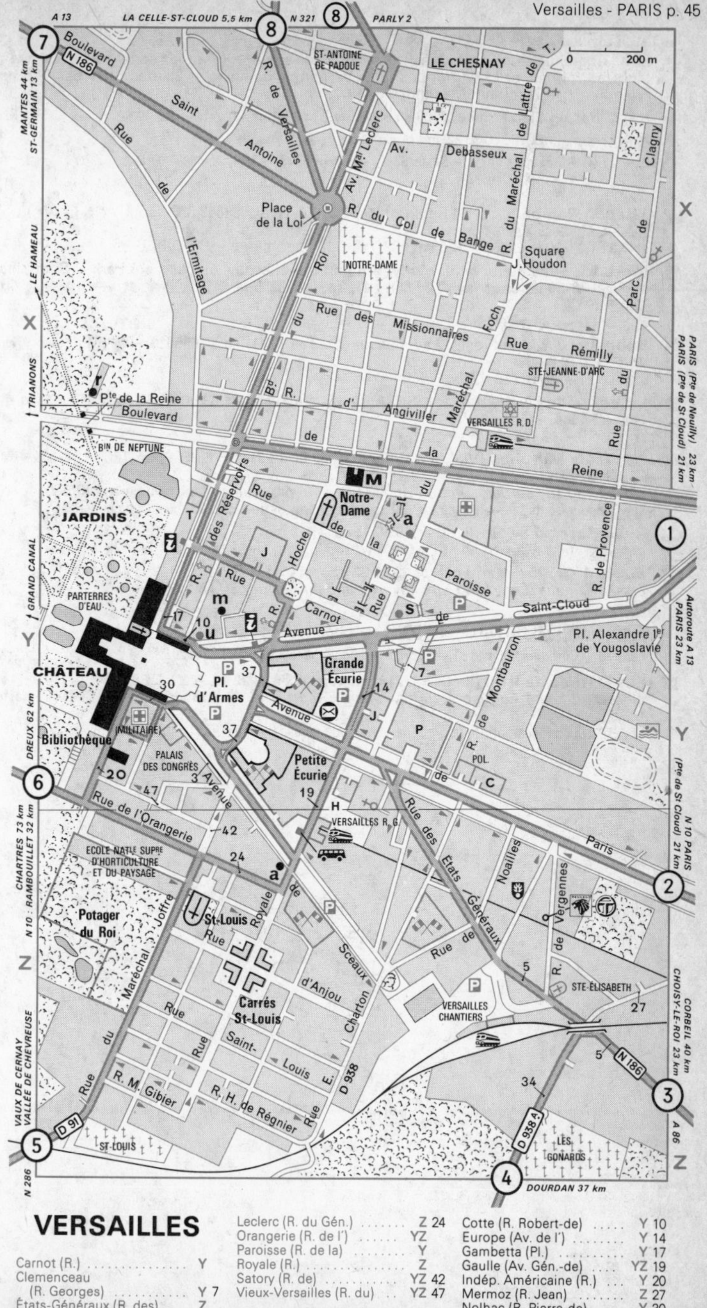

VERSAILLES

Carnot (R.) . . . . Y
Clemenceau (R. Georges) . . . . Y 7
États-Généraux (R. des) . . . Z
Foch (R. du Mar.) . . . . Y
Hoche (R.) . . . . Y

Leclerc (R. du Gén.) . . . . . . Z 24
Orangerie (R. de l') . . . . . . YZ
Paroisse (R. de la) . . . . Y
Royale (R.) . . . . Z
Satory (R. de) . . . . YZ 42
Vieux-Versailles (R. du) . . YZ 47

Chancellerie (R. de la) . . . . Y 3
Chantiers (R. des) . . . . Z 5
Cotte (R. Robert-de) . . . . . Y 10
Europe (Av. de l') . . . . Y 14
Gambetta (Pl.) . . . . Y 17
Gaulle (Av. Gén.-de) . . . . YZ 19
Indép. Américaine (R.) . . . Y 20
Mermoz (R. Jean) . . . . Z 27
Nolhac (R. Pierre-de) . . . . . Y 30
Porte de Buc (R.) . . . . Z 34
Rockefeller (Av.) . . . . Y 37

Versailles P 78000 Yvelines 101 ㉒ – pop. 95 240 – alt. 132.

See : Château*** Y – Gardens*** fountain display*** (grandes eaux) and illuminated night performances*** (grandes fêtes de nuit) in summer – Ecuries Royales* – The Trianons** – Lambinet Museum* Y **M**.

Racing Club France ✆ 39 50 59 41 by ③ : 2,5 km.

7 r. Réservoirs ✆ 39 50 36 22 and pl. d'Armes (May-September).

Paris 22 ① – Beauvais 92 ⑦ – Dreux 62 ⑥ – Évreux 85 ⑦ – Melun 59 ③ – Orléans 121 ③.

Plan on preceding page

Trianon Palace , 1 bd Reine ✆ 39 50 34 12, Telex 698863, , park – 80. AE E VISA. rest X **r**
st. : **M** 162/210 – 55 – **120 rm** 682/1 012, 10 apartments – P 720/872.

Mercure M without rest, r. Marly-le-Roi at the Chesnay, across from Parly 2 Shopping mall ✉ 78150 Le Chesnay ✆ 39 55 11 41, Telex 695205 – wc – 45. AE E VISA
st. : 30 – **78 rm** 324/350.

Bellevue M without rest, 12 av. Sceaux ✆ 39 50 13 41, Telex 695613 – wc wc . AE E VISA Z **a**
st. : 21 – **25 rm** 180/275.

Le Versailles without rest, r. Ste-Anne (Petite Place) ✆ 39 50 64 65 – wc . AE E VISA Y **m**
st. : 19 – **48 rm** 226/305.

XXXX ✿✿ **Trois Marches** (Vié), 3 r. Colbert ✆ 39 50 13 21, , « Elegant 18C hotel » – . AE E VISA Y **u**
closed 1 to 15 February, Sunday and Monday – **M** 200 (lunch) and a la carte 240/380
Spec. Méli-mélo de saumon au caviar, Crustacés étuvés au jus de carottes, Gibier (October-January).

XXX **Rescatore,** 27 av. St-Cloud ✆ 39 50 23 60 – AE VISA Y **s**
closed Saturday lunch and Sunday – **M** 165 (lunch) and a la carte 215/260.

XXX **Boule d'Or,** 25 r. Mar.-Foch ✆ 39 50 22 97 – AE E VISA Y **a**
closed Sunday dinner and Monday except Bank Holidays – **M** 145/195.

Viry-Châtillon 91170 Essonne 101 ㊱ – pop. 30 290 – alt. 36.

Paris 26 – Corbeil-Essonnes 11 – Évry 8,5 – Longjumeau 8,5 – Versailles 29.

XX ✿ **La Dariole de Viry** (Richard), 21 r. Pasteur ✆ 69 44 22 40 – . AE VISA
closed 11 July-4 August, Saturday lunch, Sunday and Bank Holidays – **st.** : **M** a la carte 185/260.
Spec. Blinis aux escargots de Bourgogne, Navarin de terre et mer au curry, Coupe "Béatrice".

and beyond...

La Ferté-sous-Jouarre 77260 S.-et-M. 56 ⑬, 196 ㉔ – pop. 7 020 – alt. 62.
See : Jouarre : crypt★ of the abbey (S : 3 km).
Paris 66 – Melun 63 – Reims 82 – Troyes 117.

XXXX ✿✿ **Auberge de Condé** (Tingaud), 1 av. Montmirail ✆ 60 22 00 07 – Ⓟ. AE ⓓ E VISA
closed February, Monday dinner and Tuesday – **M** 250 b.i./300 and a la carte
Spec. Bourse de saumon fumé au caviar, Tresse de sole et de saumon, Ris de veau aux langoustines.

Joigny 89300 Yonne 65 ④ – pop. 10 488 – alt. 101.
See : Vierge au Sourire★ in St-Thibault's Church – Côte St-Jacques ≤★ 1,5 km by D 20.
ℹ quai H.-Ragobert ✆ 86 62 11 05.
Paris 146 – Auxerre 27 – Gien 74 – Montargis 59 – Sens 30 – Troyes 76.

XXXX ✿✿✿ **A la Côte St-Jacques** (Lorain) with rm, 14 fg Paris ✆ 86 62 09 70, Telex 801458, « Fine decor », – TV wc wc ☎ Ⓟ. AE ⓓ VISA
closed 4 to 26 January – **M** (Sunday booking essential) 380/400 and a la carte – 60 – **14 rm** 350/420
Spec. Dos de saumon sauvage en vessie, Bar fumé à la crème de caviar, Trois desserts au chocolat. **Wines** Chablis.

Pontoise 95300 Val-d'Oise 196 ⑤⑥ – pop. 29 411 – alt. 27.
ℹ 6 pl. Petit Martroy ✆ 30 38 24 25.
Paris 34 – Beauvais 55 – Dieppe 135 – Mantes-la-Jolie 39 – Rouen 91.

at Cormeilles-en-Vexin NW by D 915 – ✉ **95830** Cormeilles-en-Vexin :

XXX ✿✿ **Relais Ste-Jeanne** (Cagna), on D 915 ✆ 34 66 61 56, , « Garden » – Ⓟ. AE ⓓ VISA
closed 3 to 27 August, Christmas Day, February Holidays, Tuesday dinner (except April-July), Sunday dinner and Monday – **st.** : **M** (booking essential) 250/350 and a la carte
Spec. Saumon poêlé au poivre noir, Ris de veau au coulis de truffes (June-October), Adagio chocolat et pistache.

Rheims 51100 Marne 56 ⑥⑯ – pop. 181 985 – alt. 83.
See : Cathédral★★★ : tapestries★★ – St-Remi Basilica★★ : interior★★★ – Palais du Tau★★ – Champagne cellars★ – Place Royale★ – Porte Mars★ – Hôtel de la Salle★ – Foujita Chapel★ – Library★ of Ancient College de Jésuites – Museum St-Rémi★★ – Hôtel le Vergeur Museum★ – St-Denis Museum★ – Historical centre of the French motor industry.
Envir. : Fort de la Pompelle : German helmets ★ 9 km to the SE by N 44.
18 ✆ 26 03 60 14 at Gueux to the NW by N 44 : 9,5 km.
✆ 26 88 50 50.
ℹ and Accueil de France (Information facilities and hotel reservations - not more than 5 days in advance) 1 r. Jadart ✆ 26 47 25 69, Telex 830631 – A.C. 7 bd Lundy ✆ 26 47 34 76.
Paris 142 – Bruxelles 214 – Châlons-sur-Marne 45 – Lille 209 – Luxembourg 232.

✿✿✿ **Boyer "Les Crayères"** M, 64 bd Vasnier ✆ 26 82 80 80, Telex 830959, ≤, , « Elegant mansion in park », , – TV ☎ Ⓟ – 30. AE ⓓ E VISA
closed 21 December-11 January – **M** *(closed Tuesday lunch and Monday)* (booking essential) a la carte 260/355 – 56 – **16 rm** 739/1 217
Spec. Terrine de boeuf en gelée, St-Pierre en nage de poireaux, Cervelas de volaille de Bresse. **Wines** Chouilly blanc, Mareuil rouge.

Vézelay 89450 Yonne 65 ⑮ – pop. 582 – alt. 302 – Pilgrimage (22 July).
See : Ste-Madeleine Basilica★★★ : tower ★.
Envir. : Site★ of Pierre-Perthuis SE : 6 km.
ℹ r. St-Pierre (Easter-30 September) ✆ 86 33 23 69.
Paris 217 – Auxerre 51 – Avallon 15 – Château-Chinon 60 – Clamecy 23.

at St-Père SE : 3 km by D 957 – alt. 148 – ✉ **89450** Vézelay.
See : Church of N.-Dame★.

✿✿✿ **Espérance** (Meneau) , ✆ 86 33 20 45, Telex 800005, ≤, « country garden » – rest TV ☎ Ⓟ. AE ⓓ VISA
closed early January-early February, Wednesday lunch and Tuesday – **M** (booking essential) 400 and a la carte – 65 – **17 rm** 480/900, 4 apartments 1 800
Spec. Cromesquis de foie gras, Turbot rôti, Salmigondi de pigeon. **Wines** Bourgogne aligoté, Irancy.

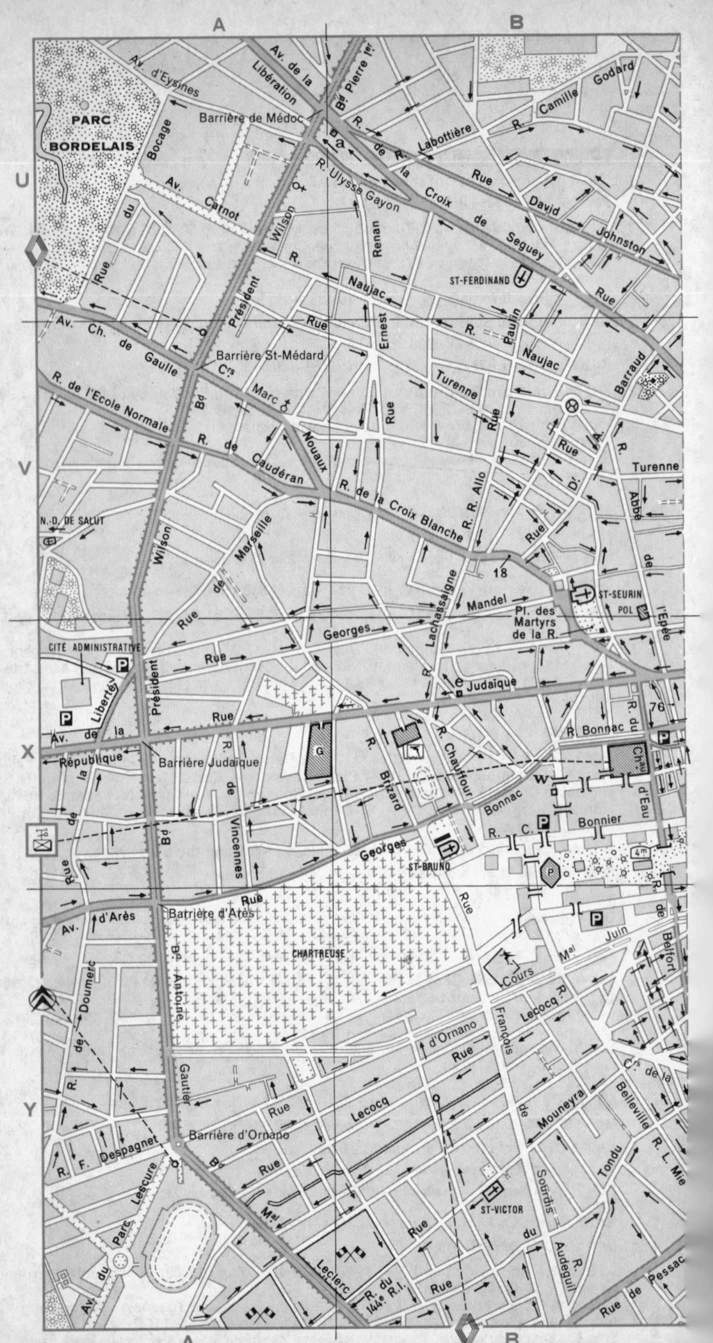

PARC BORDELAIS
Barrière de Médoc
Barrière St-Médard
ST-FERDINAND
N.-D. DE SALUT
CITÉ ADMINISTRATIVE
Barrière Judaïque
ST-SEURIN
Pl. des Martyrs de la R.
ST-BRUNO
Barrière d'Arès
CHARTREUSE
Barrière d'Ornano
ST-VICTOR

BORDEAUX

Capdeville (R.)	BV	18
Chapeau-Rouge (Cours)	DX	20
Comédie (Pl. de la)	CX	21
Docteur-Nancel-Pénard (R.)	CX	24
Duffour-Dubergier (R.)	CY	26
Esprit-des-Lois (R.)	DV	27
Gaspard-Philippe (R.)	DY	37
Hamel (R. du)	DY	43
Montbazon (R.)	CX	58
Parlement (Pl. du)	DX	65
Philippart (R. F.)	DX	69
République (Pl.)	CY	73
St-Sernin (R.)	BX	76
Tournon (Crs de)	CV	83
Tourny (Pl. de)	CV	84
Villedieu (R.)	CY	88

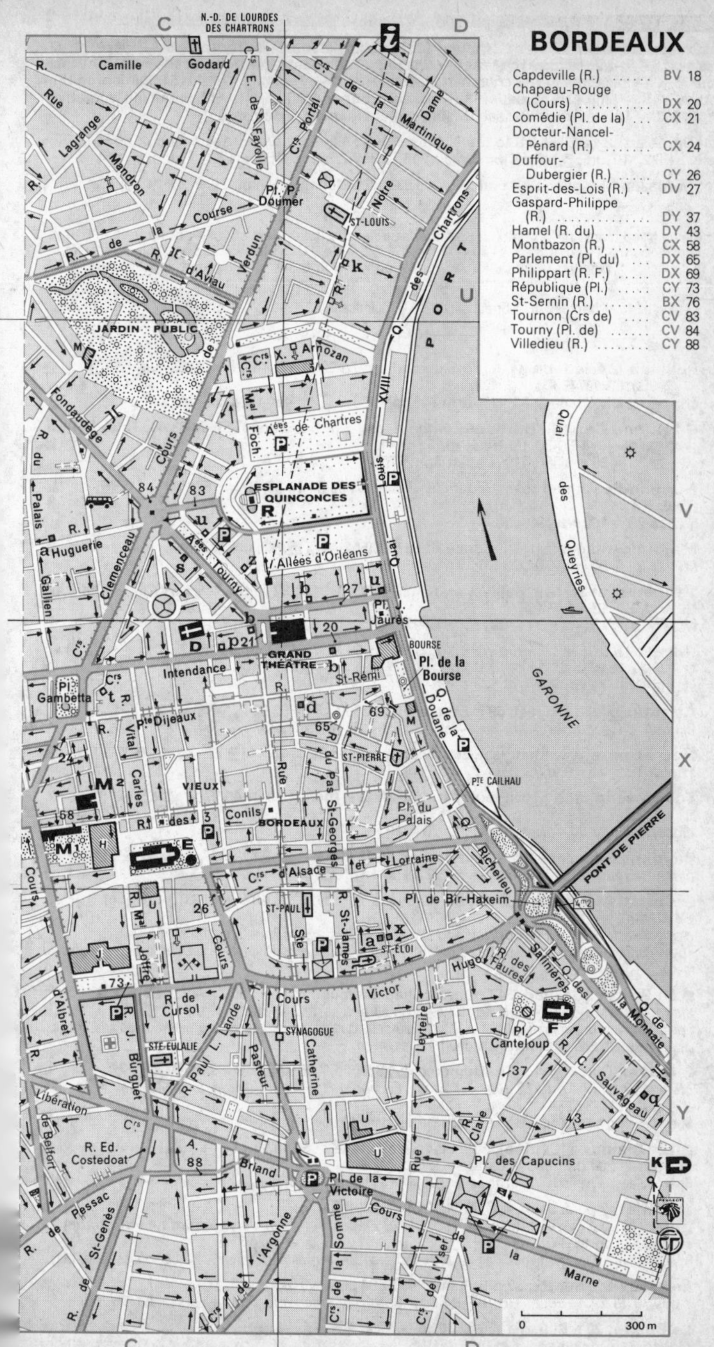

BORDEAUX P 33000 Gironde 71 ⑨ – pop. 211 197 – Greater Bordeaux 617 705 h. – alt. 5.

See : Grand Théâtre★★ CDVX – Cathedral★ and Pey Berland Belfry★ CX **E** – Place de la Bourse★ DX – St-Michel Basilica★ DY **F** – Place du Parlement★ DX **65** – Facade★ of Ste-Croix Church DY **K** – Façade★ of the church of N.-Dame CX **D** – Fountain★ of the Monument to the Girondins CV **R** – Fine Arts Museum★★ (Musée des Beaux Arts) CX **M1** – Museum of Decorative Arts★ CX **M2** – The mint★ of Pessac (Établissement monétaire de Pessac).

18 Golf Bordelais ☎ 58 28 56 04, to the NW by D 109 : 4 km ; 18 de Bordeaux Lac ☎ 56 50 92 72, to the N by D2 : 10 km ; 18 9 of Cameyrac ☎ 56 72 96 79, to the NE by N 89 : 18 km.

of Bordeaux-Mérignac : Air France ☎ 56 93 81 22 to the W :11 km.

☎ 56 92 50 50.

and Accueil de France, (Information, exchange facilities and hotel reservations - not more than 5 days in advance) 12 cours 30-juillet ☎ 56 44 28 41, Telex 570362 – Bordeaux wine Exhibition (Maison du vin de Bordeaux), 1 cours 30-juillet (Information, wine-tasting - closed Saturday afternoon and Sunday) – ☎ 56 52 82 82 CV **Z** – A.C. 8 pl. Quinconces ☎ 56 44 22 92.

Paris 579 – Lyon 548 – Nantes 325 – Strasbourg 927 – Toulouse 244.

Plan on preceding pages

Pullman Mériadeck M, 5 r. R-Lateulade ☎ 56 90 92 37, Telex 540565 – – 350. AE E VISA BX **w**
st. : rest. **Le Mériadeck M** a la carte 140 b.i/195 b.i. – 48 – **196 rm** 495/735.

Gd H. and Café de Bordeaux without rest, 2 pl Comédie ☎ 56 90 93 44, Telex 541658 – – 30-50. AE E VISA CVX **b**
st. : 30 – **95 rm** 300/410, 3 apartments 750.

Normandie without rest, 7 cours 30-Juillet ☎ 56 52 16 80, Telex 570481 – . AE E VISA CV **z**
st. : 28 – **100 rm** 190/330.

Majestic without rest, 2 r. Condé ☎ 56 52 60 44 – . E VISA DV **b**
st. : 24 – **50 rm** 210/300.

Terminus, at St-Jean Railway station, ✉ 33800, ☎ 56 92 71 58, Telex 540264 – – 60. AE E VISA
M 95 b.i./130 – 30 – **80 rm** 234/393.

Royal Médoc M without rest, 3 r. Sèze ☎ 56 81 72 42, Telex 571042 – wc wc . AE E VISA. CV **u**
st. : 27 – **45 rm** 237/277.

Atlantic M without rest, 69 r. E. Leroy, ✉ 33800, ☎ 56 92 92 22 – wc . AE VISA
closed 20 December-4 January – **st.** : 19 – **36 rm** 147/230.

Notre Dame M without rest, 36 r. N. Dame ☎ 56 52 88 24 – wc . E VISA DU **k**
st. : 18 – **21 rm** 160/220.

Tour Intendance M without rest, 16 r. Vieille Tour ☎ 56 81 46 27 – wc wc . AE VISA CX **t**
closed 24 July-24 August – **st.** : 20 – **20 rm** 145/255.

Bayonne without rest, 4 r. Martignac ☎ 56 48 00 88 – wc wc . AE E VISA
closed 15 to 31 December – **st.** : 21 – **37 rm** 109/230. CX **p**

XXXX ❀ **Christian Clément-Dubern,** 42 allées Tourny ☎ 56 48 03 44, « 18 C Decor » – AE E VISA CV **s**
closed Saturday lunch, Sunday and Bank Holidays – **st.** : **M** a la carte 220/300
Spec. Huîtres tièdes au sabayon de citron vert, Rougets au foie gras, Mignon de veau et foie gras confits au macis.

XXX ❀ **Le Rouzic** (Gautier), 34 Cours du Chapeau rouge ☎ 56 44 39 11 – AE E VISA
closed Saturday lunch and Sunday – **st.** : **M** a la carte 240/350 DX **b**
Spec. Saumon grillé aux St-Jacques (October-April), Queues de langoustines rôties aux épices douces, Lamproie à la bordelaise (March-October). **Wines** Médoc.

XXX ❀ **Clavel** (Garcia), 44 r. Ch.-Domercq, ✉ 33800, ☎ 56 92 91 52 – AE VISA.
closed 19 to 27 April, 12 July-4 August, February Holidays, Sunday and Monday – **st.** : **M** a la carte 215/310
Spec. Gratin d'huîtres au foie gras, Gaspacho de homard (June-September), Lapereau à la royale.

XXX ❀ **La Chamade** (Carrere), 20 r. Piliers de Tutelle ☎ 56 48 13 74 – . VISA DX **d**
st. : **M** 140/200 dinner a la carte
Spec. Salade "Chamade", Filet de bar en papillote au Noilly, Pavé de filet de boeuf au vin de Graves.

XXX ❀ **Ramet,** 7 pl. J. Jaurès ☎ 56 44 12 51 – . VISA DV **u**
closed 11 to 27 April, 10 to 23 August, 28 December-3 January, Saturday and Sunday – **st.** : **M** a la carte 200/310
Spec. Feuilleté d'huîtres tièdes, Ragoût de St-Jacques (October-March), Lamproie à la bordelaise (April-May).

XX **Le Vieux Bordeaux,** 27 r. Buhan ☎ 56 52 94 36 – AE VISA DY **a**
closed 1 to 29 August, 8 to 15 February, Saturday lunch and Sunday – **st.** : **M** 93/190.

XX **Le Buhan,** 28 r. Buhan ☎ 56 52 80 86 – AE E VISA. DY **x**
closed Saturday lunch – **st.** : **M** 78/185.

XX **La Jabotière,** 86 r. Bègles, ✉ 33800, ☎ 56 91 69 43 – AE ⓓ E VISA
closed Saturday lunch, Sunday dinner and Monday – **st. : M** 95/155.

XX **Chez le Chef,** 57 r. Huguerie ☎ 56 81 67 07, 🏖 – VISA CV **a**
closed Sunday dinner and Monday – **st. : M** 85/180.

X **Tupina,** 6 r. Porte de la Monnaie ☎ 56 91 56 37 – VISA DY **q**
closed Sunday and Bank Holidays – **M** a la carte 115/180.

X **l'Alhambra,** 111 bis r. Judaïque ☎ 56 96 06 91 – VISA. ✂ BX **e**
closed 14 July-15 August, Saturday lunch and Sunday – **st. : M** 160.

at Parc des Expositions : North of the town – ✉ **33300** Bordeaux :

Sofitel Aquitania Ⓜ, ☎ 56 50 83 80, Telex 570557, ≤, ⛱ – 🛗 ▤ 📺 ☎ ♿ Ⓟ – 🏛 25-600. AE ⓓ E VISA. ✂ rest
rest. **Le Flore** *(closed August, Sunday and Bank Holidays)* **M** a la carte 120/190 – **le Pub M** a la carte 90/140 🍷 – ☕ 42 – **210 rm** 435/545.

Mercure Ⓜ, ☎ 56 50 90 14, Telex 540097, 🏖, ⛱, 🎾 – 🛗 ▤ 📺 ☎ ♿ Ⓟ – 🏛 120. AE ⓓ E VISA
M a la carte 80/120 🍷 – ☕ 35 – **100 rm** 360.

Novotel-Bordeaux le Lac Ⓜ, ☎ 56 50 99 70, Telex 570274, 🏖, ⛱ – 🛗 ▤ 📺 ☎ ♿ Ⓟ – 🏛 350. AE ⓓ E VISA
M a la carte 90/160 🍷 – ☕ 34 – **173 rm** 320/330.

Mercure-Bordeaux le Lac Ⓜ, ☎ 56 50 90 30, Telex 540077, 🏖 – 🛗 ▤ 📺 🛁wc ☎ ♿ Ⓟ – 🏛 250. AE ⓓ E VISA
M 100/160 🍷 – ☕ 35 – **100 rm** 318, 3 apartments 425.

at Bouliac – ✉ **33270** Floirac :

XXX ✿✿ **Le St-James** (Amat), pl. C. Hosteins, near church ☎ 56 20 52 19, ≤, 🏖, **« shady terrace overlooking the Garonne River and Bordeaux »**, 🌳 – AE ⓓ VISA. ✂
M 120/330 and a la carte
Spec. Fondant d'aubergines au cumin, Langoustines aux ravioli d'huîtres, Civet de canard à la cuillère. **Wines** Entre-deux-Mers, 1ères Côtes de Bordeaux.

to the S :

at Talence : 6 km – ✉ **33400** Talence :

Guyenne (Hotel School) Ⓜ, av. F.-Rabelais ☎ 56 80 75 08 – 🛗 📺 🛁wc ☎ Ⓟ. VISA. ✂
closed school Holidays – **M** *(closed Saturday dinner and Sunday)* 65/95 – ☕ 20 – **27 rm** 160/200, 3 apartments 285.

to the W :

at l'Alouette : 9 km – ✉ **33600** Pessac :

✿ **La Réserve** Ⓜ 🐌, av. Bourgailh ☎ 56 07 13 28, Telex 560585, **« park »**, 🎾 – 📺 ☎ Ⓟ – 🏛 80. AE ⓓ E VISA
15 March-11 November – **M** 250/350 – ☕ 40 – **19 rm** 390/570
Spec. Foie gras frais de canard, Saumon frais, Aloyau à la bordelaise. **Wines** Graves, Médoc.

at the airport : 11 km by D 106E – ✉ **33700** Mérignac :

Novotel-Mérignac Ⓜ, ☎ 56 34 10 25, Telex 540320, 🏖, ⛱, 🌳 – ▤ rm 📺 ☎ ♿ Ⓟ – 🏛 25-200. AE ⓓ E VISA
M Grill a la carte 90/160 🍷 – ☕ 34 – **100 rm** 336/346.

Eugénie-les-Bains 40 Landes 82 ① – pop. 408 – alt. 90 – Spa (8 March-31 Oct.) – ✉ **40320** Geaune.
Bordeaux 152.

✿✿✿ **Les Prés d'Eugénie** (Guérard) Ⓜ 🐌, ☎ 58 51 19 01, Telex 540470, **« 19C mansion, elegant decor, park »**, ⛱, 🎾 – 🛗 📺 ☎ ♿ Ⓟ – 🏛 100. AE ⓓ. ✂
2 March-30 November – **M** (low-calorie menu for residents only) 160/280 – **rest. Michel Guérard M** (booking essential) 380/400 and a la carte – ☕ 70 – **28 rm** 880, 7 apartments 1 155
Spec. Boucanade de morue à la Chantilly d'ail, Lapereau "Chabrot" au bouillon de Pomerol, Corne d'abondance aux fruits glacés. **Wines** Côtes de Gascogne.

☛ *The hotels have entered into certain undertakings towards the readers of this Guide.*
Make it plain that you have the most recent Guide.

If you would like a more complete selection of hotels and restaurants, consult the MICHELIN Guides for the following countries :

Benelux, Deutschland, España Portugal, France,
Great Britain and Ireland, and Italia,

all in annual editions.

CANNES 06400 Alpes-Mar. 84 ⑨, 195 ㉟㊳ – pop. 72 787 – Casinos : Les Fleurs BZ, Palm Beach X, Municipal BZ.

See : Boulevard de la Croisette★★ BCZ – Pointe de la Croisette★ X – ≤★ from the Mount Chevalier Tower AZ **V** – La Castre Museum★ (Musée de la Castre) AZ **M** – Super Cannes Observatory ☼★★★ E : 4 km VX **B** – Tour into the Hills★ (Chemin des Collines) NE : 4 km V – The Croix des Gardes V **E** ≤★ W : 5 km then 15 mn.

9 18 Country-Club of Cannes-Mougins ✆ 93 75 79 13 by ⑤ : 9 km ; 9 18 Golf-Club of Cannes-Mandelieu ✆ 93 49 55 39 by ② : 6,5 km ; 18 Biot ✆ 93 65 08 48 by ⑤ : 14 km ; 18 Valbonne ✆ 93 42 00 08 by ⑤ : 15 km.

ℹ and Accueil de France (Information, exchange facilities and hotel reservations not more than 5 days in advance), Railway Station S.N.C.F. ✆ 93 99 19 77, Télex 470795 and Palais des Festivals et des Congrès, 1 La Croisette ✆ 93 39 24 53, Telex 470479 - A.C. r. F. Amouretti ✆ 93 39 38 94.

Paris 901 ③ – Aix-en-Provence 146 ③ – Grenoble 316 ⑤ – Marseille 158 ③ – Nice 32 ⑤ – Toulon 123 ③.

CANNES - LE CANNET - VALLAURIS

André (R. du Cdt) .... CZ
Antibes (R. d') .... BCZ
Belges (R. des) .... BZ 6
Chabaud (R.) .... CZ 15
Croisette (Bd de la) .... BCZ
Félix-Faure (R.) .... ABZ
Foch (R. du Mar.) .... BZ 25
Hôtel-de-Ville (Pl. de l') .... AZ 33
Joffre (R. du Mar.) .... BZ 35
Riouffe (R. Jean de) .... BZ 64

Alexandre-III (Bd) .... X 2
Amouretti (R. F.) .... CZ 3
Anc.-Combattants d'Afrique du Nord (Av.) .... AZ 4
Beau-Soleil (Bd) .... V 5
Bellevue (Pl.) .... V 7
Bréguières (Ch. des) .... V 8
Broussailles (Av. des) .... V 9
Buttura (R.) .... BZ 10
Carnot (Bd) .... V 13
Castre (Pl. de la) .... AZ 14
Christ-Roi (⊕) .... V 16
Clemenceau (Av. G.) .... V 17
Coteaux (Av. des) .... V 18
Dr-Pierre-Gazagnaire (R.) .... AZ 20
Dollfus (R. Jean) .... AZ 22
Ferrage (Bd de la) .... BYZ 23
Fiesole (Av.) .... V 24
Four-à-Chaux (Bd du) .... V 25
Fournas (Av. de) .... V 26
Gambetta (Bd) .... V 27
Gaulle (Pl. Gén.-de) .... BZ 28
Grasse (av. de) .... V 29
Haddad-Simon (R. J.) .... CY 30
Isnard (Pl. Paul) .... V 34
Lacour (Bd A.) .... V 36
Lattre-de-Tassigny (Av. J.-de) .... ABY 37
Leader (Bd) .... VX 38
Lérins (Av. de) .... X 39
Macé (R.) .... BZ 41
Monod (Bd Jacques) .... V 42
Montaigne (R.) .... BY 43
Mont-Chevalier (R. du) .... AZ 44
Montfleury (Bd) .... X 45
Myron-T.-Herrik (Bd) .... V 46
N.-D.-de-Bon-Voyage (⊕) .... BZ 49
N.-D.-d'Espérance (⊕) .... AZ 50
N.-D.-des-Pins (⊕) .... DZ 52
Observatoire (Bd de l') .... X 54
Oxford (Bd d') .... V 55
Pastour (R. L.) .... AZ 56
Perier (Bd du) .... V 57
Perrissol (R. L.) .... AZ 59
Pins (Bd des) .... X 60
République (Bd de la) .... X 62
Rouguière (R.) .... BZ 66
Rouvier (Bd M.) .... V 67
St-Charles (⊕) .... V 69
St-Joseph (⊕) .... AY 70
St-Nicolas (Av.) .... BY 71
St-Sauveur (R.) .... V 72
Ste-Philomène (⊕) .... V 73
Sardou (R. L.) .... V 74
Serbes (R. des) .... BZ 75
Souvenir (⊕) .... CY 76
Tapis-Vert (Av. du) .... V 77
Tuby (Bd Victor) .... AZ 78
Vallauris (Av. de) .... V 79
Victor-Hugo (R.) .... V 80
Vidal (R. du Cdt) .... CZ 82

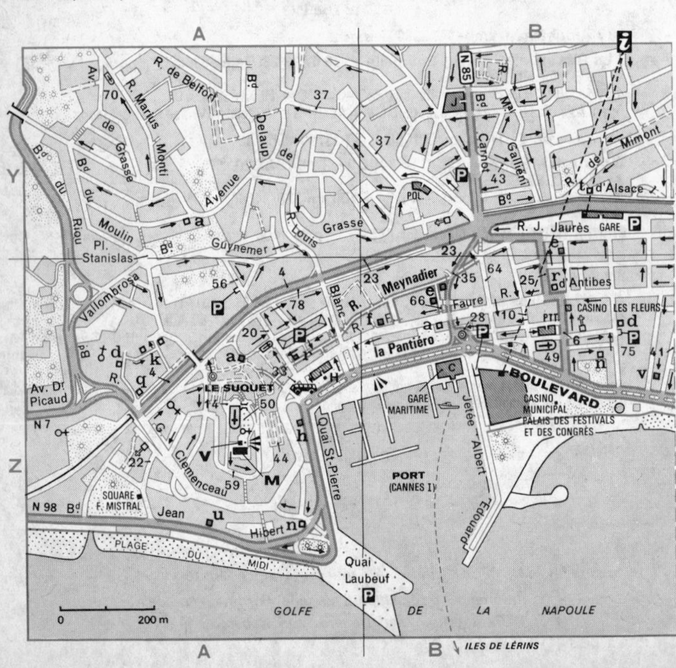

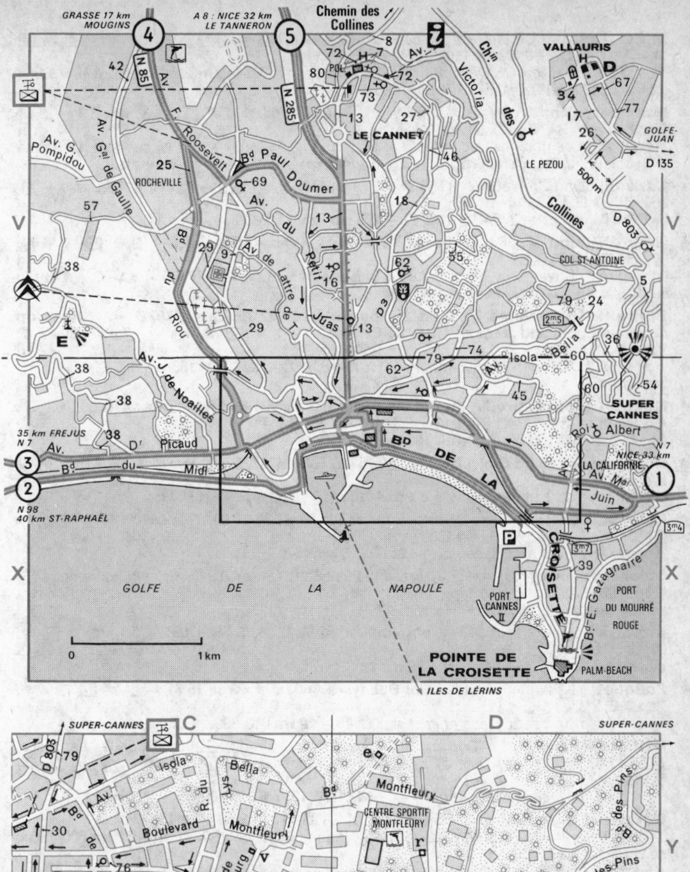

GRASSE 17 km
MOUGINS
A 8 : NICE 32 km
LE TANNERON
Chemin des Collines
VALLAURIS
LE CANNET
ROCHEVILLE
LE PEZOU
GOLFE-JUAN
D 135
500 m
COL ST ANTOINE
SUPER CANNES
35 km FREJUS
N 7
NICE 33 km
LA CALIFORNIE
N 98
40 km ST-RAPHAËL
GOLFE DE LA NAPOULE
PORT CANNES II
PORT DU MOURRÉ ROUGE
POINTE DE LA CROISETTE
PALM-BEACH
ILES DE LÉRINS
0
1 km
SUPER-CANNES
CENTRE SPORTIF MONTFLEURY
PALAIS CROISETTE
POINTE DE LA CROISETTE
PALM BEACH

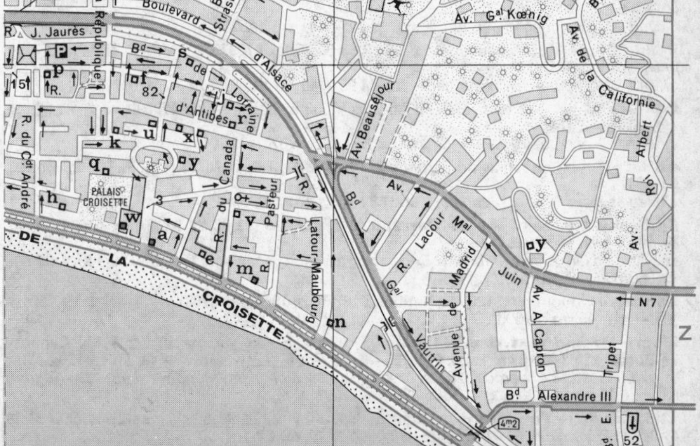

Majestic M, bd Croisette ✆ 93 68 91 00, Telex 470787, ←, ☂, ⛱, ▲, ⚑ – |‡| ▤ TV ☎ ⛟ – ⛯ 60-360. AE ⓓ E VISA. ✗ rest BZ **n**
closed 10 November-18 December – **M** a la carte 245/355 – **Grill M** a la carte 195/295 – ☕ 55 – **262 rm** 1 020/1 800, 12 apartments.

Martinez, 73 bd Croisette ✆ 93 68 91 91, Telex 470708, ←, ☂, ⛱, ▲, ⚑, ✂ – |‡| ▤ TV ☎ ♿ P – ⛯ 40-600. AE ⓓ E VISA CDZ **n**
closed 15 November-18 December and 31 January-15 March – **st. : M** see rest. **La Palme d'Or** below - **L'Orangeraie M** 195 – ☕ 70 – **421 rm** 850/2 000, 18 apartments.

Carlton, 58 bd Croisette ✆ 93 68 91 68, Telex 470720, ←, ▲ – |‡| ▤ TV ☎ ♿ ⛟ – ⛯ 250. AE ⓓ E VISA. ✗ rest CZ **e**
La Côte **M** a la carte 275/415 – ☕ 61 – **295 rm** 825/1 730, 30 apartments.

Gray d'Albion M, 38 r. Serbes ✆ 93 68 54 54, Telex 470744, ▲ – |‡| ▤ TV ☎ – ⛯ 30-200. AE ⓓ E VISA BZ **d**
M see rest. **Royal Gray** below - **Les 4 Saisons M** a la carte 125/190 – ☕ 70 – **173 rm** 890/1 505, 14 apartments.

Sofitel Méditerranée M, 2 bd J.-Hibert ✆ 93 99 22 75, Telex 470728, ←, « Roof-top swimming pool and terrace ← bay of Cannes » – |‡| ▤ TV ☎ ⛟ – ⛯ 150. AE ⓓ E VISA. ✗ rest AZ **n**
closed 20 November-21 December – **st. : M** 180/200 – ☕ 60 – **150 rm** 480/990, 4 apartments 1 450.

Novotel Montfleury M ⛰, 25 av. Beauséjour ✆ 93 68 91 50, Telex 470039, ←, ☂, « Garden », ⛱ – |‡| ▤ TV ☎ P – ⛯ 400. AE ⓓ E VISA DY **r**
M a la carte 90/160 🍷 – ☕ 50 – **180 rm** 650/850.

Gd Hôtel ⛰, 45 bd Croisette ✆ 93 38 15 45, Telex 470727, ←, ▲ – |‡| ▤ TV ☎ P. AE VISA CZ **q**
st. : M see rest. **Lamour** below – ☕ 55 – **76 rm** 670/1 390 – P 810/1 435.

Pullman Beach M without rest, 13 r. Canada ✆ 93 38 22 32, Telex 470034, ⛱ – |‡| ▤ TV ☎ ⛟ – ⛯ 30-60. AE ⓓ E VISA CZ **v**
closed November and December – ☕ 60 – **94 rm** 675/1 030.

Splendid without rest, 4 r. F.-Faure ✆ 93 99 53 11, Telex 470990, ← – |‡| kitchenette TV ☎. AE ⓓ E VISA BZ **a**
st. : 63 rm ☕ 330/660.

Victoria M without rest, 122 r. d'Antibes ✆ 93 99 36 36, Telex 470817, ⛱ – |‡| ▤ TV ☎. AE ⓓ VISA CZ **x**
closed November-January – **st. : 25 rm** ☕ 390/610.

Fouquet's M without rest, 2 rd-pt Duboys-d'Angers ✆ 93 38 75 81 – |‡| ▤ TV ☎ ⛟. AE ⓓ E VISA CZ **y**
closed 1 November-26 December – **st. :** ☕ 40 – **10 rm** 610/990.

Solhôtel and rest. Le Trident M, 61 av. Dr Picaud by ③ ✉ 06150 Cannes La Bocca, ✆ 93 47 63 00, Telex 970956, ☂, ⛱, ⚑ – |‡| kitchenette ▤ TV ☎ ⛟ – ⛯ 150. AE ⓓ E VISA
closed 1 November-15 December – **st. : M** 115 – **101 rm** ☕ 395/577 – P 575/694.

Gonnet et de la Reine, 42 bd Croisette ✆ 93 38 40 00, ← – |‡| ☎. AE VISA. ✗ CZ **h**
1 April-31 October – **st. : M** *(closed Friday)* (for residents only) – ☕ 50 – **52 rm** 500/750, 5 apartments 1 300.

Paris without rest, 34 bd d'Alsace ✆ 93 38 30 89, Telex 470995, ⛱, ⚑ – |‡| ▤ ☎ – ⛯ 40. ⓓ E VISA. ✗ CY **a**
closed 10 November-25 January – **st. :** ☕ 22 – **48 rm** 370/520.

Beau Séjour M, 5 r. Fauvettes ✆ 93 39 63 00, Telex 470975, ⛱, ⚑ – |‡| ▤ rm TV ☎ ⛟. AE ⓓ E VISA. ✗ rest AZ **d**
closed 1 November-15 December – **st. : M** 95 – **46 rm** ☕ 490/570 – P 475/710.

Century M without rest, 133 r. d'Antibes ✆ 93 99 37 64, Telex 470090 – |‡| ▤ TV ☎ ⛟. AE ⓓ E VISA CZ **r**
closed 1 December-20 January – **st. :** ☕ 25 – **35 rm** 370/480.

Abrial M without rest, 24 bd Lorraine ✆ 93 38 78 82, Telex 470761 – |‡| ▤ TV ☎ ⛟. AE ⓓ VISA CY **s**
closed 15 November-15 January – **st. : 48 rm** ☕ 270/470.

Embassy and rest. As de Carreau, 6 r. Bône ✆ 93 38 79 02, Telex 470081 – |‡| ▤ rest TV ☎. AE ⓓ E VISA CZ **j**
st. : M *(closed 20 November-15 December, lunch Monday and Tuesday)* 90/150 – **60 rm** ☕ 360/600 – P 400/500.

Canberra without rest, 120 r. d'Antibes ✆ 93 38 20 70, Telex 470817 – |‡| ▤ ☎ P. AE ⓓ VISA – **st. : 45 rm** ☕ 300/530. CZ **u**

Licorn'H. and rest. Les Saisons M, 23 av. Fr.-Tonner by ③, ✉ 06150 Cannes-La-Bocca, ✆ 93 47 18 46, Telex 470818 – |‡| ▤ rest TV 🛁wc 🚿wc ☎ P. AE ⓓ E VISA
st. : M *(closed 11 November-20 December, Sunday dinner and Monday except July-August)* 83/95 – **45 rm** ☕ 320/500 – P 365/430.

Château de la Tour ⛰, 10 av. Font-de-Veyre by ③, ✉ 06150 Cannes-La-Bocca, ✆ 93 47 34 64, Telex 470906, ⚑ – |‡| 🛁wc 🚿wc ☎ P. AE ⓓ VISA. ✗ rest
hotel : closed 15 November-1 January ; rest : closed 15 November-20 January – **st. : M** 90 – **42 rm** ☕ 260/440 – P 370/455.

Des Congrès et Festivals [M] without rest, 12 r. Teisseire ✆ 93 39 13 81 – wc wc ☎. AE ① VISA CZ **p**
closed 1 December-25 January – **st. : 20 rm** 275/430.

Ruc Hôtel without rest, 15 bd Strasbourg ✆ 93 38 64 32, Telex 270033 – wc ☎. AE E VISA CY **v**
closed 1 November-20 December – **st. : 30 rm** 260/450.

La Madone without rest, 5 av. Justinia ✆ 93 43 57 87, « fine setting », – kitchenette wc wc ☎. AE ① E VISA DZ **y**
st. : 30 – **22 rm** 360/500.

Acapulco [M], 16 bd Alsace ✆ 93 99 16 16, Telex 470929, , – wc wc ☎. AE ① E VISA BY **t**
closed 13 to 21 April – **st. : M** 95/150 – **60 rm** 550/976 – P 738/976.

Athénée [M] without rest, 6 rue Lecerf ✆ 93 38 69 54, Telex 470978 – wc wc ☎. AE ① E VISA CZ **f**
closed 1 December-15 January – **st. :** 30 – **15 rm** 253/475.

Les Orangers, 1 r. des Orangers ✆ 93 39 99 92, Telex 470873, ←, , , – wc wc ☎. AE ① E VISA. rest AZ **k**
closed November – **st. : M** 94/110 – 28 – **45 rm** 335/460 – P 440.

Host. de L'Olivier without rest, 90 r. G.-Clemenceau ✆ 93 39 53 28, , – wc wc ☎. ① VISA AZ **k**
st. : 23 rm 320/450.

Provence, 9 r. Molière ✆ 93 38 44 35, – rm wc wc ☎. AE ① E VISA. rest CZ **t**
st. : M *(closed 1 November-22 December and Sunday)* 110/135 – 20 – **30 rm** 180/350.

Univers [M] without rest, 2 r. Mar.-Foch ✆ 93 39 59 19, Telex 470972 – wc wc ☎. AE ① E VISA BZ **r**
st. : 68 rm 250/600.

Toboso without rest, 7 allée des Oliviers ✆ 93 38 20 05, – kitchenette wc ☎ Ⓟ. ① DY **e**
st. : 26 – **10 rm** 300/400.

Campanile, Aérodrome de Cannes-Mandelieu by ③ : 6 km, ✉ 06150 Cannes-La-Bocca, ✆ 93 48 69 41, Telex 461570 – wc ☎ Ⓟ – 30. VISA
st. : M 61 b.i./82 b.i. – 23 – **49 rm** 196/216.

Roches Fleuries without rest, 92 r. G.-Clemenceau ✆ 93 39 28 78, – wc wc ☎ Ⓟ. AZ **q**
closed 14 November-28 December – **st. :** 14 – **24 rm** 80/190.

Festival without rest, 3 r. Molière ✆ 93 38 69 45 – kitchenette wc ☎ CZ **k**
closed 28 November-5 January – **st. :** 18 – **17 rm** 130/300.

Cheval Blanc without rest, 3 r. de-Maupassant ✆ 93 39 88 60 – wc wc ☎ AY **a**
st. : 15 – **16 rm** 180/240.

Wagram, 140 r. d'Antibes ✆ 93 94 55 53, – rm wc wc ☎. CZ **x**
st. : M 97 – 23 – **23 rm** 179/341 – P 307/438.

XXXX ❀ **La Palme d'Or,** 73 bd Croisette ✆ 92 98 30 18 – Ⓟ. AE ① E VISA CDZ **n**
closed 15 November-18 December, 31 January-15 March, Tuesday lunch, Monday and lunch in July-August – **st. : M** a la carte 280/440
Spec. Poissons du marché, Blanc-manger de sole aux amandes, Tartelette friande d'agneau. **Wines** Bellet, Côtes de Provence.

XXXX ❀❀ **Royal Gray,** 2 r. des Etats-Unis ✆ 93 68 54 54, Telex 470744, , « Tasteful, contemporary decor » – . AE ① E VISA BZ **d**
closed 1 February-5 March, Monday (except dinner in July-August) and Sunday – **M** a la carte 340/445
Spec. Symphonie des trois salades, Filet de loup à la citronelle, Ris de veau en crépine de courgette. **Wines** Côtes de Provence.

XXX **Félix,** 63 bd Croisette ✆ 93 94 00 61, ←, – . AE E VISA CZ **m**
closed mid November-24 December, Thursday lunch in July-August and Wednesday (except dinner in July-August) – **M** a la carte 190/290.

XXX **Gaston-Gastounette,** 7 quai St-Pierre ✆ 93 39 47 92, ←, – . AE ① VISA AZ **h**
closed 5 to 21 January – **M** 165.

XXX **Le Festival,** 52 bd Croisette ✆ 93 38 04 81, – . AE ① VISA CZ **a**
closed 26 November-26 December and February Holidays – **M** a la carte 180/245.

XXX **Poêle d'Or,** 23 r. États-Unis ✆ 93 39 77 65 – . AE ① VISA BZ **v**
closed November, Tuesday lunch and Monday – **st. : M** 130.

XXX **Rescator,** 7 r. Mar.-Joffre ✆ 93 39 44 57 – . E VISA BZ **e**
closed Monday out of season – **M** 210 b.i./350 b.i..

XXX **Lamour,** 45 bd Croisette ✆ 93 99 49 60, – AE VISA CZ **q**
M 140.

XX **Blue Bar,** Former festival Centre ✆ 93 39 03 04, – . E VISA CZ **w**
closed 1 June-8 July and Tuesday except season – **M** a la carte 140/220.

XX **Le Croquant,** 18 bd J.-Hibert ✆ 93 39 39 79, ← – . AE ① E AZ **u**
closed Monday and lunch (except Sunday in winter) – **M** 90/220.

XX **La Mirabelle,** 24 r. St-Antoine ✆ 93 38 72 75 – AE E VISA AZ **a**
closed 1 to 25 December, 1 to 15 March and Tuesday – **M** (dinner only) 250 b.i./350 b.i.

XX **Caveau Provençal,** 45 r. Félix-Faure ✆ 93 39 06 33, ≤, 🏕 – ▤. AE ⊙ E VISA BZ **f**
M 78, a la carte on Sundays.

X **L'Olivier,** 9 r. Rouguière ✆ 93 39 91 63 – AE ⊙ E VISA BZ **e**
closed 15 December-15 January and Monday – **M** 65/95.

X **Le Monaco,** 15 r. 24-août ✆ 93 38 37 76 BY **e**
closed 10 November-15 December and Sunday – **st. : M** 60/80 🍷.

X **Aux Bons Enfants,** 80 r. Meynadier – 🐕 AZ **r**
closed April, 15 December-5 January, Wednesday dinner and Sunday – **st. : M** 70 🍷.

Antibes 06600 Alpes-Mar. 84 ⑨, 195 ㉟㊵
Cannes 11.

N : 4 km quartier de la Brague – ✉ **06600** Antibes :

XXXXX ✿✿ **La Bonne Auberge** (Rostang), on N 7 ✆ 93 33 36 65, Telex 470989, 🏕, « Provençal style dining room and flowered terrace » – Ⓟ. AE E VISA
closed 15 November-15 December and Monday except July-August – **M** 290/430 and a la carte
Spec. Minute de loup grillé, Fricassée de homard aux ravioles de blettes, Côtes d'agneau et paillasson de courgettes. **Wines** Bellet, Côteaux d'aix.

Mougins 06250 Alpes-Mar. 84 ⑨, 195 ㉔㊳ – pop. 10 197 – alt. 260.
Cannes 7.

XXXX ✿✿✿ **Moulin de Mougins** (Vergé) 🐌 with rm, at Notre-Dame-de-Vie SE : 2,5 km by D 3 ✆ 93 75 78 24, Telex 970732, ≤, 🏕, 🐕 – ▤ rest 📺 🛁wc ☎ Ⓟ. AE ⊙ VISA
20 March-20 November – **M** *(closed Monday except dinner from 14 July-31 August and Thursday lunch)* 430 and a la carte – ☕ 61 – **3 rm** 700/800
Spec. Poupeton de fleur de courgette aux truffes, Filets de rougets en germiny de ciboulette, Noisettes d'agneau aux truffes.

La Napoule-Plage 06 Alpes-Mar. 84 ⑧, 195 ㉞㊲ – ✉ **06210** Mandelieu-La-Napoule.
Cannes 8.

XXXX ✿✿✿ **L'Oasis** (Outhier), ✆ 93 49 95 52, Telex 461389, 🏕, « Shaded and flowered patio » – ▤. AE ⊙ E VISA
closed beginning November to mid December, Monday dinner and Thursday – **M** 380/420 and a la carte
Spec. Escalope de foie gras au gingembre, Langouste aux herbes thaï, St-Pierre au Château-Chalon. **Wines** Cassis, Bandol.

*If you would like a more complete selection of hotels and restaurants, consult the **Michelin Guides** for the following countries:*
Benelux, Deutschland, España Portugal, France,
Great Britain and Ireland, Italia.

LYONS Ⓟ **69000** Rhône 74 ⑪⑫ – pop. 418 476 Greater Lyons 1 173 797 – alt. 169.

See : Site★★★ – Old Lyons★★ (Vieux Lyon) BX : **Jewry Street★ (rue Juiverie) 65, rue St-Jean★ 92, Hotel de Gadagne★ M1 , Maison du Crible★ D – St-Jean★ : Chancel★★** BX **– Basilica of N.-D.-de-Fourvière ❋★★, ≤★** BX **– Capitals★ of the Basilica St-Martin d'Ainay** BYZ **– Lanterne tower★ of St-Paul Church** BV **– Virgin with Child★ in the St-Nizier Church** CX **– Park of the Tête d'Or★ : Rose-garden★ (roseraie) – Fountain★ of the Place des Terreaux** CV **– Traboules★ of Quartier Croix-Rousse – Arches de Chaponost★ - Montée de Garillan★** BX **– Punch and Judy Show (Théâtre de Guignol)** BX **N – Museums : Textile★★★** CZ**M2, Gallo-Roman Civilization★★ (claudian table★★★)** BX **M3, Fine-Arts★★** CV **M4 Decorative Arts★★** CZ **M5, Printing and Banking★★** CX **M6 , Guimet of Natural history★ Puppet★** BX **M1, Historic★ : lapidary★** BX **M1, Apothecary's Shop★ (Civil Hospitals)** CY **M8.**

Envir. : Rochetaillée : Automobile Museum Henri Malartre★ : 12 km.

⛳9 ⛳9 ⛳9 **Villette d'Anthon** ✆ **78 31 11 33 to the E : 21 km ;** ⛳18 **de Verger-Lyon** ✆ **78 02 84 20 to the S.**

✈ **of Lyon-Satolas** ✆ **78 71 92 21 to the E : 27 km.**

🚗 ✆ **78 92 50 50.**

ℹ and Accueil de France (Information, exchange facilities, hotel reservations - not more than 5 days in advance), pl. Bellecour ✆ 78 42 25 75, Télex 330032 Centre d'Echange de Perrache – A.C. 7 r. Grolée ✆ 78 42 51 01.

Paris 460 – Bâle 387 – Bordeaux 548 – Genève 156 – Grenoble 104 – Marseille 315 – St-Étienne 59 – Strasbourg 480 – Torino 300 – Toulouse 534.

Plan on following pages

Hotels

Town Centre (Bellecour-Terreaux) :

Sofitel M, 20 quai Gailleton 69002 78 42 72 50, Telex 330225, – 200. rest CY **k**
st. : rest. **Les Trois Dômes** (8th floor) **M** a la carte 230/330 - **Sofi Shop** (ground floor) **M** a la carte 110/140 – 59 – **194 rm** 595/975, 6 apartments 1 600/2 380.

Gd Hôtel Concorde, 11 r. Grolée 69002 78 42 56 21, Telex 330244 – – 80. rest DX **e**
st. : **Le Fiorelle** (Grill) *(closed Sunday)* **M** 105/130 – 40 – **140 rm** 330/630.

Royal, 20 pl. Bellecour 69002 78 37 57 31, Telex 310785 – rm – 40. CY **d**
st. : **M** Grill 90 – 34 – **90 rm** 248/620.

Gd H. des Beaux-Arts without rest, 75 r. Prés.-E.-Herriot 69002 78 38 09 50, Telex 330442 – . CX **t**
st. : 30 – **79 rm** 268/430.

Carlton without rest, 4 r. Jussieu 69002 78 42 56 51, Telex 310787 – . – **st. :** 32 – **89 rm** 240/435. CX **y**

La Résidence without rest, 18 r. Victor-Hugo 69002 78 42 63 28, Telex 900950 – wc wc – 40. CY **s**
st. : 18 – **63 rm** 166/200.

Globe et Cécil without rest, 21 r. Gasparin 69002 78 42 58 95, Telex 305184 – wc wc – 60. CY **b**
st. : 26 – **65 rm** 190/270.

Gd H. des Terreaux without rest, 16 r. Lanterne 69001 78 27 04 10, Telex 310273 – wc wc . CV **u**
st. : 24 – **50 rm** 89/261.

Moderne without rest, 15 r. Dubois 69002 78 42 21 83 – wc .
st. : 18,50 – **31 rm** 125/224. CX **n**

Bayard without rest, 23 pl. Bellecour 69002 78 37 39 64 – wc . CY **g**
st. : 17,50 – **15 rm** 124/170.

Perrache :

Bordeaux without rest, 1 r. Bélier 69002 78 37 58 73, Telex 330355 – . – **st. :** 33 – **83 rm** 182/400. BZ **y**

Bristol without rest, 28 cours Verdun 69002 78 37 56 55, Telex 330584 – – 45. BZ **y**
st. : 25 – **131 rm** 115/290.

Axotel and rest. Le Chalut M, 12 r. Marc-Antoine Petit 69002 78 42 17 18, Telex 380736, – wc – 25 - 130.
st. : **M** *(closed Sunday)* 80/150 – 29 – **128 rm** 205/230.

La Croix Rousse :

Lyon Métropole M, 85 quai J.-Gillet 69004 78 29 20 20, Telex 380198, , , – – 700.
Les Eaux Vives *(closed 25 December-1 January)* **M** 105/190 - **Le Grill M** 110 b.i. – 28 – **119 rm** 345/395.

Les Brotteaux :

Roosevelt M without rest, 25 r. Bossuet 69006 78 52 35 67, Telex 300295 – kitchenette – 60.
st. : 30 – **87 rm** 270/350.

Olympique without rest, 62 r. Garibaldi 69006 78 89 48 04 – wc wc . – **st. :** 15,50 – **23 rm** 162/183.

Britania without rest, 17 r. Prof.-Weill 69006 78 52 86 52, Telex 305551 – wc wc .
st. : 17 – **22 rm** 170/254.

La Part-Dieu :

Pullman Part-Dieu M, 129 r. Servient (32nd floor) 69003 78 62 94 12, Telex 380088, Lyons, Valley of the Rhône – – 300.
st. : rest. **L'Arc-en-Ciel** *(closed 12 July-18 August, Monday lunch and Sunday)* **M** a la carte 200/270 - **La Ripaille** (Grill) (ground floor) *(closed Friday dinner and Saturday)* **M** 80 b.i. /115 – 47 – **243 rm** 495/895.

Mercure M, 47 bd Vivier-Merle 69003 72 34 18 12, Telex 306469 – – 150.
M a la carte 90/150 – 33 – **124 rm** 350/405.

Athéna Part-Dieu M without rest, 45 bd Vivier-Merle 69003 72 33 70 04, Telex 306412 – wc .
st. : 25 – **122 rm** 245/300.

Créqui M without rest, 158 r. Créqui 69003 78 60 20 47 – wc .
st. : 26 – **28 rm** 234/262.

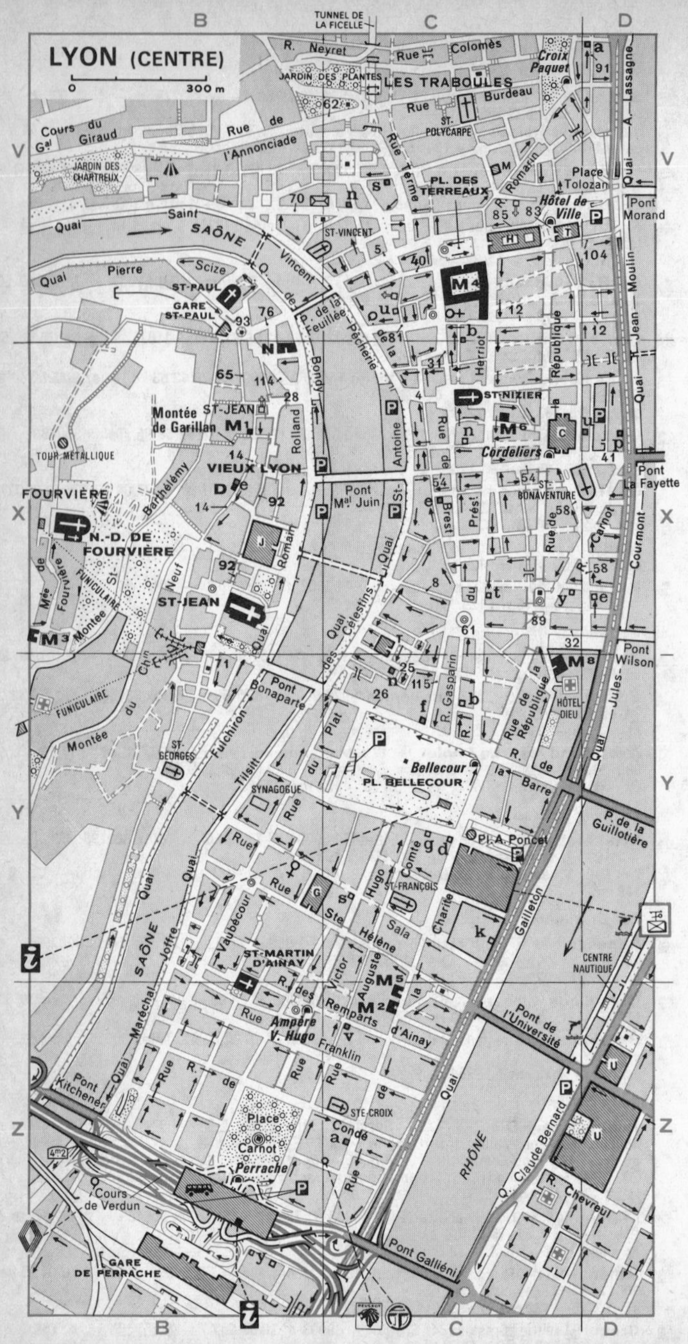

LYON (CENTRE)
0
300 m
TUNNEL DE LA FICELLE
JARDIN DES PLANTES
LES TRABOULES
Croix Paquet
PL. DES TERREAUX
Hôtel de Ville
Place Tolozan
Pont Morand
JARDIN DES CHARTREUX
SAÔNE
ST-PAUL
GARE ST-PAUL
ST-VINCENT
ST-POLYCARPE
VIEUX LYON
ST-JEAN
Montée de Garillan
TOUR MÉTALLIQUE
FOURVIÈRE
N.-D. DE FOURVIÈRE
FUNICULAIRE
ST-NIZIER
Cordeliers
ST-BONAVENTURE
Pont La Fayette
Pont Mal Juin
Pont Bonaparte
Pont Wilson
HÔTEL-DIEU
ST-GEORGES
SYNAGOGUE
Bellecour
PL. BELLECOUR
Pl. A. Poncet
P. de la Guillotière
ST-FRANÇOIS
ST-MARTIN D'AINAY
Ampère V. Hugo
CENTRE NAUTIQUE
Pont de l'Université
RHÔNE
STE-CROIX
Place Carnot
Perrache
Cours de Verdun
GARE DE PERRACHE
Pont Kitchener
Pont Galliéni
Q. Claude Bernard
R. Chevreul

STREET INDEX TO LYON TOWN PLAN

Street	Grid	No.
République (R.)	CX	
Terme (R.)	CV	
Victor-Hugo (R.)	CY	
Alnay (Remp. d')	CZ	
Albon (Pl.)	CX	4
Algérie (R. d')	CV	5
Anc.-Préfect. (R.)	CX	8
Annonciade (R.)	BV	
Barre (R. de la)	CY	
Bât-d'Argent (R.)	CV	12
Bellecour (Pl.)	CY	
Bœuf (R. du)	BX	14
Bonaparte (Pont)	BY	
Bondy (Quai de)	BX	
Brest (R. de)	CX	
Burdeau (R.)	CV	
Carnot (Pl.)	BZ	
Carnot (R.)	DX	
Célestins (Pl. des)	CY	25
Célestins (Q. des)	CX	
Chambonnet (R.)	CY	26
Change (Pl. du)	BX	28
Charité (R. de la)	CY	
Ch.-Neuf (Montée)	BX	
Chenevard (R. P.)	CX	31
Chevreul (R.)	DZ	
Childebert (R.)	CX	32
Cl.-Bernard (Quai)	CZ	
Colomès (R.)	CV	
Comte (R. A.)	CY	
Condé (R. de)	CZ	
Constantine (R.)	CV	40
Cordeliers (Pl.)	DX	41
Courmont (Quai J.)	DX	
Feuillée (P. de la)	BV	
Fourvière (Mtée de)	BX	
Franklin (R.)	CZ	
Fulchiron (Quai)	BY	
Gailleton (Quai)	CY	
Gallieni (Pont)	CZ	
Gasparin (R.)	CY	
Giraud (Crs Gén.)	BV	
Grenette (R.)	CX	54
Grolée (R.)	DX	58
Guillotière (P. de la)	DY	
Jacobins (Pl. des)	CX	61
Jardin-Plantes (R.)	CV	62
Joffre (Quai Mar.)	BZ	
Juin (Pont Mar.)	CX	
Juiverie (R.)	BX	65
Kitchener (Pont)	BZ	
La Fayette (Pont)	DX	
Lassagne (Quai A.)	DV	
Martinière (R.)	BV	70
Max (Av. Adolphe)	BY	71
Morand (Pont)	DV	
Moulin (Quai J.)	DV	
Neyret (R.)	BV	
Octavio-Mey (R.)	BV	76
Pêcherie (Quai)	CX	
Plat (R. du)	BY	
Platière (R. de la)	CV	81
Poncet (Pl. A.)	CY	
Pradel (Pl. Louis)	CV	83
Prés.-Herriot (R.)	CX	
Puits-Gaillot (R.)	CV	85
République (Pl.)	CX	89
Rom.-Rolland (Quai)	BX	
Romarin (R.)	CV	
Royale (R.)	DV	91
St-Antoine (Quai)	CX	
St-Barthélemy (Montée)	BX	
St-Jean (R.)	BX	92
St-Paul (Pl.)	BV	93
St-Vincent (Quai)	BV	
Ste-Hélène (R.)	CY	
Sala (Rue)	CY	
Scize (Quai Pierre)	BV	
Serlin (R. J.)	DV	104
Terreaux (Pl. des)	CV	
Tilsitt (Quai)	BY	
Tolozan (Pl.)	DV	
Université (P. de l')	CZ	
Vaubécour (R.)	BY	
Verdun (Cours de)	BZ	
Vernay (R. Fr.)	BX	114
Wilson (Pont)	DX	
Zola (R. Émile)	CY	115

La Guillotière :

Gd H. Helder et Institut without rest, 38 r. de Marseille 69007 78 72 09 39, Telex 306411 – wc wc. AE E VISA – **st. : 110 rm** 200/250.

Urbis Université M without rest, 51 r. Université 69007 78 72 78 42, Telex 340455 – wc wc. E VISA – 25 – **53 rm** 224/270.

Gerland :

Mercure M, 70 av. Leclerc 69007 78 58 68 53, Telex 305484, – – 450. AE E VISA
st. : M a la carte 85/150 – 33 – **194 rm** 355/380.

Monchat-Monplaisir :

Altéa Park M, 4 r. Prof.-Calmette 69008 78 74 11 20, Telex 380230, – – 30. AE VISA
st. : le Patio *(closed Saturday, Sunday and Bank Holidays)* **M** 81 b.i./100 – 31 – **72 rm** 270/312.

Lyon-Est M without rest, 104 rte Genas 69003 78 54 64 53, Telex 375974 – wc wc. AE E VISA – **st. :** 23 – **42 rm** 150/270.

à Villeurbanne :

Congrès and rest. Le Grand Camp M, pl. Cdt Rivière 69100 Villeurbanne 78 89 81 10, Telex 370216 – – 120. AE E VISA
M *(closed Sunday)* 108/150 – 32 – **132 rm** 250.

Athéna-Tolstoï, 90 cours Tolstoï 69100 Villeurbanne 78 68 81 21, Telex 330574 – wc – 200. VISA. rest
st. : M *(closed 23 December-4 January, Saturday and Sunday)* 70/115 – 24 – **137 rm** 198/243.

Restaurants

XXXXX ✿✿✿ **Paul Bocuse,** bridge of Collonges ,12 km by the banks of the River Saône (D443 D51) 69660 Collonges-au-Mont-d'Or 78 22 01 40, Telex 375382, « Tasteful decor » – . AE E VISA
M 315/465 and a la carte
Spec. Soupe aux truffes noires, Loup farci à la mousse de homard, Volaille de Bresse en vessie. **Wines** Pouilly-Fuissé, Brouilly.

XXXX **Roger Roucou Mère Guy,** 35 quai J.J. Rousseau 69350 La Mulatière 78 51 65 37, Telex 310241, – AE VISA
closed August, February Holidays, Sunday dinner and Monday – **M** 160/320.

XXX ✿ **Tour Rose** (Chavent), 16 r. Boeuf 69005 78 37 25 90, « 17C house in the old part of Lyons » – . AE E VISA BX **e**
closed Sunday – **M** 195/380
Spec. Saumon mi-cuit au fumoir, Rougets aux oursins (September-April), Aiguillettes de canard aux pommes et safran. **Wines** St-Véran, Brouilly.

XXX ✿✿ **Orsi,** 3 pl. Kléber 69006 78 89 57 68, Telex 305965, « Elegant setting » – . AE E VISA
closed August, Saturday from 1 May-21 July and Sunday – **st. : M** 180/280 and a la carte
Spec. Feuilleté du marché, Homard à la crème, Pigeonneau de Bresse en cocotte. **Wines** St-Véran, St-Amour.

XXX ⚙⚙ **Vettard,** 7 pl. Bellecour ✉ 69002 ✆ 78 42 07 59 – ▤. AE ⓓ VISA CY **f**
closed 25 July-24 August, Saturday dinner in June-July and Sunday – **M** (at rest.) 210/240 and a la carte - **Café Neuf M** a la carte 125/160 ♁
Spec. Quenelle de brochet, Loup à l'huile de basilic, Choix du boucher aux trois assaisonnements. **Wines** Chiroubles, Pouilly-Fuissé.

XXX ⚙ **Henry,** 27 r. Martinière ✉ 69001 ✆ 78 28 26 08, **mural paintings** – ▤. AE ⓓ VISA
closed Saturday lunch and Monday except Bank Holidays – **M** a la carte 190/330 CV **n**
Spec. Salade de homard au beurre de truffes, Fricassée de rougets et langoustines au chou vert, Aiguillettes de canette aux poires. **Wines** Mâcon, Fleurie.

XXX ⚙⚙ **Nandron,** 26 quai J.-Moulin ✉ 69002 ✆ 78 42 10 26 – ▤. AE ⓓ VISA DX **p**
closed 25 July-23 August, Friday dinner and Saturday – **M** 160/320 and a la carte
Spec. Quenelles de brochet, Terrine de champignons, Tourte de Canard "selon Balzac". **Wines** Brouilly, Mâcon.

XXX ⚙ **Bourillot,** 8 pl. Célestins ✉ 69002 ✆ 78 37 38 64 – ▤. AE ⓓ E VISA CY **n**
closed 28 June-28 July, 24 December-2 January, Sunday and Bank Holidays – **M** 160/310
Spec. Quenelle de brochet sauce Nantua, Volaille de Bresse, Soufflé glacé au chocolat. **Wines** Coteaux du Lyonnais, Brouilly.

XXX ⚙⚙ **Léon de Lyon** (Lacombe), 1 r. Pleney ✉ 69001 ✆ 78 28 11 33, **« typical local establishment »** – ▤. VISA CVX **b**
closed 20 December-6 January, Monday lunch and Sunday – **M** 170/350 and a la carte
Spec. Gras double émincé, Ravioli de grenouilles et mousserons (June-October), Soupe de faisan au foie gras. **Wines** Beaujolais-Village, Coteaux du Lyonnais.

XXX ⚙ **Mère Brazier,** 12 r. Royale ✉ 69001 ✆ 78 28 15 49, **« typical local establishment »** – AE ⓓ VISA DV **a**
closed August, Saturday (except dinner from 15 September to 30 June), Sunday and Bank Holidays – **M** (▤ 1st floor) 175/200
Spec. Fond d'artichaut au foie gras, Quenelle au gratin, Volaille demi-deuil. **Wines** St-Joseph, Côte de Brouilly.

XXX ⚙ **Aub. de Fond-Rose** (Brunet), 23 quai Clemenceau ✉ 69300 Caluire ✆ 78 29 34 61, terrace, **« Garden »** – Ⓟ. AE ⓓ E VISA
closed Monday from October to Easter and Sunday dinner – **M** 160/320
Spec. Marinade de rouget, Suprême de dorade aux oignons confits, Filets d'agneau en croûte. **Wines** Mâcon-Viré, Côte de Brouilly.

XXX **Cazenove,** 75 r. Boileau ✉ 69006 ✆ 78 89 82 92 – ▤. AE E VISA
closed August, Saturday and Sunday – **st. : M** a la carte 180/245.

XXX ⚙ **Daniel et Denise** (Léron), 2 r. Tupin ✉ 69002 ✆ 78 37 49 98 – ▤. AE ⓓ VISA CX **e**
closed August, Sunday, Monday lunch and Bank Holidays – **M** 120/195
Spec. Marinade de poissons tièdes aux aromates, Filets de rougets en bécasse. **Wines** Chiroubles,St-Joseph.

XXX **Le Rocher,** quartier St-Rambert, 8 quai R.-Carrié ✉ 69009 ✆ 78 83 99 72, terrace – Ⓟ. VISA
closed 13 August-3 September, 24 December-5 January, Saturday (except dinner from May to October) and Sunday – **st. : M** 100/235.

XXX ⚙ **Le Quatre Saisons** (Bertoli), 15 r. Sully ✉ 69006 ✆ 78.93.76.07 – ▤. AE ⓓ VISA
closed August, Saturday lunch and Sunday – **M** a la carte 190/275
Spec. Foie gras de canard chaud, Gibier (in season). **Wines** Chiroubles, St-Joseph.

XXX **Les Grillons,** 18 r. D.-Vincent at **Champagne-au-Mont-d'Or** ✉ 69410 **Champagne-au-Mont-d'Or,** ✆ 78 35 04 78, terrace – Ⓟ. AE ⓓ E VISA
closed 29 March-10 April, 2 to 20 November, Sunday dinner and Monday – **M** 95/245.

XXX ⚙ **Les Fantasques** (Gervais), 47 r. Bourse ✉ 69002 ✆ 78 37 36 58 – ▤. AE VISA DX **u**
closed 8 to 24 August and Sunday – **M** 160/250
Spec. Terrine de homard, Rouget en papillote, St-Jacques (in season). **Wines** Mâcon, Brouilly.

XX **Le Gourmandin,** 156 r. P.-Bert ✉ 69003 ✆ 78 62 78 77 – ▤. AE ⓓ VISA
closed 10 to 20 August, Saturday, Sunday and Bank Holidays – **st. : M** 120/280.

XX ⚙ **Chez Gervais** (Lescuyer), 42 r. P.-Corneille ✉ 69006 ✆ 78 52 19 13 – ▤. AE ⓓ E VISA
closed July, Saturday (except dinner from September to May), Sunday and Bank Holidays – **st. : M** 175 b.i./200
Spec. Salade Lyonnaise, Fricassée de volaille au vinaigre de framboises, Coupe Florence. **Wines** Mâcon blanc, Côtes du Rhône.

XX **Tante Alice,** 22 r. Remparts-d'Ainay ✉ 69002 ✆ 78 37 49 83 – ▤. AE CZ **v**
closed Easter, 24 July-24 August, 24 December-4 January, Friday dinner and Saturday – **M** 65/135 ♁.

XX **Chevallier,** 40 r. du Sergent-Blandan ✉ 69001 ✆ 78 28 19 83 – VISA CV **s**
closed July, 16 to 26 February, Tuesday and Wednesday – **st. : M** 75/136.

XX **Au Petit Col,** 68 r. Charité ✉ 69002 ✆ 78 37 25 18 – ▤. VISA CZ **a**
closed 13 July-10 August, Sunday (except lunch from 1 September to 30 Mai) and Monday – **st. : M** 75/140.

XX ⚙ **Fédora** (Judeaux), 249 r. Mérieux ✉ 69007 ✆ 78 69 46 26, terrace, garden – AE ⓓ E VISA
closed 21 December-3 January, Saturday lunch and Sunday – **M** 99/179 ♁
Spec. Charcuteries de la mer, St-Jacques au safran (October-April), Canette rôtie. **Wines** St-Joseph.

X **La Bonne Auberge "Chez Jo",** 48 av. Félix-Faure ✉ 69003 ✆ 78 60 00 57 – ▤. AE ⓓ VISA
closed August, Saturday dinner and Sunday – **st. : M** 80/130 ♁.

Environs

at Bron – pop. 41 500 – ✉ **69500** Bron :

Novotel Ⓜ, r. Lionel Terray ✆ 78 26 97 48, Telex 340781, ☂, ⛱ – ♿ ▤ TV ☎ ♿ Ⓟ – 🏛 25 - 700. AE ⓓ E VISA
M a la carte 90/160 ⚲ – ☕ 38 – **196 rm** 345.

Dau Ly 🐚 without rest, 28 r. de Prévieux ✆ 78 26 04 37 – TV ⛀wc ⛆wc ☎ 🚗 Ⓟ. AE VISA
st. : ☕ 16,50 – **22 rm** 183/222.

at Tassin-la-Demi-Lune : 5 km by D 407 – pop. 15 034 – ✉ **69160** Tassin-la-Demi-Lune :

XXX **Les Tilleuls,** 146 av. Ch.-de-Gaulle ✆ 78 34 19 58, ☂ – Ⓟ. AE VISA
closed 16 to 26 August, February Holidays, Sunday dinner and Monday except Bank Holidays – **st.** : **M** 90/230 ⚲.

to the NE :

at Crépieux-la-Pape : 7 km by N 83 and N 84 – ✉ **69140** Rillieux-la-Pape :

XXX ✿ **Larivoire** (Constantin), ✆ 78 88 50 92, ←, ☂ – Ⓟ. AE ⓓ VISA
closed 31 August-9 September, 10 February-5 March, Monday dinner and Tuesday – **st.** : **M** 130/270
Spec. Oeuf en cocotte aux langoustines, Chartreuse d'huîtres et St-Jacques (October-May), Fricassée de volaille au vinaigre. **Wines** Montagnieu, Côteaux du Lyonnais.

to the SE :

at St-Priest : 12 km by N 6 and D 148 – pop. 42 913 – ✉ **69800** St-Priest :

Moderne Ⓜ without rest, 64 rte Heyrieux ✆ 78 20 47 46 – ♿ TV ⛀wc ☎ Ⓟ. AE ⓓ VISA
closed 2 to 30 August – **st.** : ☕ 21 – **35 rm** 210/300.

at the airport of Satolas : 27 km by A 43 – ✉ **69125** Lyon Satolas Airport :

Méridien Ⓜ, 3rd floor ✆ 78 71 91 61, Telex 380480, ← – ♿ ▤ TV ☎ – 🏛 250. AE ⓓ E VISA
st. : **M** rest. see **La Gde Corbeille** below – ☕ 42 – **120 rm** 415/495.

XXX **La Gde Corbeille,** 1st floor ✆ 78 71 91 62, Telex 380480, ← – ▤. AE ⓓ VISA
closed August and Saturday – **st.** : **M** 160/200.

to the W :

at Charbonnières-les-Bains : 8 km by N 7 – pop. 3 973 – alt. 240 – Spa – ✉ **69260** Charbonnières-les-Bains :

Mercure Ⓜ, N 7 ✆ 78 34 72 79, Telex 900972, ⛱ – ▤ TV ⛀wc ☎ Ⓟ – 🏛 25 - 75. AE ⓓ E VISA
M (dinner only) a la carte 90/150 ⚲ – ☕ 32 – **60 rm** 240/300.

Beaulieu without rest, 19 av. Gén.-de-Gaulle ✆ 78 87 12 04 – ♿ ⛀wc ☎ Ⓟ – 🏛 100. AE ⓓ E VISA
st. : ☕ 18,50 – **40 rm** 145/185.

XX **Gigandon,** 5 av. Gén.-de-Gaulle ✆ 78 87 15 51 – AE VISA
closed August, Sunday dinner and Monday – **st.** : **M** 98/200.

Porte de Lyon - motorway junction A 6 N 6 Exit road signposted Limonest N : 10 km – ✉ **69570** Dardilly :

Novotel Ⓜ 🐚, ✆ 78 35 13 41, Telex 330962, ☂, ⛱, 🌳 – ♿ ▤ TV ☎ Ⓟ – 🏛 125. AE ⓓ E VISA
M Grill a la carte 90/160 ⚲ – ☕ 36 – **107 rm** 335/355.

Lyon-Nord Ⓜ, ✆ 78 35 70 20, Telex 900006, ⛱ – ♿ ▤ TV ☎ ♿ Ⓟ – 🏛 350. AE ⓓ E VISA
Grill la Braise M 60/150 ⚲ – ☕ 39 – **204 rm** 185/460.

Mercure Ⓜ, ✆ 78 35 28 05, Telex 330045, ⛱, 🎾 – ▤ rest TV ☎ Ⓟ – 🏛 250. AE ⓓ E VISA
M a la carte 110/160 ⚲ – ☕ 35 – **175 rm** 215/299.

Campanile, ✆ 78 35 48 44, Telex 310155 – TV ⛀wc ☎ Ⓟ. VISA
st. : **M** 61 b.i./82 b.i. – ☕ 23 – **43 rm** 196/216.

XX **Le Panorama,** at Dardilly-le-Haut, near the church, ✉ 69570 Dardilly, ✆ 78 47 40 19, ☂, 🌳 – AE VISA
closed July, February Holidays, Tuesday, dinner Sunday and Monday – **st.** : **M** 120/300.

Chagny 71150 S.-et-L. 69 ⑨ – pop. 5 604 – alt. 216 – Lyon 143.

Lameloise M, pl. d'Armes ✆ 85 87 08 85, Telex 801086, « Old Burgundian house, tasteful decor » – TV ☎ . E VISA. rest
closed 21 December-21 January, Thursday lunch and Wednesday – **st.** : **M** (booking essential) a la carte 250/390 – ☕ 45 – **20 rm** 280/750
Spec. Ravioli d'escargots, Pigeon de Bresse en vessie, Assiette du chocolatier. **Wines** Rully, Chassagne-Montrachet.

Condrieu 69420 Rhône 74 ⑪ – pop. 3 158 – alt. 150 – Lyon 40.

Hôt. Beau Rivage (Mme Castaing) , ✆ 74 59 52 24, Telex 308946, , « Terrace with view of Rhône River », – ☎ P. AE ⓓ E VISA
closed 5 January-15 February – **M** 190/275 and a la carte – ☕ 39 – **22 rm** 218/417, 4 apartments 565
Spec. Foie gras à l'embeurré de choux, Panaché de poisson au gingembre, Sandre à la Côte Rôtie. **Wines** Viognier, St-Joseph.

Fleurie 69820 Rhône 74 ① – pop. 1 151 – alt. 295 – Lyon 58.

XXX **Aub. du Cep** (Cortembert), pl. de l'Eglise ✆ 74 04 10 77, – AE E VISA
closed 24 to 31 March, 28 July-4 August, 22 December-12 January, Sunday dinner and Monday – **st.** : **M** (booking essential) 200/400 and a la carte
Spec. Mousseline de sandre, Fricassée de volaille au Fleurie, Entremets glacé moka nougatine. **Wines** Beaujolais blanc, Fleurie.

Mionnay 01 Ain 74 ② – pop. 796 – alt. 288 – ✉ 01390 St-André-de-Corcy – Lyon 20.

XXXX **Alain Chapel** with rm, ✆ 78 91 82 02, Telex 305605, , « flowered garden » – wc ☎ P. AE ⓓ VISA
closed January, Tuesday lunch and Monday except Bank Holidays – **M** 300/520 and a la carte – ☕ 72 – **13 rm** 600/775
Spec. Bouillon de champignons (15 April -15 July), Barbue aux pommes de terre (15 April-1 October), Poulette de Bresse en vessie. **Wines** Cheignieu, Beaujolais-Villages.

Montrond-les-Bains 42210 Loire 73 ⑱ – pop. 3 194 – alt. 356.
Lyon 68.

Host. La Poularde (Eteocle), ✆ 77 54 40 06 – TV P – 40. AE ⓓ E VISA
closed 2 to 15 January, Monday dinner and Tuesday lunch – **st.** : **M** (Sunday : booking essential) 135/370 and a la carte – ☕ 40 – **15 rm** 220/350
Spec. Trois nuances du pêcheur, Pigeonneau rôti en piccata, Tarte tiède aux fruits. **Wines** Chassagne-Montrachet, Fleurie.

Roanne SP 42300 Loire 73 ⑦ – pop. 49 638 – alt. 279.
Lyon 86.

H. des Frères Troisgros M, pl. Gare ✆ 77 71 66 97, Telex 307507 – rest TV ☎ P. AE ⓓ E VISA
closed 4 to 19 August, January, Wednesday lunch and Tuesday – **M** (booking essential) 210/390 and a la carte – ☕ 55 – **21 rm** 475/600, 5 apartments 950
Spec. Multicolore de légumes aux crabes dormeurs, Emincé de rognons de veau aux échalotes, Lingot roannais à l'huile de noix. **Wines** Beaujolais, St-Véran.

St-Étienne 42000 Loire 73 ⑲, 76 ⑨ – pop. 206 087 – alt. 517.
Lyon 63.

XXX **Pierre Gagnaire,** 3 r. G.-Teissier ✆ 77 37 57 93 – AE ⓓ VISA
closed August, February Holidays, Sunday and Monday – **st.** : **M** 170/330 and a la carte
Spec. Poêlée d'asperges et pommes de terre nouvelles au beurre de truffes (April-June), Bar aux céleris, Confit de pigeon. **Wines** St-Joseph, Coteaux du Vivarais.

Valence P 26000 Drôme 77 ⑫ – pop. 68 157 – alt. 123.
Lyon 99.

XXXX **Pic** with rm, 285 av. Victor-Hugo, Motorway exit sign-posted Valence-Sud ✆ 75 44 15 32, , « Shaded garden » – TV wc ☎ P. AE ⓓ VISA
closed 3 to 26 August, 16 to 25 February, Sunday dinner and Wednesday – **st.** : **M** (Sunday : booking essential) 350/450 and a la carte – ☕ 50 – **5 rm** 350/750
Spec. Menu Rabelais. **Wines** Côtes du Rhône.

at Pont de l'Isère – ✉ **26600** Tain-l'Hermitage :

XXX **Chabran** M with rm, N7, Motorway exit sign-posted Valence-Nord ✆ 75 84 60 09, Telex 346333, – TV wc ☎ P. VISA
closed Sunday dinner and Monday from September to Easter – **M** 190/380 and a la carte – ☕ 50 – **12 rm** 250/400
Spec. Ravioles du Royans, Poêlée de moules et supions au safran, Aiguillettes de boeuf au vieil Hermitage. **Wines** Hermitage, St-Joseph.

Vienne 38200 Isère 74 ⑪⑫ – pop. 29 050 – alt. 158.

Lyon 30.

XXXX ✿✿ **Pyramide,** bd F.-Point ✆ 74 53 01 96, **« flowered garden »** – ▤. AE ⓓ
closed 1 to 21 February – **M** (booking essential) 370/450 and a la carte
Spec. Assiette de marée, Filet de turbot au champagne, Poularde de Bresse marinière. **Wines** Côte Rôtie, St-Joseph.

Vonnas 01540 Ain 74 ② – pop. 2 505 – alt. 189.

Lyon 66.

✿✿✿ **Georges Blanc** M, ✆ 74 50 00 10, Telex 380776, – ▤ rest TV ☎ Ⓟ. AE ⓓ VISA
closed 2 January-10 February – **M** *(closed Thursday except dinner from 15 June-15 September and Wednesday except Bank Holidays)* (booking essential) 260/390 and a la carte – ☕ 50 – **23 rm** 500/1 200, 7 apartments 950/1 850
Spec. Crêpe parmentière au saumon et caviar, Bar à la marinière, Poularde de Bresse aux gousses d'ail et au foie gras. **Wines** Mâcon blanc, Chiroubles.

MARSEILLES P 13 B.-du-R. 84 ⑬ – pop. 878 689.

See : N.-D.-de-la-Garde Basilica ☀* BY – La Canebière** CV – Old Port** ABVX – Corniche Président-J.-F.-Kennedy** – Modern Port** – Palais Longchamp* DU – St-Victor Basilica* : crypt** AX – Old Major Cathedral* AU N – Pharo Parc ≤* AX – St-Laurent Belvedere ≤* AV E – Museum : Grobet-Labadié** DU M4, Cantini* : Marseilles and Moustiers pottery** (galerie de la Faïence de Marseille et de Moustiers) CX Fine Arts* and Natural History Museum* (Longchamp Palace) DU M Mediterranean Archeology* Egyptian antiquities** (Château Borely), Roman Docks* ABV M2 Old Marseilles* AV M1.**

Envir. : Corniche road of Callelongue S : 13 km.**

Exc. : Château d'If (☀***) 1 h 30.**

18 of Aix-Marseilles ✆ 42 24 20 41 to the North : 22 km.

Marseille-Marignane Air France ✆ 42 89 90 10 to the North : 28 km.

✆ 91 08 50 50.

for Corsica : Société Nationale Maritime Corse-Méditerranée, 61 bd des Dames (2e) ✆ 91 56 32 00 AU.

i and Accueil de France (Information and hotel reservations - not more than 5 days in advance), 4 Canebière, 13001, ✆ 91 54 91 11, Telex 430402 - and at St-Charles railway Station ✆ 91 50 59 18 – A.C. 143 cours Lieutaud, 13006, ✆ 91 47 86 23.

Paris 776 – Lyon 315 – Nice 187 – Torino 407 – Toulon 64 – Toulouse 404.

Plan on following pages

Sofitel Vieux Port M, 36 bd Ch.-Livon, ✉ 13007, ✆ 91 52 90 19, Telex 401270, panoramic restaurant ≤ old port, – ▤ TV ☎ ♿ Ⓟ – 100 - 450. AE ⓓ E VISA AX **n**
rest. **les Trois Forts M** a la carte 185/280 – ☕ 50 – **127 rm** 550/890, 3 apartments 2 200.

Altéa M, r. Neuve St-Martin, ✉ 13001, ✆ 91 91 91 29, Telex 401886, – ▤ TV ☎ ♿ – 400. AE ⓓ E VISA BUV **g**
st. : rest. **L'Oursinade** *(closed 31 July-2 September, Sunday and Bank Holidays)* **M** 175/240 **L'Oliveraie** (Grill) *(closed dinner Friday and Saturday)* **M** 70/95 – ☕ 45 – **200 rm** 470/590.

Pullman Beauvau without rest, **4 r. Beauvau, ✉ 13001, ✆ 91 54 91 00, Telex 401778** – ▤ TV ☎ – 30 BV **r**
71 rm.

Concorde-Prado M, **11 av. Mazargues, ✉ 13008, ✆ 91 76 51 11, Telex 420209** – ▤ TV ☎ – 80. AE ⓓ E VISA
st. : M 106/200 – ☕ 39 – **99 rm** 347/446.

Résidence Bompard without rest, **2 r. Flots-Bleus, ✉ 13007, ✆ 91 52 10 93, Telex 400430,** – kitchenette TV ☎ ♿ Ⓟ – 40. AE ⓓ VISA
st. : ☕ 25 – **47 rm** 220/295.

Gd H. Noailles, 66 Canebière, ✉ **13001, ✆ 91 54 91 48, Telex 430609** – TV ☎ – 40 - 60. AE ⓓ E VISA CV **x**
st. : M *(closed Sunday)* 80/130 – ☕ 35 – **70 rm** 250/580, 4 apartments 580 – P 450/550.

Gd H. Genève without rest, **3 bis r. Reine-Élisabeth, ✉ 13001, ✆ 91 90 51 42, Telex 440672** – TV ☎ – 25. ⓓ VISA. BV **e**
st. : ☕ 23 – **45 rm** 145/320, 4 apartments 380.

New H. Astoria M without rest, **10 bd Garibaldi, ✉ 13001, ✆ 91 33 33 50** – ▤ wc wc ☎. AE ⓓ E VISA. CV **f**
st. : ☕ 25 – **58 rm** 220/280.

Castellane M without rest, **31 r. Rouet, ✉ 13006, ✆ 91 79 27 54, Telex 402326** – TV wc ☎. AE E VISA DY **f**
st. : ☕ 27 – **55 rm** 220/290.

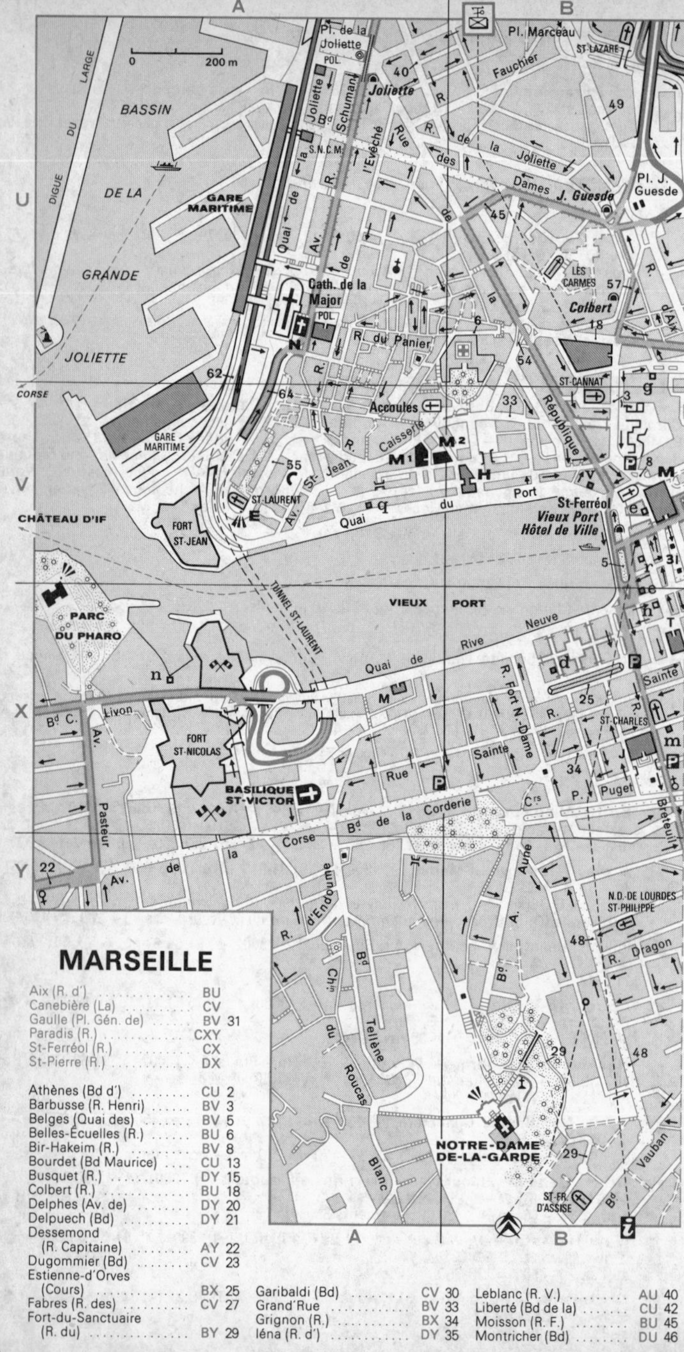

MARSEILLE

Aix (R. d') .... BU
Canebière (La) CV
Gaulle (Pl. Gén. de) .... BV 31
Paradis (R.) .... CXY
St-Ferréol (R.) CX
St-Pierre (R.) .... DX

Athènes (Bd d') .... CU 2
Barbusse (R. Henri) .... BV 3
Belges (Quai des) .... BV 5
Belles-Écuelles (R.) .... BU 6
Bir-Hakeim (R.) .... BV 8
Bourdet (Bd Maurice) .... CU 13
Busquet (R.) .... DY 15
Colbert (R.) .... BU 18
Delphes (Av. de) .... DY 20
Delpuech (Bd) .... DY 21
Dessemond (R. Capitaine) .... AY 22
Dugommier (Bd) .... CV 23
Estienne-d'Orves (Cours) .... BX 25
Fabres (R. des) .... CV 27
Fort-du-Sanctuaire (R. du) .... BY 29

Garibaldi (Bd) .... CV 30
Grand'Rue .... BV 33
Grignon (R.) .... BX 34
Iéna (R. d') .... DY 35

Leblanc (R. V.) .... AU 40
Liberté (Bd de la) .... CU 42
Moisson (R. F.) .... BU 45
Montricher (Bd) .... DU 46

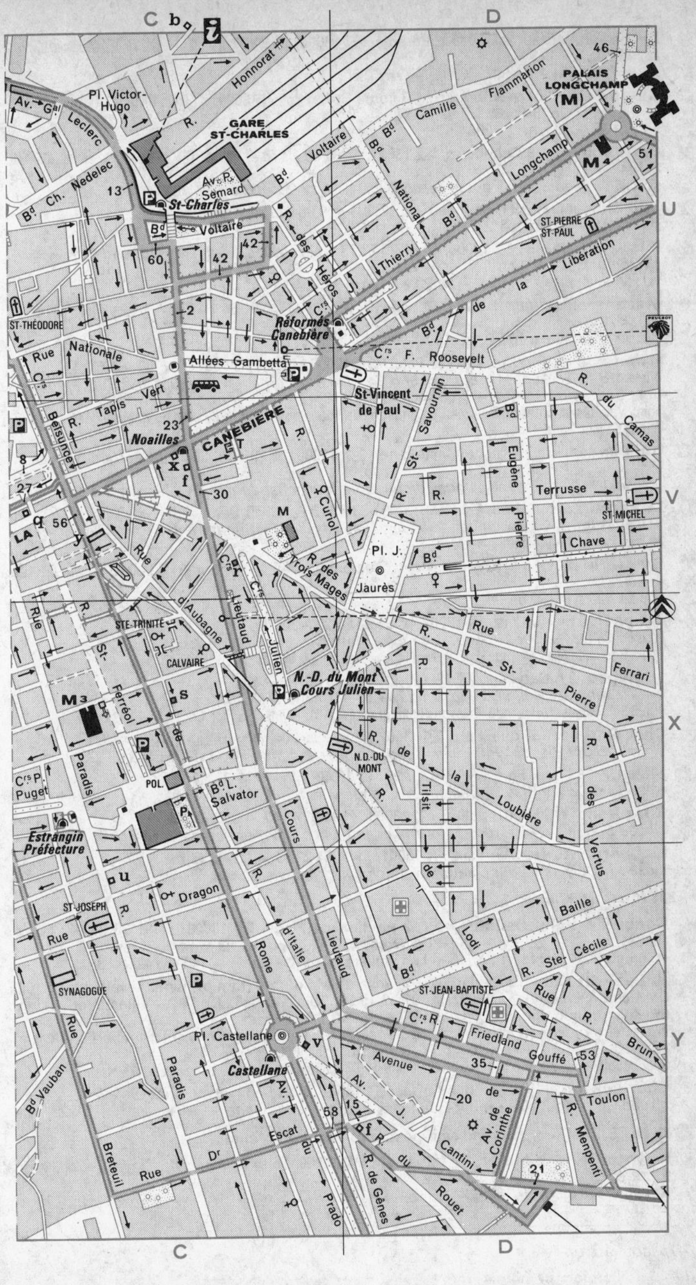

Notre-Dame (Bd)	BY	48	Sadi-Carnot (Pl.)	BU	54	Ste-Philomène (R.)	CY	58
Pelletan (Av. C.)	BU	49	St-Laurent (R.)	AV	55	Sembat (R. Marcel)	CU	60
Philipon (Bd)	DU	51	St-Louis (Crs)	CV	56	Tourette (Quai)	AU	62
Raynouard (Traverse)	DY	53	Ste-Barbe (R.)	BU	57	Vaudoyer (Av.)	AV	64

Européen without rest, 115 r. Paradis, ✉ 13006, ☎ 91 37 77 20 – wc wc. VISA — CY **u**
closed August – **st.** : 17,50 – **43 rm** 125/199.

Rome et St Pierre without rest, 7 cours St-Louis, ✉ 13001, ☎ 91 54 19 52, Telex 430641 – TV wc wc. AE E VISA — CV **y**
st. : 25 – **63 rm** 114/298.

Petit Louvre, 19 Canebière, ✉ 13001, ☎ 91 90 13 78 – TV wc wc. AE E VISA. rest — CV **q**
st. : **M** *(closed Sunday out of season)* 75/110 – 25 – **33 rm** 174/298 – P 310/370.

Sud without rest, 18 r. Beauvau, ✉ 13001, ☎ 91 54 38 50 – wc — BX **n**
st. : 18 – **24 rm** 165/235.

Ibis M, 6 r. Cassis, ✉ 13008, ☎ 91 25 73 73, Telex 400362 – TV wc – 25-40. E VISA
st. : **M** a la carte 75/115 – 20 – **118 rm** 228/249.

Martini without rest, 5 bd G.-Desplaces, ✉ 13003, ☎ 91 64 11 17 – wc. AE. — CU **b**
st. : 18 – **40 rm** 104/200.

XXX ✿ **Jambon de Parme,** 67 r. La Palud, ✉ 13006, ☎ 91 54 37 98 – AE E VISA
closed 8 to 17 August, Saturday and Sunday from 1 June-31 August and Sunday dinner from September to May – **M** a la carte 150/220 — CX **s**
Spec. Variétés de pâtes fraîches, Langoutines en papillote, Rognons et ris de veau au vinaigre de framboises. **Wines** Cassis, Bandol.

XXX **Au Pescadou,** 19 place Castellane, ✉ 13006, ☎ 91 78 36 01, Seafood – E VISA — CY **v**
closed July, August and Sunday dinner from November-June – **M** a la carte 115/225.

XXX **La Ferme,** 23 r. Sainte, ✉ 13001, ☎ 91 33 21 12 – AE VISA — BX **m**
closed August, 26 December-4 January, Saturday lunch, Sunday and Bank Holidays – **st.** : **M** a la carte 170/215.

XXX **Brasserie New-York Vieux Port,** 7 quai Belges, ✉ 13001, ☎ 91 33 60 98 – AE E VISA — BX **e**
st. : **M** 120 b.i./180 b.i.

XX ✿ **Michel,** 6 r. Catalans, ✉ 13007, ☎ 91 52 64 22 – E VISA
closed 23 December-10 January and Wednesday – **M** a la carte 250/310
Spec. Bouillabaisse, Bourride, Poissons et langoustes grillés. **Wines** Cassis, Bandol.

XX ✿ **Calypso,** 3 r. Catalans, ✉ 13007, ☎ 91 52 64 00, ← – VISA
closed February Holidays and Sunday – **M** a la carte 250/310
Spec. Bouillabaisse, Bourride, Poissons et langoustes grillés. **Wines** Bandol, Cassis.

XX **Chez Caruso,** 158 quai Port, ✉ 13002, ☎ 91 90 94 04, Italian cuisine – AE — AV **q**
closed 15 October-15 November, Sunday dinner and Monday – **st.** : **M** 180 b.i./250 b.i.

XX **Miramar,** 12 quai Port, ✉ 13002, ☎ 91 91 10 40, – AE E VISA — BV **v**
closed 1 to 22 August, 24 December-6 January and Sunday – **M** 150.

XX **Chez Benoît,** 26 cours Julien, ✉ 13006, ☎ 91 92 47 47 – VISA — CV **r**
closed Sunday from 1 April-1 November and lunch July-August – **st.** : **M** 87/150.

X **La Charpenterie,** 22 r. Paix, ✉ 13001, ☎ 91 54 22 89 – AE E VISA — BX **d**
closed 14 July-15 August, Saturday lunch and Sunday – **st.** : **M** 90/150.

at the Corniche :

Concorde-Palm Beach M, 2 promenade Plage, ✉ 13008, ☎ 91 76 20 00, Telex 401894, ←, – TV – 450. AE E VISA. rest
st. : rest. **La Réserve M** 120/180 - **Les Voiliers M** 87 – 41 – **145 rm** 425/468.

✿✿ **Le Petit Nice** (Passedat) M, anse de Maldormé (turn off when level with no 160 Corniche Kennedy) ✉ 13007, ☎ 91 52 19 39, Telex 401565, ←, « Villas overlooking the sea, refined decor », – TV . AE VISA. rest
closed 1 January-10 February – **M** *(closed Monday except dinner in summer)* a la carte 270/400 – 63 – **10 rm** 700/1 000, 8 apartments 1 600/2 000
Spec. Bouillabaisse, Loup de ligne en huile d'olive, Soupe de fruits rouges. **Wines** Bandol, Palette.

XX **Chez Fonfon,** 140 vallon des Auffes, ✉ 13007, ☎ 91 52 14 38, ← – AE VISA
closed October, 24 December-2 January, Saturday and Sunday – **M** a la carte 180/225.

to the E : 11,5 km, exit road sign-posted La Penne-St-Menet :

Novotel M, at St-Menet, ✉ 13011, ☎ 91 43 90 60, Telex 400667, – rm TV – 250. AE E VISA
M (Grill) a la carte 90/160 – 32 – **131 rm** 304/325.

Do not mix up :

Comfort of hotels	: ...
Comfort of restaurants	: XXXXX ... X
Quality of the cuisine	: ✿✿✿, ✿✿, ✿

Les Baux-de-Provence 13 B.-du-R. 84 ① – pop. 433 – alt. 280 – ✉ **13520** Maussane-les-Alpilles – Marseille 86.

in the Vallon :

XXXXX ✿✿✿ **Oustaù de Baumanière** (Thuilier) M with rm, ✆ 90 54 33 07, Telex 420203, ≤ « Tastefully decorated mansions, flowered terraces, , , , Riding club », – wc ☎ . AE E VISA
closed 20 January-6 March, Thursday lunch and Wednesday from 1 November-15 March
– **M** a la carte 280/405 – 70 – **14 rm** 725/770, 11 apartments 1 050
Spec. Soufflé de homard, Filets de rougets au basilic, Noisettes d'agneau Baumanière. **Wines** Gigondas, Côteaux des Baux.

XXX ✿ **La Riboto de Taven,** ✆ 90 97 34 23, , « Shady terrace and flowered garden near the rocks » – AE VISA
closed 10 January-26 February, Sunday dinner out of season and Monday – **st. : M** a la carte 260/370
Spec. Minute de loup à l'huile d'olive, Selle d'agneau des Alpilles truffée, Gratin de fruits au sabayon. **Wines** Côteaux des Baux, Châteauneuf-du-Pape.

XXX ✿ **La Cabro d'Or** M with rm, ✆ 90 54 33 21, Telex 401810, ≤, , « Shaded terraces, flowered garden, lake », , – wc ☎ – 80. AE E VISA
closed 15 November-20 December, Tuesday lunch and Monday from 15 October-31 March
– **st. : M** 210/250 – 48 – **22 rm** 400/630 – P 680/790
Spec. Salade du pêcheur, Filet de loup en papillote, Filet d'agneau en croûte. **Wines** Côteaux des Baux.

Carry-le-Rouet 13620 B.-du-R. 84 ⑫ – pop. 4 570.
Marseilles 27.

XXX ✿✿ **L'Escale,** ✆ 42 45 00 47, , « Terraces overlooking the Harbour, nice view », – VISA
March-October and closed Sunday dinner out of season and Monday except dinner July-August – **st. : M** (Sunday booking essential) a la carte 270/360
Spec. St-Jacques en feuille de chou (March-April), Filets de rougets à la brunoise de céleris, Homard grillé au beurre de corail. **Wines** Cassis, Côteaux d'Aix.

MONACO (Principality of) 84 ⑩, 195 ㉗㉘ – pop. 28 500 – alt. 65 – Casino.
Paris 956 – Menton 9 – Nice (by the Moyenne Corniche) 18 – San Remo 44.

Monaco Capital of the Principality – ✉ **98000** Monaco.

See : Tropical Garden★★ (Jardin exotique) : ≤★ – Observatory Caves★ (Grotte de l'Observatoire) – St-Martin Gardens★ – Early paintings of the Nice School★★ in Cathedral – Recumbent Christ★ in the Misericord Chapel – Place du Palais★ – Prince's Palace★ – Museums : oceanographic★★ (aquarium★★, ≤★★ from the terrace), Prehistoric Anthropology★ – Museum of Napoleon and Monaco History★.

Urban racing circuit - A.C. 23 bd Albert-1er ✆ 93 30 32 20, Télex 469003.

Monte-Carlo Fashionable resort of the Principality - Grand casino, Casino of Sporting Club, Casino Loews – ✉ Monte-Carlo.

See : Terrace★★ of the Grand casino – Museum of Dolls and Automata★.

18 Monte-Carlo Golf Club ✆ 93 41 09 11 to the S by N7 : 11 km.

Direction Tourisme et Congrès, 2 A bd Moulins ✆ 93 30 87 01, Télex 469760.

✿ **Paris,** pl. Casino ✆ 93 50 80 80, Telex 469925, ≤, , , – rm ☎ – 50. AE E VISA. rest
Louis XV *(closed 2 November-mid December, Tuesday and Wednesday)* **M** a la carte 340/480 and see **Grill** below – 85 – **206 rm** 1 400/1 700, 40 apartments
Spec. Velouté léger de crustacés, Salade tiède de langoustines, Gratin de fraises des bois aux pignons. **Wines** Côtes de Provence.

Hermitage, square Beaumarchais ✆ 93 50 67 31, Telex 479432, ≤, , « Dining room in Baroque style », – ☎ – 80. AE E VISA. rest
M 230/300 – 85 – **220 rm** 1 100/1 500, 20 apartments.

Loews M , av. Spélugues ✆ 93 50 65 00, Telex 479435, ≤, Casino and cabaret, – ☎ – 50-1 100. AE E VISA. rest
st. : Le Foie Gras (dinner only) **M** a la carte 320/520 - **L'Argentin** (dinner only) **M** a la carte 240/350 - **Le Pistou M** 200 - **Café de la mer M** a la carte 115/220 – 75 – **573 rm** 1 200/1 500, 68 apartments – P 1 500/1 700.

✿ **Mirabeau** M, 1 av. Princesse-Grace ✆ 93 25 45 45, Telex 479413, ≤, – ☎ – 80. AE E VISA. rest
M *(closed lunch from 28 June-6 September)* 185/285 – 75 – **96 rm** 900/1 250, 5 apartments
Spec. Poêlée de rougets en filets, Saumon grillé à la peau, Suprêmes de pigeon en coeur.

Beach Plaza M, av. Princesse-Grace, à la Plage du Larvotto ✆ 93 30 98 80, Telex 479617, ≤, , « Fashionable resort with good bathing facilities », , – ☎ – 30-300. AE E VISA.
st. : M 140/280 – 70 – **320 rm** 660/1 550, 9 apartments.

Balmoral without rest, 12 av. Costa 93 50 62 37, Telex 479436, < – AE E VISA.
st. : 35 – **68 rm** 300/550.

Louvre without rest, 16 bd Moulins 93 50 65 25, Telex 479645 – wc E VISA.
st. : **35 rm** 470/610.

Alexandra without rest, 35 bd Princesse-Charlotte 93 50 63 13, Telex 489286 – wc wc. AE E VISA.
st. : 32 – **55 rm** 357/435.

Grill de l'Hôtel de Paris, pl. Casino 93 50 80 80, « Roof-top grill (open air) with < over the Principality » – . AE E VISA.
closed June – **M** (dinner only from June-mid September) a la carte 250/400.

Toula, 20 bd de Suisse 93 50 02 02, , Italian cuisine – . AE E VISA
closed January and Sunday – **M** a la carte 250/400.

Rampoldi, 3 av. Spélugues 93 30 70 65 – . AE VISA
closed November – **M** a la carte 210/300.

Chez Gianni, 39 av. Princesse Grace 93 30 46 33, Italian cuisine – AE E VISA.
closed February Holidays and Sunday dinner – **st. : M** a la carte 175/270.

du Port, quai Albert 1er 93 50 77 21, <, , Italian cuisine – . AE E VISA
closed 2 November-8 December and Monday – **st. : M** a la carte 160/300.

at Monte-Carlo Beach (06 Alpes-Mar.) at 2,5 km – **06190** Roquebrune-Cap-Martin :

Monte-Carlo Beach H. M , 93 78 21 40, < sea and Monaco, « Fashionable resort with good bathing facilities, , » – rm – 30. AE E VISA.
rest
15 April-12 October – **M** a la carte 180/350 – 85 – **46 rm** 1 400/1 500.

NICE P **06000** Alpes-Mar. 84 ⑨⑩, 195 ㉖㉗ – pop. 338 486 – alt. at château 92 – Casino : Club.

See : Site★★ – Promenade des Anglais★★ EFZ – Old Nice★ : Château <★★ JZ, Interior★ of church of St-Martin and St-Augustin HY **D** Balustraded staircase★ of the Palais Lascaris HZ **K**, Interior★ of Ste-Reparate Cathedral HZ **L** St-Jacques Church★ HZ **N**, Decoration of St-GiaumesChapel HZ **R** – Mosaic★ by Chagall in Law Faculty DZ **U** – Cimiez : Monastery★ (Masterpieces★★ of the early Nice School in the church) HV **Q**, Roman Ruins★ HV – Museums : Marc Chagall★★ GX, Matisse★ HV **M2**, Fine Arts Museum★★ DZ **M**, Masséna★ FZ **M1**, International Naive Style Museum★ – Carnival★★★ (before Shrove Tuesday) – Mount Alban <★★ 5 km – Mount Boron <★ 3 km – St-Pons Church★ : 3 km.

Envir. : St-Michel Plateau <★★ 9,5 km.

18 Biot 93 65 08 48 : 22 km.

of Nice-Côte d'Azur 93 21 30 30 : 7 km.

93 87 50 50.

for Corsica : Société Nationale Maritime Corse-Méditerranée, Gare Maritime, quai de Commerce 93 89 89 89 JZ.

Accueil de France (hotel reservations - not more than 7 days in advance) av. Thiers 93 87 07 07, Telex 460042 ; Acropolis, Esplanade Kennedy 93 92 82 82, Telex 461045 5 av. Gustave-V 93 87 60 60 and Nice-Parking near the Airport 93 83 32 64 - A.C. 9 r. Massenet 93 87 18 17.

Paris 931 – Cannes 32 – Genova 194 – Lyon 470 – Marseille 187 – Turino 220.

Plan on following pages

Négresco, 37 prom. des Anglais 93 88 39 51, Telex 460040, <, « Public rooms and bedrooms, in period style : 16C and 18C, Empire and Napoléon III » – – 50-400. AE E VISA FZ **k**
st. : La Rotonde M a la carte 165/255 and see rest. **Chantecler** below – 75 – **140 rm** 1 200/1 900, 10 apartments.

Sofitel Splendid M, 50 bd Victor-Hugo 93 88 69 54, Telex 460938, « on 8th floor, < Nice » – – 30-100. AE E VISA. rest FYZ **g**
st. : M a la carte 120/200 – **116 rm** 550/840, 12 apartments 900/1 250 – P 650/720.

Méridien M, 1 prom. des Anglais 93 82 25 25, Telex 470361, , « Roof-top swimming pool, < bay » – – 30-400. AE E VISA FZ **d**
st. : M 160/250 – 90 – **297 rm** 900/2 200, 9 apartments.

Beach Régency M, 223 prom. des Anglais 93 83 91 51, Telex 461635, « on the roof, < the bay », – – 50-400
Le Regency - La Promenade – **305 rm**, 17 apartments.

Pullman Nice M without rest, 28 av. Notre-Dame 93 80 30 24, Telex 470662, « on 8th floor, hanging gardens on 2nd floor, < » – – 25-120. AE E VISA FXY **q**
st. : 42 – **200 rm** 430/670.

Plaza, 12 av. Verdun 93 87 80 41, Telex 460979, <, « Roof-top terrace » – – 30-550. AE E VISA. rest GZ **f**
st. : M 135 – 45 – **187 rm** 600/850 – P 720/1 390.

Continental-Masséna M without rest, 58 r. Gioffredo 93 85 49 25, Telex 470192 – – 60. AE E VISA GZ **k**
st. : **116 rm** 395/514.

La Pérouse, 11 quai Rauba-Capeu 93 62 34 63, Telex 461411, « Nice and promenade des Anglais », – – 30. AE E VISA HZ **k**
st. : **M** (coffee shop only in summer) – **63 rm** 460/860.

La Malmaison, 48 bd V.-Hugo 93 87 62 56, Telex 470410 – . AE E VISA. rest FYZ **e**
st. : **M** 100 – **50 rm** 300/450 – P 400/500.

Ambassador M without rest, 8 av. Suède 93 87 90 19, Telex 460025, – . AE E VISA FZ **x**
closed December – **st. :** 29 – **45 rm** 375/440.

Grand H. Aston M, 12 av. F.-Faure 93 80 62 52, Telex 470290, , « Roof-top terrace » – rm – 50-180. AE E VISA. rest HZ **u**
st. : M *(closed Sunday)* 220/260 – 40 – **157 rm** 720/780.

Napoléon without rest, 6 r. Grimaldi 93 87 70 07, Telex 460949 – . AE E VISA – **st. :** 20 – **80 rm** 255/410. FZ **r**

Atlantic, 12 bd Victor-Hugo 93 88 40 15, Telex 460840 – P – 30-80. AE E VISA FY **d**
st. : M 100 – 35 – **123 rm** 400/500 – P 535/770.

Park and rest. Le Passage, 6 av. de Suède 93 87 80 25, Telex 970176, – rest – 80. AE E VISA FZ **x**
st. : M *(closed Sunday)* 120 – 40 – **148 rm** 280/630 – P 535/590.

Victoria without rest, 33 bd V.-Hugo 93 88 39 60, Telex 461337, – . AE E VISA – **st. : 39 rm** 320/440. FYZ **z**

Westminster Concorde, 27 prom. des Anglais 93 88 29 44, Telex 460872, , – rest – 40-350. AE E VISA. rest FZ **m**
st. : Le Farniente *(closed 1 November-10 December)* **M** 160/200 – 50 – **110 rm** 500/900.

Gd Hôtel de Florence M without rest, 3 r. P.-Deroulède 93 88 46 87, Telex 470652 – . AE E VISA. GY **r**
st. : 57 rm 310/440.

Locarno without rest, 4 av. Baumettes 93 96 28 00, Telex 970015 – . AE E VISA DEZ **t**
st. : 22 – **48 rm** 215/350.

Lausanne without rest, 36 r. Rossini 93 88 85 94, Telex 461269 – wc wc . AE E VISA FY **t**
st. : 35 – **40 rm** 290/430.

Gounod without rest, 3 r. Gounod 93 88 26 20, Telex 461705 – wc wc . AE E VISA FYZ **g**
st. : 45 rm 350/450, 5 apartments 560.

Georges M without rest, 3 r. H.-Cordier 93 86 23 41 – wc . AE VISA DZ **e**
st. : 22 – **18 rm** 230/350.

Suisse without rest, 15 quai Rauba-Capeu, 06300, 93 62 33 00, – wc wc HZ **r**
st. : 20 – **40 rm** 195/285.

Windsor without rest, 11 r. Dalpozzo 93 88 59 35, Telex 970072, , – wc wc . AE E VISA FZ **f**
st. : 25 – **63 rm** 270/480.

Avenida without rest, 41 av. J.-Médecin 93 88 55 03 – kitchenette wc wc . AE VISA. FY **m**
st. : 18 – **34 rm** 145/215.

Brice, 44 r. Mar.-Joffre 93 88 14 44, Telex 470658, , – wc wc – 30. E VISA. rest FZ **b**
st. : M 100 – **65 rm** 270/440 – P 380/460.

Carlton without rest, 26 bd V.-Hugo 93 88 87 83 – wc wc – **29 rm**. FY **f**

New York without rest, 44 av. Mar.-Foch 93 92 04 19, Telex 470215 – wc wc . AE E VISA GY **g**
st. : 27 – **52 rm** 268/317.

Chatham without rest, 9 r. A.-Karr 93 87 80 61 – wc wc . AE E VISA FY **x**
st. : 50 rm 230/330.

Durante without rest, 16 av. Durante 93 88 84 40, – kitchenette wc wc . FY **b**
closed 31 October-7 December – 28 – **26 rm** 170/270.

Cigognes without rest, 16 r. Maccarani 93 88 65 02 – wc wc . E VISA. FY **s**
st. : 17 – **32 rm** 250/270.

Star H. M without rest, 14 r. Biscarra 93 85 19 03 – wc wc . AE E VISA GY **k**
st. : 15 – **20 rm** 120/220.

Trianon without rest, 15 av. Auber 93 88 30 69 – wc wc . AE E VISA FY **u**
18 – **32 rm** 180/242.

NICE

Félix-Faure (Av.) .... GZ 21
France (R. de) .... DFZ
Gambetta (Bd) .... EXZ
Gioffredo (R.) .... HY
Hôtel-des-Postes (R. de l') .... HY 30
Liberté (R. de la) .... GZ 35
Masséna (Espace, Pl.) .... GZ
Masséna (R.) .... GZ 43
Médecin (Av. J.) .... GY 44
Paradis (R.) .... GZ 56
Pastorelli (R.) .... GY 58
République (R.) .... JX 64

Alberti (R.) .... GHY 2
Alsace-Lorraine (Jardin d') .... EZ 3
Armée-du-Rhin (Pl.) .... JX 5
Auriol (Pont V) .... JV 7
Carnot (Bd) .... JZ 14
Desambrois (Av.) .... GHX 18
Diables-Bleus (Av. des) .... JX 19
Du Gésu (St-Jacques ⊕) .... HZ **N**
Église Russe (⊕) .... EX **X**
Gautier (Pl. P.) .... HZ 25
Ile-de-Beauté (Pl. de l') .... JZ 32
Lunel (Quai) .... JZ 37
Meyerbeer (R.) .... FZ 45
Monastère (Av. et Pl. du) .... HV 46
Moulin (Pl. J.) .... HY 47
N.-D.-de-Cimiez (⊕) .... HJV **Q**
N.-D.-du-Port (⊕) .... JY 52
Phocéens (Av. des) .... GZ 59
Rivoli (R. de) .... FZ 65
Sacré-Cœur (⊕) .... FZ 67
St-Augustin (⊕) .... HY **D**
St-Barthélémy (⊕) .... EV **C**

St-Jean-Baptiste (Av. ⊞) .... HY 73
St-Philippe (⊞) .... DY 76
St-Pierre-d'Arène (⊞) .. EZ 78

Ste-Jeanne-d'Arc (⊞) .... FV **B**
Ste-Réparate (Cath. ⊞) .... HZ **L**

Saleya (Cours) .... HZ 83
Sauvan (R. H.) .... EZ 84
Verdun (Av. de) .... FGZ 89
Wilson (Pl.) .... HY 92

XXXX ✿✿ **Chantecler** (Maximin), 37 prom. des Anglais ✆ 93 88 39 51 – ▤. AE ⓓ E VISA
closed November – **st. : M** 300/500 and a la carte FZ **k**
Spec. Courgettes aux truffes, Saumon frais au gros sel, Tian de filet d'agneau. **Wines** Cassis, Le Cannet-des-Maures.

XXX ✿ **Ane Rouge** (Vidalot), 7 quai Deux-Emmanuel, ✉ 06300, ✆ 93 89 49 63 – AE ⓓ VISA
closed 14 July-1 September, Saturday, Sunday and Bank Holidays – **M** a la carte 205/330
Spec. Huîtres plates au champagne, Homard ou langouste Ane Rouge, Ris de veau des gourmets. **Wines** Bellet, Palette. JZ **m**

XXX **La Poularde chez Lucullus,** 9 r. Deloye ✆ 93 85 22 90 – ▤. AE ⓓ E VISA GY **n**
closed 13 July-19 August and Wednesday – **M** 150/200.

XXX **Florian,** 22 r. A.-Karr ✆ 93 88 86 60 – AE E VISA FY **k**
closed 10 July-20 August, Monday lunch and Sunday – **st. : M** 150/270.

XX **Don Camillo,** 5 r. Ponchettes, ✉ 06300, ✆ 93 85 67 95, Italian cuisine – ▤. AE ⓓ E VISA – *closed July and Sunday* – **M** a la carte 120/185 HZ **h**

XX **Gourmet Lorrain** with rm, 7 av. Santa-Fior, ✉ 06100, ✆ 93 84 90 78 – ▤ TV. AE VISA FV **a**
M *(closed August, 1 to 10 January, Sunday dinner and Monday)* 135/185 – ☕ 14 – **15 rm** 120/170 – P 274/324.

XX **Bon Coin Breton,** 5 r. Blacas ✆ 93 85 17 01 – ▤. VISA GY **v**
closed August, Sunday dinner and Monday – **st. : M** 62/140.

XX **Chez Rolando,** 3 r. Desboutins ✆ 93 85 76 79, Italian cuisine – ▤. AE E VISA GZ **n**
closed Sunday and lunch July-August – **M** a la carte 120/170.

X **Rivoli,** 9 r. Rivoli ✆ 93 88 12 62 – ▤. AE ⓓ E VISA FZ **v**
closed Monday – **st. : M** 90/150 ₰.

X **La Nissarda,** 17 r. Gubernatis ✆ 93 85 26 29 – VISA HY **d**
closed 1 to 15 July, February Holidays and Wednesday – **st. : M** 70.

X **Mireille,** 19 bd Raimbaldi ✆ 93 85 27 23, one dish only : paella – ▤. VISA GX **d**
closed June, Monday and Tuesday except July-August and Bank Holidays – **st. : M** a la carte 85/95.

at the airport : 7 km – ✉ **06200** Nice :

Holiday Inn M, on N 7 ✆ 93 83 91 92, Telex 970202, 🍽, ⛱ – ▤ TV ☎ ♿ – 250. AE ⓓ E VISA
st. : M 90/250 – ☕ 70 – **151 rm** 600/850.

XXX **Ciel d'Azur,** 2nd floor in Air Terminal ✆ 93 21 36 36, Telex 970011 – ▤. AE ⓓ VISA
M 140/195.

at the Cap 3000 to the SW : 8 km – ✉ **06700** St-Laurent-du-Var :

Novotel M, ✆ 93 31 61 15, Telex 470643, 🍽, ⛱, – ▤ TV ☎ ♿ Ⓟ – 250. AE ⓓ E VISA – **M** a la carte 90/140 ₰ – ☕ 40 – **103 rm** 370/450.

at St-Pancrace N : 8 km by D 914 – alt. 302 – ✉ **06100** Nice :

XXX ✿ **Rôtisserie de St-Pancrace,** ✆ 93 84 43 69, ←, 🍽 – Ⓟ. VISA
closed 4 January-7 February and Monday except July-August – **M** a la carte 200/330
Spec. Gourmandises de la Rôtisserie, Poisson du pays rôti à l'huile d'olive, Rosette d'agneau au basilic. **Wines** Bellet, Côtes de Provence.

XX **Cicion,** ✆ 93 84 49 29, ← Nice and seaside, 🍽 – Ⓟ
closed 5 January-5 February, Wednesday and dinner (except July-August) – **M** 105/130.

St-Martin-du-Var 06670 Alpes-Mar. **84** ⑨, **195** ⑯ – pop. 1 528 alt. 122 – Nice 27.

XXX ✿✿ **Issautier** (Auberge Belle route), S : 3 km sur N 202 ✆ 93 08 10 65 – Ⓟ. AE ⓓ VISA
closed November Holidays, February Holidays, Sunday dinner and Monday – **st. : M** (booking essential) 205/310 and a la carte
Spec. Courgette avec sa fleur au fumet de champignons, Loup en feuillantine, Noisettes et côtelettes d'agneau sautées. **Wines** Bellet.

STRASBOURG

P **67000** B.-Rhin **62** ⑩ – pop. 252 264 Greater Strasbourg 409 161 alt. 139.

See : Cathédral* : Astronomical clock*, ←* CX – ←* of rue Mercière CX 53 – Old City*** BCX : la Petite France** BX, Rue du Bain-aux-Plantes** BX 7, Place de la Cathédrale* CX 17, Maison Kammerzell* CX e, Château des Rohan* CX, Cour du Corbeau* CX 18, Ponts couverts* BX B, Place Kléber* CV – Barrage Vauban ✵** BX D – Mausoleum** in St-Thomas Church CX E – Hôtel de Ville * CV H – Orangery* – Boat trips on the Ill river and the canals* CX – Guided tours of the Port* by boat – Museum : Oeuvre N.-Dame*** CX M1, Museums** in château des Rohan CX, Alsatian* CX M2, Historical * CX M3.**

⛳18 Illkirch-Graffenstaden ✆ 88 66 17 22.

✈ Strasbourg-Entzheim : Air France ✆ 88 68 86 21 by D 392 : 12 km – 🚗 ✆ 88 22 50 50.

ℹ and Accueil de France (Information and hotel reservations, not more than 5 days in advance), Palais des Congrès av. Schutzenberger ✆ 88 35 03 00, Télex 870860 ; pl. Gare ✆ 88 32 51 49 and pl. Gutenberg ✆ 88 32 57 07 – Bureau d'accueil, pont Europe (exchange facilities) ✆ 88 61 39 23 - A.C. 5 av. Paix ✆ 88 36 04 34.

Paris 488 – Bâle 145 – Bonn 360 – Bordeaux 927 – Frankfurt 218 – Karlsruhe 81 – Lille 555 – Luxembourg 221 – Lyon 480 – Stuttgart 154.

STRASBOURG

Rue	Carré	N°
Alsace (Av. d')	CV	2
Arc-en-ciel (R. de l')	CV	3
Austerlitz (R. d')	CX	4
Bains-aux-Plantes (R. du)	BX	7
Castelnau (R. Général de)	CV	16
Cathédrale (Pl. de la)	CX	17
Corbeau (Cour du)	CX	18
Corbeau (Pl. du)	CX	19
Course (Petite Rue de la)	BV	20
Desaix (Quai)	BV	22
Finkmatt (Quai)	CV	24
Finkwiller (Quai)	BX	25
Foch (R. du Mar.)	CV	26
Fossé-des-Tanneurs (R. du)	BX	27
Fossé-des-Treize (R. du)	CV	29
Francs-Bourgeois (R. des)	CX	30
Frey (Quai Ch.)	CX	32
Gutenberg (Pl. et R.)	CX	36
Haute-Montée (R.)	CV	40
Homme de fer (Pl.)	CV	41
Kuss (Pont)	BV	46
Liberté (Av. de la)	CV	47
Maire Kuss (R. du)	BV	48
Mercière (R.)	CX	53
Mésange (R. de la)	CV	54
Noyer (R. du)	BV	55
Paix (Av. de la)	CV	58
Parchemin (R. du)	CV	60
Pierre (R. du Fg de)	CV	61
Recollets (R. des)	CV	70
St-Jean (Quai)	BV	76
St-Michel (R.)	BX	77
Sébastopol (R. de)	BV	83
Temple Neuf (Pl.)	CV	88
Temple Neuf (R.)	CV	89
Turckheim (Quai)	BX	91
Vieux-Marché-aux-Poissons (R. du)	CX	94
1re Armée (R.)	CX	99

Hilton [M], av. Herrenschmidt 88 37 10 10, Telex 890363, – kitchenette – 30-450. AE VISA. rest
st. : La Maison du Boeuf (closed 1 to 21 August, *1 to 7 January and February Holidays)* **M** a la carte 200/270 - **Le Jardin M** 96 – 55 – **247 rm** 640/750, 5 apartments
Spec. Foie gras de canard, Escalope de foie d'oie poêlée aux pommes, Pot au feu de pigeonneau au foie gras. **Wines** Klevner de Heiligenstein, Pinot noir.

Sofitel [M], pl. St-Pierre-le-Jeune 88 32 99 30, Telex 870894, patio – – 100. AE E VISA. rest CV **s**
st. : Le Saint-Pierre *(closed 1 to 15 August and Sunday)* **M** a la carte 190/255 – 48 – **180 rm** 470/820, 5 apartments.

Holiday Inn [M], 20 pl. Bordeaux 88 35 70 00, Telex 890515, – – 50-600. AE E VISA
st. : La Louisiane M a la carte 160/230 – 55 – **170 rm** 495/655.

Terminus-Gruber, 10 pl. Gare 88 32 87 00, Telex 870998 – – 60. AE E VISA BV **m**
Cour de Rosemont *(closed 21 December-4 January)* **M** 110/150 – 35 – **70 rm** 345/500, 8 apartments 500/650 – P 565/780.

Novotel [M], quai Kléber 88 22 10 99, Telex 880700 – – 30-200. AE E VISA BV **k**
M a la carte 90/160 – 35 – **97 rm** 400/455.

France [M] without rest, 20 r. Jeu-des-Enfants 88 32 37 12, Telex 890084 – – 30. AE E VISA BV **v**
st. : 25 – **70 rm** 280/390.

Monopole-Métropole without rest, 16 r. Kuhn 88 32 11 94, Telex 890366, « Alsatian decor » – . AE E VISA BV **p**
closed Christmas Day-1 January – **st. :** 25 – **94 rm** 250/380.

Gd Hôtel without rest, 12 pl. Gare 88 32 46 90, Telex 870011 – . AE VISA
st. : 35 – **90 rm** 320/420, 4 apartments 480. BV **m**

des Rohan [M] without rest, 17 r. Maroquin 88 32 85 11, Telex 870047 – . VISA. – **st. :** 30 – **36 rm** 235/420. CX **u**

Nouvel H. Maison Rouge without rest, 4 r. Francs-Bourgeois 88 32 08 60, Telex 880130 – . AE E VISA CX **g**
st. : 35 – **130 rm** 270/380, 6 apartments 460/650.

Villa d'Est [M] without rest, 12 r. J.-Kablé 88 36 69 02, Telex 870669 – wc . AE E VISA
closed 22 December-2 January – 27 – **32 rm** 310/350.

La Dauphine [M] without rest, 30 r. 1re Armée 88 36 26 61, Telex 880766 – wc wc . E VISA
closed 23 December-2 January – **st. :** 23 – **45 rm** 295/310.

Hannong, 15 r. 22-Novembre 88 32 16 22, Telex 890551 – rest wc wc – 50. AE E VISA BV **f**
closed 22 to 29 December – **st. : Wyn' Bar** *(closed August, 22 to 29 December and Sunday)* **M** a la carte 130/180 – 28 – **70 rm** 250/380.

Europe without rest, 38 r. Fossé-des-Tanneurs 88 32 17 88, Telex 890220 – wc wc . AE E VISA BX **g**
st. : 21 – **60 rm** 131/350.

Bristol, 4 pl. Gare 88 32 00 83, Telex 890317 – rest wc wc . AE E VISA. rest BV **h**
st. : M 98/350 – 25 – **40 rm** 250/350.

Continental [M] without rest, 14 r. Maire Kuss 88 22 28 07, Telex 880881 – wc . AE E VISA BV **s**
st. : 19,50 – **48 rm** 215/260.

Vendôme without rest, 9 pl. Gare 88 32 45 23, Telex 890850 – wc wc . AE E VISA BV **b**
st. : 19 – **48 rm** 150/220.

XXXX **Crocodile** (Jung), 10 r. Outre 88 32 13 02 – . AE E VISA CV **x**
closed 12 July-10 August, 24 December-1 January, Sunday and Monday – **st. : M** 220/280 and a la carte
Spec. Gratin de langouste, Caille confite au foie d'oie, Noisette de sanglier à la Diane. **Wines** Riesling, Gewurztraminer.

XXX **Buerehiesel** (Westermann), Set in the Orangery Park 88 61 62 24, « Attractive Alsatian mansion in a park » – . AE E VISA
closed 7-21 Aug., 24 Dec.-7 Jan., Feb. Holidays, Tuesday (except lunch from 1 April-30 October and Wednesday) – **st. : M** 230/340 and a la carte
Spec. Fritot de foie d'oie caramélisé au soja, Matelote de poissons d'eau douce, Croustillant de caille aux pommes de terre. **Wines** Muscat, Pinot gris.

XXX **Valentin-Sorg** (14th floor), 6 pl. Homme-de-Fer 88 32 12 16, Strasbourg – AE E VISA BV **r**
closed 18 August-2 September, 16 February-4 March, Sunday dinner and Tuesday – **st. : M** 130/275
Spec. Foie chaud Fritz Kobus, Grenadins de veau aux morilles, Crêpes au kirsch. **Wines** Tokay, Riesling.

XXX ✿ **Maison Kammerzell,** 16 pl. Cathédrale ✆ 88 32 42 14, Telex 890221, « Attractive 16C Alsatian house » – AE ⓓ E VISA CX **e**
closed in February – **st.** : upstairs **M** 190/330 - **Leo Schnug** ground floor **M** 185 b.i./165
Spec. Parfait de foie gras d'oie, Flan de St-Jacques à la fondue de légumes, Pot au feu d'oie aux choux. **Wines** Klevner de Heiligenstein, Vorlauf.

XXX **Maison des Tanneurs "Gerwerstub",** 42 r. Bain-aux-Plantes ✆ 88 32 79 70, « Old Alsatian house on the banks of the River Ill » – AE ⓓ BX **t**
closed 30 June-15 July, 21 December-25 January, Sunday and Monday – **st.** : **M** a la carte 130/225.

XX **Zimmer,** 8 r. Temple-Neuf ✆ 88 32 35 01 – AE ⓓ E VISA CV **y**
closed 1 to 23 August, Saturday and Sunday – **M** 140/300.

XX **La Volière,** 1 av. Gén.-de-Gaulle ✆ 88 61 05 79 – ▤. AE ⓓ E VISA
closed 13 July-10 August, 2 to 12 January, Saturday lunch and Sunday – **st.** : **M** 148/230.

XX ✿ **La Table Gourmande** (Reix) (new location expected to be Fegersheim) , 43 rte Gén.-de-Gaulle, ✉ 67300 Schiltigheim, ✆ 88 83 61 67 – ▤. AE ⓓ E VISA
closed 2 to 17 August, 24 December-4 January, Monday dinner and Sunday – **st.** : **M** (booking essential) a la carte 210/300
Spec. Feuilleté de tourteau à l'oseille, Papillote de turbot, Confit de canard.

X **A l'Ancienne Douane,** 6 r. Douane ✆ 88 32 42 19, 🍴, « Riverside terrace » – AE ⓓ E VISA – **st.** : **M** 44/79 ₰. CX **v**

X **Strissel,** 5 pl. Grande-Boucherie ✆ 88 32 14 73, Restaurant with wine tasting, rustic decor – ▤. E VISA CX **a**
closed 8 to 30 July, February Holidays, Sunday and Monday except Bank Holidays – **st.** : **M** 37/78 ₰.

at pont de l'Europe :

🏨 **Altea Pont de l'Europe** Ⓜ 🐕, ✆ 88 61 03 23, Telex 870833, 🍴 – 📺 ☎ Ⓟ – 🏛 100-400. AE ⓓ E VISA – **st.** : **M** 52/260 ₰ – ☕ 33 – **88 rm** 310/341, 5 apartments 473.

at Illkirch-Graffenstaden 8 km – ✉ **67400** Illkirch-Graffenstaden :

🏨 **Alsace** Ⓜ, 187 rte Lyon ✆ 88 66 41 60, Telex 870706 – 🛗 🛁wc ☎ Ⓟ – 🏛 60. VISA
closed 24 December-2 January – **st.** : **M** *(closed Saturday lunch and Sunday)* 82/200 ₰ – ☕ 20 – **40 rm** 215/250 – P 285.

near Colmar interchange A 35 10 km – ✉ **67400** Illkirch-Graffenstaden :

🏨 **Novotel** Ⓜ, ✆ 88 66 21 56, Telex 890142, 🍴, 🏊, 🌳 – ▤ rest 📺 ☎ ♿ Ⓟ – 🏛 25 à 120. AE ⓓ E VISA – **M** grill a la carte approx. 90/160 ₰ – ☕ 34 – **76 rm** 315/340.

🏨 **Mercure** Ⓜ, ✆ 88 66 03 00, Telex 890277, 🍴, 🏊 – 🛗 ▤ rest 📺 ☎ ♿ Ⓟ – 🏛 25-200. AE ⓓ E VISA – **M** a la carte 100/130 ₰ – ☕ 33 – **91 rm** 315/340.

at La Wantzenau NE by D 468 – pop. 4 084 – ✉ **67610** La Wantzenau :

🏨 **Hôtel Au Moulin** Ⓜ 🐕 without rest, S : 1,5 km by D 468 ✆ 88 96 27 83, ≤, « Ancient watermill on a branch of the River Ill », 🌳 – 🛗 📺 🛁wc 🚿wc ☎ Ⓟ. AE E VISA
closed 24 December-2 January – **st.** : ☕ 30 – **19 rm** 180/280.

🏨 **Poste** Ⓜ, 21 r. Gén.-de-Gaulle ✆ 88 96 20 64, 🍴 – 🛗 ▤ rest 🛁wc 🚿wc ☎ Ⓟ – 🏛 25. AE ⓓ E VISA
closed February, Sunday dinner and Monday – **M** 120/250 ₰ – ☕ 25 – **19 rm** 200/350.

🏠 **A la Gare,** 32 r. Gare ✆ 88 96 63 44 – 🛁wc 🚿wc ☎ Ⓟ. VISA. 🚫
st. : **M** 70/130 ₰ – ☕ 20 – **19 rm** 120/180.

XXX ✿ **A la Barrière** (Aeby), 3 rte Strasbourg ✆ 88 96 20 23, 🍴 – Ⓟ. AE ⓓ E VISA
closed 12 August-4 September, February Holidays, Wednesday dinner and Thursday – **st.** : **M** (Sunday: booking essential) a la carte 210/260 ₰
Spec. Foie gras d'oie, Rouelle de saumon au citron vert, Rognon et ris de veau au Pinot. **Wines** Riesling, Gewurztraminer.

XX ✿ **Zimmer,** 23 r. Héros ✆ 88 96 62 08 – AE ⓓ E VISA
closed 1-16 August, Sunday dinner and Monday – **st.** : **M** 90/170 ₰
Spec. Terrine de foie gras, Saumon et lotte au Riesling, Filet d'agneau en croûte. **Wines** Pinot noir, Edelzwicker.

Ammerschwihr 68770 H.-Rhin 62 ⑱⑲ – pop. 1 639 – alt. 230 – Strasbourg 74.

XXX ✿✿ **Aux Armes de France** (Gaertner) with rm, ✆ 89 47 10 12 – 🛁wc ☎ Ⓟ. AE ⓓ E VISA. 🚫 rm
closed 27 July-6 August, 4 January-4 February, Thursday lunch and Wednesday – **M** (booking essential) 250/350 and a la carte – ☕ 30 – **10 rm** 240/350
Spec. Foie gras d'oie, Filet de sole aux nouilles, Canette de Barbarie aux épices et au miel. **Wines** Riesling, Gewurztraminer.

Colmar 68000 H.-Rhin 62 ⑲ – pop. 63 764 alt. 193 – Strasbourg 71.

XXXX ✿✿ **Schillinger,** 16 r. Stanislas ✆ 89 41 43 17, « Fine decor » – AE ⓓ E VISA
closed 6 July-3 August, Sunday dinner and Monday except Bank Holidays – **M** 170/320 and a la carte ₰
Spec. Foie gras frais, Caneton au citron. **Wines** Pinot Blanc.

Colroy-la-Roche 67 B.-Rhin 62 ⑧ – pop. 431 alt. 424 – ✉ **67420** Saales – Strasbourg 62.

✿✿ **Host. la Cheneaudière** M, ☎ 88 97 61 64, Telex 870438, ≤, «Fashionable country inn in a garden», – TV ☎ P. AE ① E VISA
closed January and February – **st. : M** *(closed for lunch from 1 November to 31 March except Sunday)* 190 and a la carte – ☕ 60 – **23 rm** 400/560, 5 apartments – P 650/780
Spec. Tartare de saumon sauvage, Pralines de cailles au foie gras, Gibier (season). **Wines** Pinot noir, Tokay d'Alsace.

Illhaeusern 68 H.-Rhin 62 ⑲ – pop. 557 – alt. 176 – ✉ **68150** Ribeauvillé.
Strasbourg 60.

La Clairière M without rest, rte Guémar ☎ 89 71 80 80, – TV ☎ P
closed January and February – **st. :** ☕ 32 – **24 rm** 290/450.

TOURS

Street	Grid	No.
Bordeaux (R. de)	DY	8
Commerce (R. du)	CDX	28
Grammont (Av. de)	DEZ	
Halles (Pl. et R.)	CY	
Marceau (R.)	CDY	
Nationale (R.)	DXY	
Scellerie (R. de la)	DY	91
Anatole-France (Pl.)	DX	4
Béranger (Bd)	BCDY	
Blanqui (R. A.)	EFX	
Boisdenier (R. de)	CDZ	
Boyer (R. Léon)	BY	
Bretonneau (R.)	CXY	
Briçonnet (R.)	CX	15
Buffon (R.)	DY	
Cathédrale (Pl.)	EX	18
Chanoineau (R.)	CY	20
Chanzy (R. du Gén.)	BY	
Charpentier (R. J.)	BCY	
Chevallier (R. A.)	BCZ	
Colbert (R.)	DX	
Constantine (R.)	CX	29
Corneille (R.)	DY	30
Courteline (R. G.)	BY	
Descartes (R.)	CY	33
Desmoulins (R. C.)	EFY	
Dr-Fournier (R. du)	FZ	
Docks (R. des)	EFY	
Entraigues (R. d')	BCYZ	
Foire-le-Roi (Pl.)	DX	38
Fouquet (R. Jehan)	CYZ	
Fuye (R. de la)	FYZ	
Galpin-Thiou (R.)	DEZ	
Gaulle (Av. Gén.-de)	EFZ	
George Sand (R.)	DYZ	
Gille (R. Charles)	DY	
Giraudeau (R.)	BYZ	
Grandière (R. de la)	CY	41
Gd-Marché (Pl.)	CY	42
Gd-Marché (R.)	CY	44
Grégoire-de-Tours (Pl.)	EX	47
Heurteloup (Bd)	EFY	
Jaurès (Pl. Jean)	DY	
Jolivet (R.)	FZ	
Lakanal (R.)	CZ	
Lattre-de-T. (Bd de)	EZ	
Lavoisier (R.)	DEX	54
Leclerc (Pl. du Mar.)	EY	
Lobin (R.)	FX	
Meusnier (R. du Gén.)	EXY	57
Michelet (R.)	DYZ	
Mirabeau (R.)	FXY	
Néricault-Destouches (R.)	CDY	60
N.-D. de la Riche (⊞)	BY	
Orléans (Quai d')	DEX	
Paillhou (Pl. Gaston)	CY	
Palissy (R. Bernard)	EY	
Pascal (R. Blaise)	EYZ	
Petit-Pré (R. du)	EY	
Plantin (R.)	FY	66
Plat-d'Étain (R. du)	BZ	
Plumereau (Pl.)	CY	67
Pompidou (Av. G.)	FXY	69
Pont-Neuf (Q. du)	BCX	70
Preuilly (Bd)	BY	
Proudhon (Av.)	BX	73
Rabelais (Pl.)	BZ	
Rempart (R. du)	FY	74
Renault (R. du Gén.)	BCZ	
Résistance (Pl. de la)	DY	75
Rouget-de-Lisle (R.)	BY	
Sacré-Cœur (⊞)	FZ	
St-Étienne (⊞)	DY	80
St-Gatien (Cathédrale)	EX	
St-Julien (⊞)	DX	X
St-Martin (⊞)	CY	W
St-Paul (⊞)	EZ	83

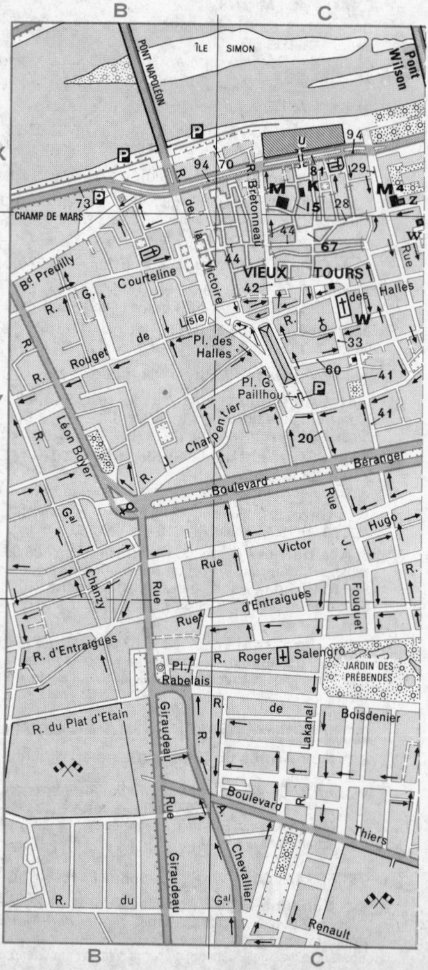

XXXXX ✿✿✿ **Aub de l'Ill** (Haeberlin), ✆ 89 71 83 23, « **Tasteful decor, set on the banks of the River Ill, ≤ over flower gardens** » – ▤. AE ⓞ
closed 29 June-8 July, February, Monday (except lunch in summer) and Tuesday – **M** (booking essential) a la carte 260/350
Spec. Terrine de saumon et St-Jacques, Saumon soufflé, Filet de chevreuil aux champignons des bois (June-January). **Wines** Riesling, Sylvaner.

Marlenheim **67520** B.-Rhin **62** ⑨ – **pop. 2 822** alt. 184 – **Strasbourg 20.**

XXX ✿✿ **Host. du Cerf** (Husser) with rm, ✆ **88 87 73 73**, ⛱, ⛱ – ⌂wc ⌂wc ☎ ⓟ – ⚠ 25. AE VISA – *closed February Holidays, Monday and Tuesday* – **st. : M** 280/350 and a la carte ⚲ – ☕ 30 – **19 rm** 190/290
Spec. Roulades de turbot aux vermicelles, Rouelles de blanc et cuisses de poularde, Millefeuille aux fruits de saison. **Wines** Edelzwicker, Vorlauf.

St-Pierre (⊞) .... FX	Simon (R. Jules) .... EY	Vaillant (R. E.) .... EFYZ
St-Saturnin (⊞) CX	Tanneurs (R. des) .... BX 94	Victoire (R. de la) ..... BXY
Ste-Jeanne d'Arc (⊞) .. CZ	Thiers (Bd et Pl.) .... CDZ	Victor-Hugo (R.) .... BCY
Salengro (R. Roger) .... CDZ	Thomas (R. A.) .... EX	Voltaire (R.) .... DXY 96
Sicard (Pl. François) .... EY 92	Ursulines (R. des) ...... EXY	Zola (R. Émile) .... DY

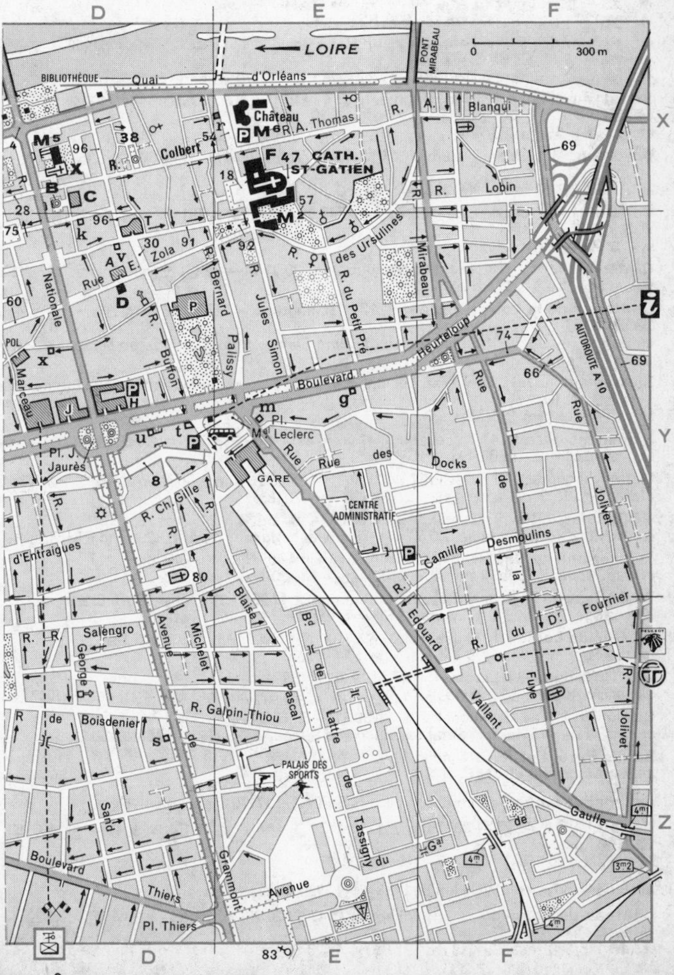

Tours P 37000 I.-et-L. 64 ⑮ – pop. 136 483 Greater Tours 251 320 – alt. 48.

See : Cathedral quarter** : Cathedral** EX, Fine Arts Museum** EXY **M2**, The Psalette* EX **F**, Historial de Touraine* EX **M6**, Place Grégoire de Tours* EX47 – Old Tours** : Place Plumereau* CY 67, hôtel Gouin* CX **M4**, rue Briçonnet* CX 15 – St-Julien quarter* : Craft Guilds Museum** (Musée du Compagnonnage) DX **M5**, Beaune-Semblançay Gardens* DX **B**, Staircase bannister* of hôtel Mame DY **D** – St-Cosme Priory* W : 3 km – Meslay Tithe Barn* (Grange de Meslay) NE : 10 km.

18 of Touraine ✆ 47 53 20 28 ; domaine de la Touche at Ballan-Miré : 14 km.

of Tours-St-Symphorien : T.A.T ✆ 47 54 21 45 NE : 7 km.

✆ 47 20 23 43.

and Accueil de France (Information, exchange facilities and hotel reservations - not more than 5 days in advance), pl. Mar.-Leclerc ✆ 47 05 58 08, Télex 750008 – Automobile Club de l'Ouest 4 pl. J.-Jaurès ✆ 47 05 50 19.

Paris 234 – Angers 109 – Bordeaux 345 – Chartres 140 – Clermont-Ferrand 299 – Limoges 204 – Le Mans 82 – Orléans 112 – Rennes 236 – St-Étienne 424.

Plan on preceding pages

Méridien M, 292 av. Grammont, ✉ 37200, ✆ 47 28 00 80, Telex 750922, ←, – 40-200. AE E VISA
st. : **M** 130 – 45 – **125 rm** 345/530, 6 apartments.

Univers and rest. la Touraine, 5 bd Heurteloup ✆ 47 05 37 12, Telex 751460 – – 30. AE E VISA DY **u**
st. : **M** *(closed Saturday)* 105/160 – 34 – **86 rm** 264/370, 3 apartments 605.

Royal M without rest, 65 av. Grammont ✆ 47 64 71 78, Telex 752006 – AE VISA DZ **s**
st. : 26 – **35 rm** 238/279.

Bordeaux, 3 pl. Mar.-Leclerc ✆ 47 05 40 32, Telex 750414 – AE E VISA. rm DY **t**
M 95/130 – **52 rm** 268/320 – P 380/550.

Central H. without rest, 21 r. Berthelot ✆ 47 05 46 44, Telex 751173 – wc wc AE E VISA DY **k**
st. : 25 – **42 rm** 120/300.

Criden M without rest, 65 bd Heurteloup ✆ 47 20 81 14 – wc AE E VISA – st. : 22 – **32 rm** 240/360 EY **g**

Châteaux de la Loire without rest, 12 r. Gambetta ✆ 47 05 10 05 – wc wc. AE E VISA DY **x**
closed 15 December-15 January, Saturday and Sunday from November to February – **st.** : 18 – **32 ch** 128/212.

Europe without rest, 12 pl. Mar.-Leclerc ✆ 47 05 42 07, « Paintings and antique furniture » – wc wc EY **m**
st. : 18 – **53 rm** 150/230.

Balzac without rest, 47 r. Scellerie ✆ 47 05 40 87 – wc wc. E VISA DY **v**
st. : 19,50 – **20 rm** 65/195.

Italia without rest, 19 r. Devilde ✉ 37100 ✆ 47 54 46 75 – wc wc. E VISA.
closed 1 to 15 September – **st.** : 20 – **20 rm** 100/185.

XXX ✿✿ **Barrier,** 101 av. Tranchée ✆ 47 54 20 39 – E VISA
closed July, February Holidays, Sunday dinner and Monday – **M** 180/290 and a la carte.

XXX **Les Jardins du Castel,** 10 r. Groison ✆ 47 41 94 40, – AE VISA
closed January, Sunday dinner and Monday – **M** 150/180.

XXX **La Rôtisserie Tourangelle,** 23 r. Commerce ✆ 47 05 71 21, – AE E VISA CX **z**
closed 6 to 28 July, 2 to 17 March, Sunday dinner and Monday – **st.** : **M** 142/280.

XXX **Au Gué de Louis XI,** 36 quai Loire ✉ 37100 ✆ 47 54 00 43 – AE E VISA
closed Sunday dinner and Monday – **st.** : **M** 86/200.

XX **Les Tuffeaux,** 19 r. Lavoisier ✆ 47 47 19 89 – E VISA EX **r**
closed 16 August-1 September, 3 to 27 January, Sunday and Monday – **st.** : **M** 154/257.

XX **Coq d'Or,** 272 av. Grammont ✆ 47 20 39 51 – AE E VISA
closed 14 July-15 August, Saturday lunch and Sunday dinner – **st.** : **M** 130/250.

XX **Relais Buré,** 1 pl. Résistance ✆ 47 05 67 74 – E VISA CXY **w**
closed Monday – **st.** : **M** 79/109.

exit road to Poitiers : interchange Tours Sud – ✉ **37170** Chambray-les-Tours :

Novotel M, ✆ 47 27 41 38, Telex 751206, – – 400. AE E VISA
M a la carte 90/160 – 35 – **125 rm** 308/355.

at Joué-lès-Tours SW : 5 km by D 86 – ✉ **37300** Joué-les-Tours :

Château de Beaulieu, rte Villandry ✆ 47 53 20 26, ←, park – wc wc – 50. E VISA
st. : **M** 145/380 – 32 – **19 rm** 300/500 – P 420/500.

Bracieux 41250 L.-et-Ch. 64 ⑱ – pop. 1 150 – alt. 81.
Tours 81.

XXXX ✿✿ **Bernard Robin,** 1 av. Chambord ✆ 54 46 41 22, ← – VISA
closed 20 December-25 January, Monday dinner and Wednesday – **st. : M** (booking essential) 175/295 and a la carte
Spec. Gelée de lapin aux herbes potagères, Carpe à la Chambord (season), Gibier (October-December). **Wines** Cheverny, Touraine-Mesland.

Montbazon 37250 I.-et-L. 64 ⑮ **G. Châteaux de la Loire** – pop. 3 011 – alt. 71.
ℹ Mairie ✆ 47 26 01 30.
Paris 247 – Châtellerault 60 – Chinon 41 – Loches 32 – Montrichard 40 – Saumur 67 – Tours 13.

✿ **Château d'Artigny** ⛰, **SW : 2 km by D 17 ✆ 47 26 24 24, Telex 750900, « Garden, park, ← River Indre, riverside annex with 8 rm », ⛱, 🎾 – 🛗 ☎ 🅟 – 🏛 80.** VISA
closed 29 December-9 January – **st. : M** 210/350 – ☕ 55 – **46 rm** 520/1 020, 7 apartments 695/1 160
Spec. Oeufs pochés et ragoût de crêtes et rognons de coq, Brouet de poissons de rivière au Vouvray, Foie gras chaud au Banyuls. **Wines** Montlouis, Chinon.

✿ **Domaine de la Tortinière** ⛰, N : 2 km by N 10 and D 287 ✆ 47 26 00 19, Telex 752186, « in a park ← valley of River Indre », ⛱, 🎾 – ☎ 🅟 – 🏛 30. E VISA. ✗ rest
15 March-15 November – **st. : M** *(closed Wednesday lunch and Tuesday in March and from 15 October to 15 November)* a la carte 205/315 – ☕ 50 – **14 rm** 350/600, 7 apartments 650/750
Spec. Saumon au gros sel, Cul de lapereau farci aux truffes, Clafoutis aux fruits de saison. **Wines** Montlouis, Saumur Champigny.

Relais de Touraine Ⓜ ⛰, N : 2 km rte Tours ✆ 47 26 06 57, ⛱, park – 🛁wc 🚿wc ☎ 🅟 – 🏛 50. E VISA
closed 2 to 15 January – **st. : M** *(closed Sunday dinner and Monday)* 120/150 – ☕ 30 – **21 rm** 250/280 – P 410.

XXX ✿ **La Chancelière,** 1 pl. Marronniers ✆ 47 26 00 67 – ▤. VISA
closed 15 to 30 November, 7 to 29 February, Sunday dinner and Monday except Bank Holidays – **st. : M** a la carte 210/300
Spec. Raviolis d'huîtres au Champagne (except July-August), Dos de saumon à la fleur de sel, Foie gras aux figues fraîches (September-December). **Wines** Chinon, Vouvray.

to W : 5 km by N 10, D 287 and D 87 – ✉ **37250** Montbazon :

XX **Moulin Fleuri** ⛰ with rm, ✆ 47 26 01 12, ←, « Terrace overlooking the River Indre », 🍽 – 🚿 🅟. AE VISA
closed 15 to 30 October, February Holidays and Monday except Bank Holidays – **st. : M** 97 – ☕ 22 – **10 rm** 83/178 – P 215/262.

Romorantin-Lanthenay <SP> 41200 L.-et-Ch. 64 ⑱ – pop. 18 187 – alt. 88.
Tours 90.

✿✿ **Gd H. Lion d'Or** Ⓜ, 69 r. Clemenceau ✆ 54 76 00 28, Telex 750990, « flowered terrace » – 🛗 TV ☎ ♿ 🅟 – 🏛 50. AE ⓞ E VISA
closed early January-mid February – **st. : M** (booking essential) 240/390 and a la carte – ☕ 60 – **10 rm** 380/600
Spec. Cuisses de grenouilles en salade de pourpier, Langoustines rôties aux épices douces, Millefeuille aux fruits de saison. **Wines** Vouvray, Bourgueil.

Germany
Deutschland

Berlin
Cologne
Düsseldorf
Frankfurt am Main
Hamburg
Hanover
Munich
Stuttgart

PRACTICAL INFORMATION

LOCAL CURRENCY

Deutsche Mark : 100 DM = 51.55 US $ (Jan. 87)

TOURIST INFORMATION

Deutsche Zentrale für Tourismus (DZT)
Beethovenstr. 69, 6000 Frankfurt 1, ✆ 069/7 57 20
Telex 4189178

Hotel booking service
Allgemeine Deutsche Zimmerreservierung (ADZ)
Beethovenstr. 69, 6000 Frankfurt 1, ✆ 069/74 07 67
Telex 416666

AIRLINES

DEUTSCHE LUFTHANSA AG : Von-Gablenz-Str. 2, 5000 Köln 21, ✆ 0221/82 61

AIR CANADA : 6000 Frankfurt, Friedensstr. 7, ✆ 069/23 40 32

AIR FRANCE : 6000 Frankfurt, Friedensstr. 11, ✆ 069/2 56 61

AMERICAN AIRLINES : 6000 Frankfurt, Wiesenhüttenplatz 26, ✆ 069/25 60 10

BRITISH AIRWAYS : 1000 Berlin 15, Kurfürstendamm 178, ✆ 030/8 82 30 67

JAPAN AIRLINES : 6000 Frankfurt, Goethestr. 9, ✆ 069/1 36 00

PAN AMERICAN : 1000 Berlin 30, Europacenter, ✆ 030/2 61 10 81

TWA : 6000 Frankfurt 90, Hamburger Allee 2, ✆ 069/70 90 97

FOREIGN EXCHANGE

Is possible in banks, saving banks and at exchange offices.
Hours of opening from Monday to Friday 8.30am to 12.30pm and 2.30pm to 4pm except Thursday 2.30pm to 6pm.

SHOPPING

In the index of street names, those printed in red are where the principal shops are found.

BREAKDOWN SERVICE

ADAC : for the addresses see text of the towns mentioned

AvD : Lyoner Str. 16, 6000 Frankfurt 71-Niederrad, ✆ 069/6 60 63 00

In Germany the ADAC, and the AvD, make a special point of assisting foreign motorists. They have motor patrols covering main roads.

TIPPING

In Germany, prices include service and taxes. You may choose to leave a tip if you wish but there is no obligation to do so.

SPEED LIMITS

The speed limit, generally, in built up areas is 50 km/h - 31 mph and on all other roads it is 100 km/h - 62mph. On motorways and dual carriageways, the recommended speed limit is 130 km/h - 80 mph.

SEAT BELTS

The wearing of seat belts is compulsory for drivers and passengers.

BERLIN

SIGHTS

West Berlin

Kurfürstendamm★★ BDX and Memorial Church (Kaiser-Wilhelm-Gedächtniskirche) DEV – Brandenburg Gate★★ (Brandenburger Tor) (East-Berlin) GU – Zoological Park★★ (Zoologischer Garten, Aquarium) EV.

Dahlem Museums (Museum Dahlem)★★★ (Painting Gallery★★, Ethnographic Museum★★) – Chateau of Charlottenburg★★ (Schloß Charlottenburg) BU (at the Knobelsdorff-Wing : Painting Collection★★, Golden Gallery★★) – Museum of Decorative Arts★ FV **M2** – Antique Museum★ (Antikenmuseum) (ancient treasure★★★) BU **M3** – Egyptian Museum★ (Ägyptisches Museum) bust of Queen Nefertiti★) BU **M4** – National Gallery★ (Nationalgalerie) FV **M6**.

Olympic Stadium★★ (Olympia-Stadion) – Radio Tower (☀★) (Funkturm) AV – Botanical Gardens★★ (Botanischer Garten).

Havel★ and Peacock Island★ (Pfaueninsel) – Wannsee★★.

Church of Maria Regina Martyrum★ (Maria-Regina-Martyrum-Kirche) BU **D** and Plötzensee Memorial (Gedenkstätte von Plötzensee) DU.

East-Berlin

Brandenburg Gate★★ (Brandenburger Tor) GU – Unter den Linden★ GUV (State Opera House★ GHU **C**, Neue Wache★ HU **D**, Arsenal★★ GHU) – Platz der Akademie★ GV.

Museum Island (Museumsinsel) (Pergamon-Museum★★★ GHU **M7** with Pergamon-Altar, National Gallery★★ HU **M8**).

Alexanderplatz★★ HU – Television Tower★★ (Fernsehturm) (☀) HU **K** – Karl-Marx-Allee★ HU – Soviet Memorial★ (Sowjetisches Ehrenmal).

BERLIN West Berlin 1000. **987** ⑰ – Pop. 1 960 000 – alt. 40 m – ☎ 030.

✈ Tegel, ☎ 41 01 31 45.

🚘 Berlin - Wannsee, ☎ 3 13 81 30.

Exhibition Grounds (Messegelände) AV, ☎ 3 03 81, Telex 182908.

ℹ Berlin Tourist-Information, Europa-Center (Budapester Straße), ☎ 2 62 60 31, Telex 18 3356 ;

ℹ Tourist Information, at Tegel Airport, ☎ 41 01 31 45.

ADAC, Berlin-Wilmersdorf, Bundesallee 29 (B 31), ☎ 8 68 61, Telex 183513.

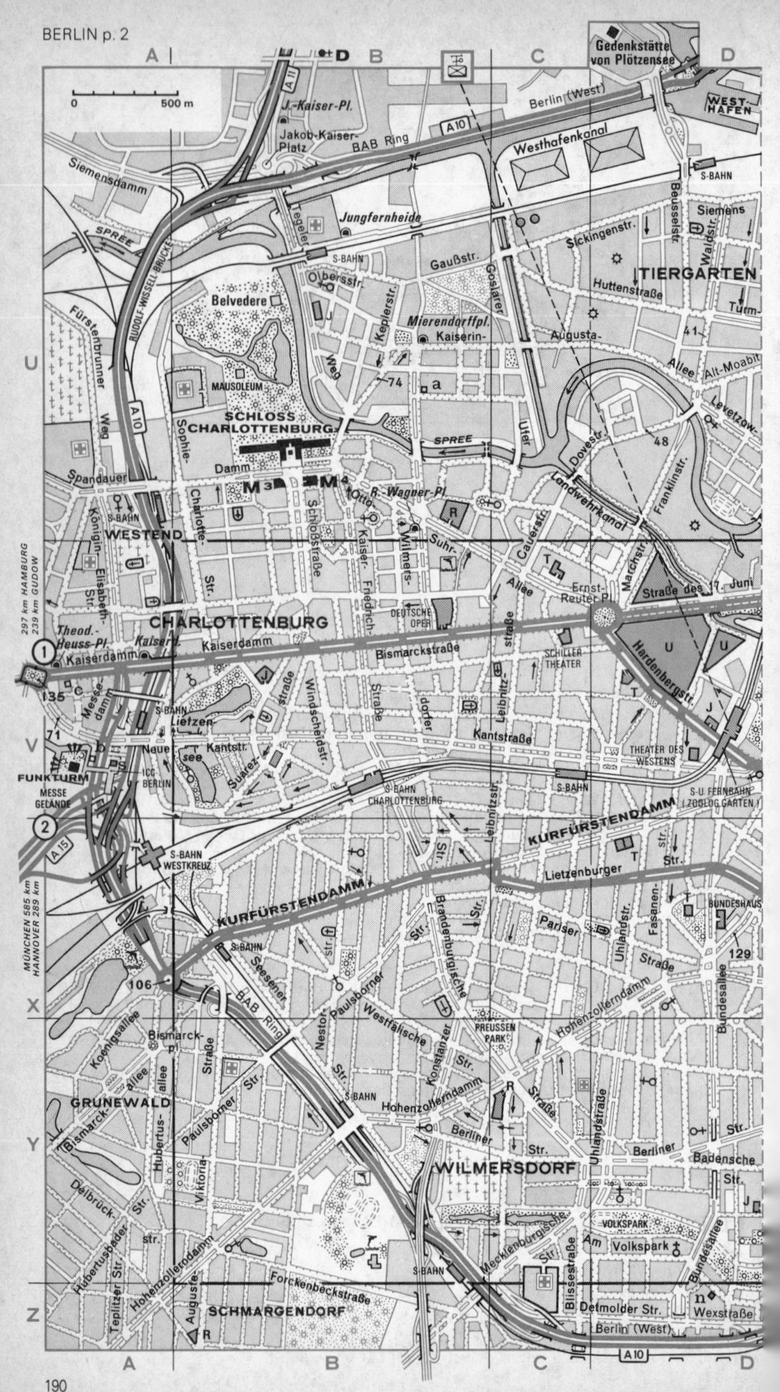

A
B
C
D
0
500 m
Gedenkstätte von Plötzensee
Berlin (West)
WEST-HAFEN
J.-Kaiser-Pl.
Jakob-Kaiser-Platz
BAB Ring
A 10
Westhafenkanal
Siemensdamm
S-BAHN
Jungfernheide
Tegeler
Siemens
SPREE
Sickingenstr.
Beusselstr.
Waldstr.
Gaußstr.
Olbersstr.
TIERGARTEN
Huttenstraße
Belvedere
Keplerstr.
Goslarer
Fürstenbrunner Weg
RUDOLF-WISSELL-BRÜCKE
Mierendorffpl.
Kaiserin-
Augusta-
Turm-
Allee
Alt-Moabit
U
MAUSOLEUM
74
a
Levetzow-
SCHLOSS CHARLOTTENBURG
Ufer
Dovestr.
48
A 10
Sophie-
SPREE
Franklinstr.
Spandauer
Damm
R.-Wagner-Pl.
Otto-
Landwehrkanal
S-BAHN
Königin-
Charlotte-
Schloßstraße
Kaiser-
Wilmers-
Suhr-
Cauerstr.
WESTEND
Elisabeth-
Str.
Friedrich-
Allee
Marchstr.
Straße des 17. Juni
Ernst-Reuter-Pl.
297 km HAMBURG
239 km GUDOW
CHARLOTTENBURG
DEUTSCHE OPER
straße
Theod.-Heuss-Pl.
Kaiserd.
Kaiserdamm
Kaiserdamm
Bismarckstraße
SCHILLER THEATER
Hardenbergstr.
1
135
Messe-damm
straße
Windscheidstr.
Straße
dorfer
Leibnitz-
S-BAHN
Lietzen-
71
Neue
see
Kantstr.
Suarez-
Kantstraße
THEATER DES WESTENS
V
FUNKTURM
ICC-BERLIN
S-BAHN CHARLOTTENBURG
S-BAHN
S-U FERNBAHN (ZOOLOG.GARTEN)
MESSE GELÄNDE
2
KURFÜRSTENDAMM
Leibnitzstr.
A 15
S-BAHN WESTKREUZ
Str.
Str.
Lietzenburger
MÜNCHEN 585 km
HANNOVER 289 km
KURFÜRSTENDAMM
Brandenburgische
Pariser
Uhlandstr.
Fasanen-
BUNDESHAUS
S-BAHN
Seesener
Straße
129
106
Paulsborner
Westfälische
Hohenzollerndamm
X
BAB Ring
Nestor-
PREUSSEN PARK
Bundesallee
Koenigsallee
Bismarck-pl.
Straße
Konstanzer
Str.
GRUNEWALD
allee
allee
Paulsborner Str.
S-BAHN
Hohenzollerndamm
R
Straße
Uhlandstraße
Bismarck-
Hubertus-
Berliner
Str.
Y
Viktoria-
Str.
Berliner
Badensche
WILMERSDORF
Str.
Delbrück-
Str.
str.
Hubertusbader
Hohenzollerndamm
VOLKSPARK
Am Volkspark
Mecklenburgische
Bundesallee
S-BAHN
Str.
Blissestraße
Forckenbeckstraße
Teplitzer Str.
Auguste-
SCHMARGENDORF
Detmolder Str.
Wexstraße
n
Z
R
Berlin (West)
A 10

BERLIN

Charlottenstraße	GUV	23
Friedrich-List-Ufer	FU	34
Friedrichstraße ..	GV	35
Goebenstraße ...	FX	39
Gotzkowskystraße	DU	41
Helmholtzstraße .	DU	48
Innsbrucker Platz ..	EZ	54
Klingelhöferstraße	EV	60
Masurenallee	AV	71
Mierendorffstraße	BU	74
Moltkestraße	FU	77
Neue Wilhelmstr. .	GU	85
Nollendorfplatz ..	EX	87
Oldenburger Str. .	EU	90
Pallasstraße	FX	96
Rathenauplatz ...	AX	106
Spichernstraße ..	DX	129
Theodor-Heuss-Platz	AV	135
Wittenbergplatz .	EX	145

Street index : See pp 5 and 8

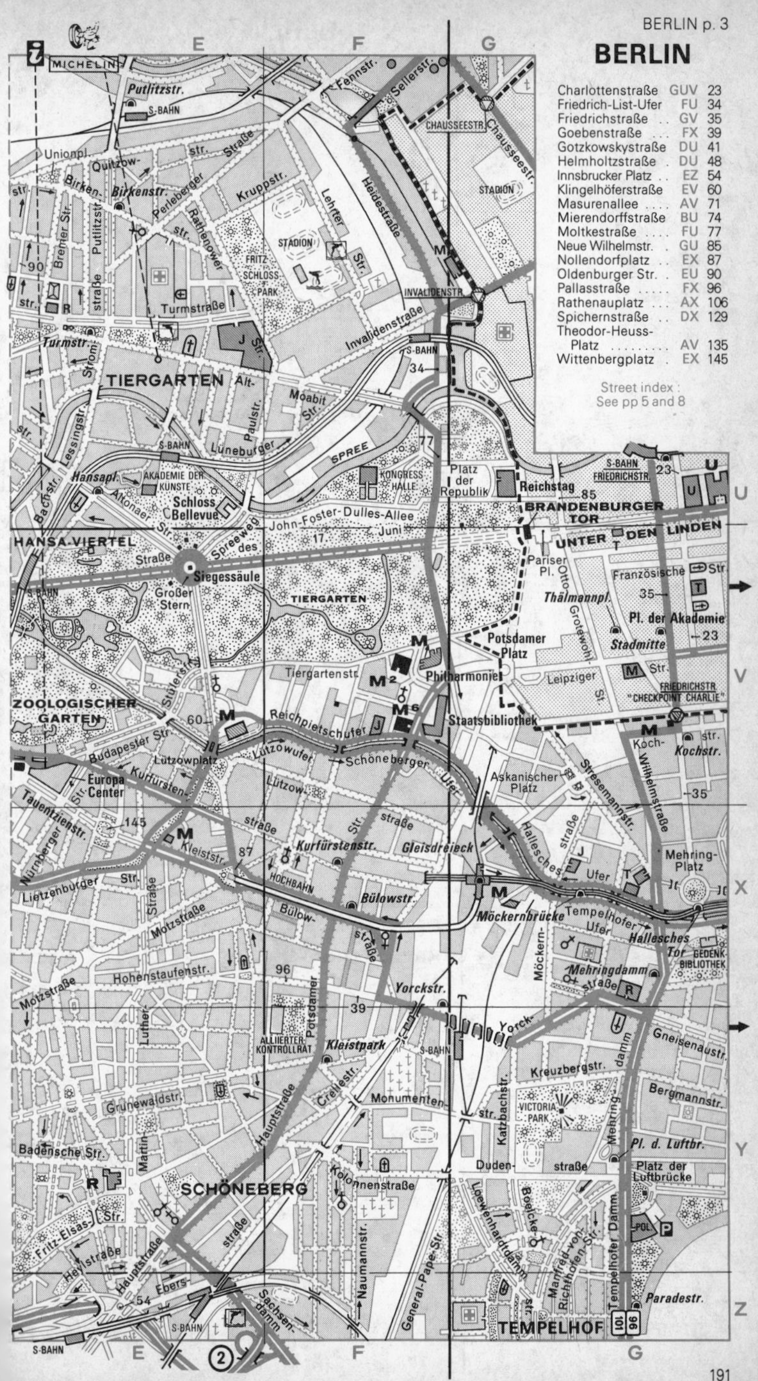

BERLIN

Street index : See pp 5 and 8

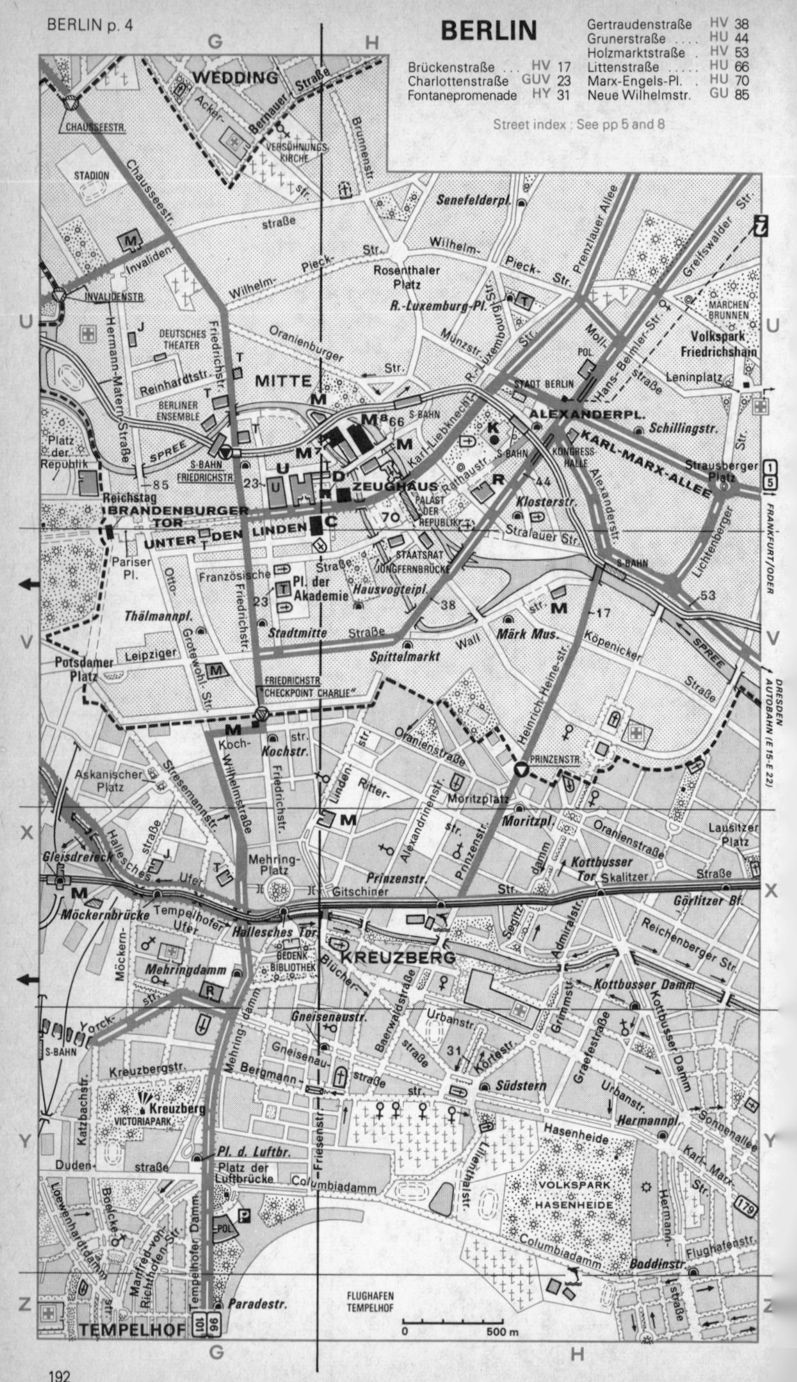

Continued p. 8

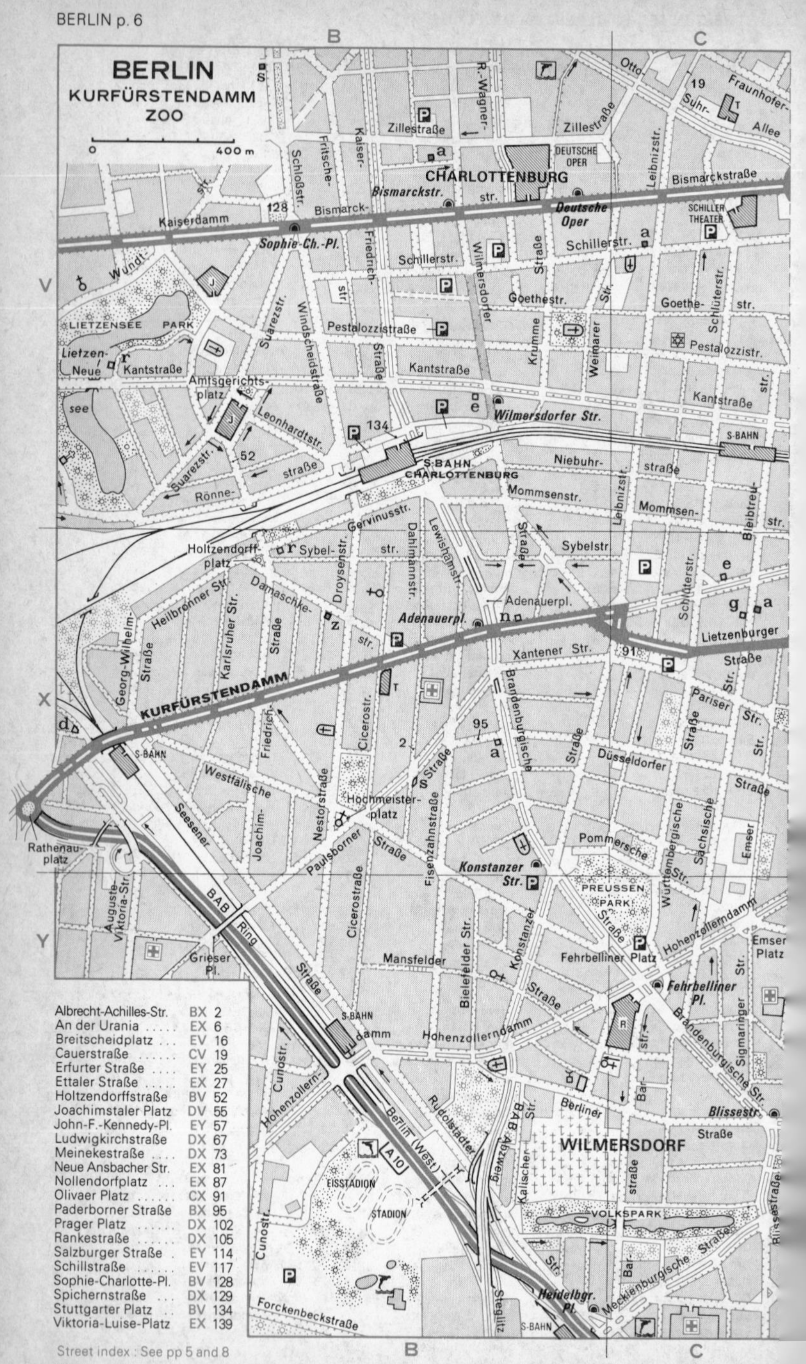

Street index : See pp 5 and 8

TIERGARTEN
Siegessäule
Großer Stern
Straße des 17. Juni
TECHNISCHE UNIVERSITÄT
Ernst-Reuter-Platz
ZOOLOGISCHER GARTEN
Landwehrkanal
KAISER-WILHELM GEDÄCHTNISKIRCHE
Europa Center
KURFÜRSTENDAMM
Budapester Str.
Kurfürstenstr.
Lützowplatz
Wittenbergpl.
Tauentzienstr.
Nollendorfpl.
Kleiststraße
BUNDESHAUS
Spichernstr.
Viktoria-Luise-Pl.
Hohenzollernpl.
Güntzelstr.
Bayerischer Platz
SCHÖNEBERG
Eisenacher Str.
Berliner Str.
Rathaus Schöneberg
Hauptstraße
VOLKSPARK
ADAC

The reference (B 15) at the end of the address is the postal district : Berlin 15

at Kurfürstendamm and near Kurfürstendamm :

Bristol-Hotel Kempinski, Kurfürstendamm 27 (B 15), 88 10 91, Telex 183553, Massage, – AE E VISA — DV **n**
Restaurants : – **Kempinski-Grill M** a la carte 63/85 – **Kempinski-Restaurant** *(closed Monday)* **M** a la carte 55/75 – **Kempinski-Eck M** a la carte 33/48 – **334 rm** 230/400 Bb.

Steigenberger Berlin, Los-Angeles-Platz 1 (B 30), 2 10 80, Telex 181444, Massage, – AE E VISA — EX **d**
Restaurants : – **Park-Restaurant** *(dinner only)* **M** a la carte 47/78 – **Berliner Stube M** a la carte 25/52 – **377 rm** 215/420 Bb.

Mondial, Kurfürstendamm 47 (B 15), 88 41 10, Telex 182839, Massage, – rest (with). AE E VISA. rest — CX **e**
M a la carte 32/60 – **75 rm** 150/240 Bb.

Am Zoo without rest, Kurfürstendamm 25 (B 15), 88 30 91, Telex 183835 – wc wc – **145 rm** Bb. — DV **z**

Arosa, Lietzenburger Str. 79 (B 15), 88 00 50, Telex 183397, (heated) – wc wc . AE E VISA. rest — DX **y**
M *(closed Sunday)* a la carte 34/55 – **90 rm** 120/205 Bb.

Kronprinz without rest (restored house of 1894), Kronprinzendamm 1 (B 31), 89 60 30, Telex 181459, beer-garden – wc . AE E VISA — BX **d**
53 rm 95/170 Bb.

Hecker's Deele, Grolmanstr. 35 (B 12), 8 89 01, Telex 184954 – rest wc . AE E — DV **e**
M a la carte 29/63 – **60 rm** 136/180.

Domus without rest, Uhlandstr. 49 (B 15), 88 20 41, Telex 185975 – wc . AE E VISA — DX **a**
closed 23 December - 1 January – **76 rm** 90/168 Bb.

Kurfürstendamm am Adenauerplatz without rest, Kurfürstendamm 68 (B 15), 88 28 41, Telex 184630 – wc wc . AE E — BX **n**
33 rm 72/195.

Berlin-Plaza, Knesebeckstr. 63 (B 15), ✆ 88 41 30, Telex 184181 – |♦| TV ⇔wc ⋔wc ☎ ⇔ P. AE ⊙ E VISA — DX **c**
M a la carte 27/43 – **131 rm** 102/150 Bb.

Bremen without rest, Bleibtreustr. 25 (B 15), ✆ 8 81 40 76, Telex 184892 – |♦| ⇔wc ☎ ⇔. AE ⊙ E — CX **g**
closed 21 to 28 December – **48 rm** 120/200.

XXX **Ristorante Anselmo**, Damaschkestr. 17 (B 31), ✆ 3 23 30 94, « Modern Italian rest. » – AE E VISA — BX **z**
closed Monday – **M** a la carte 44/77.

XXX Tessiner Stuben, Bleibtreustr. 33 (B 15), ✆ 8 81 36 11 (booking essential). — CX **a**

XX **Kopenhagen** (Danish Smörrebröds), Kurfürstendamm 203 (B 15), ✆ 8 83 25 03 – ▤. AE ⊙ E — DX **k**
M a la carte 29/55.

X **Hongkong** (Chinese rest.), Kurfürstendamm 210 (2nd floor, |♦|) (B 15), ✆ 8 81 57 56 – AE ⊙ E — DX **T**
M a la carte 27/46.

X **Friesenhof**, Uhlandstr. 185 (B 12), ✆ 8 83 60 79 – ▤. AE ⊙ E VISA — DV **m**
M a la carte 23/45.

near Memorial Church and Zoological Park :

Inter-Continental, Budapester Str. 2 (B 30), ✆ 2 60 20, Telex 184380, Massage, ≘s, ▣ – |♦| ▤ TV ♿ ⇔ P 🏔. AE ⊙ E VISA. ✻ rest — EV **a**
M a la carte 60/90 – **Brasserie M** a la carte 39/58 – **600 rm** 202/469 Bb.

Schweizerhof, Budapester Str. 21 (B 30), ✆ 2 69 60, Telex 185501, Massage, ≘s, ▣ – |♦| ▤ rest TV ♿ ⇔ P 🏔 (with ▤). AE ⊙ E VISA. ✻ rest — EV **w**
M a la carte 42/75 – **431 rm** 189/428.

Palace - Restaurant La Réserve, Budapester Str. 42 (Europa-Centre) (B 30), ✆ 26 20 11, Telex 184825 – |♦| ▤ rest TV P 🏔. ✻ rest — EV **k**
175 rm Bb.

Alsterhof, Augsburger Str. 5 (B 30), ✆ 21 99 60, Telex 183484, 🏛, Massage, ≘s, ▣ – |♦| TV ⇔ 🏔. AE ⊙ E VISA — EX **q**
M a la carte 32/62 – **141 rm** 139/220 Bb.

Berlin Penta Hotel M ⛯, Nürnberger Str. 65 (B 30), ✆ 24 00 11, Telex 182877, Massage, ≘s, ▣ – |♦| ▤ TV ♿ ⇔ P 🏔. AE ⊙ E VISA. ✻ rest — EV **t**
M a la carte 41/66 – **425 rm** 198/251 Bb.

Savoy, Fasanenstr. 9 (B 12), ✆ 31 10 30, Telex 184292 – |♦| TV. AE ⊙ E VISA. ✻ rest
M a la carte 39/66 – **130 rm** 168/280 Bb. — DV **s**

Berlin, Kurfürstenstr. 62 (B 30), ✆ 26 92 91, Telex 184332, 🏛 – |♦| ▤ rest TV P 🏔 (with ▤). AE ⊙ E VISA — EV **b**
M a la carte 35/69 (see also **Berlin Grill**) – **430 rm** 110/250 Bb.

Berlin Excelsior Hotel, Hardenbergstr. 14 (B 12), ✆ 3 19 91, Telex 184781 – |♦| ▤ rest TV P 🏔. AE ⊙ E VISA. ✻ rest — DV **b**
M a la carte 35/68 – **320 rm** 146/196 Bb.

Ambassador - Restaurant Conti-Fischstuben, Bayreuther Str. 42 (B 30), ✆ 21 90 20, Telex 184259, Massage, ≘s, ▣ – |♦| ▤ rest TV ⇔wc ⋔wc ☎ ⇔ P 🏔. AE ⊙ E VISA. ✻ rest — EV **z**
M *(closed Saturday lunch and Sunday)* a la carte 44/75 – **200 rm** 150/250 Bb.

Hamburg, Landgrafenstr. 4 (B 30), ✆ 26 91 61, Telex 184974 – |♦| TV ⇔wc ☎ ⇔ P 🏔. AE ⊙ E VISA. ✻ rest — EV **s**
M a la carte 32/61 – **240 rm** 129/184 Bb.

Sylter Hof, Kurfürstenstr. 116 (B 30), ✆ 2 12 00, Telex 183317 – |♦| TV ⇔wc ☎ P 🏔. AE ⊙ E VISA — EV **d**
M *(closed Sunday dinner)* a la carte 34/56 – **131 rm** 135/200 Bb – 25 apartments 165/320.

President without rest, An der Urania 16 (B 30), ✆ 21 90 30, Telex 184018, ≘s – |♦| ▤ TV ⇔wc ⋔wc ☎ P 🏔. AE ⊙ E VISA — EX **t**
170 rm 150/250 Bb.

Astoria without rest, Fasanenstr. 2 (B 12), ✆ 3 12 40 67, Telex 181745 – |♦| TV ⇔wc ⋔wc ☎. AE ⊙ E VISA — DV **a**
32 rm 65/150.

Remter without rest, Marburger Str. 17 (B 30), ✆ 24 60 61, Telex 183497 – |♦| TV ⇔wc ⋔wc ☎ P. ⊙ E VISA — EVX **c**
33 rm 90/140 Bb.

XXX **Berlin-Grill**, Kurfürstenstr. 62 (at Berlin Hotel) (B 30), ✆ 26 92 91 – ▤ P. AE ⊙ E VISA. ✻ — EV **b**
closed Saturday lunch and Sunday – **M** a la carte 55/85 (booking essential).

XXX **Ritz**, Rankestr. 26 (B 30), ✆ 24 72 50 – AE ⊙ E — DX **e**
closed Saturday lunch, Sunday and Bank Holidays – **M** a la carte 42/66.

XX **Bamberger Reiter**, Regensburger Str. 7 (B 30), ✆ 24 42 82 – ✻ EX **b**
closed Sunday, Monday, 1 - 19 January and 2 to 24 August – **M** (dinner only) a la carte 54/82 (booking essential).

XX **Mövenpick - Café des Artistes**, Europa-Centre (1st floor) (B 30), ✆ 2 62 70 77, ←, – . AE ⓓ E VISA EV **n**
M a la carte 40/70 – **Mövenpick-Restaurant M** a la carte 29/49.

XX **Du Pont**, Budapester Str. 1 (B 30), ✆ 2 61 88 11 – AE ⓓ E EV **x**
closed Saturday lunch, Sunday, 24 December - 2 January and Bank Holidays – **M** a la carte 45/80.

XX **Daitokai** (Japanese rest.), Tauentzienstr. 9 (Europa Centre, 1st floor) (B 30), ✆ 2 61 80 99 – AE ⓓ E VISA. ✻ EV **n**
closed Monday – **M** a la carte 36/58.

XX **Ristorante Il Sorriso** (Italian rest.), Kurfürstenstr. 76 (B 30), ✆ 2 62 13 13 – AE ⓓ E. ✻ – **M** a la carte 27/54 (booking essential for dinner) EV **r**

at Berlin-Charlottenburg :

Seehof ✈, Lietzensee-Ufer 11 (B 19), ✆ 32 00 20, Telex 182943, ←, , , – TV (with). AE ⓓ E. ✻ rest BV **r**
M a la carte 40/72 – **77 rm** 195/250 Bb.

Kanthotel without rest, Kantstr. 111 (B 12), ✆ 32 30 26, Telex 183330 – TV wc wc ☎ Ⓟ. AE ⓓ E VISA BV **e**
55 rm 124/174 Bb.

Ibis without rest, Messedamm 10 (B 19), ✆ 30 20 11, Telex 182882 – wc wc ☎ AV **b**
191 rm Bb.

Econtel without rest (modern economy-hotel), Sömmeringstr. 24 (B 10), ✆ 34 40 01 – wc ☎ Ⓟ – **205 rm** 98/144. BU **a**

Kardell, Gervinusstr. 24 (B 12), ✆ 3 24 10 66 – wc wc ☎ Ⓟ. AE ⓓ E VISA BX **r**
M *(closed Saturday lunch)* a la carte 38/65 – **33 rm** 85/150 Bb.

Am Studio without rest, Kaiserdamm 80 (B 19), ✆ 30 20 81, Telex 182825 – TV wc ☎ . AE ⓓ E VISA – **78 rm** 75/115 Bb. AV **c**

XX **La Puce**, Schillerstr. 20 (B 12), ✆ 3 12 58 31 – AE CV **a**
closed Sunday, Monday and 4 weeks July - August – **M** (dinner only) a la carte 54/72.

XX **Don Camillo** (Italian rest.), Schloßstr. 7 (B 19), BV **s**
closed 10 July - 10 August and Wednesday – **M** a la carte 36/60.

XX ✿ **Ponte Vecchio** (Tuscan rest.), Spielhagenstr. 3 (B 10), ✆ 3 42 19 99 – ⓓ BV **a**
closed Tuesday and 3 weeks July - August – **M** *(dinner only)* a la carte 43/62 (booking essential)
Spec. Cappelle di funghi porcini al forno, Pappardelle al fagiano, Sogliola ai frutti di mare.

XX **Pullman**, Messedamm 11 (Congress Centre) (B 19), ✆ 30 38 39 46, ← – ♿ . AE ⓓ E. ✻ AV **s**
closed Sunday dinner and 4 weeks July - August – **M** a la carte 29/61.

at Berlin-Dahlem by ② EZ :

Forsthaus Paulsborn ✈, Am Grunewaldsee (B 33), ✆ 8 13 80 10, – TV wc wc ☎ Ⓟ. AE ⓓ E VISA
M *(closed Monday October - April)* a la carte 32/54 – **11 rm** 85/160.

XX **Alter Krug**, Königin-Luise-Str. 52 (B 33), ✆ 8 32 50 89, « Terrace » – Ⓟ. ⓓ E VISA
closed Thursday – **M** a la carte 30/61.

at Berlin-Nikolassee by ② EZ :

XX ✿ **Frühsammer's Restaurant An der Rehwiese**, Matterhornstr. 101 (B 38), ✆ 8 03 27 20 – ⓓ VISA
M (dinner only) a la carte 54/84 (booking essential)
Spec. Zander im Wirsingblatt, Lachs im Schweinenetz gebraten, Cassoulette von grünen Linsen und Kalbsbries.

at Berlin-Reinickendorf by Sellerstr. FU :

Rheinsberg am See, Finsterwalder Str. 64 (B 26), ✆ 4 02 10 02, Telex 185972, , Massage, , , , – TV wc ☎ Ⓟ
M a la carte 32/60 – **75 rm** 69/149 Bb.

at Berlin-Siemensstadt by Siemensdamm AU :

Novotel, Ohmstr. 4 (B 13), ✆ 38 10 61, Telex 181415, (heated) – rest TV wc ☎ ♿ Ⓟ (with). AE ⓓ E VISA
M a la carte 31/55 – **119 rm** 135/178 Bb.

at Berlin-Steglitz by Hauptstr. EYZ :

Steglitz International M, Albrechtstr. 2 (B 41), ✆ 79 10 61, Telex 183545, Massage, – TV ♿ . AE ⓓ E VISA
M a la carte 29/58 – **212 rm** 120/190 Bb.

Ravenna Hotel without rest, Grunewaldstr. 8 (B 41), ✆ 7 92 80 31, Telex 184310, – wc ☎ Ⓟ. AE ⓓ E VISA – **45 rm** 80/125 Bb.

at Berlin-Waidmannslust by Sellerstr. FU :

XXX ✿ **Rockendorf's Restaurant** (elegant installation), Düsterhauptstr. 1 (B 28), ✆ 4 02 30 99 – AE ⓓ. ✻
closed Sunday, Monday, Bank Holidays, 3 weeks July - August and Christmas - New Year
M a la carte 73/110 (booking essential)
Spec. Gemüseterrine mit Gänsestopfleber und Kerbelsauce, Rehbockrücken in Himbeeressig (mid May - July), Schokoladenparfait mit Pralineneis und Minzsauce.

at Berlin-Tegel by Jakob-Kaiser-Platz BU :

Novotel Berlin Airport M, Kurt-Schumacher-Damm 202 (by airport approach) (B 51), ✆ 4 10 60, Telex 181605, ≘s, (heated) – TV wc ☎ P
187 rm Bb.

at Berlin-Wilmersdorf :

Crest Motor Hotel without rest, Güntzelstr. 14 (B 31), ✆ 87 02 41, Telex 182948 – TV wc wc ☎. AE ⓓ E VISA DY **t**
110 rm 147/194 Bb.

Franke, Albrecht-Achilles-Str. 57 (B 31), ✆ 8 92 10 97, Telex 184857 – wc ☎ P
67 rm. BX **s**

Lichtburg, Paderborner Str. 10 (B 15), ✆ 8 91 80 41, Telex 184208 – wc ☎. AE ⓓ E VISA BX **a**
M a la carte 25/37 – **62 rm** 100/153.

Atrium Hotel without rest, Motzstr. 87 (B 30), ✆ 24 40 57 – wc ☎. E EX **e**
22 rm 45/98.

XX **Medel**, Durlacher Str. 25 (B 31), , « Furnished in Tyrolean chalet-style » – AE E
M (dinner only). DZ **n**

COLOGNE (KÖLN) 5000. Nordrhein-Westfalen 987 ㉓ ㉔ – pop. 965 000 – alt. 65 m – ✆ 0221.

See : Cathedral (Dom)★★★ (Magi's Shrine★★★) DV – Roman-Germanic Museum (Römisch-Germanisches Museum)★★★ (Dionysos Mosaic) DV **M1** – Wallraf-Richartz-Museum (14 - 16 C pictures by Cologne Masters) and Museum Ludwig★★★ DV **M3** – Schnütgen-Museum★★ (Madonnas of Cologne) DX **M4** – St. Columbia (St. Kolumba)★ DX **V** – St. Alban the New (Neu St. Alban)★ – St. Maria of the Capitol (St. Maria im Kapitol) (wooden doors★★) DX **D** – Holy Apostles (St. Aposteln) (apse★) CX **N** – St. Severinus (St. Severin) (inside★) DY **K** – Rhine Park (Rheinpark)★.

Underground under construction : temporary traffic diversions and one-way system.

Köln-Bonn at Wahn (SE : 17 km), ✆ (02203) 4 01.

✆ 1 41 56 66.

Exhibition Centre (Messegelände), ✆ 82 11, Telex 8873426.

Tourist office (Verkehrsamt), Am Dom, ✆ 2 21 33 40, Telex 8883421.

ADAC, Köln 51-Bayenthal, Alteburger Str. 375, ✆ 3 79 90.

Düsseldorf 39 – Aachen 70 – Bonn 27 – Essen 68.

Plans on following pages

The reference (K 15) at the end of the address is the postal district : Köln 15

Excelsior Hotel Ernst - Restaurant Hanse Stube, Trankgasse 1 (K 1), ✆ 27 01, Telex 8882645 – rest TV (with). AE ⓓ E. ✻ rest DV **a**
M a la carte 57/98 – **146 rm** 208/450 Bb.

Dom-Hotel , Domkloster 2a (K 1), ✆ 23 37 51, Telex 8882919, « Terrace with ≤ » – TV . AE ⓓ E VISA. ✻ rest DV **d**
M a la carte 44/93 – **126 rm** 225/445 Bb.

Inter-Continental, Helenenstr. 14 (K 1), ✆ 22 80, Telex 8882162, Massage, ≘s, – TV P . AE ⓓ E VISA. ✻ rest CV **p**
M a la carte 59/100 – **300 rm** 238/461 Bb.

Consul, Belfortstr. 9 (K 1), ✆ 7 72 10, Telex 8885242, ≘s, – TV P . AE ⓓ E VISA. ✻ rest DU **v**
M a la carte 40/64 – **122 rm** 142/260 Bb.

Mondial, Bechergasse 10 (K 1), ✆ 2 06 30, Telex 8881932 – TV . ✻ rest DV **f**
204 rm Bb.

Savoy without rest, Turiner Str. 9 (K 1), ✆ 12 04 66, Telex 8886360, ≘s – TV wc wc ☎. AE E DU **s**
69 rm 115/270 Bb.

Haus Lyskirchen, Filzengraben 28 (K 1), ✆ 23 48 91, Telex 8885449, – TV wc wc ☎ . AE ⓓ E VISA DY **u**
closed 23 December - 2 January – **M** *(dinner only, closed Sunday and Bank Holidays)* a la carte 36/58 – **95 rm** 99/205 Bb.

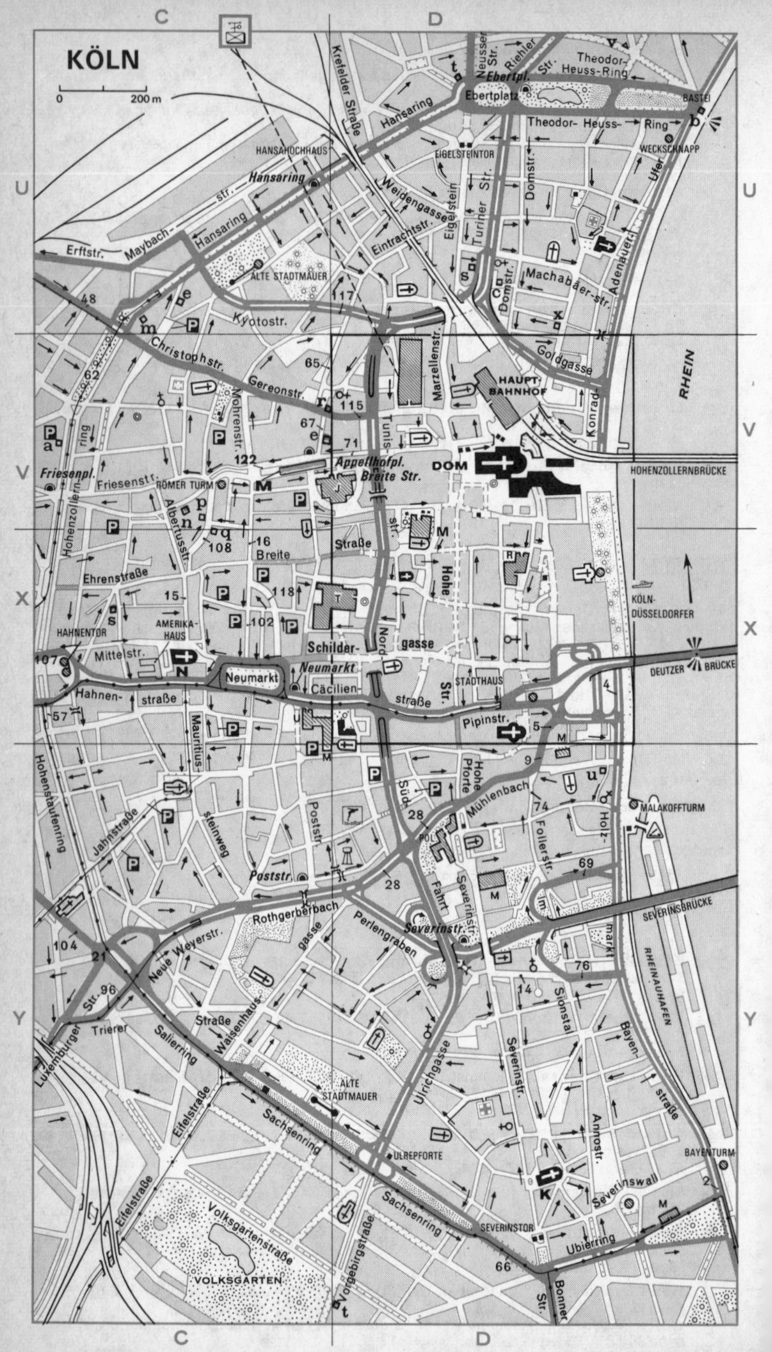
KÖLN
0
200 m
C
D
U
V
X
Y
RHEIN
HAUPT-BAHNHOF
DOM
HOHENZOLLERNBRÜCKE
DEUTZER BRÜCKE
SEVERINSBRÜCKE
RHEINAUHAFEN
KÖLN-DÜSSELDORFER
Ebertplatz
Hansaring
Neumarkt
Severinstr.
Schildergasse
VOLKSGARTEN
ALTE STADTMAUER
BAYENTURM
SEVERINSTOR
ULREPFORTE
MALAKOFFTURM
HAHNENTOR
EIGELSTEINTOR
HANSAHOCHHAUS
BASTEI
WECKSCHNAPP
RÖMER TURM
AMERIKA-HAUS
STADTHAUS

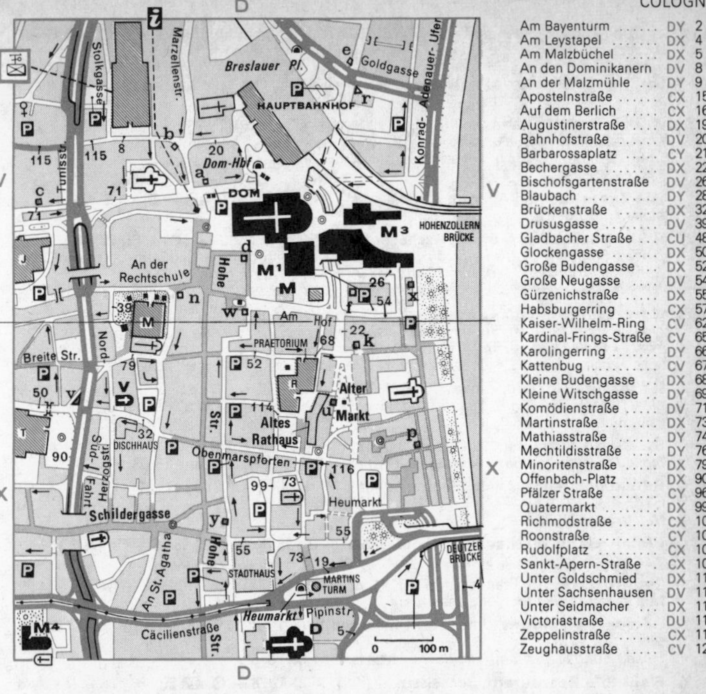

Am Bayenturm	DY	2
Am Leystapel	DX	4
Am Malzbüchel	DX	5
An den Dominikanern	DV	8
An der Malzmühle	DY	9
Apostelnstraße	CX	15
Auf dem Berlich	CX	16
Augustinerstraße	DX	19
Bahnhofstraße	DV	20
Barbarossaplatz	CY	21
Bechergasse	DX	22
Bischofsgartenstraße	DV	26
Blaubach	DY	28
Brückenstraße	DX	32
Drususgasse	DV	39
Gladbacher Straße	CU	48
Glockengasse	DX	50
Große Budengasse	DX	52
Große Neugasse	DV	54
Gürzenichstraße	DX	55
Habsburgerring	CX	57
Kaiser-Wilhelm-Ring	CV	62
Kardinal-Frings-Straße	CV	65
Karolingerring	DY	66
Kattenbug	CV	67
Kleine Budengasse	DX	68
Kleine Witschgasse	DY	69
Komödienstraße	DV	71
Martinstraße	DX	73
Mathiasstraße	DY	74
Mechtildisstraße	DY	76
Minoritenstraße	DX	79
Offenbach-Platz	DX	90
Pfälzer Straße	CY	96
Quatermarkt	DX	99
Richmodstraße	CX	102
Roonstraße	CY	104
Rudolfplatz	CX	107
Sankt-Apern-Straße	CX	108
Unter Goldschmied	DX	114
Unter Sachsenhausen	DV	115
Unter Seidmacher	DX	116
Victoriastraße	DU	117
Zeppelinstraße	CX	118
Zeughausstraße	CV	122

Bristol without rest, Kaiser-Wilhelm-Ring 48 (K 1), ☎ 12 01 95, Telex 8881146, « Antique furnished rooms » – wc wc ☎. AE ⓓ E VISA CU **m**
44 rm 99/215.

Ascot Hotel (rest. in bistro-style), Hohenzollernring 95 (K 1), ☎ 52 10 76, Telex 8883018 – TV wc wc ☎. AE ⓓ E VISA CV **a**
M a la carte 36/52 – **52 rm** 92/226 Bb.

Königshof without rest, Richartzstr. 14 (K 1), ☎ 23 45 83, Telex 8881318 – TV wc wc ☎. AE ⓓ E VISA DV **n**
95 rm 105/290 Bb.

Eden-Hotel without rest, Am Hof 18 (K 1), ☎ 23 61 23, Telex 8882889 – TV wc wc ☎. AE ⓓ E VISA DV **w**
33 rm 149/225 Bb.

Kolpinghaus International, St.-Apern-Str. 32 (K 1), ☎ 2 09 30 – wc ☎ P. AE ⓓ CVX **q**
M a la carte 22/55 – **48 rm** 80/115.

Kommerzhotel without rest, Breslauer Platz (K 1), ☎ 12 40 86, – TV wc wc ☎. AE ⓓ E VISA DV **r**
57 rm 105/190 Bb.

PLM-Hotel Baseler Hof, Breslauer Platz 2 (K 1), ☎ 1 65 40, Telex 8886982 – TV wc wc ☎. AE ⓓ E VISA DV **e**
M *(dinner only, closed Saturday, Sunday and Bank Holidays)* a la carte 38/58 – **108 rm** 135/240 Bb.

Windsor without rest, Von-Werth-Str. 36 (K 1), ☎ 13 40 31 – wc ☎. AE ⓓ E VISA CU **e**
37 rm 75/190.

Ludwig without rest, Brandenburger Str. 24 (K 1), ☎ 12 30 31, Telex 8885326 – TV wc wc ☎. AE ⓓ E VISA DU **x**
closed 23 December - 1 January – **61 rm** 95/165 Bb.

Merian-Hotel without rest, Allerheiligenstr. 1 (K 1), ☎ 12 10 25 – wc ☎. AE ⓓ E VISA DU **c**
closed 22 December - 4 January – **28 rm** 83/220 Bb.

Central Hotel without rest, An den Dominikanern 3 (K 1), ☎ 13 50 88 – TV wc wc ☎. AE ⓓ VISA DV **b**
closed 20 December - 2 January – **43 rm** 75/145 Bb.

XXXX ✿ **Chez Alex**, Mühlengasse 1 (K 1), ☎ 23 05 60, « Elegant furniture » – ▤. AE ⓓ E VISA
closed Saturday lunch, Sunday and Bank Holidays – **M** a la carte 75/110 (booking essential) DX **k**
Spec. Lasagne de homard au sabayon de truffes, Foie gras chaud aux pommes, Poularde de Bresse truffée au sel.

XXX ✿ **Rino Casati**, Ebertplatz 3 (K 1), ☎ 72 11 08 – AE ⓓ E VISA. ✱ DU **t**
closed Sunday – **M** a la carte 46/90 (booking essential)
Spec. Gemüsestrudel mit Tomatencoulis, Babysteinbutt mit Champagnersauce, Hohe Rippe mit Schalottensauce.

XXX **Die Bastei**, Konrad-Adenauer-Ufer 80 (K 1), ☎ 12 28 25, ≤ Rhein – AE ⓓ E. ✱
closed Saturday lunch – **M** a la carte 49/92. DU **b**

XXX **Franz Kellers Restaurant**, Aachener Str. 21 (K 1), ☎ 25 10 22, ☂ – Ⓟ. AE ⓓ E
closed Sunday – **M** (dinner only) a la carte 57/90 (booking essential) – **Kellers Keller** *(lunch also, closed Sunday and Saturday until 7 pm)* **M** a la carte 44/70.
by Rudolfplatz CX

XXX ✿ **Restaurant Bado - La poêle d'or**, Komödienstr. 52 (K 1), ☎ 13 41 00 – ⓓ E
closed Monday lunch, Sunday, Bank Holidays, 3 weeks July - August and Christmas - New Year – **M** a la carte 67/99 – **Bistro M** a la carte 30/47 DV **c**
Spec. Homard aux jeunes légumes, Noisette d'agneau aux courgettes, Farandole des desserts.

XX **Ristorante Alfredo**, Tunisstr. 3 (K 1), ☎ 24 43 01 – AE DX **v**
closed Saturday dinner, Sunday and 3 weeks July - August – **M** a la carte 56/74 (booking essential).

XX **St. Georg**, Magnusstr. 3 (K 1), ☎ 21 84 18, ☂ – AE ⓓ E VISA CV **n**
closed Sunday and Bank Holidays except exhibitions – **M** a la carte 58/93.

XX **Ratskeller**, Rathausplatz 1 (entrance Alter Markt) (K 1), ☎ 21 83 01, ☂ – ▤ ♿ 🏛. AE ⓓ E VISA DX **u**
M a la carte 30/70.

XX **Weinhaus im Walfisch** (17 C house), Salzgasse 13 (K 1), ☎ 21 95 75 – AE ⓓ E VISA
closed Saturday lunch, Sunday and Bank Holidays – **M** a la carte 50/87. DX **p**

XX **Em Krützche**, Am Frankenturm 1 (K 1), ☎ 21 14 32, « Terrace with ≤ » – ⓓ DV **x**
M a la carte 38/64 (booking essential).

XX **Börsen-Restaurant**, Unter Sachsenhausen 10 (K 1), ☎ 13 56 26 – ▤ 🏛. AE ⓓ E VISA. ✱ CV **r**
closed Sunday and Bank Holidays – **M** a la carte 50/75.

XX **Elsbeth's Restaurant**, Benesisstr. 57 (K 1), ☎ 21 42 78 – Ⓟ. ⓓ E. ✱ CX **s**
closed Saturday lunch and Sunday except exhibitions – **M** a la carte 34/46 (booking essential).

XX **Colonius - Turmrestaurant**, Innere Kanalstr. 100 (|$|, DM 4) (K 1), ☎ 52 20 61, ✳ Cologne, « Revolving rest. at 166 m » – ▤ Ⓟ. ⓓ E VISA. ✱ by Erftstr. CU
M a la carte 44/60.

XX **Daitokai** (Japanese rest.), Kattenburg 2 (K 1), ☎ 12 00 48 – ▤. AE ⓓ E VISA. ✱
closed Monday – **M** a la carte 38/60. CV **e**

X **La Baurie** (French rest.), Vorgebirgstr. 35 (K 1), ☎ 38 61 49 – VISA DY **t**
closed Saturday lunch and Monday – **M** a la carte 63/82.

X **China-Restaurant Tchang**, Große Sandkaul 19 (K 1), ☎ 21 76 51 – AE ⓓ E VISA
M a la carte 28/43. DX **y**

at Cologne 41-Braunsfeld by Rudolfplatz CX :

🏨 **Regent**, Melatengürtel 15, ☎ 5 49 91, Telex 8881824 – |$| ▤ rest TV ⌂wc ⌂wc ☎ Ⓟ 🏛. AE ⓓ E VISA
M a la carte 45/67 – **165 rm** 188/326 Bb.

at Cologne 21-Deutz by Deutzer Brücke DX :

XX **Restaurant im Messeturm**, Kennedy-Ufer (18th floor, |$|), ☎ 88 10 08, ≤ Cologne – ▤. AE ⓓ E. ✱
closed Saturday lunch and mid July - mid August – **M** a la carte 43/72.

at Cologne 50-Immendorf by Bonner Str. DZ :

XX **Weinstuben Bitzerhof** with rm (farmyard from 1821), Immendorfer Hauptstr. 21, ☎ (02236) 6 19 21, ☂, « Country house atmosphere » – TV ⌂wc ☎ 🚗. ✱ rm
M *(closed Sunday and Bank Holidays)* a la carte 49/71 – **3 rm** 80/130.

at Cologne 41-Lindenthal by Rudolfplatz and B 264 CX :

🏨 **Crest-Hotel Köln**, Dürener Str. 287, ☎ 46 30 01, Telex 8882516, « Garden with ☂ » – |$| ▤ rest TV ♿ 🚗 Ⓟ 🏛 (with ▤). AE ⓓ E VISA. ✱ rest
M a la carte 40/75 – **152 rm** 187/323 Bb.

🏨 **Bremer**, Dürener Str. 225, ☎ 40 50 13, Telex 8882063, ⌂s, ⌂ – |$| ▤ rest TV ⌂wc ⌂wc ☎ 🚗. AE ⓓ E VISA. ✱ rest
M a la carte 52/78 (booking essential) – **König-Pub M** a la carte 34/58 – **75 rm** 115/200 Bb.

at Cologne 51-Marienburg by Bonner Straße DY :

Marienburger Bonotel M, Bonner Str. 478, 3 70 20, Telex 8881515, – AE E VISA
M a la carte 39/69 – **91 rm** 145/275 Bb.

at Cologne 40-Marsdorf by Rudolfplatz and B 264 CX :

Novotel Köln-Westkreuz, Horbeller Str. 1, (02234) 1 60 81, Telex 8886355, (heated), – rest wc with
140 rm Bb.

at Cologne 91-Merheim by Deutzer Brücke DX :

XXXX **Goldener Pflug**, Olpener Str. 421 (B 55), 89 55 09 –
closed Saturday lunch, Sunday, Bank Holidays and 3 weeks July - August – **M** a la carte 132/180
Spec. Gänseleber mit Linsencreme, Seeteufelragout mit Senfsauce, Kalbsbries mit Trüffeln.

at Cologne 80-Mülheim by Konrad-Adenauer-Ufer DU :

Kaiser without rest, Genovevastr. 10, 62 30 57, Telex 8873546 – wc wc AE E VISA
46 rm 95/210 Bb.

XXX **Villa Hahnenburg** (former villa in a small park), Ackerstr. 146, 63 25 95, – . AE E
closed 22 December - 2 January, Sunday and Bank Holidays – **M** a la carte 44/75.

at Cologne 90- Porz-Wahnheide SE : 17 km by A 59 – 02203 :

Holiday Inn, Waldstr. 255, 56 10, Telex 8874665, , , – . rest
113 rm Bb.

Aachen 5100. Nordrhein-Westfalen 987 ㉓, 213 ㉔, 409 ⑯ – pop. 254 000 – alt. 174 m – 0241 – Köln 70.

XXXX **Gala**, Monheimsallee 44 (at Casino), 15 30 13, « Modern-elegant furniture » – . AE E VISA
closed Monday – **M** (dinner only) a la carte 75/115 (booking essential)
Spec. Maultaschen von Helgoländer Hummer, Rinderfilet mit Pumpernickelsauce, Aachener Printenauflauf.

DÜSSELDORF 4000. Nordrhein-Westfalen 987 ㉓ ㉔ – pop. 569 000 – alt. 40 m – 0211.

See : Königsallee★ – Hofgarten★ – Hetjensmuseum★ BX **M2** – Land Economic Museum (Landesmuseum Volk u. Wirtschaft)★ BV **M1** – Goethemuseum★ CV **M3** – Thyssen building (Thyssenhaus)★ CVX **E**.

Envir. : Chateau of Benrath (Schloß Benrath) (Park★) S : 10 km by Kölner Str. DXY.

Düsseldorf-Lohausen (N : 8 km), 42 11 – 3 68 04 68.

Exhibition Centre (Messegelände), 4 56 01, Telex 8584853.

Tourist office, K.-Adenauer-Platz 12 and at the Main Station, (Hauptbahnhof) 35 05 05, Telex 8587785.

ADAC, Kaiserswerther Str. 207, 43 49 51.

Amsterdam 225 – Essen 31 – Köln 39 – Rotterdam 237.

Plan on following pages

The reference (D 15) at the end of the address is the postal district : Düsseldorf 15

Breidenbacher Hof, Heinrich-Heine-Allee 36 (D 1), 1 30 30, Telex 8582630 – . AE E VISA. rest BX **a**
Restaurants : – **Grill Royal** *(closed Sunday)* **M** a la carte 65/95 – **Breidenbacher Eck M** a la carte 43/70 – **155 rm** 280/490.

Steigenberger Parkhotel, Corneliusplatz 1 (D 1), 86 51, Telex 8582331, – AE E VISA. rest CX **p**
M a la carte 54/91 – **160 rm** 239/480 Bb.

Nikko M, Immermannstr. 41 (D 1), 86 61, Telex 8582080, , Massage, , – . AE E VISA. rest DX **a**
Restaurants : – **Benkay** (Japanese rest.) **M** a la carte 30/80 – **Travellers M** a la carte 37/75 – **301 rm** 230/405 Bb.

Excelsior without rest, Kapellstr. 1 (D 30), 48 60 06, Telex 8584737 – . AE E VISA – **65 rm** 142/275 CV **a**

Savoy, Oststr. 128 (D 1), 36 03 36, Telex 8584215, Massage, , – rest – **130 rm** Bb CX **w**

Holiday Inn, Graf-Adolf-Platz 10 (D 1), 3 87 30, Telex 8586359, , – . AE E VISA CY **r**
Restaurants : – **Suppentopf** *(lunch only, closed Sunday)* **M** a la carte 26/39 – **La Rhénane M** a la carte 43/70 – **120 rm** 254/313 Bb.

Uebachs, Leopoldstr. 5 (D 1), 36 05 66, Telex 8587620 – . rest
M *(closed Sunday except exhibitions)* a la carte 43/70 – **82 rm** 147/240 Bb. DX **r**

Am Wehrhahn	DV	
Berliner Allee	CX	
Flinger Straße	BX	28
Graf-Adolf-Straße	CY	
Königsallee	CX	
Schadowstraße	CX	94
Blumenstraße	CX	7
Bolkerstraße	BX	8
Citadellstraße	BX	13
Elberfelder Straße	CX	21
Ernst-Reuter-Platz	CY	23
Fischerstraße	BV	27
Friedrich-Ebert-Straße	CX	29
Fürstenplatz	CY	30
Grabbeplatz	BX	32
Graf-Adolf-Platz	CX	33
Heinrich-Heine-Allee	BX	42
Hofgartenrampe	BV	45
Jan-Wellem-Platz	CX	51
Konrad-Adenauer-Platz	DX	59
Markplatz	BX	68
Martin-Luther-Platz	CX	69
Maximilian-Weyhe-Allee	CV	70
Mühlenstraße	BX	72
Oberbilker Markt	DY	80
Ratinger Straße	BV	88
Schadowplatz	CX	93
Schneider-Wibbel-Gasse	BX	95
Schwanenmarkt	BX	96
Tonhallenstraße	CX	99
Vagedesstraße	CV	104
Venloer Straße	CV	105

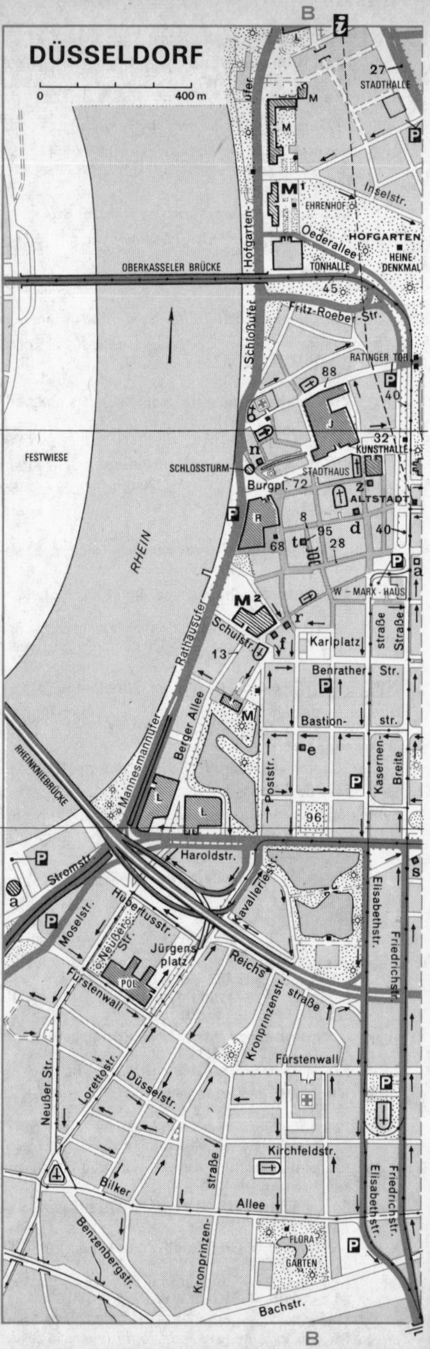

When in Europe

never be without:

the Michelin Map no 920

and

the Michelin Green Guides

Austria
England:
Scotland
The West Country
Germany
Greece
Italy
London
Paris
Portugal
Rome
Spain
Switzerland

DÜSSELDORF

0 — 400 m

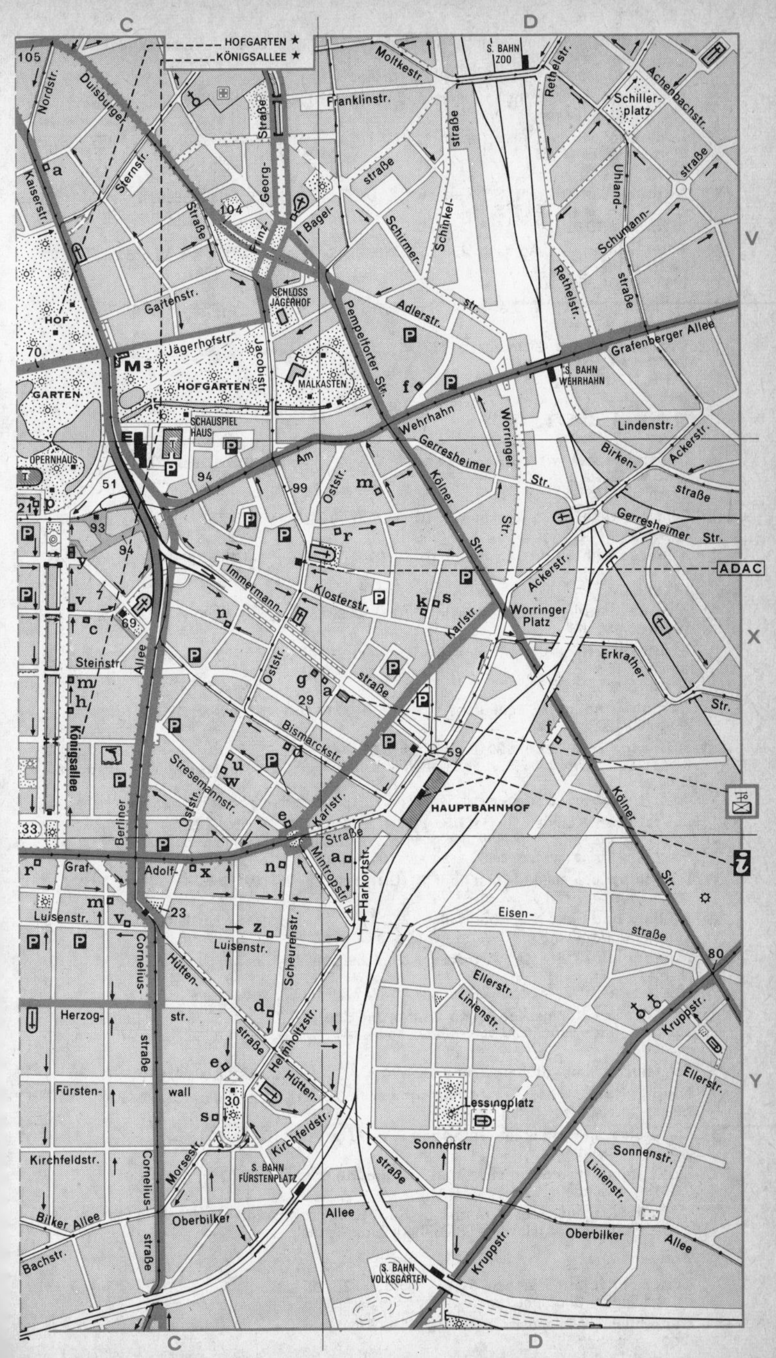
HOFGARTEN ★
KÖNIGSALLEE ★
S. BAHN ZOO
SCHLOSS JÄGERHOF
HOFGARTEN
MALKASTEN
SCHAUSPIEL HAUS
OPERNHAUS
S. BAHN WEHRHAHN
HAUPTBAHNHOF
ADAC
Worringer Platz
Lessingplatz
S. BAHN FÜRSTENPLATZ
S. BAHN VOLKSGARTEN
Königsallee
Berliner Allee
Graf-Adolf-Straße
Kölner Str.
Pempelforter Str.
Grafenberger Allee
Oberbilker Allee
Bilker Allee

Graf Adolf without rest, Stresemannplatz 1 (D 1), 36 05 91, Telex 8587844 – wc wc. AE E CX e
closed 23 December - 5 January – **100 rm** 70/185 Bb.

Ambassador without rest, Harkortstr. 7 (D 1), 37 00 03, Telex 8586286 – wc wc – **60 rm** Bb. DY a

Lindenhof without rest, Oststr. 124 (D 1), 36 09 63, Telex 8587012 – wc wc. AE E VISA CX u
43 rm 120/195.

National without rest, Schwerinstr. 16 (D 30), 49 90 62, Telex 8586597, – wc wc. AE E VISA by Duisburger Str. CV
35 rm 105/210 Bb.

Eden without rest, Adersstr. 29 (D 1), 38 10 60, Telex 8582530 – wc wc. AE E VISA CY m
106 rm 150/285 Bb.

Madison without rest, Graf-Adolf-Str. 47 (D 1), 37 02 96 – wc. CY x
24 rm Bb.

City without rest, Bismarckstr. 73 (D 1), 36 50 23, Telex 8587362 – wc wc. AE E VISA CX d
52 rm 110/180.

Börsenhotel without rest, Kreuzstr. 19a (D 1), 36 30 71, Telex 8587323 – wc wc. AE E VISA CX n
76 rm 130/240 Bb.

Central-Hotel without rest, Luisenstr. 42 (D 1), 37 90 01, Telex 8582145 – wc. AE E CY v
80 rm 140/225 Bb.

Bellevue without rest, Luisenstr. 98 (D 1), 37 70 71, Telex 8584771 – wc. CY z
23 rm Bb.

Minerva without rest, Cantadorstr. 13a (D 1), 35 09 61 – wc wc. AE E. DX m
12 rm 110/150.

Astor without rest, Kurfürstenstr. 23 (D 1), 36 06 61, – wc. AE E DX k
16 rm 75/165.

Großer Kurfürst without rest, Kurfürstenstr. 18 (D 1), 35 76 47 – wc wc. AE E DX s
22 rm 75/165.

Regina without rest, Scheurenstr. 3 (D 1), 37 04 46 – wc. AE E VISA. CY n
35 rm 90/120.

XXXX ❀ **Orangerie,** Bilker Str. 30 (D 1), 13 18 28 – AE BX e
closed Sunday except exhibitions – **M** a la carte 69/94 (booking essential) – **Bistro M** a la carte 45/70
Spec. Carpaccio von Gänseleber mit Ingwer, Pot au feu von Edelfischen, Wachteln in Madeirasauce.

XXX ❀ **Victorian,** Königstr. 3a (1st floor) (D 1), 32 02 22 – . AE E VISA CX c
closed Sunday and Bank Holidays – **M** a la carte 60/88 – **Lounge M** a la carte 36/77
Spec. Gänseleberterrine, Steinbutt mit Krustentieren, Lammgerichte.

XXX **La Scala,** Königsallee 14 (1st floor) (D 1), 32 68 32 – AE E. CX y
closed Sunday – **M** a la carte 47/74.

XXX **Müllers und Fest KD,** Königsallee 12 (D 1), 32 60 01, – AE E VISA CX y
closed Sunday and Bank Holidays – **M** a la carte 52/68.

XXX **Mövenpick - Café des Artistes,** Königsallee 60 (Kö-Galerie) (D 1), 32 03 14 – . AE E CX h
M a la carte 50/79 – **Locanda Ticinese M** a la carte 33/53.

XX **La Terrazza,** Königsallee 30 (Kö-Centre, 2nd floor,) (D 1), 32 75 40 – AE E VISA
closed Saturday until 6.30 pm, Sunday and Bank Holidays – **M** a la carte 54/76 (booking essential). CX v

XX Schneider-Wibbel-Stuben, Schneider-Wibbel-Gasse 7 (D 1), 8 00 00, BX t

XX **Nippon Kan** (Japanese rest.), Immermannstr. 35 (D 1), 35 31 35 – AE E VISA. CX g
M a la carte 40/61 (booking essential).

XX China-Sichuan-Restaurant, Graf-Adolf-Platz 7 (1st floor) (D 1), 37 96 41 BY s
(booking essential).

XX Zur Auster (rest. in bistro-style, mainly seafood), Berger Str. 9 (D 1), 32 44 04 BX r
(booking essential).

XX **Daitokai** (Japanese rest.), Mutter-Ey-Str. 1 (D 1), 32 50 54 – . AE E VISA. BX z
closed Sunday – **M** a la carte 38/60 (booking essential).

Brewery-inns :

X **Zum Schiffchen,** Hafenstr. 5 (D 1), 13 24 22 – AE E BX f
closed Sunday and Bank Holidays – **M** a la carte 27/52 (booking essential).

X Frankenheim, Wielandstr. 14 (D 1), 35 14 47 DV f
(booking essential).

X **Im Goldenen Ring**, Burgplatz 21 (D 1), ✆ 13 31 61, beer-garden – BX **n**
M a la carte 21/46.

X **Benrather Hof**, Steinstr. 1 (D 1), ✆ 32 52 18, CX **m**
M a la carte 19/43.

X **Im Goldenen Kessel**, Bolker Str. 44 (D 1), ✆ 32 60 07 BX **d**
closed 24 December - 1 January – **M** a la carte 27/37.

at Düsseldorf 31-Angermund **N : 15 km by Fischerstr.** BV :

Haus Litzbrück, Bahnhofstr. 33, ✆ (0203) 7 44 81, « Terrace », , , – . AE E
M *(closed 3 weeks July - August)* a la carte 41/69 – **23 rm** 135/205.

at Düsseldorf 13-Benrath **by Kölner Landstr.** DXY :

Rheinterrasse, Benrather Schloßufer 39, ✆ 71 20 70, « Terrace with ≤ » – wc wc . E
M a la carte 31/65 – **19 rm** 95/175 Bb.

XX **Lignano** (Italian rest.), Hildener Str. 43, ✆ 71 19 36 – AE E VISA.
closed Saturday lunch, Sunday, 31 May - 14 June and 30 August - 13 September – **M** a la carte 37/66.

XX **Pigage** with rm, Benrather Schloßallee 28, ✆ 71 40 66 – wc wc . E VISA
M *(closed Sunday except exhibitions)* a la carte 35/71 – **10 rm** 65/140.

at Düsseldorf 30-Derendorf **by Prinz-Georg-Str.** CV :

Michelangelo without rest, Roßstr. 61, ✆ 48 01 01, Telex 8588649 – wc wc
70 rm Bb.

Gildors Hotel without rest, Collenbachstr. 51, ✆ 48 80 05, Telex 8584418 – wc wc . AE E VISA
35 rm 135/210 Bb.

XXX **Amalfi** (Italian rest.), Ulmenstr. 122, ✆ 43 38 09 – AE E
closed Sunday – **M** a la carte 50/72.

at Düsseldorf 13-Eller **by Kölner Str.** DXY :

Novotel Düsseldorf Süd, Am Schönenkamp 9, ✆ 74 10 92, Telex 8584374, , (heated), – wc . AE E VISA
M a la carte 31/57 – **120 rm** 147/193 Bb.

at Düsseldorf 1-Friedrichstadt :

Esplanade, Fürstenplatz 17, ✆ 37 50 10, Telex 8582970, , – wc wc . AE E VISA. rest CY **s**
M a la carte 37/70 – **80 rm** 129/298 Bb.

Fürstenhof without rest, Fürstenplatz 3, ✆ 37 05 45, Telex 8586540 – wc wc . AE E VISA CY **e**
43 rm 125/235 Bb.

Beyer without rest, Scheurenstr. 57, ✆ 37 09 91 – wc CY **d**
19 rm.

at Düsseldorf 30-Golzheim **by Fischerstr.** BV :

Inter-Continental M, Karl-Arnold-Platz 5, ✆ 4 55 30, Telex 8584601, Massage, , – . AE E VISA. rest
M a la carte 49/82 – **310 rm** 320/455 Bb.

Düsseldorf Hilton, Georg-Glock-Str. 20, ✆ 4 37 70, Telex 8584376, , Massage, , , – . AE E VISA. rest
Restaurants : – **Hofgarten M** a la carte 34/59 – **San Francisco** (see below) – **383 rm** 219/423.

Golzheimer Krug , Karl-Kleppe-Str. 20, ✆ 43 44 53, Telex 8588919, – wc wc
27 rm Bb.

Rheinpark without rest, Bankstr. 13, ✆ 49 91 86 – wc .
30 rm 55/130.

XXXX ✿ **San Francisco**, Georg-Glock-Str. 20 (at Hilton-Hotel), ✆ 4 37 70 – . AE E VISA.
M a la carte 63/93 (booking essential for dinner)
Spec. Filet von St. Pierre mit Fenchelbutter, Gefüllte Perlhuhnbrust mit Morchelsauce, Variation vom Kalb in Kräutersauce.

XX **Fischer-Stuben-Mulfinger**, Rotterdamer Str. 15, ✆ 43 26 12, « Terrace »
closed Friday dinner and Saturday – **M** a la carte 43/74 (booking essential).

XX **Rosati** (Italian rest.), Felix-Klein-Str. 1, ✆ 4 36 05 03, – . AE E.
closed Saturday lunch and Sunday – **M** a la carte 50/70 (booking essential).

at Düsseldorf 31-Kaiserswerth by Fischerstr. BV :

Barbarossa without rest, Niederrheinstr. 365 (B 8), ✆ 40 27 19 – wc wc. AE E
33 rm 85/145.

Haus Rittendorf without rest, Friedrich-von-Spee-Str. 44, ✆ 40 40 41 – wc
10 rm 68/130.

XXX ✿✿ **Im Schiffchen** (1733 house with beautiful facade), Kaiserswerther Markt 9 (1st floor), ✆ 40 10 50 – E
closed Sunday, Bank Holidays and 4 weeks July - August – **M** (French cuisine) a la carte 90/111 (booking essential) – **Aalschokker** (German cooking) **M** a la carte 37/67.

at Düsseldorf 30-Lohausen by Fischerstr. BV :

XX **Flughafen Grill-Restaurant**, Terminal 2 (4th floor), ✆ 4 21 60 97, ← – AE E VISA.
M a la carte 38/64.

at Düsseldorf 30-Mörsenbroich by Rethelstr. DV :

Ramada-Renaissance-Hotel M, Nördlicher Zubringer 6, ✆ 6 21 60, Massage, , – . AE E VISA. rest
M a la carte 65/75 – **250 rm** 216/412 Bb.

Merkur without rest, Mörsenbroicher Weg 49, ✆ 63 40 31 – wc wc. AE E
closed 20 December - 4 January – **28 rm** 70/170 Bb.

at Düsseldorf 11-Oberkassel by Hofgartenrampe BV :

Ramada, Am Seestern 16, ✆ 59 10 47, Telex 8585575, , – . AE E VISA. rest
M a la carte 53/82 – **222 rm** 185/335 Bb.

Rheinstern Penta-Hotel, Emanuel-Leutze-Str. 17, ✆ 5 99 70, Telex 8584242, , – rest (with). AE E VISA
M a la carte 40/72 – **182 rm** 193/311 Bb.

Hanseat without rest, Belsenstr. 6, ✆ 57 50 69 – . AE E VISA
31 rm 130/220 Bb.

Arosa without rest, Sonderburgstr. 48, ✆ 55 40 11, Telex 8582242 – wc wc . AE VISA
closed 23 December - 3 January – **32 rm** 90/180.

XXX **De' Medici** (Italian rest.), Amboßstr. 3, ✆ 59 41 51 – AE E VISA
closed Saturday lunch, Sunday and Bank Holidays except exhibitions – **M** a la carte 41/70 (booking essential for dinner).

XX **Edo** (Japanese restaurants : Teppan, Robata and Tatami), Am Seestern 3, ✆ 59 10 82, « Japanese garden » – . AE E VISA.
closed Saturday lunch – **M** a la carte 42/77.

at Düsseldorf 1-Unterbilk :

XXX **Savini** (Italian rest.), Stromstr. 47, ✆ 39 39 31 – AE
closed Saturday lunch and Sunday – **M** a la carte 52/83 (booking essential).

XX **Rheinturm Top 180**, Stromstr. 20, ✆ 8 48 58, ☀ Düsseldorf and Rhein, « Revolving restaurant at 172 m », (, 4 DM) – . AE E. BY **a**
M a la carte 39/64.

Grevenbroich 4048. Nordrhein-Westfalen 987 ㉓ – pop. 57 000 – alt. 60 m – ✆ 02181.
Düsseldorf 28.

XXX ✿✿ **Zur Traube** with rm, Bahnstr. 47, ✆ 6 87 67, remarkable wine-list – wc wc . AE E
closed 23 December - 19 January, 14 to 21 April and 2 weeks July – **M** *(closed Sunday and Monday)* a la carte 63/98 (booking essential) – **5 rm** 125/270
Spec. Parfait vom Stör mit Kaviar, Mousseline von Hummer in Champagner, Gefüllte Wachtel mit Kalbsbries in Trüffeljus.

FRANKFURT AM MAIN 6000. Hessen 413 IJ 16, 987 ㉕ – pop. 612 600 – alt. 91 m – ☎ 069.

See : Zoo*** FX – Goethe's House (Goethehaus)** and Goethemuseum* DEY **M1** – Cathedral (Dom)* (Tower**, Treasure*, Choir-stalls*) EY – Tropical Garden (Palmengarten)* CV – Senckenberg-Museum* (Palaeontology department**) CX **M8** – Städel Museum (Städelsches Kunstinstitut)** (Collection** of flemish Primitives and German Masters of the 16 C) DY **M2** – Museum of Applied Arts (Museum für Kunsthandwerk)** EY **M4** – St. Catherine's Church (Katharinenkirche) (windows*) EX **A** – Henninger Turm ※* DZ.

Rhein-Main (by ⑤ : 12 km), ☎ 6 90 25 95.

at Neu-Isenburg, ☎ (06102) 85 75.

Exhibition Centre (Messegelände) (CY), ☎ 7 57 51, Telex 411558.

Tourist Information, Main Station (Hauptbahnhof), ☎ 2 12 88 49.

Subway-Station Hauptwache, B-floor, ☎ 2 12 87 08.

ADAC, Schumannstr. 4, ☎ 7 43 00.

Wiesbaden 39 ⑤ – Bonn 176 ⑤ – Nürnberg 223 ④ – Stuttgart 205 ⑤.

Plans on following pages

The reference (F 15) at the end of the address is the postal district : Frankfurt 15

Steigenberger-Hotel Frankfurter Hof, Bethmannstr. 33 (F 16), ☎ 2 02 51, Telex 411806, – 🛗 ▤ rest TV ♿ 🏛. AE ⓓ E VISA. ⚘ rest DY **e**
M *(closed Saturday)* a la carte 40/74 – **(see also rest. français and Frankfurter Stubb)** – **400 rm** 189/430 Bb.

Hessischer Hof, Friedrich-Ebert-Anlage 40 (F 97), ☎ 7 54 00, Telex 411776, « Rest. with collection of Sèvres porcelain » – 🛗 TV P 🏛. AE ⓓ E VISA. ⚘ rest CY **p**
M a la carte 54/92 – **161 rm** 225/470.

Frankfurter Intercontinental, Wilhelm-Leuschner-Str. 43 (F 1), ☎ 23 05 61, Telex 413639, < Frankfurt, Massage, ≘s, ⊠ – 🛗 ▤ TV ♿ 🏛. ⚘ rest CY **a**
Restaurants : – **Rôtisserie** – **Brasserie** – **Bierstube** – **800 rm** Bb.

CP Frankfurt Plaza M, Hamburger Allee 2, ☎ 77 07 21, Telex 412573, < Frankfurt, ≘s – 🛗 ▤ TV ♿ 🏛. AE ⓓ E VISA. ⚘ rest CX **a**
Restaurants : – **Geheimratsstube** *(closed Sunday)* **M** a la carte 45/82 – **Bäckerei M** a la carte 29/58 – **591 rm** 237/439 Bb.

Parkhotel Frankfurt, Wiesenhüttenplatz 36 (F 1), ☎ 2 69 70, Telex 412808, Massage, ≘s – 🛗 ▤ TV 🚗 P 🏛. AE ⓓ E VISA CY **k**
Restaurants : – **La Truffe** *(closed Saturday lunch, Sunday and Bank Holidays)* **M** a la carte 57/86 – **Die Parkstube** *(regional german cooking)* **M** a la carte 40/65 – **280 rm** 279/500 Bb.

Savigny, Savignystr. 14 (F 1), ☎ 7 53 30, Telex 412061 – 🛗 TV 🏛. AE ⓓ E VISA CY **f**
M a la carte 44/72 – **122 rm** 180/320 Bb.

National, Baseler Str. 50 (F 1), ☎ 23 48 41, Telex 412570 – 🛗 TV 🏛. AE ⓓ E VISA. ⚘ rest CY **x**
M a la carte 35/60 – **95 rm** 76/230 Bb.

Imperial, Sophienstr. 40 (F 90), ☎ 7 93 00 30, Telex 4189636 – 🛗 TV ⛀wc ☎ 🚗 P. AE ⓓ E VISA CV **t**
M a la carte 38/64 – **60 rm** 148/290 Bb.

Savoy, Wiesenhüttenstr. 42 (F 16), ☎ 23 05 11, Telex 416394, Massage, ≘s, ⊠ – 🛗 ▤ rest TV ⛀wc ⋒wc ☎ 🚗 🏛. AE ⓓ E VISA. ⚘ rest CY **s**
M a la carte 53/70 – **151 rm** 165/215.

Turmhotel - Restaurant Sudpfanne, Eschersheimer Landstr. 20 (F 1), ☎ 15 40 50 – 🛗 TV ⛀wc ☎ P. AE ⓓ E VISA EX **b**
M *(closed July)* a la carte 30/55 – **75 rm** 105/183 Bb.

An der Messe without rest, Westendstr. 102 (F 1), ☎ 74 79 79, Telex 4189009 – 🛗 TV ⛀wc ⋒wc ☎ 🚗. AE ⓓ E VISA CX **e**
46 rm 160/260 Bb.

Hotel Rhein Main M, Heidelberger Str. 3 (F 1), ☎ 23 23 15, Telex 413434 – 🛗 ▤ rest TV ⛀wc ☎ P. AE ⓓ E VISA CY **b**
M *(closed Sunday)* a la carte 35/67 – **48 rm** 135/270 Bb.

Palmenhof, Bockenheimer Landstr. 89 (F 1), ☎ 75 30 06 – 🛗 ⛀wc ⋒wc ☎ 🚗 🏛
45 rm Bb. CX **m**

Arcade, Speicherstr. 3 (F 1), ☎ 27 30 30 – 🛗 ▤ TV ⋒wc ☎ ♿ P. E VISA CY **e**
M *(closed Friday and Saturday)* a la carte 24/44 – **193 rm** 90/140 Bb.

Continental, Baseler Str. 56 (F 1), ☎ 23 03 41, Telex 412502 – 🛗 TV ⛀wc ⋒wc ☎ 🏛. AE ⓓ E VISA. ⚘ CY **y**
M *(closed Sunday and Bank Holidays)* a la carte 34/52 – **80 rm** 105/180.

Mozart without rest, Parkstr. 17 (F 1), ☎ 55 08 31 – 🛗 TV ⛀wc ⋒wc ☎. AE ⓓ VISA
closed 22 December - 2 January – **35 rm** 115/185. CV **p**

Falk without rest, Falkstr. 38a (F 90), ☎ 70 80 94 – 🛗 ⛀wc ⋒wc ☎ P 🏛 CV **n**
closed 22 December - 2 January – **32 rm** 90/165.

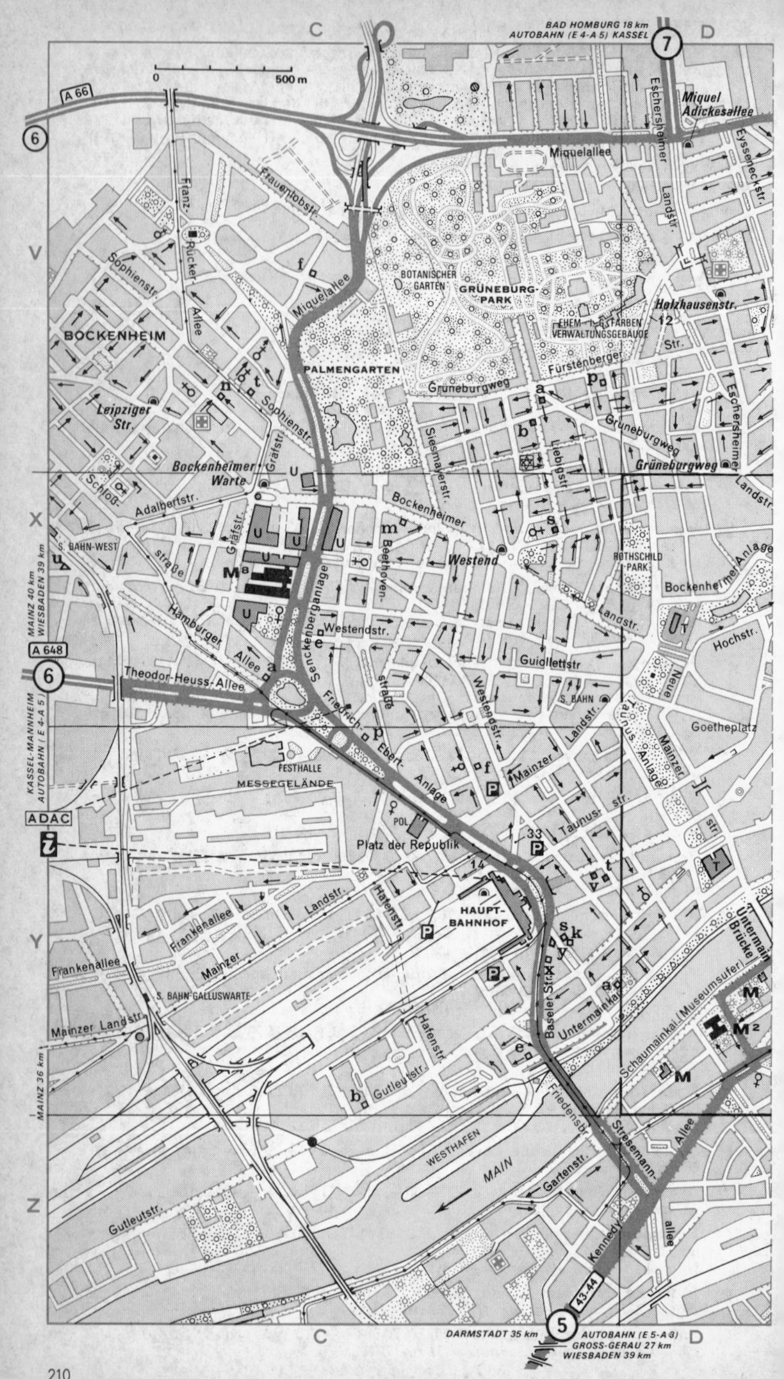
BAD HOMBURG 18 km
AUTOBAHN (E 4-A 5) KASSEL
A 66
BOCKENHEIM
Leipziger Str.
Bockenheimer Warte
BOTANISCHER GARTEN
GRÜNEBURG-PARK
PALMENGARTEN
Miquel Adickesallee
Miquelallee
Holzhausenstr.
EHEM. I.G. FARBEN VERWALTUNGSGEBÄUDE
Westend
ROTHSCHILD PARK
Grüneburgweg
Bockenheimer Anlage
Goetheplatz
Theodor-Heuss-Allee
FESTHALLE
MESSEGELÄNDE
Platz der Republik
HAUPT-BAHNHOF
ADAC
S. BAHN-WEST
S. BAHN-GALLUSWARTE
WESTHAFEN
MAIN
Untermain Brücke
Schaumainkai (Museumsufer)
Stresemann-Allee
Kennedy-allee
MAINZ 40 km
WIESBADEN 39 km
A 648
KASSEL-MANNHEIM
AUTOBAHN (E 4-A 5)
MAINZ 36 km
DARMSTADT 35 km
AUTOBAHN (E 5-A 5)
GROSS-GERAU 27 km
WIESBADEN 39 km

FRANKFURT AM MAIN

Alfred-Brehm-Platz	FX	2
Arnsburger Straße	FV	4
Bärenstraße	FX	6
Bremer Straße	DV	10
Düsseldorfer Straße	CY	14
Flößerbrücke	FY	17
Karlstraße	CY	33
Neebstraße	FV	42
Obermainbrücke	FY	45
Pfingstweidstraße	FX	47
Seehofstraße	FY	54
Siemensstraße	FY	56
Wasserweg	FY	67
Windeckstraße	FY	74

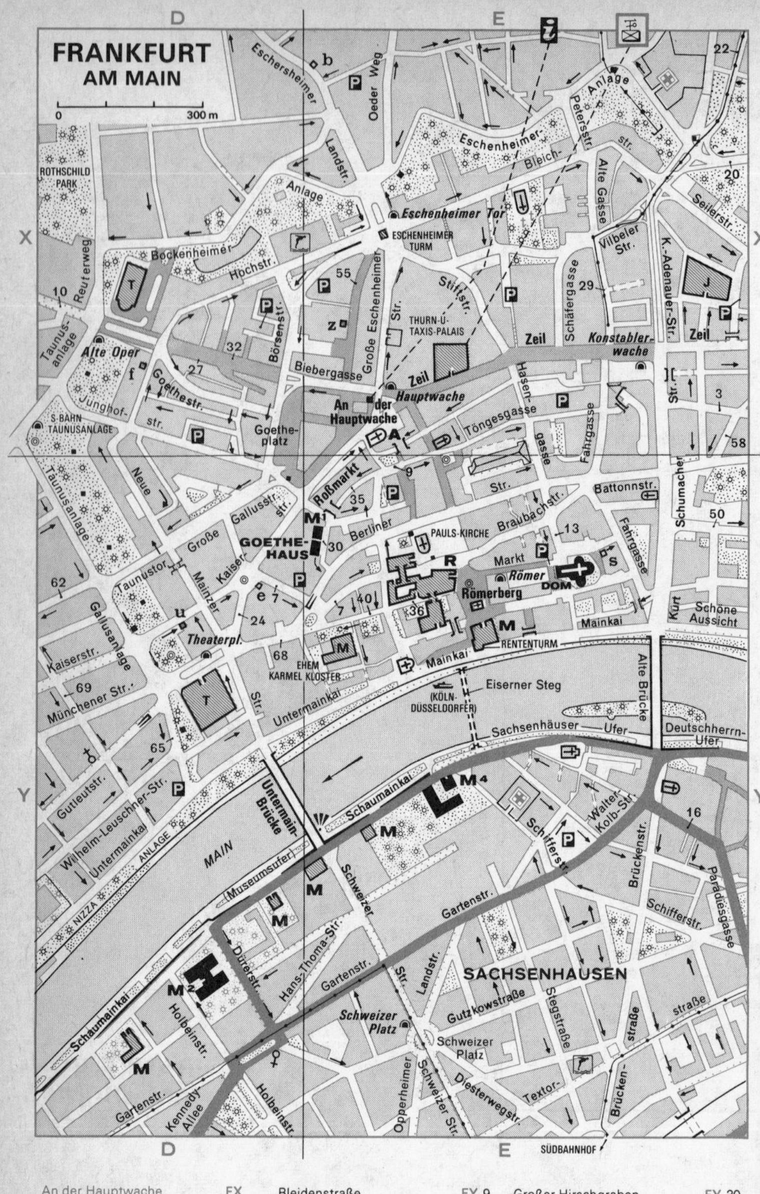

An der Hauptwache .... EX
Goethestraße .... DX
Gr. Bockenheimer Straße .... DX 27
Kaiserstraße .... DY
Münchener Straße .... DY
Roßmarkt .... EY
Schillerstraße .... EX 55
Zeil .... EX

Allerheiligenstraße .... EX 3
Bethmannstraße .... DY 7
Bleidenstraße .... EY 9
Bockenheimer Landstraße .... DX 10
Domstraße .... EY 13
Elisabethenstraße .... EY 16
Friedberger Anlage .... EX 20
Friedberger Landstraße .... EX 22
Friedensstraße .... DY 24
Große Friedberger Straße .... EX 29
Großer Hirschgraben .... EY 30
Kalbächer Gasse .... DX 32
Kleiner Hirschgraben .... EY 35
Limpurgergasse .... EY 36
Münzgasse .... EY 40
Rechneigrabenstr. .... EY 50
Stolzestraße .... EX 58
Taunusstraße .... DY 62
Untermainanlage .... DY 65
Weißfravenstraße .... DY 68
Weserstraße .... DY 69

Jaguar without rest, Theobald-Christ-Str. 19 (F 1), ✆ 43 93 01 – 37 rm. FX y

Am Zoo, Alfred-Brehm-Platz 6 (F 1), ✆ 49 07 71, Telex 4170082 – AE E VISA FX q
M *(dinner only, closed Sunday)* a la carte 25/47 – **85 rm** 79/125 Bb.

Tatra without rest, Kreuznacher Str. 37 (F 90), ✆ 77 20 71 – AE E VISA. CX u
closed 24 December - 4 January – **25 rm** 95/180 Bb.

Am Dom without rest, Kannengießergasse 3 (F 1), ✆ 28 21 41, Telex 414955 – E EY s
closed 24 December - 2 January – **30 rm** 100/210 Bb.

Admiral without rest, Hölderlinstr. 25 (F 1), ✆ 44 80 21 – AE E FX w
47 rm 75/140.

XXXX ✿ **Restaurant Français**, Bethmannstr. 33 (at Steigenberger-H. Frankfurter Hof) (F 16), ✆ 2 02 51 – AE E VISA. DY e
closed 4 weeks July - August, Sunday and Bank Holidays – **M** a la carte 57/100 (booking essential)
Spec. Hummer mit grünen Bohnenkernen, Geräucherter Wolfsbarsch mit Austern in Gurkencreme, Pochiertes Rinderfilet.

XXX **Weinhaus Brückenkeller**, Schützenstr. 6 (F 1), ✆ 28 42 38, « Old vaulted cellar with precious antiques » – AE E VISA FY a
closed Sunday and Bank Holidays except exhibitions – **M** (dinner only) a la carte 63/110 (booking essential).

XXX **Mövenpick - Baron de la Mouette**, Opernplatz 2 (F 1), ✆ 2 06 80, – AE E VISA – **M** a la carte 40/76 – **Orangerie M** a la carte 31/50 DX f

XXX **Das Restaurant im Union-International Club**, Am Leonhardsbrunn 12 (F 90), ✆ 70 30 33 – AE E VISA. CV f
closed Saturday, Sunday lunch and 10 to 31 July – **M** a la carte 44/75.

XXX ✿ **Humperdinck**, Grüneburgweg 95 (F 1), ✆ 72 21 22 – AE E VISA CV a
closed Saturday lunch, Sunday and 3 weeks June - July – **M** a la carte 68/91
Spec. Gefüllter Zander auf Petersiliensabayon, Pochierter Lammrücken auf Lauchstreifen, Pfirsichkrapfen mit Wodkasauce und Himbeersorbet.

XXX **Tse-Yang** (Chinese rest.), Kaiserstr. 67 (F 1), ✆ 23 25 41 – AE E VISA CY v
M a la carte 32/62.

XX **Le Midi**, Liebigstr. 47 (F 1), ✆ 72 14 38, – AE E VISA CV b
closed Saturday lunch, Sunday and 2 weeks August – **M** a la carte 72/96.

XX **Da Bruno** (Italian rest.), Elbestr. 15 (F 1), ✆ 23 34 16 – AE E CY t
closed Sunday, Bank Holidays and mid July - mid August – **M** a la carte 48/65.

XX Frankfurter Stubb (Rest. in the vaulted cellar of Hotel Frankfurter Hof), Bethmannstr. 33 (F 16), ✆ 21 56 79 – DY e
(booking essential).

XX **La Galleria** (Italian rest.), Theaterplatz 2 (BFG-Haus) (F 1), ✆ 23 56 80 – AE E VISA – *closed Sunday* – **M** a la carte 49/78 (booking essential) DY u

XX **Firenze** (Italian rest.), Berger Str. 30 (F 1), ✆ 43 39 56 – AE E. FX s
closed Monday except exhibitions – **M** a la carte 41/72 (booking essential).

XX Börsenkeller, Schillerstr. 11 (F 1), ✆ 28 11 15 – EX z

X **Ernos Bistro** (French rest.), Liebigstr. 15 (F 1), ✆ 72 19 97, – AE E VISA CX s
closed Saturday and Sunday except exhibitions and 15 June - 12 July – **M** a la carte 69/93 (booking essential).

at Frankfurt 80-Griesheim by ⑥ :

Ramada-Caravelle, Oeserstr. 180, ✆ 3 90 50, Telex 416812, – rest AE E VISA
M a la carte 49/76 – **236 rm** 170/331 Bb.

at Frankfurt 71-Niederrad by ⑤ :

Arabella-Hotel Frankfurt, Lyoner Str. 44, ✆ 6 63 30, Telex 416760, – AE E VISA. rest
M a la carte 40/68 – **400 rm** 175/280 Bb.

Crest-Hotel Frankfurt, Isenburger Schneise 40, ✆ 6 78 40, Telex 416717 – AE E VISA
M a la carte 43/72 – **283 rm** 208/318 Bb.

XX **Weidemann**, Kelsterbacher Str. 66, ✆ 67 59 96, – AE E VISA
closed lunch Saturday, Sunday and Bank Holidays – **M** a la carte 59/80 (booking essential).

at Frankfurt 70 - Sachsenhausen :

Holiday Inn-City Tower M, Mailänder Str. 1, ✆ 6 80 20, Telex 411805, – AE E VISA. by ④
Restaurants : – **Le Ballon M** a la carte 38/71 – **Kaffeemühle M** a la carte 31/62 – **405 rm** 228/328 Bb.

Mühlberg without rest, Offenbacher Landstr. 56, ✆ 61 30 63 – wc. AE ⓓ
closed end December - beginning January – **69 rm** 55/140. FY **h**

XX **Bistrot 77** (modern Bistro), Ziegelhüttenweg 1, ✆ 61 40 40, – AE ⓓ E EZ **a**
closed Saturday lunch, Sunday and 15 June - 7 July – **M** a la carte 63/95.

X **Henninger Turm - Museums Stubb** (DM 3), Hainer Weg 60, ✆ 6 06 36 00, ← Frankfurt, « Revolving rest. at 101 m » – FZ
closed Monday – **M** a la carte 23/52.

at Eschborn **6236** NW : 12 km :

Novotel, Philipp-Helfmann-Str. 10, ✆ (06196) 4 28 12, Telex 4072842, , (heated), – wc. AE ⓓ E by A 66 CV
M a la carte 28/45 – **227 rm** 143/187 Bb.

near Main-Taunus-Einkaufszentrum W : 14 km by ⑥ :

Holiday Inn, Am Main-Taunus-Zentrum 1, ✉ 6231 Sulzbach, ✆ (06196) 78 78, Telex 4072536, , – . AE ⓓ E VISA
M a la carte 37/64 – **291 rm** 180/240 Bb.

at Neu-Isenburg 2-Gravenbruch **6078** SE : 11 km by ④ :

Gravenbruch-Kempinski-Frankfurt M, ✆ (06102) 50 50, Telex 417673, , « Park », Massage, , (heated), , , – . AE ⓓ E VISA. rest
M *(see also* **Gourmet-Restaurant below)** a la carte 45/82 – **317 rm** 273/411 Bb.

XXXX ✿ **Gourmet-Restaurant** (at hotel Gravenbruch-Kempinski), ✆ (06102) 50 50 – . AE ⓓ E VISA.
closed Saturday, Sunday, Bank Holidays except exhibitions and 4 weeks June - July – **M** (dinner only) a la carte 65/120 (booking essential)
Spec. Hummerragout mit Nudeln, Pot au feu vom Petersfisch, Getrüffelte Perlhuhnbrust.

near Rhein-Main airport SW : 12 km by ⑤ (near motorway Flughafen exit) – ✉ **6000** Frankfurt 75 – ☎ 069 :

Sheraton M, Am Flughafen (Terminal Mitte), ✆ 6 97 70, Telex 4189294, , – . AE ⓓ E VISA. rest
Restaurants : – **Papillon** *(closed lunch Saturday, Sunday and Bank Holidays)* **M** a la carte 57/100 – **Maxwell's Bistro M** a la carte 40/70 – **Taverne** *(closed Saturday and Sunday)* **M** a la carte 30/60 – **819 rm** 281/431 Bb.

Steigenberger Airporthotel - Restaurant Pergola, Unterschweinstiege 16, ✆ 6 98 51, Telex 413112, , , free shuttle-service to the airport – . AE ⓓ E VISA
M a la carte 31/57 – **350 rm** 188/348 Bb.

XXX **Rôtisserie 5 Continents**, in the Airport, Ankunft Ausland B (Besucherhalle, Ebene 3), ✆ 6 90 34 44, ← – . AE ⓓ E VISA
M a la carte 47/78.

XX **Waldrestaurant Unterschweinstiege**, Unterschweinstiege 16, ✆ 69 25 03, « Terrace, country house atmosphere » – . AE ⓓ E VISA
M a la carte 44/74 (booking essential for buffet lunch).

on the road from Neu-Isenburg to Götzenhain by ④ : 13 km by A 661 and motorway-exit Dreieich :

XXX **Gutsschänke Neuhof**, ✉ 6072 Dreieich-Götzenhain, ✆ (06102) 32 14, « Country house atmosphere, terrace » – . AE ⓓ E VISA
M a la carte 33/74.

at Maintal **6457** by ② : 13 km :

XXX ✿ **Hessler**, Am Bootshafen 4 (Dörnigheim), ✆ (06181) 49 29 51 – .
closed Sunday, Monday and 3 weeks July - August – **M** (dinner only) a la carte 52/96 (booking essential) – **Bistro Junior** *(closed lunch Saturday and Sunday, Monday and 3 weeks July - August)* **M** a la carte 43/60
Spec. Rotbarbe in Tomaten-Basilikum-Vinaigrette, Taube auf Grünkernrisotto mit Trüffelsauce, Dreierlei von Mousse au chocolat.

Wertheim

6980. Baden-Württemberg **987** ㉕ – pop. 20 000 – alt. 142 m – ☎ 09342.
Frankfurt am Main 87.

XXXX ✿✿ **Schweizer Stuben** with rm, at Wertheim-Bettingen (E : 10 km), Geiselbrunnweg 11, ✆ 43 51, Telex 689123, ←, , , , , (indoor) – wc wc . ⓓ
closed 1 to 29 January – **M** *(closed Monday and Tuesday until 7pm)* a la carte 98/135 (remarkable wine-list, booking essential) – **16 rm** 155/350
Spec. Gugelhupf von Gänsestopfleber mit Weinbeerensauce, Goujonette von Seezunge und Krebsen, Topfengratin mit Vanilleeis und Früchten.

HAMBURG 2000. Hamburg 987 ⑤ – pop. 1 640 000 – alt. 10 m – ☎ 040.

See : Jungfernstieg★ DY – Außenalster★★★ (trip by boat★★★) EX – Hagenbeck Zoo (Tierpark Hagenbeck)★★ – Television Tower (Fernsehturm)★ (※★★) BX – Art Gallery (Kunsthalle)★★ (19C German painting) EY M1 – St. Michael's church (St. Michaelis)★ (tower ※★) BZ – Stintfang (≤★) BZ – Port (Hafen)★★ BZ.

✈ Hamburg-Fuhlsbüttel (N : 15 km), ✆ 50 80, City-Centre Airport (Air Terminal at Z0B FY), Brockesstraße, ✆ 50 85 57.

🚗 ✆ 39 18 65 56.

Exhibition Centre (Messegelände) (BX), ✆ 3 56 91, Telex 212609.

ℹ Tourist-Information, Hachmannplatz 1, ✆ 24 87 00, Telex 2163036.

ℹ Tourist-Information at the airport (Halle D), ✆ 24 87 02 40.

ADAC, Amsinckstr. 39 (H 1), ✆ 2 39 91.

Berlin 297 – Bremen 120 – Hannover 152.

Plan on following pages

The reference (H 15) at the end of the address is the postal district : Hamburg 15

near Hauptbahnhof, at St. Georg, east of the Außenalster :

Atlantic-Hotel Kempinski, An der Alster 72 (H 1), ✆ 24 80 01, Telex 2163297, ≤ Außenalster, Massage, ≘s, 🏊 – |$| ▤ rest TV 🚗 P 🅰 (with ▤). AE ⓓ E VISA. ✗ rest — EX a
M a la carte 61/100 – **300 rm** 280/420.

Europäischer Hof, Kirchenallee 45 (H 1), ✆ 24 81 71, Telex 2162493 – |$| ▤ rest TV 🚗 🅰 (with ▤). AE ⓓ E VISA — FY e
Restaurants : – **Hamburg-Restaurant M** a la carte 30/69 – **Bürgerstube M** a la carte 25/52 – **350 rm** 118/268 Bb.

Berlin, Borgfelder Str. 1 (H 26), ✆ 25 16 40, Telex 213939 – |$| ▤ rest TV 🚗 P 🅰 (with ▤). AE ⓓ E VISA. ✗ rest — by Kurt-Schumacher-Allee FY
M a la carte 45/59 – **93 rm** 115/180 Bb.

Reichshof, Kirchenallee 34 (H 1), ✆ 24 83 30, Telex 2163396 – |$| TV 🚗 🅰. AE ⓓ E VISA. ✗ rest — FY d
M a la carte 35/82 – **310 rm** 150/270 Bb.

Prem-Restaurant La Mer, An der Alster 9 (H 1), ✆ 24 54 54, Telex 2163115, « Garden » – |$| TV. AE ⓓ E VISA. ✗ rest — FX c
M *(Saturday and Sunday dinner only)* a la carte 63/85 – **48 rm** 145/290 Bb.

Ambassador, Heidenkampsweg 34 (H 1), ✆ 23 00 02, Telex 2166100, ≘s, 🏊 – |$| TV ⌂wc ☎ 🚗 P 🅰. AE ⓓ VISA
M a la carte 36/62 – **124 rm** 98/210 Bb.

Fürst Bismarck without rest, Kirchenallee 49 (H 1), ✆ 2 80 10 91, Telex 2162980 – |$| TV ⌂wc ⋒wc ☎. AE ⓓ E VISA — FY x
59 rm 80/145.

Senator, Lange Reihe 18 (H 1), ✆ 24 12 03, Telex 2174002 – |$| TV ⌂wc ⋒wc ☎ P. AE ⓓ E VISA — FY u
M (only dinner for residents) – **56 rm** 128/176 Bb.

St. Raphael, Adenauer-Allee 41 (H 1), ✆ 24 11 91, Telex 2174733 – |$| TV ⋒wc ☎ P 🅰. ✗ rest — FY m
M a la carte 27/53 – **120 rm** 105/180 Bb.

Kronprinz without rest, Kirchenallee 46 (H 1), ✆ 24 32 58, Telex 2161005 – |$| TV ⌂wc ⋒wc ☎. AE ⓓ E VISA. ✗ — FY e
73 rm 95/145 Bb.

Bellevue, An der Alster 14 (H 1), ✆ 24 80 11, Telex 2162929 – |$| ⌂wc ⋒wc ☎ P. AE ⓓ E VISA — FX t
M *(closed Saturday and Sunday July - August)* a la carte 36/68 – **80 rm** 114/200 Bb.

Aussen Alster, Schmilingskystr. 11 (H 1), ✆ 24 15 57, ≘s – |$| TV ⌂wc ⋒wc ☎. AE ⓓ E VISA — FX e
M a la carte 35/85 – **27 rm** 130/190.

Alte Wache, Adenauer-Allee 25 (H 1), ✆ 24 12 91, Telex 2162254 – |$| TV ⋒wc ☎ P 🅰
closed 24 December - 2 January – **M** (only dinner for residents) – **72 rm** 98/150. — FY s

Dänischer Hof, Holzdamm 4 (H 1), ✆ 24 55 56, Telex 2162760 – |$| ⌂wc ⋒wc ☎ P. AE ⓓ E VISA — EXY d
M (rest. for residents only) – **44 rm** 80/160.

XX **Peter Lembcke**, Holzdamm 49 (H 1), ✆ 24 32 90 – AE ⓓ E — FY t
closed Sunday, mid July - beginning August and Bank Holidays – **M** a la carte 46/81.

at Binnenalster, Altstadt, Neustadt :

✿ **Vier Jahreszeiten - Restaurant Haerlin**, Neuer Jungfernstieg 9 (H 36), ✆ 3 49 41, Telex 211629, ≤ Binnenalster – |$| TV 🚗 🅰. AE ⓓ E VISA. ✗ — DY v
M a la carte 66/100 – **175 rm** 250/516
Spec. Royal von Langustinen auf Dillsauce, Lammpiccata auf Artischocken, Limonen - Parfait in Schokoladenblättern.

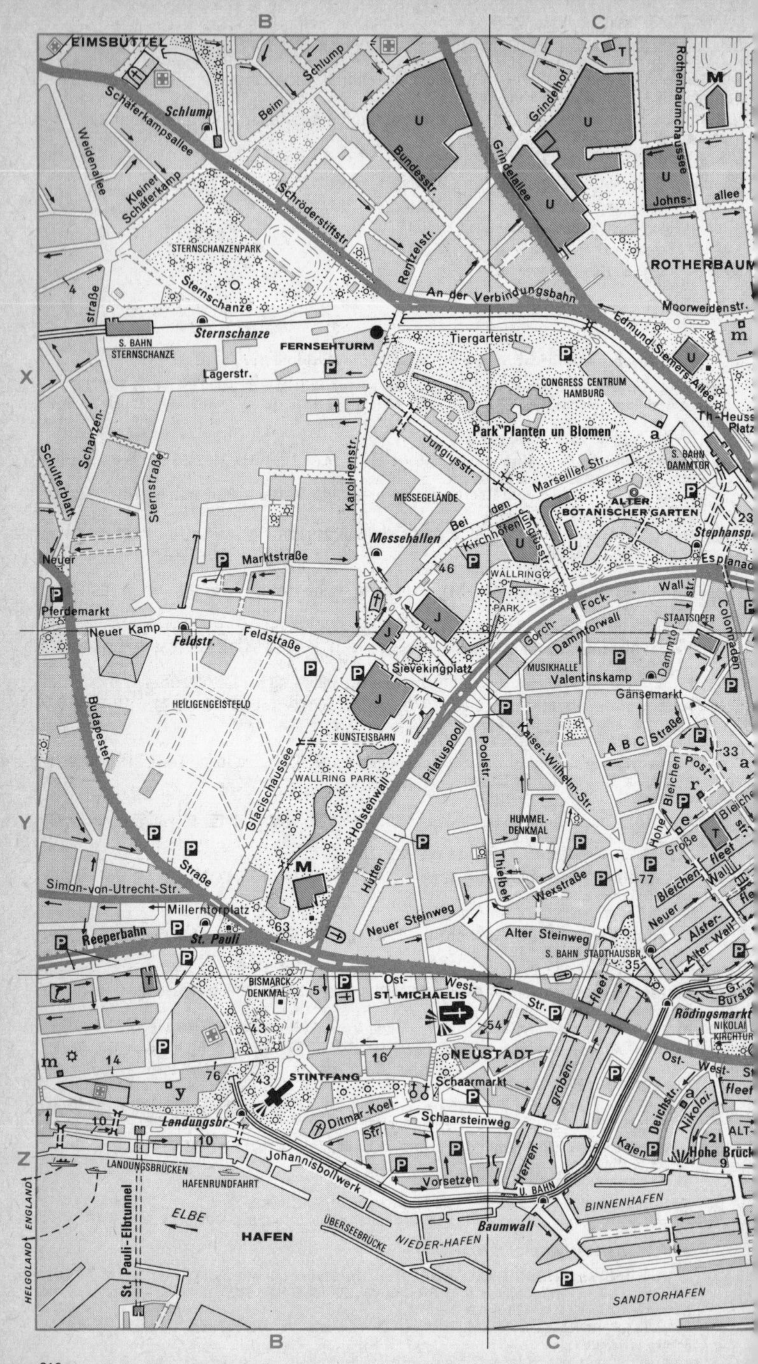
B
C
EIMSBÜTTEL
Schlump
Schäferkampsallee
Weidenallee
Kleiner Schäferkamp
Beim Schlump
Schröderstiftstr.
Bundesstr.
Rentzelstr.
Grindelhof
Grindelallee
Rothenbaumchaussee
Johnsallee
ROTHERBAUM
STERNSCHANZENPARK
Sternschanze
An der Verbindungsbahn
Moorweidenstr.
Edmund-Siemers-Allee
S. BAHN STERNSCHANZE
FERNSEHTURM
Tiergartenstr.
X
Lagerstr.
CONGRESS CENTRUM HAMBURG
Th.-Heuss-Platz
Park "Planten un Blomen"
Schanzenstr.
Schulterblatt
Sternstraße
Karolinenstr.
Jungiusstr.
MESSEGELÄNDE
Marseiller Str.
S. BAHN DAMMTOR
ALTER BOTANISCHER GARTEN
Stephansplatz
Messehallen
Bei den Kirchhöfen
Jungiusstr.
WALLRINGPARK
Esplanade
Neuer Pferdemarkt
Marktstraße
Wall
Fock
Gorch-
Dammtorwall
Dammtorstr.
STAATSOPER
Colonnaden
Neuer Kamp
Feldstr.
Feldstraße
Sievekingplatz
MUSIKHALLE
Valentinskamp
Gänsemarkt
HEILIGENGEISTFELD
KUNSTEISBAHN
Poolstr.
Kaiser-Wilhelm-Str.
ABC Straße
Budapester Straße
Glacischaussee
WALLRING PARK
Holstenwall
Pilatuspool
Post-
Hohe Bleichen
Y
HUMMEL-DENKMAL
Große Bleichen
Bleichenfleet
Thielbek
Wexstraße
Hütten
Simon-von-Utrecht-Str.
Millerntorplatz
Neuer Steinweg
Alter Steinweg
Neuer Wall
Alsterfleet
Alter Wall
Reeperbahn
St. Pauli
S. BAHN STADTHAUSBR.
BISMARCK DENKMAL
Ost-West-Str.
ST. MICHAELIS
Gr. Burstah
Rödingsmarkt
NIKOLAI KIRCHTURM
NEUSTADT
Herrengrabenfleet
STINTFANG
Schaarmarkt
Ost-West-Str.
Nikolaifleet
Ditmar-Koel-Str.
Schaarsteinweg
Deichstr.
Landungsbr.
Kajen
Hohe Brücke
ALT-
Z
LANDUNGSBRÜCKEN
HAFENRUNDFAHRT
Johannisbollwerk
Vorsetzen
U. BAHN
Baumwall
BINNENHAFEN
ELBE
HAFEN
ÜBERSEEBRÜCKE
NIEDER-HAFEN
HELGOLAND
ENGLAND
St. Pauli-Elbtunnel
SANDTORHAFEN
B
C

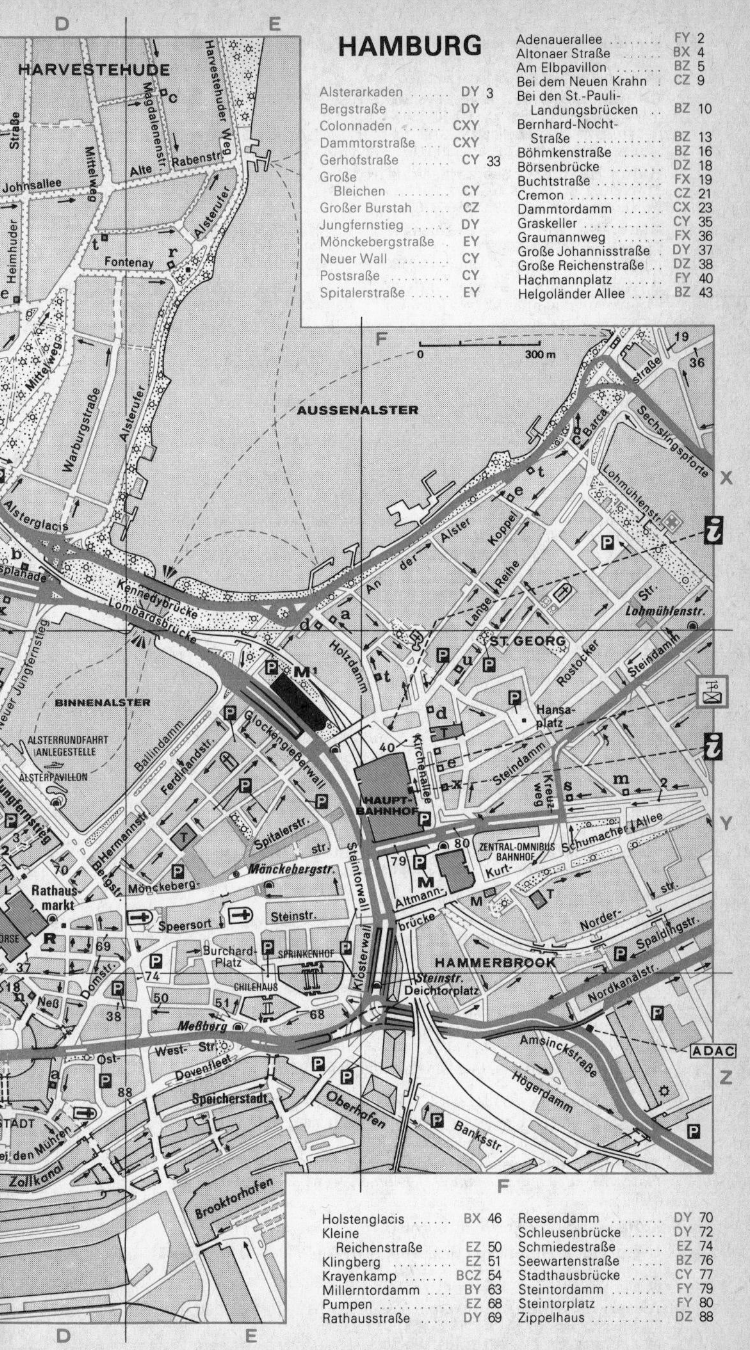
HAMBURG
Alsterarkaden DY 3
Bergstraße DY
Colonnaden CXY
Dammtorstraße CXY
Gerhofstraße CY 33
Große Bleichen CY
Großer Burstah CZ
Jungfernstieg DY
Mönckebergstraße EY
Neuer Wall CY
Postsraße CY
Spitalerstraße EY
Adenauerallee FY 2
Altonaer Straße BX 4
Am Elbpavillon BZ 5
Bei dem Neuen Krahn CZ 9
Bei den St.-Pauli-Landungsbrücken BZ 10
Bernhard-Nocht-Straße BZ 13
Böhmkenstraße BZ 16
Börsenbrücke DZ 18
Buchtstraße FX 19
Cremon CZ 21
Dammtordamm CX 23
Graskeller CY 35
Graumannweg FX 36
Große Johannisstraße DY 37
Große Reichenstraße DZ 38
Hachmannplatz FY 40
Helgoländer Allee BZ 43
Holstenglacis BX 46
Kleine Reichenstraße EZ 50
Klingberg EZ 51
Krayenkamp BCZ 54
Millerntordamm BY 63
Pumpen EZ 68
Rathausstraße DY 69
Reesendamm DY 70
Schleusenbrücke DY 72
Schmiedestraße EZ 74
Seewartenstraße BZ 76
Stadthausbrücke CY 77
Steintordamm FY 79
Steintorplatz FY 80
Zippelhaus DZ 88
HARVESTEHUDE
AUSSENALSTER
BINNENALSTER
ALSTERRUNDFAHRT ANLEGESTELLE
ALSTERPAVILLON
ST. GEORG
HAUPT-BAHNHOF
ZENTRAL-OMNIBUS BAHNHOF
HAMMERBROOK
Rathausmarkt
SPRINKENHOF
CHILEHAUS
Speicherstadt
Brooktorhafen
Zollkanal
Oberhafen
Deichtorplatz
Hansa-platz
ADAC
0 300 m

Ramada Renaissance Hotel M, Große Bleichen (H 36), ☎ 34 91 80, Massage, ≘s – |♦| ▤ TV ♿ P 🏛. AE ⦿ E VISA. ✻ rest CY **e**
M a la carte 49/87 – **211 rm** 282/385 Bb.

CP Hamburg Plaza, Marseiller Str. 2 (H 36), ☎ 3 50 20, Telex 214400, ≤ Hamburg, ≘s, ⛆ – |♦| ▤ TV ♿ 🚗 🏛. AE ⦿ E VISA. ✻ rest CX **a**
Restaurants : – **Englischer Grill** *(dinner only, closed Sunday)* **M** a la carte 44/80 – **Vierländerstube M** a la carte 35/60 – **570 rm** 200/340 Bb.

Hafen Hamburg, Seewartenstr. 9 (H 11), ☎ 31 11 30, Telex 2161319, ≤ – |♦| ⌂wc ⋔wc ☎ P 🏛. AE ⦿ E VISA BZ **y**
M a la carte 40/75 – **190 rm** 95/160 Bb.

Alster-Hof without rest, Esplanade 12 (H 36), ☎ 35 00 70, Telex 213843 – |♦| TV ⌂wc ⋔wc ☎ 🏛. AE ⦿ E VISA DX **x**
closed 22 December - 4 January – **120 rm** 110/190.

Baseler Hospiz, Esplanade 11 (H 36), ☎ 34 19 21, Telex 2163707 – |♦| ⌂wc ⋔wc ☎ 🏛
M *(closed Sunday and Bank Holidays)* a la carte 24/47 ♁ – **160 rm** 60/140. DX **x**

XXX **Zum alten Rathaus** (with entertainment-rest. Fleetenkieker), Börsenbrücke 10 (H 11), ☎ 36 75 70 DZ **n**
closed Saturday except dinner September - April and Sunday – **M** a la carte 47/75 (booking essential).

XXX **Ehmke**, Grimm 14 (H 11), ☎ 32 71 32 – AE ⦿ E VISA. ✻ DZ **a**
closed Saturday lunch and Sunday – **M** a la carte 36/72.

XXX Ratsweinkeller, Gr. Johannisstr. 2 (H 11), ☎ 36 41 53, « 1896 Hanseatic rest. » – 🏛 DY **R**

XX **Deichgraf**, Deichstr. 23 (H 11), ☎ 36 42 08 – AE ⦿ E VISA CZ **a**
closed Sunday – **M** a la carte 37/85 (booking essential).

XX **Mövenpick - Café des Artistes**, Große Bleichen 36 (ground-floor, |♦|) (H 36), ☎ 35 16 35 – AE ⦿ E VISA CY **r**
M a la carte 39/66 – **Mövenpick-Restaurant M** a la carte 27/55.

XX **Schümann's Austernkeller**, Jungfernstieg 34 (H 36), ☎ 34 62 65, « Rest. from the turn of the century with private dining rooms » – ✻ CY **a**
closed Sunday and Bank Holidays – **M** a la carte 46/118.

XX Restaurant im Finnlandhaus, Esplanade 41 (12th floor, |♦|) (H 36), ☎ 34 41 33, ≤ Hamburg, Binnen- and Außenalster – ▤. ✻ DX **b**

at Hamburg-Altona by Reeperbahn BY :

Raphael Hotel Altona, Präsident-Krahn-Str. 13 (H 50), ☎ 38 12 39 – |♦| ⋔wc ☎ P. AE ⦿ E. ✻ rest
M *(dinner only, closed Saturday and Sunday)* a la carte 25/38 – **54 rm** 58/145 Bb.

XXXX ✿ **Landhaus Scherrer**, Elbchaussee 130 (H 50), ☎ 8 80 13 25 – P. AE ⦿ E
closed Sunday, Bank Holidays and July – **M** a la carte 65/110 (booking essential) – **Bistro-Rest.** *(lunch only)* **M** a la carte 47/70
Spec. Geräucherter Steinbeißer auf Rote Beete-Sauce, Kalbskopf auf Auberginen mit Olivensauce, Roulade von Lachs und Zander im Mangoldblatt.

XXX **Fischereihafen-Restaurant Hamburg**, Große Elbstr. 143 (H 50), ☎ 38 18 16, ≤ – P. ⦿ E – **M** a la carte 37/93 (booking essential).

at Hamburg-Billstedt by Nordkanalstr. FZ :

Panorama M without rest, Billstedter Hauptstr. 44 (H 74), ☎ 73 17 01, Telex 212162, ⛆ – |♦| TV 🚗 P 🏛. AE ⦿ E VISA. ✻
closed 24 December - 2 January – **111 rm** 150/250 Bb.

at Hamburg-Blankenese W : 16 km by Reeperbahn BY :

Strandhotel ⛱, Strandweg 13 (H 55), ☎ 86 09 93, ≤, 🌳, « Villa with elegant installation, painting collection », ≘s, 🌳 – TV ⌂wc ⋔wc ☎ P. AE ⦿ E VISA
M *(closed Sunday dinner and Monday)* a la carte 42/76 – **13 rm** 128/366 Bb.

XXX **Sagebiels Fährhaus**, Blankeneser Hauptstr. 107 (H 55), ☎ 86 15 14, « Garden with ≤ » – P. AE ⦿ E VISA
closed Monday October - March – **M** a la carte 39/75.

XXX **Süllberg**, Süllbergsterrasse 2 (H 55), ☎ 86 16 86, « Terraced garden with ≤ » – P 🏛. AE ⦿ E VISA – **M** a la carte 43/76.

X **Strandhof** (Bistro-rest.), Strandweg 27 (H 55), ☎ 86 52 36, ≤, 🌳 – AE ⦿
closed Monday and 2 January - 1 February – **M** (dinner only Tuesday - Friday) a la carte 61/80.

at Hamburg-City North by Buchtstr. FX :

Crest-Hotel Hamburg, Mexicoring 1 (H 60), ☎ 6 30 50 51, Telex 2174155 – |♦| ▤ rest TV 🚗 P 🏛 (with ▤). AE ⦿ E VISA. ✻ rest
M a la carte 34/60 – **185 rm** 171/264 Bb.

Alsterkrug-Hotel, Alsterkrugchaussee 277 (H 60), ☎ 51 30 30, Telex 2173828, ≘s – |♦| TV ⋔wc ☎ 🚗 P 🏛. AE ⦿ E VISA. ✻ rest
M a la carte 38/57 – **80 rm** 134/195 Bb.

at Hamburg-Eppendorf by Grindelallee CX :

XXX ✿ **Le Canard**, Martinistr. 11 (H 20), ✆ 4 60 48 30 – AE ⓓ. ✻
closed Sunday – **M** a la carte 86/113 (booking essential)
Spec. Hummersalat, Champagnersuppe, Taubenbrust mit Weißkraut.

XX **Fisch Sellmer** (mainly seafood), Ludolfstr. 50 (H 20), ✆ 47 30 57 – Ⓟ. AE. ✻
M a la carte 39/80.

at Hamburg-Harvestehude :

Inter-Continental, Fontenay 10 (H 36), ✆ 41 41 50, Telex 211099, ≤ Hamburg and Alster, , Massage, , – | ♿ Ⓟ . AE ⓓ E VISA. ✻ rest EX r
Restaurants : – **Fontenay-Grill** *(closed Saturday lunch)* **M** a la carte 59/96 – **Hulk-Brasserie** *(buffet lunch)* **M** a la carte 40/60 – **300 rm** 262/353 Bb.

Smolka, Isestr. 98 (H 13), ✆ 47 50 50, Telex 215275 – | . AE ⓓ E VISA. ✻ rest
M *(closed Saturday dinner, Sunday and Bank Holidays)* a la carte 32/63 – **40 rm** 105/215 Bb. by Rothenbaumchaussee CX

Garden-Hotel Pöseldorf without rest, Magdalenenstr. 60 (H 13), ✆ 44 99 59, Telex 212621, « Elegantly furnished », – | wc wc ☎. AE ⓓ E VISA EX c
70 rm 133/306.

Mittelweg without rest, Mittelweg 59 (H 13), ✆ 45 32 51, Telex 2165663 – wc wc ☎ Ⓟ by Mittelweg DX
38 rm 97/174.

Abtei without rest, Abteistr. 14 (H 13), ✆ 44 29 05, Telex 2165645 – wc wc ☎. AE ⓓ E VISA by Rothenbaumchaussee CX
closed 24 December - 6 January – **14 rm** 115/230 – 4 apartments 180/250.

XX **La vite** (Italian rest.), Heimhuder Str. 5 (H 13), ✆ 45 84 01, DX e
M a la carte 44/61 (booking essential).

XX **Daitokai** (Japanese rest.), Milchstr. 1 (H 13), ✆ 4 10 10 61 – . AE ⓓ E VISA. ✻
closed Sunday – **M** a la carte 36/68 (booking essential). by Mittelweg DX

XX **Osteria Martini** (Italian rest.), Badestr. 4 (H 13), ✆ 4 10 16 51 – AE ⓓ E VISA. ✻
M a la carte 40/60 (booking essential). DX t

at Hamburg-Nienstedten W : 13 km by Reeperbahn BY :

XXX **Jacob** with rm, Elbchaussee 401 (H 52), ✆ 82 93 52, ≤, « Elbe-side setting terrace » – wc ☎ Ⓟ . AE ⓓ E
M a la carte 55/85 – **14 rm** 110/239.

XX ✿ **Landhaus Dill**, Elbchaussee 404 (H 52), ✆ 82 84 43 – Ⓟ. AE ⓓ E VISA
closed Monday, Tuesday to Friday dinner only – **M** a la carte 49/90.

at Hamburg-Rotherbaum :

Elysee Ⓜ, Rothenbaumchaussee 10 (H 13), ✆ 41 41 20, Telex 212455, Massage, , – | ♿ . AE ⓓ E VISA CX m
Restaurants : – **Piazza Romana M** a la carte 41/64 – **Brasserie M** a la carte 33/56 – **299 rm** 193/346 Bb.

XX ✿ **L'auberge française** (French rest.), Rutschbahn 34 (H 13), ✆ 4 10 25 32 – ✻
closed Saturday May - August, Sunday and July – **M** a la carte 52/82 (booking essential)
Spec. Foie d'oie poêlé sauce truffes et pommes, Rochen in Senfsauce mit Wirsing, überbackene Früchte mit Kirschcrème. by Grindelhof CX

XX **Fernsehturm-Restaurant**, Lagerstr. 2 (, 3,75 DM) (H 6), ✆ 43 80 24, ✻ Hamburg, « Revolving rest. at 132 m » – Ⓟ. AE ⓓ E VISA. ✻ BX
M a la carte 40/70 (booking essential).

at Hamburg-St. Pauli :

XX **Bavaria-Blick**, Bernhard-Nocht-Str. 99 (7th floor,) (H 4), ✆ 31 48 00, ≤ harbour – . AE ⓓ E VISA BZ m
M a la carte 41/68 (booking essential).

at Hamburg-Schnelsen by Grindelallee CX :

Novotel, Oldesloer Str. 166 (H 61), ✆ 5 50 20 73, Telex 212923, (heated) – | wc ☎ ♿ Ⓟ . AE ⓓ E VISA
M a la carte 29/53 – **124 rm** 137/182 Bb.

at Hamburg-Stellingen by Schäferkampsallee BX :

Helgoland (hospice), Kieler Str. 177 (H 54), ✆ 85 70 01 – | wc wc ☎ ♿ Ⓟ . AE ⓓ E VISA
M (rest. for residents only) – **109 rm** 107/182 Bb.

Falck, Kieler Str. 333 (H 54), ✆ 5 40 20 61, Telex 213664, – | wc wc ☎ Ⓟ
83 rm Bb.

at Hamburg-Uhlenhorst by Buchstraße FX :

Parkhotel Alster-Ruh without rest, Am Langenzug 6 (H 76), 22 45 77 – wc wc . AE E
27 rm 97/210 Bb.

Ristorante Roma (Italian rest.), Hofweg 7 (H 76), 2 20 25 54 – AE
closed Sunday lunch and Saturday – **M** a la carte 43/61.

at Hamburg-Veddel by Amsinckstr. FZ :

Carat-Hotel M, Sieldeich 9 (H 28), 78 96 60, Telex 2163354 – wc wc . AE E VISA
M a la carte 30/57 – **93 rm** 125/165 Bb.

HANOVER (HANNOVER) 3000. Niedersachsen 987 ⑮ – pop. 550 000 – alt. 55 m – 0511.

See : Herrenhausen Gardens (Herrenhäuser Gärten)★★ (Großer Garten★★, Berggarten★) CV – Kestner-Museum★ DY **M1** – Market Church (Marktkirche) (Altarpiece★★) DY **A** – Museum of Lower Saxony (Niedersächsisches Landesmuseum) (Prehistorical department★) EZ **M2** – Museum of Arts (Kunstmuseum) (Collection Sprengel★) EZ **M4**.

Hanover-Langenhagen (① : 11 km), 7 30 51 – 1 98 54 52.

Exhibition Centre (Messegelände), (by ② and B 6) 8 91, Telex 922728.

Tourist office, Ernst-August-Platz 8, 1 68 23 19 – City-Air-Terminal, Raschplatz 1PQ, 1 68 28 01.

ADAC, Hindenburgstr. 37, 8 50 01.

Berlin 289 ② – Bremen 123 ① – Hamburg 151 ①.

Plan on following pages

Maritim M, Hildesheimer Str. 34, 1 65 31, Telex 9230268, , – . rest EZ **b**
293 rm Bb.

Inter-Continental, Friedrichswall 11, 1 69 11, Telex 923656 – rest (with). AE E VISA. rest DY **a**
M a la carte 54/93 – **285 rm** 240/435 Bb.

✿ **Schweizerhof Hannover - Schu's Restaurant** M, Hinüberstr. 6, 3 49 50, Telex 923359 – . AE E VISA EX **d**
M *(closed 3 weeks June - July)* a la carte 58/94 (remarkable wine-list) – **Gourmet's Buffet M** a la carte 36/60 – **84 rm** 197/309 Bb.

Kastens Hotel Luisenhof, Luisenstr. 1, 1 24 40, Telex 922325 – . AE E VISA. rest EX **b**
M *(closed Sunday July to August)* a la carte 44/72 – **200 rm** 139/348 Bb.

Congress-Hotel am Stadtpark, Clausewitzstr. 6, 2 80 55 57, Telex 921263, , Massage, , – . AE E VISA by ②
M a la carte 29/68 – **252 rm** 119/285 Bb.

Grand Hotel Mussmann without rest, Ernst-August-Platz 7, 32 79 71, Telex 922859 – . AE E VISA EX **v**
100 rm 128/348 Bb.

Königshof M without rest, Königstr. 12, 31 20 71, Telex 922306 – wc wc . AE E EX **c**
84 rm 124/180 Bb.

Central-Hotel Kaiserhof, Ernst-August-Platz 4, 32 78 11, Telex 922810 – wc wc . AE E VISA. rest EX **a**
M a la carte 22/44 – **81 rm** 96/256 Bb.

Am Funkturm - Ristorante Milano, Hallerstr. 34, 31 70 33 (hotel) 33 23 09 (rest.) – wc wc – **40 rm** Bb. EV **s**

Hospiz Loccumer Hof, Kurt-Schumacher-Str. 16, 32 60 51 – wc wc . AE E VISA. DX **s**
M *(closed Saturday and Sunday for dinner)* a la carte 30/62 – **70 rm** 70/160 Bb.

Am Leineschloß without rest, Am Markte 12, 32 71 45, Telex 922010 – wc wc . AE E VISA DY **z**
88 rm 135/284 Bb.

Körner, Körnerstr. 24, 1 46 66, Telex 921313, , – wc wc . AE E VISA DX **e**
closed 23 December - 2 January – **M** a la carte 30/60 – **81 rm** 74/154 Bb.

Am Rathaus, Friedrichswall 21, 32 62 68, Telex 923865, – wc wc . E VISA EY **y**
M *(closed Saturday and Sunday)* a la carte 27/55 – **53 rm** 89/260 Bb.

Intercity-Hotel, Ernst-August-Platz 1, 32 74 61, Telex 921171 – rest wc (with) – **57 rm**. EX **r**

Thüringer Hof without rest, Osterstr. 37, 32 64 37 – wc wc . AE E VISA
closed 24 December - 1 January – **60 rm** 75/200. EY **e**

Atlanta without rest, Hinüberstr. 1, 34 29 39, Telex 924603 – wc wc . E. EX **t**
closed 19 to 31 December – **39 rm** 60/220 Bb.

XXXX ❀ **Landhaus Ammann** with rm, Hildesheimer Str. 185, ✆ 83 08 18, Telex 9230900, 🍽, « Elegant installation, patio with terrace » – lift TV ⇔wc ⋒wc ☎ ♿ P 🏛. AE ◉ E. ✻ rest by ③
M a la carte 60/91 (remarkable wine-list) – **Nudelstubb M** a la carte 45/73 – **14 rm** 175/320
Spec. Lachs in verschiedenen Zubereitungen, Hummer und Stubenküken in Armagnacsauce, Quarksoufflé mit Früchten.

XXX **Bakkarat im Casino am Maschsee**, Arthur-Menge-Ufer 3 (1st floor), ✆ 80 10 20, <, 🍽 – AE ◉ E VISA DZ **a**
M a la carte 45/72.

XXX ❀ **Georgenhof** ⛓ with rm, Herrenhäuser Kirchweg 20, ✆ 70 22 44, « Lower Saxony country house in park, terrace » – ⇔wc ⋒wc ☎ P by Engelbosteler Damm CV
M a la carte 49/102 (remarkable wine-list) – **17 rm** 68/190
Spec. Kalbsbriesstrudel mit Senfmousseline, Suprême vom Steinbutt mit Jakobsmuscheln, Wildentenburst in Blutsauce (October - March).

XXX ❀ **Zur Brügge's Restaurant**, Bödekerstr. 29, ✆ 31 90 05 FV **a**
closed Sunday and Bank Holidays – **M** a la carte 58/94
Spec. Atlantikhummer serviert in 2 Gängen, Rote Grütze mit Quarkeis.

XXX **Mövenpick - Baron de la Mouette**, Georgenstr. 35 (1st floor), ✆ 32 62 85 – ▤. AE ◉ E VISA EX **x**
M a la carte 42/62.

XX **Ratskeller**, Köbelinger Str. 60, ✆ 1 53 63 – 🏛 DY **n**
M a la carte 27/60.

XX ❀ **Clichy**, Weiße Kreuzstr. 31, ✆ 31 24 47 – AE EV **m**
closed Sunday, Bank Holidays and 3 weeks June - July – **M** a la carte 51/86 (booking essential)
Spec. Frikassee von Hummer und Lachs in Champagner, Täubchen auf Lauch, Lammrücken und Stopfleber in Blätterteig.

XX ❀ **Stern's Restaurant Härke-Stuben**, Marienstr. 104, ✆ 81 73 22 – AE ◉ E VISA
closed Saturday June - September – **M** a la carte 59/91 FY **b**
Spec. Kalbsbries und Artischocken in Tomatenbutter, Mastentenbrust mit Tokayersauce, Heidschnuckenrücken im Kartoffelmantel (October - December).

XX **Lila Kranz**, Kirchwender Str. 23, ✆ 85 89 21, 🍽 – ◉ E VISA FX **b**
closed Saturday lunch and 12 July - 2 August – **M** a la carte 48/68.

XX **Rôtisserie Helvetia**, Georgsplatz 11, ✆ 1 48 41 – ◉ E VISA EY **k**
M a la carte 30/55.

XX **Leineschloß**, Hinrich-Wilhelm-Kopf-Platz 1, ✆ 32 66 93, 🍽 – P 🏛 DY **k**
M a la carte 27/62.

XX **Tai-Pai** (Chinese rest.), Hildesheimer Str. 73, ✆ 88 52 30 EZ **a**
closed Monday – **M** a la carte 23/43.

XX **Mövenpick im Casino am Maschsee**, Artur-Menge-Ufer 3, ✆ 80 40 18, « Sea-setting terrace with < » – AE ◉ E VISA DZ **a**
M a la carte 27/54.

XX Mandarin-Pavillon (Chinese rest.), Marktstr. 45, ✆ 1 89 79 DY **x**

X ❀ **Goldene Gans**, Körnerstr. 3, ✆ 1 49 11 – AE ◉ E DX **t**
closed Monday – **M** (dinner only) a la carte 51/75 (booking essential)
Spec. Kulibiaka von Lachs mit Champagnerbutter, Salmi von der Taube, Lammrücken mit Thymiansauce.

X **Härke-Klause** (brewery - inn), Ständehausstr. 4, ✆ 32 11 75 – AE ◉ E EY **b**
closed Sunday and Bank Holidays – **M** a la carte 18.50/46 (also diet).

at Hanover 51-Bothfeld by Bödekerstr. FV :

🏠 **Halberstadt** without rest, Im Heidkampe 80, ✆ 64 01 18, 🌳 – TV ⇔wc ⋒wc ☎ P
closed 20 December - 5 January – **36 rm** 68/143 Bb.

XXX ❀ **Witten's Hop**, Gernsstr. 4, ✆ 64 88 44, « Country house atmosphere » – P. ✻
closed 1 to 21 January – **M** (week-days dinner only) a la carte 76/96 (remarkable wine-list).

at Hanover 51-Buchholz by Bödekerstr. FV :

🏨 **Föhrenhof**, Kirchhorster Str. 22, ✆ 6 17 21, Telex 923448, 🍽 – lift TV ⇔wc ⋒wc ☎ ♿ P 🏛. AE ◉ E VISA. ✻ rest
M a la carte 29/57 – **77 rm** 110/360 Bb.

XX **Buchholzer Windmühle**, Pasteurallee 30, ✆ 64 91 38, 🍽 – P. ✻
closed Sunday and Bank Holidays – **M** a la carte 33/59.

at Hanover 81-Döhren by ③ :

XXX **Wichmann**, Hildesheimer Str. 230, ✆ 83 16 71, « Courtyard » – P
closed Sunday, Monday and Bank Holidays – **M** a la carte 48/78.

XX **Die Insel - Maschseeterrassen**, Rudolf-von-Bennigsen-Ufer 81, ✆ 83 12 14, <, 🍽 – P 🏛. AE E
closed Monday and 2 to 21 January – **M** a la carte 29/60.

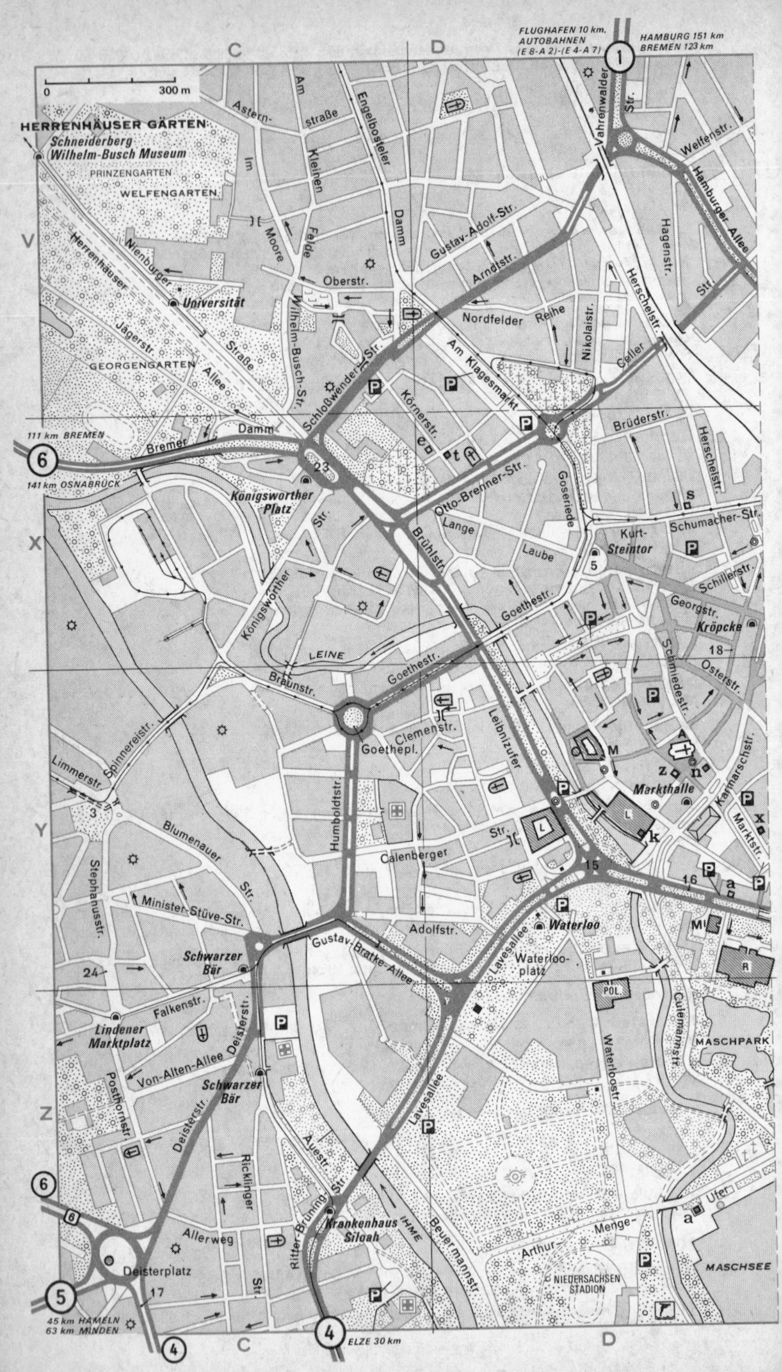

FLUGHAFEN 10 km, AUTOBAHNEN (E 8-A 2)-(E 4-A 7)
HAMBURG 151 km
BREMEN 123 km
C
D
0
300 m
HERRENHÄUSER GÄRTEN
Schneiderberg
Wilhelm-Busch Museum
PRINZENGARTEN
WELFENGARTEN
Universität
GEORGENGARTEN
Herrenhäuser Allee
Jägerstr.
Nienburger Straße
Astern-straße
Im Moore
Kleinen Felde
Engelbosteler Damm
Oberstr.
Wilhelm-Busch-Str.
Schloßwender-Str.
Gustav-Adolf-Str.
Arndtstr.
Nordfelder Reihe
Nikolaistr.
Am Klagesmarkt
Vahrenwalder Str.
Welfenstr.
Hamburger Allee
Hagenstr.
Herschelstr.
Celler Str.
Brüderstr.
V
111 km BREMEN
141 km OSNABRÜCK
Bremer Damm
Königsworther Platz
Königsworther Str.
Körnerstr.
Otto-Brenner-Str.
Goseriede
Lange Laube
Brühlstr.
Kurt-Schumacher-Str.
Steintor
Schillerstr.
Georgstr.
Kröpcke
Osterstr.
Schmiedestr.
Goethestr.
LEINE
Braunstr.
X
Spinnereistr.
Limmerstr.
Goethepl.
Clemenstr.
Leibnizufer
Humboldtstr.
Calenberger Str.
Markthalle
Karmarschstr.
Marktstr.
Y
Blumenauer Str.
Stephanusstr.
Minister-Stüve-Str.
Schwarzer Bär
Gustav-Bratke-Allee
Adolfstr.
Lavesallee
Waterloo
Waterlooplatz
POL.
Culemannstr.
MASCHPARK
Falkenstr.
Lindener Marktplatz
Von-Alten-Allee
Deisterstr.
Posthornstr.
Z
Ricklinger Str.
Auestr.
Waterloostr.
Allerweg
Deisterplatz
Ritter-Brüning-Str.
Krankenhaus Siloah
IHME
Beuermannstr.
Arthur-Menge-Ufer
NIEDERSACHSEN STADION
MASCHSEE
45 km HAMELN
63 km MINDEN
ELZE 30 km
C
D

HANNOVER

Street	Grid	No.
Bahnhofstraße	EX	7
Georgstraße	DEX	
Große Packhofstraße	DX	18
Karmarschstraße	DY	
Aegidientorplatz	EY	2
Am Küchengarten	CY	3
Am Marstall	DX	4
Am Steintor	DX	5
Bischofsholer Damm	FY	8
Braunschweiger Platz	FY	9
Emmichplatz	FX	12
Ernst-August-Platz	EX	13
Friederikenplatz	DY	15
Friedrichswall	DY	16
Göttinger Straße	CZ	17
Hans-Böckler-Allee	FY	19
Hartmannstraße	FZ	20
Joachimstraße	EX	21
Königsworther Platz	CX	23
Lindener Marktplatz	CY	24
Opernplatz	EY	25
Scharnhorststraße	FX	28
Thielenplatz	EX	29
Volgersweg	EX	30

BRAUNSCHWEIG 64 km, BERLIN 289 km
AUTOBAHN (E 4-A 7)

HILDESHEIM 31 km
KASSEL 164 km

at Hanover 42-Flughafen (Airport) by ① : 11 km :

Holiday Inn, Am Flughafen, ✆ 73 01 71, Telex 924030, – AE ⓓ E VISA
M a la carte 30/64 – **146 rm** 185/245 Bb.

at Hanover 71-Kirchrode by ② and B 65 :

Crest-Hotel Hannover, Tiergartenstr. 117, ✆ 5 10 30, Telex 922748, – wc wc . AE ⓓ E VISA
M a la carte 37/62 – **108 rm** 195/266 Bb.

at Hanover 71-Kleefeld by ② and B 65 :

Alte Mühle, Hermann-Löns-Park 3, ✆ 55 94 80, <, « Converted lower Saxony farm-house, terrace » – . AE ⓓ
closed Thursday and July – **M** a la carte 25/68.

at Hanover 72-Messe (near exhibition Centre) by ② :

Parkhotel Kronsberg, Messeschnellweg (at Exhibition Centre), ✆ 86 10 86, Telex 923448, – rest (with). AE ⓓ E VISA. rest
M a la carte 36/72 – **109 rm** 110/360 Bb.

at Langenhagen **3012** by ① : 10 km :

Grethe, Walsroder Str. 151, ✆ (0511) 73 80 11, , – wc . rest
closed 15 July - 14 August – **M** *(closed Saturday and Sunday)* a la carte 21/53 – **51 rm** 80/120 Bb.

at Langenhagen 6-Krähenwinkel **3012** by ① : 11 km :

Jägerhof, Walsroder Str. 251, ✆ (0511) 73 40 11, Telex 9218211, – wc . ⓓ E VISA
closed 23 December - 5 January – **M** *(closed Saturday lunch, Sunday and 23 December - 5 January)* a la carte 35/63 – **50 rm** 70/150 Bb.

at Ronnenberg-Benthe **3003** ⑤ : 10 km by B 65 :

Benther Berg M, Vogelsangstr. 18, ✆ (05108) 30 45, Telex 922253, , , , – rest wc (with). AE.
closed 28 December - 1 January – **M** *(closed Sunday lunch)* a la carte 37/67 – **70 rm** 83/180 Bb.

at Garbsen 1-Havelse **3008** ⑥ : 12 km by B 6 :

Wildhage, Hannoversche Str. 45, ✆ (05137) 7 50 33, – wc wc . AE ⓓ E. rest
M *(closed Sunday)* a la carte 28/55 – **25 rm** 68/140 Bb.

at Garbsen 4-Berenbostel **3008** ⑥ : 13 km by B 6 :

Landhaus Köhne am See, Seeweg 19, ✆ (05131) 9 10 85, <, « Garden terrace », , , , – rest wc wc . rm
M a la carte 28/64 – **19 rm** 76/160 Bb.

MUNICH (MÜNCHEN) 8000. Bayern **987** ㊲, **426** ④ ⑰, **413** R 22 – pop. 1 297 000 – alt. 520 m – ✆ 089.

See : Marienplatz★ KLY – Church of Our Lady (Frauenkirche)★★ (tower ※★) KY – Old Pinakothek (Alte Pinakothek)★★★ KY – German Museum (Deutsches Museum)★★ LZ **M1** – The Palace (Residenz)★ (Treasury★★ Palace Theatre★) LY – Church of Asam Brothers (Asamkirche)★ KZ **A** – National Museum of Bavaria (Bayerisches Nationalmuseum)★★ HV – New Pinakothek (Neue Pinakothek)★ GU – City Historical Museum (Münchener Stadtmuseum)★ (Moorish Dancers★★) KZ **M2** – Villa Lenbach Collections (Städt. Galerie im Lenbachhaus) (Portraits by Lenbach★) KY **M5** – Antique Collections (Staatl. Antikensammlungen)★(Etruscan trinkets★) KY **M6** – Glyptothek★ KY **M7** – German Hunting Museum (Deutsches Jagdmuseum)★ KY **M8** – Olympic Park (Olympia-Park) (Olympic Tower ※★★★) – New Town Hall (Neues Rathaus)★ LY **R** – Church of the Theatines (Theatinerkirche)★(Choir and Cupola★) LY **D** – English Garden (Englischer Garten)(view from Monopteros Temple★) HU.

Envir. : Nymphenburg★★ (castle★, park★, Amalienburg★★, Botanical Gardens★★).

München-Riem (③ : 11 km), ✆ 92 11 21 27.

✆ 12 88 44 25.

Exhibition Centre (Messegelände) (EX), ✆ 5 10 71, Telex 5212086.

Tourist office in the Main Station, ✆ 2 39 12 56.

Tourist office in the Airport München-Riem, ✆ 2 39 12 66.

Tourist-Information, Rathaus, ✆ 2 39 12 56.

ADAC, Sendlinger-Tor-Platz 9, ✆ 59 39 79.

Innsbruck 149 ⑤ – Nürnberg 165 ② – Salzburg 140 ④ – Stuttgart 219 ⑦.

Plans on following pages

The reference (M 15) at the end of the address is the postal district : Munich 15

Vier Jahreszeiten Kempinski - Restaurant Walterspiel, Maximilianstr. 17 (M 22), 23 03 90, Telex 523859, Massage, – . AE E VISA. rest LY a
M *(closed lunch Monday and Saturday)* a la carte 74/115 – **Jahreszeiten-Eck** *(closed Sunday)* **M** a la carte 43/66 – **365 rm** 266/537
Spec. Das Beste von Ente und Languste in Calvados, Seezungenröllchen auf Petersilienpüree, Gefüllter Kaninchenrücken in Sherrysauce.

Königshof, Karlsplatz 25 (M 2), 55 13 60, Telex 523616 – . AE E VISA. rest KY s
M a la carte 63/105 (remarkable wine-list) (booking essential) – **115 rm** 204/376
Spec. Entenleber in verschiedenen Zubereitungen, Hummersoufflé mit Seeigel und Corailsabayon, Entenbrust in Honig-Cidre-Sauce.

Hilton, Am Tucherpark 7 (M 22), 3 84 50, Telex 5215740, beer-garden, Massage, – . AE E VISA. rest HU n
Restaurants : – **Hilton Grill M** a la carte 64/91 – **Isar-Terrassen** (also diet) **M** a la carte 38/56 – **485 rm** 194/408.

Continental, Max-Joseph-Str. 5 (M 2), 55 79 71, Telex 522603, « Antique furniture » – . AE E VISA KY f
M a la carte 43/83 – **160 rm** 211/382 Bb.

Bayerischer Hof-Palais Montgelas, Promenadeplatz 6 (M 2), 2 12 00, Telex 523409, Massage, – rest . AE E VISA KY y
Restaurants : – **Grill M** a la carte 40/75 – **Trader Vic's** *(dinner only)* **M** a la carte 33/65 – **Palais Keller M** a la carte 25/48 – **442 rm** 185/380.

Eden-Hotel-Wolff, Arnulfstr. 4 (M 2), 55 82 81, Telex 523564 – . AE E VISA JY p
M a la carte 36/75 – **214 rm** 150/300 Bb.

Westpark-Hotel, Garmischer Str. 2 (M 2), 5 19 60, Telex 523680, – rest (with). AE E VISA by Heimeranstr. EX
M a la carte 27/60 – **258 rm** 165/280 Bb.

Excelsior, Schützenstr. 11 (M 2), 55 13 70, Telex 522419 – rest . AE E VISA JY z
M a la carte 46/70 – **118 rm** 163/306.

Drei Löwen, Schillerstr. 8 (M 2), 59 55 21, Telex 523867 – . AE E VISA – **M** *(closed Sunday)* a la carte 29/45 – **130 rm** 124/205 Bb JY e

Erzgießerei-Europe M, Erzgießereistr. 15 (M 2), 18 60 55, Telex 5214977 – wc . AE E VISA EU a
M a la carte 28/62 – **106 rm** 145/220 Bb.

Mercure M, Senefelder Str. 7 (M 2), 55 13 20, Telex 5218428 – wc . AE E VISA JY r
M a la carte 23/54 – **167 rm** 130/240 Bb.

Trustee Parkhotel M without rest, Parkstr. 31 (approach Gollierstraße) (M 2), 51 99 50, Telex 5218296 – wc . AE E VISA EV r
36 rm 155/330 Bb.

Atrium M without rest, Landwehrstr. 59 (M 2), 51 41 90, Telex 5212162, – wc wc . AE E VISA JZ d
163 rm 148/228 Bb.

Central-Hotel without rest, Schwanthalerstr. 111 (M 2), 51 08 30, Telex 5216031 – wc . AE E VISA EV s
103 rm 140/195 Bb.

Europäischer Hof without rest, Bayerstr. 31 (M 2), 55 15 10, Telex 522642 – wc wc . AE E VISA JY b
160 rm 65/160 Bb.

Intercity-Hotel, Bahnhofplatz 2 (M 2), 55 85 71, Telex 523174 – wc wc . AE E VISA JY u
M a la carte 32/58 – **209 rm** 70/178 Bb.

Metropol, Bayerstr. 43, (Entrance Goethestr.) (M 2), 53 07 64, Telex 522816 – wc wc . AE E JY k
M a la carte 25/55 – **272 rm** 71/155.

Apollo without rest, Mittererstr. 7 (M 2), 53 95 31, Telex 5212981 – wc . AE E VISA JY w
closed 23 December - 7 January – **74 rm** 160/205 Bb.

Germania, Schwanthaler Str. 28 (M 2), 5 16 80, Telex 523790 – wc wc . AE E VISA JY a
M a la carte 35/65 (mainly steaks) – **100 rm** 158/248 Bb.

Domus without rest, St.-Anna-Str. 31 (M 22), 22 17 04, Telex 529835 – wc . AE E LY b
closed 22 to 26 December – **45 rm** 130/230 Bb.

Ariston without rest, Unsöldstr. 10 (M 22), 22 26 91, Telex 522437 – wc wc . AE E LY c
closed 23 to 31 December – **61 rm** 110/180 Bb.

Straße	Feld	Nr.
Am Gasteig	HX	4
Baldeplatz	GX	14
Baumgartnerstraße	EX	17
Biedersteiner Straße	HU	25
Bonner Straße	GU	26
Denninger Straße	HU	34
Elsässer Straße	HX	42
Emil-Riedel-Straße	HV	45
Flurstraße	HX	49
Friedrichstraße	GU	52
Galileiplatz	HV	53
Gebsattelstraße	HX	55
Georgenstraße	GU	59
Giselastraße	GU	60
Gohrenstraße	HU	61
Grasserstraße	EV	63
Hackerbrücke	EV	65
Herkomerplatz	HU	71
Hiltenspergerstraße	GU	74
Hompeschstraße	HV	76
Humboldtstraße	GX	77
Innere Wiener Straße	HX	79
Johann-Fichte-Straße	HU	82
Josephsplatz	FU	83
Kaiserstraße	GU	86
Kißkaltplatz	GU	94
Kölner Platz	GU	95
Kunigundenstraße	HU	97
Kurfürstenplatz	GU	99
Lerchenfeldstraße	HV	102
Maillingerstraße	EV	109
Maria-Theresia-Straße	HV	111
Marschallstraße	HU	112
Martin-Greif-Straße	EV	115
Martiusstraße	GU	116
Maßmannstraße	FU	118
Maximiliansbrücke	HV	119
Max-Josephs-Brücke	HV	124
Max-Planck-Straße	HV	129
Messeplatz	EX	133
Metzgerstraße	HX	134
Möhlstraße	HV	137
Mozartstraße	EX	138
Münchener-Freiheit	HU	140
Oettingenstraße	HV	151
Pappenheimstraße	EV	163
Potsdamer Straße	HU	167
Prinzregentenbrücke	HV	169
Prinzregentenstraße	HV	170
Radlkoferstraße	EX	174
Regerplatz	HX	175
Rosenheimer Platz	HX	181
Sandstraße	FU	186
Schießstättstraße	EV	189
Stengelstraße	HU	201
Sternstraße	HV	202
Sternwartstraße	HV	204
Theresienhöhe	EX	207
Thiemestraße	HU	208
Tivolistraße	HU	211
Triftstraße	HV	214
Trogerstraße	HV	215
Tumblingerstraße	FX	218
Veterinärstraße	GU	221
Viktoriastraße	GU	223
Wagmüllerstraße	HV	224
Wittelsbacherstraße	GX	231
Wredestraße	EV	232
Zirkus-Krone-Straße	EV	236

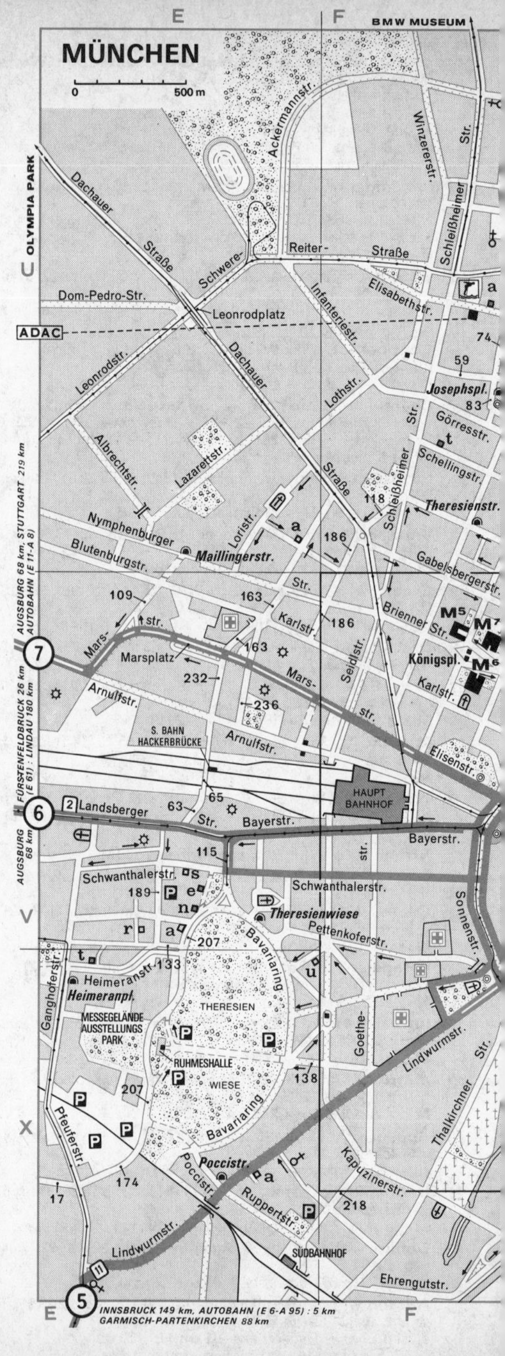

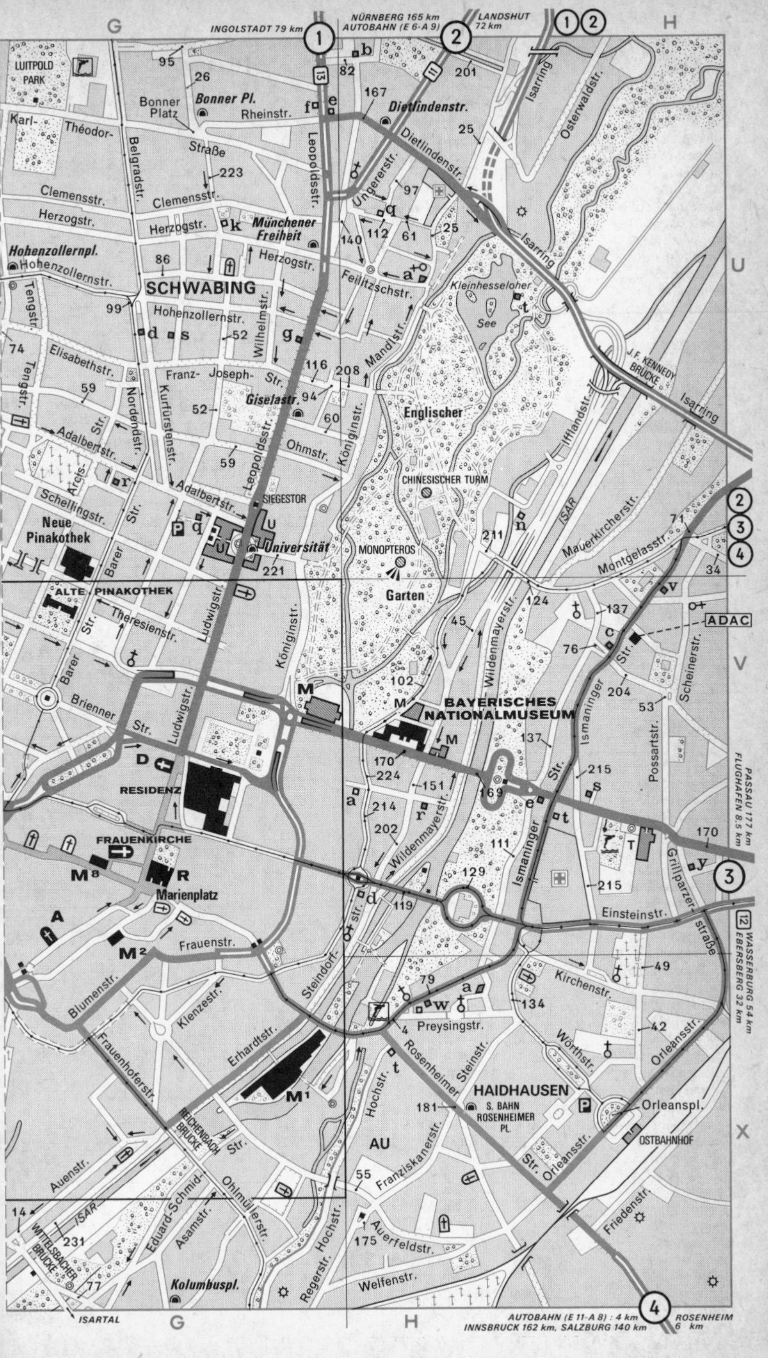
INGOLSTADT 79 km
NÜRNBERG 165 km
AUTOBAHN (E 6-A 9)
LANDSHUT 72 km
LUITPOLD PARK
Bonner Platz
Bonner Pl.
Rheinstr.
Dietlindenstr.
Karl-Théodor-Straße
Belgradstr.
Leopoldsstr.
Ungererstr.
Clemensstr.
Herzogstr.
Münchener Freiheit
Hohenzollernpl.
Hohenzollernstr.
SCHWABING
Feilitzschstr.
Isarring
Osterwaldstr.
Kleinhesseloher See
J.F. KENNEDY BRÜCKE
Tengstr.
Elisabethstr.
Franz-Joseph-Str.
Wilhelmstr.
Mandlstr.
Giselastr.
Nordendstr.
Kurfürstenstr.
Ohmstr.
Königinstr.
Englischer Garten
Ifflandstr.
Adalbertstr.
Arcisstr.
Schellingstr.
SIEGESTOR
CHINESISCHER TURM
Neue Pinakothek
Universität
MONOPTEROS
ISAR
Mauerkircherstr.
Montgelasstr.
ALTE PINAKOTHEK
Theresienstr.
Ludwigstr.
Barer Str.
Wildenmayerstr.
ADAC
Ismaninger Str.
Scheinerstr.
Brienner Str.
BAYERISCHES NATIONALMUSEUM
Possartstr.
PASSAU 177 km
FLUGHAFEN 8,5 km
RESIDENZ
FRAUENKIRCHE
Marienplatz
Grillparzerstraße
Einsteinstr.
Frauenstr.
Steindorfstr.
Kirchenstr.
WASSERBURG 54 km
EBERSBERG 32 km
Blumenstr.
Klenzestr.
Preysingstr.
Frauenhoferstr.
Erhardtstr.
Rosenheimer Str.
Steinstr.
Wörthstr.
Orleansstr.
HAIDHAUSEN
S. BAHN ROSENHEIMER PL.
Orleanspl.
OSTBAHNHOF
REICHENBACH BRÜCKE
Hochstr.
AU
Franziskanerstr.
Auenstr.
Eduard-Schmid-Str.
Ohlmüllerstr.
WITTELSBACHER BRÜCKE
Asamstr.
Auerfeldstr.
Friedenstr.
Regerstr.
Welfenstr.
Kolumbuspl.
ISARTAL
AUTOBAHN (E 11-A 8) : 4 km
INNSBRUCK 162 km, SALZBURG 140 km
ROSENHEIM 6 km

STREET INDEX TO MÜNCHEN TOWN PLANS

Continued after town plan

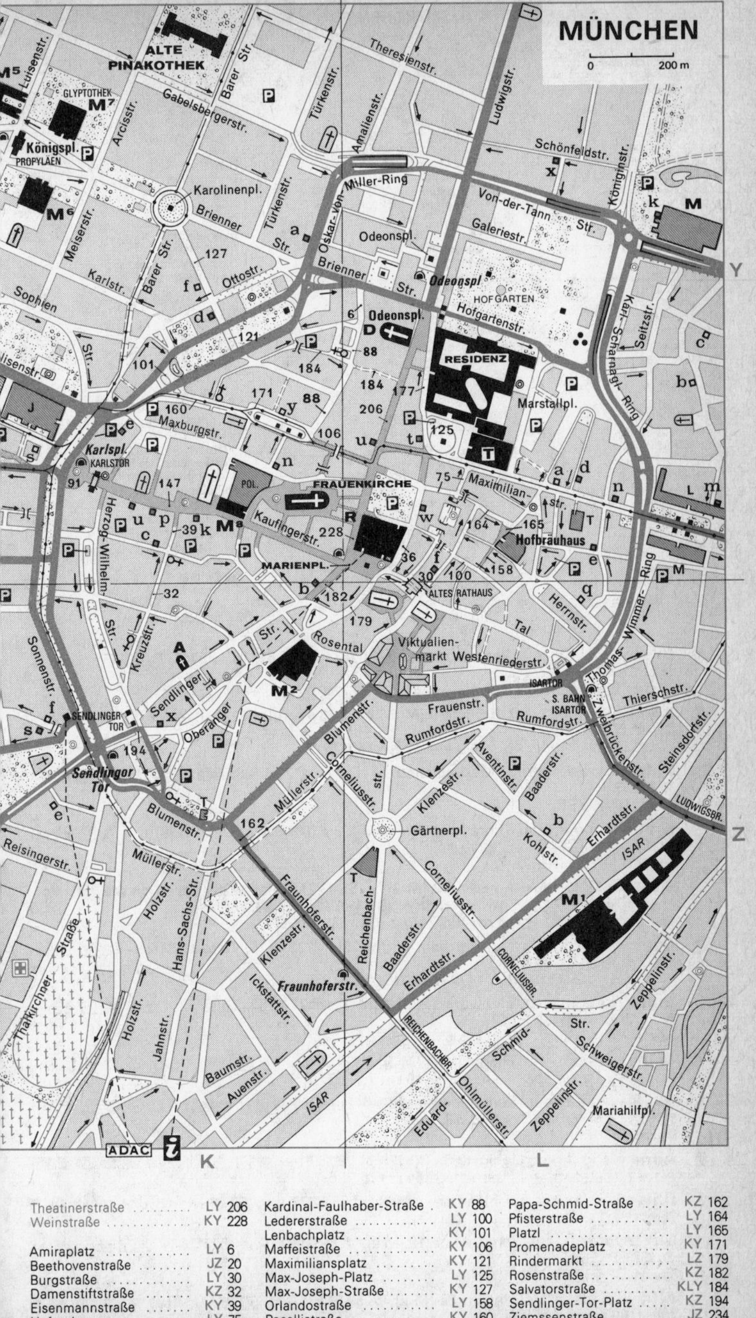

Theatinerstraße . . . . LY 206
Weinstraße . . . . KY 228

Amiraplatz . . . . LY 6
Beethovenstraße . . . . JZ 20
Burgstraße . . . . LY 30
Damenstiftstraße . . . . KZ 32
Eisenmannstraße . . . . KY 39
Hofgraben . . . . LY 75

Kardinal-Faulhaber-Straße . KY 88
Ledererstraße . . . . LY 100
Lenbachplatz . . . . KY 101
Maffeistraße . . . . KY 106
Maximiliansplatz . . . . KY 121
Max-Joseph-Platz . . . . LY 125
Max-Joseph-Straße . . . . . . KY 127
Orlandostraße . . . . LY 158
Pacellistraße . . . . KY 160

Papa-Schmid-Straße . . . . KZ 162
Pfisterstraße . . . . LY 164
Platzl . . . . LY 165
Promenadeplatz . . . . KY 171
Rindermarkt . . . . LZ 179
Rosenstraße . . . . KZ 182
Salvatorstraße . . . . KLY 184
Sendlinger-Tor-Platz . . . . KZ 194
Ziemssenstraße . . . . JZ 234

STREET INDEX TO MÜNCHEN TOWN PLANS (Concluded)

Bristol without rest, Pettenkoferstr. 2 (M 2), ☎ 59 51 51, Telex 524767 – lift TV wc ☎ garage. AE ⓓ E — KZ **f**
closed 22 December - 6 January – **57 rm** 165/240.

Admiral without rest, Kohlstr. 9 (M 5), ☎ 22 66 41, Telex 529111 – lift TV wc ☎ garage. AE ⓓ E VISA — LZ **b**
closed 22 December - 5 January – **30 rm** 150/230 Bb.

Splendid without rest, Maximilianstr. 54 (M 22), ☎ 29 66 06, Telex 522427 – lift TV wc ☎. AE E — HV **d**
40 rm 92/289 Bb.

Krone without rest, Theresienhöhe 8 (M 2), ☎ 50 40 52, Telex 5213870 – lift TV wc ☎. AE ⓓ E VISA — EV **a**
30 rm 140/220.

Deutscher Kaiser, Arnulfstr. 2 (M 2), ☎ 55 83 21, Telex 522650, rest. on the 15th floor with ≤ Munich – lift wc wc ☎ ♿ P. AE ⓓ E VISA. rest — JY **s**
M a la carte 39/60 – **168 rm** 158/241 Bb.

Concorde without rest, Herrnstr. 38 (M 22), ☎ 22 45 15, Telex 522002 – lift TV wc wc ☎ garage. AE ⓓ E VISA — LZ **q**
closed 23 to 27 December – **77 rm** 130/200 Bb.

Brack without rest, Lindwurmstr. 153 (M 2), ☎ 77 10 52, Telex 524416 – lift TV wc wc ☎ garage. AE ⓓ E VISA — EX **a**
50 rm 95/140 Bb.

Müller without rest, Fliegenstr. 1 (M 2), ☎ 26 60 63 – lift TV wc ☎ P. AE ⓓ E — KZ **e**
closed 22 December - 7 January – **40 rm** 75/156.

Mark without rest, Senefelderstr. 12 (M 2), ☎ 59 28 01, Telex 522721 – lift TV wc wc ☎ garage P. AE ⓓ E VISA — JY **v**
91 rm 100/160.

Adria without rest, Liebigstr. 8a (M 22), ☎ 29 30 81 – lift TV wc wc ☎. AE ⓓ E VISA — HV **a**
closed 23 December - 7 January – **54 rm** 65/190.

Uhland without rest, Uhlandstr. 1 (M 2), ☎ 53 92 77 – lift TV wc wc ☎ P. AE ⓓ E — EX **u**
25 rm 80/160 Bb.

Meier without rest, Schützenstr. 12 (M 2), ☎ 59 56 23, Telex 529126 – lift TV wc wc ☎. AE ⓓ E VISA — JY **x**
59 rm 118/210 Bb.

Alfa without rest, Hirtenstr. 22 (M 2), ☎ 59 84 61 – lift TV wc wc ☎ P. AE ⓓ E VISA – **80 rm** 65/195 — JY **n**

XXXX ✿✿✿ **Aubergine**, Maximiliansplatz 5 (M 2), ✆ 59 81 71 – E KY **d**
closed Sunday, Monday, Bank Holidays, 2 to 24 August and 23 December - 7 January – **M** a la carte 82/116 (booking essential)
Spec. Hummer in Rotweinbuttersauce, Kalbsbriesschnitten auf Artischockensalat, Grieß-Soufflé mit Orangenragout.

XXX ✿ **Le Gourmet**, Ligsalzstr. 46 (M 2), ✆ 50 35 97, « Small rest, elegant installation » – ⓓ E EX **t**
closed Sunday and 2 weeks January – **M** (dinner only) a la carte 79/110 (booking essential)
Spec. Schollenfilet im Reisbett, Täubchen mit Specksauce und Flan von grünen Bohnenkernen, Lammleberknödel im Schweinenetz auf warmem Radieschensalat.

XXX La Piazzetta, Oskar-v.-Miller-Ring 3 (M 2), ✆ 28 29 90, ☂, beer-garden, « Modern Italian rest, Florentine style » KY **a**

XXX **Weinhaus Schwarzwälder** (old Munich wine-restaurant), Hartmannstr. 8 (M 2), ✆ 22 72 16 – AE ⓓ E VISA KY **n**
M a la carte 42/87.

XXX ✿ **Sabitzer**, Reitmorstr. 21 (M 22), ✆ 29 85 84 – ⓓ E HV **r**
closed Saturday lunch, Bank Holidays lunch, Saturday in July - August and Sunday – **M** a la carte 69/100 (booking essential)
Spec. Wildlachs auf Gänsestopflebercrème, Lamm- und Wildgerichte, Mousse au chocolat mit Bananenschaum.

XX ✿ **Boettner** (Small old Munich rest.), Theatinerstr. 8 (M 2), ✆ 22 12 10 – ▤. AE ⓓ E VISA
closed Saturday dinner, Sunday and Bank Holidays – **M** a la carte 76/124 (booking essential) LY **u**
Spec. Hechtsoufflé mit Sauce Nantua, Hummereintopf "Hartung", Rote Grütze.

XX **El Toula**, Sparkassenstr. 5 (M 2), ✆ 29 28 69 – AE ⓓ E VISA LY **f**
closed Sunday lunch, Monday and end July - end August – **M** a la carte 69/91 (booking essential for dinner).

XX **La Belle Epoque**, Maximilianstr. 29 (M 22), ✆ 29 33 11, ☂ – AE E LY **n**
closed Saturday until 6 p.m, Sunday and 4 to 25 August – **M** a la carte 44/75 (booking essential).

XX **Chesa Rüegg**, Wurzerstr. 18 (M 22), ✆ 29 71 14, « Country house furniture » – ▤. AE ⓓ E VISA LY **d**
closed Saturday, Sunday and Bank Holidays – **M** a la carte 35/65 (booking essential).

XX **Zum Bürgerhaus**, Pettenkoferstr. 1 (M 2), ✆ 59 79 09, ☂, « Bavarian farm-house furniture » – ⓓ E VISA KZ **s**
closed Saturday until 6 p.m, Sunday and Bank Holidays – **M** a la carte 45/72 (booking essential).

XX **Weinhaus Neuner** (Typical 1852 wine-rest.), Herzogspitalstr. 8 (M 2), ✆ 2 60 39 54 – AE ⓓ E KY **c**
closed Sunday and Bank Holidays – **M** a la carte 43/72.

XX **Dallmayr**, Dienerstr. 14 (1st floor) (M 2), ✆ 2 13 51 00 – AE ⓓ LY **w**
closed dinner Saturday and August, and Sunday – **M** a la carte 35/75.

XX **Halali**, Schönfeldstr. 22 (M 22), ✆ 28 59 09 LY **x**
closed Saturday lunch, Sunday and Bank Holidays – **M** a la carte 42/64 (booking essential).

XX **Mövenpick im Künstlerhaus**, Lenbachplatz 8 (M 2), ✆ 55 78 65, ☂ – AE ⓓ E VISA KY **e**
M a la carte 35/70.

XX **Csarda Piroschka** (Hungarian rest. with gipsy-music), Prinzregentenstr. 1 (M 22), ✆ 29 54 25 – ⓟ. AE ⓓ E VISA LY **k**
closed until 6.30 p.m and Sunday – **M** a la carte 34/65 (booking essential).

XX **Austernkeller**, Stollbergstr. 11 (M 22), ✆ 29 87 87 – AE ⓓ E VISA LY **e**
closed Monday – **M** (dinner only) a la carte 42/66 (booking essential).

X **Gasthaus Glockenbach** (former old Bavarian pub), Kapuzinerstr. 29 (M 2), ✆ 53 40 43
closed Sunday, Monday and first 2 weeks mid July – **M** a la carte 43/59 (booking essential). JZ **s**

X **Goldene Stadt** (Bohemian cooking), Oberanger 44 (M 2), ✆ 26 43 82 – AE ⓓ E
closed Sunday – **M** a la carte 24/57 (booking essential for dinner). KZ **x**

X Zum Klösterl, St.-Anna-Str. 2 (M 22), ✆ 22 50 86 LY **m**
(dinner only) – (booking essential).

X Ratskeller, Marienplatz 8 (M 2), ✆ 22 03 13 LY **R**

Brewery - inns :

X **Spatenhaus-Bräustuben**, Residenzstr. 12 (M 2), ✆ 22 78 41, ☂, « Furnished in traditional alpine style » – AE E VISA LY **t**
M a la carte 29/65.

X **Augustiner - Gaststätten**, Neuhauser Str. 16 (M 2), ✆ 2 60 41 06, « Beer-garden » – ⓓ KY **p**
M a la carte 25/56.

Zum Pschorrbräu (with wine-cellar St. Michael), Neuhauser Str. 11 (M 2), 2 60 30 01, – AE E VISA KY **k**
M a la carte 21/43.

Zum Spöckmeier, Rosenstr. 9 (M 2), 26 80 88 – AE E VISA KYZ **b**
M a la carte 24/53.

Spatenhofkeller, Neuhauser Str. 26 (M 2), 26 40 10 – AE E KY **u**
M a la carte 16.50/37.

Pschorr-Keller, Theresienhöhe 7 (M 2), 50 10 88, beer-garden – . AE E EV **n**
M a la carte 22/43.

Hackerkeller und Schäfflerstuben, Theresienhöhe 4 (M 2), 50 70 04, beer-garden – E EV **e**
M a la carte 16/44.

at Munich-Bogenhausen :

Sheraton, Arabellastr. 6 (M 81), 92 40 11, Telex 522391, < Munich, beer-garden, Massage, , , – . AE E VISA. by Isarring HU
Restaurants : – **Atrium M** a la carte 36/71 – **Alt Bayern Stube** *(dinner only)* **M** a la carte 35/65 – **650 rm** 280/390 Bb.

Prinzregent M without rest, Ismaninger Str. 42 (M 80), 4 70 20 81, Telex 524403, « Elegant, rustic installation », – . AE E VISA HV **t**
closed Christmas - 6 January – **66 rm** 170/315 Bb.

Arabella-Hotel, Arabellastr. 5 (M 81), 9 23 21, Telex 529987, < Munich, Massage, , – rest . AE E VISA by Isarring HU
M a la carte 40/69 – **300 rm** 160/280 Bb.

Crest-Hotel, Effnerstr. 99 (M 81), 98 25 41, Telex 524757 – wc wc . AE E VISA. rest by Isarring HU
M a la carte 38/70 – **155 rm** 188/264 Bb.

Da Pippo (Italian rest.), Mühlbaurstr. 36 (M 80), 4 70 48 48, – E.
closed Sunday and Bank Holidays – **M** a la carte 50/75. by Prinzregentenstr. HV

Käfer-Schänke, Schumannstr. 1 (M 80), 4 16 81, , « Several rooms with rustic and elegant installations » – E. HV **s**
closed Sunday and Bank Holidays – **M** a la carte 48/90 (booking essential).

Bogenhauser Hof (former hunting lodge from 1825), Ismaninger Str. 85 (M 80), 98 55 86, HV **c**
(booking essential).

Tai Tung (Chinese rest.), Prinzregentenstr. 60 (Villa Stuck) (M 80), 47 11 00 – AE E HV **e**
M a la carte 31/55.

Mifune (Japanese rest.), Ismaninger Str. 136 (M 80), 98 75 72 – AE E. HV **v**
closed Sunday and 28 June - 5 July – **M** a la carte 28/60.

Zum Klösterl, Schneckenburger Str. 31 (M 80), 47 61 98 HV **y**

Pulcinella (Italian rest.), Hohensalzacher Str. 1 (M 81), 93 14 72, – AE E.
closed Saturday – **M** a la carte 32/62 (booking essential). by Prinzregentenstr. HV

at Munich 80-Haidhausen :

Preysing (see also **Preysing-Keller** rest. below), Preysingstr. 1, 48 10 11, Telex 529044, , – HX **w**
76 rm 135/245.

München Penta Hotel, Hochstr. 3, 4 48 55 55, Telex 529046, Massage, , – . AE E VISA HX **t**
M a la carte 44/74 – **583 rm** 183/276 Bb.

Preysing-Keller, Innere-Wiener-Str. 6, 48 10 15, « Vaulted cellar, country-house furniture » – HX **w**
closed Sunday, Bank Holidays and 23 December - 6 January – **M** (dinner only) a la carte 48/76 (remarkable wine-list, booking essential)
Spec. Ochsenschwanzsülze mit Gemüsevinaigrette, Kalbsbries auf Pilzrisotto, Rotbarbe auf Sauternes.

Rue des Halles (Rest. in Bistro-style), Steinstr. 18, 48 56 75 HX **a**
dinner only – **M** a la carte 45/61 (booking essential).

at Munich 45-Harthof by ① :

Zur Gärtnerei, Schleißheimer Str. 456, 3 13 13 73
closed Wednesday – **M** a la carte 28/53.

at Munich 83-Neu Perlach by ④ :

Orbis Hotel München M, Karl-Marx-Ring 87, 6 32 70, Telex 5213357, , – rest (with). AE E VISA. rest
M a la carte 33/70 – **185 rm** 140/205 Bb.

Novotel, Rudolf-Vogel-Bogen 3, 63 80 00, Telex 522030, , , – wc . AE E VISA
M a la carte 39/62 – **254 rm** 150/195 Bb.

at Munich 40-Schwabing :

Ramada Parkhotel, Theodor-Dambach-Straße, ✆ 36 09 90, – rest. AE E VISA by ②
M a la carte 45/56 – **260 rm** 179/332 Bb.

Holiday Inn, Leopoldstr. 194, ✆ 34 09 71, Telex 5215439, beer-garden, Massage, – . AE E VISA by ①
Restaurants : – **La Cucina M** a la carte 32/69 – **Oma's Küche M** a la carte 26/48 – **363 rm** 199/358 Bb.

Weinfurtners Garden-Hotel without rest, **Leopoldstr. 132, ✆ 36 80 04, Telex 5214315** – wc wc GU **e**
180 rm Bb.

Olympiapark-Hotel, Helene-Mayer-Ring 12, ✆ 3 51 60 71, **Telex 5215231, free entrance** to the in the recreation centre – wc . AE E VISA. rest
closed 24 December - 6 January – **M** a la carte 23/43 – **100 rm** 150/205 Bb.
by Schleißheimer Str. FU

Residence, Arthur-Kutscher-Platz 4, ✆ 38 17 80, **Telex 529788**, , – wc . AE E VISA. rest HU **q**
M a la carte 44/64 – **150 rm** 193/268.

Consul without rest, **Viktoriastr. 10**, ✆ 33 40 35 – wc GU **k**
27 rm 100/150 Bb.

Leopold, Leopoldstr. 119, ✆ 36 70 61, **Telex 5215160** – wc wc . AE E VISA GU **f**
M *(closed Saturday)* a la carte 30/56 – **85 rm** 99/155 Bb.

XXXX ✿✿✿ **Tantris**, Johann-Fichte-Str. 7, ✆ 36 20 61, , « Modern rest., fashionable decoration » – . AE E. HU **b**
closed Sunday, Bank Holidays and lunch Saturday and Monday – **M** a la carte 87/131 (booking essential)
Spec. Lachs-Terrine mit Kaviar in Gelee, Bresse-Taube auf Petersilien-Ragout mit Waldpilzen, Schokoladenblätter in Mocca-Créme.

XXX ✿ **La Mer**, Schraudolphstr. 24, ✆ 2 72 24 39, « Opulent decor » – AE E VISA.
closed Monday and late July - August – **M** (dinner only) a la carte 65/95 (booking essential). GU **r**

XXX **Savarin**, Schellingstr. 122, ✆ 52 53 11 – E FU **t**
closed Saturday lunch, Sunday, Monday and 3 weeks August – **M** a la carte 56/80.

XX **Walliser Stuben**, Leopoldstr. 33, ✆ 34 80 00, beer-garden – AE E VISA GU **g**
closed Sunday and Bank Holidays – **M** (dinner only) a la carte 38/67.

XX **Seehaus**, Kleinhesselohe 3, ✆ 39 70 72, <, « Lakeside setting, terrace » – . AE E VISA
M a la carte 25/60. HU **t**

XX **Romagna Antica** (Italian rest.), Elisabethstr. 52, ✆ 2 71 63 55, – AE E. FU **a**
closed Sunday and Bank Holidays – **M** a la carte 42/66 (booking essential).

XX **Daitokai** (Japanese rest), Nordendstr. 64 (entrance Kurfürstenstr.), ✆ 2 71 14 21 – .
AE E VISA. GU **d**
closed Sunday – **M** a la carte 36/68.

XX La Coquille, Römerstr. 15, ✆ 39 05 39 GU **s**
(dinner only) **M**.

XX **Bistro Terrine**, Amalienstr. 89 (Amalien-Passage), ✆ 28 17 80 – AE E. GU **q**
closed Sunday, Bank Holidays and 3 weeks August, Monday and Saturday dinner only – **M** a la carte 43/67 (booking essential).

XX **Restaurant 33**, Feilitzschstr. 33, ✆ 34 25 28, – AE HU **a**
M *(dinner only)* a la carte 36/59 (booking essential).

X **Ristorante Bei Grazia**, Ungererstr. 161, ✆ 36 69 31 by ②
closed Friday dinner and Saturday – **M** a la carte 28/51 (booking essential).

at Munich 50-Untermenzing by ⑦ :

Insel-Mühle (converted 16 C riverside mill), von-Kahr-Str. 87, ✆ 8 10 10, Telex 5218292, , beer-garden – wc . E VISA
M *(closed Sunday and Bank Holidays)* a la carte 46/69 – **37 rm** 130/300.

at Neuried **8027** by ⑤ :

X **Neurieder Hof**, Münchner Str. 2, ✆ (089) 7 55 82 72 – . AE E VISA
closed Monday lunch and Tuesday – **M** a la carte 29/60 (booking essential for dinner).

at Aschheim **8011** ③ : 13 km by Riem :

Zur Post, Ismaninger Str. 11 (B 471), ✆ (089) 9 03 20 27, – wc wc
M a la carte 19.50/45 – **50 rm** 45/140 Bb.

STUTTGART 7000. Baden-Württemberg 413 KL 20, 987 ㉟ – pop. 555 000 – alt. 245 m – ☎ 0711.

See: Site (Lage)★★ – Park Wilhelma DU and Killesberg Park (Höhenpark Killesberg) – Television Tower (Fernsehturm)★★ (※★★) DZ – Birkenkopf ※★★ AY – Congress- and Concert Hall (Liederhalle)★ BX – Old Castle (Altes Schloß) (Renaissance courtyard★) CX – Stuttgart State Gallery (Staatsgalerie)★ CX **M1** – Collegiate Church (Stiftskirche) (Commemorative monuments of dukes★) CX **A** – Württemberg Regional Museum (Württembergisches Landesmuseum) (Medieval art objects★★) CX **M2** – Daimler-Benz Museum★ EX **M** – Porsche-Museum★ by ⑧.

Envir.: Bad Cannstatt Spa Park (Kurpark)★ E : 4 km EU.

✈ Stuttgart-Echterdingen, by ③ ✆ 7 90 11, City Air Terminal, Stuttgart, Lautenschlagerstr. 14, ✆ 22 12 64.

Exhibition Centre (Messegelände Killesberg) (BU), ✆ 2 58 91, Telex 722584.

ℹ Tourist-Information, Klett-Passage (subway to the Main Station), ✆ 2 22 82 40, Telex 723854.

ADAC, Am Neckartor 2, ✆ 2 80 00.

Frankfurt am Main 205 ⑧ – Karlsruhe 82 ⑥ – München 219 ④ – Strasbourg 154 ⑥.

Plans on following pages

❄ **Steigenberger-Hotel Graf Zeppelin** ⛰, Arnulf-Klett-Platz 7, ✆ 29 98 81, Telex 722418, Massage, ≘s, ⛱ – 🛗 ▤ 📺 ♿ 🏋. AE ⓓ E VISA — CX **s**
M *(closed Saturday, Sunday, Bank Holidays and 20 July - 16 August)* a la carte 56/88 (booking essential) – **Bistro Zepp M** a la carte 27/42 – **280 rm** 209/400 Bb
Spec. Steinbutt in Nudelteig mit Champagnersauce, Pochiertes Kalbsfilet mit legiertem Gemüsesud, Lammrücken in Schalottensauce.

Am Schloßgarten, Schillerstr. 23, ✆ 29 99 11, Telex 722936, « Terrace with ≤ » – 🛗 ▤ rest 📺 🚗 🏋 (with ▤). AE ⓓ E VISA. ✗ rest — CX **u**
M a la carte 49/83 – **125 rm** 165/290 Bb.

Royal, Sophienstr. 35, ✆ 62 50 50, Telex 722449, 🍽 – 🛗 ▤ rest 📺 🚗 Ⓟ 🏋 — BY **b**
85 rm Bb.

Park-Hotel, Villastr. 21, ✆ 28 01 61, Telex 723405, 🍽 – 🛗 ▤ rest 📺 Ⓟ 🏋 (with ▤). AE ⓓ E VISA — DV **r**
M a la carte 41/61 – **Radiostüble** *(dinner only, closed Sunday and Bank Holidays)* **M** a la carte 25/50 – **81 rm** 150/280 Bb.

Ruff, Friedhofstr. 21, ✆ 25 01 61, Telex 721645, ⛱ – 🛗 📺 ⛀wc ⫛wc ☎ 🚗 Ⓟ 🏋. AE ⓓ E VISA — CV **a**
closed 21 December - 2 January – **M** *(closed Saturday)* a la carte 28/49 – **85 rm** 93/150 Bb.

Intercity-Hotel without rest, Arnulf-Klett-Platz 2, ✆ 29 98 01, Telex 723543 – 🛗 📺 ⛀wc ⫛wc ☎ Ⓟ 🏋. AE ⓓ E VISA — CX **p**
104 rm 78/175.

Kronen-Hotel ⛰ without rest, Kronenstr. 48, ✆ 29 96 61, Telex 723632, ≘s – 🛗 📺 ⫛wc ☎ 🚗. AE ⓓ E VISA — BX **m**
closed 20 December - 7 January – **90 rm** 93/175 Bb.

Rieker without rest, Friedrichstr. 3, ✆ 22 13 11 – 🛗 📺 ⛀wc ⫛wc ☎. AE E VISA — CX **d**
63 rm 98/164.

Unger without rest, Kronenstr. 17, ✆ 29 40 41, Telex 723995 – 🛗 📺 ⛀wc ⫛wc ☎ 🚗 🏋. AE ⓓ E VISA — CX **a**
80 rm 112/210 Bb.

Wartburg Hospiz, Lange Str. 49, ✆ 22 19 91, Telex 721587 – 🛗 ▤ rest 📺 ⛀wc ⫛wc ☎ Ⓟ 🏋 (with ▤). AE ⓓ E VISA — BX **g**
closed Easter and 23 December - 6 January – **M** *(closed Sunday and Bank Holidays)* a la carte 25/40 – **81 rm** 53/150.

Azenberg ⛰, Seestr. 116, ✆ 22 10 51, Telex 721819, ≘s, ⛱ – 🛗 ⛀wc ⫛wc ☎ 🚗 Ⓟ. AE ⓓ E VISA — AV **e**
(only dinner for residents) – **55 rm** 110/180.

Am Feuersee, Johannesstr. 2, ✆ 62 61 03 – 🛗 📺 ⫛wc ☎. AE ⓓ E VISA — AY **t**
closed 20 December - 10 January – **M** *(dinner only, closed Saturday and Sunday)* a la carte 24/45 – **38 rm** 105/160 Bb.

Wörtz-Zur Weinsteige ⛰, Hohenheimer Str. 30, ✆ 24 53 96, Telex 723821, « Terrace » – 📺 ⛀wc ⫛wc ☎. AE ⓓ E VISA — CY **p**
closed 20 December - 5 January – **M** *(closed Saturday, Sunday and Bank Holidays)* a la carte 27/64 – **25 rm** 60/192.

Mack und Pflieger without rest, Kriegerstr. 7, ✆ 29 19 27 – 🛗 ⫛wc ☎ Ⓟ — CX **h**
94 rm Bb.

Ketterer, Marienstr. 3, ✆ 29 41 51, Telex 722340 – 🛗 ⛀wc ⫛wc ☎. AE ⓓ E VISA
closed 20 to 31 December – **M** *(closed mid July - mid August, Friday and Saturday)* a la carte 22/55 – **75 rm** 98/158. — BY **y**

Münchner Hof, Neckarstr. 170, ✆ 28 30 80 – 🛗 ⛀wc ⫛wc ☎ — DV **e**
closed 24 December - 6 January – **M** *(closed Saturday lunch, Sunday and Bank Holidays)* – **18 rm** 82/145.

XXX ✿ **Alte Post**, Friedrichstr. 43, ✆ 29 30 79 – ⓓ CX **e**
closed Sunday, Bank Holidays and end July - mid August, Monday and Saturday dinner only – **M** a la carte 63/95 (booking essential)
Spec. Mousseline von Steinbutt in Caviarbutter, Reh-Medaillons in Preiselbeercreme, Ofenschlupfer mit Vanillesauce.

XXX **Da Franco** (modern rest. with italian cooking), Calwer Str. 23 (1st floor), ✆ 29 15 81 – AE E – **M** a la carte 49/67 (menu given verbally). BX **c**

XXX **Mövenpick-Rôtisserie Baron de la Mouette**, Kleiner Schloßplatz 11 (entrance Theodor-Heuss-Str.), ✆ 22 00 34 – ▤. AE ⓓ E VISA BX **a**
M a la carte 44/70 – **Chesa M** a la carte 32/55 – **Boulevard-Café M** a la carte 24/47.

XX **Der Goldene Adler**, Böheimstr. 38, ✆ 64 17 62 – AE ⓓ E VISA AY **e**
closed Monday – **M** a la carte 32/72.

XX **Schwyzer Eck**, Neckarstr. 246, ✆ 26 58 90 – Ⓟ. E DV **a**
closed Saturday and 1 to 7 January – **M** a la carte 38/72.

XX **Intercity-Restaurant**, Arnulf-Klett-Platz 2, ✆ 29 49 46 CX **v**
M a la carte 25/55.

XX **Greiner Stuben**, Arnulf-Klett-Platz 1, ✆ 29 51 21 – AE ⓓ E CX **t**
M a la carte 33/54 – **Bräustüble M** a la carte 18/37.

XX **Zeppelin-Stüble-Maukenescht** (Swabian cooking), Lautenschlagerstr. 2 (at Graf Zeppelin Hotel), ✆ 22 40 13, 🍽 – AE ⓓ E VISA CX **s**
M a la carte 24/56 (booking essential).

XX **Krämer's Bürgerstuben**, Gablenberger Hauptstr. 4, ✆ 46 54 81 – ⓓ E VISA DX **n**
closed Monday and 3 weeks July - August – **M** a la carte 40/70 (booking essential).

XX **China Garden** (Chinese rest.), Königstr. 17 (2nd floor), ✆ 22 38 66 – AE ⓓ E VISA. ✻ CX **n**
M a la carte 25/56.

at Stuttgart 50 - Bad Cannstatt :

🏨 **Spahr** Ⓜ without rest, Waiblinger Str. 63 (B 14), ✆ 55 20 00, Telex 7254608 – ⇅ TV ⛀wc ⛆wc ☎ 🚗 Ⓟ. AE ⓓ E VISA EU **a**
closed 20 December - 7 January – **59 rm** 110/205.

🏨 **Krehl's Linde**, Obere Waiblinger Str. 113, ✆ 52 75 67 – TV ⛆wc ☎ 🚗. AE EU **r**
M *(closed Sunday, Monday lunch and 1 to 24 August)* a la carte 32/61 – **25 rm** 85/200.

XX **Alt-Cannstatt**, Königsplatz 1 (Kursaal), ✆ 56 11 15, 🍽 – 🎪. AE ⓓ E EU
closed Monday – **M** a la carte 32/50.

XX **Zum Ackerbürger**, Spreuergasse 38, ✆ 56 08 93, « Historical half-timbered house from 1550 with original installation » – AE ⓓ E VISA EU **t**
closed Sunday and 3 to 20 March – **M** (dinner only) a la carte 47/69.

at Stuttgart 70 - Degerloch :

🏨 **Waldhotel Degerloch** 🐌, Guts-Muths-Weg 18, ✆ 76 50 17, Telex 7255728, 🍽, 🏊, 🎾 – ⇅ TV ⛀wc ⛆wc ☎ ♿ Ⓟ 🎪. AE ⓓ E VISA by Guts-Muths-Weg DZ
M a la carte 30/53 – **50 rm** 100/196 Bb.

XX **Turmrestaurant** (Television Tower, 144 m, ⇅ 4 DM), Jahnstr. 120, ✆ 24 61 04, ✻ Stuttgart and environs – ▤ Ⓟ. AE ⓓ E VISA DZ
M a la carte 31/58.

at Stuttgart 30 - Feuerbach :

🏨 **Europe**, Siemensstr. 26, ✆ 81 50 91, Telex 723650, 🏊 – ⇅ ▤ TV 🚗 Ⓟ 🎪. AE ⓓ E VISA. ✻ rest CU **z**
M a la carte 34/67 – **150 rm** 145/190 Bb.

XX **Lamm**, Mühlstr. 24, ✆ 85 36 15 AU **n**
closed Saturday lunch, Sunday and Bank Holidays – **M** a la carte 63/85 (booking essential).

at Stuttgart 23 - Flughafen (Airport) ④ : 15 km :

🏨 **Airport-Hotel Mövenpick**, Randstraße, ✆ 7 90 70, Telex 7245677, 🍽 – ⇅ ▤ rest TV ⛀wc ☎ Ⓟ 🎪 (with ▤). AE ⓓ E VISA
M a la carte 38/66 – **128 rm** 173/216 Bb.

XX **top air**, Randstraße (in the air-port), ✆ 79 01 21 10 – AE ⓓ E VISA
M a la carte 38/67.

at Stuttgart 80 - Möhringen ⑤ : 7 km :

🏨 **Stuttgart International**, Plieninger Str. 100, ✆ 7 20 21, Telex 7255763, entrance to the Römerbad (with 🏊, 🏊) – ⇅ ▤ rest TV ♿ 🚗 Ⓟ 🎪 (with ▤). AE ⓓ E VISA. ✻ rest
Restaurants : – **Kopenhagen** *(lunch only)* **M** a la carte 38/65 – **Paris Grill** *(dinner only)* **M** a la carte 35/75 – **Schwaben-Stube M** a la carte 17/48 – **200 rm** 167/302 Bb.

🏨 Gloria - Restaurant Möhringer Hexle, Sigmaringer Str. 59, ✆ 71 30 59, 🏊 – ⇅ TV ⛀wc ⛆wc ☎ 🚗 Ⓟ 🎪 – **70 rm** Bb.

🏨 Neotel Ⓜ without rest, Vaihinger Str. 151, ✆ 7 80 06 35, Telex 7255179 – ⇅ TV ⛀wc ⛆wc ☎ ♿ Ⓟ. E VISA – **71 rm** Bb.

🏨 **Anker**, Vaihinger Str. 76, ✆ 71 30 31 – ⇅ ⛀wc ☎ 🚗. AE ⓓ E VISA. ✻ rm
closed 20 December - 6 January – **M** *(closed Saturday and Sunday lunch)* a la carte 20/47 (Swabian specialities) 🍷 – **25 rm** 75/120 Bb.

STUTTGART

Street	Grid	No.
Albert-Schäffle-Str.	DY	
Alexanderstraße	DX	2
Am Kochenhof	ABV	
Am Kräherwald	AVX	
Am Neckartor	DV	4
Augsburger Str.	EUV	
Augustenstraße	AY	7
Badstraße	DU	
Bebelstraße	AX	
Benzstraße	EV	
Berliner Platz	BX	8
Birkenwaldstraße	BV	
Bismarckstraße	AY	9
Blumenstraße	CY	10
Böblinger Straße	AZ	
Böheimstraße	AZ	
Bolzstraße	CX	15
Botnanger Straße	AX	16
Brückenstraße	DU	17
Burgstallstraße	AZ	
Cannstatter Str.	CDV	
Charlottenplatz	CX	20
Charlottenstraße	CX	21
Daimlerstraße	EU	
Dillmannstraße	AX	22
Dobelstraße	CY	23
Eberhardstraße	CY	25
Eisenbahnstraße	EU	26
Feuerbacher-Tal-Straße	AU	
Filderstraße	BY	
Friedr.-Ebert-Str.	CU	
Friedrichstraße	CX	
Fritz-Elsas-Str.	BX	28
Gablenberger Hauptstraße	DXY	
Gänsheidestraße	DY	30
Gaußstraße	AX	
Geißeichstraße	AY	

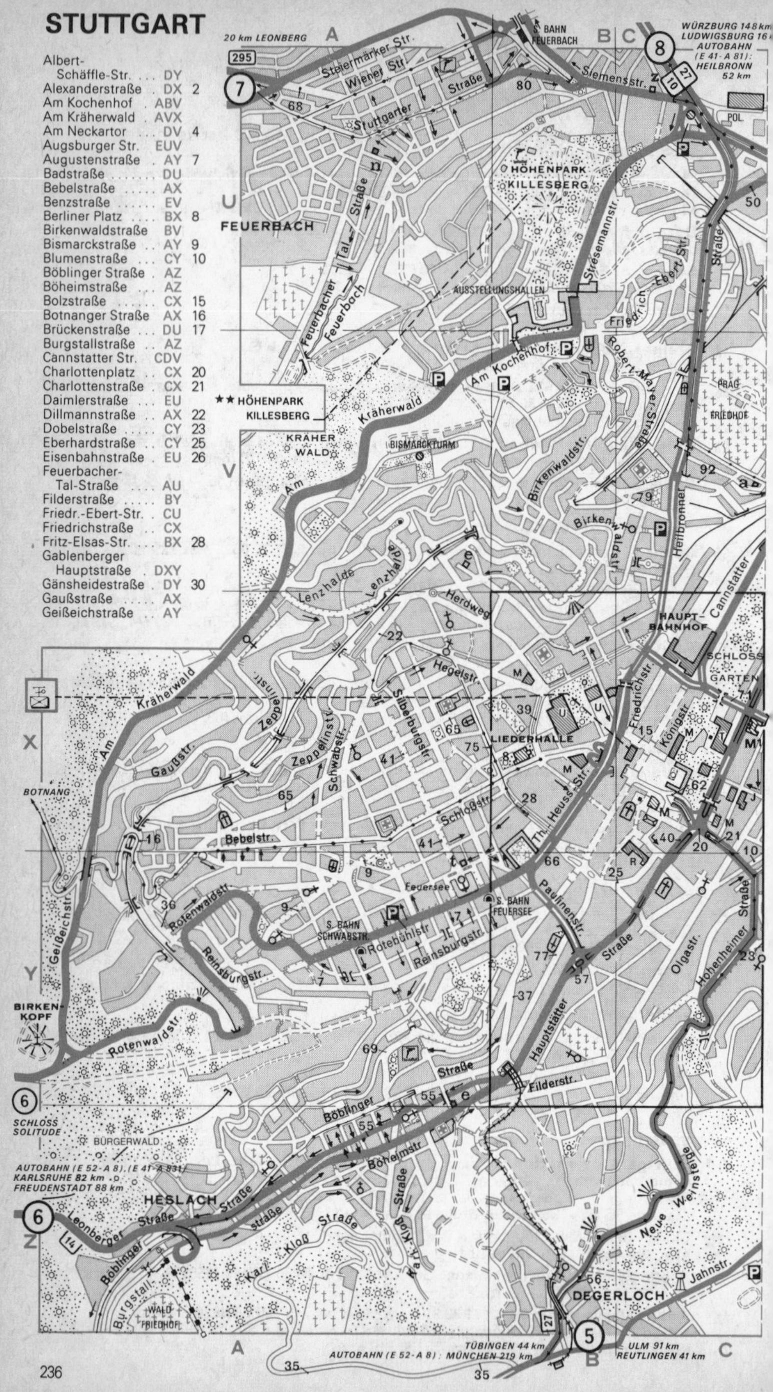

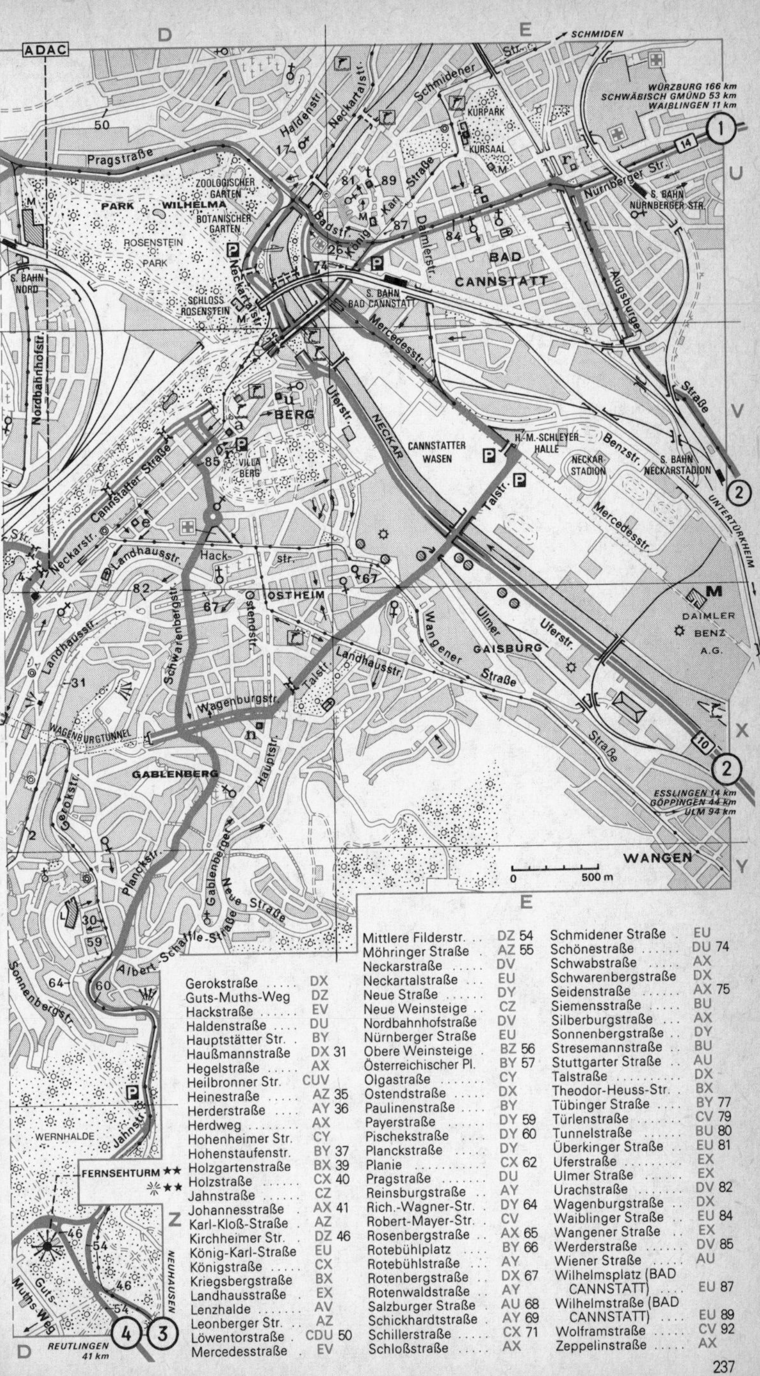

Gerokstraße	DX	
Guts-Muths-Weg	DZ	
Hackstraße	EV	
Haldenstraße	DU	
Hauptstätter Str.	BY	
Haußmannstraße	DX	31
Hegelstraße	AX	
Heilbronner Str.	CUV	
Heinestraße	AZ	35
Herderstraße	AY	36
Herdweg	AX	
Hohenheimer Str.	CY	
Hohenstaufenstr.	BY	37
Holzgartenstraße	BX	39
Holzstraße	CX	40
Jahnstraße	CZ	
Johannesstraße	AX	41
Karl-Kloß-Straße	AZ	
Kirchheimer Str.	DZ	46
König-Karl-Straße	EU	
Königstraße	CX	
Kriegsbergstraße	BX	
Landhausstraße	EX	
Lenzhalde	AV	
Leonberger Str.	AZ	
Löwentorstraße	CDU	50
Mercedesstraße	EV	
Mittlere Filderstr.	DZ	54
Möhringer Straße	AZ	55
Neckarstraße	DV	
Neckartalstraße	EU	
Neue Straße	DY	
Neue Weinsteige	CZ	
Nordbahnhofstraße	DV	
Nürnberger Straße	EU	
Obere Weinsteige	BZ	56
Österreichischer Pl.	BY	57
Olgastraße	CY	
Ostendstraße	DX	
Paulinenstraße	BY	
Payerstraße	DY	59
Pischekstraße	DY	60
Planckstraße	DY	
Planie	CX	62
Pragstraße	DU	
Reinsburgstraße	AY	
Rich.-Wagner-Str.	DY	64
Robert-Mayer-Str.	CV	
Rosenbergstraße	AX	65
Rotebühlplatz	BY	66
Rotebühlstraße	AY	
Rotenbergstraße	DX	67
Rotenwaldstraße	AY	
Salzburger Straße	AU	68
Schickhardtstraße	AY	69
Schillerstraße	CX	71
Schloßstraße	AX	
Schmidener Straße	EU	
Schönestraße	DU	74
Schwabstraße	AX	
Schwarenbergstraße	DX	
Seidenstraße	AX	75
Siemensstraße	BU	
Silberburgstraße	AX	
Sonnenbergstraße	DY	
Stresemannstraße	BU	
Stuttgarter Straße	AU	
Talstraße	DX	
Theodor-Heuss-Str.	BX	
Tübinger Straße	BY	77
Türlenstraße	CV	79
Tunnelstraße	BU	80
Überkinger Straße	EU	81
Uferstraße	EX	
Ulmer Straße	EX	
Urachstraße	DV	82
Wagenburgstraße	DX	
Waiblinger Straße	EU	84
Wangener Straße	EX	
Werderstraße	DV	85
Wiener Straße	AU	
Wilhelmsplatz (BAD CANNSTATT)	EU	87
Wilhelmstraße (BAD CANNSTATT)	EU	89
Wolframstraße	CV	92
Zeppelinstraße	AX	

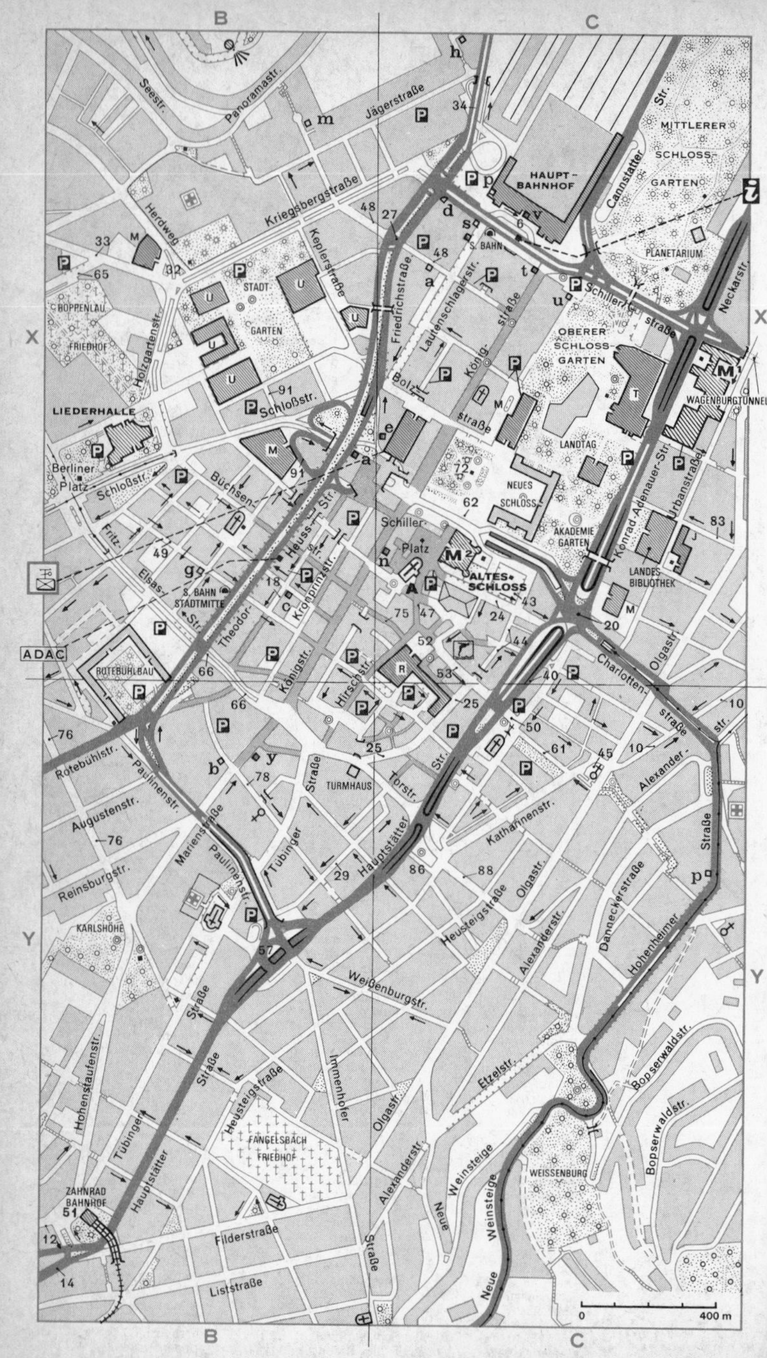

B
C
X
Y
HAUPT-BAHNHOF
MITTLERER SCHLOSS-GARTEN
OBERER SCHLOSS-GARTEN
PLANETARIUM
LANDTAG
NEUES SCHLOSS
AKADEMIE GARTEN
LANDES BIBLIOTHEK
ALTES SCHLOSS
WAGENBURGTUNNEL
STADT-GARTEN
LIEDERHALLE
HOPPENLAU FRIEDHOF
ROTEBÜHLBAU
ADAC
S. BAHN STADTMITTE
TURMHAUS
KARLSHÖHE
FANGELSBACH FRIEDHOF
WEISSENBURG
ZAHNRAD BAHNHOF
Seestr.
Panoramastr.
Jägerstraße
Kriegsbergstraße
Herdweg
Keplerstraße
Holzgartenstr.
Schloßstr.
Berliner Platz
Büchsen-
Fritz-Elsas-Str.
Theodor-Heuss-Str.
Friedrichstraße
Lautenschlagerstr.
Königstraße
Bolzstraße
Schillerstraße
Cannstatter Str.
Neckarstr.
Konrad-Adenauer-Str.
Urbanstraße
Schiller-Platz
Kronprinzstr.
Königstr.
Hirschstr.
Charlotten-straße
Olgastr.
Alexanderstr.
Rotebühlstr.
Paulinenstr.
Augustenstr.
Reinsburgstr.
Marienstraße
Tübinger Straße
Torstr.
Hauptstätter Str.
Katharinenstr.
Heusteigstraße
Danneckerstraße
Hohenheimer Straße
Weißenburgstr.
Immenhofer
Etzelstr.
Bopserwaldstr.
Hohenstaufenstr.
Filderstraße
Liststraße
Neue Weinsteige
Alexanderstr.
0
400 m

STUTTGART

Charlottenplatz CX 20
Eberhardstraße CY
Königstraße BCX
Schulstraße CX 75
Theodor-Heuss-Straße BX

Alexanderstraße CY
Arnulf-Klett-Platz CX 6
Augustenstraße BY
Blumenstraße CY 10
Böblinger Straße BY 12
Böheimstraße BY 14
Bolzstraße CX
Bopserwaldstraße CY
Büchsenstraße BX
Calwer Straße BX 18
Charlottenstraße CXY
Danneckerstraße CY
Dorotheenstraße CX 24
Eberhardstraße CY 25
Etzelstraße CY
Filderstraße BY
Friedrichsplatz CX 27
Friedrichstraße CX
Fritz-Elsas-Straße BX
Gerberstraße BY 29
Hauptstätter Straße BCY
Hegelplatz BX 32
Hegelstraße BX 33
Heilbronner Straße CX 34
Herdweg BX
Heusteigstraße BCY
Hirschstraße BXY
Hohenheimer Straße CY
Hohenstaufenstraße BY
Holzgartenstraße BX
Holzstraße CX 40
Immenhofer Straße BY
Jägerstraße BCX
Karlsplatz CX 43
Karlstraße CX 44
Katharinenplatz CY 45
Katharinenstraße CY
Keplerstraße BX
Kirchstraße CX 47
Konrad-Adenauer-Straße CX
Kriegsbergstraße BX
Kronenstraße CX 48
Kronprinzstraße BX
Lange Straße BX 49
Lautenschlagerstraße CX
Leonhardsplatz CY 50
Liststraße BY
Marienplatz BY 51
Marienstraße BY
Marktplatz CX 52
Marktstraße CX 53
Neckarstraße CX
Neue Weinsteige CY
Österreichischer Platz BY 57
Olgastraße CXY
Panoramastraße BX
Paulinenstraße BY
Pfarrstraße CY 61
Planie CX 62
Reinsburgstraße BY
Rosenbergstraße BX 65
Rotebühlplatz BX 66
Rotebühlstraße BY
Schillerplatz CX
Schillerstraße CX
Schloßplatz CX 72
Schloßstraße BX
Seestraße BX
Silberburgstraße BY 76
Sophienstraße BY 78
Tübinger Straße BY
Ulrichstraße CX 83
Urbanstraße CX
Weißenburgstraße BCY
Wilhelmsplatz CY 86
Wilhelmstraße CY 88
Willi-Bleicher-Straße BX 91

XX ✿ **Hirsch-Weinstuben**, Maierstr. 3, ℘ 71 13 75 – Ⓟ. AE ⓓ E. ✡
closed Saturday lunch, Sunday, Bank Holidays, 2 weeks July - August and 7 to 21 April –
M a la carte 30/71 (booking essential)
Spec. Terrine von Gänsestopfleber, Meeresfrüchte in Schnittlauchvinaigrette, Entenbrust in zwei Gängen serviert.

XX **Landgasthof Riedsee**, Elfenstr. 120, ℘ 71 24 84, 余 – Ⓟ. AE ⓓ E VISA
M a la carte 38/62.

at Stuttgart 50 - Mühlhausen by Neckartalstraße EU :

XXX ✿ **Öxle's Löwen**, Veitstr. 2, ℘ 53 22 26 – AE
closed lunch Monday and Saturday, Sunday and Bank Holidays – **M** a la carte 55/86
Spec. Lachsforellen- und Zanderflädle mit Sektsabayon, Krustade von Rotbarbe, Feuilleté von Kalbsfilet und weissen Trüffeln (November - February).

at Stuttgart 61 - Obertürkheim by ② :

X **Weinstube Paule**, Augsburger Str. 643, ℘ 32 14 71 – Ⓟ. AE ⓓ E
closed Thursday and last Sunday in the month – **M** a la carte 26/55 ♁.

X **Wirt am Berg**, Uhlbacher Str. 14, ℘ 32 12 26
closed Sunday, Bank Holidays, first Saturday in the month, 3 weeks July - August and 23 December - 1 January – **M** a la carte 25/52 ♁.

at Stuttgart 70 - Plieningen ④ : 13 km :

🏨 **Traube**, Brabandtgasse 2, ℘ 45 48 33, 余 – ⇔wc ⥮wc ☎ Ⓟ
closed 22 December - 6 January – **M** *(closed Saturday, Sunday and 3 weeks August)* a la carte 38/92 (booking essential) – **22 rm** 65/180.

🏨 **Fissler-Post**, Schoellstr. 4, ℘ 45 50 74 – ⥮wc ☎ ⇔ Ⓟ 🔬. AE ⓓ E VISA
M *(closed Sunday dinner)* a la carte 29/56 (booking essential) – **63 rm** 68/114.

XX **Recknagel's Nagelschmiede**, Brabandtgasse 1, ℘ 45 74 54 – Ⓟ
closed lunch Monday to Saturday, Tuesday and 22 August - 15 September – **M** a la carte 30/54.

at Stuttgart 40 - Stammheim by ⑧ :

🏨 **Novotel**, Korntaler Str. 207, ℘ 80 10 65, Telex 7252137, ≘s, ⛱ (heated) – |♦| ▤ TV ⇔wc ☎ ♿ Ⓟ 🔬. AE ⓓ E VISA
M a la carte 34/49 – **117 rm** 130/173 Bb.

***at Fellbach* 7012** by ① : 8 km – ✆ 0711 (Stuttgart) :

🏨 **Kongresshotel** Ⓜ, Tainer Str. 7, ℘ 5 85 90, Telex 7254900, ≘s – |♦| TV ⇔ Ⓟ. AE ⓓ E VISA
M (rest. see **Alt Württemberg below**) – **148 rm** 145/220 Bb.

🏨 **Am Kappelberg**, Karlstr. 37, ℘ 58 50 41, Telex 7254486, ≘s, ⛱ – |♦| ▤ TV ⇔wc ☎ ⇔ Ⓟ. AE ⓓ E
closed 22 December - 10 January and Easter (only dinner for residents) – **41 rm** 100/155 Bb.

🏨 **Alte Kelter**, Kelterweg 7, ℘ 58 90 74, 余 – ⥮wc ☎ ⇔ Ⓟ. AE E
closed January – **M** *(closed Friday)* a la carte 27/53 – **20 rm** 85/130.

XX **Alt Württemberg**, Tainer Str. 7 (Schwabenlandhalle), ✆ 58 00 88 – ▤ **P** 🏛. AE ⊙ E VISA
M a la carte 45/63.

X **Weinkeller Häussermann** (18 C vaulted cellar of 1732), Kappelbergstr. 1, ✆ 58 77 75 – ▤. AE ⊙ E VISA
closed Saturday lunch, Sunday, Bank Holidays and 24 December - 6 January – **M** a la carte 23/51.

X **Weinstube Germania** with rm, Schmerstr. 6, ✆ 58 20 37 – ⋒wc. ✂
closed 24 December - 13 January – **M** *(closed Sunday, Monday and Bank Holidays)* a la carte 23/41 – **8 rm** 30/60.

at Gerlingen **7016** ⑦ : 14 km :

🏨 **Krone**, Hauptstr. 28, ✆ (07156) 2 10 04 – |♦| TV ⇔wc ⋒wc ☎ ⇔ **P** 🏛. AE ⊙ E VISA. ✂ rest
M *(closed Wednesday dinner, Sunday, Bank Holidays and 25 July - 15 August)* a la carte 30/70 (booking essential) – **35 rm** 96/180 Bb.

🏨 **Balogh** without rest, Max-Eyth-Str. 16, ✆ (07156) 2 30 95 – |♦| ⇔wc ⋒wc ☎ ⇔ **P**. AE E
48 rm 70/135.

at Korntal-Münchingen 2 **7015** ⑧ : 9 km, near motorway exit S-Zuffenhausen :

🏨 **Mercure**, Siemensstr. 50, ✆ (07150) 1 30, Telex 723589, beer-garden, ≘s, ⊠ – |♦| ▤ TV ♿ **P** 🏛. AE ⊙ E VISA
M a la carte 26/51 – **209 rm** 151/192 Bb.

🏨 **Strohgäu Hotel**, Stuttgarter Str. 60, ✆ (07150) 60 81 – TV ⋒wc ☎ **P** 🏛. AE ⊙ E VISA
M a la carte 25/50 – **22 rm** 98/135 Bb.

at Leinfelden-Echterdingen 1 **7022** by ⑤ :

🏨 **Drei Morgen** without rest, Bahnhofstr. 39, ✆ (0711) 75 10 85 – |♦| ⋒wc ☎ ♿ ⇔ **P**. AE
25 rm 80/135 Bb.

XX **Filderämtle**, Bahnhofstr. 16 (Filderhalle), ✆ (0711) 75 02 51 – **P** 🏛. AE ⊙ E
closed Monday – **M** a la carte 22/45.

at Leinfelden-Echterdingen 2 **7022** by ⑤ :

🏨 **Lamm**, Hauptstr. 98, ✆ (0711) 79 33 26, Telex 7255686 – TV ⋒wc ☎ **P**. AE ⊙ E
M a la carte 41/66 – **20 rm** 90/120 Bb.

🏨 **Adler**, Obergasse 16, ✆ (0711) 79 35 90, ≘s, ⊠ – |♦| ⇔wc ⋒wc ☎ **P** 🏛
closed 24 December - 2 January – **M** *(closed Sunday, Monday lunch and 3 weeks July - August)* a la carte 27/59 – **19 rm** 85/130.

Baiersbronn

7292. Baden-Württemberg 413 HI 21, 987 ㉟ – pop. 14 000 – alt. 550 m – ☎ 07442.

Stuttgart 100.

XXXX ✿✿ **Restaurant Bareiss**, Gärtenbühlweg 14 (Mitteltal), ✆ 4 71, ← – ▤ **P**. ⊙. ✂
closed Monday, Tuesday, 9 June - 3 July and 28 November - 24 December – **M** a la carte 66/90 (wine-list with 350 wines)
Spec. Wachtelmaultäschchen mit Edelpilzen, St. Peters-Fisch mit Jakobsmuscheltatar, Gugelhupf vom Lachs.

XXXX ✿✿ **Schwarzwaldstube in der Traube-Tonbach** (French cuisine), Tonbachstr. 237 (Tonbach), ✆ 49 26 65, ← – **P**. AE ⊙ E. ✂
closed Thursday, Friday lunch, 6 January - 13 February and 2 to 17 July – **M** a la carte 68/96 (booking essential)
Spec. Wolfsbarsch in Rotweinbutter, Gefüllter Milchlammrücken (for 2 pers.), Mille-Feuille mit Walderdbeeren.

Bühl

7580. Baden-Württemberg 413 H 20, 987 ㉞, 242 ⑳ – pop. 23 680 – alt. 135 m – ☎ 07223.

Stuttgart 117.

XXX ✿✿ **Burg Windeck**, Kappelwindeckstr. 104 (SE : 4 km, near the castle ruins Altwindeck), ✆ 2 36 71, ← Bühl and Rhine-plain – **P**. AE ⊙ E
closed Monday, Tuesday and January - 25 February – **M** a la carte 75/120
Spec. Taubensalat mit Gänseleber, Hummer auf Linsen, Ochsenlende mit Zwiebelkruste.

Greece
Hellás

Athens

PRACTICAL INFORMATION

LOCAL CURRENCY

Greek Drachma : 100 Drs = 0.72 US $ (Jan. 87)

TOURIST INFORMATION

National Tourist Organisation (EOT) : 2 Karageorgi Servias ✆ 322 25 45 (information) and 323 71 93 (Hotel reservation). Also at East Airport ✆ 970 23 95 - Tourist Police : 7 Leoforos Singrou ✆ 171.

FOREIGN EXCHANGE

Banks are usually open on weekdays from 8am to 2pm. A branch of the National Bank of Greece is open daily from 8am to 9pm (8pm at weekends) at 2 Karageorgi Servias (Sindagma).

AIRLINES

OLYMPIC AIRWAYS : 96 Leoforos Singrou 117 41 Athens, ✆ 929 21 11 and 4 Othonos (Sindagma) 105 57 Athens, ✆ 929 24 44.
All following Companies are located near Sindagma Square :
AIR FRANCE : 4 Karageorgi Servias 105 62 Athens, ✆ 323 05 01.
BRITISH AIRWAYS : 10 Othonos 105 57 Athens, ✆ 325 06 01.
JAPAN AIRLINES : 4 Leoforos Amalias 105 57 Athens, ✆ 324 82 11.
LUFTHANSA : 4 Karageorgi Servias 105 62 Athens, ✆ 329 42 35.
PAN AM : 4 Othonos 105 57 Athens, ✆ 323 52 42.
SABENA : 8 Othonos 105 57 Athens, ✆ 323 68 21.
SWISSAIR : 4 Othonos 105 57 Athens, ✆ 323 18 71.
TWA : 8 Xenofondos 105 57 Athens, ✆ 322 64 51.

TRANSPORT IN ATHENS

Taxis : may be hailed in the street even when already engaged ; it is advised to always pay by the meter. Minimum charge : 110 Drs.
Bus : good for sightseeing and practical for short distances.
Metro : one single line of subway crossing the city from North (Kifissia) to South (Piraeus).

POSTAL SERVICES

General Post Office : 100 Eolou (Omonia) with poste restante, and also at Sindagma Square.
Telephone (OTE) : 15 and 65 Stadiou, and 85 Patission.

SHOPPING IN ATHENS

Shops are usually open from 8am to 1.30pm, and 5 to 8pm (in summer 5.30 to 8.30pm). They close on Sunday, and at 2.30pm on Monday, Wednesday and Saturday. Department Stores in Patission and Eolou. The main shopping streets are to be found in Sindagma, Kolonaki, Monastiraki and Omonia areas. Flea Market (generally open on Sunday) and Greek Handicraft in Plaka.

TIPPING

Service is generally included in hotel and restaurant bills but it is usual to tip employees.

SPEED LIMITS

The speed limit in built up areas is generally either 60 or 40 km/h (37-25 mph) ; on motorways the maximum permitted speed is 100 km/h (62 mph) and 90 km/h (56 mph) on others roads.

SEAT BELTS

The wearing of seat belts is compulsory for drivers and front seat passengers.

BREAKDOWN SERVICE

The ELPA (Automobile and Touring Club of Greece) operate a 24 hour breakdown service : phone 104.

ATHENS

SIGHTS

Views of Athens : Lycabettos (Likavitós)☼★★★ DX – Philopappos Hill (Lófos Filopápou)≤★★★ AY.

ANCIENT ATHENS

Acropolis★★★ (Akrópoli) ABY – Hephaisteion★★ (Thissío) AY and Agora★ (Arhéa Ágora) AY – Theatre of Dionysos★★ (Théatro Dionissou) BY and Odeon of Herod Atticus★ (Odío Iródou Atikoú) AY – Olympieion★★ (Naós Olimpiou Diós) BY and Hadrian's Arch★ (Píli Adrianoú) BY – Roman Forum (Romaïki Ágora) : Tower of the Winds★ BY **G**.

BYZANTINE AND TURKISH ATHENS

Pláka★★ (Old Athens) : Old Metropolitan★★ BY **A2** – Monastiráki★ (Old Turkish Bazaar) : Pandrossou Street★ BY **29**, Monastiráki Square★ BY, Kapnikaréa (Church) BY **A6**.

MODERN ATHENS

Síndagma Square★ CY : Greek guard on sentry duty – Academy, University and Library Buildings★ (Akadimia CX, Panepistimio CX, Ethniki Vivliothíki BX) – National Garden★ (Ethnikós Kípos) CY – Stadium★ (Stádio) CDY.

MUSEUMS

National Archaeological Museum★★★ (Ethnikó Arheologikó Moussío) BX – Akropolis Museum★★★ BY **M** – Museum of Cycladic and Ancient Greek Art★★ DY **M15** – Byzantine Museum★★ (Vizandinó Moussio) DY – Benaki Museum★★ (private collection of antiquities and traditional art) CDY – Museum of Traditional Greek Art★ BY **M2** – National Historical Museum★ BY **M7** – National Gallery and Soutzos Museum★★ (painting and sculpture) DY **M8**.

EXCURSIONS

Cape Sounion★★★ (Soúnio) SE : 71 km BY – Kessariani Monastery★★, E : 9 km DY – Daphne Monastery★★ (Dafní) NW : 10 km AX – Aigina Island★ (Égina) : Temple of Aphaia★★, 3 hours Rtn.

ATHENS **(ATHÍNA)** Attiki 980 ㉚ – Pop. 3 076 786 (Athens and Piraeus area) – ☎ 01.

⛳18 Glifáda (near airport) ☎ 894 68 20.

✈ S : 15 km, East Airport ☎ 96991 (International Airport - All companies except Olympic Airways), West Airport ☎ 929 21 11 (Hellinikon Airport - Olympic Airways only) – East Airport Terminal : 4 Leoforos Amalias ☎ 324 20 24, West Airport Terminal : 96 Leoforos Singrou ☎ 929 21 11.

🚗 1 Karolou ☎ 522 24 91.

ℹ Tourist Information (EOT), 2 Amerikis (Sindagma) ☎ 322 31 11 and East Airport ☎ 970 23 95.
ELPA (Automobile and Touring Club of Greece), 2 Messogion ☎ 779 16 15.

Igoumenítsa 581 – Pátra 215 – Thessaloníki 479.

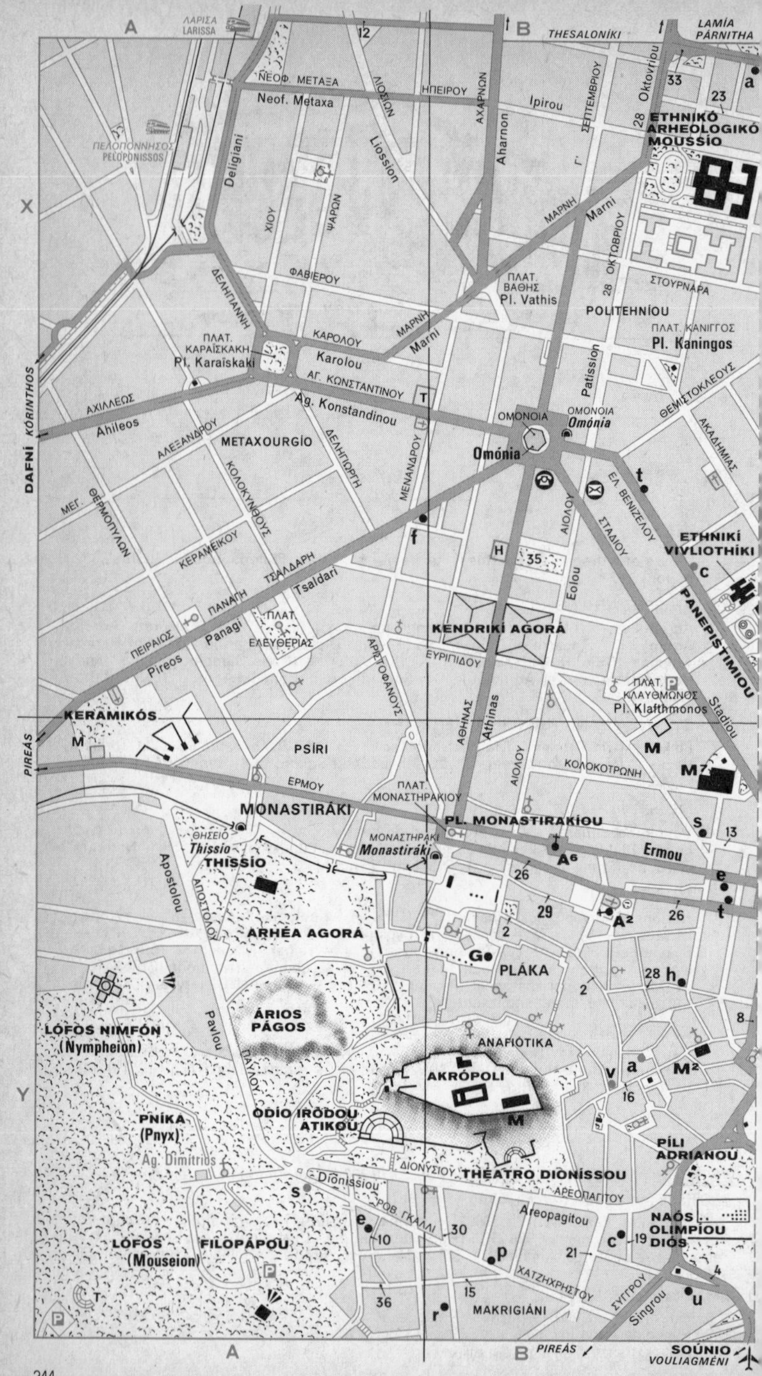
ΛΑΡΙΣΑ
LARISSA
THESALONÍKI
LAMÍA
PÁRNITHA
ΠΕΛΟΠΟΝΝΗΣΟΣ
PELOPONISSOS
ΝΕΟΦ. ΜΕΤΑΞΑ
Neof. Metaxa
ΗΠΕΙΡΟΥ
Ipirou
Deligiani
Liossion
Aharnon
Marni
Patission
ETHNIKÓ ARHEOLOGIKÓ MOUSSÍO
ΦΑΒΙΕΡΟΥ
ΣΤΟΥΡΝΑΡΑ
ΠΛΑΤ. ΒΑΘΗΣ
Pl. Vathis
POLITEHNÍOU
ΠΛΑΤ. ΚΑΝΙΓΓΟΣ
Pl. Kaningos
ΚΑΡΟΛΟΥ
Karolou
ΠΛΑΤ. ΚΑΡΑΪΣΚΑΚΗ
Pl. Karaïskaki
ΑΓ. ΚΩΝΣΤΑΝΤΙΝΟΥ
Ag. Konstandinou
ΑΧΙΛΛΕΩΣ
Ahileos
DAFNÍ
KÓRINTHOS
ΑΛΕΞΑΝΔΡΟΥ
METAXOURGÍO
ΟΜΟΝΟΙΑ
Omónia
ΘΕΜΙΣΤΟΚΛΕΟΥΣ
ΑΚΑΔΗΜΙΑΣ
ΕΛ. ΒΕΝΙΖΕΛΟΥ
ΣΤΑΔΙΟΥ
ΑΙΟΛΟΥ
ETHNIKÍ VIVLIOTHÍKI
PANEPISTIMÍOU
ΚΕΡΑΜΕΙΚΟΥ
ΤΣΑΛΔΑΡΗ
Tsaldari
ΠΑΝΑΓΗ
Panagi
ΠΕΙΡΑΙΩΣ
Pireos
ΠΛΑΤ. ΕΛΕΥΘΕΡΙΑΣ
KENDRIKÍ AGORÁ
ΕΥΡΙΠΙΔΟΥ
ΑΡΙΣΤΟΦΑΝΟΥΣ
Eolou
ΠΛΑΤ. ΚΛΑΥΘΜΩΝΟΣ
Pl. Klafthmonos
Stadiou
KERAMIKÓS
PIREÁS
PSIRI
ΑΘΗΝΑΣ
Athinas
ΚΟΛΟΚΟΤΡΩΝΗ
ΕΡΜΟΥ
ΠΛΑΤ. ΜΟΝΑΣΤΗΡΑΚΙΟΥ
MONASTIRÁKI
PL. MONASTIRAKÍOU
ΘΗΣΕΙΟ
Thissio
THISSÍO
ΜΟΝΑΣΤΗΡΑΚΙ
Monastiráki
Ermou
Apostolou
ARHÉA AGORÁ
PLÁKA
LÓFOS NIMFÓN
(Nympheion)
Pavlou
ÁRIOS PÁGOS
ANAFIÓTIKA
AKRÓPOLI
PNÍKA
(Pnyx)
ODÍO IRÓDOU ATIKOÚ
Ag. Dimítrios
ΔΙΟΝΥΣΙΟΥ
THEATRO DIONÍSSOU
Dionissíou
ΑΡΕΟΠΑΓΙΤΟΥ
Areopagitou
PÍLI ADRIANOÚ
NAÓS OLIMPÍOU DIÓS
ΡΟΒ. ΓΚΑΛΛΙ
LÓFOS (Mouseion)
FILOPÁPOU
ΧΑΤΖΗΧΡΗΣΤΟΥ
ΣΥΓΓΡΟΥ
Singrou
MAKRIGIÁNI
SOÚNIO
VOULIAGMÉNI

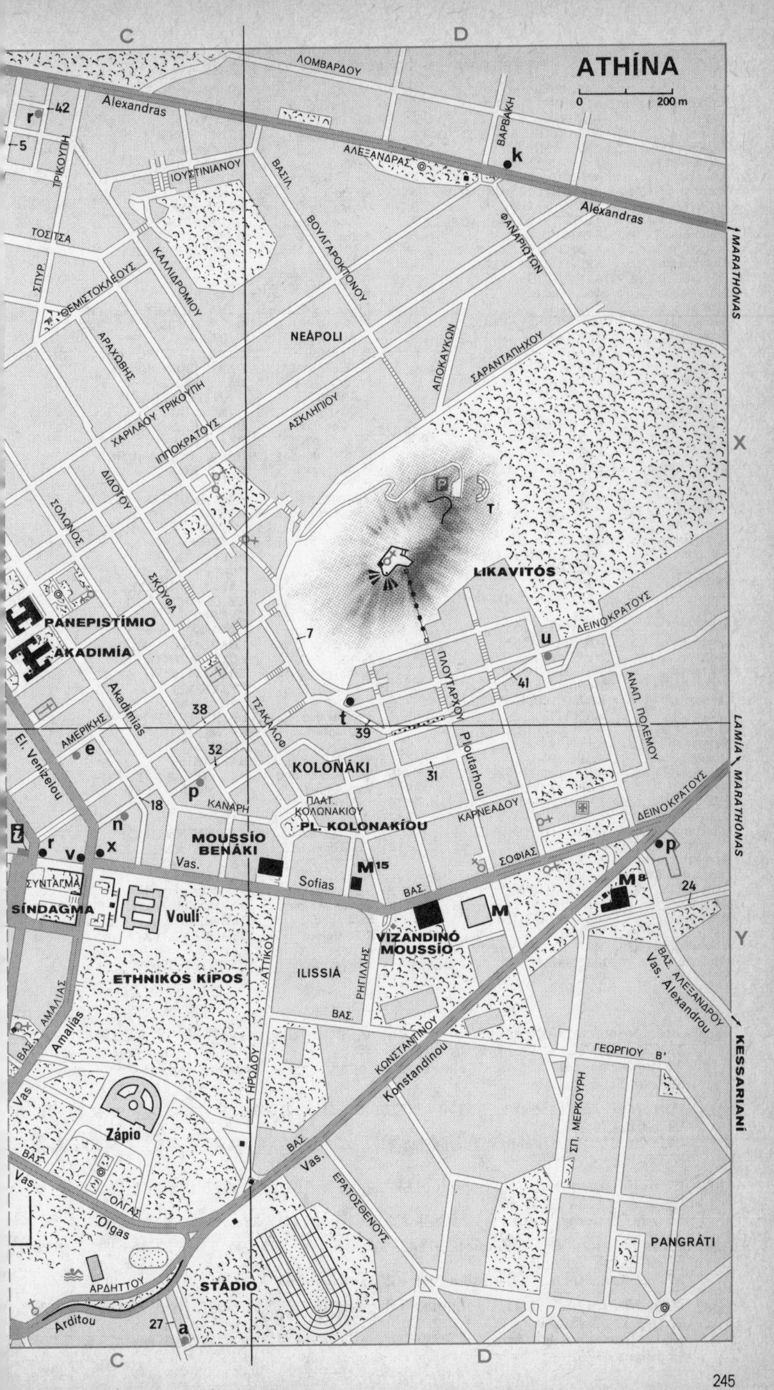
ATHÍNA
0
200 m
C
D
X
Y
Alexandras
ΛΟΜΒΑΡΔΟΥ
ΑΛΕΞΑΝΔΡΑΣ
ΒΑΡΒΑΚΗ
ΙΟΥΣΤΙΝΙΑΝΟΥ
ΤΡΙΚΟΥΠΗ
ΒΑΣΙΛ.
ΒΟΥΛΓΑΡΟΚΤΟΝΟΥ
ΦΑΝΑΡΙΩΤΩΝ
ΤΟΣΙΤΣΑ
ΣΠΥΡ.
ΘΕΜΙΣΤΟΚΛΕΟΥΣ
ΚΑΛΛΙΔΡΟΜΙΟΥ
NEÁPOLI
ΑΡΑΧΩΒΗΣ
ΑΠΟΚΑΥΚΩΝ
ΣΑΡΑΝΤΑΠΗΧΟΥ
ΧΑΡΙΛΑΟΥ ΤΡΙΚΟΥΠΗ
ΑΣΚΛΗΠΙΟΥ
ΙΠΠΟΚΡΑΤΟΥΣ
ΔΙΔΟΤΟΥ
ΣΟΛΩΝΟΣ
ΣΚΟΥΦΑ
LIKAVITÓS
ΔΕΙΝΟΚΡΑΤΟΥΣ
PANEPISTÍMIO
AKADIMÍA
Akadimias
ΑΜΕΡΙΚΗΣ
ΤΣΑΚΑΛΩΦ
ΠΛΟΥΤΑΡΧΟΥ
Ploutarhou
ΑΝΑΠ. ΠΟΛΕΜΟΥ
KOLONÁKI
ΚΑΝΑΡΗ
ΠΛΑΤ. ΚΟΛΩΝΑΚΙΟΥ
PL. KOLONAKÍOU
ΚΑΡΝΕΑΔΟΥ
El. Venizelou
MOUSSÍO BENÁKI
Vas.
Sofias
ΣΟΦΙΑΣ
ΒΑΣ.
ΣΥΝΤΑΓΜΑ
SÍNDAGMA
Vouli
VIZANDINÓ MOUSSÍO
ILISSIÁ
ΡΗΓΙΛΛΗΣ
ΑΤΤΙΚΟΥ
ETHNIKÓS KÍPOS
ΑΜΑΛΙΑΣ
Amalias
ΗΡΩΔΟΥ
ΚΩΝΣΤΑΝΤΙΝΟΥ
Konstandinou
ΒΑΣ. ΑΛΕΞΑΝΔΡΟΥ
Vas. Alexandrou
ΓΕΩΡΓΙΟΥ Β'
ΣΠ. ΜΕΡΚΟΥΡΗ
Zápio
ΕΡΑΤΟΣΘΕΝΟΥΣ
ΟΛΓΑΣ
Olgas
ΑΡΔΗΤΤΟΥ
Arditou
STÁDIO
PANGRÁTI
MARATHÓNAS
LAMÍA
KESSARIANÍ
42
5
7
41
38
39
32
31
18
24
27
r
k
u
t
e
p
n
x
v
a
T
M
M15
M8

STREET INDEX TO ATHÍNA TOWN PLAN

Street	Greek	Plan	No.
Adrianou	ΑΔΡΙΑΝΟΥ	BY	2
Ag. Konstandinou	ΑΓ. ΚΩΝΣΤΑΝΤΙΝΟΥ	AX	
Aharnon	ΑΧΑΡΝΩΝ	BX	
Ahileos	ΑΧΙΛΛΕΩΣ	AX	
Akadimias	ΑΚΑΔΗΜΙΑΣ	BCX	
Alexandras	ΑΛΕΞΑΝΔΡΑΣ	CDX	
Amerikis	ΑΜΕΡΙΚΗΣ	CXY	
Anapiron Polemou	ΑΝΑΠΗΡΩΝ ΠΟΛΕΜΟΥ	DXY	
Apokafkon	ΑΠΟΚΑΥΚΩΝ	DX	
Apostolou Pavlou	ΑΠΟΣΤΟΛΟΥ ΠΑΥΛΟΥ	AY	
Arahovis	ΑΡΑΧΩΒΗΣ	CX	
Arditou	ΑΡΔΗΤΤΟΥ	CY	
Aristofanous	ΑΡΙΣΤΟΦΑΝΟΥΣ	AX	
Asklipiou	ΑΣΚΛΗΠΙΟΥ	DX	
Ath. Diakou	ΑΘ. ΔΙΑΚΟΥ	BY	4
Athinas	ΑΘΗΝΑΣ	BXY	
Bouboulinas	ΜΠΟΥΜΠΟΥΛΙΝΑΣ	CX	5
Ddakalof	ΤΣΑΚΑΛΩΦ	DXY	
Deligiani	ΔΕΛΗΓΙΑΝΝΗ	AX	
Deligiorgi	ΔΕΛΗΓΙΩΡΓΗ	AX	
Dinokratous	ΔΕΙΝΟΚΡΑΤΟΥΣ	DX	
Dionissiou Areopagitou	ΔΙΟΝΥΣΙΟΥ ΑΡΕΟΠΑΓΙΤΟΥ	ABY	
El. Venizelou (Panepistimiou)	ΕΛ. ΒΕΝΙΖΕΛΟΥ (ΠΑΝΕΠΙΣΤΗΜΙΟΥ)	BCX	
Eolou	ΑΙΟΛΟΥ	BXY	
Eratosthenous	ΕΡΑΤΟΣΘΕΝΟΥΣ	DY	
Ermou	ΕΡΜΟΥ	ABY	
Evelpidos Rongakou	ΕΥΕΛΠΙΔΟΣ ΡΟΓΚΑΚΟΥ	DX	7
Fanarioton	ΦΑΝΑΡΙΩΤΩΝ	DX	
Favierou	ΦΑΒΙΕΡΟΥ	AX	
Filelinon	ΦΙΛΕΛΛΗΝΩΝ	BY	8
Govemster	ΓΟΥΕΜΣΤΕΡ	AY	10
Hadzihristou	ΧΑΤΖΗΧΡΗΣΤΟΥ	BY	
Harilaou Trikoupi	ΧΑΡΙΛΑΟΥ ΤΡΙΚΟΥΠΗ	CX	
Hiou	ΧΙΟΥ	AX	
Ioulianou	ΙΟΥΛΙΑΝΟΥ	AX	12
Ioustinianou	ΙΟΥΣΤΙΝΙΑΝΟΥ	CX	
Ipirou	ΗΠΕΙΡΟΥ	ABX	
Ipokratous	ΙΠΠΟΚΡΑΤΟΥΣ	CX	
Irodou Atikou	ΗΡΩΔΟΥ ΑΤΤΙΚΟΥ	DY	
Kalidromiou	ΚΑΛΛΙΔΡΟΜΙΟΥ	CX	
Kanari	ΚΑΝΑΡΗ	CY	
Kar. Servias	ΚΑΡ. ΣΕΡΒΙΑΣ	BY	13
Karneadou	ΚΑΡΝΕΑΔΟΥ	DY	
Karolou	ΚΑΡΟΛΟΥ	AX	
Kavaloti	ΚΑΒΑΛΛΟΤΙ	BY	15
Keramikou	ΚΕΡΑΜΕΙΚΟΥ	AX	
Kidathineon	ΚΥΔΑΘΗΝΑΙΩΝ	BY	16
Kolokinthous	ΚΟΛΟΚΥΝΘΟΥΣ	AX	
Kolokotroni	ΚΟΛΟΚΟΤΡΩΝΗ	BY	
Kriezotou	ΚΡΙΕΖΩΤΟΥ	CY	18
Likavitou	ΛΥΚΑΒΗΤΤΟΥ	CX	
Liossion	ΛΙΟΣΙΩΝ	BX	
Lomvardou	ΛΟΜΒΑΡΔΟΥ	DX	
Makri	ΜΑΚΡΗ	BY	19
Makrigiani	ΜΑΚΡΥΓΙΑΝΝΗ	BY	21
Marni	ΜΑΡΝΗ	ABX	
Meg. Alexandrou	ΜΕΓ. ΑΛΕΞΑΝΔΡΟΥ	AX	
Menandrou	ΜΕΝΑΝΔΡΟΥ	AX	
Metsovou	ΜΕΤΣΟΒΟΥ	BX	23
Mihalakopoulou	ΜΙΧΑΛΑΚΟΠΟΥΛΟΥ	DY	24
Mitropoleos	ΜΗΤΡΟΠΟΛΕΩΣ	BY	26
N. Theotoki	Ν. ΘΕΟΤΟΚΗ	CY	27
Navarhou Nikodimou	ΝΑΥΑΡΧΟΥ ΝΙΚΟΔΗΜΟΥ	BY	28
Neof. Metaxa	ΝΕΟΦ. ΜΕΤΑΞΑ	AX	
Omonia	ΟΜΟΝΟΙΑ	BX	
Pandrossou	ΠΑΝΔΡΟΣΟΥ	BY	29
Parthenonos	ΠΑΡΘΕΝΩΝΟΣ	BY	30
Patission (28 Oktovriou)	ΠΑΤΗΣΙΩΝ (28 ΟΚΤΩΒΡΙΟΥ)	BX	
Patr. Ioakim	ΠΑΤΡ. ΙΩΑΚΕΙΜ	DY	31
Pindarou	ΠΙΝΔΑΡΟΥ	CY	32
Pireos (Panagi Tsaldari)	ΠΕΙΡΑΙΩΣ (ΠΑΝΑΓΗ ΤΣΑΛΔΑΡΗ)	AX	
Pl. Anexartissias (Vathis)	ΠΛΑΤ. ΑΝΕΞΑΡΤΗΣΙΑΣ (ΒΑΘΗΣ)	BX	
Pl. Egiptou	ΠΛΑΤ. ΑΙΓΥΠΤΟΥ	BX	33
Pl. Eleftherias	ΠΛΑΤ. ΕΛΕΥΘΕΡΙΑΣ	AX	
Pl. Eth. Andistasseos (Kodzia)	ΠΛΑΤ. ΕΘΝ. ΑΝΤΙΣΤΑΣΕΩΣ (ΚΟΤΖΙΑ)	BX	35
Pl. Kaningos	ΠΛΑΤ. ΚΑΝΙΓΓΟΣ	BX	
Pl. Karaïskaki	ΠΛΑΤ. ΚΑΡΑΙΣΚΑΚΗ	AX	
Pl. Klafthmonos	ΠΛΑΤ. ΚΛΑΥΘΜΩΝΟΣ	BX	
Pl. Kolonakiou	ΠΛΑΤ. ΚΟΛΩΝΑΚΙΟΥ	DY	
Pl. Monastirakiou	ΠΛΑΤ. ΜΟΝΑΣΤΗΡΑΚΙΟΥ	ABY	
Ploutarhou	ΠΛΟΥΤΑΡΧΟΥ	DX	
Psaron	ΨΑΡΩΝ	AX	
Radzieri	ΡΑΤΖΙΕΡΗ	AY	36
Rigilis	ΡΗΓΙΛΛΗΣ	DY	
Rov. Gali	ΡΟΒ. ΓΚΑΛΛΙ	AY	
Sarandapihou	ΣΑΡΑΝΤΑΠΗΧΟΥ	DX	
Sindagma	ΣΥΝΤΑΓΜΑ	CY	
Singrou	ΣΥΓΓΡΟΥ	BY	
Skoufa	ΣΚΟΥΦΑ	CX	
Solonos	ΣΟΛΩΝΟΣ	CX	
Spir. Merkouri	ΣΠΥΡ. ΜΕΡΚΟΥΡΗ	DY	
Spir. Trikoupi	ΣΠΥΡ. ΤΡΙΚΟΥΠΗ	CX	
Stadiou	ΣΤΑΔΙΟΥ	BXY	
Stournara	ΣΤΟΥΡΝΑΡΑ	CX	
Themistokleous	ΘΕΜΙΣΤΟΚΛΕΟΥΣ	BCX	
Thermopilon	ΘΕΡΜΟΠΥΛΩΝ	AX	
Tossitsa	ΤΟΣΙΤΣΑ	CX	
Varvaki	ΒΑΡΒΑΚΗ	DX	
Vas. Alexandrou	ΒΑΣ. ΑΛΕΞΑΝΔΡΟΥ	DY	
Vas. Amalias	ΒΑΣ. ΑΜΑΛΙΑΣ	CY	
Vas. Georgiou B'	ΒΑΣ. ΓΕΩΡΓΟΥ Β'	DY	
Vas. Konstandinou	ΒΑΣ. ΚΩΝΣΤΑΝΤΙΝΟΥ	DY	
Vas. Olgas	ΒΑΣ. ΟΛΓΑΣ	CY	
Vas. Sofias	ΒΑΣ. ΣΟΦΙΑΣ	CDY	
Vassiliou Voulgaroktonou	ΒΑΣΙΛΕΙΟΥ ΒΟΥΛΓΑΡΟΚΤΟΝΟΥ	DX	
Voukourestiou	ΒΟΥΚΟΥΡΕΣΤΙΟΥ	CX	38
Xanthipou	ΞΑΝΘΙΠΠΟΥ	DXY	39
Xenokratous	ΞΕΝΟΚΡΑΤΟΥΣ	DX	41
Zaïmi	ΖΑΙΜΗ	CX	42
3 Septemvriou	Γ'ΣΕΠΤΕΜΒΡΙΟΥ	BX	

Intercontinental Athenaeum (Inter-Con), 89-93 Singrou, 117 45, 9023 666, Telex 221554, – by Singrou BY
M (see **Rotisserie** below) – **Cafe Pergola** (coffee shop) – **Kava Promenade** (lunch only) – **566 rm, 31 suites.**

Hilton, 46 Vas. Sofias, 106 76, 7220 201, Telex 215808, – DY **p**
M 2000/2100 **Supper club** – **Tannissia** (Taverna) – 880 – **454 rm** 13400/21735, **19 suites** 36338/162984.

Grande Bretagne, Vas. Georgiou, Sindagma, 105 63, 3230 251, Telex 219615 – CY **v**
M (see **GB Corner** below) – 900 – **330 rm** 12840/24477, **22 suites** 30218/147905.

Ledra Marriott, 115 Singrou, 117 45, SW :3 km. 9525 211, Telex 223465, – by Singrou BY
M (see **Kona Kai** below) – **Ledra Grill** – **254 rm, 4 suites.**

NJV Meridien, Vas. Georgiou, Sindagma, 105 64, 3255 301, Telex 210568 – CY **r**
M La Brasserie des Arts *4250/5000 and a la carte* – 950 – **182 rm** 14500/30489, **15 suites** 41767.

🏨 Astir Palace [M], Panepistimiou and Vas. Sofias, 106 71, ℘ 3643 112, Telex 222380 – |♦| ▤ 📺 ☎. 🏊 CY **x**
M Apokalypsis – Asteria (coffee shop) – **75 rm, 28 suites**.

🏨 **Royal Olympic,** 28-32 Diakou, 117 43, ℘ 9226 411, Telex 215753, ≤, 🏊 – |♦| ▤ ☎. 🏊. AE ⓓ E BY **u**
M Royal *1650 and a la carte* – **Templar's Grill** – **306 rm** ☐ 11000/16000, **4 suites** 22000/45000.

🏨 **Chandris,** 385 Singrou, 175 64, SW : 7 km. ℘ 9414 824, Telex 218112, 🏊 – |♦| ▤ ☎. 🏊. AE ⓓ E VISA. ✗ by Singrou BY
M Four Seasons *a la carte 1400/1800* – **371 rm** ☐ 8000/12500, **6 suites** 15000/30000.

🏨 **Holiday Inn,** 50 Mihalakopoulou, 115 28, ℘ 7248 322, Telex 218870, 🏊 – |♦| ▤ 📺 ☎ Ⓟ. 🏊. AE ⓓ E VISA. ✗ by Mihalakopoulou DY
M (buffet lunch) 1600 /dinner 3000 and a la carte – ☐ 650 – **183 rm** 9850/14700, **7 suites** 22300/37000.

🏨 **Herodion,** 4 Rov. Gali, 117 42, ℘ 9236 832, Telex 219423 – |♦| ▤ 📺 ☎ Ⓟ. AE ⓓ E VISA. ✗ BY **p**
M 1200/1280 and dinner a la carte – **90 rm** ☐ 4301/8602, **4 suites** 8823/13033.

🏨 Divani Zafolia Alexandras, 87 Alexandras, 114 74, ℘ 6449 012, Telex 214468, 🏊 – |♦| ▤ ☎ Ⓟ. 🏊 DX **k**
184 rm, 8 suites.

🏨 **Electra Palace,** 18 Nikodimou, 105 57, ℘ 3241 407, 🏊 – |♦| ▤ 📺 ☎. AE ⓓ E VISA. ✗
M 1350 and a la carte – **106 rm** ☐ 7075/9385. BY **h**

🏨 **Divanizafolia Palace,** 19-25 Parthenonos, 117 42, ℘ 9222 945, Telex 8306, 🏊 – |♦| ▤ ☎. 🏊. AE ⓓ E. ✗ BY **r**
M 1000/1200 – **200 rm** ☐ 3000/7000, **7 suites** 5000/10000.

🏨 **St. George Lycabettus,** 2 Kleomenous, 106 75, ℘ 7290 711, Telex 214253, ≤, 🏊 – |♦| ▤ ☎ Ⓟ. 🏊. AE ⓓ E VISA. ✗ DX **t**
M a la carte 2395/3000 – **139 rm** ☐ 6830/11740, **5 suites** 23480.

🏨 **Electra,** 5 Ermou, 105 63, ℘ 3223 223, Telex 216896 – |♦| ▤. AE ⓓ E VISA. ✗ BY **e**
M 1350 and a la carte – **110 rm** ☐ 7075/9385.

🏨 **Park,** 10 Alexandras, 106 82, ℘ 8832 712, Telex 214748, 🏊 – |♦| ▤ ☎ Ⓟ. ✗ BX **a**
M 1500 and a la carte – ☐ 450 – **126 rm** 5500/10200, **21 suites** 15000.

🏨 Parthenon, 3 Makri, 117 42, ℘ 9234 594, Telex 221579 – |♦| 🛁wc 🚿wc ☎ Ⓟ BY **c**
79 rm.

🏨 **Titania,** 52 Panepistimiou, 106 78, ℘ 3609 611, Telex 214673 – |♦| ▤ 🛁wc ☎ Ⓟ. AE ⓓ E VISA. ✗ BX **t**
M 477/1378 and a la carte – **398 rm** ☐ 6503/8486.

🏨 Dorian Inn, 17-19 Pireos (Panagi Tsaldari), 105 52, ℘ 5239 782, Telex 214779, 🏊 – ▤ 🛁wc ☎ AX **f**
146 rm.

🏨 Astor, 16 Kar. Servias, 105, ℘ 3255 555, Telex 214018 – |♦| ▤ 🛁wc 🚿wc ☎ BY **s**
132 rm.

🏨 Arethusa, 6-8 Mitropoleos, 105 63, ℘ 3229 431, Telex 216882 – |♦| ▤ 🛁wc 🚿wc ☎
87 rm. BY **t**

🏨 Acropolis View, 10 Govemster, off Rov. Gali, 117 42, ℘ 9217 303, Telex 219936, ≤ – |♦| ▤ 🚿wc ☎ AY **e**
32 rm.

XXXX Rotisserie (at Intercontinental H.), 89-93 Singrou, 117 45, ℘ 9023 666, Telex 221554, French rest. – ▤ by Singrou BY

XXX Kona Kai (at Ledra Marriott H.), 115 Singrou, 117 45, ℘ 9525 211, Telex 223465, « Original decor » – ▤ by Singrou BY
M (dinner only).

XXX **Athenaeum,** 8 Amerikis, International Cultural Centre, 106 71, ℘ 36 31 125. ⓓ E
closed Sunday and October-mid June – **M** a la carte 2230/4930. CY **e**

XXX **GB Corner** (at Grande Bretagne H.), Vas. Georgiou Sindagma, 105 64, ℘ 3220 251, Telex 219615, « Victorian style decor » – ▤. AE ⓓ E VISA CY **v**
M a la carte 1550/4690.

XX **Dionysos,** 43 Rov. Gali, 117 42, ℘ 9233 182, 🍴, « Woodland setting with ≤ of Acropolis » – Ⓟ. AE ⓓ E VISA AY **s**
M 2800/5000 and a la carte.

XX Gerofinikas, 10 Pindarou, 106 71, ℘ 3636 710, Greek rest. – ▤ CY **p**

XX Ideal, 46 Panepistimiou, 106 78, ℘ 3614 604, Telex 223302, Classic Greek rest. – ▤ BX **c**

XX **L'Abreuvoir,** 51 Xenocratous Kolonaki, 106 76, ℘ 7229 106, French rest.. AE ⓓ E VISA
M a la carte 2000/3090. DX **u**

X Corfu, 6 Kriezotou, 106 71, ℘ 3613 011, Greek rest. – ▤ CY **n**

"The Tavernas".

Tipical little greek restaurants, generally very modest, where it is pleasant to spend the evening, surrounded with noisy but friendly locals, sometimes with guitar or bouzouki entertainment. These particular restaurants are usually open for dinner only.

X **Myrtia,** 35 Markou Moussourou, 116 36, ℘ 7012 276, « Rustic decor, music ». AE ⓓ
closed Sunday – **M** (dinner only) 2500/2700. CY **a**

X **Kostoyanis,** Zaïmi 37, 106 82, ℘ 8220 624 CX **r**
closed Sunday – **M** (dinner only) 1000/3000.

X **Xinos,** 4 Geronda, ℘ 3221 065 BY **a**
M a la carte approx 1600.

X **Zafiris,** 4 Thespidos, ℘ 3225 460 BY **v**
M (booking essential) (dinner only) a la carte approx 1500.

at Piraeus SW : 10 km. by Singrou BY.

XX **Aglamair,** 54 Koumoundouro, ℘ 4115 511, ←, terrace, Seafood – **M** a la carte 1500/2500.

X **Dourambeis,** 29 Dilaveri, ℘ 4122 092, Seafood – **M** a la carte approx 2000.

Republic of Ireland

Dublin

PRACTICAL INFORMATION

LOCAL CURRENCY

Punt (Irish Pound) : 1 punt = 1.40 US $ (Jan. 87)

TOURIST INFORMATION

The telephone number and address of the Tourist Information office is given in the text under ℹ.

FOREIGN EXCHANGE

Banks are open 10am to 12.30pm and 1.30pm to 3pm on weekdays only.

Banks in Dublin stay open to 5pm on Thursdays and banks at Dublin and Shannon airports are open on Saturdays and Sundays.

SHOPPING IN DUBLIN

In the index of street names those printed in red are where the principal shops are found.

CAR HIRE

The international car hire companies have branches in each major city. Your hotel porter will be able to give details and help you with your arrangements.

TIPPING

Many hotels and restaurants include a service charge but where this is not the case an amount equivalent to between 10 and 15 per cent of the bill is customary. Additionally doormen, baggage porters and cloakroom attendants are generally given a gratuity.

Taxi drivers are customarily tipped between 10 and 15 per cent of the amount shown on the meter in addition to the fare.

SPEED LIMITS

The maximum permitted speed in the Republic is 55 mph (88 km/h) except where a lower speed limit is signposted.

SEAT BELTS

The wearing of seat belts is compulsory for drivers and front seat passengers.

ANIMALS

It is forbildden to bring domestic animals (dogs, cats...) into the Republic of Ireland.

DUBLIN

SIGHTS

See : National Gallery★★★ BY – Castle (State apartments★★★ *AC*) BY – Christ Church Cathedral★★ 12C BY – National Museum (Irish antiquities, Art and Industrial)★★ BY **M2** – Trinity College★ (Library★★) BY – National Museum (Zoological Collection)★ BY **M1** – Municipal Art Gallery★ BX **M3** – O'Connell Street★ (and the General Post Office) BXY – St. Stephen's Green★ BZ – St. Patrick's Cathedral (interior★) BZ – Phoenix Park (Zoological Gardens★).

Envir. : St. Doolagh's Church★ 13C (open Saturday and Sunday, afternoon only) NE : 7 m. by L 87.

DUBLIN Dublin 405 N 7 – pop. 528 882 – ☎ 01.

18 Edmondstown, Rathfarnham ☎ 907461, S : 3 m. by N 81 – 18 Elm Park, Nutley House, Donnybrook ☎ 693438, S : 3 m. – 18 Lower Churchtown Rd, Milltown ☎ 977060, S : by T 43.

✈ ☎ 379900, N : 5 ½ m. by N 1 – **Terminal :** Busaras (Central Bus Station) Store St.

⛴ to Liverpool (B & I Line) 2 daily (8 h) – to Holyhead (B & I Line) 1-2 daily (3 h 30 mn) – to the Isle of Man : Douglas (Isle of Man Steam Packet Co.) June to September 1-3 weekly (4 h 30 mn).

ℹ 14 Upper O'Connell St. ☎ 747733 – Dublin Airport ☎ 376387 and 375533.

Belfast 103 – Cork 154 – Londonderry 146.

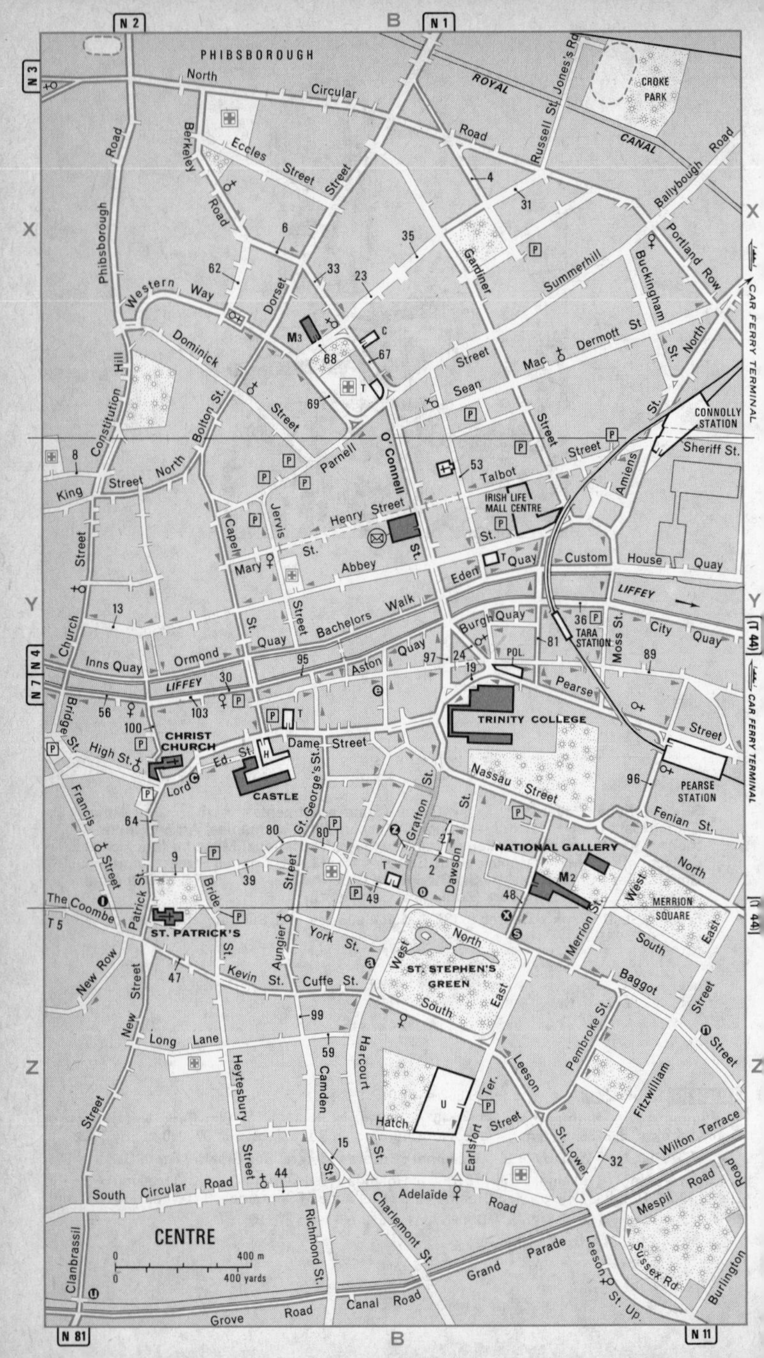

N 2
B
N 1
N 3
PHIBSBOROUGH
North Circular Road
ROYAL CANAL
CROKE PARK
Russell St.
Jones's Rd
Ballybough Road
Eccles Street
Berkeley Road
Phibsborough Road
Western Way
Dorset Street
Gardiner Street
Summerhill
Portland Row
Buckingham St.
North
Dominick Street
Sean Mac Dermott St
CAR FERRY TERMINAL
CONNOLLY STATION
Constitution Hill
Bolton St.
Parnell Street
O' Connell St.
Talbot Street
Sheriff St.
Amiens St.
King Street North
IRISH LIFE MALL CENTRE
Henry Street
Church Street
Capel St.
Jervis Street
Mary St.
Abbey St.
Eden Quay
Custom House Quay
LIFFEY
Bachelors Walk
Ormond Quay
Inns Quay
Burgh Quay
TARA STATION
Moss St.
City Quay
Aston Quay
POL.
Pearse Street
TRINITY COLLEGE
CHRIST CHURCH
Bridge St.
High St.
Lord Ed. St.
Dame Street
CASTLE
Nassau Street
PEARSE STATION
Fenian St.
Francis Street
Gt. George's St.
Grafton St.
Dawson St.
NATIONAL GALLERY
M2
M3
Merrion Sq. North
MERRION SQUARE
West
East
South
The Coombe
Patrick St.
Bride St.
ST. PATRICK'S
Aungier St.
York St.
North
ST. STEPHEN'S GREEN
South
Merrion St.
Baggot Street
New Row
New Street
Kevin St.
Cuffe St.
Long Lane
Heytesbury Street
Camden St.
Harcourt St.
Hatch Street
Earlsfort Ter.
Leeson St. Lower
Pembroke St.
Fitzwilliam Street
Wilton Terrace
South Circular Road
Adelaide Road
Mespil Road
Richmond St.
Charlemont St.
Grand Parade
Leeson St. Up.
Sussex Rd
Burlington Road
CENTRE
0 400 m
0 400 yards
Clanbrassil Street
Grove Road
Canal Road
N 81
N 11
N 7
N 4
T 44
T 5
X
Y
Z

DUBLIN

Anne Street South	BY	2
Dawson Street	BY	
Duke Street	BY	27
Grafton Street	BY	
Henry Street	BY	
Irish Life Mall Centre	BY	
O'Connell Street	BXY	
Belvidere Place	BX	4
Blessington Street	BX	6
Brunswick Street North	BY	8
Bull Alley	BY	9
Chancery Street	BY	13
Charlotte Street	BZ	15
College Street	BY	19
Denmark Street	BX	23
D'Olier Street	BY	24
Essex Quay	BY	30
Fitzgibbon Street	BX	31
Fitzwilliam Place	BZ	32
Frederick Street North	BX	33
Gardiner Place	BX	35
George's Quay	BY	36
Golden Lane	BY	39
Harrington Street	BZ	44
Kevin Street Upper	BZ	47
Kildare Street	BYZ	48
King Street South	BY	49
Malborough Street	BY	53
Merchants Quay	BY	56
Montague Street	BZ	59
Mountjoy Street	BX	62
Nicholas Street	BY	64
Parnell Square East	BX	67
Parnell Square North	BX	68
Parnell Square West	BX	69
Stephen Street	BY	80
Tara Street	BY	81
Townsend Street	BY	89
Wellington Quay	BY	95
Westland Row	BY	96
Westmoreland Street	BY	97
Wexford Street	BZ	99
Winetavern Street	BY	100
Wood Quay	BY	103

Berkeley Court, Lansdowne Rd, Ballsbridge, 601711, Telex 30554, – rest TV AE VISA.
M 14.00/17.00 **t.** and a la carte – **200 rm** 75.00/95.00 **t.** – SB (weekends only) 88.00 **st.**

Shelbourne (T.H.F.), 27 St. Stephen's Green, 766471 – TV AE VISA – **M** 17.00/19.00 **t.** and a la carte 5.50 – **167 rm, 6 suites** BZ **s**

Westbury, Grafton St., 868109, Telex 91091 – rest TV wc AE VISA BY **z**
M 13.00/16.00 **t.** and a la carte 4.10 – 6.00 – **146 rm** 70.00/98.00 **t.**, **4 suites** 225.00/275.00 **t.**

Jury's, Pembroke Rd, Ballsbridge, 605000, Telex 93723, heated, – TV AE VISA
M 16.25/17.25 **t.** and a la carte 7.00 – 7.00 – **300 rm** 69.50/82.00 **t.**, **4 suites** 150.00/250.00 **t.**

Blooms, Anglesea St., 715622, Telex 31688 – TV AE VISA. BY **e**
M 8.00/15.00 **st.** and a la carte 4.50 – 7.00 – **86 rm** 67.50/115.00 **t.**

Mount Herbert, Herbert Rd, Ballsbridge, 684321, Telex 92173, – TV wc AE VISA
M 7.50/10.95 **t.** and a la carte 3.90 – **88 rm** 15.95/39.90 **t.** – SB (weekends only) 39.00/55.00 **st.**

Le Coq Hardi with rm, 35 Pembroke Rd, 689070 – rest TV wc AE VISA.
closed Saturday lunch, Sunday, 2 weeks August, 2 weeks Christmas and Bank Holidays – **M** 12.50/22.00 **t.** and a la carte 15.70/25.50 **t.** 6.00 – **3 rm** 155.00 **st.**

Patrick Guilbaud, 46 St. James's Pl., St. James' St., off Lower Baggot St., 764192, French rest. – AE VISA BZ **n**
closed Saturday lunch, Sunday and Bank Holidays – **M** 11.80/19.50 **t.** and a la carte.

Whites on The Green, 119 St. Stephen's Green, 751975 – AE VISA BZ **a**
closed Saturday lunch, Sunday, 24 to 31 December and Bank Holidays – **M** 9.75/18.00 **t.** and a la carte 18.00/26.75 **t.** 5.00.

Ernie's, Mulberry Gdns, 693300 – AE VISA
closed Sunday, Monday, first 2 weeks July and 1 week at Christmas – **M** (dinner only) a la carte 20.25/28.75 **t.** 6.25.

Locks, 1 Windsor Terr., Portobello, 752025 – AE VISA BZ **u**
closed Saturday lunch, Sunday, 24 December-2 January and Bank Holidays – **M** 10.25 **t.** (lunch) and a la carte 16.50/19.50 **t.** 3.90.

Park, 26 Main Street, Blackrock, SE : 4 ½ m. on T 44 886177 – AE VISA
closed Saturday lunch, Sunday, Monday, 3 days at Christmas and Bank Holidays – **M** (booking essential) 7.50/19.50 **t.** 5.90.

Lord Edward, 23 Christchurch Pl., 752557, Seafood – AE VISA BY **c**
closed Saturday lunch, Sunday and Bank Holidays – **M** 11.95 **t.** (lunch) and a la carte 15.45/24.65 **t.** 4.25.

Old Dublin, 90-91 Francis St., 751173, Russian-Scandinavian rest. – AE VISA BY **i**
closed Saturday lunch, Sunday and Bank Holidays – **M** 9.50/15.00.

Bentleys, 46 Upper Baggot St., 682760 – AE VISA
closed Saturday lunch, Monday dinner, Sunday, 2 weeks July, 1 week at Christmas and Bank Holidays – **M** a la carte 13.50/18.65 **t.** 3.95.

Dobbin's, 15 Stephen's Lane, 764679, Bistro – AE VISA BZ **x**
closed Saturday lunch, Monday dinner, Sunday and Bank Holidays – **M** a la carte 13.65/22.25 **t.** 4.95.

Mitchell's Cellars, 21 Kildare St., 680367 – AE VISA
closed Saturday June-October, Sunday and Bank Holidays – **M** (lunch only) a la carte 6.65/8.05 **t.** 3.95.

Cafe de Paris, The Galleria, 6 St. Stephen's Green, 778499 – AE VISA BY **o**
closed lunch Saturday and Sunday – **M** 12.00/15.00 **st.** and a la carte 10.45/14.45 **st.** 2.35.

at Dublin Airport N : 6 ½ m. by N 1 – 01 Dublin :

Dublin International (T.H.F.), 379211, Telex 24612 – TV wc AE VISA – **M** 12.75/13.50 **st.** and a la carte 4.50 – **195 rm** 60.00/82.00 **st.**

Italy
Italia

Rome
Florence
Milan
Naples - Capri
Palerme
Taormina
Turin
Venice

PRACTICAL INFORMATION

LOCAL CURRENCY

Italian Lire : 1000 lire = 0.70 US $ (Jan. 87)

TOURIST INFORMATION

Welcome Office (Ente Provinciale per il Turismo), closed Saturday and Sunday :
– Via Parigi 5 - 00185 ROMA, ✆ 06/463748
– Via Marconi 1 - 20123 MILANO, ✆ 02/809662

See also telephone number and address of other Tourist Information offices in the text of the towns under ℹ.
American Express :
– Piazza di Spagna 38 - 00187 ROMA, ✆ 06/67641
– Via Brera 3 - 20121 MILANO, ✆ 02/85571

AIRLINES

ALITALIA : Via Bissolati 13 - 00187 ROMA, ✆ 06/46881
Piazzale Pastore o dell'Arte (EUR) - 00144 ROMA, ✆ 06/54441
Via Albricci 5 - 20122 MILANO, ✆ 02/62811
AIR FRANCE : Via Vittorio Veneto 93 - 00187 ROMA, ✆ 06/4758741
Piazza Cavour 2 - 20121 MILANO, ✆ 02/77381
PAN AM : Via Bissolati 46 - 00187 ROMA, ✆ 06/4773
Piazza Velasca 5 - 20122 MILANO, ✆ 02/877241
TWA : Via Barberini 59/67 - 00187 ROMA, ✆ 06/47211
Corso Europa 9/11 - 20122 MILANO, ✆ 02/77961

FOREIGN EXCHANGE

Money can be changed at the Banca d'Italia, other banks and authorised exchange offices (Banks close at 1.15pm and at weekends

POSTAL SERVICES

Local post offices : open Monday to Saturday 8.00am to 2.00pm

General Post Office (open 24 hours only for telegrams) :
– Piazza San Silvestro 00187 ROMA – Piazza Cordusio 20123 MILANO

SHOPPING

In the index of street names those printed in red are where the principal shops are found. In Rome, the main shopping streets are : Via del Babuino, Via dei Condotti, Via Frattina, Via Vittorio Veneto ; in Milan : Via Dante, Via Manzoni, Via Monte Napoleone, Corso Vittorio Emanuele.

BREAKDOWN SERVICE

Certain garages in the centre and outskirts of towns operate a 24 hour breakdown service. If you breakdown the police are usually able to help by indicating the nearest one.
A free car breakdown service (a tax is levied) is operated by the A.C.I. for foreign motorists carrying the fuel card (Carta Carburante). The A.C.I. also offers telephone information in English (8am to 5pm) for road and weather conditions and tourist events : 06/4212.

TIPPING

As well as the service charge, it is the custom to tip employees. The amount can vary with the region and the service given.

SPEED LIMITS

Speed limits applicable on trunk roads and motorways are according to engine capacity : 80-90 km/h or 50-56 mph (600 cc) to 110-140 km/h or 68-87 mph (over 1300 cc).

ROME

SIGHTS

Rome's most famous sights are indicated on the town plans pp. 2 to 5. For a more complete visit see the Green Guide to Italy.

ROME (ROMA) 00100 988 ㉖ – Pop. 2 826 488 – alt. 20 – ✆ 06.

18 (closed Monday) at Acquasanta ✉ 00178 Roma ✆ 783407, SE : 12 km.

9 Fioranello (closed Wednesday) at Santa Maria delle Mole ✉ 00040 Roma ✆ 608291.

18 and 9 (closed Monday) at Olgiata ✉ 00123 Roma ✆ 3789141.

✈ Ciampino SE : 15 km ✆ 4694 and Leonardo da Vinci di Fiumicino ✆ 60121 – Alitalia, via Bissolati 13 ✉ 00187 ✆ 46881 and piazzale Pastore o dell'Arte (EUR) ✉ 00144 ✆ 54441.

Termini ✆ 464923 – Tiburtina ✆ 4956626.

via Parigi 5 ✉ 00185 ✆ 463748 ; at Termini station ✆ 465461 ; on the motorways : A1 Roma North ✆ 6919958 and A2 Roma South ✆ 9464341.

A.C.I. via Cristoforo Colombo 261 ✉ 00147 ✆ 5106 and via Marsala 8 ✉ 00185 ✆ 49981, Telex 610686.

Distances from Rome are indicated in the text of the other towns listed in this Guide.

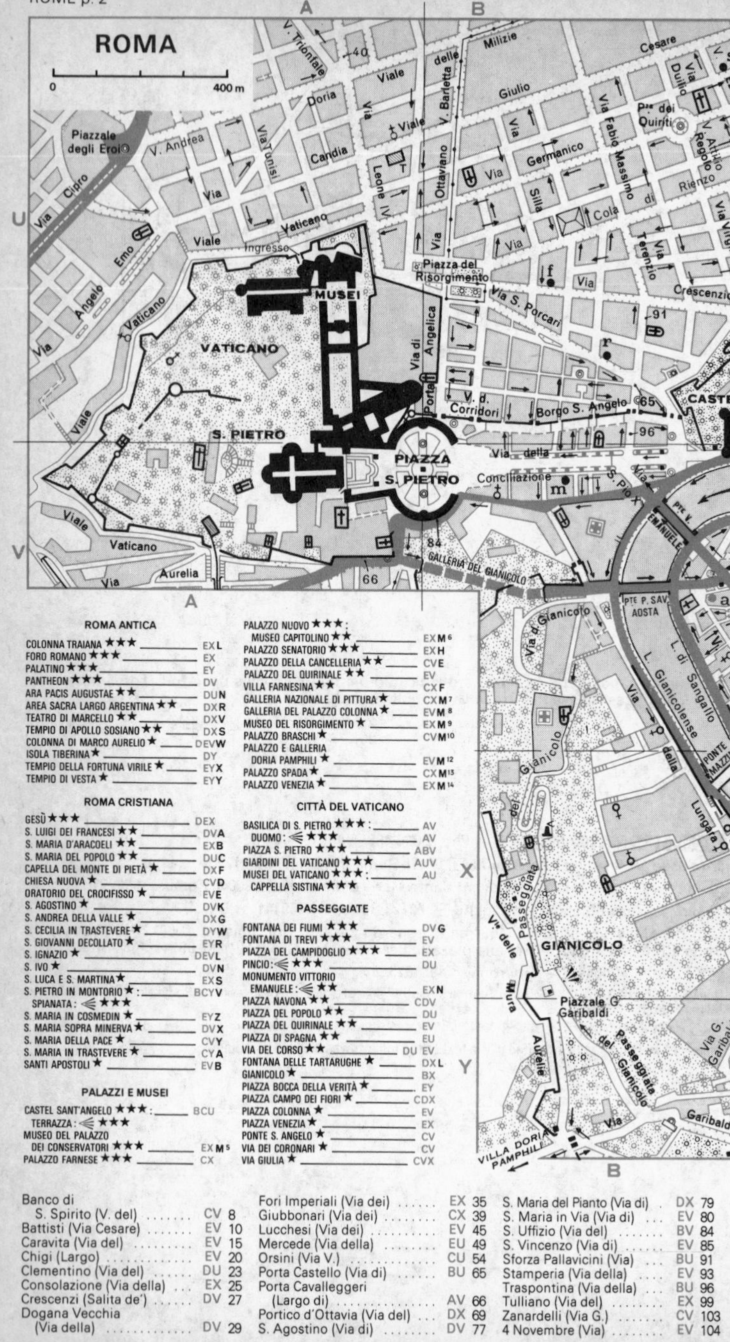

ROMA ANTICA

COLONNA TRAIANA ★★★	EX L
FORO ROMANO ★★★	EX
PALATINO ★★★	EY
PANTHEON ★★★	DV
ARA PACIS AUGUSTAE ★★	DU N
AREA SACRA LARGO ARGENTINA ★★	DX R
TEATRO DI MARCELLO ★★	DX V
TEMPIO DI APOLLO SOSIANO ★★	DX S
COLONNA DI MARCO AURELIO ★	DEV W
ISOLA TIBERINA ★	DY
TEMPIO DELLA FORTUNA VIRILE ★	EY X
TEMPIO DI VESTA ★	EY Y

ROMA CRISTIANA

GESÙ ★★★	DEX
S. LUIGI DEI FRANCESI ★★	DV A
S. MARIA D'ARACOELI ★★	EX B
S. MARIA DEL POPOLO ★★	DU C
CAPELLA DEL MONTE DI PIETÀ ★	DX F
CHIESA NUOVA ★	CV D
ORATORIO DEL CROCIFISSO ★	EV E
S. AGOSTINO ★	DV K
S. ANDREA DELLA VALLE ★	DX G
S. CECILIA IN TRASTEVERE ★	DY W
S. GIOVANNI DECOLLATO ★	EY R
S. IGNAZIO ★	DEV L
S. IVO ★	DV N
S. LUCA E S. MARTINA ★	EX S
S. PIETRO IN MONTORIO ★ :	BCY V
SPIANATA : ⋞ ★★★	
S. MARIA IN COSMEDIN ★	EY Z
S. MARIA SOPRA MINERVA ★	DV X
S. MARIA DELLA PACE ★	CV Y
S. MARIA IN TRASTEVERE ★	CY A
SANTI APOSTOLI ★	EV B

PALAZZI E MUSEI

CASTEL SANT'ANGELO ★★★ :	BCU
TERRAZZA : ⋞ ★★★	
MUSEO DEL PALAZZO DEI CONSERVATORI ★★★	EX M[5]
PALAZZO FARNESE ★★★	CX
PALAZZO NUOVO ★★★ : MUSEO CAPITOLINO ★★	EX M[6]
PALAZZO SENATORIO ★★★	EX H
PALAZZO DELLA CANCELLERIA ★★	CV E
PALAZZO DEL QUIRINALE ★★	EV
VILLA FARNESINA ★★	CX F
GALLERIA NAZIONALE DI PITTURA ★	CX M[7]
GALLERIA DEL PALAZZO COLONNA ★	EV M[8]
MUSEO DEL RISORGIMENTO ★	EX M[9]
PALAZZO BRASCHI ★	CV M[10]
PALAZZO E GALLERIA DORIA PAMPHILI ★	EV M[12]
PALAZZO SPADA ★	CX M[13]
PALAZZO VENEZIA ★	EX M[14]

CITTÀ DEL VATICANO

BASILICA DI S. PIETRO ★★★ :	AV
DUOMO : ⋞ ★★★	AV
PIAZZA S. PIETRO ★★★	ABV
GIARDINI DEL VATICANO ★★★	AUV
MUSEI DEL VATICANO ★★★ :	AU
CAPPELLA SISTINA ★★★	

PASSEGGIATE

FONTANA DEI FIUMI ★★★	DV G
FONTANA DI TREVI ★★★	EV
PIAZZA DEL CAMPIDOGLIO ★★★	EX
PINCIO : ⋞ ★★★	DU
MONUMENTO VITTORIO EMANUELE : ⋞ ★★	EX N
PIAZZA NAVONA ★★	CDV
PIAZZA DEL POPOLO ★★	DU
PIAZZA DEL QUIRINALE ★★	EV
PIAZZA DI SPAGNA ★★	EU
VIA DEL CORSO ★★	DU EV
FONTANA DELLE TARTARUGHE ★	DX L
GIANICOLO ★	BX
PIAZZA BOCCA DELLA VERITÀ ★	EY
PIAZZA CAMPO DEI FIORI ★	CDX
PIAZZA COLONNA ★	EV
PIAZZA VENEZIA ★	EX
PONTE S. ANGELO ★	CV
VIA DEI CORONARI ★	CV
VIA GIULIA ★	CVX

Banco di S. Spirito (V. del)	CV	8
Battisti (Via Cesare)	EV	10
Caravita (Via del)	EV	15
Chigi (Largo)	EV	20
Clementino (Via del)	DU	23
Consolazione (Via della)	EX	25
Crescenzi (Salita de')	DV	27
Dogana Vecchia (Via della)	DV	29
Fori Imperiali (Via dei)	EX	35
Giubbonari (Via dei)	CX	39
Lucchesi (Via dei)	EV	45
Mercede (Via della)	EU	49
Orsini (Via V.)	CU	54
Porta Castello (Via di)	BU	65
Porta Cavalleggeri (Largo di)	AV	66
Portico d'Ottavia (Via del)	DX	69
S. Agostino (Via di)	DV	77
S. Maria del Pianto (Via di)	DX	79
S. Maria in Via (Via di)	EV	80
S. Uffizio (Via del)	BV	84
S. Vincenzo (Via di)	EV	85
Sforza Pallavicini (Via)	BU	91
Stamperia (Via della)	EV	93
Traspontina (Via della)	BU	96
Tulliano (Via del)	EX	99
Zanardelli (Via G.)	CV	103
4 Novembre (Via)	EV	104

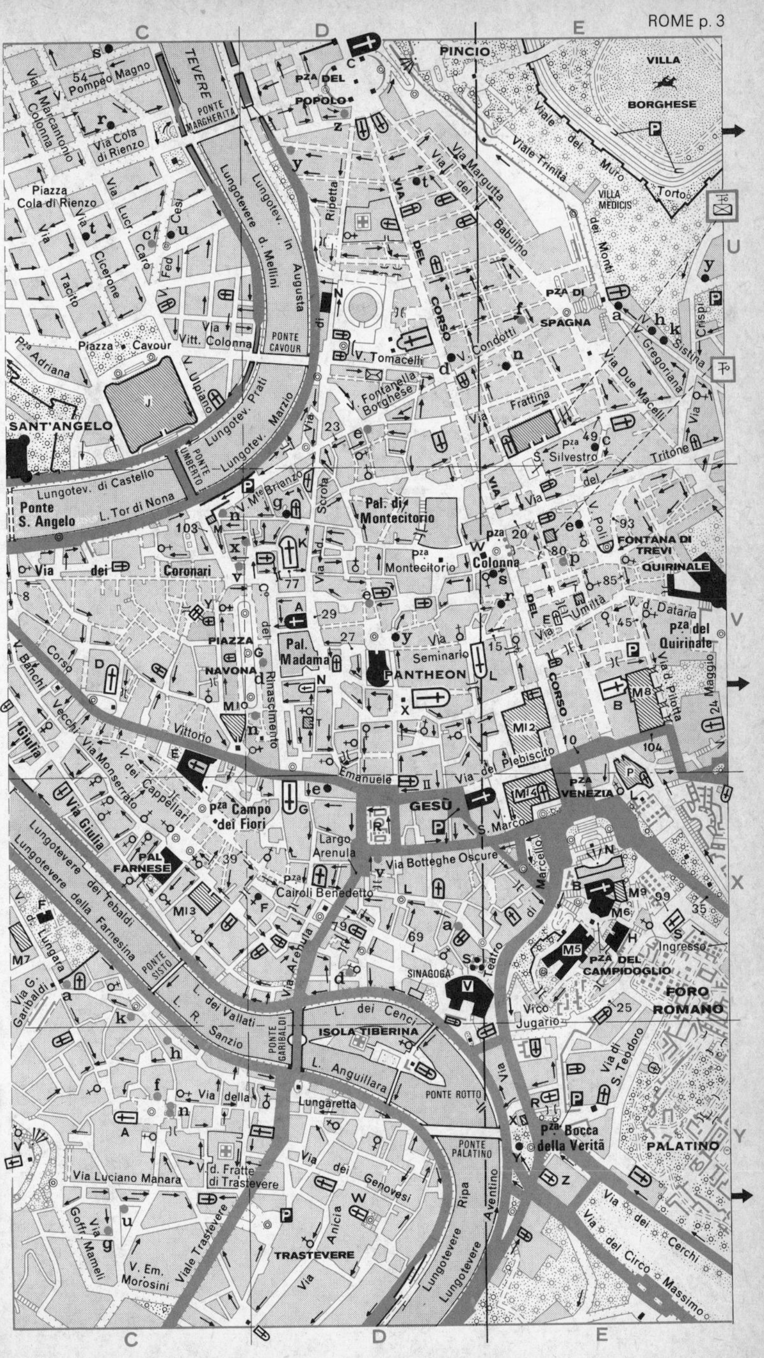
PINCIO
VILLA BORGHESE
Pza DEL POPOLO
TEVERE
PONTE MARGHERITA
Via Pompeo Magno
Via Marcantonio Colonna
Via Cola di Rienzo
Piazza Cola di Rienzo
Viale Trinità
Viale del Muro Torto
VILLA MEDICIS
Via Margutta
Via del Babuino
VIA DEL CORSO
Ripetta
Lungotevere d. Mellini
Lungotev. in Augusta
Cicerone
Tacito
Cesi
PONTE CAVOUR
Piazza Cavour
Via Vitt. Colonna
Pza Adriana
SANT'ANGELO
V. Tomacelli
V. Condotti
Pza DI SPAGNA
Via Gregoriana
Via Sistina
Crispi
Via Due Macelli
V. Fontanella Borghese
Via Frattina
Lungotev. Prati
Lungotev. Marzio
PONTE UMBERTO
Pza S. Silvestro
Via del Tritone
Lungotev. di Castello
Ponte S. Angelo
L. Tor di Nona
Pal. di Montecitorio
Pza Montecitorio
Pza Colonna
FONTANA DI TREVI
QUIRINALE
Via dei Coronari
V. d. Dataria
Pza del Quirinale
Via d. Pilotta
24 Maggio
PIAZZA NAVONA
Pal. Madama
PANTHEON
Via Seminario
V. Banchi Vecchi
Corso Vittorio Emanuele
Rinascimento
Via del Plebiscito
Pza VENEZIA
GESÙ
V. S. Marco
Via Giulia
Via Monserrato
V. dei Cappellari
Pza Campo dei Fiori
PAL. FARNESE
Largo Arenula
Via Botteghe Oscure
Pza Cairoli Benedetto
Via Arenula
Lungotevere dei Tebaldi
Lungotevere della Farnesina
PONTE SISTO
L. dei Vallati
L. R. Sanzio
PONTE GARIBALDI
L. dei Cenci
ISOLA TIBERINA
L. Anguillara
PONTE ROTTO
SINAGOGA
Via Teatro di Marcello
Pza DEL CAMPIDOGLIO
FORO ROMANO
Ingresso
Vico Jugario
Via di S. Teodoro
Pza Bocca della Verità
PALATINO
Via dei Cerchi
Via del Circo Massimo
V. d. Lungara
Via G. Garibaldi
Via della Lungaretta
Via Luciano Manara
V. d. Fratte di Trastevere
Via dei Genovesi
Via Anicia
Viale Trastevere
TRASTEVERE
Lungotevere Ripa
Lungotevere Aventino
PONTE PALATINO
Via Goffr. Mameli
V. Em. Morosini
C
D
E
U
V
X
Y

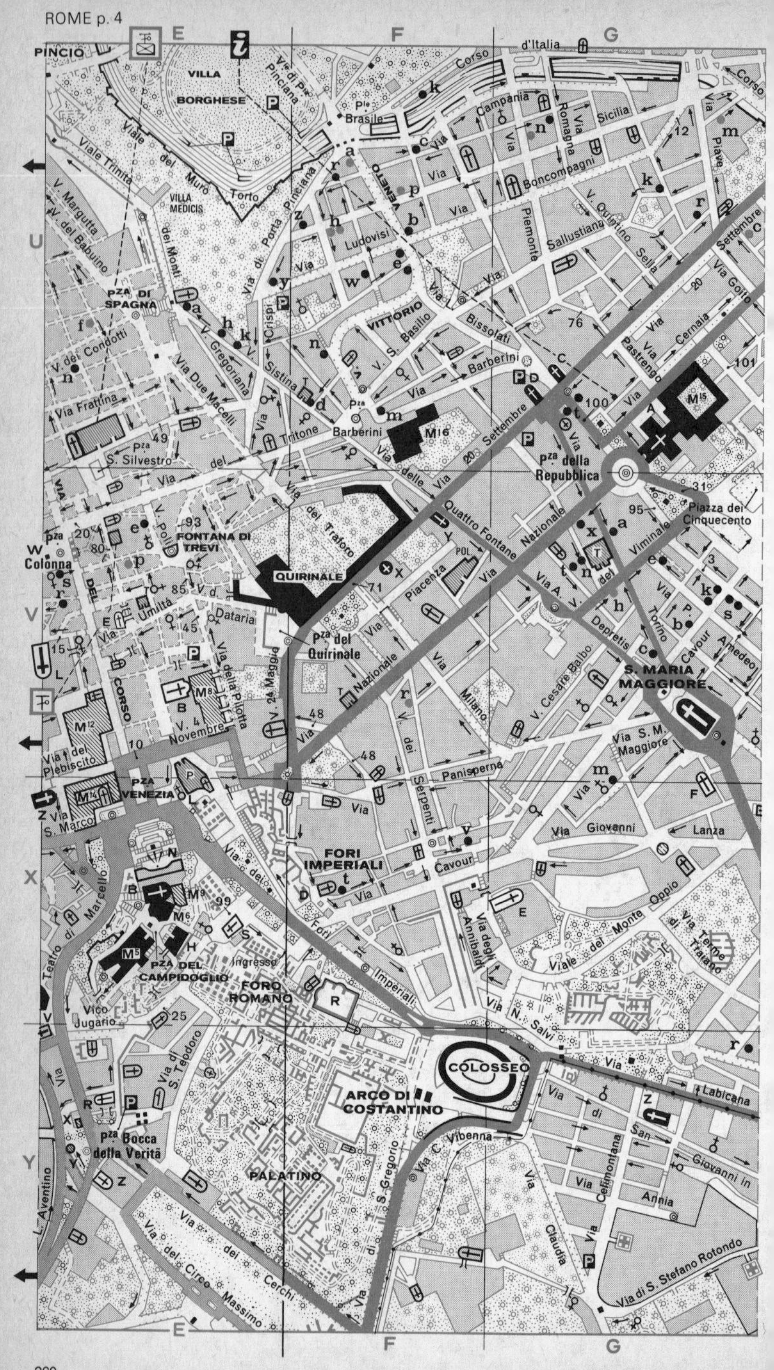
PINCIO
VILLA BORGHESE
VILLA MEDICIS
Pza DI SPAGNA
FONTANA DI TREVI
QUIRINALE
Pza del Quirinale
VITTORIO VENETO
Pza della Repubblica
Piazza dei Cinquecento
S. MARIA MAGGIORE
Pza VENEZIA
FORI IMPERIALI
Pza DEL CAMPIDOGLIO
FORO ROMANO
COLOSSEO
ARCO DI COSTANTINO
PALATINO
Pza Bocca della Verità
Via del Circo Massimo
Via dei Cerchi
Via di S. Gregorio
Via Labicana
Via di San Giovanni in Laterano
Via Nazionale
Via Cavour
Via XX Settembre
Via del Corso
Via del Tritone
Via Sistina
Via Barberini
Via Quattro Fontane
Via dei Fori Imperiali
Via Panisperna
Viale del Muro Torto
Viale Trinità dei Monti
V. Margutta
V. del Babuino
V. dei Condotti
Via Frattina
Via Due Macelli
Via Gregoriana
Via Crispi
Via di Porta Pinciana
Via Ludovisi
Via Boncompagni
Via Sallustiano
Via Piemonte
Via Bissolati
Via Quintino Sella
Via Goito
Via Cernaia
Via Pastrengo
Via Piave
Via Sicilia
Via Romagna
Via Campania
Corso d'Italia
Via del Viminale
Via Torino
Via Amedeo
Via Depretis
Via Milano
Via Piacenza
V. Cesare Balbo
Via S. M. Maggiore
Via Giovanni Lanza
Viale del Monte Oppio
Via Terme di Traiano
Via N. Salvi
Via degli Annibaldi
Via dei Serpenti
V. 24 Maggio
Via della Pilotta
V. 4 Novembre
Via del Plebiscito
Via S. Marco
Via del Teatro di Marcello
Vico Jugario
Via di S. Teodoro
L. Aventino
Via C. Vibenna
Via Claudia
Via Celimontana
Via Annia
Via di S. Stefano Rotondo
Via del Traforo
Via Dataria
Via Umiltà
Pza S. Silvestro
Pza Colonna
Ingresso
Pza Barberini
Ple Brasile
E
F
G
U
V
X
Y

ROMA

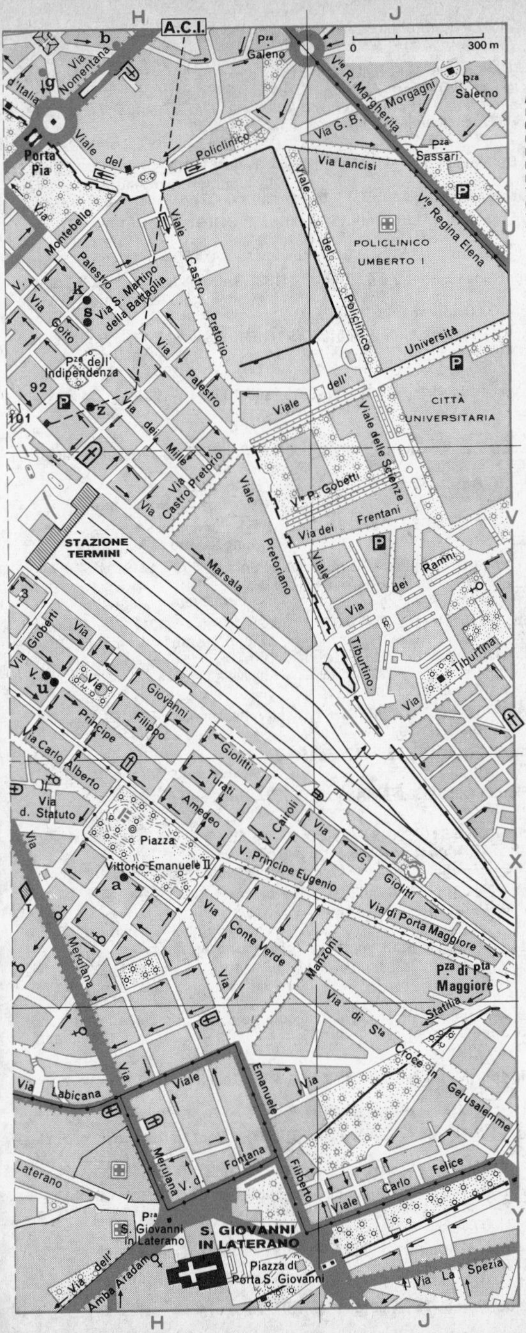

ROMA ANTICA

- ARCO DI COSTANTINO ★★★ ______ FY
- BASILICA DI MASSENZIO ★★★ ______ FX R
- COLONNA TRAIANA ★★★ ______ EX L
- COLOSSEO ★★★ ______ FGY
- FORI IMPERIALI ★★★ ______ FX
- FORO ROMANO ★★★ ______ EX
- PALATINO ★★★ ______ EFY
- TEATRO DI MARCELLO ★★ ______ EX V
- COLONNA DI MARCO AURELIO ★ ______ EV W
- TEMPIO DELLA FORTUNA VIRILE ★ ______ EY X
- TEMPIO DI VESTA ★ ______ EY Y

ROMA CRISTIANA

- GESÙ ★★★ ______ EX Z
- S. GIOVANNI IN LATERANO ★★★ ______ HY
- S. MARIA MAGGIORE ★★★ ______ GV
- S. ANDREA AL QUIRINALE ★★ ______ FV X
- S. CARLO ALLE QUATTRO FONTANE ★★ ______ FV Y
- S. CLEMENTE ★★ ______ GY Z
- S. MARIA DEGLI ANGELI ★★ ______ GU A
- S. MARIA D'ARACOELI ★★ ______ EX B
- S. MARIA DELLA VITTORIA ★★ ______ GU C
- S. SUSANNA ★★ ______ GU D
- ORATORIO DEL CROCIFISSO ★ ______ EV E
- S. IGNAZIO ★ ______ EV L
- S. GIOVANNI DECOLLATO ★ ______ EY R
- S. LUCA E S. MARTINA ★ ______ EX S
- S. MARIA IN COSMEDIN ★ ______ EY Z
- S. PIETRO IN VINCOLI ★ ______ GX E
- S. PRASSEDE ★ ______ GVX F
- SANTI APOSTOLI ★ ______ EV B

PALAZZI E MUSEI

- MUSEO NAZIONALE ROMANO ★★★ ______ GU M15
- MUSEO DEL PALAZZO DEI CONSERVATORI ★★★ ______ EX M5
- PALAZZO NUOVO ★★★ : MUSEO CAPITOLINO ★★ ______ EX M6
- PALAZZO SENATORIO ★★★ ______ EX H
- PALAZZO BARBERINI ★★ ______ FU M16
- PALAZZO DEL QUIRINALE ★★ ______ EV
- GALLERIA DEL PALAZZO COLONNA ★ ______ EV M8
- MUSEO DEL RISORGIMENTO ★ ______ EX M9
- PALAZZO E GALLERIA DORIA PAMPHILI ★ ______ EV M12
- PALAZZO VENEZIA ★ ______ EX M14

PASSEGGIATE

- FONTANA DI TREVI ★★★ ______ EV
- PIAZZA DEL CAMPIDOGLIO ★★★ ______ EX
- MONUMENTO VITTORIO EMANUELE : ⋘ ★★ ______ EX N
- PIAZZA DEL QUIRINALE ★★ ______ FV
- PIAZZA DI SPAGNA ★★ ______ EU
- VIA VITTORIO VENETO ★★ ______ FU
- PIAZZA BOCCA DELLA VERITÀ ★ ______ EY
- PIAZZA COLONNA ★ ______ EV
- PIAZZA DI PORTA MAGGIORE ★ ______ JX
- PIAZZA VENEZIA ★ ______ EX
- PORTA PIA ★ ______ HU

Amendola (Via Giovanni)	GV	3
Battisti (Via Cesare)	EV	10
Calabria (Via)	GU	12
Caravita (Via del)	EV	15
Chigi (Largo)	EV	20
Consolazione (Via della)	EX	25
Einaudi (Viale Luigi)	GV	31
Lucchesi (Via dei)	EV	45
Mazzarino (Via)	FV	48
Mercede (Via della)	EU	49
Quirinale (Via del)	FV	71
Salandra (Via A.)	GU	76
S. Maria in Via (Via di)	EV	80
S. Vincenzo (Via di)	EV	85
Solferino (Via)	HU	92
Stamperia (Via della)	EV	93
Terme Diocleziano (Via)	GV	95
Tulliano (Via del)	EX	99
Vittorio Emanuele Orlando (Via)	GU	100
Volturno (Via)	GU	101

North area Monte Mario, Stadio Olimpico, via Flaminia-Parioli, Villa Borghese, via Salaria, via Nomentana (Plans : Rome pp. 2 to 5) :

Cavalieri Hilton, via Cadlolo 101 00136 3151, Telex 610296, town, « Terraces and park », – . AE E VISA. rest
M a la carte 38/50000 and rest. **La Pergola** *(closed lunch and 1 to 20 January)* a la carte 65/90000 – 20000 – **387 rm** 300/430000 apartments 620/1662000.
by via Trionfale AU

Lord Byron, via De Notaris 5 00197 3609541, Telex 611217, – . AE E VISA
by lungotevere in Augusta DU
M see rest. **Relais le Jardin** below – 16500 – **50 rm** 300/380000 apartments 400/500000.

Aldrovandi Palace Hotel, via Aldrovandi 15 00197 841091, Telex 616141, – – . AE VISA.
by viale Trinità EU
M a la carte 48/73000 – **139 rm** 205/247000 apartments 450/700000.

Borromini without rest., via Lisbona 7 00198 841321, Telex 680485 – – .
by viale Regina Margherita JU
15000 – **75 rm** 175/210000 apartments 320/370000.

Parco dei Principi, via Frescobaldi 5 00198 841071, Telex 610517, « Small park with » – – . AE VISA. rest
by via Piemonte GU
M 32/40000 – **203 rm** 190/290000 apartments 340/440000 – P 190/250000.

Albani, without rest., via Adda 41 00198 84991, Telex 612414 – –
by via Piave GU
157 rm.

Claridge and Rest. Lo Chef, viale Liegi 62 00198 868556 and rest 8449482, Telex 610340 – wc wc – . AE VISA.
M a la carte 35/42000 – **88 rm** 145/195000, 10000 – P 145/185000.
by via Nomentana HU

Degli Aranci, via Oriani 11 00197 870202, – wc wc – . AE.
M 25/45000 – **42 rm** 90/130000.
by lungotevere in Augusta DU

Fleming and Rest. Pantagruel, piazza Monteleone di Spoleto 20 00191 3276741, Telex 610640 – wc wc – . AE VISA.
M a la carte 26/44000 – **270 rm** 81/128000.
by lungotevere in Augusta DU

XXXX **Relais Le Jardin,** via De Notaris 5 00197 3609541, Telex 611217, Elegant rest. – . AE E VISA.
by lungotevere in Augusta DU
closed Sunday – **M** (booking essential) a la carte 65/108000
Spec. Gratin di scampi su letto di spinaci, Insalata tiepida di filetto e rughetta, Carrè d'agnello farcito col suo fegato (Spring-Autumn). **Wines** Marino, Torre Ercolana.

XX **Al Fogher,** via Tevere 13/b 00198 857032, Typical Venetian rest. – . AE .
closed Sunday – **M** a la carte 34/50000.
by via Piave GU

XX Leon d'Oro, via Cagliari 25 00198 861847, Seafood –
dinner only.
by viale Regina Margherita JU

XX Nuovo Calafuria, via Flaminia 388/390 00196 3962377, Rest. and pizzeria
by Lungotevere in Augusta DU

XX **Il Caminetto,** viale dei Parioli 89 00197 803946 – . AE
closed Thursday and 12 to 18 August – **M** a la carte 26/36000.
by lungotevere in Augusta DU

X **Al Ceppo,** via Panama 2 00198 8449696, , Typical rest. – . AE VISA
closed Monday and 12 to 30 August – **M** a la carte 26/36000.
by viale Regina Margherita JU

X **Delle Vittorie,** via Monte Santo 62/64 00195 386847 – AE E VISA.
closed Sunday, 1 to 20 August and 23 December-3 January – **M** a la carte 24/41000.
by via Marcantonio Colonna CU

Middle-western area San Pietro (Vatican City), Gianicolo, corso Vittorio Emanuele, piazza Venezia, Pantheon and Quirinale, Pincio and Villa Medici, piazza di Spagna, Palatino and Fori (Plans : Rome pp. 2 and 3) :

Hassler, piazza Trinità dei Monti 6 00187 6792651, Telex 610208, town from roof-garden rest. – .
EU **a**
M a la carte 82/137000 – 20000 – **101 rm** 350/480000.

Eden, via Ludovisi 49 00187 4743551, Telex 610567, « Roof-garden rest. with town » – .
EU **y**
M a la carte 49/80000 – 13000 – **110 rm** 250/350000 apartments 650/1000000.

D'Inghilterra without rest., via Bocca di Leone 14 00187 672161, Telex 614552 – . AE E VISA.
EU **n**
15000 – **102 rm** 185/240000.

Jolly Leonardo da Vinci, via dei Gracchi 324 00192 39680, Telex 611182 – – . AE E VISA. rest
CU **r**
M 42000 – **245 rm** 155/210000.

Plaza, without rest., via del Corso 126 00186 672101, Telex 624669 – –
207 rm.
DU **d**

Gd H. de la Ville, via Sistina 69 ✉ 00187 ☏ 6733, Telex 620836 – |‡| ▤ TV ☎ 🚗 – 🏋. AE ◑ E VISA. ✂ EU **h**
M a la carte 43/66000 – **189 rm** ☕ 207/291000 apartments 455000.

Visconti Palace without rest., via Cesi 37 ✉ 00193 ☏ 3684, Telex 680407 – |‡| ▤ TV ☎ ♿ 🚗 – 🏋. AE ◑ E VISA. ✂ CU **u**
247 rm ☕ 160/220000 apartments 300000.

Cicerone, via Cicerone 55 ✉ 00193 ☏ 3576, Telex 680514 – |‡| ▤ TV ☎ 🚗 – 🏋. AE ◑ E VISA. ✂ CU **t**
M a la carte 30/46000 – **237 rm** ☕ 165/240000 apartments 340/590000 – P 190/235000.

Atlante Star, via Vitelleschi 34 ✉ 00193 ☏ 6564196, Telex 622355, « Roof-garden rest. with ≤ St. Peter's Basilica » – |‡| ▤ rm TV ☎ – 🏋. AE ◑ E VISA. ✂ rest BU **r**
M *(closed January-February)* a la carte 58/83000 – **61 rm** ☕ 240/310000 apartments 400/600000 – P 200/235000.

Delle Nazioni without rest., via Poli 7 ✉ 00187 ☏ 6792441, Telex 614193 – |‡| ▤ TV ☎. AE ◑ E VISA. ✂ EV **e**
74 rm ☕ 195/260000 apartments 300/350000.

Colonna Palace without rest., piazza Montecitorio 12 ✉ 00186 ☏ 6781341, Telex 621467 – |‡| ▤ TV ☎. AE ◑ E VISA. ✂ EV **s**
100 rm ☕ 169/231000.

Giulio Cesare without rest., via degli Scipioni 287 ✉ 00192 ☏ 310244, Telex 613010, 🌳 – |‡| ▤ TV ☎ Ⓟ – 🏋. AE ◑ VISA. ✂ CU **s**
☕ 22000 – **86 rm** 170/245000.

Columbus, via della Conciliazione 33 ✉ 00193 ☏ 6565435, Telex 620096, « Beautiful decor in 15C style building » – |‡| TV 🛁wc 🚿wc ☎ Ⓟ – 🏋. AE ◑ E VISA. ✂ rest
M a la carte 33/54000 – **107 rm** ☕ 100/154000 – P 125/175000. BV **m**

Internazionale without rest., via Sistina 79 ✉ 00187 ☏ 6793047, Telex 614333 – |‡| ▤ 🛁wc 🚿wc ☎. AE ◑ E VISA. ✂ EU **k**
35 rm ☕ 134/210000.

Gerber without rest., via degli Scipioni 241 ✉ 00192 ☏ 3595148 – |‡| 🛁wc 🚿wc ☎. AE ◑ E VISA. ✂ – **28 rm** ☕ 60/95000. BU **s**

Atlante Garden without rest., via Crescenzio 78/a ✉ 00193 ☏ 6530341 – |‡| ▤ TV 🛁wc 🚿wc ☎. AE ◑ E VISA BU **f**
43 rm ☕ 240/310000.

Della Torre Argentina without rest., corso Vittorio Emanuele 102 ✉ 00186 ☏ 6548251 – |‡| 🛁wc 🚿wc ☎ ♿. AE ◑ VISA. ✂ DX **e**
☕ 8500 – **32 rm** 65/105000.

Siena without rest., via Sant'Andrea delle Fratte 33 ✉ 00187 ☏ 6796121 – |‡| 🛁wc 🚿wc ☎. ✂ EU **c**
☕ 12500 – **21 rm** 90/127000.

Senato without rest., piazza della Rotonda 73 ✉ 00186 ☏ 6793231, ≤ Pantheon – |‡| ▤ 🛁wc 🚿wc ☎. AE ◑. ✂ DV **y**
51 rm ☕ 66/88000, ▤ 14000.

Cesàri without rest., via di Pietra 89/a ✉ 00186 ☏ 6792386 – |‡| 🛁wc 🚿wc ☎. AE ◑ E VISA – ☕ 9500 – **50 rm** 69/84000. EV **r**

Margutta without rest., via Laurina 34 ✉ 00187 ☏ 3614193 – |‡| 🛁wc 🚿wc ☎. AE ◑ E VISA – **21 rm** ☕ 50/80000. DU **t**

Portoghesi without rest., via dei Portoghesi 1 ✉ 00186 ☏ 6564231 – |‡| ▤ 🛁wc 🚿wc ☎. VISA – **27 rm** ☕ 51/85000. DV **g**

XXXX Hostaria dell'Orso, via Monte Brianzo 93 ✉ 00186 ☏ 6564250, Elegant rest. - night club, « Building and decorations in 15C style » – ▤ CV **n**
dinner only (booking essential).

XXX **El Toulà,** via della Lupa 29 ✉ 00186 ☏ 6781196, Elegant rest. – ▤. AE ◑ E VISA. ✂
closed Saturday lunch, Sunday, August and 24 to 26 December – **M** (booking essential) a la carte 50/70000 (15%). DU **e**

XXX **Ranieri,** via Mario de' Fiori 26 ✉ 00187 ☏ 6791592 – ▤. AE ◑ E VISA EU **f**
closed Sunday – **M** (booking essential) a la carte 39/73000.

XXX **4 Colonne,** via della Posta 4 ✉ 00186 ☏ 6547152 – ▤. ✂ DV **n**
closed Sunday and 5 to 31 August – **M** (booking essential) a la carte 45/54000.

XXX **Passetto,** via Zanardelli 14 ✉ 00186 ☏ 6543696 – ▤. AE ◑ VISA. ✂ CV **v**
closed Sunday – **M** a la carte 35/65000.

XX ✿ **Piperno,** Monte de' Cenci 9 ✉ 00186 ☏ 6540629, Roman rest. – ▤. ✂ DX **d**
closed Sunday dinner, Monday, Easter, 1 May, August and 23 December-2 January – **M** a la carte 43/65000
Spec. Pasta e ceci, Filetti di baccalà con carciofi, Trippa alla romana. Wines Frascati, Rosso Tapino.

XX **Mastrostefano,** piazza Navona 94 ✉ 00186 ☏ 6541669, Rest.-American bar, « Outdoor service in Summer with ≤ Bernini fountain » – ▤ DV **d**
closed Monday – **M** a la carte 40/60000.

XX **Taverna Giulia,** vicolo dell'Oro 23 ✉ 00186 ☏ 6569768, Ligurian rest. – ▤ BV **a**
closed Sunday and August – **M** (booking essential) a la carte 30/53000 (15%).

XX **Dal Bolognese,** piazza del Popolo 1 ✉ 00187 ✆ 3611426, Bolognese rest., « Collection of paintings » – ▤. AE ⓓ. ✻ DU **z**
closed Sunday dinner, Monday and August – **M** a la carte 33/49000.

XX **Squalo Bianco,** via Federico Cesi 36 ✉ 00193 ✆ 312524, Seafood – AE ⓓ. ✻ CU **c**
closed Sunday and August – **M** a la carte 35/56000.

XX **La Maiella,** piazza Sant'Apollinare 45/46 ✉ 00186 ✆ 6564174, ☂, Abruzzi rest. – ▤. AE ⓓ E VISA. ✻ CDV **x**
closed Sunday – **M** a la carte 40/55000.

XX **Vecchia Roma,** piazza Campitelli 18 ✉ 00186 ✆ 6564604, Roman and seafood rest. – ▤ – *closed Wednesday* – **M** a la carte 29/48000 (12%). DX **a**

X ✿ **La Rosetta,** via della Rosetta 9 ✉ 00187 ✆ 6561002, Seafood trattoria – ▤. AE VISA
closed Sunday, Monday lunch and August – **M** 80000 (15%) DV **e**
Spec. Tonnarelli con capesante e basilico, Rombo in salsa di ostriche, Pesce all'acqua di mare. Wines Vintage Tunina.

X **Al 59,** via Brunetti 59 ✉ 00186 ✆ 3619019, Bolognese rest. – ▤. ✻ DU **y**
closed August, Sunday and Saturday from June-July – **M** a la carte 31/52000.

X **Al Salanova,** via Florida 23 ✉ 00186 ✆ 6561409 – AE ⓓ VISA. ✻ DX **v**
closed Monday, 4 to 20 January and 4 to 20 July – **M** a la carte 24/46000 (15%).

X **Al Moro,** vicolo delle Bollette 13 ✉ 00187 ✆ 6783495, Roman trattoria – ▤. ✻ EV **p**
closed Sunday and August – **M** (booking essential) a la carte 35/72000.

Central eastern area via Vittorio Veneto, via Nazionale, Viminale, Santa Maria Maggiore, Colosseum, Porta Pia, via Nomentana, Stazione Termini, Porta San Giovanni (Plans : Rome pp. 4 and 5) :

Le Grand Hotel, via Vittorio Emanuele Orlando 3 ✉ 00185 ✆ 4709, Telex 610210 – |‡| ▤ TV ☎ ♿ – 🅰. AE ⓓ E VISA. ✻ GU **t**
M a la carte 68/103000 – ☕ 22000 – **168 rm** 325/461000.

Excelsior, via Vittorio Veneto 125 ✉ 00187 ✆ 4708, Telex 610232 – |‡| ▤ TV ☎ ♿ – 🅰. AE ⓓ E VISA. ✻ FU **b**
M a la carte 64/103000 – ☕ 21500 – **363 rm** 309/458000 apartments 889/1066000.

Ambasciatori Palace, via Vittorio Veneto 125 ✉ 00187 ✆ 474931, Telex 610241 – |‡| ▤ TV ☎ ♿ – 🅰. AE ⓓ E VISA. ✻ rest FU **e**
M Grill Bar ABC rest. a la carte 50/78000 – ☕ 18000 – **149 rm** 200/320000 apartments 600000.

Bernini Bristol, piazza Barberini 23 ✉ 00187 ✆ 463051, Telex 610554 – |‡| ▤ TV ☎ – 🅰. AE ⓓ E. ✻ rest FU **m**
M a la carte 54/89000 – ☕ 15000 – **125 rm** 250/350000 apartments 500/900000.

Jolly Vittorio Veneto, corso d'Italia 1 ✉ 00198 ✆ 8495, Telex 612293 – |‡| ▤ TV ☎ 🚗 – 🅰. AE ⓓ E VISA. ✻ rest FU **k**
M 43000 – **200 rm** ☕ 170/235000.

Mediterraneo, via Cavour 15 ✉ 00184 ✆ 464051 – |‡| ▤ TV ☎ – 🅰. AE ⓓ E VISA ✻ GV **k**
M *(closed Friday and Saturday)* 29000 – **272 rm** ☕ 167/238000 apartments 381/717000.

Regina Carlton, via Vittorio Veneto 72 ✉ 00187 ✆ 476851, Telex 620863 – |‡| ▤ TV ☎. AE ⓓ E VISA. ✻ FU **e**
M a la carte 44/68000 – ☕ 11000 – **125 rm** 165/240000 apartments 350/500000.

Victoria, via Campania 41 ✉ 00187 ✆ 473931, Telex 610212 – |‡| ▤ TV ☎ ♿. AE E. ✻ rest FU **c**
M a la carte 31/51000 – **110 rm** ☕ 160/260000.

Genova without rest., via Cavour 33 ✉ 00184 ✆ 476951, Telex 621599 – |‡| ▤ TV ☎ ♿. AE ⓓ VISA. ✻ GV **b**
91 rm ☕ 195/260000.

Londra e Cargill, piazza Sallustio 18 ✉ 00187 ✆ 473871, Telex 622227 – |‡| ▤ TV ☎ 🚗 – 🅰. AE ⓓ E VISA. ✻ GU **k**
M 40/45000 – **105 rm** ☕ 170/240000 apartments 300/500000 – P 200/210000.

Forum, via Tor de' Conti 25 ✉ 00184 ✆ 6792446, Telex 622549, « Roof-garden rest. with ≤ Imperial Forums » – |‡| ▤ TV ☎ 🚗 – 🅰. AE ⓓ E VISA. ✻ FX **t**
M (residents only) (closed Sunday) a la carte 60/98000 – ☕ 16000 – **81 rm** 180/250000 apartments 400/500000.

Massimo D'Azeglio, via Cavour 18 ✉ 00184 ✆ 460646, Telex 610556 – |‡| ▤ TV ☎ – 🅰. AE ⓓ E VISA. ✻ GV **s**
M *(closed Sunday)* 29000 – **210 rm** ☕ 144/204000.

Quirinale, via Nazionale 7 ✉ 00184 ✆ 4707, Telex 610332, ☂, 🌳 – |‡| ▤ TV ☎ ♿ – 🅰. AE ⓓ E. ✻ rest GV **x**
M 50000 – **193 rm** ☕ 176/242000 apartments 330/440000.

Eliseo, via di Porta Pinciana 30 ✉ 00187 ✆ 460556, Telex 610693, « Roof-garden rest. with ≤ Villa Borghese » – |‡| ▤ TV ☎ – 🅰. AE ⓓ E VISA. ✻ FU **r**
M (lunch only) 40000 – **53 rm** ☕ 159/244000 apartments 250/300000.

P.L.M. Etap Boston, via Lombardia 47 ✉ 00187 ✆ 473951, Telex 622247 – |‡| ▤ TV ☎ – 🅰. AE ⓓ E VISA. ✻ rest FU **z**
M 30000 – **121 rm** ☕ 145/235000 – P 178000.

Imperiale, via Vittorio Veneto 24 ✉ 00187 ℘ 4756351, Telex 621071 – |‡| ▤ TV ☎. AE ① E VISA. ✻ FU **n**
M 20/37000 – **85 rm** ☕ 140/215000 – P 130/150000.

Napoleon, piazza Vittorio Emanuele 105 ✉ 00185 ℘ 737646, Telex 611069 – |‡| ▤ ☎ – 🏃. AE ① E VISA. ✻ HX **a**
M (residents only) (closed lunch) 24000 – ☕ 11000 – **82 rm** 86/132000.

San Giorgio without rest., via Amendola 61 ✉ 00185 ℘ 4751341 – |‡| ▤ TV ☎. AE ① E VISA. ✻ GV **s**
186 rm ☕ 123/176000 apartments 299000.

La Residenza without rest., via Emilia 22 ✉ 00187 ℘ 6799592 – |‡| ▤ TV ☎ P FU **w**
27 rm ☕ 87/135000.

Mondial without rest., via Torino 127 ✉ 00184 ℘ 472861, Telex 612219 – |‡| ▤ TV ☎ 🚗 – 🏃. AE E. ✻ GV **a**
☕ 15000 – **77 rm** 132/193000.

Atlantico without rest., via Cavour 23 ✉ 00184 ℘ 485951 – |‡| ▤ TV ☎. AE ① E VISA. ✻ GV **k**
83 rm ☕ 123/176000.

Universo, via Principe Amedeo 5 ✉ 00185 ℘ 476811, Telex 610342 – |‡| ▤ TV ☎ – 🏃. AE ① E VISA. ✻ GV **e**
M 31/35000 – **207 rm** ☕ 141/215000 apartments 350000 – P 170000.

Britannia without rest., via Napoli 64 ✉ 00184 ℘ 463153, Telex 611292 – |‡| ▤ 🛁wc ⛆wc ☎. AE ① E VISA GV **t**
32 rm ☕ 120/190000.

Commodore without rest., via Torino 1 ✉ 00184 ℘ 485656, Telex 612170 – |‡| ▤ 🛁wc ⛆wc ☎. AE ① E VISA GV **c**
☕ 15000 – **62 rm** 120/180000.

Regency without rest., via Romagna 42 ✉ 00187 ℘ 4759281, Telex 622321 – |‡| ▤ TV 🛁wc ⛆wc ☎. AE ① E VISA GU **n**
☕ 10000 – **50 rm** 101/176000.

Sitea without rest., via Vittorio Emanuele Orlando 90 ✉ 00185 ℘ 4751560, Telex 614163 – |‡| ▤ 🛁wc ⛆wc ☎. AE ① E GU **t**
37 rm ☕ 120/190000.

Edera 🌿 without rest., via Poliziano 75 ✉ 00184 ℘ 7316341, Telex 621472, 🌳 – |‡| 🛁wc ⛆wc ☎ P. AE ① E VISA. ✻ GY **r**
38 rm ☕ 88/130000.

Siviglia without rest., via Gaeta 12 ✉ 00185 ℘ 4750004, Telex 612225 – |‡| 🛁wc ⛆wc ☎. AE ① VISA. ✻ HU **k**
41 rm ☕ 73/114000.

Milani without rest., via Magenta 12 ✉ 00185 ℘ 4940051, Telex 614356 – |‡| TV 🛁wc ⛆wc ☎. ✻ HU **z**
78 rm ☕ 75/119000.

Alpi without rest., via Castelfidardo 84/a ✉ 00185 ℘ 464618, Telex 611677 – |‡| ▤ TV 🛁wc ☎. AE ① E VISA HU **s**
46 rm ☕ 71/115000, ▤ 10000.

Colosseum without rest., via Sforza 10 ✉ 00184 ℘ 4751228 – |‡| ⛆wc ☎. AE ① E VISA GVX **m**
50 rm ☕ 58/100000.

Marcella without rest., via Flavia 106 ✉ 00187 ℘ 4746451, Telex 621351 – |‡| ▤ TV 🛁wc ⛆wc ☎. AE ① E. ✻ GU **r**
55 rm ☕ 115/175000.

King without rest., via Sistina 131 ✉ 00187 ℘ 4741515, Telex 626246 – |‡| ▤ 🛁wc ⛆wc ☎. AE ① E VISA FU **d**
79 rm ☕ 80/120000, ▤ 15000.

Terminal without rest., via Principe Amedeo 103 ✉ 00185 ℘ 734041 – |‡| 🛁wc ⛆wc ☎. AE. ✻ HV **u**
☕ 8000 – **35 rm** 61/97000.

Igea without rest., via Principe Amedeo 97 ✉ 00185 ℘ 7311212 – |‡| ⛆wc ☎. ✻ HV **u**
☕ 5000 – **42 rm** 40/60000.

Centro without rest., via Firenze 12 ✉ 00184 ℘ 464142, Telex 612125 – |‡| ▤ 🛁wc ⛆wc ☎. AE ① VISA. ✻ GV **n**
36 rm ☕ 90/120000.

Alba without rest., via Leonina 12 ✉ 00184 ℘ 484471 – |‡| 🛁wc ⛆wc ☎. AE ① E VISA FX **v**
26 rm ☕ 50/80000.

XXXX ✿ **Sans Souci,** via Sicilia 20/24 ✉ 00187 ℘ 493504, Elegant tavern-late night dinners – ▤. AE ① E VISA FU **p**
closed Monday and August – **M** (dinner only) (booking essential) a la carte 55/92000
Spec. Festival mediterraneo di risotti, Salmone fresco norvegese alla salsa zafferano, Filetto di bue in crosta alla salsa di tartufo nero. **Wines** Vintage Tunina, Rubesco.

XXX **Harry's Bar,** via Vittorio Veneto 150 ✉ 00187 ℘ 4745832 – ▤. AE ①. ✻ FU **a**
closed Sunday – **M** (booking essential) a la carte 44/73000.

XX **Piccolo Mondo,** via Aurora 39/d ✉ 00187 ℰ 4754595, Elegant tavern – ▤. AE ⓓ E VISA. ✻ FU **h**
closed Sunday and 10 to 25 August – **M** a la carte 38/61000 (12%).

XX **Coriolano,** via Ancona 14 ✉ 00198 ℰ 861122 – ▤ HU **g**
closed Sunday and 3 August-2 September – **M** *(booking essential)* a la carte 51/77000 (15%).

XX **Cesarina,** via Piemonte 109 ✉ 00187 ℰ 460828, Bolognese rest. – ▤. ✻ GU **n**
closed Sunday – **M** a la carte 30/48000.

XX **Loreto,** via Valenziani 19 ✉ 00187 ℰ 4742454, Seafood – ▤. ✻ GU **m**
closed Sunday and 10 to 28 August – **M** a la carte 38/58000.

X **Hostaria Costa Balena,** via Messina 5/7 ✉ 00198 ℰ 857686, Seafood trattoria – ▤. AE ⓓ E VISA HU **b**
closed Sunday and 10 to 29 August – **M** a la carte 26/43000.

X **La Matriciana,** via del Viminale 40/44 ✉ 00184 ℰ 461775 – ▤. AE ⓓ VISA GV **h**
closed Saturday and 11 to 16 August – **M** a la carte 24/38000.

X **Crisciotti-al Boschetto,** via del Boschetto 30 ✉ 00184 ℰ 4744770, 🏕, Rustic trattoria – AE ⓓ E VISA FV **r**
closed Saturday and August – **M** a la carte 20/35000 (10%).

X **Hostaria da Vincenzo,** via Castelfidardo 6 ✉ 00185 ℰ 484596 – ▤. AE ⓓ E VISA
closed Sunday and August – **M** a la carte 20/35000. GU **c**

Southern area Aventino, Porta San Paolo, Terme di Caracalla, via Appia Nuova (Plans : Rome pp. 2 to 5) :

🏨 **Sant'Anselmo** without rest., piazza Sant'Anselmo 2 ✉ 00153 ℰ 573547, 🌳 – ⊟wc ⋔wc ☎. AE. ✻ by lungotevere Aventino DY
45 rm ☕ 54/80000.

🏨 **Villa San Pio** without rest., via di Sant'Anselmo 19 ✉ 00153 ℰ 5755231, 🌳 – |‡| ⊟wc ⋔wc ☎. AE. ✻ by lungotevere Aventino DEY
59 rm ☕ 54/80000.

🏨 Santa Prisca, largo Manlio Gelsomini 25 ✉ 00153 ℰ 571917 – |‡| ▤ rest ⋔wc ☎ Ⓟ
45 rm. by lungotevere Aventino DEY

🏨 **Domus Maximi** ♨ without rest., via Santa Prisca 11/b ✉ 00153 ℰ 5782565 – ⊟wc ⋔wc ☎ by via del Circo Massimo EY
23 rm ☕ 60/90000.

XX **Da Severino,** piazza Zama 5/c ✉ 00183 ℰ 7550872 – ▤
closed Sunday dinner, Monday, 1 to 22 August and 24 to 30 December – **M** a la carte 35/50000. by via dell'Amba Aradam HY

XX **Apuleius,** via Tempio di Diana 15 ✉ 00153 ℰ 572160, « Ancient Rome style decor tavern » – ✻ by via del Circo Massimo EY
closed Sunday and 13 to 28 August – **M** a la carte 29/47000.

Trastevere area (typical district) (Plan : Rome p. 3) :

XX ✿ **Alberto Ciarla,** piazza San Cosimato 40 ✉ 00153 ℰ 5818668, 🏕 – AE ⓓ VISA. ✻
closed Sunday, 5 to 25 August and 23 December-10 January – **M** (dinner only) (booking essential) a la carte 62/82000 CY **u**
Spec. Insalate di pesce crudo, Zuppa di pasta e fagioli ai frutti di mare, Filetti di spigola alle mandorle.
Wines Vintage Tunina.

XX **Corsetti-il Galeone,** piazza San Cosimato 27 ✉ 00153 ℰ 5816311, Seafood, « Roman Atmosphere » – ▤. AE ⓓ E VISA. ✻ CY **g**
closed Wednesday – **M** a la carte 26/46000.

XX **Sabatini a Santa Maria in Trastevere,** piazza di Santa Maria in Trastevere 10 ✉ 00153 ℰ 582026, 🏕, Roman and seafood rest. – AE ⓓ VISA CY **n**
closed Wednesday – **M** a la carte 32/60000.

XX **Galeassi,** piazza di Santa Maria in Trastevere 3 ✉ 00153 ℰ 5803775, 🏕, Roman and seafood rest. – ▤. AE ⓓ E VISA. ✻ CY **f**
closed Monday and 20 December-20 January – **M** a la carte 29/50000.

XX **Sabatini,** vicolo Santa Maria in Trastevere 18 ✉ 00153 ℰ 5818307, 🏕, Typical Roman hostelry – AE ⓓ VISA CY **n**
closed Tuesday – **M** a la carte 32/60000.

XX **Checco er Carettiere,** via Benedetta 10 ✉ 00153 ℰ 5817018, 🏕, Typical Roman and seafood rest. – ▤ CX **k**
closed Sunday dinner, Monday and 10 August-10 September – **M** a la carte 32/49000.

XX **Taverna Trilussa,** via del Politeama 23 ✉ 00153 ℰ 5818918, 🏕, Typical Roman rest. – ▤. AE ⓓ VISA CY **h**
closed Sunday dinner, Monday and 30 July-28 August – **M** a la carte 21/35000.

XX **Romolo,** via di Porta Settimiana 8 ✉ 00153 ℰ 5818284, Typical trattoria, « Summer service in a cool little court-yard » – AE ⓓ E VISA CX **a**
closed Monday and August – **M** a la carte 35/50000.

Outskirts of Rome

on national road 1 - Aurelia :

Villa Pamphili, via della Nocetta 105 ✉ 00164 ℘ 5862, Telex 611675, (covered in winter), – – . AE E VISA. rest by via Garibaldi BY
M 40000 – **253 rm** 130/190000.

Holiday Inn St. Peter's, via Aurelia Antica 415 ✉ 00165 ℘ 5872, Telex 625434, , – – . AE E VISA. rest by via Garibaldi BY
M a la carte 31/55000 – 11000 – **330 rm** 149/220000.

MotelAgip, ✉ 00163 ℘ 6379001, Telex 613699, – wc – . AE E VISA. by via Aurelia AV
M 22/26000 – **222 rm** 73/117000.

Le Cigalas, via Madonna del Riposo 36 ✉ 00165 ℘ 620742, Seafood by via Aurelia AV

La Maielletta, via Aurelia Antica 270 ✉ 00165 ℘ 6374957, , Typical Abruzzi rest. – . AE . by via Aurelia AV
closed Monday – **M** a la carte 29/45000.

on the Ancient Appian way :

Cecilia Metella, via Appia Antica 125/127 ✉ 00179 ℘ 5136743, , « Shaded garden » – by via Claudia GY

Quo Vadis, via Appia Antica 38 ✉ 00179 ℘ 5136795, – .
closed Tuesday and 2 to 22 August – **M** (lunch only) a la carte 30/44000. by via Claudia GY

to E.U.R. Garden City :

Sheraton, viale del Pattinaggio ✉ 00144 ℘ 5453, Telex 614223, , – – . AE E VISA. by via di San Gregorio FY
M a la carte 45/92000 – **615 rm** 213/285000 apartments 530/990000.

Shangri Là-Corsetti, viale Algeria 141 ✉ 00144 ℘ 5916441, Telex 614664, heated, – – . AE E VISA. by via di San Gregorio FY
M a la carte 25/46000 – 9000 – **52 rm** 140/190000 apartments 220/290000.

Dei Congressi without rest., viale Shakespeare 29 ✉ 00144 ℘ 5926021, Telex 614140 – – . AE E. by via di San Gregorio FY
96 rm 100/140000.

Vecchia America-Corsetti, piazza Marconi 32 ✉ 00144 ℘ 5926601, Typical rest. and ale house – . AE E VISA by via di San Gregorio FY
closed Tuesday – **M** a la carte 24/43000.

Il Convento, via Ostiense 491 ✉ 00144 ℘ 5410115, « Outdoor service in Summer » – by via di San Gregorio FY

on the motorway to Fiumicino close to the ring-road :

Holiday Inn-Eur Parco dei Medici, viale Castello della Magliana 65 ✉ 00148 ℘ 5475, Telex 613302, , , – – . AE E VISA.
M 40000 – 13000 – **324 rm** 150/208000 apartments 458000. by viale Trastevere CY

FLORENCE (FIRENZE) 50100 P 988 ⑮ – pop. 430 748 alt. 49 – 055.

See : Monuments of Piazza del Duomo*** : Cathedral** (east end***, dome*** : **), Campanile** (**) – Baptistry** (doors***, mosaics***), Cathedral Museum** (Pietà** by Michelangelo, choristers' tribunes** by Luca della Robbia, low reliefs**, altar**) – Piazza della Signoria** : Loggia della Signoria** (Perseus*** by B. Cellini), Palazzo Vecchio*** (cabinet**) – Uffizi Gallery*** (Botticelli Room***) – Bargello Palace and Museum*** (courtyard**, works by Donatello***) – San Lorenzo*** : Church** (former sacristy**, pulpits**) – Laurentian Library**, Medici Chapels** (Princes Chapel*, New Sacristy** : Medici tombs***) – Medici Riccardi Palace** (frescoes*** by Benozzo Gozzoli, Luca Giordano Gallery**) – Santa Maria Novella** : Church* (Crucifix** by Brunelleschi, frescoes*** by Ghirlandaio, Spaniards' Chapel : frescoes**) – Ponte Vecchio* – Pitti Palace** : Palatine Gallery*** (works*** by Titian and Raphael), silverware museum*, Gallery of Modern Art* : works by the Macchiaili school – Boboli Gardens* : ** from the Citadel Belvedere ABZ – Monastery and Museum of St. Mark** (works*** by Fra Angelico) – Academy Gallery** (main gallery*** : works by Michelangelo) – Piazza della Santissima Annunziata* : Church (frescoes*), Foundlings' Hospital (portico*, medallions**) – Santa Croce** : Church** (low relief of the Annunciation** by Donatello, tomb of Leonardo Bruni**, frescoes by Giotto depicting the life of St. Francis**, Crucifix** by Donatello), Pazzi Chapel** – Excursion to the hills** : Church of San Miniato al Monte** (setting**) – Strozzi Palace** BY **F** – Church of Santa Maria del Carmine (frescoes** by Masaccio) AY **Z** San Salvi : Last Supper** – Orsanmichele* (tabernacle** by Orcagna) BCY **G.**

Exc : Medici Villas** : Villa della Pretaia (gardens*), Villa di Poggio a Caiano* by ⑥.

18 Dell'Ugolino (closed Monday), to Grassina ✉ 50015 ℘ 2051009, S : 12 km.

Galileo Galilei of Pisa to ⑦ : 95 km ℘ (050) 28088 – Alitalia, lungarno Acciaiuoli 10/12, ✉ 30123 ℘ 263051.

via Manzoni 16 ✉ 50121 ℘ 678841 – via de' Tornabuoni 15 ✉ 50123 ℘ 216544, Telex 572263. **A.C.I.** viale Amendola 36 ✉ 50121 ℘ 27841, Telex 571202 – **Roma 277** ③ – **Bologna 105** ⑧ – **Milano 298** ⑧.

FIRENZE
0
300 m
A 1
A 11
S 66
MICHELIN
★★★ S. LORENZO
★★ STA MA NOVELLA
83 km PISA
AUTOSTRADA A1
SESTO FIORENTINO
FIAT
A
B
V
X
Y
Z
Viale Francesco Redi
Via G. Galliano
Via P. Toselli
Via del Ponte alle Mosse
Via Benedetto Marcello
Via delle Porte Nuove
Viale Belfiore
V. G. Monaco
Rosselli
Via Alamanni
Via Valfonda
Viale Strozzi
V. del Romito
V. dello Statuto
Via Ridolfi
Pza della Indipendenza
PALAZZO DEI CONGRESSI
Via Guelfa
Via Nazionale
Pzale di Porta al Prato
LE CASCINE
Pza Vittorio Veneto
Vle
PTE DELLA VITTORIA
V. J. Da Diacceto
Via della Scala
Il Prato
Via Montebello
Corso Italia
AIR TERMINAL
STAZIONE
Via Palazzuolo
Lungarno Amerigo Vespucci
ARNO
V. della Fonderia
L. S. Rosa
PONTE VESPUCCI
Via de' Fossi
Via Pisana
Viale R. Sanzio
Vle Aleardi
Borgo S. Frediano
Lungarno Soderini
PTE ALLA CARRAIA
Lungarno Corsini
Lungarno Guicciardini
PONTE VECCHIO
Ariosto
Via dell'Orto
Pza del Carmine
Viale L.
Pza T. Tasso
Serragli
Maggio
Pza S. Spirito
V. de' Guicciardini
V. de' Bardi
GROTTA
Via del Campuccio
Viale F. Petrarca
Via Romana
GIARDINO DI BOBOLI
VIOTTOLONE
PZALE DELL' ISOLOTTO
FORTE DEL BELVEDERE
Pzale della Porta Romana
Via Senese
Viale Machiavelli
VIA CASSIA SIENA 68 km
AUTOSTRADA DEL SOLE (A 1) per Superstrada: SIENA 68 km
PONTE VECCHIO
PALAZZO PITTI

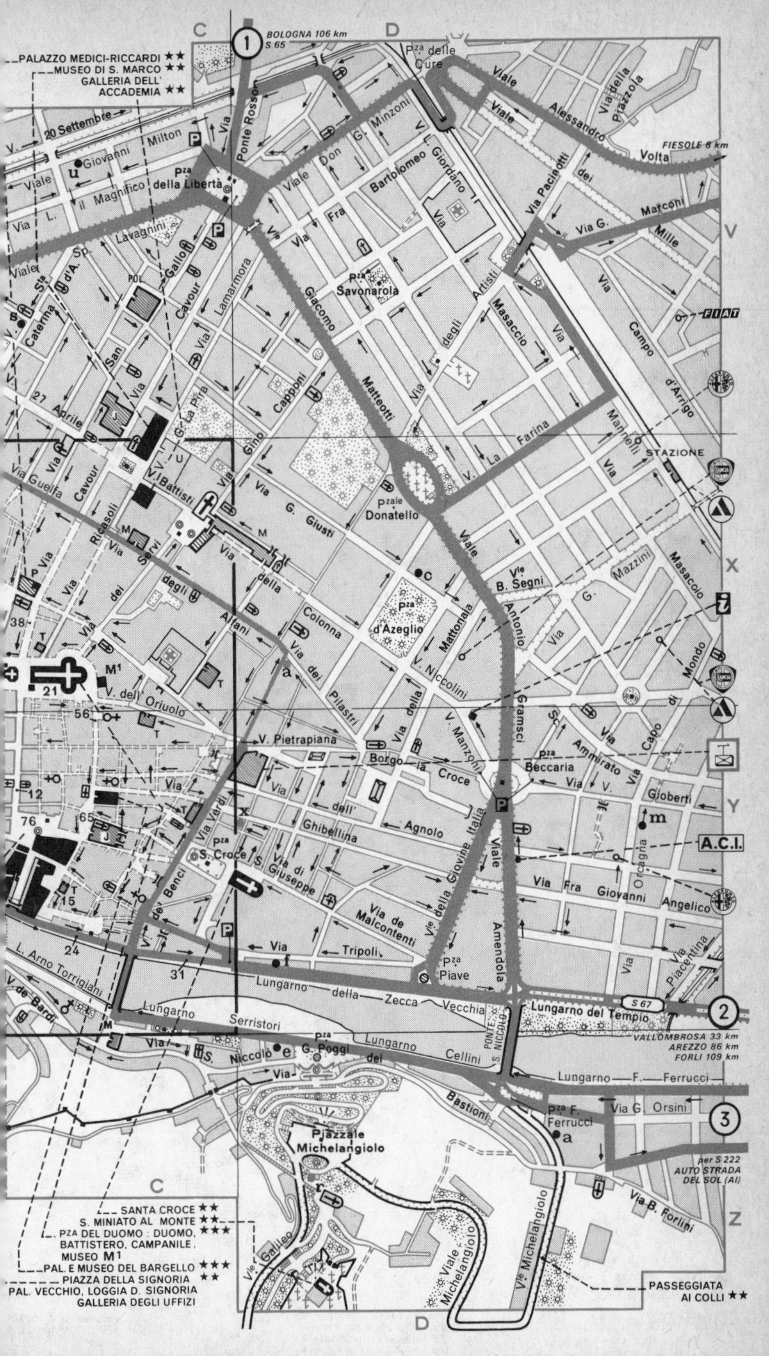
BOLOGNA 106 km
S 65
PALAZZO MEDICI-RICCARDI ★★
MUSEO DI S. MARCO ★★
GALLERIA DELL' ACCADEMIA ★★
Pza delle Cure
Viale Alessandro Volta
Via della Piazzola
FIESOLE 8 km
20 Settembre
Viale Lorenzo il Magnifico
Via Giovanni Milton
Pza della Libertà
Ponte Rosso
Viale Don G. Minzoni
Viale Fra Bartolomeo
Via L. Giordano
Via Pacinotti
Via G. Marconi
Mille
Lavagnini
Via Cavour
Via Lamarmora
Vle Giacomo Matteotti
Pza Savonarola
Via degli Artisti
Masaccio
Via Campo d'Arrigo
Via Gino Capponi
27 Aprile
Via La Farina
STAZIONE
Via Guelfa
V. Battisti
Via Ricasoli
Via dei Servi
Via G. Giusti
Pzale Donatello
Viale Antonio Gramsci
Vle B. Segni
G. Mazzini
Masaccio
Via degli Alfani
Via della Colonna
Pza d'Azeglio
Mattonaia
V. Niccolini
Via dei Pilastri
Via Capo di Mondo
V. dell' Oriuolo
V. Pietrapiana
Borgo la Croce
V. Manzoni
Pza Beccaria
Via Ammirato
V. Gioberti
Via dell' Agnolo
Ghibellina
Via Verdi
Pza S. Croce
Via di S. Giuseppe
Viale della Giovine Italia
Via Fra Giovanni Angelico
Orcagna
A.C.I.
Via de Malcontenti
Via Tripoli
Pza Piave
Viale Amendola
Via Piacentina
de Benci
L. Arno Torrigiani
Lungarno della Zecca Vecchia
Lungarno del Tempio
S 67
V. de Bardi
Lungarno Serristori
Pza G. Poggi
Lungarno Cellini
Ponte S. Niccolò
VALLOMBROSA 33 km
AREZZO 86 km
FORLI 109 km
Via S. Niccolò
Lungarno F. Ferrucci
Bastioni
Pza F. Ferrucci
Via G. Orsini
Piazzale Michelangiolo
per S 222
AUTO STRADA DEL SOL (A1)
Via B. Forlini
Viale Michelangiolo
Vle Galileo
SANTA CROCE ★★
S. MINIATO AL MONTE ★★
PZA DEL DUOMO : DUOMO, BATTISTERO, CAMPANILE, MUSEO M1 ★★★
PAL. E MUSEO DEL BARGELLO ★★★
PIAZZA DELLA SIGNORIA ★★
PAL. VECCHIO, LOGGIA D. SIGNORIA
GALLERIA DEGLI UFFIZI
PASSEGGIATA AI COLLI ★★
FIAT

FIRENZE

Calimala .... BY 10
Calzaiuoli (Via dei) .... CY
Guicciardini (Via) .... BY
Ponte Vecchio .... BY
Por Santa Maria (Via) .... BY 55
Porta Rossa (Via) .... BY
Roma (Via) .... BXY
S. Jacopo (Borgo) .... BY
Strozzi (Via degli) .... BY
Tornabuoni (Via de') .... BXY

Archibusieri (Lungarno degli) .... BY 4
Avelli (Via degli) .... BX 6
Baroncelli (Chiasso dei) .... BCY 8
Canto de' Nelli (Via) .... BX 13
Castellani (Via de') .... CY 15
Duomo (Piazza del) .... CX 21
Leoni (Via dei) .... CY 33
Medici (Lungarno A.M.Luisa de') .... CY 40
Pellicceria (Via) .... BY 49

Repubblica (Piazza della) .... BY 57
Rondinelli (Via de') .... BX 60
S. Firenze (Piazza) .... CY 65
S. Giovanni (Piazza) .... BX 67
S. Maria Nuova (Piazza di) .... CX 69
Sassetti (Via de') .... BY 73
Signoria (Piazza della) .... CY 76
Speziali (Via degli) .... BCY 77
Trebbio (Via del) .... BX 81
Uffizi (Piazzale degli) .... CY 83
Vaccchereccia (Via) .... BY 84
Vecchietti (Via de') .... BXY 85

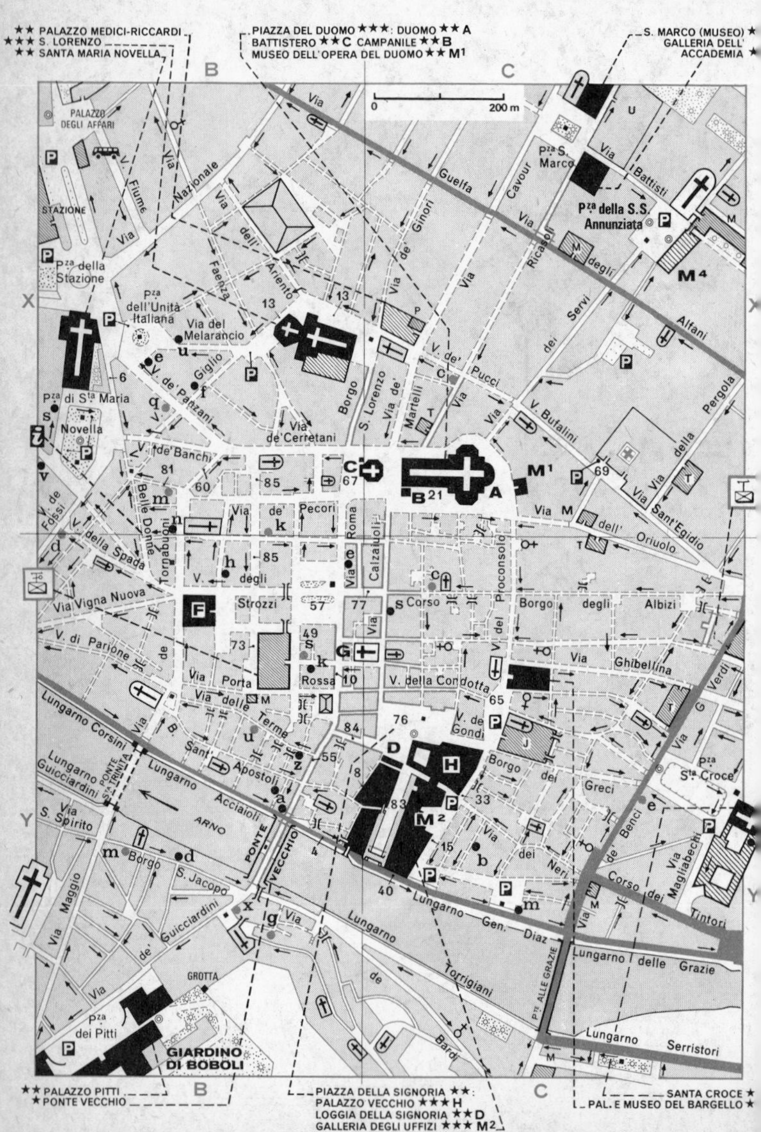

Excelsior, piazza Ognissanti 3 ✉ 50123 ✆ 264201, Telex 570022, « Rest. with summer service on terrace with ≤ » – |‡| ▤ TV ☎ ♿ – 🏛. AE ⓞ E VISA. ✻ rest AY **g**
M a la carte 78/118000 – ☕ 20000 – **205 rm** 309/488000.

Savoy, piazza della Repubblica 7 ✉ 50123 ✆ 283313, Telex 570220 – |‡| ▤ TV ☎ ♿ – 🏛. AE ⓞ E VISA. ✻ rest BY **e**
M *(dinner only)* a la carte 50/73000 – ☕ 20000 – **101 rm** 302/454000 apartments 704/904000.

Villa Medici, via Il Prato 42 ✉ 50123 ✆ 261331, Telex 570179, 🏊 – |‡| ▤ TV ☎ – 🏛. AE ⓞ E AX **g**
M rest. see Lorenzaccio below – ☕ 15000 – **107 rm** 265/450000 apartments 600/1000000.

Regency, piazza Massimo D'Azeglio 3 ✉ 50121 ✆ 245247, Telex 571058, « Beautiful garden » – |‡| ▤ TV ☎ ♿ 🚗. AE ⓞ E VISA. ✻ rest DX **c**
M *(closed Sunday)* a la carte 50/66000 – ☕ 16500 – **31 rm** 275/380000 apartments 600/800000 – P 426000.

Baglioni, piazza Unità Italiana 6 ✉ 50123 ✆ 218441, Telex 570225, « Roof-garden rest. with ≤ » – |‡| ▤ TV ☎ ♿ – 🏛. AE ⓞ E VISA. ✻ rest BX **e**
M a la carte 43/57000 – **195 rm** ☕ 171/236000.

Jolly, piazza Vittorio Veneto 4/a ✉ 50123 ✆ 2770, Telex 570191, « 🏊 on panoramic terrace » – |‡| ▤ TV ☎ – 🏛. AE ⓞ E VISA. ✻ rest AX **u**
M 39000 – **165 rm** ☕ 145/225000.

Majestic, via del Melarancio 1 ✉ 50123 ✆ 264021, Telex 570628 – |‡| ▤ TV ☎ 🚗 – 🏛. AE ⓞ E VISA. ✻ rest BX **u**
M *(closed Sunday)* 40/45000 – ☕ 17000 – **104 rm** 160/210000 apartments 300/350000 – P 150/230000.

Plaza Hotel Lucchesi, lungarno della Zecca Vecchia 38 ✉ 50122 ✆ 264141, Telex 570302, ≤ – |‡| ▤ ☎ – 🏛. AE ⓞ E VISA. ✻ rest DY **f**
M a la carte 45/55000 – **104 rm** ☕ 173/242000 apartments 349000.

Gd H. Minerva, piazza Santa Maria Novella 16 ✉ 50123 ✆ 284555, Telex 570414, 🏊 – |‡| ▤ TV ☎ ♿ – 🏛. AE E. ✻ rest BX **s**
M a la carte 35/53000 – ☕ 16000 – **107 rm** 155/205000 apartments 250/410000 – P 155/225000.

De la Ville, piazza Antinori 1 ✉ 50123 ✆ 261805, Telex 570518 – |‡| ▤ TV ☎. AE ⓞ E VISA. ✻ rest BX **n**
M (residents only) (closed lunch and Sunday) a la carte 41/60000 – **75 rm** ☕ 173/240000 apartments 310/473000.

Croce di Malta and Rest. Il Coccodrillo, via della Scala 7 ✉ 50123 ✆ 218351, Telex 570540, 🏊, 🌳 – |‡| ▤ TV ☎ – 🏛. AE E VISA. ✻ rest BX **v**
M *(closed Sunday and Monday lunch)* a la carte 36/52000 – ☕ 15000 – **98 rm** 156/206000 apartments 266000 – P 160/230000.

Etap Astoria, via del Giglio 9 ✉ 50123 ✆ 298095, Telex 571070 – |‡| ▤ TV ☎ ♿ – 🏛. AE ⓞ E VISA. ✻ rest BX **f**
M *(closed Sunday)* a la carte 37/56000 – **90 rm** ☕ 145/228000 apartment 456000 – P 154000.

Augustus without rest., piazzetta dell'Oro 5 ✉ 50123 ✆ 283054, Telex 570110 – |‡| ▤ TV ☎ ♿ – 🏛. AE ⓞ E VISA. ✻ BY **a**
☕ 12000 – **67 rm** 130/190000 apartments 264000.

Kraft, via Solferino 2 ✉ 50123 ✆ 284273, Telex 571523, « Roof-garden rest. with ≤ », 🏊 – |‡| ▤ TV ☎. AE ⓞ E VISA. ✻ rest AX **c**
M 35000 – ☕ 14000 – **66 rm** 135/190000 – P 150/190000.

Montebello Splendid, via Montebello 60 ✉ 50123 ✆ 298051, Telex 574009, 🌳 – |‡| ▤ TV ☎. AE ⓞ E. ✻ rest AX **e**
M 38/45000 – **37 rm** ☕ 160/230000 apartments 260000 – P 191000.

Londra, via Jacopo da Diacceto 16 ✉ 50123 ✆ 262791, Telex 571152 – |‡| ▤ TV ☎ ♿ 🚗 – 🏛. AE ⓞ E VISA. ✻ rest AX **n**
M a la carte 38/61000 – ☕ 16000 – **105 rm** 156/206000 – P 157/223000.

Lungarno without rest., borgo Sant'Jacopo 14 ✉ 50125 ✆ 264211, Telex 570129, ≤, « Collection of modern pictures » – |‡| ▤ TV ☎ – 🏛. AE ⓞ E VISA BY **d**
☕ 12000 – **71 rm** 130/190000.

Raffaello, viale Morgagni 19 ✉ 50134 ✆ 439871, Telex 580035 – |‡| ▤ TV ☎ 🚗 – 🏛. AE ⓞ E VISA. ✻ rest by via del Romito AV
M a la carte 29/47000 – ☕ 14500 – **141 rm** 123/172000 apartments 272000 – P 189000.

Crest and Rest. La Tegolaia, viale Europa 205 ✉ 50126 ✆ 686841, Telex 570376, 🏊 heated, 🌳 – |‡| ▤ TV ☎ ♿ Ⓟ – 🏛. AE ⓞ E VISA. ✻ rest by ③
M 25/35000 – **92 rm** ☕ 160/200000 apartments 300/400000.

Michelangelo, via Fratelli Rosselli 2 ✉ 50123 ✆ 278711, Telex 571113 – |‡| ▤ TV ☎ 🚗 – 🏛. AE ⓞ E VISA. ✻ rest AX **w**
M (residents only) 28000 – **138 rm** ☕ 145/195000 – P 148/195000.

Pierre without rest., via de' Lamberti 5 ✉ 50123 ✆ 217512, Telex 573175 – |‡| ▤ ☎. AE ⓞ VISA BY **k**
☕ 15000 – **39 rm** 160/200000 apartments 260000.

Anglo American, via Garibaldi 9 ✉ 50123 ✆ 282114, Telex 570289 – AE E VISA. rest — AX **d**
M *(closed Sunday)* 48000 – **118 rm** ☕ 170/236000 apartments 300/400000.

Principe without rest., lungarno Vespucci 34 ✉ 50123 ✆ 284848, Telex 571400, ←, – AE E VISA — AX **b**
☕ 15000 – **20 rm** 115/182000 apartment 257000.

Continental without rest., lungarno Acciaiuoli 2 ✉ 50123 ✆ 282392, Telex 580525, « Flowered terrace with ← » – wc wc. AE E VISA — BY **a**
☕ 12000 – **61 rm** 96/140000.

Alexander, viale Guidoni 101 ✉ 50127 ✆ 4378951, Telex 574026 – wc wc – — by ⑧
M a la carte 30/40000 – **88 rm** ☕ 120/170000 – P 131/166000.

Ville sull'Arno without rest., lungarno Colombo 5 ✉ 50136 ✆ 670971, Telex 573297, ←, heated – wc wc. AE VISA — by ②
☕ 12000 – **47 rm** 105/172000.

Golf without rest., viale Fratelli Rosselli 56 ✉ 50123 ✆ 293088, Telex 571630 – wc wc. AE E. — AV **k**
☕ 10000 – **39 rm** 70/106000.

Calzaiuoli without rest., via Calzaiuoli 6 ✉ 50122 ✆ 212456, Telex 580589 – wc. AE E VISA — CY **s**
☕ 7000 – **37 rm** 65/96000.

Columbus, lungarno Colombo 22/a ✉ 50136 ✆ 677251, Telex 570273 – wc wc – **99 rm.** — by ②

at Galluzzo S : 6,5 km – ✉ **50124** Firenze :

Della Signoria without rest., via delle Terme 1 ✉ 50123 ✆ 214530, Telex 571561 – wc wc. AE E VISA — BY **z**
28 rm ☕ 98/190000.

Helvetia e Bristol without rest., via de' Pescioni 2 ✉ 50123 ✆ 287814 – wc wc. AE E VISA — BY **h**
☕ 7500 – **62 rm** 65/97000.

Balestri without rest., piazza Mentana 7 ✉ 50122 ✆ 214743 – wc wc. AE VISA. — CY **m**
March-November – ☕ 12000 – **50 rm** 66/96000, 5000.

David without rest., viale Michelangiolo 1 ✉ 50125 ✆ 6811696, Telex 574553 – wc wc. AE E VISA. — DZ **a**
☕ 11000 – **25 rm** 66/98000.

Franchi without rest., via Sgambati 28 ✉ 50127 ✆ 372425, Telex 580425 – wc. AE E VISA — by ⑧
☕ 8500 – **35 rm** 55/85000.

Rapallo, via di Santa Caterina d'Alessandria 7 ✉ 50129 ✆ 472412, Telex 574251 – wc wc. AE E VISA. — CV **s**
M (residents only) a la carte 25/35000 (12%) – ☕ 8500 – **30 rm** 68/102000 – P 83/111000.

Astor, viale Milton 41 ✉ 50129 ✆ 483391, Telex 573155 – rest wc wc. AE E VISA. rest — CV **u**
M (residents only) (closed lunch) 25000 – ☕ 10000 – **25 rm** 62/91000 – dinner included 72000.

Fiorino without rest., via Osteria del Guanto 6 ✉ 50122 ✆ 210579 – wc wc — CY **b**
☕ 7000 – **23 rm** 50/72000, 3000.

Jane without rest., via Orcagna 56 ✉ 50121 ✆ 677383 – wc wc. — DY **m**
☕ 7000 – **28 rm** 42/63000.

San Remo without rest., lungarno Serristori 13 ✉ 50125 ✆ 213390 – wc wc. AE E. – **19 rm** ☕ 64/94000, 3000. — DZ **e**

Enoteca Pinchiorri, via Ghibellina 87 ✉ 50122 ✆ 242757, « Nightly service in a cool court-yard » – . AE — CDY **x**
closed Sunday, Monday lunch, August and 25 to 27 December – **M** (booking essential) a la carte 75/90000 (12%)
Spec. Inzimino di moscardini e gamberi in dolceforte, Carabaccia (zuppa di cipolle), Scottiglia (caciucco di carni), Torta di ricotta. **Wines** Bianco di Capannelle, Cannaio di Montevertine.

Sabatini, via de' Panzani 9/a ✉ 50123 ✆ 282802, Elegant traditional decor – . AE E. – *closed Monday* – **M** a la carte 43/67000 (13%). — BX **q**

Da Dante-al Lume di Candela, via delle Terme 23 r ✉ 50123 ✆ 294566 – . AE VISA. — BY **u**
closed Sunday, Monday lunch and 10 to 25 August – **M** (booking essential) a la carte 33/50000 (16%).

Harry's Bar, lungarno Vespucci 22 r ✉ 50123 ✆ 296700 – — AY **x**
closed Sunday and 10 December-15 January – **M** (booking essential) a la carte 38/53000 (16%).

Gourmet, via Il Prato 68 r ✉ 50123 ✆ 294766, Rest.-American bar – . — AX **z**
closed Sunday – **M** (booking essential) a la carte 37/58000 (15%).

XXX Lorenzaccio, via Rucellai 1/a ✉ 50123 ☎ 217100 – ▤ AX **g**

XXX **Al Campidoglio,** via del Campidoglio 8 r ✉ 50123 ☎ 287770 – ▤. AE ⓓ E VISA. ✗
closed Thursday and August – **M** a la carte 28/43000 (12%). BXY **k**

XX **Barrino,** via de' Biffi 2 r ✉ 50122 ☎ 215180, Rest.-American bar – AE ⓓ E VISA. ✗
closed lunch and Sunday – **M** (booking essential) a la carte 32/42000 (15%). CX **c**

XX **La Posta,** via de' Lamberti 20 r ✉ 50123 ☎ 212701 – ▤. AE ⓓ E VISA. ✗ BY **s**
closed Tuesday – **M** a la carte 28/52000 (13%).

XX **Buca Lapi,** via del Trebbio 1 r ✉ 50123 ☎ 213768, Typical tavern – ▤. AE VISA BX **m**
closed Sunday and Monday lunch – **M** a la carte 26/40000 (12%).

XX **La Loggia,** piazzale Michelangiolo 1 ✉ 50125 ☎ 287032, « Outdoor service in Summer with ≤ » – ▤ Ⓟ. AE ⓓ VISA. ✗ DZ **r**
closed Wednesday and 10 to 25 August – **M** a la carte 28/43000 (13%).

XX **Il Paiolo,** via del Corso 42 r ✉ 50123 ☎ 215019 – ▤. AE VISA CY **c**
closed Sunday – **M** (booking essential) a la carte 21/32000 (12%).

XX ✿ **Da Noi,** via Fiesolana 46 r ✉ 50122 ☎ 242917 – ✗ DX **a**
closed Sunday and Monday – **M** (booking essential) a la carte 36/43000
Spec. Tagliatelle di olive nere con pomodoro, origano e basilico (May-October), Rombo al cartoccio con mandorle e rosmarino, Coniglio alla maggiorana. **Wines** Arneis, Monte Vertine.

XX **13 Gobbi,** via del Porcellana 9 r ✉ 50123 ☎ 298769, Tuscan rest. – ▤. AE ⓓ VISA. ✗
closed Sunday, Monday and 26 July-24 August – **M** a la carte 27/42000 (10%). AX **v**

XX **Buca Mario,** piazza Ottaviani 16 r ✉ 50123 ☎ 214179, Typical trattoria – ▤. AE VISA. ✗
closed Wednesday and Thursday lunch – **M** a la carte 31/46000. BXY **d**

X **Celestino,** piazza Santa Felicita 4 r ✉ 50125 ☎ 296574 – ▤. AE BY **x**
closed Sunday and 30 July-23 August – **M** a la carte 24/41000 (12%).

X **Il Tirabusciò,** via de' Benci 34 r ✉ 50122 ☎ 2476225 – ▤ CY **e**
closed Thursday and Friday – **M** (booking essential) a la carte 19/30000 (12%).

X **Bordino,** via Stracciatella 9 r ✉ 50125 ☎ 213048, Typical trattoria – ▤. AE ⓓ E VISA
closed lunch, Sunday, Monday, 20 July-20 August and 23 to 31 December – **M** (booking essential) a la carte 19/30000. BY **g**

X ✿ **Cammillo,** borgo Sant'Jacopo 57 r ✉ 50125 ☎ 212427, Typical florentine trattoria – ▤. AE ⓓ E VISA BY **m**
closed Wednesday, Thursday, 1 to 20 August and 20 December-15 January – **M** a la carte 30/68000
Spec. Trippa alla fiorentina, Petti di pollo alla Cammillo, Scaloppine Capriccio. **Wines** Chianti.

on the hills S : 3 km :

Gd H. Villa Cora and Rest. Taverna Machiavelli ⛰, viale Machiavelli 18 ✉ 50125 ☎ 2298451, Telex 570604, « Floralp park with ⛱ » – 🛗 ▤ TV ☎ Ⓟ – 🏛. AE ⓓ E VISA. ✗ rest by viale Machiavelli ABZ
M 57000 (15%) – ☕ 16000 – **47 rm** 224/356000 apartments 678000.

Villa Carlotta ⛰, via Michele di Lando 3 ✉ 50125 ☎ 220530, Telex 573485, « Beautiful garden » – 🛗 ▤ TV ☎ Ⓟ – 🏛. AE ⓓ E VISA. ✗ rest AZ **a**
M a la carte 36/51000 – **26 rm** ☕ 164/227000 apartment 450000 – P 194/244000.

Villa Belvedere ⛰, via Benedetto Castelli 3 ✉ 50124 ☎ 222501, ≤ town and hills, « Garden-park with ⛱ », 🎾 – 🛗 ▤ 🛁wc ☎ ♿ Ⓟ. AE. ✗ by ④
March-November – **M** coffee shop only – ☕ 12000 – **27 rm** 118/176000.

XX **Antico Crespino,** largo Enrico Fermi 15 ✉ 50125 ☎ 221155, ≤ – AE ⓓ by ④
closed Wednesday – **M** a la carte 24/42000 (13%).

at Arcetri S : 5 km – ✉ **50125** Firenze :

X **Omero,** via Pian de' Giullari 11 r ☎ 220053, Rustic trattoria with ≤, « Summer service on terrace » – ✗ by viale Galileo CDZ
closed Tuesday and August – **M** a la carte 20/32000 (13%).

Relais Certosa, via Colle Ramole 2 ☎ 2047171, Telex 574332, ≤, ⛱ heated, 🌳, 🎾 – 🛗 ▤ TV ☎ Ⓟ – 🏛. AE ⓓ E VISA. ✗ rest by ④
M a la carte 35/55000 – **69 rm** ☕ 165/225000 apartments 250/320000.

at Candeli – ✉ **50010** :

Villa La Massa and Rest. Il Verrocchio ⛰, ☎ 630051, Telex 573555, ≤, « House and furnishing in 18C style », ⛱ heated, 🌳, 🎾 – 🛗 ▤ TV ☎ ♿ Ⓟ – 🏛. AE ⓓ E VISA. ✗ rest
M *(closed Monday, Tuesday lunch and November-March)* a la carte 50/70000 – ☕ 19000 – **43 rm** 219/384000 apartments 395/510000 – P 312/339000.

towards Trespiano N : 7 km :

Villa le Rondini ⛰, via Bolognese Vecchia 224 ✉ 50139 Firenze ☎ 400081, ≤ town, « Among the olive trees », ⛱, 🌳, 🎾 – 🛁wc 🚿wc ☎ ♿ Ⓟ – 🏛. AE ⓓ E VISA. ✗ rest
M 34000 – ☕ 12000 – **29 rm** 77/120000 – P 141000.

at Serpiolle N : 8 km – ✉ **50142** Firenze :

XX **Lo Strettoio,** ☎ 403044, 🏡, « 17C Country house among the olive trees » – ▤ Ⓟ. ✗
closed Sunday, Monday and August – **M** (booking essential) a la carte 28/40000.

MILAN (MILANO) 20100 P 988 ③, 219 ⑲ – pop. 1 515 233 alt. 122 – ✆ 02.

See : Cathedral*** (Duomo) : exterior***, interior***, walk on the roof*** – Cathedral Museum** CV M1 (Ariberto Crucifix**) – Via and Piazza Mercanti* – La Scala Opera House* : museum* – Brera Art Gallery*** – Castle of the Sforzas*** (Municipal Art Collection***, Sempione Park*) – Ambrosian Library** – Poldi-Pezzoli Museum** – Leonardo da Vinci Museum of Science and Technology* AV M1 (Leonardo da Vinci Gallery**) – Church of St. Mary of Grace* AV A (dome*, apse*, Leonardo da Vinci's Last Supper***, Crucifixion* by Montorfano) – Basilica of St. Ambrose* AV B (atrium*, pulpit*, altar front**) – Church of St. Eustorgius* BY B (Portinari Chapel**) – Church of St. Satiro CV C (dome*) – General Hospital* DX U – Church of St. Maurice* BV E (frescoes*, museum : silver plate*) – Church of St. Lawrence Major* BX F (portico*, Chapel of Sant'Aquilino*).

Envir. : Chiaravalle Abbey* (campanile*) SE : 7 km – N : Lakes : Lake Como***, Lake Maggiore***, Lake Lugano**.

18 e 9 (closed Monday) in Monza Park ✉ 20052 Monza ✆ (039) 303081, by ② : 20 km;
18 Molinetto (closed Monday) in Cernusco sul Naviglio ✉ 20063 ✆ (02) 9238500, by ⑤ : 14 km;
18 Barlassina (closed Monday) in Birago di Camnago ✉ 20030 ✆ (0362) 560621, by ① : 26 km;
18 (closed Wednesday) in Zoate di Tribiano ✉ 20067 ✆ 9060015, SE : 20 km by Strada Paullese;
9 Le Rovedine in Noverasco di Opera ✉ 20090 Opera ✆ (02) 5442730, S : 8 km by via Ripamonti.
Motor-Racing circuit in Monza Park by ② : 20 km, ✆ (039) 22366.

Forlanini of Linate E : 8 km ✆ 74852200 and Malpensa by ⑫ : 45 km ✆ 74852200 – Alitalia, corso Como 15 ✉ 20154 ✆ 62811 and via Albricci 5 ✉ 20122 ✆ 62811.

Porta Garibaldi ✆ 228274.

via Marconi 1 ✉ 20123 ✆ 809662 – Central Station ✉ 20124 ✆ 6690532.

A.C.I. corso Venezia 43 ✉ 20121 ✆ 7745 – Roma 572 ⑦ – Genève 323 ⑫ – Genova 142 ⑨ – Torino 140 ⑫.

Plans on following pages

Northern area Piazza della Repubblica, Central Station, viale Zara, Porta Garibaldi Station, Porta Volta, corso Sempione (Plans : Milan pp. 2 and 3) :

Principe di Savoia, piazza della Repubblica 17 ✉ 20124 ✆ 6230, Telex 310052, – AE VISA. DS x
M a la carte 80/125000 – 21000 – **280 rm** 339/488000 apartments 771/1420000.

Palace, piazza della Repubblica 20 ✉ 20124 ✆ 6336, Telex 311026 – AE VISA DS t
closed August – **M** rest. see **Grill Casanova** below – 25500 – **187 rm** 301/437000 apartments 649/1062000.

Excelsior Gallia, piazza Duca d'Aosta 9 ✉ 20124 ✆ 6277, Telex 311160 – AE VISA. rest DR a
M 45/70000 – **266 rm** 292/403000 apartments 587/766000.

Milano Hilton, via Galvani 12 ✉ 20124 ✆ 6983, Telex 330433 – AE VISA. rest DR t
M a la carte 56/82000 – 20500 – **339 rm** 295/368000 apartments 678/1800000.

Duca di Milano, piazza della Repubblica 13 ✉ 20124 ✆ 6284, Telex 325026 – AE VISA. rest DS x
M a la carte 50/65000 – 20000 – **60 rm** 331/472000.

Executive, viale Luigi Sturzo 45 ✉ 20154 ✆ 6294, Telex 310191 – AE VISA. rest CRS v
M 55000 – **420 rm** 205/250000 apartments 400000.

Michelangelo, via Scarlatti 33 ✉ 20124 ✆ 6755, Telex 340330 – AE VISA. rest DR c
M 50/60000 – **278 rm** 250/320000 apartments 400000.

Anderson without rest., piazza Luigi di Savoia 20 ✉ 20124 ✆ 6690141, Telex 321018 – AE VISA DR v
closed August – 12000 – **102 rm** 143/180000 apartments 210000.

Jolly Hotel Touring, via Tarchetti 2 ✉ 20121 ✆ 6335, Telex 320118 – AE VISA. rest DT v
M 40000 – **270 rm** 170/220000.

Auriga without rest., via Pirelli 7 ✉ 20124 ✆ 6592851, Telex 350146 – AE VISA. DR f
closed August – 9000 – **65 rm** 130/160000.

Atlantic without rest., via Napo Torriani 24 ✉ 20124 ✆ 6691941, Telex 321451 – AE VISA DS q
62 rm 168/231000.

Splendido, viale Andrea Doria 4 ✉ 20124 ✆ 2050, Telex 321413 – AE VISA. rest DR x
M 25/30000 – **129 rm** 210/270000 – P 130/180000.

Windsor without rest., via Galilei 2 ✉ 20124 ✆ 6346, Telex 330562 – AE DS j
13000 – **114 rm** 135/162000 apartments 195000.

Mediolanum without rest., via Mauro Macchi 1 ✉ 20124 ✆ 6705312, Telex 310448 – AE VISA DS r
52 rm 128/194000 apartments 280000.

Berna without rest., via Napo Torriani 18 ✉ 20124 ✆ 6691441, Telex 334695 – . AE E VISA. DS **a**
12000 – **83 rm** 114/156000.

Bristol without rest., via Scarlatti 32 ✉ 20124 ✆ 6694141 – . AE E DR **u**
closed August – 10000 – **71 rm** 129/173000.

Royal without rest., via Cardano 1 ✉ 20124 ✆ 6709151, Telex 333167 – . AE E VISA DR **b**
closed August – 12000 – **110 rm** 143/187000.

Europeo without rest., via Canonica 38 ✉ 20154 ✆ 344041, Telex 321237 – . AE E VISA. AS **f**
20000 – **45 rm** 115/160000.

Lancaster without rest., via Abbondio Sangiorgio 16 ✉ 20145 ✆ 315602 – wc wc. AE E VISA. AT **v**
closed July and August – 20000 – **29 rm** 105/150000.

Augustus without rest., via Napo Torriani 29 ✉ 20124 ✆ 6575741, Telex 333112 – wc wc. AE E VISA DS **h**
56 rm 82/122000.

San Carlo without rest., via Napo Torriani 28 ✉ 20124 ✆ 656336, Telex 314324 – wc wc. AE E VISA DS **s**
62 rm 85/130000.

Flora without rest., via Napo Torriani 23 ✉ 20124 ✆ 650242, Telex 312547 – wc wc. AE VISA. DS **h**
12000 – **45 rm** 73/107000.

Sempione, via Finocchiaro Aprile 11 ✉ 20124 ✆ 6570323, Telex 340498 – wc. rest DST **u**
M *(closed Saturday)* a la carte 22/37000 – 10000 – **40 rm** 80/110000 – P 110000.

Domus without rest., piazza Gerusalemme 6 ✉ 20154 ✆ 3490251, Telex 335051 – wc wc – . AE E VISA. AR **r**
10000 – **84 rm** 77/107000.

New York without rest., via Pirelli 5 ✉ 20124 ✆ 650551, Telex 325057 – wc. AE E VISA DR **f**
closed 1 to 28 August – 8000 – **71 rm** 74/106000.

San Guido without rest., via Carlo Farini 1/a ✉ 20154 ✆ 6552261 – wc wc. AE E VISA BRS **u**
8000 – **31 rm** 65/85000, 3000.

XXXX ✿ **Grill Casanova,** piazza della Repubblica 20 ✉ 20124 ✆ 650803 – . AE E VISA. DS **t**
closed August – **M** (booking essential) a la carte 65/85000
Spec. Fegatini al mirto e peperone, Risotto con scampi e rucola, Filetto di vitello con melanzane. **Wines** Masianco, Grignolino.

XXX **Romani,** via Trebazio 3 ✉ 20145 ✆ 340738 – . AE AS **m**
closed Saturday lunch, Sunday and August – **M** a la carte 24/52000.

XXX Grattacielo, via Vittor Pisani 6 ✉ 20124 ✆ 6592359, – DS **y**

XX ✿ **A Riccione,** via Taramelli 70 ✉ 20124 ✆ 6686807, Seafood – . AE E VISA
closed Monday – **M** (booking essential) a la carte 50/70000 DQ **a**
Spec. Pasta fresca con sugo di cannelli e scampi, Paella valenciana, Orata al tegame, Grigliata mista di pesce alla brace. **Wines** del Collio, Barbaresco.

XX **Ai 3 Pini,** via Tullo Morgagni 19 ✉ 20125 ✆ 6898464, « Pergola-garden » – AE VISA. DQ **n**
closed Friday lunch, Saturday and 5 to 31 August – **M** a la carte 31/50000.

XX **Da Lino Buriassi,** via Lecco angolo via Casati 12 ✉ 20124 ✆ 228227 – . AE VISA
closed Saturday lunch, Sunday and 10 to 28 August – **M** (booking essential) a la carte 27/40000. DT **g**

XX **Cavallini,** via Mauro Macchi 2 ✉ 20124 ✆ 6693174, – DS **p**
closed Saturday, Sunday, 3 to 23 August and 22 December-4 January – **M** a la carte 27/42000 (12%).

XX **Dall'Antonio,** via Cenisio 8 ✉ 20154 ✆ 384511 – . AE AR **a**
closed Sunday and August – **M** (booking essential) a la carte 36/60000.

XX ✿ **Alfredo-Gran San Bernardo,** via Borgese 14 ✉ 20154 ✆ 3319000 – AR **f**
closed Sunday, August and 21 December-19 January – **M** (booking essential) a la carte 36/48000
Spec. Risotto alla milanese ed al salto, Ossobuco in cremolata, Foiolo (trippa). **Wines** Pinot grigio, Barbera.

XX **Gianni e Dorina,** via Pepe 38, angolo via Carmagnola ✉ 20159 ✆ 606340 – . .
closed Saturday lunch, Sunday and 25 July-15 September – **M** (booking essential) a la carte 32/50000 (10%). CR **d**

XX ✿ **Casa Fontana,** piazza Carbonari 5 ✉ 20125 ✆ 6892684 – . AE. DQ **s**
closed Saturday lunch, Monday, Sunday in July, 1 to 5 January and 1 to 24 August – **M** (booking essential) a la carte 34/46000
Spec. Risotti della Casa, Rognoncini di vitello al Cognac, Filetto alla menta. **Wines** Trebbiano, Sizzano.

MILANO

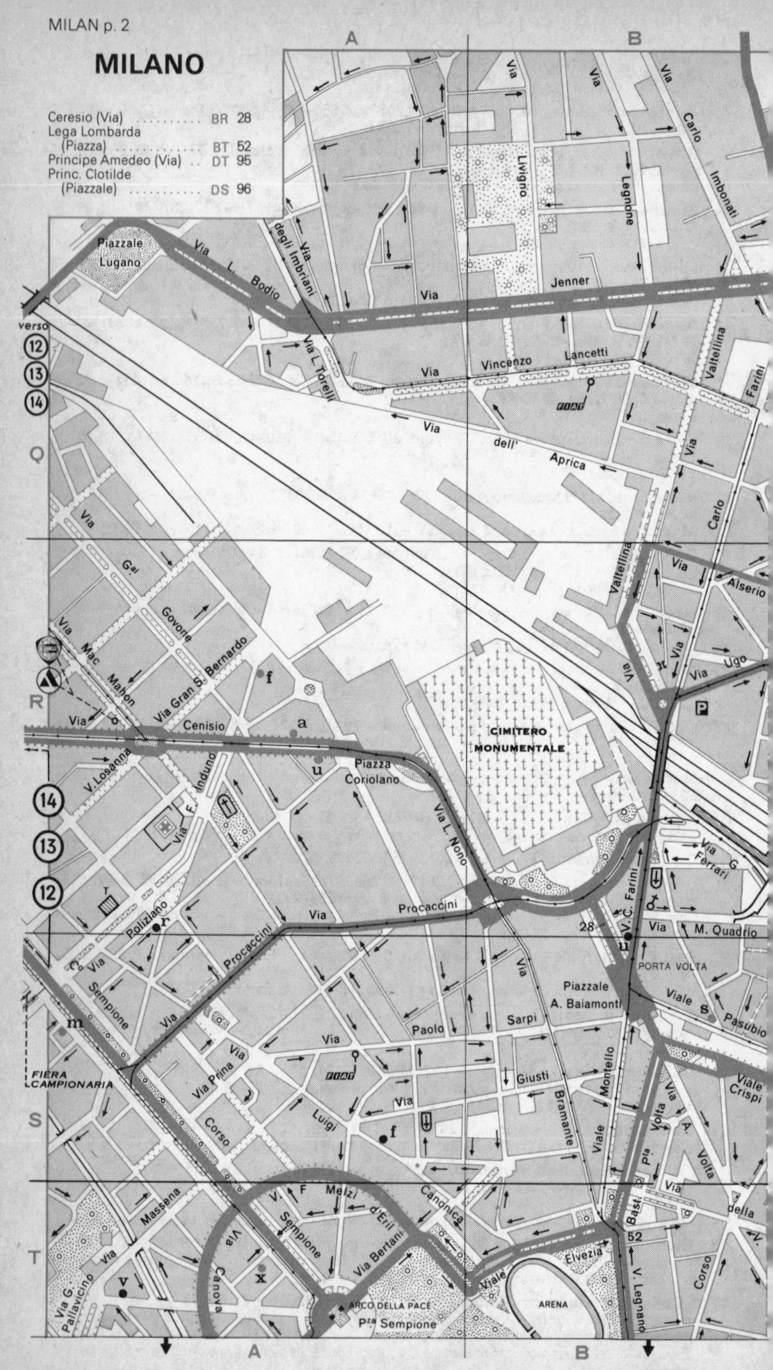

A
B
Piazzale Lugano
Via L. Bodio
Via degli Imbriani
Via Livigno
Via Legnone
Via Carlo Imbonati
Via Jenner
Via L. Torelli
Via Vincenzo Lancetti
Valtellina
Farini
Via dell' Aprica
Via Carlo
verso
12
13
14
Q
Via Gal Govone
Via Valtellina
Via Alserio
Via Ugo
Via Mac Mahon
Via Gran S. Bernardo
R
Via Cenisio
V. Losanna
Via F. Induno
Piazza Coriolano
Via L. Nono
CIMITERO MONUMENTALE
Via G. Ferrari
V. C. Farini
Via M. Quadrio
PORTA VOLTA
Piazzale A. Baiamonti
Viale Pasubio
Via Procaccini
Via Poliziano
Co Sempione
Via Sarpi
Via Paolo Giusti
FIERA CAMPIONARIA
Via Prina
Corso
Via Luigi
Via Bramante
Viale Montello
Via A. Volta
Viale Crispi
S
T
Via Massena
V. F. Melzi d'Eril
Canonica
Via Canova
Sempione
Via Bertani
Viale Elvezia
ARENA
ARCO DELLA PACE
Pza Sempione
Via G. Pallavicino
Bast.
52
V. Legnano
Corso
Via della

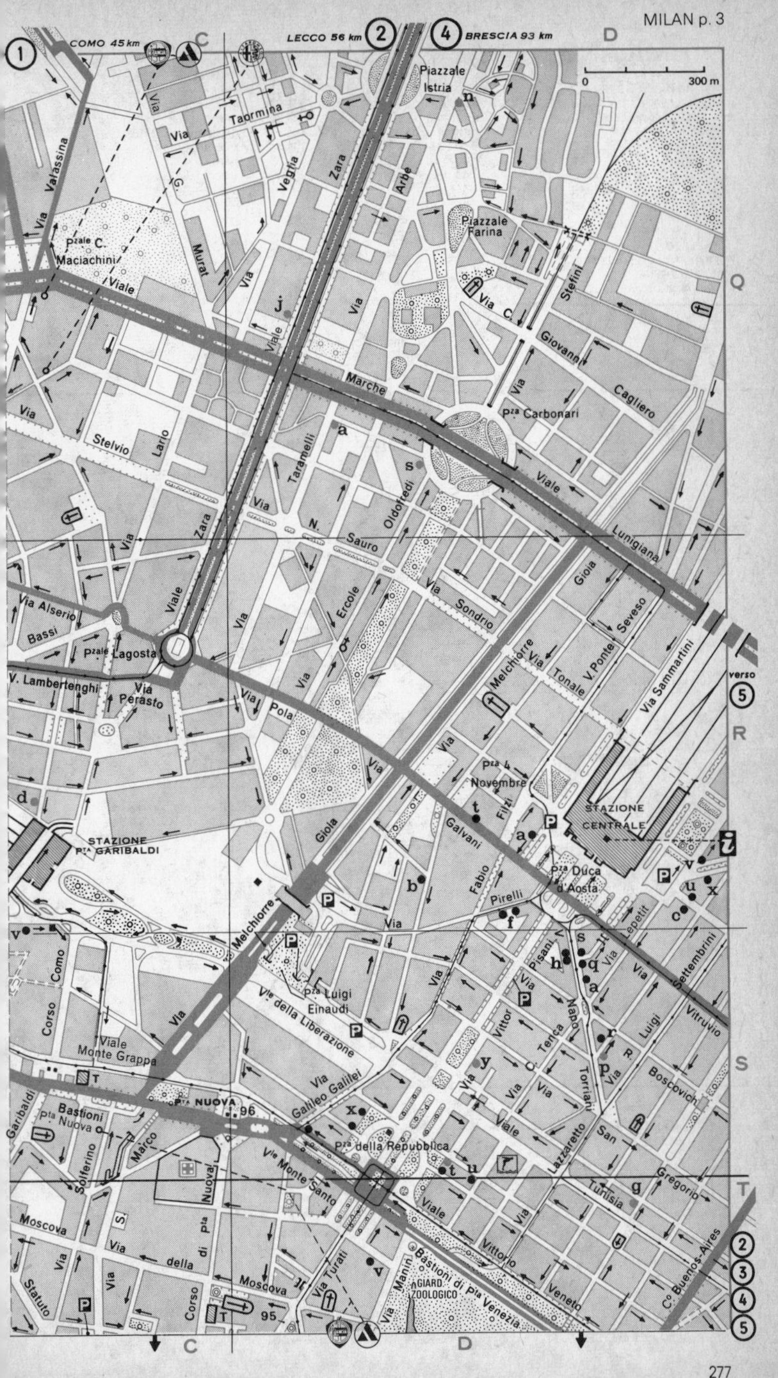

MILANO

Agnello (Via) . . . . DV 3
Arcivescovado (Via) . . . . CV 4
Augusto (Largo) . . . . DV 6
Battisti
(Via Cesare) . . . . DV 12
Beccaria
(Piazza e Via) . . . . DV 14
Borgogna (Via) . . . . DV 16
Broletto (Via) . . . . BCU 19
Cadorna (Piazzale) . . . . AU 22
Cairoli (Largo) . . . . BU 23
Cavallotti (Via Felice) . . . . . . DV 27
Concordia (Corso) . . . . DU 30
Cordusio (Piazza) . . . . CV 32
De Marchi (Via Marco) . . . . DU 35
Diaz (Piazza A.) . . . . CV 36
Festa del Perdono (Via) . . . . DV 38
Fontana (Piazza) . . . . DV 40
Generale Cantore
(Piazzale) . . . . AX 43
Giardini (Via dei) . . . . DU 44
Gonzaga (Via Maurizio) . . . . . CV 46
Laghetto (Via) . . . . DV 50
Lega Lombarda (Piazza) . . . . BT 52
Marco d'Oggiono
(Via) . . . . AX 63
Marconi (Via Guglielmo) . . . . CV 64

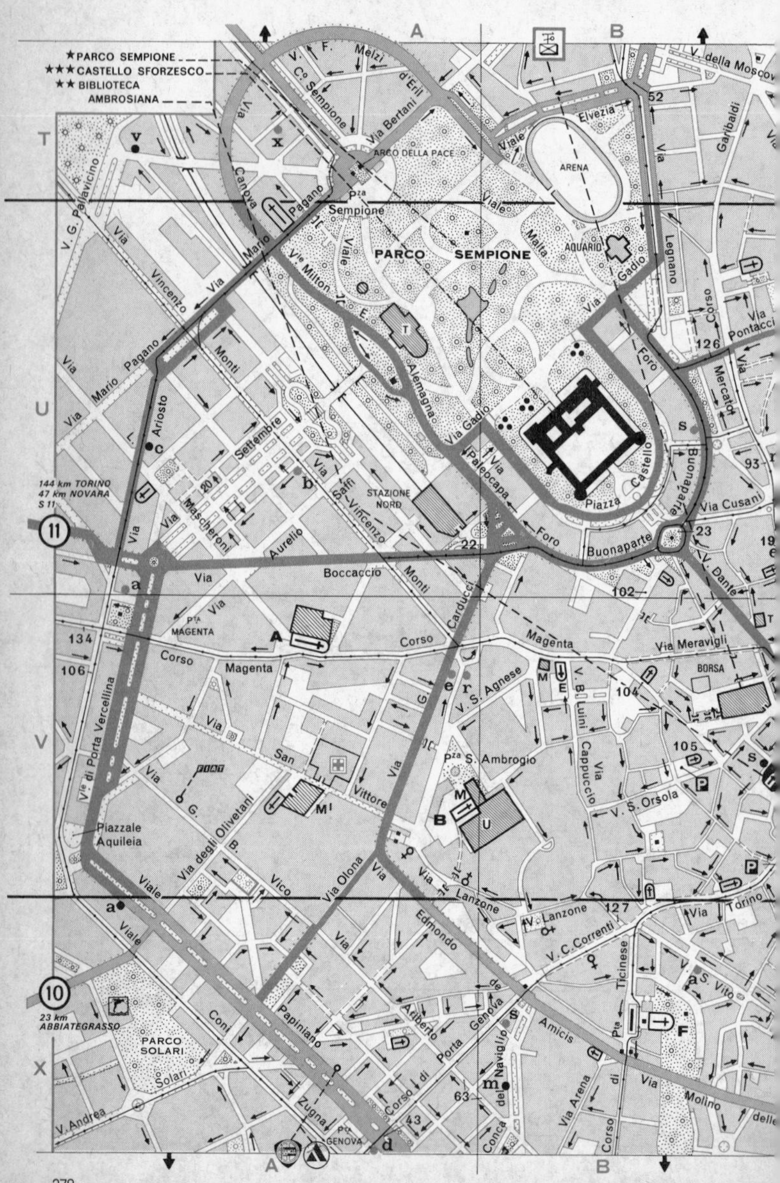

Street	Grid	No.
Mazzini (Via G.)	CV	65
Mercanti (Piazza e Via)	CV	66
Missori (Piazza)	CV	73
Orefici (Via)	CV	84
Ponte Vetero (Via)	BU	93
Porrone (Via Bassano)	CV	94
Principe Amedeo (Via)	DT	95
S. Babila (Piazza)	DV	99
S. Fedele (Piazza)	CV	100
S. Giovanni sul Muro (Via)	BU	102
S. Margherita (Via)	CV	103
S. Maria alla Porta (Via)	BV	104
S. Maria Fulcorina (Via)	BV	105
S. Michele del Carso (Viale)	AV	106
S. Paolo (Via)	DV	108
S. Prospero (Via)	CV	109
S. Protaso (Via)	CV	112
S. Stefano (Piazza)	DV	113
Scala (Piazza della)	CV	115
Tivoli (Via)	BU	126
Torchio (Via del)	BX	127
Tricolore (Piazza del)	DU	128
Vercelli (Corso)	AV	134
Verziere (Via)	DV	135
Visconti di Modrone (Via)	DV	136
5 Giornate (Piazzale)	DV	142
22 Marzo (Corso)	DV	143

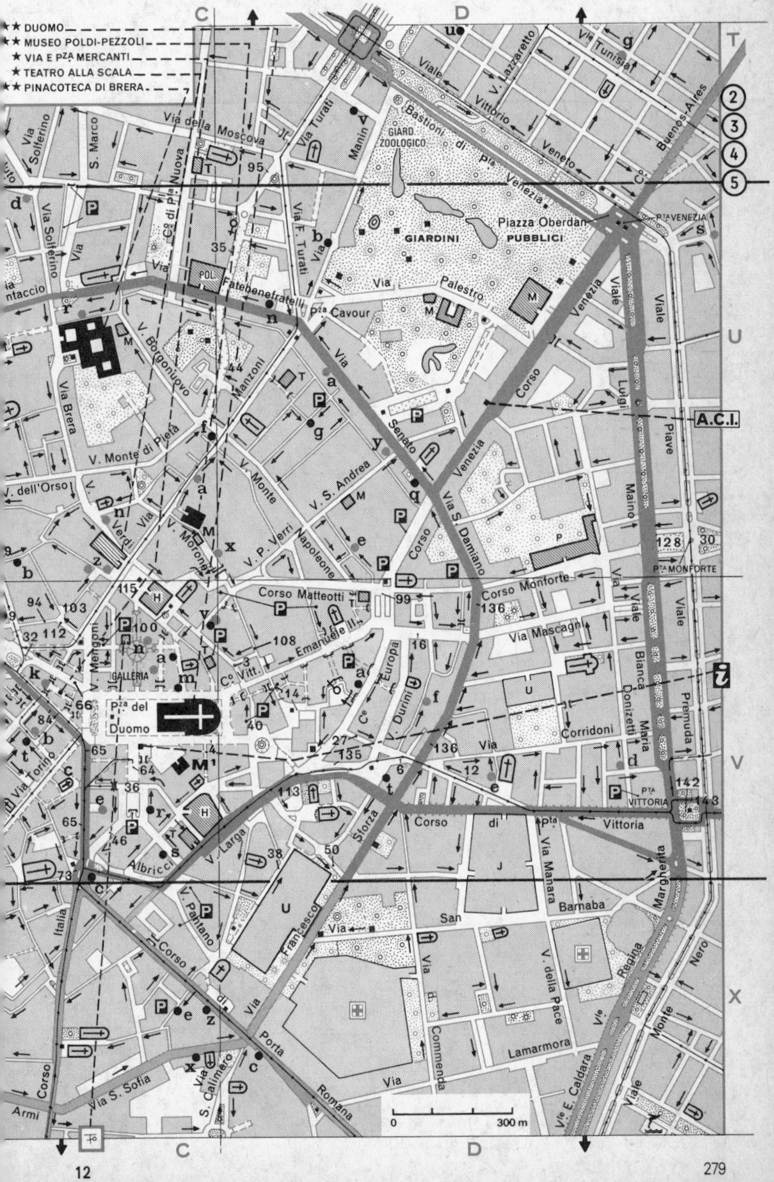

★★ DUOMO
★★ MUSEO POLDI-PEZZOLI
★ VIA E P^ZA MERCANTI
★ TEATRO ALLA SCALA
★★ PINACOTECA DI BRERA

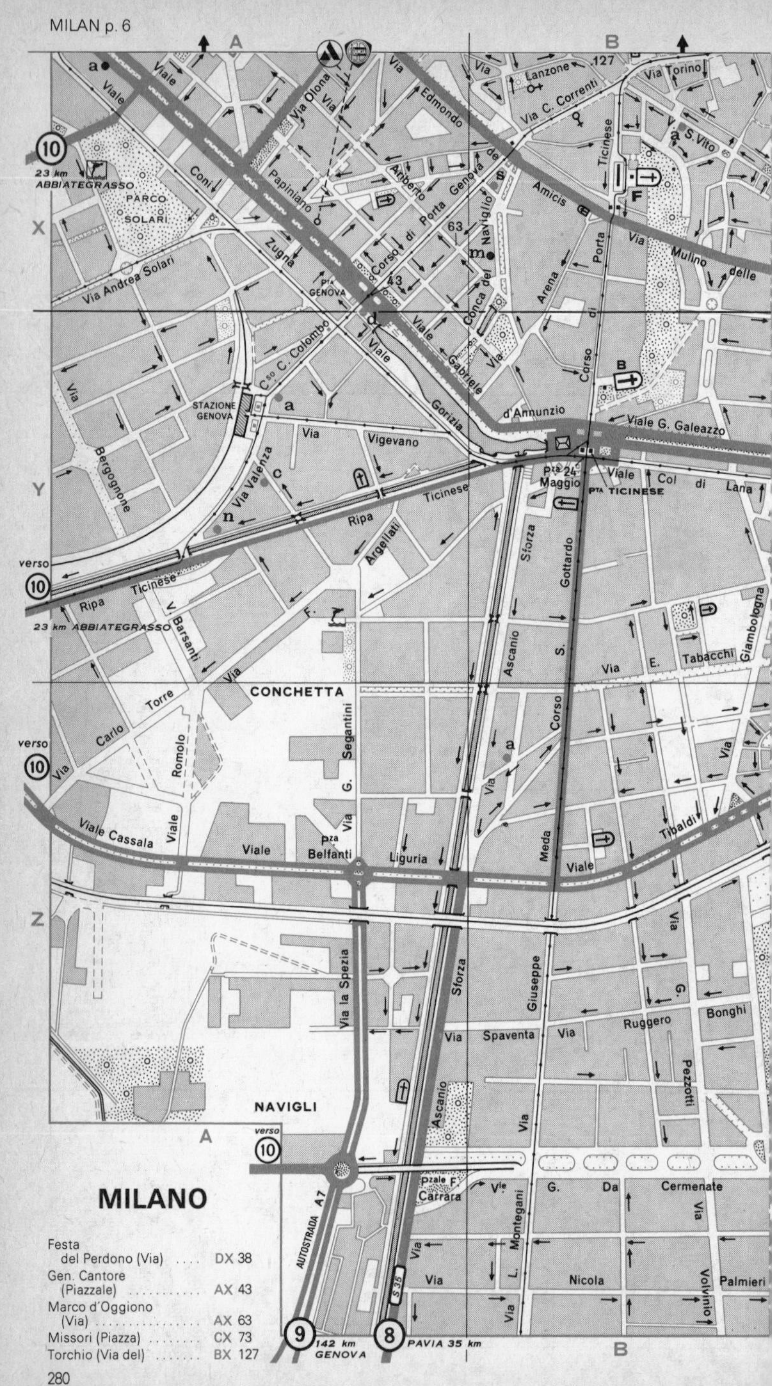

Festa del Perdono (Via) .... DX 38
Gen. Cantore (Piazzale) .... AX 43
Marco d'Oggiono (Via) .... AX 63
Missori (Piazza) .... CX 73
Torchio (Via del) .... BX 127

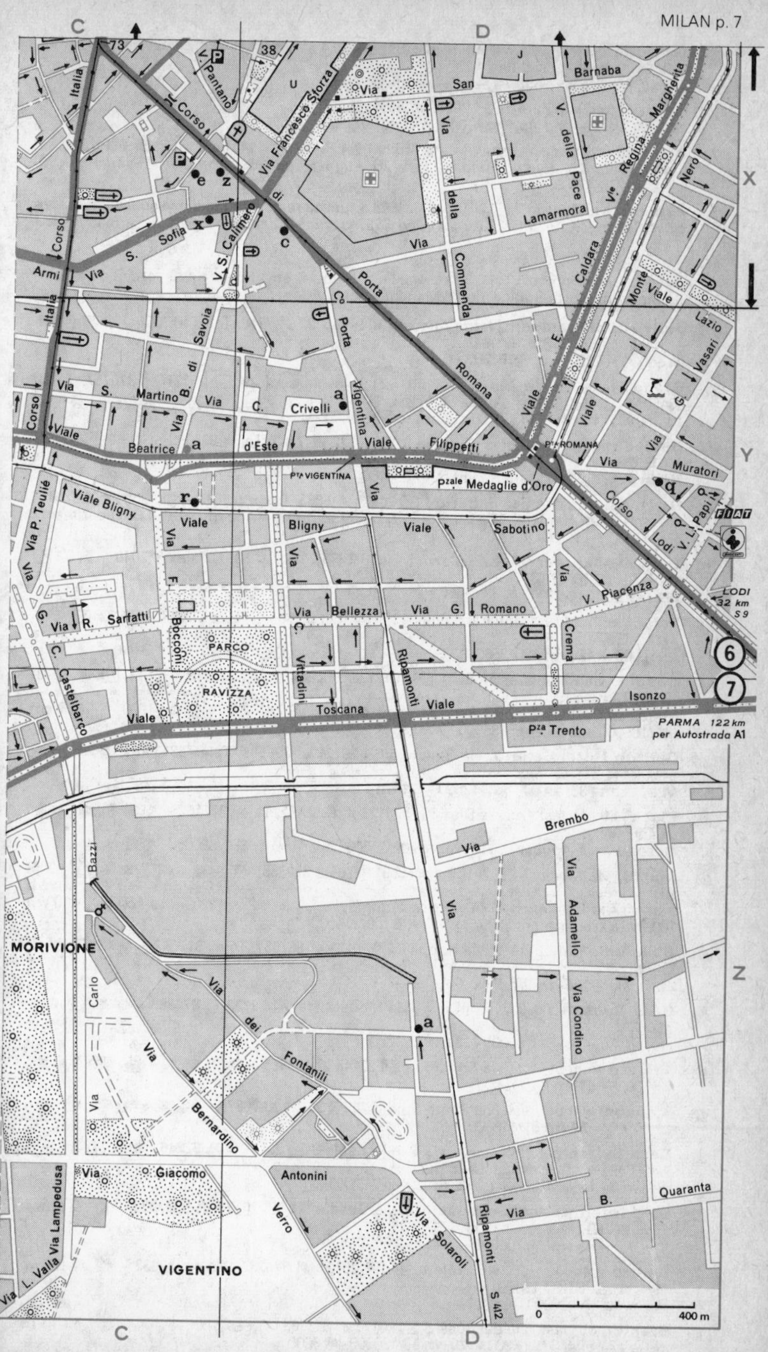

C
D
X
Y
Z
6
7
Corso Italia
Via S. Sofia
Corso di Porta Romana
Via Francesco Sforza
V. Pantano
Via San Barnaba
V. della Pace
Via della Commenda
Via Lamarmora
V.le Regina Margherita
Viale Caldara
Viale Monte Nero
Viale Lazio
Via G. Vasari
Via Muratori
Corso Lodi
V. L. Papi
V. S. Calimero
Via B. di Savoia
Via S. Martino
Via C. Crivelli
Co. Porta Vigentina
Viale Beatrice d'Este
Viale Filippetti
Pta VIGENTINA
Pzale Medaglie d'Oro
Pta ROMANA
Viale Bligny
Via P. Teulié
Viale Sabotino
Via F. Bocconi
Via Bellezza
Via G. Romano
V. Piacenza
Via Crema
Via R. Sarfatti
Via C. Vittadini
Via Ripamonti
Via Toscana
Viale Isonzo
Pza Trento
C. Castelbarco
PARCO RAVIZZA
LODI 32 km S 9
PARMA 122 km per Autostrada A1
FIAT
Via Brembo
Via Adamello
Via Condino
Via Bazzi
MORIVIONE
Via Carlo
Via del Fontanili
Via Bernardino
Via Giacomo Antonini
Via Verro
Via Solaroli
Via B. Quaranta
Via Lampedusa
Via L. Valla
VIGENTINO
S 412
0
400 m
73
38
U
J
e
z
x
c
a
r
q

X **Trattoria della Pesa,** viale Pasubio 10 ✉ 20154 ℘ 6555741, Old Milan typical trattoria with Lombardy specialities – ▤ BS **s**
closed Sunday and August – **M** a la carte 29/46000.

X **La Villetta,** viale Zara 87 ✉ 20159 ℘ 6891981, 余 DQ **j**
closed Tuesday and August – **M** a la carte 20/38000.

X **Al Vecchio Passeggero,** via Gherardini 1 ✉ 20145 ℘ 312461 – ▤. AE ⓓ VISA AT **x**
closed Saturday lunch, Sunday, 1 to 26 August and 26 December-1 January – **M** a la carte 25/42000.

X **Pechino,** via Cenisio 7 ✉ 20154 ℘ 384668, Chinese rest. with Pekinese specialities – ▤
closed Monday, 15 July-22 August and 20 December-4 January – **M** a la carte 22/34000 (12%). AR **u**

Central area Duomo, Scala, Sempione Park, Sforza Castle, Public gardens, corso Venezia, via Manzoni, North Station, corso Magenta, Porta Vittoria (Plans : Milan pp. 4 and 5) :

Jolly Hotel President, largo Augusto 10 ✉ 20122 ℘ 7746, Telex 312054 – ▤ TV ☎ ♿ – 🚗. AE ⓓ E VISA. ✗ rest DV **t**
M 50000 – **220 rm** ☐ 215/260000.

Grand Hotel et de Milan without rest., via Manzoni 29 ✉ 20121 ℘ 870757, Telex 334505 – ▤ TV ☎ – 🚗. AE ⓓ E VISA. ✗ CDU **f**
☐ 15000 – **89 rm** 200/300000 apartments 420/600000.

Galileo without rest., corso Europa 9 ✉ 20122 ℘ 7743, Telex 322095 – ▤ TV ☎. AE ⓓ E VISA. ✗ DV **a**
76 rm ☐ 230/290000 apartments 310/330000.

Gd H. Duomo, via San Raffaele 1 ✉ 20121 ℘ 8833, Telex 312086 – ▤ ☎. E VISA. ✗
closed 1 to 21 August – **M** a la carte 35/50000 – ☐ 13000 – **160 rm** 180/270000 apartments 385/420000 – P 200/250000. CV **m**

Dei Cavalieri without rest., piazza Missori 1 ✉ 20123 ℘ 8857, Telex 312040 – ▤ TV ☎ – 🚗. AE ⓓ E VISA CVX **c**
169 rm ☐ 174/227000.

Select without rest., via Baracchini 12 ✉ 20123 ℘ 8843, Telex 312256 – ▤ TV ☎ – 🚗. AE E VISA CV **s**
☐ 15000 – **120 rm** 180/250000.

Cavour, via Fatebenefratelli 21 ✉ 20121 ℘ 650983, Telex 320498 – ▤ TV ☎ ♿. AE ⓓ E VISA. ✗ rest DU **n**
M *(closed Friday dinner, Saturday and Sunday lunch)* 40000 – ☐ 13000 – **113 rm** 144/165000 apartments 185000.

Carlton Hotel Senato, via Senato 5 ✉ 20121 ℘ 798583, Telex 331306 – ▤ TV ☎ 🚗. AE E VISA. ✗ rest DU **q**
M a la carte 36/56000 – ☐ 12500 – **71 rm** 143/180000.

Plaza without rest., piazza Diaz 3 ✉ 20123 ℘ 8058452, Telex 321162 – ▤ TV ☎ – 🚗. AE ⓓ. ✗ CV **r**
closed 1 to 25 August – **118 rm** ☐ 202/255000 apartments 350/380000.

Manin, via Manin 7 ✉ 20121 ℘ 6596511, Telex 320385, 🌳 – ▤ TV ☎ – 🚗. AE E VISA. ✗ rest DU **b**
closed 7 to 23 August – **M** *(closed Saturday)* a la carte 39/54000 – ☐ 15000 – **110 rm** 139/177000 apartments 200/300000 – P 160/210000.

De la Ville without rest., via Hoepli 6 ✉ 20121 ℘ 867651, Telex 312642 – ▤ TV ☎. AE E VISA. ✗ CV **v**
☐ 14000 – **105 rm** 175/200000.

Gran Duca di York without rest., via Moneta 1/a ✉ 20123 ℘ 874863 – ▤ TV ☎ – 🚗. ✗ BV **s**
closed August – ☐ 8000 – **33 rm** 72/105000.

Ariosto without rest., via Ariosto 22 ✉ 20145 ℘ 490995 – ▤ ☎ ♿ – 🚗. AE ⓓ E VISA AU **c**
☐ 8000 – **53 rm** 84/119000.

Manzoni without rest., via Santo Spirito 20 ✉ 20121 ℘ 705700 – ☎ 🚗. ✗ DU **g**
☐ 10000 – **52 rm** 81/118000.

Casa Svizzera without rest., via San Raffaele 3 ✉ 20121 ℘ 8692246, Telex 316064 – ▤ TV wc wc ☎. AE ⓓ E VISA CV **a**
closed 28 July-24 August – **45 rm** ☐ 85/122000.

Lord Internazionale without rest., via Spadari 11 ✉ 20123 ℘ 8693028 – ▤ wc wc ☎. AE CV **t**
☐ 7500 – **46 rm** 74/106000.

Centro without rest., via Broletto 46 ✉ 20121 ℘ 875232, Telex 332632 – ▤ wc wc ☎ ♿. AE ⓓ E VISA BU **e**
54 rm ☐ 84/128000.

Star without rest., via dei Bossi 5 ✉ 20121 ℘ 871703 – ▤ wc ☎ CU **b**
closed August – ☐ 8000 – **28 rm** 95/130000, ▤ 6000.

XXXXX ✿ **Savini,** galleria Vittorio Emanuele II° ⊠ 20121 ℘ 8058343, Elegant traditional decor, « Winter garden » – ▤. AE ◑ E VISA CV **n**
closed Sunday, 10 to 19 August and 23 December-3 January – **M** (booking essential) a la carte 58/92000 (15%)
Spec. Risotto alla milanese ed al salto, Costoletta alla milanese, Filetto di San Pietro alla Ca' d'Oro. **Wines** Gavi, Franciacorta rosso.

XXXX **El Toulà,** piazza Paolo Ferrari 6 ⊠ 20121 ℘ 870302, Elegant installation – ▤. AE ◑ E VISA. 🐕 CU **z**
closed Saturday June-August, Sunday, 6 to 21 August and 23 December-6 January – **M** a la carte 57/88000 (13%).

XXXX **St. Andrews,** via Sant'Andrea 23 ⊠ 20121 ℘ 793132, Elegant installation, late night dinners – ▤. AE ◑ E VISA. 🐕 DU **y**
closed Sunday and August – **M** (booking essential) a la carte 52/77000 (15%).

XXX **Don Lisander,** via Manzoni 12/a ⊠ 20121 ℘ 790130 – ▤. AE ◑ E VISA CU **a**
closed Sunday – **M** (booking essential) a la carte 48/77000.

XXX ✿ **Peck,** via Victor Hugo 4 ⊠ 20123 ℘ 876774 – ▤. AE ◑ E VISA. 🐕 CV **b**
closed Sunday and July – **M** a la carte 35/62000
Spec. Insalata di funghi porcini e petto di cappone (March-November), Risotto alla milanese, Rognone di vitello nel suo grasso. **Wines** Torgiano, Borgo di Peuma.

XXX **Biffi Scala,** piazza della Scala ⊠ 20121 ℘ 876332, Tea-room and late night dinners – ▤. AE ◑ E VISA. 🐕 CU **z**
closed Sunday and 1 to 20 August – **M** a la carte 41/56000 (13%).

XXX **Canoviano,** via Hoepli 6 ⊠ 20121 ℘ 8058472 – ▤. 🐕 CV **v**
closed Saturday and Sunday – **M** (booking essential) a la carte 42/70000.

XXX **Suntory,** via Verdi 6 ⊠ 20121 ℘ 862210, Japanese rest. – ▤. AE ◑ E VISA. 🐕 CU **n**
closed Sunday and 10 to 17 August – **M** a la carte 45/73000.

XXX **Luciano,** via Ugo Foscolo 1 ⊠ 20121 ℘ 866818 – ▤. AE ◑ E VISA CV **a**
closed Saturday and 10 to 28 August – **M** a la carte 45/66000 (12%).

XXX **Alfio-Cavour,** via Senato 31 ⊠ 20121 ℘ 780731 – ▤. AE ◑ E VISA DU **a**
closed Saturday, Sunday lunch, August and 23 December-3 January – **M** a la carte 40/68000.

XXX **Boeucc,** piazza Belgioioso 2 ⊠ 20121 ℘ 790224, ☂ – ▤. AE. 🐕 CDU **x**
closed Saturday, Sunday lunch, August and 24 December-2 January – **M** (booking essential) a la carte 37/65000.

XXX Rigoletto, via Vincenzo Monti 33 ⊠ 20123 ℘ 4988687, Rest. and piano-bar – ▤ AU **b**

XXX **Barbarossa-da Flavio,** via Cerva 10 ⊠ 20122 ℘ 781418, Old Milan-style setting – ▤. AE ◑ VISA DV **f**
closed Saturday in July, Sunday and August – **M** a la carte 32/40000.

XXX **L'Innominato,** via Fiori Oscuri 3 ⊠ 20121 ℘ 8690552, Rest. and piano-bar – ▤. 🐕
closed Sunday, 17 to 23 April, August and 21 to 26 December – **M** (dinner only) a la carte 35/60000. CU **r**

XXX Prospero, via Chiossetto 20 ⊠ 20122 ℘ 701345 – ▤ DV **e**

XX **Kota Radja,** piazzale Baracca 6 ⊠ 20123 ℘ 468850, Chinese rest. – ▤. AE ◑ VISA
closed Sunday in August and Monday in other months – **M** a la carte 15/46000 (12%). AU **a**

XX **Bagutta,** via Bagutta 14 ⊠ 20121 ℘ 702767, ☂, Artists' meeting place, « Typical paintings and caricatures » – AE ◑ E VISA. 🐕 DU **e**
closed Sunday, 7 to 31 August and 23 December-5 January – **M** a la carte 32/50000 (12%).

XX **Rigolo,** largo Treves angolo via Solferino ⊠ 20121 ℘ 805968, Habitués' rest. – ▤. AE VISA. 🐕 CU **d**
closed Monday, Tuesday lunch and August – **M** a la carte 29/49000.

XX **Il Peschereccio,** Foro Bonaparte ang. via Sella ⊠ 20121 ℘ 861418 – ▤. AE ◑ BU **s**
closed Monday, Tuesday lunch, 1 to 21 August and 24 December-1 January – **M** (fish only) a la carte 41/54000.

XX **Al Mercante,** piazza Mercanti 17 ⊠ 20123 ℘ 8052198, « Outdoor service in summer » – ▤. AE CV **k**
closed Sunday and 1 to 22 August – **M** a la carte 25/35000.

XX **Ponvèder,** via Ponte Vetero 6 ⊠ 20121 ℘ 861977 – ▤. VISA BU **m**
closed lunch of Saturday and Sunday – **M** (booking essential) a la carte 32/40000.

XX **Boccondivino,** via Carducci 17 ⊠ 20123 ℘ 866040, Typical pork-butcher's meat, cheese and wines – ▤. AE. 🐕 AV **e**
closed Sunday and August – **M** (dinner only) (booking essential) a la carte 25/50000.

X **Trattoria dell'Angolo,** via Fiori Chiari ang via Formentini ⊠ 20121 ℘ 8058495 – ▤. AE ◑ CU **e**
closed Saturday lunch, Sunday, 1 to 7 January and 10 to 18 August – **M** a la carte 30/49000.

X **Allo Scudo,** via Mazzini 7 ⊠ 20123 ℘ 8052761, Habitués' rest. – ▤. AE ◑ CV **e**
closed Sunday and August – **M** a la carte 22/40000 (10%).

X **Al Chico,** via Sirtori 24 ⊠ 20129 ℘ 2716883, ☂, Tuscan rest. – AE ◑ E VISA DU **s**
closed Saturday lunch, Sunday, 31 July-24 August and 24 December-3 January – **M** a la carte 25/40000.

✕ Giacomo, via Donizzetti 11 ✉ 20122 ✆ 795020 DV **d**

✕ **Ai 3 Fratelli,** via Terraggio 11/13 ✉ 20123 ✆ 873281, 🏠 – ▤. 🚫 AV **r**
closed Sunday, 1 to 22 August and 24 December-5 January – **M** a la carte 19/38000.

Southern area Porta Ticinese, Porta Romana, Genova Station, Navigli, Ravizza Park, Vigentino (Plans : Milan pp. 6 and 7) :

🏨 **Lloyd** without rest., corso di Porta Romana 48 ✉ 20122 ✆ 867971, Telex 335028, « Collection of paintings by well-known artists » – |‡| ▤ TV ☎ – 🏛. AE ⓓ E VISA CX **z**
☕ 12000 – **52 rm** 130/170000.

🏨 **Ascot** without rest., via Lentasio 3 ✉ 20122 ✆ 862946, Telex 311303 – |‡| ▤ TV ☎ 🚗. AE ⓓ E VISA. 🚫 CX **e**
closed August – ☕ 13500 – **57 rm** 129/185000.

🏨 **Crivi's** without rest., corso Porta Vigentina 46 ✉ 20122 ✆ 5463341, Telex 313255 – |‡| ▤ TV ☎ 🚗 – 🏛. AE DY **a**
closed August – ☕ 13000 – **62 rm** 123/166000.

🏨 **D'Este** without rest., viale Bligny 23 ✉ 20136 ✆ 5461041, Telex 324216 – |‡| ▤ TV ☎ – 🏛. AE ⓓ E VISA CY **r**
☕ 11000 – **54 rm** 71/101000.

🏨 **Sant'Ambroeus** without rest., viale Papiniano 14 ✉ 20123 ✆ 4697451, Telex 313373 – |‡| ▤ TV ☎ – 🏛. AE ⓓ E VISA. 🚫 AX **a**
closed August and Christmas – ☕ 9000 – **52 rm** 76/110000.

🏨 **Ambrosiano** without rest., via Santa Sofia 9 ✉ 20122 ✆ 5510445 – |‡| ▤ ☎. AE ⓓ E VISA. 🚫 CX **x**
closed 16 July-23 August and 23 December-6 January – ☕ 12000 – **68 rm** 75/108000.

🏨 **Mediterraneo** without rest., via Muratori 14 ✉ 20135 ✆ 5488151, Telex 335812 – |‡| TV 🚿wc ☎ ♿ – 🏛. AE ⓓ E VISA DY **q**
closed 1 to 21 August – ☕ 7500 – **93 rm** 78/112000.

🏨 **Adriatico** without rest., via Conca del Naviglio 20 ✉ 20123 ✆ 8324141 – |‡| ▤ TV 🛁wc 🚿wc ☎. AE ⓓ E VISA BX **m**
closed 1 to 21 August – ☕ 7500 – **105 rm** 76/109000.

🏨 **Imperial** without rest., corso di Porta Romana 68 ✉ 20122 ✆ 5468241 – ▤ 🛁wc 🚿wc ☎ Ⓟ. AE E VISA. 🚫 DX **c**
☕ 12000 – **36 rm** 73/105000.

🏨 **Garden** without rest., via Rutilia 6 ✉ 20141 ✆ 537368 – 🚿wc ☎ ♿ Ⓟ DZ **a**
closed August – ☕ 5500 – **23 rm** 43/57000.

✕✕✕ Malatesta, via Bianca di Savoia 19 ✉ 20122 ✆ 5461079 – ▤ CY **a**

✕✕✕ **San Vito da Nino,** via San Vito 5 ✉ 20123 ✆ 8377029 – ▤. VISA. 🚫 BX **a**
closed Monday and August – **M** (booking essential) a la carte 50/70000 (13%).

✕✕✕ ✿ **Scaletta,** piazzale Stazione Genova ✉ 20144 ✆ 8350290 – ▤. 🚫 AY **a**
closed Sunday, Monday, 5 to 16 April, August and 24 December-7 January – **M** (booking essential) a la carte 70/80000
Spec. Patè di fegato e lumache, Ravioli di verdure, Insalata di scampi. Wines Arneis, Pergole Torte.

✕✕ ✿ **Al Porto,** piazzale Generale Cantore ✉ 20123 ✆ 8321481, Seafood – ▤. AE ⓓ
closed Sunday, Monday lunch, August and 24 December-3 January – **M** (booking essential) a la carte 36/52000 AXY **d**
Spec. Orata al pepe rosa, Scamponi gratinati, Branzino al pepe verde. Wines Tocai, Sauvignon.

✕✕ **La Cucina di Edgardo,** via Valenza 17 ✉ 20144 ✆ 8321926 – ▤. AE ⓓ E VISA. 🚫
closed Sunday and 13 to 17 August – **M** (menu surprise) (booking essential) 36000 (10%). AY **n**

✕✕ **Giordano,** via Torti angolo corso Genova 3 ✉ 20123 ✆ 8350824, Bolognese cuisine – ▤. AE ⓓ BX **s**
closed Sunday and 5 to 28 August – **M** a la carte 22/31000 (12%).

✕✕ **Al Genovese,** via Conchetta 18 ✉ 20136 ✆ 8373180, Ligurian rest. – AE BZ **a**
closed Sunday, Monday lunch and August – **M** a la carte 33/54000.

✕ **Osteria Via Pré,** via Casale 4 ✉ 20144 ✆ 8373869, Typical trattoria, Ligurian cuisine – ▤. ⓓ VISA AY **c**
closed Monday, Tuesday and August – **M** a la carte 31/42000.

Districts : Città Studi, Monforte, corso 22 Marzo, viale Corsica – E : by : Linate Airport, Idroscalo, strada Rivoltana :

🏨 **Zefiro** without rest., via Gallina 12 ✉ 20129 ✆ 7384253 – |‡| ▤ 🛁wc 🚿wc ☎ – 🏛. VISA. 🚫 by corso Concordia DU
closed August – ☕ 9000 – **55 rm** 70/100000.

🏨 **Vittoria** without rest., via Pietro Calvi 32 ✉ 20129 ✆ 5459695 – |‡| ▤ 🛁wc 🚿wc ☎. AE. 🚫 by corso 22 Marzo DV
closed 27 July-27 August and 23 December-1 January – ☕ 12000 – **18 rm** 62/92000.

🏨 **Città Studi** without rest., via Saldini 24 ✉ 20133 ✆ 744666 – |‡| ▤ 🛁wc 🚿wc ☎. AE VISA. 🚫 by corso Concordia DU
☕ 6500 – **45 rm** 45/65000.

XXXX ✿ **Giannino,** via Amatore Sciesa 8 ✉ 20135 ✆ 5452948, **Traditional style, « Original decoration; winter garden »** – Ⓟ. AE ⓓ E VISA. ✻ by corso 22 Marzo DV
closed Sunday and August – **M** a la carte 60/83000
Spec. Insalata di pesce con rucola in salsa cipollina, Tagliolini ai funghi porcini (April-November), Ossobuco con risotto alla milanese. **Wines** Gavi, Ghemme.

XXXX ✿✿✿ **Gualtiero Marchesi,** via Bonvesin de la Riva 9 ✉ 20129 ✆ 741246, **Elegant installation** – ▤. AE ⓓ. ✻ by corso 22 Marzo DV
closed holidays, Sunday, Monday lunch, August and 24 to 28 December – **M** (booking essential) a la carte 70/110000
Spec. Raviolo aperto, Gamberi saltati con piccolo ragout di melanzane in agrodolce, Costata di manzo bollita con piccole verdure di stagione e salsa alle erbe. **Wines** Prosecco, Settefilari.

XXX **Soti's,** via Pietro Calvi 2 ✉ 20129 ✆ 796838, **Elegant installation** – ▤. AE ⓓ VISA. ✻
closed Saturday lunch, Sunday and August – **M** (booking essential) a la carte 60/85000.
by corso 22 Marzo DV

XX **La Bella Pisana,** via Pasquale Sottocorno 17 ✉ 20129 ✆ 708376, ☂ – ▤. AE ⓓ E VISA
closed Sunday, Monday lunch, 4 to 31 August and 25 December-5 January – **M** a la carte 28/44000. by corso Concordia DU

XX **Hosteria del Cenacolo,** via Archimede 12 ✉ 20129 ✆ 5458962, **« Summer service in garden »** – AE. ✻ by corso 22 Marzo DV
closed Saturday lunch, Sunday and August – **M** a la carte 29/46000.

X **Il Palio di Siena,** via Turroni 4 ✉ 20129 ✆ 7387928, ☂, **Tuscan rest.** – VISA
closed Sunday dinner, Monday and August – **M** a la carte 26/42000.
by corso 22 Marzo DV

Districts : Fiera Campionaria, San Siro, Porta Magenta – NW : by ⑩ and ⑪ : Novara, Torino :

🏨🏨🏨🏨🏨 **Gd H. Brun and Rist. Ascot** ♨, via Caldera ✉ 20153 ✆ 45271 and rest. ✆ 4526279, Telex 315370 – |♦| ▤ TV ☎ ♿ 🚗 Ⓟ – 🏛. AE ⓓ E VISA. ✻ by corso Sempione AT
M *(closed Sunday)* a la carte 54/88000 – **330 rm** ☕ 215/285000 apartments 405/465000.

🏨🏨🏨🏨 **Gd H. Fieramilano,** viale Boezio 20 ✉ 20145 ✆ 3105, Telex 331426, 🚗 – |♦| ▤ TV ☎ ♿ – 🏛. AE ⓓ E VISA. ✻ rest by via Vincenzo Monti AT
M a la carte 37/60000 – **238 rm** ☕ 210/260000.

🏨🏨🏨 **Rubens** without rest., via Rubens 21 ✉ 20148 ✆ 405051, Telex 333503 – |♦| ▤ TV ☎ Ⓟ. AE ⓓ E VISA. ✻ by corso Vercelli AV
closed 1 to 21 August – **76 rm** ☕ 140/190000 apartments 225000.

🏨🏨🏨 **Capitol,** via Cimarosa 6 ✉ 20144 ✆ 4988851, Telex 316150 – |♦| ▤ TV ☎ – 🏛. AE ⓓ E. ✻ rest by corso Vercelli AV
M *(closed lunch and August)* coffee shop only – **96 rm** ☕ 140/198000.

🏨🏨🏨 Mini Hotel Tiziano, without rest., via Tiziano 6 ✉ 20145 ✆ 4988921, Telex 325420, **« Little park »** – |♦| ▤ ☎ Ⓟ – 🏛 – **54 rm** by ⑪

🏨🏨 **Green House** without rest., viale Famagosta 50 ✉ 20142 ✆ 8132451 – |♦| ▤ TV 🚿wc ☎ ♿ 🚗. AE ⓓ E VISA. ✻ by ⑩
☕ 7000 – **45 rm** 65/90000.

🏨🏨 Fiera, without rest., via Spinola 9 ✉ 20149 ✆ 432374, **« Little garden »** – |♦| 🛁wc 🚿wc ☎ 🚗 – 🏛 – **29 rm** by ⑪

🏨🏨 Mini Hotel Silva, without rest., via Silva 12 ✉ 20152 ✆ 4984449 – |♦| ▤ 🛁wc 🚿wc ☎ ♿ Ⓟ – 🏛 – **48 rm** by ⑪

🏨🏨 **Montebianco** without rest., via Monte Rosa 90 ✉ 20149 ✆ 4697941 – |♦| ▤ 🛁wc 🚿wc ☎ Ⓟ. AE ⓓ E VISA by ⑪
closed August and Christmas – ☕ 9000 – **44 rm** 112/150000.

XXX ✿ **Da Aimo,** via Montecuccoli 6 ✉ 20147 ✆ 416886 – ▤. AE. ✻ by ⑩
closed Saturday lunch, Sunday and August – **M** (booking essential) a la carte 45/87000
Spec. Melanzane ai formaggi freschi ed erbe aromatiche, Gnocchi di rucola al sugo di insalatine novelle, Animelle di vitello al rosmarino. **Wines** Malvasia Istriana, Pinot nero.

XX **La Corba,** via dei Gigli 14 ✉ 20147 ✆ 4158977, **« Summer service in garden »** – AE ⓓ VISA by ⑩
closed Sunday dinner, Monday and 8 to 24 August – **M** a la carte 35/47000.

XX **Raffaello,** via Raffaello Sanzio 8 ✉ 20149 ✆ 4814227, ☂ – AE ⓓ E VISA by ⑪
closed Friday, Saturday lunch and 5 to 22 August – **M** a la carte 28/44000.

XX **Ribot,** via Cremosano 41 ✉ 20148 ✆ 390646, **« Summer service in garden »** – Ⓟ. ✻
closed Monday and August – **M** a la carte 32/43000. by ⑪

XX **Al Primo Piatto,** via Ravizza 10 ✉ 20149 ✆ 4693206 – ▤. AE VISA by ⑪
closed Sunday – **M** a la carte 36/47000.

XX **Da Gino e Franco,** largo Domodossola 2 ✉ 20145 ✆ 312003 – ▤. ✻
closed Monday and 25 July-25 August – **M** a la carte 23/41000 (12%).
by corso Sempione AT

XX **Furio-Montebianco,** via Monte Bianco 2 ✉ 20149 ✆ 4814677, **Tuscan rest.** – ▤. AE ⓓ E VISA by ⑪
closed Monday and August – **M** a la carte 29/47000 (12%).

X **Pace,** via Washington 74 ✉ 20146 ✆ 468567, **Habitués' rest.** – ▤. ⓓ by ⑩
closed Tuesday dinner, Wednesday and 1 to 23 August – **M** a la carte 21/34000.

Districts : Sempione-Bullona, viale Certosa – NW : by ⑫ ⑬ and ⑭ : Varese, Como, Torino, Malpensa Airport :

Raffaello without rest., viale Certosa 108 ✉ 20156 ✆ 3270146, Telex 315499 – AE E VISA. by via Cenisio AR
109 rm 110/150000.

Berlino without rest., via Plana 33 ✉ 20155 ✆ 324141, Telex 312609 – wc wc. AE E VISA by via Cenisio AR
10000 – **47 rm** 75/108000.

Corallo without rest., via Cesena 20 ✉ 20155 ✆ 314074 – wc wc. AE VISA
10000 – **35 rm** 51/80000. by via Mach Mahon AR

XX La Pobbia, via Gallarate 92 ✉ 20151 ✆ 305641, Neo rustic rest., « Outdoor service in summer » – by via Cenisio AR

X **Al Vöttantott,** corso Sempione 88 ✉ 20154 ✆ 3182114, Habitués trattoria – . AE
closed Sunday and August – **M** a la carte 22/31000. by corso Sempione AS

X **Da Stefano il Marchigiano,** via Arimondi 1 angolo via Plana ✉ 20155 ✆ 390863 – AE . by via Cenisio AR
closed Friday dinner, Saturday and August – **M** a la carte 23/42000.

Abbiategrasso 20080 Milano 988 ③, 219 ⑱ – pop. 27 668 – 02.

Roma 590 – Alessandria 74 – Milano 23 – Novara 29 – Pavia 33.

at Cassinetta di Lugagnano N : 3 km – ✉ **20081 :**

XXX ✿✿ **Antica Osteria del Ponte,** ✆ 9420034 – . AE .
closed Sunday, Monday, 1 to 15 January and August – **M** (booking essential) a la carte 60/97000
Spec. Capesante e funghi porcini in salsa di soia (Autumn), Ravioli di tartufo nero (January-April), Filetti di triglia alle fave fresche (Spring). **Wines** Vintage Tunina, Tignanello.

Prices are given in local currency.
Valid for 1987 the rates shown should only vary
if the cost of living changes to any great extent.

NAPLES (NAPOLI) 80100 P 988 ㉗ – pop. 1 206 010 – h.s. April-October – 081.

See : Historic Centre★★ : New Castle★★ (triumphal arch★★) KZ, San Carlo Theatre★ KZ **T**, Piazza del Plebiscito★ JKZ, Royal Palace★ KZ – Port of Santa Lucia★★ (≤★★ of the bay) – From via Partenope ≤★★★ (at night) of the Vomero and Posillipo hills FX.

National Archaeological Museum★★★ KY : Graeco-Roman sculptures★★★; Villa Pison Gallery★★★; mosaics★★; collections★★ of small bronzes, paintings and various objets from Herculaneum and Pompeii – Carthusian Monastery of St. Martin★★ JZ : museum★ (Neapolitan cribs★★), from gallery 25 ≤★★★ of the Bay of Naples; Baroque Church (interior★★) – Capodimonte Palace and National Gallery★★ : picture gallery★★, Royal Apartments (porcelain room★★).

Spacca-Napoli quarter★★ KY : Church of Santa Chiara★ KY **C** (tomb★★ of King Robert the Wise, tomb★ of Marie de Valois, cloisters★ – Church of St. Dominic Major (caryatids★) KY **L** – Chapel of San Severo (sculptures★) KY **V** – Church of St. Lawrence Major (arch★, tomb★ of Catherine of Austria, apse★) LY **K**.

Mergellina★ (≤★★ of the bay) – Villa Floridiana★ EVX : National Museum of Ceramics★ **M2**, ≤★ – Catacombs of San Gennaro★.

Envir. : Island of Capri★★★ – Island of Ischia★★★ – Vesuvius★★★ (crater★★★, ☼★★★), E : from Herculaneum return via Torre del Greco, 27 km and 3/4 hour Rtn on foot (west side) – Pompeii★★★ (excavations), SE : 24 km – Herculaneum★★ (excavations), SE : 9 km.

Ugo Niutta of Capodichino NE : 6 km (except Sunday) ✆ 312200 – Alitalia, via Medina 41 ✉ 80133 ✆ 325325.

to Capri March-October daily (1 h 30 mn about) – Navigazione Libera del Golfo, molo Beverello ✉ 80133 ✆ 325589; to Capri (1 h 15 mn), Ischia (1 h 15 mn) and Procida (1 h), daily – Agency De Luca, molo Beverello ✉ 80133 ✆ 313882; to Cagliari Wednesday and Sunday (15 h) and Palermo daily (10 h); to Catania (15 h 15 mn) and Siracusa (18 h 45 mn), Thursday – Tirrenia Navigazione, Stazione Marittima, molo Angioino ✉ 80133 ✆ 7201111, Telex 710030; to Ischia daily (1 h 15 mn) – Libera Navigazione Lauro, via Caracciolo 11 ✆ 991889, Telex 720354.

to Capri (45 mn), Ischia (45 mn) and Procida (30 mn) daily – Agency De Luca, molo Beverello ✉ 80133 ✆ 313882; to Capri (45 mn) and Ischia (45 mn), daily – Alilauro, via Caracciolo 11 ✆ 684288, Telex 720354; to Capri daily (45 mn) – SNAV, via Caracciolo 10 ✆ 660444, Telex 720446.

via Partenope 10/a ✉ 80121 ✆ 406289 – piazza del Plebiscito (Royal Palace) ✉ 80132 ✆ 418744 – Central Station ✉ 80142 ✆ 268779 – Capodichino Airport ✉ 80133 ✆ 7805761.

A.C.I. piazzale Tecchio 49/d ✉ 80125 ✆ 614511.

Roma 219 ③ – Bari 261 ⑤.

Plans on following pages

Excelsior, via Partenope 48 ✉ 80121 ☎ 417111, Telex 710043, ≤ gulf, Vesuvius and Castel dell'Ovo – |♦| ▤ TV ☎ – 🏛. AE ⓞ E VISA. ✻ GX **w**
M a la carte 78/121000 – ☕ 16500 – **137 rm** 226/346000 apartments 500/850000.

Vesuvio, via Partenope 45 ✉ 80121 ☎ 417044, Telex 710127, « Roof-garden rest. with ≤ gulf and Castel dell'Ovo » – |♦| ▤ TV ☎ – 🏛. AE ⓞ E VISA. ✻ rest FX **n**
M a la carte 39/57000 – **170 rm** ☕ 154/218000.

Jolly, via Medina 70 ✉ 80133 ☎ 416000, Telex 720335, « Roof-garden rest. with ≤ town, gulf and Vesuvius » – |♦| ▤ TV ☎ – 🏛. AE ⓞ E VISA. ✻ rest KZ **s**
M 38000 – **278 rm** ☕ 130/165000.

Royal, via Partenope 38 ✉ 80121 ☎ 400244, Telex 710167, ≤ gulf, Posillipo and Castel dell'Ovo, 🏊 – |♦| ▤ TV ☎ ♿ 🚗 – 🏛. AE ⓞ E VISA. ✻ rest FX **n**
M a la carte 48/70000 – **287 rm** ☕ 145/190000 apartments 290000.

Britannique, corso Vittorio Emanuele 133 ✉ 80121 ☎ 660933, Telex 722281, ≤, 🌳 – |♦| ▤ TV ☎ 🚗 – 🏛. AE ⓞ E VISA. ✻ rest EX **r**
M 35000 – ☕ 12000 – **80 rm** 115/180000 apartments 220/240000, ▤ 10000 – P 125/150000.

San Germano, via Beccadelli 41 ✉ 80125 ☎ 7605422, Telex 720080, « Beautiful garden-park », 🏊 – |♦| ▤ 🚗 ⓟ – 🏛. AE ⓞ. ✻ rest by ⑧
M a la carte 22/41000 – **104 rm** ☕ 85/140000 – P 110/125000.

Serius, viale Augusto 74 ✉ 80125 ☎ 614844 – |♦| ▤ 🛁wc 🚿wc ☎ 🚗. ✻ by ⑧
M 20/25000 – ☕ 9500 – **69 rm** 62/93000, ▤ 10000 – P 101000.

Miramare without rest., via Nazario Sauro 24 ✉ 80132 ☎ 427388, ≤ – |♦| ▤ 🛁wc 🚿wc ☎. AE ⓞ E VISA GX **e**
26 rm ☕ 90/135000.

Cavour, piazza Garibaldi 32 ✉ 80142 ☎ 283122 – |♦| 🛁wc 🚿wc ☎. AE ⓞ E VISA ✻ MY **b**
M a la carte 22/33000 (18%) – **94 rm** ☕ 50/77000 – P 78/88000, low season 70/78000.

Palace Hotel, piazza Garibaldi 9 ✉ 80142 ☎ 264575, Telex 720262 – |♦| 🛁wc 🚿wc ☎ – 🏛. AE ⓞ E VISA. ✻ MY **s**
M a la carte 23/34000 (18%) – **102 rm** ☕ 56/90000 – P 80/88000, low season 70/80000.

Rex without rest., via Palepoli 12 ✉ 80132 ☎ 416388 – ▤ 🛁wc 🚿wc ☎. AE ⓞ VISA GX **r**
☕ 5000 – **40 rm** 45/70000, ▤ 5000.

Domitiana without rest., viale Kennedy 143 ✉ 80125 ☎ 610560 – |♦| 🛁wc 🚿wc ☎ ♿ – 🏛. AE ⓞ E VISA by ⑧
☕ 10000 – **40 rm** 60/97000.

XXX **La Sacrestia,** via Orazio 116 ✉ 80122 ☎ 664186, Elegant rest., « Summer service in garden-terrace with ≤ » – ▤. AE VISA. ✻ by via Caracciolo FX
closed August, Sunday in July and Wednesday in other months – **M** 38000 (14%).

XX ✿ **La Cantinella,** via Cuma 42 ✉ 80132 ☎ 404884, Typical seaside rest. – AE ⓞ VISA. ✻
closed Sunday and August – **M** a la carte 26/44000 (12%) GX **v**
Spec. Sautè di frutti di mare, Penne alla Cantinella, Pesce all'acqua pazza. **Wines** Greco di Tufo, Taurasi.

XX ✿ **Giuseppone a Mare,** via Ferdinando Russo 13-Capo Posillipo ✉ 80123 ☎ 7696002, Seaside rest. with ≤ – ⓟ. AE ⓞ E VISA. ✻ by via Caracciolo FX
closed Sunday and 23 to 31 December – **M** a la carte 25/49000 (12%)
Spec. Penne al cartoccio, Polipetti al pignatiello, Pesce all'acqua pazza. **Wines** Forastera.

XX **Sangirè,** via San Pasquale a Chiaia 56 ✉ 80121 ☎ 413259, Classic rest.-late night – ▤
dinner only – **M** (booking essential) a la carte 27/46000. FX **a**

XX **Don Salvatore,** strada Mergellina 4/a ✉ 80122 ☎ 681817, Rest. and pizzeria – ▤. AE ⓞ VISA. ✻ by via Caracciolo FX
closed Wednesday – **M** a la carte 29/50000.

X **San Carlo,** via Cesario Console 18/19 ✉ 80132 ☎ 417206 – ✻ KZ **a**
closed Sunday and August – **M** (booking essential) 40/50000.

X **Amici Miei,** via Monte di Dio 78 ✉ 80132 ☎ 405727, Habituès' rest. – AE ⓞ JZ **a**
closed Monday – **M** a la carte 15/33000 (15%).

X **Sbrescia,** rampe Sant'Antonio a Posillipo 109 ✉ 80122 ☎ 669140, Typical Neapolitan rest. with ≤ town and gulf – AE VISA. ✻ by via Caracciolo FX
closed Monday – **M** a la carte 21/38000 (12%).

When driving through towns use the plans in the **Michelin Guide.** *Features indicated include: throughroutes and by-passes; traffic junctions and major squares, new streets, car parks, pedestrian streets... All this information is revised annually.*

A complete list of cities included in this guide will be found on pp. 4 and 5.

NAPOLI

Giordano (Via L.) .... EV 64
Scarlatti (Via Alessandro) ...... EV 153

Arcoleo (Via G.) .... FX 5
Arena della Sanità (Via) .... GU 6
Artisti (Piazza degli) .... EV 9
Bernini (Via G. L.) .... EV 12
Bonito (Via G.) .... FV 13
Carducci (Via G.) .... FX 20
Chiatamone (Via) .... FX 25

Cirillo (Via D.) .... GU 27
Colonna (Via Vittoria) ...... FX 29
Crocelle (Via) .... GU 35
D'Auria (Via G.) .... FV 40
Ferraris (Via Galileo) ...... HV 54
Fontana (Via Domenico) ... EU 58
Gen. Pignatelli (Via) ...... HU 62

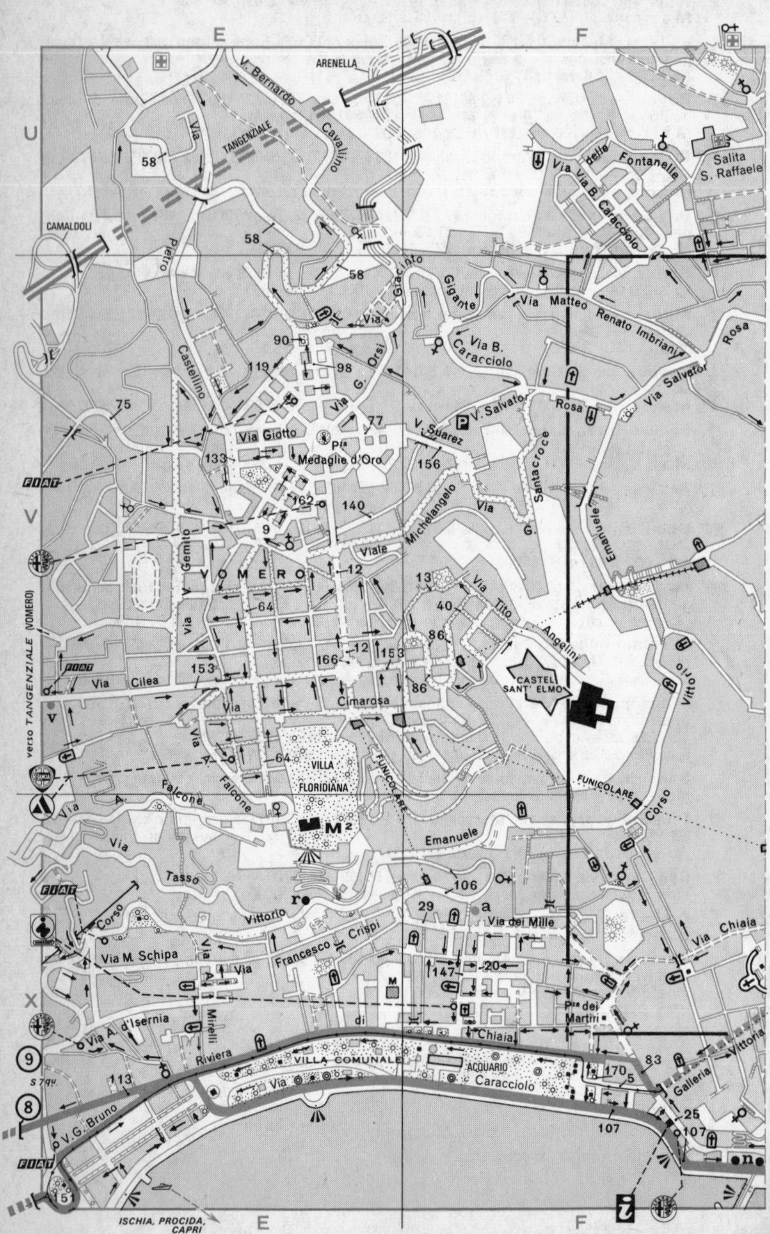

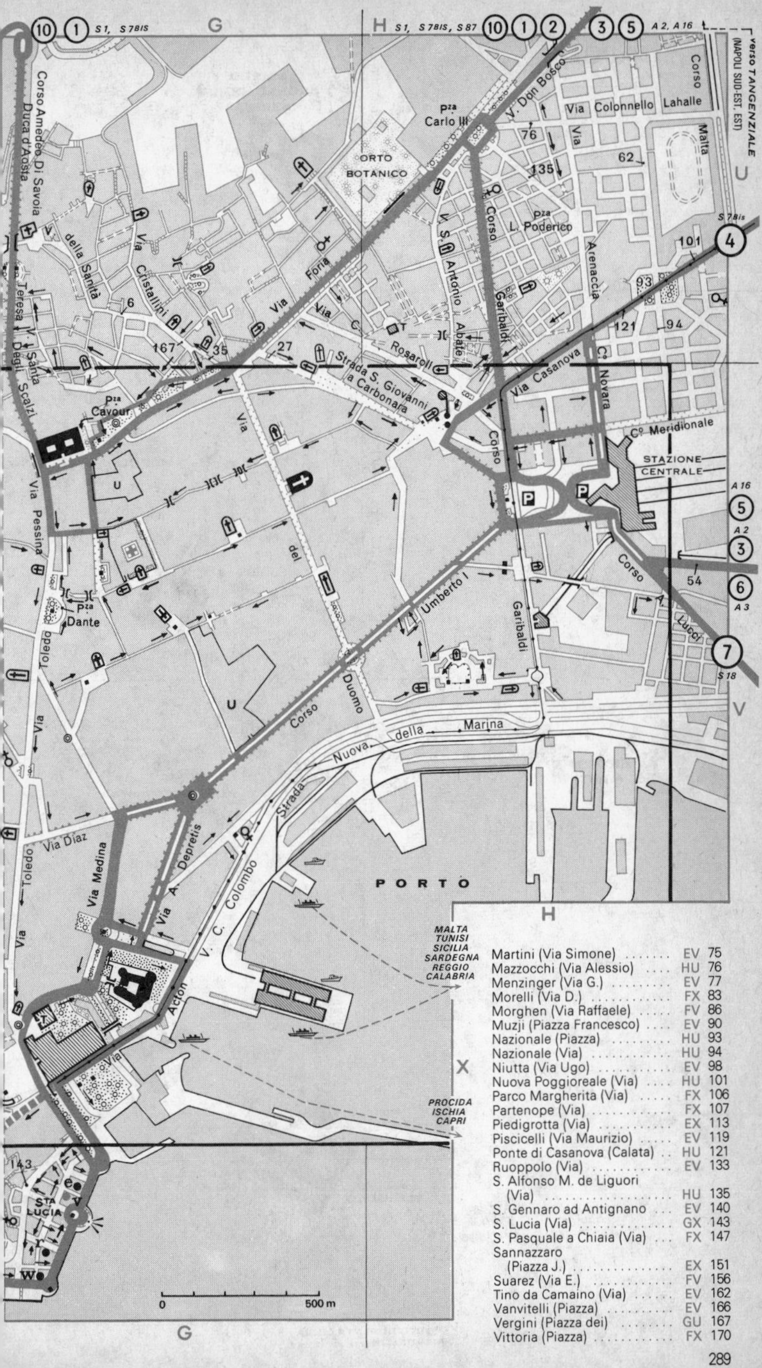
G
H
S 1, S 7BIS
S 1, S 7BIS, S 87
A 2, A 16
verso TANGENZIALE (NAPOLI SUD-EST, EST)
Corso Amedeo Di Savoia Duca d'Aosta
Pza Carlo III
ORTO BOTANICO
V. Don Bosco
Via Colonnello Lahalle
Corso Malta
Via Malta
U
della Sanità
Via Cristallini
Via Foria
V. S. Antonio Abate
Corso Garibaldi
Pza L. Poderico
Arenaccia
S 7Bis
Via S. Teresa degli Scalzi
Via C. Rosaroll
Strada S. Giovanni a Carbonara
Via Casanova
Co Novara
Co Meridionale
Pza Cavour
STAZIONE CENTRALE
A 16
A 2
A 3
S 18
Via Pessina
Via del Duomo
Corso Umberto I
Corso A. Lucci
Corso Garibaldi
Pza Dante
Toledo
Via Toledo
Via della Marina
Strada Nuova
Via Diaz
Via Medina
Via A. Depretis
V. C. Colombo
PORTO
Via Acton
MALTA TUNISI SICILIA SARDEGNA REGGIO CALABRIA
PROCIDA ISCHIA CAPRI
X
V
STA LUCIA
0
500 m

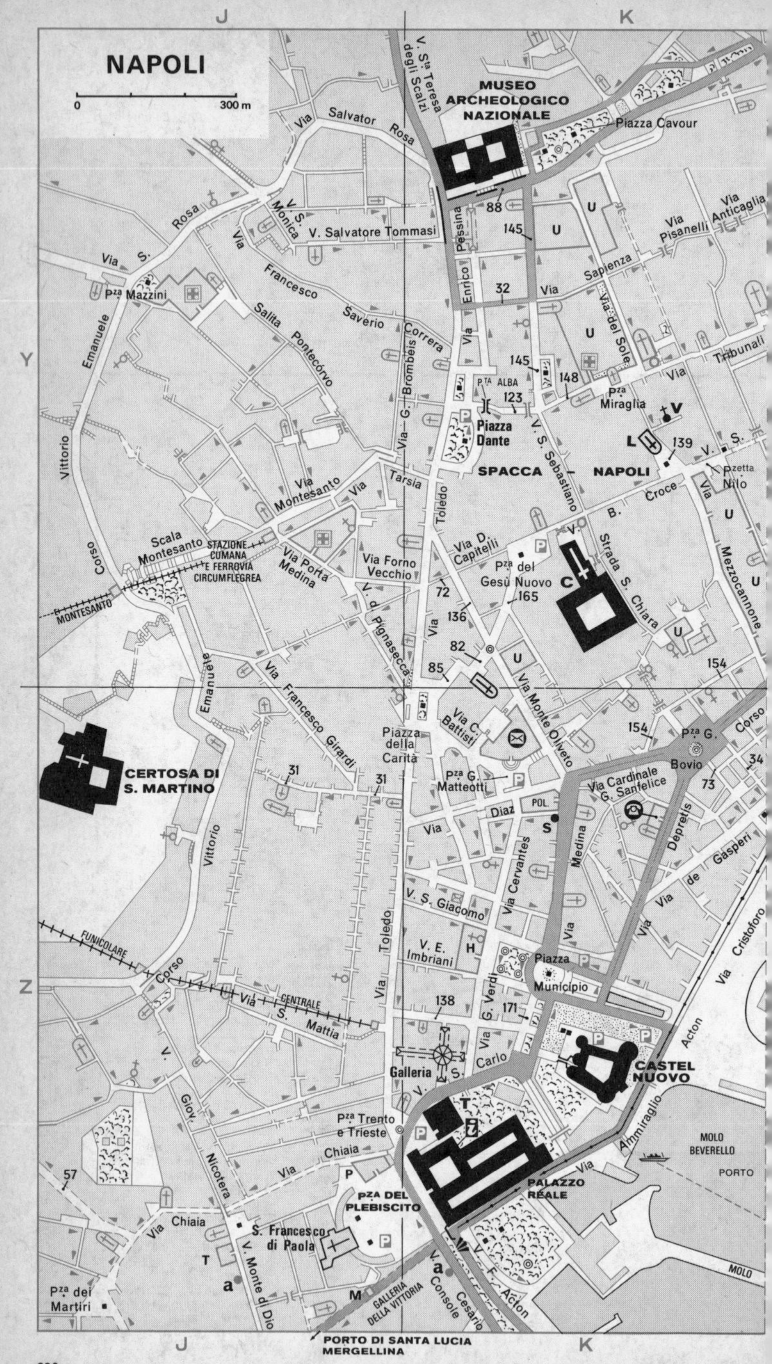
NAPOLI
0
300 m
J
K
Y
Z
MUSEO ARCHEOLOGICO NAZIONALE
Piazza Cavour
V. Sta Teresa degli Scalzi
Via Salvator Rosa
V. S. Monica
V. Salvatore Tommasi
Via Pessina
88
145
U
Via Pisanelli
Via Anticaglia
Via Sapienza
Via S. Rosa
Pza Mazzini
Via Francesco Saverio Correra
Salita Pontecórvo
Enrico
32
Via
Via del Sole
Via Tribunali
Corso Vittorio Emanuele
Via G. Brombeis
Pta ALBA
123
148
Pza Miraglia
Piazza Dante
V. S. Sebastiano
L
V
139
V. S.
Pzetta Nilo
SPACCA NAPOLI
Via Montesanto
Via Tarsia
Toledo
Via B. Croce
Scala Montesanto
STAZIONE CUMANA E FERROVIA CIRCUMFLEGREA
MONTESANTO
Via Porta Medina
Via Forno Vecchio
Via D. Capitelli
Pza del Gesù Nuovo
C
Strada S. Chiara
Via Mezzocannone
72
165
136
V. d. Pignasecca
82
85
Via Monte Oliveto
154
Via Francesco Girardi
Via C. Battisti
Piazza della Carità
Pza G. Bovio
Corso
34
73
CERTOSA DI S. MARTINO
31
Pza G. Matteotti
Via Cardinale G. Sanfelice
Via Diaz
POL.
S
Via Medina
Via Depretis
Via de Gasperi
Via Cervantes
V. S. Giacomo
FUNICOLARE
V. E. Imbriani
H
Piazza Municipio
Via Cristoforo
Corso
Via S. Mattia
CENTRALE
Via G. Verdi
138
171
Via Carlo
Galleria
V. S.
Acton
CASTEL NUOVO
T
V. Giov. Nicotera
Pza Trento e Trieste
Via Chiaia
Ammiraglio
MOLO BEVERELLO
PORTO
57
P
PZA DEL PLEBISCITO
PALAZZO REALE
Via Chiaia
S. Francesco di Paola
V. F. Acton
T
a
V. Monte di Dio
V. a Console
Cesario
Pza dei Martiri
M
GALLERIA DELLA VITTORIA
MOLO
PORTO DI SANTA LUCIA MERGELLINA

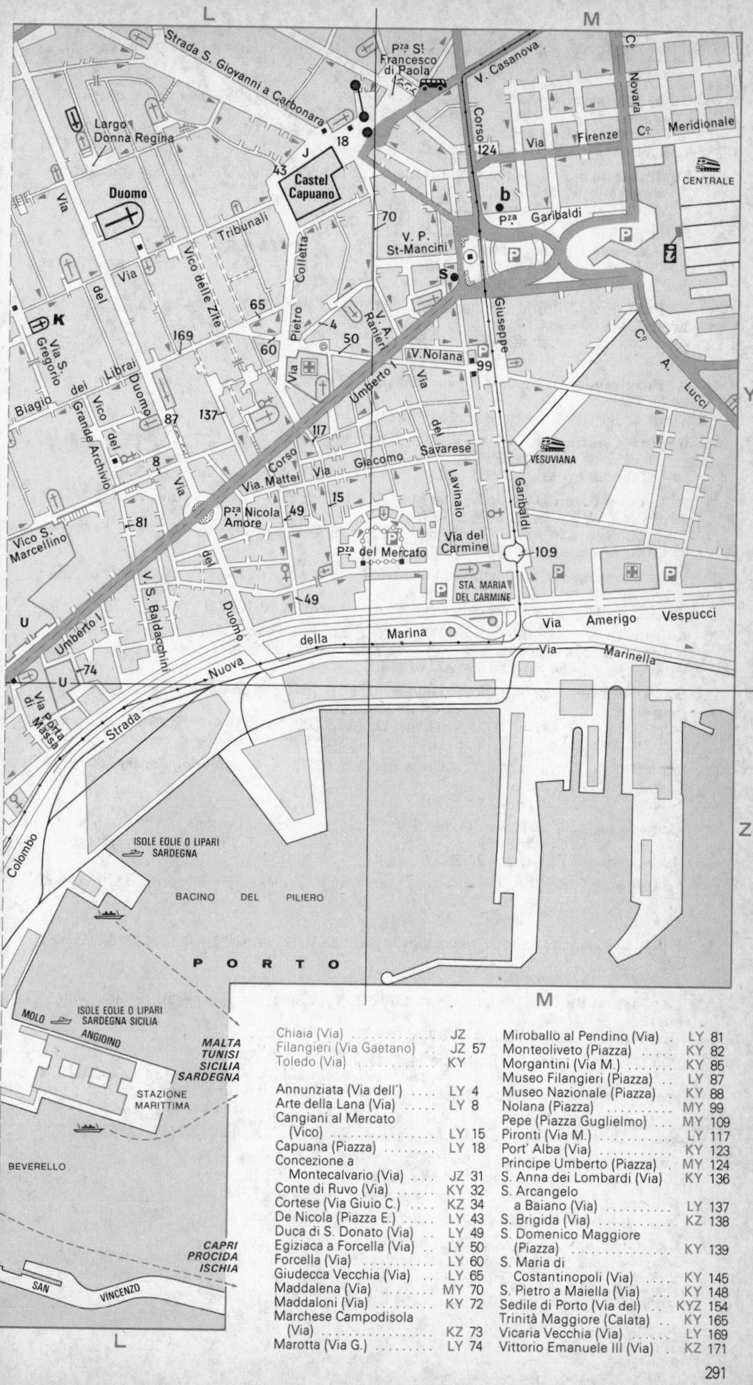

Chiaia (Via) .... JZ
Filangieri (Via Gaetano) .. JZ 57
Toledo (Via) .... KY

Annunziata (Via dell') .... LY 4
Arte della Lana (Via) ..... LY 8
Cangiani al Mercato (Vico) .... LY 15
Capuana (Piazza) .... LY 18
Concezione a Montecalvario (Via) .... JZ 31
Conte di Ruvo (Via) ...... KY 32
Cortese (Via Giuio C.) .... KZ 34
De Nicola (Piazza E.) ..... LY 43
Duca di S. Donato (Via) .. LY 49
Egiziaca a Forcella (Via) .. LY 50
Forcella (Via) .... LY 60
Giudecca Vecchia (Via) .. LY 65
Maddalena (Via) .... MY 70
Maddaloni (Via) .... KY 72
Marchese Campodisola (Via) .... KZ 73
Marotta (Via G.) .... LY 74

Miroballo al Pendino (Via) .. LY 81
Monteoliveto (Piazza) ..... KY 82
Morgantini (Via M.) .... KY 85
Museo Filangieri (Piazza) .. LY 87
Museo Nazionale (Piazza) .. KY 88
Nolana (Piazza) .... MY 99
Pepe (Piazza Guglielmo) ... MY 109
Pironti (Via M.) .... LY 117
Port' Alba (Via) .... KY 123
Principe Umberto (Piazza) . MY 124
S. Anna dei Lombardi (Via) KY 136
S. Arcangelo a Baiano (Via) .... LY 137
S. Brigida (Via) .... KZ 138
S. Domenico Maggiore (Piazza) .... KY 139
S. Maria di Costantinopoli (Via) .... KY 145
S. Pietro a Maiella (Via) ... KY 148
Sedile di Porto (Via del) .. KYZ 154
Trinità Maggiore (Calata) .. KY 165
Vicaria Vecchia (Via) ...... LY 169
Vittorio Emanuele III (Via) . KZ 171

Island of Capri 80073 Napoli 988 ㉗ – pop. 12 451 – Health and seaside resort, h.s. Easter and June-September – ☎ 081.

Gd H. Quisisana, via Camerelle 2 ☎ 8370788, Telex 710520, ≤ sea and Certosa, « Garden with » – AE E VISA.
April-October – **M** a la carte 56/86000 – **135 rm** 207/370000 apartments 480/690000 – P 245/307000, low season 218/258000.

Scalinatella without rest., via Tragara 8 ☎ 8370633, Telex 721204, ≤ sea and Certosa, heated –
15 March-October – **28 rm** 160/360000.

Luna, viale Matteotti 3 ☎ 8370433, Telex 721247, ≤ sea, Faraglioni and Certosa, « Terraces and garden with » – rm – AE E VISA. rest
April-October – **M** a la carte 40/50000 – 15000 – **48 rm** 85/195000 apartments 220/300000, 7000 – P 140/185000, low season 120/165000.

La Palma, via Vittorio Emanuele 39 ☎ 8370133, Telex 722015, – – AE E VISA. rest
April-October – **M** 40/60000 – **80 rm** 141/260000 – P 166/195000, low season 121/150000.

A' Pazziella without rest., via Giuliani 4 ☎ 8370044, ≤ sea, « Flower garden » – AE VISA.
20 rm 85/170000 apartments 130/190000.

Regina Cristina, via Serena 20 ☎ 8370303, Telex 710531, – rm wc wc – AE VISA
M 40000 – **55 rm** 72/175000, 10000 – P 115/150000, low season 100/120000.

Villa delle Sirene, via Camerelle 51 ☎ 8370102, ≤, « Lemon-grove with » – wc wc AE E VISA. rest
April-October – **M** *(closed Tuesday)* a la carte 28/42000 – **35 rm** 77/135000, 7000 – P 127000, low season 116000.

Villa Brunella, via Tragara 24 ☎ 8370279, ≤ sea and coast, « Floral terraces », – wc VISA.
19 March-5 November – **M** coffee shop only – **11 rm** 70/124000 – P 125/130000.

La Pineta without rest., via Tragara 6 ☎ 8370644, Telex 710011, ≤ sea and Certosa, « Floral terraces in pine-wood », – wc AE E VISA
April-October – **54 rm** 116/196000, 10000.

Gatto Bianco, via Vittorio Emanuele 32 ☎ 8370446, « Summer rest. service under pergola » – rm wc wc AE E VISA.
April-October – **M** 35/40000 – **44 rm** 70/130000, 8000 – P 120/145000, low season 110/120000.

Villa Sarah without rest., via Tiberio 3/a ☎ 8377817, ≤, « Shaded garden » – wc wc AE.
Easter-October – **25 rm** 48/80000.

Flora without rest., via Serena 26 ☎ 8370211, ≤ sea and Certosa, « Floral terrace » – wc AE E VISA
April-October – **25 rm** 70/125000.

La Vega without rest., via Occhio Marino 10 ☎ 8370481, ≤, « Panoramic terrace with » – wc wc AE VISA
15 March-October – **24 rm** 70/120000.

Florida without rest., via Fuorlovado 34 ☎ 8370710, – wc wc AE E VISA
10000 – **19 rm** 42/76000.

XXX **La Certosella,** via Tragara 13 ☎ 8370713, ≤, « Summer service on terrace with heated » –
April-October – **M** a la carte 42/67000.

XX ✿ **La Capannina,** via Le Botteghe 14 ☎ 8370732 – AE VISA.
15 March-10 November; closed Wednesday (except August) – **M** a la carte 29/45000 (13%)
Spec. Ravioli alla caprese, Linguine al sugo di scorfano, Grigliata mista di pesce. **Wines** Capri.

XX **La Pigna,** via Lo Palazzo 30 ☎ 8370280, ≤ gulf of Naples, – AE E VISA
Easter-October; closed Tuesday (except July-September) – **M** a la carte 30/44000 (15%).

XX **Faraglioni,** via Camerelle 75 ☎ 8370320, ≤, – AE VISA
April-October; closed Monday – **M** a la carte 31/46000 (15%).

XX **Aurora Grill,** via Le Botteghe 46 ☎ 8377642 – AE E VISA
closed Monday, January, February and March – **M** a la carte 26/40000 (12%).

X **La Sceriffa,** via Acquaviva 29 ☎ 8377953, ≤
April-October; closed Tuesday and lunch 15 July-15 September – **M** a la carte 25/38000.

X **Geranio,** viale Matteotti 8 ☎ 8370616, – AE VISA
April-15 October; closed Thursday – **M** a la carte 30/45000 (11%).

There is no paid publicity in this Guide.

PALERME (PALERMO) 90100 P 988 ㉟ – pop. 719 755 – ✆ 091.

See : Quattro Canti★ BY – Piazza Pretoria★ BY (fountain★★ **B**) – Piazza Bellini★★ BY : the Martorana★★ (mosaics★★) BYZ, Church of St. Cataldo★★ BZ – Cathedral★ (apses★, imperial crown★) AYZ – Palace of the Normans★★ (the palatine Chapel★★★ , mosaics★★★, King Roger's Room★★) AZ – Villa Bonanno★ (gardens) AZ – Church of St. John of the Hermits★★ AZ.

Capuchin Catacombs★★ AZ – Palazzo della Zisa★ AY – Regional Gallery of Sicily★★ (Abbatellis Palace★, fresco of Death Triumphant★★★, Madonna of the Annunciation★★) CY **M1** – Archaeological Museum★ (metopes from the temples at Selinus★★, the Ram★★) BY **M** – St. Lawrence Oratory★ CY **N** – Chiaramonte Palace★ (Garibaldi Gardens : magnolia fig trees★★) CY – Botanical Garden★ CDZ – Park of the Favourite N : 3 km (Ethnographic Museum : Sicilian carts★).

Envir. : Monreale★★★ by ② – Monte Pellegrino★★ N : 14 km by ③ – Ruins of Soluntum★ by ① – Bagheria : Villa Palagonia (sculptures★) by ①.

✈ Punta Raisi by ③ : 30 km ✆ 591690 – Alitalia, via della Libertà 29 ✉ 90139 ✆ 584533.

⛴ to Genova Tuesday and Friday (22 h) and to Livorno Monday, Wednesday and Friday (18 h) – Grandi Traghetti, via Mariano Stabile 179 ✆ 587939, Telex 910098; to Napoli daily (10 h), to Genova Monday, Wednesday, Friday and Sunday (23 h) and to Cagliari Monday (12 h 30 mn) – Tirrenia Navigazione, via Roma 385 ✆ 585733, Telex 910020; to Ustica daily (2 h 30 mn) – Prestifilippo Agency, via Crispi 124 ✆ 582403.

⛴ to Ustica daily (1 h 15 mn) – Prestifilippo Agency, via Crispi 124 ✆ 582403.

ℹ piazza Castelnuovo 35 ✉ 90141 ✆ 583847, Telex 910179 – Punta Raisi Airport ✆ 591405 – Central Station ✉ 90127 ✆ 233808.

A.C.I. viale delle Alpi 6 ✉ 90144 ✆ 266393.

Messina 235 ①.

Plan on following pages

Villa Igiea Gd H. ⛰, salita Belmonte 43 ✉ 90142 ✆ 543744, Telex 910092, ≤, 🌳, « Floral terraces overlooking the sea », ⛱, 🌳, 🎾 – 🛗 ▤ 📺 ☎ ♿ 🅿 – 🧑‍🏫. AE ⓓ E VISA. ✂ rest — by ③
M 55/60000 – ☕ 18000 – **118 rm** 175/300000 apartments 390/500000 – P 240/270000.

Gd H. et des Palmes, via Roma 398 ✉ 90139 ✆ 583933, Telex 911082, « Roof-garden rest. nightly » – 🛗 ▤ 📺 ☎ ♿ – 🧑‍🏫. AE ⓓ E VISA. ✂ rest — BX **g**
M *(closed Sunday)* 40000 – **183 rm** ☕ 95/125000 apartments 200/210000 – P 89000.

President, via Crispi 230 ✉ 90133 ✆ 580733, Telex 910359, ≤, « Roof-garden rest. » – 🛗 ▤ 📺 ☎ ♿ – 🧑‍🏫. ⓓ VISA. ✂ — BX **e**
M 20000 – ☕ 5500 – **129 rm** 70/85000 – P 75/90000.

Politeama Palace, piazza Ruggero Settimo 15 ✉ 90139 ✆ 322777, Telex 911053 – 🛗 ▤ 📺 ☎ – 🧑‍🏫 — AX **s**
102 rm.

Jolly, Foro Italico 22 ✉ 90133 ✆ 235842, Telex 910076, ≤, ⛱, 🌳 – 🛗 ▤ 📺 ☎ 🅿 – 🧑‍🏫. AE ⓓ E VISA. ✂ rest — DY **s**
M 35000 – **290 rm** ☕ 96/139000.

Excelsior Palace, via Marchese Ugo 3 ✉ 90141 ✆ 266155, Telex 911149 – 🛗 ▤ 📺 ☎ — AX **c**
86 rm.

Europa, via Agrigento 3 ✉ 90141 ✆ 266673 – 🛗 ▤ 📺 ☎. AE ⓓ E VISA. ✂ rest — AX **r**
M 20000 – ☕ 6500 – **73 rm** 48/75000 – P 82000.

Mediterraneo, via Rosolino Pilo 43 ✉ 90139 ✆ 581133 – 🛗 ▤ 📺 ☎ ♿ – 🧑‍🏫. AE ⓓ E VISA. ✂ rest — BX **k**
M 20000 – ☕ 6000 – **106 rm** 48/75000 apartments 150000 – P 73/82000.

MotelAgip, viale della Regione Siciliana 2620 ✉ 90145 ✆ 552033, Telex 911196 – 🛗 ▤ 🚿wc ☎ ♿ 🅿 – 🧑‍🏫. AE ⓓ E VISA. ✂ — by ③
M 22/26000 – **105 rm** ☕ 56/102000.

Metropol, via Turrisi Colonna 4 ✉ 90141 ✆ 588608 – ▤ 🛁wc 🚿wc ☎. AE ⓓ E VISA. ✂ rest — AX **a**
M (residents only) 17/18000 – ☕ 6000 – **44 rm** 35/63000, ▤ 5500 – P 62/69000.

Sausele without rest., via Vincenzo Errante 12 ✉ 90127 ✆ 6161308 – 🛗 🛁wc 🚿wc ☎ 🚗. AE E VISA — BZ **u**
☕ 6000 – **40 rm** 31/46000.

Villa Archirafi without rest., via Lincoln 30 ✉ 90133 ✆ 285827, 🌳 – 🛗 🚿wc ☎ 🅿. AE E — CZ **m**
☕ 5000 – **32 rm** 30/46000.

Touring without rest., via Mariano Stabile 136 ✉ 90139 ✆ 584444 – 🛗 ▤ 🛁wc 🚿wc ☎. AE ⓓ VISA. ✂ — BX **h**
☕ 6000 – **22 rm** 38/56000, ▤ 7000.

Liguria without rest., via Mariano Stabile 128 ✉ 90139 ✆ 581588 – 🚿wc ☎. AE ⓓ. ✂ — BX **b**
☕ 4000 – **16 rm** 22/45000.

XXXX ✿ **Charleston,** piazzale Ungheria 30 ✉ 90141 ✆ 321366 – ▤. AE ⓓ E VISA. ✂ — AY **r**
closed Sunday and 16 June-25 September – **M** a la carte 45/66000
Spec. Melanzana Charleston, Branzino in cartoccio, Parfait alla mandorla. **Wines** Regaleali, Corvo.

XXXX ✿ **Gourmand's,** via della Libertà 37/e ✉ 90139 ✆ 323431 – ▤. AE ⓓ E VISA. ✂ — AX **e**
closed Sunday – **M** a la carte 37/59000
Spec. Fettuccine Conca d'Oro, Cernia matalotta, Crêpes Gourmand's. **Wines** Chirchiaro, Bonera.

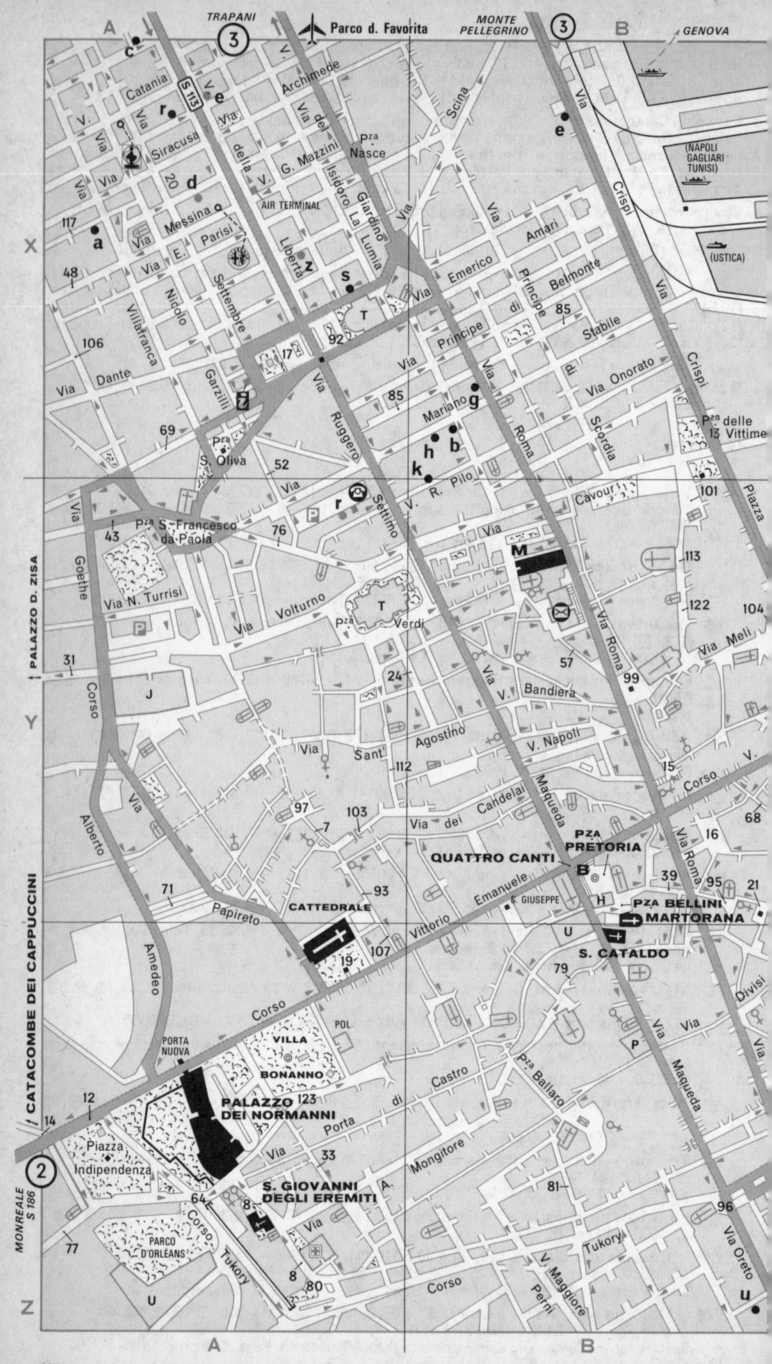
TRAPANI
Parco d. Favorita
MONTE PELLEGRINO
GENOVA
(NAPOLI CAGLIARI TUNISI)
(USTICA)
AIR TERMINAL
PALAZZO D. ZISA
CATACOMBE DEI CAPPUCCINI
MONREALE S 186
QUATTRO CANTI
Pza PRETORIA
Pza BELLINI
MARTORANA
S. CATALDO
S. GIUSEPPE
CATTEDRALE
VILLA BONANNO
PORTA NUOVA
PALAZZO DEI NORMANNI
S. GIOVANNI DEGLI EREMITI
Piazza Indipendenza
PARCO D'ORLÉANS
Pza delle 13 Vittime
Pza S. Francesco da Paola
Pza S. Oliva
Pza Verdi
Pza Nasce
Pza Ballarò
Via Roma
Via Maqueda
Corso Vittorio Emanuele
Via Crispi
Via Cavour
Via Volturno
Corso Alberto Amedeo
Corso Tukory
Via Oreto

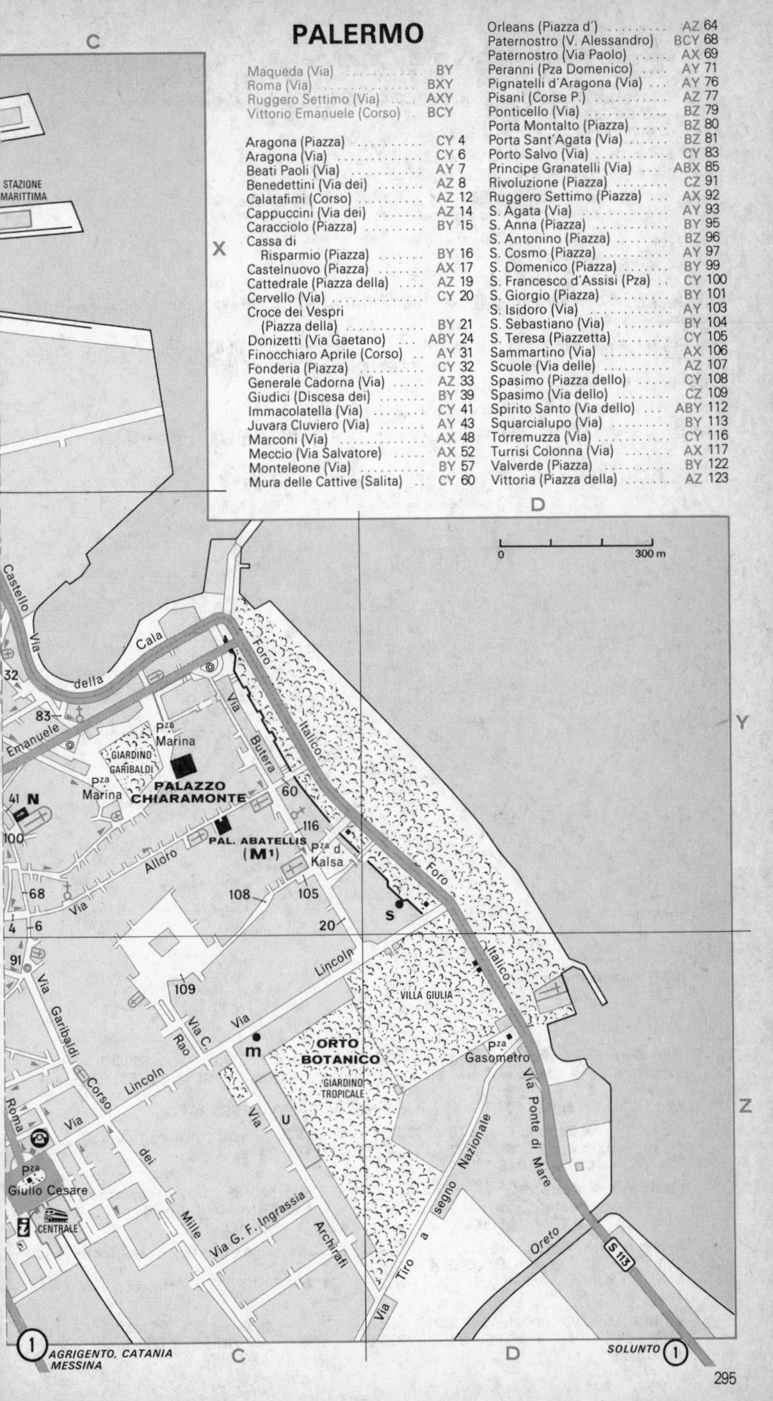

PALERMO

Maqueda (Via) . . . . BY
Roma (Via) . . . . BXY
Ruggero Settimo (Via) . . . . AXY
Vittorio Emanuele (Corso) . . BCY

Aragona (Piazza) . . . . CY 4
Aragona (Via) . . . . CY 6
Beati Paoli (Via) . . . . AY 7
Benedettini (Via dei) . . . . AZ 8
Calatafimi (Corso) . . . . AZ 12
Cappuccini (Via dei) . . . . AZ 14
Caracciolo (Piazza) . . . . BY 15
Cassa di Risparmio (Piazza) . . . . BY 16
Castelnuovo (Piazza) . . . . AX 17
Cattedrale (Piazza della) . . . . AZ 19
Cervello (Via) . . . . CY 20
Croce dei Vespri (Piazza della) . . . . BY 21
Donizetti (Via Gaetano) . . . ABY 24
Finocchiaro Aprile (Corso) . . AY 31
Fonderia (Piazza) . . . . CY 32
Generale Cadorna (Via) . . . . . AZ 33
Giudici (Discesa dei) . . . . BY 39
Immacolatella (Via) . . . . CY 41
Juvara Cluviero (Via) . . . . AY 43
Marconi (Via) . . . . AX 48
Meccio (Via Salvatore) . . . . . . AX 52
Monteleone (Via) . . . . BY 57
Mura delle Cattive (Salita) . . CY 60
Orleans (Piazza d') . . . . AZ 64
Paternostro (V. Alessandro) BCY 68
Paternostro (Via Paolo) . . . . . AX 69
Peranni (Pza Domenico) . . . . AY 71
Pignatelli d'Aragona (Via) . . . AY 76
Pisani (Corse P.) . . . . AZ 77
Ponticello (Via) . . . . BZ 79
Porta Montalto (Piazza) . . . . . BZ 80
Porta Sant'Agata (Via) . . . . . . BZ 81
Porto Salvo (Via) . . . . CY 83
Principe Granatelli (Via) . . . ABX 85
Rivoluzione (Piazza) . . . . CZ 91
Ruggero Settimo (Piazza) . . . AX 92
S. Agata (Via) . . . . AY 93
S. Anna (Piazza) . . . . BY 95
S. Antonino (Piazza) . . . . BZ 96
S. Cosmo (Piazza) . . . . AY 97
S. Domenico (Piazza) . . . . BY 99
S. Francesco d'Assisi (Pza) . . CY 100
S. Giorgio (Piazza) . . . . BY 101
S. Isidoro (Via) . . . . AY 103
S. Sebastiano (Via) . . . . BY 104
S. Teresa (Piazzetta) . . . . CY 105
Sammartino (Via) . . . . AX 106
Scuole (Via delle) . . . . AZ 107
Spasimo (Piazza dello) . . . . . CY 108
Spasimo (Via dello) . . . . CZ 109
Spirito Santo (Via dello) . . . ABY 112
Squarcialupo (Via) . . . . BY 113
Torremuzza (Via) . . . . CY 116
Turrisi Colonna (Via) . . . . . . AX 117
Valverde (Piazza) . . . . BY 122
Vittoria (Piazza della) . . . . . . AZ 123

XXX **Chamade,** via Torrearsa 22 ✉ 90139 ☎ 322204 – ▤
seasonal. AX **z**

XXX **Trattoria Trittico,** largo Montalto 7 ✉ 90147 ☎ 294809, « Outdoor summer service » – ▤ Ⓟ. AE ⓞ VISA. ✻
closed Sunday – **M** a la carte 32/48000. by ③

XXX **Friend's Bar,** via Brunelleschi 138 ✉ 90145 ☎ 201401 – ▤. AE ⓞ
closed Monday and August – **M** a la carte 27/39000. by ③

XX **Regine,** via Trapani 4/a ✉ 90141 ☎ 586566 – ▤. AE ⓞ VISA. ✻
closed Sunday and August – **M** a la carte 25/32000. AX **d**

North is at the top on all town plans.

TAORMINA 98039 Messina 988 ㊲ – pop. 10 473 alt. 250 – Health and seaside resort (at Mazzarò) – ⊛ 0942.

See : Picturesque site★★★ – Greek Theatre★★ (≤★★★) B – Public gardens★★ B – Corso Umberto★ A – Piazza 9 Aprile (≤★★) A – Belvedere★ A – Castle★ (≤★) A.

Exc : Etna★★★.

ℹ largo Santa Caterina (Corvaja palace) ☎ 23243, Telex 980062.

Catania 52 ② – Enna 135 ② – Messina 52 ① – Palermo 255 ② – Siracusa 111 ② – Trapani 359 ②.

TAORMINA

Umberto (Corso) .... A
Dionisio (Via) .... A 2
Duomo (Piazza) .... A 3
Rotabile Castelmola .... A 5
S. Antonio (Piazza) .... A 6
Vittorio Emanuele (Pza) .... B 8
9 Aprile (Piazza) .... A 9

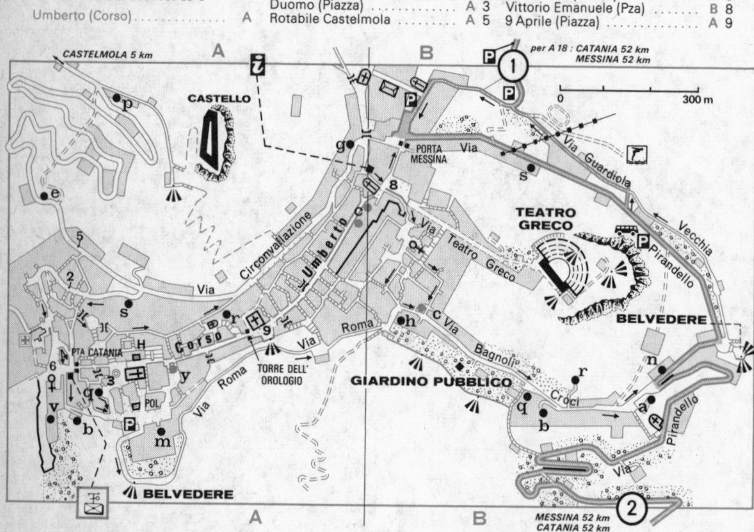

🏨 **San Domenico Palace** ⛰, piazza San Domenico 5 ☎ 23701, Telex 980013, « Floral garden with ≤ sea, coast and Etna », ⛱ heated – |♦| ▤ TV ☎ – 🏃. AE ⓞ E VISA. ✻ rest
M 60000 – **117 rm** ☕ 207/354000 apartments 474/534000 – P 250/310000. A **m**

🏨 **Jolly** ⛰, via Bagnoli Croce 75 ☎ 23312, Telex 980028, ≤ sea, coast and Etna, « ⛱ on panoramic terrace », 🪑 – |♦| ▤ Ⓟ – 🏃. AE ⓞ E VISA. ✻ rest
M 45000 – **103 rm** ☕ 115/170000. B **q**

🏨 **Excelsior Palace** ⛰, via Toselli 8 ☎ 23975, Telex 980185, ≤ sea, coast and Etna, « Little park, heated ⛱ on panoramic terrace » – |♦| ▤ TV ☎ – 🏃. ⓞ VISA. ✻ rest
March-15 November – **M** 30000 – **89 rm** ☕ 65/125000 – P 110000. A **v**

🏨 **Bristol Park Hotel,** via Bagnoli Croce 92 ☎ 23006, Telex 980005, ≤ sea, coast and Etna, ⛱ – |♦| ▤ ☎ 🚗. AE ⓞ E VISA. ✻ rest
March-October – **M** 40000 – ☕ 18000 – **54 rm** 69/138000 apartments 165000 – P 130/150000. B **r**

🏨 **Vello d'Oro,** via Fazzello 2 ☎ 23789, Telex 980186, ≤ – |♦| ▤. ⓞ VISA. ✻ rest A **r**
15 March-October – **M** *(dinner only)* 23000 – ☕ 7000 – **57 rm** 38/64000 - dinner included 62000.

Villa Paradiso, via Roma 2 ✆ 23922, ← sea, coast and Etna – |‡| ▤ TV ⇔wc ⫛wc ☎ ♿. AE ◑ E VISA. ✻ rest B **h**
closed November-18 December – **M** 27/31000 – ☕ 10000 – **33 rm** 46/89000 – P 78/96000.

Villa Fiorita without rest., via Pirandello 39 ✆ 24122, ← sea and coast, 🏊, ⛱ – |‡| ▤ TV ⇔wc ⫛wc ☏ ⌂. AE B **s**
☕ 5500 – **24 rm** 68000.

Villa Riis ⛢, via Rizzo 13 ✆ 24874, ← sea, coast and Etna, ⛱ – |‡| ▤ ⇔wc ⫛wc ☎ ♿ Ⓟ. AE E VISA. ✻ rest A **b**
April-October – **M** *(dinner only)* a la carte 26/35000 – ☕ 10000 – **30 rm** 42/85000.

Sole-Castello, Rotabile Castelmola 83 ✆ 28036, ← sea, coast and Etna, 🏊, 🎾 – |‡| ▤ ⇔wc ⫛wc ☏ ⌂ Ⓟ. ✻ A **p**
15 March-October – **M** *(dinner only)* – **57 rm** (dinner included) 60/70000.

Continental, via Dionisio 1 ✆ 23805, ⛱ – ▤ ⇔wc ⫛wc ☏. AE ◑ E VISA. ✻ rest
M *(dinner only)* 18/25000 – ☕ 7000 – **43 rm** 38/65000 - dinner included 50/60000, ▤ 4500. A **s**

Villa Belvedere without rest., via Bagnoli Croce 79 ✆ 23791, ← gardens, sea and Etna, « 🏊 on panoramic terrace », ⛱ – |‡| ⇔wc ⫛wc ☏ Ⓟ. E VISA B **b**
23 March-October – **42 rm** ☕ 51/91000.

Villa San Michele without rest., via Damiano Rosso 11 bis ✆ 24327, ← sea and bay of Naxos – |‡| ▤ ⇔wc ⫛wc ☏. AE ◑ E VISA A **q**
23 rm ☕ 47/80000.

Palazzo Santa Caterina, without rest., via Bagnoli Croce 128 ✆ 23428 – |‡| ▤ ⇔wc ☏ B **n**
22 rm.

La Campanella without rest., via Circonvallazione 3 ✆ 23381, ← – ⇔wc ⫛wc. ✻ A **g**
12 rm ☕ 35/60000.

Villa Kristina, Rotabile Castelmola ✆ 28366, ←, 🏊 – |‡| ▤ ⇔wc ⫛wc ☏ ⌂. AE ◑ E VISA. ✻ rest A **e**
closed January – **32 rm** (dinner included) 40/45000.

Villa Carlotta without rest., via Pirandello 81 ✆ 23732, ← sea and coast, ⛱ – ▤ ⇔wc ⫛wc ☎ B **a**
15 March-October – **21 rm** ☕ 33/63000, ▤ 5500.

XX **La Griglia,** corso Umberto 54 ✆ 23980 – AE ◑ VISA. ✻ A **c**
closed Tuesday – **M** a la carte 24/41000.

XX **Giova Rosy Senior,** corso Umberto 38 ✆ 24411, ⛱ – ✻ A **c**
closed Monday and 8 January-14 February – **M** a la carte 26/40000.

XX **Quattropini,** contrada Sant'Antonio ✆ 24832 – AE ◑ E VISA. ✻ 1 km by ①
closed Monday – **M** a la carte 25/35000.

X U' Bossu, via Bagnoli Croci 50 ✆ 23311 B **c**
M booking essential.

X **Ciclope,** corso Umberto ✆ 23263, ⛱ – ▤. ✻ A **y**
closed Wednesday and 10 to 31 January – **M** a la carte 20/30000.

at Capo Taormina by ② : 3 km – ✉ **98030** Mazzarò :

Grande Alb. Capotaormina, ✆ 24000, Telex 980147, ← sea and coast, 🏊, ⛵ – |‡| ▤ ☎ ⌂ Ⓟ – 🏛. AE ◑ E VISA. ✻ rest
15 April-October – **M** a la carte 63/84000 – ☕ 19000 – **210 rm** 143/226000 apartments 308/340000 – P 193000.

at Castelmola NW : 5 km A – alt. 550 – ✉ **98030** :

X **Il Faro,** contrada Pretalia ✆ 28193, ← sea and coast, ⛱ – Ⓟ. AE VISA
closed Wednesday – **M** a la carte 16/24000.

at Mazzarò by ② : 5,5 km – ✉ **98030** :

Mazzarò Sea Palace, ✆ 24004, Telex 980041, ← small bay, 🏊 heated, ⛵ – |‡| ▤ TV ☎ ⌂ – 🏛. AE ◑ VISA. ✻ rest
April-October – **M** 60000 – ☕ 20000 – **81 rm** 180/300000 apartments 500/600000 – P 230000.

Villa Sant'Andrea, ✆ 23125, Telex 980077, ← small bay, « Shaded terraces », ⛵, ⛱ – ▤ Ⓟ. AE ◑ E VISA. ✻
M 50/55000 – ☕ 15000 – **48 rm** 67/135000, ▤ 5000 – P 180000.

X **Il Pescatore,** ✆ 23460, ← sea and cliffs – Ⓟ
3 March-October; closed Monday – **M** a la carte 20/39000.

X **Il Delfino-da Angelo,** ✆ 23004, ← small bay, ⛱ – AE ◑ E VISA
15 March-October – **M** a la carte 20/31000.

X **Da Giovanni,** ✆ 23531, ← sea – AE ◑ VISA. ✻
closed Monday – **M** a la carte 27/42000.

☛ *Inclusion in the* **Michelin Guide** *cannot be achieved by pulling strings or by offering favours.*

TURIN (TORINO) 10100 P 988 ⑫ – pop. 1 035 383 alt. 239 – ☎ 011.

See : Piazza San Carlo★★ CXY – Academy of Science (Egyptian Museum★★, Sabauda Gallery★★) CX **M** – Palazzo Madama★ (Museum of Ancient Art★) CX **A** – Royal Palace★ (Royal Armoury★) CDVX – Palazzo Carignano (Risorgimento Museum★) CX **M2** – Cathedral of St. John★ (the sacred relic of the Holy Shroud★★★) CVX – Mole Antonelliana★ (※★★) DX – Carlo Biscaretti di Ruffia Motor Museum★ – Valentino Park (model medieval village★) CDZ.

Envir. : Superga : Basilica★ (≤★★★, royal tombs★) E : 10 km – Tour to the pass, Colle della Maddalena★ (≤★★) E : 10 km – Stupinigi Palace★ (or Palazzina Mauriziana) SW : 11 km.

18 and 9 I Roveri (March-November; closed Monday) at La Mandria ✉ 10070 Fiano ☎ 9235667, by ① : 18 km;

18 and 9 Torino (closed January, February and Monday), at Fiano ✉ 10070 ☎ 9235440, by ① : 20 km;

9 of Stupinigi, corso Unione Sovietica 506/A ✉ 10135 ☎ 3439975.

✈ Turin Airport by ① : 15 km ☎ 5778361 – Alitalia, via Lagrange 35 ✉ 10123 ☎ 55911.

☎ 537766.

ℹ via Roma 226 (piazza C.L.N.) ✉ 10121 ☎ 535889 – Porta Nuova Railway station ✉ 10125 ☎ 531327.

A.C.I. via Giovanni Giolitti 15 ✉ 10123 ☎ 5779.

Roma 669 ⑦ – Briançon 108 ⑪ – Chambéry 209 ⑪ – Genève 252 ③ – Genova 170 ⑦ – Grenoble 224 ⑪ – Milano 140 ③ – Nice 220 ⑨.

Plans on following pages

Jolly Principi di Piemonte, via Gobetti 15 ✉ 10123 ☎ 519693, Telex 221120 – 🛗 ▤ TV ☎ – 🏃. AE ⓓ E VISA. ⛔ rest CY **z**
M 45000 – **107 rm** ☕ 178/226000.

Turin Palace Hotel, via Sacchi 8 ✉ 10128 ☎ 515511, Telex 221411 – 🛗 ▤ TV ☎ ♿ 🚗 – 🏃. AE ⓓ E VISA. ⛔ rest CY **u**
M a la carte 41/67000 – ☕ 18000 – **125 rm** 190/230000 apartment 300000 – P 207/282000.

Jolly Hotel Ligure, piazza Carlo Felice 85 ✉ 10123 ☎ 55641, Telex 220167 – 🛗 ▤ ☎ – 🏃. AE ⓓ E VISA. ⛔ rest CY **b**
M 43000 – **156 rm** ☕ 168/214000.

Jolly Ambasciatori, corso Vittorio Emanuele 104 ✉ 10121 ☎ 5752, Telex 221296 – 🛗 ▤ TV ☎ 🚗 – 🏃. AE ⓓ E VISA. ⛔ rest BX **a**
M 43000 – **197 rm** ☕ 138/170000.

Gd H. Sitea, via Carlo Alberto 35 ✉ 10123 ☎ 5570171, Telex 220229 – 🛗 ▤ TV ☎ – 🏃. AE ⓓ E VISA. ⛔ rest CY **t**
M a la carte 38/60000 – ☕ 13000 – **116 rm** 140/180000 apartments 200000.

City without rest., via Juvarra 25 ✉ 10122 ☎ 540546, Telex 216228 – 🛗 ▤ TV ☎ – 🏃. AE ⓓ VISA. ⛔ BV **e**
closed August, Christmas and New Year's Day – ☕ 13000 – **44 rm** 140/190000.

Concord, via Lagrange 47 ✉ 10123 ☎ 5576756, Telex 221323 – 🛗 ▤ TV ☎ 🚗 – 🏃. AE ⓓ E VISA. ⛔ rest CY **s**
M 32/45000 – **140 rm** ☕ 147/184000 apartments 210000 – P 155000.

Royal, corso Regina Margherita 249 ✉ 10144 ☎ 748444, Telex 220259, ✂ – 🛗 ▤ ☎ 🚗 – 🏃 – **65 rm**. BV **u**

Stazione e Genova without rest., via Sacchi 14 ✉ 10128 ☎ 545323, Telex 224242 – 🛗 TV ⛀wc ⛆wc ☎ – 🏃. AE ⓓ E VISA. ⛔ CZ **b**
44 rm ☕ 69/102000.

Alexandra without rest., lungo Dora Napoli 14 ✉ 10152 ☎ 858327, Telex 221562 – 🛗 ▤ TV ⛀wc ⛆wc ☎ 🚗. AE ⓓ E VISA CV **c**
50 rm ☕ 93/120000.

Victoria without rest., via Nino Costa 4 ✉ 10123 ☎ 553710, Telex 212580 – 🛗 ⛀wc ⛆wc ☎. AE ⓓ VISA. ⛔ CY **v**
☕ 7000 – **65 rm** 57/79000.

Genio without rest., corso Vittorio Emanuele 47 ✉ 10125 ☎ 6505771, Telex 220308 – 🛗 TV ⛀wc ⛆wc ☎ ♿. AE ⓓ E VISA CYZ **w**
☕ 9000 – **80 rm** 58/80000.

Luxor without rest., corso Stati Uniti 7 ✉ 10128 ☎ 531529 – 🛗 TV ⛀wc ⛆wc ☎. AE ⓓ VISA CZ **s**
☕ 9000 – **63 rm** 66/95000.

Venezia without rest., via 20 Settembre 70 ✉ 10122 ☎ 513384 – 🛗 ⛀wc ⛆wc ☎ 🚗 – 🏃. AE ⓓ E VISA CX **r**
☕ 8000 – **66 rm** 57/81000.

Gran Mogol without rest., via Guarini 2 ✉ 10123 ☎ 513360 – 🛗 ⛀wc ⛆wc ☎. AE ⓓ E VISA CY **r**
closed August – ☕ 9000 – **45 rm** 58/80000.

Piemontese without rest., via Berthollet 21 ✉ 10125 ☎ 6698101 – 🛗 ⛀wc ⛆wc ☎ Ⓟ. AE ⓓ E VISA. ⛔ CZ **x**
☕ 5000 – **33 rm** 43/58000.

Cairo without rest., via La Loggia 6 ✉ 10134 ☎ 352003 – 🛗 ⛆wc ☎ Ⓟ. ⛔ by ⑩
closed 1 to 28 August – ☕ 5500 – **35 rm** 45/60000.

🏨 **Eden** without rest., via Donizetti 22 ✉ 10126 ℘ 659545 – |‡| ⇔wc ⋒wc ☎ ♿. VISA
closed August – ☐ 5000 – **27 rm** 45/60000. CZ **f**

🏨 **Cristallo** without rest., corso Traiano 28/9 ✉ 10135 ℘ 618383 – ⋒wc ☎ by ⑩
closed 3 to 26 August – ☐ 5000 – **20 rm** 43/59000.

XXXXX ❀ **Villa Sassi-El Toulà** with rm, strada al Traforo del Pino 47 ✉ 10132 ℘ 890556, « 18C Country house in a spacious park » – ▤ rest ⇔wc ⋒wc ☎ ℗ – 🏊. AE ⓓ E VISA. ✻ by ⑤
closed August – **M** *(closed Sunday)* a la carte 45/67000 – ☐ 15000 – **12 rm** 170/230000 apartment 370000 – P 220/230000
Spec. Insalata di mare tiepida, Tegoline alla Cardinale, Filetto di vitello al Salignac. **Wines** Arneis, Barbaresco.

XXXX ❀ **Del Cambio,** piazza Carignano 2 ✉ 10123 ℘ 546690, Elegant traditional decor, « 19C Decoration » – ▤. AE ⓓ VISA. ✻ CX **a**
closed Sunday and 27 July-27 August – **M** (booking essential) a la carte 38/55000 (15%)
Spec. Gamberetti all'olio di basilico, Risotto verde allo Spumante, Brasato al Barolo. **Wines** Bianco dei Roeri, Dolcetto.

XXXX **Tiffany,** piazza Solferino 16/h ✉ 10121 ℘ 540538 – ▤. ✻ CX **x**
closed Saturday lunch, Sunday and August – **M** a la carte 37/60000 (15%).

XXX ❀ **Vecchia Lanterna,** corso Re Umberto 21 ✉ 10128 ℘ 537047, Elegant installation – ▤. AE E VISA. ✻ CY **x**
closed Saturday lunch, Sunday and August – **M** (booking essential) a la carte 50/70000
Spec. Patè di fegato d'oca tartufato, Tortellone d'astaco all'essenza di gamberetti, Carrè d'agnello in salsa bigarrade. **Wines** Arneis, Brachetto.

XXX ❀ **Al Gatto Nero,** corso Filippo Turati 14 ✉ 10128 ℘ 590414, Typical Tuscan decor and cuisine – ▤. AE ⓓ. ✻ BZ **z**
closed Sunday and August – **M** a la carte 40/60000
Spec. Insalata di pesce Gatto Nero, Costata di manzo alla fiorentina, Misto mare alla brace. **Wines** bianco e rosso Montecarlo.

XXX **Al Saffi,** via Aurelio Saffi 2 ✉ 10138 ℘ 442213, Elegant installation – ▤ AV **n**
closed Sunday and August – **M** (booking essential) a la carte 45/55000.

XXX **Due Lampioni da Carlo,** via Carlo Alberto 45 ✉ 10123 ℘ 546721 – ▤. ✻ CY **n**
closed Sunday and August – **M** a la carte 41/62000.

XX **La Smarrita,** corso Unione Sovietica 244 ✉ 10134 ℘ 390657 – ▤. AE ⓓ VISA. ✻ by ⑩
closed Monday and 3 to 27 August – **M** (booking essential) a la carte 32/69000.

XX **La Cloche,** strada al Traforo del Pino 106 ✉ 10132 ℘ 894213, Typical atmosphere – ▤ ℗ – 🏊. AE ⓓ VISA. ✻ by ⑤
closed Monday – **M** (menu surprise) 33/61000.

XX **Al Dragone,** via Pomba 14 ✉ 10123 ℘ 547019 – ✻ CY **m**
closed Saturday, Sunday and August – **M** a la carte 34/45000.

XX **Due Mondi-da Ilio,** via San Pio V n° 3 ✉ 10125 ℘ 6692056 – ▤. AE VISA CZ **k**
closed Monday and 25 July-20 August – **M** a la carte 25/44000.

XX **Al Bue Rosso,** corso Casale 10 ✉ 10131 ℘ 830753 – ▤. AE ⓓ VISA DY **e**
closed Monday, Saturday lunch and August – **M** a la carte 26/41000 (10%).

XX **Montecarlo,** via San Francesco da Paola 37 ✉ 10123 ℘ 541234 – ▤. AE ⓓ VISA ✻ DY **c**
closed Saturday lunch, Sunday and August – **M** (booking essential) a la carte 33/47000.

XX **Al Camin,** corso Francia 339 ✉ 10142 ℘ 724033, Neo rustic rest. – ▤ by ⑪
closed Saturday lunch, Sunday and August – **M** a la carte 31/47000.

XX **Al Ghibellin Fuggiasco,** via Tunisi 50 ✉ 10134 ℘ 390750 – ▤. AE ⓓ E VISA BZ **b**
closed Saturday, Sunday dinner and August – **M** a la carte 25/42000.

XX **Il Papavero,** corso Raffaello 5 ✉ 10126 ℘ 6505168, 佘 – ▤. AE ⓓ VISA CZ **d**
closed Sunday and 20 June-10 July – **M** (booking essential) a la carte 30/48000.

X **Porta Rossa,** corso Appio Claudio 227 ✉ 10146 ℘ 790963, 佘 – AE VISA. ✻ by ⑪
closed Saturday lunch, Sunday and August – **M** (booking essential) a la carte 28/53000.

X **La Cuccagna,** corso Casale 371 ✉ 10132 ℘ 890069, Typical Romagnese rest. per ⑤
closed Monday and August – **M** (menu surprise) 20/30000.

X **Ostu Bacu,** corso Vercelli 226 ✉ 10155 ℘ 264579, Modern Piedmontese trattoria – ▤
closed Sunday and 13 July-15 August – **M** a la carte 30/49000. by corso Vercelli DV

X **C'era una volta,** corso Vittorio Emanuele 41 ✉ 10125 ℘ 655498, Typical Piedmontese rest. – ▤. AE ⓓ E VISA CZ **k**
closed lunch, Sunday and August – **M** (typical menu) (booking essential) 40000.

X **Da Mauro,** via Maria Vittoria 21 ✉ 10123 ℘ 8397811, Tuscan habitués' trattoria – ▤. ✻ DY **h**
closed Monday and July – **M** a la carte 16/30000.

X **Trattoria della Posta,** strada Mongreno 16 ✉ 10132 ℘ 890193, Habitués' trattoria Piedmontese cheese – ▤. ✻ by ⑤
closed Sunday dinner, Monday and 10 July-20 August – **M** a la carte 21/31000.

X **Da Giudice,** strada Valsalice 78 ✉ 10131 ℘ 6692488, « Summer service under pergola » – ℗. AE ⓓ VISA. ✻ by ⑤
closed Tuesday, Wednesday lunch and August – **M** a la carte 24/40000.

TORINO
Carlo Felice (Piazza) ..... CY 16
Roma (Via) ..... CXY
S. Carlo (Piazza) ..... CXY
Alfieri (Via) ..... CY 5
Cadorna (Lungo Po L.) ... DY 12
Carignano (Piazza) ..... CX 13
Carlo Emanuele II (Pza) .. DY 15
Casale (Corso) ..... DY 17
Castello (Piazza) ..... CX 19
Cesare Augusto (Piazza) ..... CV 23
Consolata (Via della) ..... CV 25
Diaz (Lungo Po A.) ..... DY 29
Gran Madre di Dio (Piazza) ..... DY 33
Milano (Via) ..... CV 40
Ponte Vittorio Emanuele I DY 48
Repubblica (Piazza della) ..... CV 53
S. Francesco d'Assisi (Via) ..... CX 55
Solferino (Piazza) ..... CX 64
Vitt. Emanuele II (Lgo) .. BCY 75
4 Marzo (Via) ..... CX 77
20 Settembre (Via) ..... CXY 78
A
B
A 5 AOSTA
Via Verolengo
Via Potenza
Val della Torre
Via Borgaro
Via Nole
Corso Mortara
Via Orvieto
Corso Svizzera
Riparia
Via Pianezza
Corso Livorno
Dora
Corso Appio Claudio
Via Michele Lessona
V
Via Tassoni
Co Regina Margherita
Corso Umbria
Via Svizzera
Via Nicola Fabrizi
Via San Donato
Via Cibrario
Via Giacomo Medici
Corso Francia
P^za Chiron
P^za Rivoli
S 25 : SUSA BRIANÇON
A 6-A 21
Via d'Acaja
Via Principi
Via Inghilterra
P^za Bernini
Via E. Cialdini
Via Duchessa Jolanda
P^ZA SUSA
Corso Trapani
Via Racconigi
P^za Adriano
Via Fréjus
Via Cesana
Corso Ferrucci
Via G. Cavalli
Corso Vittorio Emanuele II
Corso Vinzaglio
POL.
X
Via Frassineto
Via Nanni
Corso Francesco
Via Boggio
Via Vigone
Via Di Nanni
P^za Sabotino
Via Monginevro
Carlo
Via Castelfidardo
Corso Duca degli Abruzzi
Corso Stati
Y
Paolo
Peschiera
Via San
Corso P.
75
10
11
1
2

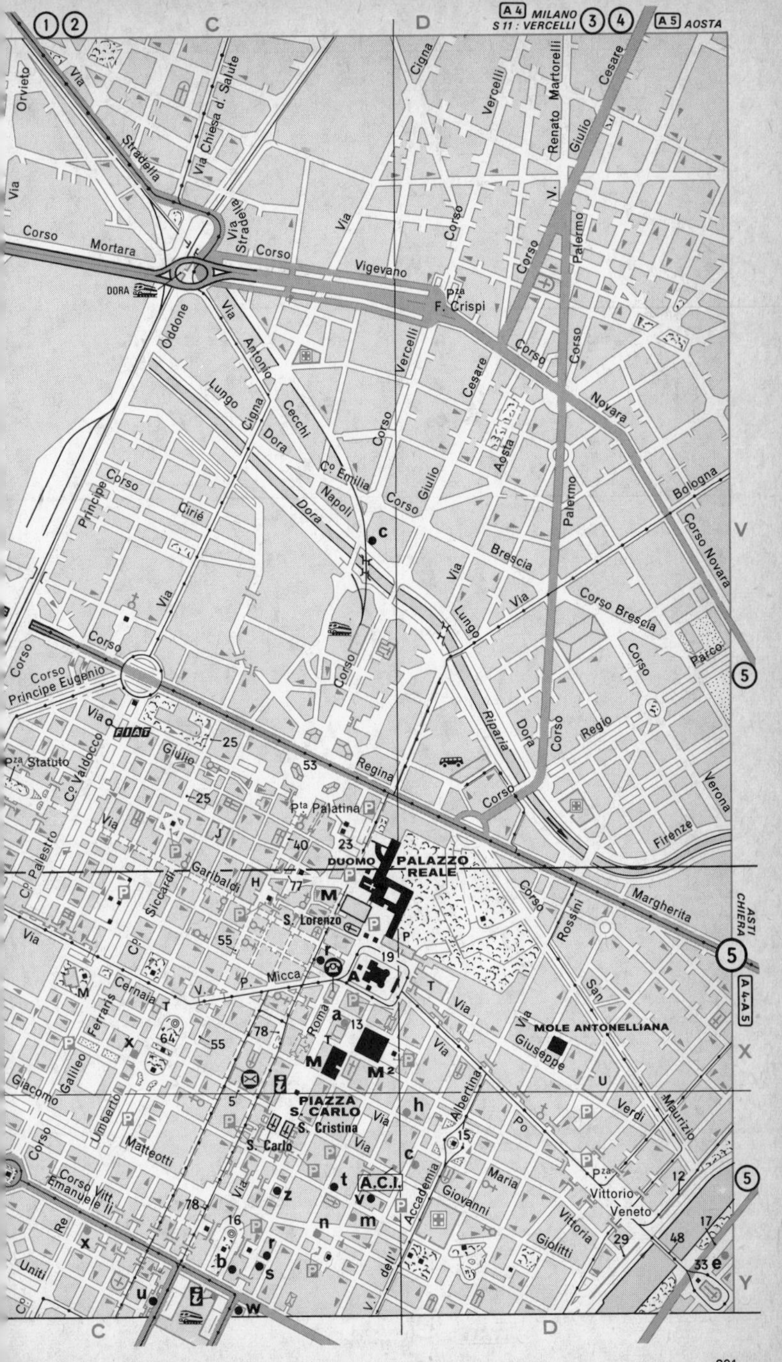
A 4 MILANO
S 11 : VERCELLI
A 5 AOSTA
C
D
V
X
Y
Via Orvieto
Via Stradella
Via Chiesa d. Salute
Cigna
Vercelli
Renato Martorelli
Giulio Cesare
Corso Mortara
DORA
Via Stradella
Corso Vigevano
Pza F. Crispi
Corso Palermo
Corso Novara
Via Oddone
Via Antonio Cecchi
Lungo Dora
Cigna
Corso Vercelli
Cesare
Aosta
Corso Giulio
Co Emilia
Corso Napoli
Dora
Corso Principe
Corso Ciriè
Via Brescia
Lungo
Via
Corso Brescia
Bologna
Corso Novara
Parco
Corso
Corso Principe Eugenio
Via
FIAT
Corso Regina
Riparia
Dora
Corso Regio
Verona
Pza Statuto
Co Valdocco
Giulio
25
53
Pta Palatina
Corso
Firenze
40
23
DUOMO
PALAZZO REALE
Co Palestro
Garibaldi
H
77
M
S. Lorenzo
Co Siccardi
Corso Margherita
Rossini
ASTI CHIERA
A 4-A 5
55
19
Via Cernaia
P. Micca
r
A
T
Via San
a
13
Roma
MOLE ANTONELLIANA
Via Giuseppe
M
x
64
78
55
Ferraris
Galileo
M²
U
Verdi
Maurizio
Giacomo
PIAZZA S. CARLO
h
Via
S. Cristina
Albertina
Po
S. Carlo
15
Corso Umberto
Matteotti
c
Maria
Pza Vittorio Veneto
12
Corso Vitt. Emanuele II
t
A.C.I.
v
Giovanni
Vittoria
17
Re
78
z
16
n
m
Accademia
48
Giolitti
29
x
r
dell'
33
e
Uniti
b
s
Co
u
w
V.
5

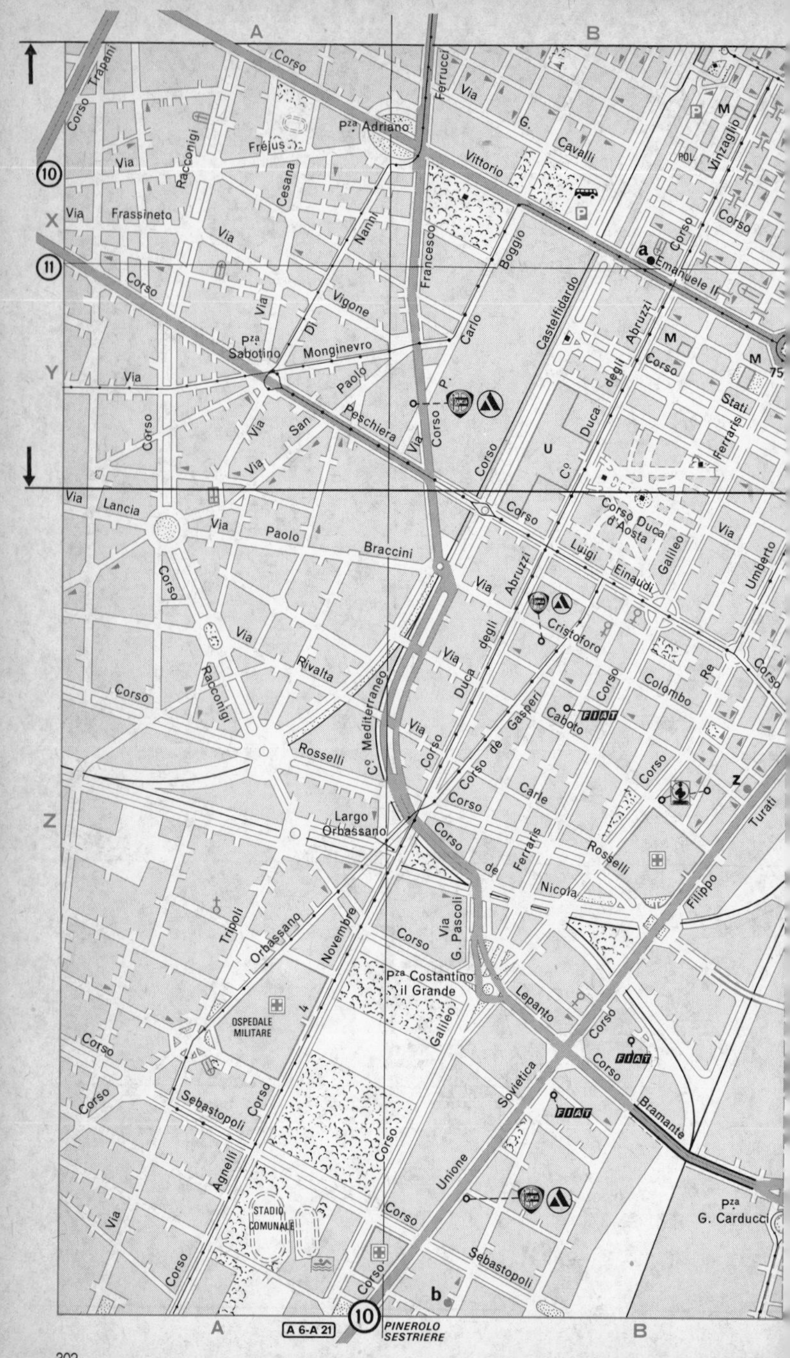

A
B
X
Y
Z
10
11
Corso Trapani
Corso
Via Racconigi
Via Frassineto
Via Frejus
Via Cesana
P^za Adriano
Corso Vittorio Emanuele II
Via Ferrucci
Via G. Cavalli
Corso Vinzaglio
POL.
P
M
Via Nanni
Corso Francesco
Via Vigone
Via Di Monginevro
P^za Sabotino
Corso Carlo Boggio
Via Castelfidardo
Corso degli Abruzzi
Corso Stati
Via Ferraris
Corso Duca
Corso Peschiera
Via San Paolo
Via P.
U
Co.
Corso Duca d'Aosta
Corso Luigi Einaudi
Via Galileo
Via Umberto
Corso Re
Via Lancia
Via Paolo Braccini
Corso Racconigi
Via Rivalta
Via Abruzzi
Via Cristoforo Colombo
Via Duca degli
Corso Caboto
Corso de Gasperi
Via Carle
Corso Turati
Corso Filippo
Corso Rosselli
Via Rosselli
C^o Mediterraneo
Largo Orbassano
Corso de Ferraris
Corso Nicola
Via G. Pascoli
Via Tripoli
Corso Orbassano
Corso 4 Novembre
P^za Costantino il Grande
Corso Galileo
Corso Lepanto
Corso Sovietica
Corso Unione
Corso Bramante
P^za G. Carducci
OSPEDALE MILITARE
Corso Sebastopoli
Corso Agnelli
STADIO COMUNALE
Via Corso
Corso Sebastopoli
FIAT
75
a
b
z
A 6-A 21
PINEROLO
SESTRIERE

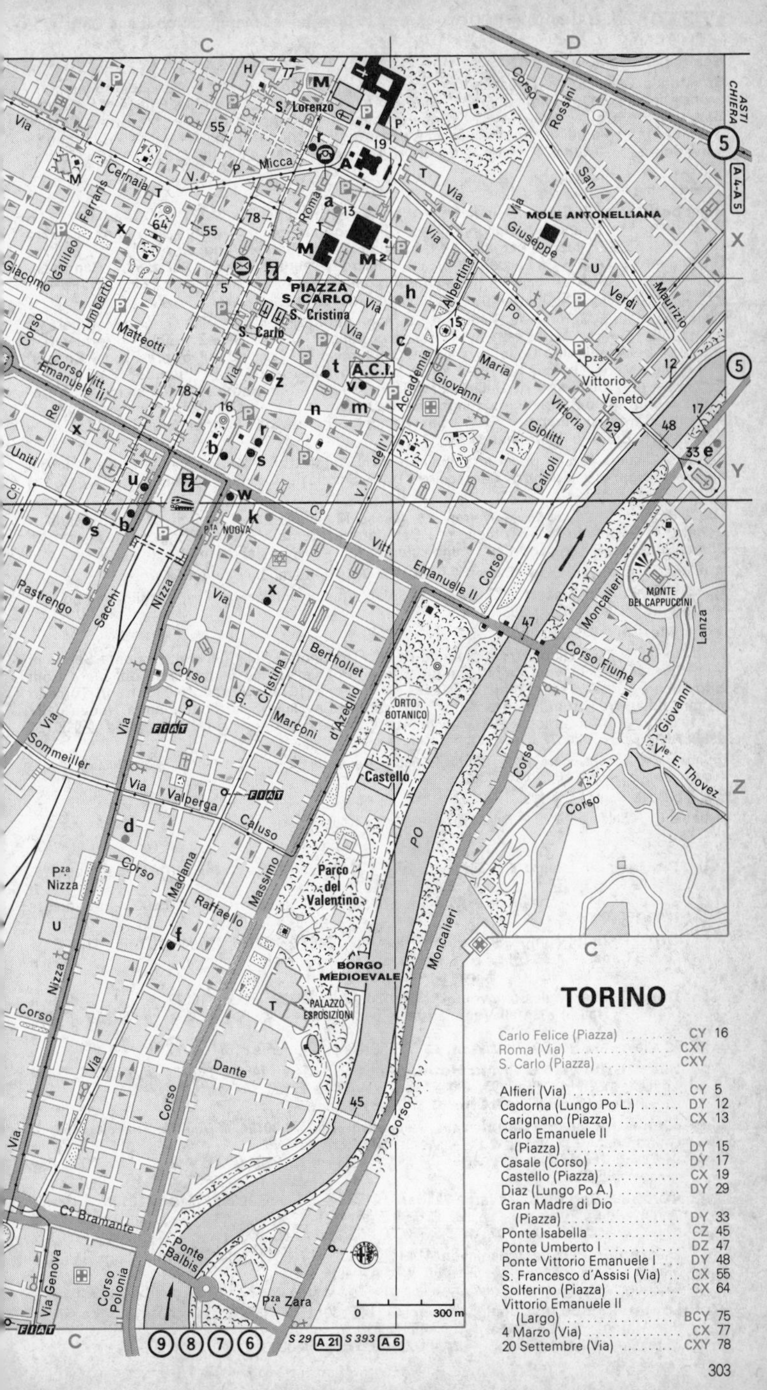

TORINO

Carlo Felice (Piazza)	CY	16
Roma (Via)	CXY	
S. Carlo (Piazza)	CXY	
Alfieri (Via)	CY	5
Cadorna (Lungo Po L.)	DY	12
Carignano (Piazza)	CX	13
Carlo Emanuele II (Piazza)	DY	15
Casale (Corso)	DY	17
Castello (Piazza)	CX	19
Diaz (Lungo Po A.)	DY	29
Gran Madre di Dio (Piazza)	DY	33
Ponte Isabella	CZ	45
Ponte Umberto I	DZ	47
Ponte Vittorio Emanuele I	DY	48
S. Francesco d'Assisi (Via)	CX	55
Solferino (Piazza)	CX	64
Vittorio Emanuele II (Largo)	BCY	75
4 Marzo (Via)	CX	77
20 Settembre (Via)	CXY	78

VENICE (VENEZIA) 30100 P 988 ⑤ – pop. 334 107 – h.s. 15 March-October and Christmas – ✆ 041.

See : St. Marks Square*** FZ :

St. Mark's Basilica*** (mosaics***, Pala d'Oro***, Treasury***, alabaster columns**, bronze horses***) – Campanile** (panorama**, loggetta**) F – Doges Palace*** (Giants' Stairway***, Golden Stairway***, Senate Chamber : Triumph of Venice***, Grand Council Chamber*** : Paradise, Apotheosis of Venice***) – Bridge of Sighs* GZ – Procuratie** (Law Courts) FZ – Clock Tower* FZ **K** - Correr Museum* FZ **M** - Libreria Vecchia* (Old Library) GZ.

Grand Canal*** :

Right bank : Palazzo Corner Spinelli** BTU **D** – Palazzo Grimani** EY **Q** – Cà Loredan** EY **H** – Cà d'Oro*** (Franchetti Gallery**) EX – Palazzo Vendramin** BT **R** – Left bank : Palazzo Dario** BV **S** – Palazzo Rezzonico** (Museum of 18th century Venetian Art*) AU – Palazzo Giustiniano** AU **X** – Cà Foscari** AU **Y** – Palazzo Bernardo** BT **Z** – Palazzo dei Camerlenghi** FX **A** – Palazzo Pesaro** (Museum of Modern Art*) EX – Academy of Fine Arts*** BV – Palazzo Venier dei Leoni (Peggy Guggenheim Collection**) BV **M2.**

Churches : Santa Maria della Salute** (Marriage at Cana***) BV – San Giorgio Maggiore** (campanile ※***, works*** by Tintoretto, stalls**) CV – San Zanipolo** (equestrian statue** by Bartolomeo Colleoni, tombs**, polyptych***, ceiling*** of the Rosary Chapel) GX – Santa Maria Gloriosa dei Frari** (works*** by Titian, triptych***, tombs***) AT – San Zaccaria* (altarpiece*** by Bellini, altarpieces**) GZ – San Sebastiano (ceiling** by Veronese) AU – Angelo Raffaele (paintings* on the organ case) AU – San Pantaleone (ceiling*) AT – Santa Maria dei Miracoli* FG **X** - San Francesco della Vigna (Madonna and Child*) DT – Church of Redentore (altarpiece*) AV.

Schools : Scuola di San Rocco*** (paintings by Tintoretto***) AT – Scuola di San Giorgio degli Schiavoni* (paintings by Carpaccio**) DT – Scuola dei Carmini* (paintings by Tiepolo**) AU.

The Lagoon : The Lido** – Murano** (Glass Museum*** – Church of Santi Maria e Donato**) – Burano** – Torcello** : Cathedral of Santa Maria Assunta** (mosaics***), Church of Santa Fosca* (portico** and columns**) – Riviera del Brenta*.

18 (closed Monday) al Lido Alberoni ✉ 30011 ✆ 731015, 15 mn by boat and 9 km.

✈ Marco Polo di Tessera, NE : 13 km ✆ 661262 (plan : Outskirts p. 3) – Alitalia, campo San Moisè 1483 ✉ 30124 ✆ 700355.

🚗 at Mestre ✆ 929472.

⛴ to Lido - San Nicolò from piazzale Roma (Tronchetto) daily (35 mn); to Punta Sabbioni from Riva degli Schiavoni daily (45 mn); to island of Pellestrina-Santa Maria del Mare from Lido Alberoni daily (1 h 15 mn); to islands of Murano (10 mn), Burano (40 mn) and Torcello (45 mn) daily, from fondamenta Nuove; to Treporti-Cavallino from Fondamenta Nuove daily (1 h 10 mn) – Information : ACTV - Venetian Transport Union, piazzale Roma ✉ 30124 ✆ 5287886, Telex 223487.

ℹ San Marco Ascensione 71/c ✉ 30124 ✆ 26356 – piazzale Roma 540/d ✉ 30125 ✆ 27402 – Santa Lucia Railway station ✉ 30121 ✆ 715016.

A.C.I. piazzale Roma ✉ 30125 ✆ 700300.

Roma 528 ① – Bologna 152 ① – Milano 267 ① – Trieste 158 ①.

Plans on following pages

Cipriani ⛵, isola della Giudecca 10 ✉ 30123 ✆ 707744, Telex 410162, ≤, ⛱ heated, 🎾, – 🛗 ▤ TV ☎ ♿ – 🏊. AE ◑ E VISA. ✻ CV **h**
27 February-10 November – **M** a la carte 90/130000 – **98 rm** ☕ 440/660000 apartments 1000/1600000.

Gritti Palace, campo Santa Maria del Giglio 2467 ✉ 30124 ✆ 794611, Telex 410125, ≤ Grand Canal – 🛗 ▤ TV ☎ ♿ – 🏊. AE ◑ E VISA. ✻ rest EZ **a**
M a la carte 80/100000 – **99 rm** ☕ 442/589000.

Danieli, riva degli Schiavoni 4196 ✉ 30122 ✆ 26480, Telex 410077, ≤ canale di San Marco, « Hall in a small Venetian-style courtyard » – 🛗 ▤ TV ☎ – 🏊. AE ◑ E VISA. ✻ rest GZ **a**
M a la carte 82/116000 – **234 rm** ☕ 308/521000 apartments 816/1111000.

Bauer Grünwald e Grand Hotel, campo San Moisè 1459 ✉ 30124 ✆ 5231520, Telex 410075, ≤ Grand Canal, 🍴 – 🛗 ▤ ♿ – 🏊. AE ◑ E VISA. ✻ rest FZ **h**
M a la carte 65/95000 – **214 rm** ☕ 215/358000 apartments 500/712000.

Monaco e Grand Canal, calle Vallaresso 1325 ✉ 30124 ✆ 700211, Telex 410450, ≤ Grand Canal – 🛗 ▤ TV ☎ ♿ – 🏊. AE VISA. ✻ rest FZ **e**
M Grand Canal Rest. a la carte 70/106000 – **75 rm** ☕ 210/320000 – ½ P 230/280000, low season 175/210000.

Europa e Regina, calle larga 22 Marzo 2159 ✉ 30124 ✆ 700477, Telex 410123, ≤ Grand Canal – 🛗 ▤ TV ☎ ♿ – 🏊. AE ◑ E VISA. ✻ rest FZ **d**
M 59000 – ☕ 20500 – **197 rm** 226/370000 apartments 653000.

Metropole, riva degli Schiavoni 4149 ✉ 30122 ✆ 705044, Telex 410340, ≤ canale di San Marco – 🛗 ▤ TV ☎ – 🏊. AE ◑ E VISA. ✻ rest DU **t**
M Zodiaco Grill *(closed Tuesday)* a la carte 40/70000 – ☕ 12000 – **64 rm** 185/258000.

Londra Palace, riva degli Schiavoni 4171 ✉ 30122 ✆ 700533, Telex 431315, ≤ canale di San Marco – 🛗 ▤ TV ☎ – 🏊. AE ◑ E VISA GZ **t**
M rest. see **Do Leoni** below – ☕ 19000 – **69 rm** 210/360000.

Etap-Park Hotel, giardini Papadopoli ✉ 30125 ✆ 5285394, Telex 410310 – ▤ ☎. AE E VISA. ✻ rest AT **k**
M a la carte 38/55000 – **100 rm** ☕ 170/280000 apartments 380000.

Splendid-Suisse, San Marco-Mercerie 760 ✉ 30124 ✆ 700755, Telex 410590 – ▤ ☎ ♿ – 🏛. AE ① E VISA. ✻ rest FY **n**
M a la carte 41/60000 – **157 rm** ☕ 210/340000 apartments 410/600000 – P 160/210000.

Luna, calle larga dell'Ascensione 1243 ✉ 30124 ✆ 5289840, Telex 410236 – ▤ ☎ – 🏛. AE VISA. ✻ FZ **p**
M 55000 – ☕ 18000 – **125 rm** 192/330000 – P 275/302000, low season 194/216000.

Saturnia-International and Rest. Il Cortile, calle larga 22 Marzo 2398 ✉ 30124 ✆ 708377, Telex 410355, « 14C Patrician building; outdoor rest. service in summer » – ▤ ☎ – 🏛. AE ① E VISA. ✻ rest EZ **n**
M *(closed Wednesday)* a la carte 48/69000 – ☕ 17000 – **97 rm** 180/270000.

Gabrielli Sandwirth, riva degli Schiavoni 4110 ✉ 30122 ✆ 5231580, Telex 410228, ≤ canale di San Marco, « Small courtyard and garden » – ▤ rest. AE ① E VISA. ✻ rest
15 March-15 November – **M** 38/55000 – **110 rm** ☕ 200/330000 – P 150/280000. DU **b**

La Fenice et des Artistes without rest., campiello de la Fenice 1936 ✉ 30124 ✆ 5232333, Telex 411150 – ▤. ✻ EZ **v**
☕ 15000 – **67 rm** 91/130000 apartments 230/260000, ▤ 10000.

Cavalletto e Doge Orseolo, calle del Cavalletto 1107 ✉ 30124 ✆ 5200955, Telex 410684, ≤ – ☎. AE VISA. ✻ FZ **f**
M 60000 – **80 rm** ☕ 155/265000.

Concordia without rest., calle larga San Marco 367 ✉ 30124 ✆ 5206866, Telex 411069 – wc ☎. AE VISA GZ **r**
60 rm ☕ 105/161000.

Santa Chiara without rest., Santa Croce 548 ✆ 706955, Telex 215621 – ▤ wc ☎ ♿. AE VISA. ✻ AT **c**
☕ 10000 – **28 rm** 90/130000.

Flora without rest., calle larga 22 Marzo 2283/a ✉ 30124 ✆ 5205844, « Small flower garden » – ▤ wc wc ☎ ♿. AE ① E VISA EZ **t**
February-15 November – **44 rm** ☕ 100/158000, ▤ 10000.

San Cassiano without rest., Santa Croce 2232 ✉ 30125 ✆ 705477, Telex 223479, ≤ – ▤ wc ☎. AE ①. ✻ EX **f**
35 rm ☕ 104/158000.

Ala without rest., campo Santa Maria del Giglio 2494 ✉ 30124 ✆ 708333, Telex 410275 – ▤ wc wc ☎. AE ① E VISA EZ **e**
80 rm ☕ 108/160000, ▤ 10000.

Casanova without rest., San Marco-Frezzeria 1284 ✉ 30124 ✆ 706855, Telex 223553 – ▤ wc wc ☎. AE VISA FZ **u**
45 rm ☕ 109/165000, ▤ 12000.

Montecarlo without rest., calle dei Specchieri 463 ✉ 30124 ✆ 707144, Telex 411098 – ▤ wc wc ☎ ♿. AE ① E VISA GY **q**
48 rm ☕ 106/160000, ▤ 10000.

San Marco, calle dei Fabbri 877 ✉ 30124 ✆ 704277, Telex 215660 – wc wc ☎. AE ① E VISA. ✻ rest FZ **r**
M *(closed Tuesday)* a la carte 33/51000 – **60 rm** ☕ 115/172000 – P 135/160000, low season 85/115000.

Bonvecchiati, calle Goldoni 4488 ✉ 30124 ✆ 5285017, Telex 410560, « Modern art picture collection » – ▤ wc wc ☎. AE E. ✻ FZ **a**
M a la carte 31/37000 – ☕ 11000 – **86 rm** 90/129000, ▤ 10000 – P 116/157000, low season 97/127000.

Scandinavia without rest., Santa Maria Formosa 5240 ✉ 30122 ✆ 5223507 – wc wc ☎. AE ① VISA GY **s**
27 rm ☕ 100/150000.

Nuovo Teson without rest., calle de la Pescaria 3980 ✉ 30122 ✆ 705555 – wc ☎. AE ① E VISA DU **s**
30 rm ☕ 54/94000.

Serenissima without rest., calle Goldoni 4486 ✉ 30124 ✆ 700011 – wc wc ☎. AE ① FYZ **w**
24 February-5 November – **34 rm** ☕ 52/92000.

Basilea without rest., rio Marin 817 ✉ 30125 ✆ 718477 – wc wc. VISA. ✻ AT **d**
30 rm ☕ 54/94000.

La Residenza without rest., campo Bandiera e Moro 3608 ✉ 30122 ✆ 5285315, « 14C building » – ▤ wc wc ☎. AE ① VISA. ✻ DU **n**
closed 8 January-15 February and 16 November-7 December – **14 rm** ☕ 49/88000, ▤ 4000.

Paganelli, riva degli Schiavoni 4687 ✉ 30122 ✆ 5224324 – ▤ rest wc wc ☎. AE E. ✻ GY **t**
M *(closed Wednesday and 15 November-16 March)* a la carte 30/48000 – **23 rm** ☕ 52/92000 – P 86/95000, low season 75/85000.

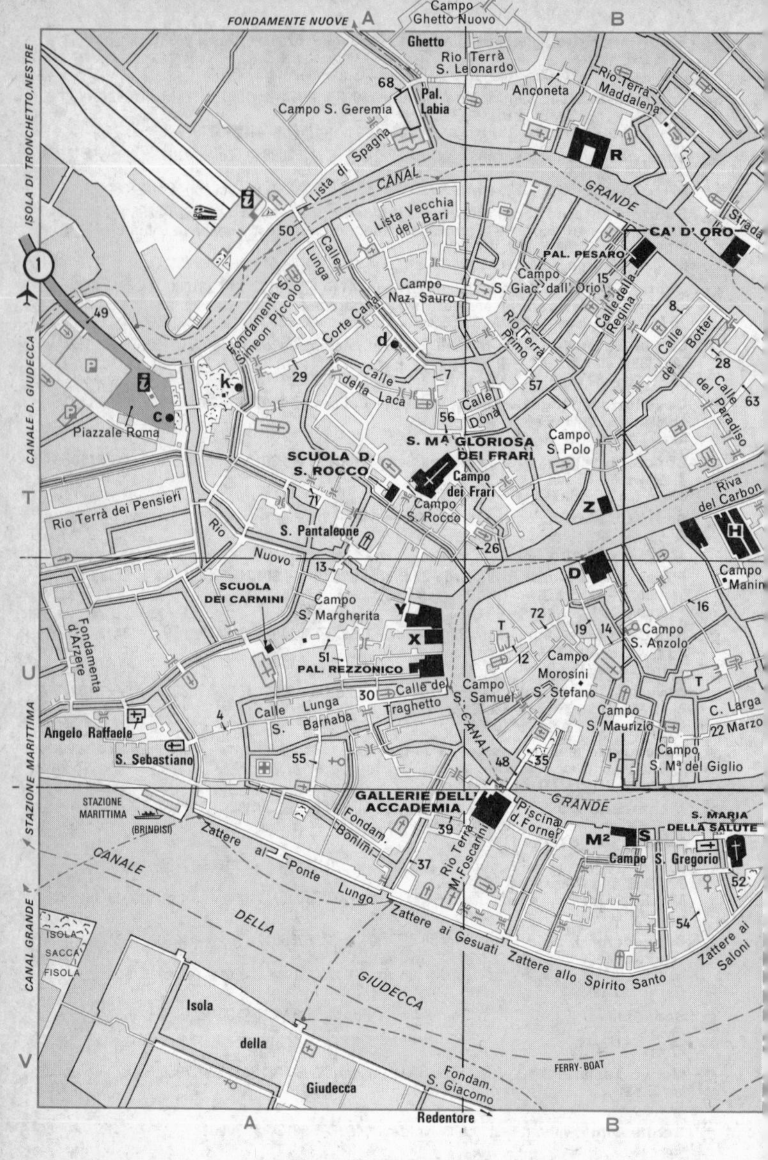

Calle larga S. Marco .... CU 23	Barbaria delle Tole .... DT 2	Calle dell'Ospedaletto ...... CT 18
Calle larga 22 Marzo .... BU	Borgoloco	Calle del Pestrin .... BU 19
Campo S. Bartolomeo .... CT 31	S. Lorenzo .... CT 3	Calle del Pistor .... CT 20
Frezzeria .... CU 40	Calle Avogaria .... AU 4	Calle delle Rasse .... CU 22
Marzaria del Capitello ..... CT 42	Calle del Caffettier .... AT 7	Calle lunga
Marzaria dell'Orologio ..... CU 43	Calle del Campanile .... BT 8	S. M. Formosa .... CT 24
Marzaria S. Salvador ...... CT 44	Calle di Canonica .... CU 9	Calle del Te Deum .... DT 25
Marzaria S. Zulian .... CT 45	Calle delle Carrozze .... BU 12	Calle del Traghetto
Piazza S. Marco .... CU	Calle della Chiesa .... AU 13	Vecchio .... BT 26
Ponte di Rialto .... CT	Calle dei Frati .... BU 14	Campo Bandiera e Moro .... DU 27
Ruga degli Orefici .... CT 62	Calle Longo .... BT 15	Campo delle Beccarie ...... BT 28
Salizzada S. Moisé .... CU 70	Calle della Mandola .... BU 16	Campo della Lana .... AT 29
Via 2 Aprile .... CT 74	Calle Larga Mazzini .... CT 17	Campo S. Barnaba .... AU 30

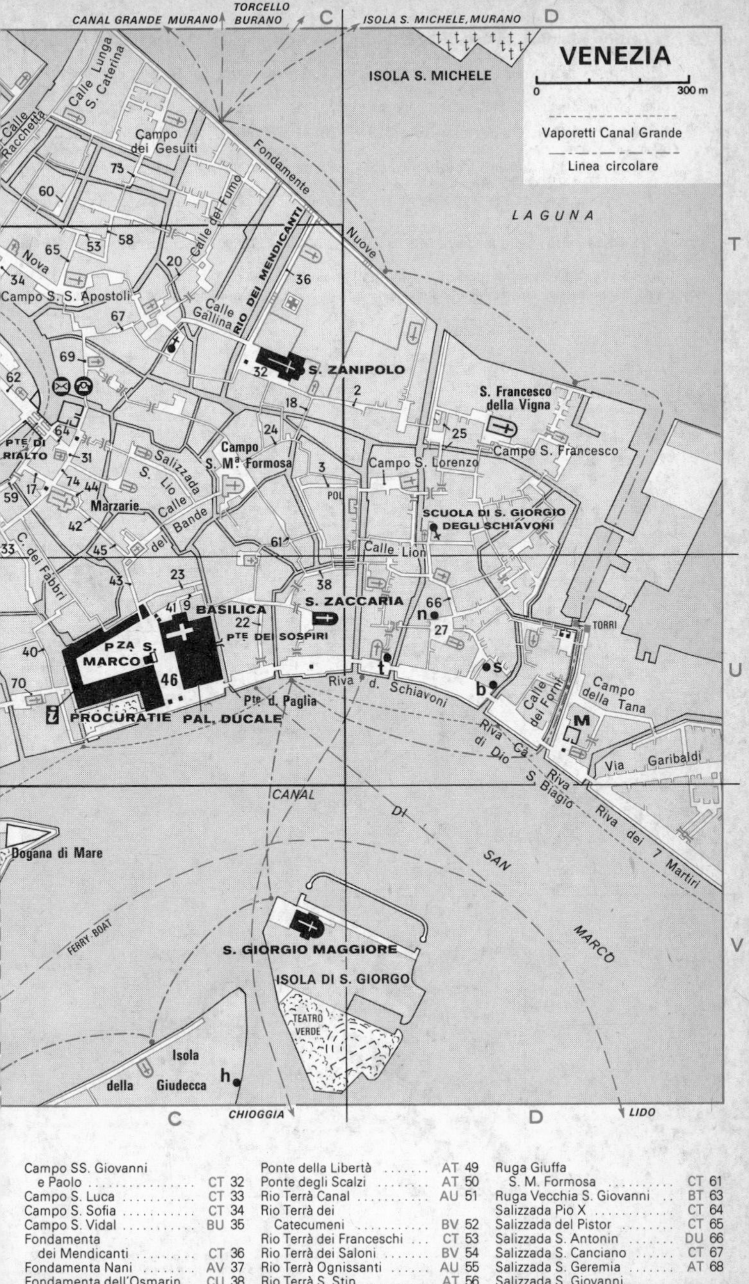
VENEZIA
0
300 m
Vaporetti Canal Grande
Linea circolare
CANAL GRANDE MURANO
TORCELLO BURANO
ISOLA S. MICHELE, MURANO
C
D
ISOLA S. MICHELE
LAGUNA
T
U
V
Calle Racchetta
Calle Lunga S. Caterina
Campo dei Gesuiti
Fondamente Nuove
Calle del Fumo
RIO DEI MENDICANTI
Nova
Campo S. S. Apostoli
Calle Gallina
S. ZANIPOLO
S. Francesco della Vigna
Campo S. Francesco
Campo S. Mª Formosa
Campo S. Lorenzo
PTE DI RIALTO
Salizzada S. Lio
Marzarie
Calle del Bande
SCUOLA DI S. GIORGIO DEGLI SCHIAVONI
Calle Lion
C. dei Fàbbri
BASILICA
S. ZACCARIA
PTE DEI SOSPIRI
PZA S. MARCO
PROCURATIE
PAL. DUCALE
Pte d. Paglia
Riva d. Schiavoni
TORRI
Campo della Tana
Calle dei Forni
Riva di Ca di Dio
Riva S. Biagio
Via Garibaldi
Riva dei 7 Martiri
CANAL DI SAN MARCO
Dogana di Mare
FERRY-BOAT
S. GIORGIO MAGGIORE
ISOLA DI S. GIORGO
TEATRO VERDE
Isola della Giudecca
CHIOGGIA
LIDO

XXXX ✻ **Antico Martini,** campo San Fantin 1983 ✉ 30124 ✆ 5224121, Elegant rest. – ▤. AE ⦿ E VISA. ⚔ EZ **x**
26 February-November; closed Tuesday and Wednesday lunch – **M** a la carte 58/99000 (15%)
Spec. Involtini di salmone, Chicche del nonno, Filetti di San Pietro alla Betty. **Wines** Malvasia, Cabernet.

XXX ✻✻ **Harry's Bar,** calle Vallaresso 1323 ✉ 30124 ✆ 5236797, American bar-rest. – ▤. AE ⦿ E VISA FZ **n**
closed Sunday dinner October-March, Monday and 5 January-3 March – **M** a la carte 65/110000 (20%)
Spec. Taglierini o risotto alle seppioline (15 July-15 October), Scampi alla Carlina, Pasticceria della Casa. **Wines** Soave, Cabernet.

XXX ✻ **La Caravella,** calle larga 22 Marzo 2397 ✉ 30124 ✆ 708901, Typical rest. – ▤. AE ⦿ E VISA. ⚔ EZ **m**
closed Wednesday – **M** (booking essential) a la carte 59/90000
Spec. Bigoli in salsa, Scampi allo Champagne, Filetto di bue Caravella. **Wines** Collio dei colli Formentini, Barchessa.

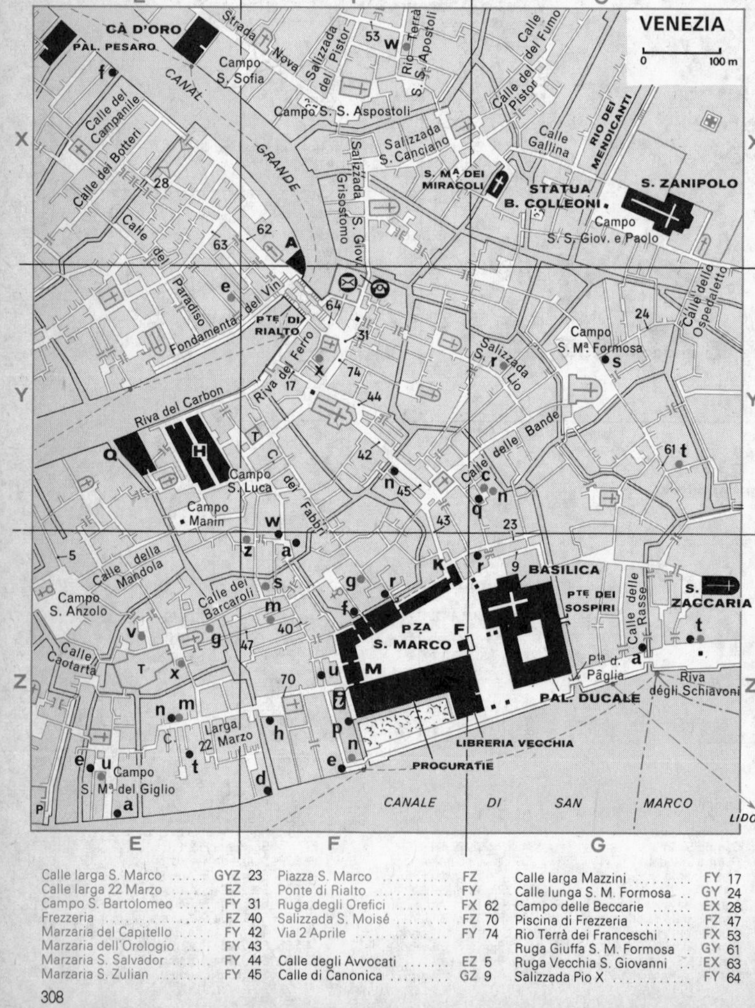

Calle larga S. Marco ...... GYZ 23	Piazza S. Marco .... FZ	Calle larga Mazzini .... FY 17
Calle larga 22 Marzo ...... EZ	Ponte di Rialto .... FY	Calle lunga S. M. Formosa .. GY 24
Campo S. Bartolomeo ..... FY 31	Ruga degli Orefici .... FX 62	Campo delle Beccarie ...... EX 28
Frezzeria .... FZ 40	Salizzada S. Moisé .... FZ 70	Piscina di Frezzeria .... FZ 47
Marzaria del Capitello ..... FY 42	Via 2 Aprile .... FY 74	Rio Terrà dei Franceschi .... FX 53
Marzaria dell'Orologio ..... FY 43		Ruga Giuffa S. M. Formosa . GY 61
Marzaria S. Salvador ...... FY 44	Calle degli Avvocati .... EZ 5	Ruga Vecchia S. Giovanni .. EX 63
Marzaria S. Zulian .... FY 45	Calle di Canonica .... GZ 9	Salizzada Pio X .... FY 64

XXX **Do Leoni,** riva degli Schiavoni 4175 ✉ 30122 ☎ 25032, Elegant rest., « Summer service on the bank of the canal » – ▤. AE ⓓ E VISA. 🚫 GZ **t**
closed Tuesday and 15 November-15 December – **M** (dinner only) (booking essential) a la carte 76/112000.

XXX **Taverna La Fenice,** San Marco 1938 ✉ 30124 ☎ 5223856, ☂, Elegant rest. – ▤. AE ⓓ E VISA. 🚫 EZ **v**
closed Sunday, Monday lunch and 12 January-23 February – **M** a la carte 44/80000 (15%).

XXX **Al Campiello,** calle dei Fuseri 4346 ✉ 30124 ☎ 706396, Rest.-American-bar-late night dinners – ▤. AE ⓓ E VISA FZ **z**
closed Monday and 8 to 22 August – **M** (booking essential) a la carte 33/57000 (13%).

XXX **Do Forni,** calle dei Specchieri 457/468 ✉ 30124 ☎ 5237729, Telex 433072, New rustic rest. – ▤. AE ⓓ E VISA GY **c**
closed Thursday and 22 November-5 December – **M** a la carte 43/63000.

XX Malamocco, campiello del Vin 4650 ✉ 30122 ☎ 27438 – ▤ GZ **n**

XX ✿ **Al Graspo de Uva,** calle dei Bombaseri 5094 ✉ 30124 ☎ 5223647, Typical tavern – ▤. AE ⓓ E VISA FY **x**
closed Monday, Tuesday and 20 December-3 January – **M** a la carte 38/62000 (16%)
Spec. Zuppa di pesce con crostoni, Trancio di cernia in salsa bragoseto, Terra, mare e bosco (pollo disossato, funghi e scampi in salsa di timo). **Wines** Pinot bianco, Cabernet.

XX **Noemi** with rm, calle dei Fabbri 909 ✉ 30124 ☎ 5225238 – ▤ rest ☎. AE ⓓ E VISA
M *(closed Sunday, Monday lunch and 10 December-5 February)* a la carte 45/65000 (15%) – ☕ 7000 – **15 rm** 32/55000. FZ **g**

XX Al Giglio, campo Santa Maria del Giglio 2477 ✉ 30124 ☎ 89456 – ▤ EZ **u**

XX **La Colomba,** piscina di Frezzeria 1665 ✉ 30124 ☎ 5221175, Typical trattoria, « Modern art picture collection » – ▤. AE ⓓ E VISA FZ **m**
closed Wednesday in November-May – **M** a la carte 49/66000 (12%).

XX **Da Ivo,** calle dei Fuseri 1809 ✉ 30124 ☎ 5285004 – ▤. AE ⓓ E VISA. 🚫 FZ **s**
closed Sunday and January – **M** (booking essential) a la carte 40/66000 (13%).

X **Madonna,** calle della Madonna 594 ✉ 30125 ☎ 5223824, Venetian trattoria – ▤. 🚫
closed Wednesday, 24 December-31 January and 4 to 17 August – **M** a la carte 22/37000 (11%). EY **e**

X **A la Vecia Cavana,** rio Terrà SS. Apostoli 4624 ✉ 30121 ☎ 5287106 – ▤. AE ⓓ E VISA
closed Tuesday – **M** a la carte 29/42000 (12%). FX **w**

X Al Barcariol, San Marco-calle dei Barcaroli ✉ 30124 ☎ 5224660 – ▤ EZ **g**

X **Da Bruno,** Castello-calle del Paradiso 5731 ✉ 30122 ☎ 5221480, Habitués' trattoria – ▤. AE GY **r**
closed Tuesday and 15 to 30 July – **M** a la carte 23/31000 (10%).

in Lido : 15 mn by boat from San Marco FZ – ✉ **30126** Venezia Lido.

ℹ Gran Viale S. M. Elisabetta 6 ☎ 765721 :

🏨🏨🏨🏨🏨 **Excelsior,** lungomare Marconi 41 ☎ 5260201, Telex 410023, ←, ⛱ heated, ▲, 🎾, 🏌18 – |‡| ▤ 📺 ☎ ♿ – 🏛. AE ⓓ E VISA. 🚫 rest
15 April-20 October – **M** a la carte 85/137000 – ☕ 18000 – **230 rm** 400/500000.

🏨🏨🏨🏨 Des Bains, lungomare Marconi 17 ☎ 765921, Telex 410142, ←, « Flower park with heated ⛱ and 🎾 », ▲, 🏌18 – |‡| ▤ 📺 ☎ Ⓟ – 🏛
seasonal – **254 rm**.

🏨🏨🏨 **Quattro Fontane** 🐚, via 4 Fontane 16 ☎ 5260227, Telex 411006, 🌳, 🎾 – ☎ Ⓟ. AE. 🚫 rest
17 April-1 October – **M** 60/75000 – ☕ 16000 – **70 rm** 150/245000 – P 205/252000, low season 180/220000.

🏨🏨🏨 **Le Boulevard and Rest. Grimod,** Gran Viale S. M. Elisabetta 41 ☎ 5261990, Telex 410185 – |‡| ▤ 📺 ☎ Ⓟ – 🏛. AE ⓓ E VISA. 🚫 rest
closed January – **M** *(closed Wednesday in October-May)* a la carte 46/68000 – **45 rm** ☕ 135/210000 – P 60/80000, low season 50/70000.

🏨🏨🏨 **Villa Mabapa,** riviera San Nicolò 16 ☎ 5260590, Telex 440170, « Summer rest. in garden », 🌳 – |‡| ▤ ☎ ♿. AE ⓓ E VISA. 🚫 rest
M *(closed 3 November-15 March)* 28/35000 – **62 rm** ☕ 140/210000 – P 130/170000, low season 110/140000.

🏨🏨 **Villa Otello** without rest., via Lepanto 12 ☎ 5260048 – |‡| 🛁wc 🚿wc ☎ Ⓟ
22 April-15 October – ☕ 10000 – **34 rm** 90/140000.

🏨🏨 **Helvetia** without rest., Gran Viale S. M. Elisabetta 4 ☎ 768403, 🌳 – |‡| 🛁wc 🚿wc ☎ Ⓟ. 🚫
April-October – **56 rm** ☕ 110/170000.

🏨 **Byron Central Hotel,** via Bragadin 30 ☎ 5260052, Telex 433109, 🌳 – |‡| ▤ 🛁wc 🚿wc ☎. AE VISA. 🚫 rest
April-15 October – **M** 25/32000 – **36 rm** ☕ 96/150000, ▤ 10000 – P 100/110000, low season 85/95000.

🏨 **Vianello,** località Alberoni ✉ 30011 Alberoni ☎ 731072, 🌳 – 🛁wc 🚿wc. 🚫 rest
15 March-15 October – **M** *(closed September-May)* 15/20000 – ☕ 5000 – **20 rm** 42/73000 – P 48/55000, low season 45/50000.

✗ **Trattoria da Ciccio,** via S. Gallo 241-in direction of Malamocco ✆ 765489, 🌂 – Ⓟ
closed Tuesday and 15 to 30 November – **M** a la carte 25/40000 (12%).

✗ **Al Vecio Cantier,** località Alberoni ✉ 30011 Alberoni ✆ 731130, 🌂
closed Monday – **M** (booking essential) a la carte 25/35000.

in Torcello **45 mn by boat from fondamenta Nuove** CT – ✉ **30012** Burano :

✗✗ ❁ **Locanda Cipriani** ⛱, ✆ 730757, Typical rest. – AE VISA. ✗
19 March-10 November; closed Tuesday – **M** a la carte 63/90000 (15%)
Spec. Risotto alla torcellana (con verdure), Scampi alla Carlina, Grigliata di pesce. **Wines** Soave, Cabernet.

✗✗ **Ostaria al Ponte del Diavolo,** ✆ 730401, 🌂 – AE
March-15 November; closed Thursday and dinner (except Saturday) – **M** a la carte 40/57000 (10%).

Norway
Norge

Oslo

PRACTICAL INFORMATION

LOCAL CURRENCY

Norwegian Kroner : 100 N-Kr = 13.52 US $ (Jan. 87)

TOURIST INFORMATION

The telephone number and address of the Tourist Information office is given in the text under ℹ.

FOREIGN EXCHANGE

In the Oslo area banks are usually open between 8.15am and 3.30pm, but in summertime, 15.5 - 31/8, they close at 3pm. Thursdays they are open till 5pm. Saturdays closed.

Most large hotels, main airports and railway stations have exchange facilities. At Fornebu Airport the bank is open from 6.30am to 10.30pm on weekdays and 7.00am to 10pm on Sundays, all the year round.

SHOPPING IN OSLO

(Knitted ware - silver ware)

Your hotel porter will be able to help you and give you information.

CAR HIRE

The international car hire companies have branches in each major city. Your hotel porter will be able to give details and help you with your arrangements.

TIPPING IN NORWAY

A service charge is included in hotel and restaurant bills and it is up to the customer to give something in addition if he wants to.

The cloakroom is sometimes included in the bill, sometimes you pay a certain amount.

Taxi drivers and baggage porters have no claim to be tipped. It is up to you if you want to give a gratuity.

SPEED LIMITS

The maximum permitted speed within congested areas is 50 km/h - 31mph. Outside congested areas it is 80 km/h - 50mph. Where there are other speed limits (lower or higher) it is signposted.

SEAT BELTS

The wearing of seat belts in Norway is compulsory for drivers and front seat passengers. All cars registered in Norway after 1/1-84 have got to have seat belts in the back seat too, and after 1/3-85 it is compulsory to use them.

ANIMALS

Very strict quarantine regulations for animals from all countries except Sweden and Finland. NO dispensations.

OSLO

SIGHTS

See : Bygdøy AZ : Viking Ships★★★ (Vikingeskipene), Folk Museum★★ (Norsk Folkemuseum), Kon-Tiki Museum★ (Kon-Tiki Museet), Fram Museum★ (Fram Museet), Maritime Museum★ (Norsk Sjøfartsmuseum) ; Frognerparken★ (Vigeland Sculptures★★) AX ; City Hall★ (Rådhuset) BY **H** ; Munch Museum★ (Munchmuseet) CY ; National Gallery★ (Nasjonalgalleriet) BY **M1** ; Akershus Castle★ (Akershus Festning) BZ ; Historical Museum★ (Historisk Museum) BY **M2**.

Outskirts : Holmenkollen★★ (NW : 10 km) : Ski Jump★, Ski Museum★ AX ; Tryvann Tower★★ (Tryvannstårnet) (NW : 14 km) : ☼★★ AX ; Sonja Henie-Onstad Centre★ (Henie-Onstads Kunstsenter) (W : 12 km) AY.

OSLO Norge 920 K 2 – pop. 447 512 – ☎ 02.

18 Oslo Golfklubb ☎ 50 44 02.

✈ Fornebu SW : 8 km ☎ 59 67 16 – SAS : Ruseløkkveien 6 ☎ Business travel : 42 75 50 (Europe and Overseas) 42 79 00 (Domestics and Scandinavia), Vacation travel : 42 77 60 – Air Terminal : Havnegata, main railway station, seaside.

⛴ Copenhagen, Frederikshavn, Kiel : contact tourist information centre (see below).

ℹ Oslo Tourist Information, City Hall, seaside ☎ 42 71 70 and Central Station – **KNA** (Kongelig Norsk Automobilklub) Royal Norwegian Automobile Club ☎ 56 26 90 – **NAF** (Norges Automobil Forbund) ☎ 42 94 00.

Hamburg 888 – København 583 – Stockholm 522.

OSLO

Street	Grid	No.
Karl Johans gate	BCY	
Grensen	CY	
Lille Grensen	CY	37
Torggata	CY	
Apotekergata	CY	2
Arbeidersamfunnets plass	CY	3
Arne Garborgs plass	CY	5
Biskop Gunnerus' gate	CY	8
Bygdøy kappellvei	AZ	9
Christian Frederiks plass	CY	10
Christiania torv	CY	13
Dronningens gate	CYZ	14
Dronning Mauds gate	BY	16
Edvard Storms gate	BX	17
Elisenbergveien	AX	19
Fredriksborgveien	AZ	20
Fridtjof Nansens plass	BY	21
Frimanns gate	CX	23
Gimleveien	AX	24
Grubbegata	CY	27
Haakon VII's gate	BY	28
Jernbanetorget	CY	31
Josefines gate	ABX	32
Kristian Augusts gate	BCY	34
Langes gate	CX	35
Lassons gate	AY	36
Løchenveien	AZ	38
Løkkeveien	ABY	39
Munchs gate	CY	41
Munkedamsveien	ABY	42
Nedre Slottsgate	CYZ	44
Nedre Vollgate	BY	45
Nygata	CY	47
Pløens gate	CY	48
Professor Aschehougs pl.	CY	49
Professor Dahls gate	AX	51
Riddervolds gate	AX	52
Roald Amundsens gate	BY	53
Ruseløkkveien	ABY	55
Rådhusplassen	BY	56
Schives gate	AX	57
Skillebekk plass	AY	59
Skovveien	AXY	60
Solli plass	AY	61
Stortingsgata	BY	62
Stortorvet	CY	63
Strandgata	CZ	64
Sven Bruns gate	BX	65
Thor Olsens gate	CX	67
Tullins gate	BX	68
Uelands gate	CX	69
Wilses gate	CX	71
Youngstorget	CY	72
Øvre Slottsgate	CY	73

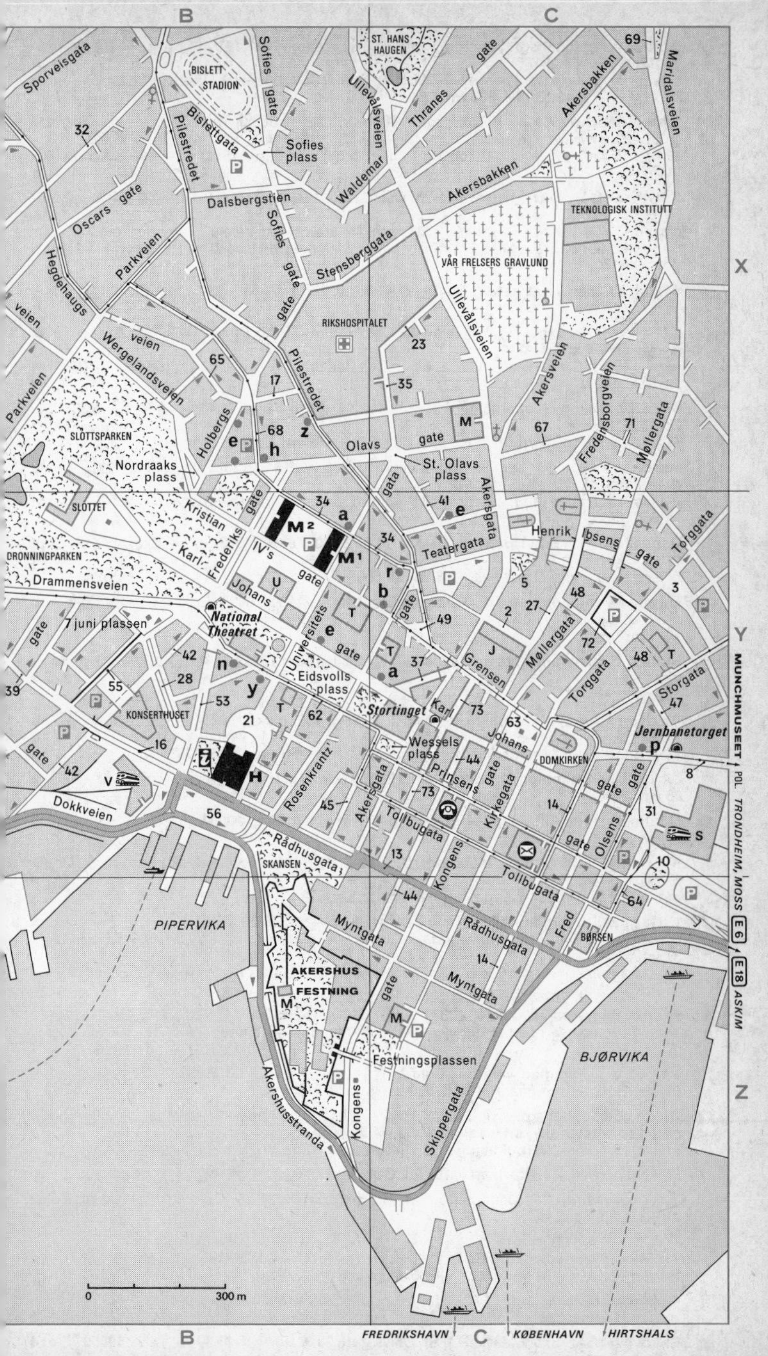

B
C
X
Y
Z
BISLETT STADION
ST. HANS HAUGEN
Sofies gate
Sofies plass
Bislettgata
Pilestredet
Sporveisgata
Oscars gate
Dalsbergstien
Ullevålsveien
Waldemar Thranes gate
Akersbakken
Maridalsveien
TEKNOLOGISK INSTITUTT
VÅR FRELSERS GRAVLUND
Stensberggata
Parkveien
Hegdehaugsveien
RIKSHOSPITALET
Wergelandsveien
Holbergs gate
Olavs gate
St. Olavs plass
Akersveien
Fredensborgveien
Møllergata
SLOTTSPARKEN
Nordraaks plass
SLOTTET
DRONNINGPARKEN
Kristian IV's gate
Frederiks gate
Karl Johans gate
Drammensveien
Akersgata
Teatergata
Henrik Ibsens gate
Torggata
7 juni plassen
National Theatret
Universitetsgata
Eidsvolls plass
Grensen
Storgata
KONSERTHUSET
Stortinget
Jernbanetorget
Wessels plass
Prinsens gate
Kirkegata
DOMKIRKEN
Dokkveien
Rosenkrantz gate
Tollbugata
Kongens gate
Olsens gate
Rådhusgata
SKANSEN
Myntgata
Fred. Olsens gate
BØRSEN
PIPERVIKA
AKERSHUS FESTNING
Festningsplassen
BJØRVIKA
Akershusstranda
Skippergata
MUNCHMUSEET
POL. TRONDHEIM, MOSS
E6
E18
ASKIM
0
300 m
FREDRIKSHAVN
KØBENHAVN
HIRTSHALS

Grand, Karl Johansgt. 31, Oslo 1, ✆ 42 93 90, Telex 71683, ≘s, ▢ – ▣ ▤ TV ☎ ⇔. ♿. AE ⊕ E VISA. ✂ CY **a**
closed 20 December-2 January – **M** (see **Grand Café** below) – **Etoile** a la carte approx. 292/437 – **Fritzuer Grill** – **308 rm** ☕ 1050/1600.

SAS Scandinavia [M], Holbergsgate 30, Oslo 1, ✆ 11 30 00, Telex 79090, ≘s, « Sky bar on 21st floor with ≤ over the city », ▢ – ▣ ▤ rest TV ☎ ♿ ⇔. AE ⊕ E VISA
M (see **Charly's** below) – **Holberg** (dinner only) a la carte 167/310 – **490 rm** ☕ 1140/1340. BX **e**

Continental, Stortingsgaten 24-26, Oslo 1, ✆ 41 90 60, Telex 71012 – ▣ TV ☎. AE ⊕ E VISA. ✂ BY **n**
closed 23 December-2 January – **M** (see **Theatercaféen** below) - **Annen Etage** *(closed Saturday, Sunday, Easter, December and Bank Holidays)* 125/450 and a la carte – **170 rm** ☕ 1000/1300.

Bristol, Kristian 4 des gate 7, Oslo 1, ✆ 41 58 40, Telex 71668 – ▣ ▤ rest TV ☎.
M (grill rest only) – **143 rm**. CY **b**

KNA Park Avenue [M], Parkveien 68, Oslo 2, ✆ 44 69 70, Telex 71763 – ▣ ▤ rest TV ☎ ♿. AE ⊕ E VISA. ✂ AY **f**
closed Easter and Christmas – **M** (buffet lunch) 155/ a la carte 156/290 – **148 rm** ☕ 1000/1120.

Sara [M], Biskop Gunnerus gate 3, Oslo 1, ✆ 42 94 10, Telex 71342 – ▣ ▤ TV ☎ Ⓟ. AE ⊕ E VISA. ✂ CY **p**
M (buffet lunch) 165/dinner a la carte 211/373 – **309 rm** ☕ 895/1095.

Ambassadeur ⛵, Camilla Colletts vei 15, Oslo 2, ✆ 44 18 35, Telex 71446, ≘s, ▢ – ▣ ▤ rest TV. AE ⊕ E VISA. ✂ AX **t**
closed Christmas and Easter – **M** *(closed Saturday and Sunday)* 150/285 – **33 rm** ☕ 850/1300.

Gabelshus ⛵, Gabelsgate 16, Oslo 2, ✆ 55 22 60, Telex 74073, ⛱ – ▣ TV ⊟wc ⥮wc ☎ Ⓟ. AE ⊕ E VISA. ✂ AY **m**
closed Easter and Christmas – **45 rm** ☕ 650/850.

Europa [M] without rest., St. Olavsgate 31, Oslo 1, ✆ 20 99 90, Telex 71512 – ▣ TV ⊟wc ⥮wc ☎. ✂ BX **h**
148 rm.

Stefan, Rosenkrantzgate 1, Oslo 1, ✆ 42 92 50, Telex 19809 – ▣ TV ⊟wc ⥮wc ☎ ♿ CY **r**
131 rm.

Carlton Rica ⛵, Parkveien 78, Oslo 2, ✆ 69 61 70, Telex 71902 – ▣ TV ⥮wc ☎. AE ⊕ E VISA AY **q**
M *(closed Saturday and Sunday)* (dinner only) 160 – **50 rm** ☕ 760/850.

Savoy, Universitetsgt. 11, Oslo 1, ✆ 20 26 55, Telex 76418 – ▣ TV ⊟wc ⥮wc ☎ BY **a**
68 rm.

Norum, Bygdøy Allé 53, ✆ 44 79 90 – ▣ ▤ rest ⊟wc ⥮wc ☎. AX **s**
59 rm.

Munch [M] without rest., Munchsgt. 5, ✆ 42 42 75, Telex 74096 – ▣ TV ⥮wc ☎ ♿. AE ⊕ E VISA. ✂ CY **e**
closed 23 December-3 January – **180 rm** ☕ 525/625.

XXX ✿ **Bagatelle,** Bygdøy Allé 3, Oslo 2, ✆ 44 63 97 – ▤. AE ⊕ E VISA AY **x**
closed lunch Saturday and Monday, Sunday, July, Easter and Christmas – **M** a la carte 375/405
Spec. Saumon et huîtres chaudes au curry, Queues de langoustines à la nage, Millefeuille au chocolat amer.

XXX **Mølla,** Sagveien 21, Oslo 4, ✆ 37 54 50, « Old water-mill » – ▤. AE ⊕ E VISA
closed Sunday and Bank Holidays – **M** (buffet lunch) 140/dinner a la carte 250/320.
by Maridalsveien CX

XXX **3 Kokker,** Drammensveien 30, Oslo 2, ✆ 44 26 50 – ▤. AE ⊕ E VISA AY **k**
closed Sunday and Easter – **M** 375 and a la carte 215/385.

XX **Blom,** Karl Johansgt. 41b, Oslo 1, ✆ 42 73 00, (Original heraldic shields collection dedicated to outstanding artistes) – ▤. AE ⊕ E VISA BY **e**
closed Sunday – **M** (buffet lunch) 85/145 and a la carte.

XX Frascati Rotisserie, Stortingsgaten 20, Oslo 1, ✆ 41 68 76 – ▤ BY **y**

XX **Theatercaféen** (at Continental H.), Stortingsgaten 24-26, Oslo 1, ✆ 41 90 60, Telex 71012 – AE ⊕ E VISA BY **n**
M a la carte 160/283.

X **La Mer,** Pilestredet 31, Oslo 1, ✆ 20 34 45, Seafood – ⊕ E VISA BX **z**
closed Sunday – **M** (dinner only) 385 and a la carte 255/360.

X **Grand Café** (at Grand H.), Karl Johansgt. 31, Oslo 1, ✆ 33 48 70 – ▤. AE ⊕ E VISA
closed 20 December-2 January – **M** a la carte 109/243. CY **a**

X Charlys (at SAS Scandinavia H.), St. Olavs gate 33, Oslo 1, ✆ 11 30 00, Telex 19090 BX **e** *at Holmenkollen* NW : 7 km by Bogstadveien – AX – and Holmenkollveien – ✉ ⊕ 02 Oslo :

Holmenkollen Park [M] ⛰, Kongeveien 26, Oslo 3, NW : 7 km by Hegdehaugsveien ✆ 14 60 90, Telex 72094, ≤ Oslo and fjord, ≘, [⛶] – |⇕| ▤ [TV] ☎ ⇔ Ⓟ. 🏛
M – Bakeriet – **200 rm**.

XXX **Frognerseteren,** Holmenkollveien 200, Oslo 3, NW : 10 km by Holmenkollveien ✆ 14 37 36, ≤ Oslo and fjord – Ⓟ. ⓓ E VISA
M a la carte 158/349.

at Fornebu Airport SW : 8 km by E 18 – AY – and Snarøyveien – ✉ ⊕ 02 Oslo :

SAS Park Royal [M] ⛰, Oslo-N-1324, Lysaker ✆ 12 02 20, Telex 78745, ≘, « Sea-side setting with private beach and tennis », park, 🎾 – |⇕| ▤ [TV] ☎ ♿ Ⓟ. 🏛. AE ⓓ E VISA
254 rm ⊐ 930/1190.

at Sandvika SW : 18km by E 18 – ✉ ⊕ 02 Oslo :

Sheraton Oslo Fjord [M], Sandviksveien 184, Oslo 1300, ✆ 54 57 00, Telex 74345, ≘ – |⇕| ▤ [TV] ☎ ♿ ⇔ Ⓟ. 🏛. AE ⓓ E VISA
M (buffet lunch) 150/dinner a la carte 195/305 – **245 rm** ⊐ 880/1270.

Portugal

Lisbon

PRACTICAL INFORMATION

LOCAL CURRENCY

Escudo : 100 Esc. = 0.68 US $ (Jan. 87)

FOREIGN EXCHANGE

Hotels, restaurants and shops do not always accept foreign currencies and the tourist is therefore advised to change cheques and currency at banks, saving banks and exchange offices - The general opening times are as follows: banks 8.30am to noon and 1 to 2.45pm (closed on Saturdays), money changers 9.30am to 6pm (usually closed on Saturday afternoons and Sundays).

SHOPPING IN LISBON

Shops and boutiques are generally open from 9am to 1pm and 3 to 7pm - In Lisbon, the main shopping streets are: Rua Augusta, Rua do Carmo, Rua Garrett (Chiado), Rua do Ouro, Rua da Prata, Av. da Roma.

TIPPING

A service charge is added to all bills in hotels, restaurants and cafés. It is usual, however, to give an additional tip for personal service ; 10 % of the fare or ticket price is also the usual amount given to taxi drivers and cinema and theatre usherettes.

SPEED LIMITS

The speed limit on motorways is 120 km/h - 74 mph, on other roads 90 km/h - 56 mph and in built up areas 60 km/h - 37 mph.

SEAT BELTS

Out of cities, it is compulsory for drivers and front seat passengers to wear seat belts.

THE FADO

The Lisbon Fado (songs) can be heard in restaurants in old parts of the town such as the Alfama, the Bairro Alto and the Mouraria. A selection of fado cabarets will be found at the end of the Lisbon restaurant list.

LISBON

SIGHTS

See : View : ★★ from the Suspension Bridge (Ponte de 25 Abril), ※ ★★ from Christ in Majesty (Cristo-Rei) S : 3,5 km.

CENTRE : POMBALINE LISBON

See : Rossio★ (square) GY – Avenida da Liberdade★ FX – Edward VII Park★ (Cold Greenhouse) EX – St. Rock★ (Igreja São Roque) FY **M**[1] – Terreiro do Paço (square) GZ.

MEDIAEVAL LISBON

See : St. George's Castle★★ (Castelo de São Jorge) GY – Cathedral★ (Sé) GZ – Santa Luzia Belvedere★ (Miradouro de Santa Luzia) JY – Alfama★★ JYZ.

MANUELINE LISBON

See : Hieronymite Monastery★★ (Mosteiro dos Jerónimos : church★★, cloister★★★) – Belém Tower★★ (Torre de Belém) – Monument to the Discoveries★ (Padrão dos Descobrimentos).

MUSEUMS

Museum of Ancient Art★★ (Museu Nacional de Arte Antiga : polyptych by Nuno Gonçalves★★★) – Calouste Gulbenkian Museum★★★ (Art collection) – Azulejo Museum★ and Church of the Mother of God★★ (Igreja da Madre de Deus) – Coach Museum★★ (Museu Nacional dos Coches) – Maritime Museum★★ (Museu de Marinha).

LISBON (LISBOA) 1100 **37** ⑫ e ⑰ – Pop. 826 140 – alt. 111 – ✪ 01.

18, 9 Estoril Golf Club W : 25 km ☎ 268 01 76 Estoril – 18 Lisbon Sports Club NW : 20 km ☎ 96 00 77 – 18 Club de Campo de Lisboa S : 15 km ☎ 24 57 17 Aroeira, Fonte da Telha.

✈ Lisboa Airport N : 8 km from city centre – T.A.P., Praça Marquês de Pombal 3, ✉ 1200, ☎ 54 40 80 and airport ☎ 88 91 81.

☎ 87 60 27 and 87 70 92.

to Madeira : E.N.M., Rua de São Julião 5, ✉ 1100, ☎ 87 01 21, and Rocha Conde de Óbidos, ✉ 1300.

Palácio Foz, Praça dos Restaudores ☎ 36 36 24, jardim de Regedor ☎ 36 35 21 and airport ☎ 89 43 23 – A.C.P. Rua Rosa Araújo 24, ✉ 1200, ☎ 56 39 31, Telex 12581 – A.C.P. Av. Barbosa do Bocage 23, ✉ 1000, ☎ 77 54 75, Telex 14070.

Madrid 653 – Bilbao 904 – Paris 1817 – Porto 325 – Sevilla 411.

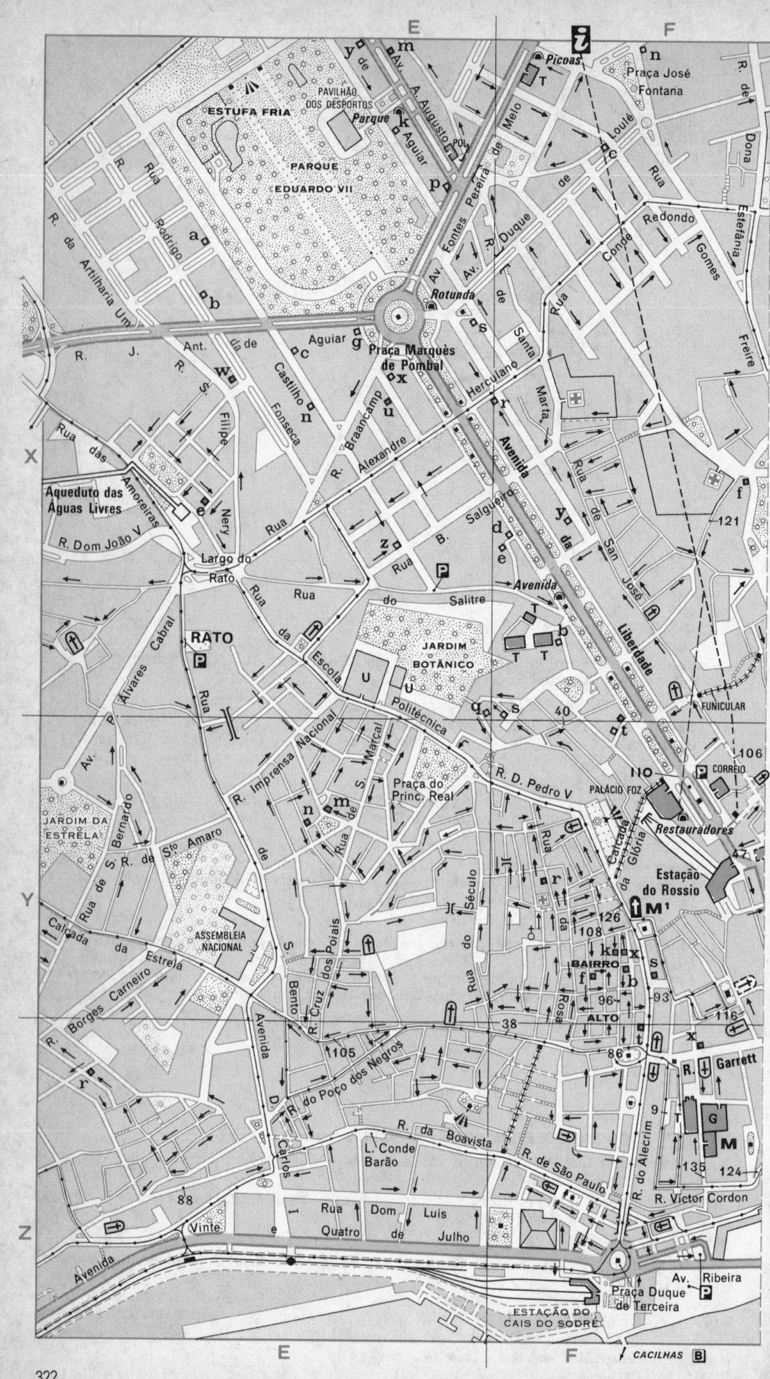
E
F
ESTUFA FRIA
PAVILHÃO DOS DESPORTOS
Parque
PARQUE EDUARDO VII
Picoas
Praça José Fontana
Rotunda
Praça Marquês de Pombal
Aqueduto das Águas Livres
Largo do Rato
RATO
JARDIM BOTÂNICO
FUNICULAR
CORREIO
PALÁCIO FOZ
Restauradores
Estação do Rossio
Praça do Princ. Real
JARDIM DA ESTRELA
ASSEMBLEIA NACIONAL
BAIRRO ALTO
L. Conde Barão
Praça Duque de Terceira
ESTAÇÃO DO CAIS DO SODRÉ
CACILHAS
X
Y
Z
Avenida da Liberdade
Rua de São Paulo
R. Victor Cordon
Rua Dom Luis
Avenida Vinte e Quatro de Julho
Av. Ribeira
Rua da Escola Politécnica
R. D. Pedro V
Rua do Salitre
Rua Alexandre Herculano
Rua Braamcamp
Av. Fontes Pereira de Melo
Rua Duque de Loulé
Rua Conde Redondo
Rua Gomes Freire
R. Dona Estefânia
Rua de Santa Marta
Rua de San José
R. da Artilharia Um
Rua das Amoreiras
R. Dom João V
Rua Rodrigo da Fonseca
R. Castilho
Av. Álvares Cabral
Rua de S. Bento
Rua do Século
Calçada da Estrela
Rua de S. Bernardo
R. de Sto Amaro
Rua Borges Carneiro
R. Imprensa Nacional
Rua de S. Marçal
R. Cruz dos Poiais
R. do Poço dos Negros
R. da Boavista
Avenida D. Carlos I
R. do Alecrim
R. Garrett
Calçada da Glória
Rua da Rosa
Av. A. Augusto de Aguiar
Rua B. Salgueiro
Rua R. Nery
R. S. Filipe
R. J. Ant. da de Aguiar

LISBOA

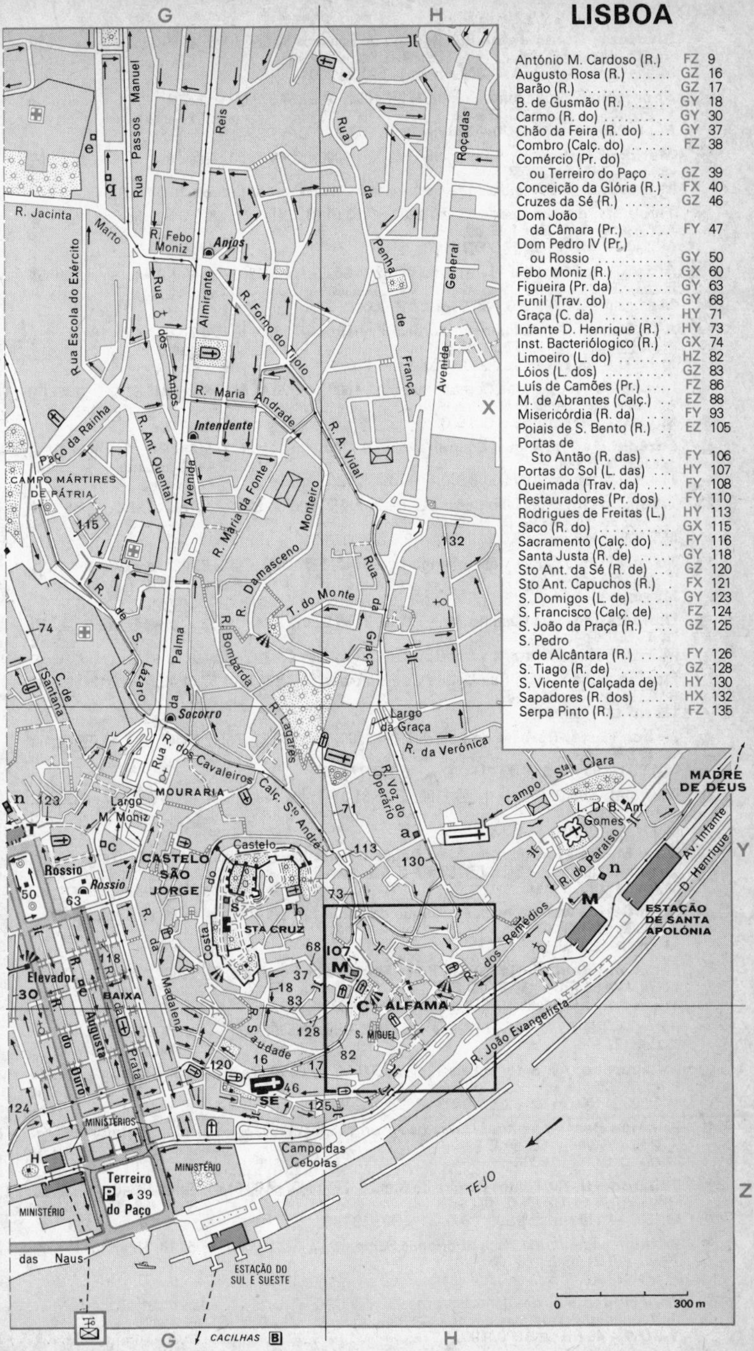

Street	Grid	No.
António M. Cardoso (R.)	FZ	9
Augusto Rosa (R.)	GZ	16
Barão (R.)	GZ	17
B. de Gusmão (R.)	GY	18
Carmo (R. do)	GY	30
Chão da Feira (R. do)	GY	37
Combro (Calç. do)	FZ	38
Comércio (Pr. do) ou Terreiro do Paço	GZ	39
Conceição da Glória (R.)	FX	40
Cruzes da Sé (R.)	GZ	46
Dom João da Câmara (Pr.)	FY	47
Dom Pedro IV (Pr.) ou Rossio	GY	50
Febo Moniz (R.)	GX	60
Figueira (Pr. da)	GY	63
Funil (Trav. do)	GY	68
Graça (C. da)	HY	71
Infante D. Henrique (R.)	HY	73
Inst. Bacteriólogico (R.)	GX	74
Limoeiro (L. do)	HZ	82
Lóios (L. dos)	GZ	83
Luís de Camões (Pr.)	FZ	86
M. de Abrantes (Calç.)	EZ	88
Misericórdia (R. da)	FY	93
Poiais de S. Bento (R.)	EZ	105
Portas de Sto Antão (R. das)	FY	106
Portas do Sol (L. das)	HY	107
Queimada (Trav. da)	FY	108
Restauradores (Pr. dos)	FY	110
Rodrigues de Freitas (L.)	HY	113
Saco (R. do)	GX	115
Sacramento (Calç. do)	FY	116
Santa Justa (R. de)	GY	118
Sto Ant. da Sé (R. de)	GZ	120
Sto Ant. Capuchos (R.)	FX	121
S. Domigos (L. de)	GY	123
S. Francisco (Calç. de)	FZ	124
S. João da Praça (R.)	GZ	125
S. Pedro de Alcântara (R.)	FY	126
S. Tiago (R. de)	GZ	128
S. Vicente (Calçada de)	HY	130
Sapadores (R. dos)	HX	132
Serpa Pinto (R.)	FZ	135

Ritz Inter-Continental, Rua Rodrigo da Fonseca 88, ⊠ 1000, ℘ 69 20 20, Telex 12589, ←, – |‡| ▤ TV ⇔ P – ♟. AE ⓓ E VISA. ✻ rest EX **b**
M a la carte 3 440/6 130 – **300 rm** ⊐ 19 500/24 200.

Sheraton Ⓜ, Rua Latino Coelho 1, ⊠ 1000, ℘ 57 57 57, Telex 12774, ←, ⛱ heated – |‡| ▤ TV ⇔ – ♟. AE ⓓ E VISA by Av. Fontes Pereira de Melo EFX
M a la carte approx. 3920 – **386 rm** ⊐ 20 000/23 000.

Meridien Lisboa Ⓜ, Rua Castillo 149, ⊠ 1000, ℘ 69 09 00, Telex 64315, ← – |‡| ▤ TV ⇔ – ♟. AE ⓓ E VISA. ✻ EX **a**
M *(closed Saturday and Sunday)* a la carte 2 200/2 900 – **331 rm** ⊐ 19 900/23 000.

Tivoli, Av. da Liberdade 185, ⊠ 1200, ℘ 53 01 81, Telex 12588, ⛱, heated, ✂ – |‡| ▤ TV ⇔ – ♟. AE ⓓ E VISA. ✻ FX **d**
M 2 400 – **342 rm** ⊐ 13 000/15 000.

Altis Ⓜ, Rua Castilho 11, ⊠ 1200, ℘ 52 24 96, Telex 42520 – |‡| ▤ TV ⇔ – ♟. AE ⓓ E VISA. ✻ EX **z**
M a la carte 2 100/3 800 – **225 rm** ⊐ 10 000/12 000.

Alfa Lisboa, Av. Columbano Bordalo Pinheiro, ⊠ 1000, ℘ 726 21 21, Telex 18477, ← – |‡| ▤ TV P – ♟. AE ⓓ E VISA. ✻ rest NW : by Av. A. Augusto de Aguiar EX
M 1 900 – **350 rm** ⊐ 15 500/18 700 – P 19 300.

Lisboa Penta, Av. dos Combatentes, ⊠ 1600, ℘ 726 45 54, Telex 18437, ⛱ – |‡| ▤ TV ⇔ P – ♟. AE ⓓ E VISA NW : by Av. A. Augusto de Aguiar EX
M 1 900 – **592 rm** ⊐ 8 500/9 500.

Lutécia, Av. Frei Miguel Contreiras 52, ⊠ 1700, ℘ 80 31 21, Telex 12457, ← – |‡| ▤ TV – ♟. AE ⓓ E VISA. ✻ N : by Av. Almirante Reis GX
M 1 900 – **150 rm** ⊐ 7 500/8 600 – P 8 100/11 300.

Tivoli Jardim, Rua Julio Cesar Machado 7, ⊠ 1200, ℘ 53 99 71, Telex 12172, ⛱ heated, ✂ – |‡| ▤ TV ⇔ P. AE ⓓ E VISA. ✻ FX **e**
M 2 000 – **119 rm** ⊐ 9 000/11 000 – P 9 200/11 700.

Novotel-Lisboa Ⓜ, av. José Malhoa-Lote 1642, ⊠ 1000, ℘ 726 60 22, Telex 40114, ←, ⛱ – |‡| ▤ TV ⇔ – ♟ NW : by Av. A. Augusto de Aguiar EX
246 rm.

Diplomático, Rua Castilho 74, ⊠ 1200, ℘ 56 20 41, Telex 13713 – |‡| ▤ TV P – ♟. AE ⓓ E VISA. ✻ EX **c**
M 1 400/1 750 – **90 rm** ⊐ 7 500/8 600 – P 8 100/11 300.

Flórida without rest., Rua Duque de Palmela 32, ⊠ 1200, ℘ 57 61 45, Telex 12256 – |‡| ▤ TV – ♟. AE ⓓ E VISA EX **x**
112 rm ⊐ 7 200/8 600.

Lisboa Plaza, Travessa do Salitre 7, ⊠ 1200, ℘ 36 39 22, Telex 16402 – |‡| ▤ TV P. AE ⓓ E VISA. ✻ FX **b**
M 1 900 – **93 rm** ⊐ 9 000/11 000 – P 9 300/12 800.

Mundial, Rua D. Duarte 4, ⊠ 1100, ℘ 86 31 01, Telex 12308, ← – |‡| ▤ P – ♟. AE ⓓ E VISA. ✻ rest GY **c**
M 1 900 – **147 rm** ⊐ 8 300/10 400.

Dom Manuel I without rest., av. Duque d'Ávila 189, ⊠ 1000, ℘ 57 61 60, Telex 43558, « Tasteful decor » – |‡| ▤ TV. AE ⓓ E VISA. ✻
64 rm ⊐ 5 900/6 600. N : by Av. Fontes Pereira de Melo EFX

Dom Carlos without rest., Av. Duque de Loulé 121, ⊠ 1000, ℘ 53 90 71, Telex 16468 – |‡| ▤. AE ⓓ VISA. ✻ EX **s**
73 rm ⊐ 5 300/6 800.

Fénix and Rest. El Bodegón, Praça Marquês de Pombal 8, ⊠ 1200, ℘ 53 51 21, Telex 12170 – |‡| ▤ TV – ♟. AE ⓓ E VISA. ✻ EX **g**
M a la carte 2 000/3 350 – **112 rm** ⊐ 7 200/8 400.

Roma, Av. de Roma 33, ⊠ 1700, ℘ 76 77 61, Telex 16586, ←, ⛱ – |‡| ▤ – ♟
263 rm. N : by Av. Almirante Reis GX

Miraparque, Av. Sidónio Pais 12, ⊠ 1000, ℘ 57 80 70, Telex 16745 – |‡| ▤ rest ⊏wc ⊓wc ☎. ✻ EX **k**
M 1 500 – **100 rm** ⊐ 4 250/4 900 – P 7 250/10 900.

Príncipe Real without rest., Rua da Alegria 53, ⊠ 1200, ℘ 36 01 16, « Tasteful decor » – |‡| ▤ ⊏wc ☎. AE ⓓ E VISA EX **q**
24 rm ⊐ 8 000/10 000.

Eduardo VII, Av. Fontes Pereira de Melo 5, ⊠ 1000, ℘ 53 01 41, Telex 18340, ← – |‡| TV ⊏wc ⊓wc ☎. AE ⓓ E VISA. ✻ EX **p**
M 1950 – **110 rm** ⊐ 6 200/7 800 – P 7 800/10 100.

Britânia without rest., Rua Rodrigues Sampaio 17, ⊠ 1100, ℘ 57 50 16, Telex 13733 – |‡| ⊏wc ☎. AE ⓓ E VISA. ✻ FX **y**
30 rm ⊐ 5 100/6 500.

York House, Rua das Janelas Verdes 32, ⊠ 1200, ℘ 66 25 44, Telex 16791, ⛱, « Former 16C Convent, Portuguese decor » – ⊏wc ⊓wc ☎. AE ⓓ E VISA. ✻ rest
M 2 000 – **48 rm** ⊐ 8 000/9 000. W : by calçada M. de Abrantes EZ

🏨 Residencia York House, without rest., Rua das Janelas Verdes 47, ⊠ 1200, ℘ 66 81 43, « English decor » – 🛁wc ☎ – **17 rm** W : by calçada M. de Abrantes EZ

🏨 **Botánico** without rest., Rua Mãe d'Água 16, ⊠ 1200, ℘ 32 03 92, Telex 12308 – |‡| ▤ 🛁wc 🚿wc ☎. AE ⊕ E VISA. 🚫🐕 FX **s**
30 rm ☕ 4 500/5 900.

🏨 **Excelsior** without rest., Rua Rodrigues Sampaio 172, ⊠ 1100, ℘ 53 71 51, Telex 14223 – |‡| 🛁wc 🚿wc ☎. AE ⊕ E VISA. 🚫🐕 EX **d**
80 rm ☕ 5 500/7 000.

🏨 **Flamingo,** Rua Castilho 41, ⊠ 1200, ℘ 53 21 91, Telex 14736 – |‡| ▤ TV 🛁wc 🚿wc ☎. AE ⊕ E VISA. 🚫🐕 EX **n**
M 2 000 – **39 rm** ☕ 6 200/7 800 – P 10 200/15 800.

🏨 Vip, without rest., Rua Fernão Lopes 25, ⊠ 1000, ℘ 57 89 23, Telex 14194 – |‡| 🛁wc ☎ **54 rm**. FX **n**

🏨 **Principe,** Av. Duque d'Ávila 201, ⊠ 1000, ℘ 53 61 51, Telex 43565 – |‡| ▤ TV 🛁wc ☎ **P**. AE ⊕ E VISA. 🚫🐕 NW : by Av. A. Augusto de Aguiar EX
M 1250 – **67 rm** ☕ 4 000/6 000 – P 5 500/6 500.

🏨 **Nazareth** 4th floor, without rest., Av. António Augusto de Aguiar 25, ⊠ 1000, ℘ 54 20 16 – |‡| 🛁wc ☎. AE ⊕ E VISA. 🚫🐕 EX **y**
32 rm ☕ 3 500/5 500.

🏨 **São Pedro** without rest., Rua Pascoal de Melo 130, ⊠ 1000, ℘ 57 87 65 – |‡| 🛁wc 🚿wc ☎ 🚗. E VISA. 🚫🐕 N : by Av. Almirante Reis GX
50 rm ☕ 4 000/4 300.

🏨 **Insulana** 2nd floor, without rest., Rua da Assunção 52, ⊠ 1100, ℘ 32 76 25 – |‡| 🛁wc 🚿wc ☎. AE ⊕ E VISA. 🚫🐕 GY **e**
32 rm ☕ 5 400.

🏨 **Dom João** without rest., Rua José Estévão 43, ⊠ 1100, ℘ 54 30 64 – |‡| 🛁wc 🚿wc ☎ 🚗. AE ⊕ E VISA. 🚫🐕 GX **e**
18 rm ☕ 3 500/6 000.

🏨 **Alicante** without rest., Av. Duque de Loulé 20, ⊠ 1000, ℘ 53 05 14 – |‡| 🛁wc 🚿wc ☎. 🚫🐕 FX **c**
36 rm ☕ 2 300/3 400.

🏨 **Imperador** without rest., Av. 5 de Outubro 55, ⊠ 1000, ℘ 57 48 84 – |‡| 🛁wc 🚿wc ☎. 🚫🐕 N : by Av. Fontes Pereira de Melo EFX
43 rm ☕ 2 800/3 650.

🏨 **Roma** 1st floor, without rest., Travessa da Glória 22-A, ⊠ 1200, ℘ 36 05 57 – TV 🛁wc 🚿wc ☎. AE E VISA. 🚫🐕 FY **t**
24 rm ☕ 3 500/4 700.

🏨 **Albergaria Pax** without rest., Rua José Estêvão 20, ⊠ 1100, ℘ 58 18 61, Telex 12862 – |‡| 🛁wc ☎. AE ⊕ E VISA. 🚫🐕 GX **q**
34 rm ☕ 4 000/5 000.

XXXX **Aviz,** Rua Serpa Pinto 12-B, ⊠ 1200, ℘ 32 53 72 – ▤. AE ⊕ E VISA. 🚫🐕 FZ **x**
M a la carte approx. 3 400.

XXXX ✿ **Tágide,** Largo da Academia Nacional de Belas Artes 18, ⊠ 1200, ℘ 32 07 20, ≤ – ▤. AE ⊕ E VISA. 🚫🐕 FZ **z**
closed Saturday dinner and Sunday – **M** a la carte 2 650/4 450
Spec. Paté de salmão, Robalo com coentras, Carne de porco com ameijoas.

XXXX **António Clara,** Av. da República 38, ⊠ 1000, ℘ 76 63 80, Telex 62506, « Former old palace » – ▤ **P**. AE ⊕ E VISA N : by Av. Fontes Pereira de Melo EFX
closed Sunday – **M** a la carte 1 850/4 600.

XXXX Clara, Campo dos Martires da Patria 49, ⊠ 1100, ℘ 55 73 41, 🌳 – ▤ FX **f**

XXXX **Tavares,** Rua da Misericórdia 37, ⊠ 1200, ℘ 32 11 12, Late 19C decor – ▤. AE E VISA. 🚫🐕 FZ **t**
closed Saturday and Sunday lunch – **M** a la carte 2 130/4 200.

XXX Cota D'Armas, Beco de São Miguel 7, ⊠ 1100, ℘ 86 86 82, 🌳, Tasteful decor and Fado cabaret at night – ▤ in Alfama

XXX **Gambrinus,** Rua das Portas de Santo Antão 25, ⊠ 1100, ℘ 32 14 66 – ▤. AE VISA. 🚫🐕 GY **n**
M a la carte 1 860/4 080.

XXX **Escorial,** Rua das Portas de Santo Antão 47, ⊠ 1100, ℘ 36 44 29, Modern decor – ▤. AE ⊕ E VISA GY **n**
M a la carte 2 140/4 280.

XXX **Pabe,** Rua Duque de Palmela 27-A, ⊠ 1200, ℘ 53 74 84, English pub style – ▤ **P**. AE ⊕ E VISA. 🚫🐕 EX **u**
M a la carte 2 150/3 750.

XXX Clube de Roma, Av. Sacadura Cabral 4A, ⊠ 1000, ℘ 77 74 33 – ▤ **P** NW : by Av. Fontes Pereira de Melo EFX

XXX ✿ **Casa da Comida,** Travessa das Amoreiras 1, ⊠ 1200, ℘ 68 53 76, « Patio with plants » – ▤. AE ⊕ E VISA. 🚫🐕 EX **e**
closed Saturday lunch and Sunday – **M** a la carte 3 100/6 300
Spec. Pregado com pimenta verde, Langosta com champagne, Pato com cepes.

XXX **Chester,** Rua Rodrigo da Fonseca 87-D, ✉ 1200, ☎ 65 73 47, Telex 13649, Meat specialities – ▤. AE ◑ E VISA. 🐕 EX **w**
closed Sunday – **M** a la carte 1 850/3 150.

XXX **Saraiva's,** Rua Eng. Canto Rosende 3, ✉ 1000, ☎ 53 19 87, Modern decor – ▤. AE ◑ E VISA. 🐕 N : by Av. A. Augusto de Aguiar EX
closed Saturday – **M** a la carte 1 720/4 200.

XXX **O Faz Figura,** Rua do Paraíso 15 B, ✉ 1100, ☎ 86 89 81, ≤, 🍽 – ▤. AE ◑ E VISA. 🐕
closed Sunday – **M** a la carte 2 000/3 000. HY **n**

XXX **Bachus,** Largo da Trindade 9, ✉ 1200, ☎ 32 28 28 – ▤. AE ◑ E VISA. 🐕 FY **s**
M a la carte 1 720/3 390.

XX **Casa do Lêao,** Castelo de São Jorge, ✉ 1100, ☎ 87 59 62, ≤ – ▤. AE ◑ E VISA. 🐕
M (lunch only) a la carte 2 100/4 150. GY **s**

XX ✿ **Conventual,** Praça das Flores 45, ✉ 1200, ☎ 60 91 96 – ▤. AE ◑ VISA EY **m**
closed Sunday – **M** a la carte 1 250/3 090.

XX **A Góndola,** Av. de Berna 64, ✉ 1000, ☎ 77 04 26, 🍽 – ▤. E VISA
closed Saturday dinner and Sunday – **M** a la carte 1 630/2 660.
N : by Av. A. Augusto de Aguiar EX

XX **Michel,** Largo de Santa Cruz do Castelo 5, ✉ 1100, ☎ 86 43 38, French rest. – ▤. AE ◑ E VISA GY **b**
closed Saturday lunch, Sunday and Bank Holidays – **M** a la carte 2 330/4 430.

XX **São Jerónimo,** Rua dos Jerónimos 12, ✉ 1300, ☎ 64 87 96 – ▤. AE ◑ E VISA
closed Sunday – **M** a la carte 1 320/2 350. W : by Av. 24 de Julho EZ

XX Petite Folie, Av. António Augusto de Aguiar 74, ✉ 1000, ☎ 52 19 48, 🍽, French rest. – VISA EX **m**

XX **Espelho d'Àgua,** Av. de Brasilia, ✉ 1300, ☎ 61 73 73, ≤, 🍽, Modern decor – ▤. AE ◑ E VISA W : by Av. 24 de Julho EZ
closed Sunday – **M** a la carte 1 520/2 980.

XX **Sancho,** Travessa da Glória 14, ✉ 1200, ☎ 36 97 80 – ▤. AE E VISA. 🐕 FXY **t**
closed Sunday – **M** a la carte 920/2 500.

XX Chez Denis, basement, Av. da República 9-A, ✉ 1000, ☎ 53 04 11, Modern decor – ▤
N : by Av. Fontes Pereira de Melo EFX

X **O Vicentinho,** Rua Voz do Operario 1 B, ✉ 1100, ☎ 86 46 95 – ▤. AE ◑ E VISA. 🐕 HY **a**
closed Sunday lunch, Monday and Bank Holidays lunch – **M** a la carte 1 250/2 360.

X **Xêlê Bananas,** Praça das Flores 29, ✉ 1200, ☎ 67 05 15, Tropical style decor – ▤. AE ◑ E VISA EY **n**
closed Sunday – **M** a la carte 1 560/3 050.

X **Sua Excelência,** Rua do Conde 42, ✉ 1200, ☎ 60 36 14 – ▤. AE ◑ E VISA
closed Wednesday, Saturday lunch, Sunday lunch and September – **M** a la carte 1 775/4 500. W : by calçada M. de Abrantes EZ

X **António,** Rua Tomàs Ribeiro 63, ✉ 1000, ☎ 53 87 80 – ▤. AE ◑ E VISA. 🐕
M a la carte 2 000/3 030. N : by Av. A. Augusto de Aguiar EX

Typical restaurants :

XX Arcadas do Faia, Rua da Barroca 56, ✉ 1200, ☎ 32 67 42, Telex 13649, Fado cabaret – ▤
M (dinner only). FY **f**

XX **A Severa,** Rua das Gáveas 51, ✉ 1200, ☎ 36 40 06, Fado cabaret at dinner – ▤. AE ◑ E VISA. 🐕 FY **b**
closed Thursday – **M** a la carte 2 050/3 450.

XX Lisboa à Noite, Rua das Gáveas 69, ✉ 1200, ☎ 36 85 57, Fado cabaret at dinner – ▤. AE ◑ E VISA. 🐕 FY **x**

XX **Sr. Vinho,** Rua do Meio - à - Lapa 18, ✉ 1200, ☎ 67 26 81, Telex 42222, Fado cabaret – ▤. AE ◑ E VISA. 🐕 EZ **r**
M (dinner only) a la carte approx. 3 000.

X **Adega Machado,** Rua do Norte 91, ✉ 1200, ☎ 36 00 95, Fado cabaret – ▤. AE ◑ E VISA. 🐕 FY **k**
closed Monday from November to March – **M** (dinner only) a la carte 1 750/2 950.

X O Forcado, Rua da Rosa 221, ✉ 1200, ☎ 36 85 79, Fado cabaret – ▤ FY **r**
M (dinner only).

X Parreirinha de Alfama, Beco do Espírito Santo 1, ✉ 1100, ☎ 86 82 09, Fado cabaret
M (dinner only). in Alfama

Spain
España

Madrid
Barcelona
Malaga - Marbella
Sevilla
Valencia

PRACTICAL INFORMATION

LOCAL CURRENCY

Peseta : 100 ptas = 0.76 US $ (Jan. 87)

TOURIST INFORMATION

The telephone number and address of the Tourist Information offices is given in the text of the towns under 🅸.

FOREIGN EXCHANGE

Banks are open from 9am to 2pm (12.30pm on Saturdays).
Exchange offices in Sevilla and Valencia airports open from 9am to 2pm, in Barcelona airport from 9am to 2pm and 7 to 11pm. In Madrid and Málaga airports, offices operate a 24 hour service.

TRANSPORT

Taxis may be hailed when showing the green light or sign "Libre" on the windscreen.
Madrid and Barcelona have a Metro (subway) network. In each station complete information and plans will be found.

SHOPPING

In the index of street names, those printed in red are where the principal shops are found.
The big stores are easy to find in town centres; they are open from 10am to 8pm.
Exclusive shops and boutiques are open from 10am to 2pm and 5 to 8pm - In Madrid they will be found in Serrano, Princesa and the Centre; in Barcelona, Passeig de Gracia, Diagonal and the Rambla de Catalunya.
Second-hand goods and antiques: El Rastro (Flea Market), Las Cortes, Serrano in Madrid; in Barcelona, Los Encantes (Flea Market), Barrio Gótico.

TIPPING

Hotel, restaurant and café bills always include service in the total charge. Nevertheless it is usual to leave the staff a small gratuity which may vary with the district and the service given. Doormen, porters and taxi-drivers are used to being tipped.

SPEED LIMITS

The maximum permitted speed on motorways is 120 km/h - 74 mph, and 90 km/h - 56 mph on other roads.

SEAT BELTS

The wearing of seat belts is compulsory for drivers and front seat passengers.

"TAPAS"

Bars serving "tapas" (typical spanish food to be eaten with a glass of wine or an aperitif) will usually be found in central, busy or old quarters of towns. In Madrid, idle your way to the Calle de la Cruz (Puerta del Sol) or to the Calle de Cuchilleros (Plaza Mayor).

MADRID

SIGHTS

See : The Prado Museum★★★ (Museo del Prado) NZ – Parque del Buen Retiro★★ HY – Paseo del Prado (Plaza de la Cibeles) NXYZ – Paseo de Recoletos NVX – Paseo de la Castellana NV – Puerta del Sol and Calle de Alcalá LMNY – Plaza Mayor★ KYZ – Royal Palace (Palacio Real)★★ KY – Descalzas Reales Convent★★ (Convento de las Descalzas Reales) KY **L** – San Antonio de la Florida (fresco by Goya★) DX **R**.

Other Museums : Archeological Museum★★ (Arqueológico Nacional) NV **M22** – Lázaro Galdiano★★ HV **M7** – The Américas Museum★ DV **M8** – Museum of Contemporary Spanish Art★ – Army Museum (del Ejército★) NY **M2**.

Envir. : El Pardo (Palacio★) NW : 13 km by C 601.

MADRID 444 y 447 K 19 – Pop. 3 188 297 – alt. 646 – ☎ 91 – Bullring.

Racecourse of the Zarzuela – 18, 18 Puerta de Hierro ☎ 216 17 45 – 9, 18 Club de Campo ☎ 207 03 95 – 18 La Moraleja by ① : 11 km ☎ 650 07 00 – 9 Club Barberán by ⑥ : 10 km ☎ 218 85 05 – 18 Las Lomas – El Bosque by ⑥ : 18 km ☎ 464 32 15 – 18 Real Automóvil Club de España by ① : 28 km ☎ 652 26 00 – 18 Nuevo Club de Madrid, Las Matas by ⑦ : 26 km ☎ 630 08 20 – 9 Somosaguas W : 10 km by Casa de Campo ☎ 212 16 47.

✈ Madrid-Barajas by ② : 13 km ☎ 222 11 65 – Iberia : pl. de Cánovas 5, ✉ 28014, ☎ 429 74 43 and Aviaco, Modesto Lafuente 76, ✉ 28003, ☎ 234 46 00.

🚘 Atocha ☎ 228 52 37 – Chamartín ☎ 733 11 22 – Príncipe Pío ☎ 248 87 16.

Shipping Companies : Cía. Trasmediterránea, Pedro Munõz Seca 2 NX, ✉ 1, ☎ 431 07 00, Telex 23189.

ℹ Princesa 1, ✉ 28008, ☎ 241 23 25, Medinaceli 2, ✉ 28006, ☎ 411 43 36 pl. Mayor 3, ✉ 28012, ☎ 266 48 74, Caballero de Gracia 7, ✉ 28013, ☎ 231 44 57 and Barajas airport ☎ 205 86 56 – R.A.C.E. José Abascal 10, ✉ 28003, ☎ 447 32 00, Telex 27341.

Paris (by Irún) 1310 ① – Barcelona 627 ② – Bilbao 397 ① – La Coruña 603 ⑦ – Lisboa 653 ⑥ – Málaga 548 ④ – Porto 599 ⑦ – Sevilla 550 ④ – Valencia 351 ③ – Zaragoza 322 ②.

Centre : Paseo del Prado, Puerta del Sol, Gran Vía, Alcalá, Paseo de Recoletos, Plaza Mayor, Leganitos (plan pp. 6 and 7) :

Palace, pl. de las Cortes 7, 28014, 429 75 51, Telex 22272 – TV – . AE E VISA. rest MY **e**
M 4 250 – 1 000 – **508 rm** 15 000/19 000.

Princesa Plaza, Serrano Jover 3, 28015, 242 21 00, Telex 44377 – TV – . AE E VISA. KV **c**
M 4 100 – 900 – **406 rm** 12 880/16 100.

Plaza without rest., coffee shop only, pl. España, 28013, 247 12 00, Telex 27383, ≤, (Summer only) – TV – . AE E VISA. KV **s**
720 – **306 rm** 9 520/11 900.

Emperador without rest., Gran Vía 53, 28013, 247 28 00, Telex 46261, – TV – . AE E VISA. KX **n**
530 – **232 rm** 7 200/9 000.

Liabeny, Salud 3, 28013, 232 53 06, Telex 49024 – TV . AE VISA. LY **e**
M 1 500 – 550 – **158 rm** 4 800/7 400.

Suecia and Rest. Bellman, Marqués de Casa Riera 4, 28014, 231 69 00, Telex 22313 – TV – . AE E VISA. MY **b**
closed August – **M** *(closed Monday, Wednesday dinner, Saturday and Sunday)* 2 400 – 675 – **64 rm** 8 375/10 275 – P 10 610/13 850.

Victoria, pl. del Angel 7, 28012, 231 60 00 – . AE E VISA LZ **u**
M 1 475 – 350 – **114 rm** 3 975/5 990 – P 5 895/6 875.

Washingtón without rest., Gran Vía 72, 28046, 266 71 00, Telex 41499 – TV KV **u**
425 – **120 rm** 4 650/8 100.

Arosa without rest., coffee shop only, Salud 21, 28013, 232 16 00, Telex 43618 – . AE E VISA LX **q**
545 – **126 rm** 5 910/8 900.

El Prado without rest., Prado 11, 28014, 429 35 68 – . AE E VISA. LZ **z**
450 – **45 rm** 6 300/8 000.

Mayorazgo, Flor Baja 3, 28013, 247 26 00, Telex 45647 – TV – . AE E VISA. KX **b**
M 2 100 – 480 – **200 rm** 5 900/8 200 – P 8 780/10 480.

El Coloso, Leganitos 13, 28013, 248 76 00, Telex 47017 – TV . AE E VISA. KX **y**
M a la carte 2 300/3 800 – 790 – **84 rm** 7 570/9 460.

Casón del Tormes without rest., Río 7, 28013, 241 97 46 – wc . VISA. KX **v**
280 – **61 rm** 3 420/5 050.

Mercator without rest., coffee shop only, Atocha 123, 28012, 429 05 00, Telex 46129 – wc . AE E VISA NZ **b**
310 – **90 rm** 3 415/5 130.

Capitol without rest., Gran Via 41, 28013, 221 83 91, Telex 41499 – TV wc . AE E VISA. KX **e**
375 – **142 rm** 6 500/9 800.

Atlántico 3rd floor, without rest., Gran Vía 38, 28013, 222 64 80 – wc . AE E VISA. LX **e**
300 – **62 rm** 3 700/5 280.

Carlos V without rest., Maestro Vitoria 5, 28013, 231 41 00, Telex 48547 – wc . AE E VISA. KY **f**
325 – **67 rm** 4 200/5 600.

California 1st floor, without rest., Gran Vía 38, 28013, 222 47 03 – wc wc . AE E VISA. LX **e**
250 – **26 rm** 2 700/4 300.

Fontela 2nd floor, without rest., Gran Vía 11, 28013, 221 64 00 – wc . AE E VISA. LX **u**
200 – **66 rm** 2 500/3 700.

Amberes 7th floor, without rest., Gran Vía 68, 28013, 247 61 00 – wc . AE VISA – 250 – **48 rm** 4 000. KX **x**

XXX **Clara's,** Arrieta 2, 28013, 242 09 45, Telex 23307, « Tasteful decor » – . E VISA. KY **s**
closed Sunday – **M** a la carte 2 800/4 675.

XXX ⊛ **El Cenador del Prado,** Prado 4, 28014, 429 15 61 – . AE E VISA. LZ **n**
closed Saturday dinner, Sunday and 5 to 20 August – **M** a la carte 2 800/3 850
Spec. Crema de melón a la hierbabuena, Patatas a la importancia con almejas, Salmón escalfado con bígaros.

XXX ⊛ **Café de Oriente,** pl. de Oriente 2, 28013, 241 39 74, Basque and French rest., Tasteful decor – . AE E VISA KY **a**
closed Saturday lunch, Sunday and August – **M** a la carte 2 450/5 850
Spec. Ensalade de bogavante al vinagre de Jerez, Blanco de rodaballo al hinojo, Tournedos al foie gras.

MADRID

Caídos de la División Azul	HS	6
Capitán Haya	GS	7
Comandante Zorita	FT	14
Costa Rica (Av. de)	HS	20
Cuatro Caminos (Glorieta de)	FU	21
Doctor Arce (Av. del)	HU	25
Doctor Fleming	GT	26
Enrique Larreta	HS	29
Estébanez Calderón	GS	30
Fray Bernardino Sahagún	HS	35
Gen. López Pozas	HS	37
Gen. Moscardó	FT	38
Jerez	HS	43
Pedro Teixeira	GT	58
Pinos Alta	FS	59
Pintor Juan Gris	FS	60
Presidente Carmona	FT	64
Raimundo Fernández Villaverde	FU	69
Ramón y Cajal (Av.)	HT	70
Reina Mercedes	FT	73
República Dominicana (Plaza)	HS	75
Rosa de Silva	FS	78
Rosario Pino	GS	79
San Amaro (Pl.)	FT	82
Segre	HT	96
Sor Angela de la Cruz	GS	99
Teruel	FT	100
Víctor Andrés Belaunde	HT	108
Víctor de la Serna	HT	110

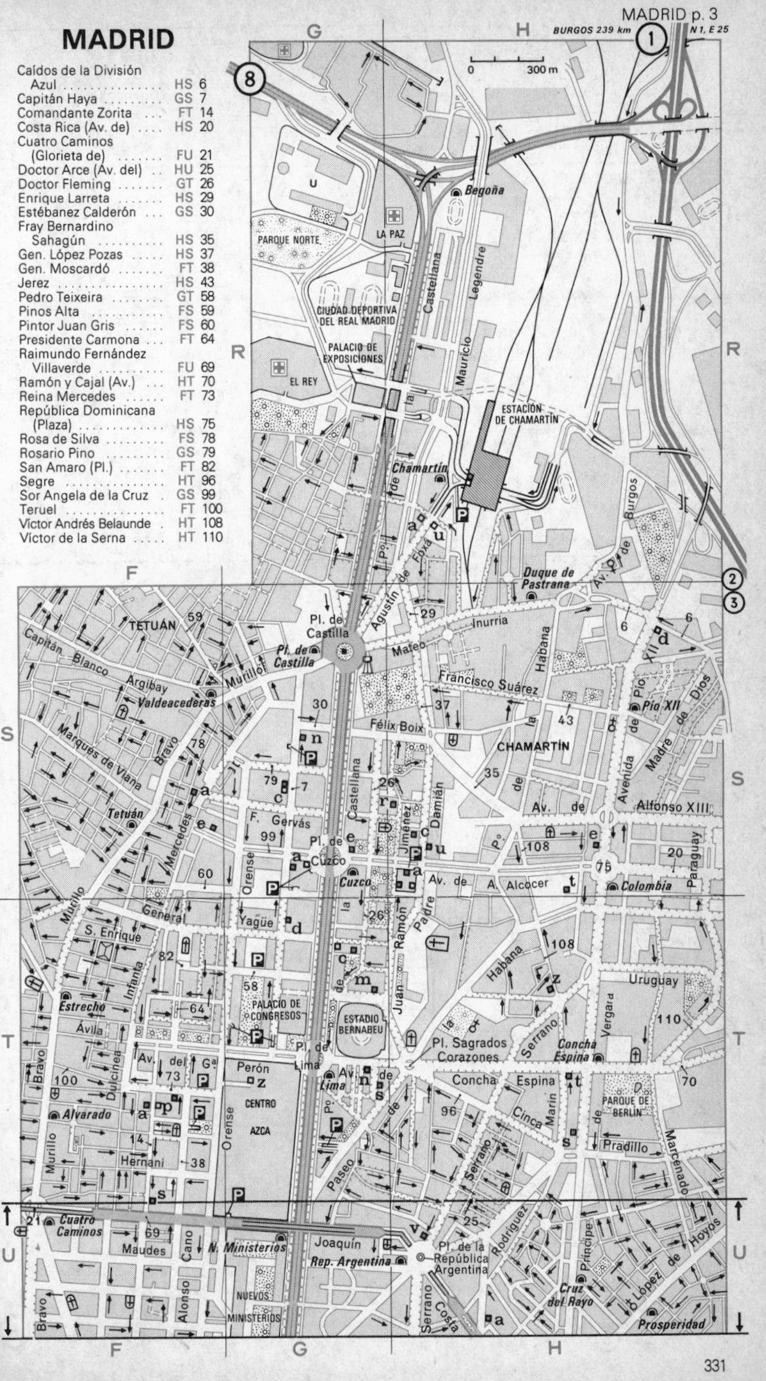

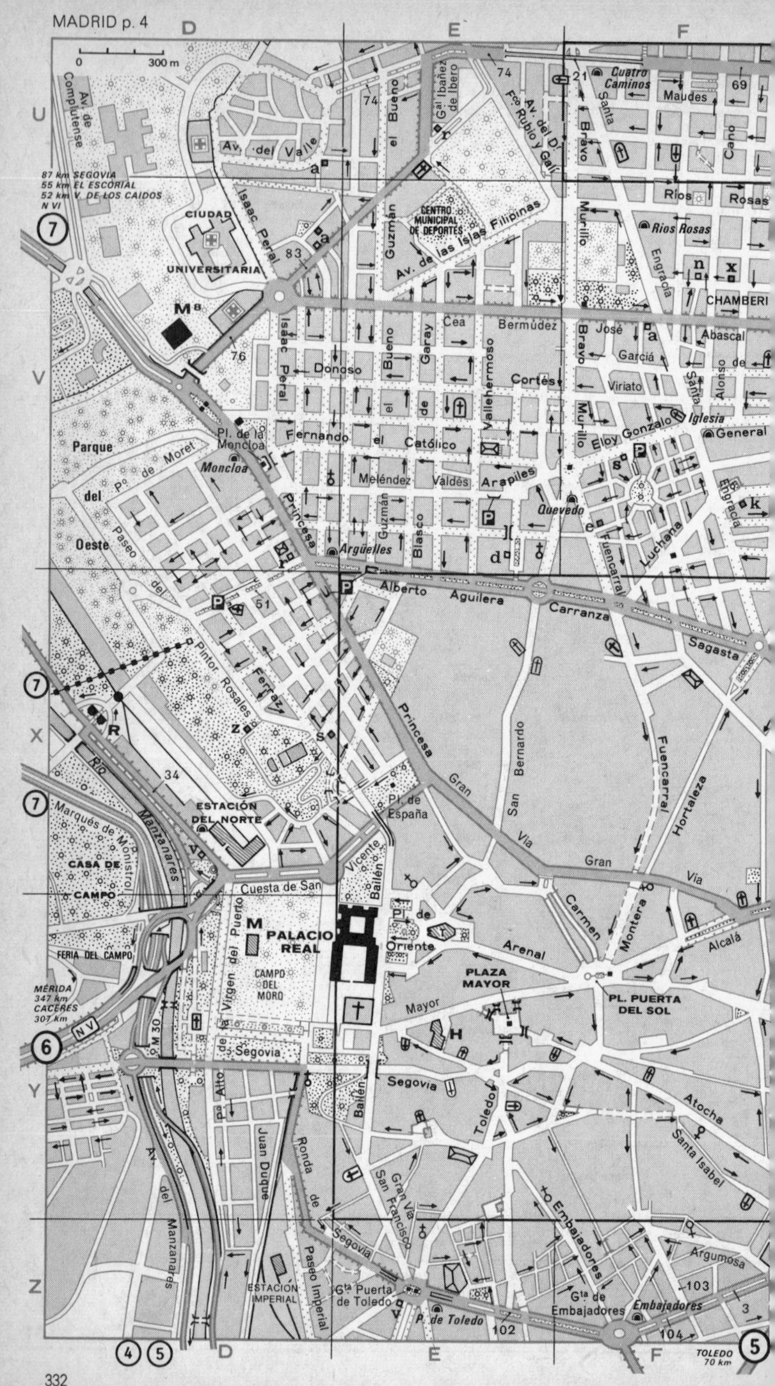
D
E
F
0 300 m
U
V
X
Y
Z
87 km SEGOVIA
55 km EL ESCORIAL
52 km V. DE LOS CAIDOS
N VI
CIUDAD UNIVERSITARIA
Av. de Complutense
Av. del Valle
Isaac Peral
CENTRO MUNICIPAL DE DEPORTES
Av. de las Islas Filipinas
Cuatro Caminos
Maudes
Ríos Rosas
CHAMBERI
Bermúdez
José Abascal
García
Cortés
Viriato
Iglesia
General
Eloy Gonzalo
Donoso
Fernando el Católico
Meléndez Valdés
Arapiles
Quevedo
Argüelles
Princesa
Pl. de la Moncloa
Moncloa
Parque del Oeste
Pº de Moret
Paseo del Pintor Rosales
Ferraz
Alberto Aguilera
Carranza
Sagasta
Fuencarral
Luchana
San Bernardo
Gran Vía
Hortaleza
Pl. de España
ESTACIÓN DEL NORTE
Río Manzanares
Marqués de Monistrol
CASA DE CAMPO
Cuesta de San Vicente
Bailén
PALACIO REAL
CAMPO DEL MORO
Pl. de Oriente
Arenal
Carmen
Montera
Alcalá
PLAZA MAYOR
PL. PUERTA DEL SOL
Mayor
FERIA DEL CAMPO
MÉRIDA 347 km
CÁCERES 307 km
N V
M 30
Virgen del Puerto
Segovia
Pº Alto
Juan Duque
Ronda de Segovia
Gran Vía San Francisco
Toledo
Atocha
Santa Isabel
Embajadores
Argumosa
Av. del Manzanares
ESTACIÓN IMPERIAL
Paseo Imperial
Gta Puerta de Toledo
P. de Toledo
Gta de Embajadores
TOLEDO 70 km

MADRID

Atocha (Ronda de)	FZ	3
Emperador Carlos V (Glorieta del)	GZ	28
Florida (Paseo de la)	DX	34
Infanta Isabel (Pas.)	GZ	42
Lagasca	HVX	44
Marqués de Salamanca (Pl.)	HV	50
Marqués de Urquijo	DX	51
Miguel Angel	GV	55
Reina Cristina (Pas.)	HZ	72
Reina Victoria (Av.)	EU	74
Reyes Católicos (Av.)	DV	76
San Francisco de Sales (Pas.)	DV	83
Toledo (Ronda de)	EZ	102
Valencia	FZ	103
Valencia (Ronda de)	FZ	104

K
L
Alberto
Aguilera
Gta Ruiz Jiménez
San Bernardo
Luchana
Gta de Bilbao
Fco
Rojas
Sta Cruz
de
Marcenado
Carranza
Bilbao
Princesa
Fuencarral
Sagasta
Divino
Pastor
Apodaca
Duque
Pl. 2 de Mayo
Barceló
V
V. Rodríguez
Conde
Amaniel
Palma
Bernardo
Palma
Tribunal
San Mateo
Noviciado
San
Reyes
TORRE DE MADRID
Reyes
Princesa
Pez
Pl. de España
Pl. de España
Ferraz
Valverde
Pez
Leganitos
Bernardo
Puebla
Fuencarral
Hortaleza
JARDINES DE SABATINI
Bailén
X
Santo Domingo
Gran Vía
Infantas
Pl. Sto Domingo
Callao
Gran
Gran Vía
Gran
Vía
Bolsa
Arrieta
Pl. Callao
Vía
PALACIO REAL
Pl. de Oriente
Pl. de Isabel II
Opera
Carmen
Y
PL. PUERTA DEL SOL
Montera
Sevilla
Alcalá
Arenal
Sol
Mayor
Pl. de Canalejas
Bailén
POL.
Carretas
Príncipe
Mayor
PLAZA MAYOR
Cruz
Sacramento
Pl. J. Benavente
Pl. de Sta Ana
Segovia
Segovia
Toledo
Concepción
Jerónima
Atocha
Huertas
Atocha
Z
Cava Baja
Colegiata
Antón Martín
Bailén
Pl. Tirso de Molina
Magdalena
Don Pedro
Cava Alta
Pl. Pta de Moros
Cra S. Francisco
Duque de Alba
Pl. de Cascorro
Embajadores
Toledo
Lavapiés
0
200 m

MADRID

XXX **Korynto,** Preciados 36, ✉ 28013, ☎ 221 59 65, Seafood – AE ⓓ E VISA. ✻ KX a
M a la carte 2 200/4 100.

XXX **Bajamar,** Gran Vía 78, ✉ 28013, ☎ 248 48 18, Telex 22818, Seafood – ▤. AE ⓓ E VISA. ✻ KV r
M a la carte 2 520/4 370.

XXX El Escuadrón, Tamayo y Baús 8, ✉ 28004, ☎ 419 28 30 – ▤ NV s

XXX **El Landó,** pl. Gabriel Miró 8, ✉ 28005, ☎ 266 76 81, Tasteful decor – ▤. AE ⓓ E VISA. ✻ KZ a
closed Sunday and August – **M** a la carte 1 995/3 905.

XXX ✿ **Irizar** 1st floor, Jovellanos 3, ✉ 28014, ☎ 231 45 69, Basque and French rest. – ▤. AE ⓓ VISA. ✻ MY d
closed Saturday lunch, Sunday, Bank Holidays dinner, 21 to 26 December and Holy-Week – **M** a la carte 2 775/4 175
Spec. Ostras gratinadas a la muselina de limón (Sept.-April), Suprema de lubina con almejas, Lomo de cordero relleno de riñones en hojaldre.

XX El Espejo, paseo de Recoletos 31, ✉ 28004, ☎ 410 25 25, « Old Parisian café style » – ▤ NV a

XX **El Descubrimiento,** pl. Colón 1, ✉ 28004, ☎ 410 28 51 – ▤. AE ⓓ E VISA. ✻ NV M
closed Sunday – **M** a la carte 1 750/3 650.

XX Platerías, pl. de Santa Ana 11, ✉ 28012, ☎ 429 70 48, Early 20C café style – ▤ LZ b

XX **Jaun de Alzate,** Princesa 18, ✉ 28008, ☎ 247 00 10 – ▤. AE ⓓ E VISA. ✻ KV a
M a la carte 3 000/4 975.

XX **La Grillade,** Jardines 3, ✉ 28013, ☎ 221 22 17 – ▤. AE ⓓ E VISA. ✻ LY p
M a la carte 1 920/4 175.

XX **Valentín,** San Alberto 3, ✉ 28013, ☎ 221 16 38 – ▤. AE ⓓ E VISA. ✻ LY h
M a la carte 2 250/4 050.

XX ✿ **Gure-Etxea,** pl. de la Paja 12, ✉ 28005, ☎ 265 61 49, Basque rest. – ▤. AE ⓓ VISA. ✻ KZ x
closed Sunday and August – **M** a la carte 2 275/3 500
Spec. Foie de canard casero, Lomo de merluza Gure-Etxea, Bacalao.

X Pazo de Monterrey, Alcalá 4, ✉ 28014, ☎ 222 30 10, Galician rest. – ▤ LY c

X **Pipó,** Augusto Figueroa 37, ✉ 28004, ☎ 221 71 18 – ▤. AE ⓓ E VISA MX c
closed Sunday and August – **M** a la carte 1 295/2 785.

X Carpanta, Bailen 20, ✉ 28005, ☎ 265 82 37 – ▤. AE ⓓ E VISA KZ b

X **Casa Lucio,** Cava Baja 35, ✉ 28005, ☎ 265 32 52, Castilian decor – ▤. AE ⓓ VISA. ✻ KZ y
closed Saturday lunch and August – **M** a la carte 2 650/4 000.

X **Esteban,** Cava Baja 36, ✉ 28005, ☎ 265 90 91 – ▤. AE ⓓ VISA. ✻ KZ y
closed Sunday and July – **M** a la carte 1 750/3 890.

X **El Mentidero de la Villa,** Santo Tomé 6, ✉ 28004, ☎ 419 55 06 – ▤. AE ⓓ E VISA MV b
M a la carte 2 345/3 925.

X Cava del Almirante, Almirante 11, ✉ 28004, ☎ 231 62 76 – ▤ MNX x

X **La Gran Tasca,** Ballesta 1, ✉ 28004, ☎ 231 00 44 – AE ⓓ E VISA. ✻ LX x
closed Sunday and June-August – **M** a la carte 2 075/4 275.

Typical atmosphere :

XXX **Café de Chinitas,** Torija 7, ✉ 28013, ☎ 248 51 35, Flamenco cabaret – ▤. AE E. ✻ KX p
closed Sunday and 24 December – **M** (dinner only) a la carte 3 175/5 575 (extra charge for show).

XX **Posada de la Villa,** Cava Baja 9, ✉ 28005, ☎ 266 18 60, Castilian decor – ▤. AE ⓓ VISA. ✻ KZ v
closed Sunday dinner – **M** a la carte 2 050/4 000.

XX **Botín,** Cuchilleros 17, ✉ 28005, ☎ 266 42 17, Old Madrid decor, Typical bodega – ▤. AE ⓓ E VISA KZ n
M a la carte 2 030/3 995.

XX **Sixto Gran Mesón,** Cervantes 28, ✉ 28014, ☎ 429 22 55, Castilian decor – ▤. AE ⓓ E VISA MZ n
closed Sunday dinner – **M** a la carte 1 600/2 925.

XX **Las Cuevas de Luis Candelas,** Cuchilleros 1, ✉ 28012, ☎ 266 54 28, Old Madrid decor - Staff in bandit costume – ▤. AE ⓓ E VISA. ✻ KZ m
M a la carte 1 700/3 725.

X **Corral de la Morería,** Morería 17, ✉ 28005, ☎ 265 11 37, Flamenco cabaret – ▤. AE ⓓ E VISA. ✻ KZ u
M (dinner only) (extra charge for show) a la carte 2 550/4 100.

X **Taberna del Alabardero,** Felipe V - 6, ✉ 28013, ☎ 247 25 77, Typical tavern – ▤. AE ⓓ E VISA KY h
M a la carte 2 200/4 175.

X **El Cosaco,** pl. de la Paja 2, ✉ 28005, ☎ 265 35 48, Russian rest. – ⓓ KZ z
M (dinner only except Sunday and Bank Holidays) a la carte 1 195/2 690.

Retiro-Salamanca-Ciudad Lineal : Castellana, Velázquez, Serrano, Goya, Príncipe de Vergara, Narváez, Don Ramón de la Cruz (plan p. 5 except where otherwise stated) :

Ritz, pl. de la Lealtad 5, 28014, 221 28 57, Telex 43986, – . AE VISA. rest — plan p. 7 NY **k**
M 8 500 – 1 500 – **156 rm** 25 000/48 000.

Villa Magna, paseo de la Castellena 22, 28046, 261 49 00, Telex 22914 – . AE E VISA. — plan p. 7 NV **x**
M 4 000 – 1 400 – **196 rm** 22 000/30 000 – P 20 650/25 900.

Wellington, Velázquez 8, 28001, 275 44 00, Telex 22700, – . AE E VISA. — HX **t**
M (see rest **El Fogón** below) – 895 – **287 rm** 9 600/15 200.

Fenix, without rest., coffee shop only, Hermosilla 2, 28001, 403 60 65, Telex 45639 – — plan p. 7 NV **c**
229 rm.

Sanvy and Rest. Belagua, Goya 3, 28001, 276 08 00, Telex 44994, – . AE E VISA. — plan p. 7 NV **r**
closed Sunday – **M** a la carte 2 150/4 500 – 700 – **141 rm** 8 700/10 900.

Convención without rest., coffee shop only, O'Donnell 53, 28009, 274 68 00, Telex 23944 – . AE E VISA. — JX **a**
530 – **790 rm** 6 640/8 375.

Los Galgos and Rest. Diabolo, Claudio Coello 139, 28006, 262 66 00, Telex 43957 – . AE E VISA — HV **a**
M *(closed Sunday)* a la carte 1 800/3 700 – 675 – **358 rm** 8 625/12 650 – P 10 865/13 165.

G. H. Velázquez, Velázquez 62, 28001, 275 28 00, Telex 22779 – . AE E VISA. — HX **s**
M 1 900 – 500 – **145 rm** 6 725/11 200 – P 7 700/10 225.

Novotel Madrid, Albacete 1, 28027, 405 46 00, Telex 41862, , – . AE E VISA.
M 2 200 – 675 – **240 rm** 7 900/9 900 – P 9 250/12 200.

G. H. Colón, Pez Volador 11, 28007, 273 59 00, Telex 22984, , – . AE E VISA. rest — JY **x**
M 1 975 – 400 – **390 rm** 4 000/5 750 – P 4 500/4 750.

Alcalá and Rest. Basque, Alcalá 66, 28009, 435 10 60, Telex 48094 – . AE E VISA. — HX **w**
M *(closed Sunday and Monday lunch)* a la carte 1 550/3 725 – 500 – **153 rm** 6 050/8 970.

Pintor, Goya 79, 28001, 435 75 45, Telex 23281 – . AE. — HX **c**
M 1 100 – 575 – **176 rm** 5 775/8 765.

Emperatriz without rest., coffee shop only, López de Hoyos 4, 28006, 413 65 11, Telex 43640 – . AE E VISA. — GV **z**
450 – **170 rm** 5 400/8 800.

Agumar without rest., coffee shop only, paseo Reina Cristina 9, 28014, 252 69 00, Telex 22814 – . AE E VISA. — HZ **a**
475 – **252 rm** 5 810/7 270.

Serrano, without rest., Marqués de Villamejor 8, 28006, 435 52 00 – — HV **b**
34 rm.

Claridge without rest., coffee shop only, pl. del Conde de Casal 6, 28007, 251 94 00, Telex 45585 – wc wc . AE E VISA — JZ **a**
350 – **150 rm** 3 150/5 050.

Abeba without rest., Alcántara 63, 28006, 401 16 50 – wc . AE E VISA. — HV **r**
350 – **90 rm** 3 700/5 825.

Don Diego 5th floor, without rest., Velázquez 45, 28001, 435 07 60 – wc . — HX **k**
395 – **58 rm** 4 100/5 820.

XXXX ❀ **Horcher,** Alfonso XII - 6, 28014, 222 07 31, « Tasteful decor » – . AE . — plan p. 7 NY **n**
closed Sunday – **M** a la carte 3 050/4 550
Spec. Ensalada de bogavante, Tartar de lubina, Ragoût de venado (October-February).

XXX **Bidasoa,** Claudio Coello 24, 28001, 431 20 81 – . AE E VISA. — HX **h**
closed Sunday and Bank Holidays – **M** a la carte 3 000/8 600.

XXX **Club 31,** Alcalá 58, 28014, 231 00 92 – . AE E VISA. — plan p. 7 NX **e**
closed August – **M** a la carte 3 700/5 400.

XXX ❀❀ **El Amparo,** Puigcerdá 8, 28001, 431 64 56, Basque and French cuisine – . AE VISA. — HX **h**
closed Saturday lunch, Sunday, Holy-Week and August – **M** a la carte 3 150/5 250
Spec. Pimientos de piquillo rellenos de bacalao, Ragoût de lenguado y vieiras con verduras, Magret de pato al vinagre de Jerez.

XXX Lucca, José Ortega y Gasset 29, 28006, 276 01 44, Modern decor, Pianist at dinner – — HV **f**

XXX **Villa y Corte de Madrid,** Serrano 110, ✉ 28006, ☎ 261 29 77, Elegant decor – ▤. AE ⊕ VISA. ✻ HV **a**
M a la carte 2 995/3 775.

XXX El Gran Chambelán, Ayala 46, ✉ 28001, ☎ 431 77 45 – ▤ HX **r**

XXX **Balzac,** Moreto 7, ✉ 28014, ☎ 239 19 22 – ▤. AE ⊕ VISA. ✻ plan p. 7 NZ **a**
closed Saturday lunch and Sunday – **M** a la carte 3 525/5 250.

XXX La Puerta de Madrid, Alcalá 79, ✉ 28009, ☎ 431 22 85 – ▤ HX **m**

XX **St.-James,** Juan Bravo 26, ✉ 28020, ☎ 275 60 10, ☂, Rice rest. – ▤. AE. ✻ HV **t**
closed Sunday – **M** a la carte 1 700/3 700.

XX **Caruso,** Serrano 70, ✉ 28001, ☎ 435 52 62 – ▤. AE ⊕ VISA. ✻ HVX **p**
closed Sunday and Bank Holidays – **M** a la carte 2 000/3 600.

XX **Schwarzwald (Selva Negra),** O'Donnel 46, ✉ 28009, ☎ 409 56 13, « Original decor » – ▤. AE ⊕ E VISA. ✻ JX **n**
M a la carte 1 775/2 975.

XX **Al Mounia,** Recoletos 5, ✉ 28001, ☎ 435 08 28, « Oriental atmosphere », North African rest. – ▤. AE ⊕ E VISA. ✻ plan p. 7 NX **s**
closed Sunday, Monday and August – **M** a la carte 2 400/2 930.

XX **La Fonda,** Lagasca 11, ✉ 28001, ☎ 403 83 07, Catalonian rest – ▤. AE ⊕ E VISA. ✻ HX **f**
M a la carte 1 900/3 000.

XX **Ponteareas,** Claudio Coello 96, ✉ 28006, ☎ 275 58 73, Galician rest – ▤. AE ⊕ E VISA. ✻ HV **w**
closed August – **M** a la carte 2 485/4 680.

XX **El Fogón,** Villanueva 34, ✉ 28001, ☎ 275 44 00, Telex 22700, « Spanish rustic style decor » – ▤. AE ⊕ E VISA. ✻ HX **t**
closed August – **M** a la carte 2 440/4 650.

XX **House of Ming,** paseo de la Castellana 74, ✉ 28001, ☎ 261 98 27, Chinese rest. – AE ⊕ E VISA. ✻ GV **f**
M a la carte 1 550/3 375.

X **Asador Velate,** Jorge Juan 91, ✉ 28009, ☎ 435 10 24, Basque rest. – ▤. AE VISA. ✻ HJX **x**
closed Sunday and August – **M** a la carte 2 275/3 925.

X ✿ **El Pescador,** José Ortega y Gasset 75, ✉ 28006, ☎ 402 12 90, Seafood – ▤. ✻ JV **t**
closed Sunday and 10 August-15 September – **M** a la carte 2 050/2 850
Spec. Sopa El Pescador, Lenguado Evaristo, Langosta a la americana.

X ✿ **La Trainera,** Lagasca 60, ✉ 28001, ☎ 276 80 35, Seafood – ▤. VISA. ✻ HX **k**
closed Sunday and August – **M** a la carte 2 050/3 850
Spec. Sopa de pescados y mariscos, Pescados y mariscos a la plancha, Langosta y bogavante a la americana.

Arganzuela, Carabanchel, Villaverde : Antonio López, paseo de Las Delicias, Santa María de la Cabeza :

🏨 **Praga** without rest., coffee shop only, Antonio López 65, ✉ 28019, ☎ 469 06 00, Telex 22823 – ⧉ ▤ 🚗. AE ⊕ E VISA. ✻ by ⑤
☕ 400 – **428 rm** 3 835/5 175.

🏨 **Aramo** without rest., coffee shop only, paseo Santa María de la Cabeza 73, ✉ 28045, ☎ 473 91 11, Telex 45885 – ⧉ ▤ TV 🚗. AE ⊕ E VISA by ⑤
☕ 400 – **105 rm** 4 500/6 500.

🏨 **Puerta de Toledo,** glorieta Puerta de Toledo 4, ✉ 28005, ☎ 474 71 00, Telex 22291 – ⧉ ▤ 🚗. AE ⊕ E VISA. ✻ plan p. 4 EZ **v**
M (rest. see **Puerta de Toledo** below) – ☕ 350 – **152 rm** 3 050/5 600.

🏨 **Carlton,** paseo de las Delicias 26, ✉ 28045, ☎ 239 71 00, Telex 44571 – ⧉ ▤. AE ⊕ VISA. ✻ plan p. 5 GZ **n**
M 1 650 – ☕ 550 – **133 rm** 6 200/9 300 – P 7 730/9 280.

XX **Puerta de Toledo,** glorieta Puerta de Toledo 4, ✉ 28005, ☎ 474 76 75, Telex 22291 – ▤. ⊕ E VISA. ✻ plan p. 4 EZ **v**
M a la carte approx. 2 100.

Moncloa : Princesa, Rosales, paseo Florida, Casa de Campo (plan p. 4 except where otherwise stated) :

🏨 **Meliá Madrid,** Princesa 27, ✉ 28008, ☎ 241 82 00, Telex 22537, ☂ – ⧉ ▤ TV – 🏔. AE ⊕ E VISA. ✻ plan p. 6 KV **t**
M 3 600 – ☕ 850 – **265 rm** 11 500/24 500 – P 13 090/18 340.

🏨 **Florida Norte** M, paseo de la Florida 5, ✉ 28008, ☎ 241 61 90, Telex 23675 – ⧉ ▤ TV 🚗. AE ⊕ E VISA. ✻ rest DX **v**
M 1 550 – ☕ 450 – **399 rm** 6 200/8 500.

🏨 **Príncipe Pío,** cuesta de San Vicente 16, ✉ 28008, ☎ 247 08 00, Telex 42183 – ⧉ ▤ 🚗 Ⓟ. ✻ rest plan p. 6 KX **d**
M 1 400 – ☕ 430 – **157 rm** 4 140/5 920 – P 5 635/6 815.

🏨 **Tirol** without rest., coffee shop only and no ☕, Marqués de Urquijo 4, ✉ 28008, ☎ 248 19 00 – ⧉ ▤ 🛁wc ☎ 🚗. VISA. ✻ DV **r**
93 rm 3 575/5 100.

XXX **Café Viena,** Luisa Fernanda 23, ✉ 28008, ℘ 248 15 91, Pianist at dinner, « Old style café » – ▤. AE ⓓ E VISA. ✻ DX **s**
closed Sunday and August – **M** a la carte 2 175/3 400.

XXX **Los Porches,** paseo Pintor Rosales 1, ✉ 28008, ℘ 247 70 53, 🏡 – ▤. AE ⓓ E VISA. ✻ DX **z**
M a la carte 2 250/4 100.

Chamberí : San Bernardo, Fuencarral, Alberto Aguilera, Santa Engracia (plan pp. 4 to 7) :

Miguel Angel Ⓜ, Miguel Angel 31, ✉ 28010, ℘ 442 00 22, Telex 44235, ⛱ – |♦| ▤ TV 🚗 – 🏛. AE ⓓ E VISA. ✻ GV **c**
M 3 800 – ☕ 950 – **300 rm** 12 800/19 000 – P 18 150/21 450.

Mindanao, paseo San Francisco de Sales 15, ✉ 28003, ℘ 449 55 00, Telex 22631, ⛱, ⛱ – |♦| ▤ TV 🚗 – 🏛. AE ⓓ E VISA. ✻ DV **a**
M 2 895 – ☕ 700 – **289 rm** 11 200/14 000 – P 16 390/24 380.

Luz Palacio, paseo de la Castellana 57, ✉ 28046, ℘ 442 51 00, Telex 27207 – |♦| ▤ TV 🚗 – 🏛. AE ⓓ E VISA. ✻ GV **p**
M 3 500 – ☕ 750 – **200 rm** 11 000/16 500 – P 14 700/17 500.

Castellana without rest., coffee shop only, paseo de la Castellana 49, ✉ 28046, ℘ 410 02 00, Telex 27686 – |♦| ▤ TV 🚗 – 🏛. AE ⓓ E VISA. ✻ GV **a**
☕ 1 200 – **320 rm** 17 500/21 000.

Escultor and Rest. Vanity, Miguel Angel 3, ✉ 28010, ℘ 410 42 03, Telex 44285 – |♦| ▤ TV 🚗. AE ⓓ VISA GV **s**
M 2 500 – ☕ 700 – **82 apartments** 6 950/11 500 – P 10 850/12 050.

Las Alondras without rest., coffee shop only, José Abascal 8, ✉ 28003, ℘ 447 40 00, Telex 49454 – |♦| ▤ TV. AE ⓓ E VISA. ✻ FV **a**
☕ 500 – **72 rm** 7 700/9 700.

Bretón, without rest., Bretón de los Herreros 29, ✉ 28003, ℘ 442 83 00 – |♦| ▤ TV 🛁wc 🚿wc ☎ – **56 rm.** FV **n**

Conde Duque without rest., coffee shop only, pl. Conde Valle de Suchil 5, ✉ 28015, ℘ 447 70 00, Telex 22058 – |♦| 🛁wc ☎ – 🏛. AE ⓓ E VISA EV **d**
☕ 350 – **138 rm** 3 325/5 665.

Zurbano, Zurbano 79, ✉ 28003, ℘ 441 45 00, Telex 27578 – |♦| ▤ 🛁wc ☎ 🚗. AE E VISA. ✻ rest GV **x**
M 1 600 – ☕ 400 – **261 rm** 5 100/6 800 – P 6 400/8 100.

Embajada, without rest., Santa Engracia 5, ✉ 28010, ℘ 447 33 00 – |♦| ▤ 🛁wc ☎ **65 rm.** MV **r**

Trafalgar without rest., Trafalgar 35, ✉ 28010, ℘ 445 62 00 – |♦| ▤ 🛁wc 🚿wc ☎. AE ⓓ E VISA. ✻ FV **s**
☕ 250 – **45 rm** 3 300/5 700.

XXXXX Fortuny, Fortuny 34, ✉ 28010, ℘ 410 77 07, 🏡, Former palace tastefully decorated-terrace – ▤ GV **n**

XXXX ✿ **Jockey,** Amador de los Ríos 6, ✉ 28010, ℘ 419 24 35, « Tasteful decor » – ▤ Ⓟ. AE ⓓ E VISA. ✻ NV **k**
closed Sunday, Bank Holidays and August – **M** a la carte 3 950/5 800
Spec. Huevos escalfados a la mousselina de trufas, Ragoût de bogavante con pasta, Pato deshuesado con higos..

XXX **Lúculo,** Génova 19, ✉ 28004, ℘ 419 40 29 – ▤. AE ⓓ VISA. ✻ NV **d**
closed Saturday lunch, Sunday, Bank Holidays, 1 week at Easter, 1 week at Christmas and 15 August – **M** a la carte 3 750/5 650.

XXX **Las Cuatro Estaciones,** General Ibañez Ibero 5, ✉ 28003, ℘ 253 63 05, Modern decor – ▤. AE ⓓ VISA. ✻ EU **r**
closed Saturday, Sunday and August-2 September – **M** a la carte 3 600/6 300.

XXX **Lur Maitea,** Fernando el Santo 4, ✉ 28010, ℘ 419 09 38, Basque rest. – ▤. AE ⓓ E VISA. ✻ MNV **u**
closed Saturday lunch, Sunday, Bank Holidays and August – **M** a la carte 2 900/4 450.

XX **Aymar,** Fuencarral 138, ✉ 28010, ℘ 445 57 67, Seafood – ▤. AE ⓓ E VISA. ✻ FV **e**
M a la carte 1 950/3 400.

XX **Las Reses,** Orfila 3, ✉ 28010, ℘ 419 10 13, Meat rest. – ▤. AE VISA. ✻ NV **e**
closed Sunday, Bank Holidays and August – **M** a la carte 2 075/3 600.

XX **L'Alsace,** Doménico Scarlatti 5, ✉ 28003, ℘ 244 40 75, « Alsatian decor » – ▤. AE ⓓ E VISA. ✻ DV **a**
M a la carte 2 000/2 900.

X **Quattrocento,** General Ampudia 18, ✉ 28003, ℘ 234 91 06, Italian rest. – ▤. AE ⓓ VISA. ✻ DU **a**
closed Sunday dinner – **M** a la carte 1 790/3 185.

X La Parra, Monte Esquinza 34, ✉ 28010, ℘ 419 54 98 – ▤ NV **z**

X **La Plaza de Chamberí,** pl. de Chamberí 10, ✉ 28010, ℘ 446 06 97, 🏡 – ▤. AE ⓓ E VISA. ✻ FV **k**
closed Sunday, Bank Holidays dinner and Holy-Week – **M** a la carte 1 770/3 450.

X **Casa Félix,** Bretón de los Herreros 39, ✉ 28003, ℘ 441 24 79 – ▤. AE E VISA. ✻ FV **x**
M a la carte 1 800/3 850.

Chamartín, Tetuán : Capitán Haya, Orense, Alberto Alcocer, paseo de la Habana (plan p. 3 except where otherwise stated) :

Eurobuilding Ⓜ, Padre Damián 23, ✉ 28036, ℰ 457 31 00, Telex 22548, « Garden with » – . AE E VISA. HS **a**
M (rest see Balthasar and **La Taberna** below) – 900 – **544 rm** 11 700/15 450.

Meliá Castilla Ⓜ, Capitán Haya 43, ✉ 28020, ℰ 270 81 00, Telex 23142, – . AE E VISA. GS **c**
850 – **1 000 rm** 11 550/14 450.

Holiday Inn, av. General Perón, ✉ 28020, ℰ 456 70 14, Telex 44709, Pianist at dinner, – . AE E VISA. rest GT **z**
M 2 250 – 950 – **313 rm** 12 075/15 625 – P 15 275/21 925.

Cuzco without rest., coffee shop only, paseo de la Castellana 133, ✉ 28046, ℰ 456 06 00, Telex 22464 – . AE E VISA. GS **a**
750 – **330 rm** 8 200/10 500.

Chamartín without rest., estación de Chamartín (railway station), ✉ 28036, ℰ 733 90 11, Telex 49201 – . AE E VISA. HR
600 – **378 rm** 6 300/8 850.

Foxá 32 Ⓜ without rest., coffee shop only, Agustín de Foxá 32, ✉ 28036, ℰ 733 10 60, Telex 49366 – . AE E VISA. HR **u**
350 – **161 rm** 5 500/6 900.

El Gran Atlanta without rest., Comandante Zorita 34, ✉ 28020, ℰ 253 59 00, Telex 45210 – . AE E VISA FT **p**
650 – **180 rm** 6 960/8 700.

Apart. Suite Foxá 25 Ⓜ without rest., Agustín de Foxá 25, ✉ 28036, ℰ 733 70 64, Telex 44911 – . AE E VISA. HR **a**
50 – **121 rm** 5 600/6 900.

Apartotel El Jardín Ⓜ without rest., carret. N I (vía de servicio), ✉ 28034, ℰ 202 83 36, – by ①
41 rm.

Aitana without rest., coffee shop only, paseo de la Castellana 152, ✉ 28046, ℰ 250 60 05, Telex 49186 – . AE VISA. GT **c**
450 – **111 rm** 5 400/8 000.

Aristos and Rest El Chaflán, av. Pío XII-34, ✉ 28016, ℰ 457 04 50, – wc . AE VISA. HS **d**
M *(closed Sunday)* a la carte 2 250/3 600 – 400 – **25 rm** 4 300/7 000.

XXXXX ✿✿✿ **Zalacaín,** Álvarez de Baena 4, ✉ 28006, ℰ 261 48 40, , « Elegant decor » – . AE . plan p. 5 GV **b**
closed Saturday lunch, Sunday, Holy-Week and August – **M** a la carte 4 850/7 525.

XXXX Balthazar, Juan Ramón Jiménez 8, ✉ 28036, ℰ 457 91 91, Telex 22548, « Tasteful classic decor » – HS **a**

XXXX Mayte Commodore, pl. República Argentina 5, ✉ 28002, ℰ 261 86 06, , « Elegant decor » – HU **v**

XXXX ✿ **El Bodegón,** Pinar 15, ✉ 28006, ℰ 262 34 15 – . AE E VISA. plan p. 5 GV **q**
closed Sunday and August – **M** a la carte 3 830/5 780
Spec. Abanico de salmón y mero a las tres compotas, Lomos de liebre con salsa de marinada (Game season), Hojaldre de chocolate con menta.

XXXX ✿ **Príncipe de Viana,** Manuel de Falla 5, ✉ 28036, ℰ 259 14 48, Basque rest. – . AE . GT **c**
closed Saturday lunch, Sunday, Holy-Week and August – **M** a la carte 3 775/5 950.

XXX **Nicolasa,** Velázquez 150, ✉ 28002, ℰ 261 99 85 – AE E VISA. HU **a**
closed Sunday and August – **M** a la carte 3 240/5 130.

XXX **Nuevo Valentín,** av. Concha Espina 8, ✉ 28036, ℰ 259 74 16, – . AE E VISA. GT **n**
M a la carte 2 250/4 250.

XXX **O'Pazo,** Reina Mercedes 20, ✉ 28020, ℰ 234 37 48, Seafood – . FT **p**
closed Sunday and August – **M** a la carte 2 150/3 800.

XXX **L'Albufera,** Capitán Haya 45, ✉ 28020, ℰ 270 80 00, Telex 23142, Pianist at dinner – . AE E VISA. GS **c**
closed August – **M** a la carte 1 220/4 600.

XXX **La Gabarra,** Santo Domingo de Silos 6, ✉ 28036, ℰ 458 78 97, Basque rest. – . AE E VISA. GT **s**
closed Saturday lunch, Sunday, Bank Holidays and August – **M** a la carte 2 650/4 450.

XXX **La Máquina,** Sor Angela de la Cruz 22, ✉ 28020, ℰ 270 61 05 – . AE E VISA. FS **e**
closed Sunday and Bank Holidays dinner – **M** a la carte 2 300/4 450.

XXX **José Luis,** Rafael Salgado 11, ✉ 28036, ℰ 250 02 42, – . AE E VISA. GT **m**
closed Sunday and August – **M** a la carte 2 200/4 100.

XXX La Boucade, Capitán Haya 30, ✉ 28020, ℰ 456 02 45 – GS **a**

XXX Cota 13, estación de Chamartín (railway station), ✉ 28036, ℰ 215 10 83, – HR

XXX **Bogavante,** Capitán Haya 20, ✉ 28020, ✆ 456 21 14, Seafood – ▤. AE ⓞ E VISA. ✗ GT **d**
closed Sunday dinner – **M** a la carte 2 600/4 200.

XXX **Itxaso,** Capitán Haya 58, ✉ 28020, ✆ 450 64 64, Basque rest. – ▤. AE ⓞ E VISA. ✗ GS **n**
closed Sunday and August – **M** a la carte 2 450/4 400.

XXX ✻ **Señorío de Bertiz,** Comandante Zorita 6, ✉ 28020, ✆ 233 27 57 – ▤. AE ⓞ E VISA. ✗ FT **s**
closed Sunday, Bank Holidays and August – **M** a la carte 2 500/4 575.

XXX **Amalur,** Padre Damián 37, ✉ 28036, ✆ 457 62 98 – ▤. AE ⓞ E VISA. ✗ HS **c**
closed Sunday, Bank Holidays, Holy-Week and 24 July-August – **M** a la carte 2 400/5 200.

XXX Señorio de Alcocer, Alberto Alcocer 1, ✉ 28036, ✆ 457 16 96 – ▤ GS **e**

XXX **Gaztelubide,** Comandante Zorita 37, ✉ 28020, ✆ 233 01 85 – ▤. AE ⓞ E VISA. ✗ FT **a**
closed Sunday dinner – **M** a la carte 2 240/4 100.

XXX **La Taberna,** Padre Damian 23, ✉ 28036, ✆ 457 78 00, Telex 22548 – ▤ 🚗. AE ⓞ E VISA. ✗ HS **a**
M a la carte 2 710/4 765.

XX El Hostal, Príncipe de Vergara 285, ✉ 28023, ✆ 259 11 94 – ▤. AE ⓞ E VISA. ✗ HS **e**

XX ✻ **Cabo Mayor,** Juan Hurtado de Mendoza 11 (back), ✉ 28036, ✆ 250 87 76, Telex 49784, « Original decor » – ▤. AE ⓞ E VISA. ✗ GHS **r**
closed Sunday and 15 August-2 September – **M** a la carte 3 150/3 800
Spec. Ensalada de salmón con maiz, Merluza a la mantequilla de limón con uvas, Pichón estofado al jerez con hongos.

XX El Faisán de Oro, Bolivia 11, ✉ 28016, ✆ 259 30 76 – ▤ HS **t**

XX **Fass,** Rodriguez Marín 84, ✉ 28022, ✆ 457 22 02, Bavarian decor, German cuisine – ▤. AE ⓞ E VISA. ✗ HT **t**
M a la carte 1 950/3 100.

XX Rugantino, Velázquez 136, ✉ 28006, ✆ 261 02 22, Italian rest. – ▤ plan p. 5 HV **e**

XX **De Funy,** Serrano 213, ✉ 28016, ✆ 259 72 25, Telex 44885, ☂, Lebanese rest., Pianist at dinner – ▤. AE ⓞ E VISA. ✗ HT **z**
M a la carte 2 000/3 750.

XX **Rheinfall,** Padre Damián 44, ✉ 28036, ✆ 457 82 88, German cuisine, « Regional decor » – ▤. AE ⓞ E VISA. ✗ HS **u**
M a la carte 2 050/3 650.

X Asador Donostiarra, Pedro Villar 14, ✉ 28020, ✆ 279 73 40, Basque rustic decor – ▤ FS **a**

X **Los Borrachos de Velázquez,** Príncipe de Vergara 205, ✉ 28002, ✆ 458 10 76, Andalusian rest. – ▤. AE ⓞ VISA. ✗ HT **s**
closed Sunday and Holy-Week – **M** a la carte 2 350/3 950.

Environs

at Ciudad Puerta de Hierro by ⑦ : 8 km by N VI and road to El Pardo – ✉ 28035 Madrid – ☎ 91 :

🏨 **Monte Real** 🔇, Arroyofresno 17 ✆ 216 21 40, Telex 22089, ☂, « Elegant decor, garden », ⛱ – |♦| ▤ 🚗 Ⓟ – 🏛. AE ⓞ E VISA
M 4 600 – ☕ 960 – **79 rm** 12 000/19 200 – P 18 800/21 200.

by ② ***: N II*** and Coslada - San Fernando Road E : 12 km – ✉ 28022 Madrid – ☎ 91 :

XX **Rancho Texano,** av. Aragón 364 ✆ 747 47 44, ☂, Grill rest., « Terrace » – ▤ Ⓟ. AE ⓞ E VISA. ✗
closed Sunday dinner – **M** a la carte 2 090/3 695.

on the road to the Airport : 12,5 km – ✉ 28042 Madrid – ☎ 91 :

🏨 **Diana** without rest., coffee shop only, Galeón 27 (Alameda de Osuna) ✆ 747 13 55, Telex 45688, ⛱ – |♦| ▤ – 🏛. AE ⓞ E VISA
☕ 385 – **271 apartments** 6 950/8 700.

at Barajas by ② : 14 km – 28042 Madrid – ☎ 91 :

🏨 **Barajas,** av. de Logroño 305 ✆ 747 77 00, Telex 22255, ☂, « Large lawn with ⛱ » – |♦| ▤ 📺 Ⓟ – 🏛. AE ⓞ E VISA. ✗ rest
M 3 025 – ☕ 750 – **230 rm** 10 500/15 200 – P 13 380/13 925.

🏨 **Alameda** Ⓜ, av. de Logroño 100 ✆ 747 48 00, Telex 43809, ⛱ – |♦| ▤ 📺 🚗 Ⓟ – 🏛. AE ⓞ E VISA. ✗ rest
M 2 750 – ☕ 650 – **145 rm** 8 700/12 200 – P 11 325/13 925.

at San Sebastián de los Reyes by ① : 17 km – ✉ 28700 San Sebastián de los Reyes – ☎ 91 :

XXX **Mesón Tejas Verdes,** carret. N I ✆ 652 73 07, ☂, « Typical Castilian tavern, garden » – ▤ Ⓟ. AE ⓞ VISA. ✗
closed Sunday dinner, Bank Holidays dinner and August – **M** a la carte 1 950/3 600.

BARCELONA 08000 443 H36 – pop. 1 754 900 – ☎ 93 – Bullring.

See : Gothic Quarter** (Barrio Gótico) : Cathedral** MR, Federic Marés Museum** (Museo F. Marés) MR, Provincial Council* (Palau de la Generalitat) MR – Montjuic* (≤*) : Museum of Catalonian Art** (Museo d'Art de Catalunya) : Romanesque and Gothic department***, ceramic Museum* – Archeological Museum (Museo Arqueológico), Spanish Village* (Pueblo Español), Joan Miró Foundation* – Zoo* (Parque Zoológico) LV – Tibidabo* (✳**) – Maritime Museum** (Drassanes i Museo Maritim) KZ **M6** – Cambo Collection (Palau de la Virreina)* JX **M7** – Picasso Museum* KV **M8** – Church of the Holy Family* (Sagrada Familia) JU **L**.

18, 9 of Prat by ⑤ : 16 km ℰ 379 02 78 – 18 of Sant Cugat by ⑦ : 20 km ℰ 674 39 58 – 18 of Vallromanas by ④ : 25 km ℰ 568 03 62.

✈ Barcelona by ⑤ : 12 km ℰ 317 01 12 – Iberia : pl. Espanya, ⊠ 08004, ℰ 325 60 00 EZ Aviaco : aeropuerto ℰ 379 24 58.

🚗 ℰ 310 00 30.

⛴ to the Balearic islands : Cía. Trasmediterránea, vía Laietana 2, ⊠ 08003, ℰ 319 82 12, Telex 54629 KX.

ℹ Gran Vía de les Corts Catalanes 658, ⊠ 08010, ℰ 301 74 43, 317 22 46 - Palacio de Congresos, pl. Neruda, ⊠ 08013, ℰ 223 24 20 and at Airport ℰ 325 58 29 – **R.A.C.C.** Santaló ⊠ 08006, ℰ 200 33 11, telex 53056.

Madrid 627 ⑥ – Bilbao 607 ⑥ – Lérida/Lleida 169 ⑥ – Perpignan 187 ② – Tarragona 109 ⑥ – Toulouse 388 ② – Valencia 361 ⑥ – Zaragoza 307 ⑥.

Plans on following pages

- Princesa Sofía Ⓜ, pl. del Papa Pius XII, ⊠ 08028, ℰ 330 71 11, Telex 51032, ≤, pool – lift ▤ TV parking – conf. – **496 rm**. — by ⑥
- **G. H. Sarriá** Ⓜ, av. de Sarriá 50, ⊠ 08029, ℰ 239 11 09, Telex 51033, ≤ – lift ▤ TV parking – conf. AE ⓓ E VISA. ✂ — EU **n**
  M 2 500 – ☕ 900 – **314 rm** 12 000/15 000.
- Avenida Palace, Gran Vía 605, ⊠ 08007, ℰ 301 96 00, Telex 54734 – lift ▤ TV – conf. ✂ rest – **211 rm** — GV **r**
- **Ritz,** Gran Vía de les Corts Catalanes 668, ⊠ 08010, ℰ 318 52 00, Telex 52739, terrace – lift ▤ TV – conf. AE ⓓ E VISA. ✂ — JU **p**
  M 5 000 – ☕ 1 250 – **161 rm** 18 000/25 000 – P 22 000/27 500.
- Presidente, av. de la Diagonal 570, ⊠ 08021, ℰ 200 21 11, Telex 52180, pool – lift ▤ TV parking – conf. – **161 rm**. — EU **u**
- Majestic, passeig de Grácia 70, ⊠ 08008, ℰ 215 45 12, Telex 52211, pool – lift ▤ TV – conf. **330 rm**. — GU **f**
- Diplomatic and Rest. La Salsa, Pau Claris 122, ⊠ 08009, ℰ 317 31 00, Telex 54701, pool – lift ▤ TV parking – conf. – **213 rm**. — GU **e**
- **Calderón,** rambla Catalunya 26, ⊠ 08007, ℰ 301 00 00, Telex 51549, pool – lift ▤ TV parking – conf. AE ⓓ E VISA. ✂ — GV **t**
  M a la carte 1 975/3 650 – ☕ 700 – **263 rm** 9 400/11 800.
- **Colón,** av. de la Catedral 7, ⊠ 08002, ℰ 301 14 04, Telex 52654 – lift ▤ – conf. AE ⓓ E VISA. ✂ rest — KV **e**
  M 2 125 – ☕ 450 – **161 rm** 7 340/9 175 – P 12 040/18 575.
- **Condes de Barcelona,** Paseo de Gracia 75, ⊠ 08008, ℰ 215 06 16 – lift ▤ TV – conf. AE ⓓ E VISA. ✂ — FGU **m**
  M 1 800 – ☕ 750 – **100 rm** 8 760/12 960 – P 8 730/11 010.
- **Hesperia** Ⓜ quiet without rest., coffee shop only, Los Vergós 20, ⊠ 08017, ℰ 204 55 51, Telex 98403 – lift ▤ TV parking – conf. AE ⓓ E VISA. ✂ — by ⑦
  ☕ 600 – **142 rm** 5 900/10 600.
- **Derby** without rest., Loreto 21, ⊠ 08029, ℰ 322 32 15, Telex 97429 – lift ▤ TV parking – conf. AE ⓓ E VISA — EV **e**
  ☕ 600 – **116 rm** 6 300/9 850.
- Cristal, Diputació 257, ⊠ 08007, ℰ 301 66 00, Telex 54560 – lift ▤ TV parking – conf. **147 rm**. — GV **t**
- **Gran Derby** Ⓜ without rest., Loreto 28, ⊠ 08029, ℰ 322 32 15, Telex 97429 – lift ▤ TV parking – conf. AE ⓓ E VISA — EV **g**
  ☕ 600 – **39 rm** 12 500/16 000.
- Nuñez Urgel, without rest., coffee shop only, Comptes de Urgell 232, ⊠ 08036, ℰ 322 41 53 – lift ▤ TV parking **121 rm**. — EV **a**
- **Royal** without rest., Ramblas 117, ⊠ 08002, ℰ 301 94 00, Telex 97565 – lift ▤ TV parking. AE ⓓ E VISA. ✂ — JX **e**
  ☕ 450 – **108 rm** 5 900/8 900.
- **Balmoral** without rest., coffee shop only, vía Augusta 5, ⊠ 08006, ℰ 217 87 00, Telex 54087 – lift ▤ TV parking – conf. AE ⓓ E VISA. ✂ — FU **n**
  ☕ 560 – **94 rm** 6 450/9 950.
- **Regente,** rambla de Catalunya 76, ⊠ 08008, ℰ 215 25 70, Telex 51939, pool – lift ▤ TV. AE ⓓ E VISA. ✂ — GU **z**
  M 1 850 – ☕ 450 – **78 rm** 6 300/9 500 – P 8 275/9 825.

Cóndor, without rest., coffee shop only, vía Augusta 127, 08006, 209 45 11, Telex 52925 – EU **z**
78 rm.

Arenas without rest., coffee shop only for dinner, Capitán Arenas 20, 08034, 204 03 00, Telex 54990 – AE E VISA. by ⑥
500 – **59 rm** 6 800/10 000.

Astoria without rest., París 203, 08036, 209 83 11, Telex 97429 – AE E VISA FU **a**
400 – **114 rm** 5 250/7 150.

G. H. Cristina without rest., coffee shop only, av. de la Diagonal 458, 08006, 217 68 00, Telex 54328 – AE E VISA FU **y**
500 – **126 rm** 6 000/8 500.

Dante without rest., Mallorca 181, 08036, 323 22 54, Telex 52588 – AE E VISA. FV **e**
450 – **81 rm** 5 000/8 700.

Numáncia without rest., coffee shop only, Numància 74, 08029, 322 44 51 – AE VISA. by ⑥
400 – **140 rm** 3 800/6 400.

Expo H., without rest., coffee shop only, Mallorca 1, 08014, 325 12 12, Telex 54147, – AE E VISA EY **m**
432 rm 6 335/7 920.

Euro-Park, without rest., coffee shop only, Aragó 325, 08009, 257 92 05 –
66 rm. JU **e**

Ficus, without rest., Mallorca 163, 08036, 253 35 00, Telex 98203 – wc wc – **74 rm**. FV **u**

Mitre without rest., Bertrán 15, 08023, 212 11 04, Telex 51531 – wc . AE E VISA by ⑦
395 – **57 rm** 4 750/6 900.

Can Putxet without rest., coffee shop only, Putxet 68, 08023, 212 51 58, Telex 98718 – wc – AE E VISA. by ⑦
M 1 000 – **125 rm** 8 500/13 900.

Gala Placidia, vía Augusta 112, 08006, 217 82 00, Telex 98820 – rest wc . AE E VISA EU **r**
M 1 200 – 475 – **31 rm** 6 000/8 500 – P 6 250/8 000.

Condado, Aribau 201, 08021, 200 23 11, Telex 54546 – rest wc wc . AE E VISA. rest EU **g**
M 1 400 – 400 – **88 rm** 4 500/6 800 – P 5 960/7 060.

Rialto without rest., coffee shop only, Fernando 42, 08002, 318 52 12, Telex 97206 – wc . AE E VISA MR **s**
360 – **103 rm** 4 775/6 960.

Pedralbes without rest., coffee shop only, Fontcubierta 4, 08007, 203 71 12, Telex 52925 – wc . AE E VISA. by ⑥
450 – **28 rm** 5 400/7 500.

Taber without rest., Aragó 256, 08007, 318 70 50, Telex 93452 – wc . AE E VISA GV **g**
65 rm 4 055/7 050.

Terminal 7th floor, without rest., coffee shop only for dinner, Provença 1, 08029, 321 53 50, Telex 98213 – wc EY **a**
75 rm.

Tres Torres without rest., Calatrava 32, 08017, 417 73 00, Telex 54990 – wc – AE E VISA by ⑦
400 – **56 rm** 4 500/6 800.

Covadonga without rest., coffee shop only, av. de la Diagonal 596, 08021, 209 55 11 – wc wc . AE E VISA EU **v**
325 – **76 rm** 3 900/6 200.

Regencia Colón without rest., Sagristans 13, 08002, 318 98 58, Telex 98175 – wc wc . AE E VISA. KV **r**
340 – **55 rm** 3 580/5 940.

Wilson, without rest., av. de la Diagonal 568, 08021, 209 25 11, Telex 54134 – wc wc – **52 rm**. EU **a**

Gótico without rest., Jaime I - 14, 08002, 315 22 11, Telex 97206 – wc . AE E VISA MR **a**
360 – **72 rm** 4 500/6 550.

Las Corts without rest., coffee shop only, Travessera de Les Corts 292, 08029, 322 08 11, Telex 59001 – wc wc – . E VISA. by ⑥
300 – **79 rm** 3 400/5 000.

Bonanova Park, without rest., Capitán Arenas 51, 08034, 204 09 00, Telex 54990 – wc wc . AE E VISA by ⑥
325 – **60 rm** 3 500/5 300.

BARCELONA

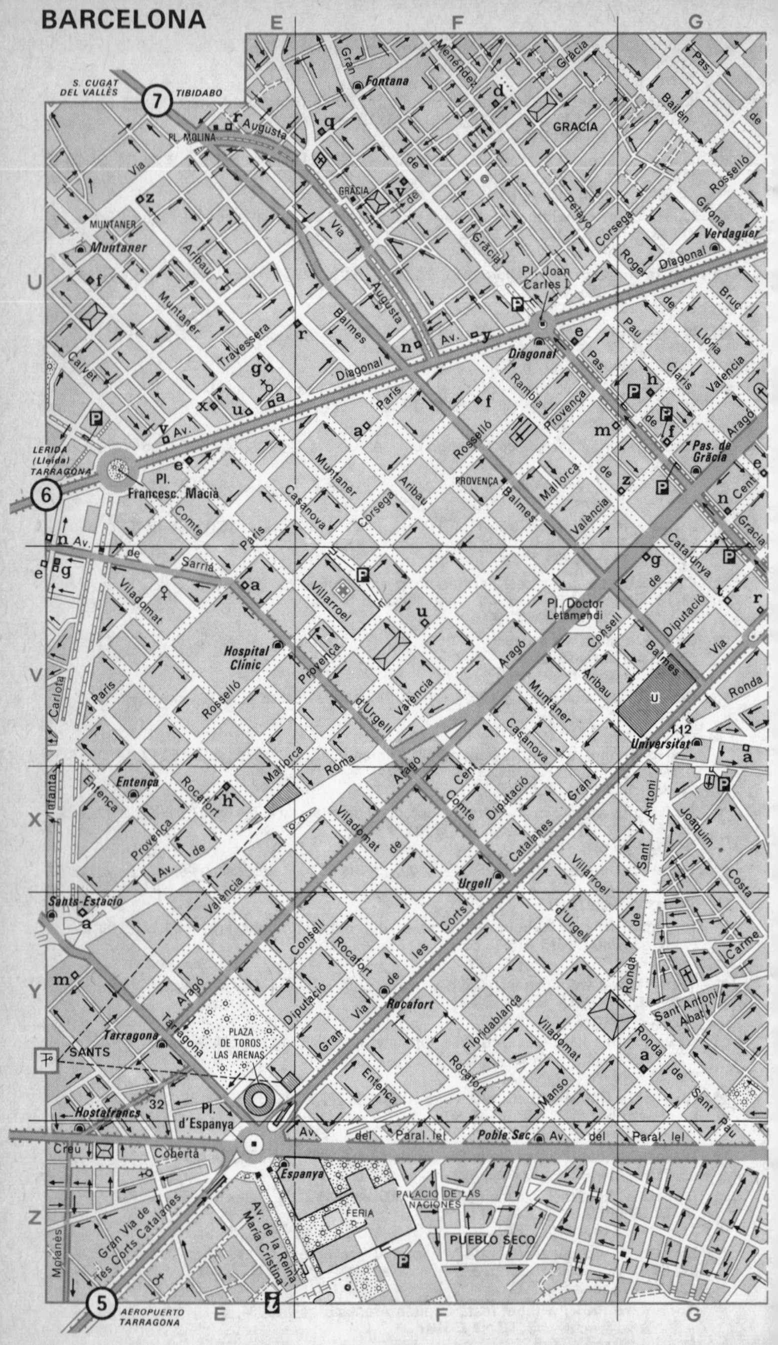
E
F
G
U
V
X
Y
Z
S. CUGAT DEL VALLÈS
TIBIDABO
7
6
5
LERIDA (Lleida) TARRAGONA
AEROPUERTO TARRAGONA
PL. MOLINA
Augusta
MUNTANER
Muntaner
Fontana
GRACIA
GRÀCIA
Verdaguer
Pl. Joan Carles I
Diagonal
Pas. de Gràcia
PROVENÇA
Pl. Francesc. Macià
Hospital Clínic
Pl. Doctor Letamendi
Universitat
Entença
Urgell
Sants-Estació
Rocafort
Tarragona
SANTS
PLAZA DE TOROS LAS ARENAS
Hostafrancs
Pl. d'Espanya
Poble Sec
Espanya
PALACIO DE LAS NACIONES
FERIA
PUEBLO SECO
Av. de la Reina Maria Cristina
Gran Via de les Corts Catalanes
Av. del Paral. lel
Sant Antoni Abat

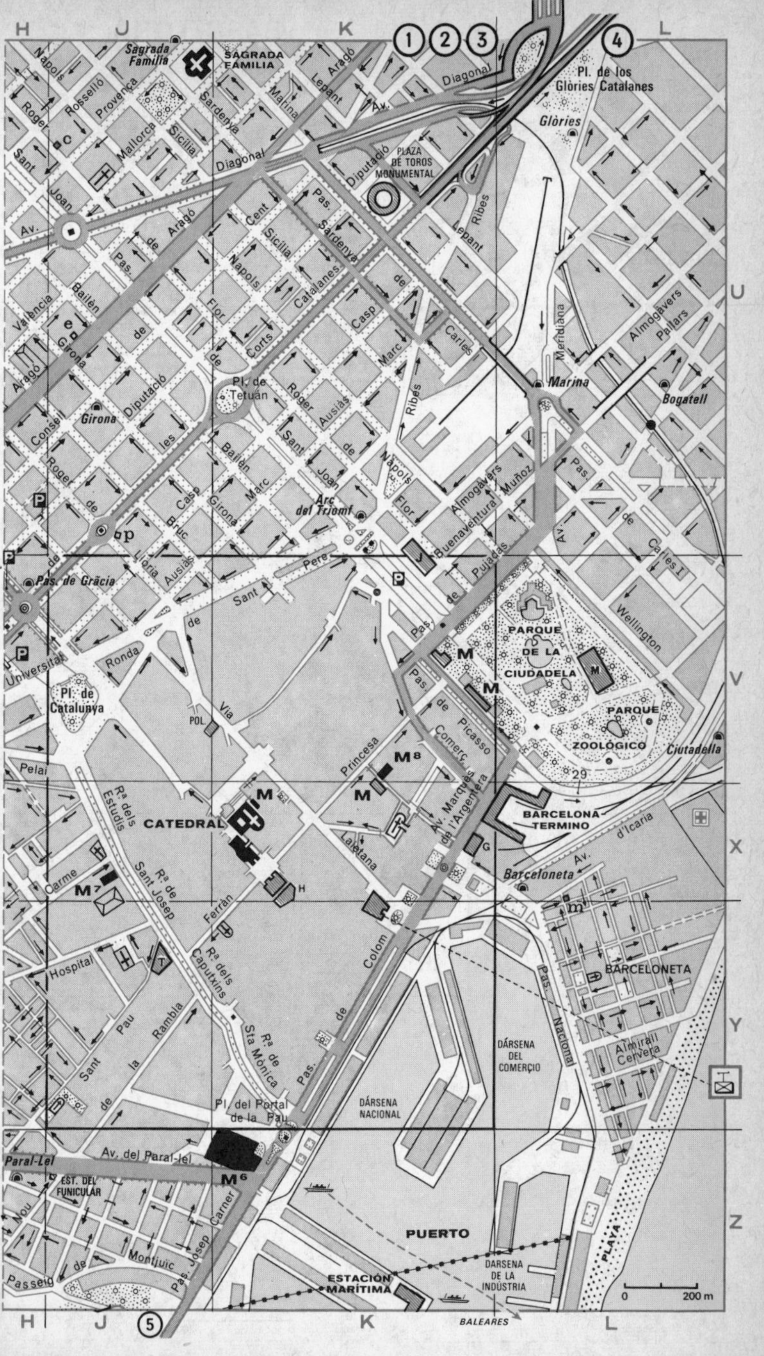
SAGRADA FAMILIA
Pl. de los Glòries Catalanes
PLAZA DE TOROS MONUMENTAL
Pl. de Tetuán
Arc del Triomf
Marina
Bogatell
Girona
Pas. de Gràcia
Pl. de Catalunya
PARQUE DE LA CIUDADELA
PARQUE ZOOLÓGICO
Ciutadella
CATEDRAL
BARCELONA TERMINO
Barceloneta
BARCELONETA
DÁRSENA DEL COMERÇIO
DÁRSENA NACIONAL
Pl. del Portal de la Pau
Paral-Lel
EST. DEL FUNICULAR
PUERTO
ESTACIÓN MARÍTIMA
DARSENA DE LA INDÚSTRIA
PLAYA
BALEARES
0
200 m

BARCELONA

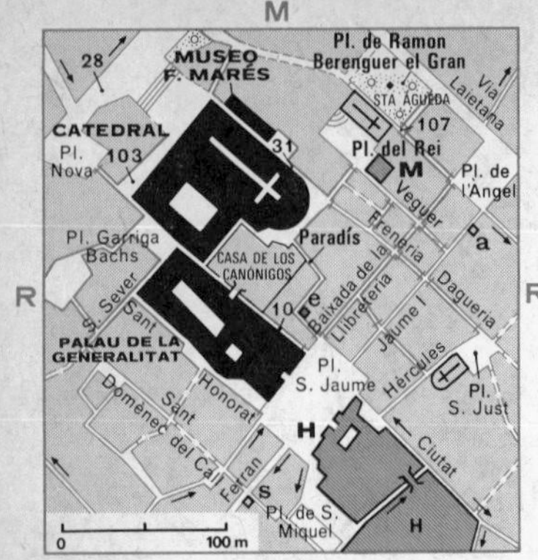

M
R
28
MUSEO F. MARÉS
Pl. de Ramon Berenguer el Gran
STA ÁGUEDA
107
Via Laietana
CATEDRAL
Pl. Nova
103
31
Pl. del Rei
M
Pl. de l'Àngel
Veguer
Pl. Garriga Bachs
Paradís
Freneria
a
CASA DE LOS CANÓNIGOS
Baixada de la Llibreteria
Daguería
S. Sever
Sant
10
e
Jaume I
PALAU DE LA GENERALITAT
Pl. S. Jaume
Hèrcules
Pl. S. Just
Domènec del Call
Sant Honorat
H
Ciutat
Ferran
s
Pl. de S. Miquel
H
0
100 m

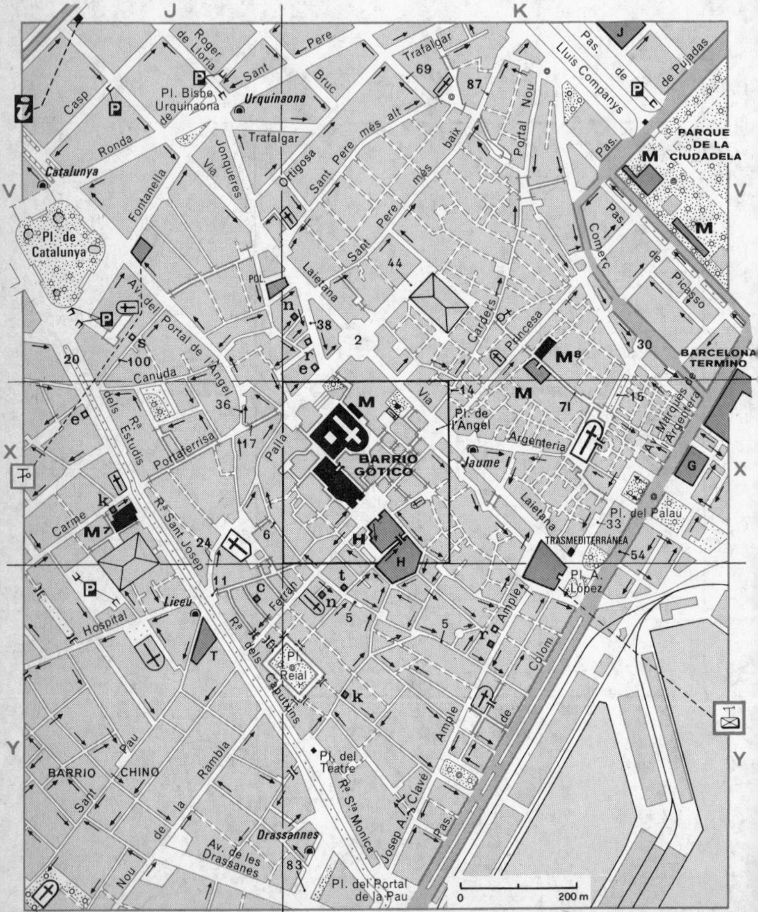

Lleó, Pelai 24, ✉ 08001, ✆ 318 13 12, Telex 98338 – |‡| ⌂wc ☎. VISA. ✻ rest GV **a**
M 900 – ☕ 230 – **42 rm** 2 200/3 690 – P 2 925/3 570.

Torelló without rest., Ample 31, ✉ 08002, ✆ 315 40 11, Telex 54606 – |‡| ⌂wc ⋒wc ☎. VISA. ✻ KY **r**
☕ 280 – **72 rm** 1 950/3 350.

Cortés, Santa Ana 25, ✉ 08002, ✆ 317 91 12, Telex 98215 – |‡| ▤ rest ⌂wc ⋒wc ☎. AE E VISA. ✻ JV **s**
M *(closed Sunday)* 675 – ☕ 325 – **56 rm** 2 500/4 150.

L'Alguer without rest., passeig Pedro Rodriguez 20, ✉ 08028, ✆ 334 60 50 – |‡| ⋒wc ☎. E VISA. ✻ by Creu Coberta EZ
☕ 285 – **33 rm** 2 320/4 050.

Classical and modern restaurants :

XXXX **Beltxenea,** Mallorca 275, ✉ 08008, ✆ 215 30 24, ☂, « Garden-terrace » – ▤. AE ⓓ E VISA. ✻ GU **h**
closed Saturday lunch and Sunday – **M** a la carte 3 200/7 725.

XXXX ✿ **Reno,** Tuset 27, ✉ 08006, ✆ 200 91 29, « Elegant classical decor » – ▤ Ⓟ. AE ⓓ E VISA. ✻ FU **r**
M a la carte 3 950/5 600
Spec. Marmita de cangrejos de río (November-May) Hojaldre de lenguado y salmón María Estuardo, Solomillo al tuétano y trufas.

XXXX ✿ **Vía Veneto,** Ganduxer 10, ✉ 08021, ✆ 200 72 44, « Early 20C style » – ▤. AE ⓓ E VISA. ✻ by ⑥
M a la carte 3 000/4 670
Spec. Ensalada de setas y langostinos al perfume de flor de tomillo, Ceps a la crema de trufas, Merluza de palangre asada al perfume de ajitos.

XXX **Finisterre,** av. de la Diagonal 469, ✉ 08036, ✆ 239 55 76 – ▤. AE ⓓ E VISA. ✻ EU **e**
M a la carte 4 350/5 800.

XXX ✿✿ **Neichel,** av. de Pedralbes 16 bis, ✉ 08034, ✆ 203 84 08 – ▤. AE ⓓ E VISA by ⑥
closed Sunday, Bank Holidays, Holy-Week, Christmas and August – **M** (booking essential) a la carte 3 200/5 400
Spec. Ensalada de gambas al vinagre del Ampurdán, Escalopa de lubina a la muselina de trufas de Huesca, Lomo de cordero en su jugo a las hierbas.

XXX **Hostal del Sol** 1st floor, passeig de Grácia 44, ✉ 08007, ✆ 215 62 25, Pianist at dinner – ▤. AE ⓓ E VISA. ✻ GU **n**
M a la carte 2 100/3 795.

XXX **El Túnel de Muntaner,** Sant Mario 22, ✉ 08022, ✆ 212 60 74 – ▤ Ⓟ. AE ⓓ E VISA
closed Sunday, Bank Holidays and August – **M** a la carte 2 550/4 800. by ⑥

XXX ✿ **Botafumeiro,** Major de Grácia 81, ✉ 08012, ✆ 218 42 30, Seafood – ▤ Ⓟ. AE ⓓ E VISA. ✻ FU **v**
closed Sunday dinner, Monday except Bank Holidays, day before Bank Holidays, Holy Week and August – **M** a la carte 2 700/5 000
Spec. Canelones de mariscos, Lubina papillot, Soufflé al Grand Marnier.

XX ✿ **La Odisea,** Copons 7, ✉ 08002, ✆ 302 36 92, Pianist at dinner – ▤. AE ⓓ E VISA
closed Saturday lunch, Sunday, Bank Holidays and August – **M** a la carte 1 990/4 125
Spec. Sopa de setas y trufas (November-April), Solomillo Villete con hortalizas al calvados, Suprema de merluza al tomate fresco. KV **n**

XX **El Gran Café,** Avinyó 9, ✉ 08002, ✆ 318 79 86, Pianist at dinner, « Early 20C style » – ▤. AE ⓓ E VISA. ✻ KY **t**
closed Sunday, Bank Holidays and August – **M** a la carte 2 050/3 675.

XX ✿ **Azulete,** Via Augusta 281, ✉ 08017, ✆ 203 59 43, ☂, « Conservatory terrace with plants » – AE ⓓ E VISA by ⑦
closed Saturday lunch, Sunday, Holy-Week, 1 to 15 August and 22 December-6 January – **M** a la carte 2 900/4 800
Spec. Brazo de gitano de pasta y verduras Arlequin, Surtido de mar, Costillas de cordero al hojaldre.

XX **Bel Air,** Córcega 286, ✉ 08008, ✆ 237 75 88, Arroces – ▤. AE ⓓ E VISA. ✻ FU **f**
closed Sunday – **M** a la carte 3 160/4 900.

XX ✿ **Ara-Cata,** Dr Ferrán 33, ✉ 08034, ✆ 204 10 53 – ▤. AE ⓓ E VISA. ✻ by ⑥
closed Saturday, Bank Holiday dinner, Holy-Week and August – **M** a la carte 2 600/4 500
Spec. Huevos Sta. Gema, Rape al Fontenac, Tournedo José Torres.

XX ✿ **Eldorado Petit,** Dolors Monserdá 51, ✉ 08017, ✆ 204 51 53, ☂, « Terrace » – ▤. AE ⓓ E VISA. ✻ by ⑦
closed Sunday – **M** a la carte 3 500/5 000
Spec. Lasaña de salmón fresco y esparragos, San Pedro al horno con romero, Carré de venado al vino tinto (Game season).

XX **Aitor,** Carbonnell 5, ✉ 08003, ✆ 319 94 88, Basque rest. – ▤. VISA LXY **m**
closed Sunday – **M** a la carte 2 200/4 450.

XX **Las Indias,** passeig Manuel Girona 38 bis, ✉ 08034, ✆ 204 48 00 – ▤. AE ⓓ VISA. ✻
closed Sunday dinner – **M** a la carte 2 275/4 200. by ⑥

XX **El Dento,** Loreto 32, ✉ 08029, ✆ 321 67 56, Seafood – ▤. AE ⓓ E VISA. ✻ EV **g**
closed Saturday and August – **M** a la carte 3 325/5 125.

XX **Quo Vadis,** Carme 7, ✉ 08001, ✆ 302 40 72 – ▤. AE ⓓ E VISA JX **k**
closed Sunday – **M** a la carte 2 650/4 400.

XX **Chévere,** rambla del Prat 14, ✉ 08012, ✆ 217 03 59 – ▤ Ⓟ. AE ⓓ E VISA. ✻ FU **q**
closed Saturday lunch, Sunday and August – **M** a la carte 1 685/3 645.

XX Cathay, Santaló 86, ✉ 08021, ✆ 209 37 86, Chinese rest. – ▤ EU **f**

XX ✿ **Jaume de Provença,** Provença 88, ✉ 08029, ✆ 230 00 29, Modern decor – ▤. AE ⓓ E VISA. ✻ EX **h**
closed Sunday dinner, Monday, Holy-Week and August – **M** a la carte 2 250/4 450
Spec. Ensalada de mariscos Mare Nostrum, Poupurri de mariscos y crustáceos con salsa americana, Riñoncitos de lechal al cava.

XX **Alt Berlín,** Diagonal 633, ✉ 08028, ✆ 339 01 66, German rest. – ▤. AE ⓓ E VISA by ⑥
M a la carte 2 250/3 545.

XX ✿ **Hostal Sant Jordi,** Travessera de Dalt 123, ✉ 08024, ✆ 213 10 37 – ▤. AE ⓓ E VISA. ✻ by Travessera de Gràcia FU
closed Sunday dinner and August – **M** a la carte 2 150/3 550
Spec. Suquet de pescados de roca, Filete en papillot con salsa de mostaza y trufas a la crema, Filete de ciervo al agridulce (October-March).

X **Can Jordi,** pasaje Marimón 18, ✉ 08021, ✆ 200 11 18 – ▤. AE ⓓ E VISA. ✻ EU **x**
closed Sunday – **M** a la carte 1 615/3 080.

X **La Balsa,** Infanta Isabel 4, ✉ 08022, ✆ 211 50 48, 🏖 – AE ⓓ VISA by ⑦
closed Sunday and Monday lunch – **M** a la carte 2 075/3 850.

Typical atmosphere restaurants :

XX La Dida, Roger de Flor 230, ✉ 08025, ✆ 207 20 04, « Regional decor » – ▤ Ⓟ JU **c**

XX **Agut d'Avignon,** Trinidad 3 (Avinyó 8), ✉ 08002, ✆ 302 60 34, « Regional decor » – ▤. AE ⓓ E VISA. ✻ KY **n**
closed Holy-Week – **M** a la carte 2 050/3 970.

XX **Font del Gat,** passeig Santa Madrona, Montjuic, ✉ 08004, ✆ 224 02 24, 🏖, Regional decor – Ⓟ. AE ⓓ. ✻ by av. Reina María Cristina EZ
M a la carte 1 950/3 800.

X **La Cuineta,** Paradís 4, ✉ 08002, ✆ 315 01 11, « In a 17C cellar » – ▤. AE ⓓ E VISA. ✻
closed Monday except Bank Holidays – **M** a la carte 2 025/3 625. MR **e**

X **Los Caracoles,** Escudellers 14, ✉ 08002, ✆ 301 20 41, Rustic regional decor – ▤. AE ⓓ E VISA. ✻ KY **k**
M a la carte 1 650/3 130.

X **Can Culleretes,** Quintana 5, ✉ 08002, ✆ 317 64 85 – ▤ JY **c**
closed Sunday dinner, Monday, and 14 July-3 August – **M** a la carte 1 150/2 300.

X **Pá i Trago,** Parlamento 41, ✉ 08015, ✆ 241 13 20 – ▤ Ⓟ. E VISA. ✻ GY **a**
closed Monday and 23 June-24 July – **M** a la carte 1 550/3 400.

X **A la Menta,** passeig Manuel Girona 50, ✉ 08034, ✆ 204 15 49, Tavern – ▤. AE ⓓ VISA. ✻ by ⑥
closed Sunday dinner – **M** (booking essential) a la carte 1 900/3 750.

X **L'Alberg,** Ramón y Cajal 13, ✉ 08012, ✆ 214 10 25, Rustic decor – ▤. E VISA. ✻
M a la carte 1 335/2 650. FU **d**

at Esplugues de Llobregat by ⑥ – ✉ 08950 Esplugues de Llobregat – ☎ 93 :

XXX **La Masía,** av. Paisos Catalans 58 ✆ 371 37 42, 🏖, « Terrace under pine-trees » – ▤ Ⓟ. AE ⓓ E VISA. ✻
M a la carte 2 450/2 700.

X ✿ **Casa Quirze,** Laureano Miró 202 ✆ 371 10 84 – ▤ Ⓟ. AE E VISA. ✻
closed Sunday dinner, Monday, Bank Holidays dinner and Holy-Week – **M** a la carte 2 400/3 250
Spec. Mousseline de rascasse, Higado de oca al vinagre de Jerez, Filete tres salsas.

at the Tibidabo by ⑦ – ✉ 08022 Barcelona – ☎ 93 :

X La Masía, ✆ 247 63 50, ≤ Town, sea and mountains.

on the road to Sant Cugat del Vallés by ⑦ : 11 km – ✉ 08023 Barcelona – ☎ 93 :

X **Can Cortés,** urbanización Ciudad Condal Tibidabo ✆ 674 17 04, ≤, 🏖, Exhibition of Catalan wines, « Old masía, rustic decor », 🏊 admis. charge – Ⓟ. AE ⓓ E VISA. ✻
M a la carte 1 150/2 150.

Argentona Barcelona 443 H37 – pop. 6 515 h. alt. 75 – ☎ 93 – Barcelona 27.

XX ✿✿ **Racó d'En Binu,** Puig i Cadafalch 14 ✆ 797 01 01 – ▤. AE E VISA
closed Sunday dinner, Monday , 1 to 20 June and 2 to 20 November – **M** a la carte 3 200/4 500
Spec. Sopa de tomate y calabacín con almendras tiernas (Summer), Langostinos Ferrer, Soufflé de limón helado.

Málaga 29000 446 V16 – pop. 503 251 – 952 – Seaside resort - Bullring.

See : Cathedral★ CY – Fine Arts Museum★ (Museo de bellas Artes) DY **M** – Alcazaba★ (museo★) DY – Gibralfaro ≤★★ DY.

Envir. : Finca de la Concepción★ by ④ : 7 km – Road from Málaga to Antequera ≤★★.

Club de Campo of Málaga by ② : 9 km ☎ 38 11 20 – of El Candado by ① : 5 km ☎ 29 46 66.

Málaga by ② : 9 km ☎ 31 19 44 – Iberia : Molina Larios 13, ✉ 29015, ☎ 31 37 31 and Aviaco : airport ☎ 31 78 58.

☎ 31 62 49.

to Melilla : Cía Trasmediterránea, Juan Díaz 4, ✉ 29015 (CZ), ☎ 22 43 93, Telex 77042.

Larios 5, ✉ 29015, ☎ 21 34 45 av. Cervantes, ✉ 29016 ☎ 22 86 00 and Airport ☎ 31 20 44 – R.A.C.E. (Automóvil Club de Málaga) pl. de las Flores 2, ✉ 29005, ☎ 21 42 60.

Madrid 548 ④ – Algeciras 133 ② – Córdoba 175 ④ – Sevilla 217 ④ – Valencia 651 ④.

Plan on next page

Centre :

Casa Curro without rest., coffee shop only, Sancha de Lara 7, ✉ 29015, ☎ 22 72 00, Telex 77366 – AE VISA. CZ **e**
400 – **104 rm** 4 000/5 800.

Bahía Málaga without rest., Somera 8, ✉ 29001, ☎ 22 43 03 – wc. VISA CZ **d**
300 – **44 rm** 3 500/5 000.

Venecia, without rest., no , Alameda Principal 9, ✉ 29001, ☎ 21 36 36 – wc
40 rm. CZ **u**

Lis without rest., Córdoba 7, ✉ 29001, ☎ 22 73 00 – wc wc. AE VISA.
250 – **53 rm** 2 035/3 200. CZ **f**

suburbs :

Las Vegas, paseo de Sancha 22, ✉ 29016, ☎ 21 77 12, Telex 79 210, ≤, – wc. AE VISA. rest by ①
M 1 550 – 350 – **73 rm** 3 300/4 950 – P 5 275/6 100.

Los Naranjos without rest., paseo de Sancha 35, ✉ 29016, ☎ 22 43 19, Telex 77030 – wc wc. AE VISA. by ①
500 – **41 rm** 6 160/7 700.

Parador Nacional de Gibralfaro, ✉ 29016, ☎ 22 19 02, , « Beautiful location with ≤ bay and town » – wc. AE VISA. DY
M 1 900 – 600 – **12 rm** 6 400/8 000 – P 7 740/10 140.

Olletas without rest, coffee shop only, Cuba 3, ✉ 29013, ☎ 25 20 00, Telex 77 151 – wc. by Cristo de la Epidemia DX
225 – **66 rm** 2 100/3 200.

Antonio Martín, paseo Marítimo 4, ✉ 29016, ☎ 22 21 13, ≤, , Large terrace by the sea – . AE VISA by ①
closed Sunday dinner in winter – **M** a la carte 1 975/3 200.

Café de París, Vélez Málaga 8, ✉ 29016, ☎ 22 50 43 – . AE VISA. by ①
closed Sunday in summer, Wednesday in winter and 10 July-2 August – **M** a la carte 1 725/3 650.

La Taberna del Pintor, Maestranza 6, ✉ 29016, ☎ 21 53 15, Typical decor, Meat – . AE VISA by ①
closed Sunday – **M** a la carte 1 200/2 450.

by the road to Cádiz by ② : 10 km – ✉ 29000 Málaga – 952 :

Guadalmar, urbanización Guadalmar ☎ 31 90 00, Telex 77099, ≤, , , – TV –
196 rm.

at Urbanización Mijas Golf by N 340 SW : 30 km – ✉ 29640 Fuengirola – 952 :

Byblos Andaluz M, ☎ 46 02 50, Telex 79713, ≤ golf course, mountains, talassotherapy facilities, , « Luxury establishment in the Andalusian style situated between two golf courses », , , , , – TV – . AE VISA. rest
M 4 900 – 1700 – **136 rm** 20 160/30 240 – P 26 320/31 360.

Hotels in categories , , , offer every modern comfort and facility - therefore no particulars are given.

wc wc

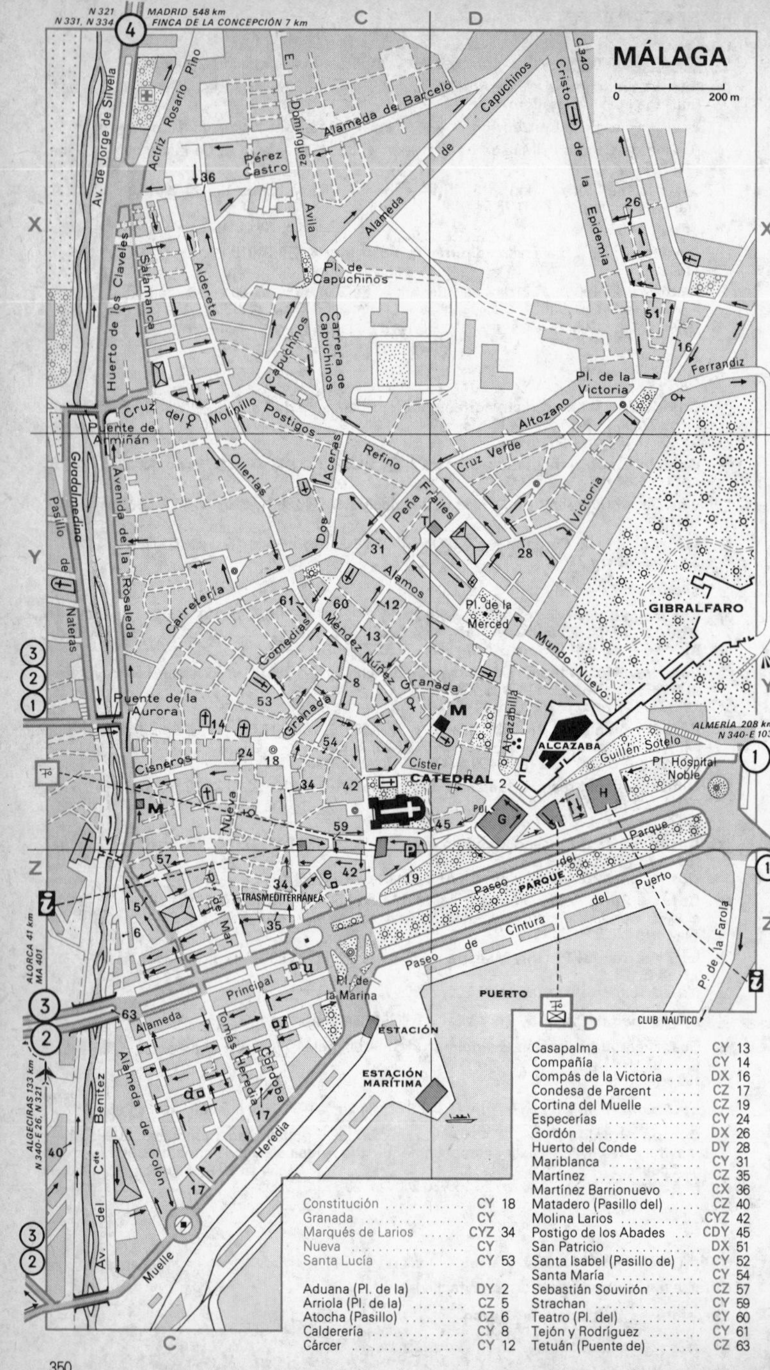

Casapalma ... CY 13
Compañía ... CY 14
Compás de la Victoria ... DX 16
Condesa de Parcent ... CZ 17
Cortina del Muelle ... CZ 19
Especerías ... CY 24
Gordón ... DX 26
Huerto del Conde ... DY 28
Mariblanca ... CY 31
Martínez ... CZ 35
Martínez Barrionuevo ... CX 36
Matadero (Pasillo del) ... CZ 40
Molina Larios ... CYZ 42
Postigo de los Abades ... CDY 45
San Patricio ... DX 51
Santa Isabel (Pasillo de) ... CY 52
Santa María ... CY 54
Sebastián Souvirón ... CZ 57
Strachan ... CY 59
Teatro (Pl. del) ... CY 60
Tejón y Rodríguez ... CY 61
Tetuán (Puente de) ... CZ 63

Constitución ... CY 18
Granada ... CY
Marqués de Larios ... CYZ 34
Nueva ... CY
Santa Lucía ... CY 53

Aduana (Pl. de la) ... DY 2
Arriola (Pl. de la) ... CZ 5
Atocha (Pasillo) ... CZ 6
Calderería ... CY 8
Cárcer ... CY 12

Marbella Málaga 446 W 15 – pop. 67 882 – ✆ 952 – Beach – Bullring.

18 Río Real-Los Monteros by ① : 5 km ✆ 77 37 76 – 18 Nueva Andalucía by ② : 5 km ✆ 78 72 00 – 18 Aloha golf, urbanización Aloha by ② : 8 km ✆ 78 23 88 – 18 golf Las Brisas, Nueva Andalucía by ② ✆ 78 03 00 – Iberia : paseo Marítimo ✆ 77 02 84.

Miguel Cano 1 ✆ 77 14 42 – **Madrid 602** ① – **Algeciras 77** ② – **Málaga 56** ①.

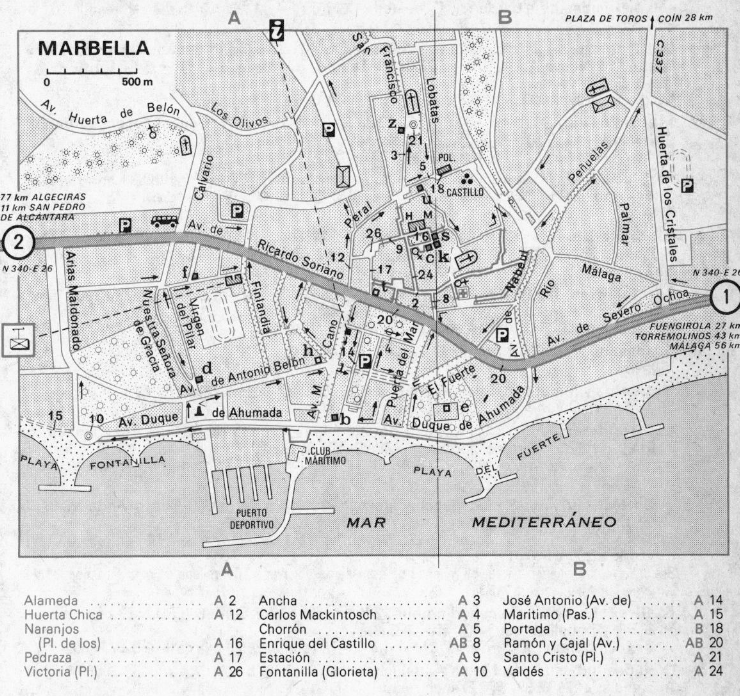

Alameda	A 2	Ancha	A 3	José Antonio (Av. de)	A 14
Huerta Chica	A 12	Carlos Mackintosch	A 4	Marítimo (Pas.)	A 15
Naranjos (Pl. de los)	A 16	Chorrón	A 5	Portada	B 18
Pedraza	A 17	Enrique del Castillo	AB 8	Ramón y Cajal (Av.)	AB 20
Victoria (Pl.)	A 26	Estación	A 9	Santo Cristo (Pl.)	A 21
		Fontanilla (Glorieta)	A 10	Valdés	A 24

El Fuerte, av. del Fuerte ✆ 77 15 00, Telex 77523, ←, « Garden with palm-trees », heated, – rest. AE E VISA. — AB **e**
M 2 200 – 650 – **262 rm** 6 500/8 500 – P 7 850/10 000.

San Cristóbal without rest., coffee shop only, Ramón y Cajal 18 ✆ 77 12 50, Telex 77712 – wc wc. E VISA — A **t**
250 – **100 rm** 2 975/4 695.

Lima without rest., av. Antonio Belón 2 ✆ 77 05 00 – wc wc. AE E VISA. — A **h**
350 – **64 rm** 3 500/5 425.

✿ **La Fonda,** pl. Santo Cristo 10 ✆ 77 25 12, « Pretty Andalusian patio » – AE E VISA. — A **z**
closed Sunday except August – **M** (dinner only) a la carte 3 230/4 625
Spec. Crepes de aguacate y gambas, Pimientos rellenos con vieiras, Pintada en hojaldre.

Gran Marisquería Santiago, av. Duque de Ahumada 5 ✆ 77 00 78, Seafood – AE E VISA. — A **b**
M a la carte 2 200/3 900.

Mena, pl. de los Naranjos 10 ✆ 77 15 97, – AE E VISA. — A **c**
closed Sunday and December-February – **M** a la carte 2 000/4 200.

Plaza, General Chinchilla 6 ✆ 77 11 11, — AB **s**

Los Naranjos, pl. de los Naranjos ✆ 77 18 19, – AE E VISA. — AB **k**
closed Sunday and 15 November-20 February – **M** a la carte 2 300/3 900.

La Esquina de Antonio, Sierra Blanca ✆ 77 44 47, — A **f**

Mamma Angela, Virgen del Pilar 26 ✆ 77 68 99, Italian rest. – — A **d**

Metropol, av. Ricardo Soriano 21 ✆ 77 77 41, – AE E VISA.
closed Sunday – **M** a la carte 1 450/2 800.

El Balcón de la Virgen, Remedios 2 ✆ 77 60 92, 16C mansion – E VISA — A **u**
closed Tuesday – **M** (dinner only in summer) a la carte 975/1 350.

on the road to Cádiz – ✉ 29600 Marbella – ☎ 952 :

Meliá Don Pepe and Grill La Farola, by ② : 1 km ☎ 77 03 00, Telex 77055, ≤ sea and mountains, Pianist at dinner, « Subtropical plants », – P –
218 rm.

Puente Romano M, by ② : 3,5 km ☎ 77 01 00, Telex 77399, « Elegant Andalusian complex in beautiful garden », heated – P – AE E VISA. rest
M 4 300 – 1300 – **196 rm** 21 000/26 000 – P 21 500/29 500.

Del Golf, urbanización Nueva Andalucía by ② : 7 km and detour : 4 km, ✉ 29660 apartado 2 Nueva Andalucía, ☎ 78 03 00, Telex 77783, ≤, 18 – P – AE E VISA.
M (dinner only) 4 000 – 1 000 – **65 rm** 13 500/19 800 – P 17 550/21 150.

Marbella Club, by ② : 3 km ☎ 77 13 00, Telex 77319, « Elegant decor ; garden », heated – P – AE E VISA.
M 4 500 – 1 250 – **100 rm** 20 000/25 000 – P 21 215/28 715.

Andalucía Plaza, urbanización Nueva Andalucía by ② : 7,5 km, ✉ 29660 apartado 21 Nueva Andalucía, ☎ 78 20 00, Telex 77086, – P –
418 rm.

Marbella Dinamar Club 24, by ② : 6 km, ✉ 29660 Nueva Andalucía, ☎ 78 05 00, Telex 77656, ≤, – P – AE E VISA
M 2 250 – 800 – **117 rm** 9 500/12 500 – P 10 750/14 000.

Las Fuentes del Rodeo, by ② : 8 km, ✉ 29660 Nueva Andalucía, ☎ 78 10 00, Telex 77340, « Garden », – P. AE E VISA. rest
M 2 000 – 500 – **110 rm** 4 000/9 000 – P 7 600/16 200.

Guadalpín, by ② : 1,5 km ☎ 77 11 00, – P
110 rm.

Nagüeles without rest, by ② : 3,5 km ☎ 77 16 88, – wc wc P.
15 March-15 October – 275 – **17 rm** 1 800/3 000.

XXX **La Meridiana,** by ② : 3,5 km and detour 1 km - camino de la Cruz - Las Lomas ☎ 77 61 90, ≤, « Terrace-garden » – P. AE E VISA
closed Thursday lunch and 12 January-11 February – **M** (dinner only in Summer) a la carte 3 150/5 200.

XXX ⚘ **Le Restaurant,** Rodeo Beach Club by ② : 8 km, ✉ 29660 Nueva Andalucía, ☎ 78 59 00, Telex 77340, French rest., « Elegant decor » – P
closed Monday in Winter and November-15 December – **M** (dinner only) a la carte 5 200/6 000
Spec. Flores de calabacin y ravioli rellenos de mousse de bogavante, Col rellena de cigalas, Solomillo de ternera a la pimienta negra y pasas.

XX **El Girasole,** by ② - 7 km and detour : 2 km - urb. Aloha, ✉ 29660 Nueva Andalucía, ☎ 78 38 59, Italian rest. – P. AE E VISA
closed Sunday and 10 January - 10 February – **M** (dinner only) a la carte 1 820/3 360.

X Orquídea, urbanización Nueva Andalucía - calle 2 - 21 B by ② : 7,7 km, ✉ 29660 Nueva Andalucía, ☎ 78 16 99, French rest.
closed Wednesday and 8 January-February – **M** (dinner only).

on the road to Málaga – ✉ 29600 Marbella – ☎ 952 :

⚘ **Los Monteros and Grill El Corzo**, by ① : 5,5 km ☎ 77 17 00, Telex 79593, ≤, Pianist at dinner, « Subtropical garden », 18 – P – AE E VISA.
M 5 000 – **170 rm** 29 600/34 000 – P 27 000/38 800
Spec. Panaché de pescados y mariscos Costa de Sol, Chuletittas de venado al vino de Málaga, Milhojas al chantilly con almendras y salsa de moras.

Don Carlos M, by ① : 10 km ☎ 83 11 40, Telex 77015, ≤, Pianist at dinner, « Large garden », heated, – P – AE E VISA.
M 3 600 – 1 450 – **236 rm** 17 000/20 500 – P 17 600/24 350.

Estrella del Mar, by ① : 9 km ☎ 83 12 75, Telex 79669, – rest P. AE E VISA. rest
March-November – **M** 1 900 – 525 – **98 rm** 4 500/7 000 – P 7 175/8 175.

XXX ⚘ **La Hacienda,** by ① : 11,5 km and detour 1,5 km ☎ 83 11 16, « Rustic decor - Patio » – P. AE E VISA.
closed Monday, Tuesday except August and November-December – **M** a la carte 4 330/5 630
Spec. Blinis de harina de garbanzos con coquinas, Pintada a la crema de uvas pasas, Escalope de pato con higos.

XX **Suizo los Altos de Marbella,** by ① : 5 km and detour 3 km ☎ 77 12 16, ≤ mountain, sea and Marbella, Regional decor – AE E VISA.
closed Monday – **M** a la carte 2 250/4 300.

Michelin puts no plaque or sign on the hotels and restaurants mentioned in this Guide.

SEVILLA 41000 P 446 T 11 12 – pop. 653 833 alt. 12 – ☎ 954 – Bullring.

See : Cathedral*** CV – Giralda*** (<**) CV – Alcazar*** (gardens**, Admiral's Apartments : Virgin of the Navigators altarpiece*) CX – Maria Luisa Park** – Fine Arts Museum** AU **M1** – Santa Cruz Quarter* CV – Pilate's House** (casa de Pilatos : azulejos**) DV **R** – Archeological Museum (Roman department*).

Envir. : Itálica <* 9 km by ⑤.

9 and Racecourse Club Pineda by ③ : 3 km ☎ 61 14 00.

✈ Sevilla - San Pablo by ① : 14 km ☎ 51 65 98 – Iberia : Almirante Lobo 2, ✉ 41002 ☎ 21 88 00.

☎ 22 03 70.

ℹ av. de la Constitución 21B ✉ 41004 ☎ 22 14 04 and paseo de Las Delicias ✉ 41012 ☎ 23 44 65 – R.A.C.E. (R.A.C. de Andalucía) av. Eduardo Dato 22, ✉ 41002 ☎ 63 13 50.

Madrid 550 ① – La Coruña 951 ⑤ – Lisboa 411 ⑤ – Málaga 217 ② – Valencia 682 ①.

Plan on following pages

Alfonso XIII, San Fernando 2, ✉ 41004, ☎ 22 28 50, Telex 72725, « Magnificent Andalusian building », – AE E VISA. CX **c**
M 3 300 – 1 100 – **148 rm** 16 000/22 000.

Los Lebreros M, Luis Morales 2, ✉ 41005, ☎ 57 94 00, Telex 72772, – AE E VISA. by Luis Montoto DV
M 2 900 (see also Rest. **La Dehesa** below) – 700 – **439 rm** 13 900/17 400 – P 15 200/20 400.

Porta Coeli M without rest., coffee shop only, av. Eduardo Dato 49, ✉ 41005, ☎ 57 00 40, Telex 72913 – AE E VISA. by E. Dato DV
600 – **246 rm** 7 000/11 000.

Macarena, San Juan de Ribera 2, ✉ 41009, ☎ 37 57 00, Telex 72815, – AE E VISA. CDT **a**
M 2 700 – **327 rm** 12 700/16 000 – P 18 700/28 200.

Inglaterra, pl. Nueva 7, ✉ 41001, ☎ 22 49 70, Telex 72244 – AE E VISA. BV **a**
M 2 100 – 450 – **120 rm** 8 300/12 300 – P 10 050/12 200.

Pasarela M without rest., av. de la Borbolla 11, ✉ 41004, ☎ 41 55 11, Telex 72486 – AE E VISA. by Av. de Portugal DX
450 – **82 rm** 7 000/10 500.

Resid. and Rest. Fernando III, San José 21, ✉ 41004, ☎ 21 73 07, Telex 72491, – AE VISA. rest CV **z**
M 1 700 – 330 – **156 rm** 4 400/6 000.

Bécquer without rest., Reyes Católicos 4, ✉ 41001, ☎ 22 89 00, Telex 72884 – AE E VISA. AV **s**
300 – **126 rm** 3 000/4 500.

América without rest., coffee shop only, Jesús del Gran Poder 2, ✉ 41002, ☎ 22 09 51, Telex 72709 – AE E VISA. BU **h**
300 – **100 rm** 3 150/5 385.

Nuevo Lar, pl. Carmen Benítez 3, ✉ 41003, ☎ 41 03 61, Telex 72816 – AE E VISA. DV **v**
M 1 300 – 500 – **137 rm** 6 700/9 500 – P 7 150/9 100.

Alcázar without rest., Menéndez Pelayo 10, ✉ 41004, ☎ 41 20 11, Telex 72360 – AE E VISA. DX **u**
300 – **93 rm** 5 670/7 525.

Doña María without rest., Don Remondo 19, ✉ 41004, ☎ 22 49 90, « Elegant classic decor - terrace with < Giralda », – AE E VISA. CV **b**
450 – **61 rm** 8 000/13 000.

Monte Carmelo without rest., Turia 9, ✉ 41011, ☎ 27 90 00 – AE VISA SW : by pl. de Cuba BX
290 – **68 rm** 3 300/5 000.

La Rábida, Castelar 24, ✉ 41001, ☎ 22 09 60 – wc wc. rest BV **d**
M 1 050 – 225 – **90 rm** 2 400/4 000 – P 3 975/4 375.

Corregidor without rest., Morgado 17, ✉ 41003, ☎ 38 51 11 – wc. AE VISA CTU **g**
325 – **69 rm** 3 900/7 000.

Venecia without rest., Trajano 31, ✉ 41002, ☎ 38 11 61 – wc wc. E VISA BU **n**
280 – **24 rm** 3 000/5 200.

Reyes Católicos without rest., Gravina 57, ✉ 41001, ☎ 21 12 00 – wc wc. AE E VISA. AV **n**
275 – **26 rm** 5 000/8 000.

Murillo and apart. Murillo without rest., Lope de Rueda 9, ✉ 41004, ☎ 21 60 95 – wc wc. AE E VISA. CV **e**
225 – **61 rm** 3 800/6 300 – **14 apartments**.

Ducal without rest., pl. Encarnación 19, ✉ 41003, ☎ 21 51 07 – wc wc. AE E VISA. CU **b**
240 – **51 rm** 3 200/4 000.

Montecarlo, Gravina 51, ✉ 41001, ✆ 21 75 03 – 🛗 ⇔wc ⋒wc ☎. AE ⓓ E VISA. ✻ AV **e**
M 1 100 – ☕ 275 – **25 rm** 3 500/6 500 – P 5 200/5 450.

Sevilla without rest., no ☕, Daoiz 5, ✉ 41003, ✆ 38 41 61 – 🛗 ▤ ⇔wc ⋒wc ☎. ✻ BCU **w**
29 rm 2 500/3 750.

XXX **Eguzki** 1st floor, Reyes Católicos 25, ✉ 41001, ✆ 21 75 85, Basque rest. – ▤. AE ⓓ E VISA. ✻
closed Sunday and August – **M** a la carte 1 800/3 550. AV **c**

XXX **San Marco,** Cuna 6, ✉ 41004, ✆ 21 24 40 – ▤. AE ⓓ E VISA. ✻ CU **x**
closed 25 July-August – **M** a la carte 2 300/3 700.

XXX **Taberna del Alabardero,** Genaro Parladí, ✉ 41013, ✆ 62 75 51 – ▤. AE ⓓ E VISA
closed Saturday lunch, Sunday and 15-31 August – **M** a la carte 2 600/3 150.

XXX **Or-Iza,** Betis 61, ✉ 41010, ✆ 22 72 11, Basque rest. – ▤. AE ⓓ VISA. ✻ BX **y**
closed Sunday and August – **M** a la carte 2 150/4 000.

XXX **Maîtres,** av. República Argentina 54, ✉ 41011, ✆ 45 68 80 – ▤. AE ⓓ E VISA. ✻
closed Sunday – **M** a la carte 1 800/3 350.
SW : by pl. de Cuba BX

XXX **Río Grande,** Betis, ✉ 41010, ✆ 27 39 56, ≤, ☂, « Large terraces on riverside » – ▤. AE ⓓ E VISA BX **r**
M a la carte 1 675/3 150.

XXX Maitres, av. San Francisco Javier 16, ✉ 41005, ✆ 65 67 52 – ▤. AE ⓓ E VISA. ✻
closed Sunday.

XXX La Dehesa, Luis Morales 2, ✉ 41005, ✆ 57 94 00, Telex 72772, Typical Andalusian decor - Grills – ▤ Ⓟ. AE ⓓ E VISA. ✻
by Luis Montoto DV

XXX **Rincón de Curro,** Virgen de Luján 45, ✉ 41011, ✆ 45 02 38 – ▤. AE ⓓ E VISA. ✻
closed Sunday dinner – **M** a la carte 1 950/3 350.
SW : by pl. de Cuba BX

XXX **Figón del Cabildo,** pl. del Cabildo, ✉ 41001, ✆ 22 01 17, ☂ – ▤. AE ⓓ E VISA. ✻ BV **e**
closed Sunday in summer and Sunday dinner in winter – **M** a la carte 1 975/3 290.

XX **Jamaica,** Jamaica 16, ✉ 41012, ✆ 61 12 44 – ▤. AE ⓓ E VISA. ✻ by ③
closed Sunday dinner – **M** a la carte 1 850/2 725.

XX La Raza, av. Isabel la Católica, ✉ 41013, ✆ 23 20 24, ≤, ☂ – ▤ CX **e**

XX **Bodegón El Riojano,** Virgen de las Montañas 12, ✉ 41011, ✆ 45 06 82 – ▤. AE ⓓ E VISA. ✻
SW : by pl. de Cuba BX
M a la carte 1 700/3 200.

XX **La Albahaca,** pl. Santa Cruz 12, ✉ 41004, ✆ 22 07 14, « Former manor house » – ▤. AE ⓓ E VISA. ✻ CV **s**
closed Sunday – **M** a la carte 1 850/3 850.

X **La Isla,** Arfe 25, ✉ 41001, ✆ 21 53 76 – ▤. AE ⓓ E VISA BV **u**
closed August – **M** a la carte 2 150/2 850.

X **Rías Baixas,** av Ciudad Jardín 6, ✉ 41005, ✆ 64 18 60, Seafood – ▤. ⓓ E VISA. ✻
closed Monday – **M** a la carte 2 000/3 500.

X **Los Alcázares,** Miguel de Mañara 10, ✉ 41004, ✆ 21 31 03, Regional decor – ▤. AE E VISA. ✻ CX **s**
closed Sunday – **M** a la carte 1 900/3 350.

X **Hostería del Laurel,** pl. de los Venerables 5, ✉ 41004, ✆ 22 02 95, Typical decor – ▤. AE VISA. ✻ CV **r**
M a la carte 1 450/2 175.

SEVILLA

Francos	CV	29
Sierpes	BUV	
Tetuán	BV	62
Adriano	ABV	2
Alemanes	CV	3
Almirante Apodaca	CU	4
Almirante Lobo	BX	6
Caballerizas	CV	12
Cabeza Rey Don Pedro	CV	13
Campana	BU	16
Concordia (Pl.)	BU	19
Demetrio de los Rios	DVX	25
Fray Ceferino González	CX	30
García de Vinuesa	BV	32
Gerona	CU	34
Jerez (Puerta de)	CX	36
Julio César	AV	37
Martín Villa	BU	42

Mateos Gago	CV	43
O'Donnell	BU	45
Pastor y Landero	AV	46
Peñuelas	DU	48
Reyes Católicos	AV	53
Rioja	BUV	54
San Laureano	AU	57
Santa María la Blanca	DV	59
Santo Tomás	CX	61
Triunfo (Pl. del)	CX	63
Velázquez	BU	65

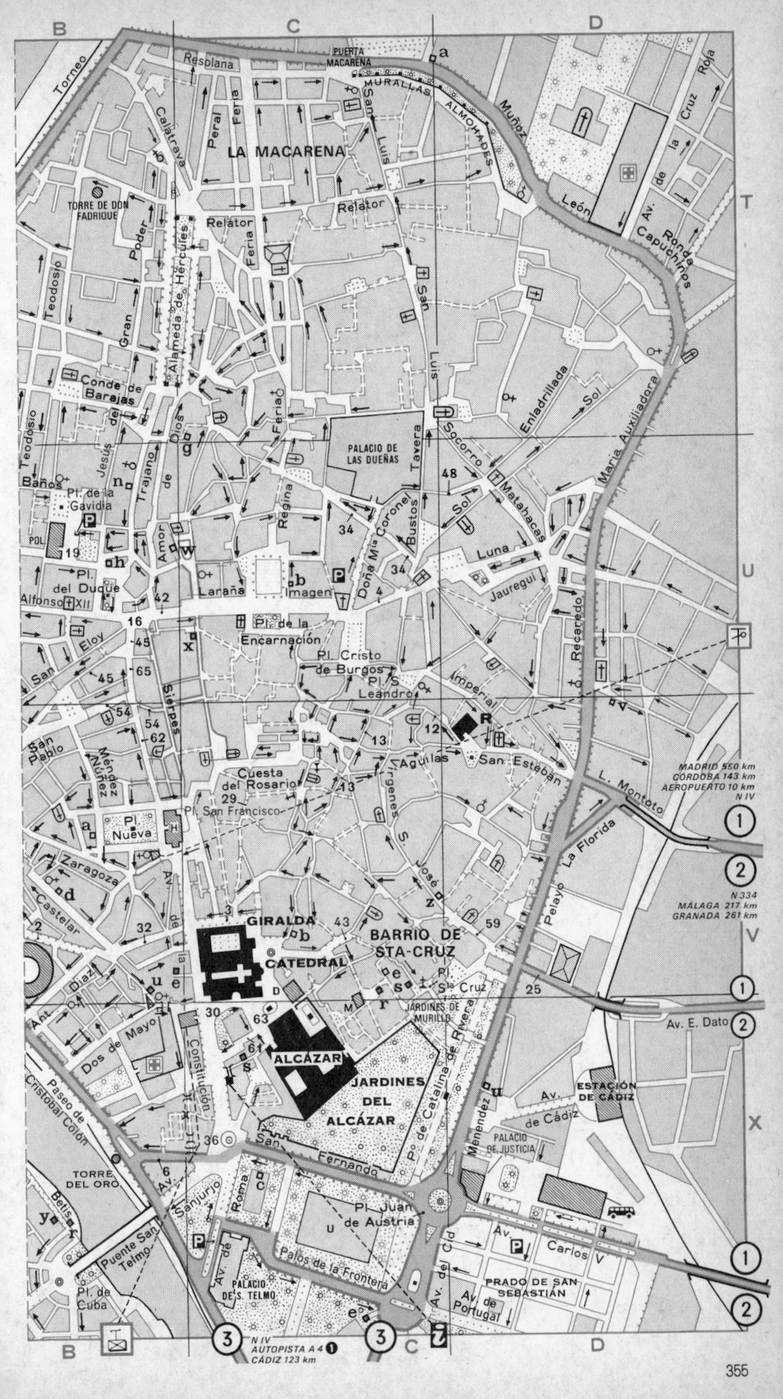
B
C
D
Torneo
Resolana
PUERTA MACARENA
MURALLAS ALMOHADES
Muñoz
León
Av. de la Cruz Roja
Ronda Capuchinos
Calatrava
Peral
Feria
San Luis
LA MACARENA
TORRE DE DON FADRIQUE
Relator
Teodosio
Gran Poder
Alameda de Hércules
Conde de Barajas
Jesús del Gran Poder
Trajano
Amor de Dios
Regina
PALACIO DE LAS DUEÑAS
Tavera
Socorro
Matahacas
Sol
Enladrillada
María Auxiliadora
Baños
Pl. de la Gavidia
POL
Pl. del Duque
Alfonso XII
Laraña
Imagen
Doña Mª Coronel
Bustos Tavera
Luna
Jauregui
Recaredo
Pl. de la Encarnación
Pl. Cristo de Burgos
Pl. S. Leandro
Imperial
San Eloy
Sierpes
San Pablo
Méndez Núñez
Cuesta del Rosario
Águilas
San Esteban
Virgenes
Pl. San Francisco
Pl. Nueva
Zaragoza
Castelar
S. José
L. Montoto
La Florida
Pelayo
MADRID 550 km
CÓRDOBA 143 km
AEROPUERTO 10 km
N IV
N 334
MÁLAGA 217 km
GRANADA 261 km
GIRALDA
CATEDRAL
BARRIO DE STA-CRUZ
Pl. Sta Cruz
JARDINES DE MURILLO
Av. de la Constitución
Díaz
Ant.
Dos de Mayo
Paseo de Cristóbal Colón
ALCÁZAR
JARDINES DEL ALCÁZAR
Pº de Catalina de Ribera
Menéndez
Av. E. Dato
Av. de Cádiz
ESTACIÓN DE CÁDIZ
PALACIO DE JUSTICIA
San Fernando
TORRE DEL ORO
Betis
Av. Sanjurjo
Av. de Roma
Pl. Juan de Austria
Av. Carlos V
Puente San Telmo
Palos de la Frontera
Av. del Cid
PRADO DE SAN SEBASTIÁN
Av. de Portugal
Pl. de Cuba
PALACIO DE S. TELMO
N IV
AUTOPISTA A 4
CÁDIZ 123 km
T
U
V
X

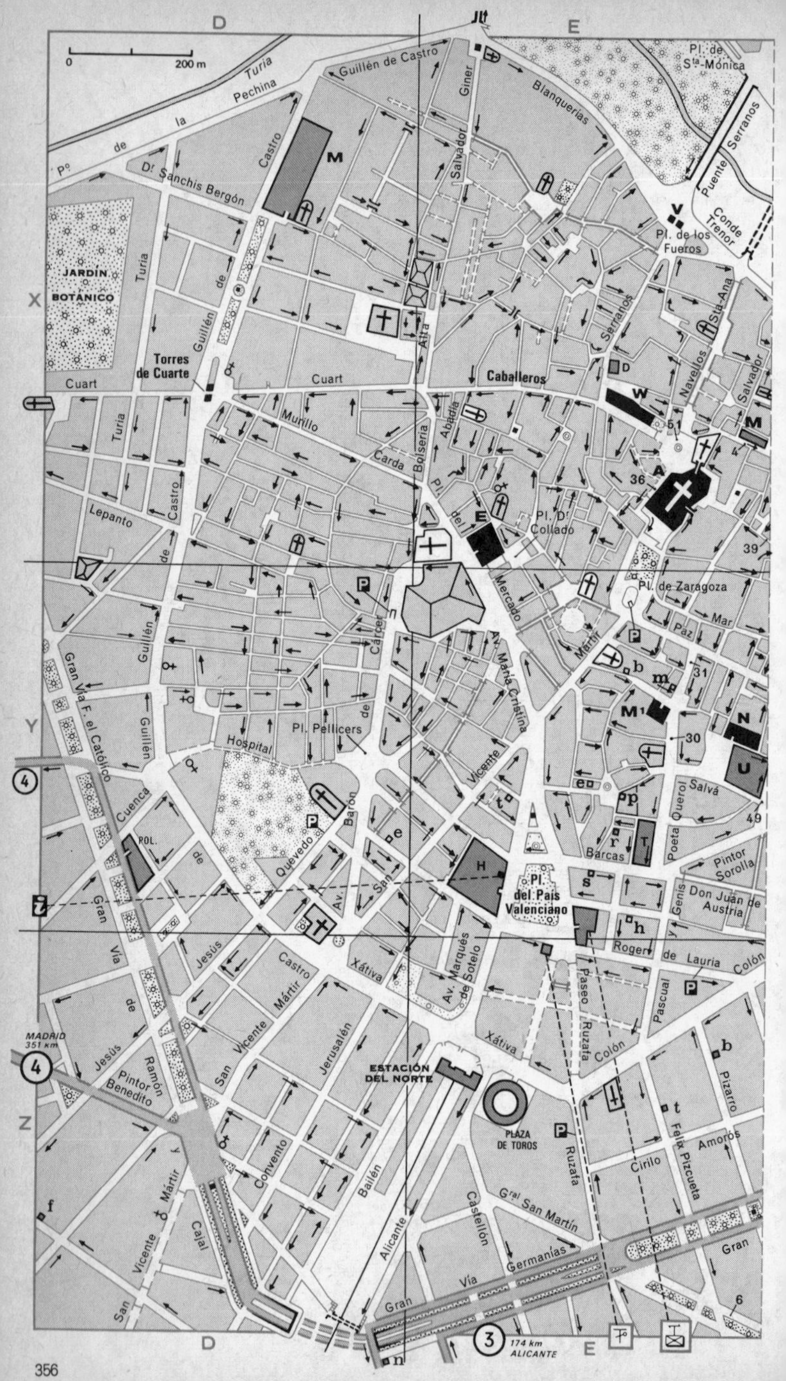
D
E
200 m
Turia
Pechina
Pº de la
Guillén de Castro
Blanquerías
Pl. de Sta-Mónica
Serranos
Puente
Conde Trenor
Pl. de los Fueros
Giner
Salvador
Castro
Dr Sanchis Bergón
JARDÍN BOTÁNICO
Turia
Guillén de
Torres de Cuarte
Cuart
Alta
Caballeros
Serranos
Sta-Ana
Navellos
Salvador
Murillo
Carda
Bolsería
Abadía
Pl. del
Pl. Dr Collado
Lepanto
Castro
Mercado
Pl. de Zaragoza
Paz
Mar
Cárcel
Av. María Cristina
Mártir
Gran Vía F. el Católico
Guillén
Pl. Pellicers
Hospital
Vicente
Cuenca
Quevedo
Barón de
Salvá
Poeta Querol
Barcas
Pintor Sorolla
Don Juan de Austria
Pl. del País Valenciano
Genís
Roger de Lauria
Colón
Gran Vía
Jesús
Castro
Xátiva
Av. Marqués de Sotelo
Av. San
Paseo Ruzafa
Pascual y
MADRID 351 km
Jesús
Pintor Benedito
Ramón
San Vicente Mártir
Jerusalén
ESTACIÓN DEL NORTE
PLAZA DE TOROS
Xátiva
Colón
Pizarro
Convento
Bailén
Castellón
Ruzafa
Cirilo Amorós
Félix Pizcueta
Grl San Martín
Mártir
Cajal
Vicente
San
Alicante
Germanías
Gran Vía
Gran
174 km ALICANTE
X
Y
Z
POL.
M
V
W
D
M
A
E
M1
N
U
H
T
51
36
39
31
30
49
6
4
3
b
m
e
p
t
r
s
h
f
n

VALENCIA

STREET INDEX

Calvo Sotelo .... EZ
País Valenciano (Pl. del) .... EY
Pascual y Genís .... EYZ
Paz .... EFY
San Vicente Mártir .... EY

Abadia .... EX
Alfonso el Magnánimo (Pl.) .... FY
Alicante .... DZ
Almirante Cadarso .... FZ
Almudín .... EX 4
Alta .... EDX
América (Pl.) .... FZ
Antiguo Reino de Valencia (Av.) .... EZ 6
Aragón (Pl. y Puente) .... FZ 7
Bailén .... DZ
Barcas .... EY
Barón de Cárcer (Av.) .... DY
Blanquerías .... EX
Boisería .... EX
Caballeros .... EX
Cánovas del Castillo (Pl.) .... FZ
Carda .... DX
Castellón .... EZ
Cirilo Amorós .... FZ
Ciscar .... FZ
Ciudadela (Pas.) .... FY
Colón .... FY
Comedias .... FY
Conde de Altea .... FZ
Conde Salvatierra .... FYZ
Conde Trénor .... EX
Convento Jerusalén .... DZ
Cuart .... DX
Cuenca .... DY
Doctor Collado (Pl.) .... EX
Doctor Sanchis Bergón .... DX
Don Juan de Austria .... EY
Félix Pizcueta .... EZ
Fueros (Pl. de los) .... EX
General Elío .... FX
General Palanca .... FY 15
General San Martín .... EZ
General Tovar .... FY
Germanías (Gran Vía) .... EZ
Gómez Ferrer (Gta de) .... FY
Grabador Esteve .... FYZ
Guillén de Castro .... DXY
Hernán Cortès .... EFZ
Hospital .... DY
Isabel la Católica .... FZ
Jesús .... DZ
Joaquín Costa .... FZ
Jorge Juan .... FZ
Lepanto .... DX
Llano del Real .... FX
Maestres .... FX
Maestro Gozalbo .... FZ
Mar .... EY
Mar (Porta de la) .... FY
Maria Cristina (Av.) .... EY
María de Molina .... EY 30
Marqués de Dos Aguas .... EY 31
Marqués de Sotelo (Av.) .... EZ
Marqués del Turia (Gran Vía) .... FZ
Mercado (Pl. del) .... EXY
Micalet .... EX 36
Murillo .... DX
Navarro Reverter (Av.) .... FY
Navellos .... EX
País Valenciano (Pl. del) .... EY
Palau .... EX 39
Pascual y Genís .... EYZ
Paz .... EFY
Pellicers (Pl.) .... DY
Pintor Benedito .... DZ
Pintor López .... FX
Pintor Sorolla .... EY
Pizarro .... EZ
Poeta Querol .... EY
Poeta Quintana .... FY 40
Quevedo .... DY
Ramón y Cajal (Gran Vía) .... DZ
Real (Puente del) .... FX
Roger de Lauria .... EZ
Ruzafa (Pas.) .... EZ
Salamanca .... FZ
Salvá .... EY
Salvador .... EX
Salvador Giner .... EX
San Pío V .... FX
San Vicente Ferrer (Pl.) .... FY 46
Santa Ana .... EX
Santa Mónica (Pl.) .... EX
Serranos .... EX
Serranos (Puente) .... EX
Sorní .... FYZ
Temple (Pl.) .... FX
Tetuán (Pl. de) .... FY
Trinidad (Calle y Puente) .... FX
Turia .... DX
Universidad .... EY 49
Virgen (Pl. de la) .... EX 51
Xativa .... DEZ
Zaragoza (Pl. de) .... EXY

VALENCIA 46000 445 N 28 29 – pop. 751 734 – alt. 13 – ☎ 96 – Bullring.

See : Fine Arts Museum** (Museo Provincial de Bellas Artes) FX **M3** – Cathedral* (Miguelete*) EX **A** – Palacio de la Generalidad* (ceilings*) EX **D** – Lonja* (silkhall*, Maritime consulate hall : ceiling*) EX **E** – Corpus Christi Collegiate Church* (Colegio del Patriarca) EY **N** – Ceramics Museum* (Museo Nacional de Cerámica) EY **M1** – Serranos Towers* EX **V** – Santo Domingo Monastery (Royal Chapel*) FY **S.**

9 of Manises by ④ : 12 km ☎ 379 08 50 – 18 Club Escorpión NW : 19 km by Liria Road ☎ 160 12 11.

Valencia - Manises Airport by ④ : 9,5 km ☎ 370 34 08 – Iberia : Paz 14, ✉ 46003, ☎ 352 05 00.

☎ 351 00 43.

To the Balearic and Canary Islands : Cía. Trasmediterránea, av. Manuel Soto Ingeniero 15, ✉ 46024, ☎ 367 06 04, Telex 62648.

Paz 46, ✉ 46003, ☎ 352 24 97 and pl. del País Valenciano 1 ✉ 46016 ☎ 351 04 17 – **R.A.C.E.** (R.A.C. de Valencia) av. Jacinto Benavente 25, ✉ 46005, ☎ 333 94 03.

Madrid 351 ④ – Albacete 183 ③ – Alicante (by coast) 174 ③ – Barcelona 361 ① – Bilbao 606 ① – Castellón de la Plana 75 ① – Málaga 654 ③ – Sevilla 676 ④ – Zaragoza 332 ①.

Plan on preceding pages

Rey Don Jaime M, av. Baleares 2, ✉ 46023, ☎ 360 73 00, Telex 64252, – AE E VISA.
M 3 250 – 750 – **314 rm** 12 000/15 000 – P 13 220/17 720.

Astoria Palace, pl. Rodrigo Botet 5, ✉ 46002, ☎ 352 67 37, Telex 62733 – AE E VISA. EY **p**
M 2 150 – 550 – **207 rm** 7 000/10 200 – P 9 950/11 850.

Reina Victoria, Barcas 4, ✉ 46002, ☎ 352 04 87, Telex 64755 – AE E VISA. rest EY **s**
M 2 300 – 520 – **92 rm** 5 460/9 140 – P 8 650/9 540.

Expo H., without rest., coffee shop only, av. Pío XII-4, ✉ 46009, ☎ 347 09 09, Telex 63212, – AE E VISA.
396 rm 8 000/10 300.

Dimar, without rest., coffee shop only, Gran Vía Marqués del Turia 80, ✉ 46005, ☎ 334 18 07, Telex 62952 – FZ **q**
95 rm.

Excelsior without rest., coffee shop only, Barcelonina 5, ✉ 46002, ☎ 351 46 12 – AE E VISA. EY **e**
270 – **64 rm** 3 550/5 300.

Oltra without rest., coffee shop only, pl. del País Valenciano 4, ✉ 46002, ☎ 352 06 12 – AE E VISA. EY **t**
335 – **93 rm** 3 750/6 025.

Lehos without rest., coffee shop only, General Urrutia (angle av. de la Plata), ✉ 46013, ☎ 334 78 00, Telex 63055, – wc wc . AE E VISA.
400 – **104 rm** 4 000/6 400.

Renasa without rest., coffee shop only, av. Cataluña 5, ✉ 46010, ☎ 369 24 50 – wc wc . AE E VISA.
300 – **73 rm** 3 300/5 500.

Inglés, Marqués de Dos Aguas 6, ✉ 46002, ☎ 351 64 26 – rest wc EY **m**
62 rm.

Continental without rest., Correos 8, ✉ 46002, ☎ 351 09 26 – wc wc . AE VISA. EY **h**
275 – **43 rm** 3 000/4 800.

Bristol without rest., Abadía San Martín 3, ✉ 46002, ☎ 352 11 76 – wc wc . AE E VISA EY **b**
closed December-15 January – 250 – **40 rm** 2 700/4 800.

Florida without rest., Padilla 4, ✉ 46001, ☎ 351 12 84 – wc wc DY **e**
250 – **45 rm** 2 500/4 800.

XXX **La Hacienda,** Navarro Reverter 12, ✉ 46004, ☎ 373 18 59 – . AE E VISA.
closed Saturday lunch, Sunday and Holy-Week – **M** a la carte 2 950/5 000. FY **y**

XXX Los Azahares, Navarro Reverter 16, ✉ 46004, ☎ 334 86 01 – FY **s**

XXX **El Condestable,** Artes Gráficas 7, ✉ 46010, ☎ 369 92 50, Castilian decor – . AE E VISA.
closed Sunday – **M** a la carte 1 900/4 450.

XXX **Ma Cuina,** Gran Vía Germanías 49, ✉ 46006, ☎ 341 77 99 – . AE VISA DZ **n**
closed Sunday – **M** a la carte 2 050/3 055.

XXX **Lionel,** Pizarro 9, ✉ 46004, ☎ 351 65 66 – . AE E VISA. EZ **b**
closed Sunday dinner – **M** a la carte 1 525/2 450.

XXX **Comodoro,** Transits 3, ✉ 46002, ☎ 351 38 15 – . AE E VISA. EY **r**
closed Sunday, Bank Holidays and August – **M** a la carte 1 450/3 400.

XX José Marí, 1 st floor, estación Marítima, ✉ 46011, ☎ 367 20 15, ←, Basque rest. – ▤.

XX **El Cachirulo,** Cronista Almela y Vives 3, ✉ 46010, ☎ 360 10 84, Aragonese rest. – ▤. VISA. ※
closed Saturday, Sunday dinner and August – **M** a la carte 1 850/3 500.

XX **El Gourmet,** Martí 3, ✉ 46005, ☎ 374 50 71 – ▤. VISA. ※ FZ **b**
closed Sunday and 15 August-15 September – **M** a la carte 1 690/2 700.

XX El Timonel, Felix Pizcueta 13, ✉ 46004, ☎ 352 63 00 – ▤ EZ **t**

XX **Casa Aurelia,** Marvá 28, ✉ 46007, ☎ 325 88 13 – ▤. AE ⓓ E VISA. ※ DZ **f**
closed Saturday lunch, Sunday and August – **M** *(lunch only)* a la carte 2 100/6 050.

XX **El Portalón,** Joaquím Costa 61, ✉ 46005, ☎ 333 79 36 – ▤. AE E VISA. ※
closed Sunday and August – **M** a la carte 1 950/3 550.

X **Marisquería Ismael,** Burriana 40, ✉ 46005, ☎ 373 57 15 – ▤. AE ⓓ E VISA. ※ FZ **e**
closed Sunday from June to September – **M** a la carte 1 815/3 450.

at Playa Puebla de Farnals by ① : 15 km – ✉ 46137 Playa Puebla de Farnals – ☎ 96 :

X **Bergamonte,** ☎ 144 16 12, ☂, « Typical Valencian "barraca" », ※ – Ⓟ. AE VISA. ※
closed Monday in winter – **M** a la carte 1 850/3 250.

at Benimamet by road C 234 NW : 8,5 km – ✉ 46080 Valencia – ☎ 96 :

Fería, av de las Ferias 2 - near the Exhibition Center ☎ 364 44 11, Telex 61079 – |‡| ▤ TV 🚗. AE ⓓ VISA. ※ rest
closed June - 10 September – **M** a la carte approx. 2 700 – ☕ 400 – **136 rm** 9 500.

on the road to the Airport by ④ : 9,5 km – ✉ 46940 Manises – ☎ 96 :

Azafata, ☎ 154 61 00, Telex 61451 – |‡| ▤ 🚗 Ⓟ – 🏛
130 rm.

Sweden
Sverige

Stockholm

PRACTICAL INFORMATION

LOCAL CURRENCY

Swedish Kronor : 100 SEK = 14.75 US $ (Jan. 87)

TOURIST INFORMATION

The Tourist Centre is situated in the Sweden House, entrance from Kungsträdgården at Hamngatan. Open Mon-Fri 9am-5pm. Sat. and Sun. 9am-2pm. Telephone weekdays 08/789 20 00, weekends to Excursion Shop 08/789 24 15, to Tourist Centre 08/789 24 18.

FOREIGN EXCHANGE

Banks are open between 9.00am and 3.00pm on weekdays only. Some banks in the centre of the city are usually open weekdays 9am to 5.30pm. Most large hotels have exchange facilities, and Arlanda airport has banking facilities between 7am to 10pm seven days a week.

SHOPPING IN STOCKHOLM

The main shopping streets in the Centre are: Hamngatan, Biblioteksgatan, Drottninggatan.

In the Old Town mainly Västerlånggatan.

THEATRE BOOKINGS

Your hotel porter will be able to make your arrangements or direct you to Theatre Booking Agents.

In addition there is a kiosk at Norrmalmstorg selling tickets for the same day's performances with a reduction of approx. 25 per cent, no booking fee.

In the summer it's open 11am-7.30pm Tues.-Sat. and 11am-5pm Sun. and Mon. During the winter 12am-7.15pm Tues.-Sat., 12am-4pm Sun., 12am-5pm Mon.

CAR HIRE

The international car hire companies have branches in Stockholm city and at Arlanda airport. Your hotel porter will be able to give details and help you with your arrangements.

TIPPING

Hotels and restaurants normally include a service charge of 15 per cent. Doormen, baggage porters etc. are generally given a gratuity.

Taxi drivers are customarily tipped about 10 per cent of the amount shown on the meter in addition to the fare.

SPEED LIMITS - SEAT BELTS

The maximum permitted speed on motorways and dual carriageways is 110 km/h - 68 mph and 90 km/h - 56 mph on other roads except where a lower speed limit is signposted.

The wearing of seat belts in Sweden is compulsory for drivers and front seat passengers.

STOCKHOLM

SIGHTS

See : Old Town★★★ (Gamla Stan) : Stortorget★★, AZ, Köpmangatan★★ AZ **35**, Österlånggatan★★ AZ ; Royal Warship Vasa★★★ (Wasavarvet) DYZ ; Skansen Open-Air Museum★★★ DY.
Royal Palace★★ (Kungliga Slottet) AZ ; Changing of the Guard★★ ; Apartments★★, Royal Armoury★★, Treasury★ ; Museum★ ; Great Church★★ (Storkyrkan) AZ ; Riddarholmen Church★★ (Riddarholmskyrkan) AZ ; Town Hall★★ (Stadshuset) BYH : ✳★★★, Djurgården DYZ : Waldemarsudde House★★, Rosendal Palace★, Thiel Gallery★ ; Gröna Lunds Tivoli★ DZ.
Kaknäs TV Tower★ (Kaknäs Tornet) ✳★★★ DY ; Gustav Adolf Square★ (Gustav Adolfs Torg) CY **16** ; Kings Gardens★ (Kungsträdgården) CY ; Riddarhouse★ (Riddarhuset) AZ ; German Church★ (Tyska Kyrkan) AZ ; Fjällgatan★ DZ ; Sergels Torg CY **54** – Hötorget★ CY 20.

Museums : Museum of National Antiquities★★★ (Historiska Museet) DY ; National Art Gallery★★ (National Museum) DY **M1** ; Nordic Museum★★ (Nordiska Museet) DY **M2** ; Museum of Far Eastern Antiquities★★ (Ostasiastiska Museet) DY **M3** ; Museum of Modern Art (Moderna Museet) DYZ **M4** ; National Maritime Museum★★ (Sjöhistoriska Museet) DY ; Halwyl Museum★ (Halwylska Museet) CY **M5** ; City Museum★ (Stads Museet) CZ **M6** ; Strindberg Museum★ BX **M7**.

Outskirts : Drottningholm Palace★★ (Drottningholms Slott) W : 12 km BY ; Apartments★★, Gardens★★, Court Theatre★, Chinese Pavilion★ ; Tours by boat★★ (in summer) : Under the Bridges★★ ; Archipelago★★ (Vaxholm, Möja, Sandhamn, Utö), Mälarenlake★ (Gripsholm, Skokloster) ; Haga Park and Pavilion of Gustav III★ (N : 4 km) BX ; Millesgården★ (E : 4 km) DX.

STOCKHOLM Sverige 920 MN2 – pop. 659 030 – ☎ 08.

18 Svenska Golfförbundet ☎ 753 02 65.

✈ Stockholm-Arlanda N : 41 km ☎ (08) 780 30 30 – SAS : Flygcity, Sveavägen 22 ☎ 780 10 00 – Air Terminal : main railway station.

Motorail for Southern Europe : SJ Travel Agency, Vasagatan 22 ☎ 762 58 15.

To Finland and excursions by boat : contact Stockholm Information Service (see below).

Stockholm Information Service, Tourist Centre, Sverigehuset, Hamngatan 27 ☎ 789 20 00 – Motormännens Riksförbund Kungl. Automobilklubben (Royal Automobile Club) ☎ 60 00 55.

Hamburg 935 – København 630 – Oslo 522.

STOCKHOLM

Street	Grid	No.
Biblioteksgatan	CY	2
Drottninggatan	BX, CY	10
Gallerian	CY	14
Hamngatan	CY	
Kungsgatan	BCY	
Sergelgatan	CY	52
Västerlånggatan	AZ	
Österlånggatan	AZ	
Birger Jarlsgatan	CXY	3
Brunkebergstorg	CY	5
Brunnsgränd	AZ	6
Bryggargatan	BY	8
Djurgårdsbron	DY	9
Erstagatan	DZ	13
Gustav Adolfs Torg	CY	16
Götgatan	CZ	17
Herkulesgatan	CY	18
Hötorget	CY	20
Järntorget	AZ	21
Järntorgsgatan	AZ	23
Kindstugatan	AZ	24
Klarabergsgatan	CY	25
Klarabergsviadukten	BY	27
Kornhamnstorg	AZ	28
Kungsbron	BY	30
Kungsträdgårdsgatan	CY	32
Källargränd	AZ	34
Köpmangatan	AZ	35
Lilla Nygatan	AZ	37
Lill-Jans Plan	CX	38
Munkbrogatan	AZ	40
Myntgatan	AZ	41
Norrbro	CY	43
Norrlandsgatan	CY	44
Nybroplan	CY	46
Odenplan	BX	47
Olof Palmes Gata	BY	48
Riddarhusgränd	AZ	49
Riddarhustorget	AZ	50
Rådhusgränd	AZ	51
Sergels Torg	CY	54
Slottskajen	AZ	55
Slussplan	AZ	56
Stadshusbron	BY	57
Stallgatan	CY	59
Storkyrkobrinken	AZ	60
Strömbron	CY	61
Strömgatan	CY	63
Södermalmstorg	CZ	64
Södra Blasieholmshamnen	CY	66
Tegelbacken	CY	67
Tegnérlunden	BX	69
Triewaldsgränd	AZ	70
Tyska Brinken	AZ	73
Vasagatan	BY	75
Östermalmstorg	DY	76
Östra Järnvägsgatan	BY	78

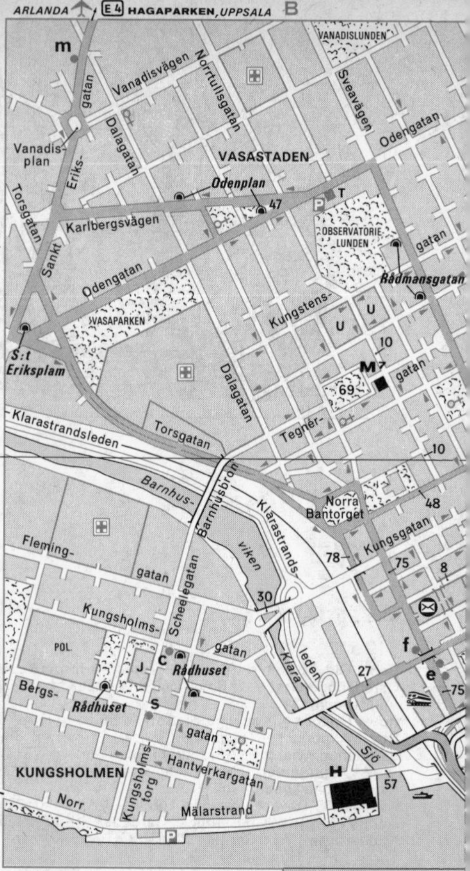

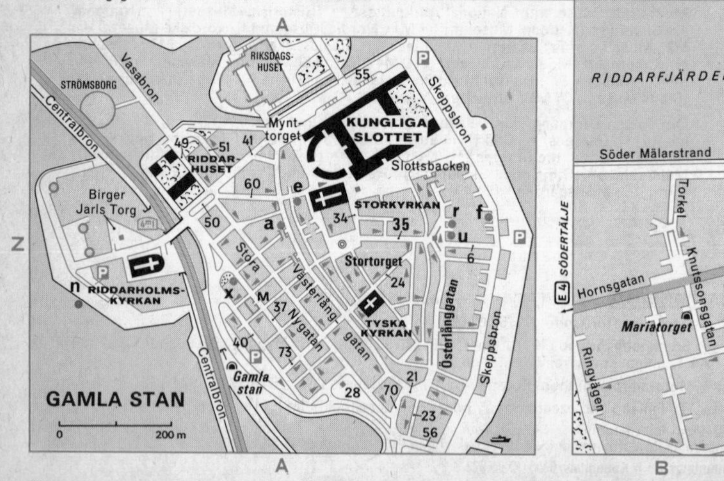

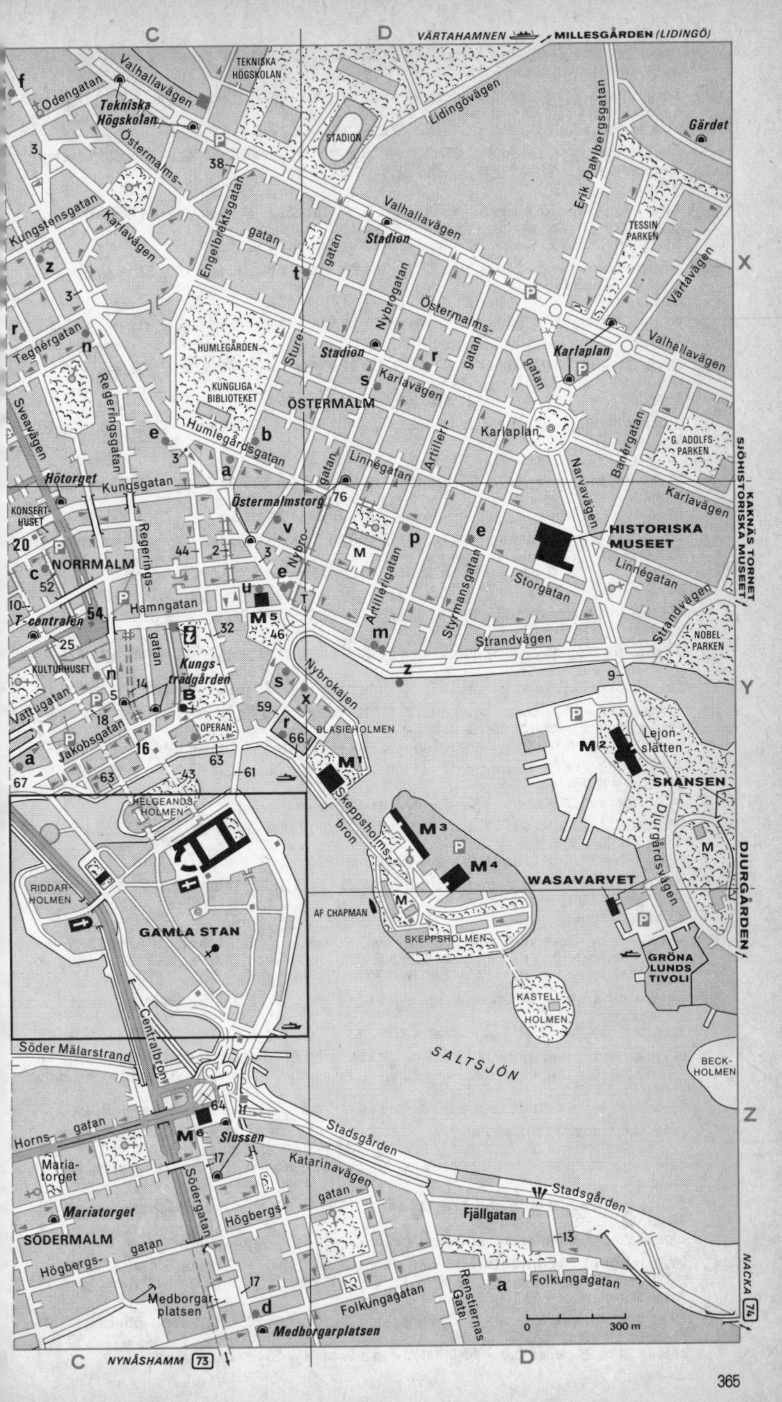
VÄRTAHAMNEN
MILLESGÅRDEN (LIDINGÖ)
TEKNISKA HÖGSKOLAN
STADION
Valhallavägen
Odengatan
Tekniska Högskolan
Östermalms-
Lidingövägen
Erik Dahlbergsgatan
Gärdet
Kungstensgatan
Karlavägen
Engelbrektsgatan
gatan
Stadion
TESSIN PARKEN
Värtavägen
Östermalms-
Nybrogatan
Sture-
Tegnérgatan
HUMLEGÅRDEN
KUNGLIGA BIBLIOTEKET
ÖSTERMALM
Karlaplan
Sveavägen
Regeringsgatan
Humlegårdsgatan
Linnégatan
Artilleri-
Narvavägen
Banérgatan
G. ADOLFS-PARKEN
SJÖHISTORISKA MUSEET
KAKNÄS TORNET
Hötorget
Kungsgatan
Östermalmstorg
KONSERT-HUSET
NORRMALM
HISTORISKA MUSEET
Storgatan
Hamngatan
Artillerigatan
Styrmansgatan
Strandvägen
T-centralen
KULTURHUSET
Kungsträdgården
Nybrokajen
NOBEL-PARKEN
Vattugatan
Jakobsgatan
OPERAN
BLASIEHOLMEN
Lejonslätten
SKANSEN
HELGEANDSHOLMEN
Skeppsholmsbron
Djurgårdsvägen
DJURGÅRDEN
RIDDARHOLMEN
GAMLA STAN
AF CHAPMAN
WASAVARVET
SKEPPSHOLMEN
GRÖNA LUNDS TIVOLI
KASTELLHOLMEN
SALTSJÖN
BECKHOLMEN
Söder Mälarstrand
Centralbron
Stadsgården
Hornsgatan
Slussen
Mariatorget
Katarinavägen
Högbergsgatan
Fjällgatan
SÖDERMALM
Södergatan
Folkungagatan
Medborgarplatsen
Renstiernas Gata
Medborgarplatsen
NACKA 74
NYNÅSHAMM 73
0
300 m

Grand H., Södra Blasieholmshamnen 8, S - 103 27, ☎ 22 10 20, Telex 19500, ←, – 335 rm. CY r

Sergel Plaza [M], Brunkebergstorg 9, S-103 27, ☎ 22 66 00, Telex 16700, « Tasteful decor » – AE E VISA CY n
M Anna Rella 140/307 and a la carte – **Plaza Café** – **407 rm** 775/1200.

Royal Viking [M], Vasagatan 1, S - 101 23, ☎ 14 10 00, Telex 13900, « Rooftop restaurant and bar » – BY f
400 rm.

Sheraton-Stockholm [M], Tegelbacken 6, S - 101 23, ☎ 14 26 00, Telex 17750, ←, – AE E VISA CY a
M (buffet lunch) 95/dinner 295 and a la carte – **460 rm** 825/1270.

Amaranten, Kungsholmsgatan 31, S - 104 20, ☎ 54 10 60, Telex 17498, – AE E VISA BY c
M a la carte 120/230 – **415 rm** 650/880.

Anglais, Humlegårdsgatan 23, S - 102 44, ☎ 24 99 00, Telex 19475 – CX a
211 rm.

SAS Strand, Nybrokajen 9, S-103 27, ☎ 22 29 00, Telex 10504, ←, « Tastefully furnished » – AE E VISA CDY x
M 150/300 and a la carte – **134 rm** 900/1500.

Stockholm Plaza [M], Birger Jarlsgatan 29, S-103 95, ☎ 14 51 20, Telex 13982, – CX e
155 rm.

Diplomat, Strandvägen 7c, S - 104 40, ☎ 63 58 00, Telex 17119, ←, – AE E VISA DY m
M *(closed Saturday dinner and Sunday)* – **132 rm** 725/1200.

Continental, Vasagatan, S - 101 21, ☎ 24 40 20, Telex 10100 – rest AE E VISA. BY e
closed 23 to 28 December – **M** (buffet lunch) 42/dinner 220 and a la carte – **250 rm** 445/1300.

Palace, S : t Eriksgatan 115, S - 100 31, ☎ 24 12 20, Telex 19877, – BX m
214 rm.

Terminus (Best Western), Vasagatan 20, S - 101 23, ☎ 22 26 40, Telex 11749, – AE E VISA. BY e
closed 23 to 27 December – **M** 105/150 and a la carte – **155 rm** 715/920.

Birger Jarl without rest., Tulegatan 8, S - 104 32, ☎ 15 10 20, Telex 11843, – wc wc AE E VISA CX z
closed 23 December-2 January – (unlicensed) – **252 rm** 575/950.

City, Slöjdgatan 7, Hötorget, S - 111 81, ☎ 22 22 40, Telex 12487, – wc AE E VISA. CY c
M (unlicensed) a la carte 103/270 – **300 rm** 595/745.

Malmen, Götgatan 49 - 51, S - 102 61, ☎ 20 81 06, Telex 19489, – wc wc AE E VISA CZ d
M 45/195 and dinner a la carte – **280 rm** 690/930.

Eden without rest., Sturegatan 10, S - 114 36, ☎ 22 31 60, Telex 10570 – wc wc AE E VISA CX b
60 rm 385/925.

Wellington (Best Western) without rest., Storgatan 6, S - 114 51, ☎ 67 09 10, Telex 17963, – wc wc AE E VISA DY p
closed 23 December-2 January – **50 rm** 630/880.

XXXX **Operakällaren** (at Opera House), S-111 86, ☎ 24 27 00, « Opulent classical decor » – AE E VISA CY
closed 4 July-2 August – **M** a la carte 275/424.

XXX ✲ **Coq Blanc,** Regeringsgatan 111, S - 111 39, ☎ 11 61 53 – AE E VISA CX n
closed Saturday except dinner September-May, Sunday, 6 July-4 August and Bank Holidays – **M** 245/300 and a la carte 225/335
Spec. Marinated tenderloin with herb sauce, Fillets of reindeer à la maison, Strawberry flambé du patron.

XXX ✲ **L'Escargot,** Scheelegatan 8, S - 112 23, ☎ 53 05 77 – AE E VISA BY s
closed Sunday and 23 December-7 January – **M** 158/475 and a la carte 166/435
Spec. La terrine de foie gras L'Escargot, Escargots beurre roquefort, Poisson et crustacés variés selon la saison.

XX **Teatergrillen,** Nybrogatan 3, S-114 34, ☎ 10 70 44, « Theatre atmosphere » – AE E VISA CY e
closed 7 April-8 September and Bank Holidays – **M** 150/700 and a la carte.

XX **Wärdshuset Stallmästaregården,** Norrtull, S-113 47, N : 2 km on E.4 ☎ 24 39 10, ←, « 17C Inn, Waterside setting », – AE E VISA by Sveavägen BX
closed Christmas – **M** 170/290 and a la carte.

XX **Clas På Hörnet** with rm, Surbrunnsgatan 20, ☎ 16 51 30, « 18C atmosphere » – wc AE E VISA. CX f
closed 24 to 26 December – **M** 115/175 and a la carte – **10 rm** 560/1300.

XX ❀ **Gourmet,** Tegnérgatan 10, S - 113 58, ☎ 31 43 98 – ▤. AE ⓓ E VISA — CX **r**
closed Saturday lunch, Sunday and Bank Holidays – **M** 150/400 and a la carte
Spec. Flambéed sea-crayfish.

XX **Riche,** Birger Jarlsgatan 4, S-114 34, ☎ 23 68 40 – ▤. AE ⓓ E VISA — CY **e**
closed Sunday lunch – **M** 150/325 and a la carte.

XX **Paul and Norbert,** Strandvägen 9, S - 114 56, ☎ 63 81 83 – AE ⓓ E VISA — DY **m**
closed Saturday, Sunday, 6 to 31 July, 23 December-6 January, 28 March-1 April and Bank Holidays – **M** (booking essential) 140/320 and a la carte.

XX ❀ **Eriks,** Strandvägskajen 17, S - 114 56, ☎ 60 60 60, Seafood, « Converted barge » – AE ⓓ E VISA — DY **z**
closed Sunday and Christmas-New Year – **M** 110/365 and a la carte 305/445
Spec. Grilled scallops with duck-liver sauce and apple, Turbot with saffron flavoured stuffing, Noilly Prat sauce and vegetables, Vanilla ice-cream with warm rosehip cream.

XX **La Brochette** (Brasserie, Ground floor), Storgatan 27, S-114 55, ☎ 62 20 00, 🍽 – ▤
closed Saturday and Sunday – **M** 80/200 and a la carte – **Ma Cave** (basement, with wine cellar) ☎ 60 25 28 – *(closed Saturday and Sunday)* 95/250 and a la carte. — DY **e**

XX **Coq Roti,** Sturegatan 19, S - 114 36, ☎ 10 25 67 – ▤. AE ⓓ E VISA — CDX **t**
closed Saturday lunch, Sunday, July and Bank Holidays – **M** 300/375 and a la carte.

XX **La Grenouille,** Grev Turegatan 16, S-114 46, ☎ 20 10 00 – ▤. AE ⓓ E VISA — CY **v**
M a la carte 195/305.

XX **Michel,** Karlavägen 73, S-114 49, ☎ 62 22 62 – AE ⓓ E VISA — DX **r**
closed Saturday lunch, Sunday, 4 July-7 August and 22 December-7 January – **M** 165/425 and a la carte.

X **Nils Emil,** Folkungagatan 122, S-116 30, ☎ 40 72 09 – ▤. AE ⓓ E VISA — DZ **a**
closed Saturday lunch, Sunday, July and Bank Holidays – **M** (booking essential) a la carte 150/270.

X **KB,** Smålandsgatan 7, S-111 46, ☎ 11 02 32 – AE ⓓ E VISA — CY **u**
closed lunch Saturday, Sunday, 15 June-8 August and Bank Holidays – **M** 70/105 and a la carte.

X ❀ **Wedholms Fisk,** Nybrokajen 17, ☎ 10 48 74 – AE ⓓ E — CY **s**
closed Sunday and July – **M** (lunch) 95 and a la carte 220/345
Spec. Seafood.

X **Ett Rum och Kök,** Nybrogatan 46, S-114 40, ☎ 61 12 02 – AE ⓓ E — DX **s**
closed Saturday, Sunday, 11 July-16 August, 23 December-8 January and Bank Holidays – **M** a la carte 200/315.

Gamla Stan (Old Stockholm) :

🏨 Reisen, Skeppsbron 12-14, S - 111 30, ☎ 22 32 60, Telex 17494, ←, 🅂 – 🛗 ▤ 📺 ☎. 🅐 — AZ **f**
125 rm.

🏨 Mälardrottningen, Riddarholmen, S - 111 28, ☎ 24 36 00, Telex 15468, ←, 🅂, « Former private motor-yacht » – ▤ 📺 🚿wc ☎ — AZ **n**
59 rm (cabins).

🏨 **Lady Hamilton** without rest., Storkyrkobrinken 5, S-111 28, ☎ 23 46 80, Telex 10434, 🅂, « Swedish rural antiques » – 🛗 📺 🛁wc 🚿wc ☎. AE ⓓ E VISA. ✻ — AZ **e**
closed 24 to 27 December – **34 rm** ☕ 860/1085.

🏨 **Lord Nelson** without rest., Västerlanggatan 22, S-111 29, ☎ 23 23 90, Telex 10434, 🅂, « Ship style installation, maritime antiques » – 🛗 📺 🚿wc ☎. AE ⓓ E VISA. ✻ — AZ **a**
closed 20 December-7 January – **31 rm** ☕ 635/920.

XXX **Eriks,** österlånggatan 17, S-111 31, ☎ 23 85 00, Seafood – ▤. AE ⓓ E VISA — AZ **u**
closed Sunday – **M** 60/295 and a la carte 230/392.

XX **Källaren Aurora,** Munkbron 11, S-111 28, ☎ 21 93 59, « In the cellars of a 17C house » – ▤. AE ⓓ E VISA — AZ **x**
closed Sunday, 24 to 28 December and Bank Holidays – **M** (dinner only) 165/287 and a la carte.

XX **Fem Små Hus,** Nygränd 10, S - 111 30, ☎ 10 87 75, « Cellars, antiques » – ▤. AE ⓓ E VISA — AZ **r**
M 96/395 and a la carte.

to the NW :

at Solna 5 km by Sveavägen – BX – and E 4 – ✉ Solna – ☎ 08 Stockholm :

XXX ❀ **Ulriksdals Wärdshus,** 171 71 Solna, N : 3 km in Ulriksdals Slottspark ☎ 85 08 15, ←, « Former inn in Royal Park », 🌳 – 🅟. AE ⓓ E VISA
closed dinner Sunday and Bank Holidays and 24 to 26 December – **M** 280 and a la carte 270/390
Spec. Partridge mousse with gele and salad, Fillets of sole, turbot and salmon with fresh asparagus in truffle sauce, Punsch parfait with peach in orange sauce.

XX **Finsmakaren,** Råsundavägen 9, 171 52 Solna, ☎ 27 67 71 – AE ⓓ E VISA
closed Saturday, Sunday, 29 June-31 July, 23 December-6 January and Bank Holidays – **M** a la carte 155/263.

at Sollentuna 15 km by Sveavägen – BX – and E4 – ✉ Sollentuna – ☎ 08 Stockholm :

XX **Edsbacka Krog,** Sollentunavägen 220, 19147, ☎ 96 33 00 – Ⓟ
closed Saturday lunch, Monday dinner, Sunday and 12 July-9 August – **M** 155/165 and a la carte.

at Arlanda Airport by Sveavägen – BX – and E4 – ☎ 0760 Arlanda :

SAS Arlandia, 190 45 Stockholm - Arlanda ☎ 618 00, Telex 13018, ≘s, ⧈, ✂ – ⧈ ▤ ⧈ ☎ ♿ Ⓟ. ⧈. AE ⓓ E VISA
M 250/460 and a la carte – **300 rm** ⊡ 730/1080.

to the E :

in Djurgården 2 km by Strandvägen – DY – ✉ ☎ 08 Stockholm :

XXX Djurgårdsbrunns Wärdshus, Djurgårdsbrunnsvägen 68, S - 115 25, ☎ 67 90 95, ←, « In Djurgården Park ».

Switzerland
Suisse
Schweiz
Svizzera

Basle
Geneva
Zürich

PRACTICAL INFORMATION

LOCAL CURRENCY

Swiss Franc : 100 F = 61.61 US $ (Jan. 87)

LANGUAGES SPOKEN

German, French and Italian are usually spoken in all administrative departments, shops, hotels and restaurants.

AIRLINES

A large number of international airlines operate out of the main Swiss airports. For general information ring the number given after the airport symbol and name in the text of each town.

POSTAL SERVICES

In large towns, post offices are open from 7.30am to noon and 1.45pm to 6.30pm, and Saturdays untill 11am. The telephone system is fully automatic.

SHOPPING

Department stores are generally open from 8am to 4pm, except on Saturdays when they close at 4 or 5pm.

In the index of street names, those printed in red are where the principal shops are found.

TIPPING

In hotels, restaurants and cafés the service charge is generally included in the prices.

SPEED LIMITS

The speed limit on motorways is 120 km/h - 74 mph, on other roads 80 km/h - 50 mph, and in built up areas 50 km/h - 31 mph.

SEAT BELTS

The wearing of seat belts is compulsory in all Swiss cantons.

BASLE (BASEL) 4000 Switzerland 66 ⑩, 216 ④ – pop. 180 463 – alt. 273 – Basle and environs from France 19-41-61, from Switzerland 061.

See : Cathedral (Münster)★★ : ≤★ CY – Zoological Garden★★★ AZ – The Port (Hafen)※★, Exposition★ CX – Fish Market Fountain★ (Fischmarktbrunnen) BY – Old Streets★ BY – Oberer Rheinweg ≤★ CY – Museums : Fine Arts★★★ (Kunstmuseum) CY, Historical★ (Historisches Museum) CY, Ethnographic (Museum für Völkerkunde)★ CY **M1** – Haus zum Kirschgarten★ CZ, Antiquities (Antikenmuseum)★ CY – ※★ from Bruderholz Water Tower 3,5 km by ⑥.

18 private ☎ 89 68 50 91 at Hagenthal-le-Bas (68-France).

Basle-Mulhouse ☎ 57.31.11 at Basle (Switzerland) by Zollfreie Strasse 8 km and at Saint-Louis (68-France) ☎ 89 69 00 00.

Blumenrain 2 ☎ 22.50.50, Télex 63318 – Automobile Club Suisse, Birsigstr. 4 ☎ 23.39.33 – T.C.S., Petrihof, Steinentorstr. 13 ☎ 23.19.55.

Paris 551 ⑧ – Bern 95 ⑤ – Freiburg 71 ① – Lyon 387 ⑧ – Mulhouse 35 ⑧ – Strasbourg 145 ①.

Plan on following pages

✿ **Trois Rois,** Blumenrain 8, ✉ 4001, ☎ 25 52 52, Telex 62937, ≤, 🍴 – |♦| ▤ TV ☎ – 80. AE ⓓ E VISA. ✗ rest — BY **a**
st. : rest. **Rôtisserie des Rois M** 88/120 ✌ - **Rhy-Deck M** a la carte 45/55 ✌ – ☕ 14 – **90 rm** 165/335, 7 apartments 480/740
Spec. Portefeuille de saumon, Escauton de ris de veau, Soufflé chaud au citron.

Hilton M, Aeschengraben 31, ✉ 4002, ☎ 22 66 22, Telex 965555, ▢ – |♦| ▤ TV ☎ ♿ – 50-300. AE ⓓ E VISA. ✗ rest — CZ **d**
st. : M a la carte 60/90 ✌ – ☕ 9,50 – **217 rm** 130/250, 10 apartments.

Plaza M, Riehenring 45, ✉ 4058, ☎ 32 33 33, Telex 64439, ▢ – |♦| ▤ TV ☎ ♿ 🚗 – 30. AE ⓓ E VISA — DX **r**
st. : rest. **Adagio** *(closed July and Sunday)* **M** 28/85 ✌ - **Grand café M** a la carte 25/50 ✌ – **243 rm** ☕ 150/270, 3 apartments 650.

Euler, Centralbahnplatz 14, ✉ 4002, ☎ 23 45 00, Telex 962215 – |♦| ▤ TV ☎ 🚗 – 120. AE ⓓ E VISA — BZ **a**
st. : M a la carte 65/95 ✌ – ☕ 12 – **55 rm** 165/271, 10 apartments 340/580.

Hôtel International M, Steinentorstrasse 25, ✉ 4001, ☎ 22 18 70, Telex 962370, ▢ – |♦| ▤ TV ☎ ♿ – 25-250. AE ⓓ E VISA. ✗ rest — BZ **b**
st. : rest. **Steinenpick M** a la carte 30/65✌ - **Rôt. Charolaise M** a la carte 60/90 ✌ – **210 rm** ☕ 270, 5 apartments 260/600.

✿ **Europe and rest. Quatre Saisons** M, Clarastrasse 43, ✉ 4058, ☎ 26 80 80, Telex 64103, 🍴 – |♦| ▤ TV ☎ 🚗 – 180. AE ⓓ E VISA. ✗ rest — CX **k**
st. : M *(closed Sunday)* a la carte 75/100 ✌ – **170 rm** ☕ 108/200.

Schweizerhof, Centralbahnplatz 1, ✉ 4002, ☎ 22 28 33, Telex 962373 – |♦| ▤ rm TV ☎ Ⓟ – 30-90. AE ⓓ E VISA — CZ **n**
st. : M a la carte 50/85 ✌ – **75 rm** ☕ 110/220.

H. Basel ⛵, Münzgasse 12, ✉ 4001, ☎ 25 24 23, Telex 64199 – |♦| ▤ rest TV ☎. AE ⓓ E VISA – **st. : M** a la carte 45/70 ✌ – **72 rm** ☕ 78/250. — BY **x**

Victoria M, Centralbahnplatz 3, ✉ 4002, ☎ 22 55 66, Telex 962362 – |♦| ▤ rest TV ☎ 🚗 – 25. AE ⓓ E VISA — CZ **n**
st. : M a la carte 40/55 ✌ – **115 rm** ☕ 90/170.

Métropol M without rest, Elisabethenanlage 5, ✉ 4051, ☎ 22 77 21, Telex 962268 – |♦| TV ☎ – 120. AE ⓓ E VISA — CZ **a**
st. : 46 rm ☕ 96/165.

Alexander M, Riehenring 85, ✉ 4058, ☎ 26 70 00, Telex 963325 – |♦| kitchenette TV ⛀wc ☎. AE ⓓ E VISA — CX **s**
st. : M a la carte 35/55 ✌ – **65 rm** 🍴 70/150 – P 110/140.

Krafft am Rhein ⛵, Rheingasse 12, ✉ 4058, ☎ 26 88 77, Telex 64360, ≤, 🍴 – |♦| ⛀wc ⛆wc ☎. AE ⓓ E VISA — CY **z**
st. : M 12/37 ✌ – **52 rm** ☕ 55/150 – P 102/150.

City, Henric Petri-Strasse 12, ✉ 4010, ☎ 23 78 11, Telex 962427 – |♦| ▤ ⛀wc ☎. AE ⓓ E VISA — CZ **f**
st. : M a la carte 45/50 ✌ – **85 rm** ☕ 70/160.

Bernina without rest, Innere Margarethenstrasse 14, ✉ 4051, ☎ 23 73 00, Telex 963813 – |♦| TV ⛀wc ⛆wc ☎. AE ⓓ E VISA — BZ **u**
st. : 35 rm ☕ 50/200.

Muenchnerhof, Riehenring 75, ✉ 4058, ☎ 26 77 80, Telex 64476 – |♦| ⛀wc ⛆wc ☎. AE ⓓ E VISA — CX **u**
st. : M 10/60 ✌ – **40 rm** ☕ 40/190.

XXXX ✿✿ **Stucki,** Bruderholzallee 42, ✉ 4059, ☎ 35 82 22, 🍴, « Flowered garden » – E VISA — by ⑥
closed 19 July-10 August, Sunday and Monday – **st. : M** 85/140 and à la carte
Spec. Ravioli au foie gras et aux truffes noires, Noix de ris de veau en crépinette, Feuilleté aux laeckerli.

XXX **Zum Schützenhaus,** Schützenmattstrasse 56, ✉ 4051, ☎ 23 67 60, 🍴 – Ⓟ. AE ⓓ E VISA – **st. : M** a la carte 65/90 ✌ — AY **e**

XXX **Terrasse,** Heltingerstrasse 104 (5th floor), ✉ 4057, ☎ 32 34 78 – |♦|. AE ⓓ E VISA — CX **v**
closed 19 July-10 August, 20 December-4 January, Saturday lunch and Sunday – **M** 60/98.

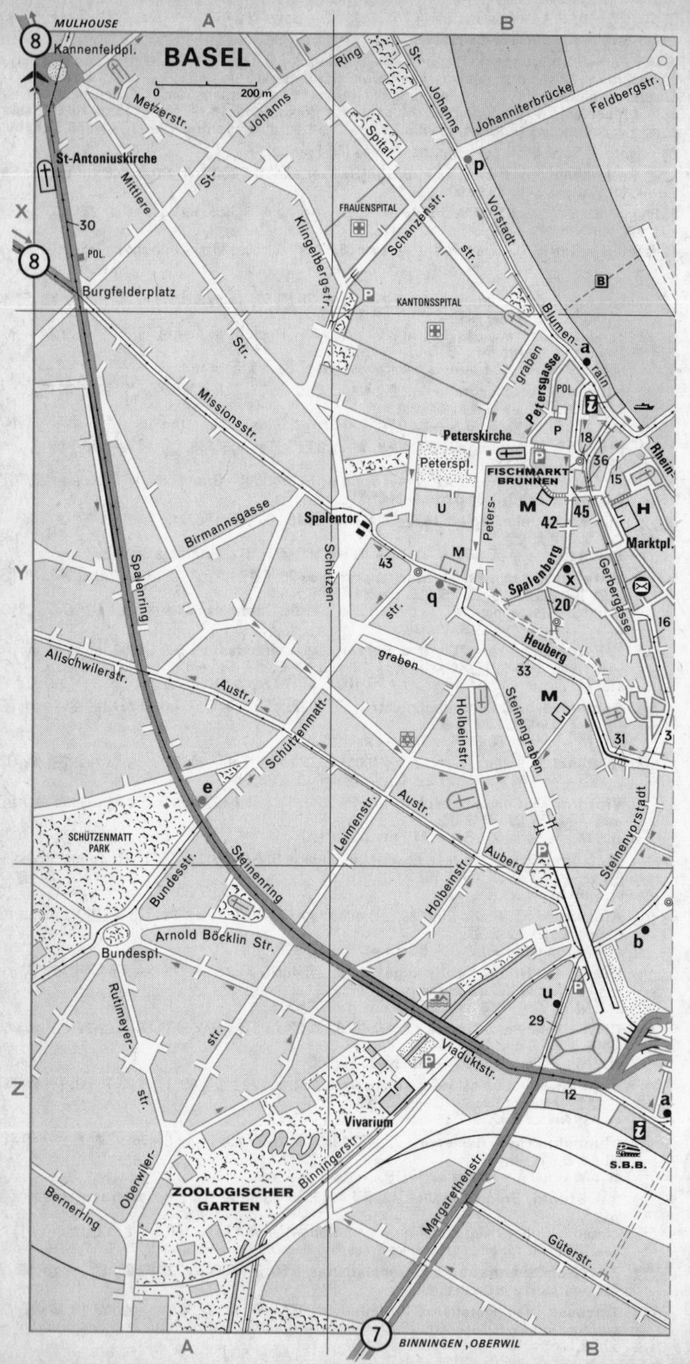
BASEL
MULHOUSE
0
200 m
Kannenfeldpl.
St-Antoniuskirche
Burgfelderplatz
Metzerstr.
Mittlere
St- Johanns
Ring
Spital-
St- Johanns
Vorstadt
Johanniterbrücke
Feldbergstr.
FRAUENSPITAL
KANTONSSPITAL
Klingelbergstr.
Schanzenstr.
Missionsstr.
Birmannsgasse
Spalenring
Spalentor
Schützen-
graben
Peterskirche
Peterspl.
FISCHMARKT-BRUNNEN
Petersgasse
Peters-
Spalenberg
Heuberg
Gerbergasse
Marktpl.
Blumen-rain
Rhein-
Allschwilerstr.
Austr.
Schützenmatt-
Holbeinstr.
Steinengraben
Steinenvorstadt
Leimenstr.
Auberg
Steinenring
SCHÜTZENMATT PARK
Bundesstr.
Bundespl.
Arnold Böcklin Str.
Rutimeyer-str.
Oberwiler-
Bernerring
Viaduktstr.
Vivarium
Binningerstr.
ZOOLOGISCHER GARTEN
Margarethenstr.
Güterstr.
S.B.B.
BINNINGEN, OBERWIL
POL.
P
U
M
H
a
b
e
p
q
u
x
12
15
16
18
20
29
30
31
33
36
42
43
45
7
8

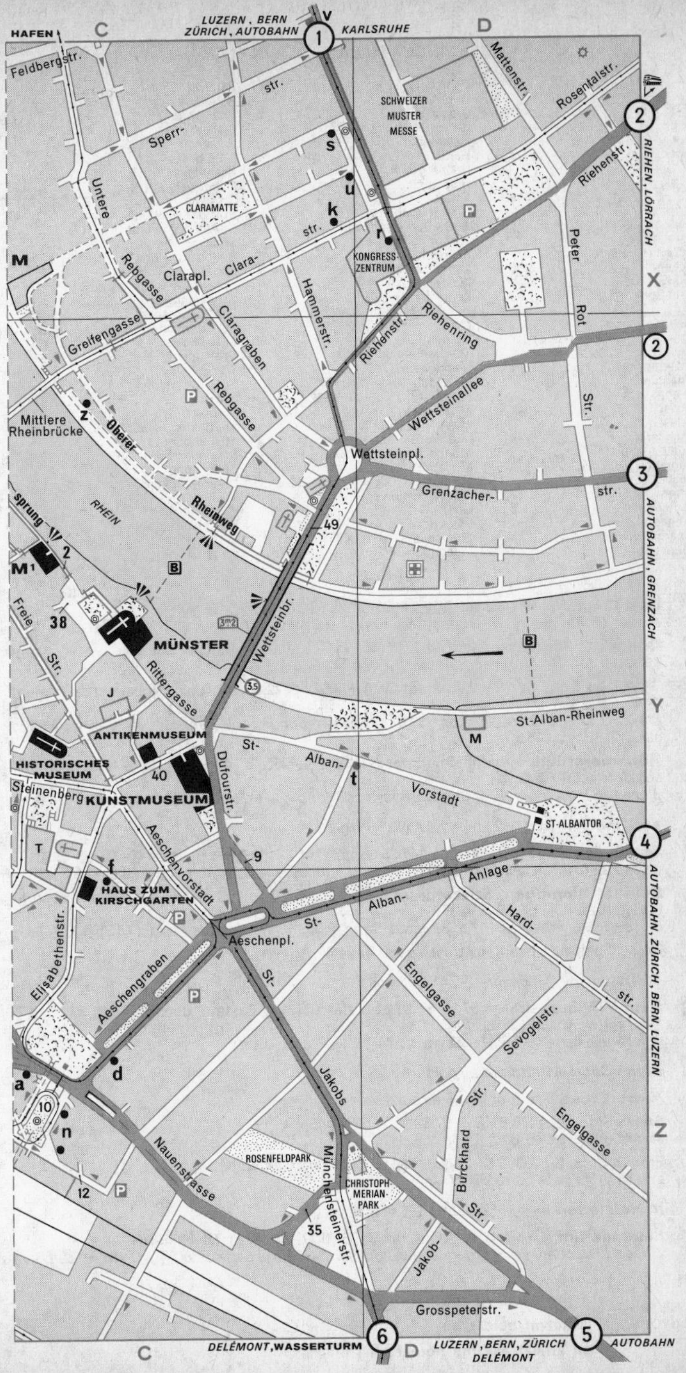
LUZERN, BERN
ZÜRICH, AUTOBAHN
KARLSRUHE
HAFEN
Feldbergstr.
Mattenstr.
Rosentalstr.
SCHWEIZER
MUSTER
MESSE
Sperr-
str.
Untere
Rebgasse
CLARAMATTE
Clarapl.
Clara-
str.
KONGRESS-
ZENTRUM
Riehenstr.
RIEHEN, LÖRRACH
Peter
Rot
Str.
Greifengasse
Claragraben
Hammerstr.
Riehenring
Rebgasse
Wettsteinallee
Mittlere
Rheinbrücke
Oberer
Rheinweg
RHEIN
Wettsteinpl.
Grenzacher-
str.
AUTOBAHN, GRENZACH
MÜNSTER
Freie
Str.
Rittergasse
Wettsteinbr.
St-Alban-Rheinweg
ANTIKENMUSEUM
HISTORISCHES
MUSEUM
Steinenberg
KUNSTMUSEUM
Dufourstr.
St-
Alban-
Vorstadt
ST-ALBANTOR
Aeschenvorstadt
HAUS ZUM
KIRSCHGARTEN
Anlage
St-
Alban-
Hard-
str.
AUTOBAHN, ZÜRICH, BERN, LUZERN
Aeschenpl.
Elisabethenstr.
Aeschengraben
Engelgasse
Sevogelstr.
St-
Jakobs
Str.
Burckhard
Engelgasse
ROSENFELDPARK
Münchensteinerstr.
CHRISTOPH-
MERIAN-
PARK
Nauenstrasse
Jakob-
Grosspeterstr.
DELÉMONT, WASSERTURM
LUZERN, BERN, ZÜRICH
DELÉMONT
AUTOBAHN

STREET INDEX TO BASEL TOWN PLAN

XX **Casanova,** Spalenvorstadt 9, ✉ 4051, ☎ 25 55 37 – AE ⓓ E VISA — BY **q**
closed 12 July-9 August, Sunday, Monday and Bank Holidays – **st. : M** 35/95 ♁.

XX **Donati,** St-Johannsvorstadt 48, ✉ 4056, ☎ 57 09 19, 🏛, Italian cuisine — BX **p**
closed 5 July-3 August and Monday – **st. : M** 23/30 ♁.

X **St Alban Eck,** St Alban Vorstadt 60, ✉ 4052, ☎ 22 03 20, Typical local establishment – AE ⓓ E VISA — CDY **t**
closed 24 December-2 January, Saturday lunch, Sunday and Bank Holidays – **st. : M** a la carte 40/65 ♁.

X **Hägemerstübli,** Hegenheimerstrasse 133, ✉ 4055, ☎ 43 94 35, 🏛, Alsatian home cooking – AE ⓓ E VISA
closed 23 December-4 January, Sunday and Monday – **st. : M** 70/90.

at Binningen by ⑦ : 2 km – ✉ **4102** Binningen :

🏠 **Schlüssel,** Schlüsselgasse 1 ☎ 47 25 66, 🏛, 🏛 – 🛗 ⇔wc ⋔wc ☎ Ⓟ. AE ⓓ E VISA
closed 22 to 29 December – **st. : M** *(closed Sunday)* a la carte 40/60 ♁ – **28 rm** ☕ 54/96.

XXX **Schloss Binningen,** Schlossgasse 5 ☎ 47 20 55, 🏛, « 16C mansion, elegantly decorated, garden » – Ⓟ. AE E VISA
closed 18 July-3 August, 1 to 8 March, Sunday dinner and Monday – **st. : M** 75/100 ♁.

XXX Holee-Schloss, Hasenrainstrasse 59 ☎ 47 24 30, ≤ – ▤.

at Riehen by ② : 5 km – ✉ **4125** Riehen :

🏠 **Ascot** Ⓜ, Baselstrasse 67 ☎ 67 39 51, Telex 62424, « Tasteful decor » – 🛗 ▤ rest 📺 ⇔wc ⋔wc ☎. AE ⓓ E VISA
st. : M a la carte 40/55 ♁ – **22 rm** ☕ 84/180 – P 129/145.

at the Basle-Mulhouse airport : by ⑧ : 8 km :

XX **Airport rest,** 5th floor in the airport, ≤.

Swiss Side, ✉ 4030 Bâle ☎ 57 32 32 – AE ⓓ E VISA
st. : M a la carte 45/60 ♁.

French Side, ✉ 68300 St-Louis ☎ 89 69 77 48 – AE ⓓ E VISA
st. : M (in FF) a la carte 95/160 ♁.

at Hofstetten by ⑦ : 12,5 km – ✉ **4114** Hofstetten :

X **Landgasthof "Rössli"** ⛰ with rm, ☎ 75 10 47, 🏛 – Ⓟ. AE ⓓ E VISA
closed 11 January-15 February and Wednesday – **M** a la carte 35/60 ♁ – **7 rm** ☕ 30/60.

Red Lion — If the name of the hotel is not in bold type, on arrival ask the hotelier his prices.

GENEVA Switzerland 74 ⑥, 217 ⑪ – pop. 157 406 – alt. 375 – Casino – Geneva and Environs : from France 19-41-22 ; from Switzerland 022.

See : The Shores of the lake ≤*** – Parks** : Mon Repos, la Perle du Lac and Villa Barton – Botanical Gardens* : alpine rock-garden** – Cathedral* : ** FY F – Reformation Monument* FYZ D – Palais des Nations* ≤** – Parc de la Grange* GY – Parc des Eaux-Vives* – Nave* of Church of Christ the King – Museums : Art and History*** GZ, Ariana**, Natural History** GZ, Petit Palais, Modern Art Museum* GZ **M1, Baur Collection*** **(in a 19C mansion)** GZ **M2**, Old Musical Instruments* GZ **M3.**

Exc. : by boat on the lake Rens. Cie Gén. de Nav., Jardin Anglais ℘ 21.25.21 – Mouettes genevoises, 8 quai du Mt-Blanc ℘ 32.29.44 – Swiss Boat, 4 quai du Mont-Blanc ℘ 32.47.47.

18 at Cologny ℘ 35.75.40 ; 18 Country Club du Bossey ℘ 50 43 75 25.

Genève-Cointrin ℘ 99.31.11.

gare Cornavin ℘ 32.53.40 and Tour de l'Ile ℘ 28.72.33 Automobile Club Suisse, 10 bd Théâtre ℘ 28.07.66 - T.C. Suisse, 9 r. P.-Fatio ℘ 37.12.12.

Paris 537 ⑦ – Bern 154 ② – Bourg-en-B. 109 ⑦ – Lausanne 63 ② – Lyon 156 ⑦ – Torino 252 ⑥.

Plan on following pages

1° - ***Right bank (Cornavin Railway Station - Les Quais - B.I.T.) :***

Richemond, Brunswick garden, ✉ 1201, ℘ **31 14 00, Telex 22598,** ≤, – rm TV ☎ – 50. AE E VISA. rest FY **u**
st. : see rest. **Le Gentilhomme** below - **L'Omnibus M** a la carte 50/95 - rest. **Le Jardin M** a la carte 55/95 – 18 – **68 rm** 270/450, 30 apartments.

Noga Hilton M, 19 quai Mt-Blanc, ✉ 1201, ℘ **31 98 11, Telex 289704,** ≤ lake and Mt-Blanc, , – TV ☎ – 850. AE E VISA. rest GY **y**
st. : see rest. **Le Cygne** below - **La Grignotière M** a la carte 50/70 - **Le Bistroquai M** a la carte 25/35 – 18 – **316 rm** 265/415, 20 apartments.

Rhône M, quai Turrettini, ✉ 1201, ℘ **31 98 31, Telex 22213,** ≤ – TV ☎ – 40-150. AE E VISA. rest EY **r**
st. : **M** a la carte 80/110 and see also rest. **Rôt. Le Neptune** below – 18 – **285 rm** 170/500, bedrooms for non smokers, 29 apartments.

Président M, 47 quai Wilson, ✉ 1211, ℘ **31 10 00, Telex 22780,** ≤ lake – TV ☎ – 25-80. AE E VISA GX **d**
st. : **M** a la carte 70/135 - **La Palmeraie M** a la carte 55/80 – 19 – **160 rm** 225/355, 30 apartments.

Les Bergues, 33 quai Bergues, ✉ 1201, ℘ **31 50 50, Telex 23383,** ≤ – rm TV ☎ – 40-350. AE E VISA. rest FY **k**
st. : see rest. **Amphitryon** below - **Le Pavillon M** a la carte 55/75 – 17 – **117 rm** 270/465, 8 apartments.

Beau Rivage, 13 quai Mont-Blanc, ✉ 1201, ℘ **31 02 21, Telex 23362,** ≤ lake, – TV ☎ – 30-200. AE E VISA. rest FY **d**
st. : see rest. **Le Chat Botté** below - **Le Quai 13 M** a la carte 45/75 – 17 – **115 rm** 230/450, 8 apartments.

Ramada Renaissance M, 19 r. Zurich, ✉ 1201, ℘ **31 02 41, Telex 289109** – TV ☎ – 150 FX **s**
La Toquade - La Cortille - Café Ragueneau – **219 rm**, 8 apartments.

Paix, 11 quai Mont-Blanc, ✉ 1201, ℘ **32 61 50, Telex 22552,** ≤ – rest TV ☎ – 80. AE E VISA. rest FY **s**
st. : **M** a la carte 70/105 – 15 – **84 rm** 160/360, 15 apartments.

Bristol M, 10 r. Mont-Blanc, ✉ 1201, ℘ **32 38 00, Telex 23739** – rest TV ☎ – 40-120. AE E VISA FY **w**
st. : **M** a la carte 60/95 – 14 – **95 rm** 190/325, 5 apartments 550.

Pullman Rotary M, 18 r. Cendrier, ✉ 1201, ℘ **31 52 00, Telex 289999,** – rest TV ☎. AE E VISA. rest FY **t**
st. : **M** 25/36 – 12 – **94 rm** 150/450 – P 70/150.

Warwick M, 14 r. Lausanne, ✉ 1201, ℘ **31 62 50, Telex 23630** – TV ☎ – 25-300. AE E VISA FY **n**
st. : **M** *(closed Saturday and Sunday)* a la carte 65/105 – **169 rm** 195/340.

Angleterre, 17 quai Mt-Blanc, ✉ 1201, ℘ **32 81 80, Telex 22668,** ≤ – rest TV ☎. AE E VISA. rest GY **t**
st. : **M** a la carte 50/75 – **60 rm** 165/360, 6 apartments 450/650.

Berne, 26 r. Berne, ✉ 1201, ℘ **31 60 00, Telex 22764** – TV ☎ – 30-100. AE E VISA. rest FY **x**
st. : **M** 25 – **84 rm** 140/220, 4 apartments 300 – P 140/230.

Cornavin without rest, 33 bd James-Fazy, ✉ 1211, ℘ **32 21 00, Telex 22853** – TV ☎. AE E VISA – **st.** : **125 rm** 110/190. EY **t**

Ambassador, 21 quai Bergues, ✉ 1201, ℘ **31 72 00, Telex 23231** – TV ☎ – 40. AE E VISA FY **p**
st. : **M** 40/45 – **91 rm** 86/230.

Amat-Carlton M, 22 r. Amat, ✉ 1202, ℘ **31 68 50, Telex 27595** – kitchenette TV ☎. AE E. rest FX **a**
st. : **M** *(closed Sunday lunch and Saturday)* a la carte 25/55 – **123 rm** 135/235.

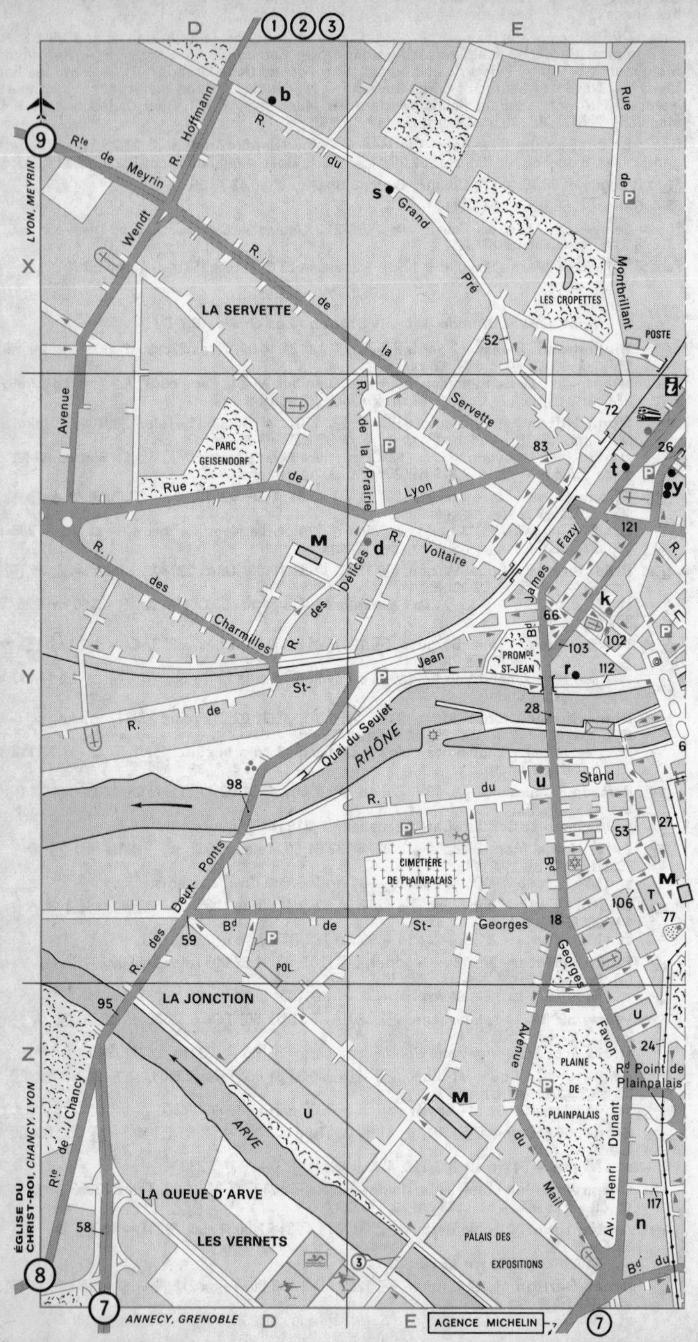

D
E
X
Y
Z
LYON, MEYRIN
ÉGLISE DU CHRIST-ROI, CHANCY, LYON
ANNECY, GRENOBLE
AGENCE MICHELIN
Rte de Meyrin
R. Hoffmann
Wendt
R. du Grand Pré
Rue de Montbrillant
LES CROPETTES
POSTE
LA SERVETTE
R. de la Servette
Avenue
PARC GEISENDORF
Rue de Lyon
R. de la Prairie
R. Voltaire
R. des Délices
R. des Charmilles
Bd James Fazy
PROMde ST-JEAN
R. de St-Jean
Quai du Seujet
RHÔNE
R. du Stand
CIMETIÈRE DE PLAINPALAIS
Bd de St-Georges
R. des Deux-Ponts
POL.
LA JONCTION
Bd Georges Favon
Avenue du Mail
PLAINE DE PLAINPALAIS
Rd Point de Plainpalais
Av. Henri Dunant
Bd du
Rte de Chancy
ARVE
LA QUEUE D'ARVE
LES VERNETS
PALAIS DES EXPOSITIONS

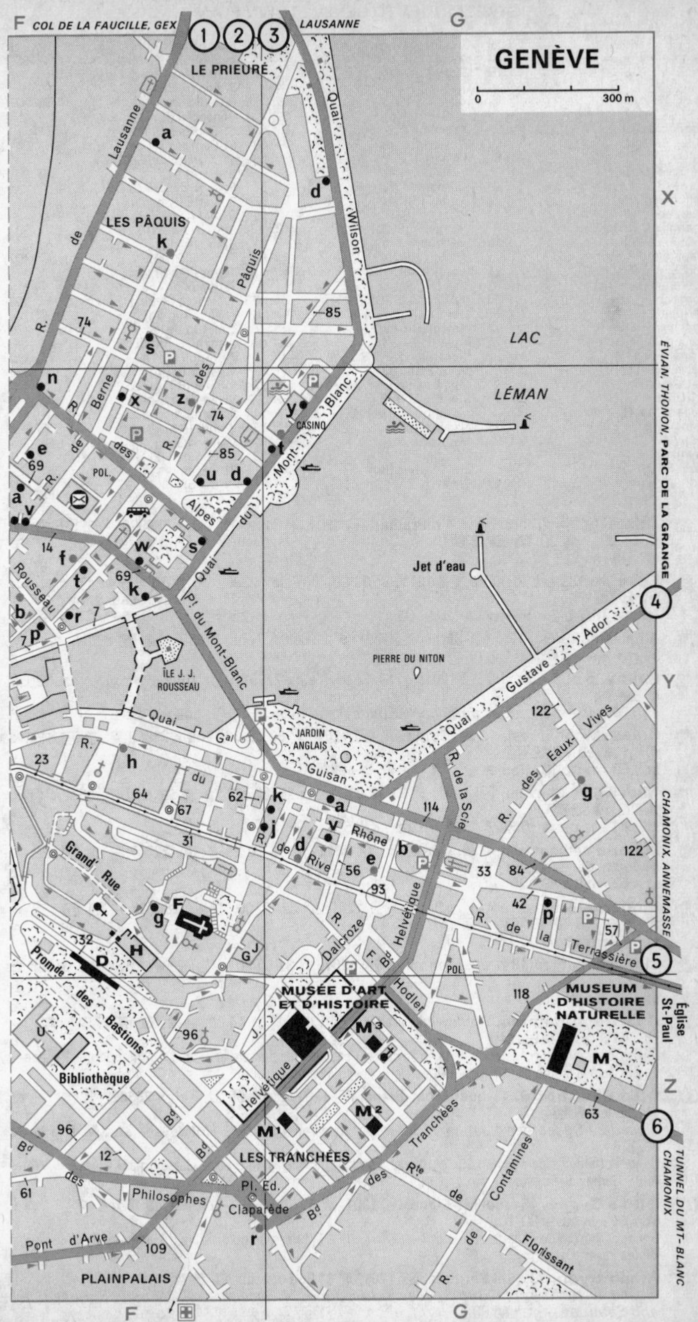
GENÈVE
0
300 m
COL DE LA FAUCILLE, GEX
LAUSANNE
LE PRIEURÉ
LES PÂQUIS
LAC
LÉMAN
CASINO
Jet d'eau
PIERRE DU NITON
ÎLE J. J. ROUSSEAU
JARDIN ANGLAIS
MUSÉE D'ART ET D'HISTOIRE
MUSEUM D'HISTOIRE NATURELLE
Bibliothèque
LES TRANCHÉES
PLAINPALAIS
ÉVIAN, THONON, PARC DE LA GRANGE
CHAMONIX, ANNEMASSE
Église St-Paul
TUNNEL DU MT-BLANC CHAMONIX
Quai Wilson
Quai du Mont-Blanc
Pt du Mont-Blanc
Quai Gustave Ador
Quai Gal Guisan
R. de Lausanne
R. de Berne
R. des Alpes
R. des Pâquis
R. Rousseau
R. du Rhône
R. de Rive
R. des Eaux-Vives
R. de la Scie
R. de la Terrassière
R. Dalcroze
Bd Helvétique
F. Bd Hodler
Grand' Rue
Promde des Bastions
Bd des Philosophes
Pl. Ed. Claparède
Pont d'Arve
Bd des Tranchées
Rte de Florissant
R. de Contamines
POL.

STREET INDEX TO GENEVE TOWN PLAN

Cristal M without rest, **4 r. Pradier, 1201, 31 34 00, Telex 289926** – wc wc – 30. AE E VISA FY **e**
st. : 79 rm 110/200.

Eden M, **135 r. Lausanne, 1211, 32 65 40, Telex 23962** – wc wc . AE E VISA by r. Lausanne FX
st. : M 19/24 – **54 rm** 120/160.

Alba without rest, **19 r. Mt-Blanc, 1201, 32 56 00, Telex 23930** – wc
54 rm. FY **a**

Savoy, 8 pl. Cornavin, **1201, 31 12 55, Telex 27951** – wc wc . AE E VISA EY **y**
st. : M *(closed Saturday dinner and Sunday)* a la carte 35/60 – **50 rm** 105/185.

Suisse without rest, **10 pl. Cornavin, 1201, 32 66 30, Telex 23868** – wc wc . AE E VISA EY **y**
st. : 60 rm 103/158.

Midi M, **pl. Chevelu, 1201, 31 78 00, Telex 23482,** – rest wc wc . AE E VISA FY **r**
st. : M a la carte 35/60 – **85 rm** 120/155.

Astoria without rest, **6 pl. Cornavin, 1211, 32 10 25, Telex 22307** – wc wc . AE E VISA EY **y**
st. : 62 rm 80/128.

Moderne without rest, **1 r. Berne, 1201, 32 81 00, Telex 289738** – wc wc . AE E VISA FY **v**
st. : 55 rm 50/120.

Lido without rest, **8 r. Chantepoulet, 1201, 31 55 30** – wc wc . AE E VISA FY **v**
st. : 31 rm 55/95.

XXXXX **Le Gentilhomme,** Brunswick garden, **1201, 31 14 00** – . AE E VISA. FY **u**
st. : M a la carte 95/140
Spec. Consommé de crustacés en gelée au caviar, Cassolette de homard et moules au champagne, Pintadeau de Bresse à la crème de foie gras. **Wines** Dardagny, Blanc de Lausanne.

XXXX **Le Chat Botté,** 13 quai Mont-Blanc, **1201, 31 65 32, Telex 23362,** ← , – . AE E VISA. FY **d**
closed 20 December-4 January, Saturday, Sunday and Bank Holidays – **st. : M** a la carte 80/110
Spec. Portefeuille de saumon à la citronelle, Fondant de volaille de Bresse, Gâteau glacé au pralin. **Wines** Aigle, Gamay de Peissy.

XXXX **Le Cygne,** 19 Quai Mt-Blanc, **1201, 31 98 11,** ← – . AE E VISA. GY **y**
st. : M a la carte 80/105
Spec. Carpaccio de canette et foie gras cru, Bar cuit à la fumée de bois, Râble de lapereau rôti à la sauge. **Wines** Pessy, Dardagny.

XXXX **Amphitryon,** 33 quai Bergues, **1201, 31 50 50** – AE E VISA. FY **k**
closed 17 to 20 April, 28 to 31 May, 6 to 8 June, 24 December-31 January, Sunday lunch and Saturday – **st. : M** 80.

XXX **Perle du Lac,** 128 r. Lausanne ✉ 1202, ☎ 31 79 35, ≤, 🏖 – Ⓟ. AE ⓓ E VISA. ✻
closed 22 December-22 January and Monday – **st. : M** a la carte 90/115.
by quai Wilson GX

XXX **Le Bouhec,** 18 r. Délices, ✉ 1203, ☎ 45 73 00 – AE ⓓ E VISA EY **d**
closed 15 July-15 August, Saturday lunch and Sunday – **st. : M** 48/115 🍷.

XXX **Tsé Yang,** 19 quai Mont-Blanc, ✉ 1201, ☎ 32 50 81, ≤, Chinese cuisine – ▤. AE ⓓ E VISA. ✻ GY **y**
st. : M a la carte 70/120.

XXX **Aub. Mère Royaume,** 9 r. Corps-Saints, ✉ 1201, ☎ 32 70 08, « Decorated in the old Genevan style » – AE ⓓ E VISA EY **k**
closed mid July-mid August, Saturday lunch and Sunday – **st. : M** a la carte 55/90 🍷.

XXX ✻ **Rôtisserie Le Neptune,** quai Turrettini, ✉ 1201, ☎ 31 98 31, 🏖 – ▤ Ⓟ. AE ⓓ E VISA. ✻ EY **r**
closed Saturday, Sunday and Bank Holidays – **st. : M** a la carte 80/120
Spec. Gravlax, Tresse de filets de sole et saumon aux morilles, Magret de canard aux baies de cassis. Wines Dardagny.

XXX Fin Bec, 55 r. Berne, ✉ 1201, ☎ 32 29 19, 🏖 – ▤ FX **k**

XX **Mövenpick-Cendrier,** 17 r. Cendrier, ✉ 1201, ☎ 32 50 30 – ▤. AE ⓓ E VISA ✻ FY **f**
st. : M a la carte 40/60 🍷.

XX **Buffet Cornavin,** 3 pl. Cornavin, ✉ 1201, ☎ 32 43 06 – AE ⓓ E VISA EY
st. : French rest. M a la carte 50/70 - **Buffet (1st class) M** a la carte 40/60 🍷.

XX **Locanda Ticinese,** 13 r. Rousseau, ✉ 1201, ☎ 32 31 70, Italian and Italo Swiss (Ticino) cuisine – AE ⓓ E VISA. ✻ FY **b**
closed 1 to 21 July, Saturday and Sunday – **st. : M** 40 🍷.

X **Boeuf Rouge,** 17 r. A.-Vincent ✉ 1201, ☎ 32 75 37, French (Lyons) cuisine FY **z**
closed Saturday and Sunday – **st. : M** a la carte 40/65 🍷.

2° - *to the N (Palais des Nations, Servette) :*

🏨🏨🏨 **Intercontinental** Ⓜ 🐕, 7 petit Saconnex, ✉ 1211 Genève 19, ☎ 34 60 91, Telex 23160, ≤, 🏖, 🏊 – 🛗 ▤ 📺 ☎ 🚗 Ⓟ – 🏛 25-600. AE ⓓ E VISA. ✻ rest by ①
st. : see rest. **Les Continents** below - **La Pergola M** a la carte 50/60 🍷 – ☕ 17 – **348 rm** 210/325, 33 apartments.

🏨 **Grand Pré** without rest, 35 r. Gd-Pré, ✉ 1202 Genève 16, ☎ 33 91 50, Telex 23284 – 🛗 📺 🛁wc 🚿wc ☎ – 🏛 30. AE ⓓ E VISA EX **s**
st. : 80 rm ☕ 120/220.

🏨 **H. des Nations** Ⓜ without rest, 62 r. Grand Pré ✉ 1202, ☎ 34 30 03, Telex 23965 – 🛗 kitchenette 📺 🛁wc ☎. AE ⓓ E VISA DX **b**
st. : 63 rm ☕ 108/166.

XXXX ✻ **Les Continents,** 7 petit Saconnex (first floor) ✉ 1211, ☎ 34 60 91 – ▤ Ⓟ. AE ⓓ E VISA. ✻ by ①
closed Sunday lunch and Saturday – **st. : M** a la carte 75/110
Spec. Ravioli de lapereau, Suprême de canard au Pinot noir, Mousse aux deux chocolats.

XXX **Fu Lung,** 30 av. G.-Motta ✉ 1202, ☎ 34 56 27, Chinese cuisine – Ⓟ. AE ⓓ E VISA
closed Saturday lunch and Sunday – **st. : M** 30/80 🍷. by rue Hoffmann DX

3° - *Left bank (Commercial Centre) :*

🏨🏨🏨 **Métropole** Ⓜ, 34 quai Gén.-Guisan ✉ 1204, ☎ 21 13 44, Telex 421550, ≤, 🏖 – 🛗 ▤ rest 📺 ☎ ♿ – 🏛 50 - 200. AE ⓓ E VISA. ✻ rest GY **a**
st. : see rest. **L'Arlequin** below- **Le Grand Quai M** 30 /52 🍷 – **129 rm** ☕ 180/310, 6 apartments.

🏨 **Armures** Ⓜ 🐕, 1 r. Puits-Saint-Pierre, Vieille Ville ✉ 1204, ☎ 28 91 72, Telex 421129 – 🛗 ▤ 📺 ☎ ♿. AE ⓓ E VISA FY **g**
closed 24 December-1 January – **st. : M** a la carte 40/60 🍷 – **28 rm** ☕ 175/380, 4 apartments 380.

🏨 **L'Arbalète,** 3 r. Tour-Maîtresse, ✉ 1204, ☎ 28 41 55, Telex 427293 – 🛗 ▤ 📺 ☎ ♿. AE ⓓ E VISA GY **v**
st. : M a la carte 35/65 🍷 – **32 rm** ☕ 200/350.

🏨 **La Cigogne,** 17 pl. Longemalle ✉ 1204, ☎ 21 42 42, Telex 421748 – 🛗 📺 ☎ – 🏛 25. AE ⓓ E VISA. ✻ rest FGY **j**
st. : M a la carte 65/95 – **50 rm** ☕ 205/340, 6 apartments 510/650.

🏨 **Century** without rest, 24 av. Frontenex ✉ 1207 ☎ 36 80 95, Telex 23223 – 🛗 kitchenette 📺 ☎ Ⓟ – 🏛 35. AE ⓓ E VISA GY **p**
st. : 125 rm ☕ 143/255, 14 apartments 255/295.

🏨 **Touring Balance,** 13 pl. Longemalle, ✉ 1204, ☎ 28 71 22, Telex 427634 – 🛗 📺 🛁wc 🚿wc ☎ – 🏛 40. AE ⓓ E VISA GY **k**
st. : M *(closed Saturday and Sunday)* 36/40 🍷 – **56 rm** ☕ 75/160 – P 145/190.

XXXX ⊛ **Parc des Eaux-Vives,** 82 quai Gustave-Ador, ✉ 1207, ☎ 35 41 40, « Pleasant setting in extensive park, attractive view » – Ⓟ. AE ⊕ E VISA by ④
closed 1 January-15 February, Saturday dinner and Monday – **st. : M** a la carte 70/140
Spec. Truite saumonée au vin de Barillet (season), Gratin de cuisses de grenouilles (season), Sabayon glacé à la williamine. **Wines** Dardagny, Aigle.

XXXX ⊛ **L'Arlequin,** 34 quai Gén.-Guisan ✉ 1204, ☎ 21 13 44 – ▤. AE ⊕ E VISA. ✻ GY **a**
closed Saturday and Sunday – **st. : M** 55/110
Spec. Trois petites salades, Blanc de turbot grillé et calamars, Filet de boeuf aux ravioli de homard. **Wines** Dardagny, Pessy.

XXX Via Veneto, 10 r. Tour Maitresse ✉ 1204, ☎ 21 65 93 – ▤ GY **d**

XXX **Roberto,** 10 r. P.-Fatio, ✉ 1204, ☎ 21 80 34, Italian cuisine – ▤. AE E VISA GY **e**
closed Saturday dinner and Sunday – **st. : M** a la carte 60/85 ♁.

XXX ⊛⊛ **Le Béarn** (Goddard), 4 quai Poste, ✉ 1204, ☎ 21 00 28 – AE ⊕ E VISA EY **u**
closed mid July-mid August, Saturday (except dinner from September-June) and Sunday – **st. : M** 95/115 and a la carte ♁
Spec. Soufflé aux truffes fraîches (December-February), Vinaigrette de queues de langoustines et son confit de courgette, Pigeon de Bresse. **Wines** Dardagny, Yvorne rouge.

XXX **Mövenpick Fusterie,** 40 r. Rhône ✉ 1204, ☎ 21 88 55, ☂ – ▤. AE ⊕ E VISA FY **h**
closed Sunday – **st. : M** a la carte 45/75 ♁.

XX **La Coupole,** 116 r. Rhône ✉ 1204, ☎ 35 65 44 – ▤ GY **b**
closed Sunday – **st. : M** 43 ♁.

XX **Sénat,** 1 r. E.-Yung, ✉ 1205, ☎ 46 58 10, ☂ – AE ⊕ E VISA FZ **r**
closed Sunday – **st. : M** 34/75 ♁.

XX La Pescaille, 15 av. H.-Dunant, ✉ 1205, ☎ 29 71 60, Seafood – ▤ EZ **n**

XX **Cavalieri,** 7 r. Cherbuliez, ✉ 1207, ☎ 35 09 56, Italian cuisine – ▤. AE ⊕ E VISA GY **g**
closed July and Monday – **st. : M** a la carte 55/80 ♁.

XX **Café Alexandre,** 7 av. Dumas ✉ 1206, ☎ 47 74 22 – ▤ BV **u**
closed 11 July-11 August, Saturday, Sunday and Bank Holidays – **st. : M** a la carte 45/70 ♁.

XX **Parc Bertrand,** 62 rte Florissant, ✉ 1206, ☎ 47 59 57, ☂ – AE E VISA
closed 23 December-5 January, Saturday dinner and Sunday – **st. : M** a la carte 55/90 ♁.
by rte Florissant GZ

Environs

by the Lakeside road, route de Lausanne :

at Bellevue by ③ : 6 km – ✉ **1293** Bellevue :

🏨 **La Réserve** Ⓜ ⛵, 301 rte de Lausanne ☎ 74 17 41, Telex 23822, ←, ☂, « Lakeside and park setting, port with mooring facilities », ⛱, 🎾 – 🛗 📺 ☎ ♿ Ⓟ – 🏛 80. AE ⊕ E VISA – **st. :** La Closerie **M** a la carte 75/105 – **59 rm** ☕ 250/360, 5 apartments.

XXX ⊛ **Tsé Fung,** 301 rte de Lausanne ☎ 74 17 41, Chinese cuisine, ☂, ⛱ – ▤ Ⓟ. AE ⊕ E VISA. ✻
st. : M a la carte 90/115
Spec. Aileron de requin impérial, Marmite mongole. **Wines** Dardagny.

at Genthod by ③ : 7 km – ✉ **1294** Genthod :

XX ⊛ **Rest. du Château de Genthod** (Leisibach), 1 rte Rennex ☎ 74 19 72, ☂, ⛱ – E VISA
closed 10-20 August, 20 December-10 January, Sunday and Monday – **st. : M** 40/70
Spec. Langoustines au beurre blanc, Saumon au Pinot noir, Parfait aux fruits.

Towards Savoy via the Lakeside :

at Cologny by ④ : 3,5 km – ✉ **1223** Cologny :

XXXX ⊛ **Aub. du Lion d'or** (Large), au Village ☎ 36 44 32, ☂, « Overlooking the lake and Geneva, terrace » – Ⓟ. AE ⊕ E VISA
closed 20 December-20 January, Saturday and Sunday – **st. : M** a la carte 85/130
Spec. Escalopines d'empereur à la fondue de poireaux, Barbue grillée aux gousses d'ail, Faisan poêlé Souvaroff (20 December-20 November). **Wines** Lully, Pinot noir.

X **Pavillon de Ruth,** 86 quai Cologny ☎ 52 14 38, ←, ☂ – Ⓟ. AE E
1 March-19 December and closed Thursday – **st. : M** a la carte 50/65 ♁.

at Vandoeuvres by ④ : 5,5 km – ✉ **1253** Vandoeuvres :

XXX **Cheval Blanc,** ☎ 50 14 01, ☂, Italian cuisine – AE E VISA. ✻
closed 1 to 21 July, Christmas-1 January, Sunday and Monday – **st. : M** a la carte 50/75 ♁.

at Vésenaz by ④ : 6 km by rte de Thonon – ✉ **1222** Vésenaz :

🏠 **La Tourelle** without rest, 26 rte Hermance ☎ 52 16 28, park – 🛁wc 🚿wc ☎ Ⓟ. AE ⊕ E VISA – *closed 20 December-15 January* – **st. : 24 rm** ☕ 100/130.

XXX **Chez Valentino,** 63 rte Thonon ☎ 52 14 40, ☂, Italian cuisine, ⛱ – Ⓟ. AE ⊕ E VISA. ✻
closed 20 December-15 January, Tuesday lunch and Monday – **st. : M** a la carte 60/95 ♁.

by route de St-Julien :

at Carouge : 3 km by r. Carouge – ✉ **1227** Carouge :

XX **Olivier de Provence,** 13 r. J.-Dalphin ☎ 42 04 50, – AE ⓓ E VISA
closed Sunday – **st. : M** a la carte 55/80.

XX **La Cassolette,** 31 r. J.-Dalphin ☎ 42 03 18
closed 17 to 26 April, 3 to 23 August, Saturday and Sunday – **st. : M** (booking essential) 52/78.

X **Aub. Communale,** 39 r. Ancienne ☎ 42 22 88,
closed Tuesday – **st. : M** a la carte 40/80 🍷.

at Troinex by ⑦ : 5 km – ✉ **1256** Troinex :

XXX ✿✿ **Vieux Moulin** (Bouilloux), 89 rte Drize ☎ 42 29 56, – P. AE E VISA
closed 1 to 15 April, 1 to 15 September, Sunday and Monday – **st. : M** (booking essential) 50/110 and a la carte
Spec. Fricassée de homard au Sauternes, Cuisse de lapereau aux chanterelles (July-August). **Wines** Chardonnay, Pinot noir.

XX **La Chaumière,** r. Fondelle ☎ 84 30 66, , – P. AE ⓓ E VISA
closed Sunday dinner and Monday – **st. : M** a la carte 60/100.

at Grand-Lancy by ⑦ : 3 km – ✉ **1212** Lancy :

XXX ✿ **Marignac** (Pelletier), 32 av. E.-Lance ☎ 94 04 24, park, – P. E VISA
closed August, Saturday lunch, Monday lunch, Sunday and Bank Holidays – **st. : M** 90/115
Spec. Soupe au foie gras de canard et jus de truffe, Couscous de poissons de mer (Easter-end September), Canard de Barbarie aux pêches. **Wines** Côteau de Lully, Dardagny.

at Plan-les-Ouates by ⑦ : 5 km – ✉ **1228** Plan-les-Ouates :

Plan-les-Ouates without rest, 135 rte St-Julien ☎ 94 92 44 – wc . AE ⓓ E VISA
closed 20 December-5 January – **st. :** 6 – **22 rm** 38/101.

at Landecy by ⑦ : 7,5 km – ✉ **1257** Landecy :

XXX ✿ **Au Fer à Cheval** (Ruprecht), 37 rte Prieur ☎ 71 10 78, – ⓓ E VISA
closed February, Wednesday lunch and Tuesday – **st. : M** 50/95
Spec. Tartare de saumon au raifort, Gigot de lapereau, Chariot de desserts.

by route de Chancy :

at Petit Lancy by ⑧ : 3 km – ✉ **1213** Petit Lancy :

✿ **Host. de la Vendée and rest. Pont Rouge,** 28 chemin Vendée ☎ 92 04 11, Telex 421304, – TV P – 80. AE ⓓ E VISA
closed 24 December-7 January – **st. : M** *(closed Easter, Saturday lunch and Sunday)* 68/100 🍷 – **34 rm** 90/200
Spec. Terrine de brochet, Filet de sole (October to March), Rognon et ris de veau. **Wines** Lully, Dardagny.

at Confignon by ⑧ : 6 km – ✉ **1232** Confignon :

XX **Aub. de Confignon,** 6 pl. Église ☎ 57 19 44, ,
closed Sunday dinner and Monday – **st. : M** 40/60 🍷.

at Cartigny by ⑧ *:* 12 km – ✉ **1236** Cartigny :

XX **L'Escapade,** 31 r. Trably ☎ 56 12 07, , – P. AE ⓓ E VISA
closed 20 December-20 January, Sunday and Monday – **st. : M** 60/100.

Towards the Jura :

at Cointrin by ⑨, route de Meyrin : 4 km – ✉ **1216** Cointrin :

Penta M, 75 av. L.-Casaï ☎ 98 47 00, Telex 27044 – TV P – 25-700. AE ⓓ E VISA. rest
st. : M 25/30 🍷 – 16 – **320 rm** 130/190, bedrooms for non smokers.

Hôtel 33, 82 av. L.-Casai ☎ 98 02 00, Telex 27991, – TV wc P. AE ⓓ E VISA
st. : M *(closed Sunday)* 20/50 🍷 – **33 rm** 87/140.

at the airport of Cointrin by ⑨ : 4 km – ✉ **1215** Genève :

XX **Rôt. Plein Ciel,** ☎ 98 22 88, ← – . AE ⓓ E VISA
st. : M a la carte 60/80.

In addition to establishments indicated by XXXXX ... X, many hotels possess good class restaurants.

ZÜRICH 8001 427 ⑥ 216 ⑱ – pop. 356 800 - alt. 441 m – ☎ 01.

See: The Quays★★ BYZ – Fraumünster cloisters★ (Alter Kreuzgang des Fraumünsters) BZ **D** – View of the town from the Zürichhorn Gardens★ V – Church of SS. Felix and Regula★ U **E** – Church of Zürich-Altstetten★ U **F** – Zoological Gardens★ (Zoo Dolder) U **K** – Museums : Swiss National Museum★★★ (Schweizerisches Landesmuseum) BY – Fine Arts Museum★★ (Kunsthaus) CZ – Rietberg Museum★★ V **M3**.

✈ Kloten ☎ 812 71 11.

ℹ Offizielles Verkehrsbüro, Bahnhofplatz 15 ✉ 8023 ☎ 211 40 00, Telex 813 744 – A.C.S. Forchstrasse 95 ✉ 8032 ☎ 55 15 00 – T.C.S. Alfred-Escher-Strasse 38 ✉ 8002 ☎ 201 25 36.

Basel 85 ⑥ – Bern 125 ⑥ – Genève 278 ⑥ – Innsbruck 288 ② – Milan 304 ⑤.

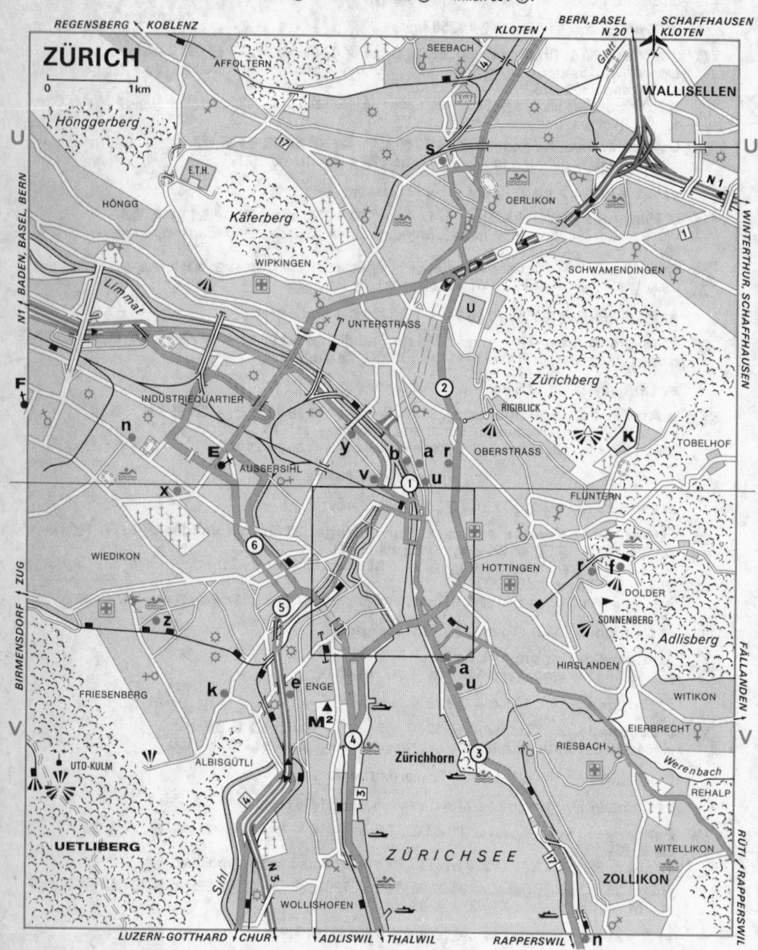

On the right bank of river Limmat (University, Fine Arts Museum) :

Dolder Grand Hotel and rest. La Rotonde ⛭, Kurhausstr. 65, ✉ 8032, ☎ 251 62 31, Telex 816416, ⩽ Zürich and lake, park, – rest ☎ AE E VISA. rest V **f**
M a la carte 65/107 – **200 rm** 220/410
Spec. Homard de nos viviers, Dodine de pintadeau La Rotonde, Emincé de filet de veau zurichoise.

Eden au Lac, Utoquai 45, ✉ 8023, ☎ 47 94 04, Telex 816339, ⩽, – ☎. AE E VISA. rest V **a**
M a la carte 47/89 – **54 rm** 170/380 Bb.

Zurich M, Neumühlequai 42, ✉ 8001, ☏ 363 63 63, Telex 56809, ←, – ☎. AE ⓓ E VISA. rest U **b**
M a la carte 41,50/63 – **221 rm** ☐ 180/300.

International M, Am Marktplatz, ✉ 8050, ☏ 311 43 41, Telex 823251, ←, – ☎. AE ⓓ E VISA U **s**
M Panorama Grill a la carte 44,50/65 – ☐ 10 – **350 rm** 150/240.

Waldhaus Dolder M, Kurhausstr. 20, ✉ 8030, ☏ 251 93 60, Telex 816460, ← Zürich and lake, park, – rest ☎ Ⓟ. AE ⓓ E VISA V **r**
M a la carte 36/58 – ☐ 10 Bb – **100 rm** 150/320.

Pullman Continental H., Stampfenbachstr. 60, ✉ 8006, ☏ 363 33 63, Telex 55393 – ☎. AE ⓓ E VISA U **a**
M a la carte 34,50/64 – ☐ 10 – **134 rm** 140/250.

Excelsior, Dufourstr. 24, ✉ 8008, ☏ 252 25 00, Telex 59295 – ☎ Ⓟ. AE ⓓ E VISA. rest CZ **f**
M a la carte 35,50/57 – **40 rm** ☐ 140/250.

Europe without rest., Dufourstr. 4, ✉ 8008, ☏ 47 10 30, Telex 816461 – ☎. AE ⓓ E VISA CZ **e**
42 rm ☐ 110/240.

Central M, Am Central 1, ✉ 8001, ☏ 251 55 55, Telex 54909, ← – ☎. AE ⓓ E VISA – **M** a la carte 33/96 – **99 rm** ☐ 200/300 Bb. BY **z**

Bellerive au Lac, Utoquai 47, ✉ 8008, ☏ 251 70 10, Telex 816398, ←, – AE ⓓ E VISA V **a**
M a la carte 32,50/63 – **57 rm** ☐ 120/220.

Opéra without rest., Dufourstr. 5, ✉ 8008, ☏ 251 90 90, Telex 816480 – wc wc ☎. AE ⓓ E VISA CZ **b**
61 rm ☐ 100/230.

Zürcherhof, Zähringerstr. 21, ✉ 8025, ☏ 47 10 40, Telex 819460 – rest wc wc ☎. AE ⓓ E VISA CY **q**
M *(closed Sunday)* a la carte 29/49 – **35 rm** ☐ 120/170 Bb.

Ambassador, Falkenstr. 6, ✉ 8008, ☏ 47 76 00, Telex 816508 – wc wc ☎. AE ⓓ E VISA CZ **a**
M a la carte 32/64 – **46 rm** ☐ 95/230.

Ammann without rest., Kirchgasse 4, ✉ 8001, ☏ 252 72 40, Telex 56208 – wc wc ☎. AE ⓓ E VISA BCZ **n**
21 rm ☐ 110/160 Bb.

Chesa Rustica, Limmatquai 70, ✉ 8001, ☏ 251 92 91, Telex 57380, ← – wc wc ☎. AE ⓓ E VISA BY **r**
– **M** *(closed 25 and 26 December)* a la carte 39/71 – **23 rm** ☐ 95/190 Bb.

Rütli M without rest., Zähringerstrasse 43, ✉ 8001, ☏ 251 54 26, Telex 816037 – wc ☎ – **47 rm**. CY **a**

Helmhaus without rest., Schiffländeplatz 30, ✉ 8001, ☏ 251 88 10, Telex 816525 – wc wc. AE ⓓ E VISA BCZ **s**
25 rm ☐ 99/175.

XXX ❀ **Agnès Amberg**, Hottingerstr. 5, ✉ 8032, ☏ 251 26 26, tasteful installation – AE ⓓ E VISA CY **d**
closed Saturday lunch, Sunday and 20 July-2 August – **M** a la carte 45/116
Spec. Terrine de foie gras caramelisé, Ragoût de homard au Sauternes, Mignon de veau, sauce Beluga.

XX **Haus Zum Rüden**, Limmatquai 42, ✉ 8001, ☏ 47 95 90, former guildhall – AE ⓓ E VISA – *closed Sunday lunch, Saturday and August* – **M** a la carte 64/104. BY **m**

XX **Jacky's Stapferstube**, Culmannstr. 45, ✉ 8033, ☏ 361 37 48, Meat specialities – Ⓟ. AE ⓓ E VISA U **r**
closed Sunday, Monday and 7 July-3 August – **M** a la carte 43/109.

XX **Kronenhalle**, Rämistrasse 4, ✉ 8001, ☏ 251 02 56, Zürich's atmosphere, paintings – AE ⓓ E VISA CZ **r**
M a la carte 46,50/85.

XX **Casa Ferlin**, Stampfenbachstr. 38, ✉ 8006, ☏ 362 35 09, Italian rest. – AE ⓓ E VISA by Stampfenbachstr. BY
closed Saturday lunch, Sunday and mid July-mid August – **M** a la carte 39/69.

XX **Bolognese**, Seegartenstr. 14, ✉ 8008, ☏ 252 37 37, Italian rest. V **u**
closed Saturday, Sunday and 21 December-15 January – **M** a la carte 24/56.

On the left bank of river Limmat (Main railway station, Business centre) :

Baur au Lac, Talstr. 1, ✉ 8022, ☏ 221 16 50, Telex 813567, « Lakeside setting, park » – ☎ Ⓟ. AE. rest BZ **a**
M a la carte 54/99 – **160 rm** ☐ 230/410.

Savoy Hotel Baur en Ville M, Paradeplatz, ✉ 8022, ☏ 211 53 60, Telex 812845 – ☎. AE ⓓ E VISA. rest BZ **e**
M a la carte 50/90 – **112 rm** ☐ 280/500.

Schweizerhof M, Bahnhofplatz 7, ✉ 8023, ☏ 211 86 40, Telex 813754 – ☎. AE ⓓ E VISA BY **a**
M *(closed Sunday)* a la carte 36/80 – **115 rm** ☐ 150/350.

Bahnhofstrasse .... BYZ
Bellevueplatz .... CZ
Limmatquai .... BYZ
Löwenstrasse .... ABY
Paradeplatz .... BZ
Poststrasse .... BZ 10
Rennweg .... BY 13
Storchengasse .... BY 19
Strehlgasse .... BY 20
Uraniastrasse .... ABY

Alfred Escher-Strasse .... AZ
Augustinergasse .... BY 2
Badenerstrasse .... AY
Bahnhofbrücke .... BY
Bahnhofplatz .... BY
Bahnhofquai .... BY
Bederstrasse .... AZ
Bleickerweg .... AZ
Brandschenkestrasse .... AZ
Bürkliplatz .... BZ
Dreikönigstrasse .... AZ
Falkenstrasse .... CZ
Freigutstrasse .... AZ
General Guisan-Quai .... ABZ
General Wille-Strasse .... AZ 3
Genferstrasse .... AZ
Gessnerallee .... AY
Gessnerbrücke .... AY
Gloriastrasse .... CY
Gotthardstrasse .... AZ
Heimplatz .... CY
Hirschengraben .... CYZ
Hirschenplatz .... BCY
Hottingerstrasse .... CZ
Kasernenstrasse .... AY
Kirchgasse .... CY
Kreuzbühlstrasse .... CZ
Leonhardstrasse .... CY
Löwenplatz .... BY
Marktgasse .... BY 5
Militärstrasse .... AY
Mühlegasse .... BCY
Münsterbrücke .... CZ
Münstergasse .... BCY
Münsterhof .... BZ
Museumstrasse .... BY 6
Neumarkt .... CY 7
Neumühlequai .... BY 9
Niederdorfstrasse .... BY
Nüschelerstrasse .... AY
Oberdorfstrasse .... CZ
Pelikanstrasse .... BY
Quaibrücke .... BZ
Rämistrasse .... CYZ
Rathausbrücke .... BY 12
Rindermarkt .... CY 14
Rudolf Brun-Brücke .... BY
St-Annagasse .... BY
St-Jakobstrasse .... AY
Sechseläutenplatz .... CZ
Seefeldstrasse .... CZ
Seestrasse .... AZ 15
Seilergraben .... CY
Selnaubrücke .... AZ
Selnaustrasse .... AYZ
Sihlbrücke .... AY
Sihlhölzlistrasse .... AZ
Sihlporte .... AY
Sihlstrasse .... ABY
Sonneggstrasse .... CY 16
Stadelhoferplatz .... CZ
Stadthausquai .... CZ
Stampfenbachstrasse .... BY 17
Stauffacherbrücke .... AY
Stauffacherplatz .... AY
Stauffacherquai .... AYZ
Stauffacherstrasse .... AY 18
Stockerstrasse .... AZ
Talstrasse .... ABYZ
Theaterplatz .... CZ
Tunnelstrasse .... AZ
Universitätstrasse .... CY 21
Usteristrasse .... BY 23
Utoquai .... CZ
Waisenhausstrasse .... BY
Walchebrücke .... BY
Weinbergstrasse .... CY
Weinplatz .... BY
Werdmühlestrasse .... BY
Werdstrasse .... AY
Zeltweg .... CZ
Zeughausstrasse .... AY
Zwingliplatz .... CY

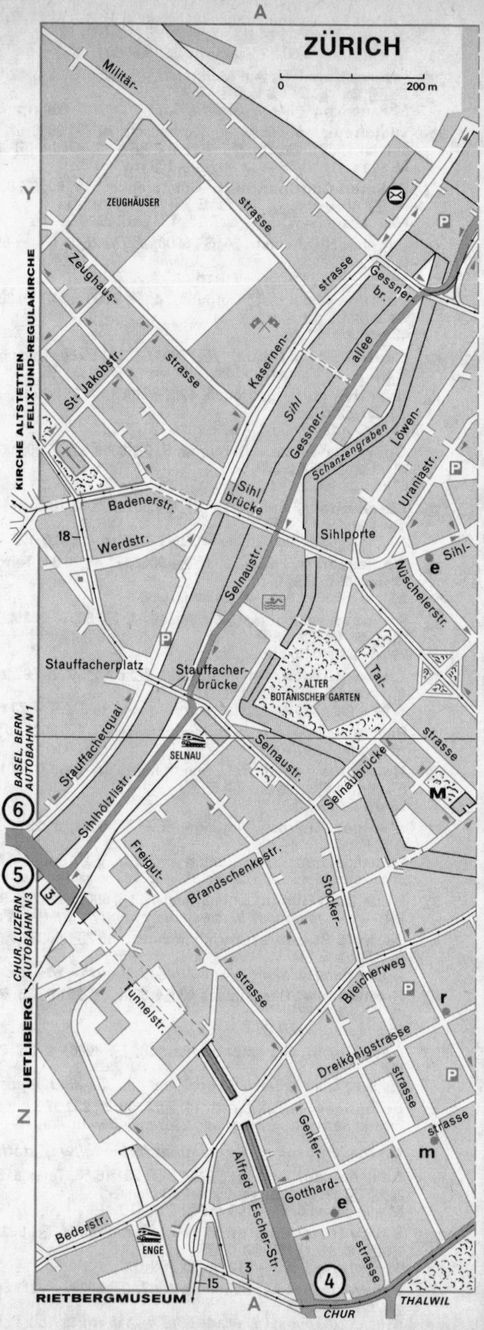

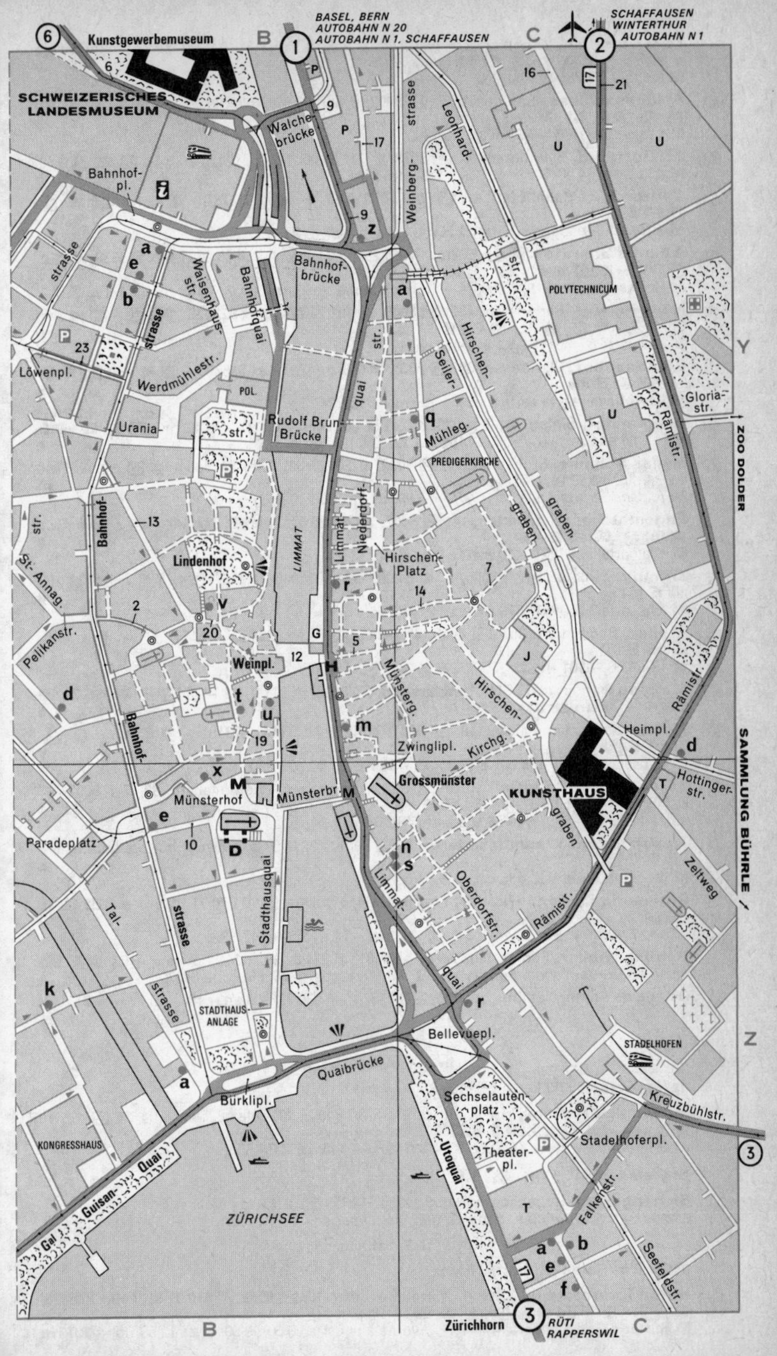

BASEL, BERN
AUTOBAHN N 20
AUTOBAHN N 1, SCHAFFAUSEN
SCHAFFAUSEN
WINTERTHUR
AUTOBAHN N 1
Kunstgewerbemuseum
SCHWEIZERISCHES LANDESMUSEUM
Walchebrücke
Weinbergstrasse
Leonhardstr.
Bahnhofpl.
Bahnhofbrücke
Waisenhausstr.
Bahnhofquai
Bahnhofstrasse
POLYTECHNICUM
Löwenpl.
Werdmühlestr.
POL.
Seilerstr.
Hirschengraben
Urania-str.
Rudolf Brun Brücke
Mühleg.
PREDIGERKIRCHE
Gloriastr.
Rämistr.
ZOO DOLDER
St-Annag.
Lindenhof
LIMMAT
Limmatquai
Niederdorfstr.
Hirschen-Platz
Pelikanstr.
Weinpl.
Münsterg.
Zwinglipl.
Kirchg.
Heimpl.
Hottingerstr.
SAMMLUNG BÜHRLE
Münsterhof
Münsterbr.
Grossmünster
KUNSTHAUS
Paradeplatz
Zeltweg
Talstrasse
Stadthausquai
Oberdorfstr.
STADTHAUS-ANLAGE
Bellevuepl.
STADELHOFEN
Quaibrücke
Bürklipl.
Sechseläutenplatz
Kreuzbühlstr.
KONGRESSHAUS
Theaterpl.
Stadelhoferpl.
Utoquai
Falkenstr.
ZÜRICHSEE
Gal Guisan-Quai
Seefeldstr.
Zürichhorn
RÜTI
RAPPERSWIL

Zum Storchen, Weinplatz 2, ✉ 8022, ☎ 211 55 10, Telex 813354, ≤, «Limmat-side setting» – AE E VISA. rest
M 55/75 – **77 rm** 140/350. BY **u**

Splügenschloss, Splügenstr. 2, ✉ 8002, ☎ 201 08 00, Telex 815553 – . AE E VISA. rest
M a la carte 37/66 – **55 rm** 140/300. AZ **e**

St. Gotthard, Bahnhofstr. 87, ✉ 8023, ☎ 211 55 00, Telex 812420 – .
M a la carte 44,50/107 – 15 – **135 rm** 160/230 Bb. BY **b**

Carlton Elite Bahnhofstr. 41, ✉ 8001, ☎ 211 65 60, Telex 812781 – rest . AE E
M *(closed Sunday)* a la carte 32,50/58 – 12 Bb – **72 rm** 125/290. BY **d**

Atlantis Sheraton M, Döltschiweg 234, ✉ 8055, ☎ 463 00 00, Telex 813338, ≤, – . AE E VISA. rest
M Rotisserie a la carte 45,50/74 – **Döltschistube** a la carte 30/52 – **163 rm** 145/335 Bb. V **z**

Nova Park M, Badenerstr. 420, ✉ 8040, ☎ 491 22 22, Telex 822822, – rest . AE E VISA. rest
M a la carte 37/55,50 – 9 – **363 rm** 133/220. U **n**

Glärnischhof, Claridenstr. 30, ✉ 8022, ☎ 202 47 47, Telex 815366 – rest . AE E VISA
M La Rotisserie a la carte 35/69 – **70 rm** 130/240 Bb. BZ **k**

Glockenhof, Sihlstr. 31, ✉ 8023, ☎ 211 56 50, Telex 812466 – rest . AE E VISA – **M** a la carte 31/51,50 – **106 rm** 122/184 Bb AY **e**

Neues Schloss, Stockerstr. 17, ✉ 8022, ☎ 201 65 50, Telex 815560 – wc wc . AE E VISA. rest
M *(closed Sunday)* a la carte 47/71 – **59 rm** 165/240 Bb. AZ **m**

Engematthof, Engimattstr. 14, ✉ 8002, ☎ 201 25 04, Telex 56327, – wc wc . AE E.
M a la carte 33/61,50 – **79 rm** 92/170 Bb. V **e**

Trümpy, Sihlquai 9, ✉ 8005, ☎ 42 54 00, Telex 822980 – wc wc . AE E VISA
M a la carte 35,50/56 – **75 rm** 110/175 Bb. U **v**

Stoller, Badenerstr. 357, ✉ 8040, ☎ 492 65 00, Telex 822460 – wc wc . AE E VISA
M 13/24,50 – **101 rm** 125/170 Bb. V **x**

Simplon without rest., Schützengasse 16, ✉ 8023, ☎ 211 61 11 – wc . AE E VISA – **75 rm** 105/175. BY **e**

Limmathaus, Limmatstr. 118, ✉ 8031, ☎ 42 52 40, Telex 823161 – wc . AE E VISA
M *(closed Sunday)* a la carte 17,50/36 – **58 rm** 58/135. U **y**

Baron de la Mouette (Mövenpick Dreikönighaus), Beethovenstr. 32, ✉ 8002, ☎ 202 09 10, Telex 59956 – . AE E VISA
closed 20 June-19 July – **M** a la carte 48/66,50. AZ **r**

Zunfthaus zur Waag, Münsterhof 8, ✉ 8001, ☎ 211 07 30, Former hatters guildhall – AE E VISA
M (booking essential) a la carte 43,50/66. BZ **x**

Rotisserie Lindenhofkeller, Pfalzgasse 4, ✉ 8001, ☎ 211 70 71, – . AE E VISA.
closed Saturday, Sunday and 8 to 31 August – **M** a la carte 42/82. BY **v**

Veltliner Keller, Schlüsselgasse 8, ✉ 8001, ☎ 221 32 28, «14C house» – AE E VISA
closed Saturday lunch, Sunday and 20 July-9 August – **M** a la carte 37/70. BY **t**

Osteria da Primo, Uetlibergstr. 166, ✉ 8045, ☎ 463 30 22, Italian rest. – V **k**

Environs

by ① to Affoltern :

at Regensdorf : 12 km – ✉ **8105** Regensdorf :

Mövenpick Holiday Inn M, im Zentrum, ☎ 840 25 20, Telex 825888 – wc . AE E VISA
M Grillroom a la carte 37,50/56,50 – 14,50 – **149 rm** 128/180 Bb.

at Dielsdorf : 15,5 km – ✉ **8157** Dielsdorf :

Bienengarten, Regensbergerstr. 9, ☎ 853 12 17, – . AE E VISA
closed Saturday lunch and mid September-October – **M** a la carte 35/61.

by ② to Schaffhausen :

at Zürich-Kloten (Airport) 10 km :

Hilton International Zürich M, Hohenbühlstr. 10, ✉ 8058, ☎ 810 31 31, Telex 825428, – . AE E. rest
M Sutter's Grill a la carte 44/79 – **Taverne** a la carte 30,50/49,50 – 12,50 Bb – **287 rm** 175/260.

Mövenpick Hotel Zürich Airport M, Walter Mittelholzerstr. 8, ✉ 8152 Glattbrugg, ✆ 810 11 11, Telex 57979 – AE E VISA
M a la carte 22/50 – 16 Bb – **330 rm** 165/220.

Airport, Oberhauserstr. 30, ✉ 8152 Glattbrugg, ✆ 810 44 44, Telex 825416 – rest wc wc. AE E VISA. rest
M a la carte 34/56 – **48 rm** 120/160 Bb.

Welcome Inn, Holbergstr. 1 (at Kloten), ✉ 8302 Kloten, ✆ 814 07 27, Telex 825527 – wc. AE E VISA
M a la carte 21/44,50 – 7,50 – **95 rm** 80/106.

Top Air, in Terminal A, ✉ 8058, ✆ 814 33 00, ← –
M a la carte 36,50/59,50.

by ③ North bank :

at Zollikon : 5 km – ✉ **8702** Zollikon :

Chez Max (Kehl), Seestr. 53, ✆ 391 88 77 – AE E VISA
closed Sunday, Monday and 14 July-4 August – **M** lunch a la carte 42/88, dinner 110/175
Spec. Oeufs de cailles brouillés à l'Alizier, Escalope de foie gras sauté, Médaillon de veau à la crème de truffes blanches.

Wirtschaft zur Höhe, Höhestr. 73, ✆ 391 59 59, – . AE E VISA
M *(closed Tuesday, last Monday of the month and 13 July to 4 August)* a la carte 42/78.

at Küsnacht : 6 km – ✉ **8700** Küsnacht :

Ermitage, Seestr. 80, ✆ 910 52 22, Telex 825707, ←, , « Attractive lakeside setting, terrace and garden » – wc
M a la carte 46/80 – **25 rm** 90/210 Bb.

Petermann's Kunststube, Seestr. 160, ✆ 910 07 15 – . AE E VISA.
closed Sunday, Monday, 22 July-10 August and 9 to 22 February – **M** a la carte 64/98
Spec. Cabri de la région au fumet de morilles (March-May), Soufflé aux écrevisses (June-October), Filet de chevreuil fumé aux truffes blanches (October-December).

by ④ to Chur-South bank :

at Rüschlikon : 9 km – ✉ **8803** Rüschlikon :

Belvoir M , Säumerstr. 37, ✆ 724 02 02, Telex 826522, ← lake, – rest wc wc . AE E VISA. rest
M a la carte 31/48 – **25 rm** 75/150.

at Gattikon : 13,5 km – ✉ **8136** Gattikon-Thalwil :

Sihlhalde, Sihlhaldenstr. 70, ✆ 720 09 27,
closed Sunday, Monday and 20 July-10 August – **M** a la carte 44/66
Spec. Ecrevisses (July-September), Gibier (season).

at Wädenswil : 22 km – ✉ **8820** Wädenswil :

Eichmühle (Wannenwetsch), Neugutstr. 933, ✆ 780 34 44 – . AE E
closed Tuesday and 20 July-8 August – **M** a la carte 41/88
Spec. La marmite du pêcheur (in winter), Daurade royale à la fondue d'orange et de citron, Salade de homard breton aux mangues.

Town plans of Basle, Geneva and Zürich : with the permission from Federal directorate for cadastral surveys, 2 January 1987.

United Kingdom

London
Birmingham
Edinburgh
Glasgow
Leeds
Liverpool
Manchester

PRACTICAL INFORMATION

LOCAL CURRENCY

Pound Sterling : £ 1 = 1.48 US $ (Jan. 87)

TOURIST INFORMATION

Tourist Information offices exist in each city included in the Guide. The telephone number and address is given in each text under ℹ.

FOREIGN EXCHANGE

Banks are open between 9.30am and 3pm on weekdays only. Most large hotels have exchange facilities, and Heathrow and Gatwick Airports have 24-hour banking facilities.

SHOPPING

In London : Oxford St./Regent St. (department stores, exclusive shops) Bond St. (exclusive shops, antiques)
Knightsbridge area (department stores, exclusive shops, boutiques)

For other towns see the index of street names : those printed in red are where the principal shops are found.

THEATRE BOOKINGS IN LONDON

Your hotel porter will be able to make your arrangements or direct you to Theatre Booking Agents.

In addition there is a kiosk in Leicester Square selling tickets for the same day's performances at half price plus booking fee. It is open 12-6.30pm.

CAR HIRE

The international car hire companies have branches in each major city. Your hotel porter will be able to give details and help you with your arrangements.

TIPPING

Many hotels and restaurants include a service charge but where this is not the case an amount equivalent to between 10 and 15 per cent of the bill is customary. Additionally doormen, baggage porters and cloakroom attendants are generally given a gratuity.

Taxi drivers are customarily tipped between 10 and 15 per cent of the amount shown on the meter in addition to the fare.

SPEED LIMITS

The maximum permitted speed on motorways and dual carriageways is 70 mph (113 km/h.) and 60 mph (97 km/h.) on other roads except where a lower speed limit is signposted.

SEAT BELTS

The wearing of seat belts in the United Kingdom is compulsory for drivers and front seat passengers.

ANIMALS

It is forbidden to bring domestic animals (dogs, cats...) into the United Kingdom.

LONDON

LONDON (Greater) 404 folds ㊷ to ㊹ – pop. 7 566 620 – ☎ 01.

✈ Heathrow, ☎ 759 4321, Telex 934892 – **Terminal** : Airbus (A1) from Victoria, Airbus (A2) from Paddington, Airbus (A3) from Euston – Underground (Piccadilly line) frequent service daily – Helicopter service to Gatwick Airport.

✈ Gatwick, ☎ 0293 (Crawley) 28822 and ☎ 01 (London) 668 4211, Telex 877725, by A 23 and M 23 – **Terminal** : Coach service from Victoria Coach Station (Flightline 777) – Railink (Gatwick Express) from Victoria (24 h service) – Helicopter service to Heathrow Airport.

✈ Stansted, at Bishop's Stortford, ☎ 0279 (Bishop's Stortford) 502380, Telex 81102, NE : 34 m. off M 11 and A 120.

BA Air Terminal : Victoria Station, ☎ 834 2323, p. 16 BX.

British Caledonian Airways, Victoria Air Terminal : Victoria Station, SW1, ☎ 834 9411, p. 16 BX.

🚗 Euston ☎ 387 8541 – King's Cross ☎ 833 2805 – Paddington ☎ 723 7000 ext 3148.

ℹ London Tourist Board, Head Office, 26 Grosvenor Gardens, SW1W 0DU, ☎ 730 3450, Telex 919 041.
National Tourist Information Centre, Victoria Station Forecourt, SW1, ☎ 730 3488.
London Visitor and Convention Bureau. Telephone Information Service, ☎ 730 3485.
British Travel Centre, 12 Regent St., Piccadilly Circus London SW1, ☎ 730 3400.
Telephone Information Service ☎ 730 0791 or Teletourist ☎ 246 8041 (English), 246 8043 (French), 246 8045 (German).

SIGHTS

HISTORIC BUILDINGS AND MONUMENTS

Palace of Westminster★★★ p. 9 NX – Tower of London★★★ p. 10 QU – Banqueting House★★ p. 9 NV – Buckingham Palace★★ p. 16 BV – Kensington Palace★★ p. 8 JV – Lincoln's Inn★★ p. 17 FV – London Bridge★★ p. 10 QV – Royal Hospital Chelsea★★ p. 15 FU – St. Jame's Palace★★ p. 13 EP – South Bank Arts Centre★★ p. 9 NV – The Temple★★ p. 5 NU – Tower Bridge★★ p. 10 QV – Albert Memorial★ p. 14 CQ – Apsley House★ p. 12 BP – George Inn★, Southwark p. 10 QV – Guildhall★ p. 6 PT – Dr Johnson's House★ p. 6 PTU **A** – Leighton House★ p. 7 GX – The Monument★ (✳★) p. 6 QU **G** – Royal Opera Arcade★ p. 13 FGN – Staple Inn★ p. 5 NT **Y**.

CHURCHES

The City Churches

St. Paul's Cathedral★★★ p. 6 PU – St. Bartholomew the Great★★ p. 6 PT **K** – St. Mary-at-Hill★★ p. 6 QU **B** – Temple Church★★ p. 5 NU – All Hallows-by-the-Tower (font cover★★, brasses★) p. 6 QU **Y** – St. Bride★ (steeple★★) p. 6 PU **J** – St. Giles Cripplegate★ p. 6 PT **N** – St. Helen Bishopsgate★ (monuments★★) p. 6 QTU **R** – St. James Garlickhythe (tower and spire★, sword rests★) p. 6 PU **R** – St. Margaret Lothbury★ p. 6 QT **s** – St. Margaret Pattens (woodwork★) p. 6 QU **N** – St. Mary Abchurch★ p. 6 QU **X** – St. Mary-le-Bow (tower and steeple★★) p. 6 PU **G** – St. Michael Paternoster Royal (tower and spire★) p. 6 PU **D** – St. Olave★ p. 6 QU **S**.

Other Churches

Westminster Abbey★★★ p. 9 MX – Southwark Cathedral★★ p. 10 QV – Queen's Chapel★ p. 13 EP – St. Clement Danes★ p. 17 FV – St. Jame's★ p. 13 EM – St. Margaret's★ p. 9 NX **A** – St. Martin in-the-Fields★ p. 17 DX – St. Paul's★ (Covent Garden) p. 17 DV – Westminster Roman Catholic Cathedral★ p. 9 MX **B**.

STREETS – SQUARES – PARKS

The City★★★ p. 6 PU – Regent's Park★★★ (Terraces★★, Zoo★★★) p. 4 KS – Bedford Square★★ p. 5 MT – Belgrave Square★★ p. 16 AV – Burlington Arcade★★ p. 13 DM – Hyde Park★★ p. 8 JU – The Mall★★ p. 13 FP – Picadilly★★ p. 13 EM – St. Jame's Park★★ p. 9 MV – Trafalgar Square★★ p. 17 DX – Whitehall★★ (Horse Guards★) p. 9 MV – Barbican★ p. 6 PT – Bond Street★ pp. 12-13 CK-DM – Charing Cross★ p. 17 DX – Cheyne Walk★ p. 8 JZ – Jermyn Street★ p. 13 EN – Piccadilly Arcade★ p. 13 DEN – Queen Anne's Gate★ p. 9 MX – Regent Street★ p. 13 EM – St. Jame's Square★ p. 13 FN – St. Jame's Street★ p. 13 EN – Shepherd Market★ p. 12 CN – Strand★ p. 17 DX – Victoria Embankment★ p. 17 EX – Waterloo Place★ p. 13 FN.

MUSEUMS

British Museum★★★ p. 5 MT – National Gallery★★★ p. 13 GM – Science Museum★★★ p. 14 CR – Tate Gallery★★★ p. 9 MY – Victoria and Albert Museum★★★ p. 15 DR – Courtauld Institute Galleries★★ p. 5 MT **M** – Museum of London★★ p. 6 PT **M** – National Portrait Gallery★★ p. 13 GM – Natural History Museum★★ p. 14 CS – Queen's Gallery★★ p. 16 BV – Wallace Collection★★ p. 12 AH – Imperial War Museum★ p. 10 PX – London Transport Museum★ p. 17 EV – Madame Tussaud's★ p. 4 KT **M** – Sir John Soane's Museum★ p. 5 NT **M** – Wellington Museum★ p. 12 BP.

ALPHABETICAL LIST OF AREAS INCLUDED

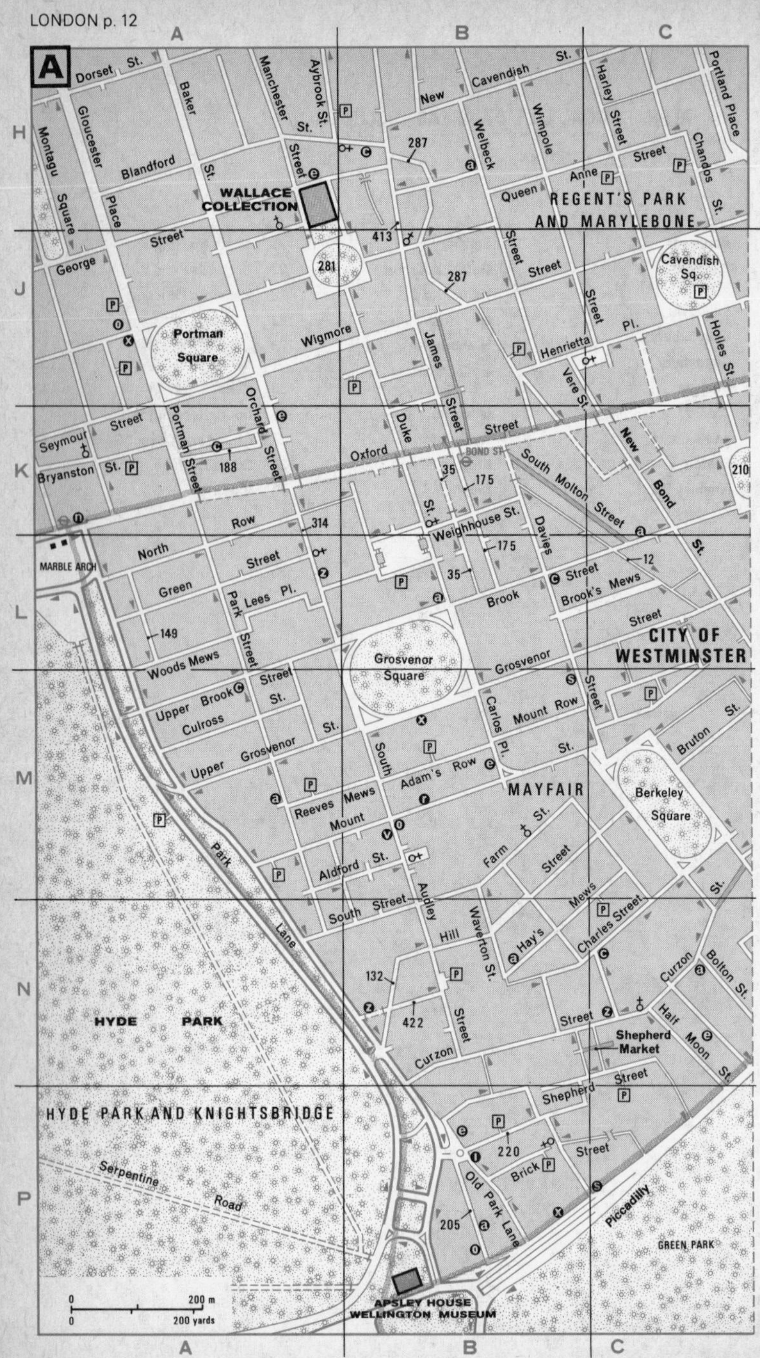
A
REGENT'S PARK AND MARYLEBONE
WALLACE COLLECTION
Portman Square
Cavendish Sq.
Grosvenor Square
Berkeley Square
CITY OF WESTMINSTER
MAYFAIR
MARBLE ARCH
HYDE PARK
HYDE PARK AND KNIGHTSBRIDGE
Shepherd Market
GREEN PARK
APSLEY HOUSE WELLINGTON MUSEUM
Oxford Street
Piccadilly
Park Lane
Serpentine Road
0 200 m
0 200 yards

Street	Grid	No.
Arlington Street	DN	6
Avery Row	CL	12
Bateman Street	FK	18
Berwick Street	FK	26
Binney Street	BL	35
Carlton Gardens	FP	74
Deanery Street	BN	132
Denman Street	FM	133
Denmark Street	GJ	134
Duke of York Street	EN	143
Duke Street ST. JAMES	EN	146
Dunraven Street	AL	149
Gerrard Street	GL	174
Gilbert Street	BL	175
Glasshouse Street	EM	179
Granville Place	AK	188
Great Castle Street	DJ	189
Greek Street	GK	198
Hamilton Place	BP	205
Hanover Square	CK	210
Hertford Street	BP	220
Leicester Square	GM	261
Manchester Square	AJ	281
Market Place	DJ	286
Marylebone Lane	BJ	287
North Audley Street	AK	314
Old Burlington Street	DM	322
Old Compton Street	GK	323
Panton Street	FM	336
Romilly Street	GL	368
Thayer Street	BJ	413
Tilney Street	BN	422
Warwick Street	EM	444

Oxford Street is closed to private traffic, Mondays to Saturdays : from 7 am to 7 pm between Portman Street and St. Giles Circus

B
A
B
C
HYDE PARK AND KNIGHTSBRIDGE
KENSINGTON GARDENS
ALBERT MEMORIAL
Kensington High St.
Kensington Road
Kensington Gore
Kensington
ROYAL ALBERT HALL
Young St.
De Vere Gardens
Palace Gate
Victoria Rd
Queen's Gate
Exhibition Road
Kensington Square
Prince Consort Rd
KENSINGTON
St. Alban's Grove
Victoria Grove
Queen's Gate Terrace
ROYAL COLLEGE OF MUSIC
IMPERIAL COLLEGE OF SCIENCE AND TECHNOLOGY
SCIENCE MUSEUM
GEOLOGICAL MUSEUM
NATURAL HISTORY MUSEUM
ROYAL COLLEGE OF ART
Gloucester Rd
Elvaston Place
Queen's Gate Place
Cornwall Gardens
Queen's Gate Gardens
Lexham Gardens
Lexham Gdns
Grenville Place
Cromwell Road
SOUTH KENSINGTON
GLOUCESTER RD
Stanhope Gardens
Ashburn Road
Knaresborough Place
Courtfield Gdns
Courtfield Road
Harrington Gardens
Wetherby Gdns
Bina Gdns
Old Brompton Rd
Onslow Gardens
Onslow Square
Sumner Place
Onslow Gdns
Cranley Gdns
Roland Gardens
Drayton Gardens
Bramham Gdns
Earl's Court Rd
Bolton Gardens
Brompton Road
Fulham Road
South Parade
EARL'S COURT
The Little Boltons
The Boltons
Redcliffe Gardens
Redcliffe Square
Finborough Road
Harcourt Ter.
Tregunter Road
Hollywood Road
Gilston Road
Evelyn Gdns
Elm Park Gdns
Elm Park Road
Beaufort St.
Old Church St.
The Vale
Elm Park
Park Walk
Ifield Road
BROMPTON CEMETERY
Q
R
S
T
U
241
242
259
357
363
360
120
421
215
59
180
101
14
99
170
300

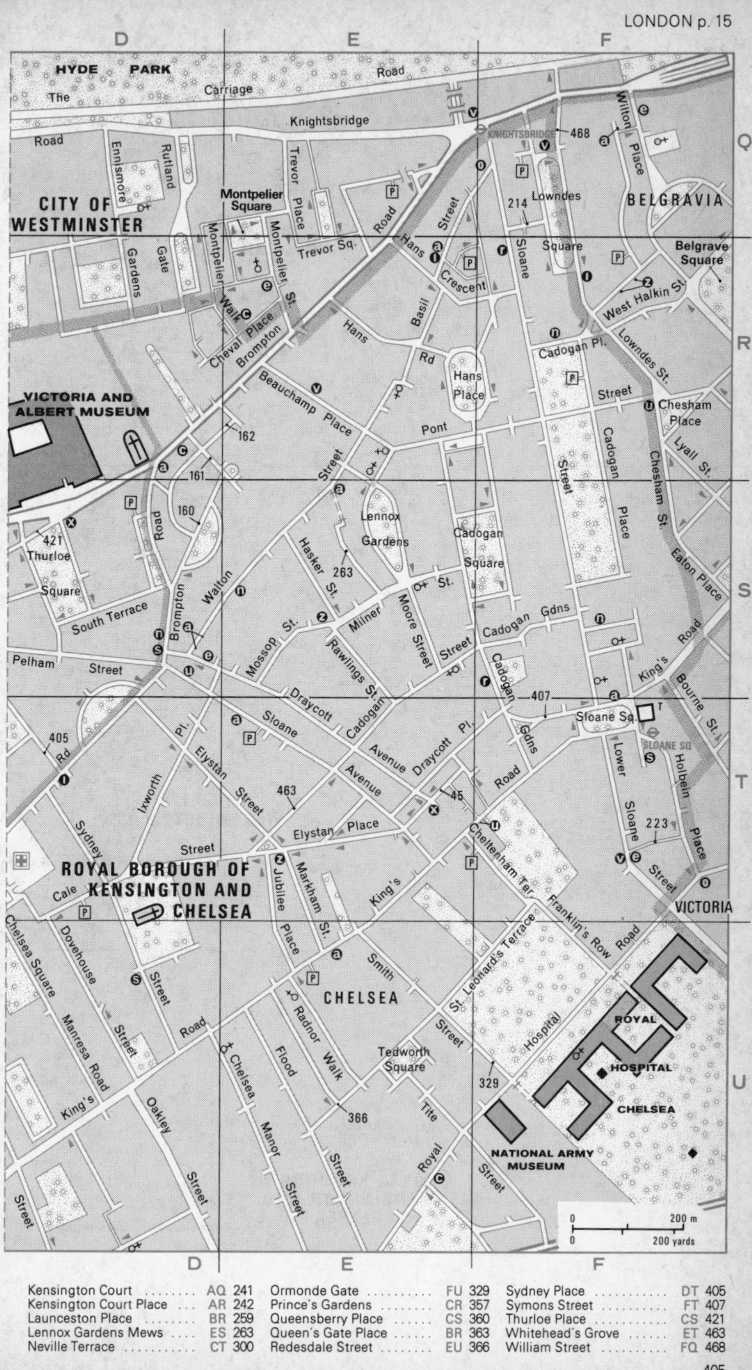

Kensington Court	AQ	241	Ormonde Gate	FU	329	Sydney Place	DT	405
Kensington Court Place	AR	242	Prince's Gardens	CR	357	Symons Street	FT	407
Launceston Place	BR	259	Queensberry Place	CS	360	Thurloe Place	CS	421
Lennox Gardens Mews	ES	263	Queen's Gate Place	BR	363	Whitehead's Grove	ET	463
Neville Terrace	CT	300	Redesdale Street	EU	366	William Street	FQ	468

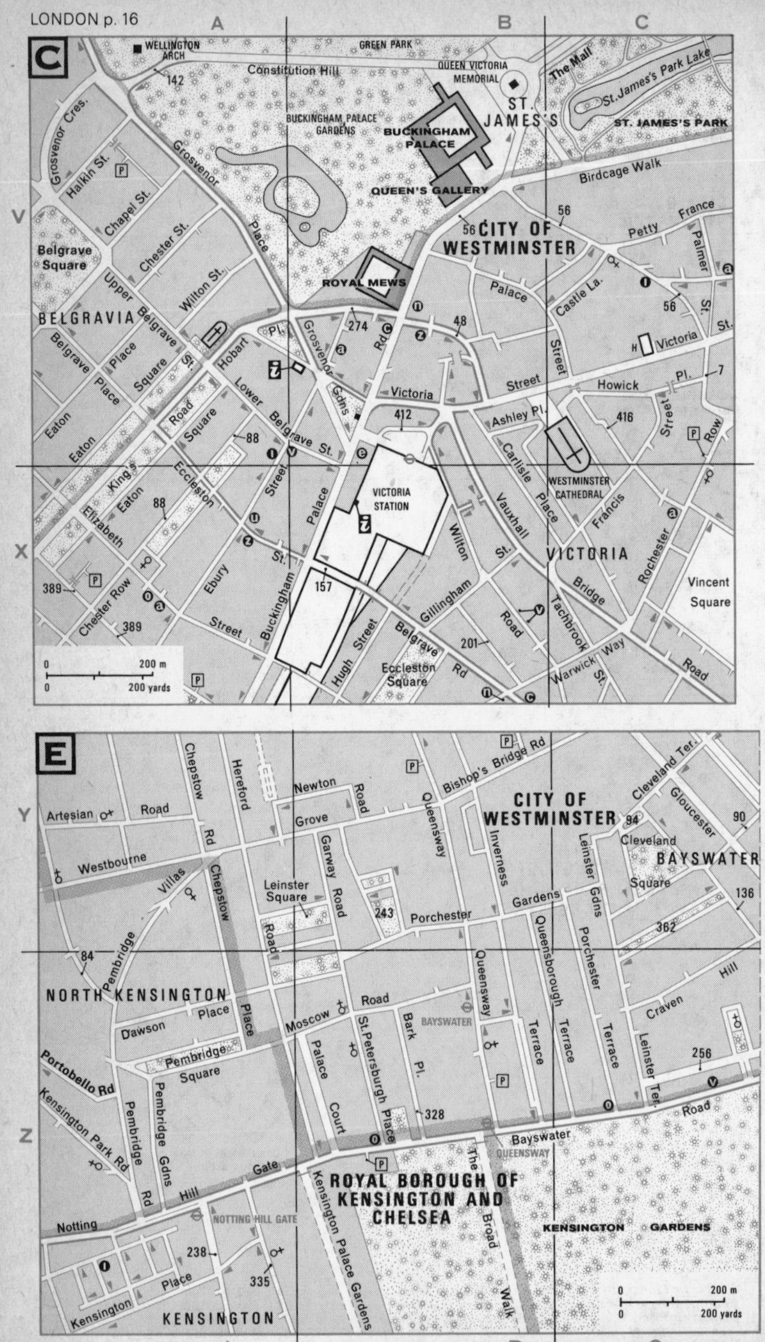
A
B
C
V
X
Y
Z
WELLINGTON ARCH
GREEN PARK
Constitution Hill
QUEEN VICTORIA MEMORIAL
The Mall
St. James's Park Lake
ST. JAMES'S
ST. JAMES'S PARK
BUCKINGHAM PALACE GARDENS
BUCKINGHAM PALACE
QUEEN'S GALLERY
Birdcage Walk
CITY OF WESTMINSTER
ROYAL MEWS
BELGRAVIA
Belgrave Square
VICTORIA STATION
WESTMINSTER CATHEDRAL
VICTORIA
Vincent Square
Eccleston Square
NORTH KENSINGTON
BAYSWATER
ROYAL BOROUGH OF KENSINGTON AND CHELSEA
KENSINGTON GARDENS
KENSINGTON
NOTTING HILL GATE
QUEENSWAY
Leinster Square
Cleveland Square
Pembridge Square
Portobello Rd
200 m
200 yards

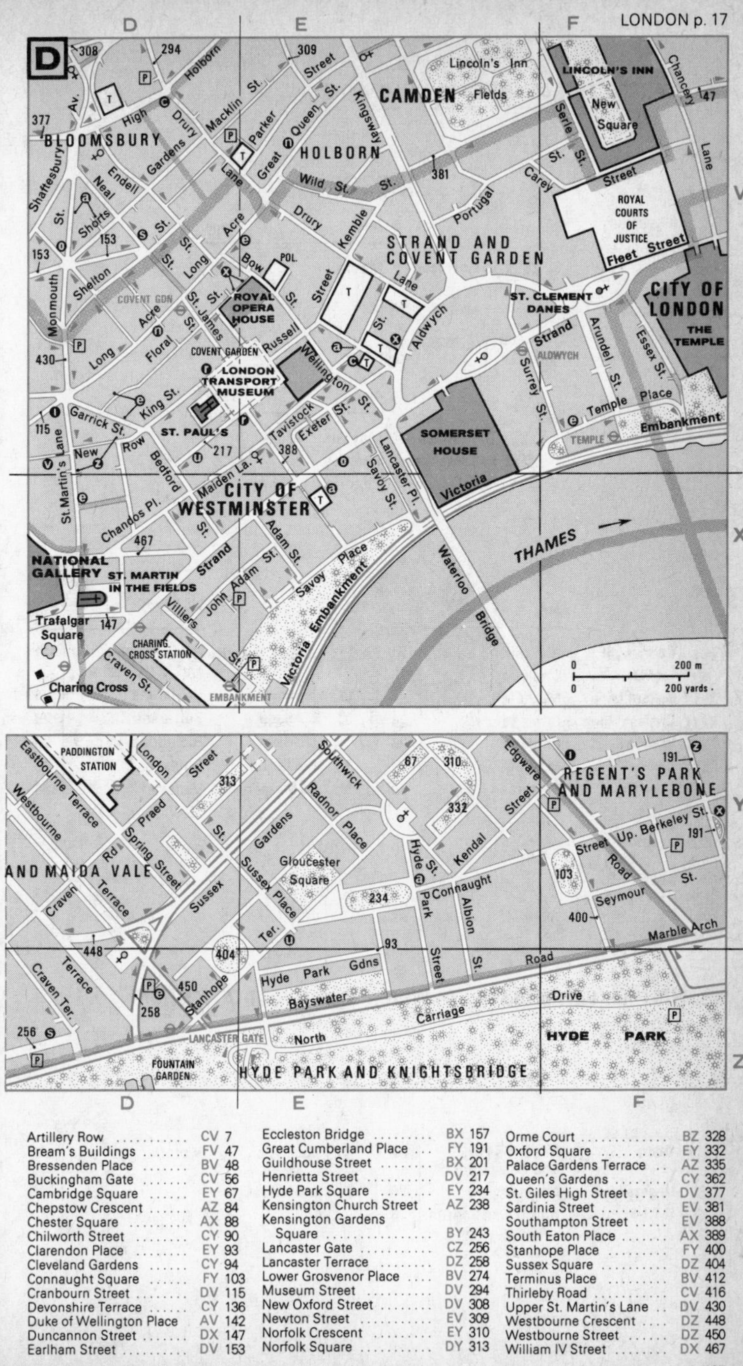

Artillery Row	CV	7
Bream's Buildings	FV	47
Bressenden Place	BV	48
Buckingham Gate	CV	56
Cambridge Square	EY	67
Chepstow Crescent	AZ	84
Chester Square	AX	88
Chilworth Street	CY	90
Clarendon Place	EY	93
Cleveland Gardens	CY	94
Connaught Square	FY	103
Cranbourn Street	DV	115
Devonshire Terrace	CY	136
Duke of Wellington Place	AV	142
Duncannon Street	DX	147
Earlham Street	DV	153
Eccleston Bridge	BX	157
Great Cumberland Place	FY	191
Guildhouse Street	BX	201
Henrietta Street	DV	217
Hyde Park Square	EY	234
Kensington Church Street	AZ	238
Kensington Gardens Square	BY	243
Lancaster Gate	CZ	256
Lancaster Terrace	DZ	258
Lower Grosvenor Place	BV	274
Museum Street	DV	294
New Oxford Street	DV	308
Newton Street	EV	309
Norfolk Crescent	EY	310
Norfolk Square	DY	313
Orme Court	BZ	328
Oxford Square	EY	332
Palace Gardens Terrace	AZ	335
Queen's Gardens	CY	362
St. Giles High Street	DV	377
Sardinia Street	EV	381
Southampton Street	EV	388
South Eaton Place	AX	389
Stanhope Place	FY	400
Sussex Square	DZ	404
Terminus Place	BV	412
Thirleby Road	CV	416
Upper St. Martin's Lane	DV	430
Westbourne Crescent	DZ	448
Westbourne Street	DZ	450
William IV Street	DX	467

STARRED ESTABLISHMENTS IN LONDON

✿✿✿

		Area	Page
XXXX	**Le Gavroche**	Mayfair	31

✿✿

		Area	Page
XXXXX	**The Terrace**	Mayfair	31
XXXX	**La Tante Claire**	Chelsea	26
XXX	**Simply Nico**	Victoria	35

✿

		Area	Page
	Connaught	Mayfair	30
	Capital	Chelsea	25
XXXXX	**90 Park Lane**	Mayfair	31
XXXX	**Chelsea Room**	Chelsea	26
XXXX	**Waltons**	Chelsea	26
XXXX	**Le Soufflé**	Mayfair	31
XXX	**Chez Nico**	Battersea	29
XXX	**Rue St. Jacques**	Regent's Park and Marylebone	32
XXX	**Suntory**	St. James's	33
XX	**L'Arlequin**	Battersea	29
XX	**Lichfield's**	Richmond	29
XX	**Ma Cuisine**	Chelsea	26
XX	**Le Mazarin**	Victoria	36

FURTHER ESTABLISHMENTS WHICH MERIT YOUR ATTENTION

M

XXX	**Odins**	Regent's Park and Marylebone	32
XX	**Bagatelle**	Chelsea	26
XX	**Hilaire**	South Kensington	28
XX	**Ken Lo's Memories of China**	Victoria	36

RESTAURANTS CLASSIFIED ACCORDING TO TYPE

Type	Area		Restaurant	Page
BISTRO	WESTMINSTER (City of)			
	Victoria	X	**Bumbles**	p. 36
DANCING	WESTMINSTER (City of)			
	Mayfair	XXX	**Tiberio**	p. 31
	St. James's	XXXXX	**Maxim's de Paris**	p. 33
SEAFOOD	CITY OF LONDON			
	City of London	XXX	**Wheeler's**	p. 24
	–	XX	**Bill Bentley's**	p. 24
	KENSINGTON & CHELSEA (Royal Borough of)			
	Chelsea	XX	**Poissonnerie de l'Avenue**	p. 26
	–	X	**Wheelers**	p. 26
	Earl's Court	XX	**Tiger Lee**	p. 27
	WESTMINSTER (City of)			
	Mayfair	XXXX	**Scott's**	p. 31
	Strand & Covent Garden	XX	**Frère Jacques**	p. 34
	–	XX	**Sheekey's**	p. 34
	–	X	**Flounders**	p. 35
	–	X	**Grimes**	p. 35
	Victoria	XX	**Hoizin**	p. 36
CHINESE	CAMDEN			
	Finchley Road	XX	**Green Cottage II**	p. 23
	Hampstead	XXX	**Zen W3**	p. 23
	Swiss Cottage	XX	**Lee Ho Fook**	p. 24
	KENSINGTON & CHELSEA (Royal Borough of)			
	Chelsea	XXX	**Zen**	p. 26
	–	XX	**Good Earth**	p. 26
	–	XX	**Good Earth**	p. 26
	Earl's Court	XX	**Tiger Lee**	p. 27
	–	X	**Crystal Palace**	p. 27
	Kensington	XX	**Mama San**	p. 27
	South Kensington	XX	**Golden Chopsticks**	p. 28
	–	XX	**Pun**	p. 28
	WESTMINSTER (City of)			
	Mayfair	XXX	**Princess Garden**	p. 31
	–	XX	**Ho-Ho**	p. 31
	–	XX	**Mr Kai**	p. 31
	Soho	XX	**Mayflower**	p. 34
	–	XX	**Poons**	p. 34
	–	X	**Diamond**	p. 34
	–	X	**Fung Shing**	p. 34
	–	X	**Gallery Rendezvous**	p. 34
	–	X	**Joy King Lau**	p. 34
	Strand & Covent Garden	X	**Happy Wok**	p. 35
	–	X	**Poons of Covent Garden**	p. 35
	Victoria	XXX	**Inn of Happiness**	p. 35
	–	XX	**Ken Lo's Memories of China**	p. 36
	–	XX	**Kym's**	p. 36
ENGLISH	KENSINGTON & CHELSEA (Royal Borough of),			
	Chelsea	XX	**English Garden**	p. 26
	–	XX	**English House**	p. 26
	WESTMINSTER (City of)			
	St. James's	XX	**Green's**	p. 33
	Strand & Covent Garden	XXX	**Simpson's-in-the-Strand**	p. 34
	Victoria	XXX	**Lockets**	p. 35
	–	X	**Tate Gallery Rest.**	p. 36

Cuisine	Area	District	Class	Restaurant	Page
FRENCH	CAMDEN				
		Bloomsbury	XXX	**Etoile (L')**	p. 23
		–	XX	**Porte de la Cité**	p. 23
		–	X	**Mon Plaisir**	p. 23
		Hampstead	XXX	**Keats**	p. 23
	CITY OF LONDON				
		City of London	XX	**Poulbot (Le)** (basement)	p. 24
		–	X	**La Bastille**	p. 24
		–	X	**La Bourse Plate**	p. 24
		–	X	**Bubb's**	p. 24
		–	X	**Gamin (Le)**	p. 24
	KENSINGTON & CHELSEA (Royal Borough of)				
		Chelsea	XXXX	✿✿ **Tante Claire (La)**	p. 26
		–	XXX	**Français (Le)**	p. 26
		–	XX	**Bagatelle**	p. 26
		–	XX	**Gavvers**	p. 26
		–	XX	✿ **Ma Cuisine**	p. 26
		–	XX	**Poissonnerie de l'Avenue**	p. 26
		–	XX	**St. Quentin**	p. 26
		–	X	**Brasserie (La)**	p. 27
		–	X	**Thierry's**	p. 27
		Kensington	XXX	**Belvedere**	p. 27
		–	XXX	**La Ruelle**	p. 27
		–	XX	**Le Crocodile**	p. 27
		–	XX	**Pomme d'Amour (La)**	p. 27
		–	XX	**La Residence**	p. 27
		North Kensington	XX	**Chez Moi**	p. 28
		–	XX	**Monsieur Thompsons**	p. 28
	WANDSWORTH				
		Battersea	XXX	✿ **Chez Nico**	p. 29
		–	XX	✿ **Arlequin (L')**	p. 29
	WESTMINSTER (City of)				
		Belgravia	XX	**Le Trou Normand**	p. 30
		Mayfair	XXXXX	✿✿ **Terrace (The)**	p. 31
		–	XXXX	✿✿✿ **Gavroche (Le)**	p. 31
		Regents Park & Marylebone	XXX	✿ **Rue St. Jacques**	p. 32
		–	X	**L'Aventure**	p. 33
		–	X	**Muscadet (Le)**	p. 33
		St. James's	XXXXX	**Maxim's de Paris**	p. 33
		–	XXXX	**A l'Ecu de France**	p. 33
		Soho	XX	**Jardin des Gourmets (Au)**	p. 33
		–	X	**Cafe Loire**	p. 34
		Strand & Covent Garden	XXXX	**Boulestin**	p. 34
		–	XX	**Chez Solange**	p. 34
		–	XX	**Interlude**	p. 34
		–	XX	**Tourment d'Amour**	p. 34
		–	X	**Cafe Pelican**	p. 35
		–	X	**Magnos Brasserie**	p. 35
		Victoria	XXX	✿✿ **Simply Nico**	p. 35
		–	XXX	**Auberge de Provence**	p. 35
		–	XX	**Ciboure**	p. 36
		–	XX	✿ **Le Mazarin**	p. 36
		–	XX	**Dolphin Brasserie**	p. 36
		–	X	**Poule au Pot (La)**	p. 36
GREEK	CAMDEN				
		Bloomsbury	XXX	**White Tower**	p. 23
HUNGARIAN	WESTMINSTER (City of)				
		Soho	XX	**Gay Hussar**	p. 36
		–	XX	**Old Budapest**	p. 34

Cuisine	Area		Restaurant	Page
INDIAN & PAKISTANI	CAMDEN			
	Bloomsbury	XX	**Lal Qila**	p. 23
	Holborn	XX	**Bhatti**	p. 24
	KENSINGTON & CHELSEA (Royal Borough of)			
	Chelsea	X	**Nayab**	p. 27
	South Kensington	XXX	**Bombay Brasserie**	p. 28
	–	XX	**Memories of India**	p. 28
	WESTMINSTER (City of)			
	Bayswater	XXX	**Bombay Palace**	p. 29
	Belgravia	XX	**Salloos**	p. 30
	Hyde Park & Knightsbridge	XXX	**Shezan**	p. 30
	Regent's Park	XX	**Gaylord**	p. 33
	Soho	XXX	**Red Fort**	p. 33
	–	XX	**Last Days of the Raj**	p. 33
	Victoria	XXX	**Kundan**	p. 35
ITALIAN	KENSINGTON & CHELSEA (Royal Borough of)			
	Chelsea	XXX	**Mario**	p. 26
	–	XX	**Eleven Park Walk**	p. 26
	–	XX	**La Finezza**	p. 26
	–	XX	**Meridiana**	p. 26
	–	XX	**Ponte Nuovo**	p. 26
	–	XX	**Toto**	p. 26
	Kensington	XX	**La Paesana**	p. 27
	WESTMINSTER (City of)			
	Bayswater & Maida Vale	XX	**San Marino**	p. 29
	Hyde Park & Knightsbridge	XX	**Montpeliano**	p. 30
	Mayfair	XXX	**Tiberio**	p. 31
	–	X	**Trattoria Fiori**	p. 32
	Regent's Park & Marylebone	XX	**La Pavona**	p. 33
	Soho	XXX	**Leonis Quo Vadis**	p. 33
	–	XX	**Rugantino**	p. 34
	–	XX	**Venezia**	p. 33
	Strand & Covent Garden	X	**Laguna**	p. 35
	Victoria	XXX	**Santini**	p. 35
	–	XX	**Villa Claudius**	p. 36
	–	X	**Fontana (La)**	p. 36
	–	X	**Mimmo d'Ischia**	p. 36
	–	X	**Villa Medici**	p. 36
JAPANESE	CITY OF LONDON			
	City of London	XX	**Aykoku Kaku**	p. 24
	–	X	**Hana Guruma Bako**	p. 24
	WESTMINSTER (City of)			
	Mayfair	XX	**Miyama**	p. 31
	–	XX	**One Two Three**	p. 31
	–	XX	**Shogun**	p. 31
	–	X	**Ikeda**	p. 32
	St. James's	XXX	✿ **Suntory**	p. 33
	Soho	XX	**Fuji**	p. 34
	Strand & Covent Garden	XX	**Azami**	p. 34
KOREAN	WESTMINSTER (City of)			
	Soho	XX	**Kaya**	p. 33
THAI	KENSINGTON & CHELSEA (Royal Borough of)			
	South Kensington	XX	**Tui**	p. 28
	WESTMINSTER (City of)			
	Soho	X	**Chiang Mai**	p. 34
VIETNAMESE	WESTMINSTER (City of)			
	Soho	X	**Nam Long**	p. 34
	–	X	**Saigon**	p. 34

LONDON AIRPORTS

Heathrow Middx. W : 17 m. by A 4, M 4 – Underground Piccadilly line direct – 404 ㊷ – ☎ 01.

✈ ☎ 759 4321, Telex 934892.

Sheraton Skyline, Bath Rd, Harlington, Hayes, UB3 5BP, ☎ 759 2535, Telex 934254, « Exotic indoor garden with ⛱ » – 🛗 ▤ TV ☎ ♿ P. 🏛. AE ⓪ VISA
M (see **Colony Room** below) – ☕ 6.90 – **355 rm** 72.80/82.90 **s.**, **5 suites** 165.00/470.00 **s.**

Heathrow Penta, Bath Rd, Hounslow, TW6 2AQ, ☎ 897 6363, Telex 934660, ≤, ⛱ – 🛗 ▤ TV ☎ ♿ P. 🏛
670 rm, **9 suites**.

Excelsior (T.H.F.), Bath Rd, West Drayton, UB7 0DU, ☎ 759 6611, Telex 24525, ⛱ heated – 🛗 ▤ TV ☎ ♿ P. 🏛. AE ⓪ VISA
M 9.25 **st.** and a la carte 🍷 3.40 – ☕ 6.75 – **573 rm** 60.00/68.00 **st.**, **7 suites**.

Holiday Inn, Stockley Rd, West Drayton, UB7 9NA, ☎ 0895 (West Drayton) 445555, Telex 934518, ⛱, 🎾 – 🛗 ▤ TV ☎ ♿ P. 🏛. AE ⓪ VISA
M 10.45 **st.** and a la carte – ☕ 5.95 – **400 rm** 60.50/71.00 **st.**, **2 suites** 156.00/231.00 **st.**

Sheraton Heathrow, Colnbrook by-pass, West Drayton, UB7 0HJ, ☎ 759 2424, Telex 934331, ⛱ – 🛗 ▤ TV ☎ ♿ P. 🏛. AE ⓪ VISA. ✻
M a la carte 9.00/19.00 **t.** – ☕ 7.00 – **405 rm** 59.00/70.00 **t.**, **5 suites** 120.00/147.00.

Skyway (T.H.F.), 140 Bath Rd, Hayes, UB3 5AW, ☎ 759 6311, Telex 23935, ⛱ heated – 🛗 ▤ rest TV ☎ ♿ P. 🏛. AE ⓪ VISA
M 12.50 **st.** and a la carte 🍷 3.00 – ☕ 6.50 – **412 rm** 50.00/60.00 **st.**

Post House (T.H.F.), Sipson Rd, West Drayton, UB7 0JU, ☎ 759 2323, Telex 934280 – 🛗 ▤ TV ☎ ♿ P. 🏛. AE ⓪ VISA
M 10.50 **st.** and a la carte 🍷 3.40 – ☕ 6.50 – **597 rm** 54.00/64.50 **st.**

Ibis, 112-114 Bath Rd, Hayes, UB3 5AL, ☎ 759 4888 – ▤ TV 🛁wc ☎ ♿ P. AE ⓪ VISA
M 7.50 **st.** and a la carte 🍷 3.50 – ☕ 5.50 – **244 rm** 39.00/44.00 **st.**

Ariel (T.H.F.), Bath Rd, Hayes, UB3 5AJ, ☎ 759 2552, Telex 21777 – 🛗 ▤ TV 🛁wc ☎ ♿ P. 🏛. AE ⓪ VISA
M 9.95 **st.** and a la carte 🍷 3.40 – ☕ 6.50 – **177 rm** 51.00/62.00 **st.**

Arlington, Shepiston Lane, Hayes, UB3 1LP, ☎ 573 6162, Group Telex 935120 – ▤ rest TV 🛁wc 🚿wc ☎ P. 🏛. AE ⓪ VISA. ✻
M *(closed lunch Saturday and Sunday)* 8.00 **t.** and a la carte – ☕ 4.00 – **80 rm** 34.00/45.00 **t.** – SB (weekends only) 56.00/76.00 **st.**

Colony Room (at Sheraton Skyline H.), Bath Rd, Harlington, Hayes, UB3 5BP, ☎ 759 2535 – ▤ P
M 16.50 **st.** (lunch) and a la carte 16.00/21.50 **st.** 🍷 4.50.

Gatwick West Sussex S : 28 m. by A 23 and M 23 – Train from Victoria : Gatwick Express 404 T 30 – ✉ West Sussex – ☎ 0293 Gatwick.

✈ ☎ 0293 (Crawley) 28822 and ☎ 01 (London) 668 4211.

Gatwick Hilton International, Gatwick Airport, RH6 0LL, ☎ 518080, Telex 877021, ⛱ – 🛗 ▤ TV ☎ ♿ P. 🏛. AE ⓪ VISA
M 10.75/16.50 **t.** and a la carte 🍷 4.65 – ☕ 6.75 – **333 rm** 72.00/88.00 **t.**, **2 suites** 150.00/250.00 **t.**

Gatwick Penta, Povey Cross Rd, ✉ Horley (Surrey), RH6 0BE, ☎ 785533, Telex 87440, 🚗 – 🛗 ▤ TV ☎ ♿ P. 🏛
260 rm, **1 suite**.

Post House (T.H.F.), Povey Cross Rd, ✉ Horley (Surrey), RH6 0BA, ☎ 771621, Telex 877351, ⛱ heated – 🛗 ▤ rest TV ☎ ♿ P. 🏛. AE ⓪ VISA
M 12.95/14.95 **st.** and a la carte 🍷 3.40 – ☕ 5.65 – **148 rm** 53.00/66.00 **st.**

Gatwick Moat House (Q.M.H.), Longbridge Roundabout, ✉ Horley (Surrey), RH6 0AB, ☎ 785599, Telex 877138 – 🛗 ▤ TV 🛁wc ☎ ♿ P. 🏛. AE ⓪ VISA
M 7.50/9.50 **t.** and a la carte 🍷 2.65 – ☕ 5.75 – **121 rm** 45.75/61.50 **st.** – SB (weekends only) 71.50 **st.**

CAMDEN Except where otherwise stated see pp. 3-6.

Bloomsbury – ✉ NW1/W1/WC1.

Russell (T.H.F.), Russell Sq., WC1B 5BE, ☎ 837 6470, Telex 24615 – 🛗 TV ☎. 🏛. AE ⓪ VISA NT **o**
M (carving rest.) 10.50 **st.** and a la carte 🍷 3.40 – ☕ 6.50 – **316 rm** 57.00/72.00 **st.**

Grafton, 130 Tottenham Court Rd, W1P 9HP, ☎ 388 4131, Telex 297234 – 🛗 ▤ rest TV ☎. 🏛. AE ⓪ VISA. ✻ LT **n**
M 10.00 **st.** and a la carte 🍷 6.00 – ☕ 6.00 – **159 rm** 59.90/79.90 **st.**

Kenilworth, 97 Great Russell St., WC1B 3LB, ✆ 637 3477, Telex 25842 – AE VISA. MT a
M 10.00 **st.** and a la carte 13.00/17.75 **st.** 3.55 – 6.00 – **180 rm** 59.90/79.90, **1 suite**.

Mountbatten, Seven Dials, WC2H 9HD, ✆ 836 4300, Telex 298087 – rest. AE VISA. p. 17 DV o
M 10.50 **t.** and a la carte 14.50/21.50 **t.** – 8.00 – **127 rm** 89.90/123.90 **st.**, **7 suites** 180.00/250.00 **st.** – SB (except summer) (weekends only) 107.00 **st.**

Bonnington, 92 Southampton Row, WC1B 4BH, ✆ 242 2828, Telex 261591 – wc. AE VISA NT s
M (buffet lunch)/dinner 8.50 **st.** and a la carte 3.20 – **242 rm** 31.35/66.00 **st.**

White Tower, 1 Percy St., W1P 0ET, ✆ 636 8141, Greek rest. – AE VISA
closed Saturday, Sunday, 3 weeks August, 1 week Christmas and Bank Holidays – **M** a la carte 12.10/21.50 **t.** 3.25. MT u

L'Etoile, 30 Charlotte St., W1P 1HJ, ✆ 636 7189, French rest. LT e

Neal Street, 26 Neal St., WC2 9PH, ✆ 836 8368 – AE VISA p. 17 DV s
closed Saturday, Sunday and Christmas-New Year – **M** a la carte 14.60/26.10 **t.** 4.35.

Seven Dials, 5 Neals Yard, off Monmouth St., WC2 9DP, ✆ 379 4955 – AE VISA p. 17 DV a
closed Saturday lunch, Sunday and Bank Holidays – **M** a la carte 12.55/16.70 **t.**

Porte de la Cité, 65 Theobalds Rd, WC1 8TA, ✆ 242 1154, French rest. – AE VISA NT c
closed Saturday, Sunday, Easter, Christmas and Bank Holidays – **M** (lunch only) 16.50 **st.** 3.00.

Lal Qila, 117 Tottenham Court Rd, W1P 9HL, ✆ 387 4570, Indian rest. LT u

Mon Plaisir, 21 Monmouth St., WC2H 9DD, ✆ 836 7243, French rest. p. 17 DV a
closed Saturday lunch, Sunday, Christmas-New Year and Bank Holidays – **M** 8.95/18.00 **t.** and a la carte 10.80/14.50 **t.** 3.20.

Euston – ✉ NW1.

Kennedy (Mt. Charlotte), 43 Cardington St., NW1 2LP, ✆ 387 4400, Telex 28250 – wc. AE VISA. LS r
M 8.50 **st.** and a la carte 3.35 – 3.50 – **320 rm** 48.50/61.00 **st.**

Finchley Road – ✉ NW1/NW3.

Charles Bernard, 5 Frognal, NW3 6AL, ✆ 794 0101, Telex 23560 – wc. AE VISA GR s
M 9.80 **st.** and a la carte 7.25/10.75 **st.** 2.60 – **57 rm** 46.00/62.10 **st.** – SB (weekends only) 58.70 **st.**

Green Cottage II, 122a Finchley Rd, NW3 5HT, ✆ 794 3833, Chinese Vegetarian rest. – JR u

Sheridans, 351 West End Lane, NW6 1LT, ✆ 794 3234 – AE VISA
closed Monday, 18 August-2 September and 1 to 15 January – **M** (dinner only and Sunday lunch) dinner a la carte 10.05/14.35 **t.** 3.40.

Hampstead – ✉ NW3.

Ladbroke Clive (Ladbroke), Primrose Hill Rd, NW3 3NA, ✆ 586 2233 – AE VISA KR a
M *(closed Saturday lunch)* 9.50 **st.** and a la carte 3.80 – 6.50 – **84 rm** 60.00/86.00 **st.** – SB (weekends only) 70.00/90.00 **st.**

Swiss Cottage, 4 Adamson Rd, NW3 3HP, ✆ 722 2281, Telex 297232, « Antique furniture collection » – wc wc. AE VISA. JR n
M 7.50/10.50 **t.** and a la carte 2.50 – **65 rm** 36.50/73.00 **t.**, **4 suites** 73.00 **t.**

Post House (T.H.F.), 215 Haverstock Hill, NW3 4RB, ✆ 794 8121, Telex 262494 – wc. AE VISA GR r
M 8.95 **st.** and a la carte 3.40 – 5.65 – **140 rm** 52.00/63.00 **st.**

Keats, 3-4 Downshire Hill, NW3 1NR, ✆ 435 3544, French rest. – AE VISA GR i
closed Sunday and last 2 weeks August – **M** (dinner only) 19.00 **st.** and a la carte 18.30/23.00 **st.** 9.00.

Zen W3, 83 Hampstead High St., NW3 1RE, ✆ 794 7863, Chinese rest. – AE VISA GR a
M a la carte 13.00/19.00 **t.**

Holborn – ✉ WC2.

Drury Lane Moat House (Q.M.H.), 10 Drury Lane, High Holborn, WC2B 5RE, ✆ 836 6666, Telex 8811395 – AE VISA. p. 17 DV c
M 11.30 **t.** and a la carte 15.35/16.60 **t.** 3.50 – 6.75 – **129 rm** 68.00/98.00 **t.**, **1 suite** 156.00 **t.** – SB (weekends only) 76.00/80.00 **st.**

XXX **L'Opera,** 32 Great Queen St., WC2B 5AA, ℘ 405 9020 – AE ⓓ VISA p. 17 EV **n**
closed Saturday lunch, Sunday and Bank Holidays – **M** 18.00/25.00 **st.** and a la carte 15.45/21.40 **t.** 3.00.

XX Hodgsons, 115 Chancery Lane, WC2, ℘ 242 2836 NT **a**

XX **Bhatti,** 37 Great Queen St., WC2, ℘ 831 0817, Indian rest. – AE ⓓ VISA
M 8.50/9.50 **t.** and a la carte 7.15/9.05 **t.** 3.15.

King's Cross – ⊠ N1.

Great Northern, N1 9AN, ℘ 837 5454, Telex 299041 – TV wc ☎. AE ⓓ VISA. MNS **s**
closed Christmas – **M** 10.00/13.00 **st.** 3.30 – **87 rm** 52.50/67.50 **st.**

Regent's Park – ⊠ NW1.

White House (Rank), Albany St., NW1 3UP, ℘ 387 1200, Telex 24111 – rest TV ☎ ♿. AE ⓓ VISA. LS **o**
M 9.00 **t.** and a la carte 10.00/20.50 **t.** – 7.00 – **580 rm** 62.00/90.00 **t.**, **9 suites** 160.00/310.00 **t.**

Swiss Cottage – ⊠ NW3.

Holiday Inn, 128 King Henry's Rd, NW3 3ST, ℘ 722 7711, Telex 267396, – TV ☎ ♿ Ⓟ. AE ⓓ VISA JR **a**
M 13.50 **t.** (lunch) and a la carte 11.60/20.20 **t.** 4.30 – 7.10 – **291 rm** 83.40/95.45 **st.**, **4 suites**.

XX **Peter's,** 65 Fairfax Rd, NW6 4EE, ℘ 624 5804 – AE ⓓ VISA JR **i**
closed Saturday lunch, Sunday dinner and 26 December – **M** 12.00 (lunch) and a la carte 12.00/15.75 **t.** 3.25.

XX Lee Ho Fook, 5-6 New College Par., Finchley Rd, NW3, ℘ 722 9552, Chinese rest. JR **c**

CITY OF LONDON Except where otherwise stated see p. 6.
St. Paul's Churchyard, EC4, ℘ 606 3030 ext 2456.

XXX **Corney and Barrow,** 109 Old Broad St., EC2N 1AP, ℘ 920 9560 – AE ⓓ VISA
closed Saturday, Sunday and Bank Holidays – **M** (lunch only) a la carte 23.25/24.55 **st.** 6.00. QT **c**

XXX Wheeler's, 33 Foster Lane, EC2V 6HD, ℘ 606 8254, Seafood PT **o**

XX **Le Poulbot** (basement), 45 Cheapside, EC2V 6AR, ℘ 236 4379, French rest. – AE ⓓ VISA – *closed Saturday, Sunday, Christmas-New Year and Bank Holidays* – **M** (lunch only) 24.50 **st.** 5.80 PU **i**

XX **Candlewick Room,** 45 Old Broad St., EC2N 1HT, ℘ 628 7929 – AE ⓓ VISA QT **n**
closed Saturday, Sunday and Bank Holidays – **M** (lunch only) 25.00 **st.** and a la carte 20.40/23.45 **t.**

XX **Corney and Barrow,** 118 Moorgate, EC2M 6UR, ℘ 628 2898 – AE ⓓ VISA
closed Saturday, Sunday and Bank Holidays – **M** a la carte 16.75/22.95 **t.** 4.00. QT **a**

XX **Corney and Barrow,** 44 Cannon St., EC4N 6JJ, ℘ 248 1700 – AE ⓓ VISA PU **r**
closed Saturday, Sunday and Bank Holidays – **M** a la carte 16.65/20.45 **t.** 4.00.

XX Aykoku Kaku, 9 Walbrook, EC4, ℘ 236 9020, Japanese rest. PQU **u**
closed Saturday and Sunday.

XX **Bill Bentley's,** Swedeland Court, 202-204 Bishopsgate, EC2M 4NR, ℘ 283 1763, Seafood – AE ⓓ VISA – *closed Saturday, Sunday and Bank Holidays* – **M** (lunch only) a la carte 14.85/18.15 **t.** 2.95 QT **e**

XX **Shares,** 12-13 Lime St., EC3M 7AA, ℘ 623 1843 – AE ⓓ VISA QU **s**
closed Saturday, Sunday and Bank Holidays – **M** (lunch only) 19.50 **t.**

XX **Bill Bentley's,** 18 Old Broad St., EC2N 1DP, ℘ 588 2655, Seafood – VISA QT **i**
closed Saturday, Sunday and Bank Holidays – **M** (lunch only) a la carte 13.45/16.25 **t.** 3.00.

X **Bubb's,** 329 Central Market, Farringdon St., EC1A 9NB, ℘ 236 2435, French rest. PT **a**
closed Saturday, Sunday, 2 weeks August, 1 week Christmas-New Year and Bank Holidays – **M** (booking essential) (lunch only) a la carte 16.45/20.50 **st.** 3.80.

X **La Bourse Plate,** 78 Leadenhall St., EC3A 3DN, ℘ 623 5159, French rest. – AE ⓓ VISA QU **v**
closed Saturday, Sunday and Bank Holidays – **M** (lunch only) 16.00 **st.** 3.40.

X **La Bastille,** 116 Newgate St., EC1A 7AE, ℘ 600 1134, French rest. – AE ⓓ VISA
closed Saturday, Sunday, last week August, 1 week Christmas and Bank Holidays – **M** *(lunch only)* 15.95. PT **z**

X **Le Gamin,** 32 Old Bailey, EC4M 7HS, ℘ 236 7931, French rest. – AE ⓓ VISA PU **a**
closed Saturday, Sunday and Bank Holidays – **M** (lunch only) 17.75 **st.** 2.80.

X Hana Guruma Bako, 49 Bow Lane, EC4M 9DL, ℘ 236 6451, Japanese rest. – PU **n**

X **Whittington's,** 21 College Hill, EC4, ℘ 248 5855 – AE ⓓ VISA PU **c**
closed Saturday, Sunday and Bank Holidays – **M** (lunch only) a la carte 12.75/16.25 **t.** 2.45.

ISLINGTON pp. 3-6.

Canonbury – ✉ N1.

✗ **Anna's Place,** 90 Mildmay Park, N1 4PR, ✆ 249 9379
closed Sunday, Monday, 2 weeks at Easter, August and 2 weeks at Christmas – **M** (booking essential) a la carte 9.85/12.95 **t.**

Finsbury – ✉ WC1/EC1/EC2.

London Ryan (Mt. Charlotte), Gwynne Pl., King Cross Rd, WC1X 9GB, ✆ 278 2480, Telex 27728 – rest wc ☎ P. AE VISA. NS **a**
M (bar lunch)/dinner 8.50 **st.** and a la carte 3.25 – 3.50 – **211 rm** 47.25/57.75 **st.**

✗✗ **Rouxl Britannia,** Triton Court, 14 Finsbury Sq., EC2A 1RR, ✆ 256 6997 – QT **x**
M Le Restaurant *(closed Saturday, Sunday and Bank Holidays)* (lunch only) 14.00 **st.** – **Le Café** *(closed Saturday, Sunday and Bank Holidays)* a la carte 6.00/16.50 **st.** 3.50.

✗✗ **Café St. Pierre,** 29 Clerkenwell Green (1st floor), EC1, ✆ 251 6606 – AE VISA
closed Saturday, Sunday, 24 December-2 January and Bank Holidays – **M** 15.00 **st.** (dinner) and a la carte 13.00/15.70 **t.** 2.50. PT **c**

Islington – ✉ N1.

✗✗ **Frederick's,** Camden Passage, N1 8EG, ✆ 359 2888, « Conservatory and walled garden » – . AE VISA PR **a**
closed Sunday, 17 and 20 April, 26 December, 1 January and Bank Holidays – **M** a la carte 12.60/16.60 **t.** 3.25.

✗✗ **Varnom's,** 2 Greenman St., N1 8SB, ✆ 359 6707 – . AE VISA
closed Saturday lunch, Sunday dinner and Monday – **M** 13.50 **t.** and a la carte 13.95/16.50 **t.** 3.00.

KENSINGTON and CHELSEA (Royal Borough of).

Chelsea – ✉ SW1/SW3/SW10 – Except where otherwise stated see pp. 14 and 15.

Hyatt Carlton Tower, 2 Cadogan Pl., SW1X 9PY, ✆ 235 5411, Telex 21944, ←, , – TV ☎ ♿ P. . AE VISA. FR **n**
M (see **Chelsea Room** below) – **Rib Room** 17.50 **t.** (lunch) and a la carte 21.80/35.50 **t.** 7.50 – 7.90 – **217 rm** 126.00/166.00 **t.**, **30 suites** 220.00/1000.00 **s.**

Sheraton Park Tower, 101 Knightsbridge, SW1X 7RN, ✆ 235 8050, Telex 917222 – TV ☎ ♿ P. . AE VISA. FQ **v**
M 10.75/16.75 **t.** and a la carte 14.60/25.25 **t.** – 8.00 – **295 rm** 127.85/161.00 **st.**, **16 suites** 316.25/345.00 **st.**

❀ **Capital,** 22-24 Basil St., SW3 1AT, ✆ 589 5171, Telex 919042 – TV ☎. AE VISA. ER **a**
M 16.50/18.50 **st.** and a la carte 27.50/32.50 **st.** 6.00 – 7.50 – **60 rm** 100.00/120.00 **st.**
Spec. Salade de pêcheurs tiède au Xérès, Carré d'agneau persillé aux herbes de Provence, Quenelles de poisson fumé.

Basil Street, 8 Basil St., SW3 1AH, ✆ 581 3311, Telex 28379 – TV ☎. . AE VISA FQ **o**
M 9.75 **t.** (lunch) and a la carte 14.45/18.75 **t.** 5.25 – 5.80 – **95 rm** 36.30/86.50 **t.**, **1 suite** 144.00 **t.**

Holiday Inn, 17-25 Sloane St., SW1X 9NU, ✆ 235 4377, Telex 919111, – TV ☎. . AE VISA. FR **r**
M a la carte 10.75/18.55 **st.** 4.50 – 5.95 – **198 rm** 93.00/118.00 **st.**, **4 suites** 245.00 **st.** – SB (weekends only) 99.00 **st.**

Cadogan Thistle (Thistle), 75 Sloane St., SW1X 9SG, ✆ 235 7141, Telex 267893 – TV ☎. . AE VISA. FR **e**
M a la carte 11.00/15.50 **t.** 3.65 – 6.75 – **68 rm** 85.00/125.00 **st.**, **5 suites** 135.00 **st.**

Royal Court (Norfolk Cap.), Sloane Sq., SW1W 8EG, ✆ 730 9191, Telex 296818 – rest TV ☎. . AE VISA. FST **a**
M 9.95/16.00 **st.** and a la carte 15.30/19.80 **t.** 3.50 – 7.25 – **98 rm** 65.00/90.00 **st.**, **5 suites** 105.00/140.00 **st.** – SB (weekends only) 87.00 **st.**

L'Hotel without rest., 28 Basil St., SW3 1AT, ✆ 589 6286, Telex 919042 – TV wc ☎. AE. ER **i**
12 rm 80.00/100.00 **st.**

Wilbraham without rest., 1-5 Wilbraham Pl., Sloane St., SW1X 9AE, ✆ 730 8296 – wc ☎. FS **n**
4.00 – **56 rm** 26.00/57.00.

Fenja without rest., 69 Cadogan Gdns, SW3 2RB, ✆ 589 1183 – wc ☎. FS **r**
16 rm.

Willett without rest., 32 Sloane Gdns, Sloane Sq., SW1W 8DJ, ✆ 824 8415 – TV wc FT **s**
17 rm 23.00/34.00 **s.**

XXXX ✿ **Chelsea Room** (at Hyatt Carlton Tower H.), 2 Cadogan Pl., SW1X 9PY, ✆ 235 5411, Telex 21944 – Ⓟ. AE VISA FR **n**
M 19.50 **t.** (lunch) and a la carte 21.00/28.00 **t.** 4.75
Spec. Foie gras aux cassis, Fricassée de turbot et homard, Mignons de bœuf Arlequin.

XXXX ✿ **Waltons,** 121 Walton St., SW3 2HP, ✆ 584 0204 – AE VISA DS **a**
closed 4 days at Easter, 3 days at Christmas and Bank Holidays – **M** 12.65/20.15 **st.** and a la carte 20.00/30.50 **t.** 3.50
Spec. Salmon-stuffed breast of chicken with basil cream sauce, Marbled terrine of turbot with a green herb sauce, Pan fried medallion of scotch beef with stilton mousse.

XXXX ✿✿ **La Tante Claire,** 68-69 Royal Hospital Rd, SW3 4HP, ✆ 352 6045, French rest. – AE EU **c**
closed Saturday, Sunday, 10 days at Easter, 3 weeks August-September, 10 days at Christmas-New Year and Bank Holidays – **M** 19.00 **st.** (lunch) and a la carte 27.80/38.50 **st.**
Spec. Frivolités de la mer, Pied de cochon farci aux morilles, mousseline de broccoli, Croustade aux pommes caramélisées.

XXX **Zen,** Chelsea Cloisters, Sloane Av., SW3 3DW, ✆ 589 1781, Chinese rest. – AE VISA ET **a**
closed 25 to 27 December – **M** a la carte 7.50/15.00 **t.**

XXX **Le Français,** 257-259 Fulham Rd, SW3 6HY, ✆ 352 4748, French rest. – AE VISA CU **a**
closed Sunday and 4 days at Christmas – **M** 17.00 **st.** 7.00.

XXX Mario, 260-262a Brompton Rd, SW3 2AS, ✆ 584 1724, Italian rest. DS **n**

XXX **Turners,** 87-89 Walton St., SW3 3HP, ✆ 584 6711 – AE VISA ES **n**
closed Monday and Bank Holidays – **M** 16.50/23.50 **st.** and a la carte 8.50.

XX **Daphne's,** 110-112 Draycott Av., SW3 3AE, ✆ 589 4257 – AE VISA DS **e**
closed Saturday lunch, Sunday and Bank Holidays – **M** a la carte 10.80/18.00 **t.** 3.50.

XX La Finezza, 62-64 Lower Sloane St., SW1, ✆ 730 8630, Italian rest. FT **v**

XX **Eleven Park Walk,** 11 Park Walk, SW10, ✆ 352 3449, Italian rest. – AE CU **r**
M 15.20/20.20 **st.** and a la carte 14.30/18.50 **t.** 2.90.

XX **English Garden,** 10 Lincoln St., SW3 2TS, ✆ 584 7272, English rest. – AE VISA ET **x**
closed 17 April and 25-26 December – **M** a la carte 14.00/26.00 **st.** 3.75.

XX **English House,** 3 Milner St., SW3 2QA, ✆ 584 3002, English rest. – AE VISA ES **z**
closed 17 April and 25-26 December – **M** 12.50/18.50 **st.** and a la carte 14.00/26.50 **st.** 3.75.

XX **Toto,** Walton House, Walton St., SW3 2JH, ✆ 589 0075, Italian rest. – AE VISA ES **a**
closed Easter and 4 days at Christmas – **M** a la carte 17.00/22.50 **t.** 3.00.

XX **Ponte Nuovo,** 126 Fulham Rd, SW3, ✆ 370 6656, Italian rest. – AE VISA CU **e**
closed Bank Holidays – **M** a la carte 10.00/18.00 **t.** 3.50.

XX **Gavvers,** 61-63 Lower Sloane St., SW1W 8DH, ✆ 730 5983, French rest. – AE VISA FT **e**
closed Sunday, 25 December-4 January and Bank Holidays – **M** (dinner only) 18.75 **st.** 2.80.

XX **Poissonnerie de l'Avenue,** 82 Sloane Av., SW3 3DZ, ✆ 589 2457, French rest., Seafood – AE VISA DS **u**
closed Sunday, 24 December-5 January and Bank Holidays – **M** a la carte 14.25/19.75 **t.** 3.50.

XX **Ménage à Trois,** 15 Beauchamp Pl., SW3 1NQ, ✆ 589 4252 – AE VISA ER **v**
closed Sunday and 25-26 December – **M** (booking essential) 10.95/30.00 **t.** and a la carte 14.40/25.00 **t.** 3.15.

XX **St. Quentin,** 243 Brompton Rd, SW3 2EP, ✆ 589 8005, French rest. – AE VISA DR **a**
closed 1 week at Christmas – **M** 9.50/12.90 **t.** and a la carte 15.30/22.40 **t.**

XX **Bagatelle,** 5 Langton St., SW10 0JL, ✆ 351 4185, French rest. – AE VISA pp. 7-10 JZ **u**
closed Sunday, 1 week Christmas and Bank Holidays – **M** 14.00 **t.** (lunch) and a la carte 19.00/21.20 **t.** 3.10.

XX **Pier 31,** 31 Cheyne Walk, SW3 5HG, ✆ 352 5006 – AE VISA pp. 7-10 KZ **c**
closed 25 and 26 December – **M** 13.00 **t.** (lunch) and a la carte 15.25/18.95 **t.** 3.25.

XX **Meridiana,** 169 Fulham Rd, SW3 6SP, ✆ 589 8815, Italian rest. – AE VISA DT **i**
M 14.50 **t.** (lunch) and a la carte 13.50/25.25 **t.** 4.50.

XX **Good Earth,** 233 Brompton Rd, SW3 2EP, ✆ 584 3658, Chinese rest. – AE VISA DR **c**
closed 24 to 27 December – **M** 15.95 **t.** and a la carte 7.25/14.15 **t.** 2.50.

XX **Good Earth,** 91 King's Rd, SW3, ✆ 352 9231, Chinese rest. – AE VISA EU **a**
closed 24 to 27 December – **M** 15.95 **t.** and a la carte 9.20/16.85 **t.** 2.50.

XX ✿ **Ma Cuisine,** 113 Walton St., SW3 2JY, ✆ 584 7585, French rest. – AE DS **a**
closed Saturday, Sunday, 1 week Easter, 15 July-15 August, and 1 week at Christmas – **M** (booking essential) a la carte 13.00/17.30 **t.** 5.55
Spec. Quiche de poireaux et saumon, Aiguillettes de bœuf paloise, Mousse brûlée.

X **Dan's,** 119 Sydney St., SW3 6NR, ✆ 352 2718 – AE VISA DU **s**
closed Saturday lunch, Sunday and 1 week at Christmas – **M** 13.50 **t.** (dinner) and a la carte approx. 11.20 **t.** 3.75.

X **Wheelers,** 33c King's Rd, SW3 4LX, ✆ 730 3023, Seafood – AE VISA FT **u**
M 9.50 **t.** (lunch) and a la carte 13.25/23.00 **t.** 3.00.

Monkey's, 1 Cale St., Chelsea Green, ☎ 352 4711 ET z

Nayab, 9 Park Walk, SW10 0AJ, ☎ 352 2137, Indian rest. – VISA BU z
closed 25-26 December, 1 January and Bank Holidays – **M** a la carte 11.75/15.65 **t.** 3.75.

Thierry's, 342 King's Rd, SW3, ☎ 352 3365, French rest. – VISA CU c
closed Sunday, Easter, 15 August-1 September, Christmas and Bank Holidays – **M** 7.00 **t.** (restricted lunch) and a la carte 2.95.

La Brasserie, 272 Brompton Rd, SW3 2AW, ☎ 584 1668, French rest. – VISA DS s
closed 24 to 26 December – **M** a la carte 10.20/13.10 **t.** 5.90.

Earl's Court – SW5/SW10 – Except where otherwise stated see pp. 14 and 15.

Barkston, 34-44 Barkston Gdns, SW5 0EW, ☎ 373 7851, Telex 8953154 – wc VISA AT c
M (buffet lunch)/dinner 12.00 **st.** and a la carte 3.95 – 5.00 – **80 rm** 40.00/50.00 **st.**

Hogarth, 27-35 Hogarth Rd, SW5 0QQ, ☎ 370 6831, Telex 8951994 – rest wc wc VISA AS a
M (bar lunch)/dinner a la carte 8.50/11.00 **st.** 3.00 – 3.50 – **85 rm** 39.50/49.50 **st.** – SB (weekends only)(November-April) 46.00/56.00 **st.**

Town House, 44-48 West Cromwell Rd, SW5 9QL, ☎ 373 4546 – wc VISA. pp. 7-10 HY o
40 rm 25.00/50.00 **st.**

Tiger Lee, 251 Old Brompton Rd, SW5 9HP, ☎ 370 2323, Chinese rest., Seafood – . VISA AU n
closed Christmas Day – **M** (dinner only) a la carte 15.50/24.00 **t.**

L'Olivier, 116 Finborough Rd, SW10, ☎ 370 4183 AU c

Brinkley's, 47 Hollywood Rd, SW10 9HY, ☎ 351 1683 – . VISA BU a
closed Sunday, Easter and Christmas – **M** (dinner only) 14.00 **t.**

Crystal Palace, 10 Hogarth Pl., SW5 0QT, ☎ 373 0754, Chinese (Peking, Szechuan) rest. – VISA pp. 7-10 HY a
M 11.50 **t.** and a la carte 2.80.

Kensington – SW7/W8/W11/W14 – Except where otherwise stated see pp. 7-10.

Royal Garden (Rank), Kensington High St., W8 4PT, ☎ 937 8000, Telex 263151, ≤ – VISA. pp. 14 and 15 AQ c
M Royal Roof *(closed Sunday)* (Dancing) 19.00/22.00 **st.** and a la carte 4.00 – 8.00 – **395 rm** 89.00/125.00 **st.**, **38 suites** 125.00/300.00 **st.**

Kensington Palace Thistle (Thistle), De Vere Gdns, W8 5RA, ☎ 937 8121, Telex 262422 – rest VISA. pp. 14 and 15 BQ a
M a la carte 15.00/20.00 **t.** 3.45 – 6.25 – **298 rm** 54.00/95.00 **st.**

Hilton International, 179-199 Holland Park Av., W11 4UL, ☎ 603 3355, Telex 919763 – VISA. GV s
M 13.50 **st.** and a la carte 17.00/20.00 **t.** 3.20 – 7.50 – **606 rm** 62.00/81.00 **t.**

London Tara (Best Western), Scarsdale Pl., W8 5SR, ☎ 937 7211, Telex 918834 – VISA. HX u
M 9.50 **t.** and a la carte 3.80 – 6.00 – **831 rm** 54.00/66.00 **st.**

Kensington Close (T.H.F.), Wrights Lane, W8 5SP, ☎ 937 8170, Telex 23914, , squash – VISA HX c
M (buffet lunch)/dinner a la carte 10.50/19.70 **st.** 3.60 – 6.25 – **529 rm** 48.00/59.00 **st.**

La Ruelle, 14 Wright's Lane, W8 6TF, ☎ 937 8525, French rest. – VISA HX i
closed Saturday, Sunday, Christmas, New Year and Bank Holidays – **M** 11.00 **st.** (lunch) and a la carte 18.40/25.20 **st.**

Belvedere, Holland House, Holland Park, ☎ 602 1238, ≤, French rest., « 19C Orangery in park », – GX x

Le Crocodile, 38c Kensington Church St., W8, ☎ 938 2501, French rest. – . VISA HV a
closed Saturday lunch and Sunday – **M** 14.00/17.95 **t.** and a la carte 4.50.

Clarke's, 124 Kensington Church St., W8, ☎ 221 9225 – . VISA HV c
closed Saturday, Sunday, 10 days Easter, 3 weeks August and 10 days Christmas – **M** 13.00/19.00 **st.** 3.50.

La Pomme d'Amour, 128 Holland Park Av., W11 4UE, ☎ 229 8532, French rest. – . VISA GV e
closed Saturday lunch, Sunday and Bank Holidays – **M** 9.75 **t.** (lunch) and a la carte 12.35/16.50 **t.** 4.25.

La Résidence, 148 Holland Park Av., W11 4UE, ☎ 221 6090, French rest. – GV z

La Paesana, 30 Uxbridge St., W8 7TA, ☎ 229 4332, Italian rest. – . VISA
closed Sunday, 17 to 20 April, 25 to 26 December and Bank Holidays – **M** a la carte 10.90/13.65 **t.** 2.40. pp. 16-17 AZ i

Mama San, 11 Russell Gdns, W14, ☎ 602 0312, Chinese rest. – GX e

North Kensington – W2/W10/W11 – Except where otherwise stated see pp. 3-6.

XXX **Leith's,** 92 Kensington Park Rd, W11 2PN, 229 4481 – . AE VISA GU **e**
closed 4 days at Christmas – **M** (dinner only) 29.50 **st.**

XX **Chez Moi,** 1 Addison Av., Holland Park, W11 4QS, 603 8267, French rest. – AE VISA pp. 7-10 GV **n**
closed Sunday, 2 weeks August, 2 weeks at Christmas and Bank Holidays – **M** (dinner only) 16.50 **t.** and a la carte 12.50/21.00 **t.** 5.50.

XX Monsieur Thompsons, 29 Kensington Park Rd, W11 2EU, 727 9957, French rest. GU **a**

South Kensington – SW5/SW7/W8 – pp.14 and 15.

Gloucester (Rank), 4-18 Harrington Gdns, SW7 4LH, 373 6030, Telex 917505 – . AE VISA. BS **r**
M 14.50/17.00 **t.** and a la carte 5.50 – 7.75 – **531 rm** 90.00/120.00 **t.**, **12 suites** 200.00/600.00 **t.**

Norfolk (Norfolk Cap.), 2-10 Harrington Rd, SW7 3ER, 589 8191, Telex 268852 – rest . AE VISA. CS **e**
M 11.75/15.00 **st.** and a la carte – 7.25 – **97 rm** 65.00/90.00 **st.**, **4 suites** 115.00/170.00 **st.**

London International (Swallow), 147c Cromwell Rd, SW5 0TH, 370 4200, Telex 27260 – . AE VISA AS **c**
M 15.00/30.00 **st.** and a la carte 6.00 – 3.50 – **416 rm** 52.00/68.00 **st.** – SB 73.00 **st.**

Rembrandt, 11 Thurloe Pl., SW7 2RS, 589 8100, Telex 295828, – . AE VISA. DS **x**
M 11.50 **st.** 3.50 – 6.75 – **200 rm** 57.00/80.00 **st.**, **1 suite** 57.00/105.00 **st.**

Gore (Best Western), 189 Queen's Gate, SW7 5EX, 584 6601, Telex 296244, « Attractive decor » – wc wc . AE VISA. BR **n**
M *(closed Saturday)* (coffee shop) a la carte 9.00/15.00 **t.** 3.00 – 6.00 – **54 rm** 54.00/110.00 **st.**

Vanderbilt, 68-86 Cromwell Rd, SW7 5BT, 589 2424, Telex 919867 – wc wc . BS **v**
230 rm.

John Howard, 4 Queen's Gate, SW7 5EH, 581 3011, Telex 8813397 – wc wc . AE VISA. BQ **i**
M 20.00/25.00 **st.** and a la carte 6.50 – 6.50 – **44 rm** 45.00/82.50 **st.**, **1 suite** 95.00/170.00 **st.**

Embassy House (Embassy), 31-33 Queen's Gate, SW7 5JA, 584 7222, Telex 8813387 – wc wc . AE VISA BR **e**
M *(closed lunch Saturday and Sunday)* (restricted lunch) 5.75/10.25 **st.** – **69 rm** 50.00/62.00 **st.**, **1 suite** 167.00 **st.**

Number Sixteen without rest., 15-17 Sumner Pl., SW7 3EG, 589 5232, Telex 266638, « Attractively furnished Victorian town houses », – wc wc . AE VISA. CT **c**
32 rm 33.00/85.00 **st.**

Alexander without rest., 9 Sumner Pl., SW7 3EE, 581 1591, Telex 917133, – wc wc . AE VISA. CT **a**
40 rm 50.00/80.00 **st.**

Number Eight without rest., Emperor's Gate, SW7 4HH, 370 7516 – wc wc . AE VISA. BS **o**
14 rm 33.00/40.00 **s.**

XXX **Bombay Brasserie,** Courtfield Close, 140 Gloucester Rd, SW7 4QH, 370 4040, Indian rest., « Raj- style decor, conservatory garden » – AE VISA BS **a**
closed 26 to 28 December – **M** (buffet lunch) 8.95/17.50 **t.** and a la carte.

XX **Reads,** 152 Old Brompton Rd, SW5 0BE, 373 2445 – . AE VISA BT **a**
closed Sunday dinner and Bank Holidays – **M** 10.50 **t.** (lunch) and a la carte 18.85/25.55 **t.**

XX **Hilaire,** 68 Old Brompton Rd, SW7 3LQ, 584 8993 – AE VISA CT **n**
closed Saturday lunch, Sunday and Bank Holidays – **M** (booking essential) 14.00/21.00 **t.** 4.00.

XX Golden Chopsticks, 1 Harrington Rd, SW7, 584 0855, Chinese rest. – CS **z**

XX **Tui,** 19 Exhibition Rd, SW7 2HE, 584 8359, Thai rest. – AE VISA CS **u**
M a la carte 10.10/15.30 **t.** 6.75.

XX **Memories of India,** 18 Gloucester Rd, SW7 4RB, 589 6450, Indian rest. – AE VISA BR **s**
M 10.50 **t.** and a la carte 4.05/8.75 **t.**

XX **Pun,** 53 Old Brompton Rd, SW7 3JX, 225 1609, Chinese rest. – . AE VISA CST **r**
M 5.50/12.80 **t.** and a la carte 3.20.

X Chanterelle, 119 Old Brompton Rd, SW7 3RN, 373 5522 BT **v**

RICHMOND-UPON-THAMES

Richmond – ✉ Surrey.

Richmond Park ✆ 876 3205.

Central Library, Little Green ✆ 940 9125.

XX ✿ **Lichfield's,** 13 Lichfield Terr., Sheen Rd, TW9 1DP, ✆ 940 5236 – ▤. AE
closed Saturday lunch, Sunday, Monday, first 2 weeks September and 1 week at Christmas – **M** (booking essential) 17.50/26.00 **st.** 3.50
Spec. Lamb with chick pea souffle, Roast duck, Iced butterscotch meringue cake.

WANDSWORTH

Battersea – ✉ SW8/SW11.

XXX ✿ **Chez Nico,** 129 Queenstown Rd, SW8 3RH, ✆ 720 6960, French rest. – VISA
closed lunch Saturday and Monday, Sunday, 4 days Easter, 3 weeks July-August, 1 week Christmas and Bank Holidays – **M** (booking essential) 14.50 **st.** (lunch) and a la carte 26.65/31.95 **st.** 6.00
Spec. Terrine de ris de veau et de morilles garnie d'une petite salade de mâche, Filets de rouget persillés au parfum de céleris, Savarin aux fruits et glace vanille, sirop de citron.

XX ✿ **L'Arlequin,** 123 Queenstown Rd, SW8 3RH, ✆ 622 0555, French rest. – ▤. AE VISA
closed Saturday, Sunday, 3 weeks August, 1 week at Christmas and Bank Holidays – **M** (booking essential) 12.50 **st.** (lunch) and a la carte 22.20/30.50 **st.** 5.00
Spec. Mi-cuit de saumon au vinaigre de framboise (February-August), Galette de pigeonneau fermier, Assiette gourmande.

XX **Alonso's,** 32 Queenstown Rd, SW8 3RX, ✆ 720 5986 – ▤. AE VISA
closed Saturday lunch and Sunday – **M** 9.75/12.75 **t.** and a la carte.

WESTMINSTER (City of)

Bayswater and Maida Vale – ✉ W2/W9 – Except where otherwise stated see pp. 16 and 17.

Royal Lancaster (Rank), Lancaster Terr., W2 2TY, ✆ 262 6737, Telex 24822, ← – ▤ rest TV ☎ & P. AE VISA. DZ **e**
M 12.50/16.95 **t.** and a la carte – 8.50 – **418 rm** 95.00/112.00 **t.**, **20 suites** 200.00/650.00 **st.**

White's (Mt. Charlotte), Bayswater Rd, 90-92 Lancaster Gate, W2 3NR, ✆ 262 2711, Telex 24771 – ▤ TV ☎ P. AE VISA CZ **v**
M 25.00 **t.** and a la carte 5.00 – 7.00 – **55 rm** 95.00/115.00 **t.**, **3 suites** 250.00 **t.** – SB (weekends only) 112.00/135.00 **st.**

London Metropole, Edgware Rd, W2 1JU, ✆ 402 4141, Telex 23711, ← – ▤ TV ☎ P. AE VISA. pp. 3-6 JT **c**
M (carving lunch)/dinner a la carte approx. 18.00 **s.** – 7.25 – **586 rm** 64.00/84.00 **st.**, **9 suites** 159.00 **st.**

Hospitality Inn (Mt. Charlotte), 104 Bayswater Rd, W2 3HL, ✆ 262 4461, Telex 22667, ← – TV ☎ P. AE VISA CZ **o**
M 6.75/9.00 **st.** and a la carte 3.50 – 6.50 – **175 rm** 55.00/85.00 **st.**, **1 suite**.

London Embassy (Embassy), 150 Bayswater Rd, W2 4RT, ✆ 229 1212, Telex 27727 – ▤ TV wc ☎ & P. AE VISA BZ **o**
M (carving rest.) 9.75 **st.** and a la carte 3.30 – 5.00 – **192 rm** 59.00/82.00 **st.**, **1 suite** 110.00 **st.**

Colonnade, 2 Warrington Cres., W9 1ER, ✆ 286 1052, Telex 298930 – TV wc wc ☎. AE VISA pp. 3-6 JT **e**
M *(closed Friday and Saturday)* (dinner only) 12.50 **t.** 2.80 – **53 rm** 35.50/55.00 **t.**

Mornington Lancaster (Best Western) without rest., 12 Lancaster Gate, W2 3LG, ✆ 262 7361, Telex 24281 – TV wc ☎. AE VISA DZ **s**
closed 22 December-2 January – 3.00 – **63 rm** 30.00/73.00 **st.**

XXX **Bombay Palace,** 50 Connaught St., Hyde Park Sq., W2, ✆ 723 8855, North Indian rest. – AE VISA EY **a**
M 9.95/10.50 **t.** and a la carte 10.50/13.50 **t.** 5.50.

XX **San Marino,** 26 Sussex Pl., W2 2TH, ✆ 723 8395, Italian rest. – AE VISA EY **u**
closed Sunday and Bank Holidays – **M** a la carte 11.75/18.35 **t.** 3.50.

Belgravia – ✉ SW1 – Except where otherwise stated see pp. 14 and 15.

Berkeley, Wilton Pl., SW1X 7RL, ✆ 235 6000, Telex 919252, – ▤ TV ☎ &. AE VISA. FQ **e**
M Restaurant *(closed Saturday)* a la carte 21.50/27.00 **st.** 3.40 – **Buttery** *(closed Sunday, August and Bank Holidays)* (buffet lunch) dinner a la carte 15.25/20.00 **st.** 3.40 – 4.50 – **160 rm** 120.00/195.00 **st.**, **26 suites**.

Lowndes Thistle (Thistle), 21 Lowndes St., SW1X 9ES, ☎ 235 6020, Telex 919065 – FR i
M a la carte 16.00/20.00 **t.** – 7.00 – **79 rm** 85.00/135.00 **st.**

Sheraton-Belgravia, 20 Chesham Pl., SW1X 8HQ, ☎ 235 6040, Telex 919020 – VISA FR u
M *(closed lunch Saturday and Bank Holidays)* 16.00/20.00 **t.** 3.50 – 7.50 – **89 rm** 90.00/120.00, **7 suites** 185.00/220.00 **t.**

Motcombs, 26 Motcomb St., SW1X 8JU, ☎ 235 6382 – VISA FR z
closed Sunday – **M** a la carte 13.85/17.60 **t.** 3.50.

Salloos, 62-64 Kinnerton St., SW1 8ER, ☎ 235 4444, Indian and Pakistani rest. – FQ a

Le Trou Normand, 27 Motcomb St., SW1, ☎ 235 1668, French rest. – VISA FR z
closed Sunday and 2 weeks at Christmas – **M** 14.50/23.50 **t.**

Hyde Park and Knightsbridge – SW1/SW7 – pp. 14 and 15.

Harrods, Knightsbridge, SW1 ☎ 730 3488.

Hyde Park (T.H.F.), 66 Knightsbridge, SW1Y 7LA, ☎ 235 2000, Telex 262057, – VISA EQ v
M 14.50/20.00 **st.** and a la carte 5.45 – 9.00 – **180 rm** 135.00/150.00 **st.**, **20 suites**.

Shezan, 16-22 Cheval Pl., Montpelier St., SW7 1ES, ☎ 589 7918, Indian and Pakistani rest. – VISA ER c
closed Sunday and Bank Holidays – **M** 9.75 **st.** and a la carte 8.75/15.00 **st.** 5.50.

Montpeliano, 13 Montpelier St., SW7 1HQ, ☎ 589 0032, Italian rest. ER e

Mayfair – W1 – pp. 12 and 13.

Claridge's, Brook St., W1A 2JQ, ☎ 629 8860, Telex 21872 – VISA BL c
M a la carte 28.50/36.20 **st.** 3.40 – **Causerie** 13.50 **st.** (lunch) and a la carte 22.30/34.80 **st.** 3.40 – 11.50 – **205 rm** 110.00/195.00 **st.**, **55 suites** 310.00/600.00 **st.**

Dorchester, Park Lane, W1A 2HJ, ☎ 629 8888, Telex 887704 – VISA BN z
M (see **The Terrace** below) – **Grill** 17.00 **t.** and a la carte 3.60 – 9.00 – **275 rm** 145.00/175.00 **st.**, **66 suites** 250.00/800.00 **st.**

Grosvenor House (T.H.F.), Park Lane, W1A 3AA, ☎ 499 6363, Telex 24871, – VISA AM a
M (see **90 Park Lane** below) – 9.50 – **468 rm** 115.00/140.00 **st.**, **50 suites**.

Inn on the Park, Hamilton Pl., Park Lane, W1A 1AZ, ☎ 499 0888, Telex 22771 – VISA BP a
M Four Seasons 20.50/22.50 **st.** and a la carte 29.50/34.50 **st.** 6.50 – **Lanes** 21.00 **st.** (lunch) and a la carte 20.50/22.50 **st.** 6.50 – 8.25 – **228 rm** 135.00/165.00 **s.**, **19 suites** 260.00/615.00 **s.**

Le Meridien, Piccadilly, W1V 0BH, ☎ 734 8000, Telex 25795, , squash – VISA EM a
M 18.15/27.50 **st.** and a la carte 6.00 – 8.60 – **284 rm** 125.00/150.00 **st.**, **19 suites** 210.00/450.00 **st.**

✿ Connaught, 16 Carlos Pl., W1Y 6AL, ☎ 499 7070 – rest BM e
M (booking essential) a la carte 23.25/40.30 **t.** 3.70 – **90 rm**, **24 suites**
Spec. Pâté de turbot froid au homard, sauce pudeur, Rendez-vous du pêcheur, sauce légère au parfum d'Armorique, Salmis de canard strasbourgeoise en surprise.

Athenaeum (Rank), 116 Piccadilly, W1V 0BJ, ☎ 499 3464, Telex 261589 – rest VISA CP s
M 17.50 **st.** (lunch) and a la carte 16.35/26.90 **st.** 4.50 – 8.00 – **112 rm** 117.00/140.00 **st.**, **6 suites** 200.00/240.00 **st.**

Brown's (T.H.F.), 29-34 Albemarle St., W1A 4SW, ☎ 493 6020, Telex 28686 – VISA DM e
M 22.00/23.00 **st.** and a la carte 4.25 – 9.25 – **125 rm** 99.00/130.00 **st.**, **5 suites**.

May Fair (Inter-Con.), Stratton St., W1A 2AN, ☎ 629 7777, Telex 262526 – VISA DN z
M 16.00/23.50 **t.** and a la carte 5.70 – 8.80 – **322 rm** 123.00/144.00, **24 suites** 273.00/700.00.

Marriott, Duke St., Grosvenor Sq., W1A 4AW, ☎ 493 1232, Telex 268101 – VISA BL a
M a la carte 17.30/26.00 **t.** – 8.00 – **228 rm** 125.00/160.00 **t.**, **9 suites** 230.00/800.00 **t.**

Inter-Continental (Inter-Con.), 1 Hamilton Pl., Hyde Park Corner, W1V 0QY, ☎ 409 3131, Telex 25853 – BP o
M (see **Le Soufflé** below) – **491 rm**, **15 suites**.

Britannia (Inter-Con.), Grosvenor Sq., W1A 3AN, ☎ 629 9400, Telex 23941 – VISA BM x
M 15.50 **t.** and a la carte 4.50 – 9.20 – **354 rm** 105.00/130.00 **s.**, **12 suites** 400.00 **s.**

Westbury (T.H.F.), New Bond St. (entrance on Conduit St.), W1A 4UH, ✆ 629 7755, Telex 24378 – TV AE VISA DM **a**
M 25.00 **st.** and a la carte 20.65/27.50 **st.** 5.45 – 8.75 – **240 rm** 95.00/110.00 **st.**, **15 suites**.

Londonderry, Park Lane, W1Y 8AP, ✆ 493 7292, Telex 263292 – TV AE VISA BP **i**
M 19.00 **st.** and a la carte 21.55/29.95 **st.** 4.10 – 8.50 – **150 rm** 132.25/161.00 **st.**, **12 suites** 207.00/400.00 **st.**

London Hilton on Park Lane, 22 Park Lane, W1A 2HH, ✆ 493 8000, Telex 24873, London – TV AE VISA BP **e**
M 19.75/26.70 **t.** and a la carte 6.50 – 9.00 – **501 rm** 110.00/157.00, **54 suites** 240.00/760.00.

Holiday Inn, 3 Berkeley St., W1X 6NE, ✆ 493 8282, Telex 24561 – TV AE VISA DN **r**
M 12.50/32.00 **st.** and a la carte 4.00 – 8.00 – **185 rm** 97.00/110.00 **st.**, **7 suites** 220.00/360.00 **st.** – SB (weekends only) 126.00/150.00 **st.**

Park Lane, Piccadilly, W1Y 8BX, ✆ 499 6321, Telex 21533 – TV AE VISA BP **x**
M 13.50/19.50 **st.** and a la carte 17.95/22.45 **st.** 4.00 – 7.50 – **323 rm** 99.95/119.95 **st.**, **54 suites** 150.00/400.00 **st.**

Chesterfield, 35 Charles St., W1X 8LX, ✆ 491 2622, Telex 269394 – TV AE VISA CN **c**
M (buffet lunch Saturday and Sunday)/a la carte 15.00/23.00 **t.** 5.00 – 7.50 – **112 rm** 95.00/115.00 **t.**, **1 suite** 200.00/350.00 **t.**

XXXXX ✲✲ **The Terrace,** (at Dorchester H.), Park Lane, W1A 2HJ, ✆ 629 8888, Telex 887704, French rest. – AE VISA BN **z**
closed Sunday – **M** (dinner only) 35.00 **st.** and a la carte 17.70/28.70 **st.** 3.60
Spec. Parfait de foies de volailles aux truffes, Symphonie de fruits de mer, Sole farcie à la brunoise de légumes gratinée.

XXXXX Mirabelle, 56 Curzon St., W1Y 8DL, ✆ 499 4636, – CN **a**

XXXXX ✲ **90 Park Lane** (T.H.F.), (at Grosvenor House H.), Park Lane, W1V 7RD, ✆ 409 1290, Telex 24871 – AE VISA AM **a**
closed Saturday lunch, Sunday and Bank Holidays – **M** 22.50/42.50 **st.** and a la carte 28.45/46.20 **st.** 7.50.

XXXX ✲✲✲ **Le Gavroche,** 43 Upper Brook St., W1P 1PS, ✆ 408 0881, French rest. – AE VISA AM **c**
closed Saturday, Sunday, 23 December-2 January and Bank Holidays – **M** (booking essential) 19.50/40.00 **st.** and a la carte 28.00/44.00 **st.** 5.60
Spec. Soufflé suissesse, Assiette du boucher, Sablé aux fraises.

XXXX ✲ **Le Soufflé** (at Inter-Continental H.), 1 Hamilton Pl., Hyde Park Corner, W1V 0QY, ✆ 409 3131, Telex 25853 – AE VISA BP **o**
M *(closed Saturday lunch)* 19.00/29.50 **st.** and a la carte
Spec. Le medley du gourmand, Le jumelé d'agneau en croûte de poivre aux deux sauces, Le soufflé aux fruits de la passion.

XXXX **Scott's,** 20 Mount St., W1Y 6HE, ✆ 629 5248, Seafood – AE VISA BM **r**
closed Sunday lunch, Christmas and Bank Holidays – **M** a la carte 20.75/36.45 **t.**

XXX **Princess Garden,** 8-10 North Audley St., W1Y 1WF, ✆ 493 3223, Chinese (Peking) rest. – AE VISA AL **z**
M 20.00/35.00 and a la carte 4.00.

XXX **Tiberio,** 22 Queen St., W1X 7PJ, ✆ 629 3561, Italian rest., Dancing – AE VISA
closed Saturday lunch and Sunday – **M** a la carte 13.50/27.75 **t.** 4.00. CN **z**

XX **Greenhouse,** 27a Hay's Mews, W1X 7RJ, ✆ 499 3331 – AE VISA BN **a**
closed Saturday lunch, Sunday, 24 December-5 January and Bank Holidays – **M** a la carte 13.60/18.70 **t.** 3.05.

XX **Langan's Brasserie,** Stratton St., W1X 5FD, ✆ 491 8822 – AE VISA DN **e**
closed Saturday lunch, Sunday and Bank Holidays – **M** (booking essential) a la carte 10.80/17.40 **t.** 4.15.

XX **Miyama,** 38 Clarges St., W1Y 7PJ, ✆ 499 2443, Japanese rest. – AE VISA
closed Saturday lunch, Sunday and Bank Holidays – **M** 7.00/24.00 **t.** and a la carte. CN **e**

XX **Mr. Kai,** 65 South Audley St., W1 5FD, ✆ 493 8988, Chinese (Peking) rest. – AE VISA BM **v**
M a la carte 20.00/30.00 **t.**

XX Shogun (at Britannia H.), Adams Row, W1, ✆ 493 1255, Telex 8813271, Japanese rest. BM **x**

XX **Ho-Ho,** 29 Maddox St., W1, ✆ 493 1228, Chinese rest. – AE VISA DL **x**
closed Sunday and Bank Holidays – **M** 8.50/18.60 **t.** and a la carte.

XX **One Two Three,** 27 Davies St., W1 1LN, ✆ 409 0750, Japanese rest. – AE VISA BM **s**
closed Saturday, Sunday and Bank Holidays – **M** 9.90/25.00 **t.** and a la carte 2.80.

Ikeda, 30 Brook St., W1Y 1AG, ✆ 629 2730, Japanese rest. – ▤. AE VISA CKL **a**
closed Saturday and Sunday – **M** 8.90/25.00 **t.** and a la carte.

Trattoria Fiori, 87-88 Mount St., W1Y 5HG, ✆ 499 1447, Italian rest. – AE VISA
closed Sunday and Bank Holidays – **M** 25.30 **t.** and a la carte 16.35/24.25 **t.** 3.50. BM **o**

Regent's Park and Marylebone – ✉ NW1/NW6/NW8/W1 – Except where otherwise stated see pp. 12 and 13.

Selfridges, Oxford St., W1 ✆ 730 3488.

Churchill, 30 Portman Sq., W1A 4ZX, ✆ 486 5800, Telex 264831 – AE VISA. AJ **x**
M a la carte 15.20/26.80 **st.** 2.85 – 7.50 – **487 rm** 120.00/135.00 **s.**, **39 suites** 220.00/525.00 **s.**

Montcalm, Great Cumberland Pl., W1A 2LF, ✆ 402 4288, Telex 28710 – AE VISA pp. 16 and 17 FY **x**
M 15.00/35.00 **st.** and a la carte 3.65 – 5.50 – **116 rm** 115.00/137.00 **st.**

Portman Inter-Continental (Inter-Con.), 22 Portman Sq., W1H 9FL, ✆ 486 5844, Telex 261526 – AJ **o**
278 rm, **8 suites**.

Holiday Inn, 134 George St., W1H 6DN, ✆ 723 1277, Telex 27983, – AE VISA pp. 16 and 17 FY **i**
M approx. 13.50 **st.** and a la carte – 7.10 – **241 rm** 105.00/127.00 **st.**, **2 suites** 300.00/500.00 **st.**

Selfridge Thistle (Thistle), 400 Orchard St., W1H 0JS, ✆ 408 2080, Telex 22361 – AE VISA. AK **e**
M a la carte 22.00/28.00 **t.** 3.95 – 6.75 – **298 rm** 90.00/125.00 **st.**

Ladbroke Westmoreland (Ladbroke), 18 Lodge Rd, NW8 7JT, ✆ 722 7722, Telex 23101 – AE VISA pp. 3-6 JS **v**
M (carving rest.) 13.00 **t.** and a la carte 3.50 – 7.50 – **347 rm** 73.00/100.00 **t.** – SB (weekends only) 75.00/95.00 **st.**

Clifton Ford, 47 Welbeck St., W1M 8DN, ✆ 486 6600, Telex 22569 – AE VISA BH **a**
M 10.50/10.75 **st.** and a la carte 4.00 – 7.50 – **220 rm** 68.00/88.00 **st.**, **2 suites** 150.00/300.00 **st.**

St. George's (T.H.F.), Langham Pl., W1N 8QS, ✆ 580 0111, Telex 27274, ← – AE VISA pp. 3-6 LT **a**
M 13.50/14.50 **st.** and a la carte 3.40 – 7.25 – **85 rm** 78.00/100.00 **st.**, **3 suites**.

Cumberland (T.H.F.), Marble Arch, W1A 4RF, ✆ 262 1234, Telex 22215 – AE VISA. AK **n**
M (carving rest.) 16.00/18.00 **st.** and a la carte 3.40 – 6.50 – **894 rm** 72.00/92.00 **st.**, **9 suites**.

Durrants, 26-32 George St., W1H 6BJ, ✆ 935 8131, Telex 894919 – wc AE VISA. AH **e**
M a la carte 13.20/17.30 **t.** 3.25 – 6.00 – **96 rm** 40.00/78.00 **st.**, **3 suites** 90.00/150.00 **st.**

Sherlock Holmes (Ladbroke), 108 Baker St., W1M 1LB, ✆ 486 6161, Telex 8954837 – wc AE VISA pp. 3-6 KT **a**
M 11.25 **t.** and a la carte 3.80 – 6.75 – **125 rm** 75.00/100.00 **t.**

Savoy Court, Granville Pl., W1H 0EH, ✆ 408 0130, Telex 8955515 – wc wc AE VISA. AK **c**
M (buffet lunch)/dinner 9.50 **t.** and a la carte 11.00/18.05 **st.** 3.00 – 6.00 – **97 rm** 52.90/74.90 **st.**

Dorset Square, 39-40 Dorset Sq., NW1 6QN, ✆ 723 7874, Telex 263964, « Attractively furnished Regency town house » – wc wc AE VISA pp. 3-6 KT **s**
M a la carte 14.50/19.50 **t.** – 8.00 – **30 rm** 55.00/90.00 **t.**

Bryanston Court, 56-60 Great Cumberland Pl., W1H 7FD, ✆ 262 3141, Group Telex 262076 – wc wc AE VISA. pp. 16 and 17 FY **z**
M *(closed Saturday, Sunday and Bank Holidays)* a la carte 9.50/13.75 **t.** 3.00 – 5.00 – **53 rm** 45.00/60.00 **st.**

Odins, 27 Devonshire St., W1N 1RS, ✆ 935 7296 – AE pp. 3-6 KT **n**
closed Saturday lunch, Sunday and Bank Holidays – **M** 12.50 **t.** (lunch) and a la carte 17.10/25.80 **t.**

❀ **Rue St. Jacques,** 5 Charlotte St., W1P 1HD, ✆ 637 0222, French rest. – ▤. AE VISA pp. 3-6 MT **c**
closed Saturday lunch, Sunday, 1 week at Christmas and Bank Holidays – **M** 15.00 **t.** (lunch) and a la carte 23.75/36.25 **t.**
Spec. Charlotte de coquilles St. Jacques, sauce légère, Le perdreau rôti aux deux sauces, Biscuit aux deux parfums.

XX **Gaylord,** 79-81 Mortimer St., W1N 7TB, ✆ 580 3615, Indian and Pakistani rest. – ▤. ⊠ AE ⓓ VISA pp. 3-6 LT **c**
M 7.75/8.50 **t.** and a la carte 🍷 3.20.

XX La Pavona, 5-7 Blandford St., W1H 3AF, ✆ 486 9696, Italian rest. – ▤ BH **c**

X Le Muscadet, 25 Paddington St., W1M 3RF, ✆ 935 2883, French rest. – ▤ KT **e**

X L'Aventure, 3 Blenheim Terr., NW8 4JS, ✆ 624 6232, French rest. JR **s**

St. James's – ✉ W1/SW1/WC2 – pp. 12 and 13.

Ritz, Piccadilly, W1V 9DG, ✆ 493 8181, Telex 267200, « Elegant restaurant in Louis XV style » – ▯ TV ☎. ⊠ AE ⓓ VISA. ✻ DN **a**
M 19.50/29.50 **st.** and a la carte 🍷 6.75 – ☕ 9.25 – **128 rm** 130.00/190.00 **st.**, **14 suites** 320.00/590.00 **st.**

Stafford 🐎, 16-18 St. James's Pl., SW1A 1NJ, ✆ 493 0111, Telex 28602 – ▯ TV ☎. 🏛. ⊠ AE ⓓ VISA. ✻ DN **u**
M 17.00/20.00 **st.** and a la carte 🍷 4.30 – ☕ 7.50 – **62 rm** 115.00/155.00 **st.**, **5 suites** 175.00/350.00 **st.**

Dukes 🐎, 35 St. James's Pl., SW1A 1NY, ✆ 491 4840, Telex 28283 – ▯ TV ☎. ⊠ AE ⓓ VISA. ✻ EP **x**
M 17.50 **t.** (lunch) and a la carte 23.00/28.00 **t.** – ☕ 8.00 – **52 rm** 110.00/145.00 **t.**, **16 suites** 200.00/450.00 **t.**

Cavendish (T.H.F.), Jermyn St., SW1Y 6JF, ✆ 930 2111, Telex 263187 – ▯ ▤ rest TV ☎ ♿ Ⓟ. 🏛. ⊠ AE ⓓ VISA EN **i**
M (bar lunch Saturday) 14.00 **st.** (lunch) and a la carte 18.00/26.25 **st.** 🍷 4.50 – ☕ 8.00 – **253 rm** 81.00/101.00 **st.**

Royal Trafalgar Thistle (Thistle), Whitcomb St., WC2H 7HG, ✆ 930 4477, Telex 298564 – ▯ ▤ rest TV ⛀wc ☎. ⊠ AE ⓓ VISA GM **r**
M a la carte 10.50/15.50 **t.** 🍷 3.85 – ☕ 6.25 – **108 rm** 60.00/95.00 **st.**

Pastoria without rest., 3-6 St. Martin's St., WC2H 7HL, ✆ 930 8641, Telex 25538 – ▯ TV ⛀wc ☎. ⊠ AE ⓓ VISA. ✻ GM **v**
☕ 6.00 – **54 rm** 60.00/80.00 **st.**

XXXXX Maxim's de Paris, 32-34 Panton St., SW1, ✆ 839 4809, French rest., Dancing – ▤ GM **a**

XXXX **A L'Ecu de France,** 111 Jermyn St., SW1Y 6HB, ✆ 930 2837, French rest. – ▤. ⊠ AE ⓓ VISA FM **z**
closed lunch Saturday and Sunday – **M** 14.75/21.75 **st.** and a la carte 🍷 5.50.

XXX ✿ **Suntory,** 72-73 St. James's St., SW1A 1PH, ✆ 409 0201, Japanese rest. – ▤. ⊠ AE ⓓ VISA EP **z**
closed Sunday and Bank Holidays – **M** 25.00 **t.** and a la carte 12.20/26.20 **t.**
Spec. Teppan-yaki, Shabu-Shabu, Tempura.

XX **Le Caprice,** Arlington House, Arlington St., SW1A 1RT, ✆ 629 2239 – ▤. ⊠ AE ⓓ VISA
closed Saturday lunch and 24 December-2 January – **M** a la carte 11.00/15.25 **t.** DN **c**

XX Green's, 36 Duke St., SW1Y 6BR, ✆ 930 4566, English rest. – ▤ EN **n**

Soho – ✉ W1/WC2 – pp. 12 and 13.

XXX **La Bastide,** 50 Greek St., W1V 5LQ, ✆ 734 3300 – ⊠ AE ⓓ VISA GK **e**
closed Saturday lunch, Sunday and Bank Holidays – **M** 12.50 **t.** and a la carte 14.60/16.40 **t.**

XXX **Red Fort,** 77 Dean St., W1V 5HA, ✆ 437 2525, Indian rest. – ⊠ AE ⓓ VISA FJK **r**
closed 25 and 26 December – **M** a la carte 7.40/14.85 **t.**

XXX **Leonis Quo Vadis,** 26-29 Dean St., W1V 6LL, ✆ 437 9585, Italian rest. – ⊠ AE ⓓ VISA
closed lunch Saturday and Sunday, 25 December, 1 January and Bank Holidays – **M** a la carte 12.20/19.65 **t.** FK **u**

XX **Au Jardin des Gourmets,** 5 Greek St., Soho Sq., W1V 5LA, ✆ 437 1816, French rest. – ⊠ AE ⓓ VISA GJ **a**
closed lunch Saturday and Bank Holidays, Sunday, Easter and Christmas – **M** 12.50/23.50 **t.** and a la carte 14.15/23.45 **t.** 🍷 2.75.

XX **L'Escargot,** 48 Greek St., W1V 5LQ, ✆ 437 2679 – ⊠ AE ⓓ VISA GK **e**
closed Saturday lunch, Sunday, Easter Christmas and Bank Holidays – **M** a la carte approx. 18.00 **t.**

XX **Gay Hussar,** 2 Greek St., W1V 6NB, ✆ 437 0973, Hungarian rest. – ▤ GJ **c**
closed Sunday – **M** 10.50 **t.** (lunch) and a la carte 14.00/19.50 **t.** 🍷 3.50.

XX **Chesa (Swiss Centre),** 2 New Coventry St., W1V 3HG, ✆ 734 1291 – ▤. ⊠ AE ⓓ VISA GM **n**
M 15.00/18.50 **st.** 🍷 1.30.

XX **Venezia,** 21 Great Chapel St., W1V 3AQ, ✆ 437 6506, Italian rest. – ⊠ AE ⓓ VISA
closed Saturday lunch, Sunday and Bank Holidays – **M** a la carte 10.80/13.50 **t.** 🍷 2.50. FJ **a**

XX **Kaya,** 22-25 Dean St., W1V 5AL, ✆ 437 6630, Korean rest. – ▤. ⊠ AE ⓓ VISA FJ **i**
closed lunch Saturday and Sunday – **M** 17.00 **t.** and a la carte 🍷 3.30.

XX **Last Days of the Raj,** 42-43 Dean St., W1V 5AR, ✆ 439 0972, Indian rest. – ▤. ⊠ AE ⓓ VISA FK **n**
M 15.00/18.00 **st.** and a la carte 9.15/12.50 **st.**

XX **Poons,** 4 Leicester St., WC2, ℘ 437 1528, Chinese rest. – ▤ GM i
closed Sunday and Christmas – **M** 6.00 **t.** and a la carte 4.20/11.00 **t.**

XX **Old Budapest,** 6 Greek St., W1, ℘ 437 2006, Hungarian rest. – EN AE VISA GJ c
closed Sunday and Bank Holidays – **M** 9.00/15.60 **t.** and a la carte 10.60/15.60 **t.** 🍷 4.50.

XX Rugantino, 26 Romilly St., W1V 5TQ, ℘ 437 5302, Italian rest. GK u

XX Mayflower, 68-70 Shaftesbury Av., W1, ℘ 734 9207, Chinese (Canton) rest. – ▤ FL o

XX Fuji, 36-40 Brewer St., W1R 3HP, ℘ 734 0957, Japanese rest. FL c

X Alastair Little, 49 Frith St., W1, ℘ 734 5183 FK o

X **Frith's,** 14 Frith St., W1V 5TS, ℘ 439 3370 – EN AE ⓓ VISA FGK s
closed Saturday lunch and Sunday – **M** 18.00 **t.**

X **Chiang Mai,** 48 Frith St., W1, ℘ 437 7444, Thai rest. – EN AE VISA FGK o
M a la carte 6.75/9.75 **st.** 🍷 2.75.

X **Fung Shing,** 15 Lisle St., WC2H 7BE, ℘ 437 1539, Chinese (Canton) rest. – EN AE ⓓ VISA – **M** 8.00/15.00 **t.** and a la carte 9.70/14.00 **t.** GL a

X **Gallery Rendez vous,** 53-55 Beak St., W1R 3LF, ℘ 734 0445, Chinese (Peking) rest. – ▤. EN AE ⓓ VISA EL a
M a la carte approx. 9.00 🍷 3.20.

X **Joy King Lau,** 3 Leicester St., WC2H 7BL, ℘ 437 1132, Chinese rest. – AE ⓓ GM e
M a la carte 12.50/20.80 **t.** 🍷 2.25.

X **Saigon,** 45 Frith St., W1V 5TE, ℘ 437 7109, Vietnamese rest. – EN AE ⓓ VISA FGK x
closed Sunday and Bank Holidays – **M** 11.00 **t.** and a la carte approx. 12.00 **t.**

X Cafe Loire, 12 Great Marlborough St., W1, ℘ 434 2666, French rest. – EN AE ⓓ VISA EK e
closed Saturday lunch, Sunday and Bank Holidays – **M** a la carte 11.65/15.60 **t.** 🍷 3.20.

X Nam Long, 40 Frith St., W1, ℘ 439 1835, Vietnamese rest. GK v

X Diamond, 23 Lisle St., WC2, ℘ 437 2517, Chinese (Canton) rest. – ▤ GL a

Strand and Covent Garden – ✉ WC2 – p. 17.

Savoy, Strand, WC2R 0EU, ℘ 836 4343, Telex 24234 – lift ▤ TV ☎. EN AE ⓓ VISA. EX a
M Grill *(closed Saturday lunch, Sunday, first 3 weeks August and Bank Holidays)* a la carte 15.75/30.25 **st.** 🍷 3.50 – **River** 16.50/25.00 **st.** and a la carte 🍷 3.30 – ☕ 8.25 – **200 rm** 120.00/195.00 **st.**, **48 suites** 230.00/450.00 **st.**

Howard, 12 Temple Pl., WC2R 2PR, ℘ 836 3555, Telex 268047 – lift ▤ TV ☎. EN AE ⓓ VISA. FV e
M a la carte 20.10/33.00 **st.** – ☕ 9.00 – **141 rm** 145.00/161.00 **st.**, **2 suites** 170.00/299.00 **st.**

Waldorf (T.H.F.), Aldwych, WC2B 4DD, ℘ 836 2400, Telex 24574 – lift ▤ rest TV ☎. EN AE ⓓ VISA EV x
closed Christmas and New Year – **M** *(closed Saturday lunch, Sunday and Bank Holidays)* 16.50/19.50 **st.** and a la carte 🍷 5.60 – ☕ 7.25 – **310 rm** 73.00/90.00 **st.**

XXXX **Boulestin,** 1a Henrietta St., WC2E 8PS, ℘ 836 7061, French rest. – ▤. EN AE ⓓ VISA EV r
closed Saturday lunch, Sunday, last 3 weeks August, 1 week Christmas and Bank Holidays – **M** 14.50 **t.** (lunch) and a la carte 19.20/25.00 **t.** 🍷 5.00.

XXX **Inigo Jones,** 14 Garrick St., WC2E 9BJ, ℘ 836 6456 – ▤. EN AE ⓓ VISA DV e
closed Saturday lunch, Sunday, 24 December-5 January and Bank Holidays – **M** 16.25 **t.** (lunch) and a la carte 🍷 5.85.

XXX **Simpson's-in-the-Strand,** 100 Strand, WC2R 0EW, ℘ 836 9112, English rest. – ▤. EN AE ⓓ VISA EV o
closed Sunday, Easter, 25 December and Bank Holidays – **M** a la carte 14.00/19.50 **st.** 🍷 3.00.

XXX **Thomas de Quincey's,** 36 Tavistock St., WC2E 7PB, ℘ 240 3972 – EN AE ⓓ VISA EV c
closed Saturday lunch, Sunday and Bank Holidays – **M** a la carte 18.55/24.95 **t.** 🍷 3.60.

XX **Interlude,** 7-8 Bow St., WC2E 7AH, ℘ 379 6473, French rest. – ▤. EN AE ⓓ VISA DEV x
closed Saturday lunch and Sunday – **M** 17.50/30.00 **st.** 🍷 3.00.

XX **Tourment d'Amour,** 19 New Row, WC2N 4LA, ℘ 240 5348, French rest. – EN AE ⓓ VISA DV z
closed Saturday lunch, Sunday and Christmas – **M** 18.00 **t.**

XX Sheekey's, 28-32 St. Martin's Court, WC2N 4AL, ℘ 240 2565, Seafood – ▤ DV v

XX **Chez Solange,** 35 Cranbourn St., WC2H 7AD, ℘ 836 5886, French rest. – ▤. EN AE ⓓ VISA DV i
closed Sunday lunch – **M** 13.00 **t.** and a la carte 14.75/20.00 **t.**

XX **Bates,** 11 Henrietta St., WC2, ℘ 240 7600 – EN AE ⓓ VISA DV u
closed Saturday lunch, Sunday and Bank Holidays – **M** 15.00 **st.** and a la carte 12.90/20.20 **t.**

XX Azami, 13-15 West St., WC2H 9BL, ℘ 240 0634, Japanese rest. pp. 12 and 13 GK z

XX **Frère Jacques,** 38 Longacre, WC2, ℘ 836 7823, Seafood – ▤. EN AE ⓓ VISA DV n
M a la carte 11.45/20.50 **t.** 🍷 3.25.

XX **Poons of Covent Garden,** 41 King St., WC2E 8JS, ✆ 240 1743, Chinese (Canton) rest. – AE ① VISA DV r
closed Sunday and 24 to 27 December – **M** a la carte 6.50/15.75 **t.** 4.50.

X Cafe Pelican, 45 St. Martins Lane, WC2N 4EJ, ✆ 379 0309, French rest., « Art deco » – ▤ DX e

X **Magnos Brasserie,** 65a Long Acre, WC2E 9JH, ✆ 836 6077, French rest. – ☒ AE ① VISA EV e
closed Saturday lunch, Sunday and 24 December-2 January – **M** 8.45 **st.** (dinner) and a la carte 13.70/20.90 **t.** 4.45.

X **Laguna,** 50 St. Martin's Lane, WC2N 4EA, ✆ 836 0960, Italian rest. – ☒ AE ① VISA
closed Sunday and Bank Holidays – **M** 7.50/8.50 and a la carte 2.35. DV z

X Flounders, 19 Tavistock St., WC2, ✆ 836 3925, Seafood – ▤ EV a

X **Happy Wok,** 52 Floral St., WC2, ✆ 836 3696, Chinese rest. – ☒ AE ① VISA DV x
closed Sunday – **M** 19.00 **t.** and a la carte 6.50/10.80 **t.**

X **Grimes,** 6 Garrick St., WC2R 9BH, ✆ 836 7008, Seafood – ☒ AE ① VISA DV e
closed Saturday lunch, Sunday, 24 to 27 December and Bank Holidays – **M** a la carte 13.35/14.85 **t.** 2.60.

Victoria – ✉ SW1 – Except where otherwise stated see p. 16.

St. James Court, Buckingham Gate, SW1 6AF, ✆ 834 6655, Telex 938075 – ▤ rest ☎. ☒ AE ① VISA CV i
M (see **Auberge de Provence** and **Inn of Happiness** below) – ☕ 8.00 – **391 rm** 95.00/135.00 **s.**, **10 suites** 140.00/165.00 **s.**

Goring, 15 Beeston Pl., Grosvenor Gdns, SW1W 0JW, ✆ 834 8211, Telex 919166 – ▤ TV ☎. ☒ AE ① VISA. BV a
M 14.00/16.00 **s.** and a la carte 5.00 – ☕ 7.00 – **90 rm** 75.00/115.00 **st.**, **4 suites** 150.00 **st.**

Royal Horseguards Thistle (Thistle), 2 Whitehall Court, SW1A 2EX, ✆ 839 3400, Telex 917096 – ▤ rest TV ☎. ☒ AE ① VISA. pp. 7-10 NV a
M a la carte 18.00/25.00 **t.** 3.50 – ☕ 6.75 – **284 rm** 70.00/100.00 **t.**, **6 suites**.

Stakis St. Ermin's (Stakis), Caxton St., SW1H 0QW, ✆ 222 7888, Telex 917731 – ▤ rest TV ☎. ☒ AE ① VISA. CV a
M (carving rest.) 11.50 **t.** and a la carte – ☕ 6.75 – **250 rm** 71.50/93.50 **t.**, **6 suites** 150.00 **t.**

Royal Westminster Thistle (Thistle), 49 Buckingham Palace Rd, SW1W 0QT, ✆ 834 1821, Telex 916821 – TV ☎. ☒ AE ① VISA. BV z
M 14.95/21.95 **t.** and a la carte 4.00 – ☕ 7.00 – **118 rm** 85.00/135.00 **st.**, **18 suites**.

Grosvenor, 101 Buckingham Palace Rd, SW1W 0SJ, ✆ 834 9494, Telex 916006 – ▤ rest TV wc ☎. BV e
365 rm.

Rubens, Buckingham Palace Rd, SW1W 0PS, ✆ 834 6600 – ▤ rest TV wc ☎. BV n
M (carving rest.) – **191 rm**.

Ebury Court, 26 Ebury St., SW1W 0LU, ✆ 730 8147 – wc ☎. ☒ VISA AV i
M a la carte 8.50/14.10 **t.** 2.10 – **39 rm** ☕ 36.00/67.00 **t.**

Hamilton House, 60-64 Warwick Way, SW1V 1SA, ✆ 821 7113 – TV wc ☎. ☒ VISA BX n
M *(closed Saturday)* (grill rest. only) (dinner only) a la carte approx. 5.80 **t.** 1.50 – **40 rm** ☕ 28.00/50.00 **st.** – SB (November-March) 44.00/52.00 **st.**

XXX ✿✿ **Simply Nico,** 48a Rochester Row, SW1, ✆ 630 8061, French rest. – ☒ AE ① VISA CX a
closed Saturday, Sunday, 3 weeks August and 1 week Christmas – **M** (booking essential) 28.00/33.00 **t.** 6.50
Spec. Terrine de foie gras et sa gelée au Sauternes, Suprême de canard au fumet de cèpes, Tulipe à la vanille.

XXX **Auberge de Provence,** (at St. James Court H.) Buckingham Gate, SW1 6AF, ✆ 834 6655, Telex 938075, French rest. – ▤. ☒ AE ① VISA CV i
M 15.00 **t.** and a la carte 13.50/21.75 **t.** 4.00.

XXX Inn of Happiness, (at St. James Court H.) Buckingham Gate, SW1 6AF, ✆ 834 6655, Telex 938075, Chinese rest. CV i

XXX **Lockets,** Marsham Court, Marsham St., SW1P 4JY, ✆ 834 9552, English rest. – ☒ AE ① VISA pp. 7-10 MY z
closed Saturday lunch, Sunday and Bank Holidays – **M** a la carte 11.65/16.65 **t.** 3.00.

XXX **Kundan,** 3 Horseferry Rd, SW1P 2AN, ✆ 834 3434, Indian and Pakistani rest. – ▤. ☒ AE ① VISA pp. 7-10 NXY a
closed Sunday and Bank Holidays – **M** 12.00/15.00 **t.** 7.50.

XXX **Santini,** 29 Ebury St., SW1W 0NZ, ✆ 730 4094, Italian rest. – ▤. ☒ AE ① VISA ABV v
closed lunch Saturday and Sunday – **M** 11.00 **t.** (lunch) and a la carte 15.90/21.50 **t.** 4.00.

XX **Ken Lo's Memories of China,** 67-69 Ebury St., SW1W 0NZ, ✆ 730 7734, Chinese rest. – ▤. AE VISA AX **u**
closed Sunday and Bank Holidays – **M** 16.50/21.50 **t.** and a la carte 12.45/17.90 **t.**

XX ❀ **Le Mazarin,** 30 Winchester St., SW1V 4UZ, ✆ 828 3366, French rest. – ▤. AE
closed Sunday, 1 week at Christmas and Bank Holidays – **M** (dinner only) 22.50 **st.** 4.00
Spec. Fricassée de poulet fermier au basilic, Tranchettes d'onglet poêlé aux échalotes, Mousse au café et ses noisettes croustillantes. pp. 7-10 LZ **i**

XX **Kym's,** 70-71 Wilton Rd, SW1V 1DE, ✆ 828 8931, Chinese(Szechuan, Hunan) rest. – ▤. AE VISA BX **v**
closed 25 and 26 December – **M** 7.50/10.50 **t.** and a la carte 8.20/12.40 **t.** 2.75.

XX **Villa Claudius,** 10a The Broadway, SW1, ✆ 222 3338, Italian rest. – AE VISA
closed Saturday, Sunday, Easter, Christmas and Bank Holidays – **M** 10.00 **t.** and a la carte 12.75/15.20 **t.** 2.75. MX **a**

XX **Dolphin Brasserie,** Dolphin Square, Chichester St., SW1V 3LX, ✆ 828 3207, French rest., « Maritime Theme » – AE VISA pp. 7-10 LZ **e**
M 12.80/18.50 **t.** 3.80.

XX **Pomegranates,** 94 Grosvenor Rd, SW1V 3LG, ✆ 828 6560 – AE VISA
closed Saturday lunch and Sunday – **M** 17.50/19.50 **t.** 3.90. pp. 7-10 LMZ **a**

XX **Eatons,** 49 Elizabeth St., SW1W 9PP, ✆ 730 0074 – AE VISA AX **a**
closed Saturday, Sunday and Bank Holidays – **M** a la carte 11.20/13.30 **s.** 3.20.

XX **Ciboure,** 21 Eccleston St., SW1W 9LX, ✆ 730 2505, French rest. – AE VISA AX **z**
closed Saturday lunch and Sunday – **M** 12.50/18.50 **t.** and a la carte 14.90/17.75 **t.**

XX **Hoizin,** 72-73 Wilton Rd, SW1V 1DE, ✆ 630 5107, Seafood – ▤. AE VISA BX **v**
closed Sunday – **M** a la carte 8.10/17.20 **t.**

X **La Fontana,** 101 Pimlico Rd, SW1W 8PH, ✆ 730 6630, Italian rest. – AE VISA
closed Bank Holidays – **M** a la carte 12.80/16.40 3.30. pp. 14 and 15 FT **o**

X La Poule au Pot, 231 Ebury St., SW1W 8UT, ✆ 730 7763, French rest. pp. 7-10 KY **n**

X **Mimmo d'Ischia,** 61 Elizabeth St., SW1W 9PP, ✆ 730 5406, Italian rest. AX **o**
M a la carte approx. 13.50 **t.** 3.60.

X **Tate Gallery Rest.,** Tate Gallery, Millbank, SW1P 4RG, ✆ 834 6754, English rest., « Rex Whistler murals » – ▤ pp. 7-10 NY **c**
closed Sunday, 17 April, 24 to 27 December, 1 January and Bank Holidays – **M** (lunch only) a la carte 8.10/16.80 **t.** 3.90.

X **Bumbles,** 16 Buckingham Palace Rd, SW1W 0QP, ✆ 828 2903, Bistro – AE VISA
closed Saturday lunch, Sunday and Bank Holidays – **M** 10.25 **t.** and a la carte 10.65/13.45 **t.** 2.50. BV **c**

X **Villa Medici,** 35 Belgrave Rd, SW1, ✆ 828 3613, Italian rest. – AE VISA BX **c**
closed Saturday lunch, Sunday and Bank Holidays – **M** a la carte 10.20/15.10 **t.** 2.70.

Bray-on-Thames Berks W : 34 m. by M 4 (junction 8-9) and A 308 – 404 R 29 – pop. 9 427 – ✉ 0628 Maidenhead

XXXX ❀❀❀ **Waterside Inn,** Ferry Rd, SL6 2AT, ✆ 20691, Telex 8813079, ←, French rest., « Thames-side setting », – Ⓟ. AE VISA
closed Tuesday lunch, Sunday dinner 19 October-Easter, Monday, 26 December-14 February and Bank Holidays – **M** 20.00/36.00 **st.** and a la carte 25.30/38.30 **st.** 5.10
Spec. Tronçonnettes de homard poêlées minute au porto blanc, Caneton Juliette (April-September), Soufflé chaud aux mirabelles (October-March).

Oxford

at Great Milton Oxon NW : 49 m. by M 40 (junction 7) and A 329 – 403 404 Q 28 – ✉ 084 46 Great Milton :

XXXX ❀❀ **Le Manoir aux Quat'Saisons** with rm, Church Rd, OX9 7PD, ✆ 8881, ←, « 15C and 16C manor house », heated, , park, – TV wc Ⓟ. AE VISA.
– *closed 24 December-22 January* – **M** *(closed Tuesday lunch, Sunday dinner and Monday)* 22.50/38.00 **st.** and a la carte 31.50/42.50 **st.** 7.50 – **10 rm** 95.00/230.00 **st.**, **1 suite** 230.00/250.00 **st.** – SB (weekdays only) 320.00 **st.**
Spec. Charlotte d'aubergines et poivrons doux aux filets mignons d'agneau, Pigeonneau de Norfolk en croûte de sel, Pomme soufflée au sabayon de cidre.

BIRMINGHAM West Midlands 403 404 O 26 – pop. 1 013 995 – ECD : Wednesday – 021.

See : Museum and Art Gallery** JZ **M1** – Museum of Science and Industry* JY **M2** – Cathedral (stained glass windows* 19C) KYZ **E.**

18 Cocks Moor Woods, Alcester Rd South, King's Heath ✆ 444 2062, S : 6 ½ m. by A 435 FX – 18 Edgbaston, Church Rd ✆ 454 1736, S : 1 m. FX – 18 Pype Hayes, Eachelhurst Rd, Walmley ✆ 361 1014, NE : 7 ½ m. – 9 Warley, Lightwoods Hill, ✆ 429 2440, W : 5 m.

Birmingham Airport : ✆ 767 7153, E : 6 ½ m. by A 45.

2 City Arcade, ✆ 643 2514 – National Exhibition Centre ✆ 780 4141 – Birmingham Airport ✆ 767 5511.

London 122 – Bristol 91 – Liverpool 103 – Manchester 86 – Nottingham 50.

Plans on following pages

Albany (T.H.F.), Smallbrook, Queensway, B5 4EW, 643 8171, Telex 337031, ←, squash – AE VISA JKZ **a**
M 9.45/8.65 **st.** and a la carte 3.40 – 6.00 – **254 rm** 55.00/65.00 **st.**, **8 suites**.

Plough and Harrow (Crest), 135 Hagley Rd, Edgbaston, B16 8LS, W : 1 ½ m. on A 456 454 4111, Telex 338074, – AE VISA. EX **a**
M (see **Plough and Harrow** below) – 7.25 – **44 rm** 68.00/83.50 **st.**, **3 suites** 110.00/145.00 **st.** – SB (weekends only) 98.00 **st.**

Midland (Best Western), 128 New St., B2 4JT, 643 2601, Telex 338419 – AE VISA. KZ **r**
M 9.50/11.50 **t.** and a la carte – **107 rm** 45.00/67.00 **t.**, **2 suites** 85.00 **t.** – SB (except Christmas)(weekends only) 56.00/61.00 **st.**

Holiday Inn, Central Sq., Holliday St., B1 1HH, 643 2766, Telex 337272, ←, – AE VISA. JZ **z**
M (buffet lunch) and a la carte 13.00/17.75 **t.** 3.20 – 6.00 – **295 rm** 52.90/59.80 **st.**, **4 suites** 145.00/260.00 **st.** – SB (weekends only) 49.00/61.00 **st.**

Strathallan Thistle (Thistle), 225 Hagley Rd, Edgbaston, B16 9RY, W : 2 m. on A 456 455 9777, Telex 336680 – rest AE VISA EX **i**
M 8.00/11.00 **t.** and a la carte 2.50 – 6.50 – **164 rm** 47.00/75.00 **st.**, **4 suites** 90.00 **st.**

Grand (Q.M.H.), Colmore Row, B3 2DA, 236 7951, Telex 338174 – AE VISA – *closed 25 to 30 December* – **M** 8.50 **st.** and a la carte – **167 rm** 58.00/68.00 **st.**, **2 suites** 90.00 **st.** – SB 55.00 **st.** JKY **c**

Royal Angus Thistle (Thistle), St Chad's, Queensway, B4 6HY, 236 4211, Telex 336889 – AE VISA. KY **s**
M approx. 10.00 **t.** and a la carte 2.75 – 5.25 – **137 rm** 47.00/75.00 **st.**, **2 suites** 85.00 **st.**

Apollo, 243-247 Hagley Rd, Edgbaston, B16 9RA, W : 2 ¼ m. on A 456 455 0271, Telex 336759 – rest wc AE VISA EX **o**
M *(closed Saturday lunch)* 12.80/14.50 **st.** and a la carte 3.00 – 5.50 – **130 rm** 44.75/58.50 **st.**, **2 suites** 59.75/64.75 **st.**

Ladbroke International (Ladbroke), New St., B2 4RX, 643 2747, Telex 338331 – wc AE VISA KZ **x**
5.75 – **191 rm** 48.00/60.00 **st.**, **4 suites** – SB (weekends only) 63.00 **st.**

Cobden, 166-174 Hagley Rd, Edgbaston, B16 9NZ, W : 2 m. on A 456 454 6621, Group Telex 339715, – wc wc AE VISA EX **n**
closed Christmas and New Year – **M** 6.00/8.50 **st.** – **210 rm** 23.50/45.00 **st.**

XXX **Plough and Harrow** (Crest), (at Plough and Harrow H.) 135 Hagley Rd, Edgbaston, B16 8LS, W : 1 ½ m. on A 456 454 4111, Telex 338074, – AE VISA EX **a**
M 16.50/22.50 **st.** and a la carte 24.75/34.75 **st.**

XXX **Jonathans',** 16-20 Wolverhampton Rd, B68 0LH, W : 4 m. by A 456 429 3757, English rest., « Victoriana », – AE VISA
closed Saturday lunch, 26 December and 1 January – **M** 7.90/16.90 **st.** and a la carte 10.30/16.30 **st.** 2.80.

XX **Rajdoot,** 12-22 Albert St., B4 7UD, 643 8805, Indian rest. – AE VISA. KZ **c**
closed lunch Sunday and Bank Holidays and 25-26 December – **M** 5.00/11.50 **t.** and a la carte 11.60/15.90 **t.** 3.00.

XX **Sloans,** Chad Sq., off Harborne Rd., Edgbaston, B15 3TQ, W : 2 ¾ m. by A 456 455 6697 – AE VISA – *closed Saturday lunch, Sunday, first week January and Bank Holidays* – **M** 19.50 **t.** and a la carte 16.60/19.50 **t.** EX **v**

XX **Henry Wong,** 283 High St., Harborne, B17 9QH, W : 3 ¾ m. by A 456 427 9799, Chinese-cantonese rest. – AE VISA EX **n**
closed Sunday, 1 week August and 24 to 26 December – **M** 8.60 **st.** (dinner) and a la carte 12.60/18.00 **st.** 5.80.

XX **Dynasty,** 93-103 Hurst St., B5 4TE, 622 1410, Chinese rest. – AE VISA KZ **e**
M 5.50/10.50 **t.** and a la carte 8.50/11.10 **t.** 2.80.

XX **Lorenzo,** 3 Park St., Digbeth, B5 5JD, 643 0541, Italian rest. – AE VISA KZ **o**
closed Saturday lunch, Monday dinner, Sunday, 3 weeks July-August and Bank Holidays – **M** a la carte 10.30/15.20 **t.** 3.10.

X **Maharaja,** 23-25 Hurst St., B5 4AS, 622 2641, Indian rest. – AE VISA KZ **i**
closed Sunday and last 2 weeks July – **M** 7.50 **t.** (dinner) and a la carte 4.55/10.00 **t.** 3.05.

at Walmley NE : 6 m. by B 4148 – Sutton Coldfield – 021 Birmingham :

Penns Hall (Embassy), Penns Lane, B76 8LH, 351 3111, Telex 335789, – AE VISA.
M a la carte 14.25/21.25 **st.** 3.35 – 5.00 – **115 rm** 48.00/57.00 **st.**, **5 suites** 80.00/95.00 **st.** – SB (weekends only) 55.00/59.00 **st.**

at Sutton Coldfield NE : 8 m. by A 38 – Sutton Coldfield – 021 Birmingham :

Belfry (De Vere), Lichfield Rd, Wishaw, B76 9PR, E : 3 m. on A 446 0675 (Curdworth) 70301, Telex 338848, ←, 18, park, squash – rest AE VISA
M 11.50 **st.** and a la carte 4.00 – **168 rm** 75.00/95.00 **st.** – SB (weekends only) 85.00/105.00 **st.**

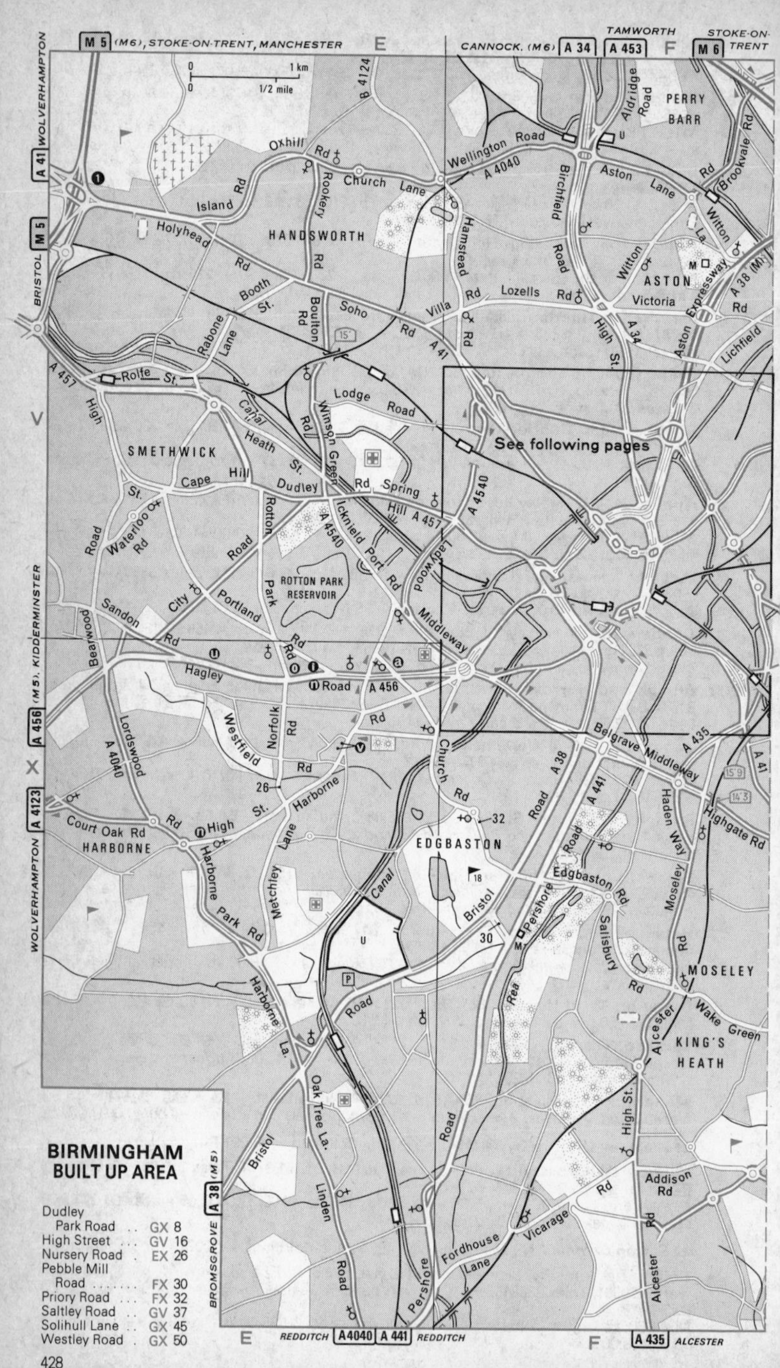

BIRMINGHAM BUILT UP AREA

Dudley Park Road ..	GX 8
High Street ...	GV 16
Nursery Road .	EX 26
Pebble Mill Road	FX 30
Priory Road ...	FX 32
Saltley Road ..	GV 37
Solihull Lane ..	GX 45
Westley Road .	GX 50

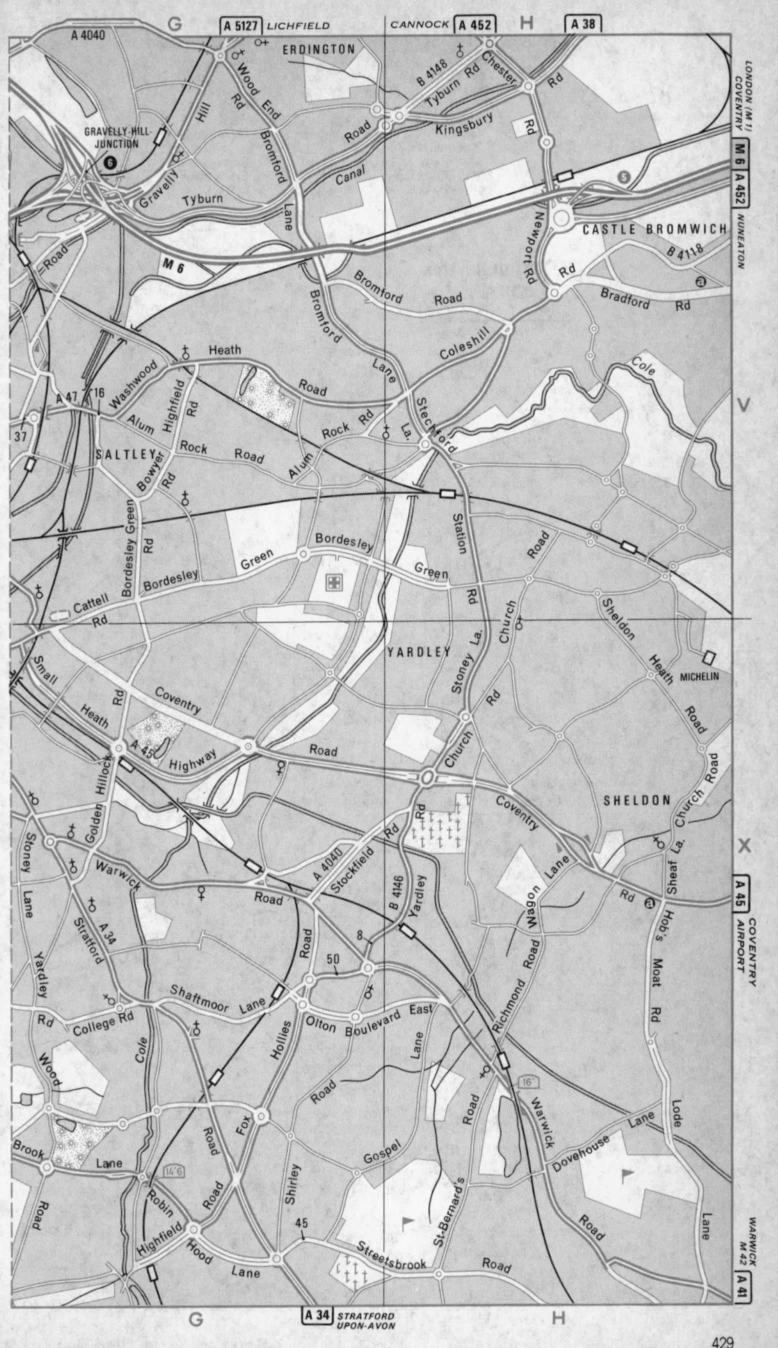
A 5127 LICHFIELD
CANNOCK A 452
A 38
A 4040
ERDINGTON
GRAVELLY HILL JUNCTION
CASTLE BROMWICH
LONDON (M 1) COVENTRY
M 6
A 452
NUNEATON
B 4148
B 4118
M 6
SALTLEY
YARDLEY
MICHELIN
SHELDON
A 47
A 45
A 45
COVENTRY AIRPORT
A 4040
B 4146
A 34
WARWICK M 42
A 41
A 34 STRATFORD UPON-AVON
Kingsbury Rd
Chester Rd
Tyburn Rd
Wood End Rd
Gravelly Hill
Bromford Lane
Canal
Tyburn Road
Newport Rd
Bromford Road
Bradford Rd
Coleshill Road
Cole
Heath Road
Washwood
Highfield Rd
Alum Rock Road
Stechford La.
Bowyer Rd
Station Rd
Bordesley Green Rd
Bordesley Green
Cattell Rd
Church Road
Sheldon Heath Road
Stoney La.
Church Rd
Small Heath
Coventry Road
Highway
Golden Hillock Rd
Church Road
Coventry Rd
Warwick Road
Stockfield Rd
Yardley Rd
Wagon Lane
Sheaf La.
Hob's Moat Rd
Stoney Lane
Yardley Rd
Stratford
Shaftmoor Lane
Olton Boulevard East
Richmond Road
College Rd
Cole
Wood
Hollies Road
Lane
Road
Fox
Road
Warwick Road
Lode Lane
Dovehouse Lane
Brook Lane
Road
Robin Hood Lane
Highfield Road
Shirley
Gospel
St. Bernard's
Streetsbrook Road
G
H
V
X

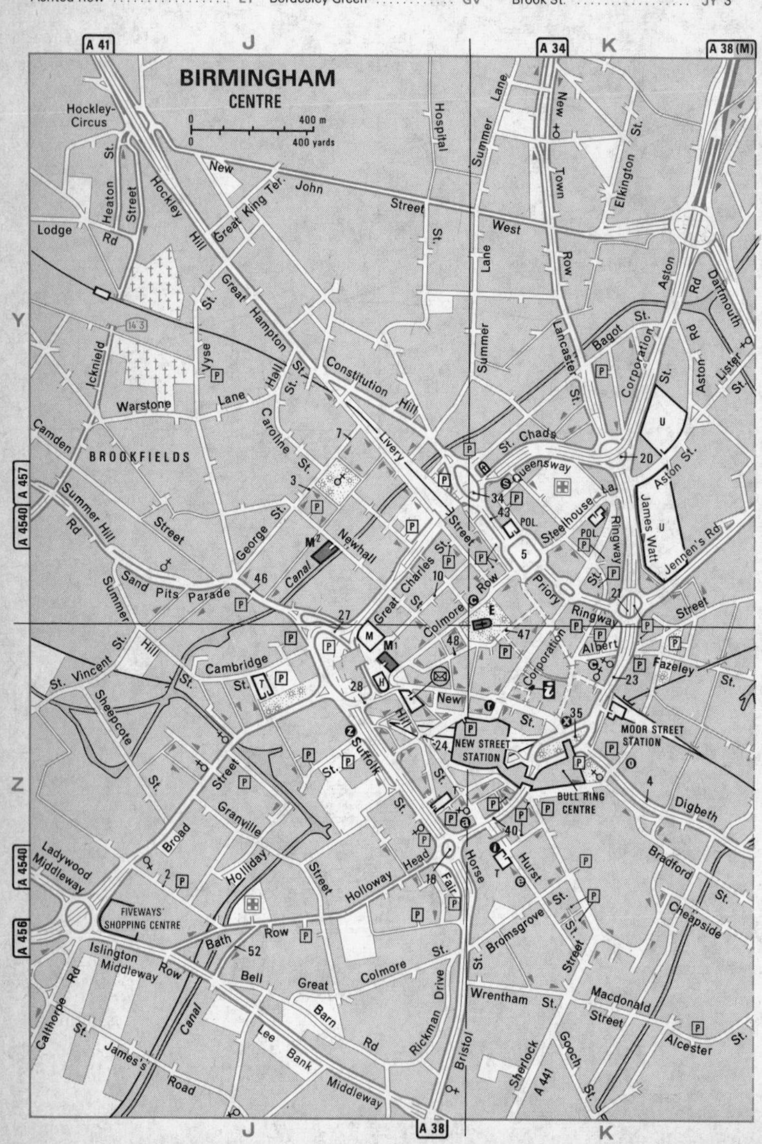

BIRMINGHAM
CENTRE
0 400 m
0 400 yards
A 41
J
A 34
K
A 38 (M)
Y
Z
A 457
A 4540
A 456
A 38
Hockley-Circus
Lodge Rd
Heaton Street
Hockley Hill
Great King Ter.
New John Street West
Hospital St.
Summer Lane
New Town Row
Elkington St.
Aston Rd
Dartmouth
Great Hampton St.
Vyse St.
Icknield
Warstone Lane
Hall St.
Constitution Hill
Lancaster St.
Bagot St.
Corporation St.
Aston Rd
Lister St.
Camden
BROOKFIELDS
Caroline St.
Livery Street
St. Chads Queensway
Summer Hill Rd
Street
George St.
Newhall
Canal
Great Charles St.
Colmore Row
Steelhouse La.
Ringway
James Watt
Aston St.
Jennen's Rd
POL.
Priory
Sand Pits Parade
Summer Hill St.
St. Vincent St.
Cambridge St.
Sheepcote St.
Albert St.
Fazeley St.
Corporation St.
New St.
Hill St.
Suffolk St.
NEW STREET STATION
MOOR STREET STATION
BULL RING CENTRE
Digbeth
Broad Street
Granville St.
Holliday Street
Holloway Head
Horse Fair
Hurst St.
Bradford St.
Ladywood Middleway
FIVEWAYS' SHOPPING CENTRE
Bath Row
Islington Row Middleway
Bromsgrove St.
Cheapside
Bell Barn Rd
Great Colmore St.
Wrentham St.
Macdonald Street
Calthorpe Rd
St. James's Road
Canal
Lee Bank Middleway
Rickman Drive
Bristol St.
Sherlock St.
A 441
Gooch St.
Alcester St.

BIRMINGHAM TOWN PLANS

Street	Grid	No.
Brookvale Rd	FV	
Bull Ring	KZ	4
Bull Ring Centre	KZ	
Calthorpe Rd	JZ	
Cambridge St.	JZ	
Camden St.	JY	
Camp Hill	LZ	
Cape Hill	EV	
Caroline St.	JY	
Cattell Rd	GV	
Cheapside	KZ	
Chester St.	LY	
Church Lane	EV	
Church Rd EDGBASTON	FX	
Church Rd SHELDON	HX	
Church Rd YARDLEY	HX	
City Rd	EV	
Coleshill Rd	HV	
College Rd	GX	
Colmore Circus	KY	5
Colmore Row	JY	
Constitution Hill	JY	
Corporation St.	KZ	
Court Oak Rd	EX	
Coventry Rd	LZ	6
Cox St.	JY	7
Curzon St.	LY	
Dartmouth Middleway	KY	
Digbeth	KZ	
Dovehouse Lane	HX	
Dudley Park Rd	GX	8
Dudley Rd	EV	
East Meadway	HV	
Edgbaston Rd	FX	
Edmund St.	JY	10
Elkington St.	KY	
Fazeley St.	KZ	
Fiveways' Shopping Centre	JZ	
Fordhouse Lane	FX	
Fox Hollies Rd	GX	
George St.	JY	
Golden Hillock Rd	GX	
Gooch St.	KZ	
Gospel Lane	HX	
Granville St.	JZ	
Gravelly Hill	GV	
Gravelly Hill Junction	GV	
Great Barr St.	LZ	
Great Charles St.	JY	
Great Colmore St.	JZ	
Great Hampton St.	JY	
Great King Ter.	JY	
Great Lister St.	LY	
Hagley Rd	EX	
Hall St.	JY	
Hampstead Rd	FV	
Harborne Lane	EX	
Harborne Park Rd	EX	
Harborne Rd	EX	
Heath Mill Lane	LZ	
Heath St.	EV	
Heaton St.	JY	
Highfield Rd	GX	
Highfield Rd	GV	
Highgate Rd	FX	
High St. ASTON	FV	
High St. BORDESLEY	LZ	14
High St. DERITEND	LZ	
High St. HARBORNE	EX	
High St. KING'S HEATH	FX	
High St. SALTLEY	GV	16
High St. SMETHWICK	EV	
Hill St.	JZ	
Hob's Moat Rd	HX	
Hockley Circus	JY	
Hockley Hill	JY	
Holliday St.	JZ	
Holloway Circus	JZ	18
Holloway Head	JZ	
Holyhead Rd	EV	
Horse Fair	JZ	
Hospital St.	JY	
Hurst St.	KZ	
Icknield Port Rd	EV	
Icknield St.	JY	
Island Rd	EV	
Islington Row Middleway	JZ	
James Watt Ringway	KY	
Jennen's Rd	KY	
Kingsbury Rd	HV	
Ladywood Middleway	EV	
Lancaster Circus	KY	20
Lancaster St.	KY	
Lawley St.	LY	
Lee Bank Middleway	JZ	
Lichfield Rd	FV	
Linden Rd	EX	
Lister St.	KY	
Livery St.	JY	
Lode Lane	HX	
Lodge Rd	EV	
Lordswood Rd	EX	
Lozells Rd	FV	
Macdonald St.	KZ	
Masshouse Circus	KY	21
Metchley Lane	EX	
Moor St. Ringway	KZ	23
Moseley Rd	FX	
Navigation St.	JZ	24
Nechell's Parkway	LY	
Newhall St.	JY	
New John St. West	JY	
Newport Rd	HV	
New St.	JZ	
New Town Row	KY	
Norfolk Rd	EX	
Nursery Rd	EX	26
Oak Tree Lane	EX	
Olton Bd East	GX	
Oxhill Rd	EV	
Paradise Circus	JY	27
Paradise St.	JZ	28
Pebble Mill Rd	FX	30
Pershore Rd	FX	
Portland Rd	EV	
Priory Ringway	KY	
Priory Rd	FX	32
Rabone Lane	EV	
Richmond Rd	HX	
Rickman Drive	JZ	
Robin Hood Lane	GX	
Rolfe St.	EV	
Rookery Rd	EV	33
Rotton Park Rd	EV	
Rupert St.	LY	
St. Bernard's Rd	HX	
St. Chads Circus	KY	34
St. Chads Ringway	KY	
St. James's Rd	JZ	
St. Martin's Circus	KZ	35
St. Vincent St.	JZ	
Salisbury Rd	FX	
Saltley Rd	GV	37
Sandon Rd	EV	
Sand Pits Parade	JY	
Sandy Lane	LZ	
Shaftmoor Lane	GX	
Sheaf Lane	HX	
Sheepcote St.	JZ	
Sheldon Heath Rd	HX	
Sherlock St.	KZ	
Shirley Rd	GX	
Smallbrook Ringway	KZ	40
Small Heath Highway	GX	
Snow Hill Ringway	KY	43
Soho Rd	EV	
Solihull Lane	GX	45
Spring Hill	EV	
Station Rd	HV	
Stechford Lane	HV	
Steelhouse Lane	KY	
Stockfield Rd	GX	
Stoney La. MOSELEY	GX	
Stoney La. SHELDON	HX	
Stratford Pl.	LZ	
Stratford Rd	GX	
Streetsbrook Rd	HX	
Suffolk St.	JZ	
Summer Hill Rd, St.	JY	
Summer Lane	KY	
Summer Row	JY	46
Temple Row	KZ	47
Tyburn Rd	GV	
Vauxhall Rd	LY	
Vicarage Rd	FX	
Victoria Rd	FV	
Villa Rd	FV	
Vyse St.	JY	
Wagon Lane	HX	
Wake Green Rd	FX	
Warstone Lane	JY	
Warwick Rd	GX	
Washwood Heath Rd	GV	
Waterloo Rd	EV	
Waterloo St.	JZ	48
Watery Lane	LZ	
Wellington Rd	FV	
Westfield Rd	EX	
Westley Rd	GX	50
Wheeley's Lane	JZ	52
Winson Green Rd	EV	
Witton Lane	FV	
Witton Rd	FV	
Wood End Rd	GV	
Wrentham St.	KZ	
Yardley Rd	HX	
Yardley Wood Rd	GX	

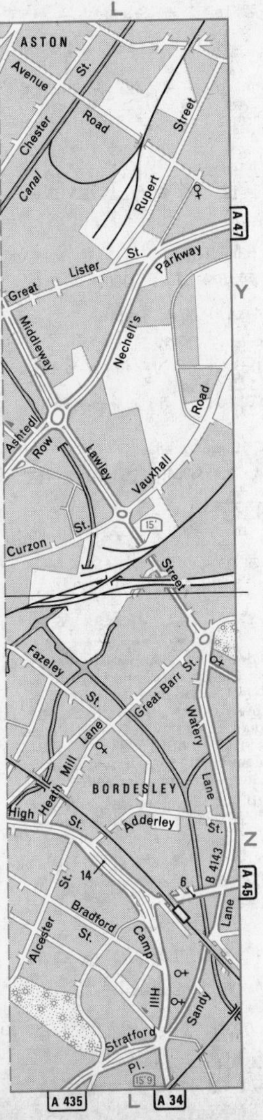

Moor Hall (Best Western), Moor Hall Drive, Four Oaks, B75 6LN, NE : 1 m. by A 453 ✆ 308 3751, Telex 335127, – wc ☎ P. AE VISA.
M 10.50/15.95 **t.** 3.95 – **50 rm** 40.00/52.00 **t.** – SB (weekends only) 52.00/56.00 **st.**

Le Bon Viveur, 65 Birmingham Rd, B72 1QF, ✆ 355 5836 – AE VISA.
closed Sunday, Monday, 3 weeks August and Bank Holidays – **M** 6.25 **t.** (lunch) and a la carte 11.80/16.35 **t.** 3.10.

at National Exhibition Centre E : 9 ½ m. on A 45 – ✉ 021 Birmingham :

Birmingham Metropole, Blackfirs Lane, Bickenhill, B40 1PP, ✆ 780 4242, Telex 336129, ←, squash – ☎ P. AE VISA
M 9.50/19.00 **st.** and a la carte 3.90 – 4.00 – **498 rm** 57.00/85.00 **st.**, **9 suites** 185.00/235.00 **st.** – SB (weekends only) 55.00 **st.**

Warwick, Blackfirs Lane, Bickenhill, B40 1PP, ✆ 780 4242, Telex 336129, squash – wc ☎ P. AE VISA
Exhibitions only – **M** (rest. see **Birmingham Metropole H.**) – 4.00 – **196 rm** 48.00/65.00 **st.**

Arden, Coventry Rd, Bickenhill, B92 0EH, S : ½ m. on A 45 ✉ Solihull ✆ 067 55 (Hampton-in-Arden) 3221, Telex 334913 – wc P. AE VISA
closed 3 days at Christmas – **M** 7.50 **st.** and a la carte 3.50 – 3.50 – **46 rm** 25.00/39.50 **st.** – SB (weekends only) 48.00 **st.**

at Sheldon SE : 6 m. on A 45 – HX – ✉ 021 Birmingham :

Wheatsheaf, 2225 Coventry Rd, B26 3EH, ✆ 742 6201 – wc ☎ P. AE VISA. HX **a**
M 6.00/6.50 **s.** and a la carte 3.75 – **84 rm** 35.00/45.00 **st.**

at Birmingham Airport SE : 7 m. on A 45 – ✉ 021 Birmingham :

Excelsior (T.H.F.), Coventry Rd, Elmdon, B26 3QW, ✆ 743 8141, Telex 338005 – P. AE VISA
M 7.50/11.25 **st.** and a la carte 3.40 – 6.00 – **141 rm** 47.00/57.00 **st.**, **3 suites**.

at West Bromwich NW : 6 m. on A 41 – ✉ West Bromwich – 021 Birmingham :

West Bromwich Moat House (Q.M.H.) Birmingham Rd, B70 6RS, W : 1 m. by A 41 ✆ 553 6111, Telex 336232 – rest wc ☎ P. AE VISA
M 8.90/9.50 **st.** and a la carte 2.95 – **181 rm** 47.00/61.00 **st.** – SB (weekends only) 46.00 **st.**

at Great Barr NW : 6 m. on A 34 – ✉ Great Barr – 021 Birmingham :

Post House (T.H.F), Chapel Lane, B43 7BG, ✆ 357 7444, Telex 338497, heated – wc P. AE VISA
M 8.50/15.00 **st.** and a la carte 3.40 – 5.65 – **204 rm** 47.00/55.00 **st.**

Barr, Pear Tree Drive, Newton Rd, B43 6HS, W : 1 m. by A 4041 ✆ 357 1141, Telex 336406, – wc ☎ P. AE VISA.
M 7.50/9.50 **st.** and a la carte 3.75 – **114 rm** 35.50/55.00 **st.** – SB (weekends only) 44.00/80.00 **st.**

EDINBURGH Midlothian (Lothian) 401 K 16 – pop. 408 822 – 031.

See : Site★★★ – International Festival★★★ (August) – Castle★★ (Site★★★, ←★★, ★★★ Great Hall : hammerbeam roof★★, Palace block : Honours of Scotland★★★) DZ – Abbey and Palace of Holyroodhouse★★ (Plasterwork ceilings★★★) – Royal Mile★★ : Gladstone's Land★ EYZ A, St. Giles' Cathedral★★ (Crown Spire★★★) EZ, Wax Museum★ EZ M1 – Canongate Tolbooth★ EY B, Victoria Street★ EZ 84 – Royal Scottish Museum★★ EZ M2 – New Town★★ : Charlotte Sq.★★★ CY 14, National Museum of Antiquities★★ EY M3, The Georgian House★ CY D – National Portrait Museum★ EY M3, Princes Street and Gardens : National Gallery of Scotland★★ DY M4 – Scott Monument★ EY F, Calton Hill EY : from Nelson Monument★★★ – Royal Botanic Gardens★★★ – Edinburgh Zoo★★ – Scottish Agricultural Museum★ – Craigmillar Castle★.

Envir. : Rosslyn Chapel★★, Apprentice Pillar★★★, S : 7 m. by A101 – 18 Silverknowes, Parkway, ✆ 336 3843, W : 4 m. – 18 Craigmillar Park, Observatory Rd ✆ 667 2837 – 18 Carrick Knowe, Glendevon Park ✆ 337 1096, W : 5 m.

✆ 333 1000, Telex 727615, W : 6 m. by A 8 – **Terminal : Waverley Bridge.** ✆ 556 1100.

Waverley Market, 3 Princes St., ✆ 557 2727 – Edinburgh Airport ✆ 333 2167.

Glasgow 46 – Newcastle-upon-Tyne 105.

Plan opposite

Caledonian, Princes St., EH1 2AB, ✆ 225 2433, Telex 72179 – ☎ P. AE VISA. CY **n**
M (rest. see **Pompadour** below) – 7.25 – **254 rm** 70.00/105.00, **7 suites** 175.00/195.00 – SB (weekends only)(October-April) 77.00 **st.**

Sheraton, 1 Festival Square, EH3 9SR, ✆ 229 9131, Telex 72398, – ☎ P. AE VISA. CDZ **v**
M 30.00 **t.** and a la carte 4.00 – 7.00 – **263 rm** 62.00/100.00 **t.**, **14 suites**.

George, 19-21 George St., EH2 2PB, ✆ 225 1251, Telex 72570 – rest ☎ P. – **195 rm**, **2 suites**. DY **z**

EDINBURGH

Street	Grid	No.
Castle Street	DY	
Frederick Street	DY	
George Street	DY	
Hanover Street	DY	
High Street	EYZ	37
Lawnmarket	EYZ	46
Princes Street	DY	
St. James Centre	EY	
Waverley Market	EY	
Bernard Terrace	EZ	3
Bread Street	DZ	6
Bristo Place	EZ	7
Candlemaker Row	EZ	9
Castlehill	DZ	10
Chambers Street	EZ	12
Chapel Street	EZ	13
Charlotte Square	CY	14
Deanhaugh Street	CY	23
Douglas Gardens	CY	25
Drummond Street	EZ	27
Forrest Road	EZ	31
Gardner's Crescent	CZ	32
George IV Bridge	EZ	33
Grassmarket	DZ	35
Home Street	DZ	38
Hope Street	CY	39
Johnston Terrace	DZ	42
King's Bridge	DZ	44
King's Stables Road	DZ	45
Leith Street	EY	47
Leven Street	DZ	48
Lothian Street	EZ	51
Mound (The)	DY	55
North Bridge	EY	61
North St. Andrew Street	EY	66
Raeburn Place	CY	69
Randolph Crescent	CY	71
St. Andrew Square	EY	73
St. Mary's Street	EY	75
Shandwick Place	CYZ	77
South Charlotte Street	DY	78
South St. David Street	DEY	79
Spittal Street	DZ	83
Victoria Street	EZ	84
Waterloo Place	EY	87
Waverley Bridge	EY	89
West Maitland Street	CZ	92

Carlton Highland, 1-29 North Bridge, EH1 1SD, 556 7277, Telex 727001, , squash – rest EY **s**
M 9.95 **t.** and a la carte 3.75 – **207 rm** 60.00/88.00 **st.**, **4 suites** 175.00 **st.**

Roxburghe (Best Western), 38 Charlotte Sq., EH2 4HG, 225 3921, Telex 727054 – DY **o**
M 8.50/11.50 **t.** and a la carte 11.90/19.50 **t.** 3.75 – **76 rm** 58.00/98.00 **st.**, **2 suites** 140.00/170.00 **st.** – SB 84.00/92.00 **st.**

Ladbroke Dragonara (Ladbroke), Bells Mills, 69 Belford Rd, EH4 3DG, 332 2545, Telex 727979 – CY **i**
M 9.75/10.95 **t.** and a la carte 3.80 – 6.25 – **146 rm** 60.50/92.50 **t.**, **3 suites** 137.50 **t.** – SB (weekends only) 72.00 **st.**

Royal Scot (Swallow), 111 Glasgow Rd, EH12 8NF, W : 4 ½ m. on A 8 334 9191, Telex 727197, –
M (carving lunch)/dinner 11.05 **st.** and a la carte 3.95 – **252 rm** 57.00/70.00 **st.**, **5 suites** 70.00/80.00 **st.** – SB (weekends only)(October-May) 58.50/70.00 **st.**

King James Thistle (Thistle), 1 Leith St., EH1 3SW, 556 0111, Telex 727200 – rest wc EY **u**
M 10.00/14.50 **t.** and a la carte 3.50 – 6.50 – **147 rm** 45.00/95.00 **st.**, **5 suites** 100.00 **st.** – SB (weekends only) 82.00 **st.**

Howard, 32-36 Gt. King St., EH3 6QH, 557 3500, Telex 727887 – wc wc DY **s**
closed 25,26 and 31 December-2 January – **M** *(closed lunch Saturday and Sunday)* 7.50/15.00 **t.** 3.50 – **25 rm** 40.00/85.00 **t.** – SB (except summer)(weekends only) 66.00/77.00 **st.**

Crest (Crest), Queens Ferry Rd, EH4 3HL, NW : 2 m. on A 90 332 2442, Telex 72541 – wc wc
M 8.25/12.25 **st.** and a la carte 3.75 – 6.15 – **118 rm** 52.00/67.00 **st.**, **1 suite** 95.00/110.00 – SB (weekends only) 64.00/72.00 **st.**

Post House (T.H.F.), Corstorphine Rd, EH12 6UA, W : 3 m. on A 8 334 8221, Telex 727103, – wc
M 7.95/11.95 **st.** and a la carte 2.95 – 5.65 – **207 rm** 52.00/65.00 **st.** **1 suite**.

Stakis Grosvenor (Stakis), Grosvenor St., EH12 5EF, 226 6001, Telex 72445 – wc wc CZ **a**
M 11.00 **st.** and a la carte 3.95 – 3.95 – **136 rm** 48.00/85.00 – SB 48.00/80.00 **st.**

XXXX **Pompadour** (at Caledonian H.), Princes St., EH1 2AB, 225 2433, Telex 72179 – . CY **n**
closed lunch Saturday and Sunday, 26 December and 1-2 January – **M** 11.50/25.00 **st.** and a la carte 24.50/32.00 **st.** 4.25.

XXX **Prestonfield House** with rm, Priestfield Rd, EH16 5UT, SE : 2 ½ m. off A 68 668 3346, Telex 727396, , « Elegant 17C mansion », , park – wc – **M** 11.00/15.90 **t.** and a la carte 17.75/29.75 **t.** 3.00 – **5 rm** 42.50/72.50 **t.**

XXX **Aye,** 80 Queen St., EH2 4NF, 226 5467, Japanese rest. – CDY **e**
closed Sunday lunch, Sunday dinner in winter and Monday – **M** 15.00/50.00 **t.** and a la carte.

XX **Cosmo,** 58a North Castle St., EH2 3LU, 226 6743, Italian rest. – DY **r**
closed Saturday lunch, Sunday and Monday – **M** a la carte 11.10/17.25 **t.** 3.30.

XX **Raffaelli,** 10-11 Randolph Pl., EH3 7TA, 225 6060, Italian rest. – CY **c**
closed Saturday lunch and Sunday – **M** a la carte 9.80/17.60 **t.** 2.40.

XX **Champany Inn Town,** 2 Bridge Rd, Colinton, EH3 0LF, SW : 4 ½ m. by A 70 on B701 441 2587 –
closed Sunday and 24 December-13 January – **M** (grill rest. only) a la carte 9.30/16.85 3.75.

XX **Merchants,** 17 Merchant St., EH1 2QD, 225 4009 – EZ **a**
closed Sunday dinner and Monday – **M** (booking essential) 6.50 **t.** and a la carte 10.75/17.00 **t.** 2.75.

XX **Martins,** 70 Rose St., North Lane, EH2 3DX, 225 3106 – DY **n**
closed Saturday lunch, Sunday, Monday, 2 weeks July and 25 December-3 January – **M** 6.50 **t.** (lunch) and a la carte 10.70/18.20 **t.** 4.50.

XX **L'Auberge,** 56 St. Mary's St., EH1 1SX, 556 5888, French rest. – EYZ **c**
closed 26 December-1 January – **M** 6.75/19.50 **t.** and a la carte 12.00/25.90 **t.** 3.20.

X **Alp-Horn,** 167 Rose St., EH2 4LS, 225 4787, Swiss rest. – DY **x**
closed Sunday, Monday, 3 weeks June-July and 2 weeks at Christmas – **M** a la carte 8.50/12.70 **t.** 3.50.

X **Verandah,** 17 Dalry Rd, EH11 2BQ, 337 5828, North Indian Rest. – CZ **z**
M 9.95 **t.** and a la carte 7.65/11.15 **t.** 2.75.

at Bonnyrigg S : 8 m. by A 7 on A 6094 – Bonnyrigg – 0875 Gorebridge :

Dalhousie Castle , EH19 3JB, SE : 1 ¼ m. on B 704 20153, Telex 72380, , « Converted 12C castle », park – .
M a la carte 13.20/21.95 **t.** 3.50 – **24 rm** 38.00/89.00 **t.**

GLASGOW Lanark. (Strathclyde) 401 402 H 16 – pop. 754 586 – ☎ 041.

See : Site★★★ – Burrell Collection★★★ – Cathedral★★★ DYZ – Tolbooth Steeple★ DZ **A** – Hunterian Art Gallery★★ (Whistler Collection★★★ Mackintosh wing★★★) CY **M2** Art Gallery and Museum Kelvingrove★★ CY – City Chambers★ DZ **C** – Glasgow School of Art★ CY **B** – Museum of Transport★★ (Scottish cars★★★, Clyde Room of Ship Models★★★) – Pollok House★ (Spanish paintings★★).

Envir. : Trossachs★★★ N : by A 739 and A 81 – Loch Lomond★★ NW : by A 82 – Clyde Estuary★ (Dumbarton Castle, Site★, Hill House Helensburgh★) by A 82 – Bothwell Castle★ and David Livingstone Centre (Museum★) SE : 9 m. by A 724.

18 Linn Park, Simshill Rd ☎ 637 5871, S : 4 m. – 18 Lethamhill, Cumbernauld Rd ☎ 770 6220 – 9 Knightswood, Lincoln Av. ☎ 959 2131, W : 4 m.

Access to Oban by helicopter.

✈ Glasgow Airport : ☎ 887 1111, Telex 778219, W : 8 m. by M 8 AV – **Terminal :** Coach service from Glasgow Central and Queen Street main line Railway Stations and from Anderston Cross and Buchanan Bus Stations – ✈ see also Prestwick.

ℹ 35-39 St. Vincent Pl. ☎ 227 4880 – Edinburgh 46 – Manchester 221.

Plan on following pages

Albany (T.H.F.), Bothwell St., G2 7EN, ☎ 248 2656, Telex 77440, ≤ – AE VISA CZ z
M 8.00/8.65 **st.** and a la carte 3.40 – 6.00 – **251 rm** 56.00/67.00 **st.**, **3 suites**.

Holiday Inn, Argyle St., Anderston, G3 8RR, ☎ 226 5577, Telex 776355, – CZ a
296 rm, **3 suites**.

One Devonshire Gardens, 1 Devonshire Gdns, G12 0UX, ☎ 339 2001 –
M (lunch by arrangement) – **8 rm**.

Stakis Grosvenor (Stakis), Grosvenor Terr., Great Western Rd, G12 0TA, ☎ 339 8811, Telex 776247 – AE VISA CY r
M 8.00/15.00 **t.** and a la carte 4.00 – 3.90 – **96 rm** 40.00/70.00 **t.**, **2 suites** 90.00/120.00 **t.** – SB 54.00/68.00 **st.**

Hospitality Inn (Mt. Charlotte), 36 Cambridge St., G3 7DS, ☎ 332 3311, Telex 777334 – AE VISA DY z
M 5.75/7.50 **st.** and a la carte 3.00 – **316 rm** 47.50/58.00 **st.**, **3 suites** 100.00 **st.**

White House without rest., 12 Cleveden Cres., G12 0PA, ☎ 339 9375 – AE VISA.
M (room service only) a la carte approx. 11.85 **t.** 2.25 – 5.75 – **32 rm** 44.30/55.80 **t.**, **11 suites** 63.30/84.50 **t.**

Tinto Firs Thistle (Thistle), 470 Kilmarnock Rd, G43 2BB, ☎ 637 2353, Telex 778329 – wc AE VISA.
M 6.50/11.25 **t.** and a la carte 3.60 – 5.95 – **27 rm** 45.00/65.00 **st.**, **2 suites** 70.00 **st.** – SB (weekends only) 62.00 **st.**

Stakis Pond (Stakis), 2-4 Shelley Road, Great Western Road, G12 2XB, ☎ 334 8161, Telex 776573, – wc AE VISA
M 5.95/8.95 **t.** and a la carte 3.50 – 3.90 – **133 rm** 42.00/65.00 **t.** – SB 44.00/64.00 **st.**

Stakis Ingram (Stakis), 201 Ingram St., G1 1DQ, ☎ 248 4401, Telex 776470 – wc DZ c
– **90 rm**.

XXX **Fountain,** 2 Woodside Cres., G3 7UL, ☎ 332 6396 – AE VISA CY c
closed Saturday lunch, Monday dinner, Sunday, 25-26 December and 1-2 January – **M** 9.00/15.00 **t.** and a la carte 13.85/17.75 **t.** 4.95.

XX **Buttery,** 652 Argyle St., G3 8UF, ☎ 221 8188 – AE VISA CZ e
closed Saturday lunch, Sunday and Bank Holidays – **M** 11.50 **st.** and a la carte 13.70/21.75 **t.**

XX **Rogano,** 11 Exchange Pl., G1 3AN, ☎ 248 4055, Seafood, « Art deco » – AE VISA – *closed Sunday and Bank Holidays* – **M** a la carte 13.75/22.35 **t.** DZ i

XX **Colonial,** 25 High St., G1 1LX, ☎ 552 1923 – AE VISA DZ a
closed Saturday lunch, Monday dinner, Sunday, 17 July-3 August, Christmas, New Year and Bank Holidays – **M** 8.25/17.95 **st.** and a la carte 12.95/19.35 **st.** 3.60.

X **Poacher's,** Ruthven Lane, off Byres Rd, G12 9BG, ☎ 339 0932 – AE VISA
closed Sunday, 1 to 2 January and Bank Holidays – **M** (restricted lunch) a la carte 9.95/17.00 **t.** 2.90.

X **Le Provençal,** 21 Royal Exchange Sq., G1 3AJ, ☎ 221 0798, French rest. – AE VISA – *closed Sunday* – **M** (restricted lunch) a la carte 7.50/15.35 **t.** 3.75 DZ e

X **Ubiquitous Chip,** 12 Ashton Lane, off Byres Rd, G12 8SJ, ☎ 334 5007, Bistro – AE VISA
closed Sunday, Christmas Day and 1 to 2 January – **M** a la carte 6.85/17.70 **t.** 2.45.

X Trattoria Sorrento, 87 Kilmarnock Rd, Shawlands, G41 3YR, ☎ 649 3002, Italian rest.

at Glasgow Airport Renfrew. (Strathclyde) W : 8 m. by M 8 – ✉ ☎ 041 Glasgow :

Excelsior (T.H.F.), Abbotsinch, PA3 2TR, ☎ 887 1212, Telex 777733 – AE VISA
M 8.95 **st.** and a la carte 3.40 – 6.00 – **290 rm** 52.00/64.00 **st.**, **7 suites**.

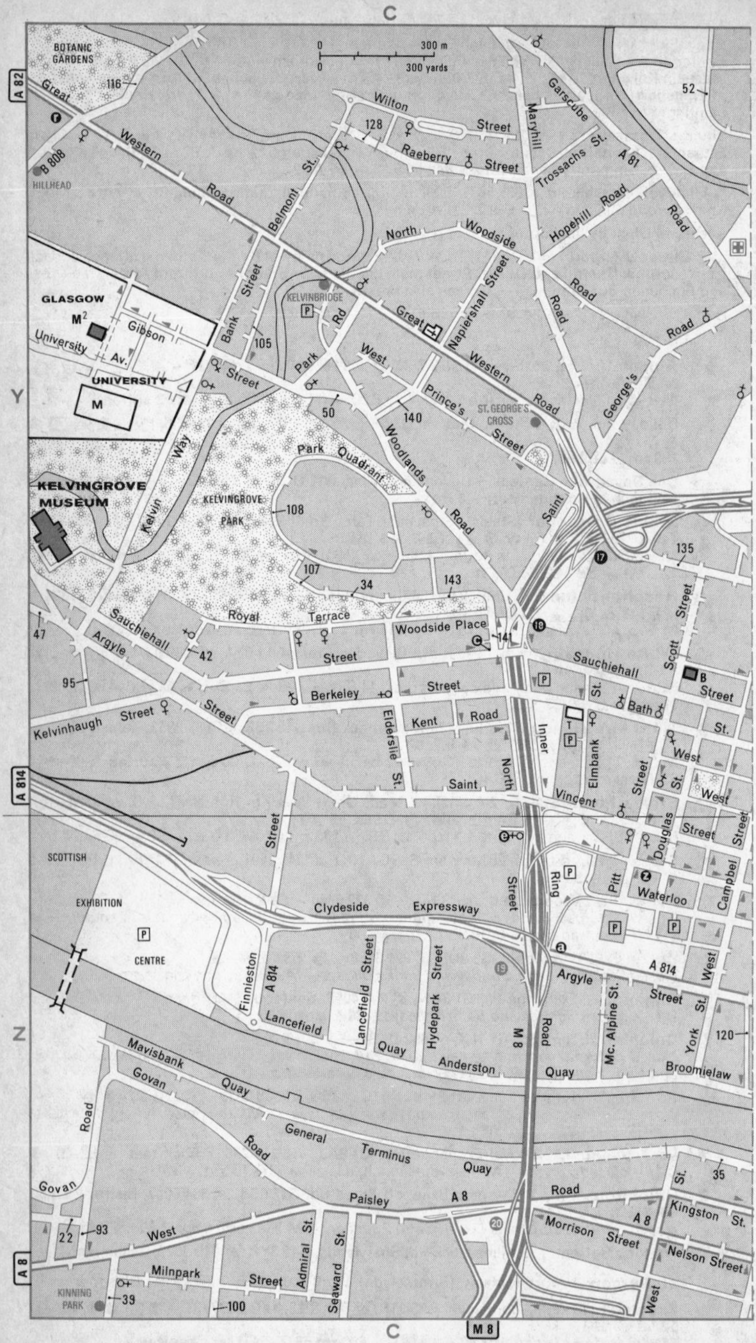

C

BOTANIC GARDENS
Great Western Road
Wilton Street
Raeberry Street
Maryhill Road
Garscube Road
Trossachs St.
A 81
Hopehill Road
North Woodside Road
Belmont St.
Bank Street
KELVINBRIDGE
Park Rd
Napiershall Street
George's Road
GLASGOW UNIVERSITY
University Av.
Gibson Street
West Prince's Street
ST. GEORGE'S CROSS
Kelvin Way
KELVINGROVE MUSEUM
KELVINGROVE PARK
Park Quadrant
Woodlands Road
Saint George's Road
Royal Terrace
Woodside Place
Sauchiehall Street
Argyle Street
Berkeley Street
Kent Road
Elderslie St.
Kelvinhaugh Street
North Street
Inner Ring Road
Elmbank St.
Bath Street
Scott Street
West Street
Saint Vincent Street
Douglas Street
Pitt Street
Waterloo Street
Campbell Street
Finnieston Street
SCOTTISH EXHIBITION CENTRE
Clydeside Expressway
Lancefield Street
Lancefield Quay
Hydepark Street
Anderston Quay
Argyle Street
A 814
Mc. Alpine St.
York St.
West St.
Broomielaw
M 8
Mavisbank Quay
Govan Road
General Terminus Quay
Paisley Road West
A 8
Kingston St.
Morrison Street
Nelson Street
Milnpark Street
Admiral St.
Seaward St.
HILLHEAD
KINNING PARK
B 808
A 82
A 814
A 8
M 8
Y
Z
0 300 m
0 300 yards
116 52 128 105 50 140 108 107 34 143 141 135 47 42 95 120 35 22 93 39 100

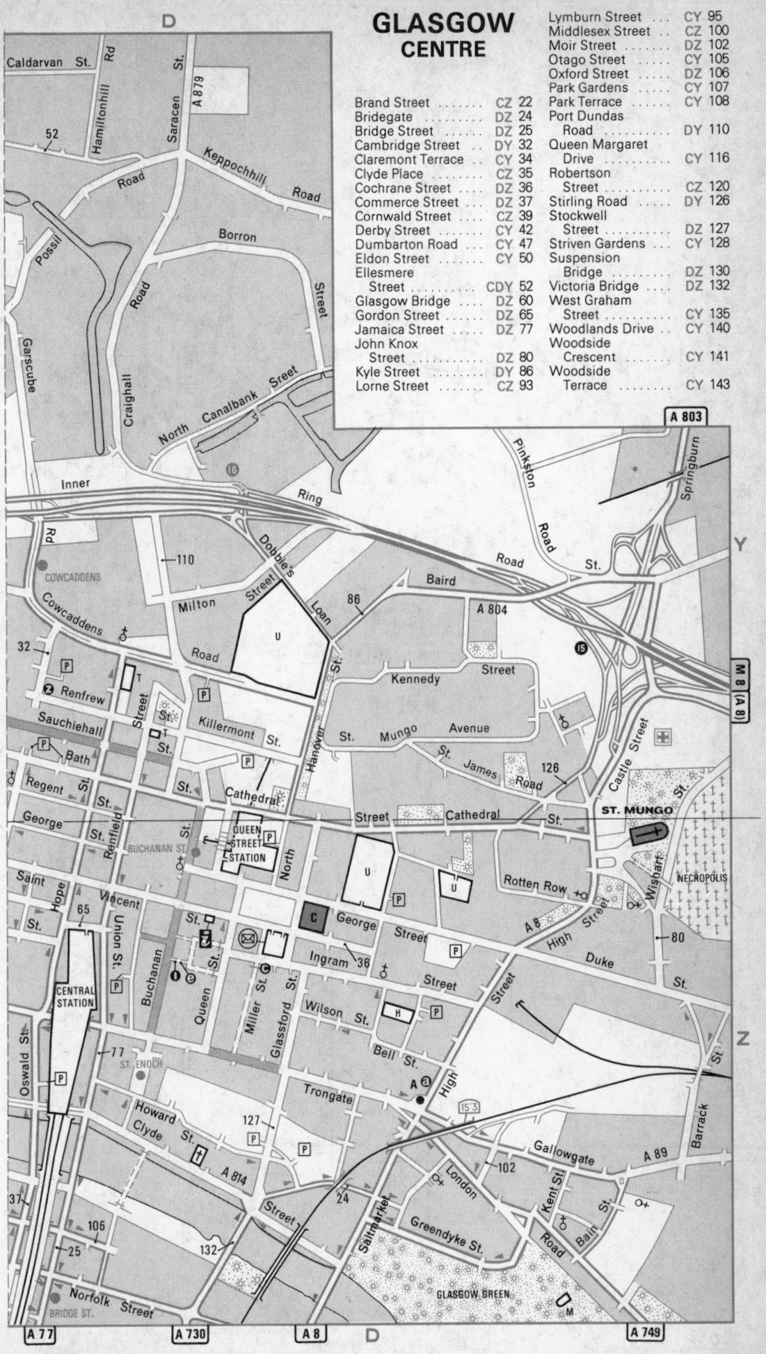
GLASGOW
CENTRE
Brand Street CZ 22
Bridegate DZ 24
Bridge Street DZ 25
Cambridge Street DY 32
Claremont Terrace CY 34
Clyde Place CZ 35
Cochrane Street DZ 36
Commerce Street DZ 37
Cornwald Street CZ 39
Derby Street CY 42
Dumbarton Road CY 47
Eldon Street CY 50
Ellesmere Street CDY 52
Glasgow Bridge DZ 60
Gordon Street DZ 65
Jamaica Street DZ 77
John Knox Street DZ 80
Kyle Street DY 86
Lorne Street CZ 93
Lymburn Street CY 95
Middlesex Street CZ 100
Moir Street DZ 102
Otago Street CY 105
Oxford Street DZ 106
Park Gardens CY 107
Park Terrace CY 108
Port Dundas Road DY 110
Queen Margaret Drive CY 116
Robertson Street CZ 120
Stirling Road DY 126
Stockwell Street DZ 127
Striven Gardens CY 128
Suspension Bridge DZ 130
Victoria Bridge DZ 132
West Graham Street CY 135
Woodlands Drive CY 140
Woodside Crescent CY 141
Woodside Terrace CY 143
D
Y
Z
A 803
A 804
M 8 (A 8)
A 77
A 730
A 8
A 749
A 879
A 814
A 89
Caldarvan St.
Hamiltonhill Rd
Saracen St.
Keppochhill Road
Possil Road
Borron Street
Garscube Rd
Craighall Road
North Canalbank Street
Inner Ring Road
Pinkston Road
Springburn
Baird St.
Dobbie's Loan
Milton Street
Cowcaddens Road
COWCADDENS
Kennedy Street
St. Mungo Avenue
St. James Road
Castle Street
ST. MUNGO
NECROPOLIS
Renfrew St.
Sauchiehall St.
Killermont St.
Hanover St.
Bath St.
Regent St.
Cathedral St.
George St.
Renfield St.
BUCHANAN ST.
QUEEN STREET STATION
North
Saint Vincent St.
Hope St.
Union St.
Buchanan St.
Queen St.
Miller St.
Glassford St.
George Street
Ingram St.
Wilson St.
Bell St.
Rotten Row
High Street
Wishart St.
Duke Street
CENTRAL STATION
Oswald St.
ST. ENOCH
Trongate
Howard St.
Clyde St.
Barrack St.
Gallowgate
London Road
Kent St.
Bain St.
Saltmarket
Greendyke St.
GLASGOW GREEN
Norfolk Street
BRIDGE ST.

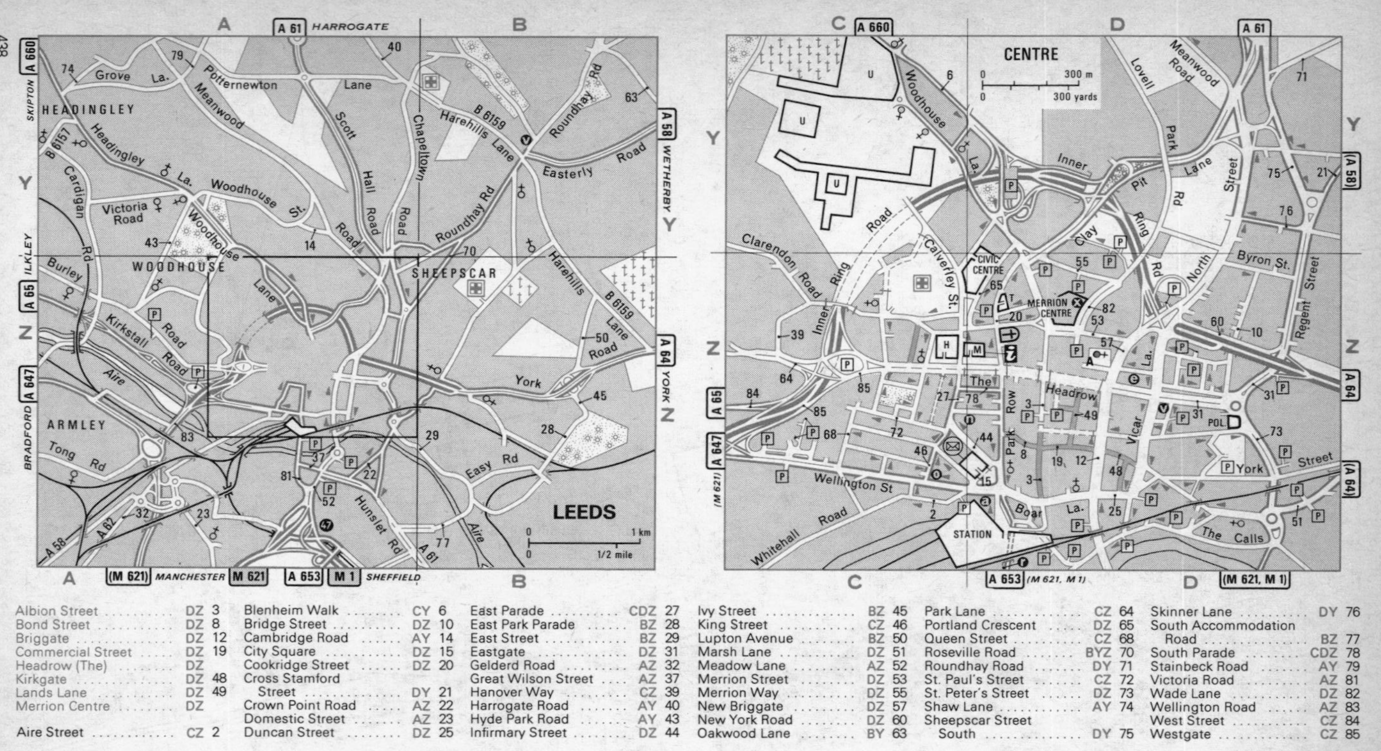

Albion Street	DZ	3
Bond Street	DZ	8
Briggate	DZ	12
Commercial Street	DZ	19
Headrow (The)	DZ	
Kirkgate	DZ	48
Lands Lane	DZ	49
Merrion Centre	DZ	
Aire Street	CZ	2
Blenheim Walk	CY	6
Bridge Street	DZ	10
Cambridge Road	AY	14
City Square	DZ	15
Cookridge Street	DZ	20
Cross Stamford Street	DY	21
Crown Point Road	AZ	22
Domestic Street	AZ	23
Duncan Street	DZ	25
East Parade	CDZ	27
East Park Parade	BZ	28
East Street	BZ	29
Eastgate	DZ	31
Gelderd Road	AZ	32
Great Wilson Street	AZ	37
Hanover Way	CZ	39
Harrogate Road	AY	40
Hyde Park Road	AY	43
Infirmary Street	DZ	44
Ivy Street	BZ	45
King Street	CZ	46
Lupton Avenue	BZ	50
Marsh Lane	DZ	51
Meadow Lane	AZ	52
Merrion Street	DZ	53
Merrion Way	DZ	55
New Briggate	DZ	57
New York Road	DZ	60
Oakwood Lane	BY	63
Park Lane	CZ	64
Portland Crescent	DZ	65
Queen Street	CZ	68
Roseville Road	BYZ	70
Roundhay Road	DY	71
St. Paul's Street	CZ	72
St. Peter's Street	DZ	73
Shaw Lane	AY	74
Sheepscar Street South	DY	75
Skinner Lane	DY	76
South Accommodation Road	BZ	77
South Parade	CDZ	78
Stainbeck Road	AY	79
Victoria Road	AZ	81
Wade Lane	DZ	82
Wellington Road	AZ	83
West Street	CZ	84
Westgate	CZ	85

LEEDS West Yorks. 402 P 22 – pop. 445 242 – ECD : Wednesday – 0532.

See : St. John's Church★ 17C DZ A.

Envir. : Temple Newsam House★ 17C (interior★★) *AC*, E : 4 m. – Kirkstall Abbey★ (ruins 12C) *AC*, NW : 3 m.

18, 18 The Lady Dorothy Wood, The Lord Irwin, Temple Newsam Rd, Halton ☏ 645624, E : 3 m. – 18 Gotts Park, Armley Ridge Rd, ☏ 638232, W : 2 m. – 18 Middleton Park, Town St., Middleton ☏ 700449, S : 3 m.

Leeds and Bradford Airport : ☏ 0532 (Rawdon) 503431, Telex 557868 NW : 8 m. by A 65 and A 658.

Central Library, Calverley St. ☏ 462453/4.

London 204 – Liverpool 75 – Manchester 43 – Newcastle-upon-Tyne 95 – Nottingham 74.

Plan opposite

Ladbroke Dragonara (Ladbroke), Neville St., LS1 4BX, ☏ 442000, Telex 557143 – rest TV ☎ P. AE VISA DZ **r**
M a la carte approx. 11.25 3.70 – 5.75 – **234 rm** 54.50/65.00 **st.**

Queens (T.H.F.), City Sq., LS1 1PL, ☏ 431323, Telex 55161 – TV wc. AE VISA DZ **a**
M 8.50/9.00 **st.** and a la carte 3.50 – 6.00 – **198 rm** 47.00/62.00 **st.**

Metropole (T.H.F.), King St., LS1 2HQ, ☏ 450841, Telex 557755 – TV wc P. AE VISA CZ **o**
M (carving rest.) 5.75/8.65 **st.** and a la carte 3.40 – 5.65 – **110 rm** 40.00/50.00 **st.**

Merrion, Merrion Centre, 17 Wade Lane, LS2 8NH, ☏ 439191, Telex 55459 – TV wc ☎ P. AE VISA DZ **x**
M 6.50/8.95 **st.** and a la carte 3.50 – 5.50 – **120 rm** 30.00/55.00 **st.** – SB (weekends only) 57.00/62.00 **st.**

XXX Gardini's Terrazza, Minerva House, 16 Greek St., LS1 5RU, ☏ 432880, Italian rest. – CDZ **n**

XXX **Mandalay,** 8 Harrison St., LS1 6PA, ☏ 446453, Indian rest. – . AE VISA DZ **e**
closed Saturday lunch and Sunday – **M** 4.75 **t.** and a la carte 8.40/11.90 **t.**

XX **Embassy,** 333 Roundhay Rd, LS8 4HT, NE : 2 ½ m. by A 58 ☏ 490562 – P. AE VISA BY **v**
closed Sunday and Bank Holidays – **M** (dinner only) 11.80 **t.** and a la carte 2.95.

XX **Shabab,** 2 Eastgate, LS2 7JL, ☏ 468988, Indian rest. – . AE VISA DZ **v**
closed Sunday lunch and Christmas Day – **M** a la carte 5.30/9.50.

at Seacroft NE : 5 ½ m. at junction of A 64 and A 6120 – 0532 Leeds :

Stakis Windmill (Stakis), Ring Rd, LS14 5QP, ☏ 732323 – rest TV wc ☎ P. AE VISA
M (grill rest. only) 5.95/10.75 **st.** 3.40 – 3.90 – **101 rm** 42.00/54.00 **st.**

at Garforth E : 6 m. at Junction of A 63 and A 642 – 0532 Leeds :

Ladbroke (Ladbroke), Wakefield Rd, LS25 1LH, ☏ 866556, Telex 556324 – TV wc ☎ P. AE VISA
M *(closed Saturday lunch)* (carving rest.) 9.95 3.70 – 5.50 – **142 rm** 44.00/53.00 **st.** – SB (weekends only) 63.00 **st.**

at Oulton SE : 6 ¼ m. at junction of A 639 and A 642 – 0532 Leeds :

Crest (Crest), The Grove, LS26 8EW, ☏ 826201, Telex 557646 – TV wc P. AE VISA
M *(closed lunch Saturday and Bank Holidays)* 6.95/11.50 **st.** and a la carte – 5.85 – **40 rm** 48.50/59.50 **st.** – SB (weekends only) 50.00/58.00 **st.**

at Horsforth NW : 5 m. by A 65 off A 6120 – 0532 Leeds :

XXX **Low Hall,** Calverley Lane, LS18 4EF, ☏ 588221, « Elizabethan manor », – P. VISA
closed Saturday lunch, Sunday, Monday, 25 to 30 December and Bank Holidays – **M** 8.50/16.00 **st.** and a la carte 16.50/24.25 **st.**

at Bramhope NW : 8 m. on A 660 – 0532 Leeds :

Post House (T.H.F.), Otley Rd, LS16 9JJ, ☏ 842911, Telex 556367, ← – rest TV wc P. AE VISA
M *(closed Saturday lunch)* 7.25/14.50 **st.** and a la carte 3.40 – 5.65 – **120 rm** 50.00/62.00 **st.**

Parkway (Embassy), Otley Rd, LS16 8AG, S : 2 m. on A 660 ☏ 672551, – TV wc P. – **39 rm**.

Ilkley West Yorks NW : 16 m. by A 660 on A 65 – 402 O 22 – pop. 13 060 – 0943.

XXX ✿ **Box Tree,** 35-37 Church St., LS29 9DR, ☏ 608484, « Ornate decor » – AE VISA
closed Sunday, Monday, 25-26 December and 1 January – **M** (dinner only) (booking essential) 17.50 **t.** and a la carte 17.00/23.00 **t.**
Spec. Terrine de fruits de mer en chemise verte au safran, Rondels d'agneau et sa garniture de legumes, Timbale de fraises "Box Tree".

LIVERPOOL CENTRE

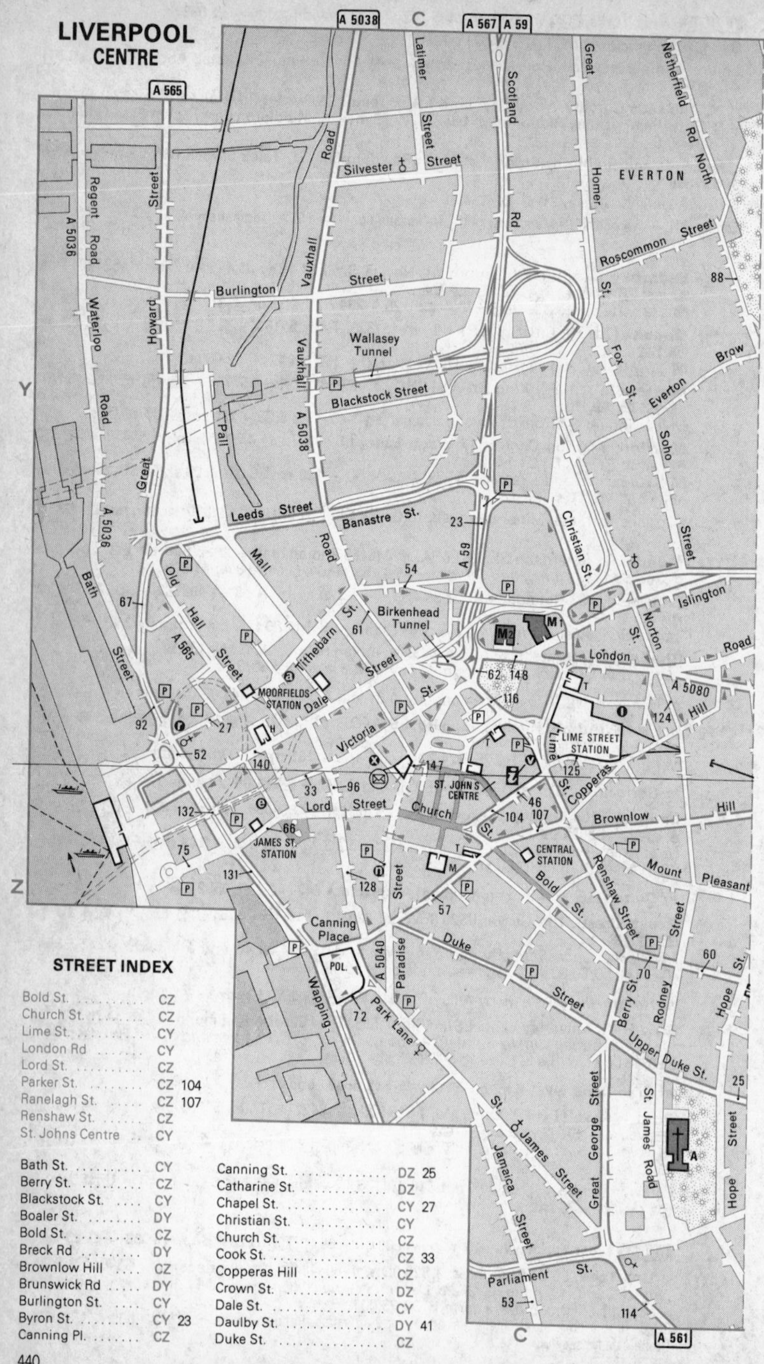

STREET INDEX

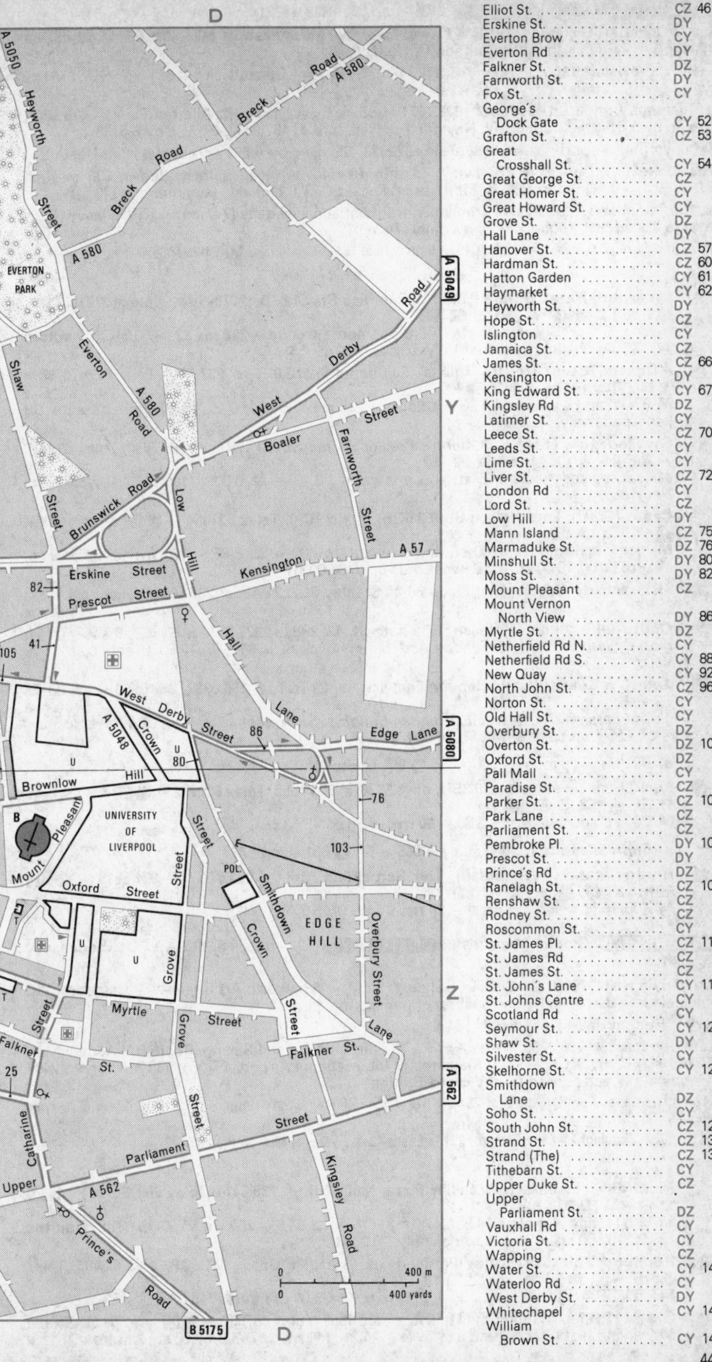

D
A 5050
Heyworth
Street
EVERTON
PARK
Breck
Road
A 580
Road
Y
A 5049
Shaw
Everton
Road
West
Derby
Road
Boaler
Street
Farnworth
Street
Brunswick
Road
Low
Hill
A 57
Erskine
Street
Prescot
Street
Kensington
82
41
105
Hall
Lane
West
Derby
Street
A 5048
Crown
86
Edge
Lane
A 5080
U
80
Brownlow
Hill
76
B
Mount
Pleasant
UNIVERSITY
OF
LIVERPOOL
Street
103
Oxford
Street
POL.
Smithdown
Crown
EDGE
HILL
Overbury
Street
U
U
Grove
Z
Myrtle
Street
Street
Grove
Street
Lane
Falkner
St.
Falkner St.
25
A 562
Catharine
Street
Street
Parliament
Upper
A 562
Kingsley
Road
Prince's
Road
0
400 m
0
400 yards
B 5175
D

LIVERPOOL Merseyside 402 403 L 23 – pop. 538 809 – ECD : Wednesday – ☎ 051.

See : Walker Art Gallery** CY **M1** – City of Liverpool Museums* CY **M2** – Anglican Cathedral* (1904) CZ **A** – Roman Catholic Cathedral* (1967) DZ **B**.

Envir. : Knowsley Safari Park** *AC*, NE : 8 m. by A 57 – Speke Hall* (16C) *AC*, SE : 7 m. by A 561.

Dunnings Bridge Rd, Bootle ☎ 928 1371 N : 5 m. by A 5036 – Allerton Park ☎ 428 1046, S : 5 m. by B 5180 – Childwall, Naylor's Rd, Gateacre ☎ 487 9982, E : 7 m. by B 5178.

Liverpool Airport : ☎ 494 0066, Telex 629323, SE : 6 m. by A 561 – **Terminal** : Pier Head.

to Ireland (Dublin) (B & I Line) 1 nightly (8 h 45 mn) – to Belfast (Belfast Car Ferries) 1 daily (9 h) – to Douglas (Isle of Man Steam Packet Co.) 1-2 weekly (summer only) (3 h).

to Birkenhead (Merseyside Transport) frequent services daily (7-8 mn) – to Wallasey (Merseyside Transport) frequent services daily (7-8 mn).

29 Lime St. ☎ 709 3631 – London 219 – Birmingham 103 – Leeds 75 – Manchester 35.

Plan on preceding pages

Liverpool Moat House (Q.M.H.), Paradise St., L1 8JD, ☎ 709 0181, Telex 627270, – AE VISA CZ **n**
closed 25 to 28 December – **M** 6.00/8.50 **t.** and a la carte – **253 rm** 48.00/59.75, **7 suites** 74.00/160.00 – SB (weekends only) 56.50/67.00 **st.**

Atlantic Tower Thistle (Thistle), 30 Chapel St., L3 9RE, ☎ 227 4444, Telex 627070, < – AE VISA CY **r**
M 9.50 **t.** and a la carte 3.20 – 6.25 – **226 rm** 47.00/70.00 **st.**, **10 suites** 70.00 **st.** – SB (weekends only) 58.00 **st.**

St. George's (T.H.F.), St. John's Precinct, Lime St., L1 1NQ, ☎ 709 7090, Telex 627630 – AE VISA CY **v**
M (carving rest.) 5.50/8.65 **st.** and a la carte 3.40 – 6.00 – **155 rm** 46.00/55.00 **st.**, **2 suites**.

Crest (Crest), Lord Nelson St., L3 5QB, ☎ 709 7050, Telex 627954 – wc AE VISA CY **i**
M (bar lunch)/dinner 13.00 **st.** and a la carte 3.00 – 5.85 – **160 rm** 45.00/55.00 **st.**, **1 suite** 60.00/85.00 **st.** – SB (weekends only) 56.00 **st.**

XXX Ristorante del Secolo, First Floor, 36-40 Stanley St., L2 6AL, ☎ 236 4004, Italian rest. CY **x**

XXX **Churchill's**, Churchill House, Tithebarn St., L2 2PB, ☎ 227 3877 – AE VISA CY **a**
closed Saturday lunch, Sunday and Bank Holidays – **M** 9.75/12.95 **t.** and a la carte 12.00/20.00 **t.** 3.25.

XX **Jenny's Seafood**, Old Ropery, Fenwick St., L2 7NT, ☎ 236 0332, Seafood – AE VISA CZ **e**
closed Saturday lunch, Monday dinner, Sunday, 25 December-2 January and Bank Holidays – **M** 9.55 **t.** and a la carte 9.65/16.60 **t.** 2.25.

at Bootle N : 5 m. by A 565 – ☎ 051 Liverpool :

Park, Park Lane West, L30 3SU, on A 5036 ☎ 525 7555, Telex 629772 – wc wc AE VISA
M 5.00 **st.** and a la carte 3.80 – **60 rm** 38.00/48.00 **st.**

at Blundellsands N : 6 ½ m. by A 565 – ☎ 051 Liverpool :

Blundellsands (Whitbread), The Serpentine, South, L23 6TN, ☎ 924 6515 – wc AE VISA.
M 7.50/10.00 **t.** and a la carte – **39 rm** 40.00/45.00 **t.**

MANCHESTER Greater Manchester 402 403 404 N 23 – pop. 437 612 – ECD : Wednesday – ☎ 061.

See : Town Hall* 19C DZ – City Art Gallery* DZ **M** – Whitworth Art Gallery* – Cathedral 15C (chancel*) DZ **B** – John Ryland's Library (manuscripts*) CZ **A**.

Envir. : Heaton Hall* (18C) *AC*, N : 5 m.

Heaton Park, ☎ 798 0295, N : by A 576 – Fairfield Golf and Sailing, Booth Rd, Audenshaw, ☎ 370 1641, E : by A 635 – Manchester International Airport ☎ (061) 489 3000 or 489 2404 – **Terminal** : Coach service from Victoria Station.

Town Hall Extension, Lloyd St. ☎ 234 3157/8 – Manchester International Airport, International Arrivals Hall ☎ 437 5233.

London 202 – Birmingham 86 – Glasgow 221 – Leeds 43 – Liverpool 35 – Nottingham 72.

Plan opposite

Piccadilly (Embassy), Piccadilly Plaza, M60 1QR, ☎ 236 8414, Telex 668765, < – AE VISA. DZ **s**
M 11.50 **t.** and a la carte 14.95/24.40 **t.** 3.75 – 6.25 – **250 rm** 65.00/75.00 **st.**, **9 suites** 150.00/180.00 **st.** – SB (weekends only) 70.00 **st.**

Portland Thistle (Thistle), Portland St., Piccadilly Gdns., M1 6DP, ☎ 228 3400, Telex 669157 – AE VISA DZ **v**
M 8.50/12.00 **t.** 5.50 – 7.95 – **219 rm** 60.00/95.00 **t.**, **1 suite** 115.00 **st.**

Grand (T.H.F.), Aytoun St., M1 3DR, ☎ 236 9559, Telex 667580 – AE VISA
M (carving rest.) 8.65 **st.** and a la carte 3.40 – **140 rm** 57.00/67.50 **st.**, **2 suites**. DZ **u**

MANCHESTER
CENTRE

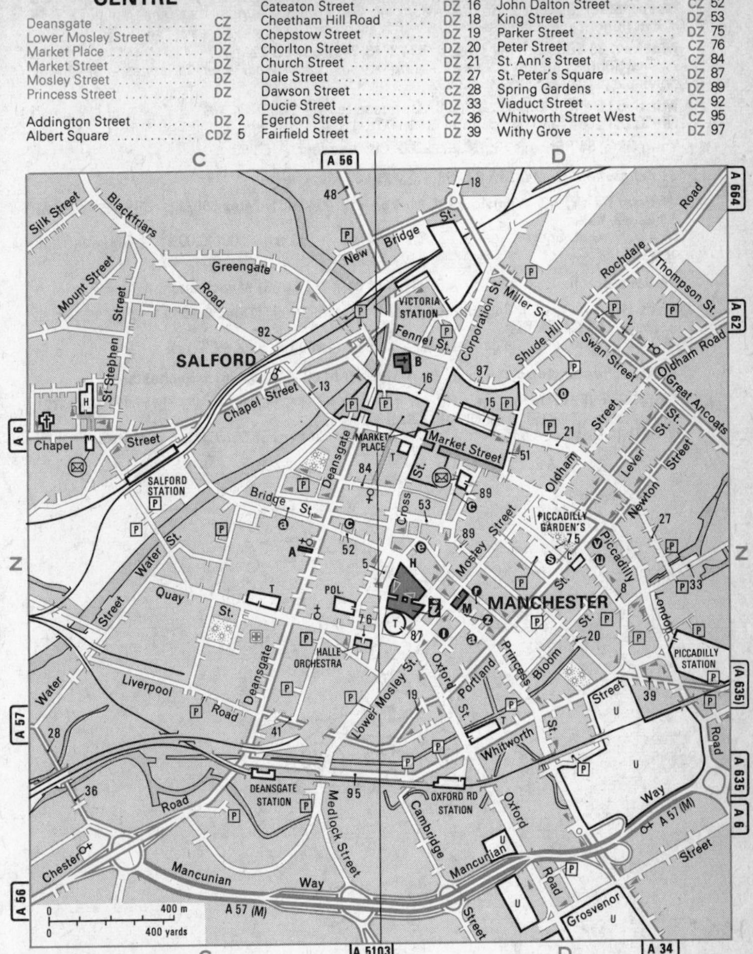

Hazeldean, 467 Bury New Rd, M7 0NX, ℰ 792 6667 – TV wc wc P. AE VISA.
closed 25 and 26 December – **M** (bar lunch Monday to Saturday)/dinner 12.00 **t.** and a la carte 3.20 – **21 rm** 27.85/45.55 **st.** – SB (weekends only) 56.10/65.85 **st.**

Terrazza, 14 Nicholas St., M1 4FE, ℰ 236 4033, Italian rest. – AE VISA DZ **r**
closed Sunday and Bank Holidays – **M** 5.95/12.50 **t.** and a la carte 7.60/13.00 **t.** 2.95.

Isola Bella, 6a Booth St., M2 4AW, ℰ 236 6417, Italian rest. – AE VISA DZ **e**
closed Sunday and Bank Holidays – **M** 18.00 **st.** and a la carte 10.40/12.80 **st.** 3.60.

Gaylord, Amethyst House, Marriott's Court, Spring Gardens, M2 1EA, ℰ 832 6037, Indian rest. – AE VISA DZ **c**
closed 25 December and 1 January – **M** 3.95/7.95 **t.** and a la carte 5.35/6.65 **t.** 3.75.

Leen Hong, 35 George St., M1 4HQ, ℰ 228 0926, Chinese rest. – AE DZ **z**
M a la carte 5.25/9.70 **t.**

Rajdoot, St. James' House, South King St., M2 6DW, ℰ 834 2176, Indian rest. – AE VISA CZ **c**
closed Sunday lunch and 25-26 December – **M** 4.00/9.50 **t.** and a la carte 2.95.

✗ **Truffles,** 63 Bridge St., M3 3BQ, ✆ 832 9393 – AE VISA — CZ **a**
closed Saturday lunch, Sunday, Monday, first 2 weeks August and Bank Holidays – **M** 9.95 **t.** (lunch) and a la carte 13.00/19.40 **t.** 2.85.

✗ **Market,** 30 Edge St., M4 1HN, ✆ 834 3743, Bistro – AE — DZ **o**
closed Sunday, Monday, 1 week spring, August and 1 week after Christmas – **M** (dinner only) a la carte 7.60/11.90 **t.** 2.50.

✗ **Mina,** 63 George St., ✆ 228 2598, Japanese rest. – AE VISA — DZ **i**
M 13.00/18.00 **t.** and a la carte 11.00/18.00 **t.** 3.00.

✗ Yang Sing, 34 Princess St., ✆ 236 2200, Chinese rest. – AE — DZ **a**

at Fallowfield S : 3 m. on B 5093 – 061 Manchester :

Willow Bank, 340 Wilmslow Rd, M14 6AF, ✆ 224 0461, Telex 668222 – TV wc. AE VISA
M 4.50/7.50 **st.** and a la carte 3.00 – 4.50 – **123 rm** 28.00/40.00 **st.** – SB (weekends only) 53.00/56.00 **st.**

at Northenden S : 6 ½ m. by A 5103 off M 56 – 061 Manchester :

Post House (T.H.F.), Palatine Rd, M22 4FH, ✆ 998 7090, Telex 669248 – TV wc. AE VISA
M 7.50/10.25 **st.** and a la carte 3.50 – 5.65 – **200 rm** 50.00/58.00 **st.**

at Manchester Airport S : 9 m. by A 5103 off M 56 – 061 Manchester :

Excelsior (T.H.F.), Ringway Rd, Wythenshawe, M22 5NS, ✆ 437 5811, Telex 668721, heated – TV. AE VISA
M 8.50/10.50 **st.** and a la carte 3.70 – 6.00 – **304 rm** 56.00/66.00 **st.**, **4 suites**.

CALENDAR OF TRADE FAIRS AND OTHER INTERNATIONAL EVENTS

AUSTRIA

Vienna	Wiener Festwochen	8 May to 14 June
Salzburg	Salzburg Festival (Festspiele)	11 to 20 April 25 July to 30 August

BENELUX

Amsterdam	Holland Festival	June
Bruges	Ascension Day Procession	Ascension
Brussels	Guild Procession (Ommegang)	first Thursday of July

DENMARK

Copenhagen	Scandinavian Furniture Fair	6 to 10 May
	HAFNIA 87 World Philatelic Exhibition	16 to 25 October
	International Boat Show 88	February 88

FINLAND

Helsinki	Nordic Fashion Fair	25 to 27 August
	Finnish Boot and Shoe Fair	26 to 27 September

FRANCE

Paris	Paris Fair	30 April to 10 May
Cannes	International Film Festival	7 to 19 May
Lyons	Lyons Fair	4 to 13 April
Marseilles	Marseilles Fair	September

GERMANY

Berlin	Berlin Fair (Grüne Woche)	30 Jan to 8 February
Frankfurt	International Fair	21 to 25 February 22 to 26 August
	International Motor Show (IAA)	10 to 20 Sept
	Frankfurt Book Fair	7 to 12 October
Hanover	Hanover Fair	1 to 8 April
Munich	Beer Festival (Oktoberfest)	19 Sept to 4 Oct

GREECE

Salonica	International Fair	September

IRELAND

Dublin	Dublin Horse Show	4 to 8 August

ITALY

Milan	Milan Fair	4 to 12 April
Palermo	Mediterranean Fair	30 May to 14 June
Turin	Automotor	13 to 18 October

NORWAY

Oslo	Nor- Shipping '87	2 to 5 June
	Fashion Week	30 Aug to 2 Sept

PORTUGAL

Lisbon	International Fair	12 to 17 May

SPAIN

Barcelona	Motor Show	2 to 10 May
Valencia	International Fair	6 to 10 May

SWEDEN

Stockholm	International Mining Exhibition	1 to 5 June
	International Fashion Fair	10 to 13 Sept
	International Technical Fair	22 to 28 October

SWITZERLAND

Geneva	Motor Show	March 88

UNITED KINGDOM

London	London International Boat Show	6 to 17 January 88
	Motor Fair	22 Oct to 1 Nov
Edinburgh	Arts Festival	9 to 31 August
Leeds	Harrogate International Toy Fair	9 to 14 Jan 88

EUROPEAN DIALLING CODES

INDICATIFS TÉLÉPHONIQUES EUROPÉENS

TELEFON-VORWAHLNUMMERN EUROPÄISCHER LÄNDER

ヨーロッパ内通話コード番号

(A)	Österreich, Autriche, Austria	43
(B)	Belgique, België, Belgium	32
(CH)	Schweiz, Suisse, Svizzera, Switzerland	41
(D)	Bundesrepublik Deutschland, RFA, West Germany	49
(DK)	Danmark, Danemark, Denmark	45
(E)	España, Espagne, Spain	34
(F)	France	33
(GB)	Great Britain, Grande-Bretagne	44
(GR)	Hellás, Grèce, Greece	30
(I)	Italia, Italie	39
(IRL)	Ireland, Irlande	353
(L)	Luxembourg	352
(MC)	Monaco	33
(N)	Norge, Norvège, Norway	47
(NL)	Nederland, Pays-Bas, Netherlands	31
(P)	Portugal	351
(S)	Sverige, Suède, Sweden	46
(SF)	Suomi, Finland	358
(YU)	Jugoslavija, Yougoslavie	38

Between certain neighbouring countries the dialling code may vary. Make enquiries.

Entre certains pays limitrophes, il existe des indicatifs spéciaux. S'informer.

Zwischen bestimmten benachbarten Ländern gibt es spezielle Vorwahlnummern. Informieren Sie sich.

いくつかの国境付近では、特別なコード番号が使われていますので、お問い合わせ下さい。

SPEED

To determine the speed at which you are travelling :

Check the time you take to cover a kilometre at constant speed ; in the table below, you will find the corresponding speed in kilometres or miles per hour. (The figures have been rounded to the nearest m.p.h.).

VITESSE

Comment déterminer la vitesse à laquelle on roule :

Chronométrer le temps employé pour parcourir un kilomètre à vitesse constante ; lire ensuite dans le tableau ci-dessous, en face du temps relevé, la vitesse correspondante en kilomètres ou en miles par heure. (Cette vitesse est calculée avec une approximation pratiquement négligeable).

GESCHWINDIGKEIT

Wie man die Geschwindigkeit bestimmt, mit der man fährt :

Messen Sie genau die Zeit, die Sie brauchen, um einen Kilometer bei gleichbleibender Geschwindigkeit zurückzulegen. Auf der untenstehenden Tabelle können Sie dann Ihre Geschwindigkeit in Kilometern oder Meilen pro Stunde ablesen. (Diese Werte weisen eine nur geringfügige Ungenauigkeit auf).

速 度

走行中に速度を測定するには:

一定の速度で1キロメートル走り、かかった時間を調べます。下記の表で該当する時間に合わせて、キロメートル数又はマイル数がわかります（当速度は概算にすぎません）。

	km	miles		km	miles		km	miles
0mn**18**s	**200**	124	**0**mn**49**s	73	45	**1**mn**30**s	**40**	25
19	189	117	**50**s	72	44,5	33	39	24
20s	**180**	112	51	**70**	43,5	35	38	23,5
21	171	106	52	69	43	37	37	23
22	164	**102**	53	68	42	**40**s	36	22,5
23	157	97	54	67	41,5	43	35	21,5
24	**150**	93	55	66	41	46	34	21
25	144	89	56	64	**39,5**	**50**s	33	20,5
26	138	86	57	63	39	53	32	**20**
27	133	82	58	62	38,5	56	31	19
28	129	**80**	59	61	38	**2**mn**00**	**30**	18,5
29	124	77	**1**mn**00**	**60**	37	5	29	18
30s	**120**	74	1	59	36,5	10	28	17,5
31	116	72	2	58	36	15	27	16,5
32	113	70	3	57	35,5	20	26	16
33	109	68	4	56	34,5	24	25	15,5
34	106	66	6	55	34	**30**s	24	15
35	103	64	7	54	33,5	35	23	14,5
36	**100**	62	8	53	33	45	22	13,5
37	97	**60**	9	52	32	55	21	13
38	95	59	**10**s	51	31,5	**3**mn**00**	**20**	12,5
39	92	57	12	**50**	31	15	19	12
40s	**90**	56	14	49	30,5	20	18	11
41	88	55	15	48	**30**	**30**s	17	10,5
42	86	53	17	47	29	45	16	**10**
43	84	52	19	46	28,5	**4**mn**00**	15	9,5
44	82	51	**20**s	45	28	15	14	8,5
45	**80**	**50**	22	44	27,5	**30**	13	8
46	78	49	24	43	26,5	**5**mn**00**	12	7,5
47	77	48	26	42	26	30	11	7
48	75	46	28	41	25,5	**6**mn**00**	**10**	6

NOTES

MANUFACTURE FRANÇAISE DES PNEUMATIQUES MICHELIN

Société en commandite par actions au capital de 700 000 000 de francs.

Place des Carmes-Déchaux - 63 Clermont-Ferrand (France)

R.C.S. Clermont-Fd B 855 200 507

Dépôt légal 4-87 - ISBN 2 06 007 077 - 5

Printed in France 3-87-37

Photocomposition : S.C.I.A. La Chapelle d'Armentières - Impression : KAPP & LAHURE, Asnières nº 6312

Michelin maps and guides are complementary publications. Use them together.

Europe

1/3000000

920
MICHELIN

EUROPE

1/3000000 - 1cm: 30 km
1 in: 47 miles (approx.)

Tourism
Roads
Relief

Index of place names

PNEU MICHELIN
46 Av de Breteuil 75341 PARIS CEDEX 07